Beyond the Worst-Case Analysis of Algorithms

There are no silver bullets in algorithm design, and no single algorithmic idea is powerful and flexible enough to solve every computational problem. Nor are there silver bullets in algorithm analysis, as the most enlightening method for analyzing an algorithm often depends on the problem and the application. However, typical algorithms courses rely almost entirely on a single analysis framework, that of worst-case analysis, wherein an algorithm is assessed by its worst performance on any input of a given size.

The purpose of this book is to popularize several alternatives to worst-case analysis and their most notable algorithmic applications, from clustering to linear programming to neural network training. Forty leading researchers have contributed introductions to different facets of this field, emphasizing the most important models and results, many of which can be taught in lectures to beginning graduate students in theoretical computer science and machine learning.

Tim Roughgarden is a professor of computer science at Columbia University. For his research, he has been awarded the ACM Grace Murray Hopper Award, the Presidential Early Career Award for Scientists and Engineers (PECASE), the Kalai Prize in Computer Science and Game Theory, the Social Choice and Welfare Prize, the Mathematical Programming Society's Tucker Prize, and the EATCS-SIGACT Gödel Prize. He was an invited speaker at the 2006 International Congress of Mathematicians, the Shapley Lecturer at the 2008 World Congress of the Game Theory Society, and a Guggenheim Fellow in 2017. His other books include *Twenty Lectures on Algorithmic Game Theory* (2016) and the *Algorithms Illuminated* book series (2017–2020).

Beyond the Worst-Case Analysis of Algorithms

Edited by

Tim Roughgarden

Columbia University, New York

CAMBRIDGE
UNIVERSITY PRESS

CAMBRIDGE
UNIVERSITY PRESS

University Printing House, Cambridge CB2 8BS, United Kingdom

One Liberty Plaza, 20th Floor, New York, NY 10006, USA

477 Williamstown Road, Port Melbourne, VIC 3207, Australia

314–321, 3rd Floor, Plot 3, Splendor Forum, Jasola District Centre, New Delhi – 110025, India

79 Anson Road, #06–04/06, Singapore 079906

Cambridge University Press is part of the University of Cambridge.

It furthers the University's mission by disseminating knowledge in the pursuit of education, learning, and research at the highest international levels of excellence.

www.cambridge.org
Information on this title: www.cambridge.org/9781108494311
DOI: 10.1017/9781108637435

First published 2021

A catalogue record for this publication is available from the British Library.

ISBN 978-1-108-49431-1 Hardback

Contents

PART THREE SEMIRANDOM MODELS

PART FOUR   SMOOTHED ANALYSIS

PART FIVE   APPLICATIONS IN MACHINE LEARNING
AND STATISTICS

Preface

There are no silver bullets in algorithm design – no one algorithmic idea is powerful and flexible enough to solve every computational problem of interest. The emphasis of an undergraduate algorithms course is accordingly on the next-best thing: a small number of general algorithm design paradigms (such as dynamic programming, divide-and-conquer, and greedy algorithms), each applicable to a range of problems that span multiple application domains.

Nor are there silver bullets in algorithm *analysis*, as the most enlightening method for analyzing an algorithm often depends on the details of the problem and motivating application. However, the focus of a typical algorithms course rests almost entirely on a single analysis framework, that of worst-case analysis, wherein an algorithm is assessed by its worst performance on any input of a given size. The goal of this book is to redress the imbalance and popularize several alternatives to worst-case analysis, developed largely in the theoretical computer science literature over the past 20 years, and their most notable algorithmic applications. Forty leading researchers have contributed introductions to different facets of this field, and the introductory Chapter 1 includes a chapter-by-chapter summary of the book's contents.

This book's roots lie in a graduate course that I developed and taught several times at Stanford University.[1] While the project has expanded in scope far beyond what can be taught in a one-term (or even one-year) course, subsets of the book can form the basis of a wide variety of graduate courses. Authors were requested to avoid comprehensive surveys and focus instead on a small number of key models and results that could be taught in lectures to second-year graduate students in theoretical computer science and theoretical machine learning. Most of the chapters conclude with open research directions as well as exercises suitable for classroom use. A free electronic copy of this book is available from the URL https://www.cambridge.org/9781108494311#resources (with the password 'BWCA_CUP').

Producing a collection of this size is impossible without the hard work of many people. First and foremost, I thank the authors for their dedication and timeliness in writing their own chapters and for providing feedback on preliminary drafts of other chapters. I thank Avrim Blum, Moses Charikar, Lauren Cowles, Anupam Gupta,

---

[1] Lecture notes and videos from this course, covering several of the topics in this book, are available from my home page (www.timroughgarden.org).

Ankur Moitra, and Greg Valiant for their enthusiasm and excellent advice when this project was in its embryonic stages. I am also grateful to all the Stanford students who took my CS264 and CS369N courses, and especially to my teaching assistants Rishi Gupta, Joshua Wang, and Qiqi Yan. The cover art is by Max Greenleaf Miller. The editing of this book was supported in part by NSF award CCF-1813188 and ARO award W911NF1910294.

Contributors

Maria-Florina Balcan
Carnegie Mellon University

Jérémy Barbay
University of Chile

Avrim Blum
Toyota Technological Institute at Chicago

Kai-Min Chung
Institute of Information Science, Academia Sinica

Daniel Dadush
Centrum Wiskunde Informatica

Sanjoy Dasgupta
University of California at San Diego

Ilias Diakonikolas
University of Wisconsin-Madison

Uriel Feige
The Weizman Institute

Fedor Fomin
University of Bergen

Vijay Ganesh
University of Waterloo

Rong Ge
Duke University

Anupam Gupta
Carnegie Mellon University

Nika Haghtalab
Cornell University

Moritz Hardt
University of California at Berkeley

Sophie Huiberts
Centrum Wiskunde Informatica

Daniel Kane
University of California at San Diego

Anna R. Karlin
University of Washington at Seattle

Elias Koutsoupias
University of Oxford

Samory Kpotufe
Columbia University

Daniel Lokshtanov
University of California at Santa Barbara

Tengyu Ma
Stanford University

Konstantin Makarychev
Northwestern University

Yury Makarychev
Toyota Technological Institute at Chicago

Bodo Manthey
University of Twente

Michael Mitzenmacher
Harvard University

Ankur Moitra
Massachusetts Institute of Technology

Eric Price
The University of Texas at Austin

Heiko Röglin
University of Bonn

Tim Roughgarden
Columbia University

Saket Saurabh
Institute of Mathematical Sciences

C. Seshadhri
University of California at Santa Cruz

Sahil Singla
Princeton University

Inbal Talgam-Cohen
Technion–Israel Institute of Technology

Salil Vadhan
Harvard University

Gregory Valiant
Stanford University

Paul Valiant
Brown University

Moshe Vardi
Rice University

Sergei Vassilvitskii
Google, Inc.

Aravindan Vijayaraghavan
Northwestern University

Meirav Zehavi
Ben-Gurion University of the Negev

CHAPTER ONE

Introduction

Tim Roughgarden

Abstract: One of the primary goals of the mathematical analysis of algorithms is to provide guidance about which algorithm is the "best" for solving a given computational problem. Worst-case analysis summarizes the performance profile of an algorithm by its worst performance on any input of a given size, implicitly advocating for the algorithm with the best-possible worst-case performance. Strong worst-case guarantees are the holy grail of algorithm design, providing an application-agnostic certification of an algorithm's robustly good performance. However, for many fundamental problems and performance measures, such guarantees are impossible and a more nuanced analysis approach is called for. This chapter surveys several alternatives to worst-case analysis that are discussed in detail later in the book.

1.1 The Worst-Case Analysis of Algorithms

1.1.1 Comparing Incomparable Algorithms

Comparing different algorithms is hard. For almost any pair of algorithms and measure of algorithm performance, each algorithm will perform better than the other on some inputs. For example, the MergeSort algorithm takes $\Theta(n \log n)$ time to sort length-n arrays, whether the input is already sorted or not, while the running time of the InsertionSort algorithm is $\Theta(n)$ on already-sorted arrays but $\Theta(n^2)$ in general.[1]

The difficulty is not specific to running time analysis. In general, consider a computational problem Π and a performance measure PERF, with PERF(A, z) quantifying the "performance" of an algorithm A for Π on an input $z \in \Pi$. For example, Π could be the Traveling Salesman Problem (TSP), A could be a polynomial-time heuristic for the problem, and PERF(A, z) could be the approximation ratio of A – i.e., the ratio of the lengths of A's output tour and an optimal tour – on the TSP instance z.[2]

---

[1] A quick reminder about asymptotic notation in the analysis of algorithms: for nonnegative real-valued functions $T(n)$ and $f(n)$ defined on the natural numbers, we write $T(n) = O(f(n))$ if there are positive constants c and n_0 such that $T(n) \leq c \cdot f(n)$ for all $n \geq n_0$; $T(n) = \Omega(f(n))$ if there exist positive c and n_0 with $T(n) \geq c \cdot f(n)$ for all $n \geq n_0$; and $T(n) = \Theta(f(n))$ if $T(n)$ is both $O(f(n))$ and $\Omega(f(n))$.

[2] In the Traveling Salesman Problem, the input is a complete undirected graph (V, E) with a nonnegative cost $c(v, w)$ for each edge $(v, w) \in E$, and the goal is to compute an ordering $v_1, v_2, \ldots, v_n$ of the vertices V that minimizes the length $\sum_{i=1}^{n} c(v_i, v_{i+1})$ of the corresponding tour (with v_{n+1} interpreted as v_1).

Or Π could be the problem of testing primality, A a randomized polynomial-time primality-testing algorithm, and $\text{PERF}(A, z)$ the probability (over A's internal randomness) that the algorithm correctly decides if the positive integer z is prime. In general, when two algorithms have incomparable performance, how can we deem one of them "better than" the other?

Worst-case analysis is a specific modeling choice in the analysis of algorithms, in which the performance profile $\{\text{PERF}(A, z)\}_{z \in \Pi}$ of an algorithm is summarized by its worst performance on any input of a given size (i.e., $\min_{z : |z| = n} \text{PERF}(A, z)$ or $\max_{z : |z| = n} \text{PERF}(A, z)$, depending on the measure, where $|z|$ denotes the size of the input z). The "better" algorithm is then the one with superior worst-case performance. MergeSort, with its worst-case asymptotic running time of $\Theta(n \log n)$ for length-n arrays, is better in this sense than InsertionSort, which has a worst-case running time of $\Theta(n^2)$.

1.1.2 Benefits of Worst-Case Analysis

While crude, worst-case analysis can be tremendously useful and, for several reasons, it has been the dominant paradigm for algorithm analysis in theoretical computer science.

1. A good worst-case guarantee is the best-case scenario for an algorithm, certifying its general-purpose utility and absolving its users from understanding which inputs are most relevant to their applications. Thus worst-case analysis is particularly well suited for "general-purpose" algorithms that are expected to work well across a range of application domains (such as the default sorting routine of a programming language).
2. Worst-case analysis is often more analytically tractable to carry out than its alternatives, such as average-case analysis with respect to a probability distribution over inputs.
3. For a remarkable number of fundamental computational problems, there are algorithms with excellent worst-case performance guarantees. For example, the lion's share of an undergraduate algorithms course comprises algorithms that run in linear or near-linear time in the worst case.[3]

1.1.3 Goals of the Analysis of Algorithms

Before critiquing the worst-case analysis approach, it's worth taking a step back to clarify why we want rigorous methods to reason about algorithm performance. There are at least three possible goals:

1. *Performance prediction.* The first goal is to explain or predict the empirical performance of algorithms. In some cases, the analyst acts as a natural scientist, taking an observed phenomenon such as "the simplex method for linear programming is fast" as ground truth, and seeking a transparent mathematical model that explains it. In others, the analyst plays the role of an engineer, seeking a theory that

---

[3] Worst-case analysis is also the dominant paradigm in complexity theory, where it has led to the development of NP-completeness and many other fundamental concepts.

gives accurate advice about whether or not an algorithm will perform well in an application of interest.

2. *Identify optimal algorithms.* The second goal is to rank different algorithms according to their performance, and ideally to single out one algorithm as "optimal." At the very least, given two algorithms A and B for the same problem, a method for algorithmic analysis should offer an opinion about which one is "better."

3. *Develop new algorithms.* The third goal is to provide a well-defined framework in which to brainstorm new algorithms. Once a measure of algorithm performance has been declared, the Pavlovian response of most computer scientists is to seek out new algorithms that improve on the state-of-the-art with respect to this measure. The focusing effect catalyzed by such yardsticks should not be underestimated.

When proving or interpreting results in algorithm design and analysis, it's important to be clear in one's mind about which of these goals the work is trying to achieve.

What's the report card for worst-case analysis with respect to these three goals?

1. Worst-case analysis gives an accurate performance prediction only for algorithms that exhibit little variation in performance across inputs of a given size. This is the case for many of the greatest hits of algorithms covered in an undergraduate course, including the running times of near-linear-time algorithms and of many canonical dynamic programming algorithms. For many more complex problems, however, the predictions of worst-case analysis are overly pessimistic (see Section 1.2).

2. For the second goal, worst-case analysis earns a middling grade – it gives good advice about which algorithm to use for some important problems (such as many of those in an undergraduate course) and bad advice for others (see Section 1.2).

3. Worst-case analysis has served as a tremendously useful brainstorming organizer. For more than a half-century, researchers striving to optimize worst-case algorithm performance have been led to thousands of new algorithms, many of them practically useful.

1.2 Famous Failures and the Need for Alternatives

For many problems a bit beyond the scope of an undergraduate course, the downside of worst-case analysis rears its ugly head. This section reviews four famous examples in which worst-case analysis gives misleading or useless advice about how to solve a problem. These examples motivate the alternatives to worst-case analysis that are surveyed in Section 1.4 and described in detail in later chapters of the book.

1.2.1 The Simplex Method for Linear Programming

Perhaps the most famous failure of worst-case analysis concerns linear programming, the problem of optimizing a linear function subject to linear constraints (Figure 1.1). Dantzig proposed in the 1940s an algorithm for solving linear programs called the *simplex method*. The simplex method solves linear programs using greedy local

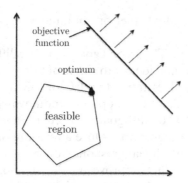

Figure 1.1 A two-dimensional linear programming problem.

search on the vertices of the solution set boundary, and variants of it remain in wide use to this day. The enduring appeal of the simplex method stems from its consistently superb performance in practice. Its running time typically scales modestly with the input size, and it routinely solves linear programs with millions of decision variables and constraints. This robust empirical performance suggested that the simplex method might well solve every linear program in a polynomial amount of time.

Klee and Minty (1972) showed by example that there are contrived linear programs that force the simplex method to run in time exponential in the number of decision variables (for all of the common "pivot rules" for choosing the next vertex). This illustrates the first potential pitfall of worst-case analysis: overly pessimistic performance predictions that cannot be taken at face value. The running time of the simplex method is polynomial for all practical purposes, despite the exponential prediction of worst-case analysis.

To add insult to injury, the first worst-case polynomial-time algorithm for linear programming, the ellipsoid method, is not competitive with the simplex method in practice.[4] Taken at face value, worst-case analysis recommends the ellipsoid method over the empirically superior simplex method. One framework for narrowing the gap between these theoretical predictions and empirical observations is *smoothed analysis*, the subject of Part Four of this book; see Section 1.4.4 for an overview.

1.2.2 Clustering and *NP*-Hard Optimization Problems

Clustering is a form of unsupervised learning (finding patterns in unlabeled data), where the informal goal is to partition a set of points into "coherent groups" (Figure 1.2). One popular way to coax this goal into a well-defined computational problem is to posit a numerical objective function over clusterings of the point set, and then seek the clustering with the best objective function value. For example, the goal could be to choose k cluster centers to minimize the sum of the distances between points and their nearest centers (the k-median objective) or the sum of the squared

---

[4] Interior-point methods, developed five years later, led to algorithms that both run in worst-case polynomial time and are competitive with the simplex method in practice.

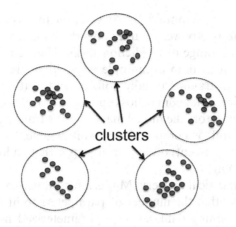

Figure 1.2 A sensible clustering of a set of points.

such distances (the k-means objective). Almost all natural optimization problems that are defined over clusterings are NP-hard.[5]

In practice, clustering is not viewed as a particularly difficult problem. Lightweight clustering algorithms, such as Lloyd's algorithm for k-means and its variants, regularly return the intuitively "correct" clusterings of real-world point sets. How can we reconcile the worst-case intractability of clustering problems with the empirical success of relatively simple algorithms?[6]

One possible explanation is that *clustering is hard only when it doesn't matter*. For example, if the difficult instances of an NP-hard clustering problem look like a bunch of random unstructured points, who cares? The common use case for a clustering algorithm is for points that represent images, or documents, or proteins, or some other objects where a "meaningful clustering" is likely to exist. Could instances with a meaningful clustering be easier than worst-case instances? Part Three of this book covers recent theoretical developments that support an affirmative answer; see Section 1.4.2 for an overview.

1.2.3 The Unreasonable Effectiveness of Machine Learning

The unreasonable effectiveness of modern machine learning algorithms has thrown the gauntlet down to researchers in algorithm analysis, and there is perhaps no other problem domain that calls out as loudly for a "beyond worst-case" approach.

To illustrate some of the challenges, consider a canonical supervised learning problem, where a learning algorithm is given a data set of object-label pairs and the goal is to produce a classifier that accurately predicts the label of as-yet-unseen objects

---

[5] Recall that a polynomial-time algorithm for an NP-hard problem would yield a polynomial-time algorithm for every problem in NP – for every problem with efficiently verifiable solutions. Assuming the widely believed $P \neq NP$ conjecture, every algorithm for an NP-hard problem either returns an incorrect answer for some inputs or runs in super-polynomial time for some inputs (or both).

[6] More generally, optimization problems are more likely to be NP-hard than polynomial-time solvable. In many cases, even computing an approximately optimal solution is an NP-hard problem. Whenever an efficient algorithm for such a problem performs better on real-world instances than (worst-case) complexity theory would suggest, there's an opportunity for a refined and more accurate theoretical analysis.

(e.g., whether or not an image contains a cat). Over the past decade, aided by massive data sets and computational power, neural networks have achieved impressive levels of performance across a range of prediction tasks. Their empirical success flies in the face of conventional wisdom in multiple ways. First, there is a computational mystery: Neural network training usually boils down to fitting parameters (weights and biases) to minimize a nonconvex loss function, for example, to minimize the number of classification errors the model makes on the training set. In the past such problems were written off as computationally intractable, but first-order methods (i.e., variants of gradient descent) often converge quickly to a local optimum or even to a global optimum. Why?

Second, there is a statistical mystery: Modern neural networks are typically over-parameterized, meaning that the number of parameters to fit is considerably larger than the size of the training data set. Overparameterized models are vulnerable to large generalization error (i.e., overfitting), since they can effectively memorize the training data without learning anything that helps classify as-yet-unseen data points. Nevertheless, state-of-the-art neural networks generalize shockingly well – why? The answer likely hinges on special properties of both real-world data sets and the optimization algorithms used for neural network training (principally stochastic gradient descent). Part Five of this book covers the state-of-the-art explanations of these and other mysteries in the empirical performance of machine learning algorithms.

The beyond worst-case viewpoint can also contribute to machine learning by "stress-testing" the existing theory and providing a road map for more robust guarantees. While work in beyond worst-case analysis makes strong assumptions relative to the norm in theoretical computer science, these assumptions are usually weaker than the norm in statistical machine learning. Research in the latter field often resembles average-case analysis, for example, when data points are modeled as independent and identically distributed samples from some underlying structured distribution. The semirandom models described in Parts Three and Four of this book serve as role models for blending adversarial and average-case modeling to encourage the design of algorithms with robustly good performance.

1.2.4 Analysis of Online Algorithms

Online algorithms are algorithms that must process their input as it arrives over time. For example, consider the online paging problem, where there is a system with a small fast memory (the cache) and a big slow memory. Data are organized into blocks called *pages*, with up to k different pages fitting in the cache at once. A page request results in either a cache hit (if the page is already in the cache) or a cache miss (if not). On a cache miss, the requested page must be brought into the cache. If the cache is already full, then some page in it must be evicted. A cache replacement policy is an algorithm for making these eviction decisions. Any systems textbook will recommend aspiring to the Least Recently Used (LRU) policy, which evicts the page whose most recent reference is furthest in the past. The same textbook will explain why: Real-world page request sequences tend to exhibit locality of reference, meaning that recently requested pages are likely to be requested again soon. The LRU policy uses the recent past as a prediction for the near future. Empirically, it typically suffers fewer cache misses than competing policies like First-In First-Out (FIFO).

Worst-case analysis, straightforwardly applied, provides no useful insights about the performance of different cache replacement policies. For every deterministic policy and cache size k, there is a pathological page request sequence that triggers a page fault rate of 100%, even though the optimal clairvoyant replacement policy (known as Bélády's furthest-in-the-future algorithm) would have a page fault rate of at most $1/k$ (Exercise 1.1). This observation is troublesome both for its absurdly pessimistic performance prediction and for its failure to differentiate between competing replacement policies (such as LRU vs. FIFO). One solution, described in Section 1.3, is to choose an appropriately fine-grained parameterization of the input space and to assess and compare algorithms using parameterized guarantees.

1.2.5 The Cons of Worst-Case Analysis

We should celebrate the fact that worst-case analysis works so well for so many fundamental computational problems, while at the same time recognizing that the cherrypicked successes highlighted in undergraduate algorithms can paint a potentially misleading picture about the range of its practical relevance. The preceding four examples highlight the chief weaknesses of the worst-case analysis framework.

1. *Overly pessimistic performance predictions.* By design, worst-case analysis gives a pessimistic estimate of an algorithm's empirical performance. In the preceding four examples, the gap between the two is embarrassingly large.
2. *Can rank algorithms inaccurately.* Overly pessimistic performance summaries can derail worst-case analysis from identifying the right algorithm to use in practice. In the online paging problem, it cannot distinguish between the FIFO and LRU policies; for linear programming, it implicitly suggests that the ellipsoid method is superior to the simplex method.
3. *No data model.* If worst-case analysis has an implicit model of data, then it's the "Murphy's Law" data model, where the instance to be solved is an adversarially selected function of the chosen algorithm.[7] Outside of security applications, this algorithm-dependent model of data is a rather paranoid and incoherent way to think about a computational problem.

   In many applications, the algorithm of choice is superior precisely because of properties of data in the application domain, such as meaningful solutions in clustering problems or locality of reference in online paging. Pure worst-case analysis provides no language for articulating such domain-specific properties of data. In this sense, the strength of worst-case analysis is also its weakness.

These drawbacks show the importance of alternatives to worst-case analysis, in the form of models that articulate properties of "relevant" inputs and algorithms that possess rigorous and meaningful algorithmic guarantees for inputs with these properties. Research in "beyond worst-case analysis" is a conversation between models and algorithms, with each informing the development of the other. It has both a scientific dimension, where the goal is to formulate transparent mathematical

---

[7] Murphy's Law: If anything can go wrong, it will.

models that explain empirically observed phenomena about algorithm performance, and an engineering dimension, where the goals are to provide accurate guidance about which algorithm to use for a problem and to design new algorithms that perform particularly well on the relevant inputs.

Concretely, what might a result that goes "beyond worst-case analysis" look like? The next section covers in detail an exemplary result by Albers et al. (2005) for the online paging problem introduced in Section 1.2.4. The rest of the book offers dozens of further examples.

1.3 Example: Parameterized Bounds in Online Paging

1.3.1 Parameterizing by Locality of Reference

Returning to the online paging example in Section 1.2.4, perhaps we shouldn't be surprised that worst-case analysis fails to advocate LRU over FIFO. The empirical superiority of LRU is due to the special structure in real-world page request sequences (locality of reference), which is outside the language of pure worst-case analysis.

The key idea for obtaining meaningful performance guarantees for and comparisons between online paging algorithms is to parameterize page request sequences according to how much locality of reference they exhibit, and then prove parameterized worst-case guarantees. Refining worst-case analysis in this way leads to dramatically more informative results. Part One of the book describes many other applications of such fine-grained input parameterizations; see Section 1.4.1 for an overview.

How should we measure locality in a page request sequence? One tried and true method is the *working set* model, which is parameterized by a function f from the positive integers $\mathbb{N}$ to $\mathbb{N}$ that describes how many different page requests are possible in a window of a given length. Formally, we say that a page sequence σ *conforms to f* if for every positive integer n and every set of n consecutive page requests in σ, there are requests for at most $f(n)$ distinct pages. For example, the identity function $f(n) = n$ imposes no restrictions on the page request sequence. A sequence can only conform to a sublinear function like $f(n) = \lceil \sqrt{n} \rceil$ or $f(n) = \lceil 1 + \log_2 n \rceil$ if it exhibits locality of reference.[8] We can assume without loss of generality that $f(1) = 1, f(2) = 2$, and $f(n + 1) \in \{f(n), f(n) + 1\}$ for all n (Exercise 1.2).

We adopt as our performance measure $\mathrm{PERF}(A, z)$ the fault rate of an online algorithm A on the page request sequence z – the fraction of requests in z on which A suffers a page fault. We next state a performance guarantee for the fault rate of the LRU policy with a cache size of k that is parameterized by a number $\alpha_f(k) \in [0, 1]$. The parameter $\alpha_f(k)$ is defined below in (1.1); intuitively, it will be close to 0 for slow-growing functions f (i.e., functions that impose strong locality of reference) and close to 1 for functions f that grow quickly (e.g., near-linearly). This performance guarantee requires that the function f is *approximately concave* in the sense that the number m_y of inputs with value y under f (that is, $|f^{-1}(y)|$) is nondecreasing in y (Figure 1.3).

---

[8] The notation $\lceil x \rceil$ means the number x, rounded up to the nearest integer.

$$
\begin{array}{c|ccccccccc}
f(n) & 1 & 2 & 3 & 3 & 4 & 4 & 4 & 5 & \cdots \\
\hline
n & 1 & 2 & 3 & 4 & 5 & 6 & 7 & 8 & \cdots
\end{array}
$$

Figure 1.3 An approximately concave function, with $m_1 = 1$, $m_2 = 1$, $m_3 = 2$, $m_4 = 3, \ldots$

Theorem 1.1 (Albers et al., 2005) *With $\alpha_f(k)$ defined as in (1.1) below:*

(a) For every approximately concave function f, cache size $k \geq 2$, and deterministic cache replacement policy, there are arbitrarily long page request sequences conforming to f for which the policy's page fault rate is at least $\alpha_f(k)$.

(b) For every approximately concave function f, cache size $k \geq 2$, and page request sequence that conforms to f, the page fault rate of the LRU policy is at most $\alpha_f(k)$ plus an additive term that goes to 0 with the sequence length.

(c) There exists a choice of an approximately concave function f, a cache size $k \geq 2$, and an arbitrarily long page request sequence that conforms to f, such that the page fault rate of the FIFO policy is bounded away from $\alpha_f(k)$.

Parts (a) and (b) prove the worst-case optimality of the LRU policy in a strong and fine-grained sense, f-by-f and k-by-k. Part (c) differentiates LRU from FIFO, as the latter is suboptimal for some (in fact, many) choices of f and k.

The guarantees in Theorem 1.1 are so good that they are meaningful even when taken at face value – for strongly sublinear f's, $\alpha_f(k)$ goes to 0 reasonably quickly with k. The precise definition of $\alpha_f(k)$ for $k \geq 2$ is

$$
\alpha_f(k) = \frac{k-1}{f^{-1}(k+1) - 2}, \tag{1.1}
$$

where we abuse notation and interpret $f^{-1}(y)$ as the smallest value of x such that $f(x) = y$. That is, $f^{-1}(y)$ denotes the smallest window length in which page requests for y distinct pages might appear. As expected, for the function $f(n) = n$ we have $\alpha_f(k) = 1$ for all k. (With no restriction on the input sequence, an adversary can force a 100% fault rate.) If $f(n) = \lceil \sqrt{n} \rceil$, however, then $\alpha_f(k)$ scales with $1/\sqrt{k}$. Thus with a cache size of 10,000, the page fault rate is always at most 1%. If $f(n) = \lceil 1 + \log_2 n \rceil$, then $\alpha_f(k)$ goes to 0 even faster with k, roughly as $k/2^k$.

1.3.2 Proof of Theorem 1.1

This section proves the first two parts of Theorem 1.1; part (c) is left as Exercise 1.4.

Part (a). To prove the lower bound in part (a), fix an approximately concave function f and a cache size $k \geq 2$. Fix a deterministic cache replacement policy A.

We construct a page sequence σ that uses only $k+1$ distinct pages, so at any given time step there is exactly one page missing from the algorithm's cache. (Assume that the algorithm begins with the first k pages in its cache.) The sequence comprises $k-1$ blocks, where the jth block consists of m_{j+1} consecutive requests for the same page p_j, where p_j is the unique page missing from the algorithm A's cache at the start of the

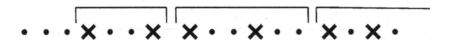

Figure 1.4 Blocks of $k - 1$ faults, for $k = 3$.

block. (Recall that m_y is the number of values of x such that $f(x) = y$.) This sequence conforms to f (Exercise 1.3).

By the choice of the p_j's, A incurs a page fault on the first request of a block, and not on any of the other (duplicate) requests of that block. Thus, algorithm A suffers exactly $k - 1$ page faults.

The length of the page request sequence is $m_2 + m_3 + \cdots + m_k$. Because $m_1 = 1$, this sum equals $(\sum_{j=1}^{k} m_j) - 1$ which, using the definition of the m_j's, equals $(f^{-1}(k + 1) - 1) - 1 = f^{-1}(k+1) - 2$. The algorithm's page fault rate on this sequence matches the definition (1.1) of $\alpha_f(k)$, as required. More generally, repeating the construction over and over again produces arbitrarily long page request sequences for which the algorithm has page fault rate $\alpha_f(k)$.

Part (b). To prove a matching upper bound for the LRU policy, fix an approximately concave function f, a cache size $k \geq 2$, and a sequence σ that conforms to f. Our fault rate target $\alpha_f(k)$ is a major clue to the proof (recall (1.1)): we should be looking to partition the sequence σ into blocks of length at least $f^{-1}(k + 1) - 2$ such that each block has at most $k - 1$ faults. So consider groups of $k - 1$ consecutive faults of the LRU policy on σ. Each such group defines a *block*, beginning with the first fault of the group, and ending with the page request that immediately precedes the beginning of the next group of faults (see Figure 1.4).

> **Claim** Consider a block other than the first or last. Consider the page requests in this block, together with the requests immediately before and after this block. These requests are for at least $k + 1$ distinct pages.

The claim immediately implies that every block contains at least $f^{-1}(k + 1) - 2$ requests. Because there are $k - 1$ faults per block, this shows that the page fault rate is at most $\alpha_f(k)$ (ignoring the vanishing additive error due to the first and last blocks), proving Theorem 1.1(b).

We proceed to the proof of the claim. Note that, in light of Theorem 1.1(c), it is essential that the proof uses properties of the LRU policy not shared by FIFO. Fix a block other than the first or last, and let p be the page requested immediately prior to this block. This request could have been a page fault, or not (cf., Figure 1.4). In any case, p is in the cache when this block begins. Consider the $k - 1$ faults contained in the block, together with the kth fault that occurs immediately after the block. We consider three cases.

First, if the k faults occurred on distinct pages that are all different from p, we have identified our $k + 1$ distinct requests (p and the k faults). For the second case, suppose that two of the k faults were for the same page $q \neq p$. How could this have happened? The page q was brought into the cache after the first fault on q and was not evicted until there were k requests for distinct pages other than q after this page fault. This gives $k + 1$ distinct page requests (q and the k other distinct requests between the two faults on q). Finally, suppose that one of these k faults was on the page p. Because p was requested just before the first of these faults, the LRU algorithm, subsequent to this request and prior to evicting p, must have received requests for k distinct pages other than p. These requests, together with that for p, give the desired $k + 1$ distinct page requests.[9]

1.3.3 Discussion

Theorem 1.1 is an example of a "parameterized analysis" of an algorithm, where the performance guarantee is expressed as a function of parameters of the input other than its size. A parameter like $\alpha_f(k)$ measures the "easiness" of an input, much like matrix condition numbers in linear algebra. We will see many more examples of parameterized analyses later in the book.

There are several reasons to aspire toward parameterized performance guarantees.

1. A parameterized guarantee is a mathematically stronger statement, containing strictly more information about an algorithm's performance than a worst-case guarantee parameterized solely by the input size.
2. A parameterized analysis can explain why an algorithm has good "real-world" performance even when its worst-case performance is poor. The approach is to first show that the algorithm performs well for "easy" values of the parameter (e.g., for f and k such that $\alpha_f(k)$ is close to 0), and then make a case that "real-world" instances are "easy" in this sense (e.g., have enough locality of reference to conform to a function f with a small value of $\alpha_f(k)$). The latter argument can be made empirically (e.g., by computing the parameter on representative benchmarks) or mathematically (e.g., by positing a generative model and proving that it typically generates easy inputs). Results in smoothed analysis (see Section 1.4.4 and Part Four) typically follow this two-step approach.
3. A parameterized performance guarantee suggests when – for which inputs, and which application domains – a given algorithm should be used. (Namely, on the inputs where the performance of the algorithm is good!) Such advice is useful to someone who has no time or interest in developing their own algorithm from scratch, and merely wishes to be an educated client of existing algorithms.[10]
4. Fine-grained performance characterizations can differentiate algorithms when worst-case analysis cannot (as with LRU vs. FIFO).
5. Formulating a good parameter often forces the analyst to articulate a form of structure in data, like the "amount of locality" in a page request sequence. Ideas for new algorithms that explicitly exploit such structure often follow soon thereafter.[11]

---

[9] The first two arguments apply also to the FIFO policy, but the third does not. Suppose p was already in the cache when it was requested just prior to the block. Under FIFO, this request does not "reset p's clock"; if it was originally brought into the cache long ago, FIFO might well evict p on the block's very first fault.

[10] For a familiar example, parameterizing the running time of graph algorithms by both the number of vertices and the number of edges provides guidance about which algorithms should be used for sparse graphs and which ones for dense graphs.

[11] The parameter $\alpha_f(k)$ showed up only in our *analysis* of the LRU policy; in other applications, the chosen parameter also guides the *design* of algorithms for the problem.

Useful parameters come in several flavors. The parameter $\alpha_f(k)$ in Theorem 1.1 is derived directly from the input to the problem, and later chapters contain many more examples of such input-based parameters. It is also common to parameterize algorithm performance by properties of an optimal solution. In parameterized algorithms (Chapter 2), the most well-studied such parameter is the size of an optimal solution. Another solution-based parameterization, popular in machine learning applications, is by the "margin," meaning the extent to which the optimal solution is particularly "pronounced"; see Exercise 1.7 for the canonical example of the analysis of the perceptron algorithm.

"Input size" is well defined for every computational problem, and this is one of the reasons why performance guarantees parameterized by input size are so ubiquitous. By contrast, the parameter $\alpha_f(k)$ used in Theorem 1.1 is specifically tailored to the online paging problem; in exchange, the performance guarantee is unusually accurate and meaningful. Alas, there are no silver bullets in parameterized analysis, or in algorithm analysis more generally, and the most enlightening analysis approach is often problem specific. Worst-case analysis can inform the choice of an appropriate analysis framework for a problem by highlighting the problem's most difficult (and often unrealistic) instances.

1.4 Overview of the Book

This book has six parts, four on "core theory" and two on "applications." Each of the following sections summarizes the chapters in one of the parts.

1.4.1 Refinements of Worst-Case Analysis

Part One of the book hews closest to traditional worst-case analysis. No assumptions are imposed on the input; as in worst-case analysis, there is no commitment to a "model of data." The innovative ideas in these chapters concern novel and problem-specific ways of expressing algorithm performance. Our online paging example (Section 1.3) falls squarely in this domain.

Chapter 2, by Fomin, Lokshtanov, Saurabh, and Zehavi, provides an overview of the relatively mature field of *parameterized algorithms*. The goal here is to understand how the running time of algorithms and the complexity of computational problems depend on parameters other than the input size. For example, for which NP-hard problems Π and parameters k is Π "fixed-parameter tractable" with respect to k, meaning solvable in time $f(k) \cdot n^{O(1)}$ for some function f that is independent of the input size n? The field has developed a number of powerful approaches to designing fixed-parameter tractable algorithms, as well as lower bound techniques for ruling out the existence of such algorithms (under appropriate complexity assumptions).

Chapter 3, by Barbay, searches for instance-optimal algorithms that for every input perform better than every other algorithm (up to a constant factor). Such an input-by-input guarantee is essentially the strongest notion of optimality one could hope for. Remarkably, there are several fundamental problems, for example, in low-dimensional computational geometry, that admit instance-optimal algorithms. Proofs of instance optimality involve input-by-input matching upper and lower bounds, and this typically requires a very fine-grained parameterization of the input space.

Chapter 4, by Roughgarden, concerns *resource augmentation*. This concept makes sense for problems that have a natural notion of a "resource," with the performance of an algorithm improving as it is given more resources. Examples include the size of a cache (with larger caches leading to fewer faults), the capacity of a network (with higher-capacity networks leading to less congestion), and the speed of a processor (with faster processors leading to earlier job completion times). A resource augmentation guarantee then states that the performance of an algorithm of interest is always close to that achieved by an all-powerful algorithm that is handicapped by slightly less resources.

1.4.2 Deterministic Models of Data

Part Two of the book proposes deterministic models of data for several NP-hard clustering and sparse recovery problems, which effectively posit conditions that are conceivably satisfied by "real-world" inputs. This work fits into the long-standing tradition of identifying "islands of tractability," meaning polynomial-time solvable special cases of NP-hard problems. Twentieth-century research on tractable special cases focused primarily on syntactic and easily checked restrictions (e.g., graph planarity or Horn satisfiability). The chapters in Part Two and some of the related application chapters consider conditions that are not necessarily easy to check, but for which there is a plausible narrative about why "real-world instances" might satisfy them, at least approximately.

Chapter 5, by Makarychev and Makarychev, studies *perturbation stability* in several different computational problems. A perturbation-stable instance satisfies a property that is effectively a uniqueness condition on steroids, stating that the optimal solution remains invariant to sufficiently small perturbations of the numbers in the input. The larger the perturbations that are tolerated, the stronger the condition on the instance and the easier the computational problem. Many problems have "stability thresholds," an allowable perturbation size at which the complexity of the problem switches suddenly from NP-hard to polynomial-time solvable. To the extent that we're comfortable identifying "instances with a meaningful clustering" with perturbation-stable instances, the positive results in this chapter give a precise sense in which clustering is hard only when it doesn't matter (cf. Section 1.2.2). As a bonus, many of these positive results are achieved by algorithms that resemble popular approaches in practice, such as single-linkage clustering and local search.

Chapter 6, by Blum, proposes an alternative condition called *approximation stability*, stating that every solution with a near-optimal objective function value closely resembles the optimal solution. That is, any solution that is structurally different from the optimal solution has significantly worse objective function value. This condition is particularly appropriate for problems like clustering, in which the objective function is only means to an end and the real goal is to recover some type of "ground-truth" clustering. This chapter demonstrates that many NP-hard problems become provably easier for approximation-stable instances.

Chapter 7, by Price, provides a glimpse of the vast literature on *sparse recovery*, where the goal is to reverse engineer a "sparse" object from a small number of clues about it. This area is more strongly associated with applied mathematics than with theoretical computer science and algorithms, but there are compelling parallels between it and the topics of the preceding two chapters. For example, consider the canonical problem in compressive sensing, in which the goal is to recover an unknown sparse signal z (a vector of length n) from a small number m of linear measurements of it. If z can be arbitrary, then the problem is hopeless unless $m = n$. But many real-world signals have most of their mass concentrated on k coordinates for small k (for an appropriate basis), and the results surveyed in this chapter show that, for such "natural" signals, the problem can be solved efficiently even when m is only modestly bigger than k (and much smaller than n).

1.4.3 Semirandom Models

Part Three of the book is about *semirandom models* – hybrids of worst- and average-case analysis in which nature and an adversary collaborate to produce an instance of a problem. For many problems, such hybrid frameworks are a "sweet spot" for algorithm analysis, with the worst-case dimension encouraging the design of robustly good algorithms and the average-case dimension allowing for strong provable guarantees.

Chapter 8, by Roughgarden, sets the stage with a review of pure average-case or *distributional analysis*, along with some of its killer applications and biggest weaknesses. Work in this area adopts a specific probability distribution over the inputs of a problem, and analyzes the expectation (or some other statistic) of the performance of an algorithm with respect to this distribution. One use of distributional analysis is to show that a general-purpose algorithm has good performance on non-pathological inputs (e.g., deterministic QuickSort on randomly ordered arrays). One key drawback of distributional analysis is that it can encourage the design of algorithms that are brittle and overly tailored to the assumed input distribution. The semirandom models of the subsequent chapters are designed to ameliorate this issue.

Chapter 9, by Feige, introduces several *planted models* and their semirandom counterparts. For example, in the planted clique problem, a clique of size k is planted in an otherwise uniformly random graph. How large does k need to be, as a function of the number of vertices, before the planted clique can be recovered in polynomial time (with high probability)? In a semi-random version of a planted model, an adversary can modify the random input in a restricted way. For example, in the clique problem, an adversary might be allowed to remove edges not in the clique; such changes intuitively make the planted clique only "more obviously optimal," but nevertheless can foil overly simplistic algorithms. One rule of thumb that emerges from this line of work, and also recurs in the next chapter, is that spectral algorithms tend to work well for planted models but the heavier machinery of semidefinite programming seems required for their semirandom counterparts. This chapter also investigates random and semirandom models for Boolean formulas, including refutation algorithms that certify that a given input formula is not satisfiable.

Chapter 10, by Moitra, drills down on a specific and extensively studied planted model, the *stochastic block model*. The vertices of a graph are partitioned into groups, and each potential edge of the graph is present independently with a probability that depends only on the groups that contain its endpoints. The algorithmic goal is to recover the groups from the (unlabeled) graph. One important special case is the planted bisection problem, where the vertices are split into two equal-size sets A and B and each edge is present independently with probability p (if both endpoints are in the same group) or $q < p$ (otherwise). How big does the gap $p - q$ need to be before the planted bisection (A, B) can be recovered, either statistically (i.e., with unbounded computational power) or with a polynomial-time algorithm? When p and q are sufficiently small, the relevant goal becomes partial recovery, meaning a proposed classification of the vertices with accuracy better than random guessing. In the semirandom version of the model, an adversary can remove edges crossing the bisection and add edges internal to each of the groups. For partial recovery, this semirandom version is provably more difficult than the original model.

Chapter 11, by Gupta and Singla, describes results for a number of online algorithms in *random-order models*. These are semirandom models in which an adversary decides on an input, and nature then presents this input to an online algorithm, one piece at a time and in random order. The canonical example here is the secretary problem, where an arbitrary finite set of numbers is presented to an algorithm in random order, and the goal is to design a stopping rule with the maximum-possible probability of stopping on the largest number of the sequence. Analogous random-order models have proved useful for overcoming worst-case lower bounds for the online versions of a number of combinatorial optimization problems, including bin packing, facility location, and network design.

Chapter 12, by Seshadhri, is a survey of the field of *self-improving algorithms*. The goal here is to design an algorithm that, when presented with a sequence of independent samples drawn from an unknown input distribution, quickly converges to the optimal algorithm for that distribution. For example, for many distributions over length-n arrays, there are sorting algorithms that make less than $\Theta(n \log n)$ comparisons on average. Could there be a "master algorithm" that replicates the performance of a distribution-optimal sorter from only a limited number of samples from the distribution? This chapter gives a positive answer under the assumption that array entries are drawn independently (from possibly different distributions), along with analogous positive results for several fundamental problems in low-dimensional computational geometry.

1.4.4 Smoothed Analysis

Part Four of the book focuses on the semirandom models studied in *smoothed analysis*. In smoothed analysis, an adversary chooses an arbitrary input, and this input is then perturbed slightly by nature. The performance of an algorithm is then assessed by its worst-case expected performance, where the worst case is over the adversary's input choice and the expectation is over the random perturbation. This analysis framework can be applied to any problem where "small random perturbations" make sense, including most problems with real-valued inputs. It can be applied to any measure of algorithm performance, but has proven most effective for running time analyses of algorithms that seem to run in super-polynomial time only on highly contrived inputs (like the simplex method). As with other semirandom models, smoothed analysis has the benefit of potentially escaping worst-case inputs, especially if they are "isolated" in the input space, while avoiding overfitting a solution to a specific distributional assumption. There is also a plausible narrative about why "real-world" inputs are captured by this framework: Whatever problem you'd like to solve, there are inevitable inaccuracies in its formulation from measurement errors, uncertainty, and so on.

Chapter 13, by Manthey, details several applications of smoothed analysis to the *analysis of local search algorithms* for combinatorial optimization problems. For example, the 2-opt heuristic for the Traveling Salesman Problem is a local search algorithm that begins with an arbitrary tour and repeatedly improves the current solution using local moves that swap one pair of edges for another. In practice, local search algorithms such as the 2-opt heuristic almost always converge to a locally optimal solution in a small number of steps. Delicate constructions show that the 2-opt heuristic, and many other local search algorithms, require an exponential number of steps to converge in the worst case. The results in this chapter use smoothed analysis to narrow the gap between worst-case analysis and empirically observed performance, establishing that many local search algorithms (including the 2-opt heuristic) have polynomial smoothed complexity.

Chapter 14, by Dadush and Huiberts, surveys the first and most famous killer application of smoothed analysis, the Spielman–Teng analysis of the *running time of the simplex method* for linear programming. As discussed in Section 1.2.1, the running time of the simplex method is exponential in the worst case but almost always polynomial in practice. This chapter develops intuition for and outlines a proof of the fact that the simplex method, implemented with the shadow vertex pivot rule, has polynomial smoothed complexity with respect to small Gaussian perturbations of the entries of the constraint matrix. The chapter also shows how to interpret the successive shortest-path algorithm for the minimum-cost maximum-flow problem as an instantiation of this version of the simplex method.

Chapter 15, by Röglin, presents a third application of smoothed analysis, to the size of *Pareto curves for multiobjective optimization problems*. For example, consider the knapsack problem, where the input consists of n items with values and sizes. One subset of the items dominates another if it has both a larger overall value and a smaller overall size, and the Pareto curve is defined as the set of undominated solutions. Pareto curves matter for algorithm design because many algorithms for multiobjective optimization problems (such as the Nemhauser–Ullmann knapsack algorithm) run in time polynomial in the size of the Pareto curve. For many problems, the Pareto curve has exponential size in the worst case but expected polynomial size in a smoothed analysis model. This chapter also presents a satisfyingly strong connection between smoothed polynomial complexity and worst-case pseudopolynomial complexity for linear binary optimization problems.

1.4.5 Applications in Machine Learning and Statistics

Part Five of the book gives a number of examples of how the paradigms in Parts One–Four have been applied to problems in *machine learning and statistics*.

Chapter 16, by Balcan and Haghtalab, considers one of the most basic problems in supervised learning, that of *learning an unknown halfspace*. This problem is relatively easy in the noiseless case but becomes notoriously difficult in the worst case in the presence of adversarial noise. This chapter surveys a number of positive statistical and computational results for the problem under additional assumptions on the data-generating distribution. One type of assumption imposes structure, such as log-concavity, on the marginal distribution over data points (i.e., ignoring their labels). A second type restricts the power of the adversary that introduces the noise, for example, by allowing the adversary to mislabel a point only with a probability that is bounded away from $1/2$.

Chapter 17, by Diakonikolas and Kane, provides an overview of recent progress in *robust high-dimensional statistics*, where the goal is to design learning algorithms that have provable guarantees even when a small constant fraction of the data points has been adversarially corrupted. For example, consider the problem of estimating the mean μ of an unknown one-dimensional Gaussian distribution $\mathcal{N}(\mu, \sigma^2)$, where the input consists of $(1 - \epsilon)n$ samples from the distribution and ϵn additional points defined by an adversary. The empirical mean of the data points is a good estimator of the true mean when there is no adversary, but adversarial outliers can distort the empirical mean arbitrarily. The median of the input points, however, remains a good estimator of the true mean even with a small fraction of corrupted data points. What about in more than one dimension? Among other results, this chapter describes a robust and efficiently computable estimator for learning the mean of a high-dimensional Gaussian distribution.

Chapter 18, by Dasgupta and Kpotufe, investigates the twin topics of *nearest neighbor search and classification*. The former is algorithmic, and the goal is to design a data structure that enables fast nearest neighbor queries. The latter is statistical, and the goal is to understand the amount of data required before the nearest neighbor classifier enjoys provable accuracy guarantees. In both cases, novel parameterizations are the key to narrowing the gap between worst-case analysis and empirically observed performance – for search, a parameterization of the data set; for classification, of the allowable target functions.

Chapter 19, by Vijayaraghavan, is about computing a *low-rank tensor decomposition*. For example, given an $m \times n \times p$ 3-tensor with entries $\{T_{i,j,k}\}$, the goal is to express T as a linear combination of the minimum-possible number of rank-one tensors (where a rank-one tensor has entries of the form $\{u_i \cdot v_j \cdot w_k\}$ for some vectors $u \in \mathbb{R}^m$, $v \in \mathbb{R}^n$, and $w \in \mathbb{R}^p$). Efficient algorithms for this problem are an increasingly important tool in the design of learning algorithms; see also Chapters 20 and 21. This problem is NP-hard in general. Jennrich's algorithm solves in polynomial time the special case of the problem in which the three sets of vectors in the low-rank decomposition (the u's, the v's, and the w's) are linearly independent. This result does not address the overcomplete regime, meaning tensors that have rank larger than dimension. (Unlike matrices, the rank of a tensor can be much larger than its smallest dimension.) For this regime, the chapter shows that a generalization of Jennrich's algorithm has smoothed polynomial complexity.

Chapter 20, by Ge and Moitra, concerns *topic modeling*, which is a basic problem in unsupervised learning. The goal here is to process a large unlabeled corpus of documents and produce a list of meaningful topics and an assignment of each document to a mixture of topics. One approach to the problem is to reduce it to nonnegative matrix factorization (NMF) – the analogue of a singular value decomposition of a matrix, with the additional constraint that both matrix factors are nonnegative. The NMF problem is hard in general, but this chapter proposes a condition on inputs, which is reasonable in a topic modeling context, under which the problem can be solved quickly in both theory and practice. The key assumption is that each topic has at least one "anchor word," the presence of which strongly indicates that the document is at least partly about that topic.

Chapter 21, by Ma, studies the computational mystery outlined in Section 1.2.3: Why are *local methods* such as stochastic gradient descent so effective in solving the *nonconvex optimization* problems that arise in supervised learning, such as computing the loss-minimizing parameters for a given neural network architecture? This chapter surveys the quickly evolving state-of-the-art on this topic, including a number of different restrictions on problems under which local methods have provable guarantees. For example, some natural problems have a nonconvex objective function that satisfies the "strict saddle condition," which asserts that at every saddle point (i.e., a point with zero gradient that is neither a minimum nor a maximum) there is a direction with strictly negative curvature. Under this condition, variants of gradient descent provably converge to a local minimum (and, for some problems, a global minimum).

Chapter 22, by Hardt, tackles the statistical mystery discussed in Section 1.2.3: *Why do overparameterized models* such as deep neural networks, which have many more parameters than training data points, so often *generalize* well in practice? While the jury is still out, this chapter surveys several of the leading explanations for this phenomenon, ranging from properties of optimization algorithms such as stochastic gradient descent (including algorithmic stability and implicit regularization) to properties of data sets (such as margin-based guarantees).

Chapter 23, by G. Valiant and P. Valiant, presents two *instance optimality* results for *distribution testing and learning*. The chapter first considers the problem of learning a discretely supported distribution from independent samples, and describes an algorithm that learns the distribution nearly as accurately as would an optimal algorithm with advance knowledge of the true multiset of (unlabeled) probabilities of the distribution. This algorithm is instance optimal in the sense that, whatever the structure of the distribution, the learning algorithm will perform almost as well as an algorithm specifically tailored for that structure. The chapter then explores the problem of identity testing: Given the description of a reference probability distribution, $\mathbf{p}$, supported on a countable set, and sample access to an unknown distribution, $\mathbf{q}$, the goal is to distinguish whether $\mathbf{p} = \mathbf{q}$ versus the case that $\mathbf{p}$ and $\mathbf{q}$ have total variation distance at least ϵ. This chapter presents a testing algorithm that has optimal sample complexity simultaneously for every distribution $\mathbf{p}$ and ϵ, up to constant factors.

1.4.6 Further Applications

The final part of the book, Part Six, gathers a number of additional applications of the ideas and techniques introduced in Parts One–Three.

Chapter 24, by Karlin and Koutsoupias, surveys alternatives to worst-case analysis in the *competitive analysis of online algorithms*. There is a long tradition in online algorithms of exploring alternative analysis frameworks, and accordingly this chapter connects to many of the themes of Parts One–Three.[12] For example, the chapter includes results on deterministic models of data (e.g., the access graph model for restricting the allowable page request sequences) and semirandom models (e.g., the diffuse adversary model to blend worst- and average-case analysis).

---

[12] Indeed, the title of this book is a riff on that of a paper in the competitive analysis of online algorithms (Koutsoupias and Papadimitriou, 2000).

Chapter 25, by Ganesh and Vardi, explores the mysteries posed by the empirical performance of *Boolean satisfiability* (SAT) *solvers*. Solvers based on backtracking algorithms such as the Davis–Putnam–Logemann–Loveland (DPLL) algorithm frequently solve SAT instances with millions of variables and clauses in a reasonable amount of time. This chapter provides an introduction to conflict-driven clause-learning (CDCL) solvers and their connections to proof systems, followed by a high-level overview of the state-of-the-art parameterizations of SAT formulas, including input-based parameters (such as parameters derived from the variable-incidence graph of an instance) and output-based parameters (such as the proof complexity in the proof system associated with CDCL solvers).

Chapter 26, by Chung, Mitzenmacher, and Vadhan, uses ideas from pseudorandomness to explain *why simple hash functions work* so well in practice. Well-designed hash functions are practical proxies for random functions – simple enough to be efficiently implementable, but complex enough to "look random." In the theoretical analysis of hash functions and their applications, one generally assumes that a hash function is chosen at random from a restricted family, such as a set of universal or k-wise independent functions for small k. For some statistics, such as the expected number of collisions under a random hash function, small families of hash functions provably perform as well as completely random functions. For others, such as the expected insertion time in a hash table with linear probing, simple hash functions are provably worse than random functions (for worst-case data). The running theme of this chapter is that a little randomness in the data, in the form of a lower bound on the entropy of the (otherwise adversarial) data-generating distribution, compensates for any missing randomness in a universal family of hash functions.

Chapter 27, by Talgam-Cohen, presents an application of the beyond worst-case viewpoint in algorithmic game theory, to *prior-independent auctions*. For example, consider the problem of designing a single-item auction, which solicits bids from bidders and then decides which bidder (if any) wins the item and what everybody pays. The traditional approach in economics to designing revenue-maximizing auctions is average-case, meaning that the setup includes a commonly known distribution over each bidder's willingness to pay for the item. An auction designer can then implement an auction that maximizes the expected revenue with respect to the assumed distributions (e.g., by setting a distribution-dependent reserve price). As with many average-case frameworks, this approach can lead to impractical solutions that are overly tailored to the assumed distributions. A semirandom variant of the model allows an adversary to pick its favorite distribution out of a rich class, from which nature chooses a random sample for each bidder. This chapter presents prior-independent auctions, both with and without a type of resource augmentation, that achieve near-optimal expected revenue simultaneously across all distributions in the class.

Chapter 28, by Roughgarden and Seshadhri, takes a beyond worst-case approach to the *analysis of social networks*. Most research in social network analysis revolves around a collection of competing generative models – probability distributions over graphs designed to replicate the most common features observed in such networks. The results in this chapter dispense with generative models and instead provide algorithmic or structural guarantees under deterministic combinatorial restrictions on a graph – that is, for restricted classes of graphs. The restrictions are motivated by the most uncontroversial properties of social and information networks, such as heavy-tailed degree distributions and strong triadic closure properties. Results for these graph classes effectively apply to all "plausible" generative models of social networks.

Chapter 29, by Balcan, reports on the emerging area of *data-driven algorithm design*. The idea here is to model the problem of selecting the best-in-class algorithm for a given application domain as an offline or online learning problem, in the spirit of the aforementioned work on self-improving algorithms. For example, in the offline version of the problem, there is an unknown distribution D over inputs, a class C of allowable algorithms, and the goal is to identify from samples the algorithm in C with the best expected performance with respect to D. The distribution D captures the details of the application domain, the samples correspond to benchmark instances representative of the domain, and the restriction to the class C is a concession to the reality that it is often more practical to be an educated client of already-implemented algorithms than to design a new algorithm from scratch. For many computational problems and algorithm classes C, it is possible to learn an (almost) best-in-class algorithm from a modest number of representative instances.

Chapter 30, by Mitzenmacher and Vassilvitskii, is an introduction to *algorithms with predictions*. For example, in the online paging problem (Section 1.2.4), the LRU policy makes predictions about future page requests based on the recent past. If its predictions were perfect, the algorithm would be optimal. What if a good but imperfect predictor is available, such as one computed by a machine learning algorithm using past data? An ideal solution would be a generic online algorithm that, given a predictor as a "black box": (i) is optimal when predictions are perfect; (ii) has gracefully degrading performance as the predictor error increases; and (iii) with an arbitrarily poor predictor, defaults to the optimal worst-case guarantee. This chapter investigates the extent to which properties (i)–(iii) can be achieved by predictor-augmented data structures and algorithms for several different problems.

1.5 Notes

This chapter is based in part on Roughgarden (2019).

The simplex method (Section 1.2.1) is described, for example, in Dantzig (1963); Khachiyan (1979) proved that the ellipsoid method solves linear programming problems in polynomial time; and the first polynomial-time interior-point method was developed by Karmarkar (1984). Lloyd's algorithm for k-means (Section 1.2.2) appears in Lloyd (1962). The phrase "clustering is hard only when it doesn't matter" (Section 1.2.2) is credited to Naftali Tishby by Daniely et al. (2012). The competitive analysis of online algorithms (Section 1.2.4) was pioneered by Sleator and Tarjan (1985). Bélády's algorithm (Section 1.2.4) appears in Bélády (1967). The working set model in Section 1.3.1 was formulated by Denning (1968). Theorem 1.1 is due to Albers et al. (2005), as is Exercise 1.5. Exercise 1.6 is folklore. The result in Exercise 1.7 is due to Block (1962) and Novikoff (1962).

Acknowledgments

I thank Jérémy Barbay, Daniel Kane, and Salil Vadhan for helpful comments on a preliminary draft of this chapter.

References

Albers, S., Favrholdt, L. M., and Giel, O. 2005. On paging with locality of reference. *Journal of Computer and System Sciences*, **70**(2), 145–175.

Bélády, L. A. 1967. A study of replacement algorithms for a virtual storage computer. *IBM Systems Journal*, **5**(2), 78–101.

Block, H. D. 1962. The perceptron: A model for brain functioning. *Reviews of Modern Physics*, **34**, 123–135.

Daniely, A., Linial, N., and Saks, M. 2012. Clustering is difficult only when it does not matter. arXiv:1205.4891.

Dantzig, G. B. 1963. *Linear Programming and Extensions*. Princeton University Press.

Denning, P. J. 1968. The working set model for program behavior. *Commuications of the ACM*, **11**(5), 323–333.

Karmarkar, N. 1984. A new polynomial-time algorithm for linear programming. *Combinatorica*, **4**, 373–395.

Khachiyan, L. G. 1979. A polynomial algorithm in linear programming. *Soviet Mathematics Doklady*, **20**(1), 191–194.

Klee, V., and Minty, G. J. 1972. How good is the simplex algorithm? In Shisha, O. (ed.), *Inequalities III*, pp. 159–175. New York: Academic Press.

Koutsoupias, E., and Papadimitriou, C. H. 2000. Beyond competitive analysis. *SIAM Journal on Computing*, **30**(1), 300–317.

Lloyd, S. P. 1962. Least squares quantization in PCM. *IEEE Transactions on Information Theory*, **28**(2), 129–136.

Novikoff, A. 1962. On convergence proofs for perceptrons. *Proceedings of the Symposium on Mathematical Theory of Automata*, vol. 12, pp. 615–622.

Roughgarden, T. 2019. Beyond worst-case analysis. *Communications of the ACM*, **62**(3), 88–96.

Sleator, D. D., and Tarjan, R. E. 1985. Amortized efficiency of list update and paging rules. *Communications of the ACM*, **28**(2), 202–208.

Exercises

Exercise 1.1 Prove that for every deterministic cache replacement policy and cache size k, there is an adversarial page request sequence such that the policy faults on every request, and such that an optimal clairvoyant policy would fault on at most a $1/k$ fraction of the requests.

[Hint: use only $k + 1$ distinct pages, and the fact that the optimal policy always evicts the page that will be requested furthest in the future.]

Exercise 1.2 Let $f : \mathbb{N} \to \mathbb{N}$ be a function of the type described in Section 1.3, with $f(n)$ denoting the maximum allowable number of distinct page requests in any window of length n.

(a) Prove that there is a nondecreasing function $f' : \mathbb{N} \to \mathbb{N}$ with $f'(1) = 1$ and $f'(n + 1) \in \{f'(n), f'(n + 1)\}$ for all n such that a page request sequence conforms to f' if and only if it conforms to f.

(b) Prove that parts (a) and (b) of Theorem 1.1 hold trivially if $f'(2) = 1$.

Exercise 1.3 Prove that the page request sequence constructed in the proof of Theorem 1.1(a) conforms to the given approximately concave function f.

$f(n)$	1	2	3	3	4	4	5	5
n	1	2	3	4	5	6	7	$\cdots$

Figure 1.5 Function used to construct a bad page request sequence for FIFO (Exercise 1.4).

Input: n unit vectors $x_1, \ldots, x_n \in \mathbb{R}^d$ with labels $b_1, \ldots, b_n \in \{-1, +1\}$.

1. Initialize t to 1 and w_1 to the all-zero vector.
2. While there is a point x_i such that $\text{sgn}(w_t \cdot x_i) \neq b_i$, set $w_{t+1} = w_t + b_i x_i$ and increment t.[13]

Figure 1.6 The perceptron algorithm.

Exercise 1.4 Prove Theorem 1.1(c).

(Hint: Many different choices of f and k work. For example, take $k = 4$, a set $\{0, 1, 2, 3, 4\}$ of five pages, the function f shown in Figure 1.5, and a page request sequence consisting of an arbitrarily large number of identical blocks of the eight page requests 10203040.)

Exercise 1.5 Prove the following analogue of Theorem 1.1(b) for the FIFO replacement policy: for every $k \geq 2$ and approximately concave function f with $f(1) = 1$, $f(2) = 2$, and $f(n + 1) \in \{f(n), f(n + 1)\}$ for all $n \geq 2$, the page fault rate of the FIFO policy on every request sequence that conforms to f is at most

$$\frac{k}{f^{-1}(k + 1) - 1}. \tag{1.2}$$

[Hint: Make minor modifications to the proof of Theorem 1.1(b). The expression in (1.2) suggests defining phases such that (i) the FIFO policy makes at most k faults per phase; and (ii) a phase plus one additional request comprises requests for at least $k + 1$ distinct pages.]

Exercise 1.6 An instance of the knapsack problem consists of n items with nonnegative values $v_1, \ldots, v_n$ and sizes $s_1, \ldots, s_n$, and a knapsack capacity C. The goal is to compute a subset $S \subseteq \{1, 2, \ldots, n\}$ of items that fits in the knapsack (i.e., with $\sum_{i \in S} s_i \leq C$) and, subject to this, has the maximum total value $\sum_{i \in S} v_i$.

One simple greedy algorithm for the problem reindexes the items in nonincreasing order of density $\frac{v_i}{s_i}$ and then returns the largest prefix $\{1, 2, \ldots, j\}$ of items that fits in the knapsack (i.e., with $\sum_{i=1}^{j} s_i \leq C$). Parameterize a knapsack instance by the ratio α of the largest size of an item and the knapsack capacity, and prove a parameterized guarantee for the greedy algorithm: The total value of its solution is at least $1 - \alpha$ times that of an optimal solution.

Exercise 1.7 The *perceptron algorithm* is one of the most classical machine learning algorithms (Figure 1.6). The input to the algorithm is n points in $\mathbb{R}^d$, with a label

---

[13] Intuitively, this update step forces the next vector to be "more correct" on x_i, by increasing $w \cdot x_i$ by $b_i(x_i \cdot x_i) = b_i$.

$b_i \in \{-1, +1\}$ for each point $\mathbf{x}_i$. The goal is to compute a *separating hyperplane*: a hyperplane with all of the positively labeled points on one side, and all of the negatively labeled points on the other. Assume that there exists a separating hyperplane, and moreover that some such hyperplane passes through the origin.[14] We are then free to scale each data point $\mathbf{x}_i$ so that $\|\mathbf{x}_i\|_2 = 1$ – this does not change which side of a hyperplane $\mathbf{x}_i$ is on.

Parameterize the input by its *margin* μ, defined as

$$\mu = \max_{\mathbf{w}: \|\mathbf{w}\|=1} \min_{i=1}^{n} |\mathbf{w} \cdot \mathbf{x}_i|,$$

where $\mathbf{w}$ ranges over the unit normal vectors of all separating hyperplanes. Let $\mathbf{w}^*$ attain the maximum. Geometrically, the parameter μ is the smallest cosine of an angle defined by a point $\mathbf{x}_i$ and the normal vector $\mathbf{w}^*$.

(a) Prove that the squared norm of $\mathbf{w}_t$ grows slowly with the number of iterations t: $\|\mathbf{w}_{t+1}\|^2 \le \|\mathbf{w}_t\|^2 + 1$ for every $t \ge 1$.

(b) Prove that the projection of $\mathbf{w}_t$ onto $\mathbf{w}^*$ grows significantly with every iteration: $\mathbf{w}_{t+1} \cdot \mathbf{w}^* \ge \mathbf{w}_t \cdot \mathbf{w}^* + \mu$ for every $t \ge 1$.

(c) Conclude that the iteration count t never exceeds $1/\mu^2$.

---

[14] The second assumption is without loss of generality, as it can be enforced by adding an extra "dummy coordinate" to the data points.

PART ONE

Refinements of Worst-Case Analysis

CHAPTER TWO
Parameterized Algorithms

Fedor V. Fomin, Daniel Lokshtanov, Saket Saurabh, and Meirav Zehavi

Abstract: Parameterized algorithmics analyzes running time in finer detail than classical complexity theory: instead of expressing the running time of an algorithm as a function of the input size only, dependence on one or more parameters of the input instance is taken into account. In this chapter we sketch some techniques and tools from this rapidly developing area.

2.1 Introduction

Worst-case running time analysis has been at the center of nearly all developments in theoretical computer science since the inception of the field. Nevertheless, this approach to measuring algorithm efficiency has its own drawbacks. It is almost never the case that the input size is the only feature of the input instance that affects the running time of an algorithm. Further, it is rarely the case that the input instances we actually want to solve look like the instances on which the algorithm performs the worst. For this reason, the running time estimates from a worst-case analysis can be overly pessimistic, and algorithms with optimized worst-case behavior often perform poorly on instances arising in applications. Real-world instances are not worst-case instances; they exhibit additional structure that can often be exploited algorithmically. Almost all areas of applications of algorithms are full of parameters. Example parameters include size, topology, shape, depth of the formula, and so on. Parameterized complexity systematically seeks to understand the contribution of such parameters to the overall complexity of the problem. That is, the goal of parameterized complexity is to find ways of solving *NP*-hard problems more efficiently than brute force: our aim is to restrict the combinatorial explosion to a parameter that is hopefully much smaller than the input size.

2.1.1 Warm-Up: Vertex Cover

Without doubt, VERTEX COVER is the most popular problem in parameterized complexity and this is why many people call it the *Drosophila melanogaster* of parameterized algorithmics. This is because VERTEX COVER is the "simplest" among all parameterized problems. By simplest we mean the following empirical fact: When designing some new algorithmic technique for a parameterized problem it is always useful to check how this technique could be applied on VERTEX COVER.

Recall that a *vertex cover* S of a graph G is a set of vertices "covering" every edge of G. In other words, the graph $G - S$ obtained from G by removing the vertices of S has no edges. In the VERTEX COVER problem, we are given a graph G and an integer k. The question is to decide whether G contains a vertex cover of size k. Moreover, most of the known algorithms, if the pair (G,k) is a yes-instance, can actually construct the corresponding vertex cover.

VERTEX COVER is an NP-complete problem, so it is very unlikely that it will admit a polynomial-time algorithm. On the contrary, deciding whether a graph has a vertex cover of size at most 2 can be clearly done in time $\mathcal{O}(n^2 \cdot m)$, which is polynomial in the input size.[1] We just try all pairs of vertices and for every pair we check whether there is an edge not covered by this pair. This running time can be easily improved to $\mathcal{O}(n^2 \cdot n)$ by making use of the following observation: A pair u, v is a vertex cover if and only if for every vertex $w \notin \{u, v\}$ its adjacency list contains no vertices but u and v. Thus if we have a vertex w whose adjacency list is longer than 2, we know that $\{u, v\}$ is not a vertex cover. Otherwise, going through all the lists takes time $\mathcal{O}(n^2 \cdot n)$. This is clearly a polynomial-time algorithm.

In general, an algorithm in which we enumerate all vertex subsets of size at most k and check whether any of them forms a vertex cover solves the problem in time $O(n^k \cdot k \cdot n)$, which is polynomial for every constant k. We also know that unless $P \neq NP$, when k is unbounded, VERTEX COVER cannot be solved in polynomial time. This sounds like the end of the story.

A bit surprisingly, this is not the end. We can show that VERTEX COVER can be solved in *linear* time for every fixed k. Moreover, VERTEX COVER can be solved in polynomial time even when $k = \mathcal{O}(\log n)$. We do it by introducing a bounded depth search tree (recursive) algorithm for the problem.

One of the simplest parameterized algorithms solving VERTEX COVER is a recursive algorithm often called the *bounded search tree* or *branching algorithm*. The algorithm is based on the following two observations: (1) For a vertex v, any vertex cover must contain either v or *all* of its neighbors $N(v)$; and (2) for a vertex v, any vertex cover must contain either v or *all* of its neighbors $N(v)$. The algorithm now proceeds recursively, where G and k will be modified before passing to a recursive call. If in some recursive branch graph G has at least one edge and parameter $k \leq 0$, this instance has no vertex cover of size k and we halt in this branch. Otherwise, we find a vertex $v \in V(G)$ of maximum degree in G. If v is of degree 0, then G has no edges and we have found a solution. Otherwise, we recursively branch on two cases by considering either v or $N(v)$ in the vertex cover. In the branch where v is in the vertex cover, we delete v and decrease the parameter k by 1. In the second branch, we add $N(v)$ to the vertex cover, delete $N(v) \cup \{v\}$ from the graph, and decrease k by $|N(v)|$. Since $|N(v)| \geq 1$, in each of the branches we decrease k by at least 1.

To analyze the running time of the algorithm, it is convenient to view this recursive algorithm as a search tree $\mathcal{T}$. The root of this tree corresponds to the initial instance (G,k), and for every node of the tree its children correspond to instances in the recursive calls. Then the running time of the algorithm is bounded by (the number of nodes in the search tree) $\times$ (time taken at each node). It is easy to implement the algorithm so the time taken at each node is bounded by $\mathcal{O}(k \cdot n)$, where

---

[1] In what follows, we will always use n and m to denote the number of vertices and the number of edges in the graph, respectively.

n is the number of vertices in G. Thus, if $\tau(k)$ is the number of nodes in the search tree, then the total time used by the algorithm is at most $\mathcal{O}(\tau(k) \cdot k \cdot n)$. Observe that in each recursive call we reduce the parameter k by at least 1. Hence the height of the tree does not exceed k, and hence $\tau(k) \leq 2^{k+1} - 1$. The above discussions bring us to the following theorem.

Theorem 2.1 VERTEX COVER *is solvable in time* $\mathcal{O}(2^k \cdot k \cdot n)$.

Since for every constant k, we have that $\mathcal{O}(2^k \cdot k \cdot n) = \mathcal{O}(n)$, the running time of Theorem 2.1 is linear for every fixed k. Also, for $k = c \log n$, we have $\mathcal{O}(2^k \cdot k \cdot n) = \mathcal{O}(2^{c \log n} \cdot \log n \cdot n) = \mathcal{O}(n^{c+1} \cdot \log n)$, which is polynomial in n.

Let us remark that $\mathcal{O}(2^k \cdot k \cdot n)$ is not the best running time bound for VERTEX COVER and the algorithm can be improved easily. For example, the following observation can be helpful. If all the vertices of a graph are of degree at most 2, then the graph is the disjoint union of cycles and paths. In this case, the minimum vertex cover can be easily found in polynomial time (how?). If, however, the graph has a vertex of degree at least 3, then branching on this vertex provides us with a better recurrence and it is possible to show that in this case the branching tree has $\mathcal{O}(1.4656^k)$ vertices. We leave the formal proof of this claim as an exercise (Exercise 2.1). The best known algorithm solves the problem in time $\mathcal{O}(1.2738^k + kn)$; it is based on a combination of kernelization (see Section 2.4) and clever branching techniques [Chen et al. (2010)].

Algorithms with running time $f(k) \cdot n^c$, for a constant c independent of both n and k, are called *fixed-parameter algorithms*, or FPT algorithms. The goal in parameterized algorithmics is to design FPT algorithms, trying to make both the $f(k)$ factor and the constant c in the bound on the running time as small as possible. FPT algorithms can be contrasted with less efficient XP algorithms (for *slice-wise polynomial*), where the running time is of the form $f(k) \cdot n^{g(k)}$, for some functions f, g. There is a huge difference in running times of the form $f(k) \cdot n^{g(k)}$ and $f(k) \cdot n^c$.

Inspired by the success we had with VERTEX COVER, it is natural to ask whether a similar improvement over brute-force is possible for every NP-hard problem, for every choice of parameter. Of course, this is not true. As an example, consider VERTEX COLORING. Here we are given as input a graph G and an integer k, and we need to decide whether G has a proper k-coloring – that is, a coloring where no two adjacent vertices obtain the same color. It is well known that VERTEX COLORING is NP-complete already for $k = 3$, so we do not hope for a polynomial-time algorithm for fixed k. Observe that even an XP algorithm with running time $f(k) \cdot n^{g(k)}$ for any functions f and g would imply that $P = NP$.

The example of VERTEX COLORING illustrates that parameterized algorithms may not be all-powerful: there are parameterized problems that do not seem to admit FPT algorithms. However, in this specific example, we could explain very precisely why we are not able to design efficient algorithms, even when the number of colors is small. From the perspective of algorithm designers such an insight is very useful; they can now stop wasting their time trying to design efficient algorithms based only on the fact that the number of colors is small and start searching for other ways to attack the problem instances. If we are trying to design a polynomial-time algorithm for a problem and failing, it is quite likely that this is because the problem is NP-hard. Is the theory of NP-hardness the right tool also for giving negative evidence for fixed-parameter tractability? In particular, if we are trying to design an $f(k) \cdot n^c$-time algorithm and fail to do so, is it because the problem is NP-hard for some fixed constant value of k, say $k = 100$? Let us look at another example, the CLIQUE problem.

In the CLIQUE problem we are given as input graph G and integer k, and the task is to decide whether G contains a clique on k vertices, that is, a set of k vertices with an edge between every pair of them. Similar to VERTEX COVER, there is a simple brute-force $n^{\mathcal{O}(k)}$-time algorithm to check whether there is a clique on at least k vertices. Can we design an FPT algorithm for this problem? After some reflection one can see that the NP-hardness of CLIQUE cannot be used to rule out an FPT algorithm for it.

Since NP-hardness is insufficient to differentiate between problems with $f(k) \cdot n^{g(k)}$-time algorithms and problems with $f(k) \cdot n^c$-time algorithms, we have to resort to stronger complexity-theoretic assumptions. The theory of *W[1]-hardness* allows us to prove (under certain complexity assumptions) that even though a problem is polynomial-time solvable for every fixed k, the parameter k has to appear in the exponent of n in the running time; that is, the problem is not FPT. This theory has been quite successful for identifying which parameterized problems are FPT and which are unlikely to be. Besides this qualitative classification of FPT versus $W[1]$-hard, more recent developments give us also (an often surprisingly tight) quantitative understanding of the time needed to solve a parameterized problem. Under reasonable assumptions about the hardness of the CNF-SAT problem, it is possible to show that there is no $f(k) \cdot n^c$, or even $f(k) \cdot n^{o(k)}$-time algorithm for finding a clique on k vertices. Thus, up to constant factors in the exponent, the naive $\mathcal{O}(n^k)$-time algorithm is optimal!

Any algorithmic theory is incomplete without an accompanying complexity theory that establishes intractability of certain problems. There is such a complexity theory providing lower bounds on the running time required to solve parameterized problems.

So the common belief is that there is no algorithm for solving CLIQUE with running time $f(k) \cdot n^{o(k)}$. But what if we seek a k-clique in a graph of maximum degree Δ where the parameter is Δ? Notice that the existence of a k-clique implies that $\Delta \geq k - 1$; thus, Δ is a weaker parameter than k, which gives hope for membership in FPT. In fact, it turns out that this can be done quite easily and efficiently when Δ is small: if we guess one vertex v in the clique, then the remaining vertices in the clique must be among the Δ neighbors of v; thus we can try all of the 2^Δ subsets of the neighbors of v and return the largest clique that we found. The total running time of this algorithm is $\mathcal{O}(2^\Delta \cdot \Delta^2 \cdot n)$, which is feasible for $\Delta = 20$ even if n is quite large. Again it is possible to use complexity theoretic assumptions on the hardness of CNF-SAT to show that this algorithm is asymptotically optimal, up to multiplicative constants in the exponent.

What the preceding algorithm shows is that the CLIQUE problem is FPT when the parameter is the maximum degree Δ of the input graph. At the same time CLIQUE is probably not FPT when the parameter is the solution size k. Thus, the classification of the problem into "tractable" or "intractable" crucially depends on the choice of parameter. This makes a lot of sense; the more we know about our input instances, the more we can exploit algorithmically! For the same problem there can be multiple

Table 2.1 Overview of the discussed problems

Problem/parameter	Good news	Bad news
VERTEX COVER/k	$\mathcal{O}(2^k \cdot k \cdot n)$-time algorithm	NP-hard (probably not in P)
CLIQUE/Δ	$\mathcal{O}(2^\Delta \cdot \Delta^2 \cdot n)$-time algorithm	NP-hard (probably not in P)
CLIQUE /k	$n^{\mathcal{O}(k)}$-time algorithm	$W[1]$-hard (probably not FPT)
VERTEX COLORING/k		NP-hard for $k = 3$ (probably not XP)

choices of parameters. *Selecting the right parameter(s) for a particular problem is an art.* We summarize the complexities of the preceding problems in Table 2.1.

Finally, we give the formal definition.

Definition 2.2 A parameterized problem $L \subseteq \Sigma^* \times \mathbb{N}$ (for alphabet Σ) is *fixed-parameter tractable* (FPT) if there exists an algorithm $\mathcal{A}$ (called a *fixed-parameter algorithm*), a computable function $f : \mathbb{N} \to \mathbb{N}$, and a constant c with the following property: given any $(x, k) \in \Sigma^* \times \mathbb{N}$, the algorithm $\mathcal{A}$ correctly decides whether $(x, k) \in L$ in time $f(k) \cdot |x|^c$ where $|x|$ denotes the length of the input x. The complexity class containing all fixed-parameter tractable problems is called FPT.

2.2 Randomization

Randomness is a powerful resource in designing algorithms and often leads to elegant algorithms, and parameterized algorithms are no exception. Consider for example the classic LONGEST PATH problem. A path is a sequence $v_1, v_2, \ldots, v_\ell$ of *distinct* vertices of a graph, such that for every i there is an edge in the graph from v_i to v_{i+1}. The number ℓ of the vertices in the path is its *length*. In the LONGEST PATH problem the input is a (directed and undirected) graph G together with an integer k, and the goal is to determine whether G contains a path P of length k. For simplicity we shall restrict our attention to undirected graphs, even though most of the discussion applies also to directed graphs.

When $k = n$ the LONGEST PATH problem is precisely the well-known HAMILTONIAN PATH problem, and therefore it is NP-complete. On the other hand, there is a simple $n^{k+\mathcal{O}(1)}$ time algorithm that tries all sequences of k vertices and checks whether any of them forms a k-path. Papadimitriou and Yannakakis (1996) posed as an open problem whether there exists a polynomial-time algorithm that determines whether a graph G on n vertices contains a path of length at least $\log n$. To achieve this it suffices to devise an algorithm with running time $c^k n^{\mathcal{O}(1)}$ for some constant c. In 1995, Alon, Yuster, and Zwick (1995) invented the *color coding* technique and gave a $(2e)^k n^{\mathcal{O}(1)}$ time randomized algorithm for LONGEST PATH (where $e \approx 2.718$), resolving the question of Papadimitriou and Yannakakis in the affirmative.

The algorithm is based on two key steps: a *random coloring* step, followed by a procedure that finds a *multicolored* path P, if such a path exists. To describe both steps we need a few definitions: a *k-coloring* of G is a function $c : V(G) \to \{1, \ldots, k\}$. Notice that a coloring simply assigns a number (color) to every vertex, and we do *not* demand that this is a proper coloring in the terminology of graph theory, where edge endpoints need to receive different colors. We will say that a path $P = v_1, v_2, \ldots, v_\ell$ is *multicolored* by a coloring c if all vertices in P receive distinct colors by c. Formally we require that for every $i \neq j$ we have $c(i) \neq c(j)$.

The first key building block of the algorithm is the insight that, for every path P of length k, a random coloring $c : V(G) \to \{1, \ldots, k\}$ with k colors will multicolor P with "not so small" probability. In particular, there are k^k ways to color $V(P)$ with k colors, and $k!$ of these colorings assign distinct colors to all vertices of P. Hence, the probability that P is multicolored is

$$\frac{k!}{k^k} \geq \frac{\sqrt{2\pi k}}{e^k} \geq e^{-k}. \tag{2.1}$$

Here the first inequality follows from Stirling's approximation.

The second building block is an efficient algorithm that determines whether G contains a path P of length k that is multicolored by a given coloring c. The algorithm uses dynamic programming. We define a function

$$f : 2^{\{1, \ldots, k\}} \times V(G) \to \{\mathsf{true}, \mathsf{false}\}$$

that takes as input a set $S \subseteq \{1, \ldots, k\}$ together with a vertex $v \in V(G)$ and outputs true if there exists a path in $G[S]$ (the subgraph of G induced by S, that is, we retain only the vertices in S and all edges between them) that uses each color of S precisely once and ends at v. Note that such a path necessarily has length $|S|$. It can be easily verified that the function f satisfies the following recurrence relation:

$$f(S, v) = \begin{cases} \mathsf{false} & \text{if } c(v) \notin S \text{ or} \\ \mathsf{true} & \text{if } \{c(v)\} = S \\ \bigvee_{u \in N(v)} f(S \setminus \{c(v)\}, u) & \text{otherwise.} \end{cases} \tag{2.2}$$

The recurrence (2.2) immediately yields an algorithm for determining whether a multicolored path exists: iterate through every set $S \subseteq \{1, \ldots, k\}$ from small to large and every vertex $v \in V(G)$. In each iteration compute $f(S, v)$ using Equation (2.2) and store the result in a table. Thus, when the algorithm computes $f(S, v)$ it can look up the value of $f(S \setminus \{c(v)\}, u)$ (which was computed in a previous iteration) in the table.

In each of the iterations the value of $f(S, v)$ is computed in at most $d(v)$ table lookups, which we assume take constant time. Thus the total time of the algorithm for determining whether a multicolored path exists is upper bounded by

$$\mathcal{O}\left(\sum_{S \subseteq \{1, \ldots, k\}} \sum_{v \in V(G)} d(v) \right) = \mathcal{O}\left(2^k (n + m) \right).$$

The final algorithm for LONGEST PATH is as follows: iterate through e^k random k-colorings c_i (here i goes from 1 to e^k). For each i check in time $\mathcal{O}\left(2^k(n+m)\right)$ whether there exists a path that is multicolored by c_i using the foregoing dynamic programming algorithm. If the algorithm finds a multicolored path, then this path has length k. However, if a path of length k exists, then the probability that *none* of the c_i's multicolors it is at most $(1 - \frac{1}{e^k})^{e^k} \leq \frac{1}{e}$. Thus, the algorithm runs in time $\mathcal{O}((2e)^k(n+m))$, always correctly returns "no" on no-instances, and returns "yes" on yes-instances with probability at least $1 - \frac{1}{e}$.

Theorem 2.3 (Alon et al., 1995)   *There exists a randomized algorithm with one-sided error for* LONGEST PATH *with running time* $\mathcal{O}((2e)^k(n+m))$.

2.2.1 Random Separation: Set Splitting

Color coding is far from being the only way to use randomness to design parameterized algorithms. A different example is the "random separation" technique. We will see how to apply random separation to design an algorithm for the SET SPLITTING problem. Here the input is a universe U, a family $\mathcal{F} = \{S_\infty, S_\in, \ldots, S_\Updownarrow\}$ of subsets of U, and an integer $k \leq m$. The goal is to find an assignment $\phi : U \to \{0,1\}$ that *splits* at least k sets in $\mathcal{F}$. Here a set $S_i \in \mathcal{F}$ is *split* by ϕ if it contains at least one element u such that $\phi(u) = 0$ and at least one element v such that $\phi(v) = 1$. The SET SPLITTING problem is also known as HYPERGRAPH MAX CUT, because when all sets S_i have cardinality 2 this is precisely the classic MAX CUT problem.

It turns out that a simple strategy yields an FPT algorithm for SET SPLITTING. In particular, we prove that if there exists an assignment ϕ that splits at least k sets in $\mathcal{F}$, then a *random* assignment ψ splits at least k sets with probability at least $\frac{1}{4^k}$. Indeed, suppose $\{S_1, S_2, \ldots, S_k\}$ are split by ϕ. For every $i \leq k$ let u_i be an element of S_i such that $\phi(u_i) = 0$ and $v_i \in S_i$ be such that $\phi(v_i) = 1$. We remark that u_i and u_j (or v_i and v_j) can be the same element even though $i \neq j$. Let $X = \bigcup_{i \leq k}\{u_i, v_i\}$, and observe that X has the following two properties. First, $|X| \leq 2k$. Second, for every assignment ψ that agrees with ϕ on X (that is, $\psi(x) = \phi(x)$ for every $x \in X$) ψ splits the sets $S_1, \ldots, S_k$ (since $\psi(u_i) = 0$ and $\psi(v_i) = 1$). The probability that ψ agrees with ϕ on X is $2^{-|X|} \geq 2^{-2k} = 4^{-k}$, as claimed.

This gives the following simple algorithm that runs in time $\mathcal{O}(4^k nm)$: try 4^k random assignments $\psi_1, \ldots, \psi_{4^k}$. If some ψ_i splits at least k sets, return that assignment. If none of the ψ_i's split at least k sets report that no assignment does. Just as for the LONGEST PATH problem, if there is an assignment that splits at least k sets, then the probability that the algorithm fails to find one is at most $(1 - \frac{1}{4^k})^{4^k} \leq 1/e$. This proves the following theorem.

Theorem 2.4   *There exists a randomized algorithm with one-sided error for* SET SPLITTING *with running time* $\mathcal{O}(4^k nm)$.

We remark that a random assignment ψ will actually split k sets with probability at least $\frac{1}{2^k}$. The proof of this claim is (slightly) more complicated, so we leave it as Exercise 2.3 (see also Chen and Lu, 2009).

2.2.2 Derandomization

It would appear that the algorithms of Theorems 2.3 and 2.4 are inherently random-ized. It turns out that the randomized step can be replaced by appropriate pseudo-random constructions without compromising (much) on the worst-case running time guarantees.

Let us first consider the algorithm for LONGEST PATH. Here we tried e^k random colorings and used the fact that if there exists a path, then with probability at least $1 - 1/e$ at least one of the colorings multicolors it. Quite remarkably one can deterministically construct a family of colorings such that this property *always* holds, instead of holding with constant probability.

Theorem 2.5 (Naor et al., 1995) *There exists an algorithm that given a universe U of size n and an integer k runs in time $e^k n^{\mathcal{O}(1)}$ and produces k-colorings $c_1, c_2, \dots c_\ell$ with $\ell = \mathcal{O}(e^{k+o(k)} \log n)$ such that for every set $S \subseteq U$ of size at most k there exists an i such that c_i multicolors S.*

Replacing the e^k random k-colorings with the $e^{k+o(k)} n^{\mathcal{O}(1)}$ k-colorings of Theorem 2.5 in the algorithm for LONGEST PATH yields a *deterministic* algorithm with running time $(2e)^{k+o(k)} n^{\mathcal{O}(1)}$.

A similar situation happens for SET SPLITTING. What we need is a family of assignments $\psi_1, \psi_2, \dots \psi_\ell$ such that for some unknown set X of size at most $2k$, at least one of the assignments ψ_i agrees with an unknown assignment ϕ on X. Since X and ϕ are unknown, what we really need is that for *every* set X of size at most $2k$ and *every* assignment $\phi_X : X \to \{0, 1\}$ at least one ψ_i agrees with ϕ_X on X. Again, this can be achieved!

Theorem 2.6 (Naor et al., 1995) *There exists an algorithm that given a universe U of size n and an integer k runs in time $2^{k+o(k)} n^{\mathcal{O}(1)}$ and produces assignments $\psi_1, \psi_2, \dots \psi_\ell$ with $\ell \leq 2^{k+o(k)} \log n$ such that for every set $X \subseteq U$ of size at most k and every assignment $\phi_X : X \to \{0, 1\}$ at least one ψ_i agrees with ϕ_X.*

Replacing the 4^k random assignments with the $4^{k+o(k)} n^{\mathcal{O}(1)}$ assignments produced by Theorem 2.6 (applied with $|X| \leq 2k$) yields a deterministic algorithm for SET SPLITTING with running time $4^{k+o(k)} n^{\mathcal{O}(1)} m$. We remark that the constructions of Theorems 2.5 and 2.6 are optimal in the sense that ℓ cannot be reduced below $\Omega(e^k \log n)$ and $\Omega(2^k \log n)$ respectively.

Theorem 2.7 *There exists a deterministic algorithm for LONGEST PATH with running time $(2e)^{k+o(k)} n^{\mathcal{O}(1)}$. There exists a deterministic algorithm for SET SPLITTING with running time $4^{k+o(k)} n^{\mathcal{O}(1)} m$.*

2.3 Structural Parameterizations

We have mostly concerned ourselves with the parameter k being the value of the objective function, or just the size of the solution. This does *not* mean that this is the only reasonable choice of parameter! For example, recall that the GRAPH COLORING problem is NP-complete for $k = 3$, where k, is the number of colors, so an FPT algorithm parameterized by k is out of the question. This does not rule out the potential for other interesting parameterized algorithms for the problem. Suppose we want to solve GRAPH COLORING, but now we know that the input instances have a relatively small vertex cover, say of size at most t. Can we use this to get an efficient algorithm?

Here is an algorithm that is FPT when parameterized by the vertex cover number t. First, compute a vertex cover X of size at most t in time $2^t(n+m)$ using the algorithm of Theorem 2.1. If $k > t$ we can find a coloring with at most $t + 1 \leq k$ colors in time $\mathcal{O}(m + n)$: just use one color of $\{1, \ldots, |X|\}$ per vertex of X and use color $|X| + 1$ for all of the remaining vertices. Because X is a vertex cover, this is a proper coloring.

Suppose now that $k \leq t$. The algorithm tries all k^t possible colorings of X. For each such choice $c_X : X \to \{1, \ldots, k\}$ it checks whether c_X can be extended to a proper coloring of G. A *necessary* condition for this to be possible is that every vertex $y \notin X$ has an available color. Formally, for every $y \notin X$ there should exist an $1 \leq i \leq k$ so that no neighbor of y has color i. Since no pair of vertices outside of X is adjacent this necessary condition is also *sufficient* – to each $y \notin X$ we can simply assign any of its available colors. This leads to an algorithm for GRAPH COLORING with running time $\mathcal{O}(k^t(n + m)) \leq \mathcal{O}(t^t(n + m))$.

Theorem 2.8 *There exists an algorithm for* GRAPH COLORING *with running time* $\mathcal{O}(t^t(n + m))$ *where t is the size of the smallest vertex cover of G.*

This algorithm is quite naive; however, quite surprisingly, one can show that it cannot be substantially improved (under appropriate complexity-theoretic assumptions). Indeed, an algorithm with running time $2^{o(t \log t)}n^{\mathcal{O}(1)}$ would contradict the Exponential Time Hypothesis (Lokshtanov et al., 2018) (see Section 2.5.2).

2.4 Kernelization

Preprocessing is a widely used technique to help cope with computationally hard problems. A natural question in this regard is how to measure the quality of preprocessing rules proposed for a specific problem; yet for a long time the mathematical analysis of polynomial time preprocessing algorithms was neglected. One central reason for this anomaly can be found in the following observation: showing that in polynomial time an instance I of an NP-hard problem can be replaced by an equivalent instance whose size is smaller than the size of I implies that $P = NP$. The situation has changed drastically with the advent of Parameterized Complexity. Roughly speaking, the objective of preprocessing rules within this framework is to reduce the input size to depend only on the parameter, where the smaller the dependency is, the better the rules are.

2.4.1 Warm-Up: the Buss Rule

Before we delve into the formal definitions, let us see a simple example. For an instance (G, k) of the VERTEX COVER problem, consider the following rule.

> **Rule I.** If G contains an isolated vertex v, then remove v from G. The resulting instance is $(G - v, k)$.

This rule takes an instance of the problem, and, if its condition is satisfied, returns an instance of the same problem of smaller size. Such a rule is called a *reduction rule*. Most importantly, this rule is *safe* in the following sense: The instance that it takes as input is a yes-instance if and only if the instance that it outputs is a yes-instance. Indeed, it is immediate to see that the removal of isolated vertices has no effect on the answer of the given instance.

Now, consider yet another reduction rule, known as the *Buss rule*.

> **Rule II.** If G contains a vertex v of degree at least $k+1$, then remove v (along with incident edges) from G, and decrement k by 1. The resulting instance is $(G - v, k - 1)$.

The safeness of this rule follows from the observation that any vertex cover of size at most k in G must contain v – indeed, any vertex cover in G that excludes v must contain all of its neighbors, and their number is strictly larger than k.

Lastly, suppose that Rules I and II have been applied exhaustively, thus neither of their conditions is satisfied, and consider the following rule.

> **Rule III.** If G contains more than k^2 edges, then return no.

Here, safeness also follows from a simple observation: As the maximum degree of a vertex in G is k (due to the exhaustive application of Rule II), any set of at most k vertices can cover at most k^2 edges. Thus, if G contains more than k^2 edges, it does not admit a vertex cover of size at most k. To strictly comply with the definition of a reduction rule, the output should be an instance of VERTEX COVER rather than yes or no. However, it is acceptable to use yes or no as abbreviations for trivial yes- or no-instances, respectively. For VERTEX COVER, concrete trivial yes- and no-instances can be, for example, the graph on an empty vertex set with $k = 0$, and the graph on two vertices connected by an edge with $k = 0$, respectively.

After the consideration of the last rule, we know that the number of edges in G is at most k^2. Furthermore, the number of vertices in G is at most $2k^2$ because G does not contain any isolated vertex (due to the exhaustive application of Rule I). We also observe that the entire process is implementable in polynomial time – each of our three rules can be applied only polynomially many times and each application runs in polynomial time. Thus, in polynomial time, we managed to reduce the size of the input instance (without even trying to solve it!) to be quadratic in k.

2.4.2 Formal Definition and Relation to Membership in FPT

The main definition in kernelization is that of a kernel, which is derived from a more general notion called *compression*.

Definition 2.9 A *compression* of a parameterized language $Q \subseteq \Sigma^* \times \mathbb{N}$ into a language $R \subseteq \Sigma^*$ is an algorithm that takes as input an instance $(x, k) \in \Sigma^* \times \mathbb{N}$, runs in time polynomial in $|x| + k$, and returns a string y such that:

1. $|y| \leq f(k)$ for some function $f(\cdot)$, and
2. $y \in R$ if and only if $(x, k) \in Q$.

If $|\Sigma| = 2$, the function $f(\cdot)$ is called the *bitsize* of the compression.

Kernelization is the special case of compression in which the projection of Q onto Σ^* equals R, that is, the source and target languages are essentially the same. Then, the algorithm is referred to as a *kernelization algorithm* or a *kernel*. Particular attention is given to the case where the function f is polynomial. In this case, we say that the problem admits *polynomial compression or kernelization*. While a polynomial kernel is obviously better than an arbitrary kernel, we have particular interest in polynomial kernels due the following characterization, which uses arbitrary (not necessarily polynomial) kernels.

In one direction, it is easy to see that if a decidable (parameterized) problem admits a kernel for some function f, then it is FPT: for any instance of the problem, we call a (polynomial-time) kernelization algorithm, and then use a decision algorithm to determine the answer to the resulting instance. Since the size of the kernel is bounded by some function f of the parameter, the running time of the decision algorithm depends only on the parameter. More surprising is the converse direction:

Theorem 2.10 *If a parameterized problem L is FPT, then it admits a kernel.*

Proof Suppose that there is an algorithm deciding if $(x, k) \in L$ in time $f(k)|x|^c$ for some computable function f and constant c. We consider two cases. In the first, $|x| \geq f(k)$, and we run the FPT algorithm on the instance in time $f(k)|x|^c \leq |x|^{c+1}$. If the FPT algorithm outputs yes, then the kernelization algorithm outputs a constant size yes-instance, and if the decision algorithm outputs no, then the kernelization algorithm outputs a constant size no-instance. In the second case, $|x| < f(k)$, and the kernelization algorithm outputs x. This yields a kernel of size $f(k)$ for the problem. $\square$

Theorem 2.10 shows that kernelization gives rise to an alternative definition of membership in FPT. So, to decide if a parameterized problem has a kernel, we can employ many known tools already given by parameterized complexity. But what if we are interested in kernels that are as small as possible? The size of a kernel obtained using Theorem 2.10 equals the dependence on k in the running time of the best known parameterized algorithm for the problem, which is often quite large (exponential or worse). Can we find better kernels? The answer is yes, we can, but not always. For many problems we can obtain polynomial kernels, but under reasonable complexity-theoretic assumptions, there exist problems in FPT that do not admit kernels of polynomial size (see Section 2.5).

In Section 2.4.1, we have already seen a polynomial (in fact, quadratic) kernel for VERTEX COVER, based on three very simple rules, where the central one is known as the Buss rule. Specifically, we proved the following theorem.

Theorem 2.11 VERTEX COVER *admits a kernel of size* $\mathcal{O}(k^2)$.

In fact, a general scheme to develop kernelization algorithms is to provide a list of reduction rules, where always the first rule in the list whose condition is satisfied is the one to be executed next; eventually, when no rule is applicable, the size of the instance should be bounded. Next, we adapt the Buss rule to a less expected context. We remark that nowadays, there is a rich toolkit to design kernels (see Notes). Moreover, extensions of kernelization are explored (see Section 2.6.1).

2.4.3 Generalization of the Buss Rule to Matrix Rank

We will now discuss a more sophisticated example of a polynomial kernel. The *rigidity* of a matrix A for a target rank r over a field $\mathbb{F}$ is the minimum Hamming distance between A and a matrix of rank at most r. Naturally, given a parameter k, the MATRIX RIGIDITY problem asks whether the rigidity of A is at most k.

Theorem 2.12 *There exists a polynomial-time algorithm that, given an instance (A, k, r) of* MATRIX RIGIDITY*, returns an equivalent instance (A', k, r) where A' has $\mathcal{O}((rk)^2)$ entries.*

Proof Sketch Given an instance (A, r, k) of MATRIX RIGIDITY, the algorithm works as follows. For $k + 1$ steps, it repeatedly selects a set of maximum size consisting of rows that are linearly independent, where if the size of this set exceeds $r + 1$, a subset of it of size $r + 1$ is used instead. Each such set of rows is removed from the input matrix, and then it is inserted into the output matrix. At the end of this greedy process, rows that remain in the input matrix are simply discarded. Afterwards, the symmetric process is executed on columns.

Clearly, the output matrix A' has at most $(r + 1)k$ rows and $(r + 1)k$ columns, and therefore $\mathcal{O}((rk)^2)$ entries. Moreover, in the forward direction, because A' is obtained by deleting rows, and then further deleting columns, of A, it is clear that if (A, k, r) is a yes-instance, then so is (A', k, r).

For the reverse direction, we only prove that the operation on rows is safe, as the safeness for columns follows similarly. To this end, let $\widehat{A}$ be the matrix obtained after the operation on rows, and suppose that $(\widehat{A}, k, r)$ is a yes-instance. Let $\widehat{B}$ be a matrix of rank at most r and Hamming distance at most k from $\widehat{A}$. Because the rows of $\widehat{A}$ were taken from A, the matrix B that consists of $\widehat{B}$ and the rows of A outside $\widehat{A}$ is at Hamming distance at most k from A. To prove that (A, k, r) is a yes-instance as well (which will be witnessed by B), we will prove that each row in A that was not inserted into $\widehat{A}$ belongs to the span of the rows of $\widehat{A}$ that also belong to $\widehat{B}$.

Notice that in each set of $r + 1$ rows inserted (in the same iteration) into $\widehat{A}$, there must be a difference between $\widehat{A}$ and $\widehat{B}$ as this set in itself is linearly independent. Since $k + 1$ iterations are performed, and the Hamming distance between $\widehat{A}$ and $\widehat{B}$ is k, there must be at least one set that is the same in both, and thus this set must have size at most r. In particular, when this set was inserted into $\widehat{A}$, it was a set of maximum size of linearly independent rows (that was not replaced by a smaller set). Thus, every row in A that was not inserted into $\widehat{A}$ belongs to the span of this set. Because this set is the same in $\widehat{A}$ and $\widehat{B}$, we conclude that B and $\widehat{B}$ have the same rank, and thus (A, k, r) is a yes-instance. $\qquad\square$

Let us point out two similarities. While in the Buss rule, we relied on the observation that in a set of $k + 1$ edges incident to the same vertex, that vertex must be picked, here we relied on the observation that in a set of $r + 1$ linearly independent rows, at least one change must be made. Further, both when arguing the correctness of Rule III, and when arguing for the existence of an "untouched" set in the reverse direction, we used an argument based on the pigeonhole principle.

When $\mathbb{F} = \mathbb{R}$, Theorem 2.12 does not yield a kernel for MATRIX RIGIDITY parameterized by $k + r$ because the bitsize to encode each entry may be unbounded in $k + r$. However, for finite fields, we have the following consequence.

Corollary 2.13 MATRIX RIGIDITY *over finite fields admits a kernel of size* $\mathcal{O}((kr)^2 f)$, *where f is the field size.*

We remark that parameterization by multiple parameters (among k, r, and f) is likely to be essential here, because it can be shown that parameterized by k alone, r alone, or f alone, MATRIX RIGIDITY is $W[1]$-hard (see Section 2.5.1).

2.5 Hardness and Optimality

2.5.1 W[1]-Hardness

In addition to a rich toolkit to design parameterized algorithms, research in parameterized complexity has also provided complementary methods to show that a problem is unlikely to be FPT. The main technique is the one of parameterized reductions analogous to those employed in the theory of NP-hardness. Here, the concept of *W[1]-hardness* replaces the one of NP-hardness, and for reductions we need not only construct an equivalent instance in FPT time, but also ensure that the size of the parameter in the new instance depends only on the size of the parameter in the original one. If there exists such a reduction transforming a problem known to be $W[1]$-hard to another problem Π, then the problem Π is $W[1]$-hard as well. Central $W[1]$-hard problems include, for example, deciding whether a nondeterministic single-tape Turing machine accepts within k steps, CLIQUE (determine whether a given graph has a clique of size k) parameterized by solution size k, and INDEPENDENT SET parameterized by solution size k (determine whether a given graph has an independent set of size k). To show that a problem Π is not XP unless $P = NP$, it is sufficient to show that there exists a fixed k such Π is NP-hard. Then, the problem is said to be *para-NP-hard*.

More formally, a central notion in this context is of a parameterized reduction, defined as follows.

Definition 2.14 Let $A, B \subseteq \Sigma^* \times \mathbb{N}$ be two parameterized problems. A *parameterized reduction* from A to B is an algorithm that, given an instance (x, k) of A, outputs an instance (x', k') of B such that (i) (x, k) is a yes-instance of A if and only if (x', k') is a yes-instance of B; (ii) $k' \leq g(k)$ for some computable function g; (iii) the running time is upper bounded by $f(k) \cdot |x|^c$ for some computable function f and constant c.

As an example of a very simple parameterized reduction, let A be CLIQUE and B be INDEPENDENT SET, and consider the following algorithm. Given an instance (G, k) of CLIQUE, the algorithm outputs the instance $(\overline{G}, k)$ of INDEPENDENT SET, where $\overline{G}$ is the complement of G (i.e., $\{u, v\} \in E(G)$ if and only if $\{u, v\} \notin E(\overline{G})$). Then, it is trivial to verify that the three properties in Definition 2.14 are satisfied. Generally, the design of parameterized reductions can often be quite technical, as we need to avoid blowing up the parameter. In many cases, it is useful to consider the "colorful version" of a W[1]-hard problem as the source of the reduction. In particular, in COLORFUL CLIQUE we are given a graph G, and a (not necessarily proper) coloring of the vertices of G in k colors, and the goal is to determine whether G has a clique on k vertices, where each vertex has a distinct color. Roughly speaking, the main reason why colors help is that they enable the reduction to consist, for each color, of a gadget for the selection of a vertex of that color, rather than k gadgets for the selection of k vertices from the entire graph. In particular, each gadget "works" on a different set of vertices. This generally simplifies the design of the gadgets that need to verify that the selected vertices form a clique.

We remark that for some choices of A and B, even when both problems are NP-hard, we do not expect to have a parameterized reduction. For example, let A be CLIQUE and B be VERTEX COVER. As already noted in Section 2.1.1, VERTEX COVER is FPT while CLIQUE is W[1]-hard. Then, although there exists a polynomial-time reduction from CLIQUE to VERTEX COVER (because both problems are NP-complete), a parameterized one would imply that CLIQUE is FPT, which is considered unlikely. We remark that known reductions from CLIQUE to VERTEX COVER blow up the parameter in the output instance, so it no longer depends only on the parameter in the input instance but on the entire input instance size. Interestingly, while we know of a parameterized reduction from INDEPENDENT SET to DOMINATING SET (through COLORFUL INDEPENDENT SET; see Notes), we do not know of a parameterized reduction from DOMINATING SET to INDEPENDENT SET. In fact, we do not expect that such a reduction exists, since INDEPENDENT SET and DOMINATING SET lie in different levels of the *W-hierarchy*. Specifically, INDEPENDENT SET is complete for the first level of this squirearchy, while DOMINATING SET is complete for the second one. For more details, we refer to the Notes.

2.5.2 ETH and SETH

To obtain (essentially) tight conditional lower bounds for the running times of algorithms, we can rely (among other hypotheses) on the *Exponential-Time Hypothesis* (ETH) and *Strong Exponential-Time Hypothesis* (SETH). To formalize the statements of ETH and SETH, first recall that given a formula φ in conjuctive normal form (CNF) with n Boolean variables and m clauses, the task of CNF-SAT is to decide whether there is a truth assignment to the variables that satisfies φ. In the p-CNF-SAT problem, each clause is restricted to have at most p literals. First, ETH asserts that 3-CNF-SAT cannot be solved in time $\mathcal{O}(2^{o(n)})$. Second, SETH asserts that for every fixed $\epsilon < 1$, there exists a (large) integer $p = p(\epsilon)$ such that p-CNF-SAT cannot be solved in time $\mathcal{O}((2 - \epsilon)^n)$. We remark that for every fixed integer p, we know that

p-CNF-SAT is solvable in time $\mathcal{O}(c^n)$ for $c < 2$ that depends on p (notice that this does not contradict SETH).

Parameterized reductions (as in Definition 2.14) can be used in conjunction with ETH or SETH to provide more fine-grained lower bounds. For an example, consider the classic reduction from 3-CNF-SAT to VERTEX COVER described by, e.g., Sipser (1996). This reduction has the following properties: Given a 3-CNF-SAT instance ϕ with n variables and m clauses, the reduction outputs in polynomial time a graph G on $3m$ vertices, such that G has a vertex cover of size at most m if and only if ϕ is satisfiable. This reduction, together with the ETH, rules out the possibility of a $2^{o(|V(G)|^{1/3})}$ time algorithm for VERTEX COVER: If such an algorithm exists, we could feed the output of the reduction into the algorithm and solve 3-CNF-SAT

$$2^{o(|V(G)|^{1/3})} \leq 2^{o((3m)^{1/3})} \leq 2^{o(n)} \text{ in time.}$$

This would contradict the ETH. In the last transition we used that the number of clauses m in a 3-SAT instance is at most $\mathcal{O}(n^3)$.

Some key points to take away from this reduction. First, good old NP-hardness reductions are by themselves sufficient to provide running time lower bounds assuming the ETH, we just had to carefully keep track how the parameters of the instance produced by the reduction depend on the parameters of the input instance. Second, the running time lower bound of $2^{o(|V(G)|^{1/3})}$ is very far off from the $2^{\Theta(n)}$ running times of the currently best known algorithms for VERTEX COVER. Luckily, Impagliazzo et al. (2001) provide a handy tool to bridge this gap.

Theorem 2.15 *Assuming the ETH,* 3-CNF-SAT *has no algorithm with running time* $2^{o(n+m)}$.

Theorem 2.15, combined with the reduction foregoing shows that VERTEX COVER can not have an algorithm with running time $2^{o(n)}$, since this would yield an algorithm for 3-CNF-SAT with running time $2^{o(m)}$, contradicting ETH. Thus, assuming the ETH, *up to constants in the exponent* the existing algorithms for VERTEX COVER (in fact even the naive 2^n time algorithm) are the best one can do!

Notice also that this gives a lower bound on the running time of FPT algorithms for VERTEX COVER when parameterized by solution size k. Indeed, since $k \leq |V(G)|$, a $2^{o(k)}|V(G)|^{\mathcal{O}(1)}$ time algorithm for VERTEX COVER would contradict the ETH. From this starting point one can get numerous lower bounds that miraculously match the running times of the best known algorithms, just by tracing the existing reductions. Of course in many cases clever new reductions have to be designed to get tight bounds (see the survey Lokshtanov et al., 2011). For example, assuming the ETH, all of the following algorithms are already best possible, up to constants in the exponent: the naive $n^{k+\mathcal{O}(1)}$ time algorithms for CLIQUE and DOMINATING SET, the $2^{\mathcal{O}(k)}n^{\mathcal{O}(1)}$ time algorithms for LONGEST PATH and SET SPLITTING from Theorems 2.3 and 2.4, and the $\mathcal{O}(t^l(n+m))$ time algorithm for GRAPH COLORING from Theorem 2.8.

All of the so-called "tight" lower bounds assuming the ETH come with the fine print "*up to constants in the exponent.*" This is of course unsatisfactory: There is a huge difference between a 2^n time algorithm and a 1.00001^n time algorithm and, so far, no one has been able to use the ETH to rule out an algorithm with running time 1.00001^n for a problem that does have an algorithm with running time 100^n. If one is willing to assume the much stronger hypothesis that is SETH, then one can pin down the precise dependence on k for some problems (Lokshtanov et al., 2011). However, so far we are lacking a result akin to Theorem 2.15 for SETH, quite severly limiting its applicability.

2.5.3 Hardness and Optimality of Kernelization

LONGEST PATH can be solved in time $2^{\mathcal{O}(k)}n^{\mathcal{O}(1)}$ (Theorem 2.7). Thus by Theorem 2.10, we deduce that LONGEST PATH admits a kernel of size $2^{\mathcal{O}(k)}$. But what about a kernel of polynomial size?

We argue that intuitively this should not be possible. Assume that LONGEST PATH admits a polynomial kernel of size k^c, where c is some fixed constant. We take many instances,

$$(G_1, k), (G_2, k), \ldots, (G_t, k),$$

of the LONGEST PATH problem, where in each instance $|V(G_i)| = n$, $1 \le i \le t$, and $k \le n$. If we make a new graph G by just taking the disjoint union of the graphs $G_1, \ldots, G_t$, we see that G contains a path of length k if and only if G_i contains a path of length k for some $i \le t$. Now run the kernelization algorithm on G. Then the kernelization algorithm would in polynomial time return a new instance (G', k') such that $|V(G')| \le k^c \le n^c$, a number potentially much smaller than t; for example, set $t = n^{1000c}$. This means that in some sense, the kernelization algorithm considers the instances $(G_1, k), (G_2, k), \ldots, (G_t, k)$ and in *polynomial time* figures out which of the instances are the most likely to contain a path of length k. More precisely, if we have to preserve the value of the OR of our instances while being forced to forget at least one of the inputs entirely, then we have to make sure that the input being forgotten was not the only one whose answer is yes (otherwise we turn a yes-instance into a no-instance). However, at least intuitively, this seems almost as difficult as solving the instances themselves, and since the LONGEST PATH problem is *NP*-complete, this seems unlikely. In 2009, a methodology to rule out polynomial kernels was developed in Fortnow and Santhanam (2008) and Bodlaender et al. (2009). The existence of polynomial kernels are ruled out, in this framework, by linking the availability of a polynomial kernel to an unlikely collapse in classical complexity. These developments deepen the connection between classical and parameterized complexity. Using this methodology one can show that LONGEST PATH does not admit a polynomial kernel unless co$NP \subseteq \frac{NP}{\text{poly}}$. In fact, in Dell and van Melkebeek (2014), the kernel lower bound methodology established in Fortnow and Santhanam (2008) and Bodlaender et al. (2009) was generalized further to provide lower bounds based on different polynomial functions for the kernel size. For an example we can show that the $\mathcal{O}(k^2)$ kernel for VERTEX COVER given by 2.11 is optimal. That is, VERTEX COVER does not have kernels of size $\mathcal{O}(k^{2-\varepsilon})$ unless co$NP \subseteq \frac{NP}{\text{poly}}$.

2.6 Outlook: New Paradigms and Application Domains

The main idea of parameterized algorithms is very general: to measure the running time in terms of both input size as well as a parameter that captures structural properties of the input instance. This idea of a multivariate algorithm analysis holds the potential to address the need for a framework for refined algorithm analysis for all kinds of problems across all domains and subfields of computer science. Indeed, parameterized complexity has permeated other algorithmic paradigms as well as other application domains. In this section we look at some of these.

2.6.1 FPT-Approximation and Lossy Kernels

Until now we have only seen decision problems in the realm of fixed parameter tractability. However, to define the notion of FPT-approximation we need to move away from decision problems and define the notion of optimization problems. However, this chapter is not the right place to do so. We will work with some ad hoc definitions and use them to show glimpses of the budding field of FPT-approximation. For the purpose of this section, we will call an approximaiton algorithm, an FPT-approximation algorithm, if its running time is $f(k) \cdot n^{\mathcal{O}(1)}$, for a parameter k (k need not be the solution size).

We will exemplify this paradigm via the PARTIAL VERTEX COVER problem. In this problem, we are given an undirected graph G and a positive integer k, and the task is to find a subset X of k vertices that covers as many edges as possible. This problem can easily be shown to be $W[1]$-hard via a reduction from the INDEPENDENT SET problem. In what follows, we give an algorithm that for every $\epsilon > 0$, runs in time $f(\epsilon, k) \cdot n^{\mathcal{O}(1)}$, and produces a $(1 + \epsilon)$-approximate solution for the problem.

A natural greedy heuristic for the problem is to *output a set X containing k vertices of the highest degree*. The case in which X could cover far fewer edges than an optimal solution is when the number of edges with both endpoints in X is proportional to the total number of edges that X covers. We will show that this case can be addressed with an FPT algorithm. Let us fix $C = 2\binom{k}{2}/\epsilon$ and and let $v_1, \ldots, v_n$ be the vertices of the graph ordered by nonincreasing degree. In the first case we assume that $d(v_1) \geq C$. Here, $d(v_i)$ denotes the degree of v_i. In this case the greedy heuristic outputs our desired solution. Indeed, $X = \{v_1, \ldots, v_k\}$ covers at least $\sum_{i=1}^{k} d(v_i) - \binom{k}{2}$ edges. The last inequality follows from the fact that any simple graph on k vertices has at most $\binom{k}{2}$ edges. Observe that optimal the solution is always upper bounded by $\sum_{i=1}^{k} d(v_i)$. Thus, the quality of the desired solution is

$$\frac{\sum_{i=1}^{k} d(v_i) - \binom{k}{2}}{\sum_{i=1}^{k} d(v_i)} \geq 1 - \frac{\binom{k}{2}}{C} \geq 1 - \frac{\epsilon}{2} \geq \frac{1}{1 + \epsilon},$$

at most $(1 + \epsilon)$ times the optimum.

We can therefore assume that $d(v_1) < C = 2\binom{k}{2}/\epsilon$. Hence, the optimal solution is upper bounded by $\sum_{i=1}^{k} d(v_i) < Ck$. That is, in this case the maximum number of edges, say t, that any set of size k can cover becomes a function of k and ϵ. What if we parameterize PARTIAL VERTEX COVER by the maximum number of edges, say t, that are covered by a set of size k? Indeed, one can show that PARTIAL VERTEX COVER is solvable in time $2^{\mathcal{O}(t)}n^{\mathcal{O}(1)}$ using the method of color coding explained in Section 2.2. We leave this as an exercise (Exercise 2.4). With this exercise in hand we can prove the following theorem.

Theorem 2.16   *For every $\epsilon > 0$, there exists an algorithm for* PARTIAL VERTEX COVER *that runs in time $f(\epsilon, k) \cdot n^{\mathcal{O}(1)}$, and produces a $(1+\epsilon)$-approximate solution for the problem.*

PARTIAL VERTEX COVER is not the only problem for which FPT-approximation algorithm exists. There are several other problem but arguably the most notable one is s-WAY CUT, parameterized by s (delete minimum number of edges such that the resulting graph has at least s connected components). The problem admits a factor 2-approximation algorithm in polynomial time. On the other hand assuming some well known complexity theory assumption it is not possible to improve this approximation algorithm. Furthermore, the problem is known to be $W[1]$-hard, parameterized by s (Downey et al., 2003). Gupta et al. (2018) obtained a $(2 - \epsilon)$-factor approximation algorithm, a fixed constant $\epsilon > 0$, running in time $f(s) \cdot n^{\mathcal{O}(1)}$. After couple of improvements, Kawarabayashi and Lin (2020) have recently obtained a nearly 5/3 factor FPT-approximation algorithm.

The area of FPT-inapproximability has also flourished. In particular, assuming FPT $\neq W[1]$, DOMINATING SET does not admit an FPT-approximation algorithm with factor $o(k)$ (Karthik et al., 2019). On the other hand, assuming a gap version of ETH, one can show that CLIQUE does not admit any FPT-approximation algorithm (Chalermsook et al., 2017).

Can we combine the theory of kernelization (Section 2.4) with FPT approximation? Unfortunately, the answer is no. Despite the success of kernelization, the basic definition has an important drawback: *It does not combine well with approximation algorithms.* This is a serious problem, since after all the ultimate goal of parameterized algorithms, or for that matter of any algorithmic paradigm, is to eventually solve the given input instance. Thus, the application of a preprocessing algorithm is always followed by an algorithm that finds a solution to the reduced instance. In practice, even after applying a preprocessing procedure, the reduced instance may not be small enough to be solved to optimality within a reasonable time bound. In these cases one gives up on optimality and resorts to approximation algorithms (or heuristics) instead. Thus it is *crucial* that the solution obtained by an approximation algorithm when run on the reduced instance provides a good solution to the original instance, or at least *some* meaningful information about the original instance.

The main reason that the existing notion of kernelization does not combine well with approximation algorithms is that the definition of a kernel is deeply rooted in decision problems, while approximation algorithms are optimization problems. This led to the new definition of *lossy kernels*, coined by Lokshtanov et al. (2017), which extends the notion of kernelization to optimization problems. The main object here is a definition of *α-approximate kernels*. We do not give the formal definition here, but, loosely speaking, an α-approximate kernel of size $g(k)$ is a polynomial time algorithm that given an instance (I, k) outputs an instance (I', k') such that $|I'| + k' \leq g(k)$ and any c-approximate solution s' to the instance (I', k') can be turned in polynomial time into a $(c \cdot \alpha)$-approximate solution s to the original instance (I, k).

We again exemplify the idea of α-approximate kernels by giving a suitable algorithm for PARTIAL VERTEX COVER. Here, we will rely on the observation that the first case in the proof of Theorem 2.16 is handled in polynomial time. We formally show this in the next theorem.

Theorem 2.17 PARTIAL VERTEX COVER *admits α-approximate kernels for every* $\alpha > 1$.

Proof We give an α-approximate kernelization algorithm for the problem for every $\alpha > 1$. Let $\epsilon = 1 - \frac{1}{\alpha}$ and $\beta = \frac{1}{\epsilon}$. Let (G, k) be the input instance. Let $v_1, v_2, \ldots, v_n$ be the vertices of G in the nonincreasing order of degree, i.e., $d_G(v_i) \geq d_G(v_j)$ for all $1 \geq i > j \geq n$. The kernelization algorithm has two cases based on the degree of v_1.

Case 1 $d_G(v_1) \geq \beta\binom{k}{2}$. In this case $S = \{v_1, \ldots, v_k\}$ is a α-approximate solution. The number of edges incident to S is at least $(\sum_{i=1}^{k} d_G(v_i)) - \binom{k}{2}$, because at most $\binom{k}{2}$ edges have both endpoints in S and they are counted twice in the sum $(\sum_{i=1}^{k} d_G(v_i))$. The value of the optimum solution is at most $\sum_{i=1}^{k} d_G(v_i)$. As in Theorem 2.16, we can show that

$$\frac{(\sum_{i=1}^{k} d_G(v_i)) - \binom{k}{2}}{\sum_{i=1}^{k} d_G(v_i)} \geq 1 - \frac{\binom{k}{2}}{d_G(v_1)} \geq 1 - \frac{1}{\beta} = \frac{1}{\alpha}.$$

The foregoing inequality implies that S is an α-approximate solution. So the kernelization algorithm outputs a trivial instance $(\emptyset, 0)$ in this case.

Case 2 $d_G(v_1) < \beta\binom{k}{2}$. Let $V' = \{v_1, v_2, \ldots, v_{k\lceil\beta\binom{k}{2}\rceil+1}\}$. In this case the algorithm outputs (G', k), where $G' = G[N_G[V']]$ (the subgraph of G induced by the vertices of V' and all of their neighbors). Let $OPT(G, k)$ denote the optimum value of the instance. We first claim that $OPT(G', k) = OPT(G, k)$. Since G' is a subgraph of G, $OPT(G', k) \leq OPT(G, k)$. Now it is enough to show that $OPT(G', k) \geq OPT(G, k)$. Toward that, we prove that there is an optimum solution that contains only vertices from the set V'. Suppose not; then consider the solution S, which is lexicographically smallest in the ordered list $v_1, \ldots v_n$. The set S contains at most $k - 1$ vertices from V' and at least one from $V \setminus V'$. Since the degree of each vertex in G is at most $\lceil\beta\binom{k}{2}\rceil - 1$ and $|S| \leq k$, we have that $|N_G[S]| \leq k\lceil\beta\binom{k}{2}\rceil$. This implies that there exists a vertex $v \in V'$ such that $v \notin N_G[S]$. Hence by including the vertex v and removing a vertex from $S \setminus V'$, we can cover at least as many edges as S can cover. This contradicts our assumption that S is lexicographically smallest. Since G' is a subgraph of G any solution of G' is also a solution of G. Thus we have shown that $OPT(G', k) = OPT(G, k)$. So the algorithm returns the instance (G', k) as the reduced instance. Since G' is a subgraph of G, in this case, the solution lifting algorithm takes a solution S' of (G', k) as input and outputs S' as a solution of (G, k). Since $OPT(G', k) = OPT(G, k)$, the correctness of the kernelization algorithm follows.

The number of vertices in the reduced instance is $O(k \cdot \lceil\frac{1}{\epsilon}\binom{k}{2}\rceil^2) = O(k^5)$. The running time of the algorithm is polynomial in the size of G. $\qquad\square$

We note that as for classical kernelization (Section 2.5.3), there are tools to rule out lossy kernelization (refer to Lokshtanov et al., 2017 for further details).

2.6.2 FPT in P

While initially the main focus of parameterized complexity was on *NP*-complete problems, the idea of going beyond the worst-case analysis by exploiting the structural properties of the input instance is applicable to problems in *P* too.

Several such algorithms can be found in the literature. For example, by the result of Fomin et al. (2018a), a maximum matching in a graph of treewidth at most k can be constructed in time $\mathcal{O}(k^4 \cdot n \log^2 n)$, while the best known worst-case running time on general graphs is $\mathcal{O}(n^{\omega})$, which is due to Mucha and Sankowski (2004). Abboud et al. (2016) proved that the DIAMETER problem can be solved in time $2^{\mathcal{O}(k \log k)} \cdot n^{1+o(1)}$ on graphs of treewidth k, but achieving running time of the form $2^{o(k)} \cdot n^{2-\varepsilon}$ for any $\varepsilon > 0$ would already contradict the SETH.

2.6.3 Application Domains

Parameterized complexity focused largely on problems on graphs in the first two decades of its existence. However, in the past decade, problems arising in different domains such as computational geometry, bioinformatics, machine learning and computational social choice theory have been considered through the lens of parameterized complexity. A plethora of parameters such as the dimension of the input, solution size, the number of input strings, patterns in people's preferences, number of candidates, and number of voters have been used as parameters in these domains. These led to numerous results in these areas and several parameterized algorithms or nonexistence of such algorithms have been proved. We refer to the following surveys for these Giannopoulos et al., 2008; Bredereck et al., 2014; Faliszewski and Niedermeier (2016); Panolan et al., 2019).

2.7 The Big Picture

Parameterized algorithms and complexity has been a spectacular success from a theoretical perspective. From the more applied perspective, only very recently, the PACE challenge kickstarted research into practical implementations for basic FPT problems like VERTEX COVER, TREEWIDTH, or STEINER TREE. (See Dell et al., 2017, 2018). These experimental contests have shown the following:

- Parameterized complexity seems particularly useful/efficient for problems arising in graph theory and networks.
- PACE implementation challenge has shown that to improve the practical performance of a parameterized algorithm one needs to fine-tune parameters and apply "time-saving optimization" tricks on top of it. Also, the algorithm that has the "best running time" (this is not unique as the running time is governed by two parameters and thus we can only talk about Pareto-optimality) may not be the best performing algorithm in practice. Thus, in practice we should use parameterized algorithms as a skeleton and optimize other parameters for performance.
- There is huge discrepancy between the running time predictions derived from theoretical analysis of parameterized algorithms (which is worst case and hence overly pessimistic) and the performance of algorithms in practice.

Every success is accompanied with its own list of failures. Unfortunately, there is lack of study of weighted discrete optimization problems, or problems over continuous domains. For example, problems arising in the field of computational geometry or mathematical programming. One reason for this is that with respect to solution size, which has become the go to parameterization in the field, the problem generally turns out to be intractable. Similarly, for problems in which input consists of vectors in $\mathbb{R}^d$, most problems turn out to be W-hard with respect to dimension d. Thus, for such problems a user should either not use parameterized complexity as a tool to design an algorithm or should avoid using so-called classical parameters. Finally, choice of a parameter is an art. One should not restrict oneself with just one parameter for the same problem. It is possible that different parameters are "small" for different families of instances of the same problem and hence together they represent wider tractability of the problem. One thing that the field must do is to interact with other fields and develop tools based on this synergy. For example, combining approximation algorithms and parameterized complexity has yielded several positive results (of course, some exciting negative results as well).

2.8 Notes

The history of parameterized algorithms can be traced back to the 1970s and 80s, including the algorithm of Dreyfus and Wagner (1971) for STEINER TREE, the algorithm of Farber et al. (1986) for ACHROMATIC NUMBER, and the celebrated result of Robertson and Seymour (1995) on DISJOINT PATHS. The foundations of parameterized complexity, the toolkit for analyzing parameterized algorithms, were laid in 1990s in the series of papers Abrahamson et al. (1995) and Downey and Fellows (1992, 1995a,b). The classic reference on parameterized complexity is the book of Downey and Fellows (1999). The new edition of this book Downey and Fellows (2013) is a comprehensive overview of the state of the art in many areas of parameterized complexity. The book by Flum and Grohe (2006) is an extensive introduction to the area with a strong emphasis on the complexity viewpoint. An introduction to basic algorithmic techniques in parameterized complexity up to 2006 is given in the book by Niedermeier (2006). The recent textbook by Cygan et al. (2015) provides a coherent account of the most recent tools and techniques in the area. The book by Fomin et al. (2019) gives a detailed overview of algorithmic and complexity techniques used in kernelization.

The reference point for branching algorithms is the work of Davis and Putnam (1960) [see also Davis et al. (1962)] on the design and analysis of algorithms to solve some satisfiability problems. Branching algorithms and techniques for their analysis are discussed in detail in the book by Fomin and Kratsch (2010). A branching algorithm with running time $\mathcal{O}(2^k(n+m))$ for VERTEX COVER appears in the book by Mehlhorn (1984). After a long sequence of improvements, the current champion algorithm runs in time $\mathcal{O}(1.2738^k + kn)$ and is due to Chen et al. (2010). The method of color coding was introduced in the seminal paper of Alon et al. (1995).

ETH and SETH were first introduced in the work of Impagliazzo and Paturi (2001), which built upon earlier work of Impagliazzo et al. (2001).

Theorem 2.10 on equivalence of kernelization and fixed-parameter tractability is due to Cai et al. (1997). The reduction rules for VERTEX COVER discussed in this chapter are attributed to Buss in Buss and Goldsmith (1993) and are often referred to as Buss kernelization in the literature. A more refined set of reduction rules for VERTEX COVER was introduced in Balasubramanian et al. (1998). The kernelization algorithm for matrix rigidity is from Fomin et al. (2018b). We refer to the following books an [Downey and Fellows (1999, 2013); Flum and Grohe (2006); Niedermeier (2006); Cygan et al. (2015); Fomin et al. (2019); Fomin and Kratsch (2010)] for detailed overview of all the techniques presented in this survey and more. We also refer the readers to the book of van Rooij et al. (2019) for an application to questions of intractability, with respect to both classical and parameterized complexity analysis, in cognitive science.

References

Abboud, Amir, Williams, Virginia Vassilevska, and Wang, Joshua R. 2016. Approximation and fixed parameter subquadratic algorithms for radius and diameter in sparse graphs. *Proceedings of the 27th Annual ACM-SIAM Symposium on Discrete Algorithms (SODA)*, pp 377–391. SIAM.

Abrahamson, Karl R., Downey, Rodney G., and Fellows, Michael R. 1995. Fixed-parameter tractability and completeness IV: On completeness for $W[P]$ and PSPACE analogues. *Annals Pure Applied Logic*, **73**(3), 235–276.

Alon, Noga, Yuster, Raphael, and Zwick, Uri. 1995. Color-coding. *Journal of the ACM*, **42**(4), 844–856.

Balasubramanian, R., Fellows, Michael R., and Raman, Venkatesh. 1998. An improved fixed-parameter algorithm for vertex cover. *Information Processing Letters*, **65**(3), 163–168.

Bodlaender, Hans L., Downey, Rodney G., Fellows, Michael R., and Hermelin, Danny. 2009. On problems without polynomial kernels. *Journal of Computer and System Sciences*, **75**(8), 423–434.

Bredereck, Robert, Chen, Jiehua, Faliszewski, Piotr, Guo, Jiong, Niedermeier, Rolf, and Woeginger, Gerhard J. 2014. Parameterized algorithmics for computational social choice: Nine research challenges. *CoRR*, abs/1407.2143.

Buss, Jonathan F., and Goldsmith, Judy. 1993. Nondeterminism within P. *SIAM Journal of Computing*, **22**(3), 560–572.

Cai, Liming, Chen, Jianer, Downey, Rodney G., and Fellows, Michael R. 1997. Advice classes of parameterized tractability. *Annals Pure Applied Logic*, **84**(1), 119–138.

Chalermsook, Parinya, Cygan, Marek, Kortsarz, Guy, Laekhanukit, Bundit, Manurangsi, Pasin, Nanongkai, Danupon, and Trevisan, Luca. 2017. From gap-ETH to FPT-inapproximability: Clique, dominating set, and more. *58th IEEE Annual Symposium on Foundations of Computer Science, FOCS 2017*, pp. 743–754. IEEE Computer Society.

Chen, Jianer, and Lu, Songjian. 2009. Improved parameterized set splitting algorithms: A probabilistic approach. *Algorithmica*, **54**(4), 472–489.

Chen, Jianer, Kanj, Iyad A., and Xia, Ge. 2010. Improved upper bounds for vertex cover. *Theoretical Computer Science*, **411**(40–42), 3736–3756.

Cygan, Marek, Fomin, Fedor V., Kowalik, Lukasz, Lokshtanov, Daniel, Marx, Dániel, Pilipczuk, Marcin, Pilipczuk, Michał, and Saurabh, Saket. 2015. *Parameterized Algorithms*. Springer.

Davis, Martin, and Putnam, Hilary. 1960. A computing procedure for quantification theory. *Journal of the ACM*, **7**, 201–215.

Davis, Martin, Logemann, George, and Loveland, Donald. 1962. A machine program for theorem-proving. *Communications of the ACM*, **5**, 394–397.

Dell, Holge, and van Melkebeek, Dieter. 2014. Satisfiability allows no nontrivial sparsification unless the polynomial-time hierarchy collapses. *Journal of the ACM*, **61**(4), 1–23:27.

Dell, Holger, Husfeldt, Thore, Jansen, Bart M. P., Kaski, Petteri, Komusiewicz, Christian, and Rosamond, Frances A. 2017. The first parameterized algorithms and computational experiments challenge. Guo, Jiong, and Hermelin, Danny (eds.), *11th International Symposium on Parameterized and Exact Computation (IPEC 2016)*, pp. 30.1–30.9. Leibniz International Proceedings in Informatics (LIPIcs), vol. 63. Schloss Dagstuhl–Leibniz-Zentrum fuer Informatik.

Dell, Holger, Komusiewicz, Christian, Talmon, Nimrod, and Weller, Mathias. 2018. The PACE 2017 Parameterized algorithms and computational experiments challenge: The second iteration. Lokshtanov, Daniel, and Nishimura, Naomi (eds.), *12th International Symposium on Parameterized and Exact Computation (IPEC 2017)*, pp. 30.1–30.12. Leibniz International Proceedings in Informatics (LIPIcs), vol. 89. Schloss Dagstuhl–Leibniz-Zentrum fuer Informatik.

Downey, Rodney G., and Fellows, Michael R. 1992. Fixed-parameter tractability and completeness. *Proceedings of the 21st Manitoba Conference on Numerical Mathematics and Computing. Congressus Numerantium*, **87**, 161–178.

Downey, Rodney G., and Fellows, Michael R. 1995a. Fixed-parameter tractability and completeness I: Basic results. *SIAM Journals of Computing*, **24**(4), 873–921.

Downey, Rodney G., and Fellows, Michael R. 1995b. Fixed-parameter tractability and completeness II: On completeness for $W[1]$. *Theoretical Computer Science*, **141**(1&2), 109–131.

Downey, Rodney G., and Fellows, Michael R. 1999. *Parameterized Complexity*. Springer-Verlag.

Downey, Rodney G., and Fellows, Michael R. 2013. *Fundamentals of Parameterized Complexity*. Texts in Computer Science. Springer.

Downey, Rodney G., Estivill-Castro, Vladimir, Fellows, Michael R., Prieto-Rodriguez, Elena, and Rosamond, Frances A. 2003. Cutting up is hard to do: The parameterized complexity of k-cut and related problems. *Electronic Notes in Theoretical Computer Science*, **78**, 209–222.

Dreyfus, Stuart E., and Wagner, Robert A. 1971. The Steiner problem in graphs. *Networks*, **1**(3), 195–207.

Faliszewski, Piotr, and Niedermeier, Rolf. 2016. Parameterization in computational social choice. In *Encyclopedia of Algorithms*, pp. 1516–1520.

Farber, Martin, Hahn, Gena, Hell, Pavol, and Miller, Donald J. 1986. Concerning the achromatic number of graphs. *Journal of Combinatorial Theory Ser. B*, **40**(1), 21–39.

Flum, Jörg, and Grohe, Martin. 2006. *Parameterized Complexity Theory*. Texts in Theoretical Computer Science. An EATCS Series. Springer-Verlag.

Fomin, Fedor V., and Kratsch, Dieter. 2010. *Exact Exponential Algorithms*. Texts in Theoretical Computer Science. An EATCS Series. Berlin: Springer-Verlag.

Fomin, Fedor V., Lokshtanov, Daniel, Saurabh, Saket, Pilipczuk, Michal, and Wrochna, Marcin. 2018a. Fully polynomial-time parameterized computations for graphs and matrices of low treewidth. *ACM Transactions on Algorithms*, **14**(3), 34:1–34:45.

Fomin, Fedor V., Lokshtanov, Daniel, Meesum, Syed Mohammad, Saurabh, Saket, and Zehavi, Meirav. 2018b. Matrix rigidity from the viewpoint of parameterized complexity. *SIAM Journal Discrete Mathematics*, **32**(2), 966–985.

Fomin, Fedor V., Lokshtanov, Daniel, Saurabh, Saket, and Zehavi, Meirav. 2019. *Kernelization. Theory of Parameterized Preprocessing*. Cambridge University Press.

Fortnow, Lance, and Santhanam, Rahul. 2008. Infeasibility of instance compression and succinct PCPs for *NP*. *Proceedings of the 40th Annual ACM Symposium on Theory of Computing (STOC)*, pp. 133–142. ACM.

Giannopoulos, Panos, Knauer, Christian, and Whitesides, Sue. 2008. Parameterized complexity of geometric problems. *Computer Journal*, **51**(3), 372–384.

Gupta, Anupam, Lee, Euiwoong, and Li, Jason. 2018. An FPT algorithm beating 2-approximation for k-cut. *Proceedings of the Twenty-Ninth Annual ACM-SIAM Symposium on Discrete Algorithms, SODA 2018*, pp. 2821–2837. SIAM.

Impagliazzo, Russell, and Paturi, Ramamohan. 2001. On the complexity of k-SAT. *Journal of Computer and System Sciences*, **62**(2), 367–375.

Impagliazzo, Russell, Paturi, Ramamohan, and Zane, Francis. 2001. Which problems have strongly exponential complexity. *Journal of Computer and System Sciences*, **63**(4), 512–530.

Karthik C. S., Laekhanukit, Bundit, and Manurangsi, Pasin. 2019. On the parameterized complexity of approximating dominating set. *Journal of ACM*, **66**(5), 33:1–33:38.

Kawarabayashi, Ken-Ichi, and Lin, Bingkai. 2020. A nearly 5/3-approximation FPT algorithm for min-k-cut. *Proceedings of the Thirty First Annual ACM-SIAM Symposium on Discrete Algorithms, SODA 2020*, pp. 990–999. *Salt Lake City, Utah, USA, January 6-8, 2020*. SIAM.

Lokshtanov, Daniel, Marx, Dániel, and Saurabh, Saket. 2011. Lower bounds based on the Exponential Time Hypothesis. *Bulletin of the EATCS*, **105**, 41–72.

Lokshtanov, Daniel, Panolan, Fahad, Ramanujan, M. S., and Saurabh, Saket. 2017. Lossy kernelization. *Proceedings of the 49th Annual ACM Symposium on Theory of Computing (STOC)*, pp. 224–237. ACM.

Lokshtanov, Daniel, Marx, Dániel, and Saurabh, Saket. 2018. Slightly Superexponential Parameterized Problems. *SIAM Journal on Computing*, **47**(3), 675–702.

Mehlhorn, Kurt. 1984. *Data Structures and Algorithms 2: Graph Algorithms and NP-Completeness*. EATCS Monographs on Theoretical Computer Science, vol. 2. Springer.

Mucha, Marcin, and Sankowski, Piotr. 2004. Maximum matchings via Gaussian elimination. *FOCS 2004*, pp. 248–255. IEEE Computer Society.

Naor, Moni, Schulman, Leonard J., and Srinivasan, Aravind. 1995. Splitters and near-optimal derandomization. *Proceedings of the 36th Annual Symposium on Foundations of Computer Science (FOCS)*, pp. 182–181. IEEE.

Niedermeier, Rolf. 2006. *Invitation to Fixed-Parameter Algorithms*. Oxford Lecture Series in Mathematics and Its Applications, vol. 31. Oxford University Press.

Panolan, Fahad, Saurabh, Saket, and Zehavi, Meirav. 2019. Parameterized computational geometry via decomposition theorems. In *Proceedings of the 13th International Conference on Algorithms and Computation (WALCOM)*, pp. 15–27. Lecture Notes in Computer Science, vol. 11355. Springer.

Papadimitriou, Christos H., and Yannakakis, Mihalis. 1996. On limited nondeterminism and the complexity of the V-C dimension. *Journal of Computer and System Sciences*, **53**(2), 161–170.

Robertson, Neil, and Seymour, Paul D. 1995. Graph minors. XIII. The disjoint paths problem. *Journal of Combinatorial Theory B*, **63**(1), 65–110.

Sipser, Michael. 1996. *Introduction to the Theory of Computation*. 1st ed. International Thomson.

van Rooij, Iris, Blokpoel, Mark, Kwisthout, Johan, and Wareham, Todd. 2019. *Cognition and Intractability: A Guide to Classical and Parameterized Complexity Analysis*. Cambridge University Press.

Exercises

Exercise 2.1 Give an algorithm for VERTEX COVER that runs in time $1.4656^k \cdot n^{O(1)}$.

Exercise 2.2 In the CLUSTER EDITING problem, we are given a graph G and an integer k, and the objective is to check whether we can turn G into a cluster graph (a disjoint union of cliques) by making at most k edge editions, where each edition is adding or deleting one edge. Obtain a $3^k n^{\mathcal{O}(1)}$-time algorithm for CLUSTER EDITING.

Exercise 2.3 Prove that a random assignment ψ splits k sets with probability at least $\frac{1}{2^k}$ (see Section 2.2.1).

Exercise 2.4 Show that PARTIAL VERTEX COVER is solvable in time $2^{\mathcal{O}(t)} n^{\mathcal{O}(1)}$, where t is the number of covered edges.

CHAPTER THREE

From Adaptive Analysis to Instance Optimality

Jérémy Barbay

Abstract: This chapter introduces the related concepts of *adaptive analysis* and *instance optimality*. The goal is to define an extremely fine-grained parameterization of a problem's instance space in order to argue that a particular algorithm for the problem is "optimal" in a very strong sense. This chapter presents two detailed case studies, for the MAXIMA SET problem and a database aggregation problem, as well as a representative list of additional techniques, results, and open problems.

3.1 Case Study 1: Maxima Sets

Suppose you have a new job and need to find a house to buy or rent. You would like to find a place close to work but not too expensive. You gather a list of possible houses, but there are too many to visit them all. Can you reduce the list of places to visit without compromising any of your criteria?

This is a two-dimensional version of a well-known problem, reinvented multiple times in various areas; we will call it the MAXIMA SET problem. In a computational geometry context, it was first considered by Kung et al. (1975). The input is a set S of n points in the plane. A point of S is called *maximal* if none of the other points in S dominates it in every coordinate. The goal in the MAXIMA SET problem is to identify all of the maximal points (i.e., the maxima set).[1] See also Figure 3.1.[2]

Several algorithms have been proposed for the MAXIMA SET problem in two dimensions.[3] These algorithms highlight the importance of analyzing an algorithm's running time as a function of *two* parameters, the usual input size n (i.e., the number of input points) and also the output size k (i.e., the number of maximal points). We next briefly review several of these algorithms, which are important precursors to the more general notions of adaptive analysis and instance optimality. This sequence of increasingly instance-adaptive running time bounds will illustrate a process of iterative refinement, culminating in a form of instance optimality.

---

[1] For the house-finding problem, the x- and y-axes correspond to the negative price and negative distance of a house (as in the house-finding problem, smaller prices and distances are better).

[2] The same problem is explored in Chapter 12 in the context of self-improving algorithms.

[3] Similar algorithms can also be used to compute the convex hull of a set of points, and indeed were originally proposed primarily for this purpose.

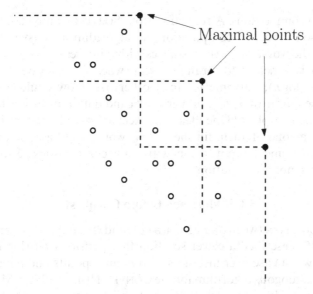

Figure 3.1 A point set and its maxima. Solid circles are the maximal points, hollow circles are the dominated points. The dashed lines indicate the "region of domination" for each of the maximal points.

3.1.1 Jarvis March (a.k.a. Gift Wrapping)

Among the n houses to consider, the cheapest and the closest are especially good candidates and can be identified with $O(n)$ comparisons. If there is only one such house (at once cheaper and closer than any other), the problem is solved. Otherwise, the cheapest and the closest must both be part of the output (they correspond to maximal points, which we will call *candidate* houses), and one can then iterate on the remaining $n - 2$ houses.

On account of a similar algorithm for the CONVEX HULL problem (Jarvis, 1973), we will call this algorithm Jarvis march. The number of house comparisons performed by the algorithm is $\Theta(nh)$ in the worst case for instances with n houses and h candidate houses selected in the end. This running time ranges from $\Theta(n)$ to $\Theta(n^2)$, depending on the output size h.

3.1.2 Graham's Scan

Another approach, which improves over the quadratic worst-case running time of Jarvis march, is to first sort the n houses by increasing price using $O(n \log n)$ comparisons and then scan the list of houses in order to eliminate all the houses that are not maxima. Scanning the sorted list requires at most $2n = O(n)$ further home comparisons: the first house of this list is the cheapest and necessarily a candidate, and any house considered after that is either a candidate (if it is closer to work than the previous most expensive candidate considered) or can be pruned (if it is at once more expensive and farther to work than the previously most expensive house considered).

As before, by analogy with a similar algorithm for the CONVEX HULL problem (Graham, 1972), we'll call this algorithm Graham's scan.[4] This algorithm performs

---

[4] Called Sweeping Line in Chapter 12.

$O(n \log n)$ house comparisons. A reduction from SORTING can be used to show that, in the comparison model of computation, no algorithm uses asymptotically fewer comparisons in the worst case over instances with n houses.

Jarvis march is superior to Graham's scan when $h = o(\log n)$, equivalent to it when $h = \Theta(\log n)$, and inferior to it otherwise. How could we know which algorithm to use, given that the number h of candidate houses is what we wanted to compute in the first place? One idea is to execute both algorithms in parallel and to stop as soon as one of them finishes.[5] This would yield a solution that runs in $O(n \cdot \min\{h, \log n\})$ time, but potentially with many comparisons performed twice. Is there a more parsimonious solution?

3.1.3 Marriage Before Conquest

Rather than choosing between `Jarvis march` and `Graham's scan`, Kirkpatrick and Seidel (1985) described a clever solution that performs $O(n \log h)$ house comparisons in the worst case over instances with n input points and h maximal points. They called the analogous algorithm for the CONVEX HULL problem Marriage Before Conquest (Kirkpatrick and Seidel, 1986), and we adopt that name here.[6]

Algorithm Marriage Before Conquest(S):

1. If $|S| = 1$ then return S.
2. Divide S into the left and right halves S_ℓ and S_r by the median x-coordinate.
3. *Discover* the point q with the maximum y-coordinate in S_r.
4. *Prune* all points in S_ℓ and S_r that are dominated by q.
5. Return the concatenation of Marriage Before Conquest(S_ℓ) and Marriage Before Conquest(S_r).

This divide-and-conquer algorithm uses as a subroutine the linear-time median finding algorithm of Blum et al. (1973). After identifying the median house price, one can partition the set of n houses into the $\lfloor n/2 \rfloor$ cheapest houses (corresponding to S_r, as cheaper is better) and the $\lceil n/2 \rceil$ most expensive houses (corresponding to S_ℓ). Given such a partition, one can find a first candidate house by selecting the house closest to work among the $\lfloor n/2 \rfloor$ least expensive houses, prune the houses dominated by this candidate, and recurse on both the set of remaining cheaper houses and the set of remaining more expensive houses.

Theorem 3.1 (Kirkpatrick and Seidel, 1985) *Given a set S of n points in the plane, the algorithm Marriage Before Conquest computes the maximal points of S in $O(n \log h)$ time, where h is the the number of maximal points.*

Proof Sketch The number of comparisons performed by the algorithm is $O(n \log h)$, as in the worst case the median divides the $h - 1$ maxima left to identify into two sets of roughly equal sizes. (In the best case, the median divides the instance into one instance with half the input points and one maximal point,

---

[5] Kirkpatrick (2009) describes this as a "Dovetailing" solution.

[6] The algorithm described here is a slight variant of that in Kirkpatrick and Seidel (1985); the original pruned only points from S_ℓ in line 4.

which is then solved recursively in linear time, and one instance with $h - 2$ maxima but only $n/2$ input points.) □

A reduction from the SORTING MULTISETS problem on an alphabet of size h shows that no algorithm in the comparison model has a running time asymptotically better than $O(n \log h)$, in the worst case over inputs with input size n and output size h.

Marriage Before Conquest is so good that its inventors titled their paper on an extension to the CONVEX HULL problem "The Ultimate Planar Convex Hull Algorithm?" (Kirkpatrick and Seidel, 1986). To answer this question (for MAXIMA SET or CONVEX HULL), one would need to prove that no algorithm can outperform Marriage Before Conquest by more than a constant factor. Haven't we already proved this? What type of optimality could one hope for beyond optimality over instances of a given input size and output size?

3.1.4 Vertical Entropy

It turns out there are natural finer-grained parameterizations of the input space for the MAXIMA SET (and CONVEX HULL) problem, which enable stronger notions of algorithm optimality. For example, consider an instance with output size $h = o(n)$, where one of the h houses in the output is cheaper and closer than the $n - h$ dominated houses. Such an instance is much easier for the Marriage Before Conquest algorithm than, say, one where each of the h candidate houses dominates exactly $(n - h)/h$ noncandidate houses. In the latter case, the algorithm might well run in $\Theta(n \log h)$ time. But in the former case, it performs only $O(n + h \log h) = o(n \log h)$ comparisons: as $h = o(n)$, the median-priced house will be among the $n - h$ dominated houses, leading to the selection of the particular one cheaper and closer than the $n - h$ noncandidate houses and the latter's immediate elimination, leaving only $h - 1$ candidate houses to process in $O(h \log h)$ time.

To better measure the difference in difficulty between such instances, Sen and Gupta (1999) defined n_i as the number of noncandidate houses dominated by the ith cheapest candidate house (and no candidate house cheaper than this one), and the *vertical entropy* of an instance as the entropy of the distribution of $\{n_i\}_{i \in [2,...,h]}$. Formally:

$$\mathcal{H}_v(n_2, \ldots, n_h) = \sum_{i=2}^{h} \frac{n_i}{n} \log \left(\frac{n}{n_i} \right). \tag{3.1}$$

Note that, by basic properties of entropy, $\mathcal{H}_v \leq \log_2 h$.

Vertical entropy yields a more fine-grained parameterization and the following result:

Theorem 3.2 (Sen and Gupta, 1999) *Given a set S of n points in the plane, the Marriage Before Conquest algorithm computes the maxima set of S in $O(n\mathcal{H}_v)$ time, where $\mathcal{H}_v$ is the vertical entropy (3.1) of S.*

Proof Sketch We claim that the number of comparisons used by the Marriage Before Conquest algorithm is $O(n \log n - \sum_{i=2}^{h} n_i \log n_i) = O(\sum_{i=2}^{h} n_i \log(n/n_i)) = O(n \mathcal{H}_v(n_2, \ldots, n_i))$. The essential idea is that, if a maximal point dominates at least n_i input points, then it will be identified by Marriage Before Conquest after at most $\log_2(n/n_i)$ rounds. (For example, if $n_i \geq n/2$, it will be identified immediately; if $n_i \geq n/4$ it will be identified after at most two levels of recursion; and so on.) Thus, the n_i input points that it dominates contribute at most n_i comparisons to at most $\log_2(n/n_i)$ partition phases. □

A reduction from the SORTING MULTISETS problem on an alphabet of size $h - 1$ and frequency distributions $\{n_i\}_{i \in [2, \ldots, h]}$ shows that no algorithm in the comparison model has a running time asymptotically better than $O(n \mathcal{H}_v)$, in the worst case over inputs with input size n and vertical entropy $\mathcal{H}_v$.

Because $\mathcal{H}_v \leq \log_2 h$, the analysis of Sen and Gupta (1999) is more fine-grained that that of Kirkpatrick and Seidel (1985). This shows that Marriage Before Conquest is even more "adaptive" than its authors gave the algorithm credit for. But does Theorem 3.2 prove that it truly is the "ultimate" algorithm for the problem?

3.1.5 (Order-Oblivious) Instance Optimality

Theorem 3.2 is insufficient to claim the "ultimateness" of the Marriage Before Conquest algorithm: one could define in a very similar way the "horizontal entropy" of an instance. There are instances with high vertical entropy and low horizontal entropy, and vice versa. One could also define a "horizontal" version of the Marriage Before Conquest algorithm, which would iteratively partition houses around the one of median distance rather than cost, which would then be optimal with respect to the horizontal entropy parameter. This section outlines a result of Afshani et al. (2017), who showed that a minor variant of the Marriage Before Conquest algorithm is indeed "ultimate," among algorithms in the comparison model that do not take advantage of the order of the input.

Central to the notion of *instance optimality* is the idea of a *certificate* of an instance.[7] Any correct algorithm for a problem implicitly certifies the correctness of its output, and the description length of this certificate is a lower bound on the algorithm's running time. In instance optimality, the goal is to define a form of certificate such that, for every instance (1) every correct algorithm implicitly defines such a certificate and (2) the protagonist algorithm (to be proved instance-optimal) runs in time at most a constant factor times the length of the shortest certificate.

In the specific case of the MAXIMA SET problem, any correct algorithm must be able to justify: (1) for each of the $n - h$ noncandidate houses, why it was discarded; and (2) for each of the h candidate houses, why it cannot be discarded. The algorithms presented in this section (Jarvis march, Graham's scan, and Marriage Before Conquest) justify their choices in the same way: (1) each noncandidate house is discarded only after the algorithm has found another house that dominates it; and (2) each candidate house is added to the output only after it has been determined that there is no cheaper house which is closer, and no closer house that is cheaper.

---

[7] A similar notion is used in Chapter 12 in the context of self-improving algorithms.

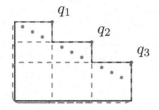

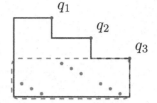

Figure 3.2 A "harder" point set for the computation of the maxima set in two dimensions.

Figure 3.3 An "easier" point set.

The next definition formalizes this idea. By the *staircase* of a point set, we mean the boundary of the union of the "regions of domination" of the maximal points (cf., Figure 3.1).

Definition 3.3 Consider a partition Π of the set S of n input points into disjoint subsets $S_1, \dots, S_t$. The partition Π is *respectful* if each subset S_k is either a singleton or can be enclosed by an axis-aligned box B_k whose interior is completely below the staircase of S. Define the *entropy* $\mathcal{H}(\Pi)$ of the partition Π to be $\sum_{k=1}^{t}(|S_k|/n)\log(n/|S_k|)$. Define the *structural entropy* $\mathcal{H}(S)$ of the input set S to be the minimum of $\mathcal{H}(\Pi)$ over all respectful partitions Π of S.

The intuition is that each nonsingleton group S_i represents a cluster of points that could conceivably be eliminated by an algorithm in one fell swoop.[8] Thus the bigger the S_i's, the easier one might expect the instance to be (Figures 3.2–3.3).

The structural entropy is always at most the vertical entropy (and similarly the horizontal entropy), as shown by taking the S_i's to be "vertical slabs" as in Figure 3.4 (with each maximal point in its own set).

The following result shows that, for every instance, the running time of the Marriage Before Conquest algorithm is bounded by the number of points times the structural entropy of the instance.

Theorem 3.4 (Afshani et al., 2017) *Given a set S of n points in the plane, the algorithm Marriage Before Conquest computes the maxima set of S in $O(n(\mathcal{H}(S)+1))$ time.*

Proof Consider the recursion tree of the algorithm (Figure 3.5) and let X_j denote the sub-list of all maximal points of S discovered during the first j recursion levels, in left-to-right order. Let $S^{(j)}$ be the subset of points of S that *survive* recursion level j, i.e., that have not been pruned during levels $0, \dots, j$ of the recursion, and let $n_j = |S^{(j)}|$. The algorithm performs $O(n_j)$ operations to refine level j into level $j+1$, and there are at most $\lceil \log n \rceil$ such levels in the computation, so the total running time is $O(\sum_{j=0}^{\lceil \log n \rceil} n_j)$. Next observe that:

---

[8] Beginning from the northeast corner of the box, travel north until you hit the staircase, and then east until you hit a maximal point q. The point q dominates all of the points in S_i.

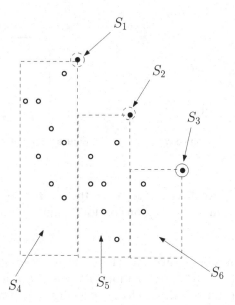

Figure 3.4 A respectful partition using vertical slabs: structural entropy generalizes vertical entropy.

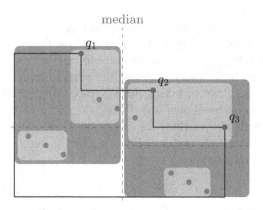

Figure 3.5 The beginning of the recursive partitioning of S. The two bottom boxes are already leaves of the recursion tree, while the two top boxes will be divided further.

(i) there can be at most $\lceil n/2^j \rceil$ points of $S^{(j)}$ with x-coordinates between any two consecutive points in X_j; and

(ii) all points of S that are strictly below the staircase of X_j have been pruned during levels $0, \ldots, j$ of the recursion.

Let Π be a respectful partition of S. Consider a nonsingleton subset S_k in Π. Let B_k be a box enclosing S_k whose interior lies below the staircase of S. Fix a level j. Suppose that the upper-right corner of B_k has x-coordinate between two consecutive points q_i and q_{i+1} in X_j. By (ii), the only points in B_k that can survive level j must have x-coordinates between q_i and q_{i+1}. Thus, by (i), the number of points in S_k that survive level j is at most $\min\{|S_k|, \lceil n/2^j \rceil\}$. (Note that the bound is trivially true if S_k is a singleton.) Because the S_k's cover the entire point set, with a double summation we have

$$\sum_{j=0}^{\lceil \log n \rceil} n_j \leq \sum_{j=0}^{\lceil \log n \rceil} \sum_{k} \min\left\{ |S_k|, \lceil n/2^j \rceil \right\}$$

$$= \sum_{k} \sum_{j=0}^{\lceil \log n \rceil} \min\left\{ |S_k|, \lceil n/2^j \rceil \right\}$$

$$\leq \sum_{k} (|S_k| \lceil \log(n/|S_k|) \rceil + |S_k| + |S_k|/2 + |S_k|/4 + \cdots + 1)$$

$$\leq \sum_{k} |S_k| (\lceil \log(n/|S_k|) \rceil + 2)$$

$$= O(n(\mathcal{H}(\Pi) + 1)).$$

This bound applies for every respectful partition of S, so it also applies with $\mathcal{H}(\Pi)$ replaced by the structural entropy $\mathcal{H}(S)$ of S. This completes the proof. $\qquad\qquad\square$

Moreover, a nontrivial adversary argument can be used to prove a matching lower bound for all *order-oblivious* algorithms (Afshani et al., 2017). Formally, the statement is: For every correct algorithm A for the MAXIMA SET problem and every set S of n points, there exists an ordering of the points in S such that A uses $\Omega(n(\mathcal{H}(S) + 1))$ comparisons to solve the corresponding instance of MAXIMA SET. Thus, any running time bound that does not reference the ordering of the points in the input (like all of the standard running time bounds for algorithms for the MAXIMA SET problem) must be $\Omega(n(\mathcal{H}(S) + 1))$.

Theorem 3.4 and the matching lower bound prove a strong form of "ultimateness" for the Marriage Before Conquest algorithm. But could we do even better by somehow taking advantage of the input order?

3.1.6 Partially Sorted Inputs

Remember the Graham's scan algorithm (Section 3.1.2), which first sorted the houses by price and then scanned the sorted list in linear time to discard noncandidate houses? This algorithm shows that the MAXIMA SET problem can be solved in *linear* time for instances in which the input is already sorted. An analogous observation holds for inputs that are partially sorted, meaning that the (ordered) input can be partitioned into a small number of sorted fragments. Here, the maxima set of each fragment can be computed in time linear in the fragment length, and the merging of all the maxima sets can in some cases be done quickly enough to obtain a better running time bound than an order-oblivious algorithm.[9]

Theorem 3.5 (Ochoa, 2019) *Consider a sequence S of n points in the plane comprising sorted fragments of lengths $r_0, \ldots, r_\rho$, with structural entropy $\mathcal{H}(S)$.*

---

[9] For further examples of algorithms that adapt to partially sorted inputs, see Exercise 3.6 and Section 3.3.1.

There is an algorithm which computes the maxima set of S in $O(n + \min\{n \log n - \sum_{i=0}^{\rho} r_i \log r_i, n\mathcal{H})\})$ time.

Perhaps techniques along the lines of Theorem 3.5 can lead to a truly instance-optimal algorithm for the MAXIMA SET problem, without any restriction to order-obliviousness?

3.1.7 Impossibility Result

The very existence of the Graham's scan algorithm implies that *no* algorithm for the MAXIMA SET problem can be truly instance optimal in the comparison model:

Theorem 3.6 (Afshani et al., 2017) *There is no instance-optimal algorithm for the MAXIMA SET problem.*

In fact, for every algorithm A for the MAXIMA SET problem, there is another algorithm B for the problem and an infinite family of inputs z such that A runs in $\Omega(n \log n)$ time on these inputs while B runs in $O(n)$ time.

Proof Sketch The intuition of the proof is very simple: For any given instance I, there is at least one competing algorithm that correctly guesses an order in which to process the input so that the Graham's scan algorithm computes the maxima set of I in linear time. Furthermore, no algorithm in the comparison model can solve *all* instances of size n in $o(n \log n)$ time (by a simple counting argument). Hence, no algorithm can compute the maxima set for every instance I in time bounded by a constant factor times that of the best algorithm for I. ☐

Theorem 3.6 shows that the "order-oblivious" qualifier (or some other restriction) is necessary for an instance optimality result for the MAXIMA SET problem. Thus, if one had to choose an "ultimate" algorithm for the problem, the Marriage Before Conquest algorithm is the best candidate around: it (or the minor variant described here) is instance optimal among order-oblivious algorithms, which would seem to be the next best thing to a truly instance-optimal algorithm (which does not exist).

3.2 Case Study 2: Instance-Optimal Aggregation Algorithms

This section considers a second case study of an instance-optimal algorithm, for the database aggregation problem for which the concept was originally defined.

3.2.1 Instance Optimality

We begin by zooming out to discuss instance optimality in general. Some measures of difficulty are finer than others. Could there be a "finest-possible" measure, so that an algorithm that is optimal with respect to that measure is automatically optimal also with respect to every other (coarser) measure? This may seem like a pipe dream for any natural computational problem, but Fagin et al. (2003) described such a result for a database aggregation problem.[10] Algorithms that are optimal with respect to such a finest-possible measure – *instance-optimal* algorithms – can be viewed as the ultimate adaptive algorithms, always as good (up to a constant factor) as every other algorithm on every input.

Consider a computational problem and cost measure, with $\text{cost}(A, z)$ denoting the cost incurred (e.g., number of operations) by the algorithm A on the input z.

Definition 3.7 (Instance Optimality)   An algorithm A for a problem is *instance optimal with approximation c with respect to the set $\mathcal{C}$ of algorithms* if for every algorithm $B \in \mathcal{C}$ and every input z,

$$\text{cost}(A, z) \leq c \cdot \text{cost}(B, z),$$

where $c \geq 1$ is a constant, independent of B and z.

The constant c in Definition 3.7 is called the *optimality ratio* of A (with respect to $\mathcal{C}$). By an *instance-optimal algorithm*, one generally means an algorithm with optimality ratio bounded by a constant.[11] This is a demanding definition, and for many problems there is no instance-optimal algorithm with respect to any reasonably rich class of algorithms $\mathcal{C}$. In Theorem 3.4, we saw an example of an instance-optimal algorithm for the MAXIMA SET problem with respect to the class of order-oblivious algorithms, and from Theorem 3.6 we learned that there is no instance-optimal algorithm for the problem with respect to the class of all comparison-based algorithms.

The rest of this section covers the original success story for instance-optimal algorithms.

3.2.2 The Setup

The problem is as follows. There is a very large set X of objects, such as Web pages. There is a small number m of attributes, such as the ranking (e.g., PageRank) of a Web page under m different search engines. To keep things simple, assume that attribute values lie in $[0, 1]$. Thus an object consists of a unique name and an element of $[0, 1]^m$.

We are also given a *scoring function* $\sigma : [0, 1]^m \rightarrow [0, 1]$ which aggregates m attribute values into a single score. We interpret higher attribute values and scores as being "better." We assume that the scoring function is *monotone*, meaning that its output is nondecreasing in each of its inputs. An obvious scoring function is the average, but clearly there are numerous other natural examples.

The algorithmic goal is, given a positive integer k, to identify k objects of X that have the highest scores (ties can be broken arbitrarily).

We assume that the data can be accessed only in a restricted way. It is presented as m sorted lists $L_1, L_2, \ldots, L_m$. Each list L_i is a copy of X, sorted in nonincreasing order

---

[10] This paper by Fagin et al. (2003) was the winner of the 2014 EATCS-SIGACT Gödel prize, a "test of time" award for papers in theoretical computer science.

[11] One drawback of this coarse definition of an instance-optimal algorithm is its Manichean nature – it does not differentiate between competing instance-optimal algorithms whose optimality ratios differ by large (constant) factors, nor does it differentiate between different problems that, even though they do not admit instance-optimal algorithms, might nevertheless differ in difficulty.

of the ith attribute value. An algorithm can access the data only by requesting the next object in one of the lists. Thus an algorithm could ask for the first (highest) object of L_4, followed by the first object of L_7, followed by the second object of L_4, and so on. Such a request reveals the name of said object along with all m of its attribute values. We charge an algorithm a cost of 1 for each such data access.[12] Thus, in the notation of Definition 3.7, we are defining the cost measure $cost(A, z)$ as the number of data accesses that the algorithm A needs to correctly identify the top k objects in the input z.

3.2.3 The Threshold Algorithm

We study the following *threshold algorithm* (TA). The algorithm is natural but perhaps not the first algorithm one would write down for the problem. The reader is encouraged to think about "more obvious" algorithms, which will probably not be instance-optimal.

Algorithm 1 The threshold algorithm (TA)

Input: a parameter k and m sorted lists.
Invariant: of the objects seen so far, S is those with the top k scores.

1. Fetch the next item from each of the m lists.
2. Compute the score $\sigma(x)$ of each object x returned, and update S as needed.
3. Let a_i denote the ith attribute value of the object just fetched from the list L_i, and set a threshold $t := \sigma(a_1, \ldots, a_m)$.
4. If all objects of S have score at least t, halt; otherwise return to step 1.

We first claim that the TA is correct – for every input, it successfully identifies the k objects with the highest scores (even if it halts well before encountering all of the objects of X).

Proof By definition, the final set S returned by the TA is the best of the objects seen by the algorithm. If an object $x \in X$ has not been seen by the TA, then its ith attribute value x_i is at most the lowest attribute value a_i of an object fetched from the list L_i (since the lists are sorted). Since σ is a monotone scoring function, $\sigma(x)$ is at most $\sigma(a_1, \ldots, a_m)$, which by definition is the final threshold t of the TA, which by the stopping rule is at most the score of every object in S. Thus every object in S has score at least as large as every object outside of S, as desired. □

---

[12] This is not the most realistic cost model, but it serves to illustrate our main points in a simple way. In the terminology of Fagin et al. (2003), this corresponds to a sequential access cost of 1 and a random access cost of 0. More generally, Fagin et al. (2003) charge some constant c_s for each data access of the type we describe and assume that accessing list L_i only reveals the value of the ith attribute; the other attribute values are then determined via $m - 1$ "random accesses" to the other lists, each of which is assumed to cost some other constant c_r. Analogous instance optimality results are possible in this more general model (Fagin et al., 2003).

The main takeaway point of the proof is: the threshold t acts as an upper bound on the best possible score of an unseen object. Once the best objects identified so far are at least this threshold, it is safe to halt without further exploration.

3.2.4 Instance Optimality of the Threshold Algorithm

The threshold algorithm is in fact *instance-optimal with optimality ratio m*.

Theorem 3.8 (Instance optimality of the TA)   *For* every *algorithm A and* every *input z,*

$$cost(TA, z) \leq m \cdot cost(A, z). \tag{3.2}$$

In words, suppose you precommit to using the TA, and you have a competitor who is allowed to pick *both* an input z *and* a (correct) algorithm A that is specifically tailored to perform well on the input z. Theorem 3.8 says that even with this extreme advantage, your opponent's performance will be only a factor of m better than yours. Recall that we view m as a small constant, which makes sense in many natural motivating applications for the problem. We will see in the text that follows that no algorithm has an optimality ratio smaller than m.

Proof (of Theorem 3.8) Consider a (correct) algorithm A and an input z. Suppose that A accesses the first $k_1, \ldots, k_m$ elements of the lists $L_1, \ldots, L_m$ en route to computing the (correct) output S on z. For each i, let b_i denote the ith attribute value of the last accessed object of L_i – the lowest such attribute value seen for an object fetched from L_i.

The key claim is that, on accord of A's correctness, every object x in A's output S must have a score $\sigma(x)$ that is at least $\sigma(b_1, \ldots, b_m)$. The reason is: For all A knows, there is an unseen object y with attribute values $b_1, \ldots, b_m$ lurking as the $(k_i + 1)$th object of list L_i for each i (recall that ties within an L_i can be broken arbitrarily). Thus, A cannot halt with $x \in S$ and $\sigma(x) < \sigma(b_1, \ldots, b_m)$ without violating correctness on some input z'. (Here z' agrees with z on the first k_i objects of each L_i, and has an object y as above next in each of the lists.)

Now, after $\max_i k_i$ rounds, the TA has probed at least as far as A into each of lists, and has discovered every object that A did (including all of S). Thus a_i, the ith attribute value of the final item fetched by the TA from the list L_i, is at most b_i. Since σ is monotone, $\sigma(a_1, \ldots, a_m) \leq \sigma(b_1, \ldots, b_m)$. Thus after at most $\max_i k_i$ rounds, the TA discovers at least k objects with a score at least its threshold, which triggers its stopping condition. Thus $cost(TA, z) \leq m \cdot \max_i k_i$; since $cost(A, z) = \sum_i k_i \geq \max_i k_i$, the proof is complete. $\square$

3.2.5 A Matching Lower Bound on the Optimality Ratio

The factor of m in Theorem 3.8 cannot be improved, for the TA or any other algorithm. We content ourselves with the case of $k = 1$ and a scoring function σ with the property that $\sigma(x) = 1$ if and only if $x_1 = x_2 = \cdots = x_m = 1$. More general lower bounds are possible (Fagin et al., 2003), using extensions of the simple idea explained here.

The guarantee of instance optimality is so strong that proving lower bounds can be quite easy. Given an arbitrary correct algorithm A, one needs to exhibit an input z and a correct algorithm A' with smaller cost on z than A. Getting to choose A' and z in tandem is what enables simple lower bound proofs.

Suppose $k = 1$. We will use only special inputs z of the following form:

- there is a unique object y with $\sigma(y) = 1$; and
- this object y appears first in exactly 1 of the lists $L_1, \ldots, L_m$. (Recall that arbitrary tie-breaking within a list is allowed.)

The lower bound follows from the following two observations. For every such input z, there is an algorithm A' with $\text{cost}(A', z) = 1$: It looks in the list containing y first, and on finding it can safely halt with y as the answer, since no other object can have a higher score. But for every fixed algorithm A, there is such an input z on which $\text{cost}(A, z) \geq m$: A must look at one of the lists last, and an adversary can choose the input z in which y is hidden in this last list.

The fact that lower bounds for instance optimality arise so trivially should give further appreciation for instance-optimal algorithms with small optimality ratios (when they exist).

3.3 Survey of Additional Results and Techniques

Many techniques have been introduced to refine worst-case analysis through parameterizations of input difficulty beyond input size. There are too many such results to list here, so we present only a selection that illustrates some key notions and techniques.

3.3.1 Input Order

We distinguish between algorithms adaptive to the *ordering* of the input versus those to the (unordered) *structure* of the input. An example of the former is the algorithm in Theorem 3.5, which adapts to partially sorted instances of the MAXIMA SET problem. For further results along these lines for adaptive sorting, see the survey of Estivill-Castro and Wood (1992) and the overview of Moffat and Petersson (1992).

3.3.2 Input Structure

An early example of adapting to (unordered) input structure is due to Munro and Spira (1976), who showed how algorithms could adapt to the frequencies of the elements in a multiset M in order to sort them with fewer comparisons than would be required in the worst case. We discuss this and a few additional examples in the text that follows.

Output size: In Section 3.1.3 we saw the concept of an *output-sensitive* algorithm, one of the most basic notions of adaptivity to input structure. Kirkpatrick and Seidel (1985) gave the first output-sensitive algorithm for computing the maximal points of a point set in d dimensions. Their algorithm's running time is $O(n(1 + \log h))$ in 2 and 3 dimensions, and $O(n(1 + \log^{d-2} h))$ for dimensions $d > 3$, where h is the number of maximal points. The next year Kirkpatrick and Seidel (1986) proved similar results for the CONVEX HULL problem, if only in two and three dimensions.

Such results were later refined for the CONVEX HULL problem by Sen and Gupta (1999) to adapt to the *vertical entropy* [cf. (3.1)] and by Afshani et al. (2017) to adapt to the structural entropy of a point set (cf., Definition 3.3). See Section 3.5.1 for recent progress and open questions for point sets in four or more dimensions.

Repetitions. For another example of (unordered) input structure, consider a multiset M of size n (e.g., $M = \{4, 4, 3, 3, 4, 5, 6, 7, 1, 2\}$ of size $n = 10$). The *multiplicity* of an element x of M is the number m_x of occurrences of x in M (e.g., $m_3 = 2$). The distribution of the multiplicities of the elements in M is the set of pairs (x, m_x) (e.g., $\{(1, 1), (2, 1), (3, 2), (4, 3), (5, 1), (6, 1), (7, 1)\}$ in M). Munro and Spira (1976) described a variant of the MergeSort algorithm that uses counters, and which takes advantage of the distribution of the multiplicities of the elements in M when sorting it. This algorithm runs in $O(n(1 + \mathcal{H}(m_1, \ldots, m_\sigma)))$ time, where σ is the number of distinct elements in M, $m_1, \ldots, m_\sigma$ are the multiplicities of the σ distinct elements, and $\mathcal{H}$ is the entropy of the corresponding distribution. They proved that this running time is the best possible in the decision tree model (up to constant factors), in the worst case over instances of size n with σ distinct elements of multiplicities $m_1, \ldots, m_\sigma$.

Miscellaneous Input Structure. Barbay et al. (2017a) proposed adaptive algorithms for three related problems where the input is a set $\mathcal{B}$ of axis-aligned boxes in d dimensions: the KLEE'S MEASURE problem (i.e., computing the volume occupied by the union of the boxes of $\mathcal{B}$); the MAXIMAL DEPTH problem (i.e., computing the maximal number of boxes of $\mathcal{B}$ that cover a common point of space); and the DEPTH DISTRIBUTION problem (i.e., for each i compute the volume of the points that are covered by exactly i boxes from $\mathcal{B}$).

3.3.3 Synergy between Order and Structure

Are there algorithms that profitably take advantage of both input order and input structure? This is the question considered by Barbay et al. (2017b). They showed that, for the problem of sorting a multiset, there is an algorithm that adapts simultaneously to partially sorted inputs (as in Section 3.1.6) and also the entropy of the distribution of elements' frequencies; for some instances, this results in a running time that is asymptotically faster than what can be achieved when taking advantage of only of one of the two aspects. They also consider data structures for answering rank and select queries, while taking advantage of the *query structure* and *query order* (in addition to the input order and input structure). Finally, Barbay and Ochoa (2018) show analogous results for the MAXIMA SET and CONVEX HULL problems (in two dimensions).

3.4 Discussion

This section compares and contrasts adaptive analysis and instance optimality with parameterized algorithms and the competitive analysis of online algorithms.

3.4.1 Comparison with Parameterized Algorithms

Both adaptive analysis and parameterized algorithms (as described in Chapter 2) analyze the running time of algorithms using parameters above and beyond the input size. One major difference between the two areas is that the former focuses on polynomial-time solvable problems (often with near-linear worst-case complexity) while the latter is focused on *NP*-hard problems.[13] Lower bounds for *NP*-hard parameterized problems are necessarily conditional (at least on $P \neq NP$, and often on stronger assumptions such as the Strong Exponential Time Hypothesis). Meanwhile, tight unconditional lower bounds are a prerequisite for instance optimality results, and these are typically known only for near-linear-time solvable problems (such as SORTING or CONVEX HULL in two or three dimensions) and restricted models of computation (comparison-based algorithms or decision trees).

Adaptive analysis is relevant more generally to polynomial-time solvable problems for which we don't know good lower bounds. For example, Barbay and Pérez-Lantero (2018) and Barbay and Olivares (2018) analyzed adaptive algorithms for various string problems (in the spirit of EDIT DISTANCE) while Barbay (2018) presented similar results for the DISCRETE FRECHET DISTANCE problem.

3.4.2 Comparison with the Competitive Analysis of Online Algorithms

An *online algorithm* is one that receives its input one piece at a time and is required to make irrevocable decisions along the way. In the competitive analysis of online algorithms (initiated by Sleator and Tarjan (1985) and covered in Chapter 24 of this book), the goal is to identify online algorithms with a good (close to 1) competitive ratio, meaning that the objective function value of the algorithm's output is guaranteed to be almost as good as what could be achieved by an all-powerful and all-knowing offline optimal algorithm.

The competitive ratio provided inspiration for the optimality ratio (Definition 3.7) and instance optimality.[14] Indeed, we can interpret a guarantee of c on the competitive ratio of an online algorithm A as a guarantee on the optimality ratio of A (where the cost(A,z) is the objective function value of the output of A for the input z) with respect to the family $\mathcal{C}$ of *all* algorithms (and in particular, the offline optimal one).

3.5 Selected Open Problems

We close our chapter with two open research directions.

3.5.1 High Dimensions

One may have more than two criteria for choosing a house: Rather than just the price and the distance to work, certainly its size, whether it has a garden, the quality of

---

[13] One superficial distinction is that in parameterized algorithms the relevant parameter value is generally given as part of the input, while in adaptive analysis it shows up only in the analysis of an algorithm. But a typical fixed-parameter tractable algorithm can be extended to handle the case where the relevant parameter is not part of the input, merely by trying all possible values for that parameter.

[14] Fagin et al. (2003) write, "We refer to c as the optimality ratio. It is similar to the competitive ratio in competitive analysis."

the neighborhood, and so on should be taken into account for such an important decision.

The results of Kirkpatrick and Seidel (1985) on the MAXIMA SET problem also covered the case of high dimensions, with the higher-dimensional analog of Marriage Before Conquest computing the maximal set of a d-dimensional point set with $d \geq 3$ in $O(n \log^{d-2} h)$ time, where as usual n and h denote the size of the input and output, respectively. Afshani et al. (2017) refined this analysis not only in dimension two (as described in Section 3.1.5), but also in dimension three, with a rather different algorithm that partitions the input based on a carefully chosen sample of points. Barbay and Rojas-Ledesma (2017) proved analogous results in $d > 3$ dimensions:

Theorem 3.9 (Barbay and Rojas-Ledesma, 2017) *Consider a set S of n points in $\mathbb{R}^d$, and let Π be a respectful partition of S into subsets $S_1, \ldots, S_t$ of sizes $n_1, \ldots, n_t$, respectively. There is an algorithm that computes the maximal points of S in*

$$O\left(n + \sum_{k=1}^{t} n_k \log^{d-2} \frac{n}{n_k}\right) \tag{3.3}$$

time.

Could there be a matching lower bound, as is the case in two and three dimensions? The (open) problem is that there is no reason to believe that the expression in (3.3) is the minimal description length of a certificate of correctness; for example, for all we know there is a bound that depends linearly on d (rather than exponentially).

3.5.2 Layers of Maxima Sets

In the MAXIMA SET problem, every point is given a binary classification (maximal or not). More generally, one could identify the maximal set S_1 of the input S (the "first layer"), followed by the maximal set S_2 of the remaining point $S \setminus S_1$ (the "second layer"), and so on.

Nielsen (1996) described this problem and an output sensitive solution (similar to that described in Section 3.1.3 for the MAXIMA SET problem). Extending this result to obtain order-oblivious instance optimality is not overly difficult, but it remains an open problem to make the algorithm adaptive to various forms of input order.

3.6 Key Takeaways

In the following we summarize what we consider to be two of the main lessons from this incomplete survey of results on adaptive analysis and instance optimality.

1. Most of the techniques used in the adaptive analysis of algorithms and data structures resemble those used in classical worst-case analysis over instances of a given input size, the difference being that the ideas are applied in a more fine-grained context.

2. The concept of instance optimality (for various computational models) can be further refined to the concept of the optimality ratio among a class of algorithms over a class of instances. Such a refinement differentiates between more pairs of algorithms than the coarser criterion of instance optimality.

3.7 Notes

We conclude with some final bibliographic remarks, to supplement those given throughout the preceding sections.

1. McQueen and Toussaint (1985) originally introduced the minor variant of Marriage Before Conquest which was proved (order-oblivious) instance optimal in Afshani et al. (2017).
2. Petersson and Moffat (1995) introduced a notion of formal reductions between measures of difficulty, which induces a partial order on difficulty measures (Estivill-Castro and Wood, 1992; Moffat and Petersson, 1992). Such a theory of reductions is similar to the reductions between pairs of problems and parameters discussed in Chapter 2 on parameterized algorithms (as reductions between parameterized problems induce a partial order on them according to difficulty), but in a context where one can prove unconditional lower bounds.
3. Barbay and Navarro (2013) formalized the notion of *compressibility* measures for the analysis of the space used by compressed data structures, inspired by difficulty measures used in the running time analysis of algorithms.

Acknowledgments

Some of the examples, definitions, and results in this chapter were inspired by similar ones in the PhD theses of Carlos Ochoa and Javiel Rojas.

References

Afshani, Peyman, Barbay, Jérémy, and Chan, Timothy M. 2017. Instance-optimal geometric algorithms. *Journal of the ACM*, **64**(1), 3:1–3:38.

Barbay, Jérémy. 2018. Adaptive computation of the discrete Fréchet distance. In *Proceedings of the 11th Symposium on String Processing and Information Retrieval (SPIRE)*, pp. 50–60.

Barbay, Jérémy, and Navarro, Gonzalo. 2013. On compressing permutations and adaptive sorting. *Theoretical Computer Science*, **513**, 109–123.

Barbay, Jérémy, and Ochoa, Carlos. 2018. Synergistic computation of planar maxima and convex hull. In *Proceedings of the 23rd Annual International Computing and Combinatorics Conference (COCOON)*, pp. 156–167.

Barbay, Jérémy, and Olivares, Andrés. 2018. Indexed dynamic programming to boost edit distance and LCSS computation. In *Proceedings of the 11th Symposium on String Processing and Information Retrieval (SPIRE)*, pp. 61–73.

Barbay, Jérémy, and Pérez-Lantero, Pablo. 2018. Adaptive computation of the swap-insert correction distance. *ACM Transactions on Algorithms*, **14**(4), 49:1–49:16.

Barbay, Jérémy, and Rojas-Ledesma, Javiel. 2017. Multivariate analysis for computing maxima in high dimensions. *CoRR*, abs/1701.03693.

Barbay, Jérémy, Pérez-Lantero, Pablo, and Rojas-Ledesma, Javiel. 2017a. Depth distribution in high dimensions. In *Proceedings of the 23rd Annual International Computing and Combinatorics Conference (COCOON)*, pp. 38–40.

Barbay, Jérémy, Ochoa, Carlos, and Satti, Srinivasa Rao. 2017b. Synergistic solutions on multiSets. In *Proceedings of the 28th Annual Symposium on Combinatorial Pattern Matching (CPM)*, pp. 31:1–31:14.

Blum, Manuel, Floyd, Robert W., Pratt, Vaughan, Rivest, Ronald L., and Tarjan, Robert E. 1973. Time bounds for selection. *Journal of Computer and System Sciences*, **7**(4), 448–461.

Estivill-Castro, Vladimir, and Wood, Derick. 1992. A survey of adaptive sorting algorithms. *ACM Computing Surveys*, **24**(4), 441–476.

Fagin, Ronald, Lotem, Amnon, and Naor, Moni. 2003. Optimal aggregation algorithms for middleware. *Journal of Computer and System Sciences*, **66**(4), 614–656.

Graham, Ron L. 1972. An efficient algorithm for determining the convex hull of a finite planar set. *Information Processing Letters*, **1**, 132–133.

Jarvis, Ray A. 1973. On the identification of the convex hull of a finite set of points in the plane. *Information Processing Letters*, **2**(1), 18–21.

Kirkpatrick, David G. 2009. Hyperbolic dovetailing. In *Proceedings of the 17th Annual European Symposium on Algorithms*, pp. 516–527. Springer Science+Business Media.

Kirkpatrick, David G., and Seidel, Raimund. 1985. Output-size sensitive algorithms for finding maximal vectors. In *Proceedings of the First International Symposium on Computational Geometry (SOCG)*, pp. 89–96. ACM.

Kirkpatrick, David G, and Seidel, Raimund. 1986. The ultimate planar convex hull algorithm? *SIAM Journal on Computing*, **15**(1), 287–299.

Kung, H T, Luccio, F, and Preparata, F P. 1975. On finding the maxima of a set of vectors. *Journal of the ACM*, **22**, 469–476.

Lucas, Édouard. 1883. *La Tour d'Hanoï, Véritable Casse-Tête Annamite*. In a puzzle game, Amiens. Jeu rapporté du Tonkin par le professeur N.Claus (De Siam).

McQueen, Mary M., and Toussaint, Godfried T. 1985. On the ultimate convex hull algorithm in practice. *Pattern Recognition Letters*, **3**(1), 29–34.

Moffat, Alistair, and Petersson, Ola. 1992. An overview of adaptive sorting. *Australian Computer Journal*, **24**(2), 70–77.

Munro, J. Ian, and Spira, Philip M. 1976. Sorting and searching in multisets. *SIAM Journal on Computing*, **5**(1), 1–8.

Nielsen, Frank. 1996. Output-sensitive peeling of convex and maximal layers. *Information Processing Letters*, **59**(5), 255–259.

Ochoa, Carlos. 2019. *Synergistic (Analysis of) Algorithms and Data Structures*. PhD thesis, University of Chile.

Petersson, Ola, and Moffat, Alistair. 1995. A framework for adaptive sorting. *Discrete Applied Mathematics*, **59**, 153–179.

Sen, Sandeep, and Gupta, Neelima. 1999. Distribution-sensitive algorithms. *Nordic Journal on Computing*, **6**, 194–211.

Sleator, D. D., and Tarjan, R. E. 1985. Amortized efficiency of list update and paging rules. *Communications of the ACM*, **28**(2), 202–208.

Exercises

Exercise 3.1 The HANOÏ TOWER problem is a classic example of recursion, originally proposed by Lucas (1883).[15] A recursive algorithm proposed in 1892 completes

---

[15] Recall the setup: The game consists of three identical rods and n disks of different sizes, which can slide onto any rod. The puzzle starts with all disks on the same rod, ordered from the biggest (at the bottom) to the

the task using $2^n - 1$ moves, and an easy argument shows that $2^n - 1$ moves are necessary. For this exercise, consider the variant in which we allow disks of equal size; everything else about the setup is the same as before. (A disk is allowed to be placed on another disk with the same size.) We call this the DISK PILE problem. In the extreme case, when all disks have the same size, the tower can be moved in a linear number of moves.

(a) Prove that there is an algorithm for DISK PILE that performs $\sum_{i \in \{1,...,s\}} n_i 2^{s-i}$ moves, where s denotes the number of distinct sizes and n_i the number of disks with size i.

(b) Prove that no algorithm can move such a tower with less than $\sum_{i \in \{1,...,s\}} n_i 2^{s-i}$ moves.

(c) What is the worst-case performance of your algorithm over all instances with a fixed value of s and a fixed total number of disks n?

(d) Which analysis is more fine-grained: the one for s and n fixed, or the one for $n_1, \ldots, n_s$ fixed?

Exercise 3.2 Given an unsorted array A and an element x, the UNSORTED SEARCH problem is to decide whether A contains at least one element with the same value as x. The cost measure is the number of times that an algorithm probes an entry of A.

(a) What is the best possible optimality ratio for the UNSORTED SEARCH problem with respect to *deterministic* algorithms over instances of size k and r elements with the same value as x?

(b) What is the best possible optimality ratio for the UNSORTED SEARCH problem with respect to *randomized* algorithms over instances of size k and r elements with the same value as x?

(c) What is the best possible optimality ratio for the UNSORTED SEARCH problems with respect to randomized algorithms over instances of size k and σ distinct elements?

Exercise 3.3 Given a sorted array A and an element x, the SORTED SEARCH problem is to decide whether A contains at least one element with the same value as x. What are the best-possible optimality ratios for the SORTED SEARCH problem with respect to deterministic and randomized algorithms over instances of size k and r elements with the same value as x?

Exercise 3.4 In the ELEMENTARY INTERSECTION problem, the input is an element x and k sorted arrays $A_1, \ldots, A_k$, and the goal is to decide whether x belongs to all k of the arrays. In the ELEMENTARY UNION problem, the input is the same but the goal is to decide whether x belongs to at least one of the k arrays.

smallest. A legal move consists of removing the topmost disk of one of the rods and placing it on top of the stack on one of the other two rods. A key constraint is that no move is allowed to place a larger disk on top of a smaller disk. The goal is to move the disks so that all are on a common rod (necessarily in sorted order) different from the one they started on.

(a) What is the best possible optimality ratio of an algorithm for the ELEMENTARY INTERSECTION problem over instances formed by k arrays of size n/k each, when ρ of those arrays contain an element of value equal to x?

(b) What is the best possible optimality ratio of an algorithm for the ELEMENTARY UNION problem over instances formed by k arrays of size n/k each, when ρ of those arrays contain an element of value equal to x?

Exercise 3.5 The algorithm Bubble Sort is well known to run in time $\Theta(n^2)$ in the worst case and $\Theta(n)$ for alreadysorted inputs. Consider the related procedures Bubble Up and `Bubble Down`, defined as follows: Bubble Up compares each pair of consecutive elements from the smallest index to the largest one, swapping them if inverted; while Bubble Up compares each pair of consecutive elements from the largest index to the smallest one, swapping them if inverted. In order to simplify the notation, suppose that the first and last elements of the array are $-\infty$ (at index 0) and $+\infty$ (at index $n+1$).

(a) Prove that a position p whose corresponding element is left unmoved by both Bubble Up and Bubble Down is a *natural pivot*: in the input array, the element is larger than all elements with smaller indices and smaller than all elements with larger indices.

(b) Prove that there is an algorithm sorting an array of n elements with η natural pivots in $O(n(1 + \log \frac{n}{\eta}))$ time.

(c) Refine the previous proof to show that there is an algorithm sorting an array of n elements with η natural pivots separated by $\eta+1$ gaps of sizes $(r_0, \ldots, r_\eta)$ in $O(n + \sum_{i=0}^{\eta} r_i \log r_i)$ time.

(d) Prove that, in the worst case over instances formed by n elements with η natural pivots separated by $\eta + 1$ gaps of sizes $(r_0, \ldots, r_\eta)$, every sorting algorithm in the comparison model runs in time $\Omega(n + \sum_{i=0}^{\eta} r_i \log r_i)$.

Exercise 3.6 The algorithm QuickSort is well known to have worst-case running time $\Theta(n^2)$ when sorting length-n arrays and using arbitrary pivots, and worst-case running time $\Theta(n \log n)$ when using median elements as pivots (using a linear-time median subroutine). Consider the implementation QuickSortWithRepetitions in which the partition induced by the median m yields *three* areas in the array: all elements of value strictly smaller than m on the left, all the elements of value strictly larger than m on the right, and all the elements of value *equal* to m in the remaining central positions.

(a) Prove that such an implementation performs $O(n(1 + \log \sigma))$ comparisons in the worst case over instances formed by n elements from an alphabet with σ distinct values.

(b) Refine the previous proof and show that such an implementation performs $O(n + \sum_{i=1}^{\sigma} n_i \log \frac{n}{n_i})$ comparisons in the worst case over instances formed by n elements taken from the alphabet $[1, \ldots, \sigma]$, where n_i is the number of occurrences of the ith value.

(c) Prove a matching lower bound (up to constant factors) that applies to all order-oblivious algorithms.

(d) Can you combine the analysis in (b) with that of natural pivots (Exercise 3.5)?

CHAPTER FOUR

Resource Augmentation

Tim Roughgarden

Abstract: This chapter introduces *resource augmentation*, in which the performance of an algorithm is compared to the best possible solution that is handicapped by fewer resources. We consider three case studies: online paging, with cache size as the resource; selfish routing, with capacity as the resource; and scheduling, with processor speed as the resource. Resource augmentation bounds also imply "loosely competitive" bounds, which show that an algorithm's performance is near-optimal for most resource levels.

4.1 Online Paging Revisited

This section illustrates the idea of resource augmentation with a familiar example, the competitive analysis of online paging algorithms. Section 4.2 discusses the pros and cons of resource augmentation more generally, Sections 4.3 and 4.4 describe additional case studies in routing and scheduling, and Section 4.5 shows how resource augmentation bounds lead to "loosely competitive" guarantees.

4.1.1 The Model

Our first case study of resource augmentation concerns the online paging problem introduced in Chapter 1. Recall the ingredients of the problem:

- There is a slow memory with N pages.
- There is a fast memory (a *cache*) that can hold only $k < N$ of the pages at a time.
- Page requests arrive online over time, with one request per time step. The decisions of an online algorithm at time t can depend only on the requests arriving at or before time t.
- If the page p_t requested at time t is already in the cache, no action is necessary.
- If p_t is not in the cache, it must be brought in; if the cache is full, one of its k pages must be evicted. This is called a *page fault*.[1]

---

[1] This model corresponds to "demand paging," meaning algorithms that modify the cache only in response to a page fault. The results in this section continue to hold in the more general model in which an algorithm is allowed to make arbitrary changes to the cache at each time step, whether or not there is a page fault, with the cost incurred by the algorithm equal to the number of changes.

We measure the performance $\text{PERF}(A, z)$ of an algorithm A on a page request sequence z by the number of page faults incurred.

4.1.2 FIF and LRU

As a benchmark, what would we do if we had clairvoyance about all future page requests? An intuitive greedy algorithm minimizes the number of page faults.

Theorem 4.1 (Bélády, 1967) *The* Furthest-In-the-Future (FIF) *algorithm, which on a page fault evicts the page to be requested furthest in the future, always minimizes the number of page faults.*

The FIF algorithm is not an online algorithm, as its eviction decisions depend on future page requests. The *Least Recently Used* (LRU) policy, which on a page fault evicts the page whose most recent request is furthest in the past, is an online surrogate for the FIF algorithm that uses the past as an approximation for the future. Empirically, the LRU algorithm performs well on most "real-world" page request sequences – not much worse than the unimplementable FIF algorithm, and better than other online algorithms such as First-In First-Out (FIFO). The usual explanation for the superiority of the LRU algorithm is that the page request sequences that arise in practice exhibit locality of reference, with recent requests likely to be requested again soon, and that LRU automatically adapts to and exploits this locality.

4.1.3 Competitive Ratio

One popular way to assess the performance of an online algorithm is through its competitive ratio:[2]

Definition 4.2 (Sleator and Tarjan, 1985) *The competitive ratio of an online algorithm A is its worst-case performance (over inputs z) relative to an optimal* offline *algorithm OPT that has advance knowledge of the entire input:*

$$\max_z \frac{\text{PERF}(A, z)}{\text{PERF}(OPT, z)}.$$

For the objective of minimizing the number of page faults, the competitive ratio is always at least 1, and the closer to 1 the better.[3]

Exercise 1.1 of Chapter 1 shows that, for every deterministic online paging algorithm A and cache size k, there are arbitrarily long page request sequences z such that A faults at every time step while the FIF algorithm faults at most once per k time steps. This example shows that every deterministic online paging algorithm has a competitive ratio of at least k. For most natural online algorithms, there is a matching upper bound of k. This state of affairs is unsatisfying for several reasons:

---

[2] See Chapter 24 for a deep dive on alternatives to worst-case analysis in the competitive analysis of online algorithms.

[3] One usually ignores any extra additive terms in the competitive ratio, which vanish as $\text{PERF}(OPT, z) \to \infty$.

1. The analysis gives an absurdly pessimistic performance prediction for LRU (and all other deterministic online algorithms), suggesting that a 100% page fault rate is unavoidable.
2. The analysis suggests that online algorithms perform worse (relative to FIF) as the cache size grows, a sharp departure from empirical observations.
3. The analysis fails to differentiate between competing policies such as LRU and FIFO, which both have a competitive ratio of k.

We next address the first two issues through a resource augmentation analysis (but not the third; see Exercise 4.2).

4.1.4 A Resource Augmentation Bound

In a *resource augmentation* analysis, the idea is to compare the performance of a protagonist algorithm (such as LRU) to an all-knowing optimal algorithm that is handicapped by "less resources." Naturally, weakening the capabilities of the offline optimal algorithm can only lead to better approximation guarantees.

Let $\text{PERF}(A, k, z)$ denote the number of page faults incurred by the algorithm A with cache size k on the page request sequence z. The main result of this section is:

Theorem 4.3 (Sleator and Tarjan, 1985) *For every page request sequence z and cache sizes $h \le k$,*

$$\text{PERF}(LRU, k, z) \le \frac{k}{k - h + 1} \cdot \text{PERF}(FIF, h, z),$$

plus an additive error term that goes to 0 with $\text{PERF}(FIF, h, z)$.

For example, LRU suffers at most twice as many page faults as the unimplementable FIF algorithm when the latter has roughly half the cache size.

Proof Consider an arbitrary page request sequence z and cache sizes $h \le k$. We first prove an upper bound on the number of page faults incurred by the LRU algorithm, and then a lower bound on the number of faults incurred by the FIF algorithm. A useful idea for accomplishing both goals is to break z into *blocks* $\sigma_1, \sigma_2, \ldots, \sigma_b$. Here σ_1 is the maximal prefix of z in which only k distinct pages are requested; the block σ_2 starts immediately after and is maximal subject to only k distinct pages being requested within it; and so on.

For the first step, note that LRU faults at most k times within a single block – at most once per page requested in the block. The reason is that once a page is brought into the cache, LRU won't evict it until k other distinct pages are requested, and this can't happen until the following block. Thus LRU incurs at most bk page faults, where b is the number of blocks. See Figure 4.1a.

For the second step, consider the FIF algorithm with a cache size $h \le k$. Consider the first block σ_1 plus the first request of the second block σ_2. Since σ_1 is maximal, this represents requests for $k + 1$ distinct pages. At least $k - h + 1$ of these pages are initially absent from the size-h cache, so no algorithm can serve all $k + 1$ pages without incurring at least $k - h + 1$ page faults. Similarly, suppose

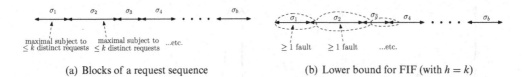

(a) Blocks of a request sequence (b) Lower bound for FIF (with $h = k$)

Figure 4.1 Proof of Theorem 4.3. In (a), the blocks of a page request sequence; the LRU algorithm incurs at most k page faults in each. In (b), the FIF algorithm incurs at least $k - h + 1$ page faults in each "shifted block."

the first request of σ_2 is the page p. After an algorithm serves the request for p, the cache contains only $h - 1$ pages other than p. By the maximality of σ_2, the "shifted block" comprising the rest of σ_2 and the first request of σ_3 includes requests for k distinct pages other than p; these cannot all be served without incurring another

$$\underbrace{k}_{\text{requests other than } p} - \underbrace{(h - 1)}_{\text{pages in cache other than } p}$$

page faults. And so on, resulting in at least $(b - 1)(k - h + 1)$ page faults overall. See Figure 4.1b.

We conclude that

$$\text{PERF}(LRU, k, z) \le bk \le \frac{k}{k - h + 1} \cdot \text{PERF}(FIF, h, z) + \frac{k}{(b - 1)(k - h + 1)}.$$

The additive error term goes to 0 as b grows large and the proof is complete. □

4.2 Discussion

Resource augmentation guarantees make sense for any problem in which there is a natural notion of a "resource," with algorithm performance improving in the resource level; see Sections 4.3 and 4.4 for two further examples. In general, a resource augmentation guarantee implies that the performance curves (i.e., performance as a function of resource level) of an online algorithm and the offline optimal algorithm are similar (Figure 4.2).

The resource augmentation guarantees in this chapter resemble worst-case analysis, in that no model of data is proposed; the difference is purely in the method of measuring algorithm performance (relative to optimal performance). As usual, this is both a feature and a bug: the lack of a data model guarantees universal applicability, but also robs the analyst of any opportunity to articulate properties of "real-world" inputs that might lead to a more accurate and fine-grained analysis. There is nothing inherently worst-case about resource augmentation guarantees, however, and the concept can equally well be applied with one of the models of data discussed in the other parts of this book.[4]

---

[4] For example, Chapter 27 combines robust distributional analysis with resource augmentation, in the context of prior-independent auctions.

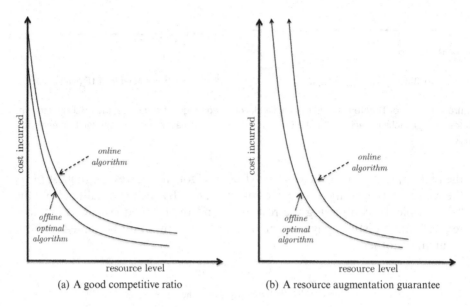

Figure 4.2 Competitive ratio guarantees vs. resource augmentation guarantees. All curves plot, for a fixed input, the cost incurred by an algorithm (e.g., number of page faults) as a function of the resource level (e.g., the cache size). In (a), a good upper bound on the competitive ratio requires that the curve for the online algorithm closely approximates that of the offline optimal algorithm pointwise over the x-axis. In (b), the vertical distance between the two curves (and the competitive ratio) grows large as the resource level approaches its minimum. A resource augmentation guarantee roughly translates to the relaxed requirement that every point of the online algorithm's performance curve has a nearby neighbor somewhere on the optimal offline algorithm's performance curve.

How should you interpret a resource augmentation guarantee like Theorem 4.3? Should you be impressed? Taken at face value, Theorem 4.3 seems much more meaningful than the competitive ratio of k without resource augmentation, even though it doesn't provide particularly sharp performance predictions (as to be expected, given the lack of a model of data). But isn't it an "apples vs. oranges" comparison? The optimal offline algorithm is powerful in its knowledge of all future page requests, but it's artificially hobbled by a small cache.

One interpretation of a resource augmentation guarantee is as a two-step recipe for building a system in which an online algorithm has good performance.

1. Estimate the resource level (e.g., cache size) such that the optimal offline algorithm has acceptable performance (e.g., page fault rate below a given target).[5] This task can be simpler than reasoning simultaneously about the cache size and paging algorithm design decisions.
2. Scale up the resources to realize the resource augmentation guarantee (e.g., doubling the cache size needed by the FIF algorithm to achieve good performance with the LRU algorithm).

---

[5] Remember: Competing with the optimal algorithm is useful only when its performance is good in some absolute sense!

A second justification for resource augmentation guarantees is that they usually lead directly to good "apples vs. apples" comparisons for most resource levels (as suggested by Figure 4.2b). Section 4.5 presents a detailed case study in the context of online paging.

4.3 Selfish Routing

Our second case study of a resource augmentation guarantee concerns a model of *selfish routing* in a congested network.

4.3.1 The Model and a Motivating Example

In selfish routing, we consider a directed flow network $G = (V, E)$, with r units of flow traveling from a source vertex s to a sink vertex t; r is called the *traffic rate*. Each edge e of the network has a flow-dependent cost function $c_e(x)$. For example, in the network in Figure 4.3a, the top edge has a constant cost function $c(x) = 1$, while the cost to traffic on the bottom edge equals the amount of flow x on the edge.

The key approximation concept in selfish routing networks is the *price of anarchy* which, as usual with approximation ratios, is defined as the ratio between two things: a realizable protagonist and a hypothetical benchmark.

Our protagonist is an *equilibrium flow*, in which all traffic is routed on shortest paths, where the length of an s–t path P is the (flow-dependent) quantity $\sum_{e \in P} c_e(f_e)$, where f_e denotes the amount of flow using the edge e. In Figure 4.3a, with one unit of traffic, the only equilibrium flow sends all traffic on the bottom edge. If $\epsilon > 0$ units of traffic were routed on the top path, that traffic would not be routed on a shortest path (incurring cost 1 instead of $1 - \epsilon$), and hence would want to switch paths.

Our benchmark is the optimal solution, meaning the fractional s–t flow that routes the r units of traffic to minimize the total cost $\sum_{e \in E} c_e(f_e) f_e$. For example, in Figure 4.3a, the optimal flow splits traffic evenly between the two paths, for a cost of $\frac{1}{2} \cdot 1 + \frac{1}{2} \cdot \frac{1}{2} = \frac{3}{4}$. The cost of the equilibrium flow is $0 \cdot 1 + 1 \cdot 1 = 1$.

The price of anarchy of a selfish routing network is defined as the ratio between the cost of an equilibrium flow and that of an optimal flow.[6] In the network in Figure 4.3a, the price of anarchy is $4/3$.

An interesting research goal is to identify selfish routing networks in which the price of anarchy is close to 1 – networks in which decentralized optimization by selfish users performs almost as well as centralized optimization. Unfortunately, without any restrictions on edges' cost functions, the price of anarchy can be arbitrarily large. To see this, replace the cost function on the bottom edge in Figure 4.3a by the function $c(x) = x^d$ for a large positive integer d (Figure 4.3b). The equilibrium flow and its cost remain the same, with all selfish traffic using the bottom edge for an overall cost of 1. The optimal flow, however, improves with d: Routing $1 - \epsilon$ units of flow on the bottom edge and ϵ units on the top edge yields a flow with cost $\epsilon + (1 - \epsilon)^{d+1}$. This cost tends to 0 as d tends to infinity and ϵ tends appropriately to 0, and hence the price of anarchy goes to infinity with d.

---

[6] It turns out that the equilibrium flow cost is uniquely defined in every selfish routing network with continuous and nondecreasing edge cost functions; see the Notes for details.

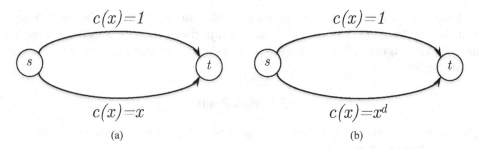

$c(x)=1$ $c(x)=1$

$c(x)=x$ $c(x)=x^d$

(a)   (b)

Figure 4.3 Two selfish routing networks. Each cost function $c(x)$ describes the cost incurred by users of an edge, as a function of the amount of traffic routed on that edge.

4.3.2 A Resource Augmentation Guarantee

Despite the negative example in the preceding section, a very general resource augmentation guarantee holds in selfish routing networks.[7]

> **Theorem 4.4** (Roughgarden and Tardos, 2002) *For every network G with nonnegative, continuous, and nondecreasing cost functions, for every traffic rate $r > 0$, and for every $\delta > 0$, the cost of an equilibrium flow in G with traffic rate r is at most $\frac{1}{\delta}$ times the cost of an optimal flow with traffic rate $(1 + \delta)r$.*

For example, consider the network in Figure 4.3b with $r = \delta = 1$ (and large d). The cost of the equilibrium flow with traffic rate 1 is 1. The optimal flow can route one unit of traffic cheaply (as we've seen), but then the network gets clogged up and it has no choice but to incur one unit of cost on the second unit of flow (the best it can do is route it on the top edge). Thus the cost of an optimal flow with double the traffic exceeds that of the original equilibrium flow.

Theorem 4.4 can be reformulated as a comparison between an equilibrium flow in a network with "faster" edges and an optimal flow in the original network. For example, simple calculations (Exercise 4.5) show that the following statement is equivalent to Theorem 4.4 with $\delta = 1$.

> **Corollary 4.5** *For every network G with nonnegative, continuous, and nondecreasing cost functions and for every traffic rate $r > 0$, the cost of an equilibrium flow in G with traffic rate r and cost functions $\{\tilde{c}_e\}_{e \in E}$ is at most that of an optimal flow in G with traffic rate r and cost functions $\{c_e\}_{e \in E}$, where each function $\tilde{c}_e$ is derived from c_e as $\tilde{c}_e(x) = c_e(x/2)/2$.*

Corollary 4.5 takes on a particularly appealing form in networks with M/M/1 delay functions, meaning cost functions of the form $c_e(x) = 1/(u_e - x)$, where u_e can be interpreted as an edge capacity or a queue service rate. (If $x \geq u_e$, interpret $c_e(x)$ as $+\infty$.) In this case, the modified function $\tilde{c}_e$ in Corollary 4.5 is

$$\tilde{c}_e(x) = \frac{1}{2(u_e - \frac{x}{2})} = \frac{1}{2u_e - x}.$$

---

[7] This result holds still more generally, in networks with multiple source and sink vertices (Exercise 4.4).

Corollary 4.5 thus translates to the following design principle for selfish routing networks with M/M/1 delay functions: to outperform optimal routing, double the capacity of every edge.

4.3.3 Proof of Theorem 4.4 (Parallel Edges)

As a warm-up to the proof of Theorem 4.4, consider the special case where $G = (V, E)$ is a network of parallel edges, meaning $V = \{s, t\}$ and every edge of E is directed from s to t (as in Figure 4.3). Choose a traffic rate $r > 0$; a cost function c_e for each edge $e \in E$ that is nonnegative, continuous, and nondecreasing; and the parameter $\delta > 0$. Let f and f^* denote equilibrium and optimal flows in G at traffic rates r and $(1 + \delta)r$, respectively. The equilibrium flow f routes traffic only on shortest paths, so there is a number L (the shortest s–t path length) such that

$$c_e(f_e) = L \quad \text{if } f_e > 0;$$
$$c_e(f_e) \geq L \quad \text{if } f_e = 0.$$

The cost of the equilibrium flow f is then

$$\sum_{e \in E} c_e(f_e)f_e = \sum_{e \in E : f_e > 0} c_e(f_e)f_e = \sum_{e \in E : f_e > 0} L \cdot f_e = r \cdot L,$$

as the total amount of flow $\sum_{e : f_e > 0} f_e$ equals the traffic rate r.

How can we bound from below the cost of the optimal flow f^*, relative to the cost rL of f? To proceed, bucket the edges of E into two categories:

$$E_1 := \text{the edges } e \text{ with } f_e^* \geq f_e;$$
$$E_2 := \text{the edges } e \text{ with } f_e^* < f_e.$$

With so few assumptions on the network cost functions, we can't say much about the costs of edges under the optimal flow f^*. The two things we *can* say are that $c_e(f_e^*) \geq L$ for all $e \in E_1$ (because cost functions are nondecreasing) and that $c_e(f_e^*) \geq 0$ for all $e \in E_2$ (because cost functions are nonnegative). At the very least, we can therefore lower bound the cost of f^* by

$$\sum_{e \in E} c_e(f_e^*)f_e^* \geq \sum_{e \in E_1} c_e(f_e^*)f_e^* \geq L \cdot \sum_{e \in E_1} f_e^*. \tag{4.1}$$

How little traffic could f^* possibly route on the edges of E_1? The flow routes $(1 + \delta)r$ units of traffic overall. It routes less flow than f on the edges of E_2 (by the definition of E_2), and f routes at most r units (i.e., its full traffic rate) on these edges. Thus

$$\sum_{e \in E_1} f_e^* = (1 + \delta)r - \sum_{e \in E_2} f_e^* \geq (1 + \delta)r - \underbrace{\sum_{e \in E_2} f_e}_{\leq r} \geq \delta r. \tag{4.2}$$

Combining the inequalities (4.1) and (4.2) shows that the cost of f^* is at least $\delta \cdot rL$, which is δ times the cost of f, as desired.

——— 79 ———

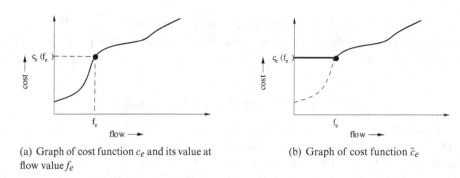

(a) Graph of cost function c_e and its value at flow value f_e

(b) Graph of cost function $\bar{c}_e$

Figure 4.4 Construction in the proof of Theorem 4.4 of the fictitious cost function $\bar{c}_e$ from the original cost function c_e and equilibrium flow value f_e.

4.3.4 Proof of Theorem 4.4 (General Networks)

Consider now the general case of Theorem 4.4, in which the network $G = (V, E)$ is arbitrary. General networks are more complex than networks of parallel edges because there is no longer a one-to-one correspondence between edges and paths – a path might comprise many edges, and an edge might participate in many different paths. This complication aside, the proof proceeds similarly to that for the special case of networks of parallel edges.

Fix a traffic rate r, a cost function c_e for each edge $e \in E$, and the parameter $\delta > 0$. As before, let f and f^* denote equilibrium and optimal flows in G at traffic rates r and $(1 + \delta)r$, respectively. It is still true that there is a number L such that all traffic in f is routed on paths P with length $\sum_{e \in P} c_e(f_e)$ equal to L, and such that all s–t paths have length at least L. The cost of the equilibrium flow is again rL.

The key trick in the proof is to replace, for the sake of analysis, each cost function $c_e(x)$ (Figure 4.4a) by the larger cost function $\bar{c}_e(x) = \max\{c_e(x), c_e(f_e)\}$ (Figure 4.4b). This trick substitutes for the decomposition in Section 4.3.3 of E into E_1 and E_2. With the fictitious cost functions $\bar{c}_e$, edge costs are always as large as if the equilibrium flow f had already been routed in the network.

By design, the cost of the optimal flow f^* is easy to bound from below with the fictitious cost functions. Even with zero flow in the network, every s–t path has cost at least L with respect to these functions. Because f^* routes $(1 + \delta)r$ units of traffic on paths with (fictitious) cost at least L, its total (fictitious) cost with respect to the $\bar{c}_e$'s is at least $(1 + \delta)rL$.

We can complete the proof by showing that the fictitious cost of f^* (with respect to the $\bar{c}_e$'s) exceeds its real cost (with respect to the c_e's) by at most rL, the equilibrium flow cost. For each edge $e \in E$ and $x \geq 0$, $\bar{c}_e(x) - c_e(x)$ is either 0 (if $x \geq f_e$) or bounded above by $c_e(f_e)$ (if $x < f_e$); in any case,

$$\underbrace{\bar{c}_e(f^*_e)f^*_e}_{\text{fictitious cost of } f^* \text{ on } e} - \underbrace{c_e(f^*_e)f^*_e}_{\text{real cost of } f^* \text{ on } e} \leq \underbrace{c_e(f_e)f_e}_{\text{real cost of } f \text{ on } e} .$$

Summing this inequality over all edges $e \in E$ shows that the difference between the costs of f^* with respect to the different cost functions is at most the cost of f (i.e., rL); this completes the proof of Theorem 4.4.

4.4 Speed Scaling in Scheduling

The lion's share of killer applications of resource augmentation concern scheduling problems. This section describes one paradigmatic example.

4.4.1 Nonclairvoyant Scheduling

We consider a model with a single machine and m jobs that arrive online. Each job j has a release time r_j and the algorithm is unaware of the job before this time. Each job j has a processing time p_j, indicating how much machine time is necessary to complete it. We assume that preemption is allowed, meaning that a job can be stopped mid-execution and restarted from the same point (with no loss) at a subsequent time.

We consider the basic objective of minimizing the total flow time[8]:

$$\sum_{j=1}^{m} \left(C_j - r_j \right),$$

where C_j denotes the completion time of job j. For an alternative formulation, note that each infinitesimal time interval $[t, t + dt]$ contributes dt to the flow time $C_j - r_j$ of every job that is *active* at time t, meaning released but not yet completed. Thus, the total flow time can be written as

$$\int_0^\infty |X_t| dt, \tag{4.3}$$

where X_t denotes the active jobs at time t.

The *shortest remaining processing time* (SRPT) algorithm always processes the job that is closest to completion (preempting jobs as needed). This algorithm makes $|X_t|$ as small as possible for all times t (Exercise 4.7) and is therefore optimal. This is a rare example of a problem in which the optimal offline algorithm is implementable as an online algorithm.

SRPT uses knowledge of the job processing times to make decisions, and as such is a *clairvoyant* algorithm. What about applications in which a job's processing time is not known before it completes, where a *nonclairvoyant* algorithm is called for? No nonclairvoyant online algorithm can guarantee a total flow time close to that achieved by SRPT (Exercise 4.8). Could a resource augmentation approach provide more helpful algorithmic guidance?

4.4.2 A Resource Augmentation Guarantee for SETF

The natural notion of a "resource" in this scheduling problem is processor speed. Thus, a resource augmentation guarantee would assert that the total flow time of some nonclairvoyant protagonist *with a faster machine* is close to that of SRPT with the original machine.

We prove such a guarantee for the *shortest elapsed time first* (SETF) algorithm, which always processes the job that has been processed the least so far. When multiple jobs are tied for the minimum elapsed time, the machine splits its processing power

---

[8] This objective is also called the total response time.

equally between them. SETF does not use jobs' processing times to make decisions, and as such is a nonclairvoyant algorithm.

Example 4.6 Fix parameters $\epsilon, \delta > 0$, with δ much smaller than ϵ. With an eye toward a resource augmentation guarantee, we compare the total flow time of SETF with a machine with speed $1 + \epsilon$ – meaning that the machine can process $(1 + \epsilon)t$ units of jobs in a time interval of length t – to that of SRPT with a unit-speed machine.

Suppose m jobs arrive at times $r_1 = 0, r_2 = 1, \ldots, r_m = m - 1$, where m is $\lfloor \frac{1}{\epsilon} \rfloor - 1$. Suppose $p_j = 1 + \epsilon + \delta$ for every job j. Under the SRPT algorithm, assuming that $\epsilon + \delta$ is sufficiently small, there will be at most two active jobs at all times (the most recently released jobs); using (4.3), the total flow time of its schedule is $O(\frac{1}{\epsilon})$. The SETF algorithm will not complete any jobs until after time m, so in each time interval $[j - 1, j]$ there are j active jobs. Using (4.3) again, the total flow time of SETF's schedule is $\Omega(\frac{1}{\epsilon^2})$.

Example 4.6 shows that SETF is not optimal, and it draws a line in the sand: The best we can hope for is that the SETF algorithm with a $(1+\epsilon)$-speed machine achieves total flow time $O(\frac{1}{\epsilon})$ times that suffered by the SRPT algorithm with a unit-speed machine. The main result of this section states that this is indeed the case.

Theorem 4.7 (Kalyanasundaram and Pruhs, 2000) *For every input and $\epsilon > 0$, the total flow time of the schedule produced by the SETF algorithm with a machine with speed $1 + \epsilon$ is at most*

$$1 + \frac{1}{\epsilon}$$

times that by the SRPT algorithm with a unit-speed machine.

Using the second version (4.3) of the objective function, Theorem 4.7 reduces to the following pointwise (over time) bound.

Lemma 4.8 *Fix $\epsilon > 0$. For every input, at every time step t,*

$$|X_t| \le \left(1 + \frac{1}{\epsilon}\right) |X_t^*|,$$

where X_t and X_t^* denote the jobs active at time t under SETF with a $(1 + \epsilon)$-speed machine and SRPT with a unit-speed machine, respectively.

In Example 4.6, at time $t = m$, $|X_t^*| = 1$ (provided ϵ, δ are sufficiently small) while $|X_t| = m \approx \frac{1}{\epsilon}$. Thus, every inequality used in the proof of Lemma 4.8 should hold almost with equality for the instance in Example 4.6. The reader is encouraged to keep this example in mind throughout the proof.

To describe the intuition behind Lemma 4.8, fix a time t. Roughly:

1. SRPT must have spent more time processing the jobs of $X_t \setminus X_t^*$ than SETF (because SRPT finished them by time t while SETF did not).

82

2. SETF performed $1 + \epsilon$ times as much job processing as SRPT, an ϵ portion of which must have been devoted to the jobs of X_t^*.

3. Because SETF prioritizes the jobs that have been processed the least, it also spent significant time processing the jobs of $X_t \setminus X_t^*$.

4. SRPT had enough time to complete all the jobs of $X_t \setminus X_t^*$ by time t, so there can't be too many such jobs.

The rest of this section supplies the appropriate details.

4.4.3 Proof of Lemma 4.8: Preliminaries

Fix an input and a time t, with X_t and X_t^* defined as in Lemma 4.8. Rename the jobs of $X_t \setminus X_t^* = \{1, 2, \ldots, k\}$ such that $r_1 \geq r_2 \geq \cdots \geq r_k$.

Consider the execution of the SETF algorithm with a $(1 + \epsilon)$-speed machine. We say that job ℓ *interferes* with job j if there is a time $s \leq t$ at which j is active and ℓ is processed in parallel with or instead of j. The *interference set* I_j of a job j is the transitive closure of the interference relation:

1. Initialize I_j to $\{j\}$.
2. While there is a job ℓ that interferes with a job of I_j, add one such job to I_j.

In Example 4.6 with $t = +\infty$, the interference set of every job is the set of all jobs (because all of the jobs are processed in parallel at the very end of the algorithm). If instead $t = m$, then $I_j = \{j, j+1, \ldots, m\}$ for each job $j \in \{1, 2, \ldots, m\}$.

The interference set of a job is uniquely defined, independent of which interfering job is chosen in each iteration of the while loop. Note that the interference set can contain jobs that were completed by SETF strictly before time t.

We require several properties of the interference sets of the jobs in $X_t \setminus X_t^*$. To state the first, define the *lifetime* of a job j as the interval $[r_j, \min\{C_j, t\}]$ up to time t during which it is active.

Proposition 4.9 *Let $j \in \{1, 2, \ldots, k\}$ be a job of $X_t \setminus X_t^*$. The union of the lifetimes of the jobs in an interference set I_j is the interval $[s_j, t]$, where s_j is the earliest release time of a job in I_j.*

Proof One job can interfere with another only if their lifetimes overlap. By induction, the union of the lifetimes of jobs in I_j is an interval. The right endpoint of the interval is at most t by definition, and is at least t because job j is active at time t. The left endpoint of the interval is the earliest time at which a job of I_j is active, which is $\min_{\ell \in I_j} r_\ell$. $\square$

Conversely, every job processed in the interval corresponding to an interference set belongs to that set.

Proposition 4.10 *Let $j \in \{1, 2, \ldots, k\}$ be a job of $X_t \setminus X_t^*$ and $[s_j, t]$ the union of the lifetimes of the jobs in j's interference set I_j. Every job processed at some time $s \in [s_j, t]$ belongs to I_j.*

Proof Suppose job ℓ is processed at some time $s \in [s_j, t]$. Since $[s_j, t]$ is the union of the lifetimes of the jobs in I_j, I_j contains a job i that is active at time s. If $i \neq \ell$, then job ℓ interferes with i and hence also belongs to I_j. $\qquad\square$

The next proposition helps implement the third step of the intuition outlined in Section 4.4.2.

Proposition 4.11 *Let $j \in \{1, 2, \ldots, k\}$ be a job of $X_t \setminus X_t^*$. Let w_ℓ denote the elapsed time of a job ℓ under SETF by time t. Then $w_\ell \leq w_j$ for every job ℓ in j's interference set I_j.*

Proof We proceed by induction on the additions to the interference set. Consider an iteration of the construction that adds a job j_1 to I_j. By construction, there is a sequence of already added jobs $j_2, j_3, \ldots, j_p$ such that $j_p = j$ and j_i interferes with j_{i+1} for each $i = 1, 2, \ldots, p - 1$. (Assume that $p > 1$; otherwise we're in the base case where $j_1 = j$ and there's nothing to prove.) As in Proposition 4.9, the union of the lifetimes of the jobs $\{j_2, j_3, \ldots, j_p\}$ forms an interval $[s, t]$; the right endpoint is t because $j_p = j$ is active at time t. By induction, $w_{j_i} \leq w_j$ for every $i = 2, 3, \ldots, p$. Thus, whenever j_1 is processed in the interval $[s, t]$, there is an active job with elapsed time at most w_j. By virtue of being processed by SETF, the elapsed time of j_1 at any such point in time is also at most w_j. The job j_1 must be processed at least once during the interval $[s, t]$ (as the job interferes with j_2), so its elapsed time by time t is at most w_j. $\qquad\square$

4.4.4 Proof of Lemma 4.8: The Main Argument

We are now prepared to implement formally the intuition outlined in Section 4.4.2.

Fix a job $j \in X_t \setminus X_t^*$; recall that $X_t \setminus X_t^* = \{1, 2, \ldots, k\}$, with jobs indexed in nonincreasing order of release time. Let I_j denote the corresponding interference set and $[s_j, t]$ the corresponding interval in Proposition 4.9. As in Proposition 4.11, let w_i denote the elapsed time of a job i under SETF at time t. All processing of the jobs in I_j (by SETF or SRPT) up to time t occurs in this interval, and all processing by SETF in this interval is of jobs in I_j (Proposition 4.10). Thus, the value w_i is precisely the amount of time devoted by SETF to the job i in the interval $[s_j, t]$.

During the interval $[s_j, t]$, the SRPT algorithm (with a unit-speed machine) spends at most $t - s_j$ time processing jobs, and in particular at most $t - s_j$ time processing jobs of I_j. Meanwhile, the SETF algorithm works continually over the interval $[s_j, t]$; at all times $s \in [s_j, t]$ there is at least one active job (Proposition 4.9), and the SETF algorithm never idles with an active job. Thus SETF (with a $(1 + \epsilon)$-speed machine) processes $(1 + \epsilon)(t - s_j)$ units worth of jobs in this interval, and all of this work is devoted to jobs of I_j (Proposition 4.10).

Now group the jobs of I_j into three categories:

1. Jobs $i \in I_j$ that belong to X_t^* (i.e., SRPT has not completed i by time t)
2. Jobs $i \in I_j$ that belong to X_t but not X_t^* (i.e., SETF has not completed i by time t, but SRPT has)

3. Jobs $i \in I_j$ that belong to neither X_t nor X_t^* (i.e., both SETF and SRPT have completed i by time t)

The SRPT algorithm spends at least as much time as SETF in the interval $[s_j, t]$ processing category-2 jobs (as the former completes them and the latter does not), as per the first step of the intuition in Section 4.4.2. Both algorithms spend exactly the same amount of time on category-3 jobs in this interval (namely, the sum of the processing times of these jobs). We can therefore conclude that the excess time $\epsilon(t - s_j)$ spent by the SETF algorithm (beyond that spent by SRPT) is devoted entirely to category-1 jobs – the jobs of X_t^* (cf., the second step of the outline in Section 4.4.2). We summarize our progress so far in a proposition.

Proposition 4.12 *For every $j = 1, 2, \ldots, k$,*

$$\sum_{i \in I_j \cap X_t^*} w_i \geq \epsilon \cdot (t - s_j).$$

The sum in Proposition 4.12 is, at least, over the jobs $\{1, 2, \ldots, j\}$.

Proposition 4.13 *For every $j = 1, 2, \ldots, k$, the interference set I_j includes the jobs $\{1, 2, \ldots, j\}$.*

Proof Recall that the jobs $\{1, 2, \ldots, k\}$ of $X_t \setminus X_t^*$ are sorted in nonincreasing order of release time. Each job $i = 1, 2, \ldots, j - 1$ is released after job j and before job j completes (which is at time t or later), and interferes with j at the time of its release (as SETF begins processing it immediately). □

Combining Propositions 4.12 and 4.13, we can associate unfinished work at time t for SETF with that of SRPT:

Corollary 4.14 *For every $j = 1, 2, \ldots, k$,*

$$\sum_{i \in I_j \cap X_t^*} w_i \geq \epsilon \cdot \sum_{\ell=1}^{j} w_\ell.$$

For example, taking $j = 1$, we can identify ϵw_1 units of time that SETF spends processing the jobs of $I_1 \cap X_t^*$ before time t. Similarly, taking $j = 2$, we can identify ϵw_2 different units of time that SETF spends processing the jobs of $I_2 \cap X_t^*$: Corollary 4.14 ensures that the total amount of time so spent is at least $\epsilon w_1 + \epsilon w_2$, with at most ϵw_1 of it already accounted for in the first step. Continuing with $j = 3, 4, \ldots, k$, the end result of this process is a collection $\{\alpha(j, i)\}$ of nonnegative "charges" from jobs j of $X_t \setminus X_t^*$ to jobs i of X_t^* that satisfies the following properties:

1. For every $j = 1, 2, \ldots, k$, $\sum_{i \in X_t^*} \alpha(j, i) = \epsilon w_j$.
2. For every $i \in X_t^*$, $\sum_{j=1}^{k} \alpha(j, i) \leq w_i$.
3. $\alpha(j, i) > 0$ only if $i \in I_j \cap X_t^*$.

Combining the third property with Proposition 4.11:

$$w_i \le w_j \text{ whenever } \alpha(j,i) > 0. \tag{4.4}$$

We can extract from the $\alpha(j,i)$'s a type of network flow in a bipartite graph with vertex sets $X_t \setminus X_t^*$ and X_t^*. Precisely, define the flow f_{ji}^+ outgoing from $j \in X_t \setminus X_t^*$ to $i \in X_t^*$ by

$$f_{ji}^+ = \frac{\alpha(j,i)}{w_j}$$

and the flow f_{ji}^- incoming to i from j by

$$f_{ji}^- = \frac{\alpha(j,i)}{w_i}.$$

If we think of each vertex h as having a capacity of w_h, then f_{ji}^+ (respectively, f_{ji}^-) represents the fraction of j's capacity (respectively, i's capacity) consumed by the charge $\alpha(j,i)$. Property (4.4) implies that the flow is *expansive*, meaning that

$$f_{ji}^+ \le f_{ji}^-$$

for every j and i.

The first property of the $\alpha(j,i)$'s implies that there are ϵ units of flow outgoing from each $j \in X_t \setminus X_t^*$, for a total of $\epsilon \cdot |X_t \setminus X_t^*|$. The second property implies that there is at most one unit of flow incoming to each $i \in X_t^*$, for a total of at most $|X_t^*|$. Because the flow is expansive, the total amount of flow incoming to X_t^* is at least that outgoing from $X_t \setminus X_t^*$, and so

$$|X_t^*| \ge \epsilon \cdot |X_t \setminus X_t^*|.$$

This completes the proof of Lemma 4.8:

$$|X_t| \le |X_t^*| + |X_t \setminus X_t^*| \le |X_t^*| \cdot \left(1 + \frac{1}{\epsilon}\right).$$

4.5 Loosely Competitive Algorithms

An online algorithm with a good resource augmentation guarantee is usually "loosely competitive" with the offline optimal algorithm, which roughly means that, for every input, its performance is near-optimal for most resource levels (cf., Figure 4.2b). We illustrate the idea using the online paging problem from Section 4.1; Exercise 4.6 outlines an analogous result in the selfish routing model of Section 4.3.

There is simple and accurate intuition behind the main result of this section. Consider a page request sequence z and a cache size k. Suppose the number of page faults incurred by the LRU algorithm is roughly the same – within a factor of 2, say – with the cache sizes k and $2k$. Theorem 4.3, with $2k$ and k playing the roles of k and h, respectively, then immediately implies that the number of page faults incurred by the LRU algorithm with cache size k is at most a constant (roughly 4) times that incurred by the offline optimal algorithm with the same cache size. In other words, in this case the LRU algorithm is competitive in the traditional sense (Definition 4.2). Otherwise, the performance of the LRU algorithm improves rapidly as the cache size is expanded from k to $2k$. But because there is a bound on the maximum fluctuation of LRU's performance (between no page faults and faulting every time step), its performance can only change rapidly for a bounded number of different cache sizes.

Here is the precise statement, followed by discussion and a proof.

Theorem 4.15 (Young, 2002) *For every $\epsilon, \delta > 0$ and positive integer n, for every page request sequence z, for all but a δ fraction of the cache sizes k in $\{1, 2, \ldots, n\}$, the LRU algorithm satisfies either:*

1. $\text{PERF}(LRU, k, z) = O(\frac{1}{\delta} \log \frac{1}{\epsilon}) \cdot \text{PERF}(FIF, k, z)$; *or*
2. $\text{PERF}(LRU, k, z) \le \epsilon \cdot |z|$.

Thus, for every page request sequence z, each cache size k falls into one of three cases. In the first case, the LRU algorithm with cache size k is competitive in the sense of Definition 4.2, with the number of page faults incurred at most a constant (i.e., $O(\frac{1}{\delta} \log \frac{1}{\epsilon})$) times the minimum possible. In the second case, the LRU algorithm has a page fault rate of at most ϵ, and thus has laudable performance in an absolute sense. In the third case neither good event occurs, but fortunately this happens for only a δ fraction of the possible cache sizes.

The parameters δ, ϵ, and n in Theorem 4.15 are used in the analysis only – no "tuning" of the LRU algorithm is needed – and Theorem 4.15 holds simultaneously for all choices of these parameters. The larger the fraction δ of bad cache sizes or the absolute performance bound ϵ that can be tolerated, the better the relative performance guarantee in the first case.

In effect, Theorem 4.15 shows that a resource augmentation guarantee like Theorem 4.3 – an apples vs. oranges comparison between an online algorithm with a big cache and an offline algorithm with a small cache – has interesting implications for online algorithms even compared with offline algorithms with the same cache size. This result dodges the lower bound on the competitive ratio of the LRU algorithm (Section 4.1.3) in two ways. First, Theorem 4.15 offers guarantees only for most choices of the cache size k; LRU might perform poorly for a few unlucky cache sizes. This is a reasonable relaxation, given that we don't expect actual page request sequences to be adversarially tailored to the choice of cache size. Second, Theorem 4.15 does not insist on good performance relative to the offline optimal algorithm – good absolute performance (i.e., a very small page fault rate) is also acceptable, as one would expect in a typical application.[9]

We proceed to the proof of Theorem 4.15, which follows closely the intuition laid out at the beginning of the section.

Proof Fix a request sequence z and values for the parameters δ, ϵ, and n. Let b be a positive integer, to be chosen in due time. The resource augmentation guarantee in Theorem 4.3 states that, ignoring additive terms,

$$\text{PERF}(LRU, k + b, z) \le \frac{k + b}{b + 1} \cdot \text{PERF}(FIF, k, z), \qquad (4.5)$$

where $k + b$ and k are playing the roles of k and h in Theorem 4.3, respectively.

---

[9] This may seem like an obvious point, but such appeals to good absolute performance are uncommon in the analysis of online algorithms.

There are two cases, depending on whether

$$\text{PERF}(LRU, k+b, z) \geq \frac{1}{2} \cdot \text{PERF}(LRU, k, z) \tag{4.6}$$

or

$$\text{PERF}(LRU, k+b, z) < \frac{1}{2} \cdot \text{PERF}(LRU, k, z).$$

Call a cache size k *good* or *bad* according to whether it belongs to the first or second case, respectively. For good cache sizes k, chaining together the inequalities (4.5) and (4.6) shows that

$$\text{PERF}(LRU, k, z) \leq 2 \cdot \frac{k+b}{b+1} \cdot \text{PERF}(FIF, k, z), \tag{4.7}$$

and hence LRU is competitive (with ratio $\frac{2(k+b)}{b+1}$) in the sense of Definition 4.2.

Consider the set of bad cache sizes; for every such size, adding b extra pages to the cache decreases the number of page faults incurred by the LRU algorithm on z by at least a factor of 2. If there are at least ℓ bad cache sizes between 1 and $t - b$ for some t, then we can find ℓ/b bad cache sizes $k_1 < k_2 < \cdots < k_{\ell/b}$ in this interval that are each at least b apart (by taking every bth bad cache size).[10] In this case, using that $\text{PERF}(LRU, k, z)$ is nonincreasing in k (Exercise 4.1), we have

$$\text{PERF}(LRU, k_{i+1}, z) < \frac{1}{2} \cdot \text{PERF}(LRU, k_i, z)$$

for each $i = 1, 2, \ldots, \ell/b$, where $k_{(\ell/b)+1}$ should be interpreted as $k_{\ell/b} + b \leq t$. Chaining all of these inequalities together yields

$$\text{PERF}(LRU, t, z) < 2^{-\ell/b} \cdot \text{PERF}(LRU, 1, z).$$

Thus, once

$$\ell \geq b \cdot \log_2 \frac{1}{\epsilon}, \tag{4.8}$$

we have a page fault rate of at most ϵ:

$$\text{PERF}(LRU, t, z) \leq \epsilon \cdot |z|, \tag{4.9}$$

where $|z|$ is the length of the request sequence z.

The time has come to instantiate the parameter b. Guided by our desire to have δn bad cache sizes between 1 and some number t force the condition that $\text{PERF}(LRU, k, z) \leq \epsilon|z|$ for all cache sizes $k \geq t$, we take $\ell = \delta n$. The inequality (4.8) then suggests taking $b = \delta n / \log_2 \frac{1}{\epsilon}$.

Cache sizes now fall into three categories:

1. Good cache sizes. By the inequality (4.7) and our choice of b,

$$\text{PERF}(LRU, k, z) = O\left(\frac{1}{\delta} \log \frac{1}{\epsilon}\right) \cdot \text{PERF}(FIF, k, z)$$

for every such cache size k.

---

[10] For clarity, we omit the appropriate ceilings and floors from fractions such as ℓ/b.

2. The smallest δn bad cache sizes in $\{1, 2, \ldots, n\}$. There is no performance guarantee for these cache sizes.
3. Bad cache sizes that are bigger than at least δn other bad cache sizes. Our choices of ℓ and b ensure that the inequality (4.9) holds for such a cache size k, with

$$\text{PERF}(LRU, k, z) \leq \epsilon |z|.$$

Cache sizes in the first and third categories meet the first and second guarantees, respectively, of Theorem 4.15. Cache sizes in the second category constitute at most a δ fraction of the possible cache sizes, so the proof is complete. $\square$

4.6 Notes

Resource augmentation was first stressed as a first-order analysis framework by Kalyanasundaram and Pruhs (2000), although there were compelling examples much earlier [such as Theorem 4.3, which was proved by Sleator and Tarjan (1985)]. The phrase "resource augmentation" was proposed shortly thereafter, by Phillips et al. (2002).

The competitive analysis of online algorithms, including the model and results in Section 4.1, was developed by Sleator and Tarjan (1985). A good general reference for the topic is the book by Borodin and El-Yaniv (1998). Theorem 4.1 is due to Bélády (1967). See Young (1991, §2.4) for empirical comparisons of the FIF, LRU, and FIFO cache replacement policies on benchmark page request sequences.

The selfish routing model described in Section 4.3 was defined by Wardrop (1952). Existence and uniqueness of equilibrium flows (see footnote 6) was proved by Beckmann et al. (1956); see also Roughgarden (2007). The price of anarchy was defined, in a different context, by Koutsoupias and Papadimitriou (1999). Theorem 4.4 and the extension in Exercise 4.4 were proved by Roughgarden and Tardos (2002). The consequent loosely competitive bound (Exercise 4.6) was proved by Friedman (2004).

Pruhs et al. (2004) is a good reference on the competitive analysis of online scheduling algorithms; it includes a figure that inspired Figure 4.2. The optimality of SRPT (Exercise 4.7) was first proved by Schrage (1968). Theorem 4.7 is by Kalyanasundaram and Pruhs (2000), as is Exercise 4.9. One solution to Exercise 4.8 appears in Motwani et al. (1994). There are several more recent and sophisticated resource augmentation guarantees for more complex scheduling problems, for example with multiple machines, jobs with different priorities, and preemptions replaced by a small number of rejections. Good entry points to this literature include Im et al. (2011), Anand et al. (2012), and Thang (2013).

The concept of a loosely competitive online algorithm is due to Young (1994) and Theorem 4.15 is from Young (2002).

Acknowledgments

I thank Jérémy Barbay, Feder Fomin, Kirk Pruhs, Nguyen Kim Thang, and Neal Young for helpful comments on a preliminary draft of this chapter.

References

Anand, S., Garg, N., and Kumar, A. 2012. Resource augmentation for weighted flow-time explained by dual fitting. In *Proceedings of the Twenty-Third Annual ACM-SIAM Symposium on Discrete Algorithms (SODA)*, pp. 1228–1241.

Beckmann, M. J., McGuire, C. B., and Winsten, C. B. 1956. *Studies in the Economics of Transportation*. Yale University Press.

Bélády, L. A. 1967. A study of replacement algorithms for a virtual storage computer. *IBM Systems Journal*, **5**(2), 78–101.

Borodin, A., and El-Yaniv, R. 1998. *Online Computation and Competitive Analysis*. Cambridge University Press.

Friedman, E. J. 2004. Genericity and congestion control in selfish routing. In *Proceedings of the 43rd Annual IEEE Conference on Decision and Control (CDC)*, pp. 4667–4672.

Im, S., Moseley, B., and Pruhs, K. 2011. A tutorial on amortized local competitiveness in online scheduling. *SIGACT News*, **42**(2), 83–97.

Kalyanasundaram, B., and Pruhs, K. 2000. Speed is as powerful as clairvoyance. *Journal of the ACM*, **47**(4), 617–643.

Koutsoupias, E., and Papadimitriou, C. H. 1999. Worst-case equilibria. In *Proceedings of the 16th Annual Symposium on Theoretical Aspects of Computer Science (STACS)*, pp. 404–413.

Motwani, R., Phillips, S., and Torng, E. 1994. Nonclairvoyant scheduling. *Theoretical Computer Science*, **130**(1), 17–47.

Phillips, C. A., Stein, C., Torng, E., and Wein, J. 2002. Optimal time-critical scheduling via resource augmentation. *Algorithmica*, **32**(2), 163–200.

Pruhs, K., Sgall, J., and Torng, E. 2004. Online scheduling. In *Handbook of Scheduling: Algorithms, Models, and Performance Analysis*, Chapter 15. CRC Press.

Roughgarden, T. 2007. Routing games. In Nisan, N., Roughgarden, T., Tardos, É., and Vazirani, V. (eds.), *Algorithmic Game Theory*, pp. 461–486. Cambridge University Press.

Roughgarden, T., and Tardos, É. 2002. How bad is selfish routing? *Journal of the ACM*, **49**(2), 236–259.

Schrage, L. 1968. A proof of the optimality of the shortest remaining processing time discipline. *Operations Research Letters*, **16**(3), 687–690.

Sleator, D. D., and Tarjan, R. E. 1985. Amortized efficiency of list update and paging rules. *Communications of the ACM*, **28**(2), 202–208.

Thang, N. K. 2013. Lagrangian duality in online scheduling with resource augmentation and speed scaling. In *21st Annual European Symposium on Algorithms (ESA)*, pp. 755–766.

Wardrop, J. G. 1952. Some theoretical aspects of road traffic research. In. *Proceedings of the Institute of Civil Engineers, Pt. II*, vol. 1, pp. 325–378.

Young, N. 2002. On-Line File Caching. *Algorithmica*, **33**(3), 371–383.

Young, N. E. 1991. *Competitive Paging and Dual-Guided Algorithms for Weighted Caching and Matching*. PhD thesis, Princeton University, Department of Computer Science.

Young, N. E. 1994. The *k*-server dual and loose competitiveness for paging. *Algorithmica*, **11**(6), 525–541.

Exercises

Exercise 4.1 Prove that for every cache size $k \geq 1$ and every page sequence z,

$$\textsc{Perf}(LRU, k + 1, z) \leq \textsc{Perf}(LRU, k, z).$$

Exercise 4.2 Prove that Theorems 4.3 and 4.15 hold also for the FIFO caching policy.

Exercise 4.3 Prove a lower bound for all deterministic online algorithms that matches the upper bound for LRU in Theorem 4.3. That is, for every choice of k and $h \leq k$, every constant $\alpha < \frac{k}{k-h+1}$, and every deterministic online paging algorithm A, there exist arbitrarily long sequences z such that $\text{PERF}(A, k, z) > \alpha \cdot \text{PERF}(\textit{FIF}, h, z)$.

Exercise 4.4 Consider a *multicommodity* selfish routing network $G = (V, E)$, with source vertices $s_1, s_2, \ldots, s_k$, sink vertices $t_1, t_2, \ldots, t_k$, and traffic rates $r_1, r_2, \ldots, r_k$. A flow now routes, for each $i = 1, 2, \ldots, k$, r_i units of traffic from s_i to t_i. In an equilibrium flow f, all traffic from s_i to t_i travels on s_i–t_i paths P with the minimum-possible length $\sum_{e \in P} c_e(f_e)$, where f_e denotes the total amount of traffic (across all source-sink pairs) using edge e.

State and prove a generalization of Theorem 4.4 to multicommodity selfish routing networks.

Exercise 4.5 Deduce Corollary 4.5 from Theorem 4.4.

Exercise 4.6 This problem derives a loosely competitive-type bound from a resource augmentation bound in the context of selfish routing (Section 4.3). Let $\pi(G, r)$ denote the ratio of the costs of equilibrium flows in G at the traffic rates r and $r/2$. By Theorem 4.4, the price of anarchy in the network G at rate r is at most $\pi(G, r)$.

(a) Use Theorem 4.4 to prove that, for every selfish routing network G and traffic rate $r > 0$, and for at least an α fraction of the traffic rates $\hat{r}$ in $[r/2, r]$, the price of anarchy in G at traffic rate $\hat{r}$ is at most $\beta \log \pi(G, r)$ (where $\alpha, \beta > 0$ are constants, independent of G and r).

(b) Prove that for every constant $K > 0$, there exists a network G with nonnegative, continuous, and nondecreasing edge cost functions and a traffic rate r such that the price of anarchy in G is at least K for every traffic rate $\hat{r} \in [r/2, r]$.
[Hint: Use a network with many parallel links.]

Exercise 4.7 Prove that the shortest remaining processing time (SRPT) algorithm is an optimal algorithm for the problem of scheduling jobs on a single machine (with preemption allowed) to minimize the total flow time.

Exercise 4.8 Prove that for every constant $c > 0$, there is no nonclairvoyant deterministic online algorithm that always produces a schedule with total flow time at most c times that of the optimal (i.e., SRPT) schedule.

Exercise 4.9 Consider the objective of minimizing the maximum idle time of a job, where the *idle time* of job j in a schedule is $C_j - r_j - \frac{p_j}{s}$, where C_j is the job's completion time, r_j is its release time, p_j is its processing time, and s is the machine speed. Show that the maximum idle time of a job under the SETF algorithm with a $(1 + \epsilon)$-speed machine is at most $\frac{1}{\epsilon}$ times that in an optimal offline solution to the problem with a unit-speed machine.
[Hint: Start from Proposition 4.11.]

PART TWO

Deterministic Models of Data

CHAPTER FIVE

Perturbation Resilience

Konstantin Makarychev and Yury Makarychev

Abstract: This chapter introduces *perturbation resilience* (also known as Bilu–Linial stability). Loosely speaking, an instance is perturbation resilient if the optimal solution remains the same when we perturb the instance. We present algorithmic and hardness results for perturbation-resilient instances. In particular, we describe *certified algorithms* that attempt to bridge the gap between the worst-case and structured instances: on one hand, they *always* find an approximate solution; on the other hand, they exactly solve perturbation-resilient instances.

5.1 Introduction

In this chapter, we discuss the notion of *perturbation resilience* (also known as stability), which was introduced by Bilu and Linial (2010). The notion of perturbation resilience aims to capture real-life instances of combinatorial optimization and clustering problems. Informally, an instance of a combinatorial optimization or clustering problem is perturbation resilient if the optimal solution remains the same when we perturb the instance.

Definition 5.1 Consider a combinatorial optimization or clustering problem. Suppose that every instance has a number of parameters; for example, if the problem is a graph partitioning problem, the parameters are edge weights; if it is a constraint satisfaction problem, they are constraint weights; if it is a clustering problem, they are distances between points. A γ-*perturbation* of an instance $\mathcal{I}$ is an instance $\mathcal{I}'$ produced by multiplying each parameter in $\mathcal{I}$ by a number between 1 and γ (the number may be different for each parameter).[1]

Definition 5.2 An instance $\mathcal{I}$ is γ-perturbation resilient if every γ-perturbation of $\mathcal{I}$ has the same optimal solution as $\mathcal{I}$ (we require that $\mathcal{I}$ have a unique optimal solution).

While the solution should not change, the *value* or *cost* of the solution may and, generally speaking, will change when we perturb the instance. The larger γ is, the

---

[1] All problems we consider are scale invariant, so equivalently we can divide the parameters by a number between 1 and γ; we will use this convention when we talk about clustering problems.

more restrictive the γ-perturbation resilience condition becomes. In particular, the instance is 1-stable if and only if it has a unique solution.

In this chapter, we also describe *certified algorithms* (see Definition 5.4), which attempt to bridge the gap between the worst-case and structured instances: on one hand, they *always* find an approximate solution; on the other, they exactly solve perturbation-resilient instances.

Motivation. The definition of perturbation resilience is particularly applicable to machine learning problems, where we are interested in finding the *true* solution/clustering/partitioning rather than in optimizing the objective function per se. Indeed, when we frame a real-life problem as a machine learning problem, we make a number of somewhat arbitrary modelling decisions (for example, when we solve a clustering problem, we choose one similarity function among a number of reasonable choices). If the optimal solution is very sensitive to these modeling choices, then, by solving the problem exactly, we will likely not find the true solution. This suggests that there is no point in solving non–perturbation-resilient instances of many machine learning problems in the first place. Additionally, empirical evidence shows that in many real-life instances, the optimal solution stands out among all feasible solutions and is thus not sensitive to small perturbations of the parameters.

Weak Perturbation Resilience. The definition of perturbation resilience is somewhat strict. Perhaps it is more natural to require that the optimal solution to a perturbed instance be *close* but not necessarily equal to the optimal solution for the original instance. This notion is captured in the definitions of (γ, N)-weak perturbation resilience.[2]

Definition 5.3 (Makarychev et al., 2014) Consider an instance $\mathcal{I}$ of a combinatorial optimization problem. Let s^* be an optimal solution and N be a set of solutions, which includes all optimal solutions. Then s^* is better than any solution s outside of N. Assume further that for every γ-perturbation $\mathcal{I}'$ of $\mathcal{I}$, s^* is a better solution for $\mathcal{I}'$ than s is. Then we say that $\mathcal{I}$ is (γ, N)-weakly perturbation-resilient or simply γ-weakly perturbation resilient. We say that an algorithm solves a weakly perturbation resilient instance $\mathcal{I}$, if given a (γ, N)-weakly perturbation-resilient instance, it finds a solution $s \in N$ (crucially, the algorithm does not know N).

One should think of set N in Definition 5.3 as the set of solutions that are close to s^* in some sense. Let us say we solve Max Cut. Then, N may be the set of cuts (S', T') that can be obtained from the optimal cut (S^*, T^*) by moving at most an ε fraction of the vertices from one side of the cut to the other. Or, N may be the set of cuts that partition some subset of the vertices V_0 (informally, the "core of the graph" or the subset of "important vertices") in the same way as (S^*, T^*). Or, it may be a set of cuts that satisfy some other structural property. Note that an instance is $(\gamma, \{s^*\})$-weakly perturbation resilient if and only if it is γ-perturbation resilient.

It would be interesting to further relax the definition of perturbation resilience. In particular, it would be more natural to require only that the optimal solution not

---

[2] We note that a related notion of weak perturbation resilience, called (γ, ε)-perturbation resilience, was introduced by (Balcan and Liang, 2016).

change if we *randomly* perturb the input. Unfortunately, we do not have any results for this weaker definition of perturbation resilience.

Certified Algorithms. Let us now define the notion of a certified approximation algorithm (Makarychev and Makarychev, 2020). The definition is inspired by the definitions of perturbation resilience and smoothed analysis (Spielman and Teng, 2004) (see also Chapters 13–15 of this book). Recall that in the smoothed analysis framework, we analyze the performance of an algorithm on a small random perturbation of the input instance. That is, we show that, after we randomly perturb the input, the algorithm can solve it with the desired accuracy in the desired time. A certified algorithm perturbs the input instance *on its own* and then solves the obtained instance exactly. Importantly, the perturbation does not have to be random or small (in fact, we will later see that for many problems the perturbation must be considerable).

Definition 5.4 A γ-certified algorithm is an algorithm that, given an instance $\mathcal{I}$ of the problem, returns a γ-perturbation $\mathcal{I}'$ of $\mathcal{I}$ and an optimal solution s^* for $\mathcal{I}'$. We will say that $\mathcal{I}'$ certifies s^*.

As we will see in Section 5.2, certified algorithms have a number of desirable properties. A γ-certified algorithm always gives a γ-approximation for the problem and its "complement," exactly solves γ-perturbation-resilient instances, and solves weakly perturbation-resilient instances. Also, one may run a certified algorithm, get a perturbed instance $\mathcal{I}'$ and an optimal solution s^* for it, then, taking into account problem-specific considerations, decide for oneself whether $\mathcal{I}'$ is similar enough to $\mathcal{I}$ and, consequently, whether s^* is a reasonably good solution for $\mathcal{I}$.

Robust Algorithms. Most algorithms for perturbation-resilient instances of combinatorial optimization problems (but not clustering problems) that we discuss in this chapter are *robust* – they never output an incorrect answer, even if the input is not γ-perturbation-resilient.

Definition 5.5 An algorithm for γ-perturbation-resilient instances is robust if the following holds: If the input instance is γ-perturbation resilient, the algorithm finds the optimal solution; if the instance is not γ-perturbation-resilient, the algorithm either finds an optimal solution or reports that the instance is not γ-perturbation resilient.

This property is very desirable, as in real life we can only assume that input instances are perturbation resilient but we cannot be completely certain that they indeed are.

Running Time. The running time of most certified algorithm we consider in this chapter will be polynomial in the size of the input and the magnitude of the parameters. Thus, we will refer to these algorithms as pseudo-polynomial-time algorithms. Specifically, the running time will be polynomial in the size of *the input* and *the ratio between the largest and the smallest parameters*. To simplify the exposition, we will additionally assume that the parameters are integers between 1 and W. However, this assumption is not crucial [see (Makarychev and Makarychev, 2020)]. In this chapter, we will also talk about other ("noncertified") algorithms for perturbation and weakly perturbation-resilient instances – these algorithms will be *true* polynomial-time algorithms, whose running time is polynomial in the input size.

Organization. We discuss results for combinatorial optimization problems in Sections 5.2–5.3 and results for clustering problems in Sections 5.5–5.7.

5.2 Combinatorial Optimization Problems

In this section, we describe properties of certified algorithm for combinatorial optimization problems.

Preliminaries We will formally define what a combinatorial optimization problem is. Our definition will capture various constraint satisfaction, graph partitioning, and covering problems. It will be instructive for us to keep in mind two examples of such problems, Max Cut and Min Uncut.

> **Definition 5.6** In *Max Cut*, given a graph $G = (V, E, w_e)$, the goal is to find a cut $(S, \bar{S})$ in G that maximizes the total weight of the cut edges. In *Min Uncut*, given a graph $G = (V, E, w_e)$, the goal is to find a cut $(S, \bar{S})$ in G that minimizes the total weight of the edges not cut by $(S, \bar{S})$.

For a given graph G, the value of a cut $(S, \bar{S})$ w.r.t. the Max Cut objective plus the cost of $(S, \bar{S})$ w.r.t. the Min Uncut objective equals the total weight of all the edges and does not depend on the specific cut $(S, \bar{S})$. In particular, an optimal solution for Max Cut is also an optimal solution for Min Uncut and vice versa. However, as we will discuss later, a good *approximate solution* for one of the problems is not necessarily a good solution for the other. We say that Max Cut and Min Uncut are *complementary* problems. Now we give a general definition of a combinatorial optimization problem.

> **Definition 5.7** An instance of *a combinatorial optimization problem* is specified by a set of feasible solutions S (the solution space), a set of constraints C, and constraint weights $w_c > 0$ for $c \in C$. Typically, the solution space S is of exponential size and is not provided explicitly. Each constraint is a map from S to $\{0, 1\}$. We say that a feasible solution $s \in S$ satisfies a constraint c in C if $c(s) = 1$.
> We consider maximization and minimization objectives.
>
> - The *maximization objective* is to maximize the total weight of the satisfied constraints: find $s \in S$ that maximizes $\mathrm{val}_\mathcal{I}(s) = \sum_{c \in C} w_c c(s)$.
> - The *minimization objective* is to minimize the total weight of the unsatisfied constraints: find $s \in S$ that minimizes $\sum_{c \in C} w_c(1 - c(s)) = w(C) - \mathrm{val}_\mathcal{I}(s)$ (where $w(C) = \sum_{c \in C} w(c)$ is the total weight of all the constraints).
>
> We say that maximization and minimization are *complementary* objectives; likewise, we call two instances that differ only in the objective *complementary* instances. Note that complementary instances have the same optimal solutions.
> Weights $\{w_c\}_{c \in C}$ are the parameters of the instance in the sense of Definition 5.1.

As is standard for maximization and minimization constraint satisfaction problems, we do not require that a feasible solution $s \in S$ satisfy all of the constraints. In other words, we assume that the constraints are "soft"; later we will consider problems with "hard" and "soft" constraints (see Theorem 5.12).

Definition 5.8 An optimization problem is a family $\mathcal{F}$ of instances. We require that all instances in $\mathcal{F}$ have the same type of the objective (either all of them have a maximization or all have a minimization objective). We assume that if an instance $(\mathcal{S}, \mathcal{C}, w)$ is in $\mathcal{F}$, then so is $(\mathcal{S}, \mathcal{C}, w')$ for any choice of positive weights w.

Let us see why this definition captures Max Cut and Min Uncut. For a given instance $G = (V, E, w)$ of Max Cut or Min Uncut, $\mathcal{S}$ is the set of all the cuts in G. For every edge $e \in E$, there is a constraint c_e; $c_e((S, \bar{S})) = 1$ if e is cut by $(S, \bar{S})$. The objective for Max Cut is to maximize $\sum_{c \in \mathcal{C}} w_c c(S, \bar{S})$. The objective for Min Uncut is to minimize $\sum_{c \in \mathcal{C}} w_c (1 - c(S, \bar{S}))$.

Consider two other examples.

Example 5.9 In *Minimum Multiway Cut*, we are given a graph $G = (V, E, w_e)$ and a set of terminals $t_1, \ldots, t_k$. The goal is to partition G into k clusters $P_1, \ldots, P_k$ such that $t_i \in P_i$ for $i \in \{1, \ldots, k\}$ so as to minimize the total weight of the cut edges. For this problem, $\mathcal{S}$ is the set of all partitions $P_1, \ldots, P_k$ such that $t_i \in P_i$ for every i. For every edge $e \in E$, there is a constraint c_e; $c_e((P_1, \ldots, P_k)) = 1$ if e is *not* cut by $(P_1, \ldots, P_k)$. The objective is to minimize $\sum_{c \in \mathcal{C}} w_c (1 - c(P_1, \ldots, P_k))$.

Example 5.10 In *Maximum Independent Set*, we are given a graph $G = (V, E, w_v)$, where w_v are positive vertex weights. The goal is to find an independent set[3] I that maximizes $w(I)$. For this problem, $\mathcal{S}$ is the set of all independents sets I in G. For every vertex $v \in V$, there is a constraint c_v; $c_v(I) = 1$ if $v \in I$. The objective is to maximize $\sum_{c \in \mathcal{C}} w_c c(I)$. The problem complementary to Maximum Independent Set is *Minimum Vertex Cover*. In Minimum Vertex Cover, the objective is to find a vertex cover $C \subset V$ that minimizes $w(C)$; equivalently, the objective is to find an independent set I that minimizes $\sum_{c \in \mathcal{C}} w_c (1 - c(I))$.

Basic Properties of Certified Algorithms Now, we discuss basic properties of certified algorithms. First, we show that certified algorithms provide an approximate solution for worst case instances and solve perturbation-resilient and weakly perturbation-resilient instances.

Theorem 5.11 *Consider a γ-certified algorithm $\mathcal{A}$.*

- *$\mathcal{A}$ finds a γ-approximate solution regardless of what the input instance is. Further, it finds a γ-approximation for both the maximization and minimization objectives.*
- *If the instance is γ-perturbation-resilient, $\mathcal{A}$ finds the optimal solution. If it is (γ, N)-weakly stable, $\mathcal{A}$ finds a solution in N.*

---

[3] Recall that a set $I \subset V$ is an *independent set* if no edge in $e \in E$ has both its endpoints in I. A set $C \subset V$ is a *vertex cover* if every edge $e \in E$ has at least one endpoint in C. Note that I is an independent set if and only if $V \setminus I$ is a set cover.

Proof   Consider an instance $\mathcal{I}$. Denote its optimal solution by s^*. Denote the instance and solution found by $\mathcal{A}$ by $\mathcal{I}'$ and s'. For each constraint $c \in \mathcal{C}$, let w_c and w'_c be its weights in $\mathcal{I}$ and $\mathcal{I}'$, respectively.

1. First, we prove that the algorithm always gives a γ-approximation for both objectives. Consider the maximization objective. The value of s' (w.r.t. weights w_c) equals

$$\sum_{c \in \mathcal{C}} w_c c(s') \geq \sum_{c \in \mathcal{C}} \frac{w'_c}{\gamma} c(s') = \frac{1}{\gamma} \sum_{c \in \mathcal{C}} w'_c c(s') \overset{(\star)}{\geq} \frac{1}{\gamma} \sum_{c \in \mathcal{C}} w'_c c(s^*) \geq \frac{1}{\gamma} \sum_{c \in \mathcal{C}} w_c c(s^*),$$

where $(\star)$ holds since s' is an optimal solution for $\mathcal{I}'$. We conclude that s' is a γ-approximate solution for the maximization objective. Similarly, we upper bound the approximation factor for the minimization objective.

$$\sum_{c \in \mathcal{C}} w_c (1 - c(s')) \leq \sum_{c \in \mathcal{C}} w'_c (1 - c(s')) \leq \sum_{c \in \mathcal{C}} w'_c (1 - c(s^*)) \leq \gamma \sum_c w_c (1 - c(s^*)).$$

2. Now, assume that $\mathcal{I}$ is γ-perturbation resilient. By the definition of perturbation resilience, $\mathcal{I}$ and $\mathcal{I}'$ have the same optimal solution. Thus, s^* is an optimal solution not only for $\mathcal{I}'$ but also for $\mathcal{I}$. Finally, assume that $\mathcal{I}$ is (γ, N)-weakly perturbation resilient. Since $\mathcal{I}$ is (γ, N) weakly perturbation resilient and $\mathcal{I}'$ is a γ-perturbation of $\mathcal{I}$, the optimal solution s' for $\mathcal{I}'$ must lie in N. □

We note that traditional approximation results for maximization and minimization objectives are often very different. For example, the algorithm for Max Cut by Goemans and Williamson (1995) gives an $\alpha_{GW} \approx 0.878$ approximation, while the best known approximation algorithm for Min Uncut gives only an $O(\sqrt{\log n})$ approximation (Agarwal et al., 2005). Similarly, Minimum Vertex Cover admits a 2-approximation algorithm, while its complement, Maximum Independent Set, does not even have an $n^{1-\delta}$ approximation if $P \neq NP$ (for every $\delta > 0$).

Consider an instance of an optimization problem. We may choose a subset of constraints $H \subset \mathcal{C}$ and require that all of them be satisfied. We call them *hard constraints* and the obtained instance an instance with hard constraints. Formally, given an instance $(\mathcal{S}, \mathcal{C}, w)$ and a subset of constraints H, we define the correspondent instance $(\mathcal{S}', \mathcal{C}', w)$ with hard constraints as follows: $\mathcal{S}' = \{a \in \mathcal{S} : c(s) = 1 \text{ for every } c \in H\}$; $\mathcal{C}' = \mathcal{C} \setminus H$; $w'(c) = w(c)$ for $c \in \mathcal{C}'$.

Theorem 5.12 (Makarychev and Makarychev, 2020)   *Assume that there is a pseudo-polynomial-time γ-certified algorithm for a problem P, where $\gamma = \gamma_n$ is at most polynomial in n. Then there is also a pseudo-polynomial-time γ-certified algorithm for a variant P' of P with hard constraints. Accordingly, the maximization and minimization variants of P' admit γ-approximation algorithms.*

We leave the proof as an exercise (see Exercise 5.3).

Remark   Constraint satisfaction problems (CSPs) with hard constraints are often much harder for approximation algorithms than those without hard constraints. More precisely, algorithms for *minimization* CSPs without hard constraints typically can also solve instances with hard constraints. However, algorithms for *maximization* CSPs often cannot solve instances with hard constraints. For example, the algorithm for Max 2-SAT by Lewin et al. (2002) gives a 0.9401 approximation. However, there is no even an $n^{1-\delta}$ approximation algorithm for Max 2-SAT with hard constraints. The latter is also true for Max 2-Horn SAT (which is a variant of Max 2-SAT in which all the constraints are Horn clauses).

5.3 Designing Certified Algorithms

In this section, we will describe a general framework for designing certified algorithms, robust algorithms for perturbation-resilient instances, and algorithms for weakly perturbation-resilient instances, as well as proving that LP or SDP relaxations for perturbation-resilient instances are integral (Makarychev et al., 2014; Makarychev and Makarychev, 2020). To use this framework, one needs to either develop a procedure for solving a certain combinatorial task (see Task 5.13 and Lemma 5.14) or design a rounding scheme (procedure) that satisfies so-called approximation and co-approximation properties (see Theorems 5.17 and 5.19 below).

General Framework Consider an optimization problem. We design a certified algorithm that (1) starts with an arbitrary solution and (2) then iteratively improves it. This approach is somewhat similar to local search, except that the improvements are not necessarily local. We show that it suffices to have a procedure for the following task.

Task 5.13 Assume that we are given an instance $\mathcal{I}(\mathcal{S}, \mathcal{C}, w)$, a partition of its constraints $\mathcal{C} = \mathcal{C}_\infty \cup \mathcal{C}_\in$, and a parameter $\gamma \geq 1$. The task is either

- *Option 1:* to find $s \in \mathcal{S}$ such that $\gamma \sum_{c \in C_1} w_c c(s) > \sum_{c \in C_2} w_c (1 - c(s))$, or
- *Option 2:* to report that for every $s \in \mathcal{S}$: $\sum_{c \in C_1} w_c c(s) \leq \sum_{c \in C_2} w_c (1 - c(s))$.

(Note that the foregoing options are not mutually exclusive.)

When we use this procedure, C_1 and C_2 will be the sets of the constraints that are currently unsatisfied and satisfied, respectively. To give some intuition what Options 1 and 2 say, imagine that $\gamma = 1$. Then Option 1 is to find a solution s such that the weight of the currently *unsatisfied* constraints *satisfied* by s is greater than the weight of the currently *satisfied* constraints *unsatisfied* by s. In other words, Option 1 is to find a solution s better than the current solution. Option 2 is to report that there is no solution better than s.

Lemma 5.14 *Assume that (1) there is a polynomial-time algorithm for Task 5.13 above and (2) there is a polynomial-time algorithm that finds some solution $s \in \mathcal{S}$. Then there exists a pseudo-polynomial-time certified algorithm for the problem.*

Before we prove Lemma 5.14, we show how to get a certified algorithm for Max Cut and Min Uncut.

Theorem 5.15 *There exists a pseudo-polynomial-time γ-certified algorithm for Max Cut and Min Uncut, where $\gamma = O(\sqrt{\log n} \log \log n)$ is the approximation factor of the algorithm for Sparsest Cut with nonuniform demands by Arora et al. (2008).*

Proof To prove the theorem, we show how to solve Task 5.13 in polynomial time. Recall that in our formulation of Max Cut, $c_e(S, \bar{S}) = 1$ if edge e is cut. Let $E_1 = \{e \in E : c_e \in C_1\}$ and $E_2 = \{e \in E : c_e \in C_2\}$; denote the total weight of the edges in E_i cut by $(S, \bar{S})$ by $w(E_i(S, \bar{S}))$. Let $\phi(S) = \frac{w(E_2(S, \bar{S}))}{w(E_1(S, \bar{S}))}$. Then our goal is to either find a cut $(S, \bar{S})$ such that $\phi(S) < \gamma$ or report that $\phi(S) \geq 1$ for every $(S, \bar{S})$. Now the problem of minimizing $\phi(S)$ over all cuts $(S, \bar{S})$ is the same as finding the sparsest cut with nonuniform demands in graph (V, E_2) with edge capacities w, demand pairs E_1, and demand weights w. We run the approximation algorithm for Sparsest Cut and get a cut $(S, \bar{S})$ that approximately – within a factor of γ – minimizes $\phi(S)$. If $\phi(S) < \gamma$, we report cut $(S, \bar{S})$; otherwise, we report that $\phi(S') \geq 1$ for every cut $(S', \bar{S}')$. $\qquad\square$

Our certified algorithm gives $\gamma_n = O(\sqrt{\log n} \log \log n)$ approximation for Max Cut and Min Uncut. Let us compare this result with known *approximation* results for Max Cut and Min Uncut. For Max Cut, we can obtain a much better approximation factor of $\alpha_{GW} \approx 0.878$ (Goemans and Williamson, 1995). However, for Min Uncut, the best known approximation factor is $O(\sqrt{\log n})$ (Agarwal et al., 2005), which is comparable to γ_n. Note that there is also a γ_n-certified algorithm with an approximation factor of α_{GW}. The algorithm first finds an α_{GW} approximation for Max Cut, and then iteratively improves it as described in Theorem 5.15. Can the bound on γ_n be improved? It turns out that the optimal value of γ_n is essentially equal to the best approximation factor α_n for Sparsest Cut with nonuniform demands [see Makarychev et al. (2014) for details].

Proof of Lemma 5.14 As stated in the introduction, we assume that all weights w_c are integers between 1 and W. We first find a feasible solution s and then iteratively improve it.

Improvement Procedure. At each iteration, we let $C_1 = \{c \in C : c(s) = 0\}$ and $C_2 = \{c \in C : c(s) = 1\}$ be the sets of unsatisfied and satisfied constraints, respectively. Define weights w' as follows: $w'_c = w_c$ if $c \in C_1$ and $w'_c = \gamma w_c$ if $c \in C_2$. We run the procedure for Task 5.13 on instance $\mathcal{I}' = (S, C, w')$. Consider two cases. Assume first that the procedure returns a solution s' such that $\gamma \sum_{c \in C_1} w'_c c(s') > \sum_{c \in C_2} w'_c (1 - c(s'))$ (Option 1). We get that $\sum_{c \in C_1} w_c c(s') > \sum_{c \in C_2} w_c (1 - c(s'))$ and thus $\text{val}_{\mathcal{I}}(s') = \sum_{c \in C_1 \cup C_2} w_c c(s') > \sum_{c \in C_2} w_c = \text{val}_{\mathcal{I}}(s)$. Therefore, solution s' improves s. We use this s' in the next iteration of the algorithm.

Assume now that the procedure reports that for every solution s': $\sum_{c \in C_1} w'_c c(s') \leq \sum_{c \in C_2} w'_c (1 - c(s'))$ (Option 2) or, equivalently, $\text{val}_{\mathcal{I}'}(s') = \sum_{c \in C_1 \cup C_2} w'_c c(s') \leq \sum_{c \in C_2} w'_c = \text{val}_{\mathcal{I}'}(s)$ We return instance $\mathcal{I}'$ and solution s.

When the algorithm terminates, it outputs an instance $\mathcal{I}'$, which is a γ-perturbation of $\mathcal{I}$, and an optimal solution s for it. Thus, the algorithm is indeed a γ-certified algorithm. It remains to bound its running time. At each iteration, the value of the solution increases by at least 1 (recall that we have assumed that all weights are integers). Therefore, the algorithm terminates in at most $\sum_{c \in C} w_c \leq |C| W$ iterations. Since each iteration requires polynomial time, the running time is polynomial in n and W. $\qquad\square$

Using Convex Relaxations We now describe how to design certified algorithms using linear or semidefinite programming relaxations (or, in fact, any polynomially tractable convex relaxations).

While our ultimate goal is to design a *certified* approximation algorithm, imagine for a moment that we simply want to design a regular approximation algorithm. One standard approach is to write a relaxation for the problem and design a rounding scheme for it. For example, to solve Maximum Independent Set (see Example 5.10), we can use the following linear programming (LP) relaxation:

$$\text{maximize} \sum_{u \in V} w_u x_u \tag{5.1}$$

subject to: $x_u + x_v \leq 1$ for $(u, v) \in E$ and $0 \leq x_u \leq 1$ for $u \in V$

Our discussion that follows applies to any combinatorial optimization problem; but it might be instructive to keep relaxation (5.1) in mind. We refer to problem solutions $s \in S$ as *combinatorial* solutions and relaxation solutions x as *fractional* solutions; we say that x is *integral* if it corresponds to a combinatorial solution $s \in S$. We assume that in the relaxation we have a variable x_c for each constraint c so that $x_c = c(s)$ for every integral solution x and corresponding combinatorial solution s.[4]

Suppose first that we design an approximation algorithm for a maximization problem. Then the relaxation is to maximize $\text{fval}(x) = \sum_{c \in C} w_c x_c$ subject to certain problem specific constraints. We solve the relaxation, find a fractional solution x, and round it to a combinatorial solution $\mathcal{R}(x)$ using a randomized rounding scheme $\mathcal{R}$. Assume that the rounding scheme satisfies the following approximation condition for some $\alpha \geq 1$:

- **Approximation Condition** The probability[5] that each constraint $c \in C$ is satisfied by $\mathcal{R}(x)$ is at least x_c/α.

Then the expected weight of the constraints satisfied by $\mathcal{R}(x)$ is at least $\frac{\text{fval}}{\alpha}$. Thus, we get a randomized α-approximation algorithm.

Suppose now that we design an algorithm for a minimization problem. Then the relaxation objective is to minimize $\sum_{c \in C} w_c(1 - x_c)$. Now, we use a rounding scheme that satisfies the following co-approximation condition for some $\beta \geq 1$:

- **Co-approximation Condition.** The probability that each constraint $c \in C$ is unsatisfied by $\mathcal{R}(x)$ is at most $\beta(1 - x_c)$.

The expected weight of the unsatisfied constraints is at most $\beta \sum_{c \in C} w_c(1 - x_c)$. We get a β-approximation algorithm. We see that approximation and co-approximation

---

[4] Note that if we do not have variables x_c in the relaxation, we can usually add them, since expressions for them appear in the relaxation objective anyway.

[5] The probability is over the random choices made by $\mathcal{R}$.

conditions play a central role in the design of traditional approximation algorithms. It turns out that they can also be used to design *certified* algorithms.

Definition 5.16 We say that a rounding scheme $\mathcal{R}$ is an (α, β)-rounding if it simultaneously satisfies the approximation and co-approximation conditions with parameters α and β.

Theorem 5.17 *Assume that there exists an (α, β)-rounding scheme $\mathcal{R}$.*
1. Assume that $\mathcal{R}$ is computable in randomized polynomial time. Let $W = \frac{\max_{c \in C} w_c}{\min_{c \in C} w_c}$ be the ratio between the maximum and the minimum weights. Then there exists a randomized[6] certified γ-approximation algorithm for the problem where $\gamma = \alpha\beta + \varepsilon$; its running time is polynomial in the instance size, W, and $1/\varepsilon$.
2. Now we make a stronger assumption. Assume that the support of $\mathcal{R}$ is of polynomial size and can be found in polynomial time and that all the weights are integers between 1 and W. Then there exists a certified γ-approximation algorithm where $\gamma = \alpha\beta$; its running time is polynomial in the instance size and W.
In both cases, the solution s^* returned by the algorithm is an optimal solution for the convex relaxation for $\mathcal{I}'$.

Proof To simplify the exposition, we will only prove Part Two. The proof of Part One is very similar but more technical. We refer the reader to Makarychev and Makarychev (2020) for details. Note that the condition that the support of $\mathcal{R}$ can be found in polynomial time is not very restrictive; most rounding schemes satisfy it.

We use Lemma 5.14 to design the algorithm. Namely, we show how to solve Task 5.13 in polynomial time. First, we solve the convex relaxation for the problem and obtain a fractional solution x. If $\sum_{c \in C_1} w_c x_c \leq \sum_{c \in C_2} w_c(1 - x_c)$, then for every s

$$\sum_{c \in C_1} w_c c(s) + \sum_{c \in C_2} w_c c(s) \leq \sum_{c \in C_1} w_c x_c + \sum_{c \in C_2} w_c x_c \leq \sum_{c \in C_2} w_c. \quad (5.2)$$

So we report that $\sum_{c \in C_1} w_c c(s) \leq \sum_{c \in C_2} w_c(1 - c(s))$ for every s (Option 2). In this case, the certified algorithm from Lemma 5.14 returns a solution s^* of value $w(C_2) = \sum_{c \in C_2} w_c$. Equation (5.2) shows that the value of every fractional solution (let alone integral) is at most $\mathrm{val}_{\mathcal{I}}(s^*) = w(C_2)$.

Assume now that $\sum_{c \in C_1} w_c x_c > \sum_{c \in C_2} w_c(1 - x_c)$. We apply rounding scheme $\mathcal{R}$ and obtain a solution $\mathcal{R}(x)$. From the approximation and co-approximation conditions, we get

$$\mathbf{E}\left[\gamma \sum_{c \in C_1} w_c c(\mathcal{R}(x)) - \sum_{c \in C_2} w_c(1 - c(\mathcal{R}(x)))\right] \geq \frac{\gamma}{\alpha} \sum_{c \in C_1} w_c x_c - \beta \sum_{c \in C_2} w_c(1 - x_c)$$

$$\overset{\text{since } \gamma = \alpha\beta}{=} \beta \left(\sum_{c \in C_1} w_c x_c - \sum_{c \in C_2} w_c(1 - x_c)\right) > 0.$$

---

[6] More precisely, the algorithm is a Las Vegas algorithm, and as such, always outputs a correct solution.

Thus for some solution s in the support of $\mathcal{R}(x)$, we have $\gamma \sum_{c \in C_1} w_c c(s) > \sum_{c \in C_2} w_c(1 - c(s))$. We find and return such a solution s. □

As an immediate corollary, we get an algorithm for solving γ-perturbation-resilient and γ-weakly perturbation-resilient instances of combinatorial optimization problems. As we will describe below (see Theorem 5.19), it is actually sufficient to make slightly weaker assumptions to get algorithms for perturbation-resilient and weakly perturbation-resilient instances. Before we state Theorem 5.19, let us discuss how we can relax the conditions in Theorem 5.17. First, it is sufficient to design a rounding scheme that only rounds an optimal fractional solution. For some problems, this may be an easier task as the optimal fractional solution may satisfy certain additional properties (e.g., be half-integral). Also, it is sufficient to design a rounding scheme that only rounds fractional solutions that are close to integral solutions.

Definition 5.18 Let us say that a fractional solution x is δ-close to integral if $x = (1 - \delta)x^{int} + \delta x^{frac}$ for some integer solution x^{int} and fractional solution x^{frac} (for LP relaxations this condition implies that each LP variable x_c is in $[0, \delta] \cup [1 - \delta, 1]$). Rounding scheme $\mathcal{R}$ is a δ-local (α, β)-rounding if it is defined and satisfies the approximation and co-approximation conditions for fractional solutions x that are δ-close to an integral solution; the rounding scheme may but does not have to be defined or satisfy the approximation and co-approximation conditions for fractional solutions that are not δ-close to integral solutions.

Remark It is sufficient to have a δ-local rounding scheme (with $\delta \geq 1/\operatorname{poly}(n)$) in Theorem 5.17. Designing such a scheme may be a considerably easer task than designing a rounding scheme for arbitrary solutions. If we have such a scheme, we proceed as follows. Denote the fractional solution corresponding to the combinatorial solution s by $x^{(s)}$. We find an optimal fractional solution x^* and then let $x = (1 - \delta)x^{(s)} + \delta x^*$. Note that x is δ-close to integral. It is easy to see that if x^* is better than $x^{(s)}$, then so is x. Then we use x in the proof of Theorem 5.17 [see Makarychev and Makarychev (2020) for details].

Now, we describe a condition under which polynomial-time algorithms for solving γ-perturbation-resilient and $(\gamma + \varepsilon, N)$-weakly stable instances of combinatorial optimization problems are guaranteed to exist. Note that we do not make any assumptions about the weights w_c.

Theorem 5.19 (Makarychev and Makarychev (2016); Angelidakis et al. (2017)) *Assume that there is an (α, β)-rounding scheme or a δ-local (α, β)-rounding scheme $\mathcal{R}$. Let $\gamma = \alpha\beta$. Then we have:*

- *The convex relaxation is integral for γ-perturbation-resilient instances. $\mathcal{R}$ does not have to be computable in polynomial-time.*
- *There exists a robust polynomial-time algorithm for solving γ-perturbation-resilient instances. The running time depends only on the size of the input. Again, $\mathcal{R}$ does not have to be computable in polynomial time (we use $\mathcal{R}$ only in the analysis of the algorithm).*

- *Assume that the support of $\mathcal{R}(x)$ is of polynomial size and can be found in polynomial time and that $\varepsilon, \delta \geq 1/\operatorname{poly}(n)$. Then there exists a polynomial-time algorithm for solving $(\gamma + \varepsilon)$-weakly perturbation-resilient instances.*

5.4 Examples of Certified Algorithms

Maximum Independent Set We now prove that there exist a $(k-1)$-certified algorithm for Maximum Independent Set (MIS) in k-colorable graphs and a robust algorithm for $(k-1)$-perturbation-resilient instances of the problem (see Example 5.10 for the definition of MIS). To get the algorithms, we follow the approach we discussed in the previous section and design an (α, β)-rounding scheme with $\alpha\beta = k - 1$.

Consider a k-colorable graph $G = (V, E, w)$. Solve relaxation (5.1) for MIS. Let x be an optimal *vertex* solution. It is known that x is half-integral (Nemhauser and Trotter, 1975). Define $V_t = \{u \in V : x_u = t\}$ for $t \in \{0, 1/2, 1\}$. Consider the following rounding scheme due to Hochbaum (1983) (the rounding scheme needs to know a proper k-coloring $(C_1, \ldots, C_k)$ of V).

Rounding scheme R

Choose $i \in \{1, \ldots, k\}$ uniformly at random.
Return $S = V_1 \cup (V_{1/2} \cap C_i)$.

Theorem 5.20 (Angelidakis et al., 2019) *$\mathcal{R}$ is an (α, β)-rounding for MIS with $\alpha = k/2$ and $\beta = 2(k-1)/k$. Given the coloring, the rounding algorithm outputs a distribution of independent sets in polynomial time; the distribution support is of polynomial size.*

Proof It is easy to see that the rounding scheme always outputs an independent set S. If $u \in V_1$, then $u \in S$ (always); if $u \in V_0$, then $u \notin S$ (always) – in these two cases there is no randomness involved, and the approximation and coapproximation conditions trivially hold. Now if $u \in V_{1/2}$, then $u \in S$ with probability $1/k$ (this happens when i is the color of u). The approximation condition holds, since $\Pr(u \in S) = 1/k = x_u/\alpha$; the co-approximation condition holds, since $\Pr(u \notin S) = \frac{k-1}{k} = \beta(1 - x_u)$. $\square$

We conclude that there exists a polynomial-time $(k-1)$-certified algorithm for MIS and a robust polynomial-time algorithm for $(k-1)$-perturbation-resilient instances. Note that the certified algorithm needs to know the k-coloring of the graph, but the robust algorithm does not; the algorithm simply solves the LP relaxation and outputs the solution, which is guaranteed to be integral (see Theorem 5.19).

Minimum Multiway Cut Now, we design certified and robust algorithms for Minimum Multiway Cut (see Example 5.9 for the definition of the problem). To simplify the exposition, we focus on the case $k = 3$. Consider the LP relaxation by Călinescu et al. (2000) for the problem. For every vertex u, there is a vector $\bar{u} = (u_1, u_2, u_3)$ in the LP. In the integral solution corresponding to a partition (P_1, P_2, P_3): $u_i = 1$, if $u \in P_i$; and $u_i = 0$, otherwise. That is, $\bar{u} = e_i$ (the ith standard basis vector) if $u \in P_i$. The objective is to minimize $\frac{1}{2} \sum_{e=(u,v) \in E} w(e) \|\bar{u} - \bar{v}\|_1$ subject to (i) $\bar{t}_j = e_j$ for all $j \in \{1, 2, 3\}$, (ii) $u_1 + u_2 + u_3 = 1$ for all $u \in V$, and (iii) $u_j \geq 0$ for all $u \in V, j \in \{1, 2, 3\}$.

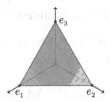 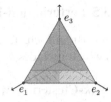

Figure 5.1 Each vector $\bar{u}$ lies in the triangle with vertices e_1, e_2, e_3. The left figure shows the 2-vertex cut of radius 3/10 with pivot $i = 3$; the right figure shows the ball cut of radius 4/5 with pivot $i = 3$.

It is easy to see that by adding auxiliary variables, we can write the objective as a linear function. Let $d(\bar{u}, \bar{v}) = \frac{1}{2}\|\bar{u} - \bar{v}\|_1$. The relaxation requires that each vector $\bar{u}$ lie in the triangle $\Delta = \text{conv}(e_1, e_2, e_3)$ with vertices e_1, e_2, e_3. Our goal is to design a δ-local (α, β)-rounding for Minimum Multiway Cut with $\alpha\beta = 4/3$ and $\delta = 1/30$. As is standard for approximation algorithms for Minimum Multiway Cut, we will consider a rounding scheme that (randomly) cuts triangle Δ into three pieces $\hat{P}_1, \hat{P}_2, \hat{P}_3$ so that $e_i \in \hat{P}_i$ and then lets $P_i = \{u : \bar{u} \in \hat{P}_i\}$ for each i. It is immediate that the rounding gives a feasible solution, since $\bar{t}_i = e_i \in \hat{P}_i$. We will describe how to cut triangle Δ so that the obtained rounding scheme is a δ-local (α, β)-rounding.

We are going to define two families of cuts, *two-vertex cuts* and *ball cuts* [introduced by Karger et al. (2004)]. Given a vertex e_i and radius $r \in (0, 1)$, let $B_r(e_i) = \{\bar{x} : d(\bar{x}, e_i) \leq r\}$ be the ball of radius r around e_i w.r.t. distance d. Geometrically, $B_r(e_i)$ is the triangle with vertices e_i, $(1-r)e_i + re_{j_1}$, and $(1-r)e_i + re_{j_2}$, where e_{j_1}, e_{j_2} are the basis vectors other than e_i. The two-vertex cut of radius $r \in (0, 1)$ with pivot $i \in \{1, 2, 3\}$, shown on Figure 5.1, is defined by $\hat{P}_j = B_r(e_j)$ for $j \in \{j_1, j_2\}$ and $\hat{P}_i = \Delta \setminus (\hat{P}_{j_1} \cup \hat{P}_{j_2})$. The ball cut of radius $r \in (0, 1)$ with pivot $i \in \{1, 2, 3\}$, shown on Figure 5.1, is defined by: $\hat{P}_i = B_r(e_i)$, every point $\bar{x} \notin \hat{P}_i$ belongs to either $\hat{P}_{j_1}$ or $\hat{P}_{j_2}$ depending on whether it lies closer to e_{j_1} or e_{j_2} w.r.t. distance d. Now we are ready to present the rounding scheme.

Rounding scheme R

Choose $r \in (0, 2/5)$ uniformly at random.
Choose pivot $i \in \{1, 2, 3\}$ uniformly at random.
With probability $1/3$, let $(\hat{P}_1, \hat{P}_2, \hat{P}_3)$ be the two-corner cut of radius r with pivot i.
Otherwise, let $(\hat{P}_1, \hat{P}_2, \hat{P}_3)$ be the ball cut of radius $1 - r$ with pivot i.
Let $P_j = \{u \in V : \bar{u} \in \hat{P}_j\}$ for $j \in \{1, 2, 3\}$.
Return partition $P = (P_1, P_2, P_3)$.

Theorem 5.21 (Angelidakis et al., 2017) $\mathcal{R}$ *is a δ-local (α, β)-rounding for Minimum Multiway Cut with $\alpha = 10/9$ and $\beta = 6/5$.*

We leave the proof as an exercise (see Exercise 5.4). We conclude that there exists a polynomial-time 4/3-certified algorithm for Multiway Cut with three terminals and a robust polynomial-time algorithm for 4/3-perturbation-resilient instances. These results generalize to $(2 - 2/k)$-perturbation-resilient instances of Multiway Cut with k terminals; see Angelidakis et al. (2017).

5.5 Perturbation-Resilient Clustering Problems

In this section, we consider k-clustering problems with the ℓ_p objective. This is a broad class of problems which includes k-means, k-medians, and k-center.

> **Definition 5.22** (k-Clustering with the ℓ_p Objective) An instance of k-clustering with the ℓ_p objective ($p \geq 1$) consists of a metric space (X, d) and a natural number k. The goal is to partition X into k disjoint clusters $C_1, \ldots, C_k$ and assign a center c_i to each cluster C_i so as to minimize the following objective function:
>
> $$\sum_{i=1}^{k} \sum_{u \in C_i} d^p(u, c_i).$$
>
> For $p = \infty$, the objective function is $\max_{\substack{i \in \{1,\ldots,k\} \\ u \in C_i}} |d(u, c_i)|$.

Note that k-medians is the k-clustering problem with the ℓ_1 objective; k-means is k-clustering with the ℓ_2 objective; and k-center is k-clustering with the ℓ_∞ objective.

Consider an instance (X, d) of k-clustering with the ℓ_p objective. In an optimal solution to this problem, each point is assigned to the closest center $c_1, \ldots, c_k$. That is, if $u \in C_i$, then $d(u, c_i) \leq d(u, c_j)$ for all $j \neq i$. This is an important property common to all so-called *clustering problems with a center-based objective*. Note that the optimal clustering $C_1, \ldots, C_k$ is determined by the centers $c_1, \ldots, c_k$. Specifically, $\{C_1, \ldots, C_k\}$ is the Voronoi partition for $c_1, \ldots, c_k$; that is, C_i is the set of points in X that are closer to c_i than to any other c_j.

Now let us assume that the distance from every point in X to its own center is less than the distances to other centers by a certain margin. Specifically, suppose that there exists an optimal clustering $C_1, \ldots, C_k$ with centers $c_1, \ldots, c_k$ that satisfies the following condition called λ-center proximity: for every $u \in C_i$, not only $d(u, c_i) \leq d(u, c_j)$ but also $\lambda d(u, c_i) < d(u, c_j)$.

> **Definition 5.23** (λ-Center Proximity) Let (X, d) be an instance of the k-clustering problem with the ℓ_p objective. Consider an optimal solution $C_1, \ldots, C_k$ with centers $c_1, \ldots, c_k$. We say that $c_1, \ldots, c_k$ satisfies the λ-center proximity condition (where $\lambda \geq 1$) if for every $u \in C_i$ and $j \neq i$, we have $\lambda d(u, c_i) < d(u, c_j)$.
>
> We say that (X, d) has an optimal solution satisfying the λ-center proximity condition if there exists an optimal solution $C_1, \ldots, C_k$ with centers $c_1, \ldots, c_k$ satisfying the λ-center proximity condition.

The optimal set of centers is not necessarily unique for a given clustering $C_1, \ldots, C_k$. Some optimal sets of centers for $C_1, \ldots, C_k$ may satisfy the λ-center proximity condition, while others do not.

In Section 5.6, we show that there exists an algorithm – a variant of the classic single-linkage clustering – that finds the optimal clustering if this clustering satisfies the 2-center proximity condition for some set of optimal centers. We note that it is NP-hard to find the optimal clustering in instances satisfying λ-center proximity condition with $\lambda < 2$ (Ben-David and Reyzin, 2014). Now we restate Definitions 5.1 and 5.2 taking into account specifics of clustering problems.

Definition 5.24 (Perturbations and Metric Perturbations) Consider a metric space (X, d). We say that a symmetric function $d' : X \times X \to \mathbf{R}^+$ is a γ-perturbation of d if for all $u, v \in X$ we have $\frac{1}{\gamma} d(u, v) \leq d'(u, v) \leq d(u, v)$. We say that d' is a *metric γ-perturbation* of d if d' is a γ-perturbation of d and a metric itself; i.e., d' satisfies the triangle inequality.

Note that a (non-metric) γ-perturbation d' may violate the triangle inequality and thus is not necessarily a metric.

Definition 5.25 (Perturbation Resilience) Consider an instance (X, d) of the k-clustering problem with the ℓ_p objective. Let $C_1, \ldots, C_k$ be the optimal clustering. Then, (X, d) is *γ-perturbation resilient* if for every γ-perturbation of d, the unique optimal clustering of (X, d') is $C_1, \ldots, C_k$. Similarly, (X, d) is *metric γ-perturbation-resilient* if for every metric γ-perturbation of d, the unique optimal clustering of (X, d') is $C_1, \ldots, C_k$.

The definition of metric γ-perturbation resilience is less restrictive than that of γ-perturbation resilience: if an instance is γ-perturbation resilient, it is also *metric* γ-perturbation resilient but not the other way around. In particular, every algorithm that solves metric γ-perturbation-resilient instances also solves γ-perturbation-resilient instances.

Note that in the definition of γ-perturbation resilience we do not require that the optimal centers of the clusters $C_1, \ldots, C_k$ are the same for distance functions d and d'. If we added this requirement we would get a much stronger definition of γ-perturbation resilience or metric γ-perturbation resilience (see Exercise 5.7).

Perturbation resilience is a stronger notion than center proximity: Every γ-perturbation-resilient instance satisfies the γ-center proximity condition. We prove this implication in Theorem 5.27. The converse statement does not hold, and thus these notions are not equivalent (see Exercise 5.10).

In this chapter, we present two results on γ-perturbation resilience. First, we give a dynamic programming algorithm that finds an exact solution to any 2-center proximity instance of the k-clustering problem (see Theorem 5.29). Since every metric 2-perturbation-resilient instance satisfies the 2-center proximity condition (see Theorem 5.27), our algorithm also works for metric 2-perturbation-resilient instances. Then, we discuss a connection between perturbation resilience and local search and show that the standard local search algorithm for k-medians is a $(3 + \varepsilon)$-certified algorithm. Thus, this algorithm returns the optimal clustering for γ-perturbation-resilient instances and gives a $(3 + \varepsilon)$-approximation for arbitrary instances.

Open Question 5.26 Suppose we replace the requirement that d' be a γ-perturbation of d with the requirement that d' be a *metric γ-perturbation* of d in the definition of a γ-certified algorithm (see Definition 5.4). Can we design a $(3 + \varepsilon)$-certified algorithm according to the new definition?

5.5.1 Metric Perturbation Resilience Implies Center Proximity

We show that metric perturbation resilience implies center proximity.

Theorem 5.27 (Awasthi et al., 2012, and Angelidakis et al., 2017) *Let (X,d) be a metric γ-perturbation-resilient instance of the k-clustering problem with the ℓ_p objective ($p \geq 1$). Consider the unique optimal solution $\mathcal{C} = (C_1, \ldots, C_k)$ and an optimal set of centers $\{c_1, \ldots, c_k\}$ (which is not necessarily unique). Then, centers $c_1, \ldots, c_k$ satisfy the γ-center proximity property.*

Proof Consider an arbitrary point p in X. Let c_i be the closest center to p in $\{c_1, \ldots, c_k\}$ and c_j be another center. We need to show that $d(p, c_j) > \gamma d(p, c_i)$. Suppose that $d(p, c_j) \leq \gamma d(p, c_i)$. Let $r^* = d(p, c_i)$. Define a new metric d'. Consider the complete graph $G = (X, E)$ on the metric space X. Let the length $\mathrm{len}(u,v)$ of every edge (u,v) be $d(u,v)$. Then, $d(u,v)$ is the shortest path metric on G. We now shorten edge (p, c_j) while preserving the lengths of all other edges. Specifically, we let $\mathrm{len}'(p, c_j) = r^*$ and $\mathrm{len}'(u,v) = d(u,v)$ for $(u,v) \neq (p, c_j)$. Let d' be the shortest path metric on graph G with edge lengths $\mathrm{len}'(u,v)$. Observe that $d'(u,v) = d(u,v)$ unless there is a shortcut that goes along the edge (p, c_j). That is, the distance $d'(u,v)$ between any two points u and v equals the length of the shortest of the following three paths: (1) $u \to v$, (2) $u \to p \to c_j \to v$, and (3) $u \to c_j \to p \to v$. Thus,

$$d'(u,v) = \min\left(d(u,v), d(u,p) + r^* + d(c_j, v), d(u, c_j) + r^* + d(p,v)\right).$$

Note that $\mathrm{len}(u,v)/\gamma \leq \mathrm{len}'(u,v) \leq \mathrm{len}(u,v)$. Hence, $d(u,v)/\gamma \leq d'(u,v) \leq d(u,v)$ and thus $d'(u,v)$ is a γ-perturbation. Thus, the optimal clustering of X for d' is the same as for d. Namely, it is $C_1, \ldots, C_k$. However, generally speaking, the optimal centers for clusters $C_1, \ldots, C_k$ may differ for metrics d and d' (for some γ-perturbations they do!). Nevertheless, we claim that c_i and c_j are optimal centers for clusters C_i and C_j with respect to metric d'. This leads to a contradiction with our assumption that $d(p, c_j) \leq \gamma d(p, c_i)$, because p must be closer to its own center c_i than to c_j and, consequently, we must have $d(p, c_i) = d'(p, c_i) < d'(p, c_j) = d(p, c_i)$.

Therefore, to finish the proof we need to show that c_i and c_j are optimal centers for clusters C_i and C_j with respect to the metric d'. To this end, we prove that the metric d' equals d within clusters C_i and C_j, and, hence any optimal center for C_i w.r.t. d is also an optimal center w.r.t d' and vice versa. $\square$

Lemma 5.28 *For all $u, v \in C_i$, we have $d(u,v) = d'(u,v)$. Also, for all $u, v \in C_j$, we have $d(u,v) = d'(u,v)$.*

Proof To prove that $d'(u,v) = d(u,v)$, we need to show that $d(u,v) < \min(d(u,p) + r^* + d(c_j, v), d(u, c_j) + r^* + d(p, v))$. Assume without loss of generality that $d(u,p) + r^* + d(c_j, v) \leq d(u, c_j) + r^* + d(p, v)$. Then,

$$d(u,p) + r^* + d(c_j, v) = \underbrace{\left(d(u,p) + d(p, c_i)\right)}_{\geq d(u, c_i)} + d(c_j, v) \geq d(u, c_i) + d(c_j, v).$$

1. If $u, v \in C_i$, then the closest center to v is c_i and, particularly, $d(c_j, v) > d(c_i, v)$. Thus, $d(u, p) + r^* + d(c_j, v) > d(u, c_i) + d(c_i, v) \geq d(u, v)$.

2. If $u, v \in C_j$, then the closest center to u is c_j and, particularly, $d(u, c_i) > d(u, c_j)$. Thus, $d(u, p) + r^* + d(c_j, v) > d(u, c_j) + d(c_j, v) \geq d(u, v)$. $\qquad \square$

5.6 Algorithm for 2-Perturbation-Resilient Instances

In this section, we prove that a variant of the single-linkage clustering algorithm finds the exact optimal solution for instances of clustering problems with the ℓ_p objective satisfying the 2-center proximity condition (or, more formally: instances that have an optimal solution $C_1, \ldots, C_k$ with centers $c_1, \ldots, c_k$ that satisfy the 2-center proximity condition).

Single-linkage clustering is a classic algorithm that works as follows. Given a metric space (X, d) on n points, it creates n clusters each containing a single point from X. Then, at every step it picks the two closest clusters and merges them. The distance between clusters is usually defined as the distance between the two closest points in the clusters i.e., $d(C', C'') = \min_{u \in C', v \in C''} d(u, v)$. Thus, at every step the number of clusters decreases by 1. The algorithm stops when only k clusters remain.

Single-linkage clustering is a fairly simple and relatively fast algorithm. However, it fails to find an optimal clustering when the clusters are not isolated from each other. It is also very fragile to noise because adding just a few extra points to the dataset X can drastically alter the output. We cannot use single-linkage clustering as is for perturbation-resilient instances, since this algorithm may output a very bad clustering even if the instance is γ-perturbation-resilient with arbitrarily large γ (see Exercise 5.11) and for this reason will use a dynamic programming-based postprocessing step.

Theorem 5.29 (Angelidakis et al., 2017) *There exists a polynomial-time algorithm that given an instance (X, d) of k-clustering with the ℓ_p objective outputs an optimal solution if (X, d) has an optimal solution satisfying the 2-center proximity condition.*

Algorithm Consider the complete graph G on X, in which every edge (u, v) has length $d(u, v)$. Our algorithm first constructs the minimum spanning tree (MST) T in G and then clusters T using dynamic programming. To construct the MST, we can use one of many known algorithms, particularly Kruskal's algorithm which is essentially a variant of single-linkage clustering. We describe the dynamic program later in this section. Now we show that if an instance has an optimal solution satisfying the 2-center proximity condition then all clusters in that solution must form connected components in the minimum spanning tree.

Theorem 5.30 *Consider an instance (X, d) of k-clustering with the ℓ_p objective. Let $C_1, \ldots, C_k$ be an optimal clustering with centers $c_1, \ldots, c_k$ satisfying the 2-center proximity condition; and let $T = (X, E)$ be the minimum spanning tree (MST) in the complete graph on X with edge lengths $d(u, v)$. Then, each cluster C_i is a subtree of T (i.e., for every two vertices $u, v \in C_i$, the unique shortest path from u to v in T completely lies within C_i).*

We will need the following lemma.

Lemma 5.31 *Consider an instance (X, d) of the k-clustering problem with the ℓ_p objective. Suppose that $C_1, \ldots, C_k$ is an optimal clustering for (X, d) and $c_1, \ldots, c_k$ is an optimal set of centers. If $c_1, \ldots, c_k$ satisfy the 2-center proximity property, then for every two distinct clusters C_i and C_j and all points $u \in C_i$ and $v \in C_j$, we have $d(u, c_i) < d(u, v)$.*

Proof Since $c_1, \ldots, c_k$ satisfy the 2-center proximity property, we have $2d(u, c_i) < d(u, c_j)$ and $2d(v, c_j) < d(v, c_i)$. Thus, by the triangle inequality, $2d(u, c_i) < d(u, v) + d(v, c_j)$ and $2d(v, c_j) < d(v, u) + d(u, c_i)$. We sum these inequalities with coefficients 2/3 and 1/3 and obtain the desired bound: $d(u, c_i) < d(u, v)$. □

Proof of Theorem 5.30 Since T is a tree, it suffices to show that for every $u \in C_i$, all points on the unique path in T from u to c_i lie in C_i. Consider an arbitrary point $u \in C_i$ and denote the path from u to c_i by $u_1, \ldots, u_M$, where $u_1 = u$ and $u_M = c_i$. We prove by induction on m that all u_m ($m = 1, \ldots, M$) are in C_i. The point $u_1 = u$ is in C_i. Also, $u_M \in C_i$ because $u_M = c_i$ is the center of C_i. Suppose that $u_m \in C_i$ and $m < M - 1$, we show that $u_{m+1} \in C_i$. By the MST cycle property, (u_M, u_m) is the longest edge in the cycle $u_m \to u_{m+1} \to \cdots \to u_M \to u_m$ (since all edges in the cycle but edge (u_M, u_m) belong to the MST). Particularly, $d(u_m, c_i) \equiv d(u_m, u_M) \geq d(u_m, u_{m+1})$. By the induction hypothesis $u_m \in C_i$. Therefore, by Lemma 5.31, u_{m+1} also belongs to C_i (because if u_{m+1} was not in C_i we would have $d(u_m, c_i) < d(u_m, u_{m+1})$). □

Dynamic Program We now describe a dynamic program for finding the optimal clustering in the MST. Let us choose an arbitrary vertex r in X as a root for the MST T. Denote by T_u the subtree rooted at vertex u. We define two types of subproblems OPT and OPT_{AC}:

1. Let $\text{OPT}(u, m)$ be the optimal cost of partitioning subtree T_u into m clusters that are subtrees of T.
2. Let $\text{OPT}_{AC}(u, m, c)$ be the optimal cost of partitioning subtree T_u into m clusters subject to the following constraint: vertex u and all points in its cluster must be assigned to the center c.

The cost of k-clustering X equals $OPT(r, k)$. For simplicity, we assume that the MST is a binary tree (the general case can be handled by transforming any tree to a binary tree by adding "dummy" vertices). Let left(u) be the left child of u and right(u) be the right child of u.

We write recurrence relations on OPT and OPT_{AC}. To compute $\text{OPT}(u, m)$ we need to find the optimal center for u and return $\text{OPT}(u, m, c)$. Thus,

$$\text{OPT}(u, m) = \min_{c \in X} \text{OPT}_{AC}(u, m, c).$$

To find $\text{OPT}_{AC}(u, m, c)$, we find the optimal solutions for the left and right subtrees and combine them. To this end, we need to guess the number of clusters m_L and m_R in the left and right subtrees. We present formulas for $\text{OPT}_{AC}(u, m, c)$ in the four possible cases.

1. If both children $\text{left}(u)$ and $\text{right}(u)$ are in the same cluster as u, then

$$\min_{\substack{m_L, m_R \in \mathbf{Z}^+ \\ m_L + m_R = m+1}} d(c, u) + \text{OPT}_{AC}(\text{left}(u), c, m_L) + \text{OPT}_{AC}(\text{right}(u), c, m_R).$$

2. If $\text{left}(u)$ is in the same cluster as u, but $\text{right}(u)$ is in a different cluster, then

$$\min_{\substack{m_L, m_R \in \mathbf{Z}^+ \\ m_L + m_R = m}} d(c, u) + \text{OPT}_{AC}(\text{left}(u), c, m_L) + \text{OPT}(\text{right}(u), m_R).$$

3. If $\text{right}(u)$ is in the same cluster as u, but $\text{left}(u)$ is in a different cluster, then

$$\min_{\substack{m_L, m_R \in \mathbf{Z}^+ \\ m_L + m_R = m}} d(c, u) + \text{OPT}(\text{left}(u), m_L) + \text{OPT}_{AC}(\text{right}(u), c, m_R).$$

4. If u, $\text{left}(u)$, and $\text{right}(u)$ are in different clusters, then

$$\min_{\substack{m_L, m_R \in \mathbf{Z}^+ \\ m_L + m_R = m-1}} d(c, u) + \text{OPT}(\text{left}(u), m_L) + \text{OPT}(\text{right}(u), m_R).$$

We compute the values of $\text{OPT}_{AC}(u, m, c)$ in the four cases above and choose the minimum among them.

The sizes of the DP tables for OPT and OPT_{AC} are $O(n \times k)$ and $n \times k \times n) = O(n^2 k)$, respectively. It takes $O(n)$ and $O(k)$ time to compute each entry in the tables OPT and OPT_{AC}, respectively. Thus, the total running time of the DP algorithm is $O(n^2 k^2)$. The running time of Prim's MST algorithm is $O(n^2)$.

5.7 $(3 + \varepsilon)$-Certified Local Search Algorithm for k-Medians

A common heuristic for clustering as well as for related problems such as Facility Location is local search (see also Chapter 13). Sometimes, local search algorithms are used on their own and sometimes to process the output of other algorithms. It is known that local search gives a $(3 + \varepsilon)$-approximation for k-medians and a $(9 + \varepsilon)$-approximation for k-means (Arya et al., 2004; Kanungo et al., 2004), where $\varepsilon > 0$ is arbitrary. The running time is exponential in $1/\varepsilon$. We will see that local search is a $(3 + \varepsilon)$-certified algorithm k-medians.

Below, we will focus on the k-medians problem though similar results hold for any clustering problems with the ℓ_p objective. Consider an arbitrary set of centers $c_1, \ldots, c_k$. The optimal clustering $C_1, \ldots, C_k$ for this set of centers is defined by the Voronoi partition; i.e., $u \in C_i$ if and only if c_i is the closest center to u (ties between centers are broken arbitrarily). Denote by $\text{cost}(c_1, \ldots, c_k)$ its cost.

We now describe a 1-local search algorithm. The algorithm maintains a set of k centers $c_1, \ldots, c_k$. It starts with an arbitrary set of centers $c_1, \ldots, c_k$. Then, at every step, it considers all possible swaps $c_i \to u$, where c_i is a center in the current set of centers, and u is a point outside of this set. If we can improve the solution by swapping c_i with u, we perform this swap. In other words, if for some pair (c_i, u), we have $\text{cost}(c_1, \ldots, c_{i-1}, u, c_{i+1}, \ldots, c_k) < \text{cost}(c_1, \ldots, c_k)$, then we replace the center c_i with u. The algorithm terminates when no swap $c_i \to u$ can improve the solution. We call the obtained set of centers *1-locally optimal* and denote it by L. A more powerful (alas less practical) version of the local search algorithm considers swaps of size up to ρ instead of 1. We call this algorithm the ρ-local search algorithm. Its running time is exponential in ρ.

Theorem 5.32 (Cohen-Addad and Schwiegelshohn, 2017 and Balcan and White, 2017) *The ρ-local search algorithm for k-medians outputs the optimal solution on $(3 + O(1/\rho))$-perturbation-resilient instances[7].*

This result follows from the following theorem.

Theorem 5.33 *The ρ-local search algorithm for k-medians is $(3 + O(1/\rho))$-certified.*

Proof Consider an arbitrary metric space (X, d). Suppose that the local search algorithm outputs a clustering with centers $L = \{l_1, \ldots, l_k\}$. We show that there exists a γ-perturbation of d – a distance function $d' : X \times X \to \mathbf{R}^+$ for which L is the optimal solution (where $\gamma = 3 + O(1/\rho)$). We note that, generally speaking, d' does not have to satisfy the triangle inequality and thus (X, d') is not necessarily a metric space.

We define d' as follows: If l_i is the closest center to u in L, then $d'(u, l_i) = d(u, l_i)/\gamma$; otherwise, $d'(u, l_i) = d(u, l_i)$. Consider an arbitrary set of centers $S = \{s_1, \ldots, s_k\}$. We need to show that the cost of the k-median clustering with centers in L is at most the cost of the k-median clustering with centers in S with respect to the new distance function d' and thus L is an optimal solution for d'. Let $l(u)$ and $s(u)$ be the closest centers to point u in L and S respectively with respect to d; and let $l'(u)$ and $s'(u)$ be the closest centers to point u in L and S respectively with respect to d'. Our goal is to prove that

$$\sum_{u \in X} d'(u, l'(u)) \le \sum_{u \in X} d'(u, s'(u)). \tag{5.3}$$

Observe that for every point $u \in X$, we have $d(u, v) = d'(u, v)$ for all v but $v = l(u)$. Thus, $l'(u) = l(u)$ and $d'(u, l'(u)) = d(u, l(u))/\gamma$. Consequently, the left-hand side of (5.3) equals $\sum_{u \in X} d(u, l(u))/\gamma$. Similarly, $s'(u) = s(u)$ and $d'(u, s'(u)) = d(u, s(u))$ if $l(u) \notin S$. However, if $l(u) \in S$, then $d'(u, s'(u)) = \min\left(d(u, s(u)), d(u, l(u))/\gamma\right)$ as, in this case, the optimal center for u in S w.r.t. d' can be $l(u)$.

Let us split all vertices in X into two groups $A = \{u : l(u) \in S\}$ and $B = \{u : l(u) \notin S\}$. Then, for $u \in A$, we have $d'(u, s'(u)) = \min\left(d(u, s(u)), d(u, l(u))/\gamma\right)$;

---

[7] In contrast to Theorem 5.29, Theorem 5.32 requires that the instance be perturbation resilient, not only *metric* perturbation resilient.

and for $u \in B$, we have $d'(u, s'(u)) = d(u, s(u))$. Thus, inequality (5.3) is equivalent to

$$\sum_{u \in X} \frac{d(u, l(u))}{\gamma} \leq \sum_{u \in A} \min \left(d(u, s(u)), \frac{d(u, l(u))}{\gamma} \right) + \sum_{u \in B} d(u, s(u)),$$

which after multiplying both parts by γ can be written as

$$\sum_{u \in X} d(u, l(u)) \leq \sum_{u \in A} \min \left(\gamma d(u, s(u)), d(u, l(u)) \right) + \sum_{u \in B} \gamma d(u, s(u)). \qquad (5.4)$$

For $u \in A$, we have $d(u, s(u)) \leq d(u, l(u))$, since both $s(u)$ and $l(u)$ are in S and $s(u) = \arg\min_{v \in S} d(u, v)$. Thus, $\min \left(\gamma d(u, s(u)), d(u, l(u)) \right) \geq d(u, s(u))$. Consequently, inequality (5.4) follows from the following theorem. $\qquad \square$

Theorem 5.34 (Local Approximation; Cohen-Addad and Schwiegelshohn, 2017) *Let L be a ρ-locally optimal set of centers with respect to a metric d and S be an arbitrary set of k centers. Define sets A and B as above. Then, $\sum_{u \in X} d(u, l(u)) \leq \sum_{u \in A} d(u, s(u)) + \gamma \sum_{u \in B} d(u, s(u))$, for some $\gamma = 3 + O(1/\rho)$.*

We refer to Cohen-Addad and Schwiegelshohn (2017) for the proof.

5.8 Notes

In the first article on the subject, Bilu and Linial (2010) defined perturbation resilience, explained its importance, and gave an algorithm for $O(n)$-perturbation-resilient instances of Max Cut.[8] Bilu et al. (2013) gave an algorithm for $O(\sqrt{n})$-perturbation-resilient instances of Max Cut. Mihalák et al. (2011) designed a greedy algorithm for 1.8-perturbation-resilient instances of TSP. Then, Makarychev et al. (2014) designed a general framework for solving perturbation-resilient instances of combinatorial optimization problems (which we described in this chapter). The framework provides a general recipe for designing algorithms for perturbation-resilient and weakly perturbation-resilient instances, as well as proving that LP and SDP relaxations for perturbation-resilient instances are integral. This framework was used to design algorithms for several optimization problems, including algorithms for $O(\sqrt{\log n} \log \log n)$-perturbation-resilient instances of Max Cut (Makarychev et al., 2014), $(2 - 2/k)$-perturbation-resilient instances of Minimum Multiway Cut (Angelidakis et al., 2017), $(1 + \varepsilon)$-perturbation-resilient instances of *planar* Maximum Independent Set, and $(k - 1)$-perturbation-resilient instances of Maximum Independent Set in k-colorable graphs (Angelidakis et al., 2019). Makarychev and Makarychev (2020) introduced certified algorithms and showed how to design them using the framework we discussed above.

There are a number of negative results for perturbation-resilient instances. Most of the negative results show that there are no robust algorithms for γ-perturbation-resilient instances and no polynomial-time γ-certified algorithms. The assumption that the algorithms are certified or robust is crucial. In fact, that there is no

---

[8] Note that Bilu and Linial, as well as many other authors, refer to "perturbation resilience" as "stability."

polynomial-time algorithm, robust or otherwise, for perturbation-resilient instances is very challenging; to do so, one needs to get a reduction that maps known "hard instances" of some problem to perturbation-resilient instances of the problem at hand. Nevertheless, we know that there is no polynomial-time algorithm for ∞-perturbation-resilient instances of Max k-Cut (for every $k \geq 3$) if $RP \neq NP$ (Makarychev et al., 2014), and there is no polynomial-time algorithm for $o(\sqrt{n})$-perturbation-resilient instances of Maximum Independent Set if finding a planted clique in a random graph is hard (Angelidakis et al., 2019). Note that there are strong negative results for some very basic problems: there are no polynomial-time $n^{1-\delta}$-certified algorithms for Set Cover, Min Vertex Cover/Maximum Independent Set, Max 2-Horn SAT; also, there are no polynomial-time *robust* algorithms for $n^{1-\delta}$-perturbation-resilient instances of these problems. The result for Max 2-Horn SAT is particularly striking, since maximization and minimization variants of the problem admit a constant-factor approximation. The negative results suggest that one should study algorithms for special families of perturbation-resilient instances. This was done by Angelidakis et al. (2019), who gave an algorithm for *planar* $(1 + \varepsilon)$-perturbation-resilient instances of Maximum Independent Set. This result is particularly interesting, as it holds when the perturbation resilience parameter $\gamma = 1 + \varepsilon$ is arbitrarily close to 1.

The study of perturbation-resilient instances of clustering problems was initiated by Awasthi et al. (2012), who gave an algorithm for finding the optimal clustering for 3-perturbation-resilient instances. Similarly to the algorithm we discussed in this chapter, their algorithm first runs single-linkage clustering and then recovers the optimal solution using dynamic programming. However, the dynamic program used in their algorithm is quite different from the one we presented here – it is simpler and faster but requires that the input be more perturbation-resilient. Balcan and Liang (2016) designed an algorithm for $(1 + \sqrt{2})$-perturbation-resilient instances $(1 + \sqrt{2} \approx 2.414)$. Balcan et al. (2016) gave algorithms for 2-perturbation-resilient instances of symmetric and asymmetric k-center and obtained matching hardness results. Angelidakis et al. (2017) offered the definition of *metric* γ-perturbation resilience and presented an algorithm for metric 2-perturbation-resilient instances of k-medians and k-means, which we discussed in this chapter (see Theorem 5.29). Ben-David and Reyzin (2014) showed that it is NP-hard to find the optimal clustering for instances of k-medians satisfying the $(2 - \varepsilon)$-center proximity condition.

Cohen-Addad and Schwiegelshohn (2017) observed that the local search algorithm finds the optimal clustering for $(3 + \varepsilon)$-perturbation-resilient instances. In their paper, they used a slightly different model from the one we discussed in this chapter. Theorem 5.32 is due to Balcan and White (2017). Very recently, Friggstad et al. (2019) designed an algorithm for solving $(1 + \varepsilon)$-perturbation-resilient instances of Euclidean k-means and k-medians (where the points lie in a *fixed* dimensional Euclidean space). As was noted in Makarychev and Makarychev (2020), their algorithm is also $(1 + \varepsilon)$-certified.

We also refer the reader to the survey by Makarychev and Makarychev (2016) for a more detailed though somewhat outdated overview of known results for perturbation-resilient instances. Finally, we note that this chapter is based in part on Makarychev and Makarychev (2020).

References

Agarwal, Amit, Charikar, Moses, Makarychev, Konstantin, and Makarychev, Yury. 2005. $O(\sqrt{\log n})$ approximation algorithms for Min UnCut, Min 2CNF Deletion, and directed cut problems. In *Proceedings of the Symposium on Theory of Computing*, pp. 573–581.

Angelidakis, Haris, Makarychev, Konstantin, and Makarychev, Yury. 2017. Algorithms for stable and perturbation-resilient problems. In *Proceedings of the Symposium on Theory of Computing*, pp. 438–451.

Angelidakis, Haris, Awasthi, Pranjal, Blum, Avrim, Chatziafratis, Vaggos, and Dan, Chen. 2019. Bilu-Linial stability, certified algorithms and the Independent Set problem. In *Proceedings of the European Symposium on Algorithms*, pp. 7:1–16.

Arora, Sanjeev, Lee, James, and Naor, Assaf. 2008. Euclidean distortion and the sparsest cut. *Journal of the American Mathematical Society*, **21**(1), 1–21.

Arya, Vijay, Garg, Naveen, Khandekar, Rohit, Meyerson, Adam, Munagala, Kamesh, and Pandit, Vinayaka. 2004. Local search heuristics for k-median and facility location problems. *SIAM Journal on Computing*, **33**(3), 544–562.

Awasthi, Pranjal, Blum, Avrim, and Sheffet, Or. 2012. Center-based clustering under perturbation stability. *Information Processing Letters*, **112**(1–2), 49–54.

Balcan, Maria Florina, and Liang, Yingyu. 2016. Clustering under perturbation resilience. *SIAM Journal on Computing*, **45**(1), 102–155.

Balcan, Maria-Florina, and White, Colin. 2017. Clustering under local stability: Bridging the gap between worst-case and beyond worst-case analysis. *arXiv preprint arXiv:1705.07157*.

Balcan, Maria-Florina, Haghtalab, Nika, and White, Colin. 2016. k-center Clustering under perturbation resilience. *Proceedings of ICALP*, **68**, 1–68:14.

Ben-David, Shalev, and Reyzin, Lev. 2014. Data stability in clustering: A closer look. *Theoretical Computer Science*, **558**, 51–61.

Bilu, Yonatan, and Linial, Nathan. 2010. Are stable instances easy? *Proceedings of ICS*, 2010, 332–341.

Bilu, Yonatan, Daniely, Amit, Linial, Nati, and Saks, Michael. 2013. On the practically interesting instances of MAXCUT. *Proceedings of STACS*, 2013, 526–537.

Călinescu, Gruia, Karloff, Howard, and Rabani, Yuval. 2000. An improved approximation algorithm for MULTIWAY CUT. *Journal of Computer System Sciences*, **60**(3), 564–574.

Cohen-Addad, Vincent, and Schwiegelshohn, Chris. 2017. On the local structure of stable clustering instances. In *Proceedings of the Symposium on Foundations of Computer Science*, pp. 49–60.

Friggstad, Zachary, Khodamoradi, Kamyar, and Salavatipour, Mohammad R. 2019. Exact algorithms and lower bounds for stable instances of Euclidean K-means. In *Proceedings of the Symposium on Discrete Algorithms*, pp. 2958–2972.

Goemans, Michel X, and Williamson, David P. 1995. Improved approximation algorithms for maximum cut and satisfiability problems using semidefinite programming. *Journal of the ACM (JACM)*, **42**(6), 1115–1145.

Hochbaum, Dorit S. 1983. Efficient bounds for the stable set, vertex cover and set packing problems. *Discrete Applied Mathematics*, **6**(3), 243–254.

Kanungo, Tapas, Mount, David M, Netanyahu, Nathan S, Piatko, Christine D, Silverman, Ruth, and Wu, Angela Y. 2004. A local search approximation algorithm for k-means clustering. *Computational Geometry*, **28**(2–3), 89–112.

Karger, David R, Klein, Philip, Stein, Cliff, Thorup, Mikkel, and Young, Neal E. 2004. Rounding algorithms for a geometric embedding of minimum multiway Cut. *Mathematics of Operations Research*, **29**(3), 436–461.

Lewin, Michael, Livnat, Dror, and Zwick, Uri. 2002. Improved Rounding Techniques for the MAX 2-SAT and MAX DI-CUT Problems. In *Proceedings of the Conference on Integer Programming and Combinatorial Optimization*, pp. 67–82.

Makarychev, Konstantin, and Makarychev, Yury. 2016. Bilu-Linial stability. Hazan, T., Papandreou, G., and Tarlow, D. (eds.), *Perturbations, Optimization, and Statistics*. MIT Press.

Makarychev, Konstantin, and Makarychev, Yury. 2020. *Certified algorithms: Worst-case analysis and beyond. Proceeding of ITCS*, 49, 1–4: 14.

Makarychev, Konstantin, Makarychev, Yury, and Vijayaraghavan, Aravindan. 2014. Bilu-Linial stable instances of max cut and minimum multiway cut. In *Proceedings of the Symposium on Discrete Algorithms*, pp. 890–906.

Mihalák, Matúš, Schöngens, Marcel, Šrámek, Rastislav, and Widmayer, Peter. 2011. On the complexity of the metric TSP under stability considerations. In *SOFSEM 2011: Theory and Practice of Computer Science*, pp. 382–393.

Nemhauser, George L, and Trotter, Leslie Earl. 1975. Vertex packings: Structural properties and algorithms. *Mathematical Programming*, **8**(1), 232–248.

Spielman, Daniel A, and Teng, Shang-Hua. 2004. Smoothed Analysis of Algorithms: Why the simplex algorithm usually takes polynomial time. *Journal of the ACM*, **51**(3), 385–463.

Exercises

Exercise 5.1 Consider an instance $\mathcal{I}$ of a maximization constraint satisfaction problem (such as Max 3SAT or Max 2CSP), in which the constraints are individually satisfiable. Assume that $\mathcal{I}$ has a unique optimal solution. Show that $\mathcal{I}$ is ∞-perturbation resilient iff there is a solution that satisfies all the constraints.

Exercise 5.2 Give examples of α-approximation algorithms for combinatorial optimization and clustering problems that are not α-certified.

Exercise 5.3 Prove Theorem 5.12. [Hint: Assign very large weights to $c \in H$.]

Exercise 5.4 Prove Theorem 5.21.

Exercise 5.5 Consider a maximization optimization problem P. Assume that every instance $\mathcal{I} = (\mathcal{S}, \mathcal{C}, w)$ has value at least $\alpha \cdot w(\mathcal{C})$ for some $\alpha \leq 1$ (for example, $\alpha = 1/2$ for Max Cut, $\alpha = 1/2^k$ for Boolean k-CSP). Prove that every γ-perturbation-resilient instance $\mathcal{I} = (\mathcal{S}, \mathcal{C}, w)$ has a solution of value at least $\frac{\gamma}{\gamma + 1/\alpha} w(\mathcal{C})$.

Exercise 5.6 Consider a maximization problem P. Assume that it does not admit an α-approximation ($\alpha > 1$); more precisely, there is a Karp-reduction from 3-SAT to P that maps a yes-instance to an instance whose optimal solution has value at least $c \cdot w(\mathcal{C})$, and a no-instance to an instance whose optimal solution has value less than $\frac{c \cdot w(\mathcal{C})}{\alpha}$. Prove that then there is no polynomial-time algorithm for deciding whether an instance $\mathcal{I}$ of P is α-perturbation-resilient (if $NP \neq \mathbf{co}NP$).

Exercise 5.7 Show that there are no instances (X, d) of k-clustering problems with $|X| > k$ and $\gamma \geq 2$ satisfying the following strong version of the γ-perturbation resilience condition: For every metric γ-perturbation d' of d there is only one set of optimal centers, and this set of centers is the same as for metric (X, d).

Exercise 5.8 Consider a γ-perturbation-resilient instance (X, d) of the k-clustering problem with the ℓ_p objective. Show that a γ-certified solution to (X, d) is an optimal solution for this problem.

Exercise 5.9 Show that a γ-certified solution to an arbitrary instance of the k-clustering problem with the ℓ_p objective is a γ^p approximation to the optimal solution.

Exercise 5.10 Give an example of an instance (X, d) of k-medians that is not γ-perturbation-resilient, but whose unique optimal solution satisfies the γ-center proximity property.

Exercise 5.11 Give an example of a 100-perturbation-resilient instance for which the single-linkage clustering is suboptimal.

CHAPTER SIX

Approximation Stability and Proxy Objectives

Avrim Blum

Abstract: This chapter introduces *approximation stability*, an input condition motivated by the common practice of using the score of a solution under an easy-to-measure objective function as proxy for true solution quality, in problems in which the true goal is to find a solution that "looks like" an unknown target solution. An instance is approximation-stable if all solutions with near-optimal values for the proxy objective are close in solution space to the desired target solution, and it turns out that such instances have a number of surprising algorithmic properties. This chapter describes the approximation-stability notion, presents a variety of algorithmic guarantees under this condition, and discusses implications for the use of approximation ratio as a yardstick for problems of solution discovery.

6.1 Introduction and Motivation

Many algorithmic problems, while posed as a task of optimizing a measurable objective function, are motivated by an underlying goal of *approximating a desired (target) solution*. An example would be clustering a dataset of points that represent images of people by optimizing a k-means or k-median objective, when the true goal is to cluster the images based on who is in them.[1] Another example would be searching for a Nash or approximate-Nash equilibrium in a game with the hope that the solution found will approximately predict how people will play. Implicit in formulations such as these is a hope that a solution that optimizes or nearly optimizes the measurable *proxy* objective (the k-means or k-median score in the case of clustering, or the maximum incentive to deviate in the case of equilibria) will indeed be close to the solution one is hoping to recover.

Approximation stability formalizes and makes explicit this connection. An instance is approximation stable if all near-optimal solutions to the proxy objective are indeed close to the desired target solution (see Section 6.2 for a formal definition with parameters). An instance is not approximation stable if being near-optimal for the proxy objective is *not* a sufficient condition for being close to the target. Any

---

[1] For a clustering $C_1, \ldots, C_k$ of a point set S, its k-median score is $\sum_{i=1}^{k} \min_{c_i} \sum_{x \in C_i} d(x, c_i)$. Its k-means score is $\sum_{i=1}^{k} \min_{c_i} \sum_{x \in C_i} d(x, c_i)^2$.

given instance might or might not be approximation stable. If it is, this motivates use of the proxy objective. If it is not, then it means the motivation for using the proxy objective, at least by itself without additional conditions, is somewhat suspect and perhaps should be reexamined.

The results surveyed in this chapter show the following surprising type of statement for a variety of well-studied objectives: Instances satisfying approximation stability at levels that would seem too weak to be helpful can in fact be solved to high accuracy using structural properties inherent in the stability condition itself. As an example, suppose a clustering instance is stable with respect to the k-median objective in the sense that every clustering whose k-median score is within a factor 1.1 of optimal is ϵ-close to the target solution. For instance, in the case of clustering images by who is in them, this would mean that every 1.1-approximation to the k-median score correctly clusters a $1 - \epsilon$ fraction of the images. (In Section 6.2 we will define this as $(1.1, \epsilon)$-approximation stability to the k-median objective.) At first glance, this condition seems too weak to be useful since we do not have any efficient algorithms that achieve a 1.1-approximation to the k-median score. The best approximation guarantee known for k-median is roughly a factor of 2.7 (Li and Svensson, 2016), and in fact achieving a 1.1-approximation is known to be NP-hard (Guha and Khuller, 1999; Jain et al., 2002). Nonetheless, as we will see in the text that follows, we can give a natural, efficient algorithm guaranteed to find a clustering that is $O(\epsilon)$-close to the target in any instance satisfying this condition. Curiously, the k-median problem remains NP-hard to approximate *even on such stable instances*, so the algorithm approximates the solution without necessarily approximating the objective (Balcan et al., 2009b, 2013).[2]

Interesting Parameter Ranges We will define an instance to be (c, ϵ) approximation stable for a given objective function if every c-approximation to the objective is ϵ-close to the target solution. Notice that if c is greater than or equal to the best known approximation factor for the objective, then we immediately have an efficient algorithm to find solutions that are ϵ-close to the target for such instances. So, such large values of c are not so interesting. Instead, we will be interested in the case that c is much smaller than the best known approximation factor for the given objective. We will then be asking the question: Even though we do not have a c-approximation to the given objective, can we *do as well as if* we had a generic such approximation algorithm, with respect to the goal of finding a solution that is close to the desired target?

6.2 Definitions and Discussion

We now formally present the main property studied in this chapter, namely that of (c, ϵ)-approximation stability.

First, consider some optimization problem, such as MAX-SAT or k-median clustering. An optimization problem is defined by an objective function Φ, such as the number of clauses satisfied for the MAX-SAT problem or the k-median cost for the k-median problem. For any given problem instance, there is some space of possible solutions to that instance, and the objective function Φ assigns a score to

---

[2] If one also makes the assumption that cluster sizes are roughly balanced, then this hardness goes away, and in fact one can give efficient algorithms to approximate k-median to the desired 1.1 factor, and thereby get ϵ-close to the target solution. See Section 6.3.

each one. For example, for the MAX-SAT problem, an instance would be a formula on n variables, the solution space would be the set $\{0,1\}^n$ of all possible Boolean assignments to the variables, and the objective value for a proposed solution is the number of clauses satisfied. For the k-median problem, an instance would be a set S of n points in some metric space $\mathcal{M} = (X, d)$, the solution space would be the set of all k-clusterings $\{C_1, \ldots, C_k\}$ of S, and the objective value for a proposed solution would be the k-median score $\sum_{i=1}^{k} \min_{c_i \in X} \sum_{x \in C_i} d(x, c_i)$. In addition to the objective score, we are also interested in the distance between solutions in the solution space. So we will assume we are given some natural distance measure $dist(\cdot, \cdot)$ over possible solutions, such as normalized Hamming distance for the case of truth assignments to variables (normalized to the range $[0, 1]$), or the fraction of points that would have to be reassigned in one clustering in order to make it match another clustering, in the case of clustering problems. Lastly, we assume there is some unknown *target* solution we are hoping to get close to, such as a correct clustering of images based on who is in them, or in the case of MAX-SAT that there is some truth assignment that corresponds to "correct" behavior. We then say that an instance satisfies approximation stability if all near-optimal solutions according to the given objective are close to the target solution according to the given distance measure on solutions. Formally,

Definition 6.1 Consider a problem defined by an objective function Φ, and with distance function *dist* on its solution space. An instance I satisfies (c, ϵ)-*approximation stability* with respect to an (unknown) target solution y_T if all solutions y of I having $\Phi(I, y)$ within a factor c of the optimal objective value for I satisfy $dist(y, y_T) \leq \epsilon$.

For example, an instance of the k-median problem satisfies (c, ϵ)-approximation stability if all clusterings that have k-median score at most c times that of the optimal k-median clustering agree with the target clustering on at least a $1 - \epsilon$ fraction of points.

It is often helpful to think of approximation stability in its contrapositive form: any solution that is ϵ-*far* from the target must be expensive, costing more than c times the minimum objective cost. A schematic illustration of approximation-stability is given in Figure 6.1.

Removing the Target Solution One can also define a nearly identical notion of approximation stability without reference to any target solution, by just asking that all near-optimal solutions be close *to each other*. Specifically, if all near-optimal solutions are within distance ϵ of a target solution then they are all within distance 2ϵ of each other by the triangle inequality, and if all near-optimal solutions are within distance ϵ of each other and the target is also a near-optimal solution, then clearly they are within distance ϵ of the target.

Target versus Optimal Approximation stability does not require that the target solution be the same as the solution with optimal objective value (see Figure 6.1). For example, for the problem of clustering, we will typically refer to the target clustering as $\mathcal{C}_T$ and the optimal clustering for the objective as $\mathcal{C}^*$. However, it can be helpful to think of the two as equal on first reading.

Determining if an Instance Is Stable Because approximation stability refers to distance to an unknown target, there is no way for an algorithm to tell if an instance

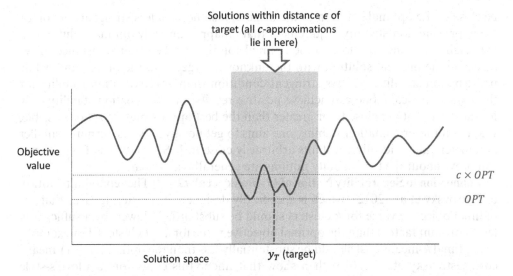

Figure 6.1 A schematic view of approximation stability. Note that the target y_T need not have the optimum objective value, but all near-optimal solutions must be close to y_T.

is indeed approximation stable. However, if one has an oracle that will report if a solution is "good enough," and if one has an algorithm that finds good solutions on stable instances, then one can just run the algorithm: If the oracle reports success, then one has found a good solution (in which case one probably doesn't care if the instance was actually stable); if it reports failure, then one knows the instance wasn't stable.

Algorithmic Structure For a given stability notion, it is natural to ask what kinds of algorithms that notion motivates. In the case of clustering, we will see that approximation stability motivates "ball growing" approaches, where one increases a threshold τ, connecting together all pairs of distance $\leq \tau$, and then forms cluster cores based on dense components in this graph. One can then make a second pass to assign non-core points to clusters based on their distance to the cluster cores from the first pass. In the case of Nash equilibria, approximation stability does not seem to necessarily motivate new algorithms, but rather leads to improved bounds for existing algorithms that aim to find solutions of small support.

Connection to Perturbation Stability Perturbation stability, discussed in Chapter 5, asks that modifying the instance (e.g., changing the distances between data points) by up to a factor of c should not change the optimal solution to the given objective (e.g., should not change how points are clustered in the optimal k-median clustering). One can also define a relaxed version of perturbation stability that allows the optimal solution to change by up to an ϵ fraction of points (Balcan and Liang, 2016). This relaxed version has an interesting connection to approximation stability. In particular, for many problems of interest, if one modifies an instance by changing distances by up to a factor of c, then the cost of any given solution changes by at most some function of c (e.g., for k-median clustering, the cost of any given solution would change by at most a factor of c and for k-means clustering, the cost of any given solution would change by at most a factor of c^2). This implies that an optimal solution to a perturbed instance is also a near-optimal solution to the original instance. Thus, the perturbation-stability requirement that optimal solutions to perturbed instances be close to the optimal solution to the original instance is a less stringent version of the approximation-stability requirement that *all* approximately optimal solutions to the original instance be close to the optimal solution to the original instance (if we associate the optimal solution with the unknown target). On the other hand, while perturbation stability is a less stringent condition than approximation stability for the same c, typically one can achieve positive results for perturbation stability only for factors c that are close to or greater than the best approximation ratios possible, whereas for approximation stability one aims to get positive results for much smaller parameter values, ideally constants arbitrarily close to 1. So the types of results one can prove about the two stability notions are generally incomparable.

Connection to Separability Notion of Ostrovsky et al. (2012) The separability notion of Ostrovsky et al. (2012), which is specifically designed for clustering, asks that the optimal objective value for k clusters should be substantially lower (by a sufficiently large constant factor) than the optimal objective value for $k-1$ clusters. For example, the optimal k-means cost should be substantially less than the optimal $(k-1)$-means cost. Ostrovsky et al. (2012) then show that under this condition, a Lloyd's-style algorithm will succeed in finding a near-optimal solution. They also show that if a clustering instance satisfies this property for a sufficiently large constant factor, then it also has the property that all near-optimal k-means clusterings are close together, namely approximation stability. Therefore, algorithms designed for approximation stability (such as given in this chapter) will also succeed under their separability condition. In the other direction, the Ostrovsky et al. (2012) separation condition for a small separation constant is a weaker condition than approximation stability in the case that all target clusters are large. That is because approximation stability asks that *all* clusterings that are ϵ-far from the target be more expensive than optimal by at least a factor of c, whereas this condition only asks that clusterings having at most $k-1$ clusters (which are ϵ-far from the target if all target clusters have at least ϵn points) be expensive.

Proxy Objectives An ideal proxy objective would both (a) be something one has reason to believe is optimized by the target and not by any solution far from the target and (b) be efficiently optimizable. If (b) does not hold but either one has a good approximation algorithm or one has an algorithm under approximation stability, then it would be enough to satisfy a somewhat stronger version of (a) in which solutions far from the target are not even near-optimal. Thus, algorithms that work under approximation stability can help broaden the set of proxy objectives one might reasonably consider for a given problem.

More broadly, a general approach to finding a desired target solution is to identify properties that one believes the target solution should have, and then use them to identify the target or a close approximation to it. In the context of clustering, Balcan et al. (2008) and Daniely et al. (2012) even more broadly consider properties that are not (even in principle) sufficient to uniquely identify the target solution, but do allow for a small set of candidate solutions, that one could then present to a user for further refinement using other criteria. An example of such a property is that most data points x should be closer on average to points in their own target cluster than to points in any other target cluster, by some additive (Balcan et al., 2008) or multiplicative (Daniely et al., 2012) gap γ. Ackerman and Ben-David (2009) consider an intriguing property called "center perturbation clusterability" that is a bit like an inverse of approximation stability. They consider center-based clusterings (a clustering is defined by k centers, with each data point assigned to its nearest center) and ask that all clusterings whose centers are close to the optimal centers should have a cost within a small factor of the optimal cost. One could also hope to *learn* relevant properties from past data, using techniques such as in Chapter 29.

6.3 The k-Median Problem

The k-median problem is a particularly clean objective for studying approximation-stability, and many of the ideas used for it can be extended to other clustering formulations such as k-means and min-sum clustering. So, we focus on it here.

We now show how one can design an efficient clustering algorithm with the guarantee that if an instance is $(1.1, \epsilon)$-approximation stable for the k-median objective, it will find a solution that is $O(\epsilon)$-close to the target, or even ϵ-close to the target if all target clusters are large compared to ϵn. That is, it performs nearly as well (in terms of distance to the target) as would be guaranteed by a generic 1.1-factor approximation to the k-median objective, even though approximating k-median to such a level is *NP*-hard. More generally, if the instance is $(1 + \alpha, \epsilon)$-stable then the algorithm will find a solution that is $O(\epsilon/\alpha)$-close to the target, or even ϵ-close to the target if all target clusters are large compared to $\epsilon n/\alpha$. Note that $1/\epsilon$, $1/\alpha$, and k need not be constants (and in fact, one should not think of k as a constant since we do not want to view an algorithm that "tries all possible k-tuples of centers" as efficient). For example, we might have $\mathcal{C}_T$ consist of $n^{0.1}$ clusters of size $n^{0.9}$, $\epsilon = 1/n^{0.2}$ and $\alpha = 1/n^{0.09}$ (this would correspond to the case of large target clusters in Theorem 6.2).

We begin with a formal definition of the k-median problem, state the main results, and then give algorithms and proofs.

6.3.1 Definitions

Let $\mathcal{M} = (X, d)$ be a metric space with point set X and distance function d. A k-*clustering* of a point set $S \subseteq X$ is a partition $\mathcal{C}$ of S into k clusters $\{C_1, \ldots, C_k\}$. The k-*median cost* of a clustering is the total distance of all points to the best "center" of their clustering. That is,

$$\Phi_{kmedian}(\mathcal{C}) = \sum_{i=1}^{k} \min_{c_i \in X} \sum_{x \in C_i} d(x, c_i). \tag{6.1}$$

As mentioned earlier, we define the *distance* $dist(\mathcal{C}, \mathcal{C}')$ between two clusterings of the same point set S as the fraction of points that would need to be reassigned in one of the clusterings to make it equal to the other (up to reindexing of the clusters, since the names of the clusters do not matter). Formally, the distance between $\mathcal{C} = \{C_1, \ldots, C_k\}$ and $\mathcal{C}' = \{C'_1, \ldots, C'_k\}$ is

$$dist(\mathcal{C}, \mathcal{C}') = \min_{\sigma} \frac{1}{n} \sum_{i=1}^{k} |C_i \setminus C'_{\sigma(i)}|, \tag{6.2}$$

where the minimum is taken over all bijections $\sigma : \{1, \ldots, k\} \to \{1, \ldots, k\}$. This distance is a metric on clusterings (see Exercise 6.1).

We say that two clusterings C and C' are ϵ-close if $dist(C, C') < \epsilon$. Note that if C and C' are ϵ-close and all clusters C_i have size at least $2\epsilon n$, then the bijection σ minimizing $\frac{1}{n} \sum_{i=1}^{k} |C_i \setminus C'_{\sigma(i)}|$ has the property that for all i, $|C_i \cap C'_{\sigma(i)}| > \frac{1}{2}|C_i|$. This implies for instance that such σ is unique, and we can say that C and C' *agree on x* if $x \in C_i \cap C'_{\sigma(i)}$ for some i, and C and C' *disagree on x* otherwise.

6.3.2 Some Interesting Results

We now present some interesting results known about k-median clustering under approximation stability. We will then go into more detail into the algorithm and proof for one of them.

Theorem 6.2 k-Median, Large Clusters Case (Balcan et al., 2013) *There is an efficient algorithm that will produce a clustering that is ϵ-close to the target clustering C_T whenever the instance satisfies $(1 + \alpha, \epsilon)$-approximation stability for the k-median objective and each cluster in C_T has size at least $(4 + 15/\alpha)\epsilon n + 2$.*

The proof of Theorem 6.2 by Balcan et al. (2013) focuses on the distance of the clustering produced to the target C_T, though Schalekamp et al. (2010) point out that under the assumptions of the theorem, the algorithm additionally achieves a good k-median approximation as well. So, in this case, the k-median approximation problem itself has become easier under approximation stability. However, interestingly, once we allow small clusters, finding an approximation to the objective becomes as hard as in the general case, and yet we can still find a solution that is close to the target clustering.

Theorem 6.3 k-Median: General Case (Balcan et al., 2013) *There is an efficient algorithm that will produce a clustering that is $O(\epsilon + \epsilon/\alpha)$-close to the target clustering C_T whenever the instance satisfies $(1 + \alpha, \epsilon)$-approximation-stability for the k-median objective.*

Theorem 6.4 Hardness of Approximation (Balcan et al., 2013) *For k-median, k-means, and min-sum objectives, for any $c > 1$, the problem of finding a c-approximation can be reduced in polynomial time to the problem of finding a c-approximation under (c, ϵ)-approximation-stability. Therefore, a polynomial-time algorithm for finding a c-approximation under (c, ϵ)-approximation stability implies a polynomial-time algorithm for finding a c-approximation in general.*

As noted previously, α and ϵ may be sub-constant. However, in the case that $1/\alpha = O(1)$, Awasthi et al. (2010b) give an improvement to Theorem 6.2, needing a minimum cluster size of only ϵn to produce a solution that is ϵ-close to the target. Their result also holds under the separability notion of Ostrovsky et al. (2012) at the $1 + \alpha$ separation level, and further was used as a building block by Li and Svensson (2016) in the current best k-median approximation.[3] So it is interesting that results

---

[3] Li and Svensson (2016) give a bi-criteria algorithm that for some constant c_0 finds a k-clustering C_k whose k-median cost is not too much greater than the cost of the optimal $k - c_0$ clustering $C^*_{k-c_0}$. To convert this to a true approximation, one then considers two cases. Case (a) is that $C^*_{k-c_0}$ is not too much more expensive than

based on non-worst-case stability notions can also have application to worst-case approximation bounds.

6.3.3 Algorithms and Proofs

We now present the algorithm and main ideas for the proof of Theorem 6.2.

First, a small amount of notation. Given a clustering instance specified by a metric space $\mathcal{M} = (X, d)$ and a set of points $S \subseteq X$, fix an optimal k-median clustering $\mathcal{C}^* = \{C_1^*, \ldots, C_k^*\}$, and let c_i^* be the center point (a.k.a. "median") for C_i^*. Note that $\mathcal{C}^*$ may not be exactly the same as the target $\mathcal{C}_T$. For $x \in S$, define

$$w(x) = \min_i d(x, c_i^*)$$

to be the contribution of x to the k-median objective in $\mathcal{C}^*$ (i.e., x's "weight"). Similarly, let $w_2(x)$ be x's distance to its second-closest center point among $\{c_1^*, c_2^*, \ldots, c_k^*\}$. Also, let OPT denote the k-median cost of $\mathcal{C}^*$ and define

$$w_{avg} = \frac{1}{n} \sum_{i=1}^{n} w(x) = \frac{OPT}{n}.$$

That is, w_{avg} is the average weight of the points. Finally, let $\epsilon^* = dist(\mathcal{C}_T, \mathcal{C}^*)$. By the approximation stability assumption, $\epsilon^* \le \epsilon$. (The reader may wish to think of $\epsilon^* = 0$ and $\mathcal{C}^* = \mathcal{C}_T$ on first read.)

The way that approximation stability will be used is via the following key lemma, which gives us two important properties of approximation-stable instances.

Lemma 6.5 *If the instance $(\mathcal{M}, S)$ is $(1 + \alpha, \epsilon)$-approximation stable for the k-median objective, then*

a. *If each cluster in $\mathcal{C}_T$ has size at least $2\epsilon n$, then less than $(\epsilon - \epsilon^*)n$ points $x \in S$ on which $\mathcal{C}_T$ and $\mathcal{C}^*$ agree have $w_2(x) - w(x) < \frac{\alpha w_{avg}}{\epsilon}$.*

b. *For any $t > 0$, at most $t(\epsilon n / \alpha)$ points $x \in S$ have $w(x) \ge \frac{\alpha w_{avg}}{t\epsilon}$.*

Proof To prove Property (a), assume to the contrary. Then one could take $\mathcal{C}^*$ and move $(\epsilon - \epsilon^*)n$ points x on which $\mathcal{C}_T$ and $\mathcal{C}^*$ agree to their second-closest clusters, increasing the objective by at most αOPT. Moreover, this new clustering $\mathcal{C}' = \{C_1', \ldots, C_k'\}$ has distance at least ϵ from $\mathcal{C}_T$, because we begin at distance ϵ^* from $\mathcal{C}_T$ and each move increases this distance by $\frac{1}{n}$ (here we use the fact that because each cluster in $\mathcal{C}_T$ has size at least $2\epsilon n$, the optimal bijection between $\mathcal{C}_T$ and $\mathcal{C}'$ remains the same as the optimal bijection between $\mathcal{C}_T$ and $\mathcal{C}^*$). Hence we have a clustering that is not ϵ-close to $\mathcal{C}_T$ with cost only $(1 + \alpha)OPT$, a contradiction.

---

the optimal k-clustering C_k^*, in which case the solution C_k found is itself a good approximation to C_k^*. Case (b) is that there is a large gap between the cost of $C_{k-c_0}^*$ and the cost of C_k^*. But in that case, running the algorithm of Awasthi et al. (2010b) on values $k, k-1, k-2, \ldots, k-c_0+1$ is guaranteed to produce at least one low-cost k'-clustering for $k' \le k$. So, running both procedures guarantees a good approximation.

Property (b) simply follows from the definition of the average weight w_{avg}, and Markov's inequality. $\qquad\square$

Note: one can also prove that a slightly weaker version of Property (a) of Lemma 6.5 holds in the case that C_T may have small clusters. The small clusters case is trickier because reassigning points need not always increase the distance between the clusterings (e.g., think of just swapping all points in two clusters). So, the argument is more involved. See Section 6.3.4.

Let us now use Lemma 6.5 to define the notion of a *critical distance* and of *good* and *bad* points. Specifically,

Definition 6.6 Define the **critical distance** $d_{crit} = \frac{\alpha w_{avg}}{5\epsilon}$; note that this is $1/5$ the value in property (a) of Lemma 6.5. Define point $x \in S$ to be **good** if both $w(x) < d_{crit}$ and $w_2(x) - w(x) \geq 5d_{crit}$, else define x to be **bad**. Let $X_i \subseteq C_i^*$ be the good points in the optimal cluster C_i^*, and let $B = S \setminus (\cup X_i)$ be the bad points.

We now show that if an instance is approximation stable, there cannot be too many bad points:

Proposition 6.7 *If the instance $(\mathcal{M}, S)$ is $(1 + \alpha, \epsilon)$-approximation stable for the k-median objective and each cluster in C_T has size at least $2\epsilon n$, then $|B| < (1 + 5/\alpha)\epsilon n$.*

Proof By Lemma 6.5(a), the number of points on which C^* and C_T agree where $w_2(x) - w(x) < 5d_{crit}$ is at most $(\epsilon - \epsilon^*)n$, and there can be at most $\epsilon^* n$ additional such points where C^* and C_T disagree. Setting $t = 5$ in Lemma 6.5(b) bounds the number of points that have $w(x) \geq d_{crit}$ by $(5\epsilon/\alpha)n$. $\qquad\square$

Let us now see one way we can use the critical distance and definition of good and bad points to help with clustering. To do this we begin by defining the notion of a *threshold graph*.

Definition 6.8 (Threshold Graph) Define the τ-*threshold graph* $G_\tau = (S, E_\tau)$ to be the graph produced by connecting all pairs $\{x, y\} \in \binom{S}{2}$ with $d(x, y) < \tau$.

Lemma 6.9 (Threshold Graph Lemma) *For a $(1 + \alpha, \epsilon)$-approximation-stable instance, the threshold graph G_τ for $\tau = 2d_{crit}$ has the following properties:*

(i) *For all x, y in the same X_i, the edge $\{x, y\}$ is in the graph G_τ.*
(ii) *For $x \in X_i$ and $y \in X_j$ for $j \neq i$, $\{x, y\}$ is not an edge in G_τ. Moreover, such points x, y do not share any neighbors in G_τ.*

Proof For part (i), since x, y are both good, they are at distance less than d_{crit} to their common cluster center c_i^*, by definition. Hence, by the triangle inequality, the distance $d(x, y)$ satisfies

$$d(x, y) \leq d(x, c_i^*) + d(c_i^*, y) < 2 \times d_{crit} = \tau.$$

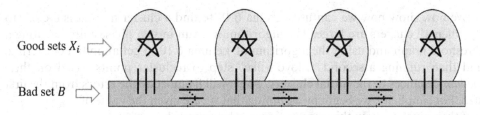

Figure 6.2 The high-level structure of a threshold graph.

For part (ii), note that the distance from any good point x to any other cluster center, and in particular to y's cluster center c_j^*, is at least $5d_{crit}$. Again by the triangle inequality,

$$d(x,y) \geq d(x,c_j^*) - d(y,c_j^*) \geq 5d_{crit} - d_{crit} = 2\tau.$$

Since each edge in G_τ is between points at distance less than τ, the points x, y cannot share any common neighbors. □

Hence, the graph G_τ for the foregoing value of τ is fairly simple to describe: each X_i forms a clique, and its neighborhood $N_{G_\tau}(X_i) \setminus X_i$ lies entirely in the bad set B with no edges going between X_i and $X_{j \neq i}$, or between X_i and $N_{G_\tau}(X_{j \neq i})$. See Figure 6.2 for an illustration.

We now show how we can use this structure to find a clustering of error at most ϵ. We do this in two steps, beginning with the following lemma.

Lemma 6.10 *There is a deterministic polynomial-time algorithm that given a graph $G = (S, E)$ satisfying properties (i), (ii) of Lemma 6.9 and given an upper bound b on the number of bad points such that each $|X_i| \geq b + 2$, outputs a k-clustering with each X_i contained in a distinct cluster.*

Proof Construct a graph $H = (S, E')$ where we place an edge $\{x, y\} \in E'$ if x and y have at least b common neighbors in G. By property (i), each X_i is a clique of size $\geq b + 2$ in G, so each pair $x, y \in X_i$ has at least b common neighbors in G and hence $\{x, y\} \in E'$. Now consider $x \in X_i \cup N_G(X_i)$, and $y \notin X_i \cup N_G(X_i)$: we claim there is no edge between x, y in this new graph H. First, x and y cannot share neighbors that lie in X_i (since $y \notin X_i \cup N_G(X_i)$), nor in some $X_{j \neq i}$ (since $x \notin X_j \cup N_G(X_j)$ by property (ii)). Hence the common neighbors of x, y all lie in B, which has size at most b. Moreover, at least one of x and y must itself belong to B for them to have any common neighbors at all (again by property (ii)) – hence, the number of distinct common neighbors is at most $b - 1$, which implies that $\{x, y\} \notin E'$.

Thus each X_i is contained within a distinct component of the graph H. Note that the component containing some X_i may also contain some vertices from B; moreover, there may also be components in H that contain only vertices from B. But since the X_i's are larger than B, we can obtain the claimed clustering by taking the largest k components in H and adding the vertices of all other smaller components in H to any of these, using this as the k-clustering. □

We now show how we can use Lemma 6.10 to find a clustering that is ϵ-close to C_T when all clusters are large. The algorithm will run in two phases: first creating a threshold graph and using the algorithm of Lemma 6.10 to get an initial clustering, and then running a second "Lloyd's-like" step to recluster points based on their *median* distances to the initial clusters, which will fix most of the errors from the first step. For simplicity, we begin by assuming that we are given the value of $w_{avg} = \frac{OPT}{n}$, and then we show how this assumption can be removed.

Theorem 6.11 (Large Clusters, Known w_{avg})   *There is an efficient algorithm such that if the given clustering instance $(\mathcal{M}, S)$ is $(1+\alpha, \epsilon)$-approximation-stable for the k-median objective and each cluster in C_T has size at least $(3+10/\alpha)\epsilon n+2$, then given w_{avg} it will find a clustering that is ϵ-close to C_T.*

Proof   Let us define $b := (1+5/\alpha)\epsilon n$. By assumption, each cluster in the target clustering has at least $(3 + 10/\alpha)\epsilon n + 2 = 2b + \epsilon n + 2$ points. Since the *optimal k-median clustering* C^* differs from the target clustering by at most $\epsilon^* n \leq \epsilon n$ points, each cluster C_i^* in C^* must have at least $2b + 2$ points. Moreover, by Proposition 6.7(i), the bad points B have $|B| \leq b$, and hence for each i,

$$|X_i| = |C_i^* \setminus B| \geq b + 2.$$

Now, given w_{avg}, we can construct the graph G_τ with $\tau = 2d_{crit}$ (which we can compute from the given value of w_{avg}), and apply Lemma 6.10 to find a k-clustering C' where each X_i is contained within a distinct cluster. Note that this clustering C' differs from the optimal clustering C^* only in the bad points, and hence, $dist(C', C_T) \leq \epsilon^* + |B|/n \leq O(\epsilon + \epsilon/\alpha)$. However, our goal is to get ϵ-close to the target, which we do as follows.

Call a point x "red" if it is a bad point of the type given in part (a) of Lemma 6.5 (i.e., $w_2(x) - w(x) < 5d_{crit}$), "yellow" if it is not red but is a bad point of the type given in part (b) of Lemma 6.5 with $t = 5$ (i.e., $w(x) \geq d_{crit}$), and "green" otherwise. So, the green points are those in the sets X_i, and we have partitioned the bad set B into red points and yellow points. Let $C' = \{C_1', \ldots, C_k'\}$ and recall that C' agrees with C^* on the green points, so without loss of generality we may assume $X_i \subseteq C_i'$. We now construct a new clustering C'' that agrees with C^* on both the green and yellow points. Specifically, for each point x and each cluster C_j', compute the median distance $d_{median}(x, C_j')$ between x and all points in C_j'; then insert x into the cluster C_i'' for $i = \text{argmin}_j d_{median}(x, C_j')$. Since each non-red point x satisfies $w_2(x) - w(x) \geq 5d_{crit}$, and all green points g satisfy $w(g) < d_{crit}$, this means that any non-red point x must satisfy the following two conditions: (1) for a green point g_1 in the *same* cluster as x in C^* we have

$$d(x, g_1) \leq w(x) + d_{crit},$$

and (2) for a green point g_2 in a *different* cluster than x in C^* we have

$$d(x, g_2) \geq w_2(x) - d_{crit} \geq w(x) + 4d_{crit}.$$

Therefore, $d(x, g_1) < d(x, g_2)$. Since each cluster in C' has a strict majority of green points (even with point x removed) all of which are clustered as in C^*, this means that for a non-red point x, the median distance to points in its correct cluster with respect to C^* is less than the median distance to points in any incorrect cluster. Thus, C'' agrees with C^* on all non-red points. Therefore, every point where C'' and C_T disagree must be either (i) a point where C^* and C_T disagree or (ii) a red point where C^* and C_T agree. Since there are at most $\epsilon^* n$ of the former and at most $(\epsilon - \epsilon^*)n$ of the latter by Lemma 6.5, this implies $dist(C'', C_T) \leq \epsilon$ as desired. For convenience, the above procedure is given as Algorithm 1. □

Algorithm 1 k-median algorithm: Large clusters (given a guess w of w_{avg})

Input: $w, \epsilon \leq 1, \alpha > 0, k$.

Step 1: Construct the τ-threshold graph G_τ with $\tau = 2d_{crit} = \frac{1}{5}\frac{\alpha w}{\epsilon}$.

Step 2: Apply the algorithm of Lemma 6.10 to find an initial clustering C'. Specifically, construct graph H by connecting x, y if they share at least $b = (1 + 5/\alpha)\epsilon n$ neighbors in G_τ and let $C'_1, \ldots, C'_k$ be the k largest components of H.

Step 3: Produce clustering C'' by reclustering according to smallest median distance in C'. That is, $C''_i = \{x : i = \arg\min_j d_{median}(x, C'_j)\}$.

Step 4: Output the k clusters $C''_1, \ldots, C''_k$.

We now extend the preceding argument to the case where we are not given the value of w_{avg}.

Theorem 6.12 (Large Clusters, Unknown w_{avg}) *There is an efficient algorithm such that if the given instance $(\mathcal{M}, S)$ is $(1 + \alpha, \epsilon)$-approximation stable for the k-median objective, and each cluster in C_T has size at least $(4 + 15/\alpha)\epsilon n + 2$, the algorithm will produce a clustering that is ϵ-close to C_T.*

Proof The algorithm for the case that we are not given the value w_{avg} is the following: we run steps 1 and 2 of Algorithm 1 repeatedly for different guesses w of w_{avg}, starting with $w = 0$ (so the graph G_τ is empty) and at each step increasing w to the next value such that G_τ contains at least one new edge (so we have at most n^2 different guesses to try). If the current value of w causes the k largest components of H to miss more than $b := (1 + 5/\alpha)\epsilon n$ points, or if any of these components has size $\leq b$, then we discard this guess w, and try again with the next larger guess for w. Otherwise, we run Algorithm 1 to completion and let C'' be the clustering produced.

Note that we still might have $w < w_{avg}$, but this just implies that the resulting graphs G_τ and H can have only fewer edges than the corresponding graphs for the correct w_{avg}. Hence, some of the X_i's might not have fully formed into connected components in H. However, if the k largest components together miss at most b points, then this implies we must have at least one component for each X_i, and therefore exactly one component for each X_i. So, we never misclassify the good points lying in these largest components. We might misclassify all the bad points (at most b of these), and might fail to cluster at most b of the points in the actual X_i's (i.e., those not lying in the largest k

components), but this nonetheless guarantees that each cluster C_i' contains at least $|X_i| - b \geq b + 2$ correctly clustered green points (with respect to C^*) and at most b misclassified points. Therefore, as shown in the proof of Theorem 6.11, the resulting clustering C'' will correctly cluster all non-red points as in C^* and so is at distance at most $(\epsilon - \epsilon^*) + \epsilon^* = \epsilon$ from C_T. For convenience, this procedure is given as Algorithm 2. $\qquad\square$

Algorithm 2 k-median algorithm: Large clusters (unknown w_{avg})

Input: $\epsilon \leq 1, \alpha > 0, k$.
For $j = 1, 2, 3 \ldots$ do:

Step 1: Let τ be the jth smallest pairwise distance in S. Construct τ-threshold graph G_τ.
Step 2: Run step 2 of Algorithm 1 to construct graph H and clusters $C_1', \ldots, C_k'$.
Step 3: If $\min(|C_1'|, \ldots, |C_k'|) > b$ and $|C_1' \cup \ldots \cup C_k'| \geq n(1 - \epsilon - 5\epsilon/\alpha)$, run step 3 of Algorithm 1 and output the clusters $C_1'', \ldots, C_k''$ produced.

6.3.4 Handling Small Clusters

Small target clusters introduce additional challenges. One is that modifying a clustering C by reassigning ϵn points into different clusters may no longer produce a clustering C' that is ϵ-far from C. For example, if two clusters C_i and C_j in C are both small, then moving all points from C_i into C_j and moving all points from C_j into C_i produces the exact same clustering as at the start. However, it turns out that any set of ϵn reassignments must contain a subset of size at least $\epsilon' n$ for $\epsilon' \geq \epsilon/3$ that indeed create a clustering C' that is ϵ'-far from the original C (Balcan et al., 2013). This allows for a slightly weaker analog of Lemma 6.5 to be shown. Another challenge is that in growing the threshold τ, it can be difficult to tell when to stop. In particular, if we grow the threshold until the kth largest cluster produced has more than b points, we may have gone too far – merging two large clusters and producing a high-error solution. However, this can be addressed by first running any constant-factor k-median approximation to get an estimate $\tilde{w}_{avg}$ for w_{avg}, and then using that quantity inside the algorithm. Finally, there may be some clusters that are dominated by bad points. Nonetheless, this can be handled as well, though we can no longer run the reclustering phase (step 3) of algorithm 1, resulting in a solution that is $O(\epsilon + \epsilon/\alpha)$-close to the target rather than ϵ-close. The formal guarantee is in Theorem 6.3.

6.4 k-Means, Min-Sum, and Other Clustering Objectives

Similar results to those presented for the k-median problem are also known for the k-means and min-sum clustering objectives. The k-means score of a clustering is defined similarly to the k-median score, except we square the distances:

$$\Phi_{kmeans}(C) = \sum_{i=1}^{k} \min_{c_i \in X} \sum_{x \in C_i} d(x, c_i)^2. \tag{6.3}$$

In min-sum clustering, the objective value is the sum of all pairwise intra-cluster distances.

$$\Phi_{minsum}(\mathcal{C}) = \sum_{i=1}^{k} \sum_{x \in C_i} \sum_{y \in C_i} d(x,y). \tag{6.4}$$

For example, in a uniform metric space, all clusterings have the same k-median or k-means cost, but the min-sum objective would be optimized by making all clusters equal in size.

For the k-means problem, there is an analogous result to Theorem 6.3:

Theorem 6.13 k-Means: General Case (Balcan et al., 2013)   *There is an efficient algorithm that will produce a clustering that is $O(\epsilon + \epsilon/\alpha)$-close to the target clustering $\mathcal{C}_T$ whenever the instance satisfies $(1+\alpha, \epsilon)$-approximation stability for the k-means objective.*

The min-sum objective is more challenging to analyze because the contribution of any given data point to the overall cost depends on the size of the cluster it is in. In fact, unlike the k-median and k-means problems that have constant-factor approximation algorithms, the best approximation guarantee known for the min-sum objective is an $O(\log^{1+\delta}(n))$ factor (Bartal et al., 2001).

Balcan et al. (2013) give a bound for min-sum clustering of the form in Theorem 6.13 given earlier but only under the assumption that all target clusters have size at least $c\epsilon n/\alpha$ for a sufficiently large constant c. Balcan and Braverman (2009) extend this to general cluster sizes, so long as one is given up-front a constant-factor approximation to the objective; else their algorithm produces a list of $O(\log \log n)$ solutions such that at least one solution will be $O(\epsilon + \epsilon/\alpha)$-close to the target clustering.

6.5 Clustering Applications

Voevodski et al. (2012) consider clustering applications in computational biology, and show that approximation stability can be a useful guide in designing algorithms for them, especially when those settings come with additional constraints. Specifically, in the application considered by Voevodski et al. (2012), one is not given the distances between all data points up front. Instead, one can make a limited number of one-versus-all queries: proposing a query point and running a procedure that returns its distance to all other points in the dataset. They design an algorithm that, assuming (c, ϵ)-approximation stability for the k-median objective, finds a clustering that is ϵ-close to the target by using only $O(k)$ such one-versus-all queries in the large cluster case, and furthermore is faster than the algorithm we presented here. They then use their algorithm to cluster biological datasets in the Pfam (Finn et al., 2010) and SCOP (Murzin et al., 1995) databases, where the points are proteins and distances are inversely proportional to their sequence similarity. The Pfam and SCOP databases are used in biology to observe evolutionary relationships between proteins and to find close relatives of particular proteins. Voevodski et al. (2012) show that their algorithms are not only fast on these datasets, but also achieve high accuracy. In particular, for one of these sources they obtain clusterings that almost exactly match the given classification, and for the other, the accuracy of their algorithm is comparable to that of the best known (but slower) algorithms using the full distance matrix.

6.6 Nash Equilibria

We now consider the problem of finding approximate Nash equilibria from the perspective of approximation stability.

Let (R, C) denote a 2-player, n-action bimatrix game. Here, R is the payoff matrix for the row player and C is the payoff matrix for the column player. A (mixed) strategy is a probability distribution over n actions, which we will represent as a column vector. Let Δ_n denote the strategy space, that is, the set of vectors in $[0, 1]^n$ whose entries sum to 1. The goal of each player is to maximize its expected payoff. A pair of strategies (p, q) (p for the row player and q for the column player) is a *Nash equilibrium* if neither player has any incentive to deviate; that is,

- For all $p' \in \Delta_n$, $p'^T R q \leq p^T R q$.
- For all $q' \in \Delta_n$, $p^T C q' \leq p^T C q$.

A pair of strategies (p, q) is an *approximate* Nash equilibrium if no player has a *large* incentive to deviate. More formally, assume the matrices R, C have all entries in the range $[0, 1]$. We then say that (p, q) is an α-*approximate* equilibrium if

- For all $p' \in \Delta_n$, $p'^T R q \leq p^T R q + \alpha$.
- For all $q' \in \Delta_n$, $p^T C q' \leq p^T C q + \alpha$.

We say that (p, q) is a *well-supported* α-approximate Nash equilibrium if only actions whose payoffs are within α of the best response to the opponent's strategy have positive probability. That is, if i is in the support of p, then $e_i^T R q \geq \max_j e_j^T R q - \alpha$, and similarly if i is in the support of q then $p^T C e_i \geq \max_j p^T C e_j - \alpha$, where e_i is the unit vector with 1 in coordinate i.

Finding approximate equilibria in general $n \times n$ bimatrix games appears to be a challenge computationally. Lipton et al. (2003) show that there always exist α-approximate equilibria with support over at most $O((\log n)/\alpha^2)$ actions, which leads to an $n^{O(\log n/\alpha^2)}$-time algorithm for computing α-approximate equilibria. This is the fastest general algorithm known, and Rubinstein (2016) shows that under the Exponential Time Hypothesis for PPAD, there is no algorithm with running time $n^{O(\log^{1-\delta} n)}$ for any constant $\delta > 0$. The associated structural statement is also known to be existentially tight (Feder et al., 2007). The smallest value of α for which an α-approximate equilibrium is known to be computable in polynomial time is 0.3393 (Tsaknakis and Spirakis, 2007).

However, one reason we might wish to find an approximate Nash equilibrium is to predict how people will play. If we imagine that people will indeed play an approximate Nash equilibrium, but beyond that we wish to make no additional assumptions on player behavior, then for play to be predictable in principle this requires that all approximate equilibria be close together. That is, if we anticipate people will play an α-approximate equilibrium and wish to predict mixed strategies up to, say, a variation distance ϵ, then we will want the game to satisfy (α, ϵ)-approximation stability.[4]

Awasthi et al. (2010a) show that games satisfying (α, ϵ)-approximation stability indeed have additional useful structural properties. Specifically, if $\epsilon \leq 2\alpha - 6\alpha^2$, then there must exist an $O(\alpha)$-equilibrium where each player's strategy has support size $O(1/\alpha)$. For constant α this implies a polynomial-time algorithm for computing $O(\alpha)$-equilibria. For general α, ϵ such games must have an α-equilibrium of support size $O((\frac{\epsilon^2}{\alpha^2}) \log(1 + \frac{1}{\epsilon}) \log(n))$; this does not lead to a polynomial-time algorithm, but at least gives a substantial reduction in the dependence on α when $\epsilon = O(\alpha)$, for instance. Note also that α and ϵ need not be constants, so this gives a quasi-polynomial time algorithm for finding, say, $1/poly(n)$-approximate equilibria in games that are sufficiently stable at that value of α. This is especially interesting because it is known to be PPAD-hard to find $1/poly(n)$-approximate equilibria in general games. See Balcan and Braverman (2017) for further discussion.

An Example As a simple example of an approximation-stable game, consider the prisoner's dilemma (with payoffs scaled to $[0, 1]$):

$$R = \begin{bmatrix} 0.75 & 0 \\ 1 & 0.25 \end{bmatrix} \quad C = \begin{bmatrix} 0.75 & 1 \\ 0 & 0.25 \end{bmatrix}.$$

Here, the only Nash equilibrium is to both play action 2 (defecting), resulting in a payoff of 0.25 to each, even though both playing action 1 (cooperating) would produce payoff 0.75 to each. This game is (α, ϵ)-approximation stable for $\alpha = \epsilon/4$ for any $\epsilon < 1$ because if any player puts an ϵ probability mass on action 1, then (no matter what the other player is doing) that player will have incentive $\epsilon/4$ to deviate. Further examples of natural approximation-stable games are given in Exercises 6.4 and 6.5.

Approximation Stability and Perturbation Stability Balcan and Braverman (2017) prove an interesting connection between approximation stability and perturbation stability (discussed in Chapter 5) for the Nash equilibrium problem. Specifically, they show that if (p, q) is a *well-supported* approximate Nash equilibrium in game (R, C), then there must exist a nearby game (R', C') such that (p, q) is an (exact) Nash equilibrium in (R', C'), and vice versa. This implies that assuming that all well-supported approximate equilibria are close together is the same as assuming that all exact equilibria in slightly perturbed games are close together. In addition, they extend the above general support-size statement to this assumption, as well as to a reversal of quantifiers when the total number of equilibria is polynomial in n (assuming that for each equilibrium in a perturbed game there exists a close equilibrium in the original game, rather than assuming that there exists an equilibrium in the original game that is close to all equilibria in perturbed games).

6.7 The Big Picture

We now step back and reflect on how approximation stability may be useful and what it can tell us. First, approximation stability allows us to formalize what typically are informal motivations for objective functions that can be measured from the data, when the true goal is to find an unknown target solution. If an algorithm

---

[4] For concreteness, we define the distance between the strategy pair (p, q) and the strategy pair (p', q') as $\max[d(p, p'), d(q, q')]$ where $d(., .)$ is variation distance.

can be designed for approximation-stable instances, it means that this algorithm will perform well on any instances for which that motivation is well justified, possibly even bypassing approximation-hardness barriers with respect to the true goal.

Second, approximation stability provides an interesting implication through its contrapositive. Suppose an algorithm designed for approximation stability does *not* perform well on typical instances from a given domain, e.g., as in the domains considered by Schalekamp et al. (2010). This means that those instances are not approximation stable, which in turn means that if an algorithm is to perform well on them, it will not be due solely to its ability to achieve a good approximation to the given objective function. Instead, one should aim to look for other criteria or algorithmic properties, perhaps in concert with performance on the objective. That is, approximation stability can help motivate and provide guidance in the search for additional theoretical guarantees beyond approximation ratio.

Third, approximation stability can provide a useful design guide for algorithms in practice. As seen in the work of Voevodski et al. (2012) described earlier on clustering protein sequences from limited information, if one is in a new situation and unsure about what kind of algorithm would be best, asking "can we design an algorithm that operates under our given constraints and would do well if the input was sufficiently approximation stable?" can help in producing highly practical methods, regardless of whether stability is indeed perfectly satisfied in the instances.

6.8 Open Questions

One problem for which an approximation stability result would be quite interesting is *sparsest cut*. Given a graph $G = (V, E)$, the sparsest cut problem asks to find the cut $(S, V \setminus S)$ that minimizes $\frac{|E(S, V \setminus S)|}{\min(|S|, |V \setminus S|)}$. This problem is *NP*-hard and the best approximation known is a factor $O(\sqrt{\log n})$ (Arora et al., 2009). One common motivation for sparsest cut is that nodes might represent objects of two types (say, images of cats and of dogs), edges might represent similarity, and the hope is that the correct partition (cats on one side and dogs on the other) would in fact be a sparse cut. Notice that this is a problem of recovering a target solution. From this perspective, a natural question then is: suppose an instance satisfies (c, ϵ) approximation stability for sparsest cut, even for a large constant c. Can one use this to efficiently find a solution that is $O(\epsilon)$-close to the target? If so, then this would be achieving the benefits of a constant-factor approximation even if we do not in general know how to achieve a constant-factor approximation.

Another type of problem for which approximation stability could be quite interesting to consider is phylogenetic tree reconstruction. Here, the goal is to reconstruct an unknown evolutionary tree for a given set of current objects (species, languages, etc.), by optimizing some quantity over the current objects. Typically, the quantity being optimized is motivated by a specific postulated probabilistic model for how mutations occur. However, it would be interesting to obtain guarantees under nonprobabilistic stability assumptions as well.

Finally, the MAX-SAT problem could be interesting to consider in this context. The MAX-SAT problem is sometimes used to model solution discovery problems, including problems of learning and clustering (Berg et al., 2018), so approximation-stability results would be of interest here as well.

6.9 Relaxations

Balcan et al. (2009a) consider a relaxation of (c, ϵ)-approximation stability that allows for the presence of noisy data: data points for which the (heuristic) distance measure does not reflect cluster membership well, which could cause stability over the full dataset to be violated. Specifically, they define and analyze a notion of (v, c, ϵ)-approximation stability, which requires that the data satisfy (c, ϵ) approximation stability only after a v fraction of the data points have been removed.

It would also be interesting to consider relaxations that place an assumption only on c-approximations satisfying some additional condition that natural approximation algorithms tend to provide. For example, suppose we require only that c-approximations that are also local optima under some reasonable locality notion must be ϵ-close to the target. Can one extend positive results like those described earlier to weaker assumptions of this form as well?

6.10 Notes

The notion of approximation stability for clustering first appeared in Balcan et al. (2008), though its implications were not studied in detail until Balcan et al. (2009b). The terminology used in this chapter follows Balcan et al. (2013). The approximation-stability results for clustering and Nash equilibria described in this chapter are primarily from Balcan et al. (2013), Awasthi et al. (2010a), and Balcan and Braverman (2017). Empirical work described on clustering biological sequences is from Voevodski et al. (2012). Other work on approximation stability, not discussed here, includes work analyzing k-means++ under approximation stability (Agarwal et al., 2015) and on correlation clustering (Balcan and Braverman, 2009).

References

Ackerman, Margareta, and Ben-David, Shai. 2009. Clusterability: A theoretical study. *Artificial Intelligence and Statistics*, 1–8.

Agarwal, Manu, Jaiswal, Ragesh, and Pal, Arindam. 2015. k-Means++ under approximation stability. *Theoretical Computer Science*, **588**, 37–51.

Arora, Sanjeev, Rao, Satish, and Vazirani, Umesh. 2009. Expander flows, geometric embeddings and graph partitioning. *Journal of the ACM (JACM)*, **56**(2), 5.

Awasthi, Pranjal, Balcan, Maria-Florina, Blum, Avrim, Sheffet, Or, and Vempala, Santosh. 2010a. On Nash-equilibria of approximation-stable games. In *International Symposium on Algorithmic Game Theory*, pp. 78–89. Springer.

Awasthi, Pranjal, Blum, Avrim, and Sheffet, Or. 2010b. Stability yields a PTAS for k-median and k-means clustering. In *2010 IEEE 51st Annual Symposium on Foundations of Computer Science*, pp. 309–318. IEEE.

Balcan, Maria-Florina, and Braverman, Mark. 2009. Finding low error clusterings. In *Proceedings of the 22nd Annual Conference on Learning Theory*.

Balcan, Maria-Florina, and Braverman, Mark. 2017. Nash equilibria in perturbation-stable games. *Theory of Computing*, **13**(1), 1–31.

Balcan, Maria-Florina, and Liang, Yingyu. 2016. Clustering under perturbation resilience. *SIAM Journal on Computing*, **45**(1), 102–155.

Balcan, Maria-Florina, Blum, Avrim, and Vempala, Santosh. 2008. A Discriminative Framework for Clustering via Similarity Functions. In *Proceedings of the 40th ACM Symposium on Theory of Computing*, pp. 671–680.

Balcan, Maria-Florina, Röglin, Heiko, and Teng, Shang-Hua. 2009a. Agnostic clustering. In *International Conference on Algorithmic Learning Theory*, pp. 384–398. Springer.

Balcan, Maria-Florina, Blum, Avrim, and Gupta, Anupam. 2009b. Approximate clustering without the approximation. In *Proceedings of the Twentieth Annual ACM-SIAM Symposium on Discrete Algorithms*, pp. 1068–1077. Society for Industrial and Applied Mathematics.

Balcan, Maria-Florina, Blum, Avrim, and Gupta, Anupam. 2013. Clustering under approximation stability. *Journal of the ACM (JACM)*, **60**(2), 8.

Bartal, Yair, Charikar, Moses, and Raz, Danny. 2001. Approximating min-sum k-clustering in metric spaces. In *Proceedings on 33rd Annual ACM Symposium on Theory of Computing*.

Berg, Jeremias, Hyttinen, Antti, and Järvisalo, Matti. Applications of MaxSAT in data analysis. In *Proceedings of Pragmatics of SAT* 2015 and 2018, pp. 50–64.

Daniely, Amit, Linial, Nati, and Saks, Michael. 2012. Clustering is difficult only when it does not matter. *arXiv preprint arXiv:1205.4891*.

Feder, Tomas, Nazerzadeh, Hamid, and Saberi, Amin. 2007. Approximating Nash equilibria using small-support strategies. *Proceeding of the 8th ACM-EC*, pp. 352–354.

Finn, R.D., Mistry, J., Tate, J., et al. 2010. The Pfam protein families database. *Nucleic Acids Research*, **38**, D211–222.

Guha, Sudipto, and Khuller, Samir. 1999. Greedy strikes back: Improved facility location algorithms. *Journal of Algorithms*, **31**(1), 228–248.

Jain, Kamal, Mahdian, Mohammad, and Saberi, Amin. 2002. A new greedy approach for facility location problems. In *Proceedings of the Thiry-Fourth Annual ACM Symposium on Theory of Computing*, pp. 731–740. ACM.

Li, Shi, and Svensson, Ola. 2016. Approximating k-median via pseudo-approximation. *SIAM Journal on Computing*, **45**(2), 530–547.

Lipton, Richard J., Markakis, Evangelos, and Mehta, Aranyak. 2003. Playing large games using simple strategies. In *Proceedings of 4th ACM-EC*, pp. 36–41.

Murzin, A.G., Brenner, S. E., Hubbard, T., and Chothia, C. 1995. SCOP: A structural classification of proteins database for the investigation of sequences and structures. *Journal of Molecular Biology*, **247**, 536–540.

Ostrovsky, Rafail, Rabani, Yuval, Schulman, Leonard J, and Swamy, Chaitanya. 2012. The effectiveness of Lloyd-type methods for the k-means problem. *Journal of the ACM (JACM)*, **59**(6), 28.

Rubinstein, Aviad. 2016. Settling the complexity of computing approximate two-player Nash equilibria. In *2016 IEEE 57th Annual Symposium on Foundations of Computer Science (FOCS)*, pp. 258–265. IEEE.

Schalekamp, Frans, Yu, Michael, and van Zuylen, Anke. 2010. Clustering with or without the approximation. In *Proceedings of the 16th Annual International Computing and Combinatorics Conference*.

Tsaknakis, Haralampos, and Spirakis, Paul G. 2007. An optimization approach for approximate Nash equilibria. Workshop on Internet and Network Economics, pp. 42–56.

Voevodski, Konstantin, Balcan, Maria-Florina, Röglin, Heiko, Teng, Shang-Hua, and Xia, Yu. 2012. Active clustering of biological sequences. *Journal of Machine Learning Research*, **13**(Jan), 203–225.

Exercises

Exercise 6.1 Prove that Equation 6.2 defining the distance between k-clusterings is a metric. Specifically, show that (a) $dist(\mathcal{C}, \mathcal{C}')$ is symmetric and (b) it satisfies the triangle inequality. Note: the trickier property here is (a).

Exercise 6.2 What is the expected distance $dist(C, C')$ between two *random* k-clusterings C, C' of a set of n points, in the limit as $n \rightarrow \infty$?

Exercise 6.3 Consider k-median clustering for $k = 2$. Give an example of a set of points satisfying $(1.4, 0)$ approximation stability (i.e., all c-approximations for $c \leq 1.4$ are identical to the target clustering) but not $(1.6, 0.3)$ approximation-stability (i.e., there exists a c-approximation for $c \leq 1.6$ that has distance at least 0.3 from the target clustering). Is your example 1.6-perturbation resilient (Chapter 5)?

Exercise 6.4 Consider the *matching pennies* game (with payoffs scaled to $[0, 1]$):

$$R = \begin{bmatrix} 1 & 0 \\ 0 & 1 \end{bmatrix} \quad C = \begin{bmatrix} 0 & 1 \\ 1 & 0 \end{bmatrix}.$$

The unique Nash equilibrium of this game is for both players to play $(0.5, 0.5)$, giving each an expected payoff of 0.5. Prove that this game is $(3/16, 1/4)$-approximation stable. That is, for any strategy pair (p, q) such that at least one of p or q puts more than $3/4$ probability on one of its two actions, at least one player must have at least a $3/16$ incentive to deviate (there must be some action they can play in which their expected gain is larger than their current expected gain by at least $3/16$).

Exercise 6.5 Consider the game of *rock-paper-scissors* (with payoffs scaled to $[0, 1]$):

$$R = \begin{bmatrix} 0.5 & 0 & 1 \\ 1 & 0.5 & 0 \\ 0 & 1 & 0.5 \end{bmatrix} \quad C = \begin{bmatrix} 0.5 & 1 & 0 \\ 0 & 0.5 & 1 \\ 1 & 0 & 0.5 \end{bmatrix}.$$

Prove that this game is $(\alpha, 4\alpha)$-approximation stable for any $\alpha < 1/6$.

CHAPTER SEVEN

Sparse Recovery

Eric Price

Abstract: Many real-world signals are approximately *sparse*, meaning that a small fraction of the coordinates contain almost all the signal mass; examples include images, audio, and any signals drawn from Zipfian, power-law, or log-normal distributions. If a signal $x \in \mathbb{R}^n$ is approximately k-sparse, then ideally the complexity of estimating or manipulating x should scale primarily with k rather than n.

Such *sparse recovery* algorithms are possible for a variety of different problem variants, corresponding to different modalities of measuring x and different guarantees on the estimation error. In this chapter we will consider streaming algorithms, compressed sensing, and sparse Fourier transforms, as well as extensions to low-rank matrix recovery.

7.1 Sparse Recovery

Imagine that you are tallying the results of an election by hand, and would like to find the top few candidates. You might maintain a sheet of paper recording the count for each candidate, while you pass through the giant stack of ballots. But write-in candidates make this challenging in a large election: the recording sheet would run out of space from votes for "candidates" like Batman or Bart Simpson. You would be fine ignoring such joke candidates with very few votes, but you don't want to miss a significant write-in candidate – and you don't want to miss him or her even if all his or her votes happened late in the day, at the bottom of the stack of ballots, after your tally sheet has run out of space. An algorithm due to Misra and Gries (1982), to be covered in the next section, offers a solution that uses only a small amount of space, at the cost of giving an *approximate* answer. If there are only k "real" candidates, and all the other candidates are rare, the approximation error will be small.

This property, that a small fraction of coordinates contains a large fraction of the mass, has been empirically observed for signals in many different domains. It follows from popular rules of thumb such as Zipf's law and the 80/20 rule, as well as popular generative models that yield power law or lognormal distributions. In Figure 7.1 we show a few examples of this phenomenon: in music (the Fourier transform of a short snippet), images (represented in a basis such as the Haar wavelet), and networks (number of inlinks per page). These different domains vary in how quickly

---

140

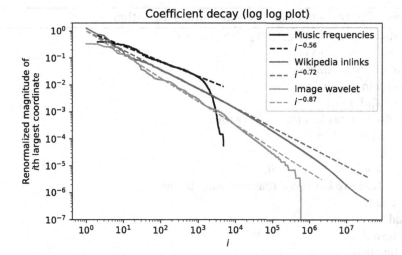

Figure 7.1 Coefficient decay in three example signals of different domains. In each example, the *i*th largest coordinate has magnitude decaying as $i^{-\alpha}$ for some $\alpha \in (0.5, 1)$. The audio data contain the frequencies in a 1/10 second clip of a popular music video; the image data are the Haar wavelet representation of one frame of this video; the graph data are the number of inlinks per page on English Wikipedia.

the coefficients decay, but they all have the same qualitative behavior: the *i*th largest coordinate has magnitude roughly proportional to $i^{-\alpha}$ for some $\alpha \in (0.5, 1)$ for small *i*, followed by even faster decay for large *i*.

None of the results presented in this chapter rely on any distributional assumptions on signals, and require only that the signal to be recovered or manipulated is (approximately) sparse. This assumption is analogous to the stability definitions of Chapters 5 and 6, except with "meaningful solutions" now identified with "(approximate) sparsity." Most of the algorithms in this chapter provide input-by-input guarantees, parameterized by how close the unknown signal is to being *k*-sparse. As with the parameterized guarantees in Chapters 1 and 2, these will be nontrivial only when the parameter is small (i.e., when the signal is approximately *k*-sparse).

Outline of the Chapter. In Section 7.2 we give a streaming algorithm for sparse recovery. In Section 7.3 we present two *linear sketching* algorithms for the problem. Linear sketching algorithms have several advantages over other streaming algorithms, and the second algorithm also achieves a stronger "ℓ_2" approximation guarantee for sparse recovery. In Section 7.4 we turn to *compressive sensing* algorithms. Compressive sensing is essentially the same problem as sparse recovery with linear sketching, but studied by a different community for a different purpose, leading to significant differences in techniques and subtler differences in goals. Section 7.5 contains a lower bound that matches the algorithms of Sections 7.3 and 7.4. Section 7.6 presents some more involved results in the area. Finally, Section 7.7 shows how sparse recovery techniques extend to low-rank matrix estimation.

Notation. For any $x \in \mathbb{R}^n$ and $k \in [n]$, we use $H_k(x)$ to denote the *k*-sparse vector in $\mathbb{R}^n$ that sets all but the largest *k* entries (in magnitude) of x to zero.

Algorithm 1 FREQUENTELEMENTS heavy hitters algorithm

1: **function** FREQUENTELEMENTS(STREAM, k)
2:    $d \leftarrow$ DICTIONARY()
3:    **for** u in STREAM **do**
4:      **if** u in d **then**
5:        $d[u]$ += 1
6:      **else if** d has less than k keys **then**
7:        $d[u] \leftarrow 1$
8:      **else**
9:        $d[u'] \mathrel{-}= 1 \quad \forall u' \in d$.
10:       Remove keys of d that now map to zero
11:      **end if**
12:    **end for**
13:    **return** d
14: **end function**

7.2 A Simple Insertion-Only Streaming Algorithm

The election counting example is one example of a *data stream*. An (insertion-only) data stream consists of a long series of items

$$u_1, u_2, u_3, \ldots, u_N \in [n].$$

This stream represents the count vector $x \in \mathbb{R}^n$ given by

$$x_i = |\{j : u_j = i\}|.$$

The goal of sparse recovery (also known as heavy hitters) in this context is to approximate x while scanning through u, while storing much less than n or $N = \|x\|_1$ space (where $\|x\|_p := (\sum_i x_i^p)^{1/p}$ is the ℓ_p-norm).

The straightforward method for estimating x is to store it in a dictionary (a.k.a. associative array or map). We would start with an empty dictionary d, and for every element u that appears in the stream we increment $d[u]$ (with newly added elements set to 1). The problem with this method is that the space used is the total number of distinct elements in the stream, which could be as large as n.

The FREQUENTELEMENTS algorithm, presented in Algorithm 1 and due to Misra and Gries (1982), is a simple twist on the straightforward approach. The only difference is that we pick a parameter k (think, perhaps, $k = \sqrt{n}$) and, if incrementing $d[u]$ would make d have more than k keys, we instead *subtract* 1 from the counter of every key in the dictionary – and if that brings a counter to zero, the corresponding key is removed. The space usage is then $\Theta(k)$ words and the error in the final count of every element is, at most, the total number of times this subtraction occurs. Since each subtraction removes k from the sum of the values in d, while each addition adds only 1 and the sum of values remains nonnegative, the subtraction step can happen at most a $1/(k + 1)$ fraction of the stream steps. Thus:

Lemma 7.1 *The estimates $\widehat{x}_u = d[u]$ given by the* FREQUENTELEMENTS *algorithm satisfy*

142

$$x_u - \frac{1}{k+1}\|x\|_1 \le \widehat{x}_u \le x_u$$

for every element u.

One can also get a more refined bound that is significantly stronger in a sparse setting. If a few elements really do dominate the stream, those elements will end up with large values, which further constrains the number of deletions. One way to bound this is to consider as a potential function the sum of the entries of d that do not correspond to the $k/2$ largest entries of x. This potential is nonnegative at all times, only increases by 1 at a time, and does so at most $\|x - H_{k/2}(x)\|_1 \le \|x\|_1$ times; on the other hand, each subtraction removes at least $k/2$ from this potential, so the total number of subtractions is at most $\|x - H_{k/2}(x)\|_1 \cdot \frac{2}{k}$. Thus:

Lemma 7.2 *The estimates $\widehat{x}_u = d[u]$ given by the FREQUENTELEMENTS algorithm satisfy*

$$x_u - \frac{2}{k}\|x - H_{k/2}(x)\|_1 \le \widehat{x}_u \le x_u$$

for every element u.

Which of Lemmas 7.1 and 7.2 more accurately characterizes the performance of FREQUENTELEMENTS depends on the sparsity of x. The sparsity-aware bound of Lemma 7.2 gives a better asymptotic bound on the error in terms of k when the frequencies decay faster than Zipf's law (in which the ith most common element having frequency proportional to $1/i$). When the frequencies decay slower, however, $\|x - H_{k/2}(x)\|_1 \approx \|x\|_1$ for $k \ll n$ so Lemma 7.1's better constant factors give a better bound.

7.3 Handling Deletions: Linear Sketching Algorithms

The FREQUENTELEMENTS algorithm is designed for *insertion-only* streams, where items arrive in sequence and never leave. A more general, and more challenging, setting is that of *turnstile* streams, where items can be both inserted and deleted. The name evokes an amusement park: you want to study the people who are currently inside the park, while only tracking people as they enter and leave through turnstiles. An important subclass is the *strict* turnstile stream, wherein the final vector x has nonnegative values (e.g., people cannot leave without arriving).

In Algorithm 2 we present two algorithms for solving sparse recovery in turnstile streams: COUNTMINSKETCH (Cormode and Muthukrishnan, 2005) and COUNTSKETCH (Charikar et al., 2002). The two algorithms are almost identical, with COUNTSKETCH having a few more pieces; these extra parts are displayed in gray, and should be ignored to read the COUNTMINSKETCH algorithm.

It turns out that almost every turnstile streaming algorithm can be implemented as a *linear sketch*. In a linear sketch, you store $y = Ax$ for some (possibly randomized) matrix $A \in \mathbb{R}^{m \times n}$. This can easily be maintained under streaming updates: when an element is inserted or deleted, you simply add or subtract the corresponding column of A from the sketch y. The space used by the linear sketch is m words to store y, plus the size of the random seed to produce A; and for the algorithms we will consider, the

---

Algorithm 2 CountMinSketch in black / CountSketch in black and gray

---

1: **function** CountMinSketch/CountSketch(Stream, B, R)
2:     Pick $h_1, \ldots, h_R : [n] \to [B]$ pairwise independent hash functions.
3:     Pick $s_1, \ldots, s_R : [n] \to \{-1, 1\}$ pairwise independent hash functions.
4:     $y_i^{(r)} \leftarrow 0 \quad \forall i \in [B], r \in [R]$
5:     **for** (u, a) in Stream **do** $\triangleright$ (Corresponding to stream update $x_u \leftarrow x_u + a$)
6:         **for** $r \in [R]$ **do**
7:             $y_{h_r(u)}^{(r)}$ += $a \cdot s_r(u)$.
8:         **end for**
9:     **end for**
10:    **for** $u \in [n]$ **do**
11:        $\widehat{x}_u \leftarrow \min_{r \in [R]} y_{h_r(u)}$. $\triangleright$ (CountMinSketch only)
12:        $\widehat{x}_u \leftarrow \operatorname{median}_{r \in [R]} y_{h_r(u)} \cdot s_r(u)$. $\triangleright$ (CountSketch only)
13:    **end for**
14:    **return** $\widehat{x}$
15: **end function**

---

seed is small so this is essentially m. Another benefit of linear sketching algorithms over insertion-only streaming is *mergability*: you can split the stream into pieces (say, multiple routers), sketch the pieces individually, then add up the results to get the sketch for the full stream. One can observe that CountMinSketch/CountSketch are linear sketches. In particular, the final value stored in each coordinate $y_j^{(r)}$ is

$$y_j^{(r)} = \sum_{u=1}^{n} 1_{h_r(u)=j} s_r(u) \cdot x_u, \tag{7.1}$$

which is a linear function of x.

7.3.1 The Count-Min Sketch: An ℓ_1 Guarantee

The idea behind CountMinSketch is that if we had unlimited space, we'd just store a single hash table with the counts for all items in the stream. If we instead store a hash table of much smaller size $B = O(k)$, there will be collisions. Standard methods for resolving those collisions, like linked lists, would again need linear space in the number of distinct items. But what happens if we don't resolve collisions at all, and just store in each hash cell the total number of elements that hash there?

Given such a "hash table," we can estimate the count for an item by the value in the cell it hashes to. For strict turnstile streams, this is an overestimate of the true answer: it contains the true count plus the counts of colliding elements. But any other element has only a $1/B$ chance of colliding in the hash table, so the expected error is at most $\|x\|_1 / B$. This would be a decent bound comparable to Lemma 7.1, except that it is only in expectation for each element. Almost surely *some* element will have much higher error – indeed, there is no way to distinguish between the heavy hitters and the (small fraction, but still numerous) other elements that happen to collide with them.

To fix this, CountMinSketch repeats the process with $R = O(\log n)$ different hash tables. Since each hash table gives an overestimate, the final estimate of an element is the minimum estimate from any repetition. This achieves the following:

Theorem 7.3 *If x has nonnegative entries, then* CountMinSketch, *when run with $B \geq 4k$ and $R \geq 2\log_2 n$, returns an $\widehat{x}$ that satisfies*

$$x_u \leq \widehat{x}_u \leq x_u + \frac{1}{k}\|x - H_k(x)\|_1$$

for all u with $1 - 1/n$ probability.

The statement is very similar to the FrequentElements bound in Lemma 7.2. It is an overestimate rather than an underestimate, but otherwise the error bound is identical up to scaling k by 2. Unlike FrequentElements, CountMinSketch can handle deletions, but this comes at a cost: CountMinSketch uses $O(k \log n)$ words of space rather than $O(k)$, it is randomized, and the time required for computing $\widehat{x}$ at the end of the stream is $O(n \log n)$ rather than $O(k)$ because every coordinate x_u must be estimated to find the largest k. The first two issues cannot be avoided for "typical" values of $k \in (n^{0.01}, n^{0.99})$. In Section 7.5 we will show that $\Omega(k \log n)$ words of space are necessary to handle deletions, and randomization is needed to achieve $o(\min(k^2, n))$ words (Ganguly, 2008). The recovery time, however, can be improved; see the bibliographic notes for details.

Proof of Theorem 7.3. Define $\widehat{x}^{(r)}$ by $\widehat{x}_u^{(r)} = y_{h_r(u)}$ for each u, so that $\widehat{x}_u = \min_r \widehat{x}_u^{(r)}$. Let $H \subseteq [n]$ contain the largest k coordinates of x, known as the "heavy hitters". Then

$$0 \leq \widehat{x}_u^{(r)} - x_u = \underbrace{\sum_{\substack{h_r(v)=h_r(u) \\ v \neq u}} x_v}_{} = \underbrace{\sum_{\substack{v \in H \\ h_r(v)=h_r(u) \\ v \neq u}} x_v}_{E_H} + \underbrace{\sum_{\substack{v \notin H \\ h_r(v)=h_r(u) \\ v \neq u}} x_v}_{E_L}. \qquad (7.2)$$

For u to be estimated badly, either E_H or E_L must be large. E_H represents the error u receives from colliding with heavy hitters. This is usually zero, because there aren't too many heavy hitters. E_L is the error from non–heavy-hitters. This is likely nonzero, but is small in expectation. Formally, we have that

$$\Pr[E_H > 0] \leq \Pr[\exists v \in H \setminus \{u\} : h_r(v) = h_r(u)] \leq \frac{k}{B} \leq \frac{1}{4} \qquad (7.3)$$

by our choice of $B \geq 4k$. We also have that

$$\mathbb{E}[E_L] = \sum_{\substack{v \in [n] \setminus H \\ v \neq u}} x_v \cdot \Pr[h(v) = h(u)] \leq \sum_{v \in [n] \setminus H} x_v \cdot \frac{1}{B} = \|x - H_k(x)\|_1 / B. \quad (7.4)$$

Hence by Markov's inequality,

$$\Pr[E_L > \|x - H_k(x)\|_1 / k] \leq \frac{k}{B} \leq \frac{1}{4};$$

so by a union bound, independently for each r

$$\Pr[\widehat{x}_u^{(r)} - x_u > \|x - H_k(x)\|_1/k] \leq \frac{1}{2}. \tag{7.5}$$

Therefore because $R \geq 2\log_2 n$,

$$\Pr[\widehat{x}_u - x_u > \|x - H_k(x)\|_1/k] \leq \frac{1}{2^R} \leq \frac{1}{n^2}.$$

Taking a union bound over u gives the result. □

Negative Entries and COUNTMEDIANSKETCH. The COUNTMINSKETCH algorithm relies on the strict turnstile assumption that the final vector x has only nonnegative coordinates. If the entries of x may be negative, one can simply replace the min on line 11 with a median and increase B and R by constant factors. By increasing B, the failure event (7.5) will have failure probability $2k/B < 1/2$. Then a Chernoff bound can show that with high probability *most* iterations r will not fail, and hence the median estimate is good. This algorithm is known as the COUNTMEDIANSKETCH, and achieves the same $\frac{1}{k}\|x - H_k(x)\|_1$ error guarantee as Theorem 7.3 but with two-sided error.

7.3.2 Count-Sketch: The ℓ_2 Guarantee

The gray lines in Algorithm 2 describe the modifications required to produce the COUNTSKETCH algorithm, which is like COUNTMEDIANSKETCH but with random signs introduced. This changes the error for a single r from (7.2) to

$$\widehat{x}_u^{(r)} - x_u = \sum_{\substack{h_r(v)=h_r(u) \\ v \neq u}} x_v s_r(v) s_r(u).$$

For fixed h_r, this is now a random variable in s_r, and because s_r is pairwise independent and mean zero, all the cross terms in $\mathbb{E}_{s_r}[(\widehat{x}_u^{(r)} - x_u)^2]$ disappear. In particular, (7.4) becomes

$$\mathbb{E}_{h_r, s_r}[E_L^2] = \sum_{\substack{v \in [n] \setminus H \\ v \neq u}} x_v^2 \cdot \Pr[h(v) = h(u)] \leq \|x - H_k(x)\|_2^2/B.$$

If $B \geq 16k$, applying Markov's inequality and a union bound with the k/B chance that $E_H > 0$ shows that in each repetition

$$\Pr\left[(\widehat{x}_u^{(r)} - x_u)^2 > \|x - H_k(x)\|_2^2/k\right] < 1/8.$$

The chance this happens in at least $R/2$ of the R repetitions is then at most

$$\binom{R}{R/2} \cdot (1/8)^{R/2} < 2^R/8^{R/2} = 1/2^{R/2} \leq 1/n^2$$

for $R \geq 4\log_2 n$. If that failure event doesn't happen, the median is a good estimate, giving the following theorem:

Theorem 7.4 CountSketch, *when run with* $B \geq 16k$ *and* $R \geq 4\log_2 n$, *returns an* $\widehat{x}$ *that satisfies*

$$(\widehat{x}_u - x_u)^2 \leq \frac{1}{k}\|x - H_k(x)\|_2^2$$

for all u *with* $1 - 1/n$ *probability.*

At first glance, the bounds on $|\widehat{x}_u - x_u|$ given for CountMinSketch (Theorem 7.3) and CountSketch (Theorem 7.4) may seem incomparable—while $\|x - H_k(x)\|_2 \leq \|x - H_k(x)\|_1$, the denominator is only $\sqrt{k}$ for CountSketch rather than k for CountMinSketch. However, as shown in Exercise 7.1, this is misleading: up to constant factors, the ℓ_2 bound of Theorem 7.4 is stronger than the ℓ_1 bound of Theorem 7.3 for every vector x. For many natural vectors x, this difference is quite significant; we now examine it in detail.

7.3.3 Discussion of Recovery Guarantees

To better understand how much better ℓ_2 recovery guarantees are than ℓ_1 ones, we consider power-law (or "Zipfian") distributions where the ith largest element has frequency proportional to $i^{-\alpha}$. We also suppose the stream is distributed over a number of elements $n \gg k$ (which is finite so the sum of frequencies is still finite for $\alpha < 1.0$). For sharply decaying distributions of $\alpha > 1.0$, the ℓ_1 guarantee is

$$\|\widehat{x} - x\|_\infty \leq \frac{1}{k}\sum_{i=k+1}^{n} x_i \approx \frac{1}{k}x_1 \cdot \sum_{i=k+1}^{n} i^{-\alpha} \approx \frac{1}{\alpha - 1}x_k,$$

while the ℓ_2 guarantee for $\alpha > 0.5$ is

$$\|\widehat{x} - x\|_\infty \leq \sqrt{\frac{1}{k}\sum_{i=k+1}^{n} x_i^2} \approx \sqrt{\frac{1}{k}x_1^2 \cdot \sum_{i=k+1}^{n} i^{-2\alpha}} \approx \frac{1}{\sqrt{2\alpha - 1}}x_k.$$

When $\alpha > 1.0$, these two guarantees are identical up to constant factors. But for intermediate decay of $0.5 < \alpha < 1.0$, the ℓ_1 guarantee is much worse:

$$\|\widehat{x} - x\|_\infty \leq \frac{1}{k}\sum_{i=k+1}^{n} x_i \approx \frac{1}{k}x_1 \cdot \sum_{i=k+1}^{n} i^{-\alpha} \approx \frac{1}{k}x_1\frac{1}{1 - \alpha}n^{1-\alpha}$$

That is, unless $k > n^{1-\alpha}$, the ℓ_1 guarantee gives *no* nontrivial estimates (indeed, the all-zeros vector would satisfy it). Even above that threshold, the ℓ_1 guarantee remains a $(n/k)^{1-\alpha}$ factor worse than the ℓ_2 guarantee. For slow decay of $\alpha < 0.5$, the ℓ_2 guarantee becomes

$$\|\widehat{x} - x\|_\infty \leq \sqrt{\frac{1}{k}\sum_{i=k+1}^{n} x_i^2} \approx \sqrt{\frac{1}{k}x_1^2 \cdot \sum_{i=k+1}^{n} i^{-2\alpha}} \approx x_1\frac{1}{\sqrt{1 - 2\alpha}}\sqrt{\frac{n}{k}}n^{-\alpha}.$$

which is trivial until $k > n^{1-2\alpha}$, and remains a $\sqrt{n/k}$ factor better than the ℓ_1 bound for larger k.

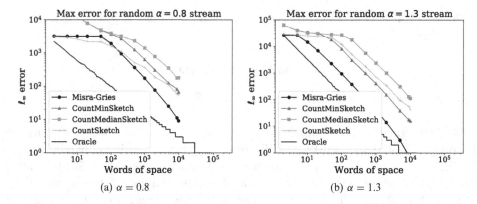

Figure 7.2 Comparison of error as a function of space for sparse recovery algorithms on random power law distribution streams, where the ith most common element has frequency proportional to $i^{-\alpha}$, with 10^5 items drawn over a 10^4 size domain. FREQUENTELEMENTS is assumed to use two words per entry of its table (one for the key, one for the value). ORACLE stores exactly the largest entries of the stream (with two words per entry). For $\alpha < 1$, the ℓ_2 bound of COUNTSKETCH gives significant benefit; for $\alpha > 1$, it performs worse than COUNTMINSKETCH due to constant factor inefficiency. In both cases, FREQUENTELEMENTS uses roughly an order of magnitude less space than COUNTMINSKETCH due to avoiding the $O(\log n)$ factor.

The intermediate regime of $\alpha \in (0.5, 1.0)$ is the most relevant one in practice, as observed in the examples illustrated in Figure 7.1 as well as more generally (see, for example, Clauset et al. (2009)). Therefore the ℓ_2 guarantee is significantly more desirable than the ℓ_1 one.

In Figure 7.2 we illustrate these calculations with the empirical performance of the algorithms we have seen so far on such power-law distributions. The results closely match what one would expect from the theoretical bounds we have shown. For $\alpha = 0.8$, but not $\alpha = 1.3$, COUNTSKETCH's ℓ_2 bound is more important than COUNTMINSKETCH's constant factors, and in certain parameter regimes even enough to beat the $\Theta(\log n)$ factor savings in FREQUENTELEMENTS.

7.4 Uniform Algorithms

The sparse recovery algorithms described in the preceding sections originated in the computer science community in the context of streaming algorithms. Another body of work designed to solve very similar problems comes from the statistics and signal processing communities, where it is known as *compressed sensing* or *compressive sampling* (Donoho et al., 2006; Candes et al., 2006). The motivation for compressed sensing is situations where one has a physical process that can cheaply observe linear measurements of a signal of interest – for example, MRI machines inherently sample Fourier measurements of the desired image; the single-pixel camera architecture takes pictures by applying brief masks during exposure; genetic testing companies can mix blood samples before testing; and radio telescopes sample from the Fourier spectrum based on their geometry. Without any assumption on the signal structure, learning an arbitrary $x \in \mathbb{R}^n$ would require n linear measurements, but a structural assumption such as sparsity can allow for fewer measurements – ideally leading to faster MRIs, higher-resolution photos, and cheaper genetic testing.

The high-level goal in compressed sensing is thus essentially identical to that of turnstile streaming sparse recovery: estimating approximately k-sparse vectors x from a small number of linear measurements $y = Ax$. (We say that x is k-sparse if it has at most k nonzero coordinates, and approximately k-sparse if it is "close" to a k-sparse vector.) But the emphasis is somewhat different, leading to different solutions.

Most notably, compressed sensing algorithms are designed to work even if the observation matrix A is not fully under the control of the algorithm designer. The observation matrix may have to satisfy a number of complicated constraints coming from how the physical sensing apparatus works; but as long as A is "good enough" in a formal sense, the recovery algorithms will work. Moreover, this allows for a degree of modularity: one can mix and match different algorithms and matrices, since essentially any "good enough" matrix construction will work with any algorithm. This modularity is in sharp contrast to most methods from the streaming community: it makes no sense to try and use (say) the COUNTSKETCH measurement matrix with the faster (Larsen et al., 2016) recovery algorithm, because the algorithms are intimately tied to their matrices.

7.4.1 The Restricted Isometry Property

The simplest approach to determining if A is "good enough" is that of *incoherence*:

Definition 7.5 Let $A \in \mathbb{R}^{m \times n}$ have columns $a_1, \ldots, a_n$ of ℓ_2 norm 1. The *coherence μ* of A is

$$\mu := \max_{i \neq j} |\langle a_i, a_j \rangle|.$$

If $\mu = 0$, then A has orthonormal columns so it is invertible and recovery is certainly possible. But our goal is to have $m \ll n$, so A cannot have orthonormal columns. The interesting thing is that even if μ is somewhat larger – up to $\Theta(1/k)$ – then sparse recovery is possible with a variety of algorithms. Unfortunately, every matrix with $m < n/2$ has coherence $\mu > \sqrt{\frac{1}{2m}}$, so achieving "good enough" incoherence would require $\Omega(k^2)$ linear measurements. For the polynomially large values of k typically considered, this is rather more than the $O(k \log n)$ measurements we saw with streaming algorithms, suggesting the need for a different definition of "good enough." One popular definition is the Restricted Isometry Property:

Definition 7.6 For any k, the restricted isometry constant $\delta_k = \delta_k(A)$ of a matrix $A \in \mathbb{R}^{m \times n}$ is the smallest $\delta \geq 0$ such that

$$(1 - \delta)\|x\|_2^2 \leq \|Ax\|_2^2 \leq (1 + \delta)\|x\|_2^2 \qquad \text{for all } k\text{-sparse } x.$$

An equivalent formulation is that

$$\|(A^\top A - I)_{S \times S}\| \leq \delta \qquad \text{for all } S \subset [n], |S| \leq k, \tag{7.6}$$

where $\| \cdot \|$ denotes the spectral norm.

We (informally) say that A satisfies the Restricted Isometry Property (RIP) if $\delta_{Ck} < c$ for some sufficiently large constant $C \geq 1$ and sufficiently small $c < 1$. The algorithmic results that follow show that the RIP (with sufficiently good constants C, c) implies that approximate k-sparse recovery is possible. One can show that $\delta_k \leq (k-1)\mu$, so this subsumes the incoherence-based results that require $\mu < \Theta(1/k)$, but the RIP bound is possible with only $m = O(k \log(n/k))$.

The Gaussian Ensemble. A simple way to construct an RIP matrix with good parameters is by taking i.i.d. Gaussian entries of the appropriate variance.

Theorem 7.7 *Let $0 < \varepsilon < 1$ and $k > 1$ be parameters. If $A \in \mathbb{R}^{m \times n}$ has i.i.d. Gaussian entries of variance $1/m$, and $m > C\frac{1}{\varepsilon^2} k \log \frac{n}{k}$ for a sufficiently large constant C, then A has RIP constant $\delta_k < \varepsilon$ with $1 - e^{-\Omega(\varepsilon^2 m)}$ probability.*

The proof is based on applying a union bound to a net. We start with a lemma that shows how to bound an operator norm – which is a supremum over a continuous set – by the maximum over a finite set:

Lemma 7.8 *There exists a set $T \subset \mathbb{R}^n$ of 3^n unit vectors such that, for any symmetric matrix $M \in \mathbb{R}^{n \times n}$,*

$$\|M\| \leq 4 \max_{x \in T} x^\top M x.$$

Since $\|M\| = \sup_{\|x\|_2 = 1} x^\top M x$, this lemma loses at most a factor of 4. The proof is given as Exercise 7.5.

The other key lemma we need is the distributional Johnson–Lindenstrauss Lemma, which shows for any specific x that $\|Ax\|_2 \approx \|x\|_2$ with high probability:

Lemma 7.9 (Johnson–Lindenstrauss) *For any $x \in \mathbb{R}^n$ and $\varepsilon \in (0, 1)$, if $A \in \mathbb{R}^{m \times n}$ has i.i.d. Gaussian entries of variance $1/m$, then*

$$\Pr[|\|Ax\|_2^2 - \|x\|_2^2| > \varepsilon \|x\|_2^2] < 2e^{-\Omega(\varepsilon^2 m)}.$$

Proof of Theorem 7.7 Let $T \subset \mathbb{R}^k$ be the set of size 3^k given by Lemma 7.8 such that, for every set $S \subseteq [n]$ of size k,

$$\|(A^\top A - I)_{S \times S}\| \leq 4 \max_{x \in T} x^\top (A^\top A - I)_{S \times S} x.$$

By Lemma 7.9 applied with $\varepsilon' = \varepsilon/4$ and $n' = k$, we have for each S and $x \in T$ that

$$x^\top (A^\top A - I)_{S \times S} x \leq \frac{\varepsilon}{4} \|x\|_2^2 \leq \frac{\varepsilon}{4}$$

with probability at least $1 - 2e^{-\Omega(\varepsilon^2 m)}$. Taking a union bound over all S and $x \in T$, we have that

$$\delta_k \leq 4 \max_S \max_{x \in T} x^\top (A^\top A - I)_{S \times S} x$$

is bounded by ε with probability at least $1 - 2\binom{n}{k} 3^k e^{-\Omega(\varepsilon^2 m)}$. If $m \geq O(\frac{1}{\varepsilon^2} k \log \frac{n}{k})$, this is $1 - e^{-\Omega(\varepsilon^2 m)}$. $\qquad \square$

Gaussian matrices are just one way of constructing RIP matrices. Another example, with an essentially identical proof to the above, is a matrix with i.i.d. $\{\pm 1\}$ entries. We discuss more involved examples in Section 7.6 and the bibliographic notes.

7.4.2 Postmeasurement vs. Premeasurement Noise

In streaming algorithms, it makes sense to suppose that $y = Ax$ is stored exactly: we see all of x eventually, and have complete control of the observations. But for the motivating applications for compressed sensing, where y represents a physical observation of some signal, one expects noise in the observation. Therefore we will aim for algorithmic guarantees in the presence of *postmeasurement* noise: if

$$y = Ax^* + e$$

for an *exactly k*-sparse x^* and arbitrary noise vector e, the recovered $\widehat{x}$ will satisfy

$$\|\widehat{x} - x^*\|_2 \leq C\|e\|_2 \tag{7.7}$$

for some constant C.

Of course, signals such as images are unlikely to be exactly sparse, so a more realistic setting would have both postmeasurement noise e and premeasurement noise $x - H_k(x)$. For RIP matrices, however, such a result is actually implied by the postmeasurement guarantee (7.7) by treating the premeasurement noise $x - H_k(x)$ as postmeasurement noise $A(x - H_k(x))$; see Exercise 7.2.

7.4.3 Iterative Methods

We now turn to algorithms that perform sparse recovery with RIP matrices. This can be done with either iterative methods or convex programming. The iterative methods are generally simpler and faster, but often require more measurements (by a constant factor). We will present a simple recovery algorithm, known as IterativeHardThresholding.

For intuition, suppose that there is no noise, so $y = Ax^*$. Recall that, since A satisfies the RIP, $A^\top A$ approximates the identity on any $O(k) \times O(k)$ submatrix. Therefore

$$A^\top y = A^\top Ax^* \approx x^*,$$

where the approximation is good over $O(k)$-sized subsets. In particular, we will show

$$\|H_k(A^\top y) - x^*\|_2 \leq O(\delta_{2k})\|x^*\|_2 \ll \|x^*\|_2.$$

This means that $x^{(1)} = H_k(A^\top y)$ is a good first step in recovering x^*: it is most of the way there. (The operation H_k, which thresholds to the largest k entries, is known as "hard" thresholding because of the discontinuity in treatment between elements just above and just below the threshold.) But $x^{(1)}$ still has some residual error $x^* - x^{(1)}$. To reduce this, we can compute $y - Ax^{(1)} = A(x^* - x^{(1)})$, which is effectively a measurement of this residual. We then repeat the procedure of multiplying by $A^\top$ and thresholding, getting a new estimate of x^*:

$$x^{(2)} = H_k(x^{(1)} + A^\top(y - Ax^{(1)})).$$

Algorithm 3 Iterative Hard Thresholding (IHT)

1: **function** ITERATIVEHARDTHRESHOLDING(y, A, k)
2:    $x^{(0)} \leftarrow 0$
3:    **for** $r \leftarrow 0, 1, 2, \ldots, R - 1$ **do**
4:        $x^{(r+1)} \leftarrow H_k \left(x^{(r)} + A^\top (y - Ax^{(r)}) \right)$
5:    **end for**
6:    **return** $x^{(R)}$
7: **end function**

In Lemma 7.11 we show that this ITERATIVEHARDTHRESHOLDING procedure works even with noise: if $y = Ax^* + e$ for an exactly k-sparse vector x^*, the residual error geometrically converges to the noise level $O(\|e\|_2)$. To establish this, we first show that the thresholding step does not increase the ℓ_2 distance by more than a constant factor:

Lemma 7.10 *Let $x, z \in \mathbb{R}^n$ so that x is k-sparse with support S and $T \subseteq [n]$ consists of the largest k terms of z. Then*

$$\|x - z_T\|_2^2 \leq 3 \|(x - z)_{S \cup T}\|_2^2.$$

Proof For every $i \in S \setminus T$ we can assign a unique $j \in T \setminus S$ such that $|z_j| \geq |z_i|$. Therefore

$$x_i^2 \leq (|x_i - z_i| + |z_i|)^2 \leq (|x_i - z_i| + |z_j|)^2 \leq 2(x_i - z_i)^2 + 2z_j^2.$$

Adding in the terms for $i \in T$ gives the result. □

Lemma 7.11 *In each iteration of* ITERATIVEHARDTHRESHOLDING,

$$\|x^{(r+1)} - x^*\|_2 \leq \sqrt{3} \delta_{3k} \|x^{(r)} - x^*\|_2 + \sqrt{6} \|e\|_2.$$

Proof Define

$$x' := x^{(r)} + A^\top (y - Ax^{(r)}) = x^* + (A^\top A - I)(x^* - x^{(r)}) + A^\top e.$$

Let $S = \text{supp}(x^{(r+1)}) \cup \text{supp}(x^{(r)}) \cup \text{supp}(x^*)$, so $|S| \leq 3k$. Note that the RIP implies that

$$\|A_S^\top\|^2 = \|(A^\top A)_{S \times S}\| \leq 1 + \delta_{3k}.$$

Therefore we have

$$\|(x' - x^*)_S\|_2 \leq \|((A^\top A - I)(x^* - x^{(r)}))_S\|_2 + \|(A^\top e)_S\|_2$$
$$\leq \|(A^\top A - I)_{S \times S}\| \|x^* - x^{(r)}\|_2 + \|A_S^\top\| \cdot \|e\|_2$$
$$\leq \delta_{3k} \|x^* - x^{(r)}\|_2 + \sqrt{1 + \delta_{3k}} \cdot \|e\|_2.$$

Finally, since $\delta_{3k} < 1$ and $x^{(r+1)} = H_k(x')$ we have by Lemma 7.10 that

$$\|x^{(r+1)} - x^*\|_2 \leq \sqrt{3}\|(x^* - x')_S\|_2 \leq \sqrt{3}\delta_{3k}\|x^{(r)} - x^*\|_2 + \sqrt{6}\|e\|_2. \qquad \square$$

If $\delta_{3k} < 1/\sqrt{3}$, this iteration will eventually converge to $O(\|e\|_2)$. If $\delta_{3k} < \frac{1}{4\sqrt{3}} \approx$ 0.144, we will have

$$\|x^{(r+1)} - x^*\|_2 \leq \max\left(\frac{1}{2}\|x^{(r)} - x^*\|_2, \sqrt{24}\|e\|_2\right)$$

and hence the residual error $\|x^{(r+1)} - x^*\|_2$ will converge geometrically to at most $\sqrt{24}\|e\|_2$:

Theorem 7.12 *If $\delta_{3k} < 0.14$, the output $x^{(R)}$ of* IterativeHardThresholding *will have*

$$\|x^{(R)} - x^*\|_2 \leq \sqrt{24}\|e\|_2$$

after $R = \log_2 \frac{\|x^*\|_2}{\|e\|_2}$ iterations.

Uniformity vs. Nonuniformity. The foregoing argument relies on the fact that RIP works uniformly for *all* sparse vectors, even ones that depend on the matrix A (as the residuals $x^* - x^{(r)}$ do). As a result, the theorem also applies to $y = Ax^* + e$ for every x^* and e. This stands in contrast to the nonuniform randomized guarantee of CountMinSketch: for each matrix A, there are many vectors x that will cause CountMinSketch to violate its ℓ_1 guarantee. For RIP-based algorithms, while the matrix A is typically randomized and as such might fail to satisfy the RIP, as long as A satisfies the RIP the recovery guarantee will hold on every input.

Uniformity is very convenient in proofs because it allows us to ignore any possible dependencies between the error and the measurement matrix. However, some properties cannot be achieved uniformly: the ℓ_2 bound achieved by CountSketch is one (Cohen et al., 2009).

7.4.4 L1 Minimization

Another method for performing compressed sensing from an RIP matrix is L1 minimization, also known as basis pursuit or, in its Lagrangian form, the LASSO. The intuition is that, since the true x^* is k-sparse, one would like to find the *sparsest* vector $\widehat{x}$ that approximately matches the measurements; here we say $\widehat{x}$ "matches" the measurements if $\|y - A\widehat{x}\|_2 \leq R$ for some external estimate R on the noise $\|e\|_2$. However, finding the sparsest $\widehat{x}$ is a hard nonconvex optimization problem, so we settle for minimizing its convex relaxation $\|\widehat{x}\|_1$. Remarkably, and in contrast to minimizing $\|\widehat{x}\|_p$ for $p > 1$, this tends to yield sparse solutions.

Algorithm 4 L1 minimization

1: **function** L1Minimization(y, A, R)
2: $\quad \widehat{x} \leftarrow \arg\min_{\|y - Ax'\|_2 \leq R} \|x'\|_1$
3: $\quad$ **return** $\widehat{x}$
4: **end function**

Theorem 7.13 *There exists a constant $C > 0$ such that the following holds. Let $A \in \mathbb{R}^{m \times n}$ have RIP constant $\delta_{2k} < 0.62$. Then for any k-sparse $x \in \mathbb{R}^n$ and any $e \in \mathbb{R}^m$, and any $R \geq \|e\|_2$, the L1 minimization result $\widehat{x} = \text{L1MINIMIZATION}$ $(Ax + e, A, R)$ satisfies*

$$\|\widehat{x} - x^*\|_2 \leq CR.$$

See Candes et al. (2006), or the presentation in Foucart and Rauhut (2013), for a proof. Up to constant factors, this is essentially the same result as Iterative Hard Thresholding.

7.5 Lower Bound

A linear sparse recovery algorithm consists of a distribution on random matrices $A \in \mathbb{R}^{m \times n}$ and an algorithm for recovering $\widehat{x}$ from A and $y = Ax$. In the preceding sections we have given various such algorithms that achieve various guarantees, the weakest of which is the ℓ_1/ℓ_1 guarantee:

$$\|\widehat{x} - x\|_1 \leq O(1) \cdot \|x - H_k(x)\|_1.$$

Both COUNTMINSKETCH and COUNTSKETCH achieved this with $O(k \log n)$ linear measurements, and ITERATIVEHARDTHRESHOLDING and L1MINIMIZATION achieve this with $O(k \log \frac{n}{k})$ Gaussian linear measurements; for $k < n^{0.99}$, the two bounds are equivalent. We now show that this many measurements are necessary for any linear sketching algorithm.

Theorem 7.14 (Do Ba et al., 2010) *Any ℓ_1/ℓ_1 linear sparse recovery algorithm with constant approximation factor and constant success probability requires $\Omega(k \log \frac{n}{k})$ linear measurements.*

Proof Sketch The proof is based on communication complexity. Roughly speaking, we will produce a distribution on x that contains a lot of information, then show how to extract that information from Ax using the ℓ_1/ℓ_1 sparse recovery algorithm. This implies Ax also contains a lot of information, so m must be fairly large.

We pick a large "codebook" $T \subseteq \{0, 1\}^n$ of k-sparse binary vectors of minimum Hamming distance $k/2$. One can construct such a T of size $2^{\Omega(k \log \frac{n}{k})}$ using a greedy construction (see Exercise 7.6).

Now, suppose we have an algorithm that can perform ℓ_1/ℓ_1 sparse recovery with approximation factor C. Set $R = \Theta(\log n)$, and for any $x_1, x_2, \ldots, x_R \in T$ take

$$x = x_1 + \varepsilon x_2 + \varepsilon^2 x_3 + \cdots + \varepsilon^R x_R$$

for $\varepsilon = \frac{1}{4C+6}$ a small constant. The idea of the proof is the following: given $y = Ax$, we can recover $\widehat{x}$ such that

$$\|\widehat{x} - x_1\|_1 \leq \|x - x_1\|_1 + \|\widehat{x} - x\|_1 \leq (C + 1)\|x - x_1\|_1$$
$$\leq (C + 1)k \frac{\varepsilon}{1 - \varepsilon} < k/4$$

and so, because T has minimum distance $k/2$, we can exactly recover x_1 by rounding $\widehat{x}$ to the nearest element of T. But then we can repeat the process on $\frac{1}{\varepsilon}(Ax - Ax_1)$ to find x_2, then x_3, up to x_R, for $R \lg |T| = \Omega(Rk \log(n/k))$ bits total. Thus Ax must contain this many bits; but if the entries of A are rational numbers with poly(n) bounded numerators and denominators, then each entry of Ax can be described in $O(R + \log n)$ bits, so

$$m \cdot O(R + \log n) \geq \Omega(Rk \log(n/k))$$

or $m \geq \Omega(k \log(n/k))$.

There are two issues that make the aforementioned outline not totally satisfactory, which we only briefly address how to resolve here. First, the theorem statement makes no supposition on the entries of A being polynomially bounded. To resolve this, we perturb x with a tiny (polynomially small) amount of additive Gaussian noise, after which discretizing Ax at an even tinier (but still polynomial) precision has negligible effect on the failure probability. The second issue is that the above outline requires the algorithm to recover all R vectors, so it applies only if the algorithm succeeds with $1 - 1/\log n$ probability rather than constant probability. This is resolved by using a reduction from the communication complexity of the *augmented indexing* problem. $\qquad \square$

7.6 Different Measurement Models

7.6.1 A Hybrid Result: The RIP-1 and Sparse Matrices

Sparse matrices are much more convenient to store and manipulate than dense ones. Unfortunately, sparse matrices cannot satisfy the standard RIP (see Exercise 7.3). However, they can satisfy an ℓ_1 version of it:

Definition 7.15 For any k, the RIP-1 constant $\delta_k^{(1)}$ of a matrix $A \in \mathbb{R}^{m \times n}$ is the smallest $\delta \geq 0$ such that

$$(1 - \delta)\|x\|_1 \leq \frac{1}{d}\|Ax\|_1 \leq \|x\|_1 \qquad \text{for all } k\text{-sparse } x$$

for some scale factor d.

We (informally) say that A satisfies the RIP-1 if $\delta_{Ck}^{(1)} < c$ for some sufficiently good constants $C \geq 1$, $c < 1$. The definition of the RIP-1 differs from the standard RIP in that it uses the ℓ_1 norm and that it includes a scale factor d. The scale factor is convenient, because the prototypical RIP-1 matrix is the adjacency matrix of an *unbalanced bipartite expander graph*:

Definition 7.16 A (k, ε) unbalanced bipartite expander is a bipartite graph $G = (A, B, E)$ with left degree d such that, for any set $S \subseteq A$ of vertices on the left with size $|S| \leq k$, the neighborhood $N(S) \subseteq B$ has size $|N(S)| \geq (1 - \varepsilon)d|S|$.

A random bipartite graph of left degree $d = \Theta(\log n)$, n right vertices, and $m = \Theta(\frac{1}{\varepsilon^2}k \log n)$ left vertices is an expander with high probability. There also exist explicit constructions, albeit with slightly worse parameters. Bipartite expansion is closely connected to the RIP-1:

Lemma 7.17 (Berinde et al., 2008a) *A binary matrix $A \in \{0,1\}^{m \times n}$ with d ones per column has RIP-1 constant $\delta_k^{(1)} < \varepsilon$ if and only if it is the adjacency matrix of a $(k, \Theta(\varepsilon))$-bipartite expander.*

Just like with the standard RIP, sparse recovery from RIP-1 matrices is possible through either linear programming or iterative methods. One such iterative method is SPARSEMATCHINGPURSUIT (Berinde et al., 2008b), shown in Algorithm 5.

Algorithm 5 Sparse Matching Pursuit (SMP)

1: **function** SPARSEMATCHINGPURSUIT(y, A, k)
2:    $x^{(0)} \leftarrow 0$
3:    **for** $r \leftarrow 0, 1, 2, \ldots, R-1$ **do**
4:       $u_i \leftarrow \text{median}_{A_{ji}=1}(y - Ax^{(r)})_j \quad \forall i \in [n]$
5:       $x^{(r+1)} \leftarrow H_k\left(x^{(r)} + H_{2k}(u)\right)$
6:    **end for**
7:    **return** $x^{(R)}$
8: **end function**

Theorem 7.18 *Let $A \in \mathbb{R}^{m \times n}$ be a binary matrix with RIP-1 constant $\delta_{Ck}^{(1)} < c$ for sufficiently large constant C and small constant c. Then for any $x \in \mathbb{R}^n$, the result $\widehat{x}$ of either SMP or L1 minimization has*

$$\|\widehat{x} - x\| \leq O(1) \cdot \|x - H_k(x)\|_1.$$

The SPARSEMATCHINGPURSUIT algorithm is very similar to ITERATIVEHARD THRESHOLDING. In fact, if the H_{2k} threshold were removed and the median replaced by a mean, the algorithm would be identical to ITERATIVEHARDTHRESHOLDING on $A/\sqrt{d}$ for d-regular graphs A. It seems plausible that ITERATIVEHARDTHRESHOLDING also works in this setting, but we are not aware of such a result.

Alternatively, one can view SPARSEMATCHINGPURSUIT as an iterative version of COUNTMEDIANSKETCH. If the random hash functions used in COUNTMEDIAN SKETCH were fully independent, not just pairwise independent, then the associated matrix A would be a near-optimal RIP-1 matrix with high probability. Furthermore, the first iterate $x^{(1)}$ of SPARSEMATCHINGPURSUIT is identical to the (thresholded to top k) result of COUNTMEDIANSKETCH, which achieves the ℓ_1/ℓ_1 result with high probability for each x. By iteratively refining the estimates, SPARSEMATCHINGPURSUIT can achieve the ℓ_1/ℓ_1 result uniformly for all x.

Relative to algorithms previously considered in this chapter, the RIP-1 algorithm combines the uniform guarantees of RIP-based algorithms with the sparse matrices and fast algorithms of COUNTMIN and COUNTSKETCH. The downside is that the Theorem 7.18 recovery guarantee is weaker than all the others: it depends on the ℓ_1 not the ℓ_2 norm of the tail, and only bounds the ℓ_1 not the ℓ_2 or ℓ_∞ error of the result.

7.6.2 Fourier Measurements

An important subclass of linear measurements is that of *Fourier measurements*, where A consists of rows of a Fourier matrix. In this section we will focus on the unidimensional discrete Fourier matrix $F \in \mathbb{C}^{n \times n}$ given by

$$F_{ij} = \frac{1}{\sqrt{n}} e^{2\pi \mathrm{i} ij/n},$$

although similar results exist for other Fourier-related matrices such as Hadamard or multidimensional discrete Fourier matrices. In this context, we consider the measurement matrix $A = F_\Omega$ that consists of a subset $\Omega \subset [n]$ of rows of the discrete Fourier matrix. The goal is to find conditions on Ω and algorithms under which sparse recovery is possible and efficient.

This problem is of interest to both the streaming and compressed sensing communities, but as with previous sections of this chapter there are differences in emphasis.

Compressed Sensing. The main compressed sensing motivation for Fourier measurements is that physical processes such as MRIs, radio astronomy, and wireless communication naturally yield Fourier measurements of the signal. The secondary motivation is that subsampled Fourier matrices make compressed sensing algorithms more efficient: they can be stored in $O(m)$ words rather than the $O(mn)$ required by i.i.d. Gaussian matrices, and the running time for recovery algorithms – being dominated by the cost of multiplying a vector by A or $A^\top$ – becomes $\widetilde{O}(n)$ rather than $\widetilde{O}(mn)$ by using the Fast Fourier Transform (FFT).

Fortunately, subsampled Fourier matrices satisfy the RIP with relatively few rows:

Theorem 7.19 (Haviv and Regev, 2017) *Let $0 < \varepsilon < 1$ and $k > 1$ be parameters. Let $\Omega \subset [n]$ by a random subset of size m. If $m > C\frac{1}{\varepsilon^2} k \log n \log^2 k$ for a sufficiently large constant C, then $\sqrt{\frac{n}{m}} F_\Omega$ satisfies $\delta_k < \varepsilon$ with high probability.*

Therefore, with an extra $O(\log^2 k)$ factor in measurements, standard recovery algorithms such as IterativeHardThresholding and L1Minimization give sparse recovery from Fourier measurements. We do not know if the extra $\log^2 k$ factor relative to Gaussian matrices' $O(k \log(n/k))$ is necessary. For the case of *Hadamard* matrices, the same theorem applies but we do know at least one extra $\log k$ is necessary (Błasiok et al., 2019).

Sublinear Algorithms. The streaming and sublinear algorithms community became interested in sparse recovery with Fourier measurements for a different reason: it gives the prospect of a faster Fourier transform than the FFT, one that can approximate the Fourier transform of a signal in *sublinear* time.

Theorem 7.20 (Hassanieh et al., 2012) *There exists an algorithm to compute $\widehat{x}$ using $O(k \log(n/k) \log(n/\delta))$ time and queries to Fx such that*

$$\|\widehat{x} - x\|_2 \leq 2\|x - H_k(x)\|_2 + \delta \|x\|_2$$

with $9/10$ probability.

One can also optimize the number of queries at the expense of time, down to $O(k \log(n/\delta))$ queries with $O(k \log^{O(1)} n)$ time (Kapralov, 2017).

The basic approach for these results is to try to simulate streaming algorithms like COUNTSKETCH using Fourier measurements. We pick a "filter" $g \in \mathbb{C}^n$ that is sparse in both Fourier ("frequency") domain and regular ("time") domain: Fg is $B = O(k)$-sparse, while g is approximately n/B-sparse. We can use our queries to Fx to compute the sparse result of pointwise multiplication $Fx \cdot Fg$. By the Fourier convolution theorem,

$$F^{-1}(Fx \cdot Fg) = x * g.$$

We can use a B-dimensional inverse FFT on $Fx \cdot Fg$ to quickly compute $(x * g)_j$ at B different positions j. If g is chosen carefully, the result can be shown to behave similarly to the linear observations (7.1) in COUNTSKETCH: we can approximately "hash" the coordinates down to B cells, and observe the sum within each cell.

7.7 Matrix Recovery

A natural extension of sparse recovery is that of *low-rank matrix recovery*. Rather than estimating a k-sparse vector $x \in \mathbb{R}^n$, we consider estimating a rank-k matrix X. For this brief overview, we only consider positive semidefinite matrices $X \in \mathbb{R}^{n \times n}$. Let the eigenspectrum of X be $\lambda = \lambda(X) \in \mathbb{R}^n$, sorted in decreasing order: $\lambda_1 \geq \lambda_2 \geq \cdots \geq \lambda_n \geq 0$. Then X having rank k is equivalent to λ being k-sparse. Low-rank matrix recovery shares much motivation with sparse recovery, since the matrix spectra often do empirically decay. Moreover, the techniques used in sparse recovery often extend to the matrix case. Such techniques include:

Algorithm 6 FREQUENTDIRECTIONS matrix heavy hitters algorithm

---

1: **function** FREQUENTDIRECTIONS(STREAM, k)
2: $\quad \widehat{X} \leftarrow 0 \in \mathbb{R}^{n \times n}$
3: $\quad$ **for** u in STREAM **do**
4: $\quad\quad \widehat{X} \mathrel{+}= uu^\top$
5: $\quad\quad$ **if** $\widehat{X}$ has rank $k + 1$ **then**
6: $\quad\quad\quad$ Compute the eigendecomposition $\widehat{X} = \sum_{i=1}^{k+1} \lambda_i v_i v_i^\top$
7: $\quad\quad\quad$ Set $\widehat{X} \leftarrow \sum_{i=1}^{k} (\lambda_i - \lambda_{k+1}) v_i v_i^\top$
8: $\quad\quad$ **end if**
9: $\quad$ **end for**
10: $\quad$ **return** $\widehat{X}$
11: **end function**

Insertion-Only. Suppose that the matrix X is received as a series of rank one updates, $X = \sum u_i u_i^\top$ for a stream of vectors $u_i \in \mathbb{R}^n$. This setting is much like insertion-only streaming algorithms, and a simple extension of FREQUENTELEMENTS due to Liberty (2013), known as FREQUENTDIRECTIONS, achieves a result analogous to Lemma 7.1. The idea is to keep track of a rank-k approximation $\widehat{X}$ to X (which can be stored in kn space). On any update $u_i u_i^\top$, first the update is added to $\widehat{X}$, then this updated matrix – which could have rank up to $k + 1$ – is "shrunk" back down to rank k by subtracting $s_i := \lambda_{k+1}(\widehat{X})$ from every eigenvalue. As shown in Exercise 7.4, one can prove bounds for this algorithm analogous to the FREQUENTELEMENTS bounds of Lemmas 7.1 and 7.2: both

$$X - \frac{1}{k+1}\|\lambda\|_1 \mathbf{I} \preceq \widehat{X} \preceq X \qquad (7.8)$$

and a sparsity-aware bound

$$X - \frac{2}{k}\|\lambda - H_{k/2}(\lambda)\|_1 \mathbf{I} \preceq \widehat{X} \preceq X. \qquad (7.9)$$

L1 Minimization. The foregoing algorithm relies on "insertion-only"–like updates to X. With more general updates, one would like an algorithm that can reconstruct an estimate of X from linear measurements $\mathcal{A} : \mathbb{R}^{n \times n} \to \mathbb{R}^m$.

The natural analogue of L1 minimization is to minimize the *nuclear norm*, which for positive semidefinite matrices equals the trace:

$$\|\widehat{X}\|_* := \|\lambda(\widehat{X})\|_1 = \mathrm{Tr}(\widehat{X}) = \sum_{i=1}^{n} \lambda_i.$$

This nuclear norm minimization problem

$$\min_{\mathcal{A}(\widehat{X})=y} \|\widehat{X}\|_*$$

is a semidefinite program, and it turns out that this leads to an ℓ_1/ℓ_1 bound for recovery:

$$\|X - \widehat{X}\|_* \leq O(1)\|\lambda - H_k(\lambda)\|_1$$

if $\mathcal{A}$ is a "good" set of observations, as Gaussian linear measurements are w.h.p. once $m \geq O(kn)$.

Note that just as in the vector case, this ℓ_1/ℓ_1 bound from $L1$ minimization is weaker than the ℓ_∞/ℓ_1 achieved by FREQUENTELEMENTS/FREQUENTDIRECTIONS. Unlike the vector case, however, here L1 minimization does not lose an additional $\log(n/k)$ factor in the sample/space complexity.

Streaming Algorithms. Nuclear norm minimization requires solving a semidefinite program, which is polynomial time but still not that efficient. It also uses a dense linear sketch $\mathcal{A}(X)$, which takes $m = O(kn)$ time to update whenever a single entry of X is updated.

One alternative is to store

$$Y = X\Omega \qquad \text{and} \qquad W = \Psi X$$

for random Gaussian matrices $\Omega \in \mathbb{R}^{n \times 2k+1}, \Psi \in \mathbb{R}^{4k+3 \times n}$. These can be updated in $O(k)$ time under single-entry updates to X. Moreover, there is a relatively fast algorithm to compute a good approximation $\widehat{X}$ to X from Y and W: if Y has SVD $Q\Sigma R^\top$ for $Q \in \mathbb{R}^{n \times 2k+1}$,

$$\widehat{X} := Q(\Psi Q)^+ W$$

satisfies

$$\mathbb{E}[\|X - \widehat{X}\|_F^2] \le 4\|\lambda - H_k(\lambda)\|_2^2.$$

This is an ℓ_2/ℓ_2 bound on the eigenvalues of the approximation, which is stronger than the ℓ_1/ℓ_1 bound from L1 minimization (although the latter is a uniform bound).

7.8 Notes

For much more detail on compressed sensing, in both the vector and matrix case, we recommend the book by Foucart and Rauhut (2013). For a survey on sparse recovery from the perspective of streaming algorithms, see Gilbert and Indyk (2010). An empirical study of power-law distributions can be found in Clauset et al. (2009).

Algorithms similar to CountMinSketch or CountSketch but with sublinear recovery time can be found in Cormode and Hadjieleftheriou (2008), Gilbert et al. (2012), and Larsen et al. (2016).

Alternative RIP Matrices. The sample complexity m required for subsampled Fourier matrices to satisfy the RIP has been the focus of a long line of improvements (Candes et al., 2006; Rudelson and Vershynin, 2008; Cheraghchi et al., 2013; Bourgain, 2014; Haviv and Regev, 2017). Partial circulant matrices are another construction of RIP matrices with similar benefits to subsampled Fourier matrices: they use $O(n)$ bits of randomness, they can be multiplied with a vector in $O(n \log n)$ time, and they satisfy the RIP with $O(k \log^c n)$ measurements (Krahmer et al., 2014). The best deterministic construction of RIP matrices uses $m = k^{2-\varepsilon}$ rows for a very small constant $\varepsilon > 0$ Bourgain et al. (2011). The lower bound on sparsity of RIP matrices given in Exercise 7.3 is due to Chandar (2010).

Matrix Recovery. Nuclear norm minimization for low-rank matrix recovery was first shown for exactly low-rank matrices by Recht et al. (2010), and extended to the robust case by Candes and Plan (2011). The streaming algorithm we present is from Tropp et al. (2017), based on Upadhyay (2018) and Clarkson and Woodruff (2009).

References

Berinde, Radu, Gilbert, Anna C, Indyk, Piotr, Karloff, Howard, and Strauss, Martin J. 2008a. Combining geometry and combinatorics: A unified approach to sparse signal recovery. In *2008 46th Annual Allerton Conference on Communication, Control, and Computing*, pp. 798–805. IEEE.

Berinde, Radu, Indyk, Piotr, and Ruzic, Milan. 2008b. Practical near-optimal sparse recovery in the l1 norm. In *2008 46th Annual Allerton Conference on Communication, Control, and Computing*, pp. 198–205. IEEE.

Błasiok, Jarosław, Lopatto, Patrick, Luh, Kyle, and Marcinek, Jake. 2019. An improved lower bound for sparse reconstruction from subsampled Hadamard matrices. In *Foundations of Computer Science*, pp. 1564–1567.

Bourgain, Jean. 2014. An improved estimate in the restricted isometry problem. In *Geometric Aspects of Functional Analysis*, pp. 65–70. Springer.

Bourgain, Jean, Dilworth, Stephen, Ford, Kevin, Konyagin, Sergei, Kutzarova, Denka, et al. 2011. Explicit constructions of RIP matrices and related problems. *Duke Mathematical Journal*, **159**(1), 145–185.

Candes, Emmanuel J, and Plan, Yaniv. 2011. Tight oracle inequalities for low-rank matrix recovery from a minimal number of noisy random measurements. *IEEE Transactions on Information Theory*, **57**(4), 2342–2359.

Candes, Emmanuel J, Romberg, Justin K, and Tao, Terence. 2006. Stable signal recovery from incomplete and inaccurate measurements. *Communications on Pure and Applied Mathematics*, **59**(8), 1207–1223.

Chandar, Venkat Bala. 2010. *Sparse Graph Codes for Compression, Sensing, and Secrecy*. Ph.D. thesis, Massachusetts Institute of Technology.

Charikar, Moses, Chen, Kevin, and Farach-Colton, Martin. 2002. Finding frequent items in data streams. *International Colloquium on Automata, Languages, and Programming*, pp. 693–703. Springer.

Cheraghchi, Mahdi, Guruswami, Venkatesan, and Velingker, Ameya. 2013. Restricted isometry of Fourier matrices and list decodability of random linear codes. *SIAM Journal on Computing*, **42**(5), 1888–1914.

Clarkson, Kenneth L, and Woodruff, David P. 2009. Numerical linear algebra in the streaming model. In *Proceedings of the Forty-First Annual ACM Symposium on Theory of Computing*, pp. 798–805. ACM.

Clauset, Aaron, Shalizi, Cosma Rohilla, and Newman, Mark EJ. 2009. Power-law distributions in empirical data. *SIAM Review*, **51**(4), 661–703.

Cohen, A., Dahmen, W., and DeVore, R. 2009. Compressed sensing and best k-term approximation. *Journal of the American Mathematical Society*, **22**(1), 211–231.

Cormode, Graham, and Hadjieleftheriou, Marios. 2008. Finding frequent items in data streams. *Proceedings of the VLDB Endowment*, **1**(2), 1530–1541.

Cormode, Graham, and Muthukrishnan, Shan. 2005. An improved data stream summary: the count-min sketch and its applications. *Journal of Algorithms*, **55**(1), 58–75.

Do Ba, Khanh, Indyk, Piotr, Price, Eric, and Woodruff, David P. 2010. Lower bounds for sparse recovery. In *Proceedings of the Twenty-First Annual ACM-SIAM Symposium on Discrete Algorithms*, pp. 1190–1197. SIAM.

Donoho, David L, et al. 2006. Compressed sensing. *IEEE Transactions on Information Theory*, **52**(4), 1289–1306.

Foucart, Simon, and Rauhut, Holger. 2013. *A Mathematical Introduction to Compressive Sensing*. Springer.

Ganguly, Sumit. 2008. Lower bounds on frequency estimation of data streams. In *International Computer Science Symposium in Russia*, pp. 204–215. Springer.

Gilbert, Anna, and Indyk, Piotr. 2010. Sparse recovery using sparse matrices. *Proceedings of the IEEE*, **98**(6), 937–947.

Gilbert, Anna C, Li, Yi, Porat, Ely, and Strauss, Martin J. 2012. Approximate sparse recovery: optimizing time and measurements. *SIAM Journal on Computing*, **41**(2), 436–453.

Hassanieh, H., Indyk, P., Katabi, D., and Price, E. 2012. Nearly optimal sparse Fourier transform. In *Proceedings of the 44th Symposium on Theory of Computing Conference*, pp. 563–578.

Haviv, Ishay, and Regev, Oded. 2017. The restricted isometry property of subsampled Fourier matrices. *Geometric Aspects of Functional Analysis*, pp. 163–179. Springer.

Kapralov, Michael. 2017. Sample efficient estimation and recovery in sparse FFT via isolation on average. In *2017 IEEE 58th Annual Symposium on Foundations of Computer Science (FOCS)*, pp. 651–662. IEEE

Krahmer, Felix, Mendelson, Shahar, and Rauhut, Holger. 2014. Suprema of chaos processes and the restricted isometry property. *Communications on Pure and Applied Mathematics*, **67**(11), 1877–1904.

Larsen, Kasper Green, Nelson, Jelani, Nguyên, Huy L, and Thorup, Mikkel. 2016. Heavy hitters via cluster-preserving clustering. In *2016 IEEE 57th Annual Symposium on Foundations of Computer Science (FOCS)*, pp. 61–70. IEEE.

Liberty, Edo. 2013. Simple and deterministic matrix sketching. In *Proceedings of the 19th ACM SIGKDD International Conference on Knowledge Discovery and Data Mining.* ACM.

Misra, Jayadev, and Gries, David. 1982. Finding repeated elements. *Science of Computer Programming,* **2**(2), 143–152.

Recht, Benjamin, Fazel, Maryam, and Parrilo, Pablo A. 2010. Guaranteed minimum-rank solutions of linear matrix equations via nuclear norm minimization. *SIAM Review,* **52**(3), 471–501.

Rudelson, M., and Vershynin, R. 2008. On sparse reconstruction from Fourier and Gaussian measurements. *CPAM,* **61**(8), 1025–1171.

Tropp, Joel A, Yurtsever, Alp, Udell, Madeleine, and Cevher, Volkan. 2017. Practical sketching algorithms for low-rank matrix approximation. *SIAM Journal on Matrix Analysis and Applications,* **38**(4), 1454–1485.

Upadhyay, Jalaj. 2018. The price of privacy for low-rank factorization. *Advances in Neural Information Processing Systems,* pp. 4176–4187.

Exercises

Exercise 7.1 Comparison of COUNTSKETCH and COUNTMINSKETCH guarantees.

(a) For any vector $x \in \mathbb{R}^n$, show that

$$\|x - H_k(x)\|_2 \leq \frac{1}{\sqrt{k}}\|x\|_1.$$

(b) Show that if $\widehat{x}$ is the result of COUNTSKETCH for $k' = 2k$, then

$$\|\widehat{x} - x\|_\infty \leq \frac{1}{k}\|x - H_k(x)\|_1.$$

Compare this bound to the Theorem 7.3 bound for COUNTMINSKETCH.

Exercise 7.2 Premeasurement noise and RIP-based methods.

(a) Show that, if A has RIP constant δ_k,

$$\|A(x - H_k(x))\|_2 \leq \frac{(1 + \delta_k)}{\sqrt{k}}\|x\|_1$$

for any vector $x \in \mathbb{R}^n$.

(b) Show that the result $\widehat{x}$ of L1MINIMIZATION or ITERATIVEHARDTHRESHOLDING from $y = Ax$ satisfies

$$\|\widehat{x} - x\|_2 \leq \frac{O(1)}{\sqrt{k}}\|x - H_k(x)\|_1$$

if A satisfies a sufficiently strong RIP.

(c) Use the Johnson–Lindenstrauss Lemma to show that, if A has i.i.d. Gaussian entries of variance $1/m$, the result $\widehat{x}$ of L1MINIMIZATION or ITERATIVEHARDTHRESHOLDING from $y = Ax$ will satisfy

$$\|\widehat{x} - x\|_2 \leq O(1)\|x - H_k(x)\|_2$$

with $1 - e^{-\Omega(m)}$ probability. Note that this is a *nonuniform* bound. How does it compare to the bound in (b)?

Exercise 7.3 In this problem we show that matrices that satisfy the RIP cannot be very sparse. Let $A \in \mathbb{R}^{m \times n}$ have $\delta_k < 1/2$ for $m < n$. Suppose that the average column sparsity of A is d, i.e., A has nd nonzero entries. Furthermore, suppose that $A \in \{0, \pm\alpha\}^{m \times n}$ for some parameter α.

(a) By looking at the sparsest column, give a bound for α in terms of d.
(b) By looking at the densest row, give a bound for α in terms of n, m, d and k.
(c) Conclude that either $d \geq k/C$ or $m \geq n/C$ for a universal constant C.
(d) [Optional] Extend the result to general settings of the nonzero $A_{i,j}$.

Exercise 7.4 Consider the matrix FREQUENTELEMENTS-like algorithm FREQUENT DIRECTIONS described in Algorithm 6.

(a) Use the potential function $\mathrm{Tr}(\widehat{X})$ to show that $\sum_i s_i \leq \frac{1}{k+1}\|\lambda\|_1$, where s_i is the eigenvalue shrinkage after the ith update. Conclude that FREQUENTELEMENTS achieves (7.8).
(b) Now let Π be the orthogonal projection matrix onto the span of all but the top $k/2$ eigenvectors of X. Using $\mathrm{Tr}(\Pi\widehat{X})$ as a potential function, prove that FREQUENTDIRECTIONS also satisfies the bound (7.9).

Exercise 7.5 Prove Lemma 7.8. Choose T to be a 1/2-cover of the unit ℓ_2 ball $\mathcal{B}$, meaning that $T \subset \mathcal{B}$ and, for every $x \in \mathcal{B}$, there exists an x' in T such that $\|x' - x\|_2 \leq \frac{1}{2}$. (This will give a set T satisfying the lemma of *at most* unit norm elements, but scaling them up to unit norm only makes the result more true.)

Exercise 7.6 Construct the codebook T used in the proof of Theorem 7.14. First construct a code of Hamming distance $k/4$ over $[n/k]^k$, then embed this into $\{0, 1\}^n$.

PART THREE

Semirandom Models

CHAPTER EIGHT

Distributional Analysis

Tim Roughgarden

Abstract: In *distributional* or *average-case analysis*, the goal is to
design an algorithm with good-on-average performance with respect
to a specific probability distribution. Distributional analysis can
be useful for the study of general-purpose algorithms on "non-
pathological" inputs, and for the design of specialized algorithms
in applications where there is detailed understanding of the relevant
input distribution. For some problems, however, pure distributional
analysis encourages "overfitting" an algorithmic solution to a particular distributional assumption and a more robust analysis framework is called for. This chapter presents numerous examples of the
pros and cons of distributional analysis, highlighting some of its
greatest hits while also setting the stage for the hybrids of worst- and
average-case analysis studied in later chapters.

8.1 Introduction

Part One of this book covered refinements of worst-case analysis that do not impose
any assumptions on the possible inputs. Part Two described several deterministic
models of data, where inputs to a problem were restricted to those with properties
that are plausibly shared by all "real-world" inputs. This chapter, and a majority
of the remaining chapters in the book, consider models that include a *probability
distribution* over inputs.

8.1.1 The Pros and Cons of Distributional Analysis

In its purest form, the goal in distributional analysis is to analyze the average
performance of algorithms with respect to a specific input distribution, and perhaps
also to design new algorithms that perform particularly well for this distribution.
What do we hope to gain from such an analysis?

- In applications in which the input distribution is well understood (e.g., because
  of lots of recent and representative data), distributional analysis is well suited
  both to predict the performance of existing algorithms and to design algorithms
  specialized to the input distribution.
- When there is a large gap between the empirical and worst-case performance of
  an algorithm, an input distribution can serve as a metaphor for "nonpathological"

inputs. Even if the input distribution cannot be taken literally, a good average-case bound is a plausibility argument for the algorithm's empirical performance. The three examples in Section 8.2 are in this spirit.

- Optimizing performance with respect to a specific input distribution can lead to new algorithmic ideas that are useful much more broadly. The examples in Sections 8.3 and 8.4 have this flavor.

And what could go wrong?

- Carrying out an average-case analysis of an algorithm might be analytically tractable only for the simplest (and not necessarily realistic) input distributions.
- Optimizing performance with respect to a specific input distribution can lead to "overfitting," meaning algorithmic solutions that are overly reliant on the details of the distributional assumptions and have brittle performance guarantees (which may not hold if the distributional assumptions are violated).
- Pursuing distribution-specific optimizations can distract from the pursuit of more robust and broadly useful algorithmic ideas.

This chapter has two goals. The first is to celebrate a few classical results in the average-case analysis of algorithms, which constitute some of the earliest work on alternatives to worst-case analysis. Our coverage here is far from encyclopedic, with the discussion confined to a sampling of relatively simple results for well-known problems that contribute to the chapter's overarching narrative. The second goal is to examine critically such average-case results, thereby motivating the more robust models of distributional analysis outlined in Section 8.5 and studied in detail later in the book.

8.1.2 An Optimal Stopping Problem

The pros and cons of distributional analysis are evident in a famous example from optimal stopping theory, which is interesting in its own right and also relevant to some of the random-order models described in Chapter 11. Consider a game with n stages. Nonnegative prizes arrive online, with v_i denoting the value of the prize that appears in stage i. At each stage, an algorithm must decide between accepting the current prize (which terminates the game) and proceeding to the next stage after discarding it. This involves a difficult trade-off, between the risk of being too ambitious (and skipping over what turns out to be the highest-value prize) and not ambitious enough (settling for a modest-value prize instead of waiting for a better one).

Suppose we posit specific distributions $D_1, D_2, \ldots, D_n$, known in advance to the algorithm designer, such that the value v_i of the stage-i prize is drawn independently from D_i. (The D_i's may or may not be identical.) An algorithm learns the realization v_i of a prize value only at stage i. We can then speak about an *optimal* algorithm for the problem, meaning an online algorithm that achieves the maximum-possible expected prize value, where the expectation is with respect to the assumed distributions $D_1, D_2, \ldots, D_n$.

The optimal algorithm for a given sequence of prize value distributions is easy enough to specify, by working backward in time. If an algorithm finds itself at stage n without having accepted a prize, it should definitely accept the final prize. (Recall all prizes have nonnegative values.) At an earlier stage i, the algorithm should accept the stage-i prize if and only if v_i is at least the expected prize value obtained by the (inductively defined) optimal strategy for stages $i + 1, i + 2, \ldots, n$.

8.1.3 Discussion

The solution above illustrates the primary advantages of distributional analysis: an unequivocal definition of an "optimal" algorithm, and the possibility of a crisp characterization of such an algorithm (as a function of the input distributions).

The disadvantages of average-case analysis are also on display, and there are several reasons why one might reject this optimal algorithm.

1. The algorithm takes the distributional assumptions literally and its description depends in a detailed way on the assumed distributions. It is unclear how robust the optimality guarantee is to misspecifications of these distributions, or to a reordering of the distributions.
2. The algorithm is relatively complicated, in that it is defined by n different parameters (one threshold for each stage).
3. The algorithm does not provide any qualitative advice about how to tackle similar problems (other than "work backwards").

The third point is particularly relevant when studying a problem chosen as a deliberate simplification of a "real-world" problem that is too messy to analyze directly. In this case, an optimal solution to the simpler problem is useful only inasmuch as it suggests a plausibly effective solution to the more general problem.

For our optimal stopping problem, could there be nontrivial guarantees for simpler, more intuitive, and more robust algorithms?

8.1.4 Threshold Rules and the Prophet Inequality

Returning to the optimal stopping problem of Section 8.1.2, a *threshold stopping rule* is defined by a single parameter, a threshold t. The corresponding online algorithm accepts the first prize i with value satisfying $v_i \geq t$ (if any). Such a rule is clearly suboptimal, as it doesn't even necessarily accept the prize at stage n. Nevertheless, the following *prophet inequality* proves that there is a threshold strategy with an intuitive threshold that performs approximately as well as a fully clairvoyant prophet.[1]

Theorem 8.1 (Samuel-Cahn, 1984) *For every sequence* $\mathbf{D} = D_1, D_2, \ldots, D_n$ *of independent prize value distributions, there is a threshold rule that guarantees expected reward at least* $\frac{1}{2}\mathbf{E}_{\mathbf{v} \sim \mathbf{D}}[\max_i v_i]$, *where* $\mathbf{v}$ *denotes* $(v_1, \ldots, v_n)$.

This guarantee holds, in particular, for the threshold t at which there is a 50/50 chance that the rule accepts one of the n prizes.

Proof Let z^+ denote $\max\{z, 0\}$. Consider a threshold strategy with threshold t (to be chosen later). The plan is to prove a lower bound on the expected value

---

[1] See Chapter 11 for an analogous result for a related problem, the *secretary problem*.

of this strategy and an upper bound on the expected value of a prophet such that the two bounds are easy to compare.

What value does the t-threshold strategy obtain? Let $q(t)$ denote the probability of the failure mode in which the threshold strategy accepts no prize at all; in this case, it obtains zero value. With the remaining probability $1 - q(t)$, the rule obtains value at least t. To improve this lower bound, consider the case where exactly one prize i satisfies $v_i \geq t$; then, the rule also gets "extra credit" of $v_i - t$ above and beyond its baseline value of t.[2]

Formally, we can bound the expected value obtained by the t-threshold strategy from below by

$$(1 - q(t)) \cdot t$$

$$+ \sum_{i=1}^{n} \mathbf{E_v}\big[v_i - t \mid v_i \geq t, v_j < t \,\forall j \neq i\big] \cdot \mathbf{Pr}[v_i \geq t] \cdot \mathbf{Pr}\big[v_j < t \,\forall j \neq i\big] \quad (8.1)$$

$$= (1 - q(t)) \cdot t + \sum_{i=1}^{n} \underbrace{\mathbf{E_v}[v_i - t \mid v_i \geq t] \cdot \mathbf{Pr}[v_i \geq t]}_{=\mathbf{E_v}[(v_i - t)^+]} \cdot \underbrace{\mathbf{Pr}\big[v_j < t \,\forall j \neq i\big]}_{\geq q(t)} \quad (8.2)$$

$$\geq (1 - q(t)) \cdot t + q(t) \sum_{i=1}^{n} \mathbf{E_v}\big[(v_i - t)^+\big], \quad (8.3)$$

where we use the independence of the D_i's in (8.1) to factor the two probability terms and in (8.2) to drop the conditioning on the event that $v_j < t$ for every $j \neq i$. In (8.3), we use that $q(t) = \mathbf{Pr}\big[v_j < t \,\forall j\big] \leq \mathbf{Pr}\big[v_j < t \,\forall j \neq i\big]$.

Now we produce an upper bound on the prophet's expected value $\mathbf{E_{v \sim D}}[\max_i v_i]$ that is easy to compare to (8.3). The expression $\mathbf{E_v}[\max_i v_i]$ doesn't reference the strategy's threshold t, so we add and subtract it to derive

$$\mathbf{E_v}\Big[\overset{n}{\underset{i=1}{\max}} \, v_i\Big] = \mathbf{E_v}\Big[t + \overset{n}{\underset{i=1}{\max}}(v_i - t)\Big]$$

$$\leq t + \mathbf{E_v}\Big[\overset{n}{\underset{i=1}{\max}}(v_i - t)^+\Big]$$

$$\leq t + \sum_{i=1}^{n} \mathbf{E_v}\big[(v_i - t)^+\big]. \quad (8.4)$$

Comparing (8.3) and (8.4), we can complete the proof by setting t so that $q(t) = \frac{1}{2}$, with a 50/50 chance of accepting a prize.[3] $\square$

The drawback of this threshold rule relative to the optimal online algorithm is clear: it does not guarantee as much expected value. Nonetheless, this solution possesses several attractive properties that are not satisfied by the optimal algorithm:

---

[2] The difficulty when two prizes i and j exceed the threshold is that this extra credit is either $v_i - t$ or $v_j - t$ (whichever appeared earlier). The proof avoids reasoning about the ordering of the distributions by crediting the rule only with the baseline value of t in this case.

[3] If there is no such t because of point masses in the D_i's, then a minor extension of the argument yields the same result (Exercise 8.1).

1. The threshold rule recommended by Theorem 8.1 depends on the prize value distributions $D_1, D_2, \ldots, D_n$ only inasmuch as it depends on the number t for which there is a 50/50 probability that at least one realized value exceeds t. For example, reordering the distributions arbitrarily does not change the recommended threshold rule.
2. A threshold rule is simple in that it is defined by only one parameter. Intuitively, a single-parameter rule is less prone to "overfitting" to the assumed distributions than a more highly parameterized algorithm like the (n-parameter) optimal algorithm.[4]
3. Theorem 8.1 gives flexible qualitative advice about how to approach such problems: Start with threshold rules, and don't be too risk-averse (i.e., choose an ambitious enough threshold that receiving no prize is a distinct possibility).

8.2 Average-Case Justifications of Classical Algorithms

Distributional assumptions can guide the design of algorithms, as with the optimal stopping problem introduced in Section 8.1.2. Distributional analysis can also be used to analyze a general-purpose algorithm, with the goal of explaining mathematically why its empirical performance is much better than its worst-case performance. In these applications, the assumed probability distribution over inputs should not be taken literally; rather, it serves as a metaphor for "real-world" or "non-pathological" inputs. This section gives the flavor of work along these lines by describing one result for each of three classical problems: sorting, hashing, and bin packing.

8.2.1 QuickSort

Recall the QUICKSORT algorithm from undergraduate algorithms which, given an array of n elements from a totally ordered set, works as follows:

- Designate one the n array entries as a "pivot" element.
- Partition the input array around the pivot element p, meaning rearrange the array entries so that all entries less than p appear before p in the array and all entries greater than p appear after p in the array.
- Recursively sort the subarray comprising the elements less than p.
- Recursively sort the subarray comprising the elements greater than p.

The second step of the algorithm is easy to implement in $\Theta(n)$ time. There are many ways to choose the pivot element, and the running time of the algorithm varies between $\Theta(n \log n)$ and $\Theta(n^2)$, depending on these choices.[5] One way to enforce the best-case scenario is to explicitly compute the median element and use it as the pivot. A simpler and more practical solution is to choose the pivot element uniformly at random; most of the time, it will be close enough to the median that

---

[4] See Chapter 29 on data-driven algorithm design for a formalization of this intuition.

[5] In the best-case scenario, every pivot element is the median element of the subarray, leading to the recurrence $T(n) = 2T(\frac{n}{2}) + \Theta(n)$ with solution $\Theta(n \log n)$. In the worst-case scenario, every pivot element is the minimum or maximum element of the subarray, leading to the recurrence $T(n) = T(n-1) + \Theta(n)$ with solution $\Theta(n^2)$.

both recursive calls are on significantly smaller inputs. A still simpler solution, which is common in practice, is to always use the first array element as the pivot element. This deterministic version of QUICKSORT runs in $\Theta(n^2)$ time on already sorted arrays, but empirically its running time is $\Theta(n \log n)$ on almost all other inputs. One way to formalize this observation is to analyze the algorithm's expected running time on a random input. As a comparison-based sorting algorithm, the running time of QUICKSORT depends only on the relative order of the array entries, so we can assume without loss of generality that the input is a permutation of $\{1, 2, \ldots, n\}$ and identify a "random input" with a random permutation. With any of the standard implementations of the partitioning subroutine, the average-case running time of this deterministic QUICKSORT algorithm is at most a constant factor larger than its best-case running time.

Theorem 8.2 (Hoare, 1962) *The expected running time of the deterministic QuickSort algorithm on a random permutation of $\{1, 2, \ldots, n\}$ is $O(n \log n)$.*

Proof We sketch one of the standard proofs. Assume that the partitioning subroutine only makes comparisons that involve the pivot element; this is the case for all of the textbook implementations. Each recursive call is given a subarray consisting of the elements from some interval $\{i, i+1, \ldots, j\}$; conditioned on this interval, the relative order of its elements in the subarray is uniformly random.

Fix elements i and j with $i < j$. These elements are passed to the same sequence of recursive calls (along with $i + 1, i + 2, \ldots, j - 1$), up to the first call in which an element from $\{i, i+1, \ldots, j\}$ is chosen as a pivot element. At this point, i and j are either compared to each other (if i or j was the chosen pivot) or not (otherwise); in any case, they are never compared to each other again in the future. With all subarray orderings equally likely, the probability that i and j are compared is exactly $\frac{2}{j-i+1}$. By the linearity of expectation, the expected total number of comparisons is then $\sum_{i=1}^{n-1} \sum_{j=i+1}^{n} \frac{2}{j-i+1} = O(n \log n)$, and the expected running time of the algorithm is at most a constant factor larger. □

8.2.2 Linear Probing

A hash table is a data structure that supports fast insertions and lookups. Under the hood, most hash table implementations maintain an array A of some length n and use a hash function h to map each inserted object x to an array entry $h(x) \in \{1, 2, \ldots, n\}$. A fundamental issue in hash table design is how to resolve collisions, meaning pairs x, y of distinct inserted objects for which $h(x) = h(y)$. *Linear probing* is a specific way of resolving collisions:

1. Initially, all entries of A are empty.
2. Store a newly inserted object x in the first empty entry in the sequence $A[h(x)]$, $A[h(x) + 1], A[h(x) + 2], \ldots$, wrapping around to the beginning of the array, if necessary.
3. To search for an object x, scan the entries $A[h(x)], A[h(x) + 1], A[h(x) + 2], \ldots$ until encountering x (a successful search) or an empty slot (an unsuccessful search), wrapping around to the beginning of the array, if necessary.

That is, the hash function indicates the starting position for an insertion or lookup operation, and the operation scans to the right until it finds the desired object or an empty position. The running time of an insertion or lookup operation is proportional to the length of this scan.

The bigger the fraction α of the hash table that is occupied (called its *load*), the fewer empty array entries and the longer the scans. To get calibrated, imagine searching for an empty array entry using independent and uniformly random probes. The number of attempts until a success is then a geometric random variable with success probability $1-\alpha$, which has expected value $\frac{1}{1-\alpha}$. With linear probing, however, objects tend to clump together in consecutive slots, resulting in slower operation times. How much slower?

Nontrivial mathematical guarantees for hash tables are possible only under assumptions that rule out data sets that are pathologically correlated with the table's hash function; for this reason, hash tables have long constituted one of the killer applications of average-case analysis. Common assumptions include asserting some amount of randomness in the data (as in average-case analysis), in the choice of hash function (as in randomized algorithms), or both (as in Chapter 26). For example, assuming that the data and hash function are such that every hash value $h(x)$ is an independent and uniform draw from $\{1, 2, \ldots, n\}$, the expected time of insertions and lookups scales with $\frac{1}{(1-\alpha)^2}$.[6]

8.2.3 Bin Packing

The *bin packing* problem played a central role in the early development of the average-case analysis of algorithms; this section presents one representative result.[7] Here, the average-case analysis is of the solution quality output by a heuristic (as with the prophet inequality), not its running time (unlike our QUICKSORT and linear probing examples).

In the bin packing problem, the input is n items with sizes $s_1, s_2, \ldots, s_n \in [0, 1]$. Feasible solutions correspond to ways of partitioning the items into bins so that the sum of the sizes in each bin is at most 1. The objective is to minimize the number of bins used. This problem is *NP*-hard, so every polynomial-time algorithm produces suboptimal solutions in some cases (assuming $P \neq NP$).

Many practical bin packing heuristics have been studied extensively from both worst-case and average-case viewpoints. One example is the *first-fit decreasing* (FFD) algorithm:

- Sort and reindex the items so that $s_1 \geq s_2 \geq \cdots s_n$.
- For $i = 1, 2, \ldots, n$:
  - If there is an existing bin with room for item i (i.e., with current total size at most $1 - s_i$), add i to the first such bin.
  - Otherwise, start a new bin and add i to it.

---

[6] This result played an important role in the genesis of the mathematical analysis of algorithms. Donald E. Knuth, its discoverer, wrote: "I first formulated the following derivation in 1962...Ever since that day, the analysis of algorithms has in fact been one of the major themes in my life."

[7] See Chapter 11 for an analysis of bin packing heuristics in random-order models.

For example, consider an input consisting of 6 items with size $\frac{1}{2} + \epsilon$, 6 items with size $\frac{1}{4} + 2\epsilon$, 6 jobs with size $\frac{1}{4} + \epsilon$, and 12 items with size $\frac{1}{4} - 2\epsilon$. The FFD algorithm uses 11 bins while an optimal solution packs them perfectly into 9 bins (Exercise 8.3). Duplicating this set of 30 jobs as many times as necessary shows that there are arbitrarily large inputs for which the FFD algorithm uses $\frac{11}{9}$ times as many bins as an optimal solution. Conversely, the FFD algorithm never uses more than $\frac{11}{9}$ times the minimum-possible number of bins plus an additive constant (see the Notes for details).

The factor of $\frac{11}{9} \approx 1.22$ is quite good as worst-case approximation ratios go, but empirically the FFD algorithm usually produces a solution that is extremely close to optimal. One approach to better theoretical bounds is distributional analysis. For bin-packing algorithms, the natural starting point is the case where item sizes are independent draws from the uniform distribution on $[0, 1]$. Under this (strong) assumption, the FFD algorithm is near-optimal in a strong sense.

Theorem 8.3 (Frederickson, 1980) *For every $\epsilon > 0$, for n items with sizes distributed independently and uniformly in $[0, 1]$, with probability $1 - o(1)$ as $n \to \infty$, the FFD algorithm uses less than $(1 + \epsilon)$ times as many bins as an optimal solution.*

In other words, the typical approximation ratio of the FFD algorithm tends to 1 as the input size grows large.

We outline a two-step proof of Theorem 8.3. The first step shows that the guarantee holds for a less natural algorithm that we call the *truncate and match* (TM) algorithm. The second step shows that the FFD algorithm never uses more bins than the TM algorithm.

The truncate and match algorithm works as follows:

- Pack every item with size at least $1 - \frac{2}{n^{1/4}}$ in its own bin.[8]
- Sort and reindex the remaining k items so that $s_1 \geq s_2 \geq \cdots \geq s_k$. (Assume for simplicity that k is even.)
- For each $i = 1, \ldots, k/2$, put items i and $k - i + 1$ into a common bin if possible; otherwise, put them in separate bins.

To explain the intuition behind the TM algorithm, consider the expected order statistics (i.e., expected minimum, expected second-minimum, etc.) of n independent samples from the uniform distribution on $[0, 1]$. It can be shown that these split $[0, 1]$ evenly into $n + 1$ subintervals; the expected minimum is $\frac{1}{n+1}$, the expected second-minimum $\frac{2}{n+1}$, and so on. Thus at least in an expected sense, the first and last items together should fill up a bin exactly, as should the second and second-to-last items, and so on. Moreover, as n grows large, the difference between the realized order statistics and their expectations should become small. Setting aside a small number of the largest items in the first step then corrects for any (small) deviations from these expectations with negligible additional cost. See Exercise 8.4 for details.

We leave the second step of the proof of Theorem 8.3 as Exercise 8.5.

---

[8] For clarity, we omit ceilings and floors. See Exercise 8.4 for the motivation behind this size cutoff.

Lemma 8.4 *For every bin packing input, the FFD algorithm uses at most as many bins as the TM algorithm.*

The description of the general-purpose FFD algorithm is not tailored to a distributional assumption, but the proof of Theorem 8.3 is fairly specific to uniform-type distributions. This is emblematic of one of the drawbacks of average-case analysis: Often, it is analytically tractable only under quite specific distributional assumptions.

8.3 Good-on-Average Algorithms for Euclidean Problems

Another classical application domain for average-case analysis is in computational geometry, with the input comprising random points from some subset of Euclidean space. We highlight two representative results for fundamental problems in two dimensions, one concerning the running time of an always-correct convex hull algorithm and one about the solution quality of an efficient heuristic for the *NP*-hard Traveling Salesman Problem.

8.3.1 2D Convex Hull

A typical textbook on computational geometry begins with the *2D convex hull* problem. The input consists of a set S of n points in the plane (in the unit square $[0, 1] \times [0, 1]$, say) and the goal is to report, in sorted order, the points of S that lie on the convex hull of S.[9] There are several algorithms that solve the 2D convex hull problem in $\Theta(n \log n)$ time. Can we do better – perhaps even linear time – when the points are drawn from a distribution, such as the uniform distribution on the square?

Theorem 8.5 (Bentley and Shamos, 1978) *There is an algorithm that solves the 2D convex hull problem in expected $O(n)$ time for n points drawn independently and uniformly from the unit square.*

The algorithm is a simple divide-and-conquer algorithm. Given points $S = \{p_1, p_2, \ldots, p_n\}$ drawn independently and uniformly from the plane:

- If the input S contains at most five points, compute the convex hull by brute force. Return the points of S on the convex hull, sorted by their x-coordinates.
- Otherwise, let $S_1 = \{p_1, \ldots, p_{n/2}\}$ and $S_2 = \{p_{(n/2)+1}, \ldots, p_n\}$ denote the first and second halves of S. (Assume for simplicity that n is even.)
- Recursively compute the convex hull C_1 of S_1, with its points sorted by their x-coordinates.
- Recursively compute the convex hull C_2 of S_2, with its points sorted by their x-coordinates.
- Merge C_1 and C_2 into the convex hull C of S. Return C, with the points of C sorted by their x-coordinates.

---

[9] Recall that the *convex hull* of a set of points is the smallest convex set containing them, or equivalently the set of all convex combinations of points from S. In two dimensions, imagine the points as nails in a board, and the convex hull as a taut rubber band that encloses them.

For every set S and partition of S into S_1 and S_2, every point on the convex hull of S is on the convex hull of either S_1 or S_2. Correctness of the algorithm follows immediately. The last step is easy to implement in time linear in $|C_1| + |C_2|$; see Exercise 8.6. Because the subproblems S_1 and S_2 are themselves uniformly random points from the unit square (with the sorting occurring only after the recursive computation completes), the expected running time of the algorithm is governed by the recurrence

$$T(n) \leq 2 \cdot T(\tfrac{n}{2}) + O(\mathbf{E}[|C_1| + |C_2|]).$$

Theorem 8.5 follows immediately from this recurrence and the following combinatorial bound.

Lemma 8.6 (Rényi and Sulanke, 1963) *The expected size of the convex hull of n points drawn independently and uniformly from the unit square is $O(\log n)$.*

Proof Imagine drawing the input points in two phases, with $\frac{n}{2}$ points S_i drawn in phase i for $i = 1, 2$. An elementary argument shows that the convex hull of the points in S_1 occupies, in expectation, at least a $1 - O(\frac{\log n}{n})$ fraction of the unit square (Exercise 8.7). Each point of the second phase thus lies in the interior of the convex hull of S_1 (and hence of $S_1 \cup S_2$) except with probability $O(\frac{\log n}{n})$, so the expected number of points from S_2 on the convex hull of $S_1 \cup S_2$ is $O(\log n)$. By symmetry, the same is true of S_1. $\square$

8.3.2 The Traveling Salesman Problem in the Plane

In the *Traveling Salesman Problem* (TSP), the input consists of n points and distances between them, and the goal is to compute a tour of the points (visiting each point once and returning to the starting point) with the minimum-possible total length. In *Euclidean* TSP, the points lie in Euclidean space and all distances are straight-line distances. This problem is *NP*-hard, even in two dimensions. The main result of this section is analogous to Theorem 8.3 in Section 8.2.3 for the bin packing problem— a polynomial-time algorithm that, when the input points are drawn independently and uniformly from the unit square, has approximation ratio tending to 1 (with high probability) as n tends to infinity.

The algorithm, which we call the *Stitch* algorithm, works as follows:

- Divide the unit square evenly into $s = \frac{n}{\ln n}$ subsquares, each with side length $\sqrt{(\ln n)/n}$.[10]
- For each subsquare $i = 1, 2, \ldots, s$, containing the points P_i:
  - If $|P_i| \leq 6\log_2 n$, compute the optimal tour T_i of P_i using dynamic programming.[11]
  - Otherwise, return an arbitrary tour T_i of P_i.

---

[10] Again, we ignore ceilings and floors.

[11] Given k points, label them $\{1, 2, \ldots, k\}$. There is one subproblem for each subset S of points and point $j \in S$, whose solution is the minimum-length path that starts at the point 1, ends at the point j, and visits every point of S exactly once. Each of the $O(k2^k)$ subproblems can be solved in $O(k)$ time by trying all possibilities for the final hop of the optimal path. When $k = O(\log n)$, this running time of $O(k^2 2^k)$ is polynomial in n.

- Choose an arbitrary representative point from each nonempty set P_i, and let R denote the set of representatives.
- Construct a tour T_0 of R by visiting points from left-to-right in the bottommost row of subsquares, right to left in the second to bottom row, and so on, returning to the starting point after visiting all the points in the topmost row.
- Shortcut the union of the subtours $\cup_{i=0}^{s} T_i$ to a single tour T of all n points, and return T.[12]

This algorithm runs in polynomial time with probability 1 and returns a tour of the input points. As for the approximation guarantee:

Theorem 8.7 (Karp, 1977) *For every $\epsilon > 0$, for n points distributed independently and uniformly in the unit square, with probability $1 - o(1)$ as $n \to \infty$, the Stitch algorithm returns a tour with total length less than $(1 + \epsilon)$ times that of an optimal tour.*

Proving Theorem 8.7 requires understanding the typical length of an optimal tour of random points in the unit square and then bounding from above the difference between the lengths of the tour returned by the Stitch algorithm and of the optimal tour. The first step is not difficult (Exercise 8.8).

Lemma 8.8 *There is a constant $c_1 > 0$ such that, with probability $1 - o(1)$ as $n \to \infty$, the length of an optimal tour of n points drawn independently and uniformly from the unit square is at least $c_1 \sqrt{n}$.*

Lemma 8.8 implies that proving Theorem 8.7 reduces to showing that (with high probability) the difference between the lengths of Stitch's tour and the optimal tour is $o(\sqrt{n})$.

For the second step, we start with a simple consequence of the Chernoff bound (see Exercise 8.9).

Lemma 8.9 *In the Stitch algorithm, with probability $1 - o(1)$ as $n \to \infty$, every subsquare contains at most $6 \log_2 n$ points.*

It is also easy to bound the length of the tour T_0 of the representative points R in the Stitch algorithm (see Exercise 8.10).

Lemma 8.10 *There is a constant c_2 such that, for every input, the length of the tour T_0 in the Stitch algorithm is at most*

$$c_2 \cdot \sqrt{s} = c_2 \cdot \sqrt{\frac{n}{\ln n}}.$$

---

[12] The union of the $s + 1$ subtours can be viewed as a connected Eulerian graph, which then admits a closed Eulerian walk (using every edge of the graph exactly once). This walk can be transformed to a tour of the points with only smaller length by skipping repeated visits to a point.

The key lemma states that an optimal tour can be massaged into subtours for all of the subsquares without much additional cost.

Lemma 8.11 *Let T^* denote an optimal tour of the n input points, and let L_i denote the length of the portion of T^* that lies within the subsquare $i \in \{1, 2, \ldots, s\}$ defined by the Stitch algorithm. For every subsquare $i = 1, 2, \ldots, s$, there exists a tour of the points P_i in the subsquare of length at most*

$$L_i + 6\sqrt{\frac{\ln n}{n}}. \tag{8.5}$$

The key point in Lemma 8.11 is that the upper bound in (8.5) depends only on the size of the square, and not on the number of times that the optimal tour T^* crosses its boundaries.

Before proving Lemma 8.11, we observe that Lemmas 8.8–8.11 easily imply Theorem 8.7. Indeed, with high probability:

1. The optimal tour has length $L^* \geq c_1\sqrt{n}$.
2. Every subsquare in the Stitch algorithm contains at most $6 \ln n$ points, and hence the algorithm computes an optimal tour of the points in each subsquare (with length at most (8.5)).
3. Thus, recalling that $s = \frac{n}{\ln n}$, the total length of Stitch's tour is at most

$$\sum_{i=1}^{s}\left(L_i + 6\sqrt{\frac{\ln n}{n}}\right) + c_2 \cdot \sqrt{\frac{n}{\ln n}} = L^* + O\left(\sqrt{\frac{n}{\ln n}}\right) = (1 + o(1)) \cdot L^*.$$

Finally, we prove Lemma 8.11.

Proof (Lemma 8.11) Fix a subsquare i with a nonempty set P_i of points. The optimal tour T^* visits every point in P_i while crossing the boundary of the subsquare an even number $2t$ of times; denote these crossing points by $Q_i = \{y_1, y_2, \ldots, y_{2t}\}$, indexed in clockwise order around the subsquare's perimeter (starting from the lower left corner). Now form a connected Eulerian multigraph $G = (V, E)$ with vertices $V = P_i \cup Q_i$ by adding the following edges:

- Add the portions of T^* that lie inside the subsquare (giving points of P_i a degree of 2 and points of Q_i a degree of 1).
- Let M_1 (respectively, M_2) denote the perfect matching of Q_i that matches each y_j with j odd (respectively, with j even) to y_{j+1}. (In M_2, y_{2t} is matched with y_1.) Add two copies of the cheaper matching to the edge set E and one copy of the more expensive matching (boosting the degree of points of Q_i to 4 while also ensuring connectivity).

The total length of the edges contributed by the first ingredient is L_i. The total length of the edges in $M_1 \cup M_2$ is at most the perimeter of the subsquare, which is $4\sqrt{\frac{\ln n}{n}}$. The second copy of the cheaper matching adds at most $2\sqrt{\frac{\ln n}{n}}$ to the total length of the edges in G. As in footnote 12, because G is connected and

Eulerian, we can extract from it a tour of $P_i \cup Q_i$ (and hence of P_i) that has total length at most that of the edges of G, which is at most $L_i + 6\sqrt{\frac{\ln n}{n}}$. $\square$

8.3.3 Discussion

To what extent are the two divide-and-conquer algorithms of this section tailored to the distributional assumption that the input points are drawn independently and uniformly at random from the unit square? For the convex hull algorithm in Section 8.3.1, the consequence of an incorrect distributional assumption is mild; its worst-case running time is governed by the recurrence $T(n) \le 2T(\frac{n}{2}) + O(n)$ and hence is $O(n \log n)$, which is close to linear. Also, analogs of Lemma 8.6 (and hence Theorem 8.5) can be shown to hold for a number of other distributions.

The Stitch algorithm in Section 8.3.2, with its fixed dissection of the unit square into equal-size subsquares, may appear hopelessly tied to the assumption of a uniform distribution. But minor modifications to it result in more robust algorithms, for example by using an *adaptive* dissection, which recursively divides each square along either the median x-coordinate or the median y-coordinate of the points in the square. Indeed, this idea paved the way for later algorithms that obtained polynomial-time approximation schemes (i.e., $(1 + \epsilon)$-approximations for arbitrarily small constant ϵ) even for the *worst-case* version of Euclidean TSP (see the Notes).

Zooming out, our discussion of these two examples touches on one of the biggest risks of average-case analysis: distributional assumptions can lead to algorithms that are unduly tailored to the assumptions. On the other hand, even when this is the case, the high-level ideas behind the algorithms can prove useful much more broadly.

8.4 Random Graphs and Planted Models

Most of our average-case models so far concern random numerical data. This section studies random combinatorial structures, and specifically different probability distributions over graphs.

8.4.1 Erdős-Rényi Random Graphs

This section reviews the most well-studied model of random graphs, the *Erdős-Rényi* random graph model. This model is a family $\{\mathcal{G}_{n,p}\}$ of distributions, indexed by the number n of vertices and the edge density p. A sample from the distribution $\mathcal{G}_{n,p}$ is a graph $G = (V, E)$ with $|V| = n$ and each of the $\binom{n}{2}$ possible edges present independently with probability p. The special case of $p = \frac{1}{2}$ is the uniform distribution over all n-vertex graphs. This is an example of an "oblivious random model," meaning that it is defined independently of any particular optimization problem.

The assumption of uniformly random data may have felt like cheating already in our previous examples, but it is particularly problematic for many computational problems on graphs. Not only is this distributional assumption extremely specific, it also fails to meaningfully differentiate between different algorithms.[13] We illustrate this point with two problems that are discussed at length in Chapters 9 and 10.

---

[13] It also fails to replicate the statistical properties commonly observed in "real-world" graphs; see Chapter 28 for further discussion.

Example: Minimum Bisection. In the *graph bisection* problem, the input is an undirected graph $G = (V, E)$ with an even number of vertices, and the goal is to identify a bisection (i.e., a partition of V into two equal-size groups) with the fewest number of crossing edges.

To see why this problem is algorithmically uninteresting in the Erdős–Rényi random graph model, take $p = \frac{1}{2}$ and let n tend to infinity. In a random sample from $\mathcal{G}_{n,p}$, for every bisection $(S, \bar{S})$ of the set V of n vertices, the expected number of edges of E crossing it is $\frac{n^2}{8}$. A straightforward application of the Chernoff bound shows that, with probability $1 - o(1)$ as $n \to \infty$, the number of edges crossing *every* bisection is $(1 \pm o(1)) \cdot \frac{n^2}{8}$ (Exercise 8.11). Thus even an algorithm that computes a *maximum* bisection is an almost optimal algorithm for computing a minimum bisection!

Example: Maximum Clique. In the *maximum clique* problem, the goal (given an undirected graph) is to identify the largest subset of vertices that are mutually adjacent. In a random graph in the $\mathcal{G}_{n,1/2}$ model, the size of the maximum clique is very likely to be $\approx 2 \log_2 n$.[14] To see heuristically why this is true, note that for an integer k, the expected number of cliques on k vertices in a random graph of $\mathcal{G}_{n,1/2}$ is exactly

$$\binom{n}{k} 2^{-\binom{k}{2}} \approx n^k 2^{-k^2/2},$$

which is 1 precisely when $k = 2 \log_2 n$. That is, $2 \log_2 n$ is approximately the largest k for which we expect to see at least one k-clique.

On the other hand, while there are several polynomial-time algorithms (including the obvious greedy algorithm) that compute, with high probability, a clique of size $\approx \log_2 n$ in a random graph from $\mathcal{G}_{n,1/2}$, no such algorithm is known to do better. The Erdős–Rényi model fails to distinguish between different efficient heuristics for the Maximum Clique problem.

8.4.2 Planted Graph Models

Chapters 5 and 6 study deterministic models of data in which the optimal solution to an optimization problem must be "clearly optimal" in some sense, with the motivation of zeroing in on the instances with a "meaningful" solution (such as an informative clustering of data points). *Planted graph models* implement the same stability idea in the context of random graphs, by positing probability distributions over inputs which generate (with high probability) graphs in which an optimal solution "sticks out." The goal is then to devise a polynomial-time algorithm that recovers the optimal solution with high probability, under the weakest possible assumptions on the input distribution. Unlike an oblivious random model such as the Erdős–Rényi model, planted models are generally defined with a particular computational problem in mind.

Algorithms for planted models generally fall into three categories, listed roughly in order of increasing complexity and power.

---

[14] In fact, the size of the maximum clique turns out to be incredibly concentrated; see the Notes.

1. *Combinatorial approaches.* We leave the term "combinatorial" safely undefined, but basically it refers to algorithms that work directly with the graph, rather than resorting to any continuous methods. For example, an algorithm that looks only at vertex degrees, subgraphs, shortest paths, etc., would be considered combinatorial.
2. *Spectral algorithms.* Here "spectral" means an algorithm that computes and uses the eigenvectors of a suitable matrix derived from the input graph. Spectral algorithms often achieve optimal recovery guarantees for planted models.
3. *Semidefinite programming* (SDP). Algorithms that use semidefinite programming have proved useful for extending guarantees for spectral algorithms in planted models to hold also in semirandom models (see Chapters 9 and 10).

Example: Planted Bisection. In the planted bisection problem, a graph is generated according to the following random process (for a fixed vertex set V, with $|V|$ even, and parameters $p, q \in [0, 1]$):

1. Choose a partition (S, T) of V with $|S| = |T|$ uniformly at random.
2. Independently for each pair (i, j) of vertices inside the same cluster (S or T), include the edge (i, j) with probability p.
3. Independently for each pair (i, j) of vertices in different clusters, include the edge (i, j) with probability q.[15]

Thus the expected edge density inside the clusters is p, and between the clusters is q.

The difficulty of recovering the planted bisection (S, T) clearly depends on the gap between p and q. The problem is impossible if $p = q$ and trivial if $p = 1$ and $q = 0$. Thus the key question in this model is: how big does the gap $p - q$ need to be before exact recovery is possible in polynomial time (with high probability)?

When p, q, and $p - q$ are bounded below by a constant independent of n, the problem is easily solved by combinatorial approaches (Exercise 8.12); unfortunately, these do not resemble algorithms that perform well in practice.

We can make the problem more difficult by allowing p, q, and $p - q$ to go to 0 with n. Here, semidefinite programming-based algorithms work for an impressively wide range of parameter values. For example:

Theorem 8.12 (Abbe et al., 2016; Hajek et al., 2016) *If $p = \frac{\alpha \ln n}{n}$ and $q = \frac{\beta \ln n}{n}$ with $\alpha > \beta$, then:*

(a) If $\sqrt{\alpha} - \sqrt{\beta} \geq \sqrt{2}$, there is a polynomial-time algorithm that recovers the planted partition (S, T) with probability $1 - o(1)$ as $n \to \infty$.
(b) If $\sqrt{\alpha} - \sqrt{\beta} < \sqrt{2}$, then no algorithm recovers the planted partition with constant probability as $n \to \infty$.

In this parameter regime, semidefinite programming algorithms provably achieve information-theoretically optimal recovery guarantees. Thus, switching from the $p, q, p - q = \Omega(1)$ parameter regime to the $p, q, p - q = o(1)$ regime is valuable not because we literally believe that the latter is more faithful to "real-world" instances, but rather because it encourages better algorithm design.

---

[15] This model is a special case of the stochastic block model studied in Chapter 10.

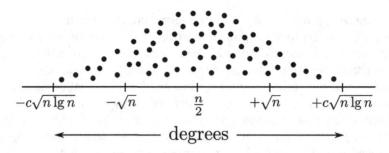

$$-c\sqrt{n\lg n} \qquad -\sqrt{n} \qquad \frac{n}{2} \qquad +\sqrt{n} \qquad +c\sqrt{n\lg n}$$

$\longleftarrow$ degrees $\longrightarrow$

Figure 8.1 Degree distribution of an Erdős–Rényi random graph with edge density $\frac{1}{2}$, before planting the k-clique Q. If $k = \Omega(\sqrt{n\lg n})$, then the planted clique will consist of the k vertices with the highest degrees.

Example: Planted Clique. The *planted clique* problem with parameters k and n concerns the following distribution over graphs.

1. Fix a vertex set V with n vertices. Sample a graph from $\mathcal{G}_{n,1/2}$: Independently for each pair (i,j) of vertices, include the edge (i,j) with probability $\frac{1}{2}$.
2. Choose a random subset $Q \subseteq V$ of k vertices.
3. Add all remaining edges between pairs of vertices in Q.

Once k is significantly bigger than $\approx 2\log_2 n$, the likely size of a maximum clique in a random graph from $\mathcal{G}_{n,1/2}$, the planted clique Q is with high probability the maximum clique of the graph. How big does k need to be before it becomes visible to a polynomial-time algorithm?

When $k = \Omega(\sqrt{n\log n})$, the problem is trivial, with the k highest-degree vertices constituting the planted clique Q. To see why this is true, think first about the sampled Erdős–Rényi random graph, before the clique Q is planted. The expected degree of each vertex is $\approx n/2$, with standard deviation $\approx \sqrt{n}/2$. Textbook large deviation inequalities show that, with high probability, the degree of every vertex is within $\approx \sqrt{\ln n}$ standard deviations of its expectation (Figure 8.1). Planting a clique Q of size $a\sqrt{n\log n}$, for a sufficiently large constant a, then boosts the degrees of all of the clique vertices enough that they catapult past the degrees of all of the vertices not in the clique.

The "highest degrees" algorithm is not very useful in practice. What went wrong? The same thing that often goes wrong with pure average-case analysis – the solution is brittle and overly tailored to a specific distributional assumption. How can we change the input model to encourage the design of algorithms with more robust guarantees?

One idea is to mimic what worked well for the planted bisection problem, and to study a more difficult parameter regime that forces us to develop more useful algorithms. For the planted clique problem, there are nontrivial algorithms, including spectral algorithms, that recover the planted clique Q with high probability provided $k = \Omega(\sqrt{n})$ (see the Notes).

8.4.3 Discussion

There is a happy ending to the study of both the planted bisection and planted clique problems: with the right choice of parameter regimes, these models drive us toward nontrivial algorithms that might plausibly be useful starting points for the design of practical algorithms. Still, both results seem to emerge from "threading the needle" in the parameter space. Could there be a better alternative, in the form of input models that explicitly encourage the design of robustly good algorithms?

8.5 Robust Distributional Analysis

Many of the remaining chapters in this book pursue different hybrids of worst- and average-case analysis, in search of a "sweet spot" for algorithm analysis that both encourages robustly good algorithms (as in worst-case analysis) and allows for strong provable guarantees (as in average-case analysis). Most of these models assume that there is in fact a probability distribution over inputs (as in average-case analysis), but that this distribution is a priori *unknown* to an algorithm. The goal is then to design algorithms that work well no matter what the input distribution is (perhaps with some restrictions on the class of possible distributions). Indeed, several of the average-case guarantees in this chapter can be viewed as applying simultaneously (i.e., in the worst case) across a restricted but still infinite family of input distributions:

- The $\frac{1}{2}$-approximation in the prophet inequality (Theorem 8.1) for a threshold-t rule applies simultaneously to all distribution sequences $D_1, D_2, \ldots, D_n$ such that $\mathbf{Pr}_{\mathbf{v}\sim\mathbf{D}}[\max_i v_i \geq t] = \frac{1}{2}$ (e.g., all possible reorderings of one such sequence).
- The guarantees for our algorithms for the bin packing (Theorem 8.3), convex hull (Theorem 8.5), and Euclidean TSP (Theorem 8.7) problems hold more generally for all input distributions that are sufficiently close to uniform.

The general research agenda in robust distributional analysis is to prove approximate optimality guarantees for algorithms for as many different computational problems and as rich a class of input distributions as possible. Work in the area can be divided into two categories, both well represented in this book, depending on whether an algorithm observes one or many samples from the unknown input distribution. We conclude this chapter with an overview of what's to come.

8.5.1 Simultaneous Near-Optimality

In *single-sample* models, an algorithm is designed with knowledge only of a class $\mathcal{D}$ of possible input distributions, and receives only a single input drawn from an unknown and adversarially chosen distribution from $\mathcal{D}$. In these models, the algorithm cannot hope to learn anything non-trivial about the input distribution. Instead, the goal is to design an algorithm that, for every input distribution $D \in \mathcal{D}$, has expected performance close to that of the optimal algorithm specifically tailored for D. Examples include:

- The semirandom models in Chapters 9–11 and 17 and the smoothed analysis models in Chapters 13–15 and 19. In these models, nature and an adversary collaborate to produce an input, and each fixed adversary strategy induces a particular input distribution. Performing well with respect to the adversary in these models is equivalent to performing well simultaneously across all of the induced input distributions.

- The effectiveness of simple hash functions with pseudorandom data (Chapter 26). The main result in this chapter is a guarantee for universal hashing that holds simultaneously across all data distributions with sufficient entropy.
- Prior-independent auctions (Chapter 27), which are auctions that achieve near-optimal expected revenue simultaneously across a wide class of valuation distributions.

8.5.2 Learning a Near-Optimal Solution

In *multisample* models, an algorithm observes multiple samples from an unknown input distribution $D \in \mathcal{D}$, and the goal is to efficiently identify a near-optimal algorithm for D from as few samples as possible. Examples include:

- Self-improving algorithms (Chapter 12) and data-driven algorithm design (Chapter 29), where the goal is to design an algorithm that, when presented with independent samples from an unknown input distribution, quickly converges to an approximately best-in-class algorithm for that distribution.
- Supervised learning (Chapters 16 and 22), where the goal is to identify the expected loss-minimizing hypothesis (from a given hypothesis class) for an unknown data distribution given samples from that distribution.
- Distribution testing (Chapter 23), where the goal is to make accurate inferences about an unknown distribution from a limited number of samples.

8.6 Notes

The prophet inequality (Theorem 8.1) is due to Samuel-Cahn (1984). The pros and cons of threshold rules versus optimal online algorithms are discussed also by Hartline (in preparation). QUICKSORT and its original analysis are due to Hoare (1962). The $(1 - \alpha)^{-2}$ bound for linear probing with load α and random data, as well as the corresponding quote in Section 8.2.2, are in Knuth (1998). A good (if outdated) entry point to the literature on bin packing is Coffman et al. (1996). The lower bound for the FFD algorithm in Exercise 8.3 is from Johnson et al. (1974). The first upper bound of the form $\frac{11}{9} \cdot OPT + O(1)$ for the number of bins used by the FFD algorithm, where OPT denotes the minimum-possible number of bins, is due to Johnson (1973). The exact worst-case bound for FFD was pinned down recently by Dósa et al. (2013). The average-case guarantee in Theorem 8.3 is a variation on one by Frederickson (1980), who proved that the expected difference between the number of bins used by FFD and an optimal solution is $O(n^{2/3})$. A more sophisticated argument gives a tight bound of $\Theta(n^{1/2})$ on this expectation (Coffman et al., 1991).

The linear expected time algorithm for 2D convex hulls (Theorem 8.5) is by Bentley and Shamos (1978). Lemma 8.6 was first proved by Rényi and Sulanke (1963); the proof outlined here follows Har-Peled (1998). Exercise 8.6 is solved by Andrews (1979). The asymptotic optimality of the Stitch algorithm for Euclidean TSP (Theorem 8.7) is due to Karp (1977), who also gave an alternative solution based on the adaptive dissections mentioned in Section 8.3.3. A good general reference for this topic is Karp and Steele (1985). The worst-case approximation schemes mentioned in Section 8.3.3 are due to Arora (1998) and Mitchell (1999).

The Erdős–Rényi random graph model is from Erdős and Rényi (1960). The size of the maximum clique in a random graph drawn from $\mathcal{G}_{n,1/2}$ was characterized by Matula (1976); with high probability it is either k or $k + 1$, where k is an integer roughly equal to $2 \log_2 n$. Grimmett and McDiarmid (1975) proved that the greedy algorithm finds, with high probability, a clique of size roughly $\log_2 n$ in a random graph from $\mathcal{G}_{n,1/2}$. The planted bisection model described here was proposed by Bui et al. (1987) and is also a special case of the stochastic block model defined by Holland et al. (1983). Part (b) of Theorem 8.12 and a weaker version of part (a) were proved by Abbe et al. (2016); the stated version of part (a) is due to Hajek et al. (2016). The planted clique model was suggested by Jerrum (1992). Kucera (1995) noted that the "top-k degrees" algorithm works with high probability when $k = \Omega(\sqrt{n \log n})$. The first polynomial-time algorithm for the planted clique problem with $k = O(\sqrt{n})$ was the spectral algorithm of Alon et al. (1998). Barak et al. (2016) supplied evidence, in the form of a sum-of-squares lower bound, that the planted clique problem is intractable when $k = o(\sqrt{n})$.

The versions of the Chernoff bound stated in Exercises 8.4(a) and 8.9 can be found, for example, in Mitzenmacher and Upfal (2017).

Acknowledgments

I thank Anupam Gupta, C. Seshadhri, and Sahil Singla for helpful comments on a preliminary draft of this chapter.

References

Abbe, E., Bandeira, A. S., and Hall, G. 2016. Exact recovery in the stochastic block model. *IEEE Transactions on Information Theory*, **62**(1), 471–487.

Alon, N., Krivelevich, M., and Sudakov, B. 1998. Finding a large hidden clique in a random graph. *Random Structures & Algorithms*, **13**(3–4), 457–466.

Andrews, A. M. 1979. Another efficient algorithm for convex hulls in two dimensions. *Information Processing Letters*, **9**(5), 216–219.

Arora, S. 1998. Polynomial time approximation schemes for Euclidean Traveling Salesman and other geometric problems. *Journal of the ACM*, **45**(5), 753–782.

Barak, B., Hopkins, S. B., Kelner, J. A., Kothari, P., Moitra, A., and Potechin, A. 2016. A nearly tight sum-of-squares lower bound for the planted clique problem. In *Proceedings of the 57th Annual IEEE Symposium on Foundations of Computer Science (FOCS)*, pp. 428–437.

Bentley, J. L., and Shamos, M. I. 1978. Divide and conquer for linear expected time. *Information Processing Letters*, **7**(2), 87–91.

Bui, T. N., Chaudhuri, S., Leighton, F. T., and Sipser, M. 1987. Graph bisection algorithms with good average case behavior. *Combinatorica*, **7**(2), 171–191.

Coffman, Jr., E. G., Courcoubetis, C., Garey, M. R., Johnson, D. S., McGeoch, L. A., Shor, P. W., Weber, R. R., and Yannakakis, M. 1991. Fundamental discrepancies between average-case analyses under discrete and continuous distributions: A bin packing case study. In *Proceedings of the 23rd Annual ACM Symposium on Theory of Computing (STOC)*, pp. 230–240.

Coffman, Jr., E. G., Garey, M. R., and Johnson, D. S. 1996. Approximation algorithms for bin packing: A survey. In Hochbaum, D. (ed.), *Approximation Algorithms for NP-Hard Problems*, pp. 46–93. PWS.

Dósa, G., Li, R., Hanc, X., and Tuza, Z. 2013. Tight absolute bound for first fit decreasing bin-packing: $FFD(L) \leq 11/9OPT(L) + 6/9$. *Theoretical Computer Science*, **510**, 13–61.

Erdős, P., and Rényi, A. 1960. On the evolution of random graphs. *Publications of the Mathematical Institute of the Hungarian Academy of Sciences*, **5**, 17–61.

Frederickson, G. N. 1980. Probabilistic analysis for simple one- and two-dimensional bin packing algorithms. *Information Processing Letters*, **11**(4–5), 156–161.

Grimmett, G., and McDiarmid, C. J. H. 1975. On colouring random graphs. *Mathematical Proceedings of the Cambridge Philosophical Society*, **77**, 313–324.

Hajek, B., Wu, Y., and Xu, J. 2016. Achieving exact cluster recovery threshold via semidefinite programming: Extensions. *IEEE Transactions on Information Theory*, **62**(10), 5918–5937.

Har-Peled, S. 1998. *On the Expected Complexity of Random Convex Hulls*. Technical Report 330/98. School of Mathematical Sciences, Tel Aviv University.

Hartline, J. D. *Mechanism Design and Approximation*. Cambridge University Press, Book in preparation.

Hoare, C. A. R. 1962. Quicksort. *The Computer Journal*, **5**(1), 10–15.

Holland, P. W., Lasket, K., and Leinhardt, S. 1983. Stochastic blockmodels: First steps. *Social Networks*, **5**(2), 109–137.

Jerrum, M. 1992. Large cliques elude the metropolis process. *Random Structures and Algorithms*, **3**(4), 347–359.

Johnson, D. S. 1973. *Near-Optimal Bin Packing Algorithms*. PhD thesis, MIT.

Johnson, D. S., Demers, A., Ullman, J. D., Garey, M. R., and Graham, R. L. 1974. Worst-case performance bounds for simple one-dimensional packing Algorithms. *SIAM Journal on Computing*, **3**(4), 299–325.

Karp, R. M. 1977. Probabilistic analysis of partitioning algorithms for the Traveling-Salesman Problem in the plane. *Mathematics of Operations Research*, **2**(3), 209–224.

Karp, R. M., and Steele, J. M. 1985. Probabilistic analysis of heuristics. In Lawler, E. L., Lenstra, J. K., Rinnooy Kan, A. H. G., and Shmoys, D. B. (eds.), *The Traveling Salesman Problem*, pp. 181–205. John Wiley & Sons.

Knuth, D. E. 1998. *The Art of Computer Programming: Sorting and Searching*, 2nd ed., vol. 3. Addison-Wesley.

Kucera, L. 1995. Expected complexity of graph partitioning problems. *Discrete Applied Mathematics*, **57**(2–3), 193–212.

Matula, D. W. 1976. *The Largest Clique Size in a Random Graph*. Technical Report 7608. Department of Computer Science, Southern Methodist University.

Mitchell, J. S. B. 1999. Guillotine subdivisions approximate polygonal subdivisions: A simple polynomial-time approximation scheme for geometric TSP, k-MST, and related problems. *SIAM Journal on Computing*, **28**(4), 1298–1309.

Mitzenmacher, M., and Upfal, E. 2017. *Probability and Computing*, 2nd ed. Cambridge. University Press.

Rényi, A., and Sulanke, R. 1963. Über die konvexe Hülle von *n* zugällig gewählten Punkten. *Zeitschrift für Wahrscheinlichkeitstheorie und Verwandte Gebiete*, **2**, 75–84.

Samuel-Cahn, E. 1984. Comparison of threshold stop rules and maximum for independent nonnegative random variables. *Annals of Probability*, **12**(4), 1213–1216.

Exercises

Exercise 8.1 Extend the prophet inequality (Theorem 8.1) to the case in which there is no threshold t with $q(t) = \frac{1}{2}$, where $q(t)$ is the probability that no prize meets the threshold.

[Hint: Define t such that $\Pr[\pi_i > t$ for all $i] \leq \frac{1}{2} \leq \Pr[\pi_i \geq t$ for all $i]$. Show that at least one of the two corresponding strategies – either taking the first prize with value at least t, or the first with value exceeding t – satisfies the requirement.]

Exercise 8.2 The prophet inequality (Theorem 8.1) provides an approximation guarantee of $\frac{1}{2}$ relative to the expected prize value obtained by a prophet, which is at least (and possibly more than) the expected prize value obtained by an optimal online algorithm. Show by examples that the latter quantity can range from 50% to 100% of the former.

Exercise 8.3 Prove that for a bin packing instance consisting of 6 items with size $\frac{1}{2}+\epsilon$, 6 items with size $\frac{1}{4}+2\epsilon$, 6 jobs with size $\frac{1}{4}+\epsilon$, and 12 items with size $\frac{1}{4}-2\epsilon$, the first-fit decreasing algorithm uses 11 bins and an optimal solution uses 9 bins.

Exercise 8.4 This exercise and the next outline a proof of Theorem 8.3. Divide the interval $[0, 1]$ evenly into $n^{1/4}$ intervals, with I_j denoting the subinterval $[\frac{j-1}{n^{1/4}}, \frac{j}{n^{1/4}}]$ for $j = 1, 2, \ldots, n^{1/4}$. Let P_j denote the items with size in I_j.

(a) One version of the Chernoff bound states that, for every sequence $X_1, X_2, \ldots, X_n$ of Bernoulli (0–1) random variables with means $p_1, p_2, \ldots, p_n$ and every $\delta \in (0, 1)$,

$$\Pr[|X - \mu| \geq \delta\mu] \leq 2e^{-\mu\delta^2/3},$$

where X and μ denote $\sum_{i=1}^{n} X_i$ and $\sum_{i=1}^{n} p_i$, respectively. Use this bound to prove that

$$|P_j| \in \left[n^{3/4} - \sqrt{n}, n^{3/4} + \sqrt{n} \right] \text{ for all } j = 1, 2, \ldots, n^{1/4} \qquad (8.6)$$

with probability 1-o(1) as $n \to \infty$.

(b) Assuming (8.6), prove that the sum $\sum_{i=1}^{n} s_i$ is at least $\frac{1}{2}n - c_1 n^{3/4}$ for some constant $c_1 > 0$. What does this imply about the number of bins used by an optimal solution?

(c) Assuming (8.6), prove that in the third step of the TM algorithm, every pair of items i and $k - i + 1$ fits in a single bin.

(d) Conclude that there is a constant $c_2 > 0$ such that, when property (8.6) holds, the TM algorithm uses at most $\frac{1}{2}n + c_2 n^{3/4} = (1+o(1)) \cdot OPT$ bins, where OPT denotes the number of bins used by an optimal solution.

Exercise 8.5 Prove Lemma 8.4.

Exercise 8.6 Give an algorithm that, given a set S of n points from the square sorted by x-coordinate, computes the convex hull of S in $O(n)$ time.

[Hint: compute the lower and upper parts of the convex hull separately.]

Exercise 8.7 Prove that the convex hull of n points drawn independently and uniformly at random from the unit square occupies a $1 - O(\frac{\log n}{n})$ fraction of the square.

Exercise 8.8 Prove Lemma 8.8.

[Hint: Chop the unit square evenly into n subsquares of side length $n^{-1/2}$, and each subsquare further into 9 mini-squares of side length $\frac{1}{3} \cdot n^{-1/2}$. For a given subsquare, what is the probability that the input includes one point from its center mini-square and none from the other 8 mini-squares?]

Exercise 8.9 Another variation of the Chernoff bound states that, for every sequence $X_1, X_2, \ldots, X_n$ of Bernoulli (0–1) random variables with means $p_1, p_2, \ldots, p_n$ and every $t \geq 6\mu$,

$$\mathbf{Pr}[X \geq t] \leq 2^{-t},$$

where X and μ denote $\sum_{i=1}^{n} X_i$ and $\sum_{i=1}^{n} p_i$, respectively. Use this bound to prove Lemma 8.9.

Exercise 8.10 Prove Lemma 8.10.

Exercise 8.11 Use the Chernoff bound from Exercise 8.4(a) to prove that, with probability approaching 1 as $n \to \infty$, every bisection of a random graph from $\mathcal{G}_{n,p}$ has $(1 \pm o(1)) \cdot \frac{n^2}{8}$ crossing edges.

Exercise 8.12 Consider the planted bisection problem with parameters $p = c_1$ and $q = p - c_2$ for constants $c_1, c_2 > 0$. Consider the following simple combinatorial algorithm for recovering a planted bisection:

- Choose a vertex v arbitrarily.
- Let A denote the $\frac{n}{2}$ vertices that have the fewest common neighbors with v.
- Let B denote the rest of the vertices (including v) and return (A, B).

Prove that, with high probability over the random choice of G (approaching 1 as $n \to \infty$), this algorithm exactly recovers the planted bisection.

[Hint: compute the expected number of common neighbors for pairs of vertices on the same and on different sides of the planted partition. Use the Chernoff bound.]

Exercise 8.13 Consider the planted clique problem (Section 8.4.2) with planted clique size $k \geq c \log_2 n$ for a sufficiently large constant c. Design an algorithm that runs in $n^{O(\log n)}$ time and, with probability $1 - o(1)$ as $n \to \infty$, recovers the planted clique.

CHAPTER NINE

Introduction to Semirandom Models

Uriel Feige

Abstract: This chapter introduces *semirandom models*, in which input instances are generated by a process that combines random components with adversarial components. These models may bridge the gap between worst case assumptions on input instances, that often are too pessimistic, and purely random "average case" assumptions, which might be too optimistic. We discuss several semirandom frameworks. We present algorithmic paradigms that have been proved effective in handling semirandom instances, and explain some principles used in their analysis. We also discuss computational hardness results for the semirandom setting.

9.1 Introduction

In semirandom models, input instances are generated by a process that combines random components with adversarial components. There are different ways by which these components can be combined, and indeed, many different semirandom models have been proposed. In this section we present several such models. In Section 9.2 we explain considerations that motivate the introduction of semirandom models. In Section 9.3 we survey some representative past work on semirandom models. In Section 9.4 we list some open questions.

9.1.1 Examples of Semirandom Models

In distributional models (see Chapter 8 in this book) the input instance is generated by a random process. In semirandom models, generation of input instances involves both a random component and an adversarial (worst-case) component. We present here examples of semirandom models, and contrast them with related distributional models that have no adversarial component. In all models considered in this chapter, the algorithm that is faced with a computational problem (3SAT, 3-coloring, minimum bisection, maximum independent set, in our examples) gets to see only the resulting input instance, but not the way by which it was generated.

In our first example, the adversary first chooses a tentative input instance, and then the final input instance is generated by applying a small random perturbation to the tentative input instance. Semirandom models of this nature are studied in the area of *smoothed analysis* (see Part Four in this book).

3SAT

>**Worst case.** The input is an arbitrary 3CNF formula ϕ. A 3CNF formula is a collection of clauses, in which each clause contains three literals, where a literal is a Boolean variable or a negation of a Boolean variable. A satisfying assignment is a truth assignment to the Boolean variables such that in every clause at least one literal is set to *true*. The goal is to determine whether ϕ is satisfiable, namely, whether there is a satisfying assignment.

>**Distributional.** Given positive integer parameters n (for the number of variables) and m (the number of clauses), one generates independently at random m clauses, where each clause contains three variables chosen uniformly at random from the $\binom{n}{3}$ triples of variables, and the polarity of the variables in each clause (determining whether the literal associated with the variable is negated) is chosen uniformly at random. The goal is to determine whether the resulting 3CNF formula ϕ is satisfiable.

>**Semirandom.** Given integer parameters n and m and a parameter p (where $0 < p < 1$), an adversary generates a 3CNF formula ϕ' containing m clauses of its choice. This completes the adversarial part of the construction. Thereafter, for each literal in ϕ', its polarity is flipped independently with probability p. The goal is to determine whether the resulting 3CNF formula ϕ is satisfiable.

In our next example, a tentative input instance is first generated in a distributional manner, and thereafter an adversary is allowed to modify the tentative input instance in some restricted way. Often, the forms of modification that are allowed are meant to capture modifications under which the resulting final instance should not be more difficult to solve than the original tentative instance. We refer to such an adversary as a *monotone adversary*.

Minimum Bisection

>**Worst case.** The input is an arbitrary graph $G(V,E)$ with an even number n of vertices. The goal is to output a set $S \subset V$ of cardinality $\frac{n}{2}$ for which the number $|E(S, V \setminus S)|$ of cut edges is minimized.

>**Distributional.** Given an even integer n and parameters $\frac{1}{n} \le p < q \le 1 - \frac{1}{n}$ one generates a graph $G(V,E)$ (with $|V| = n$) as follows. A subset $S \subset V$ of size $\frac{n}{2}$ is chosen at random. For every pair of vertices (u,v) with $u \in S$ and $v \in V \setminus S$, the edge (u,v) is included in E independently with probability p. For other pairs (u,v) of distinct vertices (either both vertices in S or both not in S) the edge (u,v) is included in E independently with probability q. The resulting graph $G(V,E)$ is the input graph, and the goal is to output the minimum bisection. The set S is referred to as the *planted bisection*. If $q - p$ is sufficiently large then with high probability the unique minimum bisection is S.

>**Semirandom.** Given n, p, q, first one generates a random input graph exactly as explained earlier. This completes the random component of the construction. Thereafter, an adversary may observe the random graph and remove from the cut $(S, V \setminus S)$ arbitrary edges of its choice, and add elsewhere (within S or within $V \setminus S$) arbitrary edges of its choice. The goal is to output the minimum bisection in the resulting input graph. If S was the minimum bisection in the random graph, it remains so in the semirandom graph.

In the following example, one of the random steps in a distributional model is replaced by an adversarial step. We refer here to such models as *separable*, as we separate between the components generated at random and those generated by the adversary. The semirandom model presented for 3SAT, in the special case in which $p = \frac{1}{2}$, is one such separable model, as the choice of variables is completely adversarial, whereas the choice of polarities is completely random. We now present a separable model for 3-coloring.

3-Coloring

Worst case. The input is an arbitrary graph $G(V, E)$. The goal is to legally 3-color its vertices, if possible. A legal 3-coloring is a partition of V into three sets of vertices, referred to as color classes, where the subgraph induced on each color class is an independent set.

Distributional. Given parameters n and $0 < p < 1$, first, a graph $G(V, E')$ is generated as an Erdos–Renyi $G_{n,p}$ random graph (where there are n vertices, and every edge is present independently with probability p). Thereafter, every vertex independently at random is associated with one of the colors, c_1, c_2, or c_3. This association is referred to as the planted 3-coloring. All monochromatic edges (edges whose endpoints are associated with the same color) are removed. The resulting graph is the input graph $G(V, E)$. The goal is to output a legal 3-coloring. If p is sufficiently large (e.g., $p \geq \frac{2 \log n}{n}$ suffices) then with high probability the planted 3-coloring is the unique legal 3-coloring of $G(V, E)$.

Semirandom. Given parameters n and $0 < p < 1$, the input graph $G(V, E)$ is generated as follows. First, a graph $G(V, E')$ is generated as a $G_{n,p}$ random graph. This completes the random component of the construction. Thereafter, an adversary observes the random graph and associates with each vertex one of the three colors, c_1, c_2, or c_3, with the only restriction being that every color class is of size $\frac{n}{3}$ (rounded up or down to an integer value). All monochromatic edges (with respect to this planted 3-coloring) are removed. The goal is to output a legal 3-coloring for the resulting input graph $G(V, E)$. Here, even if p is fairly large (but not larger than $\frac{1}{3}$), $G(V, E)$ may have legal 3-colorings that differ from the planted one.

Our final example (for this section) gives a semirandom model that is a variation on a distributional planted model. In the underlying distributional planted model, with high probability the planted solution is the unique optimal solution. In contrast, in the semirandom model the planted solution might be far from optimal. The algorithmic goal in the semirandom setting is to find a solution that is as good as the planted one.

Maximum Independent Set (MIS)

Worst case. The input is an arbitrary graph $G(V, E)$. The goal is to output a set $S \subset V$ of maximum cardinality that induces an independent set (namely, $(u, v) \notin E$ for every $u, v \in S$).

Distributional. Given parameters n, k, and p (where $k < n$ are positive integers and $0 < p < 1$), first, a graph $G(V, E')$ is generated as a $G_{n,p}$ random graph. Thereafter, a random set $S \subset V$ of k vertices is turned into an independent set by removing from E' all edges of the form (u, v) for $u, v \in S$. This S is referred to as the *planted independent set*. The resulting graph $G(V, E)$ is the input graph, and the goal is to output an independent set of maximum size. If k is sufficiently large (e.g., for $p = \frac{1}{2}$ it suffices to take $k = 3 \log n$) then with high probability the unique independent set of maximum size is S.

Semirandom. Given parameters n, k, and p, the input graph $G(V, E)$ (with $|V| = n$) is generated as follows. First, a graph with a planted independent set S is generated exactly as in the distributional model. This completes the random component of the construction. Thereafter, all edges within $V \setminus S$ are removed. Finally, an adversary observes the random graph (whose only edges are between S and $V \setminus S$) and may add to it arbitrary edges of its choice, as long as none of the added edges has both endpoints inside S. Hence the adversary has complete control over the subgraph induced on $V \setminus S$, and acts as a monotone adversary with respect to the edges between S and $V \setminus S$. The goal is to output an independent set of size at least k in the resulting input graph $G(V, E)$. Note that regardless of the edges added by the adversary, S itself is a feasible solution, but depending on the edges (not) added by the adversary, there might be other feasible solutions.

9.2 Why Study Semirandom Models?

A semirandom model involves a random component and an adversarial component. As we have seen in Section 9.1.1 (and we will see additional examples later), there are many different roles that we can delegate to the adversary when constructing the input instance. In the text that follows we discuss some of the considerations involved in proposing a semirandom model. As semirandom models are often conceived as refinements of distributional models, we shall also discuss some of the motivations for studying distributional models, with emphasis on those motivations that apply also to semirandom models.

In the discussion that follows, it will be convenient to distinguish between two classes of distributional models. We shall refer to one class as that of *oblivious random models*, and to the other as *planted models*.

In oblivious random models, the input is generated by a random process that is independent of the optimization problem that one is interested in solving. The distributional model given for 3SAT in Section 9.1.1 is an example of an oblivious random model, and the model applies without change to other constraint satisfaction problems such as 3AND or *not-all-equal* 3SAT. An example of an oblivious random model for graph problems is the Erdos–Renyi $G_{n,p}$ random graph model. This model applies to any graph problem, though the range of interest for the parameter p might depend on the optimization problem of interest. For example, for maximum clique one might choose $p = \frac{1}{2}$, for Hamiltonicity one might choose $p = \frac{\log n}{n}$, whereas for 3-coloring one might choose $p = \frac{4}{n}$.

In planted models, the input is generated by a random process that depends on the optimization problem that one is interested in. For example, the planted distributional models considered in Section 9.1.1 for the three graph problems – minimum bisection, 3-coloring, and maximum independent set – are different from each other. In planted models, the planted solution is often the unique optimal solution.

9.2.1 Average Case Analysis

Distributional models are sometimes assumed to represent input instances that may occur in practice. The extent to which one can defend such assumptions depends on the setting.

In some settings, distributional models exactly capture the set of interesting input instances. Most notably, this happens in settings related to cryptography, in which participants in a cryptographic scheme are instructed to generate various inputs to the scheme at random. For example, in public key cryptographic schemes such as RSA, a participant is instructed to generate its public key by privately picking two large random primes p and q, computing $n = pq$, and publishing n as the public key. Factoring algorithms that are tailored for this specific distributional setting have far-reaching consequences for the underlying cryptographic scheme.

In some settings, distributional models are conjectured to be a good approximation of reality. For example, studies in statistical physics often involve random graph models that have a geometric nature: the vertices of the graph lie in a low dimensional space, and only vertices that are geometrically close to each other may be connected by edges. The random aspect of the model can be either in the location of the vertices, or in the choice of which of the possible edges are indeed edges.

However, in many settings, the relation between distributional models and typical instances that occur in practice is less clear. For example, in the study of social networks, one often considers distributions over graphs that are generated by a random process such as preferential attachment. These distributions may capture some of the typical aspects of social networks (such as typical degree sequences), though for any given social network of interest, there may be other important aspects (such as the relative frequencies of various small subgraphs) that are not captured well by the underlying distributional model.

Oblivious random models typically exhibit a multitude of nearly optimal solutions, with pairs of nearly optimal solutions that are very different from each other. As argued in Chapters 5 and 6, in some settings, an optimal solution to an optimization problems is most useful when it is basically unique, and of significantly better value than those solutions that significantly differ from it. In these cases, planted models can serve as the basis for average case analysis of instances of interest, as the planted solution is often the unique optimal solution. But also here, the planted models capture only some aspects of "interesting" input instances, and may not capture other aspects.

Summarizing the foregoing discussion, distributional models, whether oblivious or planted, are sometimes meant to represent average case analysis, but in many cases there is a major difficulty of characterizing the "right" distributional model for the set of problems that may appear in practice. In such settings, it is important that algorithms that are designed for inputs generated by the distributional model will be robust, and work well also for inputs that are generated by other processes. A way of addressing this concern is through the use of semirandom models. In these models, the exact distribution of input instances is not known to the algorithm, as some aspects of the input instance are left to the discretion of an adversary. Consequently, algorithms designed for semirandom models avoid the danger of "overfitting" to a particular input distribution, and they are expected to be more robust than algorithms that are designed for distributional models. This is one of the major reasons for introducing semirandom models such as the monotone adversary (e.g., for minimum bisection in Section 9.1.1). In Section 9.3 we will see examples of how such models direct the design of algorithms toward algorithms that are more robust.

Another contribution of semirandom models is in providing refinements of *average case analysis*, clarifying what it is that one actually averages over. In semirandom models, some aspects of the input instance are chosen by an adversary, and the random distribution is over some other aspects. For example, in smoothed models (e.g., for 3SAT in Section 9.1.1), the algorithm needs to work well on average not only when the average is taken as a global average over all input instances, but also when one takes a local average around any particular tentative input instance, regardless of what this tentative input instance is. Another example is random-order models for online algorithms (see Chapter 11), where an adversary may select a worst-case instance, and only the order of arrival is random.

9.2.2 Recovering a Signal Contaminated by Noise

Randomness in generation of input instances can sometimes be thought of as representing "noise" that makes finding an otherwise obvious solution more difficult. For example, for error correction of encoded messages transmitted over a noisy channel, the source of difficulty in decoding is the errors introduced into the encoded message by the noisy channel. In the absence of noise, decoding the transmitted message is trivial. With noise, decoding typically involves two aspects. One is information theoretic – does the noisy message contain sufficient information in order to uniquely recover the transmitted message (with high probability)? The other is algorithmic, designing an efficient algorithm for recovering encoded messages from their noisy received message.

Noise is often modeled as being random. For example, in a binary symmetric channel (BSC) each transmitted bit is flipped independently with probability $p < \frac{1}{2}$. However, it is also reasonable to model noise as being semirandom. For example, one may assume that each transmitted bit i is flipped with probability $p_i \leq p$ rather than exactly p, where the value of p_i is determined by an adversary. If a decoding algorithm works in the former model but not in this latter model, this may be a sign of "overfitting" the algorithm to the model. Noise is also often modeled as being fully adversarial. In Hamming's model, within a block of bits, the total fraction of bits flipped is at most p, but an adversary may decide which bits are flipped. Decoding in the information theoretic sense is more difficult in the Hamming model than in the BSC model (the transmission rate under which unique decoding is possible is smaller in the Hamming model). Also, decoding in the algorithmic sense appears to be more difficult in the Hamming model. This last statement is supported by the observation that for every $p < \frac{1}{2}$ and $p' < p$, if block sizes are sufficiently large, every decoding algorithm for the Hamming model with p fraction of errors works also in the BSC model when the error probability is p'.

In analogy to the coding setting, planted models can also be viewed as representing an ideal object contaminated by noise. Under this view, the goal is typically to recover the ideal object. Solving an optimization problem associated with the object may serve as a means toward this end, but is not the goal by itself. This view is different from that taken in most of this chapter, where the goal is typically to solve an optimization problem, and a solution is accepted even if it does not correspond to the planted object.

As an example, for the MIS problem, the ideal object is an independent set of size k in an otherwise complete graph. This ideal object is contaminated by noise, where noise corresponds to removing some of the edges of the graph. If every edge is removed independently with the same probability (in analogy to independent noise), one gets the standard distributional model for planted independent set (but with the goal of finding the planted independent set, rather than that of finding a maximum independent set). Semirandom models for MIS correspond to models in which the noise is not independent, and this makes recovering the ideal object more difficult.

9.2.3 A Model for Worst-Case Instances

To make progress (e.g., achieve a better approximation ratio) in the design of algorithms for a difficult computational problem, it is useful to have an understanding of which are the most difficult instances of the problem. For some problems, distributional models are conjectured to produce input instances that are essentially as difficult as worst-case instances. For example, it is conjectured that 3SAT on random 3CNF formulas with dn clauses (for some large constant d – such formulas are unlikely to be satisfiable) are essentially as difficult to refute as adversarially chosen 3CNF formulas with dn clauses. For some other problems, such as the dense k-subgraph problem (given an input graph and a parameter k, find the induced subgraph on k vertices with the highest average degree), distributional models appear to capture the limitations of currently known algorithms, and progress on distributional instances played a key role in improving the approximation ratio also for worst-case instances (see Bhaskara et al., 2010).

There are problems whose approximability is not well understood (examples include sparsest cut, unique games) and (natural) distributional models produce instances on which known algorithms perform much better than the best approximation ratios known for worst-case instances. In such cases, it is instructive to consider semirandom instances, and try to extend the good performance of algorithms to the semirandom instances (as done in Kolla et al., 2011). Success in this effort may suggest that known algorithmic approaches might also suffice in order to handle worst-cases instances (even though we might be lacking the analysis to support this), whereas failure may help clarify what aspects of input instances are those that create difficulties for currently known algorithms.

9.2.4 NP-Hardness

The theory of NP-completeness has great value in informing us that certain problems do not have polynomial-time algorithms (unless $P = NP$), and hence that we should not waste efforts in trying to design polynomial-time algorithms for them (unless we are seriously trying to prove that $P = NP$). This theory has been extended to proving NP-hardness of approximation results. This plays a key role in directing research on approximation algorithms to those problems (such as sparsest cut) for which there still is hope for substantial improvements, and away from problems (such as max-3SAT) for which there is only negligible room for improvements. Unfortunately, the theory of NP-completeness has not been successfully extended (so far) to distributional problems, and hence it is difficult to judge whether our failure to find good algorithms for a distributional problem (in those cases where we fail) is because there really is no good algorithm for handling the instances generated by the distribution, or because we are not using the right algorithmic tools for the distributional problem. This makes it difficult to classify which distributional problems are easy and which are hard.

One of the advantages of semirandom models is that their adversarial component offers us possibilities for proving NP-hardness results. Consequently, it is not rare that for semirandom models, for certain ranges of parameters we have polynomial-time algorithms, and we also have NP-hardness results that explain why the algorithmic results do not extend to other ranges of the parameters. Hence research on algorithms for semirandom models can be guided by the theory of NP-completeness toward problems or which there is hope to make progress, and away from problems for which progress is hopeless. This aspect is missing in research on algorithms for distributional problems.

9.3 Some Representative Work

In this section we shall present some key insights that emerged in the study of semirandom input models. In doing so, we shall provide some historical perspective of how these ideas developed (though not necessarily in historical order).

9.3.1 Preliminary Results on Semirandom Models

Blum and Spencer (1995), following earlier work by Blum (1990), motivated and introduced several semirandom models for the k-coloring problem. One of these models, referred to in their work as the *colorgame* model, is a *monotone adversary* model for k-coloring. In this model, the set of vertices is partitioned into k equal sized color classes. Thereafter for every pair of vertices u, v in different color classes, an edge (u, v) is introduced independently with probability p. The edges introduced in this stage are referred to as *random edges*. Finally, the adversary may introduce arbitrary additional edges between color classes, referred to as *adversarial edges*. The goal is to design polynomial-time algorithms that k-color the resulting graph, for a wide range of values of k and p. As in all semirandom models, the coloring algorithm is not told which edges are random and which are adversarial.

For $k = 3$ Blum and Spencer propose the following algorithm. Let $N(v)$ denote the set of neighbors of a vertex v. Two vertices u and v are said to be *linked* if the subgraph induced on $N(u) \cap N(v)$ includes at least one edge. Observe that in every legal 3-coloring, two linked vertices must both be colored by the same color, because in every legal coloring their common neighborhood requires at least two colors. Consequently, two linked vertices u and v may be *merged*, namely, replaced by a single vertex w, with $N(w) = N(u) \cup N(v)$. The new graph is 3-colorable if and only if the original graph is 3-colorable. Any two vertices that were linked in the original graph are also linked in the new graph, but there may be vertices that were not linked in the original graph and become linked in the new graph. Repeatedly merging linked vertices whenever possible (in an arbitrary order – all orders give the same final outcome), the algorithm is successful if the final resulting graph is a triangle. In this case the graph has a unique 3-coloring: for every vertex t of the triangle, the set of vertices that were merged in order to give t forms a color class. Observe that the algorithm is monotone in the following sense: if it is successful for a graph G, then it also successful for every 3-colorable graph G' that can be obtained from G by adding edges to G. This follows because any sequence of merge operations that is performed in G can also be performed in G'. The only edge addition that can prevent a merge between linked vertices u and v is to add the edge (u, v), but this is not allowed because the resulting graph will not be 3-colorable.

Blum and Spencer proved that when $p > n^{-0.6+\epsilon}$ there is high probability (over the choice of the random edges, regardless of the choice of the adversarial edges) that the algorithm indeed 3-colors the graph. At this low edge density, initially most pairs of vertices do not have any common neighbors and hence cannot possibly be linked, and the crux of the proof is in showing that as the algorithm progresses, more pairs of vertices become linked. The algorithm can be adapted to k-coloring of k-colorable semirandom graphs (two vertices are linked if their common neighborhood contains a K_{k-1}), though the required value of p increases to $n^{-\delta_k+\epsilon}$, for $\delta_k = \frac{2k}{k(k+1)-2}$.

Blum and Spencer also considered an *unbalanced* k-colorable semirandom model in which the sizes of different color classes can differ significantly, and showed an *NP*-hardness result for coloring such graphs.

Theorem 9.1 (Blum and Spencer, 1995) *For every $k \geq 4$ and every $\epsilon > 0$, if $p \leq n^{-\epsilon}$ then it is NP-hard to k-color graphs that are produced by the monotone adversary unbalanced semirandom model for k-coloring.*

Proof We sketch the proof for $k = 4$. Suppose that $p = n^{-3\epsilon}$ for some $0 < \epsilon < 1$. Let H be an arbitrary graph on $3n^\epsilon$ vertices for which one wishes to find a 3-coloring. This problem is *NP*-hard, but can be reduced to the problem of 4-coloring a semirandom graph with unbalanced color classes. This is done by creating a graph G^* that is composed of a disjoint union of H and an independent set I of size $n - 3n^\epsilon$, and connecting every vertex $u \in H$ and $v \in I$ by an edge (u, v). Every 4-coloring of G^* must 3-color H, and moreover, deriving the 3-coloring for H from the 4-coloring of G^* can be done in polynomial time. Hence if 3-coloring H is *NP*-hard, so is 4-coloring G^*.

However, G^* can be obtained with high probability as the outcome of the unbalanced semirandom 4-coloring model. Suppose for simplicity of the presentation that the three color classes of H are of equal size. Then consider the unbalanced 4-coloring semirandom model with one "large" color class of size $n-3n^\epsilon$ and three "small" color classes, each of size n^ϵ. With high probability, all random edges in the construction of the input graph will have at least one of their endpoints in the large color class, and no edges between the small color classes. If this high-probability event happens, then the monotone adversary can add between the three small color classes a set of edges that make the subgraph induced on them isomorphic to H, and also add all missing edges between the large color class and each of the small color classes, and this results in the graph G^*. As we argued that it is *NP*-hard to 4-color G^*, it is *NP*-hard to 4-color graphs in the unbalanced semirandom 4-coloring model. $\square$

9.3.2 Planted Clique/MIS with a Monotone Adversary

In this section we shall discuss algorithms for a semirandom model for the maximum independent set (MIS) problem. The model and associated algorithms can easily be adapted to the clique problem as well, due to the fact that a set S of vertices forms a clique in G if and only if it forms an independent set in the complement graph $\bar{G}$

The following is a standard distributional model $G_{n,k,\frac{1}{2}}$ for MIS, often referred to as planted MIS, or hidden MIS (and in analogy, planted/hidden clique – see Chapter 8). One first generates a random $G_{n,\frac{1}{2}}$ graph G'. In G', one selects a set S of k vertices at random, and removes all edges within S. The result is the input graph G. The goal is to design a polynomial-time algorithm that with high probability (over the choice of G) solves the MIS problem. For sufficiently large k (k slightly above $2\log n$ suffices), there is high probability (over the random choice $G \in G_{n,k,\frac{1}{2}}$) that S is the unique MIS in G, and in this case the goal of solving MIS coincides with a goal of finding S.

When $k \geq c\sqrt{n\log n}$ for a sufficiently large constant c, the vertices of S are (almost surely) simply those of lowest degree in G. When $k \geq c\sqrt{n}$, recovering S (with high probability) is more challenging, but there are several known algorithms that manage to do so. Perhaps the simplest of these is the following algorithm of Feige and Ron (2010). The highest degree vertices in the (residual) graph are removed from the graph in an iterative fashion, until only an independent set remains. Feige and Ron prove that with high probability this independent set I is a relatively large subset of S. Moreover, S can be recovered by adding to I those vertices not connected to any vertex in I.

Alon et al. (1998) developed a *spectral* algorithm for recovering S. It is easier to present their algorithm in the planted clique model rather than planted MIS. It is well known that for the adjacency matrix A of a random $G_{n,\frac{1}{2}}$ graph, almost surely the largest eigenvalue satisfies $\lambda_1(A) \simeq \frac{n}{2}$, whereas all other eigenvalues are not larger than roughly $\sqrt{n}$. A standard argument based on *Rayleigh quotients* implies that planting a clique of size $k > c\sqrt{n}$ (for sufficiently large constant c) in a random graph should create an eigenvalue of value roughly $\frac{k}{2}$. Hence for the input graph G, we expect its adjacency matrix A_G to satisfy $\lambda_2(A_G) \simeq \frac{k}{2} > \sqrt{n}$. Alon et al. (1998) proved that with high probability, the set K of k largest entries in the eigenvector with eigenvalue λ_2 have an overlap of size at least $\frac{5k}{6}$ with set S. Iteratively removing from K pairs of vertices that do not form an edge results in a clique K' of size at least $\frac{2k}{3}$. It is not hard to prove that necessarily $K' \subset S$, and that all other vertices of S are precisely those vertices that are neighbors with all vertices of K'.

To evaluate the robustness of these algorithmic techniques, the distributional $G_{n,k,\frac{1}{2}}$ model for MIS can be extended into a semirandom model by introducing a monotone adversary. The adversary, who has unbounded computational power, may observe G, and add to it edges of his choice, provided that S remains an independent set. This gives the semirandom graph $\hat{G}$. Observe that if S is a MIS (the unique MIS, respectively) in G, then necessarily S is a MIS (the unique MIS, respectively) in $\hat{G}$ as well. The goal is to design a polynomial-time algorithm that with high probability (over the choice of $G \in G_{n,k,\frac{1}{2}}$, for every $\hat{G}$ that may be generated from G) finds S.

The iterative algorithm that is based only on degrees of vertices can easily be fooled by the adversary (that in particular has the power to make all vertices of S have substantial higher degree than all the remaining vertices). Likewise, the spectral algorithm can also be fooled by the adversary, and it too will not find S in $\hat{G}$. However, with additional machinery, the spectral algorithm can be salvaged. An algorithm that does work in the semirandom model is based on semidefinite programming. At a high level, one may think of semidefinite programs (SDPs) as a technique that combines spectral techniques with linear programming. This is because SDPs involve two types of constraints: spectral (requiring a certain matrix to have no negative eigenvalues), and linear (as in linear programming).

We present here the algorithm of Feige and Krauthgamer (2000) for the semi-random MIS model. It is based on the ϑ function of Lovasz (which will be defined shortly). Given a graph G, $\vartheta(G)$ can be computed (up to arbitrary precision) in polynomial time, and it provides an upper bound (that might be far from tight) on $\alpha(G)$ (the size of the MIS in G). The key technical lemma in Feige and Krauthgamer (2000) is the following.

Lemma 9.2 *Let $k \geq c\sqrt{n}$ for sufficiently large c. For $G \in G_{n,k,\frac{1}{2}}$, with probability at least $1 - \frac{1}{n^2}$ (over choice of G) it holds that $\vartheta(G) = \alpha(G)$.*

Though Lemma 9.2 is stated for $G \in G_{n,k,\frac{1}{2}}$, it applies also for $\hat{G}$ generated by the semirandom model. This is because ϑ is a monotone function – adding edges to G can only cause ϑ to decrease. But ϑ cannot decrease below $\alpha(\hat{G})$, and hence equality is preserved.

Given Lemma 9.2, finding S in $\hat{G}$ is easy. The failure probability is small enough to ensure that with high probability, for every vertex $v \in S$ it holds that $\vartheta(\hat{G} \setminus v) = k - 1$, and for every vertex $v \notin S$ it holds that $\vartheta(\hat{G} \setminus v) = k$ (here $\hat{G} \setminus v$ refers to the graph obtained from $\hat{G}$ by removing vertex v and all its incident edges). This gives a polynomial-time test that correctly classifies every vertex of $\hat{G}$ as either in S or not in S. As we shall see, in fact it holds that all vertices can be tested simultaneously just by a single computation of $\vartheta(\hat{G})$.

Let us now provide some details about the contents of Lemma 9.2. The ϑ function has many equivalent definitions. One of them is the following. An *orthonormal representation* of $G(V, E)$ associates with each vertex $i \in V$ a unit vector $x_i \in R^n$, such that x_i and x_j are orthogonal ($x_i \cdot x_j = 0$) whenever $(i,j) \in E$. Maximizing over all orthonormal representations $\{x_i\}$ of G and over all unit vectors d (d is referred to as the *handle*) we have

$$\vartheta(G) = \max_{d, \{x_i\}} \sum_{i \in V} (d \cdot x_i)^2.$$

The optimal orthonormal representation and the associated handle that maximize the above formulation for ϑ can be found (up to arbitrary precision) in polynomial time by formulating the problem as an SDP (details omitted). To see that $\vartheta(G) \geq \alpha(G)$, observe that for any independent set S the following is a feasible solution for the SDP: choose $x_i = d$ for all $i \in S$, and choose all remaining vectors x_j for $j \notin S$ to be orthogonal to d and to each other. Observe also that ϑ is indeed monotone as explained above (adding edges to G adds constraints on the orthonormal representation, and hence the value of ϑ cannot increase).

Now we explain how Lemma 9.2 can be used in order to recover the planted independent set S. Applying a union bound over less than n subgraphs, the lemma implies that with probability at least $1 - \frac{1}{n}$ (over the choice of $G \in G_{n,k,\frac{1}{2}}$) $\vartheta(G') = \alpha(G') = \alpha(G) - 1$ for every subgraph G' that can be obtained from G by removing a single vertex of S. The foregoing equalities imply that for every vertex $i \in S$, it holds that in the optimal SDP solution $d \cdot x_i \geq 1 - \frac{1}{2n}$. Otherwise, by dropping i from G without changing the SDP solution we get that $\vartheta(G \backslash \{i\}) > \vartheta(G) - 1 + \frac{1}{2n} > \alpha(G) - 1$, contradicting the foregoing equality (with $G' = G \backslash \{i\}$). No vertex $i \notin S$ can have $d \cdot x_j \geq 1 - \frac{1}{2n}$, as together with the contribution of the vertices from S, the value of $\vartheta(G)$ would exceed $|S| = \alpha(G)$, contradicting Lemma 9.2. We thus conclude that with high probability (over the choice of $G \in G_{n,k,\frac{1}{2}}$), for $\hat{G}$ generated in the semirandom model, the vertices of S are precisely those that have inner product larger than $1 - \frac{1}{2n}$ with the handle d.

We now explain how Lemma 9.2 is proved. Its proof is based on a dual (equivalent) formulation of the ϑ function. In this formulation, given a graph $G(V, E)$

$$\vartheta(G) = \min_{M}[\lambda_1(M)],$$

where M ranges over all n by n symmetric matrices in which $M_{ij} = 1$ whenever $(i, j) \notin E$, and $\lambda_1(M)$ denotes the largest eigenvalue of M. As a sanity check, observe that if G has an independent set S of size k, the minimum of the foregoing formulation cannot possibly be smaller than k, because M contains a k by k block of "1" entries (a Rayleigh quotient argument then implies that $\lambda_1(M) \geq k$). Given $G \in G_{n,k,\frac{1}{2}}$ with an independent set S of size k, Feige and Krauthgamer (2000) construct the following matrix M. As required, M is symmetric, and $M_{i,j} = 1$ for all vertices i, j for which $(i, j) \notin E$ (including the diagonal of M). It remains to set the values of $M_{i,j}$ for pairs of vertices i, j for which $(i, j) \in E$ (which can happen only if at least one of i or j is not in S). This is done as follows. If both i and j are not in S, then $M_{ij} = -1$. If $i \notin S$ and $j \in S$ then $M_{i,j} = -\frac{k - d_{i,S}}{d_{i,S}}$, where $d_{i,S}$ is the number of neighbors that vertex i has in the set S. This value of M_{ij} roughly equals -1, and is chosen so that $\sum_{j \in S} M_{ij} = 0$ for every $i \notin S$. Finally, if $i \in S$ and $j \notin S$, then symmetry of M dictates that $M_{ij} = M_{ji}$. For this matrix M, the vector $v_S \in \{0, 1\}^n$, which has entries of value 1 at coordinates that correspond to vertices of S and 0 elsewhere, serves as an eigenvector of eigenvalue k. Feige and Krauthgamer (2000) prove that with high probability (over choice of G) it holds that this matrix M has no eigenvalue larger than k. This establishes that $\vartheta(G) = k$. The same M applies also to any graph $\hat{G}$ derived from G by a monotone adversary, because adding edges to G only removes constraints imposed on M.

Summarizing, the spectral algorithm of Alon et al. (1998) can find the planted independent set in the distributional model $G_{n,p,\frac{1}{2}}$. The way to extend it to the semirandom model is by use of semidefinite programming, based on computing the ϑ function. More generally, a useful rule of thumb to remember is that semidefinite programming can often serve as a robust version of spectral algorithms.

Another advantage of the SDP approach, implicit in the preceding discussion, is that it not only finds the planted independent set, but also certifies its optimality: the solution to the dual SDP serves as a proof that $\hat{G}$ does not contain any independent set of size larger than k.

9.3.3 Refutation Heuristics

In Section 9.3.2 we presented algorithms that search for solutions in various random and semirandom models. Once a solution is found, the algorithm terminates. A complementary problem is that of determining that an input instance does not have any good solutions. For example, when attempting to verify that a given hardware design or a given software code meets its specification, one often reduces the verification task to that of determining satisfiability of a Boolean formula. A satisfying assignment for the Boolean formula corresponds to a bug in the design, and the absence of satisfying assignments implies that the design meets the specifications. Hence one would like an algorithm that certifies that no solution (satisfying assignment, in this case) exists. Such algorithms are referred to as *refutation algorithms*.

For NP-hard problems such as SAT, there are no polynomial-time refutation algorithms unless $P = NP$. Hence it is natural to consider random and semirandom models for refutation tasks. However, refutation tasks involve a difficulty not present in search tasks. NP-hard problems do not possess polynomial size witnesses for their unsatisfiability (unless $NP = coNP$). Consequently it is not clear what a refutation algorithm should be searching for, and what evidence a refutation algorithm can gather that would ensure that the input instance cannot possibly have a solution.

Recall the distributional model for 3SAT presented in Section 9.1.1. In that model, the input is a random 3CNF formula ϕ with n variables and m clauses, and the goal is to determine whether it is satisfiable. Standard use of Chernoff bounds and a union bound over all possible assignments shows that when $m > cn$ (for some sufficiently large constant c) then almost surely ϕ is not satisfiable. Hence, if we trust that the formula was indeed generated according the the distributional model, and are willing to tolerate a small probability of error, then a refutation algorithm can simply output *not satisfiable*, and will with high probability (over choice of ϕ) be correct. However, this approach is not satisfactory for multiple reasons, one of which being that it provides no insights as to how to design refutation algorithms in practice. Consequently, we shall be interested in algorithms that for a given distributional model D have the following properties.

1. For every input formula ϕ, the algorithm A correctly determines whether ϕ is satisfiable or not.
2. With high probability (over choice of $\phi \in D$), the algorithm A produces its output in polynomial time.

We can completely trust the output of such an algorithm A. However, on some instances, A might run for exponential time, and we might need to terminate A before obtaining an answer. If most inputs generated by D are not satisfiable, then it is appropriate to refer to A as a *refutation heuristic*.

Before addressing refutation heuristics for SAT, it is useful to consider refutation heuristics for a different NP-hard problem, that of MIS. Consider the $G_{n,\frac{1}{2}}$ distributional model for MIS, and fix $k = \frac{n}{5}$. We refer to graphs G for which $\alpha(G) \geq k$ as *satisfiable*. For this setting we offer the following refutation heuristic, based on the ϑ function discussed in Section 9.3.2.

Refutation Heuristic for MIS Compute $\vartheta(G)$. If $\vartheta(G) < k$ output *not satisfiable*. If $\vartheta(G) \geq k$ use exhaustive search to find the MIS in G. If its size is at least k output *satisfiable*, and if its size is less than k output *not satisfiable*.

The output of the refutation heuristic is always correct because $\vartheta(G) \geq \alpha(G)$ for every graph G. For most input graphs G generated from $G_{n,\frac{1}{2}}$ the algorithm runs in polynomial time, because for such graphs $\vartheta(G) = O(\sqrt{n})$ with high probability (an indirect way of proving this is by combining Lemma 9.2 with monotonicity of the ϑ function), and ϑ can be computed up to arbitrary precision in polynomial time.

This refutation heuristic extends without change to $G_{n,p}$ models with $p \geq \frac{c}{n}$ for a sufficiently large constant c, because also for such graphs $\vartheta(G) < \frac{n}{5}$ with high probability. See Coja-Oghlan (2005).

Given that we have a refutation heuristic for MIS we can hope to design one for 3SAT as well, by reducing 3SAT to MIS. However, the standard "textbook" reductions from 3SAT to MIS, when applied to a random 3SAT instance, do not give a random $G_{n,p}$ graph. Hence the refutation heuristic for MIS might not terminate in polynomial time for such graphs. This difficulty is addressed by Friedman et al. (2005), who design a different reduction for 3SAT to MIS. They also design a simpler reduction from 4SAT to MIS, and this is the reduction that we choose to explain here.

We consider a random 4CNF formula ϕ with $m = cn^2$ clauses, for large enough c. Partition ϕ it into three subformulas. ϕ^+ contains only those clauses in which all literals are positive, ϕ^- contains only those clauses in which all literals are negative, and ϕ' contains the remaining clauses. We completely ignore ϕ', and construct two graphs, G^+ based on ϕ^+, and G^- based on ϕ^-. We describe the construction of G^+, and the construction of G^- is similar.

The vertex set V of G^+ contains $\binom{n}{2}$ vertices, where each vertex is labeled by a distinct pair of distinct variables. For every clause in ϕ^+ (that we assume contains four distinct variables), put an edge in G^+ between the vertex labeled by the first two variables in the clause and the vertex labeled by the last two variables in the clause.

Lemma 9.3 *If ϕ is satisfiable, then at least one of the two graphs G^+ and G^- has an independent set of size at least $\binom{n/2}{2} \simeq |V|/4$.*

Proof Consider an arbitrary satisfying assignment for ϕ, let S^+ be the set of variables assigned to true, and let S^- be the set of variables assigned to false. Consider the set of $\binom{|S^-|}{2}$ vertices in G^+ labeled by pairs of vertices from S^-. They must form an independent set because ϕ cannot have a clause containing only variables from S^- in which all literals are positive. Likewise, G^- has an independent set of size at least $\binom{|S^+|}{2}$. As $\max[|S^+|, |S^-|] \geq n/2$, the proof follows. $\qquad\square$

Observe that if ϕ is random then both G^+ and G^- are random graphs, each with roughly $m/16 \simeq c|V|/8$ edges, and hence average degree roughly $c/4$. (Clarification: the exact number of edges in each of the graphs is not distributed exactly as in the $G_{n,p}$ model. However, given the number of edges, the locations of the edges are random and independent, exactly as in the $G_{n,p}$ model. This suffices for the bounds of Coja-Oghlan [2005] on the ϑ function to apply.) For large enough c, the refutation Heuristic for MIS will with high probability take only polynomial time to certify that neither G^+ nor G^- have independent sets larger than $|V|/5$, and thus establish that ϕ cannot have a satisfying assignment.

The refutation heuristic for 4SAT can be extended to kSAT, refuting random kCNF formulas for all k, provided that $m > cn^{k/2}$. Doing so for even values of k is fairly straightforward. The extension to odd k (including $k = 3$, 3SAT) is significantly more difficult. For some of the latest results in this respect, see Allen et al. (2015) and references therein.

It is an open question whether there are refutation heuristics that can refute random 3CNF formulas with significantly fewer than $n^{3/2}$ clauses. The answer to this question may have implications to the approximability of various NP-hard problems such as minimum bisection and dense k-subgraph (see Feige (2002) for details), as well as to problems in statistics and machine learning (see for example Daniely et al. [2013]).

9.3.4 Monotone Adversary for Locally Optimal Solutions

Recall the semirandom model for the MIS problem presented in Section 9.1.1. That model, referred here as the FK model (as introduced by Feige and Kilian [2001]) is more challenging than the model presented in Section 9.3.2, as the monotone adversary has complete control on the subgraph induced on $V \setminus S$. That subgraph might contain independent sets larger than S, and hence S need not be the MIS in G. Consequently, there is no hope of developing algorithms that solve MIS in the FK model, as the solution might lie within $V \setminus S$, and the graph induced on $V \setminus S$ might be a "worst case" instance for MIS. Likewise, recovering S unambiguously is also not a feasible task in this model, because the adversary may plant in $V \setminus S$ other independent sets of size k that are statistically indistinguishable from S itself. Consequently, for simplicity, we set the goal in this model to be that of outputting one independent set of size at least k. However, we remark that the algorithms for this model meet this goal by outputting a list of independent sets, one of which is S. Hence the algorithms might not be able to tell which of the independent sets that they output is S itself, but they do find S.

The FK model attempts to address the following question: what properties of an independent set make finding the independent set easy? Clearly, being the largest independent set in a graph is not such a property, as MIS is NP-hard. Instead, the FK model offers a different answer that can be phrased as follows: if the independent set S is a strong local maximum, then S can be found. The term *strong local maximum* informally means that for every independent set S' in G, either $|S' \cap S|$ is much smaller than $|S|$, or the size $|S'|$ is much closer to $|S' \cap S|$ than to $|S|$. The strong local optimality of S is implied (with high probability) by the random part of the FK model, and adding edges to G (by the monotone adversary) preserves the property of being a strong local minimum.

Another motivation for the FK model comes from the graph coloring problem. Every color class is an independent set, but need not be the largest independent set in the graph. Algorithms for finding independent sets in the FK model easily translate to graph coloring algorithms in various random and semirandom models for the graph coloring problem.

Algorithms for the FK model are based on semidefinite programming. However, Lemma 9.2 need not hold in this model. The subgraph induced on $V \setminus S$ can cause the ϑ function to greatly exceed k – this is true even if this subgraph does not contain any independent set larger than k. Consequently, in the FK model, the algorithm presented in Section 9.3.2 need not find neither S, nor any other independent set in G of size at least k.

Feige and Kilian (2001) make more sophisticated use of semidefinite programming, and in a certain regime for the parameters of the FK model, they obtain the following result.

Theorem 9.4 (Feige and Kilian, 2001) *Let $k = \alpha n$, and let $\epsilon > 0$ be an arbitrary positive constant. Then in the FK model (in which $|S| = k$, edges between S and $V \setminus S$ are introduced independently with probability p, and the adversary may add arbitrary edges $(u, v) \notin S \times S$) the following results hold:*

- *If $p \geq (1 + \epsilon)\frac{\ln n}{\alpha n}$ then there is a random polynomial-time algorithm that with high probability outputs an independent set of size k.*
- *If $p \leq (1 - \epsilon)\frac{\ln n}{\alpha n}$ then the adversary has a strategy such that unless $NP \subset BPP$, every random polynomial-time algorithm fails with high probability to output an independent set of size k.*

The algorithm in the proof of Theorem 9.4 has five phases that are sketched in the following list (with most of the details omitted).

1. Make repeated use of the ϑ function to extract from the graph $t \leq O(\log n)$ sets of vertices $S_1, \ldots, S_t$, with the property that most vertices of S are among the extracted vertices.
2. Make repeated use of the random hyperplane rounding technique of Goemans and Williamson (1995) so as to find within each set S_i a relatively large independent set I_i.
3. It can be shown that with high probability, there will be *good* indices $i \in [t]$ for which $|I_i \cap S| \geq \frac{3}{4}|I_i|$. "Guess" (by trying all possibilities – there are only polynomially many of them) which are the good indices. Take the union of the corresponding I_i, and remove a maximal matching from the corresponding induced subgraph. The resulting set I of vertices that remains forms an independent set (due to the maximality of the matching). Moreover, as every matching edge must contain at least one vertex not from S, it follows that (for the correct guess) most of the vertices of I are from S.
4. Setting up a certain matching problem between I and $V \setminus I$, identify a set of M vertices to remove from I, resulting in $I' = I \setminus M$. It can then be shown that $I' \subset S$.
5. Consider the subgraph induced on the nonneighbors of I' (this subgraph includes I' itself), find in it a maximal matching, and remove the vertices of the matching. This gives an independent set, and if it is larger than I', it replaces I'. It can be shown that this new I' maintains the invariant that it is a subset of S. Repeat this process until there is no further improvement in the size of I'. If at this point $|I'| \geq k$, then output I'.

In phase 3 the algorithm tries out polynomially many guesses, and several of them may result in outputting independent sets of size at least k. Feige and Kilian (2001) prove that when $p \geq (1+\epsilon)\frac{\ln n}{\alpha n}$, there is high probability that the planted independent set S is among those output by the algorithm. However, when $p \leq (1 - \epsilon)\frac{\ln n}{\alpha n}$, the monotone adversary has a strategy that may cause the algorithm to fail. The algorithm does manage to complete the first three phases and to find a fairly large independent set, but of size somewhat smaller than k. The difficulty is in the fourth and fifth phases of the algorithm. This difficulty arises because there is likely to be a small (but not negligible) set of vertices $T \subset (V \backslash S)$ that has no random edge to S. The adversary may then choose a pattern of edges between T and S that on the one hand makes the largest independent set in $S \cup T$ be S itself, and on the other hand makes it difficult for the algorithm to determine which vertices of I (the result of the third phase) belong to T. These vertices prevent extending I to a larger independent set. Moreover, these considerations can be used to derive the NP-hardness result stated in the second part of Theorem 9.4, along lines similar to those used in the proof of Theorem 9.1.

We end this section with an open question.

Question: *What is the smallest value of k (as a function of n) such that an independent set of size k can be efficiently found in the FK model when $p = \frac{1}{2}$?*

McKenzie et al. (2020) show that an algorithm based on semidefinite programming works when $k \geq \Omega(n^{2/3})$. In analogy to the results stated in Section 9.3.2, one may hope to design an algorithm that works for $k \geq \Omega(\sqrt{n})$, though such an algorithm is not known at the moment, and neither is there a hardness result that suggests that no such algorithm exists.

9.3.5 Separable Semirandom Models

In Sections 9.3.2 and 9.3.4 we discussed semirandom graph models in which some of the edges in the input graph are generated at random, and others are generated by an adversary. Hence when generating an input instance, both the random decisions and the adversarial decisions refer to the same aspect of the input instance, to the edges. In this and subsequent sections we discuss classes of semirandom models that we refer to as *separable*. In these models, certain aspects of the input instance are random, and certain other aspects are adversarial. Such models help clarify which aspects of a problem contribute to its computational difficulty.

Recall the 3SAT semirandom model of Section 9.1.1, with n variables, m clauses, and probability p of flipping the polarity of a variable. When setting $p = \frac{1}{2}$, it provides a conceptually simple separable model for 3SAT. One may think of a 3CNF formula as having two distinct aspects: one is the choice of variables in each clause, and the other is the polarity of each variable. In the distributional model, both the choice of variables and the choice of their polarities are random. In the separable semirandom model, the choice of variables is left to the complete discretion of the adversary, whereas given the set of variables in each clause, the polarities of variables are set completely at random (each variable appearance is set independently to be positive with probability $\frac{1}{2}$ and negative with probability $\frac{1}{2}$). As in the distributional model for 3SAT, when $m > cn$ (for some sufficiently large constant c) then almost surely the resulting input formula is not satisfiable. As discussed in Section 9.3.3, when $m > cn^{3/2}$, there are refutation heuristics for the distributional model. As stated, these heuristics do not apply to the separable semirandom model. To appreciate some of the difficulties, observe that for the heuristic described in Section 9.3.3 for refuting

4SAT, the graphs G^+ and G^- referred to in Lemma 9.3 will not be random in the semirandom model. Nevertheless, if one allows a modest increase in the number of clauses to $m \geq cn^{3/2}\sqrt{\log \log n}$, then there are ways of adapting the known refutation heuristics for 3SAT to the semirandom model (see Feige, 2007). This suggests that the key aspect that is required for efficient refutation of random 3CNF formulas (with sufficiently many clauses) is randomness in the polarity of the variables. Randomness in the choice of variables does not seem to play a significant role. To test this conclusion, it makes sense to study also a complementary separable semirandom model for 3SAT, in which the choice of variables in each clause is random, whereas the choice of their polarities is adversarial. We do not know if the known refutation heuristics can be adapted to this other separable semirandom model.

9.3.6 Separable Models for Unique Games

An instructive use of separable semirandom models is provided by Kolla et al. (2011). They consider instances of *unique games*. A unique game instance is specified by a graph $G(V, E)$ with n vertices, a set $[k]$ of labels, and for every $(u, v) \in E$ – a permutation π_{uv} on $[k]$. Given an assignment of a label $L(v) \in [k]$ to each vertex $v \in V$, the value of the game is the fraction of edges (u, v) for which $L(v) = \pi_{uv}(L(u))$. One seeks an assignment of labels that maximizes the value of the game. This problem is *NP*-hard, and the *unique games conjecture* (UGC) of Khot (2002) states that for every $\epsilon > 0$, there is some k such that it is *NP*-hard to distinguish between unique games of value at least $1 - \epsilon$ and unique games of value at most ϵ. Because of its many consequences for hardness of approximation, much effort has been spent both in attempts to prove and in attempts to refute the UGC. Such efforts could presumably be guided toward promising avenues if we knew how to design instances of unique games with value $1 - \epsilon$ for which no known algorithm can find a solution of value greater than ϵ. Given n, k and ϵ, the design of such unique games instance involves four aspects:

1. A choice of input graph $G(V, E)$
2. A function $L : V \rightarrow [k]$ assigning labels to the vertices, and a choice of permutations π_{uv} that cause the value of the assignment to be 1
3. A choice of $\epsilon|E|$ edges E' to corrupt
4. A choice of alternative permutations π'_{uv} for $(u, v) \in E'$ (where possibly $L(v) \neq \pi'_{uv}(L(u))$)

If an adversary controls all aspects of the input instance, then we get a worst-case unique games instance. There are four separable semirandom models that weaken the adversary in a minimal way. Namely, for each model three of the above aspects are controlled by the adversary, where the remaining one is random. One may ask which of these semirandom models generates a distribution over inputs on which UGC might be true. Somewhat surprisingly, Kolla et al. (2011) prove that none of them do (if the input graph has sufficiently many edges).

Theorem 9.5 (Kolla et al., 2011) *For arbitrary $\delta > 0$, let k be sufficiently large, let $\epsilon > 0$ (the fraction of corrupted edges) be sufficiently small, and suppose that* *the number of edges in G is required to be at least $f(k, \delta)n$ (for some explicitly given function f). Then there is a randomized polynomial-time algorithm that given an instance generated in any one of the above four separable semirandom models, finds with high probability a solution of value at least $1 - \delta$.*

The probability in Theorem 9.5 is taken both over the random choices made in the generation of the semirandom input instance, and over the randomness of the algorithm.

For lack of space we do not sketch the proof of Theorem 9.5. However, we do wish to point out that when only the third aspect (the choice of E') is random, the adversary is sufficiently strong to foil all previously known approaches for approximating unique games. To handle this case, Kolla et al. (2011) introduce the so-called *crude SDP* and develop techniques that exploit its solutions in order to find approximate solutions for unique games. One of the goals of semirandom models is to bring about the development of new algorithmic techniques, and the separable model for unique games has served this purpose well.

9.3.7 The Hosted Coloring Framework

We discuss here two separable semirandom models for 3-coloring. Recall the 3-coloring distributional model of Section 9.1.1. The key parameter there is p – the probability with which edges are introduced between vertices of different color classes. When p is constant, the 3-coloring can be recovered using the fact that for graphs of degree $\Omega(n)$, 3-coloring can be solved in polynomial time even on worst case instances. (Here is a sketch of how this can be done. A greedy algorithm finds a dominating set S of size $O(\log n)$ is such a graph. "Guess" (that is, try all possibilities) the true color of every vertex in S. For each vertex not in S, at most two possible colors remain legal. Hence the problem of extending the correct 3-coloring of S to the rest of the graph can be cast as a 2SAT problem, and 2SAT is solvable in polynomial time.) As p decreases, finding the planted coloring becomes more difficult. In fact, if there is an algorithm that finds the planted 3-coloring (with high probability) for $p = p_0$, then the same algorithm can be applied for every $p_1 > p_0$, by first subsampling the edges of the graph, keeping each edge with probability $\frac{p_0}{p_1}$.

Blum and Spencer (1995) design a combinatorial algorithm that finds the planted 3-coloring (w.h.p.) when $p \geq n^{\epsilon-1}$ for $\epsilon > 0$. Their algorithm is based on the following principle. For every two vertices u and v one computes the size of the intersection of the distance r neighborhood of u and the distance r neighborhood of v, where $r = \Theta(\frac{1}{\epsilon})$ and r is odd. For some threshold t that depends on p and r, it holds with high probability that vertices u and v are in the same color class if and only if the size of the intersection is above t. For example, if $p = n^{-0.4}$ one can take $r = 1$ and $t = \frac{n}{2}p^2$, because vertices of the same color classes are expected to have $p^2\frac{2n}{3}$ common neighbors, whereas vertices of different color classes are expected to have only $p^2\frac{n}{3}$ common neighbors.

Alon and Kahale (1997) greatly improved over the results of Blum and Spencer (1995). They designed a spectral algorithm (based on the eigenvectors associated with the two most negative eigenvalues of the adjacency matrix of G) that finds the planted 3-coloring (w.h.p.) whenever $p \geq \frac{c\log n}{n}$ (for sufficiently large constant c).

Moreover, enhancing the spectral algorithm with additional combinatorial steps, they also manage to 3-color the input graph (w.h.p.) whenever $p \geq \frac{c}{n}$ (for sufficiently large constant c). At such low densities, the planted 3-color is no longer the unique 3-coloring of the input graph (for example, the graph is likely to have isolated vertices that may be placed in any color class), and hence the algorithm does not necessarily recover the planted 3-coloring (which is statistically indistinguishable from many other 3-colorings of the graph).

David and Feige (2016) introduced the hosted 3-coloring framework for the 3-coloring problem. In their models, there is a class $\mathcal{H}$ of host graphs. To generate an input graph G, one first selects a graph $H \in \mathcal{H}$, and then plants in it a balanced 3-coloring (by partitioning the vertex set into three roughly equal parts and removing all edges within each part). The resulting graph G is given as input to a polynomial-time algorithm that needs to 3-color G. The distributional 3-coloring model is a special case of the hosted 3-coloring framework, in which $\mathcal{H}$ is the class of $G_{n,p}$ graphs, a member $H \in \mathcal{H}$ is chosen at random, and then a balanced 3-coloring is planted at random. Other models within the hosted 3-coloring framework may assign parts (or even all, if the class $\mathcal{H}$ is sufficiently restricted) of the graph generation process to the discretion on an adversary.

In one separable semirandom model within the framework, $\mathcal{H}$ is the class of d-regular spectral expander graphs. Namely, for every graph $H \in \mathcal{H}$, except for the largest eigenvalue of its adjacency matrix, every other eigenvalue has absolute value much smaller than d. A graph $H \in \mathcal{H}$ is chosen by an adversary, and the planted 3-coloring is chosen at random. David and Feige (2016) show that the 3-coloring algorithm of Alon and Kahale (1997) can be modified to apply to this case. This shows that random planted 3-colorings can be found even if the host graph is chosen by an adversary, provided that the host graph is an expander.

In another separable semirandom model within the framework, a host graph H is chosen at random from $\mathcal{H} = G_{n,p}$, but the planted balanced 3-coloring is chosen by an adversary, after seeing H. Somewhat surprisingly, David and Feige (2016) show that for a certain range of values for p, corresponding to the random graph having average degree somewhat smaller than $\sqrt{n}$, 3-coloring the resulting graph is NP-hard. We explain here the main idea of the NP-hardness result (substantial additional work is required in order to turn the following informal argument into a rigorous proof). Let $\mathcal{Q}$ be a carefully chosen class of graphs on which 3-coloring is NP-hard. First one shows that given any 3-colorable graph $Q \in \mathcal{Q}$ on n^{ϵ} vertices, if p is sufficiently large ($p \geq n^{-2/3}$ is required here), then H is likely to contain many copies of Q. The computationally unbounded adversary can find a copy of Q in H, and plant in H a 3-coloring that leaves this copy of Q unmodified (by having the planted coloring agree on Q with some existing 3-coloring of Q). Moreover, if p is not too large ($p \leq n^{-1/2}$ is required here), the planting can be made in such a way that Q becomes separated from the rest of H (due to the fact that edges that are monochromatic under the planted 3-coloring are removed from H). Any algorithm that 3-colors G can infer from it in polynomial time a 3-coloring for Q, because it is easy to find Q within G. As 3-coloring Q was assumed to be difficult, so is 3-coloring G.

In general, results in the hosted 3-coloring framework help clarify which aspects of randomness in the planted coloring model are the key to successful 3-coloring algorithms.

9.4 Open Problems

As is evident from Section 9.3, there are many different semirandom models. We presented some of them, and some others are discussed more extensively in other chapters of this book. Some of the more creative models, such as the permutation-invariant random edges (PIE) model of Makarychev et al. (2014), were not discussed because of lack of space.

We also attempted to provide an overview of some of the algorithmic techniques that are used in handling semirandom models. Further details can be found in the references. Moreover, we provided brief explanations as to how hardness results are proved in semirandom model. We believe that having hardness results (and not just algorithms) is a key component in building a complexity theory for semirandom models.

There are many open questions associated with distributional and semirandom models. Some were mentioned in previous sections. Here we list a few more. The first two refer to improving the parameters under which algorithms are known to work. Similar questions can be asked for other problems. The other two questions relate to less standard research directions.

- Recall that Alon and Kahale (1997) design a 3-coloring for the distributional model for 3-coloring, provided that $p \geq cn$ for a sufficiently large constant c. Can the algorithm be extended to hold for all p? In this context, it is worth mentioning that for a different NP-hard problem, that of Hamiltonicity, there is a polynomial-time algorithm that works in the $G_{n,p}$ model for all values of p. That is, regardless of the value of p, with high probability over the choice of the input random graph G, if G is not Hamiltonian then the algorithm provides a witness for this fact (the witness is simply a vertex of degree less that 2), whereas if the graph is Hamiltonian the algorithm produces a Hamiltonian cycle (using the extension–rotation technique). See Bollobás et al. (1987) for details.
- In Theorem 9.5 (concerning unique games), can one remove the requirement that the number of edges is sufficiently high?
- Consider the following semirandom model for the MIS problem. First an adversary selects an arbitrary n vertex graph $H(V, E)$. Thereafter, a random subset $S \subset V$ of size k is made into an independent set by removing all edges induced by S, thus making S a random planted independent set. The resulting graph G (but not H) and the parameter k (size of S) are given as input, and the task is to output an independent set of size at least k. Is there a polynomial-time algorithm that with high probability (over the random choice of S) outputs an independent set of size at least k? Is there a proof that this problem is NP-hard?
- Recall that there are refutation heuristics for 3SAT when the random 3CNF formula has more than $n^{3/2}$ clauses. The following questions may serve as a first step toward refuting sparser formulas.

  Given an initial random 3CNF formula ϕ with n^{δ} clauses, one can set the polarities of all variables to be positive, and then the resulting formula is satisfiable. The question is how one should set the polarities of the variables so that the resulting formula ϕ' can be certified in polynomial time to be not satisfiable. When $\delta > \frac{3}{2}$, this can be done by setting the polarities at random, as then the refutation heuristic of Section 9.3.3 can be used. For $\frac{7}{5} < \delta < \frac{3}{2}$, with high probability over the choice of ϕ, there are settings of the polarities (not necessarily by a polynomial-time procedure) under which refutation can be achieved in polynomial time. (Hint: break ϕ' into a prefix with random polarities, and a suffix whose polarities form a 0/1 string that encodes the refutation witness of Feige et al. (2006) for the prefix.) For $\delta < \frac{7}{5}$, it is an open question whether there is any setting of the polarities (whether done in polynomial time or exponential time) under which polynomial-time refutation becomes possible.

Acknowledgments

The work of the author is supported in part by the Israel Science Foundation (grant No. 1388/16). I thank Ankur Moitra, Tim Roughgarden, and Danny Vilenchik for their useful comments.

References

Allen, Sarah R., O'Donnell, Ryan, and Witmer, David. 2015. How to refute a random CSP. In *IEEE 56th Annual Symposium on Foundations of Computer Science, FOCS*, pp. 689–708.

Alon, Noga, and Kahale, Nabil. 1997. A spectral technique for coloring random 3-colorable graphs. *SIAM Journal on Computing*, **26**(6), 1733–1748.

Alon, Noga, Krivelevich, Michael, and Sudakov, Benny. 1998. Finding a large hidden clique in a random graph. *Random Structures & Algorithms*, **13**(3-4), 457–466.

Bhaskara, Aditya, Charikar, Moses, Chlamtac, Eden, Feige, Uriel, and Vijayaraghavan, Aravindan. 2010. Detecting high log-densities: an $O(n^{1/4})$ approximation for densest k-subgraph. In *Proceedings of the 42nd ACM Symposium on Theory of Computing, STOC*, pp. 201–210.

Blum, Avrim. 1990. Some tools for approximate 3-coloring (extended abstract). In *31st Annual Symposium on Foundations of Computer Science*, Volume II, pp. 554–562. IEEE.

Blum, Avrim, and Spencer, Joel. 1995. Coloring random and semirandom k-colorable graphs. *Journal of Algorithms*, **19**(2), 204–234.

Bollobás, Béla, Fenner, Trevor I., and Frieze, Alan M. 1987. An algorithm for finding Hamilton cycles in a random graph. *Combinatorica*, **7**(4), 327–341.

Coja-Oghlan, Amin. 2005. The Lovász number of random graphs. *Combinatorics, Probability & Computing*, **14**(4), 439–465.

Daniely, Amit, Linial, Nati, and Shalev-Shwartz, Shai. 2013. More data speeds up training time in learning halfspaces over sparse vectors. In *Advances in Neural Information Processing Systems 26: 27th Annual Conference on Neural Information Processing Systems 2013*, pp. 145–153.

David, Roee, and Feige, Uriel. 2016. On the effect of randomness on planted 3-coloring models. In *Proceedings of the 48th Annual ACM SIGACT Symposium on Theory of Computing, STOC 2016*, pp. 77–90.

Feige, Uriel. 2002. Relations between average case complexity and approximation complexity. In *Proceedings on 34th Annual ACM Symposium on Theory of Computing*, pp. 534–543.

Feige, Uriel. 2007. Refuting smoothed 3CNF formulas. In *48th Annual IEEE Symposium on Foundations of Computer Science, FOCS*, pp. 407–417.

Feige, Uriel, and Kilian, Joe. 2001. Heuristics for semirandom graph problems. *Journal of Computer and System Sciences*, **63**(4), 639–671.

Feige, Uriel, and Krauthgamer, Robert. 2000. Finding and certifying a large hidden clique in a semirandom graph. *Random Struct. Algorithms*, **16**(2), 195–208.

Feige, Uriel, and Ron, Dorit. 2010. Finding hidden cliques in linear time. In *21st International Meeting on Probabilistic, Combinatorial, and Asymptotic Methods in the Analysis of Algorithms (AofA'10)*, pp. 189–204.

Feige, Uriel, Kim, Jeong Han, and Ofek, Eran. 2006. Witnesses for non-satisfiability of dense random 3CNF formulas. In *47th Annual IEEE Symposium on Foundations of Computer Science, FOCS 2006*, pp. 497–508.

Friedman, Joel, Goerdt, Andreas, and Krivelevich, Michael. 2005. Recognizing more unsatisfiable random k-SAT instances efficiently. *SIAM Journal of Computing*, **35**(2), 408–430.

Goemans, Michel X., and Williamson, David P. 1995. Improved approximation algorithms for maximum cut and satisfiability problems using semidefinite programming. *Journal of ACM*, **42**(6), 1115–1145.

Khot, Subhash. 2002. On the power of unique 2-prover 1-round games. In *Proceedings on 34th Annual ACM Symposium on Theory of Computing*, pp. 767–775.

Kolla, Alexandra, Makarychev, Konstantin, and Makarychev, Yury. 2011. How to play unique games Against a semirandom adversary: Study of semirandom models of unique games. In *IEEE 52nd Annual Symposium on Foundations of Computer Science, FOCS 2011*, pp. 443–452.

Makarychev, Konstantin, Makarychev, Yury, and Vijayaraghavan, Aravindan. 2014. Constant factor approximation for balanced cut in the PIE model. In *Symposium on Theory of Computing, STOC 2014*, pp. 41–49.

McKenzie, Theo, Mehta, Hermish, and Trevisan, Luca. 2020. A new algorithm for the robust semirandom independent set problem. In *Proceedings of the 2020 ACM-SIAM Symposium on Discrete Algorithms (SODA)*, pp. 738–746.

CHAPTER TEN

Semirandom Stochastic Block Models

Ankur Moitra

Abstract: This chapter introduces *semirandom stochastic block models* and explores semirandom models in other machine learning applications.

10.1 Introduction

The stochastic block model was introduced by Holland et al. (1983) and has been a mainstay in statistics ever since. Furthermore, it has found a wide range of applications in biology, physics, and computer science. The model defines a procedure for generating a random graph with a planted community structure that proceeds as follows:

(a) First, each of the n nodes is independently assigned to one of the k communities, where p_i is the probability of being assigned to community i.

(b) Next, edges are sampled independently based on the community assignments: If nodes u and v belong to communities i and j respectively, the edge (u, v) occurs with probability $W_{i,j}$ independent of all other edges, where W is a $k \times k$ symmetric matrix whose entries are between zero and one.

The goal is to recover the community structure, either exactly or approximately, from observing the graph. But how could we go about doing that?

Let's build some intuition by starting from a special case. Suppose there are just two communities and that $W_{1,1} = W_{2,2} = p$ and $W_{1,2} = W_{2,1} = q$. Furthermore, suppose that $p > q$, which is called the *assortative* case and is natural in applications such as finding communities in a social network, where we would expect members of the same community to be more likely to be friends with each other. Finally consider the sparsity of a cut, defined as

$$\phi(U) = \frac{|E(U, V \setminus U)|}{\min(|U|, |V \setminus U|)},$$

where V is the set of all nodes and $|E(U, V \setminus U)|$ is the number of edges with one endpoint in U and the other outside of U. It is easy to see that for sufficiently large n the cut that is the sparsest *in expectation* is exactly the one that puts all the nodes from one community on one side and the rest on the other side. With a bit more work (and with some restrictions on the parameters) it can be shown that this is true with high probability too: *For sufficiently large n, the cut that is the sparsest is (with high probability) the same as the planted community structure that was used to generate the graph.* Thus, recovering the planted community structure reduces to computing the sparsest cut in a random graph sampled from the model.

But it turns out that there is a wrench in our plan: Finding the sparsest cut (or even approximating it) is known to be *NP*-hard. Nevertheless it turns out that there are ways around it. For example, we could write down a semidefinite programming relaxation (and we will do that later). Somewhat surprisingly, the relaxation turns out to be exact in the case of the stochastic block model.

Moreover, there are all sorts of algorithms that succeed in recovering the planted community structure. Historically, the first algorithms that were shown to work used degree counting – i.e., counting the number of common neighbors between two nodes – to decide if they belong to the same or different communities. This is similar in spirit to the top degree algorithm that was introduced in Section 8.4.2 in Chapter 8 for the planted clique problem. There are also spectral algorithms that write down the adjacency matrix of the graph and use the top eigenvectors to find the planted community structure. There are even approaches based on Markov chains and ones based on belief propagation. Since it was first introduced, the stochastic block model has become a sort of test bed for different algorithmic techniques, with an emphasis on getting algorithms that succeed in the widest possible range of parameters. In this chapter, we will take a different perspective and will study how robust various algorithms are to changes in the model.

First we will define the notion of a monotone adversary. This definition will make sense only in the assortative case.

Definition 10.1 A monotone adversary is given the graph G along with the planted community structure that was used to generate it and is allowed to make the following modifications:

(a) It can add an edge (u, v) between any pair of nodes u and v that belong to the same community.
(b) It can remove an edge (u, v) between any pair of nodes u and v that are in different communities.

What's a bit strange is that the types of changes the monotone adversary is allowed to make seem to be helpful, in the sense that they make the planted community more obvious. It turns out that coping with a monotone adversary is actually quite challenging and many natural algorithms break. It is also important to note that there is no budget to the number of changes that the adversary can make. But then again, his goal is to further obfuscate the community structure; so if he simply made all of these changes and added all the edges within each community and removed all edges between communities it would be trivial to find the community structure. Our adversary will have to be more subtle.

To get a feel for what this adversary can do, let's study two algorithms, one that he can break and one that he cannot. Suppose there are two communities and they have exactly the same size. This is called the planted bisection model. Also set $p = \frac{1}{2}$ and $q = \frac{1}{4}$ for the intra- and interconnection probabilities respectively. Then it is easy to see that for any pair of nodes from the same community, the expected number of common neighbors they have is

$$p^2 \times \frac{n}{2} + q^2 \times \frac{n}{2} = \frac{5}{32} \times n.$$

Instead, if they come from different communities, the expected number of common neighbors is

$$pq \times n = \frac{4}{32} \times n.$$

Hence if we choose a threshold $T = \frac{9}{64} \times n$ and n is sufficiently large, the pairs of nodes with at least T common neighbors will be exactly those pairs of nodes from the same community. This is our first algorithm.

Also consider the minimum bisection problem:

$$\min_{|U| = \frac{n}{2}} |E(U, V \setminus U)|.$$

As before (when we considered the sparsest cut), it is easy to see that for sufficiently large n the bisection that cuts the fewest edges will (with high probability) be the same as the planted community structure. Let's solve the minimum bisection problem by brute-force search. This is our second algorithm. Any idea which of the two algorithms continues to work in the presence of a monotone adversary?

Lemma 10.2 *Minimum bisection succeeds against a monotone adversary with $p = \frac{1}{2}$ and $q = \frac{1}{4}$*

Proof First, consider any edge that the adversary adds. Its endpoints belong to the same community so adding the edge does not increase the number of edges cut in the planted bisection. Moreover adding the edge cannot decrease the number of edges cut in any other bisection. Second, consider any edge that the adversary removes. Its endpoints belong to different communities so removing it reduces the number of edges cut in the planted bisection by one. Removing it can decrease the number of edges cut in any other bisection by at most one. So, either way, if at the beginning (before the adversary makes any changes) the planted bisection was the unique solution to the minimum bisection, it is afterwards as well. □

There are many ways to break the degree counting algorithm. The adversary could add all the edges within one of the two communities, say the first one. Then the number of common neighbors for two nodes from the first community is larger than the number for nodes in different communities, which itself is larger than the number for nodes that are both in the second community. Now if we knew this is what the adversary was doing, we could in turn try to fix our degree counting algorithm. But the goal is to find algorithms that do not need to be fixed in this kind of vicious cycle. We want to design algorithms that work without exploiting some kind of brittle structure present in the graphs sampled from the generative model.

10.2 Recovery via Semidefinite Programming

As before, let G be a random graph on n nodes with a planted bisection where the probability of including an edge with both endpoints on the same side is p and otherwise the probability is q. In this section, we will give an algorithm for recovering the planted bisection that is based on semidefinite programming and succeeds with high probability. Later, we will show that it continues to work against a monotone adversary.

10.2.1 A Certificate of Optimality

First we define the relaxation we will work with. We will use the standard notation $X \succeq 0$ to denote the constraint that X is symmetric and has nonnegative eigenvalues – i.e., it is positive semidefinite. Now consider

$$\begin{aligned} \min \quad & \frac{m}{2} - \sum_{(u,v) \in E} \frac{X_{u,v}}{2} \\ \text{s.t.} \quad & \sum_{u,v} X_{u,v} = 0 \\ & X_{u,u} = 1 \text{ for all } u \\ & X \succeq 0, \end{aligned}$$

where E are the edges in G.

To see that this is indeed a relaxation for the minimum bisection problem, consider any bisection $(U, V \setminus U)$ and define a corresponding length n vector s where $s_u = 1$ if $u \in U$ and $s_u = -1$ otherwise. Now set $X = ss^\top$. It is easy to check that $X_{u,u} = 1$ and $X \succeq 0$. Moreover a straightforward computation gives the equation

$$\frac{m}{2} - \sum_{(u,v) \in E} \frac{X_{u,v}}{2} = |E(U, V \setminus U)|,$$

which shows that the objective value in the semidefinite program is exactly the number of edges crossing the bisection. Finally, if we let $\vec{1}$ be the vector of all ones, then

$$\sum_{u,v} X_{u,v} = \vec{1}^\top X \vec{1} = \left(\sum_u s_u \right)^2 = 0$$

because U is a bisection.

We will now prove the following main theorem of Boppana (1987), refined in Feige and Kilian (2001):

Theorem 10.3 *If $(p - q)n \geq C\sqrt{pn \log n}$ for some universal constant C, then with high probability over the generation of the random graph G, the value of the semidefinite programming relaxation is exactly the size of its minimum bisection.*

The approach is to guess a feasible solution to the dual program that certifies that there is no feasible solution to the primal that achieves a value that is strictly smaller than the minimum bisection. The dual takes the form:

$$\max \quad \frac{m}{2} + \frac{\sum_u y_u}{4}$$
$$\text{s.t.} \quad M \triangleq -A - y_0 J - Y \succeq 0.$$

Here m is the number of edges in G, A is the adjacency matrix, J is the matrix of all ones, and Y is the diagonal matrix whose values along the diagonal are the variables y_u, one for each node in the graph. There is also a special variable y_0.

To get some intuition for this dual let us check weak duality. Consider a primal and dual feasible pair (X, M). Let $\langle X, M \rangle = \sum_{u,v} X_{u,v} M_{u,v}$ denote the matrix inner product. First using the fact that $X \succeq 0$ and $M \succeq 0$ and standard facts about the cone of positive semidefinite matrices, we have that

$$\langle X, M \rangle \geq 0.$$

Now using the expression for M we can write

$$-\langle X, A \rangle - \langle X, y_0 J \rangle - \langle X, Y \rangle \geq 0.$$

We can rewrite the first term using the computation

$$\langle X, A \rangle = 2 \sum_{(u,v) \in E} X_{u,v}.$$

The second term is zero because X is feasible. The third term is equal to $\sum_u y_u$ because $X_{u,u} = 1$ and Y is diagonal. Rearranging, adding $2m$ to both sides and dividing by four gives us

$$\frac{m}{2} - \frac{\sum_{(u,v) \in E} X_{u,v}}{2} \geq \frac{m}{2} + \frac{\sum_u y_u}{4}.$$

The left-hand side is the objective function of the primal and the right-hand side is the objective function of the dual, as desired.

The main insight of Feige and Kilian (2001) is to guess a solution to the dual based on the planted bisection. The first time you see a trick like this, you might feel like you've been cheated. After all, finding the planted bisection is what we're after so how can you assume you know it when you guess a solution to the dual? The point is that you can pretend to know whatever you want, and if at the end of the day you construct a solution that really is feasible, you know that when you solve the dual program to optimality the lower bound you get will be at least as good. To foreshadow what we will talk about later, this is also the main insight behind *why* semidefinite programs are robust to a monotone adversary. When you're working in the dual, you can pretend to know what the monotone adversary has done as well. This knowledge can help you adapt your lower bound to however the instance has been modified.

Anyways, let o_u be the number of neighbors of u that are on the opposite side of the bisection as u. Similarly let s_u be the number of neighbors of u on the same side. The idea is to set $y_0 = 1$ and each $y_u = o_u - s_u$. For this setting of the variables, it is easy to compute that

$$\frac{m}{2} + \frac{\sum_u y_u}{4} = |E(U, V \setminus U)|,$$

where U is the planted bisection. What remains is to show that with high probability this construction is feasible – i.e.,

$$M = -A + J - Y \succeq 0.$$

The way that Feige and Kilian (2001) proved this bound was by applying the trace method. Specifically, they computed the expected trace of even powers of M to get a handle on the distribution of its eigenvalues. Instead, we will give a heuristic argument why one would expect this bound to be true.

10.2.2 Some Random Matrix Theory

First we review some classic random matrix theory. In a seminal work, Wigner (1993) studied the distribution of the eigenvalues of a random matrix A whose entries are independent and identically distributed and mean zero.

Theorem 10.4 *Suppose that Z is an $n \times n$ random symmetric matrix whose diagonal entries are zero and whose off-diagonal entries $Z_{i,j}$ are independent and identically distributed with mean zero and variance σ^2. Then the distribution of the eigenvalues of Z converges in law to the semicircle of radius $R = 2\sigma\sqrt{n}$ – i.e., the distribution*

$$\frac{2}{\pi R^2} \sqrt{R^2 - x^2}.$$

Now there are some weaknesses to using this semicircle law. While it tells us what the distribution converges to, there could be $o(n)$ eigenvalues that are anywhere outside the semicircle. However, it turns out that there are other related approaches for showing essentially the same bounds on the spectral radius that hold with high probability. See, for example, Füredi and Komlós (1981). There are even extensions that allow the entries of Z to have different distributions, as long as they remain independent; see Bandeira et al. (2016).

Our goal is to understand the spectrum of A, which, recall is the adjacency matrix of G. Its diagonal entries are zero and its off diagonal entries are Bernoulli random variables with either mean p or mean q depending on whether or not the pair of nodes corresponding to the row and column are on the same side of the planted bisection. First, notice that the entries in A do not have mean zero. This drastically changes what we should expect its spectrum to look like. Intuitively, we should expect one large eigenvalue that behaves like the average degree and its corresponding eigenvector should be close to the all 1's vector. If G were regular, this would be exactly true. In terms of the contribution to M, the large eigenvalue in A is cancelled out by the J term whose eigenvector is also the all ones vector but has a much larger eigenvalue of n rather than $\frac{p+q}{2}n$.

Now that we have discussed the top eigenvalue of A, let's talk about the others. It is reasonable to expect them to behave like they do in a random matrix whose entries are mean zero. It turns out there are generalizations of Theorem 10.4 that allow for the entries to be independent but not identically distributed. In fact, what we need is even a little stronger than that because we need bounds on the spectral radius rather than merely characterizing what the limiting distribution of the spectrum looks like.

In any case, we should expect $\lambda_2(A) \lesssim 2\sqrt{pn}$ because the entries of A have variance at most p.

Finally, the eigenvalues of Y are its diagonals, which are distributed as the difference between a binomial with mean $\frac{q}{2}n$ and one with mean $\frac{p}{2}n$. And putting it all together,

$$\lambda_{min}(-A + J - Y) \gtrsim -\lambda_2(A) - \lambda_{min}(Y) \gtrsim \frac{p-q}{2}n - 2\sqrt{pn} \geq 0.$$

If G were regular, the tilde in the first inequality could be removed.

10.3 Robustness Against a Monotone Adversary

In this section, we will show that the semidefinite programming relaxation continues to be exact even in the presence of a monotone adversary. In fact, Feige and Kilian (2001) gave an elegant abstraction of what makes the relaxation robust. Let $h(G)$ denote the optimal value of the relaxation on G and let $b(G)$ denote the size of the minimum bisection.

Definition 10.5 We say that a function h is *robust with respect to a monotone adversary* if for any graph G, $h(G) = b(G)$ implies that $h(H) = b(H)$, where H is obtained from G by either removing an edge that crosses the minimum bisection or adding an edge that does not cross it.

Note that this is a slightly different notion of a monotone change because it is with respect to the minimum bisection (as opposed to the planted bisection). However, for the stochastic block model, in the regime of parameters we are interested in, the minimum bisection and the planted one will be the same with high probability. It turns out that verifying some bounded monotonicity properties of h is enough to guarantee that it is robust. In particular Feige and Kilian (2001) prove:

Proposition 10.6 *Suppose that h satisfies the properties*

(1) For all graphs G, $h(G) \leq b(G)$ and
(2) If H is obtained by adding an edge to G then $h(G) \leq h(H) \leq h(G) + 1$

Then h is robust with respect to a monotone adversary.

Proof Suppose G is a graph for which $h(G) = b(G)$ and H is obtained by adding an edge with both endpoints on the same side of the minimum bisection. Invoking the properties of h we have

$$h(G) \leq h(H) \leq b(H) = b(G) = h(G).$$

The first inequality follows from the monotonicity property. The second inequality follows from the lower bound property. The first equality follows because adding the edge does not change the value of the minimum bisection. And the last equality is by assumption. This implies $h(H) = b(H)$, as desired.

Now suppose instead that H is obtained by removing an edge that crosses the minimum bisection. Again invoking the properties of h we have

$$h(G) - 1 \leq h(H) \leq b(H) = b(G) - 1.$$

The first inequality follows from the bounded monotonicity property. The second inequality follows from the lower bound property. The equality follows because removing the edge decreases the value of the minimum bisection by one. This implies $h(H) = b(H)$ and completes the proof. $\quad\square$

Now all that remains is to verify that the relaxation satisfies the properties in the proposition. First, $h(G) \leq b(G)$ holds because it is a relaxation of the minimum bisection. Second, if H is obtained by adding an edge (u, v) to G then the change in the objective function in the relaxation is that we have added a term $\frac{1}{2} - \frac{X_{u,v}}{2}$. Because $X \succeq 0$ and $X_{u,u} = X_{v,v} = 1$ it follows that $|X_{u,v}| \leq 1$ (otherwise the determinant of the 2×2 submatrix indexed by u and v would be negative). Thus for any feasible X the net change in the objective function is between zero and one, as desired. Hence we have the following main result:

Theorem 10.7 *If $(p - q)n \geq C\sqrt{pn \log n}$ for some universal constant C, the semidefinite programming relaxation recovers the exact value of the minimum bisection in the semirandom planted bisection model.*

Alternatively, it is easy to see that the explicit dual certificate that Feige and Kilian (2001) construct tracks the number of edges cut in the planted bisection (if you remove an edge crossing the cut, it decreases in value by one and if you add an edge that does not cross the cut it stays the same) and continues to be feasible.

To summarize, what we have learned is that while there are many sorts of algorithms that recover the planted partition in the stochastic block model, some of them break when we allow monotone changes. However, semidefinite programs do not. Once you can show that they work and get the exact value of the planted bisection, they continue to track it after monotone changes. You can see this either by making a bounded monotonicity argument using the constraints of the relaxation or by directly reasoning about the choice of the dual certificate. Generally, we do not know many other ways to obtain algorithms that work in semirandom models. Most of the analyses work by passing the dual and involve convex programs in some intrinsic way.

10.4 Information Theoretic Limits of Exact Recovery

10.4.1 Planted Bisection

In this section, we will study the information theoretic limits of exact recovery in the planted bisection model. So far our approach has been to approximate the minimum bisection and in some range of parameters the relaxation works and moreover the minimum bisection really is the planted bisection. But if p and q are sufficiently close, the minimum bisection will not be the planted bisection. This motivates the question: In what range of parameters is it information theoretically possible to recover the planted bisection (or partition) exactly? And can we design algorithms that work down to this limit?

It turns out that the answer is yes! First, Abbe et al. (2015) gave sharp bounds on the threshold for exact recovery:

Theorem 10.8 *Let n be the number of nodes and set* $p = \frac{a \log n}{n}$ *and* $q = \frac{b \log n}{n}$. *Then in the planted bisection model if*

$$\frac{a+b}{2} - \sqrt{ab} > 1,$$

then it is possible to recover the planted bisection exactly with high probability. And if

$$\frac{a+b}{2} - \sqrt{ab} < 1$$

it is information-theoretically impossible to recover the planted bisection exactly with probability $1 - o(1)$ *for sufficiently large n.*

Moreover, they showed that almost the same semidefinite programming relaxation works close to the information theoretic threshold. They use the Goemans–Williamson relaxation

$$\min \quad \frac{m}{2} - \sum_{(u,v) \in E} \frac{X_{u,v}}{2}$$
$$X_{u,u} = 1 \text{ for all } u$$
$$X \succeq 0.$$

This is almost the same as our earlier relaxation, except that we have removed the constraint that $\sum_{u,v} X_{u,v} = 1$. This was later improved by Hajek et al. (2016) to get all the way down to the threshold.

Theorem 10.9 *When* $\frac{a+b}{2} - \sqrt{ab} > 1$, *the unique solution to the Goemans–Williamson relaxation is the rank one matrix* $X = ss^\top$, *where s is the* ± 1 *indicator vector of the planted bisection.*

The proof uses many of the same ideas we have seen before, including a similar choice for the dual certificate (except that there is no longer a y_0). However, it requires a sharper bound on the spectrum of the associated random matrix in order to reach the information theoretic limit exactly.

We remark that just as before, the fact that we have a semidefinite programming algorithm that works down to the information theoretic threshold actually gives us more – it gives us an algorithm that works even against a monotone adversary. This is a somewhat surprising corollary because it means that there are no gaps between what can be done in a random versus a semirandom model, at least when it comes to exact recovery.

Corollary 10.10 *The threshold for recovery in the planted bisection model and the semirandom planted bisection model are the same, and can both be solved by semidefinite programming.*

10.4.2 General Stochastic Block Models

So far we have only talked about planted bisection problems. With considerably more work, Abbe and Sandon (2015) were able to pin down the sharp information theoretic limits of exact recovery in a general stochastic block model – with k communities of potentially different sizes and a general $k \times k$ symmetric matrix of connection probabilities. It turns out that there is a nice information theoretic interpretation of the threshold through what is called the Chernoff–Hellinger divergence. In fact, even in the planted bisection model, the bound corresponds to the threshold where you would expect each of the n nodes to have more neighbors on the same side of the bisection than on the opposite side.

The algorithm of Abbe and Sandon (2015) uses the local neighborhoods around each node in a highly complex way to guess which community it belongs to and then performs a cleanup phase to refine these estimates. However, the algorithm breaks down in a semirandom model in much the same way that the degree counting algorithm we gave in Section 2.1 did. Perry and Wein (2017) gave a semidefinite relaxation for the multicommunity case. For example in the case of k communities of known sizes $s_1, \ldots, s_k$ they solve the semidefinite program:

$$
\begin{aligned}
\max \ & \langle A, X \rangle \\
\text{s.t.} \ & \langle J, X \rangle = \tfrac{k}{k-1} \sum_i s_i^2 - \tfrac{1}{k-1} n^2 \\
& X_{u,u} = 1 \text{ for all } u \\
& X \geq \tfrac{-1}{k-1} \\
& X \succeq 0.
\end{aligned}
$$

This is the standard relaxation of the maximum k-cut problem. They show that it achieves exact recovery down to the information theoretic limit, and once again the results extend to the semirandom model. At this juncture it is natural to wonder if the thresholds for recovery for all sorts of problems are the same in the random and semirandom models. Later we will see examples where they are not, where being robust to a monotone adversary really is at odds with reaching the information theoretic limits of an average-case model.

10.5 Partial Recovery and Belief Propagation

So far we have focused on the problem of exact recovery, and necessarily we needed the average degree to be logarithmic. After all, if it is not at least logarithmic, with high probability the graph we generate will have isolated nodes and it is impossible to figure out to which community they belong. In this section, we will switch gears and will study settings where the average degree is constant but we relax our goal. We will want to find a bisection that is merely $\frac{1}{2} + \epsilon$ correlated with the true bisection. What this means is if the nodes on one side of the planted bisection are given a hidden color of red, and the others are given blue, we want to find a bisection where one side has at least a $\frac{1}{2} + \epsilon$ fraction of its nodes colored red and the other has at least a $\frac{1}{2} + \epsilon$ fraction colored blue. *If we can do this with probability $1 - o(1)$ for some ϵ that is bounded away from zero independently of n, we say that we have solved partial recovery.*

Suppose $p = \frac{a}{n}$ and $q = \frac{b}{n}$ are the intra- and interconnection probabilities respectively. Then Decelle et al. (2011) made a striking conjecture:

Conjecture 1 If $(a - b)^2 > 2(a + b)$, there is a polynomial-time algorithm to solve partial recovery in the planted bisection model. Moreover, if $(a - b)^2 < 2(a+b)$, then it is information theoretically impossible to solve partial recovery.

10.5.1 Belief Propagation

The conjecture was based on deep but nonrigorous ideas originating from statistical physics, and was first derived heuristically as a stability criterion for belief propagation. Belief propagation is an iterative algorithm for performing probabilistic and causal reasoning. In our setting, each node maintains a belief of the probability that it belongs to each particular community. In each step, it broadcasts its beliefs to all of its neighbors in the graph. After hearing the messages from all the other nodes, it updates its own beliefs and the process continues until convergence.

To be more precise, let ϕ_u^i be node u's belief that he belongs to community i. For technical reasons it is important to also have an estimate $\phi_{u \leftarrow v}^i$ of the community that node u belongs to if node v were not there. The assumption underneath belief propagation is that the neighbors of u are independent conditioned on the state of u. This is not exactly true but sparse random graphs locally look like trees and it is true on trees. Accordingly the update rule we follow is to set

$$\phi_{u \leftarrow v}^i \propto \prod_{w \neq v: (w,u) \in E} \sum_{j=1}^{2} \phi_{w \rightarrow u}^j p_{i,j},$$

where $p_{i,j}$ is the probability that there is an edge between a pair of nodes, one in community i the other in community j. We normalize the right-hand side so that $\phi_{u \leftarrow v}^i$ is a distribution. After we reach convergence, we compute the marginal as

$$\phi_u^i \propto \prod_{v: (u,v) \in E} \sum_{j=1}^{2} \phi_{w \rightarrow u}^j p_{i,j}$$

There is also some effect from missing edges – if nodes u and v do not share an edge then they are somewhat less likely to be in the same community. However, this can be treated as a global interaction that is omitted here.

In general, we will reach a fixed point of the belief propagation equations. However, there is a trivial fixed point. Intuitively, if each node knows nothing about which community it belongs to, it will never learn anything from its neighbors that will cause it to update its beliefs. This manifests itself by noticing that if all the messages are initialized to $\frac{1}{2}$, the next round of messages will also be $\frac{1}{2}$, and so on. The trick is that in some range of parameters that fixed point will be unstable. If we perturb away from the trivial fixed point, we will not come back to it. In fact, the trivial fixed point is unstable if and only if $(a - b)^2 > 2(a + b)$. The motivation behind the conjecture of Decelle et al. (2011) is the hope that if belief propagation does not get stuck at the trivial fixed point, the solution it ultimately reaches ought to solve the partial recovery problem. And yet this is only half of the conjecture, because the conjecture also posits that when the trivial fixed point is stable, not only does belief propagation fail to solve partial recovery, but the problem itself ought to be information theoretically impossible.

Amazingly, the conjecture is true! Mossel et al. (2018) and Massoulié (2014) proved that partial recovery is solvable if and only if $(a - b)^2 > 2(a + b)$. In fact, the algorithms that they gave were derived from belief propagation. Massoulié (2014) used spectral properties of logarithmic length no-return walks to recover the planted bisection. Mossel et al. (2018) used non-backtracking walks instead.

Theorem 10.11 *There is a polynomial-time algorithm that, when $(a - b)^2 > 2(a + b)$, solves partial recovery in the planted bisection model. Moreover, if $(a - b)^2 < 2(a + b)$, then it is information theoretically impossible to solve partial recovery.*

The upper bound was proved independently in Mossel et al. (2018) and Massoulié (2014). The lower bound (which also handles the case of equality, which was not a part of the original conjecture) was proved in Mossel et al. (2018).

While the algorithms that achieved the sharp information-theoretic threshold for exact recovery were (for the most part) based on semidefinite programming and their guarantees immediately extended to the semirandom model, this is not true here. The spectrum of the non-backtracking random walk matrix cannot be naturally incorporated into a convex program,[1] and it is an essential part of belief propagation (that was the basis for the conjecture in the first place) in that the message that node u sends to node v does not depend on the message from node v to node u in the previous step. The intuition is that you do not want a node to become more confident about its beliefs because of having its own earlier beliefs reflected back to itself.

There is another way to think about why non-backtracking walks are natural. In a sparse random graph, even if the average degree is constant, there are bound to be some nodes with degree $\Theta\left(\frac{\log n}{\log \log n}\right)$. Now consider the adjacency matrix. Apart from the top eigenvector, the other eigenvectors corresponding to large eigenvalues will be *localized* – they will have their weight concentrated around a high degree node and its neighbors. Hence they do not reveal anything interesting about the planted community structure. In contrast, the non-backtracking walk matrix damps the effect of high degree nodes because once the walk leaves a high-degree node it cannot immediately return and the high-degree nodes are all typically far apart from each other.

10.6 Random versus Semirandom Separations

In the exact recovery problem, everything that could be solved in the random model could also be solved in the semirandom model all the way down to the same information theoretic limit. In this section, we will show that there is a gap between what is possible in the random versus semirandom model for partial recovery.

---

[1] The problem is the matrix is not symmetric!

10.6.1 Information Theoretic Limits in Semirandom Models

Moitra et al. (2016) prove:

Theorem 10.12 *There is a δ > 0 (depending on a and b) so that if*

$$(a - b)^2 \le (2 + \delta)(a + b),$$

partial recovery in the semirandom planted bisection model is information theoretically impossible.

This is the first such separation between a random and a corresponding semi-random model. This result needs some digestion. What it means is that seemingly helpful changes such as adding edges within a community and removing edges between different communities can actually hurt. They can break belief propagation. But in fact, something stronger is true. Any algorithm that reaches the information theoretic limit for partial recovery can be broken by one fixed monotone adversary (because he can move the information theoretic threshold).

Guédon and Vershynin (2016) gave a semidefinite program for solving partial recovery, but not down to the information theoretic limit (more on that later). As we saw earlier, when semidefinite programs work for an average-case problem such as community detection in the stochastic block model, their analysis tends to carry over to monotone changes. So when algorithms derived through belief propagation are able to reach the information theoretic limits but semidefinite relaxations are seemingly not able to, it could be owing to the fact that belief propagation is a sharp prediction on one type of distribution and semidefinite programs are working with families of distributions – those that can be obtained from the stochastic block model under monotone changes.

Another implication is that reaching the sharp information theoretic threshold is not always the right thing to aim for. Sometimes it is possible to reach the threshold only by exploiting the structure of the noise – i.e., assumptions from the generative model about how often nodes on different sides of the community are connected to each other. So there is a tension between reaching a sharp threshold for partial recovery and being robust to a monotone adversary. You can have one but not both, unlike in the case of exact recovery.

10.6.2 The Broadcast Tree Model

We will explain the intuition behind this separation in a simpler model that in many senses is a precursor to the stochastic block model. It is called the broadcast tree model:

Definition 10.13 In the broadcast tree model with two colors, we start from a d-ary tree (where $d = \frac{a+b}{2}$) of height n and color the root node either red or blue uniformly at random. Each child is given the same color as its parent with probability $\frac{a}{a+b}$ and the opposite color otherwise. We are given the colors of the leaves and the goal is to guess the color of the root correctly with probability at least $\frac{1}{2} + \epsilon$, where ϵ is independent of n.

In the stochastic block model (where we think of the sides of the bisection as being associated with the colors red and blue), the local neighborhood around a node looks like a tree. Each node has a Poisson number of neighbors with expectation $d = \frac{a+b}{2}$. Moreover, each neighbor has probability $\frac{a}{a+b}$ of having the same color, and otherwise is the opposite color. We call the preceding problem partial recovery, in analogy with the stochastic block model. In fact, the threshold where partial recovery is possible will also look familiar:

Theorem 10.14 *In the two-color broadcast tree model, partial recovery is possible if and only if $(a-b)^2 > 2(a+b)$.*

In fact, when $(a-b)^2 > 2(a+b)$, a simple algorithm works: Look at the colors of the leaves and take majority vote. Kesten and Stigum (1966) proved not just this but a general central limit theorem for Markov branching processes. Evans et al. (2000) showed that when $(a-b)^2 \le 2(a+b)$ partial recovery is information theoretically impossible through a careful coupling argument. The intuition is that the mutual information between the color of any leaf and the root is

$$\left(\frac{a-b}{a+b}\right)^{2n}$$

and there are d^n leaves, so if $(a-b)^2 < 2(a+b)$ we might expect that there is not enough information in the leaves asymptotically as the height increases. However, mutual information is not subadditive in this way and a more careful argument is needed. This threshold is called the Kesten–Stigum bound.

Nevertheless, let's think about what kind of effect a monotone adversary could have around the local neighborhood of a node in the stochastic block model and find some way to map this onto the broadcast tree model. A monotone adversary could remove an edge between a red and blue node, thereby removing the corresponding subtree from the local neighborhood. (Adding edges within a community is more difficult to reason about because we are adding subtrees; but what kind of subtrees ought we be allowed to add?) Now the intuition in the broadcast tree model is this: Suppose the root is colored red. Then even among the children of the root we are somewhat likely to have a blue child where in his subtree there are more red leaves than blue leaves. Thus his descendants vote the opposite way that he would for the color of the root, but nevertheless help get the correct answer. The point is algorithms that work down to the Kesten–Stigum bound need to exploit this quirk of our generative model. Without doing so, they would not actually reach the information theoretic threshold. By carefully cutting edges like this where the descendants end up voting the correct way but opposite to the root of the subtree, we can actually move the information theoretic threshold.

Now you may be wondering whether there is *any* algorithm that solves partial recovery in the semirandom model. Moitra et al. (2016) showed that the analysis of Guédon and Vershynin (2016) carries over with some simple modifications:

Theorem 10.15 *There is a constant $C > 2$ so that if $a > 20$ and*

$$(a-b)^2 \le C(a+b)$$

then partial recovery in the semirandom planted bisection model can be solved in polynomial time.

There is also an algorithm for solving partial recovery in the broadcast tree model: Instead of taking the majority vote of the leaves, we take the recursive majority. Interestingly, these methods are sometimes preferred in practice over the majority, and perhaps one explanation is that they trade off reaching the sharp information theoretic limit with better robustness properties. In a related direction, Makarychev et al. (2016) give an algorithm for community detection that can tolerate a linear number of edge insertions or deletions. Their algorithm even extends to settings where there are more than two communities.

Finally, we mention that in a remarkable paper, Montanari and Sen (2016) showed that the Goemans–Williamson relaxation almost achieves the Kesten–Stigum bound for the following distinguishing problem: We are given a graph that is generated from either (1) an Erdos–Renyi model with average degree $\frac{a+b}{2}$ or (2) the planted bisection model. Our goal is to tell which model the graph was generated from. This is still a challenging problem. First, the average degree in the two models is the same. Second, the information theoretic lower bounds that show that partial recovery beneath the Kesten–Stigum bound is impossible actually do so by showing that even distinguishing problem is impossible – i.e., you can't tell whether there is any planted bisection.

The main result of Montanari and Sen (2016) is

Theorem 10.16 *The Goemans–Williamson relaxation can be used to solve the distinguishing problem with probability $1 - o(1)$ provided that*

$$(a - b)^2 > (2 + o(1))(a + b)$$

The $o(1)$ failure probability goes to zero as a function of n but the $o(1)$ term relating a and b goes to zero as a and b increase (but not as a function of n).

So the gap in performance between belief propagation and the semidefinite programming relaxation goes to zero as the degree goes to infinity. The analysis in Montanari and Sen (2016) is based on guessing a locally computable solution to the relaxation. It in turn uses intuition from belief propagation about the way that the color of a node ought to depend on its local neighborhood through what is called the Gaussian wave. Their analysis is highly sophisticated, and it might be possible to show that it continues to work in a semirandom model but this is not known. In exact recovery, we got robustness to a monotone adversary just from the fact that the relaxation was exact with high probability and satisfied a bounded monotonicity property. However, in partial recovery the relaxation is not exact anymore.

10.7 Above Average-Case Analysis

In this section, we will explore some applications of semirandom models in machine learning. Most of this book and even the name "beyond worst-case analysis" put the emphasis on finding models where we can get provably guarantees that are better than those that we have on worst-case inputs. In Chapter 17, by assuming a generative model on the uncorrupted data, we are able to get computationally efficient estimators that are provably resilient to contamination. In Chapter 16, we place structural assumptions on either the input distribution or the locations where the labels are the noisiest to get better algorithms for some basic problems in supervised learning.

In contrast, here we will focus on some average-case settings where we can rigorously analyze various algorithms by making generative assumptions on their input. We have already seen some examples – such as when we wanted to find well-connected sets of nodes in a graph, we assumed there was a planted partition and that the graph was generated from the stochastic block model. Despite the fact that our starting point is an average-case model instead of a worst-case one, I argue that the types of models we have seen in beyond worst-case analysis can still be important things to think about. Instead of using semirandom models as a way around worst-case hardness, we can think of them as a way to move "above average-case analysis" and stress test whether our algorithms continue to work when we make changes to the model.

It turns out that just like how in community detection there were many algorithms that worked in an average-case model but only semidefinite programming hierarchies survived attacks by monotone adversaries, so too in many other classic problems in machine learning we might expect that some of the standard algorithms are robust and others are not.

10.7.1 Matrix Completion

To see the same principle applied more broadly, let's talk about the matrix completion problem. This is a classic problem in unsupervised learning where the goal is to fill in the missing entries of a low rank matrix from some partial observations.

Definition 10.17 There is an unknown $n \times m$ matrix M of rank at most r and we observe p of its entries $M_{i,j}$ chosen uniformly at random. Moreover, M is μ-incoherent (roughly, this measures how uncorrelated the singular vectors of M are with the standard basis). The goal is to fill in the missing entries of M, and to do so while keeping p as small as possible.

We will omit a precise definition of incoherence because it is not needed for our discussion. However, the picture to keep in mind is if M were diagonal then by virtue of being rank at most r it would have at most r nonzeros. If we observe p entries of M that are chosen uniformly at random, we need p to be about mn – i.e., the number of entries of M – to see all of the diagonal entries to be able to complete M correctly. The notion of incoherence precludes this possibility by ensuring that the entries of M are spread out in an appropriate sense.

In any case, the natural approach to try is to look for the matrix X that has the smallest rank that agrees with all the observed entries. More precisely, let $\Omega \subseteq [n] \times [m]$ be the set of observed entries. Then we could attempt to solve:

$$\min \text{rank}(X)$$
$$\text{s.t. } X_{i,j} = M_{i,j} \text{ for all } (i,j) \in \Omega.$$

This problem is NP-hard. However, inspired by results in compressed sensing that find sparse solutions to linear systems by using the ℓ_1-relaxation, we could use an

ℓ_1-relaxation of the rank. In particular, the rank of a matrix is the number of nonzero singular values. The *nuclear norm*, denoted by $\|X\|_*$, is the sum of the singular values. Now we can introduce the relaxation we will be interested in

$$\min \|X\|_*$$

$$\text{s.t.} \quad X_{i,j} = M_{i,j} \text{ for all } (i,j) \in \Omega.$$

This is now a convex program that we can solve efficiently. (An easy way to see this is to use the dual formulation of the nuclear norm as $\|X\|_* = \max_{B:\|B\|\leq 1}\langle X, B\rangle$ and to incorporate the objective function into the constraints and use the ellipsoid method. However, there are much faster algorithms for solving this convex program.) In a seminal work, Candès and Tao (2010) showed the following:

Theorem 10.18 *Suppose M is a rank r n × m matrix that is μ-incoherent and that we observe p of its entries, chosen uniformly at random. Then if $p \geq C\mu^2 r(n + m)\log^2(n+m)$ for a universal constant C, with high probability the solution to the convex program is exactly M.*

What is amazing about this result is that there are about $nr + mr$ parameters in a rank r $n \times m$ matrix. So if our number of observations is just a polylogarithmic factor larger, we can fill in all the missing entries of M exactly. Moreover, there is an efficient algorithm that does it!

10.7.2 Alternating Minimization

There are still some disadvantages to the convex programming approach. First, actually solving the convex program might be too computationally expensive at large scale. Second, the answer we are looking for takes up $nr + mr$ space so in principle we might not want to write it down as an $n \times m$ matrix – it could be too large to store in memory. It turns out there is another approach to matrix completion, one that is often preferred in practice, which is called alternating minimization. Let U be an $n \times r$ matrix and let V be an $m \times r$ matrix. Then alternating minimization iterates the following steps until convergence:

(a) $U \leftarrow \arg\min_U \sum_{(i,j)\in\Omega} |(UV_{i,j}^\top - M_{i,j}|^2$
(b) $V \leftarrow \arg\min_V \sum_{(i,j)\in\Omega} |(UV_{i,j}^\top - M_{i,j}|^2$

Each step is a least squares problem and can be solved efficiently. Note that compared to the convex programming approach, we have a different set of problems when it comes to the analysis. The output is necessarily rank r but we are attempting to solve a nonconvex problem iteratively so we need to explain why we do not get stuck in a spurious local minimum. Keshavan et al. (2010) and Jain et al. (2013) gave the first analysis of alternating minimization and showed that it provably works under similar conditions. In fact, it is possible to rigorously analyze iterative methods for various other related nonconvex problems. See Chapter 21. In any case, there are some aspects of the results in Keshavan et al. (2010) and Jain et al. (2013) that are quantitatively worse than those that we obtained through nuclear norm minimization. The bounds for alternating minization have a worse dependence on the condition number of M. In fact, the convex programming approach has no dependence whatsoever on the condition number! Nevertheless the results are stronger in that alternating minimization runs much faster and needs much less space because it keeps track of the answer in a factorized form.

10.7.3 Semirandom Matrix Completion

Now we can introduce a semirandom model for matrix completion suggested in Moitra (2015):

Definition 10.19   As before, let M be a rank r $n \times m$ matrix that is μ-incoherent. Suppose p entries $\Omega \subseteq [n] \times [m]$ are chosen uniformly at random. A monotone adversary is given M and Ω and chooses $\Omega' \supseteq \Omega$. Finally, we observe $M_{i,j}$ for all $(i,j) \in \Omega'$.

In much the same way that the monotone adversary in the stochastic block model was just making the communities better internally connected, and less connected to each other, so too this monotone adversary seems to be quite benign. We are trying to fill in the missing entries of M and he is showing us more of M. However, it turns out that among the convex programming approach and the alternating minimization approach, one will continue to work and one will break with the addition of a monotone adversary.

Claim 10.20   *Nuclear norm minimization is robust to a monotone adversary.*

Here is an easy way to see why: When a monotone adversary shows you more of the matrix, the new observations just become additional constraints (that are satisfied by M). *But why does the analysis of alternating minimization break down?* Let M_Ω denote the unknown matrix where we zero out all of the entries outside of Ω. Then a key step in the analysis of alternating minimization is that M_Ω (when appropriately rescaled) should be a good spectral approximation to M. This is true because of the matrix Chernoff bound and because M is assumed to be incoherent. But when a monotone adversary can reveal more entries of M it is no longer true. For example, in the case when $M = J$ (recall, J is the matrix of all ones) then M_Ω is the adjacency matrix of a random bipartite graph and is spectrally close (when rescaled) to the complete bipartite graph. But a monotone adversary can plant a dense subgraph and mess up this key property.

So, while in theoretical computer science, beyond worst-case analysis generally means giving better algorithms (or approximation algorithms) than you otherwise would, in theoretical machine learning it can mean giving you new axes (beyond average-case models) on which to compare algorithms. In the average-case model, alternating minimization gets similar performance guarantees but is much faster and more space efficient. But when we move to a semirandom model and test out how brittle it is, we really see the difference between these two algorithms.

Cheng and Ge (2018) explicitly break several nonconvex methods for matrix completion in the semirandom model. They show an example where all local minima of the nonconvex objective are far from the ground truth matrix. They show that singular value decomposition based initialization also fails to get close. Finally Cheng and Ge (2018) give an efficient preprocessing step that can make nonconvex methods robust to a monotone adversary. The intuition again can be explained in the setting where $M = J$. In the random model, our observation can be described as the adjacency matrix of a random bipartite graph. In the semirandom model, an adversary has added additional edges. But the resulting graph still contains an expanding subgraph, and by reweighting the edges we can make it look more random.

In a related work, Ling et al. (2019) considered synchronization problems where the goal is to find the phase offsets of some coupled oscillators. It is known that there are semidefinite programs that provably work under various conditions on the topology of the graph describing which pairs of oscillators have nonzero interaction terms. There are also nonconvex methods for solving semidefinite programs when you are guaranteed that there is a low-rank solution. Ling et al. (2019) show that a monotone adversary that can add more edges to the network can create spurious local minima.

In summary, while algorithms based on semidefinite programming sometimes inherit appealing robustness properties automatically, other times it is possible to modify nonconvex methods to make them robust too. Perhaps there are other examples waiting to be discovered, where you can teach an old dog (nonconvex methods) a new trick (like being robust to a monotone adversary) without adding too much computational overhead.

10.8 Semirandom Mixture Models

There are other interesting settings where incorporating ideas from semirandom models can help us probe the brittleness of our modeling assumptions. Starting with Dasgupta (1999) a long line of work in theoretical computer science has sought efficient algorithms for learning the parameters of a Gaussian mixture model, culminating in Moitra and Valiant (2010) and Belkin and Sinha (2010). The goal is to give algorithms that take a polynomial number of samples and run in polynomial time, that work under the minimal possible assumptions. The first works assumed the centers of the components are far apart, and later works assumed only that their pairwise total variation distance was bounded away from zero. Let $\mathcal{N}(\mu, \Sigma)$ denote the d-dimensional gaussian with mean μ and covariance Σ. Awasthi and Vijayaraghavan (2018) introduced a semirandom Gaussian mixture model:

Definition 10.21 First, samples $x_1, \ldots, x_m$ are drawn from a mixture of k Gaussians

$$w_1 \mathcal{N}(\mu_1, \Sigma_1) + \cdots + w_k \mathcal{N}(\mu_k, \Sigma_k)$$

in d dimensions. Then a monotone adversary is allowed to inspect the samples and move each sample x_i to a point x_i' as follows: Suppose x_i was drawn from the jth component. Then x_i' must be on the segment connecting x_i and μ_j.

Algorithms like in Moitra and Valiant (2010) and Belkin and Sinha (2010) that are based on the method of moments rely on brittle algebraic properties. They break in the semirandom model. However, clustering based algorithms (which make fairly strong assumptions about how far the centers of the components are from each other) continue to work. Awasthi and Vijayaraghavan (2018) prove:

Theorem 10.22 *Suppose a polynomial number of points are generated from a semirandom Gaussian mixture model where each covariance satisfies $\Sigma_i \preceq \sigma I$ and moreover*

$$\|\mu_i - \mu_j\| \gtrsim \sqrt{d}\sigma$$

for all $i \neq j$. There is an algorithm that with high probability clusters points into which component they were generated from.

Specifically, they use Lloyd's algorithm. In fact, Awasthi and Vijayaraghavan (2018) show that the separation criteria, while substantially stronger than what is needed when the data actually come from a Gaussian mixture model, is in fact somewhat close to optimal: Let Δ be a parameter. Then there is a semirandom Gaussian mixture model with separation $\Delta\sigma$ for which any algorithm will misclassify at least kd/Δ^4 total points. The fact that it continues to work in a semirandom model suggests some theoretical justification for why it is widely used across so many domains. An interesting open question is to give a similar analysis for heuristics such as the expectation–maximization algorithm.

References

Abbe, Emmanuel, and Sandon, Colin. 2015. Community detection in general stochastic block models: Fundamental limits and efficient algorithms for recovery. In *2015 IEEE 56th Annual Symposium on Foundations of Computer Science*, pp. 670–688. IEEE.

Abbe, Emmanuel, Bandeira, Afonso S, and Hall, Georgina. 2015. Exact recovery in the stochastic block model. *IEEE Transactions on Information Theory*, **62**(1), 471–487.

Awasthi, Pranjal, and Vijayaraghavan, Aravindan. 2018. Clustering semi-random mixtures of Gaussians. In Proceedings of the 35th *International Conference on Machine Learning* (ICML) 2018. Proceedings of Machine Learning Research, vol. 80, pp. 5055–5064.

Bandeira, Afonso S, Van Handel, Ramon, et al. 2016. Sharp nonasymptotic bounds on the norm of random matrices with independent entries. *The Annals of Probability*, **44**(4), 2479–2506.

Belkin, Mikhail, and Sinha, Kaushik. 2010. Polynomial learning of distribution families. In *2010 IEEE 51st Annual Symposium on Foundations of Computer Science*, pp. 103–112. IEEE.

Boppana, Ravi B. 1987. Eigenvalues and graph bisection: An average-case analysis. *28th Annual Symposium on Foundations of Computer Science (SFCS 1987)*, pp. 280–285. IEEE.

Candès, Emmanuel J., and Tao, Terence. 2010. The power of convex relaxation: Near-optimal matrix completion. *IEEE Transactions on Information Theory*, **56**(5), 2053–2080.

Cheng, Yu, and Ge, Rong. 2018. Non-convex matrix completion against a semi-random adversary. In 31st *Conference on Learning Theory (COLT 2018)*, Proceedings of Machine Learning Research, vol. 75, pp. 1362–1394.

Dasgupta, Sanjoy. 1999. Learning mixtures of Gaussians. *40th Annual Symposium on Foundations of Computer Science (Cat. No. 99CB37039)*, pp. 634–644. IEEE.

Decelle, Aurelien, Krzakala, Florent, Moore, Cristopher, and Zdeborová, Lenka. 2011. Asymptotic analysis of the stochastic block model for modular networks and its algorithmic applications. *Physical Review E*, **84**(6), 066106.

Evans, William, Kenyon, Claire, Peres, Yuval, Schulman, Leonard J, et al. 2000. Broadcasting on trees and the Ising model. *The Annals of Applied Probability*, **10**(2), 410–433.

Feige, Uriel, and Kilian, Joe. 2001. Heuristics for semirandom graph problems. *Journal of Computer and System Sciences*, **63**(4), 639–671.

Füredi, Zoltán, and Komlós, János. 1981. The eigenvalues of random symmetric matrices. *Combinatorica*, **1**(3), 233–241.

Guédon, Olivier, and Vershynin, Roman. 2016. Community detection in sparse networks via Grothendiecks inequality. *Probability Theory and Related Fields*, **165**(3-4), 1025–1049.

Hajek, Bruce, Wu, Yihong, and Xu, Jiaming. 2016. Achieving exact cluster recovery threshold via semidefinite programming. *IEEE Transactions on Information Theory*, **62**(5), 2788–2797.

Holland, Paul W, Laskey, Kathryn Blackmond, and Leinhardt, Samuel. 1983. Stochastic blockmodels: First steps. *Social Networks*, **5**(2), 109–137.

Jain, Prateek, Netrapalli, Praneeth, and Sanghavi, Sujay. 2013. Low-rank matrix completion using alternating minimization. In *Proceedings of the Forty-Fifth Annual ACM Symposium on Theory of Computing*, pp. 665–674. ACM.

Keshavan, Raghunandan H, Montanari, Andrea, and Oh, Sewoong. 2010. Matrix completion from a few entries. *IEEE Transactions on Information Theory*, **56**(6), 2980–2998.

Kesten, Harry, and Stigum, Bernt P. 1966. A limit theorem for multidimensional Galton-Watson processes. *The Annals of Mathematical Statistics*, **37**(5), 1211–1223.

Ling, Shuyang, Xu, Ruitu, and Bandeira, Afonso S. 2019. On the landscape of synchronization networks: A perspective from nonconvex optimization. *SIAM Journal on Optimization*, **29**(3), 1879–1907.

Makarychev, Konstantin, Makarychev, Yury, and Vijayaraghavan, Aravindan. 2016. Learning communities in the presence of errors. In 29th *Conference on Learning Theory (COLT 2016)*, Proceedings of Machine Learning Research, vol. 49.

Massoulié, Laurent. 2014. Community detection thresholds and the weak Ramanujan property. In *Proceedings of the Forty-Sixth Annual ACM Symposium on Theory of Computing*, pp. 694–703. ACM.

Moitra, Ankur. 2015. CAREER: Algorithmic aspects of machine learning. Available at: https://thmatters.files.wordpress.com/2016/07/ankur-moitra-proposal.pdf.

Moitra, Ankur, and Valiant, Gregory. 2010. Settling the polynomial learnability of mixtures of Gaussians. In *2010 IEEE 51st Annual Symposium on Foundations of Computer Science*, pp. 93–102. IEEE.

Moitra, Ankur, Perry, William, and Wein, Alexander S. 2016. How robust are reconstruction thresholds for community detection? In *Proceedings of the Forty-Eighth Annual ACM Symposium on Theory of Computing*, pp. 828–841. ACM.

Montanari, Andrea, and Sen, Subhabrata. 2016. Semidefinite programs on sparse random graphs and their application to community detection. In *Proceedings of the Forty-Eighth Annual ACM Symposium on Theory of Computing*, pp. 814–827. ACM.

Mossel, Elchanan, Neeman, Joe, and Sly, Allan. 2018. A proof of the block model threshold conjecture. *Combinatorica*, **38**(3), 665–708.

Perry, Amelia, and Wein, Alexander S. 2017. A semidefinite program for unbalanced multisection in the stochastic block model. In *2017 International Conference on Sampling Theory and Applications (SampTA)*, pp. 64–67. IEEE.

Wigner, Eugene P. 1993. Characteristic vectors of bordered matrices with infinite dimensions i. In *The Collected Works of Eugene Paul Wigner*, pp. 524–540. Springer-Verlag.

Exercises

Exercise 10.1 Consider the planted bisection model from earlier in the chapter: There are two communities A and B that each have size $\frac{n}{2}$. Each pair of nodes from the same community are connected with probability $p = \frac{1}{2}$ and each pair of nodes from different communities are connected with probability $q = \frac{1}{4}$. This exercise and the next explore deterministic criteria for recovering the planted bisection against a monotone adversary.

Suppose we are given a bisection (S, T) with the following properties:

(a) For each node $u \in S$, u has strictly more neighbors in S than in T.
(b) Similarly for each node $u \in T$, u has strictly more neighbors in T than in S.

Show that there is a monotone adversary that can create a bisection (S, T) with this property but that is *uncorrelated* with the planted bisection.[2]

Exercise 10.2 Show that if you can find a bisection (S, T) with the property that the induced graphs on S and T respectively both have edge expansion at least $\frac{1}{3}$ that S and T are with high probability *highly correlated* with the planted bisection. In particular show that the symmetric difference between S and either A or B has at size $O(1)$ and similarly for T.

Exercise 10.3 This exercise considers semirandom models in another popular setup in machine learning. Specifically, we will consider compressed sensing where there is an unknown k-sparse vector x in n dimensions. The usual setting is that we observe $Ax = b$, where A is an $m \times n$ matrix and m is much smaller than n. We want to recover x exactly despite the fact that A is not invertible. It turns out that if A satisfies the *restricted isometry property* you can get away with $m = Ck \log n/k$, and one of the many algorithms for finding x is to solve ℓ_1 minimization:

$$\min \|x\|_1$$

$$\text{s.t. } Ax = b$$

Consider the following semirandom model: Suppose a monotone adversary can add additional rows to A to form $\widetilde{A}$ and that we get $\widetilde{A}x = \widetilde{b}$. Show that if ℓ_1 minimization succeeds in recovering x, then it continues to succeed against a monotone adversary.[3]

---

[2] Here, by uncorrelated, we mean that each set S and T has the same number of nodes from each of the two communities.

[3] It turns out that one can still recover x approximately even when it is not k-sparse in the sense that one can recover a k-sparse approximation to it. This is called *stable recovery*. Even for this more general problem, ℓ_1 minimization works against a monotone adversary (whereas many iterative algorithms do not), but to fully set up this problem would be too much of a digression…

CHAPTER ELEVEN

Random-Order Models

Anupam Gupta and Sahil Singla

Abstract: This chapter introduces the *random-order model* in online algorithms. In this model, the input is chosen by an adversary, then randomly permuted before being presented to the algorithm. This reshuffling often weakens the power of the adversary and allows for improved algorithmic guarantees. We show such improvements for two broad classes of problems: packing problems where we must pick a constrained set of items to maximize total value, and covering problems where we must satisfy given requirements at minimum total cost. We also discuss how random-order model relates to other stochastic models used for non-worst-case competitive analysis.

11.1 Motivation: Picking a Large Element

Suppose we want to pick the maximum of a collection of n numbers. At the beginning, we know this cardinality n, but nothing about the range of numbers to arrive. We are then presented distinct nonnegative real numbers $v_1, v_2, \ldots, v_n$ one by one; upon seeing a number v_i, we must either immediately pick it, or discard it forever. We can pick at most one number. The goal is to maximize the expected value of the number we pick, where the expectation is over any randomness in our algorithm. We want this expected value to be close to the maximum value $v_{\max} := \max_{i \in \{1,2,\ldots,n\}} v_i$. Formally, we want to minimize the *competitive ratio*, which is defined as the ratio of $v_{\max}$ to our expected value. Note that this maximum $v_{\max}$ is independent of the order in which the elements are presented, and is unknown to our algorithm until all the numbers have been revealed.

If we use a deterministic algorithm, our value can be arbitrarily smaller than $v_{\max}$, even for $n = 2$. Say the first number $v_1 = 1$. If our deterministic algorithm picks v_1, the adversary can present $v_2 = M \gg 1$; if it does not, the adversary can present $v_2 = 1/M \ll 1$. Either way, the adversary can make the competitive ratio as bad as it wants by making M large.

Using a randomized algorithm helps only a little: a naïve randomized strategy is to select a uniformly random position $i \in \{1, \ldots, n\}$ up-front and pick the ith number v_i. Since we pick each number with probability $1/n$, the expected value is $\sum_i v_i/n \geq v_{\max}/n$. This turns out to be the best we can do, as long the input sequence is controlled by an adversary and the maximum value is much larger than the others. Indeed, one strategy for the adversary is to choose a uniformly random index j, and present the request sequence $1, M, M^2, \ldots, M^j, 0, 0, \ldots, 0$ – a rapidly ascending chain of j numbers followed by worthless numbers. If M is very large, any good algorithm must pick the last number in the ascending chain upon seeing it. But this is tantamount to guessing j, and random guessing is the best an algorithm can do. (This intuition can be made formal using Yao's minimax lemma.)

These bad examples show that the problem is hard for two reasons: the first reason being the large range of the numbers involved, and the second being the adversary's ability to carefully design these difficult sequences. Consider the following way to mitigate the latter effect: what if the adversary chooses the n numbers, but then the numbers are shuffled and presented to the algorithm in a uniformly random order? This random-order version of the problem above is commonly known as the *secretary problem*: the goal is to hire the best secretary (or at least a fairly good one) if the candidates for the job appear in a random order.

Somewhat surprisingly, randomly shuffling the numbers changes the complexity of the problem drastically. Here is the elegant 50%-algorithm:

---

1. Reject the first $n/2$ numbers, and then
2. Pick the first number after that which is bigger than all the previous numbers (if any).

Theorem 11.1 *The 50%-algorithm gets an expected value of at least $v_{max}/4$.*

Proof Assume for simplicity all numbers are distinct. The algorithm definitely picks v_{max} if the highest number is in the second half of the random order (which happens with probability $1/2$), and also the second-highest number is in the first half (which, conditioned on the first event, happens with probability at least $1/2$, the two events being positively correlated). Hence, we get an expected value of at least $v_{max}/4$. (We get a stronger guarantee: we pick the highest number v_{max} itself with probability at least $1/4$, but we will not explore this expected-value-versus-probability direction any further.) $\square$

11.1.1 The Model and a Discussion

The secretary problem, with the lower bounds in the worst-case setting and an elegant algorithm for the random-order model, highlights the fact that sequential decision-making problems are often hard in the worst case not merely because the underlying *set* of requests is hard, but also because these requests are carefully woven into a difficult-to-solve *sequence*. In many situations where there is no adversary, it may be reasonable to assume that the ordering of the requests is benign, which leads us to the random-order model. Indeed, one can view this as a *semirandom* model from Chapter 9, where the input is first chosen by an adversary and then randomly perturbed before being given to the algorithm.

Let us review the *competitive analysis* model for worst-case analysis of online algorithms (also discussed in Chapter 24). Here, the adversary chooses a sequence of requests and presents them to the algorithm one by one. The algorithm must take actions to serve a request before seeing the next request, and it cannot change past decisions. The actions have rewards, say, and the *competitive ratio* is the optimal reward for the sequence (in hindsight) divided by the algorithm's reward. (For problems in which we seek to minimize costs instead of maximize rewards, the competitive ratio is the algorithm's cost divided by the optimal cost.) Since the algorithm can never outperform the optimal choice, the competitive ratio is always at least 1.

Now given any online problem, the *random-order model* (henceforth the *RO model*) considers the setting where the adversary first chooses a *set S* of requests (and not a sequence). The elements of this set are then presented to the algorithm in a uniformly random order. Formally, given a set $S = \{r_1, r_2, \ldots, r_n\}$ of $n = |S|$ requests, we imagine nature drawing a uniformly random permutation π of $\{1, \ldots, n\}$, and then defining the input sequence to be $r_{\pi(1)}, r_{\pi(2)}, \ldots, r_{\pi(n)}$. As before, the online algorithm sees these requests one by one, and has to perform its irrevocable actions for $r_{\pi(i)}$ before seeing $r_{\pi(i+1)}$. The length n of the input sequence may also be revealed to the algorithm at the beginning, depending on the problem. The competitive ratio (for maximization problems) is defined as the ratio between the optimum value for S and the expected value of the algorithm, where the expectation is now taken over both the randomness of the reshuffle π and that of the algorithm. (Again, we use the convention that the competitive ratio is at least 1, and hence have to flip the ratio for minimization problems.)

A strength of the RO model is its simplicity and that it captures other commonly considered stochastic input models. Indeed, since the RO model does not assume the algorithm has any prior knowledge of the underlying set of requests (except perhaps the cardinality n), it captures situations in which the input sequence consists of independent and identically distributed (i.i.d.) random draws from some fixed and unknown distribution. Reasoning about the RO model avoids overfitting the algorithm to any particular properties of the distribution, and makes the algorithms more general and robust by design.

Another motivation for the RO model is aesthetic and pragmatic: the simplicity of the model makes it a good starting point for designing algorithms. If we want to develop an online algorithm (or even an offline one) for some algorithmic task, a good step is to first solve it in the RO model and then extend the result to the worst-case setting. This can be useful either way: in the best case, we may succeed in getting an algorithm for the worst-case setting using the insights developed in the RO model. Else the extension may be difficult, but still we know a good algorithm under the (mild?) assumption of random-order arrivals.

Of course, the assumption of uniform random orderings may be unreasonable in some settings, especially if the algorithm performs poorly when the random-order assumption is violated. There have been attempts to refine the model to require less randomness from the input stream, while still getting better-than-worst-case performance. We discuss some of these in Section 11.5.2, but much remains to be done.

11.1.2 Roadmap

In Section 11.2 we discuss an optimal algorithm for the secretary problem. In Section 11.3 we give algorithms to choose multiple items instead of just a single one, and other maximization packing problems. In Section 11.4 we discuss minimization problems. In Section 11.5 we present some specializations and extensions of the RO model.

11.2 The Secretary Problem

We saw the 50% algorithm based on the idea of using the first half of the random order sequence to compute a threshold that weeds out "low" values. This idea of choosing a good threshold will be a recurring one in this chapter. The choice of waiting for half of the sequence was for simplicity: a right choice is to wait for $1/e \approx 37\%$ fraction, which gives us the 37%-algorithm:

---

1. Reject the first n/e numbers, and then
2. Pick the first number after that (if any) which is bigger than all the previous numbers.

(Although n/e is not an integer, rounding it to the nearest integer does not impact the guarantees substantively.) Call a number a *prefix-maximum* if it is the largest among the numbers revealed before it. Notice being the maximum is a property of just the set of numbers, whereas being a prefix-maximum is a property of the random sequence and the current position. A *wait-and-pick* algorithm is one that rejects the first m numbers, and then picks the first prefix-maximum number.

Theorem 11.2 *As $n \to \infty$, the 37%-algorithm picks the highest number with probability at least $1/e$. Hence, it gets expected value at least $v_{\max}/e$. Moreover, n/e is the optimal choice of m among all wait-and-pick algorithms.*

Proof If we pick the first prefix-maximum after rejecting the first m numbers, the probability we pick the maximum is

$$\sum_{t=m+1}^{n} \Pr[v_t \text{ is max}] \cdot \Pr[\text{max among first } t-1 \text{ numbers falls in first } m \text{ positions}]$$

$$\overset{(\star)}{=} \sum_{t=m+1}^{n} \frac{1}{n} \cdot \frac{m}{t-1} = \frac{m}{n}(H_{n-1} - H_{m-1}),$$

where $H_k = 1 + \frac{1}{2} + \frac{1}{3} + \cdots + \frac{1}{k}$ is the kth harmonic number. The equality $(\star)$ uses the uniform random order. Now using the approximation $H_k \approx \ln k + 0.57$ for large k, we get the probability of picking the maximum is about $\frac{m}{n} \ln \frac{n-1}{m-1}$ when m, n are large. This quantity has a maximum value of $1/e$ if we choose $m = n/e$. $\qquad \square$

Next we show we can replace any strategy (in a comparison-based model) with a wait-and-pick strategy without decreasing the probability of picking the maximum.

Theorem 11.3 *The strategy that maximizes the probability of picking the highest number can be assumed to be a wait-and-pick strategy.*

Proof Think of yourself as a player trying to maximize the probability of picking the maximum number. Clearly, you should reject the next number v_i if it is not prefix-maximum. Otherwise, you should pick v_i only if it is prefix-maximum and the probability of v_i being the maximum is more than the probability of you picking the maximum in the remaining sequence. Let us calculate these probabilities.

We use Pmax to abbreviate "prefix-maximum," For position $i \in \{1, \ldots, n\}$, define

$$f(i) = \Pr[v_i \text{ is max} \mid v_i \text{ is Pmax}] \overset{(\star)}{=} \frac{\Pr[v_i \text{ is max}]}{\Pr[v_i \text{ is Pmax}]} \overset{(\star\star)}{=} \frac{1/n}{1/i} = \frac{i}{n},$$

where equality $(\star)$ uses that the maximum is also a prefix-maximum, and $(\star\star)$ uses the uniform random ordering. Note that $f(i)$ increases with i.

Now consider a problem in which the numbers are again being revealed in a random order but we must reject the first i numbers. The goal is to still maximize the probability of picking the highest of the n numbers. Let $g(i)$ denote the probability that the optimal strategy for this problem picks the global maximum.

The function $g(i)$ must be a nonincreasing function of i, else we could just ignore the $(i + 1)^{st}$ number and set $g(i)$ to mimic the strategy for $g(i + 1)$. Moreover, $f(i)$ is increasing. So from the preceding discussion, you should not pick a prefix-maximum number at any position i where $f(i) < g(i)$, since you can do better on the suffix. Moreover, when $f(i) \geq g(i)$, you should pick v_i if it is prefix-maximum, since it is worse to wait. Therefore, the approach of waiting until f becomes greater than g and thereafter picking the first prefix-maximum is an optimal strategy. □

Theorems 11.2 and 11.3 imply for $n \to \infty$ that no algorithm can pick the maximum with probability more than $1/e$. Since we placed no bounds on the number magnitudes, this can also be used to show that for any $\varepsilon > 0$, there exist an n and numbers $\{v_i\}_{i \in \{1, \ldots, n\}}$ where every algorithm has expected value at most $(1/e + \varepsilon) \cdot \max_i v_i$.

11.3 Multiple-Secretary and Other Maximization Problems

We now extend our insights from the single-item case to settings where we can pick multiple items. Each item has a value, and we have constraints on what we can pick (e.g., we can pick at most k items, or pick any acyclic subset of edges of a graph). The goal is to maximize the total value. (We study minimization problems in Section 11.4.) Our algorithms can be broadly classified as being *order-oblivious* or *order-adaptive*, depending on the degree to which they rely on the random-order assumption.

11.3.1 Order-Oblivious Algorithms

The 50%-strategy for the single-item secretary problem has an interesting property: if each number is equally likely to lie in the first or the second half, we pick $v_{\max}$ with probability $1/4$ even if the arrival sequence within the first and second halves is chosen by an adversary. To formalize this property, define an *order-oblivious* algorithm as one with the following two-phase structure: In the first phase (of some length m) the algorithm gets a uniformly random subset of m items, but is not allowed to pick any of these items. In the second phase, the remaining items arrive in an adversarial order, and only now can the algorithm pick items while respecting any constraints that exist. (For example, in the secretary problem, only one item may be picked.) Clearly, any order-oblivious algorithm runs in the random-order model with the same (or better) performance guarantee, and hence we can focus our attention on designing such algorithms. Focusing on order-oblivious algorithms has two benefits. First, such algorithms are easier to design and analyze, which becomes crucial when the underlying constraints become more difficult to reason about. Second, the guarantees of such algorithms can be interpreted as holding even for adversarial arrivals, as long as we have offline access to some samples from the underlying distribution (discussed in Section 11.5). To make things concrete, let us start with the simplest generalization of the secretary problem.

The Multiple-Secretary Problem: Picking k Items

We now pick k items to maximize the expected sum of their values: the case $k = 1$ is the secretary problem from the previous section. We associate the items with the set $[n] = \{1, \ldots, n\}$, with item $i \in [n]$ having value $v_i \in \mathbb{R}$; all values are distinct. Let $S^\star \subseteq [n]$ be the set of k items of largest value, and let the total value of the set $S^\star$ be $V^\star := \sum_{i \in S^\star} v_i$.

It is easy to get an algorithm that gets expected value $\Omega(V^\star)$, e.g., by splitting the input sequence of length n into k equal-sized portions and running the single-item algorithm separately on each of these, or by setting threshold τ to be the value of (say) the $\lceil k/3 \rceil$th-highest value item in the first 50% of the items and picking the first k items in the second half whose values exceed τ (see Exercise 11.1). Since both these algorithms ignore a constant fraction of the items, they lose at least a constant factor of the optimal value in expectation. But we may hope to do better. Indeed, the 50% algorithm obtains a (noisy) estimate of the threshold between the maximum value item and the rest, and then picks the first item above the threshold. The simplest extension of this idea would be to estimate the threshold between the top k items, and the rest. Since we are picking $k \gg 1$ elements, we can hope to get accurate estimates of this threshold by sampling a smaller fraction of the stream.

The following (order-oblivious) algorithm formalizes this intuition. It gets an expected value of $V^\star(1 - \delta)$, where $\delta \to 0$ as $k \to \infty$. To achieve this performance, we get an accurate estimate of the kth largest item in the entire sequence after ignoring only δn items, and hence can start picking items much earlier.

---

1. Set $\varepsilon = \delta = O\left(\frac{\log k}{k^{1/3}}\right)$.
2. *First phase:* ignore the first δn items.
   Threshold $\tau \leftarrow$ value of the $(1 - \varepsilon)\delta k^{th}$-highest valued item in this ignored set.
3. *Second phase:* pick the first k items seen that have value greater than τ.

Theorem 11.4 *The order-oblivious algorithm above for the multiple-secretary problem has expected value $V^\star(1 - O(\delta))$, where $\delta = O\left(\frac{\log k}{k^{1/3}}\right)$.*

Proof The δn items ignored in the first phase contain in expectation δk items from $S^\star$, so we lose expected value $\delta V^\star$. Now a natural threshold would be the δk^{th}-highest value item among the ignored items. To account for the variance in

---

239

how many elements from $S^\star$ fall among the ignored elements, we set a slightly higher threshold of the $(1 - \varepsilon)\delta k$th-highest value.

Let $v' := \min_{i \in S^\star} v_i$ be the lowest value item we actually want to pick. There are two failure modes for this algorithm: (i) the threshold is too low if $\tau < v'$, as then we may pick low-valued items, and (ii) the threshold is too high if fewer than $k - O(\delta k)$ items from $S^\star$ fall among the last $(1 - \delta)n$ items that are greater than τ. Let us see why both these bad events happen rarely.

- *Not too low*: For event (i) to happen, fewer than $(1 - \varepsilon)\delta k$ items from $S^\star$ fall in the first δn locations: i.e., their number is less than $(1 - \varepsilon)$ times its expectation δk. This has probability at most $\exp(-\varepsilon^2 \delta k)$ by Chernoff–Hoeffding concentration bound (see the aside in the text that follows). Notice if $\tau \geq v'$ then we never run out of budget k.
- *Not too high*: For event (ii), let v'' be the $(1 - 2\varepsilon)k^{th}$-highest value in $S^\star$. We expect $(1 - 2\varepsilon)\delta k$ items above v'' to appear among the ignored items, so the probability that more than $(1 - \varepsilon)\delta k$ appear is $\exp(-\varepsilon^2 \delta k)$ by Chernoff–Hoeffding concentration bound. This means that $\tau \leq v''$ with high probability, and moreover most of the high-valued items appear in the second phase (where we will pick them whenever event (i) does not happen, as we don't run out of budget).

Finally, since we are allowed to lose $O(\delta V^\star)$ value, it suffices that the error probability $\exp(-\varepsilon^2 \delta k)$ be at most $O(\delta) = 1/\operatorname{poly}(k)$. This requires us to set $\varepsilon^2 \delta k = \Omega(\log k)$, and a good choice of parameters is $\varepsilon = \delta = O\left(\frac{\log k}{k^{1/3}}\right)$. $\qquad\square$

An aside: the familiar Chernoff–Hoeffding concentration bounds (Exercise 8.3(a) in Chapter 8) are for sums of bounded *independent* random variables, but the RO model has correlations (e.g., if one element from $S^\star$ falls in the first δn locations, another is slightly less likely to do so). The easiest fix to this issue is to ignore not the first δn items but instead a random number of items with the number drawn from a Binomial(n, δ) distribution with expectation δn. In this case each item has probability δ of being ignored, independent of others. A second way to achieve independence is to imagine each arrival happening at a uniformly and independently chosen time in $[0, 1]$. Algorithmically, we can sample n i.i.d. times from Uniform$[0, 1]$, sort them in increasing order, and assign the ith time to the ith arrival. Now, rather than ignoring the first δn arrivals, we can ignore arrivals happening before time $\delta \in [0, 1]$. Finally, a third alternative is to not strive for independence, but instead directly use concentration bounds for sums of exchangeable random variables. Each of these three alternatives offers different benefits, and one alternative might be much easier to analyze than the others, depending on the problem at hand.

The loss of $\approx V^\star/k^{1/3}$ in Theorem 11.4 is not optimal. We will see an order-adaptive algorithm in the next section that achieves an expected value of $V^\star\left(1 - O\left(\sqrt{\log k/k}\right)\right)$. That algorithm will not use a single threshold; instead it will adaptively refine its threshold as it sees more of the sequence. But first, let us discuss a few more order-oblivious algorithms for other combinatorial constraints.

Maximum-Weight Forest

Suppose the items arriving in a random order are the n edges of a (multi-)graph $G = (V, E)$, with edge e having a value/weight v_e. The algorithm knows the graph at the beginning, but not the weights. When the edge e arrives, its weight v_e is revealed, and we decide whether to pick the edge or not. Our goal is to pick a subset of edges with large total weight that form a forest (i.e., do not contain a cycle). The target $V^\star$ is the total weight of a maximum-weight forest of the graph: offline, we can solve this problem using, e.g., Kruskal's greedy algorithm. This *graphical secretary* problem generalizes the secretary problem: Imagine a graph with two vertices and n parallel edges between them. Since any two edges form a cycle, we can pick at most one edge, which models the single-item problem.

As a first step toward an algorithm, suppose all the edge values are either 0 or v (but we don't know in advance which edges have what value). A greedy algorithm is to pick the next weight-v edge whenever possible, i.e., when it does not create cycles with previously picked edges. This returns a max-weight forest, because the optimal solution is a maximal forest among the subset of weight-v edges, and every maximal forest in a graph has the same number of edges. This suggests the following algorithm for general values: if we know some value v for which there is a subset of acyclic edges, each of value v, with total weight $\geq \frac{1}{\alpha} \cdot V^\star$, then we can get an α-competitive solution by greedily picking value-v edges whenever possible.

How do we find such a value v that gives a good approximation? The RANDOM-THRESHOLD algorithm that follows uses two techniques: *bucketing* the values and *(randomly) mixing* a collection of algorithms. We assume that all values are powers of 2; indeed, rounding values down to the closest power of 2 loses at most a factor of 2 in the final guarantee.

---

1. Ignore the first $n/2$ items and let $\hat{v}$ be their highest value.
2. Select a uniformly random $r \in \{0, \dots, \log n\}$, and set threshold $\tau := \hat{v}/2^r$.
3. For the second $n/2$ items, greedily pick any item of value at least τ that does not create a cycle.

Theorem 11.5 *The order-oblivious* RANDOM-THRESHOLD *algorithm for the graphical secretary problem gets an expected value* $\Omega\left(\frac{V^\star}{\log n}\right)$.

Here is the main proof idea: either most of the value is in a single item (say $v_{\max}$), in which case when $r = 0$ (with probability $1/\log n$) this mimics the 50%-algorithm. Else, we can assume that $v_{\max}$ falls in the first half, giving us a good estimate without much loss. Now, very little of $V^\star$ can come from items of value less than $v_{\max}/n$ (since there are only n items). So we can focus on $\log n$ buckets of items whose values lie in $[v_{\max}/2^{i+1}, v_{\max}/2^i)$. These buckets, on average, contain value $V^\star/\log n$ each, and hence picking a random one does well.

An Improved Algorithm for Max-Weight Forests. The RANDOM-THRESHOLD algorithm above used relatively few properties of the max-weight forest. Indeed, it extends to downward-closed set systems with the property that if all values are 0 or v then picking the next value-v element whenever possible gives a near-optimal solution. However, we can do better using properties of the underlying graph. Here is a

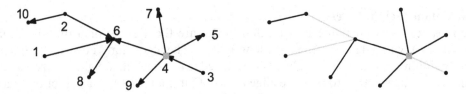

Figure 11.1 The optimal tree: the numbers on the left are those given by $\widehat{\pi}$. The gray box numbered 4 is the root. The edges in the right are those retained in the claimed solution.

constant-competitive algorithm for graphical secretary where the main idea is to decompose the problem into several disjoint single-item secretary problems.

---

1. Choose a uniformly random permutation $\widehat{\pi}$ of the vertices of the graph.
2. For each edge $\{u, v\}$, direct it from u to v if $\widehat{\pi}(u) < \widehat{\pi}(v)$.
3. Independently for each vertex u, consider the edges directed *towards* u and run the order-oblivious 50%-algorithm on these edges.

Theorem 11.6 *The algorithm for the graphical secretary problem is order-oblivious and gets an expected value at least $V^\star/8$.*

Proof The algorithm picks a forest; i.e., there are no cycles (in the undirected sense) among the picked edges. Indeed, the highest numbered vertex (w.r.t. $\widehat{\pi}$) on any such cycle would have two or more incoming edge picked, which is not possible.

However, since we restrict to picking only one incoming edge per vertex, the optimal max-weight forest $S^\star$ may no longer be feasible. Despite this, we claim there is a forest with the one-incoming-edge-per-vertex restriction, and expected value $V^\star/2$. (The randomness here is over the choice of the permutation $\widehat{\pi}$, but not of the random order.) Since the 50%-algorithm gets a quarter of this value (in expectation over the random ordering), we get the desired bound of $V^\star/8$.

To prove the claim, root each component of $S^\star$ at an arbitrary node, and associate each non-root vertex u with the unique edge $e(u)$ of the undirected graph on the path towards the root. The proposed solution chooses for each vertex u, the edge $e(u) = \{u, v\}$ if $\widehat{\pi}(v) < \widehat{\pi}(u)$, i.e., if it is directed *into* u (Figure 11.1). Since this event happens with probability $1/2$, the proof follows by linearity of expectation. $\qquad\square$

This algorithm is order-oblivious because the 50%-algorithm has the property. If we don't care about order-obliviousness, we can instead use the 37%-algorithm and get expected value at least $V^\star/2e$.

The Matroid Secretary Problem

One of the most tantalizing generalizations of the secretary problem is to *matroids*. (A matroid defines a notion of *independence* for subsets of elements, generalizing linear-independence of a collection of vectors in a vector space. For example, if we define a subset of edges to be independent if they are acyclic, these form a "graphic" matroid.) Suppose the n items form the ground set elements of a known matroid, and we can pick only subsets of items that are independent in this matroid. The weight/value $V^\star$ of the max-weight independent set can be computed offline by the obvious generalization of Kruskal's greedy algorithm. The open question is to get an expected value of $\Omega(V^\star)$ online in the RO model. The approach from Theorem 11.5 gives expected value $\Omega(V^\star/\log k)$, where k is the largest size of an independent set (its *rank*). The current best algorithms (which are also order-oblivious) achieve an expected value of $\Omega(V^\star/\log\log k)$. Moreover, we can obtain $\Omega(V^\star)$ for many special classes of matroids by exploiting their special properties, like we did for the graphic matroid earlier; see the Notes for references.

11.3.2 Order-Adaptive Algorithms

The foregoing order-oblivious algorithms have several benefits, but their competitive ratios are often worse than *order-adaptive* algorithms where we exploit the randomness of the entire arrival order. Let us revisit the problem of picking k items.

The Multiple-Secretary Problem Revisited
In the order-oblivious case of Section 11.3.1, we ignored the first $\approx k^{-1/3}$ fraction of the items in the first phase, and then chose a fixed threshold to use in the second phase. The length of this initial phase was chosen to balance two competing concerns: we wanted the first phase to be short, so that we ignore few items, but we wanted it to be long enough to get a good estimate of the kth largest item in the entire input. The idea for the improved algorithm is to run in multiple phases and use time-varying thresholds. Roughly, the algorithm uses the first $n_0 = \delta n$ arrivals to learn a threshold for the next n_0 arrivals, then it computes a new threshold at time $n_1 = 2n_0$ for the next n_1 arrivals, and so on.

As in the order-oblivious algorithm, we aim for the $(1-\varepsilon)k$th-largest element of $S^\star$ – that ε gives us a margin of safety so that we don't pick a threshold lower than the kth-largest (a.k.a. smallest) element of $S^\star$. But we vary the value of ε. In the beginning, we have low confidence, so we pick items cautiously (by setting a high ε_0 and creating a larger safety margin). As we see more elements we are more confident in our estimates, and can decrease the ε_j values.

---

1. Set $\delta := \sqrt{\frac{\log k}{k}}$. Denote $n_j := 2^j \delta n$ and ignore first $n_0 = \delta n$ items.
2. For $j \in [0, \log 1/\delta]$, phase j runs on arrivals in *window* $W_j := (n_j, n_{j+1}]$

   - Let $k_j := (k/n)n_j$ and let $\varepsilon_j := \sqrt{\delta/2^j}$.
   - Set threshold τ_j to be the $(1 - \varepsilon_j)k_j$th-largest value among the first n_j items.
   - Choose any item in window W_j with value above τ_j (until budget k is exhausted).

Theorem 11.7 *The order-adaptive algorithm for the multiple-secretary problem has expected value* $V^\star\left(1 - O\left(\sqrt{\frac{\log k}{k}}\right)\right)$.

Proof As in Theorem 11.4, we first show that none of the thresholds τ_j are "too low" (so we never run out of budget k). Indeed, for τ_j to lie below

$v' := \min_{i \in S^\star} v_i$, less than $(1 - \varepsilon_j)k_j$ items from $S^\star$ should fall in the first n_j items. Since we expect k_j of them, the probability of this is at most $\exp(-\varepsilon_j^2 k_j) = \exp(-\delta^2 k) = 1/\operatorname{poly}(k)$.

Next, we claim that τ_j is not "too high": it is with high probability at most the value of the $(1 - 2\varepsilon_j)k$th highest item in $S^\star$ (thus all thresholds are at most $(1 - 2\varepsilon_0)k^{th}$ highest value). Indeed, we expect $(1 - 2\varepsilon_j)k_j$ of these highest items to appear in the first n_j arrivals, and the probability that more than $(1 - \varepsilon_j)k_j$ appear is $\exp(-\varepsilon_j^2 k_j) = 1/\operatorname{poly}(k)$.

Taking a union bound over all $j \in [0, \log 1/\delta]$, with high probability all thresholds are neither too high nor too low. Condition on this good event. Now any of the top $(1 - 2\varepsilon_0)k$ items will be picked if it arrives after first the n_0 arrivals (since no threshold is too high and we never run out of budget k), i.e., with probability $(1 - \delta)$. Similarly, any item that is in top $(1 - 2\varepsilon_{j+1})k$, but not in top $(1 - 2\varepsilon_j)k$, will be picked if it arrives after n_{j+1}, i.e., with probability $(1 - 2^{j+1}\delta)$. Thus if $v_{\max} = v_1 > \ldots > v_k$ are the top k items, we get an expected value of

$$\sum_{i=1}^{(1-2\varepsilon_0)k} v_i(1 - \delta) + \sum_{j=0}^{\log 1/\delta - 1} \sum_{i=(1-2\varepsilon_j)k}^{(1-2\varepsilon_{j+1})k} v_i(1 - 2^{j+1}\delta).$$

This is at least $V^\star(1 - \delta) - V^\star/k\left(\sum_{j=0}^{\log 1/\delta} 2\varepsilon_{j+1}k \cdot 2^{j+1}\delta\right)$ because the negative terms are maximized when the top k items are all equal to $V^\star/k$. Simplifying, we get $V^\star(1 - O(\delta))$, as claimed. $\qquad\square$

The logarithmic term in δ can be removed (see the Notes), but the loss of $\sqrt{k}$ is essential. Here is a sketch of the lower bound. By Yao's minimax lemma, it suffices to give a distribution over instances that causes a large loss for any deterministic algorithm. Suppose each item has value 0 with probability $1 - \frac{k}{n}$, else it has value 1 or 2 with equal probability. The number of nonzero items is therefore $k \pm O(\sqrt{k})$ with high probability, with about half 1's and half 2's, i.e., $V^\star = 3k/2 \pm O(\sqrt{k})$. Ideally, we want to pick all the 2's and then fill the remaining $k/2 \pm O(\sqrt{k})$ slots using the 1's. However, consider the state of the algorithm after $n/2$ arrivals. Since the algorithm doesn't know how many 2's will arrive in the second half, it doesn't know how many 1's to pick in the first half. Hence, it will either lose about $\Theta(\sqrt{k})$ 2's in the second half, or it will pick $\Theta(\sqrt{k})$ too few 1's from the first half. Either way, the algorithm will lose $\Omega(V^\star/\sqrt{k})$ value.

Solving Packing Integer Programs

The problem of picking a max-value subset of k items can be vastly generalized. Indeed, if each item i has size $a_i \in [0, 1]$ and we can pick items having total size k, we get the knapsack problem. More generally, suppose we have k units each of d different resources, and item i is specified by the amount $a_{ij} \in [0, 1]$ of each resource $j \in \{1, \ldots, d\}$ it uses if picked; we can pick any subset of items/vectors that can be supported by our resources. Formally, a set of n different d-dimensional vectors $\mathbf{a}_1, \mathbf{a}_2, \ldots, \mathbf{a}_n \in [0, 1]^d$ arrive in a random order, each having an associated value v_i. We can pick any subset of items subject to the associated vectors summing to at most

k in each coordinate. (All vectors and values are initially unknown, and on arrival of a vector we must irrevocably pick or discard it.) We want to maximize the expected value of the picked vectors. This gives a packing integer program:

$$\max \sum_i v_i x_i \quad \text{s.t.} \quad \sum_i x_i \mathbf{a}_i \leq k \cdot \mathbf{1} \text{ and } x_i \in \{0, 1\},$$

where the vectors arrive in a random order. Let $V^\star := \max_{\mathbf{x} \in \{0,1\}^d} \{\mathbf{v} \cdot \mathbf{x} \mid A\mathbf{x} \leq k\mathbf{1}\}$ be the optimal value, where $A \in [0, 1]^{d \times n}$ has columns $\mathbf{a}_i$. The multiple-secretary problem is modeled by A having a single row of all ones. By extending the approach from Theorem 11.7 considerably, one can achieve a competitive ratio of $(1 - O(\sqrt{(\log d)/k}))$. In fact, several algorithms using varying approaches are known, each giving this competitive ratio.

We now sketch a weaker result. To begin, we allow the variables to be fractional ($x_i \in [0, 1]$) instead of integers ($x_i \in \{0, 1\}$). Since we assume the capacity k is much larger than $\log d$, we can use randomized rounding to go back from fractional to integer solutions with a little loss in value. One of the key ideas is that learning a threshold can be viewed as learning optimal dual values for this linear program (LP).

Theorem 11.8 *There exists an algorithm to solve packing LPs in the RO model to achieve expected value $V^\star \left(1 - O\left(\sqrt{\frac{d \log n}{k}}\right)\right)$.*

Proof Sketch The proof is similar to that of Theorem 11.7. The algorithm uses windows of exponentially increasing sizes and (re-)estimates the optimal duals in each window. Let $\delta := \sqrt{\frac{d \log n}{k}}$; we will motivate this choice soon. As before, let $n_j = 2^j \delta n$, $k_j = (k/n)n_j$, $\varepsilon_j = \sqrt{\delta/2^j}$, and the window $W_j = (n_j, n_{j+1}]$. Now, our thresholds are the d-dimensional optimal dual variables τ_j for the linear program:

$$\max \sum_{i=1}^{n_j} v_i x_i \quad \text{s.t.} \quad \sum_{i=1}^{n_j} x_i \mathbf{a}_i \leq (1 - \varepsilon_j) k_j \cdot \mathbf{1} \text{ and } x_i \in [0, 1]. \quad (11.1)$$

Having computed τ_j at time n_j, the algorithm picks an item $i \in W_j$ if $v_i \geq \tau_j \cdot \mathbf{a}_i$. In the 1-dimensional multiple-secretary case, the dual is just the value of the $(1 - \varepsilon_j)k_j^{th}$ largest-value item among the first n_j, matching the choice in Theorem 11.7. In general, the dual τ_j can be thought of as the price-per-unit-consumption for every resource; we want to select i only if its value v_i is more than the total price $\tau_j \cdot \mathbf{a}_i$.

Let us sketch why the dual vector τ_j is not "too low": i.e., the dual τ_j computed is (with high probability) such that the set $\{\mathbf{a}_i \mid \tau_j \cdot \mathbf{a}_i \leq v_i, i \in [n]\}$ of all columns that satisfy the threshold τ_j is still feasible. Indeed, suppose a price vector τ is *bad*, and using it as threshold on the entire set causes the usage of some resource to exceed k. If τ it is an optimal dual at time n_j, the usage of that same resource by the first n_j items is at most $(1 - \varepsilon_j)k_j$ by the LP (11.1). A Chernoff–Hoeffding bound shows that this happens with probability at most $\exp(-\varepsilon_j^2 k_j) = o(1/n^d)$, by our choice of δ. Now the crucial idea is to prune the (infinite) set of dual vectors to at most n^d by considering only a subset of vectors using which the algorithm makes different decisions. Roughly, there are

n choices of prices in each of the d dimensions, giving us n^d different possible bad dual vectors; a union-bound now gives the proof. □

As mentioned earlier, a stronger version of this result has an additive loss $O(\sqrt{\frac{\log d}{k}})V^\star$. Such a result is interesting only when $k \gg \log d$, so this is called the "large budget" assumption. How well can we solve packing problems without such an assumption? Specifically, given a downwards-closed family $\mathcal{F} \subseteq 2^{[n]}$, suppose we want to pick a subset of items having high total value and lying in $\mathcal{F}$. For the information-theoretic question where computation is not a concern, the best known upper bound is $\Omega(V^\star/\log^2 n)$, and there are families where $\Omega(V^\star/\frac{\log n}{\log\log n})$ is not possible (see Exercise 11.2). Can we close this gap? Also, which downward-closed families $\mathcal{F}$ admit efficient algorithms with good guarantees?

Max-Weight Matchings

Consider a bipartite graph on n agents and m items. Each agent i has a value $v_{ij} \in \mathbb{R}_{\geq 0}$ for item j. The maximum-weight matching problem is to find an assignment $M : [n] \to [m]$ to maximize $\sum_{i \in [n]} v_{iM(i)}$ such that no item j is assigned to more than one agent, i.e., $|M^{-1}(j)| \leq 1$ for all $j \in [m]$. In the online setting, which has applications to allocating advertisements, the m items are given up-front and the n agents arrive one by one. On arriving, agent i reveals their valuations v_{ij} for $j \in [m]$, whereupon we may irrevocably allocate one of the remaining items to i. Let $V^\star$ denote the value of the optimal matching. The case of $m = 1$ with a single item is exactly the single-item secretary problem.

The main algorithmic technique in this section almost seems naïve at first glance: after ignoring the few first arrivals, we make each subsequent decision based on an optimal solution of the arrivals until that point, *ignoring* all past decisions. For the matching problem, this idea translates to the following:

Ignore the first n/e agents. When agent $i \in (n/e, n]$ arrives:

1. Compute a max-value matching $M^{(i)}$ for the first i arrivals (ignoring past decisions).
2. If $M^{(i)}$ matches the current agent i to item j, and if j is still available, then allocate j to agent i; else, give nothing to agent i.

(We assume that the matching $M^{(i)}$ depends only on the identities of the first i requests and is independent of their arrival order.) We show the power of this idea by proving that it gives optimal competitiveness for matchings.

Theorem 11.9 *The algorithm gives a matching with expected value at least $V^\star/e$.*

Proof There are two insights into the proof. The first is that the matching $M^{(i)}$ is on a random subset of i of the n requests, and so has an expected value at least $(i/n)V^\star$. The ith agent is a random one of these and so gets expected value $V^\star/n$.

The second idea is to show, like in Theorem 11.2, that if agent i is matched to item j in $M^{(i)}$, then j is free with probability $\frac{n}{ei}$. Indeed, condition on the set, but not the order, of first i agents (which fixes $M^{(i)}$) and the identity of the ith agent (which fixes j). Now for any $k \in (n/e, i)$, the item j was allocated to the kth agent with probability at most $\frac{1}{k}$ (because even if j is matched in $M^{(k)}$, the probability of the corresponding agent being the kth agent is at most $1/k$). The arrival order of the first $k - 1$ agents is irrelevant for this event, so we can do this argument for all $s < k$: the probability j was allocated to the sth agent, conditioned on j not being allocated to the kth agent, is at most $\frac{1}{s}$. So the probability that j is available for agent i is at least $\prod_{n/e < k < i} \left(1 - \frac{1}{k}\right) \approx \frac{n}{ei}$. Combining these two ideas and using linearity of expectation, the expected total matching value is at least $\sum_{i=1+n/e}^{n} \left(n/ei \cdot V^\star/n\right) \approx V^\star/e$. $\qquad\square$

This approach can be extended to combinatorial auctions where each agent i has a submodular (or an XOS) valuation v_i and can be assigned a subset $S_i \subseteq [m]$ of items; the goal is to maximize total welfare $\sum_i v_i(S_i)$. Also, this approach of following the current solution (ignoring past decisions) extends to solving packing LPs: the algorithm solves a slightly scaled-down version of the current LP at each step i and sets the variable x_i according to the obtained solution.

11.4 Minimization Problems

We now study *minimization* problems in the RO model. In these problems the goal is to minimize some notion of cost (e.g., the length of augmenting paths, or the number of bins) subject to fulfilling some requirements. All the algorithms in this section are order-adaptive. We use OPT to denote both the optimal solution on the instance S and its cost.

11.4.1 Minimizing Augmentations in Online Matching

We start with one reason why the RO model might help for online discrete minimization problems. Consider a problem to be "well-behaved" if there is always a solution of cost $\approx OPT$ to serve the remaining requests. This is clearly true at the beginning of the input sequence, and we want it to remain true over time – i.e., poor choices in the past should not cause the optimal solution on the remaining requests to become much more expensive. Moreover, suppose that the problem cost is "additive" over the requests. Then satisfying the next request, which by the RO property is a random one of i remaining requests, should cost $\approx OPT/i$ in expectation. Summing over all n requests gives an expected cost of $\approx OPT(\frac{1}{n}+\frac{1}{n-1}+\cdots+\frac{1}{2}+1) = O(\log n)\,OPT$. (This general idea is reminiscent of that for max-weight matchings from Section 11.3.2, albeit in a minimization setting.)

To illustrate this idea, we consider an online bipartite matching problem. Let $G = (U, V, E)$ be a bipartite graph with $|U| = |V| = n$. Initially the algorithm does not know the edge set E of the graph, and hence the initial matching $M_0 = \emptyset$. At each time step $t \in [1, n]$, all edges incident to the tth vertex $u_t \in U$ are revealed. If the previous matching M_{t-1} is no longer a maximum matching among the current set of edges, the algorithm must perform an augmentation to obtain a maximum

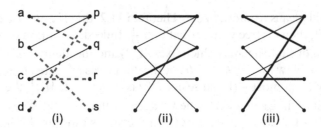

Figure 11.2 (i) The graph G with a perfect matching shown by dashed edges. (ii) An intermediate matching M_2. (iii) The matching M_3 after the next request arrives at d.

matching M_t. We do not want the matchings to change too drastically, so we define the cost incurred by the algorithm at step t to be the length of the augmenting path $M_{t-1} \triangle M_t$. The goal is to minimize the total cost of the algorithm. (For simplicity, assume G has a perfect matching and $OPT = n$, so we need to augment at each step.) A natural algorithm is *shortest augmenting path* (see Figure 11.2):

When a request $u_t \in U$ arrives:

1. Augment along a shortest alternating path P_t from u_t to some unmatched vertex in V.

Theorem 11.10 *The shortest augmenting path algorithm incurs in total $O(n \log n)$ augmentation cost in expectation in the RO model.*

Proof Fix an optimal matching M^*, and consider some time step during the algorithm's execution. Suppose the current maximum matching M has size $n-k$. As a thought experiment, if all the remaining k vertices in U are revealed at once, the symmetric difference $M^* \triangle M$ forms k node-disjoint alternating paths from these remaining k vertices to unmatched nodes in V. Augmenting along these paths would gives us the optimal matching. The sum of lengths of these paths is at most $|M^*| + |M| \leq 2n$. (Observe that the cost of the optimal solution on the remaining requests does increase over time, but only by a constant factor.) Now, since the next vertex is chosen uniformly at random, its augmenting path in the above collection – and hence the *shortest* augmenting path from this vertex – has expected length at most $2n/k$. Now summing over all k from n down to 1 gives a total expected cost of $2n(\frac{1}{n} + \frac{1}{n-1} + \cdots + \frac{1}{2} + 1) = 2nH_n = O(n \log n)$, hence proving the theorem. $\qquad\square$

This $O(\log n)$-competitiveness guarantee happens to be tight for this matching problem in the RO model; see Exercise 11.3.

11.4.2 Bin Packing

In the classical bin-packing problem (which you may recall from Chapter 8), the request sequence consists of items of sizes $s_1, s_2, \ldots, s_n$; these items need to be packed into bins of unit capacity. (We assume each $s_i \leq 1$.) The goal is to minimize the number of bins used. One popular algorithm is BEST FIT:

When the next item (with size s_t) arrives:

1. If the item does not fit in any currently used bin, put it in a new bin. Else,
2. Put into a bin where the resulting empty space is minimized (i.e., where it fits "best").

BEST FIT uses no more than $2\,OPT$ bins in the worst case. Indeed, the sum of item sizes in any two of the bins is strictly more than 1, else we would never have started the later of these bins. Hence we use at most $\lceil 2\sum_i s_i \rceil$ bins, whereas OPT must be at least $\lceil \sum_i s_i \rceil$, since each bin holds at most unit total size. A more sophisticated analysis shows that BEST FIT uses $1.7\,OPT + O(1)$ bins on any request sequence, and this multiplicative factor of 1.7 is the best possible.

The examples showing the lower bound of 1.7 are intricate, but a lower bound of $3/2$ is much easier to show and also illustrates why BEST FIT does better in the RO model. Consider $n/2$ items of size $1/2^- := 1/2 - \varepsilon$, followed by $n/2$ items of size $1/2^+ := 1/2 + \varepsilon$. While the optimal solution uses $n/2$ bins, BEST FIT uses $3n/4$ bins on this adversarial sequence, since it pairs up the $1/2^-$ items with each other, and then has to use one bin per $1/2^+$ item. On the other hand, in the RO case, the imbalance between the two kinds of items behaves very similar to a symmetric random walk on the integers. (It is exactly such a random walk, but conditioned on starting and ending at the origin). The number of $1/2^+$ items that occupy a bin by themselves can now be bounded in terms of the maximum deviation from the origin (see Exercise 11.4), which is $O(\sqrt{n \log n}) = o(OPT)$ with high probability. Hence on this instance BEST FIT uses only $(1 + o(1))\,OPT$ bins in the RO model, compared to $1.5\,OPT$ in the adversarial order. On general instances, we get:

Theorem 11.11 *The* BEST FIT *algorithm uses at most* $(1.5 + o(1))\,OPT$ *bins in the RO setting.*

The key insight in the proof of this result is a "scaling" result, saying that any εn-length subsequence of the input has an optimal value εOPT, plus lower-order terms. The proof uses the random order property and concentration-of-measure. Observe that the worst-case example does not satisfy this scaling property: the second half of that instance has optimal value $n/2$, the same as for the entire instance. (Such a scaling property is often the crucial difference between the worst-case and RO moels: e.g., we used this in the algorithm for packing LPs in Section 11.3.2.)

The exact performance of BEST FIT in RO model remains unresolved: the best known lower bound uses $1.07\,OPT$ bins. Can we close this gap? Also, can we analyze other common heuristics in this model? For example, FIRST FIT places the next request in the bin that was started the earliest and can accommodate the item. Exercise 11.5 asks you to show that the NEXT FIT heuristic does not benefit from the random ordering, and has a competitive ratio of 2 in both the adversarial and RO models.

11.4.3 Facility Location

A slightly different algorithmic intuition is used for the *online facility location* problem, which is related to the k-means and k-median clustering problems. In this problem, we are given a metric space (V, d) with point set V, and distances $d : V \times V \to \mathbb{R}_{\geq 0}$ satisfying the triangle inequality. Let $f \geq 0$ be the cost of opening a facility; the algorithm can be extended to cases where different locations have different facility costs. Each request is specified by a point in the metric space, and let $R_t = \{r_1, \ldots, r_t\}$ be the (multi)-set of request points that arrive by time t. A solution at time t is a set $F_t \subseteq V$ of "facilities" whose opening cost is $f \cdot |F_t|$, and whose connection cost is the sum of distances from every request to its closest facility in F_t, i.e., $\sum_{j \in R_t} \min_{i \in F_t} d(j, i)$. An open facility remains open forever, so we require $F_{t-1} \subseteq F_t$. We want the algorithm's total cost (i.e., the opening plus connection costs) at time t to be at most a constant times the optimal total cost for R_t in the RO model. Such a result is impossible in the adversarial arrival model, where a tight $\Theta(\frac{\log n}{\log \log n})$ worst-case competitiveness is known.

There is a tension between the two components of the cost: opening more facilities increases the opening cost, but reduces the connection cost. Also, when request r_t arrives, if its distance to its closest facility in F_{t-1} is more than f, it is definitely better (in a greedy sense) to open a new facility at r_t and pay the opening cost of f, than to pay the connection cost more than f. This suggests the following algorithm:

When a request r_t arrives:

1. Let $d_t := \min_{i \in F_{t-1}} d(r_t, i)$ be its distance to the closest facility in F_{t-1}.
2. Set $F_t \leftarrow F_{t-1} \cup \{r_t\}$ with probability $p_t := \min\{1, d_t/f\}$, and $F_t \leftarrow F_{t-1}$ otherwise.

Observe that the choice of p_t approximately balances the expected opening cost $p_t \cdot f \leq d_t$ with the expected connection cost $(1 - p_t)d_t \leq d_t$. Moreover, since the set of facilities increases over time, a request may be reassigned to a closer facility later in the algorithm; however, the analysis works even assuming the request r_t is permanently assigned to its closest facility in F_t.

Theorem 11.12 *The foregoing algorithm is $O(1)$-competitive in the RO model.*

The insight behind the proof is a charging argument that first classifies each request as "easy" (if they are close to a facility in the optimal solution, and hence cheap) or "difficult" (if they are far from their facility). There are an equal number of each type, and the random permutation ensures that easy and difficult requests are roughly interleaved. This way, each difficult request can be paired with its preceding easy one, and this pairing can be used to bound their cost.

11.5 Related Models and Extensions

There have been other online models related to RO arrival. Broadly, these models can be classified either as "adding more randomness" to the RO model by making further stochastic assumptions on the arrivals, or as "limiting randomness" where the arrival sequence need not be uniformly random. The former lets us exploit the increased stochasticity to design algorithms with better performance guarantees; the latter help us quantify the robustness of the algorithms, and the limitations of the RO model.

11.5.1 Adding More Randomness

The RO model is at least as general as the *i.i.d. model*, which assumes a probability distribution $\mathcal{D}$ over potential requests where each request is an independent draw from the distribution $\mathcal{D}$. Hence, all the foregoing RO results immediately translate to the i.i.d. model. Is the converse also true – i.e., can we obtain identical algorithmic results in the two models? The next case study answers this question negatively, and then illustrates how to use the knowledge of the underlying distribution to perform better.

Steiner Tree in the RO Model

In the online Steiner tree problem, we are given a metric space (V, d), which can be thought of as a complete graph with edge weights $d(u, v)$; each request is a vertex in V. Let $R_t = \{r_1, \ldots, r_t\}$ be the (multi)-set of request vertices that arrive by time t. When a request r_t arrives, the algorithm must pick some edges $E_t \subseteq \binom{V}{2}$, so that edges $E_1 \cup \cdots \cup E_t$ picked until now connect R_t into a single component. The cost of each edge $\{u, v\}$ is its length $d(u, v)$, and the goal is to minimize the total cost.

The first algorithm we may imagine is the greedy algorithm, which picks a single edge connecting r_t to the closest previous request in R_{t-1}. This greedy algorithm is $O(\log n)$-competitive for any request sequence of length n in the worst case. Surprisingly, there are lower bounds of $\Omega(\log n)$, not just for adversarial arrivals, but also for the RO model. Let us discuss how the logarithmic lower bound for the adversarial model translates to one for the RO model.

There are two properties of the Steiner tree problem that make this transformation possible. The first is that duplicating requests does not change the cost of the Steiner tree, but making many copies of a request makes it likely that one of these copies will appear early in the RO sequence. Hence, if we take a fixed request sequence σ, duplicate the ith request C^{n-i} times (for some large $C > 1$), apply a uniform random permutation, and remove all but the first copy of each original request, the result looks close to σ with high probability. Of course, the sequence length increases from n to $\approx C^n$, and hence the lower bound goes from being logarithmic to being doubly logarithmic in the sequence length.

We now use a second property of Steiner tree: the worst-case examples consist of n requests that can be given in $\log n$ batches, with the ith batch containing $\approx 2^i$ requests – it turns out that giving so much information in parallel does not help the algorithm. Since we don't care about the relative ordering within the batches, we can duplicate the requests in the ith *batch* C^i times, thereby making the resulting request sequences of length $\leq C^{1+\log n}$. It is now easy to set $C = n$ to get a lower bound of $\Omega(\frac{\log n}{\log \log n})$, but a careful analysis allows us to set C to be a constant, and get an $\Omega(\log n)$ lower bound for the RO setting.

Steiner Tree in the i.i.d. Model

Given this lower bound for the RO model, what if we make stronger assumptions about the randomness in the input? What if the arrivals are i.i.d. draws from a probability distribution? We now have to make an important distinction, whether the distribution is known to the algorithm or not. The lower bound of the previous section can easily be extended to the case where arrivals are from an *unknown* distribution, so our only hope for a positive result is to consider the i.i.d. model with *known* distributions. In other words, each request is a random vertex of the graph, where vertex v is requested with a known probability $p_v \geq 0$ (and $\sum_v p_v = 1$). Let $\mathbf{p} = (p_1, p_2, \ldots, p_{|V|})$ be the vector of these probabilities. For simplicity, assume that we know the length n of the request sequence. The *augmented greedy* algorithm is the following:

1. Let A be the (multi-)set of $n-1$ i.i.d. samples from the distribution $\mathbf{p}$, plus the first request r_1.
2. Build a minimum spanning tree T connecting all the vertices in A.
3. For each subsequent request r_i (for $i \geq 2$): connect r_i to the closest vertex in $A \cup R_{i-1}$ using a direct edge.

Note that our algorithm requires minimal knowledge of the underlying distribution: it merely takes a set of samples that are stochastically identical to the actual request sequence and builds the "anticipatory" tree connecting this sample. Now the hope is that the real requests will look similar to the samples, and hence will have close-by vertices to which they can connect.

Theorem 11.13 *The augmented greedy algorithm is 4-competitive for the Steiner tree problem in the setting of i.i.d. requests with known distributions.*

Proof Since set A is drawn from the same distribution as the actual request sequence R_n, the expected optimal Steiner tree on A also costs OPT. The minimum spanning tree to connect up A is known to give a 2-approximate Steiner tree (Exercise 11.6), so the expected cost for T is $2OPT$.

Next, we need to bound the expected cost of connecting r_t to the previous tree for $t \geq 2$. Let the samples in A be called $a_2, a_3, \ldots, a_n$. Root the tree T at r_1, and let the "share" of a_t from T be the cost of the first edge on the path from a_t to the root. The sum of shares equals the cost of T. Now, the cost to connect r_t is at most the expected minimum distance from r_t to a vertex in $A \setminus \{a_t\}$. But r_t and a_t are from the same distribution, so this expected minimum distance is bounded by the expected distance from a_t to its closest neighbor in T, which is at most the expected share of a_t. Summing, the connection costs for the r_t requests is at most the expected cost of T, i.e., at most $2OPT$. This completes the proof. □

This proof extends to the setting where different requests are drawn from different known distributions; see Exercise 11.6.

11.5.2 Reducing the Randomness

Do we need the order of items to be uniformly random, or can weaker assumptions suffice for the problems we care about? This question was partially addressed in Section 11.3.1 where we saw order-oblivious algorithms. Recall: these algorithms assume a less-demanding arrival model, where a random fraction of the adversarial input set S is revealed to the algorithm in a first phase, and the remaining input set arrives in an adversarial order in the second phase. We now discuss some other models that have been proposed to reduce the amount of randomness required from the input. While some remarkable results have been obtained in these directions, there is still much to explore.

Entropy of the Random Arrival Order

One principled way of quantifying the randomness is to measure the entropy of the input sequences: a uniformly random permutation on n items has entropy $\log(n!) = O(n \log n)$, whereas order-oblivious algorithms (where each item is put randomly in either phase) require at most $\log \binom{n}{n/2} \le n$ bits of entropy. Are there arrival order distributions with even less entropy for which we can give good algorithms?

This line of research was initiated by Kesselheim et al. (2015), who showed the existence of arrival-order distributions with entropy only $O(\log \log n)$ that allow e-competitive algorithms for the single-item secretary problem (and also for some simple multiple-item problems). Moreover, they showed tightness of their results – for any arrival distribution with $o(\log \log n)$ entropy no online algorithm can be $O(1)$-competitive. This work also defines a notion of "almost k-wise uniformity," which requires that the induced distribution on every subset of k items be close to uniform. They show that this property and its variants suffice for some of the algorithms, but not for all.

A different perspective is the following: since the performance analysis for an algorithm in the RO model depends only on certain randomness properties of the input sequence (which are implied by the random ordering), it may be meaningful in some cases to (empirically) verify these specific properties on the actual input stream. For example, Bahmani et al. (2010) used this approach to explain the experimental efficacy of their algorithm computing personalized pageranks in the RO model.

Robustness and the RO Model

The RO model assumes that the adversary first chooses all the item values, and then the arrival order is perturbed at random according to some specified process. While this is a very appealing framework, one concern is that the algorithms may overfit the model. What if, as in some other semirandom models, the adversary gets to make a small number of changes *after* the randomness has been added? Alternatively, what if some parts of the input must remain in adversarial order, and the remainder is randomly permuted? For instance, say the adversary is allowed to specify a single item that must arrive at some specific position in the input sequence, or it is allowed to change the position of a single item after the randomness has been added. Most current algorithms fail when faced with such modest changes to the model. For example, the 37%-algorithm picks nothing if the adversary presents a large item in the beginning. Of course, these algorithms were not designed to be robust: but can we get analogous results even if the input sequence is slightly corrupted?

One approach is to give "best-of-both-worlds" algorithms that achieve a good performance when the input is randomly permuted, and which also have a good worst-case performance in all cases. For instance, Mirrokni et al. (2012) and Raghvendra (2016) give such results for online ad allocation and min-cost matching, respectively.

Since the secretary problem has poor performance in the worst case, we may want more refined guarantees, that the performance degrades with the amount of corruption. Here is a different semirandom model for the multiple-secretary problem from Section 11.3.1. In the *Byzantine* model, the adversary not only chooses the values of all n items; it also chooses the relative or absolute order of some εn of these items. The remaining $(1 - \varepsilon)n$ "good" items are then randomly permuted within the remaining positions. The goal is now to compare to the top k items among only these good items. Some preliminary results are known for this model (Bradač et al., 2019), but many questions remain open. In general, getting robust algorithms for secretary problems, or other optimization problems considered in this chapter, remains an important direction to explore.

11.5.3 Extending Random-Order Algorithms to Other Models

Algorithms for the RO model can help in designing good algorithms for similar models. One such example is for the *prophet* model, which is closely related to the optimal stopping problem in Section 8.1.4 of Chapter 8. In this model, we are given n independent prize-value distributions $D_1, \ldots, D_n$, and then presented with draws $v_i \sim D_i$ from these distributions in *adversarial* order. The threshold rule from Chapter 8, which picks the first prize with value above some threshold computable from just the distributions, gets expected value at least $\frac{1}{2} \mathbb{E}[\max_i v_i]$. Note the differences between the prophet and RO models: the prophet model assumes more about the values – namely, that they are drawn from the given distributions – but less about the ordering, since the items can be presented in an adversarial order. Interestingly, order-oblivious algorithms in the RO model can be used to get algorithms in the prophet model.

Indeed, suppose we only have limited access to the distributions D_i in the prophet model: we can get information about them only by drawing a few samples from each distribution. (Clearly we need at least one sample from the distributions, else we would be back in the online adversarial model.) Can we use these samples to get algorithms in this limited-access prophet model for some packing constraint family $\mathcal{F}$? The next theorem shows we can convert order-oblivious algorithms for the RO model to this setting using only a single sample from each distribution.

Theorem 11.14 *Given an α-competitive order-oblivious online algorithm for a packing problem $\mathcal{F}$, there exists an α-competitive algorithm for the corresponding prophet model with unknown probability distributions, assuming we have access to one (independent) sample from each distribution.*

The idea is to choose a random subset of items to be presented to the order-oblivious algorithm in the first phase; for these items we send in the sampled values available to us, and for the remaining items we use their values among the actual arrivals. The details are left as Exercise 11.7.

11.6 Notes

The classical secretary problem and its variants have long been studied in optimal stopping theory; see Ferguson (1989) for a historical survey. In computer science, the RO model has been used, e.g., for computational geometry problems, to get fast and elegant algorithms for problems like convex hulls and linear programming; see Seidel (1993) for a survey in the context of the *backwards analysis* technique. The secretary problem has gained broader attention due to connections to strategyproof mechanism design for online auctions (Hajiaghayi et al., 2004; Kleinberg, 2005). Theorem 11.3 is due to Gilbert and Mosteller (1966).

Section 11.3.1: The notion of an order-oblivious algorithm was first defined by Azar et al. (2014). The order-oblivious multiple-secretary algorithm is folklore. The matroid secretary problem was proposed by Babaioff et al. (2018); Theorem 11.5 is an adaptation of their $O(\log r)$-competitive algorithm for general matroids. Theorem 11.6, due to Korula and Pál (2009), extends to a $2e$-competitive order-adaptive algorithm. The current best algorithm is 4-competitive (Soto et al., 2018). The only lower bound known is the factor of e from Theorems 11.2 and 11.3, even for arbitrary matroids, whereas the best algorithm for general matroids has competitive ratio $O(\log\log \text{rank})$ (Lachish, 2014; Feldman et al., 2015). See the survey by Dinitz (2013) for work leading up to these results.

Section 11.3.2: The order-adaptive algorithms for multiple-secretary (Theorem 11.7) and for packing LPs (Theorem 11.8) are based on the work of Agrawal et al. (2014). The former result can be improved to give $(1 - O(\sqrt{1/k}))$-competitiveness (Kleinberg, 2005). Extending work on the AdWords problem (see the monograph by Mehta (2012)), Devanur and Hayes (2009) studied packing LPs in the RO model. The optimal results have $(1 - O(\sqrt{(\log d_{\text{nnz}})/k}))$-competitiveness (Kesselheim et al., 2018), where d_{nnz} is the maximum number of non-zeros in any column; these are based on the solve-ignoring-past-decisions approach we used for max-value matchings. Rubinstein (2016) and Rubinstein and Singla (2017) gave $O(\text{poly} \log n)$-competitive algorithms for general packing problems for subadditive functions. Theorem 11.9 (and extensions to combinatorial auctions) appear in Kesselheim et al. (2013).

Section 11.4: Theorem 11.10 about shortest augmenting paths is due to Chaudhuri et al. (2009). A worst-case result of $O(\log^2 n)$ was given by Bernstein et al. (2018); closing this gap remains an open problem. The analysis of BEST FIT in Theorem 11.11 is by Kenyon (1996). Theorem 11.12 for facility location is by Meyerson (2001); see Meyerson et al. (2001) for other network design problems in the RO setting. The tight nearly-logarithmic competitiveness for adversarial arrivals is due to Fotakis (2008).

Section 11.5.1: Theorem 11.13 for Steiner tree is by Garg et al. (2008). Grandoni et al. (2013) and Dehghani et al. (2017) give algorithms for set cover and k-server in the i.i.d. or prophet models. The gap between the RO and i.i.d. models (with *unknown* distributions) remains an interesting direction to explore. Correa et al. (2019) show that the single-item problem has the same competitiveness in both models; can we show similar results (or gaps) for other problems?

Section 11.5.2: Kesselheim et al. (2015) study connections between entropy and the RO model. The RO model with corruptions was proposed by Bradač et al. (2019), who also give $(1 - \varepsilon)$-competitive algorithms for the multiple-secretary problem with weak estimates on the optimal value. A similar model for online matching for mixed (stochastic and worst-case) arrivals was studied by Esfandiari et al. (2018). Finally, Theorem 11.14 to design prophet inequalities from samples is by Azar et al. (2014).

Acknowledgments

We thank Tim Roughgarden, C. Seshadhri, Matt Weinberg, and Uri Feige for their comments on an initial draft of this chapter.

References

Agrawal, Shipra, Wang, Zizhuo, and Ye, Yinyu. 2014. A dynamic near-optimal algorithm for online linear programming. *Operations Research*, **62**(4), 876–890.

Azar, Pablo D., Kleinberg, Robert, and Weinberg, S. Matthew. 2014. Prophet inequalities with limited information. In ACM-SIAM Symposium on Discrete Algorithms (SODA), 1358–1377.

Babaioff, Moshe, Immorlica, Nicole, Kempe, David, and Kleinberg, Robert. 2018. Matroid secretary problems. *Journal of the ACM*, **65**(6), 35:1–35:26.

Bahmani, Bahman, Chowdhury, Abdur, and Goel, Ashish. 2010. Fast incremental and personalized PageRank. *PVLDB*, **4**(3), 173–184.

Bernstein, Aaron, Holm, Jacob, and Rotenberg, Eva. 2018. Online bipartite matching with amortized $O(\log^2 n)$ replacements. In *ACM-SIAM Symposium on Discrete Algorithms (SODA)*, pp. 947–959.

Bradač, Domagoj, Gupta, Anupam, Singla, Sahil, and Žužic, Goran. 2019. Robust algorithms for the secretary problem. *Proceedings of the 11th Innovations in Theoretical Computer Science Conference (ITCS)*, pp. 32: 1–32:26.

Chaudhuri, Kamalika, Daskalakis, Constantinos, Kleinberg, Robert D., and Lin, Henry. 2009. Online bipartite perfect matching with augmentations.

Correa, José R., Dütting, Paul, Fischer, Felix A., and Schewior, Kevin. 2019. Prophet Inequalities for I.I.D. Random variables from an unknown distribution. *ACM Conference on Economics and Computation (EC)*, pp. 3–17.

Dehghani, Sina, Ehsani, Soheil, Hajiaghayi, MohammadTaghi, Liaghat, Vahid, and Seddighin, Saeed. 2017. Stochastic k-server: How should uber work? *International Colloquium on Automata, Languages, and Programming (ICALP)*, pp. 126:1–126:14.

Devanur, Nikhil R., and Hayes, Thomas P. 2009. The adwords problem: Online keyword matching with budgeted bidders under random permutations. *ACM Conference on Electronic Commerce (EC)*, pp. 71–78.

Dinitz, Michael. 2013. Recent advances on the matroid secretary problem. *SIGACT News*, **44**(2), 126–142.

Esfandiari, Hossein, Korula, Nitish, and Mirrokni, Vahab S. 2018. Allocation with traffic spikes: mixing adversarial and stochastic models. *ASM Transactions on Economics and Computing*, **6**(3–4), 14:1–14.23.

Feldman, Moran, Svensson, Ola, and Zenklusen, Rico. 2015. A simple $O(\log \log(\text{rank}))$-competitive algorithm for the matroid secretary problem. *ACM-SIAM Symposium on Discrete Algorithms (SODA)*, 1189–1201.

Ferguson, Thomas S. 1989. Who solved the secretary problem? *Statistical Science*, **4**(3), 282–289.

Fotakis, Dimitris. 2008. On the Competitive ratio for online facility location. *Algorithmica*, **50**(1), 1–57.

Garg, Naveen, Gupta, Anupam, Leonardi, Stefano, and Sankowski, Piotr. 2008. Stochastic analyses for online combinatorial optimization problems. In *ACM-SIAM Symposium on Discrete Algorithms (SODA)*, 942–951.

Gilbert, John P., and Mosteller, Frederick. 1966. Recognizing the maximum of a sequence. *Journal of the American Statistical Association*, **61**(313), 35–73.

Grandoni, Fabrizio, Gupta, Anupam, Leonardi, Stefano, Miettinen, Pauli, Sankowski, Piotr, and Singh, Mohit. 2013. Set covering with our eyes closed. *SIAM Journal on Computing*, **42**(3), 808–830.

Hajiaghayi, Mohammad Taghi, Kleinberg, Robert D., and Parkes, David C. 2004. Adaptive limited-supply online auctions. *ACM Conference on Electronic Commerce (EC)*, pp. 71–80

Kenyon, Claire. 1996. Best-fit bin-packing with random order. In *ACM-SIAM Symposium on Discrete Algorithms (SODA)*, 359–364.

Kesselheim, Thomas, Radke, Klaus, Tönnis, Andreas, and Vöcking, Berthold. 2013. An optimal online algorithm for weighted bipartite matching and extensions to combinatorial auctions. In *European Symposium on Algorithms (ESA)*, pp. 589–600.

Kesselheim, Thomas, Radke, Klaus, Tönnis, Andreas, and Vöcking, Berthold. 2018. Primal beats dual on online packing LPs in the random-order model. *SIAM Journal on Computing*, 47(5), 1939–1964.

Kesselheim, Thomas, Kleinberg, Robert D., and Niazadeh, Rad. 2015. Secretary problems with non-uniform arrival order. In *ACM Symposium on Theory of Computing (STOC)*, pp. 879–888.

Kleinberg, Robert. 2005. A multiple-choice secretary algorithm with applications to online auctions. In *ACM-SIAM Symposium on Discrete Algorithms (SODA)*, pp. 630–631.

Korula, Nitish, and Pál, Martin. 2009. Algorithms for secretary problems on graphs and hypergraphs. *International Colloquium on Automata, Languages, and Programming (ICALP)*, pp. 508–520.

Lachish, Oded. 2014. O(log log Rank) Competitive ratio for the matroid secretary problem. *FOCS*, pp. 326–335.

Mehta, Aranyak. 2012. Online matching and ad allocation. *Foundations and Trends in Theoretical Computer Science*, **8**(4), 265–368.

Meyerson, Adam. 2001. Online facility location. In *IEEE Symposium on Foundations of Computer Science (FOCS)*, pp. 426–431.

Meyerson, Adam, Munagala, Kamesh, and Plotkin, Serge A. 2001. Designing networks incrementally. In *IEEE Symposium on Foundations of Computer Science (FOCS)*, pp. 406–415.

Mirrokni, Vahab S., Gharan, Shayan Oveis, and Zadimoghaddam, Morteza. 2012. Simultaneous approximations for adversarial and stochastic online budgeted allocation. In *ACM-SIAM Symposium on Discrete Algorithms (SODA)*, pp. 1690–1701.

Raghvendra, Sharath. 2016. A robust and optimal online algorithm for minimum metric bipartite matching. In *Proceedings of the International Conference on Approximation Algorithms for Combinatorial Optimization Problems and on Randomization and Computation (APPROX-RANDOM)*.

Rubinstein, Aviad. 2016. Beyond matroids: secretary problem and prophet inequality with general constraints. In *ACM Symposium on Theory of Computing (STOC)*, pp. 324–332.

Rubinstein, Aviad, and Singla, Sahil. 2017. Combinatorial prophet inequalities. In *ACM-SIAM Symposium on Discrete Algorithms (SODA)*, pp. 1671–1687.

Seidel, Raimund. 1993. Backwards analysis of randomized geometric algorithms. In *New Trends in Discrete and Computational Geometry*. Algorithms and Combinatorics, Vol. 10. Springer-Verlag.

Soto, José A., Turkieltaub, Abner, and Verdugo, Victor. 2018. Strong algorithms for the ordinal matroid secretary problem. In *ACM-SIAM Symposium on Discrete Algorithms (SODA)*, pp. 715–734.

Exercises

Exercise 11.1 Show that both algorithms proposed above Theorem 11.4 for the multiple secretary problem achieve expected value $\Omega(V^*)$.

Exercise 11.2 Show why for a general packing constraint family $\mathcal{F}$, i.e., $A \in \mathcal{F}$ and $B \subseteq A$ implies $B \in \mathcal{F}$, no online algorithm has $o(\frac{\log n}{\log\log n})$-competitiveness. [Hint: Imagine n elements in a $\sqrt{n} \times \sqrt{n}$ matrix and $\mathcal{F}$ consists of subsets of columns.]

Exercise 11.3 Consider a cycle on $2n$ vertices, and hence it has a perfect matching. Show that the shortest augmenting path algorithm for minimizing augmentations in online matching from Section 11.4.1 has $\Omega(n \log n)$ cost in expectation.

Exercise 11.4 Suppose $n/2$ items of size $1/2^- := 1/2 - \varepsilon$ and $n/2$ items of size $1/2^+ := 1/2 + \varepsilon$ are presented in a random order to the BEST FIT bin packing heuristic from Section 11.4.2. Define the imbalance I_t after t items to be the number of $1/2^+$ items minus the number of $1/2^-$ items. Show that the number of bins that have only a single item (and hence waste about $1/2$ space) is at most $(\max_t I_t) - (\min_t I_t)$. Use a Chernoff–Hoeffding bound to prove this is at most $O(\sqrt{n \log n})$ with probability $1 - 1/\operatorname{poly}(n)$.

Exercise 11.5 In the NEXT FIT heuristic for the bin packing problem from Section 11.4.2, the next item is added to the current bin if it can accommodate the item, otherwise we put the item into a new bin. Show that this algorithm has a competitive ratio of 2 in both the adversarial and RO models.

Exercise 11.6 Show that for a set of requests in a metric space, the minimum spanning tree on this subset gives a 2-approximate solution to the Steiner tree. Also, extend the Steiner tree algorithm from the i.i.d. model to the prophet model, where the n requests are drawn from n independent (possibly different) known distributions $\mathbf{p}^t$ over the vertices.

Exercise 11.7 Prove Theorem 11.14.

Exercise 11.8 Suppose the input consists of $(1 - \varepsilon)n$ good items and εn bad items. The adversary decides all n item values, and also the locations of bad items. The good items are then randomly permuted in the remaining positions. If v^* denotes the value of the largest good item, show there is no online algorithm with expected value $\Omega(v^*/(\varepsilon n))$. [Hint: There is only one non-zero good item and all the bad items have values much smaller than v^*. The bad items are arranged as the single-item adversarial arrival lower bound instance.]

CHAPTER TWELVE

Self-Improving Algorithms

C. Seshadhri

Abstract: Self-improving algorithms provide a framework that interpolates between worst-case and average-case analysis. In this setting, inputs are assumed to be generated from an unknown distribution $\mathcal{D}$. A self-improving algorithm starts off as a vanilla worst-case algorithm. As it processes more inputs from $\mathcal{D}$, it tunes itself to become optimal for inputs from $\mathcal{D}$. In this chapter, we discuss self-improving algorithms for sorting and 2D coordinate-wise maxima.

12.1 Introduction

In many scenarios, an algorithm is designed to be used repeatedly, on inputs coming from some "source." For example, we may wish to sort the stock prices of commodities every morning. Or, design a routing algorithm for a truck delivery service that is used every day. Instead of just being a standard worst-case algorithm, the ideal algorithm should attempt to exploit structure in the inputs. On the other hand, it is highly unlikely that the inputs come from a closed-form source that we can completely describe.

Suppose one posits that the inputs are generated iid from a distribution $\mathcal{D}$. This distribution is unknown to the algorithm designer. Worst-case analysis takes the pessimistic view that because it is impossible to describe $\mathcal{D}$, the algorithm should simply do as well as possible for the worst possible inputs. Average-case analysis would take the optimistic route of trying to describe $\mathcal{D}$ (to the best extent possible), tailoring the algorithm for that distribution. The model of *self-improving algorithms* is an attempt to bridge the pessimism of worst-case analysis with the optimism of average-case analysis. It was first formulated in the context of sorting, by Ailon et al. (2011). A self-improving algorithm starts off with minimal assumptions on the input distribution $\mathcal{D}$, tries to learn about $\mathcal{D}$, and optimizes the running time for *this* $\mathcal{D}$.

Let us begin with some formalism. There is a fixed, but unknown distribution $\mathcal{D}$ that generates iid inputs denoted $I_1, I_2, \ldots$. Given input I_t, our aim is to compute $f(I_t)$, for some fixed function $f(\cdot)$. (For example, $f(I)$ might denote the sorted version of an input array I.) The self-improving algorithm does not know $\mathcal{D}$, and gains information about $\mathcal{D}$ as it sees more inputs (as t increases).

259

A self-improving algorithm has two phases:

- Learning phase: Initially, the self-improving algorithm simply computes $f(I_t)$ using a worst-case algorithm. As t increases (more inputs are seen), it learns more information about $\mathcal{D}$ and stores a summary of it in a data structure T.
- Limiting phase: In this phase, the algorithm uses the data structure T to compute $f(I_t)$ faster.

The aim is to build a small data structure T in a short learning phase, to attain a faster running time in the limiting phase. We note that the concept of a self-improving algorithm is valid for any algorithmic performance measure (such as solution quality), but all the killer applications concern running time.

Note that there is a natural offline/online view of the setting. The self-improving algorithm can be thought of as an online algorithm. The corresponding offline algorithm would know $\mathcal{D}$. The "online" self-improving algorithm should ideally perform competitively with the "offline" optimal version (which knows $\mathcal{D}$).

Since I_t is a random variable, it is more meaningful to talk of the *expected* running time in the limiting phase. Typically, every algorithm has some bad input, which may have some negligible (but nonzero) probability. Thus, in general, beating the worst-case running time seems to require averaging over a distribution of inputs.

While we consider the distribution $\mathcal{D}$ to be fixed and the inputs to be independent draws, one could imagine richer settings. One might consider $\mathcal{D}$ to itself evolve over time, or for the inputs to be generated by a Markov process where I_t depends on the previous I_{t-1}. All the results known so far take the fixed $\mathcal{D}$ view.

12.1.1 The Question of Sorting

Let us test out the self-improving model on the problem of comparison-based sorting. Let $\mathcal{D}$ be a distribution on real-valued arrays[1] of length n. A classical worst-case algorithm, such as MERGESORT, can sort in worst-case $O(n \lg n)$ time. Our aim is to sort $I \sim \mathcal{D}$, in better than $O(n \lg n)$ time. Let us begin with the "offline" setting. When $\mathcal{D}$ is known, can we beat the $n \lg n$ time lower bound for sorting?

The tools of information theory can be used to give a fairly satisfying answer to this question. This answer will form the basis of the self-improving sorter analysis. To maintain the flow of this chapter, we defer the formal definitions and theorems from information theory to Section 12.2. A reader unfamiliar with the definition of entropy and the notion of optimal search trees may wish to read Section 12.2 before this section.

The question of sorting in $o(n \lg n)$ time was first addressed by Fredman (1976), for the special case of sorting within subsets of permutations. Let $[n]$ denote the set $\{1, 2, \ldots, n\}$. Consider an input array I of length n, with indexing starting from 1. On sorting I, each element ends up a potentially new position. Let $\pi(I)$ be the array of final positions after sorting.[2] So the ith element of $\pi(I)$ is the index of the ith element of I after sorting I. For example, suppose $I = [5, 3, 42, 7]$. Then $\pi(I)$ is $[2, 1, 4, 3]$.

---

[1] The results hold for any total order, but it is convenient to assume that the domain of reals.

[2] If elements in I are repeated, we can define $\pi(I)$ for a stable sorting of I.

We will refer to $\pi(I)$ as the permutation induced by I. Suppose there was a known set Γ of permutations, and we are guaranteed that $\pi(I) \in \Gamma$.

Theorem 12.1 *Fix a set Γ of permutations. There is an algorithm that sorts any array I such that $\pi(I) \in \Gamma$, using (worst case) $\lg|\Gamma| + 2n$ comparisons.*

Proof Let $I = (x_1, x_2, \ldots, x_n)$, and for each $k \leq n$, let $I_{\leq k} = (x_1, x_2, \ldots, x_k)$. We will perform insertion sort, as follows. In the kth iteration, $\pi(I_{\leq k})$ has been determined. We need to determine the position of x_{k+1} in the sorted version of $I_{\leq k}$.

We describe a preprocessing step that does *not* involve any comparisons of the elements of I. The purpose of this step is to construct the "right" search tree to find x_{k+1}. We will construct a large table, indexed by every permutation τ over $[k]$, for all $k \leq n$. Fix some such permutation τ over $[k]$. Consider permutations σ (over $[n]$) such that the subarray of the first k elements of σ induce the permutation τ. (In other words, if $\sigma_{\leq k}$ denotes the subarray of the first k elements of σ, then $\pi(\sigma_{\leq k}) = \tau$.) Let the set of such permutations be denoted Γ_τ. Furthermore, partition Γ_τ into sets $\Gamma_\tau^1, \Gamma_\tau^2, \ldots, \Gamma_\tau^{k+1}$ as follows. The set Γ_τ^i consists of permutations σ where the $(k+1)$th element is at position i, after sorting the first $(k+1)$ elements of σ. Equivalently, $\pi(\sigma_{\leq k+1})$ has i as the $(k+1)$th element. Consider the distribution on $[k+1]$ where the probability of i is $|\Gamma_\tau^i|/|\Gamma_\tau|$, and let T be an optimal search tree for this distribution (refer to Lemma 12.9). Note that leaves of T are labeled with $[k+1]$. We can construct T to be such that: if $|\Gamma_\tau^i|/|\Gamma_\tau| \in [1/2^d, 1/2^{d-1})$, then, in T, the depth of the leaf labeled i is at most $d + 2$.

Now, we describe how to insert x_{k+1} into the sorted order of $x_{\leq k}$ (denote the latter as y). Having determined $\pi(x_k)$, we get the appropriate search tree T as described earlier. Each internal node of T denotes a comparison with some $i \in [k]$. (A comparison with $k + 1$ would be superfluous, since it is the largest element in $[k + 1]$.) The algorithm processes this node by comparing x_{k+1} with y_i. Thus, by walking down the tree T, the algorithm will correctly determine x_{k+1}'s position in y, and determine $\pi(I_{\leq k+1})$.

What is the expected search time for this iteration? Suppose the search reached the leaf node labeled i. The search time is at most $\lg(|\Gamma_\tau|/|\Gamma_\tau^i|) + 2$. Note that τ is the permutation induced by the first k elements of the input I, and i is the position of x_{k+1} in this permutation. Let us define $\Gamma^{(k)}$ to be the set of permutations extending $\pi(I_{\leq \ell})$. Then this search time is at most $\lg(|\Gamma^{(k)}|/|\Gamma^{(k+1)}|) + 2$. Summing over all k and noting that $\Gamma_1 = \Gamma$, the total number of comparisons is at most $\sum_{k=1}^{n}[\lg(|\Gamma^{(k)}|/|\Gamma^{(k+1)}|) + 2] = \lg|\Gamma| + 2n$, as desired. $\square$

Note that $|\Gamma| \leq n!$, so $\lg|\Gamma| \leq \lg n! = O(n \lg n)$. But if $|\Gamma| = 2^{O(n)}$, then linear time sorting is possible.

The algorithm given in the proof runs in exponential time, even though the number of comparisons performed is $O(n \lg n)$. For every prefix permutation τ, the algorithm needs to compute an optimal search tree by going over all of Γ_τ.

For arbitrary distributions, the entropy of the induced distributions on permutations determines the minimum expected number of comparisons for sorting.

Theorem 12.2 *Consider any distribution $\mathcal{D}$ on real arrays of length n. There is a sorting algorithm (that is correct on every input) whose expected comparison complexity on input $I \sim \mathcal{D}$ is $H(\pi(I)) + O(n)$. Moreover, any comparison based algorithm must make at least $H(\pi(I))$ comparisons in expectation.*

The algorithm is analogous to the previous one, but the analysis needs some information theoretic manipulations. Details are given in Exercise 12.2. The lower bound is a direct consequence of Shannon's encoding theorem, Theorem 12.7.

Theorem 12.2 provides the optimal "offline" bound, which is the benchmark bound that a self-improving algorithm must shoot for. Moreover, the proof hints at the role of entropy optimal search trees in beating the $n \lg n$ sorting bound. Let us now state the desired behavior of a self-improving sorter.

- Training phase: Every input is sorted in $\Theta(n \lg n)$ time using a vanilla sorting algorithm, such as MERGESORT. As the number of inputs grows, the self-improving sorter builds some data structure T.
- Limiting phase: The expected running time is now $O(H(\pi(I))+n)$, or at least close to it. The algorithm uses T to speed up the computation.

There are a number of complexity parameters[3] to optimize.

- Limiting run time: Making this smaller than the worst-case complexity is the whole point of self-improving algorithms. As mentioned earlier, our ideal for sorting is $O(H(\pi(I))+n)$ time. We stress that the running time is an expectation over $I \sim \mathcal{D}$.
- Size of the data structure T.
- Training phase length: This is the number of instances seen to build T. There is a natural tradeoff here: a longer learning phase would lead to more information about $\mathcal{D}$, which is presumably useful for reducing the limiting run time.

To see the path toward a self-improving sorter, let us begin by ignoring the training phase length. We effectively assume the self-improving algorithm could learn $\mathcal{D}$ exactly.

Furthermore, suppose we only cared for the limiting running time. In this case, Theorem 12.2 gives us the desired self-improving algorithm, for any $\mathcal{D}$. Observe that the search tree constructed in the proof of Theorem 12.1 (and Theorem 12.2) could be precomputed in the training phase. Using this search tree, every input inducing a permutation in Γ can be sorted in $\lg |\Gamma|+O(n)$ time. The catch is that the search tree, as described, requires storage exponential in n. As explained later, lower bounds for self-improving algorithms imply that exponential storage is necessary for any algorithm that achieves the bound of Theorem 12.2.

---

[3] A less important complexity parameter is the total time required to build T. Ideally, one would hope that (in the case of sorting) the time to construct T would simply be the length of the training phase times the worst-case sorting time. In all the self-improving algorithms discussed, such a statement will hold. For the sake of exposition, we will ignore this aspect.

The next step is to find classes of distributions where T can be made smaller, even assuming that $\mathcal{D}$ is known. The final step is to show that T can be built by seeing a few instances from $\mathcal{D}$, thereby bounding the training phase length.

We now state the main results on self-improving sorters from Ailon et al. (2011). We require the self-improving algorithm to always gives the correct output on all inputs, regardless of what happens in the training phase. The guarantees on the limiting run time are probabilistic. The training phase depends on the random inputs seen, and it may fail with some small probability. For convenience, we use *with high probability (whp)* to denote events with probability at least $1 - 1/n$.

We require that the input distribution $\mathcal{D}$ be a *product distribution* $\prod_{i \in [n]} \mathcal{D}_i$. Therefore, for all $i \in [n]$, the ith entry of the input comes from an independent distribution $\mathcal{D}_i$.

Theorem 12.3 *For any $\varepsilon \in (0, 1]$, there exists a self-improving sorter for product distributions where the following guarantees hold whp. (i) Limiting run time of $O(\varepsilon^{-1} H(\pi(I)) + n)$, (ii) Data structure size of $O(n^{1+\varepsilon})$, (iii) Training phase length of $O(n^{\varepsilon})$, and (iv) Training run time of $O(n \lg n)$.*

There appear to be two dissatisfying aspects of this theorem. First, the restriction to product distributions, and second, the superlinear sized data structure. There are lower bounds showing that both are necessary.

Theorem 12.4 *Any self-improving sorter for arbitrary distributions that has a limiting run time of $O(H(\pi(I)) + n)$ requires $2^{\Omega(n \lg n)}$ storage.*

Theorem 12.4 shows that Fredman's construction from Theorems 12.1 and 12.2 are space optimal. One can build on the proof ideas of this lower bound to show that self-improving sorters for product distributions require superlinear storage.

Theorem 12.5 *Fix any $\varepsilon \in (0, 1]$. Any self-improving sorter for arbitrary product distributions that has a limiting run time at most $\varepsilon^{-1}(H(\pi(I)) + n)$ requires $n^{1+\varepsilon}$ storage.*

A weaker version of Theorem 12.3, with a quadratic-sized data structure, is proved in Section 12.3. Theorem 12.4 is proven in Section 12.3.3, which can be read independently of the other sections. Before describing the self-improving algorithm, we delve into basic information theory.

12.2 Information Theory Basics

Information theory plays a central role in the analysis of self-improving algorithms. To prove optimality for a self-improving algorithm, one needs a lower bound on the performance of the best possible algorithm. In many cases, information theory provides the perfect tools to express such lower bounds. Much of the material in this section is standard and can be found in the classic textbook of Cover and Thomas (2006).

Information theory begins with the concept of *Shannon entropy.*

Definition 12.6 For a discrete random variable X over finite universe $\mathcal{X}$, the Shannon entropy is $H(X) = - \sum_{u \in \mathcal{X}} \Pr[X = u] \lg \Pr[X = u]$.

A *unique binary encoding* of $\mathcal{X}$ is a one-to-one function $f : \mathcal{X} \to \{0, 1\}^*$. (For convenience, we simply say "encoding.") For a random variable X, an important quantity of student is the *encoding length* $|f(X)|$, where size is the string length. Thus, for the random variable X, one could ask for the encoding function f that minimizes the encoding length of X. Somewhat abusing notation, we will refer to *encodings of* X, though it really refers to encodings of the universe $\mathcal{X}$. This notation allows us to ignore the universe $\mathcal{X}$.

Shannon's classic encoding theorem, stated as Theorem 12.7 relates the encoding length to the entropy.

Theorem 12.7 (Cover and Thomas, 2006, Theorem 5.4.1) *Any encoding of a random variable X has expected length at least $H(X)$. Furthermore, there exists an encoding of expected length at most $H(X) + 1$.*

Our primary application of this theorem is to *comparison trees*. Most standard sorting algorithms work by comparing individual elements of the input array I ("is $I[a] \leq I[b]$?"). One can imagine "unrolling" the algorithm, to represent it as a binary tree, where each node is a comparison. This tree is called a comparison tree. To "run" the comparison tree on an input, we apply the comparison at a node, and move to an appropriate child depending on the answer. The leaves of the comparison tree contain the answer, which for sorting would be the induced permutation $\pi(I)$. Note that this abstraction of sorting ignores the data movement, and only considers the comparisons required to sort.

Let us describe comparison trees more abstractly. Let $\mathcal{U}$ be an arbitrary universe, and let $\mathcal{X}$ be a finite set. A comparison-based algorithm $\mathcal{A}$ to compute a function $X : \mathcal{U} \to \mathcal{X}$ is a rooted binary tree $\mathcal{A}$ such that (i) every internal node of $\mathcal{A}$ represents a comparison of the form "$f(I) \leq g(I)$?", where $f, g : \mathcal{U} \to \mathbf{R}$ are *arbitrary* functions on the input universe $\mathcal{U}$; and (ii) the leaves of $\mathcal{A}$ are labeled with outputs from $\mathcal{X}$ such that for every input $I \in \mathcal{U}$, following the appropriate path for I leads to the correct output $X(I)$. In our setting, $\mathcal{U}$ is the set of array, $\mathcal{X}$ is the set of permutations, and the functions f, g typically pick out specific elements of the input.

If $\mathcal{A}$ has maximum depth d, we say that $\mathcal{A}$ needs d comparisons (in the worst case). For a distribution $\mathcal{D}$ on $\mathcal{U}$, the *expected number of comparisons* (with respect to $\mathcal{D}$) is the expected length of a path from the root to a leaf in $\mathcal{A}$, where the leaves are sampled according to the distribution that $\mathcal{D}$ induces on $\mathcal{X}$ via X.

In a binary tree, all nodes have a binary encoding given by the path to the node from the root. Edges to left/right children are encoded as 0/1, thereby giving a string representation for paths. Thus, the comparison tree implicitly gives a binary encoding of (the labels on) the leaves, and the depth corresponds to the encoding length. A direct consequence of Theorem 12.7 is the following theorem.

Theorem 12.8 *Let $\mathcal{D}$ be a distribution on a universe $\mathcal{U}$ and let $X : \mathcal{U} \to \mathcal{X}$ be a random variable. Then any comparison-based algorithm to compute X needs at least $H(X)$ expected comparisons.*

A special, useful case of comparison trees are *search trees* for discrete random variables X over an ordered universe. Each comparison is of the form "$X \leq v$?" for some v in the universe $\mathcal{X}$[4].

We can give an explicit construction of a near optimal search tree for a random variable. The proof is given as Exercise 12.1.

Lemma 12.9 *Let X be a discrete real-valued random variable with support size k. There exists a search tree that determines the value of X and has the following properties.*

- *The tree makes expected $H(X) + 2$ comparisons.*
- *The maximum number of comparisons is at most $2 \lg k$.*
- *If an element x (in the range of X) has probability in $[2^{-d}, 2^{-d+1})$, then the depth of x in T is at most $d + 2$.*
- *Given an explicit description of X, the search tree can be computed in $O(k \lg k)$ time.*

The following lemma is an important tool in the analysis of self-improving algorithms and was first discovered in that context. To get some context, consider the self-improving sorter. On an input I, it makes some number of comparisons to determine $\pi(I)$. Our goal is to upper bound this number by $H(\pi(I))$. We will describe a random variable Z (which is a deterministic function of I), such that the comparisons will correspond to searching in the optimal search tree for Z. Thus, the number of comparisons performed by the self-improving algorithm will be $H(Z)$. The following lemma asserts that if Z can be computed with few comparisons from $\pi(I)$, then $H(Z)$ cannot be much larger than $H(\pi(I))$.

To formalize, we think of computing Z from I, with the random variable $\pi(I)$ as advice. The lemma is stated in terms of general random variables.

Lemma 12.10 *Let $\mathcal{D}$ be a distribution on a universe $\mathcal{U}$, and let $X : \mathcal{U} \to \mathcal{X}$ and $Y : \mathcal{U} \to \mathcal{Y}$ be two random variables. Suppose that the function f defined by $f : (I, Y(I)) \mapsto X(I)$ can be computed by a comparison-based algorithm performing C comparisons on average over $\mathcal{D}$. Then $H(X) \leq H(Y) + C + 1$.*

Proof Abusing notation, let $\mathcal{X}$ and $\mathcal{Y}$ denote the ranges of the functions X and Y respectively. Thus, one can think of X as a distribution over $\mathcal{X}$ (and analogously for $\mathcal{Y}$). The proof strategy is to get an encoding of $\mathcal{X}$, whose expected length, under X, is an upper bound of $H(X)$. The encoding of $\mathcal{X}$ uses the optimal encoding of the set $\mathcal{Y}$, under distribution Y, and the outcomes of the comparison-based algorithm that computes X.

Let s be the optimal encoding (with shortest expected length) of Y. For convenience, let the expected code length of s be L_s. By Theorem 12.7, $H(Y) \leq L_s \leq H(Y) + 1$.

---

[4] We note a technical distinction between the usual concept of binary search trees (BSTs) with our definition here. In standard BSTs, a node leads to three possibilities ($<$, $=$, $>$) while our notion only has two possibilities ($\leq$, $>$). Standard BSTs technically give ternary encodings, while our notion is more suitable to standard definitions of entropy.

Using f, we can convert s into a unique encoding t of $\mathcal{X}$. Indeed, for every $I \in \mathcal{U}$, $X(I)$ can be uniquely identified by a string $t(I)$ that is the concatenation of $s(Y(I))$ and additional bits that represent the outcomes of the comparisons for the algorithm to compute $f(I, Y(I))$. Thus, for every element $x \in \mathcal{X}$, we can define $t(x)$ as the lexicographically smallest string $t(I)$ for which $X(I) = x$, and we obtain a unique encoding t for $\mathcal{X}$. Let $c(I)$ denote the number of comparisons made for $(I, Y(I))$ and let the expected code length of t be L_t. Observe that

$$L_t = \mathbf{E}_{\mathcal{D}}[|t(X(I))|] \le \mathbf{E}_{\mathcal{D}}[c(I) + s(Y(I))] = C + L_s \le H(Y) + C + 1.$$

By Theorem 12.7 again, $L_t \ge H(X)$, completing the proof. $\square$

Finally, we recall the well-known property of the joint entropy of independent random variables. The joint entropy of random variables $X_1, X_2, \ldots, X_k$ can be thought of as the entropy of a single k-tuple random variable $(X_1, X_2, \ldots, X_k)$.

Claim 12.11 (Cover and Thomas, 2006, Theorem 2.6.6) *Let $H(X_1, \ldots, X_n)$ be the joint entropy of independent random variables $X_1, \ldots, X_n$. Then $H(X_1, \ldots, X_n) = \sum_i H(X_i)$.*

12.3 The Self-Improving Sorter

The sorting algorithm is a version of bucket sort. Essentially, the training phase identifies a linear set of disjoint intervals (buckets) such that the expected number of input numbers within a bucket is constant. The sorting algorithm uses an optimal search tree to search for each input number in these buckets. The buckets are sorted using insertion sort. Since the buckets are disjoint, the final sorted order can be determined in linear time.

We start by describing the data structures T that will be learned. Given specific conditions on the data structures, we can complete the analysis of the limiting phase. Lastly, we show how T is built in the training phase.

In general, expectations are taken over $I \sim \mathcal{D}$. We will use $i \in [n]$ to refer to the ith entry of an input, which is distributed as $\mathcal{D}_i$. We will assume that all the $\mathcal{D}_i$'s are continuous, so two numbers have zero probability of being identical. This is mostly a technical convenience, and can be removed using tie-breaking rules.

The data structures that form T will be parameterized by $\alpha > 1$.

- **The B_j buckets** This is a sequence $-\infty = b_1 \le b_2 \le b_2 \ldots b_n \le b_{n+1} = \infty$. We will refer to the interval $(b_j, b_{j+1}]$ as the *jth bucket B_j*. Note that the buckets partition **R**. We require that the expected number of input numbers falling into any bucket is constant (the choice of 10 is just for concreteness).

  Property B: For all $j \in [n]$, $\mathbf{E}[|I \cap B_j|] \le 10$.

- **The T_i-trees** For each $i \in [n]$, T_i is an "α-approximate" search tree with leaves corresponding to the buckets.

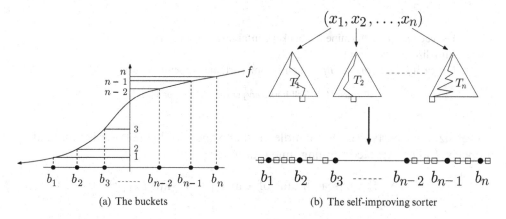

(a) The buckets   (b) The self-improving sorter

Figure 12.1 (a) The construction of the ideal buckets. (b) A pictorial description of the limiting phase. In this figure, we use empty squares to denote the x_is.

Definition 12.12 For any $i \in [n]$, let X_i be the random variable denoting the bucket that contains $x \sim \mathcal{D}_i$. Denote by H_i the Shannon entropy of X_i, $H(X_i)$.

Property T: For all $i \in [n]$, $\mathbf{E}_{x \sim \mathcal{D}_i}[\text{search time of } x \text{ in } T_i] \leq \alpha(H_i + 1)$.

If the distributions are known, one can construct "ideal" buckets such that $\mathbf{E}[|I \cap B_j|] = 1$, and construct tress with $\alpha = 1$. Consider the function $f(v) := \mathbf{E}[|I \cap (-\infty, v)|]$, the number of input numbers at most v. (This is the sum of CDFs of $\mathcal{D}_i$.) Recall that the distributions $\mathcal{D}_i$ are continuous. Then f is a continuous[5], monotone function going from 0 to n. The bucket boundaries are simply defined by $f^{-1}(1), f^{-1}(2)$, etc. Refer to Figure 12.1a. Given the buckets and knowledge of the $\mathcal{D}_i$'s, Lemma 12.9 provides us with the T_i trees (with $\alpha = 1$).

12.3.1 The Limiting Phase

The limiting phase is quite straightforward (also refer to Figure 12.1b). For convenience, we use i to denote an input number, and j to denote a bucket. We denote the input by $I = (x_1, x_2, \ldots, x_n)$.

Theorem 12.13 *Assume that properties B and T hold. Then the expected running time of* SISLimiting(I) *is* $O(\alpha(H(\pi(I)) + n))$.

The expected running time can be split into the time required for determining the buckets, and the total running time of insertion sort on each bucket (quadratic in

---

[5] Without continuity, B_j buckets might not exist. since there could be an individual number that repeatedly appears in an input. Of course, this would only make sorting easier. We could find all such numbers and place them into special buckets, where further sorting is not needed.

SISLimiting(I)

1. For each $i \in [n]$, determine the bucket containing x_i using T_i.
2. Initialize empty output.
3. For each $j \in [n]$, sort $I \cap B_j$ using insertion sort, and append to output.

Figure 12.2 Self-improving sorter: limiting phase.

bucket size). Property B gives a handle on the former, while the latter is bounded by property T. The expected running time is at most:

$$\sum_{i\in[n]} \mathbf{E}_{x\sim\mathcal{D}_i}[\text{search time of } x \text{ in } T_i] + \sum_{j\in[n]} \mathbf{E}[|I \cap B_j|^2]$$

$$\leq \sum_{i\in[n]} \alpha H_i + \alpha n + \sum_{j\in[n]} \mathbf{E}[|I \cap B_j|^2]. \tag{12.1}$$

As we show in Lemma 12.14, $\sum_i H_i \leq H(\pi(I)) + O(n)$ and for all j, $\mathbf{E}[|I \cap B_j|^2] = O(1)$. These bounds complete the proof of Theorem 12.13.

The following lemma is what connects the sum of search times to the optimal sorting time of $H(\pi(I))$. The full independence of the $\mathcal{D}_i$'s is crucially used in this proof. The lemma applies for any choice of buckets (not just buckets constructed by the self-improving sorter).

Lemma 12.14 $\sum_i H_i \leq H(\pi(I)) + 2n$.

Proof Let X_i be the random variable denoting the bucket that x_i falls into. Since the X_is are independent, by Claim 12.11 the joint entropy $H(X_1, X_2, \ldots, X_n)$ is exactly $\sum_{i\in[n]} H(X_i) = \sum_{i\in[n]} H_i$.

Let X be the random variable $(X_1, X_2, \ldots, X_n)$. We apply Lemma 12.10, with $Y = \pi(I)$. We need to give a comparison-based algorithm that computes X given $(I, \pi(I))$. The "advice" $\pi(I)$ allows the algorithm to sort I for free. The desired comparison-based algorithm uses $\pi(I)$ to sort I (for no extra comparisons) and then merge the sorted list with $[b_1, b_2, \ldots, b_{n+1} = \infty]$. The merging requires at most $2n$ comparisons, after which the bucket of every x_i in I is determined. Thus, $H(X) \leq H(\pi(I)) + 2n$. $\square$

The next claim is proven by property B and only requires pairwise independence of the $\mathcal{D}_i$'s. (Proof in Exercise 12.7.)

Claim 12.15 *For all $j \in [n]$, $\mathbf{E}[|I \cap B_j|^2] = O(1)$.*

12.3.2 The Training Phase

The training phase uses independent inputs $I_1, I_2, \ldots, I_t$ to construct a data structure. Instead of directly proving the full Theorem 12.3 here, it is instructive to get a quadratic sized T (the $\varepsilon = 1$ case). The size of T will be $O(n^2)$ and the training phase

Bucket

1. Merge $\lambda = \lceil c \ln n \rceil$ independent inputs into a single sorted array L of length λn.
2. Output $L(\lambda), L(2\lambda), \ldots, L(\lambda n)$ as the bucket boundaries.

Figure 12.3 Self-improving sorter: constructing buckets.

Tree

1. Take $\ell = \lceil cn^2 \ln n \rceil$ independent inputs. For each $i \in [n]$, let S_i denote the set of ℓ independent draws from $\mathcal{D}_i$.
2. For each $i \in [n]$:
    1. For each $j \in [n]$, let $\hat{p}_{ij}$ be the fraction of numbers in S_i that are contained in B_j.
    2. Output, as T_i, the search tree over the buckets given by Lemma 12.9 applied to the distribution $\{\hat{p}_{ij}\}$ (varying over j).

Figure 12.4 Self-improving sorter: constructing search trees.

will last $O(n^2 \lg n)$ rounds. We split the training phase into $\lambda + \ell$ rounds, where the first λ rounds are used to learn the buckets, and the latter ℓ are used to learn the trees.

We use c to denote a sufficiently large constant, required to get sufficient concentration in the application of Chernoff–Hoeffding bounds. (Refer to Chap. 8, Exercise 8.3 for more details on Chernoff bounds.)

The "ideal" buckets would each contain λ elements from the union of λ inputs. So we simply construct the empirical buckets with respect to λ inputs. We require $\lambda = \Omega(\lg n)$ for taking a union bound over the n buckets.

Once the buckets are constructed, we can simply estimate the distribution of X_i (see Definition 12.12) to construct approximately optimal search trees. We will of course need to prove that these trees are approximate optimal with respect to the original distribution.

Claim 12.16 *The B_j-buckets satisfy property B with probability at least $1 - 1/n^2$.*

Proof Consider the ideal buckets given in Figure 12.1a. We will denote these with primed variables, to distinguish from the buckets constructed by the algorithm. The ideal buckets are given by a sequence $-\infty = b'_0 \leq b'_1 \leq b'_2 \leq \cdots \leq b'_n = \infty$ with the following property. Let the jth ideal bucket be $B'_j = (b'_{j-1}, b'_j]$. For every j, $\mathbf{E}[|I \cap B'_j|] = 1$. Observe that the expected size $\mathbf{E}[|L \cap B'_j|]$ is exactly λ. Note that $|L \cap B'_j|$ can be expressed as a sum of independent Bernoulli random variables (Exercise 12.7). By a multiplicative Chernoff bound (Dubhashi and Panconesi, 2009, Part 2, Theorem 1.1), for each $j \in [n]$, $\Pr[|L \cap B'_j| < \lambda/2] \leq \exp(-\lambda/8) = \exp(-(c/8)\lg n) \leq 1/n^3$ (for sufficiently large c). By a union bound over the ideal buckets, with probability at least $1 - 1/n^2$, all ideal buckets contain at least $\lambda/2$ points of L. Each bucket constructed in Bucket contains λ contiguous points of L. These constructed buckets contain at most two ideal buckets, and intersects at most four ideal buckets. (Each endpoint might lie in a different ideal bucket.) Thus, for every constructed bucket B_j, $\mathbf{E}[|I \cap B_j|] \leq 4$. $\square$

Claim 12.17 *The T_i-trees constructed by the algorithm (refer to Figure 12.4) satisfy Property T with probability at least $1-1/n^2$. Formally, the expected search time in T_i is at most $2H_i + 5$.*

Proof First, fix $i,j \in [n]$. Let p_{ij} be the probability that $x \sim \mathcal{D}_i$ lands in bucket B_j. Let $\hat{p}_{ij}$ be the fraction of entries in S_i that land in B_j. Observe that $\mathbf{E}[\hat{p}_{ij}] = p_{ij}$, and by the Hoeffding bound (Dubhashi and Panconesi, 2009, Part 2, Theorem 1.1), $\Pr[|p_{ij} - \hat{p}_{ij}| > 1/2n] \leq 2\exp(-2\ell/n^2)$. By the choice of ℓ, this probability is at most $1/n^5$.

We take a union bound over all i,j. Thus, with probability at least $1 - 1/n^3$, for all $i,j \in [n]$, $|\hat{p}_{ij} - p_{ij}| \leq 1/2n$. Henceforth, assume this holds.

Let us fix a choice of i. Note that T_i is the optimal search tree with respect to $\hat{p}_{ij}$, but the expected search time needs to be computed according to $x \sim \mathcal{D}_i$. We apply the properties of the optimal search tree given in Lemma 12.9. If $x \in B_j$, then the search time is the depth of B_j in T_i, which is at most $\lceil \lg \hat{p}_{ij}^{-1} \rceil \leq \lg \hat{p}_{ij}^{-1} + 1$. The maximum search time is at most $2\lg n$. Let us partition the support $[n]$ into $H := \{j | p_{ij} \geq 1/n\}$ and $L := [n] \setminus H$. The expected search time in T_i is at most:

$$\sum_{j \in L} p_{ij}(2\lg n) + \sum_{j \in H} p_{ij}(\lg \hat{p}_{ij}^{-1} + 1)$$

$$= 2\sum_{j \in L} p_{ij} \lg(1/p_{ij}) + \sum_{j \in H} p_{ij} \lg(1/p_{ij}) + \sum_{j \in H} p_{ij} \lg(p_{ij}/\hat{p}_{ij}) + 1$$

$$= 2H_i + 1 + \sum_{j \in H} p_{ij} \lg(p_{ij}/\hat{p}_{ij}).$$

Thus, we get the desired optimal time of $2H_i + 1$, with an additional "error" term. The error term is the Kullback–Leibler (KL) divergence between the true distribution and the estimated version. Using that fact that $|\hat{p}_{ij} - p_{ij}| \leq 1/2n$ and that $p_{ij} \geq 1/n$ for $j \in H$, we can upper bound the error term by 4 (Exercise 12.3). □

Reducing the Storage of T to n^ε The hint to reducing the size of the trees is given in the end of the previous proof. Indeed, it is overkill to estimate all of the p_{ij}s so accurately. We only need to get the search time to within a constant factor of H_i, which can be obtained with a cruder estimate of p_{ij}s. Intuitively, suppose (for a fixed i) we knew only the buckets B_j where $p_{ij} \geq n^{-\varepsilon}$. There are at most n^ε such "heavy" buckets. We could store the optimal search tree for just these buckets using n^ε storage. For the remaining buckets, we can simply perform binary search.

Consider $x \sim \mathcal{D}_i$. Recall that the optimal time to find x in B_j is approximately $\lg 1/p_{ij}$. If x landed in a heavy bucket, then the search time is identical to the optimal time. If not, then the search takes $\lg n$ time. Since the bucket is not heavy, the optimal time is $\lg 1/p_{ij} \geq \lg n^{-\varepsilon} = \varepsilon \lg n$. Thus, this construction satisfies property T, with the factor $\alpha = 1/\varepsilon$.

We leave the formal description of the tree construction and the optimality proof to Exercise 12.6.

12.3.3 The Lower Bound for Self-Improving Sorters

The self-improving sorter described in the previous section crucially uses the independence of the $\mathcal{D}_i$ distributions. In this section, we investigate the connections between the (in)dependence of the $\mathcal{D}_i$ distributions and the storage required by the self-improving algorithm.

The next result shows that if the $\mathcal{D}_i$'s are arbitrarily correlated, then any self-improving algorithm requires exponential storage. This result will also imply the storage required for Fredman's construction in Theorem 12.1 is essentially optimal (up to exponential factors).

We require the following definition.

Definition 12.18 For a parameter $\gamma > 1$, a comparison tree for sorting is γ-optimal for distribution $\mathcal{D}$, if the expected number of comparisons for sorting an input from $\mathcal{D}$ is at most $\gamma(H(\pi(I)) + n)$.

A self-improving sorter is γ-optimal for $\mathcal{D}$ if: assuming the input distribution is $\mathcal{D}$, the limiting run time is at most $\gamma(H(\pi(I)) + n)$.

The lower bounds are basically counting arguments. We ignore the running time or length of the training phase, and abstract it away as follows. In the training phase, the self-improving algorithm has unrestricted access to $\mathcal{D}$. At the end of the training phase, it is allowed only s bits of storage. In the limiting phase, it cannot change these bits.

One can view the s bits of storage as (implicitly) storing a γ-optimal comparison tree for small γ. Focus on distributions $\mathcal{D}$ that are uniform over subsets of permutations, as in Theorem 12.1. There are $2^{\Omega(n!)}$ such distributions. If a self-improving sorter works for all distributions, then the s bits of storage must be able to encode a γ-optimal comparison tree for all these $2^{\Omega(n!)}$ distributions. If $2^s \ll 2^{\Omega(n!)}$, then the *same setting* of s bits must work for many distributions. We will show that this is not possible, and thus s must be $\Omega(n!)$. The lower bound is surprisingly robust even for fairly large γ.

Theorem 12.19 *Let $\gamma \in (1, (\lg n)/10)$. A self-improving sorter that is γ-optimal for all distributions requires $\Omega(2^{(n \lg n)/6\gamma})$ bits of storage.*

Proof Set $h = (6\gamma)^{-1} n \lg n$. For every subset Π of 2^h permutations, let $\mathcal{D}_\Pi$ denote the uniform distribution on Π. The total number of such distributions is $\binom{n!}{2^h} > (n!/2^h)^{2^h}$.

By definition, a γ-optimal comparison tree sorter for $\mathcal{D}_\Pi$ makes $\gamma(n + h)$ expected comparisons on inputs from $\mathcal{D}_\Pi$. Fix any such sorter $\mathcal{A}$. By Markov's inequality, at least half of the permutations in Π are sorted by $\mathcal{A}$ in at most $2\gamma(n + h)$ comparisons. But, within $2\gamma(n + h)$ comparisons, the procedure $\mathcal{A}$ can only sort a set P of at most $2^{2\gamma(n+h)}$ permutations. Therefore, if $\mathcal{A}$ is

γ-optimal for distribution $\mathcal{D}_{\Pi'}$, then Π' must have half its elements from P. This limits the number of such Π' to

$$\binom{n!}{2^h/2}\binom{2^{2\gamma(n+h)}}{2^h/2} < (n!)^{2^{h-1}}2^{\gamma(n+h)2^h}.$$

Consider a set of comparison trees, such that for every $\mathcal{D}_\Pi$, there is some tree in this set that is γ-optimal. The size of this set is at least

$$(n!/2^h)^{2^h}/((n!)^{2^{h-1}}2^{\gamma(n+h)2^h}) > (n!)^{2^{h-1}}2^{-2^h(h(\gamma+1)+\gamma n)}.$$

The self-improving sorter must have enough storage to uniquely encode every comparison tree in this set. Thus, its storage s must be at least the logarithm of the above bound. Plugging in the choice of $h = (6\gamma)^{-1}n\lg n$ and using $\gamma < (\lg n)/10$, we can bound $s = \Omega(2^h)$ (Exercise 12.8). $\qquad\square$

A refinement of this argument proves the time-space tradeoff for self-improving algorithms for product distributions.

Theorem 12.20 *Let $\gamma > 1$. A self-improving sorter that is γ-optimal for product distributions requires $n^{1+\Omega(\gamma)}$ storage.*

12.4 Self-Improving Algorithms for 2D Maxima

The problem of 2D coordinate-wise maxima is a classic computational geometry problem. The input is a set of n points P in $\mathbf{R}^2$, represented as an array of coordinate pairs. For a point x, we use $x(1), x(2)$ to denote the coordinates. A point x *dominates* point y if $x(1) \geq y(1)$ and $x(2) \geq y(2)$. A point that is not dominated by any other point in P is called *maximal* (or a maximum). The problem is to find the set of maxima in P.

(We will use left/right and above/below to denote relative positions in the plane.) The maxima form a "staircase" such that all other points of P lie below the staircase. This is also called the *Pareto frontier*. Conventionally, the algorithm must also output the maxima in sorted order along the staircase. This is equivalent to a sorted order (in either coordinate). Refer to Figure 12.5a. All points in the shaded region are dominated by the maxima.

The problem of computing the set of maxima can be reduced to sorting, using the sweep line approach. Begin by sorting P from right to left. Imagine a vertical sweep line ℓ processing points from right to left. We will maintain the invariant that all maximal points to the right of ℓ have been determined (in sorted order). Suppose the sweep line now processes the point x. Since all maximal points to the right of x have been found, we also know the highest such maximal point y. If x is lower than y, x is dominated by y (and can be removed). Otherwise, x is maximal, and is added to the output. The sweep line then processes the next point, to the left of x. Observe that, after the initial sorting, the algorithm runs in $O(n)$ time.

Clarkson et al. (2014) designed self-improving algorithms for 2D maxima. The input is an array of points $(x_1, x_2, \ldots, x_n)$, where $x_i \sim \mathcal{D}_i$. Each $\mathcal{D}_i$ is a distribution over $\mathbf{R}^2$ and independent. Why can't we simply run a self-improving sorter over the

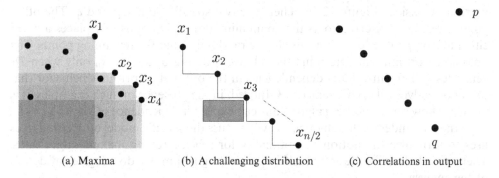

(a) Maxima   (b) A challenging distribution   (c) Correlations in output

Figure 12.5 (a) The staircase formed by maxima. (b) Points that lie in the gray region are easy to discard, but those lying near the staircase require more time. (c) If a distribution generates p instead of q, the output changes dramatically.

1-coordinates and run the linear time sweeping procedure to get the maxima? The answer to this gets to tricky issues in defining optimality for maxima computation.

Consider Figure 12.5a. Suppose, for $i \in [1,4]$, $\mathcal{D}_i$ generates the fixed point x_i. The other $(n - 4)$ distributions generate a uniform at random point from the darkest grey region. Observe that the 1-coordinates of the latter points can have any of $(n - 4)!$ permutations with equal probability. Thus, the entropy of the sorted order of 1-coordinates of the input is $\Theta(n \lg n)$, which is the limiting time of the self-improving sorter. On the other hand, the output is simply (x_1, x_2, x_3, x_4). Indeed, the classic output sensitive 2D maxima algorithm of Kirkpatrick and Seidel (1986) finds the maxima in $O(n \lg h)$ time, where h is the number of maximal points. (Here, $h = 4$.) This raises the issue of accurately describing the "right" optimal limiting running time.

Consider Figure 12.5b. For $i \leq n/2$, $\mathcal{D}_i$ generates the fixed point x_i, all of which are maximal. For $i > n/2$, $\mathcal{D}_i$ behaves as follows. It first generates a point on the staircase. With probability $1/n$, it perturbs this point *above* the staircase. With the remaining probability, it moves it slightly below the staircase. The final algorithm must be correct on all inputs. For each x_i ($i > n/2$), determining maximality seems equivalent to determining fairly precisely its position with respect to $x_1, \ldots, x_{n/2}$. This would require $\Omega(\lg n)$ time for each such point, and $\Omega(n \lg n)$ time seems unavoidable overall.

Contrast this with the situation where with probability $1 - 1/n$, $\mathcal{D}_i$ ($i > n/2$) generates a point in the grey region. With the remaining probability, it generates a point above the staircase, as in the previous setting. Clearly, one can determine in $O(1)$ time whether x_i lies in the gray region, by simply comparing with x_3. In expectation, at most one of these points lies above the staircase, for which we can determine maximality in $O(\lg n)$ by binary search. Overall, there is a $O(n)$ algorithm in this scenario. The takeaway is that the positioning of nonmaximal points affect the optimal running time. Similar considerations appear in *instance optimal algorithms*, as discussed in Chapter 3.

The Correlations For the sorting analysis, it was crucial that we could relate the optimal running time to independent searches over the buckets. This independence is exploited in the optimality analysis of Theorem 12.13. Intuitively, one number of the input does not affect the relative order of other numbers. But this is not true for maxima. Consider Figure 12.5a. There are two specific points, p and q. The other points are simply referred to as the "remaining points." Suppose $\mathcal{D}_1$ places a point either at p or q. Other distributions choose randomly from the remaining points. The optimal algorithm will determine the relative ordering of $x_2, \ldots, x_n$ only when $\mathcal{D}_1$ generates q. This introduces dependencies in the optimal algorithm's behavior that prevents analyses like Theorem 12.13. Indeed, in the presence of such examples, it is not clear how self-improving algorithms can exploit independence of the $\mathcal{D}_i$'s.

In the remainder of this chapter, we will discuss the specific model of decision trees uses to formalize the notion of optimality for self-improving maxima algorithms. Then, we will describe the actual self-improving algorithm. We do not give any details of the analysis.

12.4.1 Certificates and Linear Decision Trees

We need to make precise the notion of an optimal algorithm for 2D maxima, over a distribution $\mathcal{D}$. Unlike sorting, where we leverage information theory for this purpose, our approach here is less general. As the previous section shows, there are a number of challenges that maxima pose, and we do not know if there is a self-improving algorithm that is optimal with respect to *any* possible algorithm.

Let us first address the output sensitivity issue. Even though the actual output size may be small, additional work is necessary to determine which points appear in the output. We also want to consider algorithms that give a correct output on *all* instances, not just those in the support of $\mathcal{D}$. For example, suppose for all inputs in the support of $\mathcal{D}$, there was a set of (say) three points that always formed the maxima. The optimal algorithm just for $\mathcal{D}$ could always output these three points. But such an algorithm is not a legitimate maxima algorithm, since it would be incorrect on other inputs.

To handle these issues, we demand that any algorithm must provide a simple proof that the output is correct. This is formalized through *certificates*.

Definition 12.21 Let $P \subseteq \mathbf{R}^2$ be finite. A *maxima certificate* γ for P consists of (i) the indices of the maximal points in P, sorted from left to right; and (ii) a *per-point certificate* for each non-maximal point $p \in P$, i.e., the index of an input point that dominates p. A certificate γ is *valid* for P if γ satisfies conditions (i) and (ii) for P.

A correct algorithm might not produce a certificate, but most known algorithms implicitly provide such a certificate. Clearly, the simple sweep-line algorithm does so; a point x is removed from consideration iff the algorithm discovers an input point y that dominates it. Note that certificates are not unique, and this is one of the challenges for designing optimal maxima algorithms. In Figure 12.5a, the darker the region, the more certificates for nonmaximality. The optimal algorithm likely needs to discover the "fastest" certificate. Our notion of optimality crucially depends on the definition of certificates. Again, we point the reader to Chapter 3 on instance optimal algorithms, where similar notions appear.

Linear Comparison Trees For sorting, the notion of optimal limiting time was defined with respect to any comparison tree. Intuitively, one operation only generated one bit of information. For 2D maxima, we do not know how to compete with such a powerful model. Instead, we consider a weaker model, where nodes in the comparison tree correspond to *linear queries*.

Definition 12.22 A *linear comparison tree* (LCT) $\mathcal{T}$ is a rooted binary tree. Each node v of $\mathcal{T}$ is labeled with a query of the form "is p above ℓ_v?" Here, p is an input point and ℓ_v a line. The line ℓ_v can be obtained in four ways, in increasing order of complexity: (i) a fixed line independent of the input (but dependent on v); (ii) a line with a fixed slope (dependent on v) passing through a given input point; (iii) a line through an input point and a fixed point q_v, dependent on v; and (iv) a line through two distinct input points.

Given an input P, an *evaluation* of a linear comparison tree $\mathcal{T}$ on P is the node sequence that starts at the root and chooses in each step the child according to the outcome of the current comparison on P.

This model does not capture queries that involve relationships of more than three points. Nonetheless, the model is powerful enough to capture standard computational geometry algorithms, as those described by de Berg et al. (2008). Typically, 2D maxima algorithms only compare coordinates between individual points, which is captured by query (ii). (The slope of the line is either zero or infinity.) The final self-improving algorithm will also only use query (ii).

Now for the key definition that formalizes our desired limiting running time.

Definition 12.23 An LCT $\mathcal{T}$ *computes the maxima of a planar point set* if every leaf v of $\mathcal{T}$ is labeled with a maxima certificate that is valid for every input that reaches v (on evaluation by $\mathcal{T}$).

The *depth* d_v of node v in $\mathcal{T}$ is the length of the path from the root of $\mathcal{T}$ to v. Let $v(P)$ be the leaf reached by the evaluation of $\mathcal{T}$ on input P. The *expected depth* of $\mathcal{T}$ over $\mathcal{D}$ is defined as

$$d_{\mathcal{D}}(\mathcal{T}) = \mathbf{E}_{P \sim \mathcal{D}}[d_{v(P)}].$$

Finally, we have the benchmark limiting running time to aim for.

Definition 12.24 Let **T** be the set of LCTs that compute 2D maxima. For a distribution $\mathcal{D}$, define $OPTMAX(\mathcal{D})$ as $\inf_{\mathcal{T} \in \mathbf{T}} d_{\mathcal{D}}(\mathcal{T})$.

Thus, for inputs drawn from $\mathcal{D}$, it is the expected depth of the best LCT computing 2D maxima. The limiting running time of our self-improving algorithm will run in time $O(OPTMAX(\mathcal{D}) + n)$.

12.4.2 The Self-Improving Algorithm

Rather surprisingly, the data structures built in the learning phase are *identical* to those used for sorting. These will be built using the 1-coordinate of the input points. Somewhat counterintuitively, despite $OPTMAX(\mathcal{D})$ potentially being defined by a tree that makes arbitrary line comparisons, our optimal self-improving algorithm purely uses vertical lines (compares 1-coordinates).

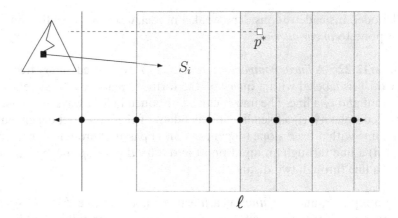

Figure 12.6 A pictorial description of the self-improving algorithm for 2D maxima.

Recall the buckets used in the self-improving sorter. The bucket boundaries are every λth element of a merged (sorted) list of 1-coordinates of λ inputs. It will be convenient to interpret any interval B of 1-coordinates as the 2D region $B \times \mathbf{R}$. We will refer to the latter as a *slab*. Using the notation of $b_1 \leq b_2 \leq b_3 \ldots \leq b_{n+1}$ for the bucket boundaries, a slab is defined as $(b_j, b_k] \times \mathbf{R}$ for $j < k$. If $k = j + 1$, we refer to this as a *leaf slab*. Note that all internal nodes of the T_i-trees can be interpreted as placing a point in a slab. Refer to Figure 12.6. The black circles denote the b_j's, and the region between two vertical lines is a slab.

The self-improving algorithm (in the limiting phase) can be thought of as a refinement of the sweep line algorithm discussed at the beginning of Section 12.4. The key idea is to interleave the sorting of 1-coordinates with the maxima discovery. The searching is conservative, in that we only search for points that have the potential of being the next maximal point.

Let us revisit the self-improving sorting algorithm, and imagine that searches in the different T_i's are proceeding in parallel. Consider some snapshot in time. The search for (the 1-coordinate of) each x_i is at some node in T_i; equivalently each x_i has been placed in some slab. Some of these searches have reached leaf slabs, and the corresponding points has been placed in leaf slabs. By the properties of the buckets, the expected number of points falling in each leaf slab is $O(1)$. We can afford to sort the 1-coordinates of all points placed in leaf slabs and find the maxima among them. By choosing the searching ordering carefully, we can ensure the following. At any time, there is a slab boundary such that all maxima to the right of this boundary have been discovered. Whenever we advance the search for any point, we first check if it is dominated by any of the discovered maxima. If so, we can remove this point and save the (remaining) time to search for it. This is precisely the savings over the self-improving sorter.

We describe the limiting phase of the self-improving algorithm. For the sake of exposition, we defer the details of data structure implementations to Exercises 12.10 and 12.11. The important variables are

- ℓ: This is the equivalent of the vertical sweep line. It only takes as values the slab boundaries. Initially, it is set to $b_{n+1} = \infty$ and will only decrease. Abusing notation, we will say "decrement ℓ" to mean moving ℓ from b_i to b_{i-1}.

SIMaxima

While $\ell > b_1$:

1. Find the rightmost slab boundary r, among all the active S_is. Find an arbitrary active slab S_j with right slab boundary r.
2. If $r = \ell$:
   1. If x_j is dominated by p^*: mark x_j as inactive and nonmaximal (certified by p^*).
   2. Else, if S_j is L (the leaf slab with ℓ as the right boundary): the search of x_j has completed, so mark x_j as inactive.
   3. Else: advance the search for x_j by one step (thereby updating S_j).
3. Else ($r < \ell$):
   1. Sort all points in L by 1-coordinate, and update the set of maxima and p^*.
   2. Decrement ℓ.

Figure 12.7 Self-improving maxima.

- Active/inactive points: These are points currently being searched. Inactive points are either classified as maximal or are assigned a certificate of nonmaximality.
- L: This is the leaf slab whose right boundary is ℓ.
- p^*: This is the leftmost maximal point to the right of ℓ. It is also the highest point to the right of ℓ.
- S_i slabs: This represents the current snapshot of the searches. Each active point x_i is currently placed in a slab S_i, which corresponds to a node in T_i. Initially, this slab is simply $(b_1, b_{n+1}]$. Every step of a search updates the slab.

The algorithm is described in Figure 12.7. Refer to Figure 12.6, showing a snapshot of the algorithm. All maximal points in the grey region have been determined, and p^* is the leftmost such maximal point. All points below the dashed line can be certified as nonmaximal. The lightly shaded slab S_i corresponds to the current state of the search of a point x_i.

At every stage, the active points have not yet been placed in leaf slabs, but are known to be to the left of ℓ. Our aim is to find all the (potential maxima) points in the leaf slab L, with the minimum amount of searching. Among all the right slab boundaries of the S_i slabs (recall that these are only for the active points), let r denote the rightmost slab boundary. If $r < \ell$, then there is no active point in L. Equivalently, all points in L have already been found. So the set of maxima can be updated with the points in L, ℓ can be decremented, and the sweep has progressed. The real work happens when $r = \ell$, so there are active points potentially in ℓ. In this case, the algorithm finds an arbitrary active point x_j, whose corresponding slab S_j has right boundary ℓ. If x_j is dominated by p^*, then the search for x_j can be terminated immediately. Otherwise, the search for x_j proceeds one step. The optimality of the self-improving algorithm hinges on the termination of searches for nonmaximal points.

12.5 More Self-Improving Algorithms

We give a short summary of other results on self-improving algorithms.

Self-Improving 2D Delaunay Triangulations The Delaunay triangulation and its dual, the Voronoi diagram, are fundamental constructs in computational geometry. They can be built in $O(n \lg n)$ time for n points in $\mathbf{R}^2$. One of the first generalizations of the self-improving sorter was for Delaunay triangulations (given in Ailon et al., 2011). Conceptually, it follows the sorting paradigm almost exactly, where each step/data structure of the algorithm is replaced with a more complex geometric object. The bucket boundaries are replaced by an ε-net for disks; the buckets themselves by a Delaunay triangulation of this ε-net; the search trees are distribution-optimal search trees for points in the plane. Simple operations like merging lists of sorted numbers or sorting within buckets become fairly complex procedures. There is no challenge of output sensitivity (as there is for 2D maxima), so one can achieve optimality with respect to arbitrary comparison trees.

Self-Improving 2D Convex Hulls Getting self-improving algorithms for 2D convex hulls is surprisingly tricky, because of complicated dependencies on the output structure. Conceptually, the approach is similar to that of 2D maxima. As with the latter, the optimality is shown only with respect to LCTs. The slab structure and search trees used are identical. The main new idea is to learn a nested sequence of convex polygons, such that the probability that a point is on the convex hull is related to its position in these nested polygons. The number of comparisons made by the final algorithm is optimal, but the data structure operations add an additive overhead of $O(n \lg \lg n)$ time. Thus, the final running time is slightly suboptimal. The first paper by Clarkson et al. (2010) on this problem claimed the optimal additive term of $O(n)$, but had a serious error. The final result was obtained by Clarkson et al. (2014), in conjunction with the 2D maxima result.

Self-Improving Sorters, Beyond Product Distributions This is a natural and compelling question, in light of the exponential storage lower bound for arbitrary distributions. Recent work by Cheng et al. (2020) studied two richer classes of distributions: mixtures of m product distributions and linearly correlated classes. The former is an important generalization, and provides an interpolation between vanilla product distributions ($m = 1$) and arbitrary distributions ($m = n!$). The limiting time and storage are $O(\varepsilon^{-1}(H(\pi(I) + n)))$ and $O(m^{\varepsilon} n^{1+\varepsilon} + mn)$ respectively, matching the $m = 1$ bound of Theorem 12.3. But the training phase lasts for $O(mn)$ rounds, which is significantly larger than the n^{ε} bound of Theorem 12.3.

12.6 Critique of the Self-Improving Model

The Successes The self-improving framework has something new to say about classic problems such as sorting, 2D Delaunay triangulations, and convex hulls. Computational geometers regularly study assumptions under which the classic $O(n \lg n)$ running time bound can be beaten. The series of current results share a common set of techniques, which makes for an underlying theory (instead of just a collection of results).

The Shortcomings All of the current results are for $O(n \lg n)$ time problems, and that is no coincidence. For all these problems, we have nuanced understanding of the lower bounds, which give an analytic handle on the optimality of the limiting phase. All the running time improvements come from faster search, which can be related to entropy-like expressions. A similar issue appears in Chapter 3 for instance-optimal algorithms.

This pinpoints a major roadblock in designing self-improving graph algorithms. For problems such as shortest paths, routing, flows, etc., we do not have a good handle on lower bounds with respect to a distribution on inputs. A somewhat subtle issue is that for approximation problems, concentration inequalities suggest "trivial" self-improving algorithms. In the training phase, the algorithm precomputes solutions for all the sampled inputs. In the limiting phase, the algorithm simply tries out all of these candidate solutions, and outputs the best option. As an example, consider the minimum spanning tree (MST) problem over n vertices, where each edge weight is generated from an independent distribution. Our aim is to solve the problem in $o(n^2)$ time. Under certain assumptions, Goemans and Vondrák (2006) prove that there is a set of $O(n \lg n)$ edges that contain the MST with high probability. Thus, the self-improving algorithm would simply find these edges in the training phase. In the limiting phase, it could run an MST algorithm on this subset. Unfortunately, to get a zero failure probability, the algorithm would be forced to look at all edges to find unlikely events (going back to the vanilla algorithm). It seems challenging to find graph problems that lead to compelling self-improving algorithms.

Connections to Other Models Chapter 3 discusses *instance optimal algorithms*. This is philosophically quite different from self-improving algorithms, since instance optimality is about specific inputs that are easy, rather than input distributions that are easy. Nonetheless, for the 2D maxima problem, there is a striking similarity between the challenges and techniques: the important of output-sensitive algorithms, the notion of certificates of output, and the appearance of entropy (like) terms in the analysis. Could there be some formal connection between these models?

Chapter 29 is on *data-driven algorithm selection*. In this setting, there is a fixed class of algorithms and a distribution $\mathcal{D}$ on inputs. Suppose we selected an algorithm from this class by first sampling a few inputs (the training data) and outputting the best algorithm for the training data from the class. How well does this generalize? Here, the connections with self-improving algorithms are direct. The self-improving sorter implicitly constructs a class of potential algorithms through the data structure T (the buckets and search trees). The training phase essentially selects an algorithm from this class, based on the inputs seen thus far. The optimality argument of the self-improving algorithm can be thought of as a proof of generalization.

The most intriguing connection is with Chapter 30, combining machine learning (ML) models (from, say, deep learning) with algorithms, to adapt to their input. This is uncannily similar to the self-improving framework. The following example was first introduced by Kraska et al. (2018), though Lykouris and Vassilvitskii (2018) give the following formalization. Take the simple example of (repeatedly) searching among a set of n objects. The standard solution is to store these objects sorted by an index and, of course, do binary search. Suppose one had a predictor for the position of a query element, based on some other features of the object. This could be used to speed up the search, presumably by searching around the predicted position using finger search trees. If the prediction is accurate, we beat binary search. Otherwise, we wish to do no worse than it. This is analogous to the self-improving sorter. The buckets and trees can be thought of as predictors for the positions of elements, which are sufficiently accurate if the distribution is learned correctly. Lykouris and Vassilvitskii (2018) have results for online caching in this setting. Practically, the most compelling aspect of their work is that the algorithms designed are oblivious to the predictor (unlike self-improving algorithms, where the "predictors" are explicitly constructed through the data structures). The connection between these models is an exciting direction for future work.

The Path Forward We provide a list of open problems and directions in self-improving algorithms.

1. Get a self-improving sorter for mixtures of m product distributions, with $o(mn)$ length training phase (refer to Cheng et al., 2020).
2. Get a self-improving 2D convex hull algorithm that has running time $O(OPT + n)$. The current bound is $O(OPT + n \lg \lg n)$, given by Clarkson et al. (2014).
3. Get optimality for self-improving 2D convex hulls and maxima, with respect to general comparison trees, not just LCTs. This will likely require a new set of techniques.
4. Get self-improving algorithms for 2D convex hulls and maxima, where the input distribution is a mixture of product distributions. Given the recent results for sorting, this appears to be a promising direction for future work.
5. Get self-improving algorithms for higher dimensional Delaunay triangulations and convex hulls. This seems like an excellent candidate to go beyond $O(n \lg n)$ problems. One would likely have to extend the current toolkit significantly, especially to deal with the variable output complexity.
6. Design self-improving graph algorithms. This would be an exciting development for the self-improving model, and may require a rethink of the current framework. Currently, we require the algorithm to be always correct, which may be too restrictive. Likely candidates for problems are spanning subgraphs, shortest paths, and routing/flow problems.
7. Consider settings where the inputs come from a Markov distribution. Currently, we think of the input distribution $\mathcal{D}$ as fixed, generating independent inputs. One could think of there being an unknown Markov process that generates inputs to the algorithm. It would be interesting to come up with even a toy problem in this setting that leads to some new algorithmic techniques.
8. Explore the connection of self-improving algorithms to recent applied work on algorithms with predictors. In terms of branching out of theory, this appears to be the most significant direction.

Acknowledgments

The author would like to thank Jérémy Barbay, Anupam Gupta, Akash Kumar, Tim Roughgarden, and Sahil Singla for their valuable comments on this chapter. This chapter reads significantly better because of their suggestions.

References

Ailon, Nir, Chazelle, Bernard, Clarkson, Kenneth L., Liu, Ding, Mulzer, Wolfgang, and Seshadhri, C. 2011. Self-improving algorithms. *SIAM Journal on Computing*, **40**(2), 350–375.

Cheng, Siu-Wing, Jin, Kai, and Yan, Lie. 2020. Extensions of self-improving sorters. *Algorithmica*, **82**, 88–102.

Clarkson, K. L., Mulzer, W., and Seshadhri, C. 2010. Self-improving algorithms for convex hulls. *ACM-SIAM Symposium on Discrete Algorithms (SODA)*, pp. 1546–1565.

Clarkson, Kenneth L., Mulzer, Wolfgang, and Seshadhri, C. 2014. Self-improving algorithms for coordinatewise maxima and convex hulls. *SIAM Journal on Computing*, **43**(2), 617–653.

Cover, Thomas M., and Thomas, Joy A. 2006. *Elements of Information Theory*, 2nd ed. Wiley-Interscience.

de Berg, Mark, Cheong, Otfried, van Kreveld, Marc, and Overmars, Mark. 2008. *Computational Geometry*. Springer.

Dubhashi, D. P., and Panconesi, A. 2009. *Concentration of Measure for the Analysis of Randomized Algorithms*. Cambridge University Press.

Fredman, Michael L. 1976. How good is the information theory bound in sorting? *Theoretical Computer Science*, **1**(4), 355–361.

Goemans, Michel X., and Vondrák, Jan. 2006. Covering minimum spanning trees of random subgraphs. *Random Structures and Algorithms*, **29**(3), 257–276.

Kirkpatrick, David G., and Seidel, Raimund. 1986. The ultimate planar convex hull algorithm? *SIAM Journal on Computing*, **15**(1), 287–299.

Kraska, Tim, Beutel, Alex, Chi, Ed H., Dean, Jeffrey, and Polyzotis, Neoklis. 2018. The case for learned index structures. *International Conference on Management of Data (SIGMOD)*, pp. 489–504.

Lykouris, Thodoris, and Vassilvitskii, Sergei. 2018. Competitive caching with machine learned advice. In *International Conference on Machine Learning (ICML)*, pp. 3302–3311.

Exercises

Exercise 12.1 Consider a discrete distribution $\mathcal{D}$ on $[n]$. Construct a search tree whose expected search time is $O(H(\mathcal{D}) + 1)$. [Hint: do binary search, but split the probability mass in half. But what if half is not possible? To bound the maximum depth, switch to vanilla binary search after some comparisons.]

Exercise 12.2 In this exercise, we will prove Theorem 12.2. This will require some setup.

1. The conditional entropy $H(Y|X)$ is defined as $\sum_{x \in \mathcal{X}} \Pr[X = x] H(Y|X = x)$. Prove the chain rule: $H(Y|X) = H(X, Y) - H(X)$.
2. The key to generalizing the proof of Theorem 12.1 is in defining the random variables Z_i as follows. Let Z_i be the position of x_i when inserted into the sorted order of $I_{\leq i-1}$. Follow the algorithm in the proof of Theorem 12.1, appropriately generalized to the setting of Theorem 12.2. Prove that the insertion of x_{k+1} can be done in expected $H(Z_{k+1}|Z_1, Z_2, \ldots, Z_k)$ comparisons.
3. Now complete the proof of Theorem 12.2 using the chain rule.

Exercise 12.3 Complete the proof of Claim 12.17. Prove that $\sum_{j \in H} p_{ij} \lg(p_{ij}/\widehat{p}_{ij}) \leq 4$. Recall that $\forall j \in H$, $p_{ij} \geq 1/n$ and that for all j, $|p_{ij} - \widehat{p}_{ij}| \leq 1/2n$. [Hint: use the Taylor approximation $\ln(1 - x) \leq 2x$ for $x \in (0, 1)$.]

Exercise 12.4 The construction of **Tree** and the proof of Claim 12.17 are overkill, in that $O(n^2 \lg n)$ inputs are not necessary. The next few exercises will demonstrate why, and will lead to the $n^{1+\varepsilon}$ storage construction. One does not need to approximate p_{ij}s to additive accuracy $\Theta(1/n)$. Suppose one obtained $\hat{p}_{ij}$s with the following property. If $p_{ij} > 1/2n$, then $\hat{p}_{ij} = \Theta(p_{ij})$. If $p_{ij} \leq 1/2n$, then $\hat{p}_{ij} = O(1/n)$. Show that the search trees constructed in Exercise 12.1 with $\{\hat{p}_{ij}\}$ are $O(1)$-optimal search trees with respect to the original distribution.

Exercise 12.5 Use Exercise 12.4 to prove Claim 12.17 when the training phase length is $O(n \lg n)$ (as opposed to $O(n^2 \lg n)$) independent inputs.

Exercise 12.6 The previous exercises set us up to construct T_is of size n^ε, for any $\varepsilon > 0$. Let a bucket B_j be heavy for i if $p_{ij} \geq n^{-\varepsilon}$, and call a search heavy if it leads to a heavy bucket. First, show that $O(n^\varepsilon \lg n)$ independent inputs can be used to build T_is (for all i, each of size $O(n^\varepsilon)$) that are $O(1)$-optimal for heavy searches. Next, use these trees to perform searches that $O(1/\varepsilon)$-optimal. (Hint: if a search is not heavy, perform standard binary search.)

Exercise 12.7 Let $Y_1, Y_2, \ldots, Y_r$ be pairwise independent Bernoulli random variables. Prove that $E[(\sum_{i \leq r} Y_i)^2] = O(E[\sum_{i \leq r} Y_i]^2 + E[\sum_{i \leq r} Y_i])$. Use this fact to prove Claim 12.15. (Hint: write $|I \cap B_j|$ as a sum of Bernoulli random variables.)

Exercise 12.8 Complete the proof of Theorem 12.19 by showing the following statement. Let $h = (6\gamma)^{-1} n \lg n$ and $\gamma < (\lg n)/10$. Then $\lg[(n!)^{2^{h-1}} 2^{-2^h(h(\gamma+1)+\gamma n)}] = \Omega(2^h)$.

Exercise 12.9 Consider maximal certificates as defined in Definition 12.21. Suppose we additionally required that when the certificates says "x_i dominated by x_j," then x_j be maximal. Thus, only maximal points are allowed to certify that other points are nonmaximal. Show that there is a linear time procedure that, given a maximal certificate, constructs one with this condition.

Exercise 12.10 Consider storing a universe of objects with keys in $[n]$. We need a data structure that support find-max (finding an object with maximum key), delete, and decrement-key operations. For the latter two, assume you have a pointer to the object. Initially, all objects have key n, and there are at most n objects. Design a data structure that runs in total $O(n+z)$ time, where z is the number of operations performed.

Exercise 12.11 Use the data structure in Exercise 12.10 to implement the self-improving maxima algorithm of Figure 12.7. Suppose the total search time (operations in T_i's) is t. Prove that the total running time is $O(t + n)$.

PART FOUR

Smoothed Analysis

CHAPTER THIRTEEN

Smoothed Analysis of Local Search
Bodo Manthey

Abstract: Local search is a powerful paradigm for finding good solutions to intractable combinatorial optimization problems. However, for many local search heuristics there exist worst-case instances on which they are extremely slow or provide solutions that are far from optimal.

Smoothed analysis is a semirandom input model that has been invented to bridge the gap between poor worst-case and good empirical performance of algorithms. In smoothed analysis, an adversary picks an arbitrary input, which is then slightly randomly perturbed. In particular, smoothed analysis has been applied successfully to local search algorithms in a variety of cases.

We use the 2-opt heuristic for the traveling salesman problem and the k-means method for clustering as examples to explain how local search heuristics can be analyzed in the framework of smoothed analysis. For both algorithms, as for many other local search algorithms, the worst-case running time is exponential in the input size, but polynomial in the framework of smoothed analysis.

13.1 Introduction

Large-scale optimization problems appear in many areas, ranging from engineering to the sciences. Unfortunately, many of these problems are computationally intractable. Thus, finding optimal solutions is very time consuming. In practice, however, heuristics are often successful in finding close-to-optimal solutions surprisingly quickly. One particularly popular class of such heuristics are local search heuristics, which are often appealing because of their speed and because they are very easy to implement.

A *local search heuristic* for a combinatorial optimization problem is initialized with some solution of the given instance. Then it searches in the neighborhood of the current solution for a solution with better objective value. If successful, the local search heuristic replaces the current solution with this better solution. We call this a *local improvement step* of the local search heuristic. Then the local search heuristic does the same search again. Here, the neighborhood of a solution are all solutions that can be obtained by slightly modifying this solution. What this means exactly depends on the problem and the local search heuristic.

A local search heuristic terminates if there is no better solution in the neighborhood of the current solution. We call such a solution a *local optimum*. Note that local optima are not necessarily globally optimal solutions.

What is striking for many local search algorithms is the discrepancy between worst-case and observed performance: on the one hand, there often exist instances on which they take an exponential number of iterations before reaching a local optimum. It is also often quite easy to come up with instances on which they can converge to local optima that are much worse than global optima. From the complexity-theoretic perspective, finding a local optimum with respect to a given local search algorithm is *PLS*-complete for many such algorithms. (*PLS* stands for "polynomial local search" and captures the difficulty of finding local optima of optimization problems with respect to a "neighborhood." Although weaker than *NP*-completeness, *PLS*-completeness is widely considered to be a strong evidence of intractability (Schäffer and Yannakakis, 1991).)

On the other hand, this pessimistic view does not seem to reflect reality, where local search algorithms are popular because of their speed. The worst-case examples that show exponential running time are usually fragile constructions that hardly ever occur in practice. Sometimes, local search heuristics even achieve good empirical approximation performance. But even if not, their speed allows to rerun them a number of times with different initializations, which often results in much better performance.

This discrepancy makes local search heuristics a prime candidate for an "analysis beyond the worst case." In particular, smoothed analysis has been applied quite successfully to explain the empirical performance of local search algorithms.

Smoothed analysis is a semirandom input model that has been invented by Spielman and Teng (2004) in order to explain the empirical performance of the simplex method for linear programming. It is a hybrid of worst-case and average-case analysis and interpolates between these two: an adversary specifies an instance, and then this instance is slightly randomly perturbed. The smoothed performance of an algorithm is the maximum expected performance that the adversary can achieve, where the expectation is taken over the random perturbation.

If worst-case instances are isolated in the input space, then it is potentially very unlikely that we obtain such bad instances after perturbation. In principle, smoothed analysis can be applied to any measure of performance, but it has been most successful for the analysis of running times of algorithms that are super-polynomial in the worst-case but fast in practice, such as the two local search heuristics that we discuss in this chapter.

In the following, we explain smoothed analysis of local search algorithms mainly by means of the 2-opt heuristic for the traveling salesman problem (TSP) and the k-means method for clustering. We will mostly focus on the running time of these algorithms and only briefly touch upon their approximation performance.

13.2 Smoothed Analysis of the Running Time

The goal in this section is to show bounds for the *smoothed number of iterations* of local search algorithms, which is the maximum expected number of iterations, where the expectation is taken over the random perturbation.

We start this section with a simple analysis of the running time of the 2-opt heuristic for the TSP. After that, we sketch how to improve the bound obtained. Finally, we analyze the k-means method as an example of a local search algorithm where the analysis is much less straightforward than for 2-opt.

13.2.1 Main Ideas

The main idea behind all smoothed analyses of running times of local search heuristics that have been conducted so far is the following "potential function" approach, where the objective function plays the role of the potential:

- We prove that the objective value of the initial solution is not too big.
- We prove that it is unlikely that iterations improve the objective value by only a small amount.

If the objective value is at most v in the beginning and there is no iteration that decreases it by less than ε, then the number of iterations can be at most v/ε.

Note that this approach is still quite pessimistic: first, it is unlikely that we always make the minimal possible improvement. It is more likely that some iterations cause a much larger improvement. Second, often there are several local improvement steps possible. In this case, the foregoing approach assumes that we always make the worst possible choice.

The main advantage of this approach is that it decouples the iterations. If we would analyze iterations depending on earlier iterations, then we would face dependencies that are very hard to deal with.

13.2.2 A Simple Bound for 2-Opt

To illustrate a smoothed analysis of the running time of a local search heuristic, we take the 2-opt heuristic for the TSP as an example. More specifically, we consider the TSP in the Euclidean plane, where the distance between two points $a, b \in \mathbb{R}^2$ is given by $\|a - b\|^2$, i.e., the squared Euclidean distance between the two points. This means that – given a set $Y \subseteq \mathbb{R}^2$ of n points – the goal is to compute a Hamiltonian cycle (also called a tour) H through Y that minimizes

$$\sum_{\{a, b\} \in H} \|a - b\|^2.$$

In other words, we want to find a cyclic ordering of the points that minimizes the sum of squared distances of consecutive points.

We chose this problem for two reasons. First, for points in the plane, the concept of "small perturbations" is quite natural. Second, the choice of squared Euclidean distances (compared to the – more natural – Euclidean distances) is because this makes the smoothed analysis of the running time relatively compact, in contrast to many other cases of smoothed analysis, which are quite involved technically.

TSP and the 2-Opt Heuristic

The 2-opt heuristic for the TSP performs so-called *2-opt steps* to improve a given initial tour as long as possible. A *2-opt step* is the following operation: let H be an

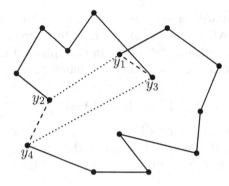

Figure 13.1 An example of a 2-opt step, where the edges $\{y_1, y_2\}$ are replaced by $\{y_1, y_3\}$ and $\{y_2, y_4\}$.

arbitrary Hamiltonian tour through the point set Y. Assume that H contains edges $\{y_1, y_2\}$ and $\{y_3, y_4\}$, where the four distinct points y_1, y_2, y_3, and y_4 appear in this order in H. Assume further that $\|y_1 - y_2\|^2 + \|y_3 - y_4\|^2 > \|y_1 - y_3\|^2 + \|y_2 - y_4\|^2$. Then we replace $\{y_1, y_2\}$ and $\{y_3, y_4\}$ by $\{y_1, y_3\}$ and $\{y_2, y_4\}$ to obtain a shorter Hamiltonian tour. See Figure 13.1 for an example.

Initialized with an arbitrary Hamiltonian tour H through the point set Y, the 2-opt heuristic performs 2-opt steps until a local minimum is reached.

Model and Approach

We use the following probabilistic input model for the analysis of 2-opt: an adversary specifies a set $X = \{x_1, \ldots, x_n\} \subseteq [0,1]^2$ consisting of n points from the unit square. Then we obtain the actual input Y by perturbing each point x_i by a random variable g_i:

$$Y = \{y_i = x_i + g_i \mid i \in \{1, \ldots, n\}\}.$$

We assume that $g_1, \ldots, g_n$ are independent and follow a 2-dimensional Gaussian distribution with standard deviation σ and mean 0. We call the instance Y a σ-*perturbed point set*.

We mainly exploit two properties of Gaussian distributions in our smoothed analysis. First, their maximum density is bounded. Second, a 2-dimensional Gaussian distribution can be viewed as superposition of two 1-dimensional Gaussian distributions in any two orthonormal directions.

Our approach is as described earlier. First, we show that the initial tour has a length of $O(n)$ with high probability. Second, we show that the probability that there exists any 2-opt step that decreases the objective function by less than ε is bounded from above by ε times a polynomial in n and $1/\sigma$. Finally, we combine these two ingredients together with the worst-case upper bound of $n!$ for the number of iterations to obtain a smoothed polynomial bound for the number of iterations.

Technical Preliminaries and Assumptions

In the following, we assume that $\sigma \leq \frac{1}{2\sqrt{n \ln n}}$. This is without loss of generality by Exercise 13.2.

The following lemma is a standard tail bound for Gaussian random variables. A proof can be found in many textbooks on probability theory.

Lemma 13.1 (Tail Bound for Gaussians) *Let X be a random variable with Gaussian distribution with mean $\mu \in \mathbb{R}$ and standard deviation $\sigma > 0$. Then*

$$\mathbb{P}(X \geq \mu + \sigma t) = \mathbb{P}(X \leq \mu - \sigma t) \leq \frac{1}{t\sqrt{2\pi}} \cdot \exp\left(-\frac{t^2}{2}\right).$$

Lemma 13.2 (Interval Lemma for Gaussians) *Let X be distributed according to a Gaussian distribution with arbitrary mean and standard deviation $\sigma > 0$. Let $t \in \mathbb{R}$, and let $\varepsilon > 0$. Then*

$$\mathbb{P}\big(X \in (t, t + \varepsilon]\big) \leq \frac{\varepsilon}{2\sigma}.$$

Proof This follows from the fact that the density of a Gaussian random variable with standard deviation σ is bounded from above by $\frac{1}{2\sigma}$. $\qquad\square$

Upper Bound for the Initial Tour

The following lemma gives a quite trivial upper bound for the length of an initial tour.

Lemma 13.3 *We have $L_{\text{init}} \leq 18n$ with a probability of at least $1 - \frac{1}{n!}$.*

Proof If $Y \subseteq [-1, 2]^d$, then the longest distance between any two points in Y (measured in squared Euclidean distance) is at most 18. Thus, any tour has a length of at most $18n$ in this case.

If $Y \not\subseteq [-1, 2]^2$, then there exists an i such that $\|g_i\|_\infty \geq 1$. Thus, there must exist an $i \in \{1, \ldots, n\}$ and a coordinate $j \in \{1, 2\}$ such that the absolute value of the jth entry of g_i is at least 1. We use Lemma 13.1 with $\sigma \leq \frac{1}{2\sqrt{n \ln n}}$ and $t = 1/\sigma$. This yields that the probability for a single entry to be of absolute value at least 1 is bounded from above by

$$\frac{1}{2\sqrt{2\pi n \ln n}} \cdot \exp(-2n \ln n) \leq n^{-2n} \leq (n!)^{-2}.$$

A union bound over the n choices of i and the two choices of j and the (very loose) bound $2n \leq n!$ yields the lemma. $\qquad\square$

For the remainder of this section, let $\Delta_{a,b}(c) = \|c - a\|^2 - \|c - b\|^2$. The improvement of a 2-opt step, where $\{y_1, y_2\}$ and $\{y_3, y_4\}$ are replaced by $\{y_1, y_3\}$ and $\{y_2, y_4\}$, can thus be written as $\Delta_{y_2, y_3}(y_1) - \Delta_{y_2, y_3}(y_4)$.

Let $\Delta_{\min}$ be the smallest positive improvement by any possible 2-opt step. For the analysis of $\Delta_{\min}$, the following lemma is useful.

Lemma 13.4 *Let $a, b \in \mathbb{R}^2$ with $a \neq b$, and let $c \in \mathbb{R}^2$ be drawn according to a Gaussian distribution with standard deviation σ. Let $I \subseteq \mathbb{R}$ be an interval of length ε. Then*

$$\mathbb{P}\big(\Delta_{a,b}(c) \in I\big) \leq \frac{\varepsilon}{4\sigma \cdot \|a - b\|}.$$

Proof Since Gaussian distributions are rotationally symmetric and translation invariant, we can assume without loss of generality that $a = (0, 0)$ and $b = (\delta, 0)$ with $\delta = \|a - b\|$. Let $c = (c_1, c_2)^{\mathrm{T}}$. Then $\Delta_{a,b}(c) = (c_1^2 + c_2^2) - ((c_1 - \delta)^2 + c_2^2) = 2c_1\delta - \delta^2$. Since δ^2 is a constant (independent of a, b, and c), we have $\Delta_{a,b}(c) \in I$ if and only if $2c_1\delta$ falls into an interval of length ε. This is equivalent to c_1 falling into an interval of length $\frac{\varepsilon}{2\delta}$.

Since c_1 is a 1-dimensional Gaussian random variable with a standard deviation of σ, the lemma follows from Lemma 13.2. $\qquad\square$

With this lemma, we can bound the probability that any improving 2-opt step yields only a small improvement.

Lemma 13.5 $\mathbb{P}(\Delta_{\min} \leq \varepsilon) = O\big(\frac{n^4 \varepsilon}{\sigma^2}\big).$

Proof Consider any four distinct points $y_1, y_2, y_3, y_4 \in Y$ and the 2-opt step, where the two edges $\{y_1, y_2\}$ and $\{y_3, y_4\}$ are replaced by $\{y_1, y_3\}$ and $\{y_2, y_4\}$. We prove that the probability that this 2-opt step yields a positive improvement of at most ε is bounded by $O(\varepsilon/\sigma^2)$. Then the lemma follows by a union bound over the choices of the four points $y_1, y_2, y_3, y_4 \in Y$.

The improvement caused by this 2-opt step equals $\Delta_{y_2, y_3}(y_1) - \Delta_{y_2, y_3}(y_4)$. We use the principle of deferred decision: first, let an adversary fix the position of y_2, y_3, and y_4 arbitrarily. This fixes $\alpha = \Delta_{y_2, y_3}(y_4)$ as well as the distance $\delta = \|y_2 - y_3\|$ between y_2 and y_3. Thus, the improvement caused by this 2-opt step is only in the interval $(0, \varepsilon]$ if $\Delta_{y_2, y_3}(y_1) \in (\alpha, \alpha + \varepsilon]$, which is an interval of size ε. The probability that this happens is bounded from above by $\frac{\varepsilon}{4\sigma\delta}$ according to Lemma 13.4.

Let f be the probability density function of $\delta = \|y_2 - y_3\|$. Then the probability that the 2-opt step considered yields an improvement of at most ε is bounded from above by

$$\int_{\delta=0}^{\infty} \frac{\varepsilon}{4\sigma\delta} \cdot f(\delta)\, \mathrm{d}\delta.$$

Now we observe that the distribution of $1/\delta$ is stochastically dominated by $1/X$, where X is chi-distributed. This is because $\frac{\varepsilon}{4\sigma\delta}$ is decreasing in δ. Thus, the "worst-case" is that x_3 – the unperturbed version of y_3 – is located exactly at y_2. The chi-distribution describes the length of a vector that is distributed according to a Gaussian distribution with mean 0. In the 2-dimensional case, the density of the chi-distribution is given by $\frac{x}{\sigma^2} \cdot \exp\big(-\frac{x^2}{2\sigma^2}\big)$.

From this observation, we obtain that we can replace f by the density function of the chi-distribution to get an upper bound for the probability that we have an improvement of at most ε:

$$\int_{\delta=0}^{\infty} \frac{\varepsilon}{4\sigma\delta} \cdot \frac{\delta}{\sigma^2} \cdot \exp\left(-\frac{\delta^2}{2\sigma^2}\right) \, d\delta = \int_{\delta=0}^{\infty} \frac{\varepsilon}{4\sigma^3} \cdot \exp\left(-\frac{\delta^2}{2\sigma^2}\right) \, d\delta = O\left(\frac{\varepsilon}{\sigma^2}\right).$$

To finish the proof, we take a union bound over the $O(n^4)$ choices for the points y_1, y_2, y_3, and y_4. $\qquad\square$

The previous lemma can be turned into a tail bound for the number of iterations that 2-opt needs to converge to a local optimum, which yields our first theorem.

Theorem 13.6 *Let $Y \subseteq \mathbb{R}^2$ be a σ-perturbed point set, and let $\sigma \leq \frac{1}{2\sqrt{n \ln n}}$. Then the expected maximum number of iterations that the 2-opt heuristic needs to compute a locally optimal TSP tour with respect to squared Euclidean distances is bounded from above by $O(n^6 \log n/\sigma^2)$.*

Proof If 2-opt runs for at least t steps, then we must have $L_{\text{init}} \geq 18n$ or $\Delta_{\min} \leq 18n/t$. The probability that any of these events happens is at most $\frac{1}{n!} + O\left(\frac{n^5}{\sigma^2 t}\right)$ by Lemmas 13.3 and 13.5, where the probability is taken over the random perturbation.

Since no TSP tour shows up twice in any run of 2-opt, we know that the number of iterations is upper-bounded by $n!$. Let T be the random variable that is the maximum possible number of iterations that 2-opt can need on the (random) point set Y. Then

$$\mathbb{E}(T) = \sum_{t=1}^{n!} \mathbb{P}(T \geq t) \leq \sum_{t=1}^{n!} \left(\frac{1}{n!} + O\left(\frac{n^5}{\sigma^2 t}\right)\right) = O\left(\frac{n^6 \log n}{\sigma^2}\right). \qquad\square$$

13.2.3 Possibilities for Improving the Bound

Very roughly, the analysis of the running time of 2-opt in the previous section worked as follows:

- We have used the objective function as a potential function, and we have proved a (very simple) upper bound for the length of any initial tour.
- We have divided the possible steps that the algorithm can take into classes. In our case, every 2-opt step is exactly described by four points, namely the four endpoints of the edges involved. The rest of the tour does not play a role.
- For each such class, we have proved that it is unlikely that any iteration of this class yields only a small improvement.
- By taking a union bound over all classes, we turned this into a tail bound for the number of iterations and used this to obtain a bound on the expected number of iterations.

This immediately gives the following options for improving the bound:

- We could show a smaller bound for the length of the initial tour. This would immediately improve the bound.
- We could try to divide the possible iterations of the 2-opt heuristic into fewer classes. Then it would suffice to take the union bound over fewer classes.
- We could try to prove a stronger upper bound for the probability that any iteration of a class yields a small improvement. This would yield a stronger tail bound for the number of iterations and therefore improve the final bound.

In fact, avoiding the naive application of the union bound and instead cleverly partitioning the iterations into groups that can be analyzed simultaneously is usually the key ingredient of a smoothed analysis. In the remainder of this subsection, we sketch ideas how to improve the bound for the smoothed number of iterations of 2-opt.

Improving the Initial Tour Length

So far, we did not make any assumptions on how the initial tour was constructed. In practice, however, one would probably start with some reasonable approximation instead of an arbitrary (bad) tour. For instance, one can find an initial tour of length $O(1)$ (Yukich, 1998), which immediately decreases our bound by a linear factor. (This holds only for squared Euclidean distances in 2-dimensional space. For standard Euclidean distances, one can guarantee only bounds of length $O(\sqrt{n})$.)

Linked Pairs of 2-Opt Steps

The idea behind analyzing so-called "linked pairs of 2-opt steps" is the observation that taking into account only the smallest possible improvement is quite pessimistic. In order to improve the bound, we consider pairs of 2-opt steps that share some vertices. The two 2-opt steps of such a pair do not have to be executed next to each other in a run of 2-opt. This improvement does not fall directly into one of the three possibilities of improvement mentioned earlier. Indeed, we prove a stronger upper bound for the probability that a class yields a small improvement, but not for single iterations. Instead, we consider two iterations, which increases the number of classes. It turns out that the stronger upper bound more than compensates the increase of the number of different classes.

Sharing only a single vertex leaves the edges of the two 2-opt steps disjoint and, thus, does not help to improve the bound. It turns out that the case in which all four vertices are identical for both 2-opt steps is quite difficult to analyze because of dependencies. Hence, we restrict ourselves to pairs of 2-opt steps that overlap in two or three vertices. As at most six vertices are involved in such pairs, the number of such pairs is at most $O(n^6)$. While this is worse than the number of simple 2-opt steps, which is $O(n^4)$, it is compensated by the fact that the probability that both 2-opt steps yield only a small improvement is much smaller than in the case of a single 2-opt step. Basically, although the improvements obtained from the two 2-opt steps from such a pair are not independent, we can analyze them as if they were. The following lemma, whose formal proof we omit, summarizes this.

Lemma 13.7 *The probability that there exists a linked pair of 2-opt steps that have two or three vertices in common and such that both 2-opt steps improve the tour, but only by at most $\varepsilon > 0$, is at most $O\left(\frac{n^6 \varepsilon^2}{\sigma^4}\right)$.*

Crucial for this approach to work is that we encounter sufficiently many linked pairs of 2-opt steps in any run of 2-opt. The following lemma basically states that every sufficiently long sequence of 2-opt steps must contain a constant fraction of 2-opt steps that form disjoint linked pairs. We omit its proof, which is not difficult, but a bit technical.

Lemma 13.8 (Röglin and Schmidt, 2018) *Every sequence of t consecutive 2-opt steps contains at least $(2t - n)/7$ disjoint linked pairs of 2-opt steps that share either two or three vertices.*

Theorem 13.9 *Let $Y \subseteq \mathbb{R}^2$ be a σ-perturbed point set, and let $\sigma \leq \frac{1}{2\sqrt{n \ln n}}$. Then the expected maximum number of iterations that the 2-opt heuristic needs to compute a locally optimal TSP tour with respect to squared Euclidean distances is $O(n^4/\sigma^2)$.*

Proof Let T be the random variable that is the maximum possible number of iterations that 2-opt can need on the (random) point set Y. By Lemma 13.8, there exist constants $c_1, c_2 > 0$ such that every sequence of at least $t \geq c_1 n^2$ iterations contains at least $c_2 t$ disjoint pairs of linked 2-opt steps sharing two or three vertices.

Then $T \geq t$ only if $t \leq c_1 n^2$ or if $L_{\text{init}} \geq 18n$ or if there is a pair of linked 2-opt steps that yields an improvement of at most $\frac{18n}{c_2 t}$. Thus, there exist constants $c_3, c_4 > 0$ such that, by Lemma 13.7, we have

$$\mathbb{E}(T) \leq c_1 n^2 + \sum_{t \geq c_1 n^2} \mathbb{P}(T \geq t) \leq c_1 n^2 + \sum_{t \geq c_1 n^2} \min\left\{1, c_3 \cdot \frac{n^8}{t^2 \sigma^4}\right\}$$

$$\leq c_4 \cdot \frac{n^4}{\sigma^2} + \sum_{t \geq c_4 n^4/\sigma^2} c_3 \cdot \frac{n^8}{t^2 \sigma^4} = O\left(\frac{n^4}{\sigma^2}\right). \qquad \square$$

With the preceding discussion about the initial tour length, we can even improve the bound of Theorem 13.9 to $O(n^3/\sigma^2)$.

13.2.4 A Bound for the k-Means Method

The second example of a local search heuristic whose running time we want to analyze in the framework of smoothed analysis is the k-means method for clustering.

Description of the k-Means Method

Before doing the smoothed analysis, let us first describe k-means clustering and the k-means method.

We are given a finite set $X \subseteq \mathbb{R}^d$ of n data points and the number $k \in \mathbb{N}$ of clusters. The goal of k-means clustering is to partition these points into k clusters $C_1, \ldots, C_k$.

In addition to the clusters, we want to compute cluster centers $c_1, \ldots, c_k \in \mathbb{R}^d$ that are the representatives of their clusters. The centers do not have to be data points. The goal of k-means clustering is to find clusters and centers that minimize the sum of squared distances of data points to cluster centers:

$$\sum_{i=1}^{k} \sum_{x \in C_i} \|x - c_i\|^2.$$

If we already know the cluster centers, then this specifies (up to tie-breaking) a clustering: every point is assigned to a cluster whose center is closest to it. The other way round, if we have clusters $C_1, \ldots, C_k$, then each cluster center c_i should be chosen as the center of mass

$$\mathrm{cm}(C_i) = \frac{1}{|C_i|} \cdot \sum_{x \in C_i} x$$

of C_i. This is a direct consequence of the following lemma, the proof of which we leave as Exercise 13.4.

Lemma 13.10 *Let $C \subseteq \mathbb{R}^d$ be a finite set of points, let $c = \mathrm{cm}(C)$ be the center of mass of C, and let $z \in \mathbb{R}^d$ be arbitrary. Then*

$$\sum_{x \in C} \|x - z\|^2 = \sum_{x \in C} \|x - c\|^2 + |C| \cdot \|c - z\|^2.$$

The key idea of the k-means method is to exploit that clustering and centers mutually imply each other: the k-means method alternates between optimizing the clustering based on the given centers and optimizing the centers based on the given clustering. More formally, it works as follows:

1. Choose initial cluster centers $c_1, \ldots, c_k$.
2. Construct a clustering $C_1, \ldots, C_k$ from the current cluster centers.
3. Set $c_i = \mathrm{cm}(C_i)$ for all $i \in \{1, \ldots, k\}$.
4. If anything changed in steps 13.2.4 or 13.2.4, return to step (13.2.4).

The k-means method is one of the most popular clustering algorithms. Its popularity stems from two facts: first, it is very simple. Second, it is very fast on practical data sets. This second fact allows one to rerun it several times with different initializations in order to obtain a good clustering.

However, in contrast to practical performance, the worst-case running time of the k-means method is exponential in the number k of clusters. We can choose $k = \Theta(n)$, which shows that the worst-case number of iterations can be exponential. This lower bound construction works already in the Euclidean plane, i.e., if $d = 2$ is fixed.

The only known worst-case upper bound for the number of iterations is based on counting the number of different clusterings and the trivial fact that no clustering occurs twice in a run of the k-means method. The number of different clusterings of n points in d-dimensional space into k clusters, where clusters have to be separated by hyperplanes, is upper-bounded by n^{3kd}.

Model and Approach

In the following, we apply smoothed analysis to the running time of the k-means method. More specifically, our goal is to prove an upper bound that is polynomial in n^k and $1/\sigma$, which removes a factor of d from the exponent compared to the worst-case running time. While such a bound surely does not explain the observed performance of the algorithm, it conveys the basic ideas of the analysis. To keep the analysis relatively simple, we combine the first $\text{poly}(n^k, 1/\sigma)$ bound with techniques that were used later in the proof of a truly polynomial bound.

In comparison to the 2-opt heuristic, we have to address two technical challenges in the smoothed analysis of the k-means method:

- Iterations of the 2-opt heuristic can be compactly represented by the four vertices involved. For the k-means method, such a compact representation of iterations is much less obvious.
- In order to obtain a polynomial bound for the smoothed running time of the 2-opt heuristic, it was sufficient to consider the improvement caused by a single iteration. This does not seem to be the case for the k-means method.

The model that we use for the smoothed analysis is the same as for the 2-opt heuristic: an adversary specifies a set $X \subseteq [0, 1]^d$ of n points. Then these points are perturbed by independent Gaussian random variables of standard deviation σ. We call the resulting point set $Y \subseteq \mathbb{R}^d$ again a σ-perturbed point set, and we run the k-means method on this point set Y.

Again, restricting X to the unit hypercube is just a matter of scaling and does not restrict generality. And again, we restrict our analysis to the case $\sigma \leq 1$ because of Exercise 13.2.

In the following, we also make the (natural) assumption that $k, d \leq n$. In many applications, k and d are even considered to be constant. Using the upper bound of n for k and d sometimes simplifies calculations.

The main idea is similar to the 2-opt heuristic: we use the objective function as a potential function and show that it has to decrease sufficiently quickly. However, as noted already at the beginning of this section, there are two issues that make this more difficult than for the 2-opt heuristic: first, a compact description of iterations does not seem to exist for the k-means method. Second, we cannot rule out that there are iterations in which the objective function decreases by only a negligible amount. This makes it necessary to consider longer sequences of iterations, similar to the analysis of linked pairs of 2-opt steps. But while the analysis of linked pairs of 2-opt steps was necessary only to improve the bound, here this seems unavoidable.

For the first issue, it turns out that we can describe iterations by $O(kd)$ points sufficiently precisely. For the second issue, considering sequences of 2^k iterations suffices in order to make it unlikely that all of them yield only a small improvement.

Decrease of the Objective Function

In order to analyze the decrease of the objective function, we first have to understand what causes it to decrease. The objective function gets smaller (1) by moving cluster centers and (2) by reassigning data points.

Lemma 13.10 implies that moving a cluster center c_i by a distance of ε to the center of mass of its point set C_i decreases the objective value by $\varepsilon^2 \cdot |C_i| \geq \varepsilon^2$.

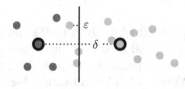

Figure 13.2 If we reassign the leftmost light point – which is at a distance of ε from the bisecting hyperplane – to the dark cluster, then this decreases the objective function by $2\varepsilon\delta$, where δ is the distance between the two centers.

For a hyperplane H and a point z, we denote by $\mathrm{dist}(z, H)$ the Euclidean distance of z to H. For analyzing the decrease of the objective value caused by reassigning a point, we need the notion of a bisecting hyperplane: for two points $x, y \in \mathbb{R}^d$ with $x \neq y$, we call a hyperplane H the bisector of x and y if H is orthogonal to $x - y$ and $\mathrm{dist}(x, H) = \mathrm{dist}(y, H)$. This means that

$$H = \left\{ z \in \mathbb{R}^d \mid 2z^{\mathrm{T}}(x - y) = (x + y)^{\mathrm{T}}(x - y) \right\}.$$

The decrease of the objective function caused by reassigning a data point to a different cluster depends on the distance of this point from the corresponding bisecting hyperplane and the distance between the two cluster centers involved. The following lemma makes this more precise – see also Figure 13.2. We leave its proof as Exercise 13.5.

Lemma 13.11 *Let c_i and c_j be two cluster centers with bisector H, and let $y \in C_i$. If $\|y - c_j\| < \|y - c_i\|$; then reassigning y to C_j decreases the objective value by*

$$2 \cdot \mathrm{dist}(y, H) \cdot \|c_i - c_j\|.$$

The rough idea for the smoothed analysis is as follows: if many points are reassigned to a new cluster, then it is unlikely that all of them are close to their corresponding bisecting hyperplane. If only a few points are reassigned, then at least one cluster center must move significantly. This hope turns out to be wrong for a single iteration, so we have to consider longer sequences of iterations.

Dense Iterations

We call an iteration of the k-means method *dense* if there is at least one cluster that gains or loses in total at least $2kd$ points. According to Lemma 13.11, we have to show that in a dense iteration, it is unlikely that all these points are close to their corresponding bisecting hyperplanes or that centers are too close to each other.

We call the point set Y ε-*separated* if, for all hyperplanes $H \subseteq \mathbb{R}^d$, there are fewer than $2d$ points $y \in Y$ with $\mathrm{dist}(y, H) \leq \varepsilon$. The following lemma quantifies the minimal improvement caused by any dense iteration, provided that Y is ε-separated.

Lemma 13.12 *If Y is ε-separated, then the potential decreases by at least $2\varepsilon^2/n$ in every dense iteration.*

Proof Since the iteration is dense, there must be a cluster C_i that exchanges at least $2kd$ points with other clusters in this iteration. Hence, there must be another cluster C_j with which C_i exchanges at least $2d + 1$ points. Since Y is ε-separated, at least one point $y \in Y$ that switches between C_i and C_j is at a distance of at least ε from the hyperplane bisecting $c_i = \mathrm{cm}(C_i)$ and $c_j = \mathrm{cm}(C_j)$, where C_i and C_j are the clusters before the switch.

In order to bound the decrease of the objective value from below by $2\varepsilon^2/n$, we need a lower bound of ε/n for $\|c_i - c_j\|$. There exists a hyperplane H' (the bisector from the previous iteration) that separates C_i from C_j. Among all at least $2d + 1$ points that want to switch in the current iteration, at least one point y must be at a distance of at least ε from H', since Y is ε-separated. Assume without loss of generality that $y \in C_i$. Then, since (i) $|C_i| \leq n$; (ii) y is at least ε away from H', since Y is ε-separated; and (iii) all points of C_i are on the same side of H', the center of mass $c_i = \mathrm{cm}(C_i)$ must be at least ε/n away from H'. Hence, $\frac{\varepsilon}{n} \leq \mathrm{dist}(c_i, H') \leq \|c_i - c_j\|$. (Note that this argument does not work with the bisector of c_i and c_j instead of H', as some points are on the "wrong side" of this bisector.) □

A simple union bound together the following lemma yields an upper bound for the probability that Y is not ε-separated (Lemma 13.14).

Lemma 13.13 *Let $P \subseteq \mathbb{R}^d$ be any finite set of at least d points, and let $H \subseteq \mathbb{R}^d$ be an arbitrary hyperplane. Then there exists a hyperplane $H' \subseteq \mathbb{R}^d$ that contains at least d points of P such that*

$$\max_{p \in P}\big(\mathrm{dist}(p, H')\big) \leq 2d \cdot \max_{p \in P}\big(\mathrm{dist}(p, H)\big).$$

We skip the proof of Lemma 13.13 and refer to Arthur and Vassilvitskii's paper (Arthur and Vassilvitskii, 2009, Lemma 5.8). The intuition of this lemma is as follows: if there is any hyperplane H such that all points of some set $P \subseteq \mathbb{R}^d$ are close to H, then there is also a hyperplane H' that contains d points of P and all other points in P are close to H'. Lemma 13.13 is useful because of the dependency between the location of the bisecting hyperplanes and the data points. Using it, we can use d points to fix some hyperplane and then use the independent randomness of another d points to show that they are not close to this hyperplane.

Lemma 13.14 *The probability that Y is not ε-separated is at most $n^{2d} \cdot \left(\frac{2d\varepsilon}{\sigma}\right)^d$.*

Proof According to Lemma 13.13, it suffices to show that the probability that there are two disjoint sets P and P' consisting of d points of Y each such that all points of P' are $(2d\varepsilon)$-close to the hyperplane through P is bounded by $n^{2d} \cdot \left(\frac{2d\varepsilon}{\sigma}\right)^d$.

Fix any sets P and P' of d points. Using the principle of deferred decisions, we fix the position of the points in P arbitrarily. Then the probability that all points of P' are within distance $2d\varepsilon$ of the hyperplane through P is at most $(2d\varepsilon/\sigma)^d$, because perturbations of the points in P' are independent and the probability that a point is within a distance of $2d\varepsilon$ of a fixed hyperplane is bounded from above by $2d\varepsilon/\sigma$ by Lemma 13.2. The lemma follows by a union bound over the at most n^{2d} choices for P and P'. □

By combining Lemmas 13.12 and 13.14, we obtain the following result about dense iterations.

Lemma 13.15 *For $d \geq 2$ and $\sigma \leq 1$, the probability that there exists a dense iteration in which the potential decreases by less than ε is bounded from above by*

$$\left(\frac{2n^{3.5}\sqrt{\varepsilon}}{\sigma} \right)^d.$$

Proof According to Lemma 13.12, if there is a dense iteration in which the potential decreases by less than ε, then Y is not $\sqrt{n\varepsilon/2}$-separated. By Lemma 13.14 and $d \leq n$, this happens with a probability of at most

$$n^{2d} \cdot \left(\frac{2d\sqrt{n\varepsilon/2}}{\sigma} \right)^d \leq \left(\frac{2dn^{2.5}\sqrt{\varepsilon}}{\sigma} \right)^d \leq \left(\frac{2n^{3.5}\sqrt{\varepsilon}}{\sigma} \right)^d. \qquad \square$$

Sparse Iterations

We call an iteration *sparse* if every cluster gains or loses in total at most $2kd$ points.

Let C_i^t be the set of points in the ith cluster in iteration t of the k-means method. We define an *epoch* to be a sequence of consecutive iterations $t, t+1, \ldots, t+\ell$ in which no cluster assumes more than two different point sets. This means that $|\{C_i^a \mid t \leq a \leq t+\ell\}| \leq 2$ for all $i \in \{1, 2, \ldots, k\}$. A trivial upper bound for the length of every epoch is given in the following lemma. In fact, it is possible to show that the length of every epoch is at most 3 (see Exercise 13.6), but this is not needed for the bound that we aim for.

Lemma 13.16 *The length of every epoch is bounded by 2^k.*

Proof After 2^k iterations, at least one cluster must have assumed a third set of points. Otherwise, a clustering would show up a second time. This is impossible as the objective value strictly decreases in every iteration. $\qquad \square$

We call a set $Y \subseteq \mathbb{R}^d$ of data points η-*coarse* for some number $\eta > 0$ if, for all triples $P_1, P_2, P_3 \subseteq Y$ of different subsets with $|P_1 \triangle P_2| \leq 2kd$ and $|P_2 \triangle P_3| \leq 2kd$, we have $\| \mathrm{cm}(P_i) - \mathrm{cm}(P_{i+1}) \| > \eta$ for at least one $i \in \{1, 2\}$. Here, "$\triangle$" denotes the symmetric difference of two sets.

Lemma 13.17 *Assume that Y is η-coarse and consider a sequence of 2^k consecutive iterations of the k-means method. If each of these iterations is sparse, then the potential decreases by at least η^2.*

Proof After 2^k iterations, at least one cluster has assumed a third configuration (Lemma 13.16). Since the iterations are sparse, there are sets P_1, P_2, and P_3 such that $|P_1 \triangle P_2|, |P_2 \triangle P_3| \leq 2kd$ such that this cluster switches from point set P_1 to P_2 and later to P_3 (directly from P_2 or after switching back to P_1 – not necessarily in consecutive iterations). Since the instance is η-coarse, we have

$\| \operatorname{cm}(P_1) - \operatorname{cm}(P_2) \| > \eta$ or $\| \operatorname{cm}(P_2) - \operatorname{cm}(P_3) \| > \eta$. Thus, the corresponding cluster center must have moved by at least η in one iteration, which decreases the potential by at least η^2 according to Lemma 13.10. □

Lemma 13.18 *The probability that Y is not η-coarse is bounded from above by* $(7n)^{4kd} \cdot (4nkd\eta/\sigma)^d$.

Proof Let $P_1, P_2, P_3 \subseteq Y$ be three sets with $|P_1 \triangle P_2| \leq \ell$ and $|P_2 \triangle P_3| \leq \ell$. Let $A = P_1 \cap P_2 \cap P_3$, and let B_1, B_2, and B_3 be sets such that $P_i = A \cup B_i$ for $i \in \{1, 2, 3\}$ and B_1, B_2, and B_3 are disjoint to A. We have $|B_1 \cup B_2 \cup B_3| \leq 2\ell$ and $B_1 \cap B_2 \cap B_3 = \emptyset$.

We perform a union bound over the choices of the sets B_1, B_2, and B_3. The number of possible choice for these sets is upper-bounded by $7^{2\ell} \cdot \binom{n}{2\ell} \leq (7n)^{2\ell}$: we select 2ℓ elements of Y. Then we choose for each element in which of the three sets it should belong. None of these elements belongs to all sets, but there can be elements that belong to no set. We need this possibility, since we can have $|B_1 \cup B_2 \cup B_3| < 2\ell$.

For $i \in \{1, 2, 3\}$, we have

$$\operatorname{cm}(P_i) = \frac{|A|}{|A| + |B_i|} \cdot \operatorname{cm}(A) + \frac{|B_i|}{|A| + |B_i|} \cdot \operatorname{cm}(B_i).$$

Hence, for $i \in \{1, 2\}$, we can write $\operatorname{cm}(P_i) - \operatorname{cm}(P_{i+1})$ as

$$\operatorname{cm}(P_i) - \operatorname{cm}(P_{i+1}) = \left(\frac{|A|}{|A| + |B_i|} - \frac{|A|}{|A| + |B_{i+1}|} \right) \cdot \operatorname{cm}(A)$$

$$+ \frac{|B_i|}{|A| + |B_i|} \cdot \operatorname{cm}(B_i) - \frac{|B_{i+1}|}{|A| + |B_{i+1}|} \cdot \operatorname{cm}(B_{i+1}).$$

We distinguish three cases. The first case is that $|B_i| = |B_{i+1}|$ for some $i \in \{1, 2\}$. Then the preceding equation simplifies to

$$\operatorname{cm}(P_i) - \operatorname{cm}(P_{i+1}) = \frac{|B_i|}{|A| + |B_i|} \cdot \operatorname{cm}(B_i) - \frac{|B_i|}{|A| + |B_i|} \cdot \operatorname{cm}(B_{i+1})$$

$$= \frac{1}{|A| + |B_i|} \cdot \left(\sum_{y \in B_i \setminus B_{i+1}} y - \sum_{y \in B_{i+1} \setminus B_i} y \right).$$

Since $B_i \neq B_{i+1}$ and $|B_i| = |B_{i+1}|$, there exists a point $y \in B_i \setminus B_{i+1}$.

We use the principle of deferred decisions. We first fix all points in $(B_i \cup B_{i+1}) \setminus \{y\}$ arbitrarily. Then $\| \operatorname{cm}(P_i) - \operatorname{cm}(P_{i+1}) \| \leq \eta$ is equivalent to the event that y assumes a position in a hyperball of radius $(|A| + |B_i|) \cdot \eta \leq n\eta$. The probability that this happens is bounded from above by the maximum density of a Gaussian distribution times the volume of the hyperball, which is at most $(n\eta/\sigma)^d \leq (2n\eta\ell/\sigma)^d$.

The second case is that $A = \emptyset$. This case is in fact identical to the first case.

The third case is that $|B_1| \neq |B_2| \neq |B_3|$. We denote by $\mathcal{B}(c,r) = \{x \in \mathbb{R}^d \mid \|x - c\| \leq r\}$ the hyperball of radius r around c. For $i \in \{1,2\}$, let

$$r_i = \left(\frac{|A|}{|A| + |B_i|} - \frac{|A|}{|A| + |B_{i+1}|} \right)^{-1} = \frac{(|A| + |B_i|) \cdot (|A| + |B_{i+1}|)}{|A| \cdot (|B_{i+1}| - |B_i|)}$$

and

$$Z_i = \frac{|B_{i+1}|}{|A| + |B_{i+1}|} \operatorname{cm}(B_{i+1}) - \frac{|B_i|}{|A| + |B_i|} \operatorname{cm}(B_i).$$

We observe that the event $\| \operatorname{cm}(P_i) - \operatorname{cm}(P_{i+1})\| < \eta$ is equivalent to the event that $\operatorname{cm}(A) \in \mathcal{B}_i = \mathcal{B}(r_i Z_i, |r_i|\eta)$. Consequently, a necessary condition that the event $\| \operatorname{cm}(P_i) - \operatorname{cm}(P_{i+1})\| < \eta$ occurs for both $i \in \{1,2\}$ is that the hyperballs $\mathcal{B}_1$ and $\mathcal{B}_2$ intersect.

The two hyperballs intersect if and only if their centers are at a distance of at most $(|r_1| + |r_2|) \cdot \eta$ of each other. Hence,

$$\mathbb{P}\big(\| \operatorname{cm}(P_1) - \operatorname{cm}(P_2)\| \leq \eta \text{ and } \| \operatorname{cm}(P_2) - \operatorname{cm}(P_3)\| \leq \eta\big)$$
$$\leq \mathbb{P}\left(\|r_1 Z_1 - r_2 Z_2\| \leq \big(|r_1| + |r_2|\big)\eta\right).$$

With some tedious but not too insightful calculations, we can see that the probability of this event is bounded as desired. $\qquad\square$

The main technical problem in the proof of Lemma 13.18 is that we cannot control the position of $\operatorname{cm}(A)$. The reason is that there are too many possible choices for points in A. Because of this, we cannot simply apply a union bound over all possibilities for A.

The first case in the proof of Lemma 13.18 shows that for the case that the same number of points leaves and enters a cluster, it is already quite likely that the potential decreases significantly. In this case, no epochs are needed. The reason is that the influence of $\operatorname{cm}(A)$ cancels out in $\operatorname{cm}(P_i) - \operatorname{cm}(P_{i+1})$ if $|B_i| = |B_{i+1}|$. In this way, the difficulty that we have to say something about $\operatorname{cm}(A)$ disappears.

If $|B_i| \neq |B_{i+1}|$, then $\operatorname{cm}(A)$ shows up with different coefficients in $\operatorname{cm}(C_i)$ and $\operatorname{cm}(C_{i+1})$ and, hence, with a nonzero coefficient in $\operatorname{cm}(P_i) - \operatorname{cm}(P_{i+1})$. This implies that for any position of $\operatorname{cm}(B_i)$ and $\operatorname{cm}(B_{i+1})$, there exists a location for $\operatorname{cm}(A)$ such that $\operatorname{cm}(P_i)$ and $\operatorname{cm}(P_{i+1})$ are close. However, this is possible only if $\operatorname{cm}(A)$ assumes a position in some hyperball of a certain radius. The center of this hyperball depends only on $\operatorname{cm}(B_i)$ and $\operatorname{cm}(B_{i+1})$. We conclude that we can have $\| \operatorname{cm}(P_1) - \operatorname{cm}(P_2)\| \leq \eta$ and $\| \operatorname{cm}(P_2) - \operatorname{cm}(P_3)\| \leq \eta$ simultaneously only if these hyperballs intersect.

Lemmas 13.17 and 13.18 imply the following.

Lemma 13.19 *The probability that there is a sequence of 2^k consecutive sparse improving iterations such that the potential decreases by less than ε over this sequence is at most*

$$(7n)^{4kd} \cdot \left(\frac{4nkd\sqrt{\varepsilon}}{\sigma} \right)^d \leq \left(\frac{c_{\text{sparse}} n^{4k+4} \sqrt{\varepsilon}}{\sigma} \right)^d$$

for some sufficiently large constant c_{sparse}.

Putting Everything Together

To get a smoothed bound for the number of iterations, we need an upper bound for the objective function of the initial clustering. The proof of the following lemma is almost identical to the proof of Lemma 13.3 and therefore omitted. Here we exploit our assumption that $\sigma \leq 1$.

Lemma 13.20 *Let $\sigma \leq 1$, let $D = 10\sqrt{kd \ln n}$, and let Y be a σ-perturbed point set. Then $\mathbb{P}(Y \nsubseteq [-D, D]^d) \leq n^{-3kd}$.*

A consequence of Lemma 13.20 is that after the first iteration, the potential is bounded by $ndD^2 = c_{\text{init}}nd^2k \ln n \leq c_{\text{init}}n^5$ for some constant c_{init}. (The upper bound of $c_{\text{init}}n^5$ is very poor, but simplifies the bounds.)

Theorem 13.21 *For $d \geq 2$, the smoothed number of iterations of the k-means method is at most $O(2^k n^{14k+12}/\sigma^2)$.*

Proof We choose $\varepsilon = \sigma^2 \cdot n^{-14k-8}$. By Lemma 13.15, the probability that there is a dense iteration that decreases the potential by at most ε is at most cn^{-3kd} for some constant $c > 0$. By Lemma 13.19, the probability that there is a sequence of 2^k consecutive sparse iterations that decrease the potential in total by at most ε is also at most $c'n^{-3kd}$ for some constant $c' > 0$. By Lemma 13.20, the probability that the initial potential is more than $O(n^5)$ is also at most n^{-3kd}.

If any of these events happens nevertheless, we bound the number of iterations by its worst-case bound of n^{3kd} (Inaba et al., 2000). This contributes only $O(1)$ to the expected value. Otherwise, the number of iterations is bounded by $O(2^k n^{14k+13}/\sigma^2)$. $\qquad\square$

Toward a Truly Polynomial Bound

The bound obtained in Theorem 13.21 is still quite poor. In particular, it has the number k of clusters in the exponent. It can be shown that the smoothed number of iterations of k-means is bounded by a polynomial in n and $1/\sigma$ (without k or d in the exponent). The idea for this improved analysis is to refine the partitioning of iterations into more types, not only into sparse and dense iterations. However, the analysis becomes technically quite involved, while the analysis presented here already conveys the key ideas.

13.3 Smoothed Analysis of the Approximation Ratio

Local search heuristics are popular not only because they are fast, but also because they succeed relatively often in finding local optima that are not much worse than global optima. In order to understand this theoretically, we would like to analyze the ratio of the objective value of the local optimum found and of a global optimum. However, there are several issues to this:

- Which local optimum the heuristic finds depends on the initial solution. In fact, a local search heuristic is fully specified only if we also say how the initial solution is computed. For the running time, we have avoided this issue by taking a worst-case approach, i.e., analyzing the maximum running time if we always make the worst possible choice.

For the approximation ratio, we avoid this issue in the same way by comparing the global optimum with the worst local optimum. However, the downside of this is that we obtain approximation ratios much worse than the results obtained by using quite simple heuristics to construct the initial solution, rendering the results purely theoretical.

- While local search heuristics often perform very well with respect to speed, their performance in terms of approximation ratio is somewhat mixed. In fact, worst-case examples for the approximation ratio are often quite robust against small perturbations.
- A pure technical issue is that, in order to analyze the approximation ratio, we have to analyze the ratio of two random variables, namely the length of an optimal tour and the length of the tour computed by the algorithm, that are highly dependent.

We consider again the 2-opt heuristic for the TSP, but this time, we use the (standard) Euclidean distances to measure the tour length.

We do not give full proofs in the remainder of this section, as most proofs are too lengthy and technical to be presented here. Instead, we restrict ourselves to giving some intuition of the proof ideas.

13.3.1 A Simple Bound for the Approximation Ratio of 2-Opt

We call a TSP tour through a point set *2-optimal* if it cannot be shortened by a 2-opt step. For a point set Y, we denote by $\mathrm{WLO}(Y)$ (worst local optimum) the length of the longest 2-optimal tour through Y. We denote by $\mathrm{TSP}(Y)$ the length of the shortest TSP tour.

Our goal here is to prove a smoothed approximation ratio of $O(1/\sigma)$. This means that $\mathbb{E}(\mathrm{WLO}(Y)/\mathrm{TSP}(Y)) = O(1/\sigma)$. The idea to prove this is as follows:

- Prove that $\mathrm{TSP}(Y) = \Omega(\sigma \cdot \sqrt{n})$ with high probability.
- Prove that $\mathrm{WLO}(Y) = O(\sqrt{n})$ with high probability.
- If either bound does not hold (which happens only with negligible probability), then we use the trivial upper bound of $n/2$ for the approximation ratio.

The following lower bound for the length of an optimal tour is given without a proof (see also Chapter 8). It follows from concentration of measure results for Euclidean optimization problems.

Lemma 13.22 *There exists a constant $c > 0$ such that $\mathrm{TSP}(Y) \geq c \cdot \sigma \sqrt{n}$ with a probability of at least $1 - \exp(-c'n)$.*

In particular, Lemma 13.22 implies that $\mathbb{E}(\mathrm{TSP}(Y)) = \Omega(\sigma\sqrt{n})$, which we leave as Exercise 13.3.

Next, we state an upper bound for the length of any locally optimal tour. The key insight here is that if a tour is too long, then it must contain two almost parallel edges that are not too far away. These edges can then be replaced by a 2-opt step. Hence, the original tour was not locally optimal.

Lemma 13.23 *Let $Y \subseteq [a,b]^2$ be a set of n points for some $a < b$, and let T be any 2-optimal tour through Y. Then the length $L(T)$ of T is bounded from above by $O((b-a) \cdot \sqrt{n})$.*

Combining Lemma 13.23 with the fact that not too many points can be too far outside of the unit hypercube, we obtain the following lemma.

Lemma 13.24 *There exist constants $c, c' > 0$ such that, for all $\sigma \leq 1$, the following holds: the probability that there exists a 2-optimal tour T through Y that has a length of more than $c \cdot \sqrt{n}$ is bounded by $\exp(-c'\sqrt{n})$.*

The upper bound for the length of local optima plus the lower bound for the length of optimal tours together with the trivial worst-case bound of $n/2$ of 2-opt's approximation ratio yield the following result.

Theorem 13.25 *Let $Y \subseteq \mathbb{R}^2$ be σ-perturbed point set. Then*

$$\mathbb{E}\left(\frac{\mathrm{WLO}(Y)}{\mathrm{TSP}(Y)}\right) = O\left(\frac{1}{\sigma}\right).$$

13.3.2 Improved Smoothed Approximation Ratio of 2-Opt

In the previous section, we have sketched a bound of $O(1/\sigma)$ for the smoothed approximation ratio of 2-opt. This bound is still far away from explaining the observed approximation performance of 2-opt, which usually finds a solution only a few percent worse than the optimal solution.

The most striking reason that the bound is so poor is the following: we have analyzed the objective value of the globally optimal and locally optimal solution completely independently. The obvious advantage of this is that it avoids all dependencies between the two quantities. The obvious disadvantage is that it only yields a very poor bound: both the upper bound for the length of a locally optimal solution and the lower bound for the length of a globally optimal solution are tight, but the former is achieved if the unperturbed points are spread evenly over $[0,1]^d$, whereas the latter is achieved by putting all unperturbed points at exactly the same location.

By taking the positions of the unperturbed points into account, it is possible to improve the smoothed approximation ratio of 2-opt to $O(\log(1/\sigma))$.

This seems to be almost tight, as there exist instances X of n points such that $\mathbb{E}\left(\frac{\mathrm{WLO}(Y)}{\mathrm{TSP}(Y)}\right) = \Omega\left(\frac{\log n}{\log \log n}\right)$ for $\sigma = O(1/\sqrt{n})$. The idea to prove this smoothed lower bound for the approximation ratio is to show that the known worst-case lower bound example for the ratio WLO / TSP of $\Omega(\log n / \log \log n)$ can be made robust against perturbations with $\sigma = O(1/\sqrt{n})$.

However, even the improved bound of $O(\log(1/\sigma))$ requires σ to be constant to achieve some constant approximation ratio. Such results are also easily obtained by many simple heuristics for the TSP.

13.4 Discussion and Open Problems

13.4.1 Running Time

Both smoothed analyses that we have presented in Section 13.2 have in common that they are based on analyzing the smallest possible improvement of either a single iteration or a few iterations.

This has been extended to longer sequences of iterations for the flip heuristic for the Max-Cut problem. An instance of Max-Cut is given by an undirected graph $G = (V, E)$ with edge weights $w : E \to [-1, 1]$. The goal is to find a partition $\sigma : V \to \{-1, 1\}$ of the vertices of maximum cut weight

$$\frac{1}{2} \cdot \sum_{e = \{u, v\} \in E} w(e) \cdot \left(1 - \sigma(u)\sigma(v)\right).$$

The flip heuristic for MaxCut starts with an arbitrary partition. Then it iteratively flips the sign of a vertex if this would increase the cut weight, until it has converged to a local optimum.

The flip heuristic for MaxCut has been a notoriously difficult problem for a few years because it eluded a smoothed analysis despite its simplicity. In order to make the smoothed analysis of its running time possible, it was necessary to consider much longer sequences of iterations, namely sequences of length linear in the number of vertices. The main challenge then was to find enough independent randomness in such sequences.

In summary, the feature that all smoothed analyses of the running time of local search heuristics have in common seems to be that it is unlikely that iterations cause only very small improvements. In contrast, the worst-case constructions to show an exponential lower bound for the running time of these heuristics are quite fragile. They are usually based on implementing a "binary counter," where each bit is represented by some small gadget. The gadgets for the different bits are scaled versions of each other, which implies that all but the gadgets for the most significant bits are tiny and easily break under small perturbations.

We conclude this section with three open problems: first, prove that the Lin-Kernighan heuristic for the TSP has polynomial smoothed running time. This heuristic has incredible performance in practice, much better than 2-opt. However, it seems to be difficult to find a compact representation of the iterations. The reason for this is that each iteration replaces an unbounded number of edges.

Second, devise general techniques for the smoothed analysis of local search heuristics. Despite all the similarities, each smoothed analysis of a local search heuristic so far is tailored to the specific algorithm. Is it possible to develop a general framework or general conditions that imply smoothed polynomial running time?

Third, all smoothed analyses of local search heuristics use the decrease of the objective function by showing that it is unlikely that any iteration (or all iterations in some sequence) yields only a small improvement. This still seems to be rather pessimistic, as it is unlikely that a local search heuristic performs very often iterations that yield only the smallest possible improvement. Is it possible to do a smoothed analysis "beyond the smallest improvement" in order to get improved bounds? In particular, the polynomial bounds obtained in the smoothed analyses of the k-means method and the flip heuristic for MaxCut have quite large degree. We assume that considerably improving these bounds requires new ideas.

13.4.2 Approximation Ratio

Given the relatively strong results for local search heuristics with respect to running time and the quite poor results with respect to approximation ratio, the question arises why this is the case. In fact, the results for the approximation ratio that we have presented here are only of purely theoretical interest, as – in case of the TSP – even a simple insertion heuristic achieves an approximation ratio of 2 in the worst case.

For the k-means method, the situation is different: the approximation performance of the k-means method is not very good in the first place. In fact, the main reason why the k-means method is so popular is its speed. This allows us to run it many times on the same data set with different initializations. The hope is that for at least one initialization, we get a good clustering. In general, only very poor guarantees are possible, even in the framework of smoothed analysis (Exercise 13.8).

Thus, the question arises if smoothed analysis is the right tool for analyzing the approximation ratio of algorithms. The few successes – although nontrivial – are merely of theoretical interest. A reason for this could be that the worst-case examples for the approximation ratio seem to be much more robust against small perturbations.

We conclude this section with three open problems: first, prove a nontrivial bound for the approximation performance of the Lin–Kernighan heuristic for the TSP mentioned in the previous section.

Second, apply smoothed analyses to "hybrid heuristics." The smoothed analysis so far have only been applied to "pure" local search heuristics. However, in particular the approximation ratio depends heavily on a good initialization. Hence, we have to take into account two algorithms (the initialization and the actual heuristic) instead of only one. Is it possible to show improved bounds in this setting? For instance, the k-means method as described in this chapter has a poor approximation performance. Is it possible to prove a good approximation performance, when initialized cleverly?

Third, find a meaningful way to do smoothed analysis of approximation ratios or devise a different approach toward "approximation ratio beyond the worst case" that really explains the approximation performance of such heuristics in practice. One of the strong points of smoothed analysis is that it is a relatively problem-independent semirandom input model. Essentially the only property that is needed for a smoothed analysis is that the concept of "small perturbations" make sense for the problem considered. However, this advantage is also a disadvantage: because of problem independence, smoothed analysis completely ignores any structure that interesting instances might have. Thus, in order to address this question, it might be necessary to come up with more problem-specific input models for "non-worst-case" instances.

13.5 Notes

Smoothed analysis has been introduced by Spielman and Teng (2004) in order to explain the performance of the simplex method for linear programming. Arthur and

Vassilvitskii (2009) were the first to apply smoothed analysis to local search heuristics, namely to the k-means method and to the Iterative Closest Point (ICP) algorithm.

The original smoothed analysis of 2-opt, both for running time and approximation ratio and including the concept of linked pairs, was done by Englert et al. (2014) (see Röglin and Schmidt (2018) for a corrected version of Lemma 13.8). They also provided a Euclidean instance on which 2-opt needs an exponential number of iterations to compute a local optimum. Furthermore, they provided a smoothed analysis of 2-opt for TSP in (non-Euclidean) general graphs (Englert et al., 2016). The analysis of the running time under Gaussian noise using squared Euclidean distances presented here follows a simplified proof by Manthey and Veenstra (2013). The improved smoothed analysis of the approximation ratio is due to Künnemann and Manthey (2015). The absolute length of locally optimal tours is by Chandra et al. (1999). They also proved a worst-case bound of $O(\log n)$ for the approximation ratio of 2-opt. The high-probability statement in Lemma 13.22 follows from Rhee's isoperimetric inequality (Rhee, 1993). Johnson and McGeoch provide experimental evidence for the performance of 2-opt and the Lin–Kernighan heuristic (Johnson and McGeoch, 1997, 2002).

Arthur and Vassilvitskii (2009) proved a bound polynomial in n^k and $1/\sigma$ for the smoothed running time of the k-means method and a polynomial bound for the so-called ICP algorithm. The bound for the k-means method has been improved to a polynomial bound by Arthur et al. (2011). The proof presented here combines the two proofs to simplify the argument. A weaker bound can be obtained for more general distance measures (Manthey and Röglin, 2013). Vattani (2011) provided an example in 2-dimensional space for which k-means needs exponential time to compute a local optimum. The upper bound for the worst-case running time is by Inaba et al. (2000).

The first smoothed analysis of the running time of the flip heuristic for the Max-Cut problem for graphs of bounded degree has been done by Elsässer and Tscheuschner (2011) (see Exercise 13.9). Etscheid and Röglin (2014) proved a quasi-polynomial bound in general graphs. For the special case of complete graphs, this has been improved by Angel et al. (2017) to a polynomial bound with high probability.

References

Angel, Omer, Bubeck, Sébastien, Peres, Yuval, and Wei, Fan. 2017. Local max-cut in smoothed polynomial time. In *Proceedings of the 49th Annual ACM Symposium on Theory of Computing (STOC)*, pp. 429–437. ACM.

Arthur, David, and Vassilvitskii, Sergei. 2009. Worst-case and smoothed analysis of the ICP algorithm, with an application to the k-means method. *SIAM Journal on Computing*, **39**(2), 766–782.

Arthur, David, Manthey, Bodo, and Röglin, Heiko. 2011. Smoothed analysis of the k-means method. *Journal of the ACM*, **58**(5).

Chandra, Barun, Karloff, Howard, and Tovey, Craig. 1999. New results on the old k-opt algorithm for the traveling salesman problem. *SIAM Journal on Computing*, **28**(6), 1998–2029.

Elsässer, Robert, and Tscheuschner, Tobias. 2011. Settling the complexity of local max-cut (almost) completely. In *Proceedings of the 38th International Colloqium on Automata, Languages and Programming (ICALP)*. Lecture Notes in Computer Science, vol. 6755. Springer.

Englert, Matthias, Röglin, Heiko, and Vöcking, Berthold. 2014. Worst case and probabilistic analysis of the 2-opt algorithm for the TSP. *Algorithmica*, **68**(1), 190–264.

Englert, Matthias, Röglin, Heiko, and Vöcking, Berthold. 2016. Smoothed analysis of the 2-opt algorithm for the general TSP. *ACM Transactions on Algorithms*, **13**(1), 10:1–10:15.

Etscheid, Michael, and Röglin, Heiko. 2017. Smoothed analysis of local search for the maximum-cut problem. ACM Transactions on Algorithms, **13**(2), 25:1–25:12.

Inaba, Mary, Katoh, Naoki, and Imai, Hiroshi. 2000. Variance-based k-clustering algorithms by Voronoi diagrams and randomization. *IEICE Transactions on Information and Systems*, **E83-D**(6), 1199–1206.

Johnson, David S., and McGeoch, Lyle A. 1997. The traveling salesman problem: A case study. In Emile Aarts and Jan Karel Lenstra (eds), *Local Search in Combinatorial Optimization*. John Wiley & Sons.

Johnson, David S., and McGeoch, Lyle A. 2002. Experimental analysis of heuristics for the STSP. In Gregory Gutin and Abraham P. Punnen (eds.), *The Traveling Salesman Problem and Its Variations*, pp. 215–310. Kluwer Academic Publishers.

Künnemann, Marvin, and Manthey, Bodo. 2015. Towards understanding the smoothed approximation ratio of the 2-opt heuristic. *Proceedings of the 42nd International Colloquium on Automata, Languages and Programming (ICALP)*, pp. 369–443. Lecture Notes in Computer Science, vol. 9134. Springer.

Manthey, Bodo, and Röglin, Heiko. 2013. Worst-case and smoothed analysis of k-means clustering with Bregman Divergences. *Journal of Computational Geometry*, **4**(1), 94–132.

Manthey, Bodo, and Veenstra, Rianne. 2013. Smoothed analysis of the 2-opt heuristic for the TSP: Polynomial bounds for Gaussian noise. *Proceedings of the 24th Annual International Symposium on Algorithms and Computation (ISAAC)*. Lecture Notes in Computer Science, vol. 8283. Springer.

Rhee, WanSoo T. 1993. A matching problem and subadditive Euclidean functionals. *The Annals of Applied Probability*, **3**(3), 794–801.

Röglin, Heiko, and Schmidt, Melanie. 2018. *Randomized Algorithms and Probabilistic Analysis*. Technical Report, University of Bonn.

Schäffer, Alejandro A., and Yannakakis, Mihalis. 1991. Simple local search problems that are hard to solve. *SIAM Journal on Computing*, **20**(1), 56–87.

Spielman, Daniel A., and Teng, Shang-Hua. 2004. Smoothed analysis of algorithms: Why the simplex algorithm usually takes polynomial time. *Journal of the ACM*, **51**(3), 385–463.

Vattani, Andrea. 2011. k-Means requires exponentially many iterations even in the plane. *Discrete and Computational Geometry*, **45**(4), 596–616.

Yukich, Joseph E. 1998. *Probability Theory of Classical Euclidean Optimization Problems*. Lecture Notes in Mathematics, vol. 1675. Springer.

Exercises

Exercise 13.1 Consider the following probabilistic model for the TSP: given a finite set V of n vertices, the distance $d(u, v)$ between any $u, v \in V$ is drawn independently and uniformly at random from the interval $[0, 1]$.

Prove that the expected number of iterations that the 2-opt heuristic needs on such instances is at most $O(n^6 \log n)$.

Exercise 13.2 In the analysis of the 2-opt heuristic and the k-means method, we have restricted ourselves to "reasonably small" σ and claimed that this does not pose any severe restriction. Justify this by showing that the smoothed number of iterations for both algorithms is monotonically decreasing in σ.

More formally, let $T(n, \sigma)$ denote the smoothed number of iterations of either local search algorithm on instances of n points perturbed by Gaussians of standard deviation σ. Show that $T(n, \sigma)$ is nonincreasing in σ.

Exercise 13.3 Let $X \subseteq \mathbb{R}^2$ be a set of n points in the Euclidean plane and let Y be a perturbation of X as described in Section 13.2.2.

Prove that $\mathbb{E}(\text{TSP}(Y)) = \Omega(\sigma \cdot \sqrt{n})$.

[*Hint:* For any $y \in Y$, estimate the distance to a closest neighbor of y in $Y \setminus \{y\}$.]

Exercise 13.4 Prove Lemma 13.10.

Exercise 13.5 Prove Lemma 13.11.

Exercise 13.6 Prove the following stronger version of Lemma 13.16: the length of every epoch is bounded by 3.

Exercise 13.7 Consider the following variant of the k-means method, which we call "lazy k-means": in every iteration, only one point is reassigned to a new cluster. Ties are broken arbitrarily. After reassigning a single point, the two cluster centers involved are adjusted.

Show that the smoothed running time of lazy k-means is bounded by a polynomial in n and $1/\sigma$, without any exponential dependency on d or k.

[Hint: Consider epochs and adjust the concept of η-coarseness appropriately. In order to avoid a factor of 2^k, you have to use the result of Exercise 13.6.]

Exercise 13.8 For the approximation ratio of the k-means method, we consider the ratio of objective value of the worst local optimum divided by objective value of a global optimum.

(a) Give a simple instance that shows that the approximation ratio of the k-means method cannot be bounded by a constant.

(b) Let $\sigma \ll 1$. Show that the smoothed approximation ratio of k-means is not $o(1/\sigma^2)$. Here, smoothed approximation ratio refers again to the expected ratio of the worst local optimum to a global optimum.

Exercise 13.9 For graphs with maximum degree $O(\log n)$, proving a smoothed polynomial bound for the flip heuristic for Max-Cut is much easier than for general graphs.

For a graph $G = (V, E)$, let Δ be the maximal degree of G, let $n = |V|$, and let $m = |E|$. Let $\phi \geq 1$, and let $f_e : [0, 1] \to [0, \phi]$ be a density function for $e \in E$. Let w_e be drawn according to f_e. We consider the flip heuristic for Max-Cut on the instance (G, w). Let $\delta_{\min}$ be the smallest possible improvement caused by any possible iteration of the flip heuristic. Let T be the maximum number of iterations that the flip heuristic needs on the instance (G, w).

(a) Prove that $\mathbb{P}(\delta_{\min} \leq \varepsilon) \leq 2^\Delta n\phi\varepsilon$.

(b) Prove that $\mathbb{P}(T \geq t) \leq 2^\Delta nm\phi/t$ for all $t \in \mathbb{N}$ with $t \geq 1$.

(c) Prove that $\mathbb{E}(T) = O(2^\Delta n^2 m\phi)$.

CHAPTER FOURTEEN

Smoothed Analysis of the Simplex Method

Daniel Dadush and Sophie Huiberts

Abstract: In this chapter, we give a technical overview of smoothed analyses of the shadow vertex simplex method for linear programming. We first review the properties of the shadow vertex simplex method and its associated geometry. We begin the smoothed analysis discussion with an analysis of the successive shortest path algorithm for the minimum-cost maximum-flow problem under objective perturbations, a classical instantiation of the shadow vertex simplex method. Then we move to general linear programming and give an analysis of a shadow vertex based algorithm for linear programming under Gaussian constraint perturbations.

14.1 Introduction

We recall that a linear program (LP) in n variables and m constraints is of the form

$$\max c^{\mathsf{T}} x \qquad (14.1)$$
$$Ax \le b,$$

where $x \in \mathbb{R}^n$ are the decision variables. The data of the LP are the objective $c \in \mathbb{R}^n$, the constraint matrix $A \in \mathbb{R}^{m \times n}$, and the corresponding right-hand side vector $b \in \mathbb{R}^m$. We shall refer to $P = \{x \in \mathbb{R}^n : Ax \le b\}$ as the feasible polyhedron. Throughout the chapter, we will assume that the reader is familiar with the basics of linear programming and polyhedral theory (the reader may consult the excellent book by Matousek and Gärtner (2007) for a reference).

The simplex method, introduced by Dantzig in 1947, is the first procedure developed for algorithmically solving LPs. It is a class of local search based LP algorithms, which solve LPs by moving from vertex to vertex along edges of the feasible polyhedron until an optimal solution or unbounded ray is found. The methods differ by the rule they use for choosing the next vertex to move to, known as the pivot rule. Three popular pivot rules are Dantzig's rule, which chooses the edge for which the objective gain per unit of slack is maximized (with respect to the current tight constraints), and Goldfarb's steepest edge rule together with its approximate cousin, Harris' Devex rule, which chooses the edge whose angle to the objective is minimized.

Organization In Section 14.2, we give a detailed overview the shadow vertex simplex method and its associated geometry. In Section 14.3, we analyze the successive shortest path algorithm for minimum-cost maximum-flow under objective perturbations. In Section 14.4, we give an analysis for general LPs under Gaussian constraint perturbations.

14.2 The Shadow Vertex Simplex Method

The shadow vertex simplex algorithm is a simplex method that, given two objectives c, d and an initial vertex v maximizing c, computes a path corresponding to vertices that are optimal (maximizing) for any intermediary objective $\lambda c + (1 - \lambda)d, \lambda \in [0, 1]$.

While the shadow vertex rule is not generally used in practice, e.g., the steepest descent rule is empirically far more efficient, it is much easier to analyze from the theoretical perspective, as it admits a tractable characterization of the vertices it visits. Namely, a vertex can be visited only if it optimizes an objective between c and d, which can be checked by solving an LP.

In what follows, we overview the main properties of the shadow vertex simplex method together with how to implement it algorithmically. For this purpose, we will need the following definitions.

Definition 14.1 (Optimal Face) For $P \subseteq \mathbb{R}^n$ a polyhedron and $c \in \mathbb{R}^n$, define $P[c] := \{x \in P : c^\mathsf{T} x = \sup_{z \in P} c^\mathsf{T} z\}$ to be the face of P maximizing c. If $\sup_{z \in P} c^\mathsf{T} z = \infty$, then $P[c] = \emptyset$ and we say that P is unbounded w.r.t. c.

Note that, in this notation, if $P[c] = P[d] \neq \emptyset$, for $d \in \mathbb{R}^n$, then $P[c] = P[\lambda c + (1 - \lambda)d]$ for all $\lambda \in [0, 1]$.

Definition 14.2 (Tangent Cone) Let $P = \{x \in \mathbb{R}^n : Ax \leq b\}$, $A \in \mathbb{R}^{m \times n}$, $b \in \mathbb{R}^m$, be a polyhedron. For $x \in P$, define $\mathrm{tight}_P(x) = \{i \in [m] : a_i^\mathsf{T} x = b_i\}$ to be the tight constraints at x. The tangent cone at x w.r.t. P is $T_P(x) := \{w \in \mathbb{R}^n : \exists \varepsilon > 0 \text{ s.t. } x + \varepsilon w \in P\}$, the set of movement directions around x in P. In terms of the inequality representation, $T_P(x) := \{w \in \mathbb{R}^n : A_B w \leq 0\}$ where $B = \mathrm{tight}_P(x)$.

The Structure of the Shadow Path The following lemma provides the general structure of any shadow path, which will generically induce a valid simplex path.

Lemma 14.3 (Shadow Path) *Let $P \subseteq \mathbb{R}^n$ be a polyhedron and $c, d \in \mathbb{R}^n$. Then there exists a unique sequence of faces $P(c, d) := (v_0, e_1, v_1, \ldots, e_k, v_k)$ of P, $k \geq 0$, known as the shadow path of P w.r.t. (c, d), and scalars $0 = \lambda_0 < \lambda_1 < \cdots < \lambda_k < \lambda_{k+1} = 1$ such that*

1. *For all $1 \leq i \leq k$, we have $e_i = P[(1 - \lambda_i)c + \lambda_i d] \neq \emptyset$, and moreover $e_1, \ldots, e_k$ are distinct faces of P.*
2. *For all $0 \leq i \leq k$ and $\lambda \in (\lambda_i, \lambda_{i+1})$, $v_i = P[(1 - \lambda)c + \lambda d]$.*
3. *For all $0 < i < k$, the faces satisfy $v_i = e_i \cap e_{i+1} \neq \emptyset$, and if $k \geq 1$ then $v_0 \subset e_1$ and $v_k \subset e_k$.*

Furthermore, the first face is $v_0 = P[c][d]$, the face of $P[c]$ maximizing d, and the last face is $v_k = P[d][c]$. For every $i \in [k]$, we have $v_{i-1} = e_i[c] = e_i[-d]$ and $v_i = e_i[-c] = e_i[d]$.

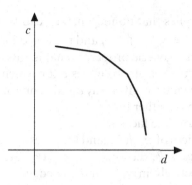

Figure 14.1 In (c, d) space, a shadow path starts at the highest vertex and moves to the rightmost vertex if it exists.

Note that, as a set, the shadow path $P(c, d)$ exactly corresponds to the set of faces $\{P[(1 - \lambda)c + \lambda d] : \lambda \in (0, 1)\}$ optimizing an objective in (c, d). Lemma 14.3 shows that these faces have a useful connectivity structure that we will exploit algorithmically.

Definition 14.4 (Shadow Path Properties) Given a polyhedron P, $c, d \in \mathbb{R}^n$, letting $P(c, d) = (v_0, e_1, v_1, \ldots, e_k, v_k)$, we use $P_V(c, d)$ to denote the subsequence of nonempty faces of $(v_0, v_1, \ldots, v_k)$ and $P_E(c, d) = (e_1, e_2, \ldots, e_k)$. We call each face $F \in P(c, d)$ a shadow face. We define the shadow path $P(c, d)$ to be nondegenerate if $\dim(v_0) \leq 0$ and $e_1, \ldots, e_k$ are edges of P. Note that this automatically enforces that $v_1, \ldots, v_{k-1}$ are vertices of P and that $\dim(v_k) \leq 0$. We say that $P(c, d)$ is proper if $P[c][d] \neq \emptyset$.

We are interested in the case when shadow paths are proper and nondegenerate. For a proper nondegenerate path $P(c, d) = (v_0, \ldots, e_k, v_k)$, the set $v_0 \cup \cup_{i=1}^{k} e_i$ is a connected polygonal path that begins at the vertex $v_0 = P[c][d]$ and follows edges of P, and thus forms a valid simplex path. The final face v_k will be nonempty iff P is bounded w.r.t. d. In this case, $v_k = P[d][c]$ is the vertex of $P[d]$ maximizing c. If $v_k = \emptyset$, then e_k will be an unbounded edge of the form $e_k = v_{k-1} + [0, \infty) \cdot w_k$ for which $w_k^\mathsf{T} d > 0$, yielding a certificate of the unboundedness of P w.r.t. d.

A useful way to interpret the shadow path is via a 2-dimensional projection induced by c, d. We index this projection by $\pi_{c,d}$, where $\pi_{c,d}(z) := (d^\mathsf{T} z, c^\mathsf{T} z)$, and define $e_x := (1, 0), e_y := (0, 1)$ to be the generators of the x- and y- axes in $\mathbb{R}^2$ respectively. Under this map, the faces of the shadow path trace a path along the upper hull of $\pi_{c,d}(P)$. The projection interpretation is the reason why Borgwardt (1977) called the parametric objective method the shadow vertex simplex method (*schatteneckenalgoritmus*), which is the most common name for it today.

Lemma 14.5 *Let P be a polyhedron, $c, d \in \mathbb{R}^n$. For $P(c, d) = (v_0, e_1, v_1, \ldots, e_k, v_k)$, the shadow path satisfies $\pi_{c,d}(P)(e_y, e_x) = (\pi_{c,d}(v_0), \ldots, \pi_{c,d}(e_k), \pi_{c,d}(v_k))$. Furthermore, the shadow path $\pi_{c,d}(P)(e_y, e_x)$ is nondegenerate and $P(c, d)$ is nondegenerate iff $\dim(v_0) = \dim(\pi_{c,d}(v_0))$ and $\dim(e_i) = \dim(\pi_{c,d}(e_i)) = 1$ for all $i \in [k]$.*

311

Lemma 14.5 in fact implies that nondegeneracy can be restated as requiring $\pi_{c,d}$ to be a bijection between $S = v_0 \cup \bigcup_{i=1}^{k} e_i$ and its projection $\pi_{c,d}(S)$. Nondegeneracy of a shadow path is in fact a generic property. That is, given any pointed polyhedron $P \subseteq \mathbb{R}^n$ and objective d, the set of objectives c for which $P(c,d)$ is degenerate has measure 0 in $\mathbb{R}^n$. As a consequence, given any c and d, one may achieve nondegeneracy by infinitessimally perturbing either c or d.

Under the $\pi_{c,d}$ projection, the faces $v_0, \ldots, v_k$, except possibly v_0, v_k which may be empty, always map to vertices of $\pi_{c,d}(P)$, and the faces $e_1, \ldots, e_k$ always map to edges of $\pi_{c,d}(P)$. Assuming $v_0, v_k \neq \emptyset$, then $\pi_{c,d}(v_0), \pi_{c,d}(v_k)$ are the vertices of maximum y and x coordinate respectively in $\pi_{c,d}$, and the edges $\pi_{c,d}(e_1), \ldots, \pi_{c,d}(e_k)$ follow the upper hull of $\pi_{c,d}(P)$ between $\pi_{c,d}(v_0)$ and $\pi_{c,d}(v_k)$ from left to right. In this view, one can interpret the multipliers $\lambda_1 < \cdots < \lambda_k \in (0,1)$ from Lemma 14.3 in terms of the slopes of $e_1, \ldots, e_k$ under $\pi_{c,d}$. Precisely, if we define the c,d slope $s_{c,d}(e_i) := c^\top(x_1 - x_0)/d^\top(x_1 - x_0)$, $i \in [k]$, where $x_1, x_0 \in e_i$ are any two points with $d^\top x_1 \neq d^\top x_0$, then $s_{c,d}(e_i) = -\lambda_i/(1 - \lambda_i)$. This follows directly from the fact that the objective $(1 - \lambda_i)c + \lambda_i d$, $\lambda_i \in (0,1)$, is constant on e_i. From this, we also see that $0 > s_{c,d}(e_1) > \cdots > s_{c,d}(e_k)$, i.e., the slopes are negative and strictly decreasing.

The Shadow Vertex Simplex Algorithm A shadow vertex pivot, i.e., a move across an edge of P, will correspond to moving in a direction of largest (c,d) slope from the current vertex. Computing these directions will be achieved by solving linear programs over the tangent cones. In the context of the successive shortest path algorithm, these LPs are solved via a shortest path computation, while in the Gaussian constraint perturbation model, they are solved explicitly by computing the extreme rays of the tangent cone. An abstract implementation of the shadow vertex simplex method is provided in Algorithm 1. While there is technically freedom in the choice of the maximizer on line 3, under nondegeneracy the solution will in fact be unique. We state the main guarantees of the following algorithm.

Theorem 14.6 *Algorithm 1 is correct and finite. On input $P, c, d, v_0 \in P[c][d] \neq \emptyset$, the vertex–edge sequence $v_0, e_1, v_1, \ldots, e_k, v_k$ computed by the algorithm visits every face of $P(c,d)$ and the computed multipliers $\lambda_1, \ldots, \lambda_k \in (0,1)$ form a nondecreasing sequence that satisfies $e_i \subseteq P[(1 - \lambda_i)c + \lambda_i d]$ for every $i \in [k]$. If $P(c,d)$ is nondegenerate, then $(v_0, e_1, v_1, \ldots, e_k, v_k) = P(c,d)$. Furthermore, the number of simplex pivots performed is then $|P_E(c,d)|$, and the complexity of the algorithm is that of solving $|P_V(c,d)|$ tangent cone programs.*

In regard to slopes, the value of the program on line 3 equals the (c,d)-slope $s_{c,d}(e_{i+1})$.

While Algorithm 1 still works in the presence of degeneracy, one can no longer characterize the number of pivots by $|P_E(c,d)|$, though this always remains a lower bound. This is because it may take multiple pivots to cross a single face of $P_E(c,d)$, or equivalently, there can be a consecutive block $[i,j]$ of iterations where $\lambda_i = \cdots = \lambda_j$.

As is evident from the theorem and the algorithm, the complexity of each iteration depends on the difficulty of solving the tangent cone programs on line 3. One instance in which this is easy, is when the inequality system is *nondegenerate*.

Algorithm 1 The shadow vertex simplex algorithm

Require: $P = \{x \in \mathbb{R}^n : Ax \le b\}$, $c, d \in \mathbb{R}^n$, initial vertex $v_0 \in P[c][d] \ne \emptyset$.
Ensure: Return vertex of $P[d][c]$ if non-empty or $e \in \text{edges}(P)$ unbounded w.r.t. d.

  1: $i \leftarrow 0$
  2: **loop**
  3:    $w_{i+1} \leftarrow$ vertex of $\operatorname{argmax}\{c^\mathsf{T} w : w \in T_P(v_i), d^\mathsf{T} w = 1\}$ or $\emptyset$ if infeasible
  4:    **if** $w_{i+1} = \emptyset$ **then**
  5:       **return** v_i
  6:    **end if**
  7:    $\lambda_{i+1} \leftarrow -w_{i+1}^\mathsf{T} c / (1 - w_{i+1}^\mathsf{T} c)$
  8:    $s_{i+1} \leftarrow \sup\{s \ge 0 : v_i + s w_{i+1} \in P\}$
  9:    $e_{i+1} \leftarrow v_{i+1} + [0, s_{i+1}] \cdot w_{i+1}$
10:    $i \leftarrow i + 1$
11:    **if** $s_i = \infty$ **then**
12:       $v_i \leftarrow \emptyset$
13:       **return** e_i
14:    **else**
15:       $v_i \leftarrow v_{i-1} + s_i w_i$
16:    **end if**
17: **end loop**

Definition 14.7 (Nondegenerate Inequality System) We say that the system $Ax \le b$, $A \in \mathbb{R}^{m \times n}$, $b \in \mathbb{R}^m$, $m \ge n$, describing a polyhedron P is *nondegenerate* if P is pointed and if for every vertex $v \in P$ the set $\text{tight}_P(v)$ is a *basis* of A.

When the description of P is clear, we say that P is nondegenerate to mean that its describing system is. We call $B \subseteq [m]$, $|B| = n$, a *basis* of A if A_B, the submatrix corresponding to the rows in B, is invertible. A basis B is feasible if $A_B^{-1} b_B$ is a vertex of P. For a nondegenerate polyhedron P and $v \in \text{vertices}(P)$, the extreme rays of the tangent cone at v are simple to compute. More precisely, letting $B = \text{tight}_P(v)$ denote the basis for v, the extreme rays of the tangent cone $T_P(v)$ are generated by the columns of $-A_B^{-1}$. Knowing this explicit description of the extreme rays of $T_P(v)$, the program on line 3 is easy to solve because w_{i+1} is always a scalar multiple of a generator of an extreme ray.

The Shadow Plane and the Polar In the previous subsection, we examined the shadow path $P(c, d)$ induced by two objectives, c, d. This is enough for the result we prove in Section 14.3. For the sake of Section 14.4, we generalize the shadow path slightly by examining the shadow on the plane $W = \text{span}(c, d)$. Letting π_W denote the orthogonal projection onto W, we will work with $\pi_W(P)$, the shadow of P on W. This will be useful to capture somewhat more global shadow properties. In particular, it will allow us to relate to the geometry of the corresponding polar, and allow us to get bounds on the lengths of shadow paths having knowledge of W, but not of the exact objectives $c, d \in W$ whose shadow path we will follow.

313

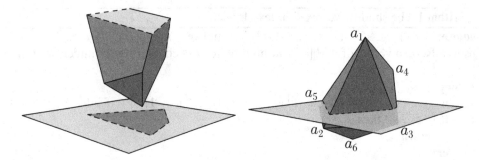

Figure 14.2 On the left, we see a polyhedron P projected on a plane W. The boundary of the projection uniquely lifts into the polyhedron. On the right, we see the corresponding polar polytope $Q = P^\circ$ with the intersection $Q \cap W$ marked. Every facet of Q intersected by W is intersected through its relative interior.

Definition 14.8 (Shadow on W) Let $P \subseteq \mathbb{R}^n$ be a polyhedron and let $W \subseteq \mathbb{R}^n$ be a 2-dimensional linear subspace. We define the shadow faces of P w.r.t. W by $P[W] = \{P[c] : c \in W \setminus \{0\}\}$, that is the set of faces of P optimizing a nonzero objective in W. Let $P_V[W], P_E[W]$ denote the set of faces in $P[W]$ projecting to vertices and edges of $\pi_W(P)$ respectively. We define $P[W]$ to be nondegenerate if every face $F \in P[W]$ satisfies $\dim(F) = \dim(\pi_W(F))$.

The following lemma provides the straightforward relations between shadow paths on W and the number of vertices of $\pi_W(P)$.

Lemma 14.9 *Let $P \subseteq \mathbb{R}^n$ be a polyhedron, $W \subseteq \mathbb{R}^n$, $\dim(W) = 2$. Then for $c, d \in W$, if the path $P(c,d)$ is nondegenerate and proper, then the number of pivots performed by Algorithm 1 on input $P, c, d, P[c][d]$ is bounded by $|P_V[W]| = |\mathrm{vertices}(\pi_W(P))|$. Furthermore, if $P[W]$ is nondegenerate and $\mathrm{span}(c,d) = W$, then $P(c,d)$ is nondegenerate.*

Moving to the polar view, we assume that we start with a polyhedron of the form $P = \{x \in \mathbb{R}^n : Ax \leq 1\}$. Define the polar polytope as $Q = \mathrm{conv}(a_1, \ldots, a_m)$, where $a_1, \ldots, a_m$ are the rows of the constraint matrix A. We use a slightly different definition of the polar polytope than is common. The standard definition takes the polar to be

$$P^\circ := \{y \in \mathbb{R}^n : y^\mathsf{T} x \leq 1, \forall x \in P\} = \mathrm{conv}(Q, 0).$$

We have $P^\circ \neq Q$ exactly when P is unbounded. We depict a polyhedron and its polar polytope in Figure 14.2.

The following lemma, which follows from relatively standard polyhedral duality arguments, tells us that one can control the vertex count of the shadow using the corresponding slice of the polar. It provides the key geometric quantity we will bound in Section 14.4. Proving the lemma is Exercise 14.2.

Lemma 14.10 *Let $P = \{x \in \mathbb{R}^n : Ax \leq 1\}$ be a polyhedron with a nondegenerate shadow on W and Q its polar polytope. Then*

$$|\mathrm{vertices}(\pi_W(P))| \leq |\mathrm{edges}(Q \cap W)|.$$

If P is bounded then the inequality is tight.

14.3 The Successive Shortest Path Algorithm

In this section, we will study the classical successive shortest path (SSP) algorithm for the minimum-cost maximum-flow problem under objective perturbations.

The Flow Polytope Given a directed graph $G = (V, E)$ with source $s \in V$ and sink $t \in V$, a vector of positive arc capacities $u \in \mathbb{R}_+^E$, and a vector of arc costs $c \in (0, 1)^E$, we want to find a flow $f \in \mathbb{R}_+^E$ satisfying

$$\sum_{ij \in E} f_{ij} - \sum_{ji \in E} f_{ji} = 0, \forall i \in V \setminus \{s, t\} \tag{14.2}$$

$$0 \leq f_{ij} \leq u_{ij}, \forall ij \in E$$

that maximizes the amount of flow shipped from s to t, and among such flows minimizes the cost $c^\mathsf{T} f$. We denote the set of feasible flows, that is, those satisfying (14.2), by P.

For simplicity of notation in what follows, we assume that G does not have bidirected arcs, that is E contains at most one of any pair $\{ij, ji\}$. To make the identification with the shadow vertex simplex method easiest, we consider only the case in which every shortest s–t path is unique.

The SSP Algorithm We now describe the algorithm. For this purpose, we introduce some notation. Letting $\overleftarrow{ij} = ji$, we define the reverse arcs $\overleftarrow{E} := \{ji : ij \in E\}$, and extend c to $\overleftarrow{E}$ by letting $c_{ji} = -c_{ij}$ for $ji \in \overleftarrow{E}$. For $w \in \{-1, 0, 1\}^E$, we define its associated subgraph $R = \{a \in E : w_a = 1\} \cup \{\overleftarrow{a} : a \in E, w_a = -1\}$ and vice versa, noting that $c^\mathsf{T} w = \sum_{a \in R} c_a$. Given a feasible flow $f \in P$, the *residual graph* $N[f]$ has the same node set V and arc set $A[f] = F[f] \cup R[f] \cup B[f]$, where $F[f] = \{a \in E : f_a = 0\}$, $R[f] = \{\overleftarrow{a} : a \in E : f_a = u_a\}$, $B[f] = \{a, \overleftarrow{a} : a \in E, 0 < f_a < u_a\}$ are called forward, reverse, and bidirected arcs w.r.t. f respectively. The combinatorial description of the SSP algorithm is:

1. Initialize f to 0 on E.
2. While $N[f]$ contains an s-t path: compute a shortest s-t path R in $N[f]$ with respect to the costs c with associated vector $w_R \in \{-1, 0, 1\}^E$. Augment f along R until a capacity constraint becomes tight, that, is update $f \leftarrow f + s_R w_R$ where $s_R = \max\{s \geq 0 : f + s_R w_R \in P\}$. Repeat.
3. Return f.

We recall that a shortest s–t path is well defined if and only if $N[f]$ does not contain negative cost cycles.

For the SSP algorithm to take many iterations to find the optimum solution, the difference between the path lengths in each iteration should be very small. As long as the costs are not adversarially chosen, it seems unlikely that this should happen. That is what we formalize and prove in the remainder of this chapter.

The SSP as Shadow Vertex We now show that the SSP algorithm corresponds to running the shadow vertex simplex algorithm on P applied to the starting objective being $-c$ and the target objective d being the flow from s to t, that is $d^\mathsf{T} f := \sum_{sj \in E} f_{sj}$. This correspondence will also show correctness of the SSP.

To see the link to the shadow vertex simplex algorithm, we reinterpret prior observations polyhedrally. Firstly, it is direct to check that the face $P[d]$ is the set of maximum s–t flows. In particular, the maximum-flow of minimum cost is then $P[d][-c]$. Since the arc costs are positive on E, any nonzero flow $f \in P$ must incur positive cost. Therefore, the zero flow is the unique cost minimizer, that is, $\{0\} = P[-c] = P[-c][d]$. Thus, by Theorem 14.6, one can run the shadow vertex simplex algorithm on the flow polytope P, objectives $-c, d$ and starting vertex 0 and get a vertex $v \in P[d][-c]$ as output.

To complete the identification, one need only show that the tangent cone LPs correspond to shortest s–t path computations. This is a consequence of the following lemma, whose proof is left as Exercise 14.3.

Lemma 14.11 *For $f \in P$ with residual graph $N[f]$, the following hold:*

1. *The tangent cone can be explicitly described using flow conservation and tight capacity constraints as $T_P(f) := \{w \in \mathbb{R}^A : \sum_{ij \in A} w_{ij} - \sum_{ji \in A} w_{ji} = 0 \ \forall i \in V \setminus \{s, t\}, w_a \geq 0 \ \forall a \in F[f], w_a \leq 0 \ \forall a \in R[f]\}$.*

2. *If $N[f]$ does not contain negative cost cycles, then any vertex solution to the program $\inf\{c^\mathsf{T} w : w \in T_P(f), d^\mathsf{T} w = \delta\}$, $\delta \in \{\pm 1\}$ corresponds to a minimum-cost s-t path for $\delta = 1$ and t-s path for $\delta = -1$, which by convention has cost ∞ if no such path exists.*

3. *If f is a shadow vertex and the shadow path is nondegenerate, the value of the above program for $\delta = 1$ equals the slope $s_{c,d}(e)$ of the shadow edge e leaving f and the value of the program for $\delta = -1$ equals the slope $s_{c,d}(e')$ of the shadow edge e' entering f.*

It will be useful to note here that since we interpolate from $-c$, that is minimizing cost, the shadow $P(-c, d)$ will in fact follow edges of the lower hull of $\pi_{c,d}(P)$ from left to right. In particular, the (c, d) slopes (cost per unit of flow) of the corresponding edges will all be positive and form an increasing sequence. The (c, d) slope of a shadow edge is always equal to the cost of some s–t path $\overleftrightarrow{E}$. Since any such path uses at most $n - 1$ edges of cost between $(-1, 1)$, the slope of any shadow edge is strictly less than $n - 1$, which will be crucial to the analysis in the next section. By the correspondence of slopes with multipliers, the slope bound implies the rather strong property that any maximizer of $-c + \frac{n-1}{n}d$ in P, is already on the optimal face $P[d][-c]$.

14.3.1 Smoothed Analysis of the SSP

As shown by Zadeh (1973), there are inputs where the SSP algorithm requires an exponential number of iterations to converge. In what follows, we explain the main result of Brunsch et al. (2015), which shows that exponential behavior can be remedied by slightly perturbing the edge costs.

The perturbation model is known as the one-step model, which is a general model where we only control the support and maximum density of the perturbations. Precisely, each edge cost c_e will be a continuous random variable supported on $(0, 1)$, whose maximum density is upper bounded by a parameter $\phi \geq 1$. The upper bound on ϕ is equivalent to the statement that for any interval $[a,b] \subseteq [0,1]$, the inequality $\Pr[c_e \in [a,b]] \leq \phi|b-a|$, known as the interval lemma, holds. Note that as $\phi \to \infty$, the cost vector c can concentrate on a single vector and thus converge to a worst-case instance. The main result of this section is as follows.

Theorem 14.12 (Brunsch et al., 2015) *Let $G = (V,E)$ be a graph with n nodes and m arcs, a source $s \in V$ and sink $t \in V$, and positive capacities $u \in \mathbb{R}_+^E$. Then for a random cost vector $c \in (0,1)^E$ with independent coordinates having maximum density $\phi \geq 1$, the expected number of iterations of the SSP algorithm on G is bounded by $O(mn\phi)$.*

As with many smoothed analysis results, we want to quantify some form of "expected progress" per iteration, and the difficulty lies in identifying enough "independent randomness" such that not all randomness is used up in the first iteration.

To prove the theorem, we will upper bound the expected number of edges on the random shadow path followed by the SSP. The main idea will be to bound the expected number of times an arc of G can used by the s–t paths found by the SSP algorithm.

For the analysis, we maintain the notation from the previous section together with the following definitions. For $f \in P$, we identify the tight constraints $\text{tight}_P(f)$ with arcs in $\overleftrightarrow{E}$, namely $a \in \text{tight}_P(f)$ iff $a \in E$ and $f_{ij} = 0$ or $a \in \overleftarrow{E}$ and $f_{ij} = u_{ij}$. Similarly, we define $P_a = \{f \in P : a \in \text{tight}_P(f)\}$. To identify (c,d) slopes, for any $f \in P$, we use $p_{s,t}(f), p_{t,s}(f) \in \mathbb{R} \cup \{\pm\infty\}$ to denote the cost of the shortest s–t and t–s path in $N[f]$. Similarly, for $a \in \overleftrightarrow{E}$, we use $p_{s,t}^{a\pm}(f), p_{t,s}^{a\pm}(f)$ to denote the corresponding minimum-cost paths not using arc a (superscript $a-$) and using arc a (superscript $a+$).

Proof of Theorem 14.12 To prove the theorem, we show that $\mathbb{E}_c[|P_E(-c,d)|]$, the expected shadow vertex count, is bounded by $O(mn\phi)$. Since the cost vector c is generic, the shadow path $P(-c,d)$ is nondegenerate with probability 1. By Theorem 14.6, this will establish the desired bound on the number of shadow vertex pivots.

Let $(v_0, e_1, v_1, \ldots, e_k, v_k)$ denote the random shadow path $P(-c,d)$, and similarly for $a \in \overleftrightarrow{E}$, let $(v_0^a, e_1^a, v_1^a, \ldots, e_{k_a}^a, v_{k_a}^a)$ be the shadow path $P_a(-c,d)$, which we may assume to be nondegenerate with probability 1. Note that since P is a polytope, each shadow path is either $\emptyset$ (if the corresponding facet is infeasible) or contains no empty faces. By the natural extension of Lemma 14.11 to facets of P, we have that for $a \in \overleftrightarrow{E}$ and $i \in [k_a]$, the (c,d) slope of edge e_i^a is equal to $s_{c,d}(e_i^a) = p_{s,t}^{a-}(v_{i-1}^a) = -p_{t,s}^{a-}(v_i^a)$, i.e., the corresponding shortest path length restricted to not using arc a.

Since each vertex $v_{i-1} \subset e_i$, $i \in [k]$, is contained in its outgoing edge, there must exist a tight constraint $a \in \text{tight}_P(v_{i-1})$ such that $a \notin \text{tight}_P(e_i)$. This yields the following direct inequality:

$$|P_E(-c,d)| = \sum_{i=1}^{k} 1 \leq \sum_{a \in \overleftrightarrow{E}} \sum_{i=1}^{k} 1[a \in \text{tight}_P(v_i), a \notin \text{tight}_P(e_i)]. \qquad (14.3)$$

Fixing $a \in \overleftrightarrow{E}$, we now show that the corresponding term in (14.3) is bounded on expectation over c by $O(n\phi)$. For $i \in [k]$, since the (c,d) slope satisfies $s_{c,d}(e_i) = p_{s,t}(v_{i-1})$, we know that $a \in \mathrm{tight}_P(v_{i-1}) \setminus \mathrm{tight}_P(e_i)$ implies that the minimum-cost s-t path in $N[v_i]$ uses arc a. In particular, $p_{s,t}(v_{i-1}) = p_{s,t}^{a+}(v_{i-1})$. Since $-p_{t,s}(v_{i-1})$ is the (c,d) slope of the incoming edge at v_{i-1}, by the increasing property of slopes we also have the inequality $-p_{t,s}(v_{i-1}) \le p_{s,t}^{a+}(v_{i-1})$. Putting this information together,

$$\sum_{i=1}^{k} \mathbb{1}[a \in \mathrm{tight}_P(v_{i-1}), a \notin \mathrm{tight}_P(e_i)]$$

$$\le \sum_{i=0}^{k-1} \mathbb{1}[a \in \mathrm{tight}_P(v_i), -p_{t,s}(v_i) \le p_{s,t}^{a+}(v_i) \le p_{s,t}(v_i)]$$

$$\le \sum_{i=0}^{k-1} \mathbb{1}[a \in \mathrm{tight}_P(v_i), -p_{t,s}^{a-}(v_i) \le p_{s,t}^{a+}(v_i) \le p_{s,t}^{a-}(v_i)],$$

where last inequality follows from the trivial inequalities $p_{s,t}^{a-}(v_i) \ge p_{s,t}(v_i)$ and $p_{t,s}^{a-}(v_i) \ge p_{t,s}(v_i)$. We now make the link to the shadow of P_a. Since v_i is a shadow face in $P(-c,d)$, $a \in \mathrm{tight}_P(v_i)$ implies that v_i is also a shadow face of $P_a(-c,d)$. By this containment and the characterization of edge slopes in $P_a(-c,d)$ as shortest path lengths, we have that

$$\sum_{i=0}^{k-1} \mathbb{1}[a \in \mathrm{tight}_P(v_i), -p_{t,s}^{a-}(v_i) \le p_{s,t}^{a+}(v_i) \le p_{s,t}^{a-}(v_i)]$$

$$= \sum_{i=0}^{k-1} \mathbb{1}[v_i \in P_a(-c,d), -p_{t,s}^{a-}(v_i) \le p_{s,t}^{a+}(v_i) \le p_{s,t}^{a-}(v_i)]$$

$$\le \sum_{i=0}^{k_a} \mathbb{1}[-p_{t,s}^{a-}(v_i^a) \le p_{s,t}^{a+}(v_i^a) \le p_{s,t}^{a-}(v_i^a)]$$

$$\le 2 + \sum_{i=1}^{k_a-1} \mathbb{1}[s_{c,d}(e_i^a) \le p_{s,t}^{a+}(v_i^a) \le s_{c,d}(e_{i+1}^a)].$$

We may now usefully take an expectation with respect to c_a. The crucial observation here is that by independence of the components of c, the shadow path $P_a(-c,d)$ is independent of the cost c_a, noting that the flow along arc a is fixed in P_a. Furthermore, expressing $a = pq \in \overleftrightarrow{E}$, we may usefully decompose $p_{s,t}^{a+}(v_i^a) = c_a + r_{s,t}^{a+}(v_i^a)$, where $r_{s,t}^{a+}(v_i^a)$ is the sum of the cost of the shortest s-p and q-t paths in $N[v_i^a]$. Noting that $N[v_i^a]$ does not contain $\overleftarrow{a}$, we see that $r_{s,t}^{a+}(v_i^a)$ is clearly independent of c_a. Using that edge slopes satisfy $0 < s_{c,d}(e_1^a) < \cdots < s_{c,d}(e_{k_a}^a) \le n-1$, where the last inequality follows as before

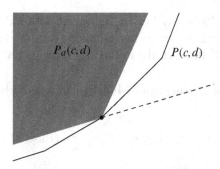

Figure 14.3 Any vertex of $P(c, d)$ is a vertex of some $P_a(c, d)$, and the outgoing edge on $P(c, d)$ has slope between the slopes of the adjacent edges of $P_a(c, d)$.

by the correspondence with s–t path lengths, together with the interval lemma, we bound the expectation as follows:

$$\mathbb{E}_{c_a}\left[\sum_{i=1}^{k_a-1} 1[s_{c,d}(e_i^a) \le p_{s,t}^{a+}(v_i^a) \le s_{c,d}(e_{i+1}^a)]\right]$$

$$= \sum_{i=1}^{k_a-1} \Pr_{c_a}[c_a + r_{s,t}^{a+}(v_i^a) \in [s_{c,d}(e_i^a), s_{c,d}(e_{i+1}^a)]]$$

$$\le \sum_{i=1}^{k_a-1} \phi\left(s_{c,d}(e_{i+1}^a) - s_{c,d}(e_i^a)\right)$$

$$= \phi\left(s_{c,d}(e_{k_a}^a) - s_{c,d}(e_1^a)\right) \le (n-1)\phi.$$

Putting it all together, using that $|\overleftrightarrow{E}| = 2m$, we derive the desired expected bound

$$\mathbb{E}_c[|P_E(-c, d)|] \le \sum_{a \in \overleftrightarrow{E}} \mathbb{E}_c\left[\sum_{i=1}^{k} 1[a \in \text{tight}_P(v_{i-1}), a \notin \text{tight}_P(e_i)]\right]$$

$$\le 4m + \sum_{a \in \overleftrightarrow{E}} \mathbb{E}_c\left[\sum_{i=1}^{k_a-1} 1[s_{c,d}(e_i^a) \le p_{s,t}^{a+}(v_i^a) \le s_{c,d}(e_{i+1}^a)]\right]$$

$$\le 4m + 2m\phi(n-1) = O(mn\phi). \qquad \square$$

14.4 LPs with Gaussian Constraints

The Gaussian constraint perturbation model in this section was the first smoothed complexity model to be studied and was introduced by Spielman and Teng (2004). While not entirely realistic, since it does not preserve for example the sparsity structure seen in most real-world LPs, it does show that the worst-case behavior of the simplex method is very brittle. Namely, it shows that a shadow vertex simplex method efficiently solves most LPs in any big enough neighborhood around a base LP. At a very high level, this because an average shadow vertex pivot covers a significant fraction of the "distance" between the initial and target objective.

The Gaussian Constraint Perturbation Model In this perturbation model, we start with any base LP

$$\max c^{\mathsf{T}}x, \ \bar{A}x \le \bar{b}, \qquad \text{(Base LP)}$$

$\bar{A} \in \mathbb{R}^{m \times n}, \bar{b} \in \mathbb{R}^m, c \in \mathbb{R}^n \setminus \{0\}$, where the rows of $(\bar{A}, \bar{b})$ are normalized to have ℓ_2 norm at most 1. From the base LP, we generate the smoothed LP by adding Gaussian perturbations to both the constraint matrix $\bar{A}$ and the right-hand side $\bar{b}$. Precisely, the data of the smoothed LP are $A = \bar{A} + \hat{A}, b = \bar{b} + \hat{b}$, and c, where the perturbations $\hat{A}, \hat{b}$ have i.i.d. mean 0, variance σ^2 Gaussian entries. The goal is to solve

$$\max c^{\mathsf{T}}x, \ Ax \le b. \qquad \text{(Smoothed LP)}$$

Note that we do not need to perturb the objective in this model, though we do require that $c \ne 0$. The base LP data must be normalized for this definition to make sense, since otherwise one could scale the base LP data up to make the effective perturbation negligible.

As noted earlier, the strength of the shadow vertex simplex algorithm lies in it being easy to characterize whether a basis is visited given the starting and final objective vectors. There is no dependence on decisions made in previous pivot steps. To preserve this independence, we have to be careful with how we find our initial vertex and objective. On the one hand, if we start out knowing a feasible basis $B \subset [m]$ of the smoothed LP, we cannot just set $d = \sum_{i \in B} a_i$, where $a_1, \ldots, a_m$ denote the rows of A. This would cause the shadow plane span(c, d) to depend on A and make our calculations rather more difficult. On the other hand, we cannot choose our starting objective d independently of A, b and find the vertex optimizing it, because that is the very problem that we aim to solve. We resolve this by analyzing the expected shadow vertex count on a plane that is independent of A, b and designing an algorithm that uses the shadow vertex simplex method as a subroutine only on objectives that lie inside such prespecified planes.

Smoothed Unit LPs As a further simplification of the probabilistic analysis, we restrict our shadow bounds to LPs with right-hand side equal to 1 and only A perturbed with Gaussian noise:

$$\max c^{\mathsf{T}}x, \ Ax \le 1. \qquad \text{(Smoothed Unit LP)}$$

This assumption guarantees that 0 is a feasible solution. In the rest of this subsection, we reduce solving (Smoothed LP) to solving (Smoothed Unit LP) and show how to solve (Smoothed Unit LP).

The next theorem is the central technical result of this section and will be proven in subsection 14.4.2. The bound carries over to the expected number of pivot steps of the shadow vertex simplex method on a smoothed unit LP with c, d in a fixed plane using Lemma 14.9 and Lemma 14.10.

Theorem 14.13 *Let $W \subset \mathbb{R}^n$ be a fixed 2-dimensional subspace, $m \geq n \geq 3$ and let $a_1, \ldots, a_m \in \mathbb{R}^n$ be independent Gaussian random vectors with variance σ^2 and expectations of norm at most 1. Then the expected number of edges is bounded by*

$$\mathbb{E}[|\text{edges}(\text{conv}(a_1, \ldots, a_m) \cap W)|]$$
$$= O(n^2 \sqrt{\ln m} \, \sigma^{-2} + n^{2.5} \ln m \, \sigma^{-1} + n^{2.5} \ln^{1.5} m).$$

The linear programs we solve and their shadows are nondegenerate with probability 1, so Theorem 14.13 will also bound the expected number of pivot steps of a run of the shadow vertex simplex method.

First, we describe an algorithm that builds on this shadow path length bound to solve general smoothed LPs. After that, we will sketch the proof of Theorem 14.13.

Two-Phase Interpolation Method Given data A, b, c, define the Phase I Unit LP:

$$\max c^\mathsf{T} x \qquad\qquad \text{(Phase I Unit LP)}$$
$$Ax \leq 1$$

and the Phase II interpolation LP with parametric objective for $\gamma \in (-\infty, \infty)$

$$\max c^\mathsf{T} x + \gamma \lambda \qquad\qquad \text{(Int. LP)}$$
$$Ax + (1 - b)\lambda \leq 1$$
$$0 \leq \lambda \leq 1.$$

We claim that, if we can solve smoothed unit LPs, then we can use the pair (Phase I Unit LP) and (Int. LP) to solve general smoothed LPs.

Writing P for the feasible set of (Int. LP) and e_λ for the basis vector in the direction of increasing λ, the optimal solution to (Phase I Unit LP) corresponds to $P[-e_\lambda][c]$. Assuming that (Smoothed LP) is feasible, its optimal solution corresponds to $P[e_\lambda][c]$. Both (Phase I Unit LP) and (Int. LP) are unit LPs. We first describe how to solve (Smoothed LP) given a solution to (Phase I Unit LP).

If (Smoothed LP) is unbounded (i.e., the system $c^\mathsf{T} x > 0, Ax \leq 0$ is feasible), this will be detected during Phase I as (Unit LP) is also unbounded.

Let us assume for the moment that (Smoothed LP) is bounded and feasible (i.e., has an optimal solution). We can start the shadow vertex simplex method from the vertex $P[-e_\lambda][c]$ at objective $\gamma e_\lambda + c$, for some $\gamma < 0$ small enough, and move to maximize e_λ to find $P[e_\lambda][c]$.

If (Smoothed LP) is infeasible but bounded, then the shadow vertex run will terminate at a vertex having $\lambda < 1$. Thus, all cases can be detected by the two-phase procedure.

We bound the number of pivot steps taken to solve (Int. LP) given a solution to (Unit LP), and after that we describe how to solve (Unit LP).

Consider polyhedron $P' = \{(x, \lambda) \in \mathbb{R}^{n+1} : Ax + (1 - b)\lambda \leq 1\}$, the slab $H = \{(x, \lambda) \in \mathbb{R}^{d+1} : 0 \leq \lambda \leq 1\}$ and let $W = \text{span}(c, e_\lambda)$. In this notation, $P = P' \cap H$ is the feasible set of (Int. LP) and W is the shadow plane of (Int. LP). We bound the number of vertices in the shadow $\pi_W(P)$ of (Int. LP) by relating it to $\pi_W(P')$.

The constraint matrix of P' is $(A, 1 - b)$, so the rows are Gaussian distributed with variance σ^2 and means of norm at most 2. After rescaling by a factor 2 we satisfy all the conditions for Theorem 14.13 to apply.

Since the shadow plane contains the normal vector e_λ to the inequalities $0 \le \lambda \le 1$, these constraints intersect the shadow plane W at right angles. It follows that $\pi_W(P' \cap H) = \pi_W(P') \cap H$. Adding two constraints to a 2D polyhedron can add at most two new edges, hence the constraints on λ can add at most four new vertices. By combining these observations, we directly derive the following lemma.

Lemma 14.14 *If (Unit LP) is unbounded, then (Smoothed LP) is unbounded. If (Unit LP) is bounded, then given an optimal solution to (Unit LP) one can solve (Smoothed LP) using an expected $O(n^2 \sqrt{\ln m}\, \sigma^{-2} + n^{2.5} \ln m\, \sigma^{-1} + n^{2.5} \ln^{1.5} m)$ shadow vertex simplex pivots over (Int. LP).*

Given the Lemma 14.14, our main task is now to solve (Unit LP), i.e., either to find an optimal solution or to determine unboundedness. The simplest algorithm that can operate using only predetermined shadow planes is Borgwardt's dimension-by-dimension (DD) algorithm.

DD Algorithm The DD algorithm solves Unit LP by iteratively solving the restrictions:

$$\max\ {c^k}^\mathsf{T} x \qquad \text{(Unit LP}_k\text{)}$$
$$Ax \le 1$$
$$x_i = 0,\ \forall i \in \{k+1, \ldots, n\},$$

where $k \in \{1, \ldots, n\}$ and $c^k := (c_1, \ldots, c_k, 0, \ldots, 0)$. We assume that $c_1 \neq 0$ without loss of generality. The crucial observation in this context is that the optimal vertex v^* of (Unit LP$_k$), $k \in \{1, \ldots, n-1\}$, is generically on an edge w^* of the shadow of (Unit LP$_{k+1}$) with respect to c^k and e_{k+1}. To initialize the (Unit LP$_{k+1}$) solve, we move to a vertex v_0 of the edge w^* and compute an objective $d \in \text{span}(c^k, e_{k+1})$ uniquely maximized by v_0. Noting that $c^{k+1} \in \text{span}(c^k, e_{k+1})$, we then solve (Unit LP$_{k+1}$) by running the shadow vertex simplex method from v_0 with starting objective d and target objective c^{k+1}.

We note that Borgwardt's algorithm can be applied to any LP with a known feasible point as long as appropriate nondegeneracy conditions hold (which occur with probability 1 for smoothed LPs). Furthermore, (Unit LP$_1$) is trivial to solve, since the feasible region is an interval whose endpoints are straightforward to compute. By combining these arguments, we get the following theorem.

Theorem 14.15 *Let S_k, $k \in \{2, \ldots, n\}$, denote the shadow of (Unit LP$_k$) on $W_k = \text{span}(c_{k-1}, e_k)$. Then, if each (Unit LP$_k$) and shadow S_k is nondegenerate for $k \in \{2, \ldots, n\}$, the DD algorithm solves (Unit LP) using at most $\sum_{k=2}^n |\text{vertices}(S_k)|$ number of pivots.*

To bound the number of vertices of S_k, we first observe that the feasible set of (Unit LP$_k$) does not depend on coordinates $k+1, \ldots, n$ of the constraints vectors. Ignoring those, it is clear that there is an equivalent unit LP to (Unit LP$_k$) in just k variables. This equivalent unit LP has Gaussian distributed rows with variance σ^2 and means of norm at most 1.

Using Theorem 14.15 with the shadow bounds in Theorem 14.13, for $k \geq 3$, and Theorem 14.18 (proven in Section 14.4.1), for $k = 2$, we get the following complexity estimate for solving (Smoothed Unit LP).

Corollary 14.16 *The program (Smoothed Unit LP) can be solved by the DD algorithm using an expected number of shadow vertex pivots bounded by*

$$\sum_{k=2}^{n} \mathbb{E}[|\text{edges}(\text{conv}(a_1, \ldots, a_m) \cap W_k)|]$$

$$= O(n^3 \sqrt{\ln m}\, \sigma^{-2} + n^{3.5} \sigma^{-1} \ln m + n^{3.5} \ln^{3/2} m).$$

14.4.1 The Shadow Bound in Two Dimensions

As a warm-up before the proof sketch of Theorem 14.13, we look at the easier 2-dimensional case. We bound the expected complexity of the convex hull of Gaussian perturbed points. The proof is much simpler than the shadow bound in higher dimensions but it contains many of the key insights we need.

First, we state a simple lemma. Proving this lemma is Exercise 14.4.

Lemma 14.17 *Let $X \in \mathbb{R}$ be a random variable with $\mathbb{E}[X] = \mu$ and $\text{Var}(X) = \tau^2$. Then X satisfies*

$$\frac{\mathbb{E}[X^2]}{\mathbb{E}[|X|]} \geq (|\mu| + \tau)/2.$$

Theorem 14.18 *For points $a_1, \ldots a_m \in \mathbb{R}^2$ independently Gaussian distributed, each with covariance matrix $\sigma^2 I_2$ and $\|\mathbb{E}[a_i]\| \leq 1$ for all $i \in [m]$, the convex hull $Q := \text{conv}(a_1, \ldots, a_m)$ has $O(\sigma^{-1} + \sqrt{\ln m})$ edges in expectation.*

Proof We will prove that, on average, the edges of Q are long and the perimeter of Q is small. This is sufficient to bound the expected number of edges.

For $i, j \in [m], i \neq j$, let $E_{i,j}$ denote the event that a_i and a_j are the endpoints of an edge of Q. By linearity of expectation we have the following equality:

$$\mathbb{E}[\text{perimeter}(Q)] = \sum_{1 \leq i < j \leq m} \mathbb{E}[\|a_i - a_j\| \mid E_{i,j}] \Pr[E_{i,j}].$$

We lower bound the right-hand side by taking the minimum over all conditional expectations and get

$$\sum_{1 \leq i < j \leq m} \mathbb{E}[\|a_i - a_j\| \mid E_{i,j}] \Pr[E_{i,j}] \geq \min_{k \neq l} \mathbb{E}[\|a_k - a_l\| \mid E_{k,l}] \sum_{1 \leq i < j \leq m} \Pr[E_{i,j}].$$

Dividing on both sides, we can estimate the expected number of edges

$$\mathbb{E}[|\text{edges}(Q)|] = \sum_{1 \leq i < j \leq m} \Pr[E_{i,j}] \leq \frac{\mathbb{E}[\text{perimeter}(Q)]}{\min_{k \neq l} \mathbb{E}[\|a_k - a_l\| \mid E_{k,l}]}. \tag{14.4}$$

We are left to bound the numerator and denominator on the right-hand side. For the first, we observe that Q is convex and thus has perimeter at most that of any containing disc. This yields the bound

$$\mathbb{E}[\text{perimeter}(Q)] \leq \mathbb{E}[2\pi \max_i \|a_i\|] \leq 2\pi(1 + 6\sigma\sqrt{\ln m}), \qquad (14.5)$$

using standard Gaussian tail bounds.

We are left to lower bound the denominator. Fix $k = 1, l = 2$ without loss of generality. The quantity of interest is

$$\mathbb{E}[\|a_1 - a_2\| \mid E_{1,2}] = \frac{\int_{\mathbb{R}^2}\int_{\mathbb{R}^2}\|a_1 - a_2\|\Pr[E_{1,2}]\mu_1(a_1)\mu_2(a_2)\mathrm{d}a_1\mathrm{d}a_2}{\int_{\mathbb{R}^2}\int_{\mathbb{R}^2}\Pr[E_{1,2}]\mu_1(a_1)\mu_2(a_2)\mathrm{d}a_1\mathrm{d}a_2},$$

where μ_i is the probability density of a_i and the probability of $E_{1,2} := E_{1,2}(a_1, \ldots, a_n)$ is taken over the randomness in $a_3, a_4, \ldots, a_m$. To get control on the event $E_{1,2}$, we perform a change of coordinates from $a_1, a_2 \in \mathbb{R}^2$ to $t \in [0, \infty], \theta \in \mathbb{S}^1, h_1, h_2 \in \mathbb{R}$ satisfying

$$a_1 = t\theta + R_\theta(h_1)$$
$$a_2 = t\theta + R_\theta(h_2),$$

where $R_\theta : \mathbb{R} \to \theta^\perp$ is the isometric linear embedding of $\mathbb{R}$ into the linear subspace orthogonal to θ, with $R_\theta(1)$ having positive first coordinate. This transformation is uniquely defined and continuous whenever a_1 and a_2 are linearly independent and θ has nonzero first coordinate, which happens with probability 1. The Jacobian of this transformation is $|h_1 - h_2|$ and we can rewrite the above fraction as

$$\frac{\int_0^\infty \int_{\mathbb{S}^1} \int_{-\infty}^\infty \int_{-\infty}^\infty |h_1 - h_2|^2 \Pr[E_{1,2}]\mu_1(t\theta + R_\theta(h_1))\mu_2(t\theta + R_\theta(h_2))\mathrm{d}h_1\mathrm{d}h_2\mathrm{d}\theta\mathrm{d}t}{\int_0^\infty \int_{\mathbb{S}^1} \int_{-\infty}^\infty \int_{-\infty}^\infty |h_1 - h_2| \Pr[E_{1,2}]\mu_1(t\theta + R_\theta(h_1))\mu_2(t\theta + R_\theta(h_2))\mathrm{d}h_1\mathrm{d}h_2\mathrm{d}\theta\mathrm{d}t}.$$

The event $E_{1,2}$ is equivalent to asking that either $\theta^\mathsf{T} a_i \leq t$ for all $i = 3, 4, \ldots, m$ or $\theta^\mathsf{T} a_i \geq t$ for all $i = 3, 4, \ldots, m$. This makes $E_{1,2}$ a function of only $a_3, \ldots, a_m$ and θ and t, i.e. its value does not depend on h_1, h_2.

Now, we use that $\frac{\int g(p)h(p)\mathrm{d}p}{\int g(p)\mathrm{d}p} \geq \inf_p h(p)$ for any positive integrable g, h and find

$$\mathbb{E}[\|a_1 - a_2\| \mid E_{1,2}]$$
$$\geq \inf_{t,\theta} \frac{\int_{-\infty}^\infty \int_{-\infty}^\infty |h_1 - h_2|^2 \mu_1(t\theta + R_\theta(h_1))\mu_2(t\theta + R_\theta(h_2))\mathrm{d}h_1\mathrm{d}h_2}{\int_{-\infty}^\infty \int_{-\infty}^\infty |h_1 - h_2| \mu_1(t\theta + R_\theta(h_1))\mu_2(t\theta + R_\theta(h_2))\mathrm{d}h_1\mathrm{d}h_2}$$
$$= \inf_{t,\theta} \frac{\int_{-\infty}^\infty z^2 \left(\int_{-\infty}^\infty \mu_1(R_\theta(h_1))\mu_2(R_\theta(h_1 - z))\mathrm{d}h_1\right)\mathrm{d}z}{\int_{-\infty}^\infty |z| \left(\int_{-\infty}^\infty \mu_1(R_\theta(h_1))\mu_2(R_\theta(h_1 - z))\mathrm{d}h_1\right)\mathrm{d}z},$$

substituting $z = h_1 - h_2$ and simplifying. For fixed t, θ, we can reinterpret the last fraction as $\mathbb{E}[Z^2]/\mathbb{E}[|Z|]$ for Z a random variable with probability density proportional to

$$\int_{-\infty}^\infty \mu_1(R_\theta(h_1))\mu_2(R_\theta(h_1 - z))\mathrm{d}h_1.$$

This is the same probability density as that of the difference of two independent Gaussian random variables each of variance σ^2, which means that Z has variance $2\sigma^2$. If we apply Lemma 14.17 to Z, we deduce $\mathbb{E}[\|a_1 - a_2\| \mid E_{1,2}] \geq \sigma/\sqrt{2}$. We conclude that the expected total number of edges is bounded from above by

$$\mathbb{E}[\text{edges}(Q)] \leq 2\pi \frac{1 + 6\sigma\sqrt{\ln m}}{\sigma/\sqrt{2}} \leq 9\sigma^{-1} + 54\sqrt{\ln m}. \qquad \square$$

14.4.2 The Shadow Bound in Higher Dimensions

In this section we sketch the proof of Theorem 14.13. For the remainder of this section, let $a_1, \ldots, a_m \in \mathbb{R}^n$ be independent variance σ^2 Gaussian random vectors, $Q := \text{conv}(a_1, \ldots, a_m)$ and $W \subseteq \mathbb{R}^n$ be a fixed 2D plane.

Our task is to bound $\mathbb{E}[|\text{edges}(Q \cap W)|]$. The strategy will be the same as in Theorem 14.18, namely to relate the perimeter and expected minimum edge length. A first observation is that an edge of $Q \cap W$ w.p. 1 takes the form $\text{conv}(a_i : i \in B) \cap W$, where $B \subseteq [m]$, $|B| = n$, and $\text{conv}(a_i : i \in B)$ is a facet of Q (see Figure 14.2). From here, an identical argument as for (14.4) yields the following edge counting lemma.

Lemma 14.19 *For a basis $B \subseteq [m]$, $|B| = n$, let E_B denote the event that $\text{conv}(a_i : i \in B) \cap W$ is an edge of $Q \cap W$. Then, the following bound holds:*

$$\mathbb{E}[|\text{edges}(Q \cap W)|] \leq \frac{\mathbb{E}[\text{perimeter}(Q \cap W)]}{\min_{B \subseteq [m], |B| = n} \mathbb{E}[\text{length}(\text{conv}(a_i : i \in B) \cap W) \mid E_B]}.$$

The numerator in Lemma 14.19 can be bounded along the same lines as in Theorem 14.18.

Lemma 14.20 $\mathbb{E}[\text{perimeter}(Q \cap W)] \leq \mathbb{E}[\text{perimeter}(\pi_W(Q))] \leq O(1 + \sigma\sqrt{\ln m})$.

We now restrict our attention to lower bounding $\mathbb{E}[\text{length}(\text{conv}(a_i : i \in B) \cap W) \mid E_B]$ for a fixed basis $B \subseteq [m]$, where w.l.o.g. we may assume that $B = \{1, \ldots, n\}$.

Just like we did in the proof of Theorem 14.18, we perform a change of variables. The first part of the new parameterization of $a_1, \ldots, a_n$ consists of their containing affine subspace H, described by $\theta \in \mathbb{S}^{n-1}, t \geq 0$ satisfying

$$\text{aff}(a_1, \ldots, a_n) =: H = \{x \in \mathbb{R}^n : \theta^\mathsf{T} x = t \quad \text{for all } i \in [n]\}.$$

This is depicted in Figure 14.4, with $\text{conv}(a_i : i \in B) \cap W$ marked by the line segment K.

To describe the location of the points inside the hyperplane H, we use a family of orthonormal embeddings $R := R_\theta : \mathbb{R}^{n-1} \to \theta^\perp$, where the points $b_1, \ldots, b_n$ satisfy $t\theta + R_\theta(b_i) = a_i, \forall i \in [n]$. A simple choice for R_θ is $R_\theta(b) := (b, 0) - (e_n + \theta)$ $(\theta^\mathsf{T}(b, 0))/(1 + \theta_n)$, which first sends $b \to (b, 0) \in (e_n)^\perp$ and composes it with the rotation which sends e_n to θ and fixes $\text{span}(e_n, \theta)^\perp$. The properties of this change of variables are given in Theorem 14.21.

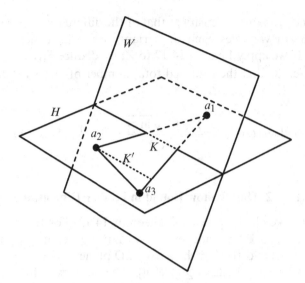

Figure 14.4 The vectors $a_1, \ldots, a_n$ are conditioned for $\mathrm{conv}(a_1, \ldots, a_n)$ to intersect W and lie in H. The short dotted line segment $K = W \cap H \cap \mathrm{conv}(a_1, a_2, a_3)$ is the edge of $Q \cap W$ induced by the basis and the longer dotted line segment K' is the longest chord of the simplex parallel to the line $H \cap W$. We aim to lower bound the expected length of the line segment K.

Theorem 14.21 *The change of variables is well defined with probability 1 and has Jacobian $(n-1)!\,\mathrm{vol}(\mathrm{conv}(b_1, \ldots, b_n))$. If we fix θ, t then the induced probability density function of $b_1, \ldots, b_n$ is proportional to $\mathrm{vol}(\mathrm{conv}(b_1, \ldots, b_n)) \prod_{i=1}^{n} \mu_i(Rb_i)$, where μ_i is the probability density function of a_i for each $i \in [n]$.*

Define the line $\ell \subset \mathbb{R}^{n-1}$ to satisfy $H \cap W = t\theta + R\ell$. In this notation we get $\mathrm{conv}(a_1, \ldots, a_n) \cap W = t\theta + R(\mathrm{conv}(b_1, \ldots, b_n) \cap \ell)$. The event E_B holds when $\theta^\top a_i > t$ for all $i = n+1, \ldots, m$ or $\theta^\top a_i < t$ for all $i = n+1, \ldots, m$ (i.e., $\mathrm{conv}(a_1, \ldots, a_n)$ is a facet of Q), which we denote by $E_{B,f}$, and $\mathrm{conv}(b_i : i \in B) \cap \ell$ has positive length, which we denote by $E_{B,l}$. Just like in the 2-dimensional case, after conditioning on θ, t, the events $E_{B,f}$ and $E_{B,l}$ become independent. In particular, after this conditioning, $E_{B,l}$ only depends on $b_1, \ldots, b_n$ and $E_{B,f}$ is independent of $b_1, \ldots, b_n$.

Given this independence, we may restrict our attention to proving a lower bound on $\mathbb{E}[\mathrm{length}(\mathrm{conv}(b_1, \ldots, b_n) \cap \ell) \mid E_{B,l}]$, where $b_1, \ldots, b_n$ are conditioned on a fixed θ and t. To analyze the expected edge length, we will need the following concepts.

Definition 14.22 Let $\omega \in \mathbb{R}^n$, $\|\omega\|_2 = 1$ and $p \in \omega^\perp$ such that $\ell = p + \mathbb{R}\omega$ and let $\mathcal{L} := \mathrm{conv}(b_i : i \in B) \cap \ell$. For any $q \in \omega^\perp$, define the set of convex combinations

$$C(q) := \left\{ \lambda \in \mathbb{R}_+^n : \sum_{i=1}^{n} \lambda_i = 1, \sum_{i=1}^{n} \lambda_i \pi_\omega^\perp(b_i) = q \right\},$$

whose ℓ_1 diameter we denote by $\|C(q)\|_1$, which is 0 by convention if $C(q) = \emptyset$. Let $\gamma := \|C(p)\|_1$. Define $z \in \mathbb{R}^n$ to be the unique up to sign solution to $\sum_{i=1}^{n} z_i \pi_{\omega^\perp}(b_i) = 0$ with $\|z\|_1 = 1$ (uniqueness holds w.p. 1).

Some preliminary remarks on the above definitions. ω is the direction of the line ℓ and $\{p\} = \pi_{\omega^\perp}(\ell)$ is its intersection with $\omega^\perp$. $\mathcal{L}$ is the tentative edge whose expected length we wish to lower bound. The set $C(q)$, $q \in \omega^\perp$, is a line segment in the direction of z, noting that the difference of any two points in $C(q)$ must be a multiple of z. In particular, if $C(p) \neq \emptyset$, one may express $C(p) = [\lambda_0, \lambda_0 + \gamma z]$, for some convex combination λ_0, where $\gamma := \|C(p)\|_1$ as above. One may equivalently define

$$C(p) = \left\{ \lambda \in \mathbb{R}_+^n : \sum_{i=1}^n \lambda_i = 1, \ \sum_{i=1}^n \lambda_i b_i \in \mathcal{L} \right\},$$

that is, $C(p)$ is the set of convex combination representing the edge $\mathcal{L}$. It is now direct to see that $\mathcal{L}$ has positive length iff $\gamma > 0$, that is, $E_{B,l}$ is equivalent to $\gamma > 0$.

The following lemma, whose proof is Exercise 14.6, encapsulates the properties of $C(q)$ that we will need.

Lemma 14.23 *Let* $y := \sum_{i=1}^n |z_i| \pi_{\omega^\perp}(b_i)$ *and* $h_1 = \omega^\mathsf{T} b_1, \ldots, h_n = \omega^\mathsf{T} b_n$. *Then the following hold:*

1. $\|C(q)\|_1$ *is a nonnegative concave function of* $q \in \mathrm{conv}(\pi_{\omega^\perp}(b_i) : i \in [n])$.
2. $\max_{q \in \mathrm{conv}(\pi_{\omega^\perp}(b_i):i\in[n])} \|C(q)\|_1 = \|C(y)\|_1 = 2$.
3. $\mathrm{length}(\mathcal{L}) = \gamma \left| \sum_{i=1}^n z_i h_i \right|$.

The factors on the right-hand side in the last item of Lemma 14.23 have identifiable meanings. The sum $2\left|\sum_{i=1}^n z_i h_i\right|$ is the length of the longest chord of $\mathrm{conv}(b_1, \ldots, b_n)$ parallel to ℓ. In Figure 14.4, this longest chord is represented by the line segment K'. It is the analogue of $h_1 - h_2$ from the 2-dimensional case. The remaining term, $\gamma/2$, is the ratio of the length of the edge $\mathcal{L}$ to the length of the longest chord. In Figure 14.4 this is the ratio of the length of the line segment K to the length of the line segment K'. We note that this term has no analogue in 2 dimensions and so lower bounding it will require new ideas. We can now lower bound the expected length of $\mathcal{L}$ as follows:

$$\mathbb{E}\left[\gamma \left| \sum_{i=1}^n z_i h_i \right| \ \Big| \ \gamma > 0 \right] \geq \mathbb{E}[\gamma \mid \gamma > 0] \inf_{\pi_{\omega^\perp}(b_i):i\in[n]} \mathbb{E}\left[\left| \sum_{i=1}^n z_i h_i \right| \ \Big| \ \pi_{\omega^\perp}(b_i) : i \in [n] \right],$$

$$(14.6)$$

noting that $(\pi_{\omega^\perp}(b_i) : i \in [n])$ determine z and γ.

We first lower bound the latter term, the expected maximum chord length, for which we will need the induced probability density on $h_1, \ldots, h_n$. This is given by the following lemma, whose proof is a straightforward manipulation of the Jacobian in Theorem 14.21.

Lemma 14.24 *For any fixed values of the projections* $\pi_{\omega^\perp}(b_1), \ldots, \pi_{\omega^\perp}(b_n)$, *the inner products* $h_1, \ldots, h_n$ *have joint probability density proportional to*

$$\left| \sum_{i=1}^n z_i h_i \right| \prod_{i=1}^n \mu_i(R(h_i\omega)).$$

Using Lemma 14.24 and an analoguous argument to that in Theorem 14.18, we can express $\mathbb{E}\big[|\sum_{i=1}^{n} z_i h_i| \mid \pi_{\omega^\perp}(b_i) : i \in [n]\big]$ as the ratio $\mathbb{E}[(\sum_{i=1}^{n} z_i x_i)^2]/\mathbb{E}[|\sum_{i=1}^{n} z_i x_i|]$, where $x_1, \ldots, x_n$ are independent and each x_i is distributed according to $\mu_i(R(x_i\omega))$. Since $\sum_{i=1}^{n} z_i x_i$ has variance $\sigma^2 \|z\|_2^2 \geq \sigma^2 \|z\|_1^2/n = \sigma^2/n$, we may apply Lemma 14.17 to deduce the following lower bound.

Lemma 14.25 *Fixing* $\pi_{\omega^\perp}(b_1), \ldots, \pi_{\omega^\perp}(b_n)$, *we have* $\mathbb{E}[|\sum_{i=1}^{n} z_i h_i|] \geq \sigma/(2\sqrt{n})$.

The remaining task is to lower bound $\mathbb{E}[\gamma \mid \gamma > 0]$. This will require a number of new ideas and some simplifying assumptions, which we sketch below.

The main intuitive observation is that $\gamma > 0$ is small essentially only when $p \in \mathrm{conv}(\pi_{\omega^\perp}(b_i) : i \in [n])$ is close to the boundary of the convex hull. To show that this does not happen on average, the main idea will be to show that for any configuration $\pi_{\omega^\perp}(b_1), \ldots, \pi_{\omega^\perp}(b_n)$ for which γ is tiny, there is a nearly equiprobable one for which γ is lower bounded a function of n, m, and σ. Here the move to the improved configuration will correspond to pushing the "center" y of $\mathrm{conv}(\pi_{\omega^\perp}(b_i) : i \in [n])$ toward p, where y is as in Lemma 14.23.

To be able to argue near-equiprobability, we will make the simplifying assumption that the original densities $\mu_1, \ldots, \mu_m$ are L-log-Lipschitz, for $L = \Theta(\sqrt{n \ln m}/\sigma)$, where we recall that $f : \mathbb{R}^n \to \mathbb{R}_+$ is L-log-Lipschitz if $f(x) \leq f(y)e^{L\|x-y\|}$, $\forall x, y$. While a variance σ^2 Gaussian is not *globally* log-Lipschitz, it can be checked that is L-log-Lipschitz within distance $\sigma^2 L$ of its mean. By standard Gaussian tail bounds the probability that any a_i is at distance $\sigma^2 L = \Omega(\sigma\sqrt{n \ln m})$ from its mean is at most $m^{-\Omega(n)}$. Since an event occurring w.p. less than $\binom{m}{n}^{-1}$ contributes at most 1 to $E[|\mathrm{edges}(Q \cap W)|]$, noting that $\binom{m}{n}$ is a deterministic upper bound, it is intuitive that we can assume L-log-Lipschitzness "wherever it matters," though a rigorous proof of this is beyond the scope of this chapter.

Using log-Lipschitzness, we will only be able to argue that close-by configurations are equiprobable. For this to make a noticeable impact on γ, we will need $\pi_{\omega^\perp}(b_1), \ldots, \pi_{\omega^\perp}(b_n)$ to not be too far apart to begin with. For this purpose, we let E_D denote the event that $\max_{i,j} \|\pi_{\omega^\perp}(b_i) - \pi_{\omega^\perp}(b_j)\| \leq D$, for $D = \Theta(1 + \sigma\sqrt{n \ln m})$. It is useful to note that the original $a_1, \ldots, a_m$, which are farther apart, already satisfy this distance requirement w.p. $1 - m^{-\Omega(n)}$ using similar tail bound arguments as above.

With these concepts, we will be able to lower bound $\mathbb{E}[\gamma \mid \gamma > 0, E_D]$ in Lemma 14.26. For this to be useful, we would like

$$\mathbb{E}[\gamma \mid \gamma > 0] \geq \mathbb{E}[\gamma \mid \gamma > 0, E_D]/2. \tag{14.7}$$

While this may not be true in general, the main reason it can fail is if the starting basis B has probability less than $m^{-\Omega(n)}$ of forming an edge to begin with, in which case it can be safely ignored anyway. We henceforth assume inequality (14.7).

Lemma 14.26 *With* $L = \Theta(\sqrt{n \ln m}/\sigma), D = \Theta(1 + \sigma\sqrt{n \ln m})$ *we have that* $\mathbb{E}[\gamma \mid \gamma > 0, E_D] \geq \Omega(\frac{1}{nDL})$.

Proof Sketch Let us start by fixing $s_i := \pi_{\omega^\perp}(b_i) - \pi_{\omega^\perp}(b_1)$ for all $2 \leq i \leq n$, for which the condition $\|s_i\| \leq D$, $\|s_i - s_j\| \leq D$, for all $i, j \in \{2, \ldots, n\}$ holds. Note that this condition is equivalent to E_D. Let $S = \mathrm{conv}(0, s_2, \ldots, s_n)$ denote the resulting shape of the projected convex hull. Let us now additionally fix $h_1, \ldots, h_n$ arbitrarily.

At this point, the only degree of freedom left is in the position of $\pi_{\omega^\perp}(b_1)$. The condition $\gamma > 0$ is now equivalent to $p \in \pi_{\omega^\perp}(b_1) + S \Leftrightarrow \pi_{\omega^\perp}(b_1) \in p - S$. From here, the conditional density μ of $\pi_{\omega^\perp}(b_1)$ satisfies

$$\mu \propto \mu_1(R(\pi_{\omega^\perp}(b_1))) \prod_{i=2}^{n} \mu_i(R(\pi_{\omega^\perp}(b_1) + s_i)),$$

where we note that fixing $h_1, \ldots, h_n, s_2, \ldots, s_n$ makes the Jacobian in Theorem 14.21 constant.

As we mentioned earlier, we assume that $\mu_1, \ldots, \mu_n$ are L-log-Lipschitz everywhere. This makes μ be nL-log-Lipschitz. Since $p - S$ has diameter at most D and γ is a concave function of $\pi_{\omega^\perp}(b_1)$ with maximum 2 by Lemma 14.23, we can use Lemma 14.27 to finish the sketch. $\qquad\square$

The final lemma is Exercise 14.7.

Lemma 14.27 *For a random variable $x \in S \subset \mathbb{R}^n$ having L-log-Lipschitz density supported on a convex set S of diameter D and $f : S \to \mathbb{R}_+$ concave, one has*

$$\mathbb{E}[f(x)] \geq e^{-2} \frac{\max_{y \in S} f(y)}{\max(DL, n)}.$$

Putting together Lemmas 14.19, 14.20, 14.25, 14.26, and inequality 14.7, we get the desired result

$$\mathbb{E}[|\text{edges}(Q \cap W)|] \leq \frac{O(1 + \sigma\sqrt{\ln m})}{\frac{\sigma}{2\sqrt{n}} \cdot \Omega(\frac{1}{nDL})}$$
$$= O(n^2\sigma^{-2}\sqrt{\ln m}(1 + \sigma\sqrt{n \ln m})(1 + \sigma\sqrt{\ln m})).$$

14.5 Discussion

We saw smoothed complexity results for linear programming in two different perturbation models. In the first model, the feasible region was highly structured and "well-conditioned," namely a flow polytope, and only the objective was perturbed. In the second model, the feasible region was a general linear program whose constraint data was perturbed by Gaussians.

While the latter model is the more general, the LPs it generates differ from real-world LPs in many ways. Real-world LPs are often highly degenerate, due to the combinatorial nature of many practical problems, and sparse, typically only 1% of the constraint matrix entries are nonzero. The Gaussian constraint perturbation model has neither of these properties. Second, it is folklore that the number of pivot steps it takes to solve an LP is roughly linear in m or n. At least from the perspective of the shadow vertex simplex method, this provably does not hold for the Gaussian constraint perturbation model. Indeed, Borgwardt (1987) proved that as $m \to \infty$ and n is fixed, the shadow bound for Gaussian unit LPs (where the means are all 0) is $\Theta(n^{1.5}\sqrt{\ln m})$.

There are plenty of concrete open problems in this area. The shadow bound of Theorem 14.13 is likely to be improvable, as it does not match the known $\Theta(n^{1.5}\sqrt{\ln m})$ bound for Gaussian unit LPs mentioned earlier. Already in two dimensions, the correct bound could be much smaller, as discussed in Devillers et al. (2016). In the i.i.d. Gaussian case, the edge counting strategy in Lemma 14.19 is exact, but our lower bound on the expected edge length is much smaller than the true value. In the smoothed case, the edge counting strategy seems too lossy already when $n = 2$.

The proof of Theorem 14.13 also works for any log-Lipschitz probability distribution with sufficiently strong tail bounds. However, nothing is known for distributions with bounded support or distributions that preserve some meaningful structure of the LP, such as most zeroes in the constraint matrix. One difficulty in extending the current proof lies in it considering even very unlikely hyperplanes for the basis vectors to lie in.

In practice the shadow vertex pivot rule is outperformed by the commonly used most-negative reduced cost rule, steepest edge rule, and Devex rule. However, there are currently no theoretical explanations for why these rules would perform well. The analyses discussed here do not extend to such pivot rules, due to making heavy use of the local characterization of whether a given vertex is visited by the algorithm.

We note that a major reason for the popularity of the simplex method is its unparalleled effectiveness at solving sequences of related LPs, where after each solve a column or row may be added or deleted from the current program. In this context, the simplex method is easy to "warm start" from either the primal or dual side, and typically only a few additional pivots solve the new LP. This scenario occurs naturally in the context of integer programming, where one must solve many related LP relaxations within a branch and bound tree or during the iterations of a cutting plane method. Current theoretical analyses of the simplex method don't say anything about this scenario.

14.6 Notes

The shadow vertex simplex method was first introduced by Gass and Saaty (1955) to solve bi-objective linear programming problems and is also known as the parametric simplex algorithm.

Families of LPs on which the shadow vertex simplex method takes an exponential number of steps were constructed by Murty (1980), Goldfarb (1983, 1994), Amenta and Ziegler (1998), and Gärtner et al. (2013). One such construction is the subject of Exercise 14.1. A very interesting construction was given by Disser and Skutella (2018), who gave a flow network on which it is NP-complete to decide whether the SSP algorithm will ever use a given edge. Hence, the shadow vertex simplex algorithm implicitly spends its exponential running time to solve hard problems.

The first probabilistic analysis of the simplex method is due Borgwardt, see (Borgwardt, 1987), who studied the complexity of solving $\max c^\mathsf{T} x, Ax \leq 1$ when the rows of A are sampled from a spherically symmetric distribution. He proved a tight shadow bound of $\Theta(n^2 m^{1/(n-1)})$, which is valid for any such distribution, as well as the tight limit for the Gaussian distribution mentioned earlier. Both of these bounds can be made algorithmic, losing a factor n, using Borgwardt's DD algorithm.

The smoothed analysis of the SSP algorithm is due to Brunsch et al. (2015). They also proved that the running time bound holds for the SSP algorithm as applied to the minimum-cost flow problem, and they showed a nearly matching lower bound.

The first smoothed analysis of the simplex method was by Spielman and Teng (2004), who introduced the concept of smoothed analysis and the perturbation model of Section 14.4. They achieved a bound of $O(n^{55}m^{86}\sigma^{-30} + n^{70}m^{86})$. This bound was subsequently improved by Deshpande and Spielman (2005), Vershynin (2009), Schnalzger (2014), and Dadush and Huiberts (2018).

In this chapter, we used the DD algorithm for the Phase I unit LP, traversing $n - 1$ shadow paths. Another algorithm for solving (Phase I Unit LP), which traverses an expected $O(1)$ shadow paths, can bring the smoothed complexity bound down to $O(n^2\sigma^{-2}\sqrt{\ln m} + n^3 \ln^{3/2} m)$. This procedure, which is a variant of an algorithm of Vershynin (2009), as well as a rigorous proof of Theorem 14.13, can be found in Dadush and Huiberts (2018).

The 2-dimensional convex hull complexity of Gaussian perturbed points from Theorem 14.18 was studied before by Damerow and Sohler (2004), Schnalzger (2014), and Devillers et al. (2016). The best general bound among them is $O(\sqrt{\ln n} + \sigma^{-1}\sqrt{\ln n})$, asymptotically slightly worse than the bound in Theorem 14.18.

The DD algorithm was first used for smoothed analysis by Schnalzger (2014). The edge counting strategy based on the perimeter and minimum edge length is due to Kelner and Spielman (2006). They proved that an algorithm based on the shadow vertex simplex method can solve linear programs in weakly polynomial time. The two-phase interpolation method used here was first introduced and analyzed in the context of smoothed analysis by Vershynin (2009). The coordinate transformation in Theorem 14.21 is called a Blaschke–Petkantschin identity. It is a standard tool in the study of random convex hulls.

The number of pivot steps in practice is surveyed by Shamir (1987). More recent experiments such as Makhorin (2017) remain bounded by a small linear function of $n + m$, though a slightly super-linear function better fits the data according to Andrei (2004).

References

Amenta, Nina, and Ziegler, Günter M. 1998. Deformed products and maximal shadows. *Contemporary Mathematics*, **223**, 57–90.

Andrei, Neculai. 2004. On the complexity of MINOS package for linear programming. *Studies in Informatics and Control*, **13**(1), 35–46.

Borgwardt, Karl-Heinz. 1977. *Untersuchungen zur Asymptotik der mittleren Schrittzahl von Simplexverfahren in der linearen Optimierung*. Ph.D. thesis, Universität Kaiserslautern.

Borgwardt, Karl-Heinz. 1987. *The Simplex Method: A Probabilistic Analysis*. Algorithms and Combinatorics: Study and Research Texts, vol. 1. Springer-Verlag.

Brunsch, Tobias, Cornelissen, Kamiel, Manthey, Bodo, Röglin, Heiko, and Rösner, Clemens. 2015. Smoothed analysis of the successive shortest path algorithm. *SIAM Journal on Computing*, **44**(6), 1798–1819. Preliminary version in SODA '13.

Dadush, Daniel, and Huiberts, Sophie. 2018. A friendly smoothed analysis of the simplex method. In *Proceedings of the 50th Annual ACM SIGACT Symposium on Theory of Computing*. ACM, pp. 390–403.

Damerow, Valentina, and Sohler, Christian. 2004. Extreme points under random noise. In *European Symposium on Algorithms*, pp. 264–274. Springer.

Deshpande, Amit, and Spielman, Daniel A. 2005. Improved smoothed analysis of the shadow vertex simplex method. *Proceedings of the 46th Annual IEEE Symposium on Foundations of Computer Science*, pp. 349–356. FOCS '05.

Devillers, Olivier, Glisse, Marc, Goaoc, Xavier, and Thomasse, Rémy. 2016. Smoothed complexity of convex hulls by witnesses and collectors. *Journal of Computational Geometry*, **7**(2), 101–144.

Disser, Yann, and Skutella, Martin. 2018. The simplex algorithm is NP-mighty. *ACM Transactions on Algorithms (TALG)*, **15**(1), 5.

Gärtner, Bernd, Helbling, Christian, Ota, Yoshiki, and Takahashi, Takeru. 2013. Large shadows from sparse inequalities. *arXiv preprint arXiv:1308.2495*.

Gass, Saul, and Saaty, Thomas. 1955. The computational algorithm for the parametric objective function. *Naval Research Logistics Quarterly*, **2**, 39–45.

Goldfarb, Donald. 1983. *Worst case complexity of the shadow vertex simplex algorithm*. Technical report. Columbia University, New York.

Goldfarb, Donald. 1994. *On the Complexity of the Simplex Method*, pp. 25–38. Springer Netherlands.

Kelner, Jonathan A., and Spielman, Daniel A. 2006. A randomized polynomial-time simplex algorithm for linear programming. In *Proceedings of the 38th Annual ACM Symposium on Theory of Computing*, pp. 51–60. STOC '06. ACM, New York.

Makhorin, Andrew. 2017. GLPK (GNU Linear Programming Kit) documentation.

Matousek, Jiri, and Gärtner, Bernd. 2007. *Understanding and Using Linear Programming*. Springer Science+Business Media.

Murty, Katta G. 1980. Computational complexity of parametric linear programming. *Mathematical Programming*, **19**(2), 213–219.

Schnalzger, Emanuel. 2014. *Lineare Optimierung mit dem Schatteneckenalgorithmus im Kontext probabilistischer Analysen*. PhD thesis, Universität Augsburg. Original in German. English translation by K.H. Borgwardt available at www.math.uni-augsburg.de/prof/opt/mitarbeiter/Ehemalige/borgwardt/Downloads/Abschlussarbeiten/Doc_Habil.pdf.

Shamir, Ron. 1987. The efficiency of the simplex method: A survey. *Management Science*, **33**(3), 301–334.

Spielman, Daniel A., and Teng, Shang-Hua. 2004. Smoothed analysis of algorithms: why the simplex algorithm usually takes polynomial time. *Journal of ACM*, **51**(3), 385–463 (electronic).

Vershynin, Roman. 2009. Beyond Hirsch conjecture: walks on random polytopes and smoothed complexity of the simplex method. *SIAM Journal on Computing*, **39**(2), 646–678. Preliminary version in FOCS '06.

Zadeh, Norman. 1973. A bad network problem for the simplex method and other minimum cost flow algorithms. *Mathematical Programming*, **5**, 255–266.

Exercises

Exercise 14.1 In this exercise we show that the projection of an LP can have 2^n vertices on instances with n variables and $2n$ constraints. The Goldfarb cube in dimension n is the LP

$$\max x_n$$
$$0 \le x_1 \le 1$$
$$\alpha x_1 \le x_2 \le 1 - \alpha x_1$$
$$\alpha(x_{k-1} - \beta x_{k-2}) \le x_k \le 1 - \alpha(x_{k-1} - \beta x_{k-2}) \text{ for } 3 \le k \le n,$$

where $\alpha < 1/2$ and $\beta < \alpha/4$.

(a) Prove that the LP has 2^n vertices.
(b) Prove that every vertex is optimal for some range of linear combinations $\alpha e_{n-1} + \beta e_n$. [Hint: A vertex maximizes an objective if that objective can be written as a nonnegative linear combination of the constraint vectors of tight constraints.]
(c) Show that it follows that the shadow vertex simplex method has worst-case running time exponential in n.
(d) Can you adapt the instance such that the expected shadow vertex count remains exponential when the shadow plane is randomly perturbed?
(e) Define *zero-preserving* perturbations to perturb only the nonzero entries of the constraint matrix. Do the worst-case instances still have shadows with exponentially many vertices after Gaussian zero-preserving perturbations of variance $O(1)$ are applied?

Exercise 14.2 Prove Lemma 14.10. Specifically, show that if a basis $B \subset [m]$ induces the optimal vertex of P for some objective c, then B induces a facet of Q intersecting the ray $c\mathbb{R}_{++}$. Then, prove that this fact implies the lemma.

Exercise 14.3 Prove Lemma 14.11.

Exercise 14.4 Prove Lemma 14.17.

Exercise 14.5 Verify that the Jacobian of the coordinate transformation in Theorem 14.18 is $|h_1 - h_2|$.

Exercise 14.6 Prove Lemma 14.23.

Exercise 14.7 Prove Lemma 14.27. [Hint: Let $y = \mathrm{argmax}_{y \in S} f(y)$ and define $S' := y + \alpha(S - y)$. Prove that $\Pr[x \in S'] \geq e^{-2}$ for $\alpha = 1 - \frac{1}{\max(DL,n)}$, and that $f(x) \geq (1 - \alpha)f(y)$ for all $x \in S'$.]

CHAPTER FIFTEEN

Smoothed Analysis of Pareto Curves in Multiobjective Optimization

Heiko Röglin

Abstract: In a multiobjective optimization problem a solution is called Pareto-optimal if no criterion can be improved without deteriorating at least one of the other criteria. Computing the set of all Pareto-optimal solutions is a common task in multiobjective optimization to filter out unreasonable trade-offs.

For most problems the number of Pareto-optimal solutions increases only moderately with the input size in applications. However, for virtually every multiobjective optimization problem there exist worst-case instances with an exponential number of Pareto-optimal solutions. In order to explain this discrepancy, we analyze a large class of multiobjective optimization problems in the model of smoothed analysis and prove a polynomial bound on the expected number of Pareto-optimal solutions.

We also present algorithms for computing the set of Pareto-optimal solutions for different optimization problems and discuss related results on the smoothed complexity of optimization problems.

15.1 Algorithms for Computing Pareto Curves

Suppose you would like to book a flight to your favorite conference. Your decision is then probably guided by different factors, such as the price, the number of stops, and the arrival time. Usually you won't find a flight that is optimal in every respect and you have to choose the best trade-off. This is characteristic for many decisions faced every day by people, companies, and other economic entities.

The notion of "best trade-off" is hard to formalize and often there is no consensus on how different criteria should be traded off against each other. However, there is little disagreement that in a reasonable outcome no criterion can be improved without deteriorating at least one of the other criteria. Outcomes with this property are called *Pareto-optimal* and they play a crucial role in multicriteria decision making as they help to filter out unreasonable solutions. In this section we discuss algorithms for computing the set of Pareto-optimal solutions for different problems.

15.1.1 Knapsack Problem

The *knapsack problem* is a well-known *NP*-hard optimization problem. An instance of this problem consists of a set of items, each with a profit and a weight, and a capacity. The goal is to find a subset of the items that maximizes the total profit among all subsets whose total weight does not exceed the capacity. Let $p = (p_1, \ldots, p_n)^T \in \mathbb{R}^n_{\geq 0}$ and $w = (w_1, \ldots, w_n)^T \in \mathbb{R}^n_{\geq 0}$ denote the profits and weights, respectively, and let $W \in \mathbb{R}_{\geq 0}$ denote the capacity. Formally the knapsack problem can be stated as follows:

$$
\begin{aligned}
\text{maximize} \quad & p^T x = p_1 x_1 + \cdots + p_n x_n \\
\text{subject to} \quad & w^T x = w_1 x_1 + \cdots + w_n x_n \leq W, \\
& \text{and } x = (x_1, \ldots, x_n)^T \in \{0, 1\}^n.
\end{aligned}
$$

The knapsack problem has attracted a great deal of attention, both in theory and in practice. Theoreticians are interested in the knapsack problem because of its simple structure; it can be expressed as a binary program with one linear objective function and one linear constraint. On the other hand, knapsack-like problems often occur in applications, and practitioners have developed numerous heuristics for solving them. These heuristics work very well on random and real-world instances and they usually find optimal solutions quickly even for very large instances.

In the following, we assume that an arbitrary instance $\mathcal{I}$ of the knapsack problem is given. We use the term *solution* to refer to a vector $x \in \{0, 1\}^n$, and we say that a solution is *feasible* if $w^T x \leq W$. We say that a solution x *contains item i* if $x_i = 1$ and that it *does not contain item i* if $x_i = 0$.

One naive approach for solving the knapsack problem is to enumerate all feasible solutions and to select the one with maximum profit. This approach is not efficient, as there are typically exponentially many feasible solutions. In order to decrease the number of solutions that have to be considered, we view the knapsack problem as a bicriteria optimization problem and restrict the enumeration to only the Pareto-optimal solutions.

Definition 15.1 A solution y *dominates* a solution x if $p^T y \geq p^T x$ and $w^T y \leq w^T x$, with at least one of these inequalities being strict. A solution x is called *Pareto-optimal* if it is not dominated by any other solution. The *Pareto set* or *Pareto curve* is the set of all Pareto-optimal solutions.

Once the Pareto set is known, the given instance of the knapsack problem can be solved optimally in time linear in the size of this set due to the following observation.

Lemma 15.2 *There always exists an optimal solution that is also Pareto-optimal.*

Proof Take an arbitrary optimal solution x and assume that it is not Pareto-optimal. There cannot be a solution y with $p^T y > p^T x$ and $w^T y \leq w^T x$ because then y would be a better solution than x. Hence, if x is not Pareto-optimal then it is dominated by a solution y with $p^T y = p^T x$ and $w^T y < w^T x$. Then either y is Pareto-optimal or we repeat the argument to find a solution z with $p^T z = p^T y$

and $w^T z < w^T y$. This construction terminates after a finite number of iterations with an optimal solution that is also Pareto-optimal. $\square$

We denote the Pareto set by $\mathcal{P} \subseteq \{0,1\}^n$. It can happen that there are two or more Pareto-optimal solutions with the same profit and the same weight. Then $\mathcal{P}$ is assumed to contain only one of these solutions, which can be chosen arbitrarily. Due to the previous lemma the solution

$$x^\star = \arg\max_{x \in \mathcal{P}} \{p^T x \mid w^T x \leq W\},$$

is an optimal solution of the given instance of the knapsack problem.

In the following we present an algorithm invented by Nemhauser and Ullmann (1969) to compute the Pareto set of a given instance of the knapsack problem. We will refer to this algorithm, which is based on dynamic programming, as the *Nemhauser–Ullmann algorithm*. For each $i \in \{0, 1, \ldots, n\}$ it computes the Pareto set $\mathcal{P}_i$ of the restricted instance $\mathcal{I}_i$ that contains only the first i items of the given instance $\mathcal{I}$. Then $\mathcal{P}_n = \mathcal{P}$ is the set we are looking for. Let

$$\mathcal{S}_i = \{x \in \{0,1\}^n \mid x_{i+1} = \ldots = x_n = 0\}$$

denote the set of solutions that do not contain the items $i + 1, \ldots, n$. Formally, solutions of the instance $\mathcal{I}_i$ are binary vectors of length i. We will, however, represent them as binary vectors of length n from $\mathcal{S}_i$. For a solution $x \in \{0,1\}^n$ and an item $i \in \{1, \ldots, n\}$ we denote by x^{+i} the solution that is obtained by adding item i to solution x:

$$x_j^{+i} = \begin{cases} x_j & \text{if } j \neq i, \\ 1 & \text{if } j = i. \end{cases}$$

Furthermore, for a set $\mathcal{S} \subseteq \{0,1\}^n$ of solutions let

$$\mathcal{S}^{+i} = \{y \in \{0,1\}^n \mid \exists x \in \mathcal{S} : y = x^{+i}\}.$$

If for some $i \in \{1, \ldots, n\}$, the set $\mathcal{P}_{i-1}$ is known then the set $\mathcal{P}_i$ can be computed with the help of the following lemma. For the lemma we assume a consistent tie-breaking between solutions that have the same profit and the same weight. In particular, if $p^T x = p^T y$ and $w^T x = w^T y$ for two solutions x and y and the tie-breaking favors x over y then it should also favor x^{+i} over y^{+i} for any i.

Lemma 15.3 *For every $i \in \{1, \ldots, n\}$, the set $\mathcal{P}_i$ is a subset of $\mathcal{P}_{i-1} \cup \mathcal{P}_{i-1}^{+i}$.*

Proof Let $x \in \mathcal{P}_i$. Based on the value of x_i we distinguish two cases.

First we consider the case $x_i = 0$. We claim that in this case $x \in \mathcal{P}_{i-1}$. Assume for contradiction that $x \notin \mathcal{P}_{i-1}$. Then there exists a solution $y \in \mathcal{P}_{i-1} \subseteq \mathcal{S}_{i-1} \subseteq \mathcal{S}_i$ that dominates x. Since $y \in \mathcal{S}_i$, solution x cannot be Pareto-optimal among the solutions in $\mathcal{S}_i$. Hence, $x \notin \mathcal{P}_i$, contradicting the choice of x.

Now we consider the case $x_i = 1$. We claim that in this case $x \in \mathcal{P}_{i-1}^{+i}$. Since $x \in \mathcal{S}_i$ and $x_i = 1$, there exists a solution $y \in \mathcal{S}_{i-1}$ such that $x = y^{+i}$. We need to show that $y \in \mathcal{P}_{i-1}$. Assume for contradiction that there exists a solution

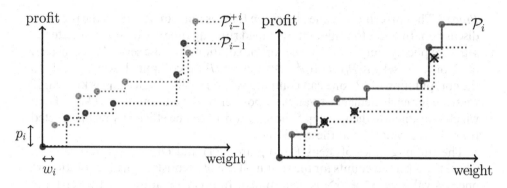

Figure 15.1 Illustration of one iteration of the for-loop of the Nemhauser–Ullmann algorithm: The set $\mathcal{P}_{i-1}^{+i}$ is a copy of the set $\mathcal{P}_{i-1}$ that is shifted by (w_i, p_i). The set $\mathcal{P}_i$ is obtained by removing dominated solutions.

$z \in \mathcal{P}_{i-1}$ that dominates y. Then $p^T z \geq p^T y$ and $w^T z \leq w^T y$ and one of these inequalities is strict. By adding item i to the solutions y and z, we obtain $p^T z^{+i} \geq p^T y^{+i}$ and $w^T z^{+i} \leq w^T y^{+i}$, with one of these inequalities being strict. Hence, the solution z^{+i} dominates the solution $x = y^{+i}$. Since $z^{+i} \in \mathcal{S}_i$, this implies $x \notin \mathcal{P}_i$, contradicting the choice of x. $\qquad\qquad\square$

Due to the previous lemma, the Pareto set $\mathcal{P}_i$ can be computed easily if the Pareto set $\mathcal{P}_{i-1}$ is already known. For this one only needs to compute the set $\mathcal{P}_{i-1} \cup \mathcal{P}_{i-1}^{+i}$ and remove solutions from this set that are dominated by other solutions from this set. Using additionally that $\mathcal{P}_0 = \mathcal{S}_0 = \{0^n\}$, we obtain the following algorithm to solve the knapsack problem optimally (see Figure 15.1 for an illustration).

Algorithm 1 Nemhauser–Ullmann algorithm

1: $\mathcal{P}_0 := \{0^n\}$;
2: **for** $i = 1, \ldots, n$ **do**
3: $\quad \mathcal{Q}_i := \mathcal{P}_{i-1} \cup \mathcal{P}_{i-1}^{+i}$;
4: $\quad \mathcal{P}_i := \{x \in \mathcal{Q}_i \mid \nexists y \in \mathcal{Q}_i : y \text{ dominates } x\}$;
5: **return** $x^\star := \arg\max_{x \in \mathcal{P}_n} \{p^T x \mid w^T x \leq W\}$;

In line 4 a tie-breaking is assumed so that $\mathcal{P}_i$ does never contain two solutions with identical profits and weights.

Observe that all steps of the Nemhauser–Ullmann algorithm except for line 5 are independent of the capacity W. In order to speed up the algorithm, one could remove solutions with weights larger than W already from $\mathcal{Q}_i$ in line 3.

We analyze the running time of the Nemhauser–Ullmann algorithm using the model of a unit-cost RAM. In this model, arithmetic operations such as adding and comparing two numbers can be performed in constant time regardless of their bit-lengths. We use this model for the sake of simplicity and in order to keep the focus on the important details of the running time analysis.

Theorem 15.4 *The Nemhauser–Ullmann algorithm solves the knapsack problem optimally. There exists an implementation with running time $\Theta(\sum_{i=0}^{n-1} |\mathcal{P}_i|)$.*

Proof The correctness of the algorithm follows immediately from the previous discussion. In order to achieve the claimed running time, we do not compute the sets $\mathcal{P}_i$ explicitly, but only the values of the solutions in these sets. That is, instead of $\mathcal{P}_i$ only the set $\mathrm{val}(\mathcal{P}_i) := \{(p^T x, w^T x) \mid x \in \mathcal{P}_i\}$ is computed. Analogously to the computation of $\mathcal{P}_i$, one can compute $\mathrm{val}(\mathcal{P}_i)$ easily if $\mathrm{val}(\mathcal{P}_{i-1})$ is known. If we store for each element of $\mathrm{val}(\mathcal{P}_i)$ a pointer to the element of $\mathrm{val}(\mathcal{P}_{i-1})$ from which it originates, then in step 5 the solution $x^\star$ can be efficiently reconstructed from the sets $\mathrm{val}(\mathcal{P}_i)$ and these pointers.

The running times of steps 1 and 5 are $O(1)$ and $O(n + |\mathcal{P}|)$, respectively, where the term n accounts for the running time of reconstructing the solution $x^\star$ once its value $(p^T x^\star, w^T x^\star)$ is determined. In every iteration i of the for-loop, the running time of step 3 to compute $\mathrm{val}(\mathcal{Q}_i)$ is $\Theta(|\mathcal{P}_{i-1}|)$ because on a unit-cost RAM the set $\mathrm{val}(\mathcal{P}_{i-1}^{+i})$ can be computed in time $\Theta(|\mathcal{P}_{i-1}|)$ from the set $\mathrm{val}(\mathcal{P}_{i-1})$.

In a straightforward implementation, the running time of step 4 is $\Theta(|\mathcal{Q}_i|^2) = \Theta(|\mathcal{P}_{i-1}|^2)$ because we need to compare every pair of values from $\mathrm{val}(\mathcal{Q}_i)$ and each comparison takes time $O(1)$. Step 4 can be implemented more efficiently. For this, we store the values in each set $\mathrm{val}(\mathcal{P}_i)$ sorted in nondecreasing order of weights. If $\mathrm{val}(\mathcal{P}_{i-1})$ is sorted in this way, then, without any additional computational effort, the computation of the set $\mathrm{val}(\mathcal{Q}_i)$ in step 3 can be implemented such that $\mathrm{val}(\mathcal{Q}_i)$ is also sorted: The sorted set $\mathrm{val}(\mathcal{P}_{i-1}^{+i})$ can be computed in time $\Theta(|\mathcal{P}_{i-1}|)$. Then, in order to compute the set $\mathrm{val}(\mathcal{Q}_i)$, only the two sorted sets $\mathrm{val}(\mathcal{P}_{i-1})$ and $\mathrm{val}(\mathcal{P}_{i-1}^{+i})$ need to be merged in time $\Theta(|\mathcal{P}_{i-1}|)$. If the set $\mathrm{val}(\mathcal{Q}_i)$ is sorted, step 4 can be implemented to run in time $\Theta(|\mathcal{Q}_i|)$ as a sweep algorithm going once through $\mathrm{val}(\mathcal{Q}_i)$ in nondecreasing order of weights (see Exercise 15.1). □

Theorem 15.4 ensures that the Nemhauser–Ullmann algorithm solves the knapsack problem efficiently if all Pareto sets $\mathcal{P}_i$ have polynomial size.[1] As the knapsack problem is NP-hard, it is not surprising that there are instances with exponentially many Pareto-optimal solutions. If one sets $p_i = w_i = 2^i$ for each item $i \in \{1, \dots, n\}$ then even every solution from $\{0, 1\}^n$ is Pareto-optimal.

15.1.2 Shortest Path Problem

Shortest path problems often come naturally with multiple objectives. Think for example of automotive navigation systems in which one can usually choose between the shortest, cheapest, and fastest route. Let us consider the *bicriteria single-source shortest path problem*. An instance of this problem is described by a directed graph $G = (V, E)$ with costs $c : E \to \mathbb{R}_{>0}$, weights $w : E \to \mathbb{R}_{>0}$, and a source vertex $s \in V$. The goal is to compute for each $v \in V$ the set $\mathcal{P}^v$ of Pareto-optimal s–v paths according to the following definition.

---

[1] Let us remark that the sizes of the Pareto sets are in general not monotone and there are instances where $|\mathcal{P}_{i+1}| < |\mathcal{P}_i|$ for some i. Hence, it does not suffice if only the Pareto set $\mathcal{P} = \mathcal{P}_n$ has polynomial size. However, we are not aware of any class of instances where $|\mathcal{P}_n|$ is polynomially bounded while $|\mathcal{P}_i|$ is superpolynomial for some i.

Definition 15.5 For an s–v path P we denote by $w(P) = \sum_{e \in P} w(e)$ its weight and by $c(P) = \sum_{e \in P} c(e)$ its costs. An s–v path P_1 *dominates* an s–v path P_2 if $w(P_1) \leq w(P_2)$ and $c(P_1) \leq c(P_2)$, with at least one of these inequalities being strict. An s–v path P is called *Pareto-optimal* if it is not dominated by any other s–v path.

A well-known algorithm for the single-criterion single-source shortest path problem (with only weights but no costs on the edges) is the Bellman–Ford algorithm. It stores a distance label for each vertex which is initially set to infinity for each vertex except the source s for which it is set to zero. Then it performs a sequence of relax operations on the edges as shown in the following pseudocode.

Algorithm 2 Bellman–Ford algorithm

1: $\text{dist}(s) = 0$;
2: **for** $v \in V \setminus \{s\}$ **do** $\text{dist}(v) = \infty$;
3: **for** $i = 1, \dots, |V| - 1$ **do**
4:     **for** each $(u, v) \in E$ **do**
5:         RELAX(u, v);
6: **procedure** RELAX(u, v)
7:     **if** $\text{dist}(v) > \text{dist}(u) + w(u, v)$ **then**
8:         $\text{dist}(v) := \text{dist}(u) + w(u, v)$;

It can be shown that after termination the distance label $\text{dist}(v)$ of each vertex v equals the length of the shortest s–v path in G. By standard methods one can adapt the algorithm so that for each vertex the actual shortest s–v path is computed. One can also easily adapt this algorithm to the bicriteria shortest path problem if one replaces each distance label $\text{dist}(v)$ by a list L_v of s–v paths. Initially L_s contains only the trivial path of length 0 from s to s and all other lists L_v are empty. In every relax operation for an edge (u, v) a new set $L_u^{+(u, v)}$ is obtained from L_u by appending the edge (u, v) to each path from L_u. Then the paths from $L_u^{+(u, v)}$ are added to L_v. Finally L_v is cleaned up by removing all paths from L_v that are dominated by other paths from this list. This is shown in the following pseudocode.

Algorithm 3 Bicriteria Bellman–Ford algorithm

1: $L_s = \{\text{path of length 0 from } s \text{ to } s\}$;
2: **for** $v \in V \setminus \{s\}$ **do** $L_v = \emptyset$;
3: **for** $i = 1, \dots, |V| - 1$ **do**
4:     **for** each $(u, v) \in E$ **do**
5:         RELAX(u, v);
6: **procedure** RELAX(u, v)
7:     Obtain $L_u^{+(u, v)}$ from L_u by appending the edge (u, v) to each path from L_u.
8:     $L_v := L_v \cup L_u^{+(u, v)}$;
9:     Remove dominated paths from L_v.

Analogously to the Nemhauser–Ullmann algorithm, the running time of the bicriteria Bellman–Ford algorithm depends crucially on the sizes of the lists L_v

that appear throughout the algorithm. We have to look at the algorithm in slightly more detail to give an upper bound on its running time. The algorithm performs $M := (|V| - 1) \cdot |E|$ relax operations, which we denote by $R_1, \ldots, R_M$. For a relax operation R_k that relaxes the edge (u, v), we define $u(R_k) = u$ and $v(R_k) = v$. Let $k \in [M]$ and consider the first k relax operations. These define for every vertex $v \in V$ a set S_v^k of s–v paths that can be discovered by the first k relax operations. To be more precise, S_v^k contains exactly those s–v paths that appear as a subsequence in $(u(R_1), v(R_1)), \ldots, (u(R_k), v(R_k))$. In the single-criterion version, after k relax operations the distance label $\text{dist}(v)$ contains the length of the shortest path in S_v^k. In the bicriteria version, the list L_v contains after k relax operations all paths from S_v^k that are Pareto-optimal within this set (i.e., that are not dominated by other paths from this set). We will denote the list L_v after k relax operations by L_v^k in the following.

Theorem 15.6 *After termination of the bicriteria Bellman–Ford algorithm the list L_v equals for every vertex $v \in V$ the set of Pareto-optimal s–v paths. There exists an implementation with running time $\Theta\left(\sum_{k=1}^{M}\left(|L_{u(R_k)}^{k-1}| + |L_{v(R_k)}^{k-1}|\right)\right)$.*

Proof The correctness of the algorithm follows by an inductive argument along the lines of the analysis of the single-criterion version (see Exercise 15.4). The analysis of the running time is similar to the proof of Theorem 15.4. The dominating factor is the time to remove dominated paths from L_v in line 9 of the pseudocode. A naive implementation has running time $\Theta(|L_{u(R_k)}^{k-1}| \cdot |L_{v(R_k)}^{k-1}|)$ for the kth relax operation, while the running time $\Theta(|L_{u(R_k)}^{k-1}| + |L_{v(R_k)}^{k-1}|)$ can be achieved by sweeping through the lists when they are sorted in nondecreasing order of weight. $\square$

While in applications where the bicriteria shortest path problem occurs, it has been observed that the number of Pareto-optimal solutions is usually not very large, one can easily construct instances of the bicriteria shortest path problem in which the number of Pareto-optimal paths is exponential in the size of the graph (see Exercise 15.3).

The reader might wonder why we adapted the Bellman–Ford algorithm and not Dijkstra's algorithm to the bicriteria single-source shortest path problem. Indeed there is a generalization of Dijkstra's algorithm to the bicriteria shortest path problem due to Hansen (1979), which also performs a sequence of operations similar to the relax operations of the Bellman–Ford algorithm. However, in contrast to the Bellman–Ford algorithm the sequence of relax operations is not fixed beforehand but it depends on the actual costs and weights of the edges. For this reason, it is not clear how to analyze the expected running time and in particular the analysis that we present in Section 15.2 does not apply to the generalization of Dijkstra's algorithm.

15.1.3 Multiple Objectives and Other Optimization Problems

For the sake of simplicity, we have discussed only problems with two objectives above. However, one can easily adapt the definition of Pareto-optimal solutions and both presented algorithms to more than two objectives. Consider the multidimensional knapsack problem, a version of the knapsack problem in which every item still has a single profit but instead of a single weight, it has a weight vector from $\mathbb{R}_{\geq 0}^{d-1}$ for some $d \geq 2$, and also the capacity is a vector from $\mathbb{R}_{\geq 0}^{d-1}$. This problem gives rise to a multiobjective optimization problem with d objectives: maximize the profit $p^T x$ and minimize for each $i \in [d-1]$ the ith weight $(w^{(i)})^T x$. Similarly it is often natural to consider multiobjective shortest path problems with more than two objectives.

In order to compute the Pareto set of an instance of the multidimensional knapsack problem or the multiobjective shortest path problem, no modification to the pseudocode of the Nemhauser–Ullmann algorithm (Algorithm 1) and the bicriteria Bellman–Ford algorithm (Algorithm 3) are necessary. However, the implementation and the analysis of the running time have to be adapted. The crucial difference is that the removal of dominated solutions from Q_i and L_v cannot be implemented in time linear in the sizes of these sets anymore because the sweeping approach, which assumes that the solutions are sorted with respect to one of the objectives, fails for more than two objectives. If one uses the naive implementation, which pairwisely compares the solutions, then the running times of the algorithms become $\Theta(\sum_{i=0}^{n-1} |\mathcal{P}_i|^2)$ and $O(\sum_{i=1}^{M} |L_{u(R_i)}^{i-1}| \cdot |L_{v(R_i)}^{i-1}|)$, respectively.

Asymptotically one can do better by using known algorithms for the maximum vector problem to filter out the dominated solutions. In this problem a set of m vectors in $\mathbb{R}^k$ is given and one wants to compute the set of Pareto-optimal vectors among them. The fastest known algorithm for this problem is due to Kung et al. (1975). It relies on divide and conquer and its running time is $O(m \log^{k-2} m)$. For d objectives this yields running times of $\Theta\left(\sum_{i=0}^{n-1} |\mathcal{P}_i| \log^{d-2}(|\mathcal{P}_i|)\right)$ and

$$O\left(\sum_{i=1}^{M} (|L_{u(R_i)}^{i-1}| + |L_{v(R_i)}^{i-1}|) \cdot \log^{d-2}(|L_{u(R_i)}^{i-1}| + |L_{v(R_i)}^{i-1}|)\right)$$

for the Nemhauser–Ullmann algorithm and the Bellman–Ford algorithm, respectively.

The Nemhauser–Ullmann algorithm and the Bicriteria Bellman–Ford algorithm are only two examples of many algorithms in the literature for computing Pareto sets of various multiobjective optimization problems. Similar algorithms exist, for example, for the multiobjective network flow problem. As a rule of thumb, algorithms that solve the single-criterion version of an optimization problem by dynamic programming can usually be adapted to compute the Pareto set of the multiobjective version.

On the other hand, there are also problems for which it is unknown if there exist algorithms that compute the Pareto set in time polynomial in its size and the sizes of the Pareto sets of appropriate subproblems. The multiobjective spanning tree problem is one such example, where the best known way to compute the Pareto set is essentially to first compute the set of all spanning trees and then to remove the dominated ones. An even stronger requirement is that of an efficient output-sensitive algorithm, which computes the Pareto set in time polynomial in its size and the input size. Bkler et al. (2017) show that such an algorithm exists for the multiobjective version of the minimum-cut problem and that no such algorithm exists for the bicriteria shortest path problem, unless $P = NP$. For many other multiobjective problems, including the knapsack problem and the multiobjective spanning tree problem, it is an open question whether efficient output-sensitive algorithms exist.

15.1.4 Approximate Pareto Curves

For virtually every multiobjective optimization problem the number of Pareto-optimal solutions can be exponential in the worst case. One way of coping with this problem is to relax the requirement of finding the complete Pareto set. A solution x is ε-*dominated* by a solution y if y is worse than x by at most a factor of $1 + \varepsilon$ in each objective (i.e., $w(y)/w(x) \leq 1 + \varepsilon$ for each criterion w that is to be minimized and $p(x)/p(y) \leq 1 + \varepsilon$ for each criterion p that is to be maximized). We say that $\mathcal{P}_\varepsilon$ is an ε-*approximation of a Pareto set* $\mathcal{P}$ if for any solution in $\mathcal{P}$, there is a solution in $\mathcal{P}_\varepsilon$ that ε-dominates it.

In his pioneering work, Hansen (1980) presents an approximation scheme for computing ε-approximate Pareto sets of the bicriteria shortest path problem. Papadimitriou and Yannakakis (2000) show that for any instance of a multiobjective optimization problem, there is an ε-approximation of the Pareto set whose size is polynomial in the input size and $1/\varepsilon$ but exponential in the number of objectives. Furthermore, they define the *gap version* of a multiobjective optimization problem with d objectives as follows: given an instance of the problem and a vector $b \in \mathbb{R}^d$, either return a solution whose objective vector dominates b or report (correctly) that there does not exist any solution whose objective vector is better than b by more than a $(1 + \varepsilon)$ factor in all objectives. They show that an FPTAS for approximating the Pareto set of a multiobjective optimization problem exists if and only if the gap version of the problem can be solved in polynomial time. In particular, this implies that if the exact single-criterion version of a problem (i.e., the question "Is there a solution with weight exactly x?") can be solved in pseudopolynomial time, then its multiobjective version admits an FPTAS for approximating the Pareto set. This is the case, for example, for the spanning tree problem, the all-pair shortest path problem, and the perfect matching problem.

Vassilvitskii and Yannakakis (2005) show how to compute ε-approximate Pareto sets whose size is at most three times as large as the smallest such set for bicriteria problems whose gap versions can be solved in polynomial time. Diakonikolas and Yannakakis (2007) improve this factor to two and show that this is the best possible that can be achieved in polynomial time, unless $P = NP$.

15.2 Number of Pareto-optimal Solutions

Both for the knapsack problem and the bicriteria shortest path problem, the number of Pareto-optimal solutions increases only moderately with the input size in applications. This is in contrast to the exponential worst-case behavior (see Exercise 15.3). To explain this discrepancy, we will analyze the number of Pareto-optimal solutions in the framework of smoothed analysis. First we will focus on the knapsack problem but we will see afterwards that the proven bound also holds for a much larger class of problems including the bicriteria shortest path problem and many other natural bicriteria optimization problems. We will then also briefly discuss known results for problems with more than two objectives.

15.2.1 Knapsack Problem

Let us consider the knapsack problem. In a worst-case analysis the adversary is allowed to choose the profits $p_1, \ldots, p_n$ and the weights $w_1, \ldots, w_n$ exactly (he can also choose the capacity but the number of Pareto-optimal solutions is independent of this). This makes him very powerful and makes it possible to choose an instance in which every solution is Pareto-optimal. In order to limit the power of the adversary to construct such artificial instances that do not resemble typical inputs, we add some randomness to his decisions.

Let $\phi \geq 1$ be a parameter. In the following analysis, we assume that the adversary can still determine the profits exactly while for each weight it can only choose an interval of length $1/\phi$ from which it is chosen uniformly at random independently of the other weights. This means that the adversary can specify each weight only with a precision of $1/\phi$. We normalize the weights and restrict the adversary to intervals that are subsets of $[0, 1]$. This normalization is necessary to ensure that the effect of the noise cannot be ruled out by scaling all weights in the input by some large number.

Observe that the parameter ϕ measures the strength of the adversary. If $\phi = 1$ then all weights are chosen uniformly at random from $[0, 1]$, which resembles an average-case analysis. On the other hand, in the limit for $\phi \to \infty$ the adversary can determine the weights (almost) exactly and the model approaches a classical worst-case analysis. Hence, it is not surprising that the bound that we will prove for the expected number of Pareto-optimal solutions grows with ϕ. However, we will see that it grows only polynomially with n and ϕ, which implies that already a small amount of random noise suffices to rule out the worst case and to obtain a benign instance in expectation.

Theorem 15.7 *Consider an instance $\mathcal{I}$ of the knapsack problem with arbitrary profits $p_1, \ldots, p_n \in \mathbb{R}_{\geq 0}$ in which every weight w_i is chosen uniformly at random from an arbitrary interval $A_i \subseteq [0, 1]$ of length $1/\phi$ independently of the other weights. Then the expected number of Pareto-optimal solutions in $\mathcal{I}$ is bounded from above by $n^2\phi + 1$.*

The rest of this section presents the proof of Theorem 15.7 in detail. Here is a brief summary. Since all weights take values between 0 and 1, all solutions have weights between 0 and n. We divide the interval $[0, n]$ uniformly into a large number k of subintervals of length n/k each. For large enough k it is unlikely that there exist two Pareto-optimal solutions whose weights lie in the same subinterval because the weights are continuous random variables. Assuming that this does not happen, the number of Pareto-optimal solutions equals the number of subintervals that contain a Pareto-optimal solution. The most important and nontrivial step is then to bound, for each subinterval, the probability that it contains a Pareto-optimal solution. Once we have proven an upper bound for this, the theorem follows by summing up this upper bound over all subintervals due to linearity of expectation.

Before we prove the theorem, we state one simple but crucial property of the random variables that we consider.

Lemma 15.8 *Let X be a random variable that is chosen uniformly at random from some interval A of length $1/\phi$. Furthermore let I be an interval of length ε. Then $\Pr[X \in I] \leq \phi\varepsilon$.*

Proof Since X is chosen uniformly at random from A, we obtain

$$\Pr[X \in I] = \frac{|A \cap I|}{|A|} \le \frac{|I|}{|A|} \le \frac{\varepsilon}{1/\phi} = \phi\varepsilon. \qquad \square$$

Proof of Theorem 15.7 Every solution $x \in \{0,1\}^n$ has a weight $w^T x$ in the interval $[0, n]$ because each weight w_i lies in $[0, 1]$. We partition the interval $(0, n]$ uniformly into $k \in \mathbb{N}$ intervals $I_0^k, \ldots, I_{k-1}^k$ for some large number k to be chosen later. Formally, let $I_i^k = (ni/k, n(i+1)/k]$. We say that the interval I_i^k is *nonempty* if there exists a Pareto-optimal solution $x \in \mathcal{P}$ with $w^T x \in I_i^k$.

We denote by X^k the number of nonempty intervals I_i^k plus one. The term $+1$ accounts for the solution 0^n, which is always Pareto-optimal and does not belong to any interval I_i^k. Nevertheless, the variable X^k can be much smaller than $|\mathcal{P}|$ because many Pareto-optimal solutions could lie in the same interval I_i^k. We will ensure that every interval I_i^k contains at most one Pareto-optimal solution with high probability by choosing k sufficiently large. Then, with high probability, $|\mathcal{P}| = X^k$.

In the following, we make this argument more formal. For $k \in \mathbb{N}$, let $\mathcal{F}_k$ denote the event that there exist two different solutions $x, y \in \{0, 1\}^n$ with $|w^T x - w^T y| \le n/k$. Since each interval I_i^k has length n/k, every interval I_i^k contains at most one Pareto-optimal solution if $\mathcal{F}_k$ does not occur.

Lemma 15.9 *For every $k \in \mathbb{N}$, $\Pr[\mathcal{F}_k] \le \frac{2^{2n+1} n\phi}{k}$.*

Proof There are 2^n choices for x and y each. We prove the lemma by a union bound over all these choices. Let $x, y \in \{0, 1\}^n$ with $x \ne y$ be fixed. Then there exists an index i with $x_i \ne y_i$. Assume without loss of generality that $x_i = 0$ and $y_i = 1$. We use the principle of deferred decisions and assume that all weights w_j except for w_i are already fixed. Then $w^T x - w^T y = \alpha - w_i$ for some constant α that depends on x and y and the fixed profits w_j. It holds that

$$\Pr\left[|w^T x - w^T y| \le \frac{n}{k}\right] \le \sup_{\alpha \in \mathbb{R}} \Pr_{w_i}\left[|\alpha - w_i| \le \frac{n}{k}\right]$$

$$= \sup_{\alpha \in \mathbb{R}} \Pr_{w_i}\left[w_i \in \left[\alpha - \frac{n}{k}, \alpha + \frac{n}{k}\right]\right] \le \frac{2n\phi}{k},$$

where the last inequality follows from Lemma 15.8[2]. Now a union bound over all choices for x and y concludes the proof. $\qquad \square$

The most nontrivial part in the analysis is the following lemma, which states for an arbitrary interval an upper bound for the probability that it contains a Pareto-optimal solution. We defer the proof of this lemma to the end of this section.

---

[2] Formally, we condition on the outcome of the w_j with $j \ne i$. This outcome determines the value of α. Then we apply the law of total probability, but instead of integrating over all possible outcomes of the w_j with $j \ne i$, we derive an upper bound by looking only at the worst choice for α.

Lemma 15.10 *For every $t \geq 0$ and every $\varepsilon > 0$,*

$$\Pr[\exists x \in \mathcal{P} \mid w^T x \in (t, t + \varepsilon]] \leq n\phi\varepsilon.$$

The following lemma is the main building block in the proof of the theorem.

Lemma 15.11 *For every $k \in \mathbb{N}$, $\mathbf{E}\left[X^k\right] \leq n^2\phi + 1$.*

Proof Let X_i^k denote a random variable that is 1 if the interval I_i^k is nonempty and 0 otherwise. Then

$$X^k = 1 + \sum_{i=0}^{k-1} X_i^k$$

and by linearity of expectation

$$\mathbf{E}\left[X^k\right] = \mathbf{E}\left[1 + \sum_{i=0}^{k-1} X_i^k\right] = 1 + \sum_{i=0}^{k-1} \mathbf{E}\left[X_i^k\right]. \tag{15.1}$$

Since X_i^k is a 0–1 random variable, its expected value can be written as

$$\mathbf{E}\left[X_i^k\right] = \Pr[X_i^k = 1] = \Pr[\exists x \in \mathcal{P} \mid w^T x \in I_i^k]. \tag{15.2}$$

Using that each interval I_i^k has length n/k, Lemma 15.10 and (15.2) imply

$$\mathbf{E}\left[X_i^k\right] \leq \frac{n^2\phi}{k}.$$

Together with (15.1) this implies

$$\mathbf{E}\left[X^k\right] = 1 + \sum_{i=0}^{k-1} \mathbf{E}\left[X_i^k\right] \leq 1 + k \cdot \frac{n^2\phi}{k} = n^2\phi + 1. \qquad \square$$

With the help of Lemmas 15.9 and 15.11, we can finish the proof of the theorem as follows:

$$\mathbf{E}[|\mathcal{P}|] = \sum_{i=1}^{2^n} \left(i \cdot \Pr[|\mathcal{P}| = i]\right)$$

$$= \sum_{i=1}^{2^n} \left(i \cdot \Pr[|\mathcal{P}| = i \wedge \mathcal{F}_k] + i \cdot \Pr[|\mathcal{P}| = i \wedge \neg \mathcal{F}_k]\right)$$

$$\stackrel{(1)}{=} \sum_{i=1}^{2^n} \left(i \cdot \Pr[\mathcal{F}_k] \cdot \Pr[|\mathcal{P}| = i \mid \mathcal{F}_k]\right) + \sum_{i=1}^{2^n} \left(i \cdot \Pr[X^k = i \wedge \neg \mathcal{F}_k]\right)$$

$$\leq \Pr[\mathcal{F}_k] \cdot \sum_{i=1}^{2^n} \left(i \cdot \Pr[|\mathcal{P}| = i \mid \mathcal{F}_k]\right) + \sum_{i=1}^{2^n} \left(i \cdot \Pr[X^k = i]\right)$$

$$\overset{(2)}{\leq} \frac{2^{2n+1}n\phi}{k} \cdot \sum_{i=1}^{2^n} \left(2^n \cdot \Pr[|\mathcal{P}| = i \mid \mathcal{F}_k]\right) + \mathbf{E}\left[X^k\right]$$

$$\overset{(3)}{\leq} \frac{2^{3n+1}n\phi}{k} + n^2\phi + 1. \tag{15.3}$$

Let us comment on some of the steps in the previous calculation.

- The upper bound 2^n on the indices of the sums follows because $|\mathcal{P}|$ can never exceed the total number of solutions, which is 2^n.
- The rewriting of the first term in (1) follows from the definition of the conditional probability and the rewriting of the second term follows because $X^k = |\mathcal{P}|$ when the event $\neg\mathcal{F}_k$ occurs.
- (2) follows from Lemma 15.9 and the definition of the expected value.
- (3) follows from the identity $\sum_{i=1}^{2^n} \Pr[|\mathcal{P}| = i \mid \mathcal{F}_k] = 1$ and Lemma 15.11.

Since (15.3) holds for every $k \in \mathbb{N}$, it must be $\mathbf{E}[|\mathcal{P}|] \leq n^2\phi + 1$. $\qquad\square$

It only remains to prove Lemma 15.10. An easy way to derive an upper bound for the probability that there exists a Pareto-optimal solution in the interval $(t, t + \varepsilon]$ is to apply a union bound over all solutions. Since there is an exponential number of solutions, this does not lead to a useful bound. The key improvement in the proof of Lemma 15.10 is to apply the union bound only over the n dimensions.

Proof of Lemma 15.10 Fix $t \geq 0$ and $\varepsilon > 0$. First of all we define a random variable $\Lambda(t)$. In order to define $\Lambda(t)$, we define the *winner* $x^\star$ to be the most valuable solution satisfying $w^T x \leq t$, i.e.,

$$x^\star = \arg\max\{p^T x \mid x \in \{0, 1\}^n \text{ and } w^T x \leq t\}.$$

For $t \geq 0$, such a solution $x^\star$ must always exist. We say that a solution x is a *loser* if it has a higher profit than $x^\star$. By the choice of $x^\star$, losers do not satisfy the constraint $w^T x \leq t$ (hence their name). We denote by $\hat{x}$ the loser with the smallest weight (see Figure 15.2), i.e.,

$$\hat{x} = \arg\min\{w^T x \mid x \in \{0, 1\}^n \text{ and } p^T x > p^T x^\star\}.$$

If there does not exist a solution x with $p^T x > p^T x^\star$, then $\hat{x}$ is undefined, which we denote by $\hat{x} = \perp$. Based on $\hat{x}$, we define the random variable $\Lambda(t)$ as

$$\Lambda(t) = \begin{cases} w^T\hat{x} - t & \text{if } \hat{x} \neq \perp, \\ \infty & \text{if } \hat{x} = \perp. \end{cases}$$

The random variable $\Lambda(t)$ satisfies the following equivalence:

$$\Lambda(t) \leq \varepsilon \iff \exists x \in \mathcal{P} : w^T x \in (t, t + \varepsilon]. \tag{15.4}$$

To see this, assume that there exists a Pareto-optimal solution whose weight lies in $(t, t + \varepsilon]$, and let y denote the Pareto-optimal solution with the smallest weight in $(t, t + \varepsilon]$. Then $y = \hat{x}$ and hence $\Lambda(t) = w^T\hat{x} - t \in (0, \varepsilon]$. Conversely,

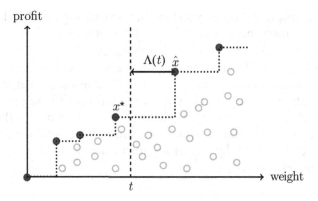

Figure 15.2 Definitions of the winner $x^\star$, the loser $\hat{x}$, and the random variable $\Lambda(t)$.

if $\Lambda(t) \le \varepsilon$, then $\hat{x}$ must be a Pareto-optimal solution whose weight lies in the interval $(t, t + \varepsilon]$. Together this yields equivalence (15.4). Hence,

$$\Pr[\exists x \in \mathcal{P} \mid w^T x \in (t, t + \varepsilon]] = \Pr[\Lambda(t) \le \varepsilon]. \tag{15.5}$$

It only remains to bound the probability that $\Lambda(t)$ does not exceed ε. In order to analyze this probability, we define a set of auxiliary random variables $\Lambda^1(t), \ldots, \Lambda^n(t)$ such that $\Lambda(t)$ is guaranteed to always take a value also taken by at least one of the auxiliary random variables. Then we analyze the auxiliary random variables and use a union bound to conclude the desired bound for $\Lambda(t)$.

Let $i \in [n]$ be fixed. The random variable $\Lambda^i(t)$ is defined similarly to $\Lambda(t)$, but only solutions that do not contain item i are eligible as winners and only solutions that contain item i are eligible as losers. We make this more formal in the following. For $j \in \{0, 1\}$, we define

$$\mathcal{S}^{x_i = j} = \{x \in \{0, 1\}^n \mid x_i = j\},$$

and we define $x^{\star, i}$ to be

$$x^{\star, i} = \arg\max\{p^T x \mid x \in \mathcal{S}^{x_i = 0} \text{ and } w^T x \le t\}.$$

That is, $x^{\star, i}$ is the winner among the solutions that do not contain item i. We restrict our attention to losers that contain item i and define

$$\hat{x}^i = \arg\min\{w^T x \mid x \in \mathcal{S}^{x_i = 1} \text{ and } p^T x > p^T x^{\star, i}\}.$$

If there does not exist a solution $x \in \mathcal{S}^{x_i = 1}$ with $p^T x > p^T x^{\star, i}$, then $\hat{x}^i$ is undefined, i.e., $\hat{x}^i = \bot$. Based on $\hat{x}^i$, we define the random variable $\Lambda^i(t)$ as

$$\Lambda^i(t) = \begin{cases} w^T \hat{x}^i - t & \text{if } \hat{x}^i \ne \bot, \\ \infty & \text{if } \hat{x}^i = \bot. \end{cases}$$

Lemma 15.12 *For every choice of profits and weights, either $\Lambda(t) = \infty$ or there exists an index $i \in [n]$ such that $\Lambda(t) = \Lambda^i(t)$.*

Proof Assume that $\Lambda(t) \neq \infty$. Then there exist a winner $x^\star$ and a loser $\hat{x}$. Since $x^\star \neq \hat{x}$, there must be an index $i \in [n]$ with $x_i^\star \neq \hat{x}_i$. Since all weights are nonnegative and $w^T x^\star < w^T \hat{x}$, there must even be an index $i \in [n]$ with $x_i^\star = 0$ and $\hat{x}_i = 1$. We claim that for this index i, $\Lambda(t) = \Lambda^i(t)$. In order to see this, we first observe that $x^\star = x^{\star,i}$. This follows because $x^\star$ is the solution with the highest profit among all solutions with weight at most t. Since it belongs to $\mathcal{S}^{x_i=0}$, it is in particular the solution with the highest profit among all solutions that do not contain item i and have weight at most t. Since $x^\star = x^{\star,i}$, by similar arguments it follows that $\hat{x} = \hat{x}^i$. This directly implies that $\Lambda(t) = \Lambda^i(t)$. □

Lemma 15.13 *For every $i \in [n]$ and every $\varepsilon \geq 0$,*

$$\Pr[\Lambda^i(t) \in (0, \varepsilon]] \leq \phi\varepsilon.$$

Proof In order to prove the lemma, it suffices to exploit the randomness of the weight w_i. We apply the principle of deferred decisions and assume that all other weights are fixed arbitrarily. Then the weights of all solutions from $\mathcal{S}^{x_i=0}$ and hence also the solution $x^{\star,i}$ are fixed because w_i does not influence the solutions in $\mathcal{S}^{x_i=0}$ and the profits $p_1, \ldots, p_n$ are fixed. If the solution $x^{\star,i}$ is fixed, then also the set of losers $\mathcal{L} = \{x \in \mathcal{S}^{x_i=1} \mid p^T x > p^T x^{\star,i}\}$ is fixed. Since, by definition, all solutions from $\mathcal{L}$ contain item i the identity of the solution $\hat{x}^i$ does not depend on w_i. (Of course, the weight $w^T \hat{x}^i$ depends on w_i. However, which solution will become $\hat{x}^i$ is independent of w_i.) This implies that, given the fixed values of the weights w_j with $j \neq i$, we can rewrite the event $\Lambda^i(t) \in (0, \varepsilon]$ as $w^T \hat{x}^i - t \in (0, \varepsilon]$ for a fixed solution $\hat{x}^i$. For a constant $\alpha \in \mathbb{R}$ depending on the fixed values of the weights w_j with $j \neq i$, we can rewrite this event as $w_i \in (\alpha, \alpha + \varepsilon]$. By Lemma 15.8, the probability of this event is bounded from above by $\phi\varepsilon$. □

Combining Lemmas 15.12 and 15.13 yields

$$\Pr[\Lambda(t) \leq \varepsilon] \leq \Pr\left[\exists i \in [n]: \Lambda^i(t) \in (0, \varepsilon]\right] \leq \sum_{i=1}^{n} \Pr[\Lambda^i(t) \in (0, \varepsilon]] \leq n\phi\varepsilon.$$

Together with (15.5) this proves the lemma. □

Theorem 15.7 implies the following result on the running time of the Nemhauser–Ullmann algorithm.

Corollary 15.14 *Consider an instance $\mathcal{I}$ of the knapsack problem with arbitrary profits $p_1, \ldots, p_n \in \mathbb{R}_{\geq 0}$ in which every weight w_i is chosen uniformly at random from an arbitrary interval $A_i \subseteq [0, 1]$ of length $1/\phi$ independently of the other weights. Then the expected running time of the Nemhauser–Ullmann algorithm is $O(n^3\phi)$.*

Proof It follows from Theorem 15.4 that the expected running time of the Nemhauser–Ullmann algorithm is bounded from above by

$$O\left(\mathbf{E}\left[\sum_{i=0}^{n-1}|\mathcal{P}_i|\right]\right),$$

where $\mathcal{P}_i$ denotes the Pareto set of the restricted instance that consists only of the first i items. Using linearity of expectation and Theorem 15.7, we obtain that this term is bounded from above by

$$O\left(\sum_{i=0}^{n-1}\mathbf{E}[|\mathcal{P}_i|]\right) = O\left(\sum_{i=0}^{n-1}(i^2\phi + 1)\right) = O(n^3\phi). \qquad \square$$

The decision to add randomness only to the weights is arbitrary. Of course if both the profits and the weights are chosen independently uniformly at random from intervals of length $1/\phi$ then the upper bound still applies. With minor modifications, the analysis can also be adapted to the case that only the profits are random while the weights are adversarial.

15.2.2 General Model

Theorem 15.7 can be extended in several ways. First of all, the noise model can be generalized to a much wider class of distributions. In fact the only property that we used about the random weights is Lemma 15.8, which says that the probability to fall into any interval of length ε is at most $\phi\varepsilon$. This is true for every random variable that is described by a probability density function that is bounded from above by ϕ. Hence instead of allowing the adversary to choose an interval of length $1/\phi$ for each weight w_i, we could also allow it to choose a density function $f_i : [0,1] \to [0,\phi]$ according to which w_i is chosen independently of the other weights. This includes as a special case the uniform distribution in an interval of length $1/\phi$ but it also allows different types of random noise. Observe that we have restricted the density functions to $[0,1]$ to normalize the weights.

In the following we will use the term *ϕ-perturbed random variable* to refer to a random variable described by a density $f : \mathbb{R} \to [0,\phi]$. If we replace all occurrences of Lemma 15.8 in the proof of Theorem 15.7 by the following lemma then Theorem 15.7 follows also for general ϕ-perturbed weights from $[0,1]$.

Lemma 15.15 *Let X be a ϕ-perturbed random variable that is described by a density function $f : [0,1] \to [0,\phi]$. For any interval I of length ε, $\Pr[X \in I] \le \phi\varepsilon$.*

Proof The lemma follows by the following simple calculation:

$$\Pr[X \in I] = \int_I f(x)\,dx \le \int_I \phi\,dx = \phi\varepsilon. \qquad \square$$

Next we state an even more general version of Theorem 15.7. The first generalization compared to Theorem 15.7 is that an arbitrary set $\mathcal{S} \subseteq \{0,1\}^n$ of solutions is given. In the case of the knapsack problem, every vector from $\{0,1\}^n$ is a solution, i.e., $S = \{0,1\}^n$. The second generalization is that the adversarial objective function p does not have to be linear. In fact, it can be an arbitrary function that maps every solution to some real value. The third generalization is that we extend the range of the ϕ-perturbed weights from $[0,1]$ to $[-1,1]$.

Theorem 15.16 *Let $S \subseteq \{0,1\}^n$ and $p : S \to \mathbb{R}$ be arbitrary. Let $w_1, \ldots, w_n$ be arbitrary ϕ-perturbed numbers from the interval $[-1,1]$. Then the expected number of solutions $x \in S$ that are Pareto-optimal with respect to the objective functions $p(x)$ and $w^T x$ is $O(n^2\phi)$. This upper bound holds regardless of whether the objective functions are to be maximized or minimized.*

We will not prove Theorem 15.16, but let us remark that its proof is very similar to the proof of Theorem 15.7. In fact we never used in the proof that $S = \{0,1\}^n$ and that p is linear. The fact that all weights w_i are positive was used only to argue that there must be an index i with $x_i^\star = 0$ and $\hat{x}_i = 1$. For general w_i, it could also be the other way round. Handling this issue is the only modification of the proof that is not completely straightforward.

To illustrate the power of Theorem 15.16, let us discuss its implications on graph problems. For a given graph with m edges $e_1, \ldots, e_m$, one can identify every vector $x \in \{0,1\}^m$ with a subset of edges $E' = \{e_i \mid x_i = 1\}$. Then x is the so-called incidence vector of the edge set E'. If, for example, there is a source vertex s and a target vertex v given, one could choose the set S of feasible solutions as the set of all incidence vectors of paths from s to v in the given graph. This way, Theorem 15.16 implies that the expected number of Pareto-optimal s–v paths in the bicriteria shortest-path problem is $O(m^2\phi)$. Similarly, one could choose S as the set of incidence vectors of all spanning trees of a given graph. Then the result implies that in expectation there are only $O(m^2\phi)$ Pareto-optimal spanning trees in the bicriteria spanning tree problem. In the traveling salesman problem (TSP) we are given an undirected graph with edge weights and the goal is to find a shortest tour (i.e., Hamiltonian cycle) that visits every vertex exactly once. As for the bicritera shortest path problem, Theorem 15.16 implies that in expectation there are only $O(m^2\phi)$ Pareto-optimal tours in the bicriteria version of the TSP.

For the bicriteria Bellman–Ford algorithm we obtain the following corollary.

Corollary 15.17 *Consider an instance of the bicriteria shortest-path problem with arbitrary costs and nonnegative ϕ-perturbed weights from the interval $[0,1]$. Let n and m denote the number of vertices and edges, respectively. Then the expected running time of the bicriteria Bellman–Ford algorithm is $O\left(nm^3\phi\right)$.*

Proof We can use Theorem 15.16 to bound the expected size of each list L_v^i that occurs throughout the algorithm by $O(m^2\phi)$, where m denotes the number of edges in the graph. Using linearity of expectation and Theorem 15.6 yields that the expected running time is

$$\Theta\left(\sum_{i=1}^{M} \left(\mathbf{E}\left[|L_{u(R_i)}^{i-1}|\right] + \mathbf{E}\left[|L_{v(R_i)}^{i-1}|\right]\right)\right).$$

Using that the expected length of each list is $O(m^2\phi)$ and $M = (n-1)\cdot m$ implies the claimed bound. $\qquad\qquad\qquad\qquad\qquad\qquad\qquad\qquad\qquad\qquad\qquad\qquad$ □

Let us finally remark that Theorem 15.16 can also be adapted to the setting where the set S of feasible solutions is an arbitrary subset of $\{0, \ldots, k\}^n$ for some $k \in \mathbb{N}$. Then the expected number of Pareto-optimal solutions is $O(n^2 k^2 \phi)$. This is useful to model, for example, the bounded knapsack problem, in which a number of identical copies of every item is given.

15.2.3 Multiobjective Optimization Problems

Even though Theorem 15.16 is quite general, it still has one severe restriction: it only applies to optimization problems with two objective functions. The extension to optimization problems with more than two objectives is rather challenging and requires different methods. In this section, we summarize the main results.

In Theorem 15.16 one of the objective functions is assumed to be arbitrary while the other is linear with ϕ-perturbed coefficients. We consider now optimization problems with one arbitrary objective function and d linear objective functions with ϕ-perturbed coefficients. Röglin and Teng (2009) were the first to study this model. They proved an upper bound of $O((n^2\phi)^{f(d)})$ for the expected number of Pareto-optimal solutions where f is a rapidly growing function (roughly $2^d d!$). This has been improved by Moitra and O'Donnell (2012) to $O(n^{2d}\phi^{d(d+1)/2})$. Brunsch and Röglin (2015) improved the upper bound further to $O(n^{2d}\phi^d)$ under the assumption that all density functions are unimodal, where a function $f : \mathbb{R} \to \mathbb{R}$ is called unimodal if there exists some $x \in \mathbb{R}$ such that f is monotonically increasing on $(-\infty, x]$ and monotonically decreasing on $[x, \infty)$.

The cth moment of a random variable X is the expected value $\mathbf{E}[X^c]$ if it exists. Brunsch and Röglin (2015) also prove upper bounds on the moments of the number of Pareto-optimal solutions. In particular they show that for any constant c the cth moment is bounded from above by $O((n^{2d}\phi^{d(d+1)/2})^c)$ and $O((n^{2d}\phi^d)^c)$ for general and unimodal densities, respectively. Upper bounds for the moments give rise to non-trivial tail bounds. Consider the case $d = 1$. Then the cth moment is bounded from above by $b_c(n^2\phi)^c$ for some constant b_c depending on c. Applying Markov's inequality to the cth moment yields for every $\alpha \geq 1$

$$\Pr[|\mathcal{P}| \geq \alpha \cdot (n^2\phi)] = \Pr[|\mathcal{P}|^c \geq \alpha^c(n^2\phi)^c] = \Pr\left[|\mathcal{P}|^c \geq \frac{\alpha^c}{b_c} \cdot b_c(n^2\phi)^c\right] \leq \frac{b_c}{\alpha^c},$$

while applying Markov's inequality directly to $|\mathcal{P}|$ yields only a bound of (roughly) $1/\alpha$. Upper bounds for the moments are also important for another reason: If the running time of an algorithm depends polynomially but not linearly on the number of Pareto-optimal solutions (like the running time of the Nemhauser–Ullmann algorithm for more than two objective functions), then Theorem 15.16 cannot be used to derive any bound on its expected running time. This is because a bound on $\mathbf{E}[|\mathcal{P}|]$ does not imply any bound on, for example, $\mathbf{E}[|\mathcal{P}|^2]$. Only with the result of Brunsch and Röglin about the moments of $|\mathcal{P}|$ a polynomial bound follows for the expected running time of these algorithms.

Improving earlier work of Brunsch et al. (2014), Brunsch (2014) shows lower bounds for the expected number of Pareto-optimal solutions of $\Omega(n^2\phi)$ for $d = 1$ and $\Omega(n^{d-1.5}\phi^d)$ for $d \geq 2$. Hence the upper bound in Theorem 15.16 for the bicriteria case is asymptotically tight.

A ϕ-perturbed number is nonzero with probability 1. This implies that each of the d objective functions depends on all the variables. This limits the expressibility of the model because there are many examples of problems in which some objective function depends only on a certain subset of the variables. Brunsch and Röglin (2015) discuss this subtle issue in more detail and they also give concrete examples. To circumvent this problem, they introduce *zero-preserving perturbations*. In their model, the adversary can decide for each coefficient whether it should be a ϕ-perturbed number or is deterministically set to zero. For this model they prove upper bounds of $O(n^{O(d^3)}\phi^d)$ and $O((n\phi)^{O(d^3)})$ for unimodal and general ϕ-perturbed coefficients, respectively, for the expected number of Pareto-optimal solutions.

15.3 Smoothed Complexity of Binary Optimization Problems

The results on the expected number of Pareto-optimal solutions imply that the knapsack problem can be solved in expected polynomial time on instances with ϕ-perturbed weights or ϕ-perturbed profits (Corollary 15.14). A natural question is whether or not similar results also hold for other *NP*-hard optimizations problems. Does, for example, the TSP admit an algorithm with expected polynomial running time if all distances are ϕ-perturbed? Instead of studying each problem separately, we will now present a general characterization due to Beier and Vöcking (2006) of which combinatorial optimization problems can be solved efficiently on instances with ϕ-perturbed numbers.

While most smoothed analyses in the literature focus on the analysis of specific algorithms, this section instead considers *problems* in the sense of complexity theory. We will study *linear binary optimization problems*. In an instance of such a problem Π, a linear objective function $c^T x = c_1 x_1 + \cdots + c_n x_n$ is to be minimized or maximized over an arbitrary set $\mathcal{S} \subseteq \{0,1\}^n$ of feasible solutions. The problem Π could, for example, be the TSP and the coefficients c_i could be the edge lengths. (See also the discussion in Section 15.2.2 on how graph problems can be encoded as binary optimization problems.) One could also encode the knapsack problem as a linear binary optimization problem. Then $\mathcal{S}$ contains all subsets of items whose total weight does not exceed the capacity.

We will study the *smoothed complexity* of linear binary optimization problems, by which we mean the complexity of instances in which the coefficients $c_1, \ldots, c_n$ are ϕ-perturbed numbers from the interval $[-1, 1]$. We will assume without loss of generality that the objective function $c^T x$ is to be minimized. Since ϕ-perturbed numbers have infinite encoding length with probability 1, we have to discuss the machine model that we will use in the following. One could change the input model and assume that the ϕ-perturbed coefficients are discretized by rounding them after a polynomial number, say n^2, of bits. The effect of this rounding is so small that it does not influence our results. We will, however, not make this assumption explicit and use, for the sake of simplicity, the continuous random variables in our probabilistic analysis. When defining the input size we will not take the encoding length of the coefficients c_i into account. Instead we assume that the coefficients $c_1, \ldots, c_n$ contribute in total only n to the input length.

To state the main result, let us recall two definitions from computational complexity. We call a linear binary optimization problem *strongly NP-hard* if it is already *NP*-hard when restricted to instances with integer coefficients c_i in which the largest absolute value $C := \max_i |c_i|$ of any of the coefficients is bounded by a polynomial in the input length. The TSP is, for example, strongly *NP*-hard because it is already *NP*-hard when all edges have length either 1 or 2. The knapsack problem, on the other hand, is not strongly *NP*-hard because instances in which all profits are integers and polynomially bounded in the input size can be solved by dynamic programming in polynomial time.

A language L belongs to the complexity class *ZPP* (zero-error probabilistic polynomial time) if there exists a randomized algorithm A that decides for each input x in expected polynomial time whether or not x belongs to L. That is, A always produces the correct answer but its running time is a random variable whose expected value is bounded polynomially for every input x. Let us point out that the expectation is only with respect to the random decisions of the algorithm and not with respect to a randomly chosen input. It is yet unclear whether or not $P = ZPP$. In any case, languages that belong to *ZPP* are generally considered to be easy to decide and *NP*-hard problems are believed to not lie in *ZPP*.

Theorem 15.18 *Let Π be a linear binary optimization problem that is strongly NP-hard. Then there does not exist an algorithm for Π whose expected running time is polynomially bounded in N and ϕ for instances with ϕ-perturbed coefficients from $[-1, 1]$, where N denotes the input length, unless $NP \subseteq ZPP$.*

The main idea of the proof of this theorem can be summarized as follows: An algorithm A for Π with expected running time polynomial in N and ϕ can be used to solve worst-case instances of Π with polynomially bounded numbers optimally in expected polynomial time. Given such a worst-case instance, one could add a small amount of random noise to all the numbers and then solve the resulting instance with A in expected time polynomial in N and ϕ. If this random noise is small enough ($\phi = \Theta(C)$) then it does not change the optimal solution. This way, we obtain an algorithm that solves worst-case instances with polynomially bounded numbers in expected polynomial time, implying that $NP \subseteq ZPP$.

Theorem 15.18 shows that ϕ-perturbed instances of strongly *NP*-hard optimization problems are not easier to solve than worst-case instances. Hence, these problems stay hard also in the model of smoothed analysis. One consequence of this result is that there is no hope that the TSP can be solved efficiently when the edge lengths are randomly perturbed. This is in clear contrast to the knapsack problem, which is easy to solve on randomly perturbed inputs. We will now state a more general positive result. We say that a linear binary optimization problem Π can be solved in *pseudo-linear time* if there exists an algorithm whose running time on instances with integer coefficients is bounded from above by $p(N) \cdot C$, where p denotes a polynomial, N denotes the input length, and C denotes the largest absolute value of any of the coefficients.

Theorem 15.19 *A linear binary optimization problem Π that can be solved in pseudo-linear time in the worst case can be solved in expected polynomial time (with respect to the input length and ϕ) on instances with ϕ-perturbed numbers from $[-1, 1]$.*

Let A_p be an algorithm that solves integral instances of Π in pseudo-linear time. In the proof of Theorem 15.19, the algorithm A_p is used to construct an algorithm A that solves instances with ϕ-perturbed numbers in expected polynomial time. Algorithm A first rounds all ϕ-perturbed coefficients after some number b of bits after the binary point. Then it uses the algorithm A_p to solve the rounded instance. One can prove that for $b = \Theta(\log n)$ rounding all coefficients does not change the optimal solution with high probability. This is based on the observation that in instances with ϕ-perturbed numbers usually the best solution is significantly better than the second best solution and hence it stays optimal even after rounding all coefficients (see Exercise 15.8). For $b = \Theta(\log n)$ the running time of A_p to solve the rounded instance optimally is polynomial. This yields an algorithm that always runs in polynomial time and solves ϕ-perturbed instances of Π with high probability correctly. It is possible to adapt this approach to obtain an algorithm that always computes the optimal solution and whose expected running time is polynomial.

15.4 Conclusions

We have proven bounds on the expected number of Pareto-optimal solutions and we have studied the complexity of linear binary optimization problems in the framework of smoothed analysis. Our results are in many cases consistent with empirical observations. The knapsack problem is, for example, easy to solve in applications and has few Pareto-optimal solutions while solving large-scale TSP instances optimally is computationally still expensive despite a lot of progress that has been made in the last decades and great speedups in the common solvers.

The models that we considered in this chapter are very general, in particular because the set S of feasible solutions can be arbitrarily chosen, both in Section 15.2 and in Section 15.3. However, this generality is also a drawback of our results because the adversary is still rather powerful and can exactly determine the combinatorial structure of the problem. Often problems are easier in applications than in the worst case because the instances obey certain structural properties. Depending on the problem and application, input graphs might be planar or have small degree, distances might satisfy the triangle inequality etc. Such structural properties are not considered in our general model. Hence, often it is advisable to look in more detail into the instances that are really relevant in applications instead of only assuming that some coefficients are random.

An illustrative experimental study of the multiobjective shortest path problem is due to Müller-Hannemann and Weihe (2006). They consider a graph that is obtained from the daily train schedule of the German railway network and observe that the number of Pareto-optimal train connections in view of travel time, fare, and number of train changes is very small (for no pair of nodes there were more than 8 Pareto-optimal connections in the experiments). This is much smaller than suggested by Theorem 15.16. One possible explanation is that in this and many other applications, the objective functions are not independent but to some degree correlated, which might reduce the number of Pareto-optimal solutions. It would be interesting to find a formal model for correlated objective functions that explains the extremely small number of Pareto-optimal solutions observed in this setting.

15.5 Notes

The bicriteria Bellman–Ford algorithm was described by Corley and Moon (1985). The analysis of its running time presented in this chapter can also be found in Beier (2004). Beier and Vöcking (2004) initiated the study of the number of Pareto-optimal solutions in the framework of smoothed analysis. The proof of Theorem 15.7 in this chapter follows an improved and simplified analysis due to Beier et al. (2007). This analysis also generalizes the original work of Beier and Vöcking to integer optimization problems. The bound stated in Beier et al. (2007) is $O(n^2 k^2 \log(k)\phi)$ if $S \subseteq \{0, \ldots, k\}^n$. It has been improved to $O(n^2 k^2 \phi)$ by Röglin and Rösner (2017).

The results in Section 15.3 can be found in Beier and Vöcking (2006). Theorems 15.18 and 15.19 do not give a complete characterization of the smoothed complexity of linear binary optimization problems because Theorem 15.19 applies only to pseudo-linear and not to general pseudo-polynomial algorithms. Beier and Vöcking circumvent this problem by introducing a notion of polynomial smoothed complexity that is not based on expected running times (similar to polynomial average-case complexity). Later Röglin and Teng (2009) showed that all problems that can be solved in pseudo-polynomial time in the worst case can be solved in expected polynomial time on ϕ-perturbed instances, which completes the characterization.

References

Beier, René. 2004. *Probabilistic Analysis of Discrete Optimization Problems*. PhD thesis, Universität des Saarlandes.

Beier, René, and Vöcking, Berthold. 2004. Random knapsack in expected polynomial time. *Journal of Computer and System Sciences*, **69**(3), 306–329.

Beier, René, and Vöcking, Berthold. 2006. Typical properties of winners and losers in discrete optimization. *SIAM Journal on Computing*, **35**(4), 855–881.

Beier, René, Röglin, Heiko, and Vöcking, Berthold. 2007. The smoothed number of Pareto optimal solutions in bicriteria integer optimization. In *Proceedings of the 12th International Conference on Integer Programming and Combinatorial Optimization (IPCO)*, pp. 53–67.

Brunsch, Tobias. 2014. *Smoothed Analysis of Selected Optimization Problems and Algorithms*. PhD thesis, Universität Bonn.

Brunsch, Tobias, and Röglin, Heiko. 2015. Improved smoothed analysis of multiobjective optimization. *Journal of the ACM*, **62**(1), 4:1–4:58.

Brunsch, Tobias, Goyal, Navin, Rademacher, Luis, and Röglin, Heiko. 2014. Lower bounds for the average and smoothed number of Pareto-optima. *Theory of Computing*, **10**, 237–256.

Bkler, Fritz, Ehrgott, Matthias, Morris, Christopher, and Mutzel, Petra. 2017. Output-sensitive complexity of multiobjective combinatorial optimization. *Journal of Multi-Criteria Decision Analysis*, **24**(1-2), 25–36.

Corley, H. William, and Moon, I. Douglas. 1985. Shortest paths in networks with vector weights. *Journal of Optimization Theory and Application*, **46**(1), 79–86.

Diakonikolas, Ilias, and Yannakakis, Mihalis. 2007. Small approximate Pareto sets for bi-objective shortest paths and other problems. *Proceedings of the 10th International*

Workshop on Approximation Algorithms for Combinatorial Optimization Problems (APPROX), pp. 74–88.

Hansen, Pierre. 1980. Bicriterion path problems. In *Multiple Criteria Decision Making: Theory and Applications*. Lecture Notes in Economics and Mathematical Systems, vol. 177, pp. 109–127. Springer-Verlag.

Kung, H. T., Luccio, Fabrizio, and Preparata, Franco P. 1975. On finding the maxima of a set of vectors. *Journal of the ACM*, **22**(4), 469–476.

Moitra, Ankur, and O'Donnell, Ryan. 2012. Pareto optimal solutions for smoothed analysts. *SIAM Journal on Computing*, **41**(5), 1266–1284.

Müller-Hannemann, Matthias, and Weihe, Karsten. 2006. On the cardinality of the Pareto set in bicriteria shortest path problems. *Annals of Operations Research*, **147**(1), 269–286.

Nemhauser, George L., and Ullmann, Zev. 1969. Discrete dynamic programming and capital allocation. *Management Science*, **15**(9), 494–505.

Papadimitriou, Christos H., and Yannakakis, Mihalis. 2000. On the approximability of trade-offs and optimal access of Web sources. In *Proceedings of the 41st Annual IEEE Symposium on Foundations of Computer Science (FOCS)*, pp. 86–92.

Röglin, Heiko, and Rösner, Clemens. 2017. The smoothed number of Pareto-optimal solutions in non-integer bicriteria optimization. *Proceedings of the 14th Annual Conference on Theory and Applications of Models of Computation (TAMC)*, pp. 543–555.

Röglin, Heiko, and Teng, Shang-Hua. 2009. Smoothed analysis of multiobjective optimization. In *Proceedings of the 50th Annual IEEE Symposium on Foundations of Computer Science (FOCS)*, pp. 681–690.

Vassilvitskii, Sergei, and Yannakakis, Mihalis. 2005. Efficiently computing succinct trade-off curves. *Theoretical Computer Science*, **348**(2–3), 334–356.

Exercises

Exercise 15.1 Implement the Nemhauser–Ullmann algorithm so that your implementation achieves a running time of $\Theta(\sum_{i=0}^{n-1} |\mathcal{P}_i|)$.

Exercise 15.2 Find an instance of the knapsack problem with $|\mathcal{P}_{i+1}| < |\mathcal{P}_i|$ for some i.

Exercise 15.3 Construct instances for the bicriteria shortest path problem with an exponential number of Pareto-optimal s–v paths for some vertices s and v.

Exercise 15.4 Prove that the bicriteria Bellman–Ford algorithm is correct, i.e., that after termination the list L_v equals for every vertex $v \in V$ the set of Pareto-optimal s–v paths

Exercise 15.5 A famous algorithm for the single criterion all-pairs shortest path problem is the Floyd–Warshall algorithm. Adapt this algorithm to the bicriteria all-pairs shortest path problem (given a graph G with costs and weights, compute for each pair (u, v) of vertices the set of Pareto-optimal u–v paths in G). State a bound on its running time in the same fashion as Theorem 15.6. What is the expected running time if the weights are ϕ-perturbed?

Exercise 15.6 The concept of zero-preserving perturbations could also be applied to the bicriteria case with one adversarial objective function and one linear objective function with ϕ-perturbed coefficients. Show that, in contrast to the multiobjective case, for bicriteria optimization problems it does not increase the expressibility. For this, show that zero-preserving perturbations for the bicriteria case can be simulated by ϕ-perturbed coefficients if the set S of feasible solutions is adapted appropriately. Why does this simulation not work for problems with three or more objectives?

Exercise 15.7 Prove that the expected number of Pareto-optimal points among n points drawn independently and uniformly at random from the unit square is $O(\log n)$.

Exercise 15.8 Given an instance $\mathcal{I}$ of some linear binary optimization problem Π with a set $S \subseteq \{0, 1\}^n$ of feasible solutions, the winner gap is defined as

$$\Delta = c^T x^{\star\star} - c^T x^{\star},$$

where

$$x^{\star} = \arg\min\{c^T x \mid x \in S\} \quad \text{and} \quad x^{\star\star} = \arg\min\{c^T x \mid x \in S \setminus \{x^{\star}\}\}$$

denote the best and second best solution of $\mathcal{I}$, respectively. Let $\mathcal{I}$ be an instance of Π with ϕ-perturbed coefficients $c_1, \ldots, c_n$. Prove that, for every $\varepsilon > 0$,

$$\Pr[\Delta \leq \varepsilon] \leq 2n\phi\varepsilon.$$

[Hint: This statement follows by similar arguments as Lemma 15.10.]

PART FIVE

Applications in Machine Learning and Statistics

CHAPTER SIXTEEN

Noise in Classification

Maria-Florina Balcan and Nika Haghtalab

Abstract: This chapter considers the computational and statistical aspects of learning linear thresholds in the presence of noise. When there is no noise, several algorithms exist that efficiently learn near-optimal linear thresholds using a small amount of data. However, even a small amount of adversarial noise makes this problem notoriously hard in the worst case. We discuss approaches for dealing with these negative results by exploiting natural assumptions on the data-generating process.

16.1 Introduction

Machine learning studies automatic methods for making accurate predictions and useful decisions based on previous observations and experience. From the application point of view, machine learning has become a successful discipline for operating in complex domains such as natural language processing, speech recognition, and computer vision. Moreover, the theoretical foundations of machine learning have led to the development of powerful and versatile techniques, which are routinely used in a wide range of commercial systems in today's world. However, a major challenge of increasing importance in the theory and practice of machine learning is to provide algorithms that are robust to adversarial noise.

In this chapter, we focus on *classification* where the goal is to learn a classification rule from labeled examples only. Consider, for example, the task of automatically classifying social media posts as either appropriate or inappropriate for publication. To achieve this one can examine past social media posts and their features – such as the author, bag of words, and hashtags –and whether they were appropriate for publication. These data can be used to learn a classifier that best decides whether a newly posted article is appropriate for publication, e.g., by finding the best parameters for a linear classifier that makes such predictions. While classification is one of the most commonly used paradigms of machine learning in practice, from the worst-case perspective, it is often computationally hard and requires an amount of information that is seldom available. One of the main challenges in classification is the presence of *noise* in data sets. For example, a labeler may be making mistakes when deciding whether a post is appropriate for publication. It is also possible that the correct decision is not a linear separator or even that there is no perfect classification rule. The latter can happen when, for example, one appropriate post and one inappropriate post map to the same feature vector. Indeed, when the noise in classification is adversarially designed, classification is believed to be hard. On the other hand, there is an increasing need for learning algorithms that can withstand intentionally adversarial behavior in their environment, e.g., a large fraction of inappropriate social media posts are made with the intention to pass through the deployed classifier. Therefore, it is essential to provide a theoretical grounding for the performance of learning algorithms in the presence of real-life adversaries.

In this chapter, we go beyond the worst case in studying noise in classification with a focus on learning linear threshold classifiers. Learning linear thresholds is a canonical problem in machine learning that serves as a backbone for several other learning problems, such as support vector machines and neural networks. In the absence of noise, several computationally efficient algorithms exist that can learn highly accurate linear thresholds. However, introducing even a small amount of adversarial noise makes this problem notoriously intractable with a runtime that is prohibitively large in the number of features. In this chapter, we present some of the recent progress on learning linear thresholds in the presence of noise under assumptions on the data-generating process. The first approach considers restrictions on the marginal distribution of instances, e.g., log-concave or Gaussian distributions. The second approach additionally considers how the true classification of instances match those expressed by the most accurate classifier one is content with, e.g., assuming that the Bayes optimal classifier is also a linear threshold. At a technical level, many of the results in this chapter contribute to and draw insights from high-dimensional geometry to limit the effects of noise on learning algorithms.

We describe the formal setup in Section 16.2. In Section 16.3, we overview the classical worst-case and best-case results on computational and statistical aspects of classification. In Section 16.4 we showcase general assumptions on the marginal distribution of instances that lead to improved computational performance. In Section 16.5 we obtain further computational and statistical improvements by investigating additional assumptions on the nature of the label noise. We end this chapter by putting the work into a broader context.

16.2 Model

We consider an instance space $\mathcal{X}$ and a set of labels $\mathcal{Y} = \{-1, +1\}$. A *classifier* is a function $f : \mathcal{X} \to \mathcal{Y}$ that maps an instance $x \in \mathcal{X}$ to its classification y. For example, x can represent a social media post and y can indicate whether the post was appropriate for publication. We consider a set of classifiers $\mathcal{F}$. We denote the Vapnik–Chervonenkis (VC) dimension of $\mathcal{F}$, which measures the expressibility of $\mathcal{F}$, by $\dim(\mathcal{F})$.[1] We further consider a distribution $\mathcal{D}$ over $\mathcal{X} \times \mathcal{Y}$. While $\mathcal{D}$ is assumed to be unknown, we assume access to a set S of i.i.d. samples from $\mathcal{D}$. For a classifier f, we represent its *expected* and *empirical error*, respectively, by $\mathrm{err}_{\mathcal{D}}(f) = \Pr_{(x,y) \sim \mathcal{D}}[y \neq f(x)]$ and $\mathrm{err}_S(f) = \frac{1}{|S|} \sum_{(x,y) \in S} \mathbf{1}_{(y \neq f(x))}$. *Classification* is the task of learning a classifier with near optimal error from a set of classifiers $\mathcal{F}$, i.e., finding f such that $\mathrm{err}_{\mathcal{D}}(f) \leq \mathrm{opt} + \epsilon$, where $\mathrm{opt} = \min_{f^* \in \mathcal{F}} \mathrm{err}_{\mathcal{D}}(f^*)$. Classification is considered under a number of settings. *Agnostic learning* refers to a setting in

---

[1] VC dimension is the size of the largest $X \subseteq \mathcal{X}$ that can be labeled in all possible ways using functions in $\mathcal{F}$.

which no additional assumptions are made regarding the set of classifiers $\mathcal{F}$ or the distribution of instances $\mathcal{D}$. *Realizable learning* refers to a setting where there is $f^* \in \mathcal{F}$ such that $\text{err}_{\mathcal{D}}(f^*) = 0$, in which case, one is looking for a classifier f with $\text{err}_{\mathcal{D}}(f) \leq \epsilon$.

In parts of this chapter, we work with the class of linear threshold classifiers. That is, we assume that the input space is $\mathcal{X} = \mathbb{R}^d$ for some $d \in \mathbb{N}$ and refer to an instance by its d-dimensional vector representation $\vec{x} \in \mathbb{R}^d$. A *homogeneous linear threshold* classifier, also called a *halfspace through the origin*, is a function $h_{\vec{w}}(\vec{x}) = \text{sign}(\vec{w} \cdot \vec{x})$ for some unit vector $\vec{w} \in \mathbb{R}^d$. The VC dimension of the class of d-dimensional homogeneous linear thresholds is $\dim(\mathcal{F}) = d$.

16.3 The Best Case and the Worst Case

In this section, we review the computational and statistical aspects of classification at the opposite ends of the difficulty spectrum – the realizable and agnostic settings.

16.3.1 Sample Complexity

It is well known that to find a classifier of error ϵ in the realizable setting, all one needs to do is to take a set of $\tilde{\Theta}(\dim(\mathcal{F})/\epsilon)$ i.i.d. samples from $\mathcal{D}$ and choose $f \in \mathcal{F}$ that perfectly classifies all of these samples.[2] Formally, for any $\epsilon, \delta \in (0, 1)$, there is

$$m_{\epsilon,\delta}^{real} \in O\left(\frac{1}{\epsilon}\left(\dim(\mathcal{F})\ln\left(\frac{1}{\epsilon}\right) + \ln\left(\frac{1}{\delta}\right)\right)\right)$$

such that with probability $1 - \delta$ over $S \sim \mathcal{D}^{m_{\epsilon,\delta}^{real}}$, if $\text{err}_S(f) = 0$ then $\text{err}_{\mathcal{D}}(f) \leq \epsilon$.

In most applications of machine learning, however, either the perfect classifier is much more complex than those included in $\mathcal{F}$ or there is no way to perfectly classify instances. This is where agnostic learning comes in. With no assumptions on the performance of classifiers one instead chooses $f \in \mathcal{F}$ with least empirical error. One way to make this work is to estimate the error of all classifiers within ϵ with high probability over the draw of the samples. This is called *uniform convergence* and requires $\Theta(\dim(\mathcal{F})/\epsilon^2)$ samples. More formally, for any $\epsilon, \delta \in (0, 1)$, there is

$$m_{\epsilon,\delta} \in O\left(\frac{1}{\epsilon^2}\left(\dim(\mathcal{F}) + \ln\left(\frac{1}{\delta}\right)\right)\right)$$

such that with probability $1 - \delta$ over the sample set $S \sim \mathcal{D}^{m_{\epsilon,\delta}}$, for all $f \in \mathcal{F}$, $|\text{err}_{\mathcal{D}}(f) - \text{err}_S(f)| \leq \epsilon$. These sample complexities are known to be nearly tight. We refer the reader to Anthony and Bartlett (1999) for more details.[3]

It is evident from these results that in the worst case agnostic learning requires significantly, i.e., about a factor of $1/\epsilon$, more data than realizable learning. Unfortunately, such large amount of data may not be available in many applications

---

[2] We use notation $\tilde{\Theta}$ to hide logarithmic dependence on $1/\epsilon$ and $1/\delta$.

[3] Informally speaking, the VC dimension of a function class controls the number of samples needed for learning. This is because if the number of samples is much smaller than the VC dimension, it is possible to have two functions that perform identically on the training set but there is a large gap between their performance on the true distributions. The surprising aspect of these results is that the VC dimension also characterizes the number of samples sufficient for learning.

and domains, e.g., medical imaging. On the other hand, day-to-day applications of machine learning rarely resemble worst-case instances of agnostic learning. In Section 16.5, we show how the sample complexity of agnostic leaning significantly improves when we make additional assumptions on the nature of the noise.

16.3.2 Computational Complexity

Given a sufficiently large sample set, the computational complexity of classification is concerned with whether one can efficiently compute a classifier of good quality on the samples. In the realizable setting, this involves computing a classifier f that makes no mistakes on the sample set. More generally, in the agnostic setting one needs to compute a classifier $f \in \mathcal{F}$ of (approximately) least error. This can be done in $\text{poly}(|\mathcal{F}|)$ runtime. However, in most cases $\mathcal{F}$ is infinitely large or, even in cases that it is finite, it is exponential in the natural representation of the problem, e.g., the set of all linear threshold functions, decision trees, boolean functions, etc. In this section, we focus on a setting where $\mathcal{F}$ is the set of homogeneous linear thresholds, which is one of the most popular classifiers studied in machine learning.

Consider the realizable setting where $f_{\vec{w}} \in \mathcal{F}$ exists that is consistent with the set S sampled from $\mathcal{D}$, i.e., $y = \text{sign}(\vec{w} \cdot \vec{x})$ for all $(\vec{x}, y) \in S$. Then such a vector $\vec{w} = \frac{\vec{v}}{\|\vec{v}\|_2}$ can be computed in time $\text{poly}(d, |S|)$ by finding a solution $\vec{v}$ to the following linear program with a dummy objective

$$\begin{aligned} & \text{minimize}_{\vec{v} \in \mathbb{R}^d} && 1 \\ & \text{subject to} && y(\vec{v} \cdot \vec{x}) \geq 1, && \forall(\vec{x}, y) \in S. \end{aligned} \qquad (16.1)$$

Can one use this linear program in the agnostic case? The answer depends on how much noise, measured by the error of the optimal classifier, exists in the data set. After all, if the noise is so small that it does not appear in the sample set, then one can continue to use the above linear program. To see this more formally, let $\mathcal{O}_{\mathcal{F}}$ be an *oracle* for the realizable setting that takes sample set S and returns a classifier $f \in \mathcal{F}$ that is perfect on S if one exists. Note that the aforementioned linear program achieves this by returning $\vec{w}$ that satisfies the constraints or certifying that no such vector exists. In the following algorithm, we apply this oracle that is designed for the realizable setting to the agnostic learning problem where the noise level is very small. Interestingly, these guarantees go beyond learning linear thresholds and apply to any learning problem that is efficiently solvable in the realizable setting.

Algorithm 1 Efficient agnostic learning for small noise

Input: Sampling access to $\mathcal{D}$, set of classifiers $\mathcal{F}$, oracle $\mathcal{O}_{\mathcal{F}}$, ϵ, and δ.

1. Let $m = m_{\frac{\epsilon}{4}, 0.5}^{real}$ and $r = m^2 \ln(2/\delta)$.
2. For $i = 1, \dots, r$, take a sample set S_i of m i.i.d. samples from $\mathcal{D}$. Let $f_i = \mathcal{O}_{\mathcal{F}}(S_i)$ or $f_i = $ "none" if there is no perfect classifier for S_i.
3. Take a fresh sample set S of $m' = \frac{1}{\epsilon} \ln(r/\delta)$ i.i.d. samples from $\mathcal{D}$.
4. Return f_i with minimum $\text{err}_S(f_i)$.

Theorem 16.1 (Kearns and Li, 1988) *Consider an agnostic learning problem with distribution $\mathcal{D}$ and set of classifiers $\mathcal{F}$ such that $\min_{f \in \mathcal{F}} \text{err}_{\mathcal{D}}(f) \leq c\epsilon/\dim(\mathcal{F})$ for a sufficiently small constant c. Algorithm 1 makes $\text{poly}(\dim(\mathcal{F}), \frac{1}{\epsilon}, \ln(\frac{1}{\delta}))$ calls to the realizable oracle $\mathcal{O}_{\mathcal{F}}$, and with probability $1 - \delta$, returns a classifier f with $\text{err}_{\mathcal{D}}(f) \leq \epsilon$.*

Proof Sketch It is not hard to see that step 2 of the algorithm returns at least one classifier $f_i \in \mathcal{F}$, which perfectly classifies S_i of size $m = \tilde{\Theta}(\dim(\mathcal{F})/\epsilon)$ with high probability, and therefore has error at most $\epsilon/4$ on $\mathcal{D}$. Since $m = \Theta(\epsilon^{-1}\dim(\mathcal{F})\ln(1/\epsilon))$, for a fixed i, the probability that S_i is perfectly labeled by the optimal classifier is $(1 - c\epsilon/\dim(\mathcal{F}))^m \geq \frac{1}{m^2}$. Repeating this $r = m^2 \ln(2/\delta)$ times, with probability at least $1 - \frac{\delta}{2}$ at least one sample set is perfectly labeled by the optimal classifier

We use the Chernoff bound to estimate the error within a multiplicative factor of 2.[4] With probability $1 - \delta$ over the choice of m' samples S, any such classifier f_i with $\text{err}_{\mathcal{D}}(f_i) \leq \epsilon/4$ has $\text{err}_S(f_i) \leq \epsilon/2$ and any such classifier with $\text{err}_{\mathcal{D}}(f_i) > \epsilon$ has $\text{err}_S(f_i) > \epsilon/2$. Therefore, Algorithm 1 returns a classifier of error ϵ. $\qquad\square$

Theorem 16.1 shows how to efficiently learn a d-dimensional linear threshold in the agnostic setting when the noise level is $O\left(\frac{\epsilon}{d}\right)$. At its heart, Theorem 16.1 relies on the fact that when the noise is small, linear program (16.1) is still feasible with a reasonable probability. On the other hand, significant noise in agnostic learning leads to unsatisfiable constraints in linear program (16.1). Indeed, in a system of linear equations where one can satisfy $(1 - \epsilon)$ fraction of the equations, it is *NP*-hard to find a solution that satisfies $\Theta(1)$ fraction of them. Guruswami and Raghavendra (2009) use this to show that even if there is a near-perfect linear threshold $f^* \in \mathcal{F}$ with $\text{err}_{\mathcal{D}}(f^*) \leq \epsilon$, finding any classifier in $\mathcal{F}$ with error $\leq \frac{1}{2} - \Theta(1)$ is *NP*-hard. Agnostic learning of linear thresholds is hard even if the algorithm is allowed to return a classifier $f \notin \mathcal{F}$. This setting is called *improper* learning and is generally simpler than the problem of learning a classifier from $\mathcal{F}$. But, even in improper learning, when the optimal linear threshold has a small constant error opt, it is hard to learn a classifier of error $O(\text{opt})$ (Daniely, 2016), assuming that refuting Random Constraint Satisfaction Problems is hard under a certain regime.

These hardness results demonstrate a gap between what is efficiently learnable in the agnostic setting and the realizable setting, even if one has access to unlimited data. In Sections 16.4 and 16.5, we circumvent these hardness results by simple assumptions on the shape of the marginal distribution or the nature of the noise.

16.4 Benefits of Assumptions on the Marginal Distribution

In this section, we show how additional assumptions on the marginal distribution of $\mathcal{D}$ on instance space $\mathcal{X}$ improve the computational aspects of classification.

---

[4] Here, a multiplicative approximation rather than an additive one needs fewer samples than is discussed in Section 16.3.1.

A commonly used class of distributions in the theory and practice of machine learning is the class of *log-concave* distributions, which includes the Gaussian distribution and uniform distribution over convex sets. Formally,

Definition 16.2 A distribution $\mathcal{P}$ with density p is log-concave if $\log(p(\cdot))$ is concave. It is isotropic if its mean is at the origin and has a unit covariance matrix.

Throughout this section, we assume that the marginal distribution of $\mathcal{D}$ is log-concave and isotropic. Apart from this we make no further assumptions and allow for arbitrary label noise. Let us first state several useful properties of isotropic log-concave distributions. We refer the interested reader to (Lovász and Vempala, 2007; Balcan and Long, 2013; Awasthi et al., 2017b) for the proof of these properties.

Theorem 16.3 *Let $\mathcal{P}$ be an isotropic log-concave distribution over $\mathcal{X} = \mathbb{R}^d$.*

1. *All marginals of $\mathcal{P}$ are also isotropic log-concave distributions.*
2. *For any r, $\Pr[\|\vec{x}\| \geq r\sqrt{d}] \leq \exp(-r + 1)$.*
3. *There are constants $\overline{C}_1$ and $\underline{C}_1$, such that for any two unit vectors $\vec{w}$ and $\vec{w}'$, $\underline{C}_1 \theta(\vec{w}, \vec{w}') \leq \Pr_{\vec{x} \sim \mathcal{P}}[\operatorname{sign}(\vec{w} \cdot \vec{x}) \neq \operatorname{sign}(\vec{w}' \cdot \vec{x})] \leq \overline{C}_1 \theta(\vec{w}, \vec{w}')$, where $\theta(\vec{w}, \vec{w}')$ is the angle between vectors $\vec{w}$ and $\vec{w}'$.*
4. *There are constants $\overline{C}_2$ and $\underline{C}_2$, such that for any unit vector $\vec{w}$ and γ, $\underline{C}_2 \gamma \leq \Pr_{\vec{x} \sim \mathcal{P}}\left[|\vec{x} \cdot \vec{w}| \leq \gamma\right] \leq \overline{C}_2 \gamma$.*
5. *For any constant C_3 there is a constant C_3' such that for any two unit vectors $\vec{w}$ and $\vec{w}'$ such that $\theta(\vec{w}, \vec{w}') \leq \alpha < \pi/2$, we have $\Pr_{\vec{x} \sim \mathcal{P}}[|\vec{x} \cdot \vec{w}| \geq C_3'\alpha$ and $\operatorname{sign}(\vec{w} \cdot \vec{x}) \neq \operatorname{sign}(\vec{w}' \cdot \vec{x})] \leq \alpha C_3$.*

Part 1 of Theorem 16.3 is useful in establishing the other properties of log-concave distributions. For example, projection of $\vec{x}$ on any orthonormal subspace is equivalent to the marginal distribution over the coordinates of the new subspace and thus forms an isotropic log-concave distribution. This allows one to prove the rest of Theorem 16.3 by analyzing the projections of $\vec{x}$ on the relevant unit vectors $\vec{w}$ and $\vec{w}'$. Part 1 and the exponential tail property of log-concave distributions (as expressed in Part 2) are used in Section 16.4.1 to show that linear thresholds can be approximated using low degree polynomials over log-concave distributions.

Part 3 allows one to bound the error of a candidate classifier in terms of its angle to the optimal classifier. In addition, the exponential tail of log-concave distributions implies that a large fraction of the distribution is in a band around the decision boundary of a classifier (Part 4). Furthermore, the exponential tail property – when applied to regions that are progressively farther from the origin and are captured within the disagreement region – implies that only a small part of the disagreement between a candidate classifier and the optimal classifier falls outside of this band (Part 5). Sections 16.4.2 and 16.5.2 use these properties to localize the learning problem near a decision boundary of a candidate classifier and achieve strong computational results for learning linear thresholds.

16.4.1 Computational Improvements via Polynomial Regression

One of the reasons behind the computational hardness of agnostic learning is that it involves a nonconvex and nonsmooth function, sign($\cdot$). Furthermore, sign($\cdot$) cannot be approximated *uniformly over all* $\vec{x}$ by low degree polynomials or other convex and smooth functions that can be efficiently optimized. However, one only needs to approximate sign($\cdot$) in *expectation* over the data-generating distribution. This is especially useful when the marginal distribution has exponential tail, e.g., log-concave distributions, because it allows one to focus on approximating sign($\cdot$) close to its decision boundary, at the expense of poorer approximations far from the boundary, but without reducing the (expected) approximation factor overall.

This is the idea behind the work of Kalai et al. (2008) that showed that if $\mathcal{D}$ has a log-concave marginal, then one can learn a classifier of error opt + ϵ in time poly $\left(d^{\kappa(1/\epsilon)} \right)$, for a fixed function κ. Importantly, this result establishes that a low-degree polynomial threshold approximates sign($\cdot$) in expectation. We state this claim below and refer the interested reader to Kalai et al. (2008) for its proof.

Theorem 16.4 (Kalai et al., 2008) *There is a function κ such that for any log-concave (not necessarily isotropic) distribution $\mathcal{P}$ on $\mathbb{R}$, for any ϵ and θ, there is a polynomial $q : \mathbb{R} \to \mathbb{R}$ of degree $\kappa(1/\epsilon)$ such that $\mathbb{E}_{z \sim \mathcal{P}} \left[|q(z) - \text{sign}(z - \theta)| \right] \leq \epsilon$.*

This result suggests a learning algorithm that fits a polynomial, in L_1 distance, to the set of samples observed from $\mathcal{D}$. This algorithm is formally presented in Algorithm 2. At a high level, for a set S of labeled instances, our goal is to compute a polynomial $p : \mathbb{R}^d \to \mathbb{R}$ of degree $\kappa(1/\epsilon)$ that minimizes $\mathbb{E}_{(\vec{x}, y) \sim S} \left[|p(\vec{x}) - y| \right]$. This can be done in time poly($d^{\kappa(1/\epsilon)}$), by expanding each d-dimensional instance $\vec{x}$ to a poly($d^{\kappa(1/\epsilon)}$)-dimensional instance $\vec{x}'$ that includes all monomials with degree at most $\kappa(1/\epsilon)$ of $\vec{x}$. We can then perform an L_1 regression on $(\vec{x}', y)$s to find p in time poly($d^{\kappa(1/\epsilon)}$) – for example by using a linear program. With p in hand, we then choose a threshold θ so as to minimize the empirical error of sign $\left(p(\vec{x}) - \theta \right)$. This allows us to use Theorem 16.4 to prove the following result.

Algorithm 2 L_1 Polynomial regresssion

Input: Set S of poly $\left(\frac{1}{\epsilon} d^{\kappa(1/\epsilon)} \right)$ samples from $\mathcal{D}$

1. Find polynomial p of degree $\kappa(1/\epsilon)$ that minimizes $\mathbb{E}_{(\vec{x}, y) \sim S} \left[|p(\vec{x}) - y| \right]$.
2. Let $f(\vec{x}) = \text{sign} \left(p(\vec{x}) - \theta \right)$ for $\theta \in [-1, 1]$ that minimizes the empirical error on S.

Theorem 16.5 (Kalai et al., 2008) *The L_1 Polynomial regression algorithm (Algorithm 2) achieves $\text{err}_{\mathcal{D}}(f) \leq \text{opt} + \epsilon/2$ in expectation over the choice of S.*

Proof Let $f(\vec{x}) = \text{sign}(p(\vec{x}) - \theta)$ be the outcome of Algorithm 2 on sample set S. It is not hard to see that the empirical error of f is at most half of the L_1 error of p, i.e., $\text{err}_S(f) \leq \frac{1}{2} \mathbb{E}_S \left[|y - p(\vec{x})| \right]$, where $\mathbb{E}_S$ denotes expectation taken with respect to the empirical distribution $(\vec{x}, y) \sim S$. To see this, note that $f(\vec{x})$

is wrong only if θ falls between $p(\vec{x})$ and y. If we were to pick θ uniformly at random from $[-1, 1]$, then in expectation $f(\vec{x})$ is wrong with probability $|p(\vec{x}) - y|/2$. But θ is specifically picked by the algorithm to minimize $\mathrm{err}_S(f)$; therefore, it beats the expectation and also achieves $\mathrm{err}_S(f) \le \frac{1}{2}\mathbb{E}_S[|y - p(\vec{x})|]$.

Next, we use Theorem 16.4 to show that there is a polynomial p^* that approximates the optimal classifier in expectation over a log-concave distribution. Let $h^* = \mathrm{sign}(\vec{w}^* \cdot \vec{x})$ be the optimal linear threshold for distribution $\mathcal{D}$. Note that $\vec{w}^* \cdot \vec{x}$ is a one-dimensional isotropic log-concave distribution (By Theorem 16.3 part 1). Let $p^*(\vec{x}) = q(\vec{x} \cdot \vec{w}^*)$ be a polynomial of degree $\kappa(2/\epsilon)$ that approximates h^* according to Theorem 16.4, i.e., $\mathbb{E}_{\mathcal{D}}[|p^*(\vec{x}) - h^*(\vec{x}))|] \le \epsilon/2$. Then, we have

$$\mathrm{err}_S(f) \le \frac{1}{2}\mathbb{E}_S[|y - p(\vec{x})|] \le \frac{1}{2}\mathbb{E}_S[|y - p^*(\vec{x})|]$$

$$\le \frac{1}{2}\left(\mathbb{E}_S[|y - h^*(\vec{x})|] + \mathbb{E}_S[|p^*(\vec{x}) - h^*(\vec{x})|]\right).$$

Consider the expected value of the final expression $\frac{1}{2}(\mathbb{E}_S[|y - h^*(\vec{x})|] + \mathbb{E}_S[|p^*(\vec{x}) - h^*(\vec{x})|])$ over the draw of a set S of m samples from $\mathcal{D}$. Since $|y - h^*(\vec{x})| = 2$ whenever $y \ne h^*(\vec{x})$, we have $\mathbb{E}_{S \sim \mathcal{D}^m}[\frac{1}{2}\mathbb{E}_S[|y - h^*(\vec{x})|]] = \mathrm{opt}$. Moreover, $\mathbb{E}_{S \sim \mathcal{D}^m}[\frac{1}{2}\mathbb{E}_S[|p^*(\vec{x}) - h^*(\vec{x})|]] \le \epsilon/4$ since $\mathbb{E}_{\vec{x} \sim \mathcal{D}}[|p^*(\vec{x}) - h^*(\vec{x})|] \le \epsilon/2$. So, the expected value of the final expression is at most $\mathrm{opt} + \epsilon/4$. The expected value of the initial expression $\mathrm{err}_S(f)$ is the expected empirical error of the hypothesis produced. Using the fact that the VC dimension of the class of degree-$\kappa(1/\epsilon)$ polynomial thresholds is $O\left(d^{\kappa(1/\epsilon)}\right)$ and Algorithm 2 uses $m = \mathrm{poly}\left(\epsilon^{-1}d^{\kappa(1/\epsilon)}\right)$ samples, the expected empirical error of h is within $\epsilon/4$ of its expected true error, proving the theorem. $\qquad\square$

Note that Theorem 16.5 bounds the error in expectation over $S \sim \mathcal{D}^m$, rather than with high probability. This is because $|p^*(\vec{x}) - h^*(\vec{x})|$ is small in expectation but unbounded in the worst case. However, this is sufficient to show that a single run of the Algorithm 2 has $\mathrm{err}_{\mathcal{D}}(f) \le \mathrm{opt} + \epsilon$ with probability $\Omega(\epsilon)$. To achieve a high-probability bound, we run this algorithm $O(\frac{1}{\epsilon}\log\frac{1}{\delta})$ times and evaluate the outcomes on a separate sample of size $\tilde{O}(\frac{1}{\epsilon^2}\log\frac{1}{\delta})$. This is formalized as follows.

Corollary 16.6 *For any ϵ and δ, repeat Algorithm 2 on $O\left(\epsilon^{-1}\ln(1/\delta)\right)$ independently generated sample sets S_i to learn f_i. Take an additional $\tilde{O}\left(\epsilon^{-2}\ln(1/\delta)\right)$ samples from $\mathcal{D}$ and return f_i^* that minimizes the error on this sample set. With probability $1 - \delta$, this classifier has $\mathrm{err}_{\mathcal{D}}(f_i^*) \le \mathrm{opt} + \epsilon$.*

An interesting aspect of Algorithm 2 is that it is *improper*, i.e., it uses a *polynomial threshold* function to learn over the class of linear threshold functions. Furthermore, this algorithm runs in polynomial time and learns a classifier of error $O(\mathrm{opt})$ when $\mathrm{opt} = \mathrm{err}_{\mathcal{D}}(h^*)$ is *an arbitrarily small constant*. As discussed in Section 16.3.2, no computationally efficient algorithm could have obtained this guarantee for general distributions (Daniely, 2016). This highlights the need to use structural properties of log-concave distributions for obtaining improved learning guarantees.

While L_1 polynomial regression is an extremely powerful algorithm and can obtain error of opt $+ \epsilon$ in poly($d^{\kappa(1/\epsilon)}$) time for any value of ϵ, its runtime is polynomial only when ϵ is a constant. There is a different simple and efficient algorithm, called *Averaging*, that achieves nontrivial learning guarantees for any ϵ that is sufficiently larger than opt. The averaging algorithm (Servedio, 2001) returns the average of label weighted instances[5]

$$\text{classifier } h_{\vec{w}} \text{ where } \vec{w} = \frac{\mathbb{E}_S[y\vec{x}]}{\|\mathbb{E}_S[y\vec{x}]\|}. \qquad \text{(Averaging Algorithm)}$$

The idea behind the averaging algorithm is simple – if a distribution is realizable and symmetric around the origin (such as a Gaussian) then $\mathbb{E}[y\vec{x}]$ points in the direction of the perfect classifier. However, even a small amount of adversarial noise can create a vector component that is orthogonal to $\vec{w}^*$. Nevertheless, Kalai et al. (2008) show that the averaging algorithm recovers $\vec{w}^*$ within angle ϵ when opt is sufficiently smaller than ϵ.

Theorem 16.7 (Based on Kalai et al., 2008) *Consider a distribution $\mathcal{D}$ with a Gaussian and unit variance marginal. There is a constant c such that for any δ and $\epsilon > c \, \text{opt} \sqrt{\ln(1/\text{opt})}$, there is $m \in O\left(\frac{d^2}{\epsilon^2} \ln\left(\frac{d}{\delta}\right)\right)$ such that with probability $1 - \delta$, the outcome of the averaging algorithm on a set of m samples has $\text{err}_{\mathcal{D}}(h_{\vec{w}}) \le \text{opt} + \epsilon$. Furthermore the averaging algorithm runs in time $\text{poly}(d, \frac{1}{\epsilon})$.*

This theorem shows that when $\epsilon \in \Omega(\text{opt} \sqrt{\ln(1/\text{opt})})$ one can efficiently learn a linear threshold of error opt $+ \epsilon$. In the next section, we present a stronger algorithm that achieves the same learning guarantee for $\epsilon \in \Omega(\text{opt})$ based on an adaptive localization technique that limits the power of adversarial noise further.

16.4.2 Computational Improvements via Localization

One of the challenges we face in designing computationally efficient learning algorithms is that an algorithm's sensitivity to noise is not the same throughout the distribution. This is often a byproduct of the fact that easy-to-optimize surrogate loss functions, which approximate the nonconvex sign function, have nonuniform approximation guarantee over the space. This poses a challenge since an adversary can corrupt a small fraction of the data in more sensitive regions and degrade the quality of the algorithm's outcome disproportionately. Identifying and removing these regions typically require knowing the target classifier and therefore cannot be fully done as a preprocessing step. However, when a reasonably good classifier is known in advance it may be possible to approximately identify these regions and *localize* the problem to learn a better classifier. This is the idea behind the work of Awasthi et al. (2017b) which creates an adaptive sequence of carefully designed optimization problems based on localization both on the instance space and the hypothesis space, i.e., focusing on the data close to the current decision boundary and on classifiers close to the current guess. Localization on instances close to the

---

[5] Interestingly, the averaging algorithm is equivalent to L_2 polynomial regression of degree 1 over the Gaussian distribution.

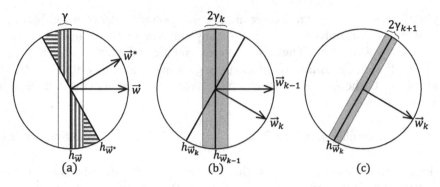

Figure 16.1 Demonstrating localization and margin-based analysis. Part (a) demonstrates the partition of disagreement of $h_{\vec{w}}$ and $h_{\vec{w}*}$ to instances within the band and outside the band. Parts (b) and (c) demonstrate the search for $\vec{w}_k$ within α_k angle of $\vec{w}_{k-1}$ that has error of at most c_0 and the band in the subsequent iteration of step (2) of Algorithm 3.

current decision boundary reduces the impact of adversarial noise on the learning process, while localization on the hypothesis space ensures that the history is not forgotten. Using this, Awasthi et al. (2017b) learns a linear separator of error $\mathrm{opt} + \epsilon$ for $\epsilon \in \Omega(\mathrm{opt})$ in time $\mathrm{poly}(d, \frac{1}{\epsilon})$ when $\mathcal{D}$ has an isotropic log-concave marginal.

Key Technical Ideas. At its core, localization leverages the fact that a large fraction of the disagreement between a reasonably good classifier and the optimal classifier is close to the decision boundary of the former classifier over an isotropic log-concave distribution. To see this, consider Figure 16.1a that demonstrates the disagreement between classifiers $h_{\vec{w}}$ and $h_{\vec{w}*}$ as wedges of the distribution with total probability,

$$\mathop{\mathrm{err}}_{\mathcal{D}}(h_{\vec{w}}) - \mathop{\mathrm{err}}_{\mathcal{D}}(h_{\vec{w}*}) \le \Pr\left[h_{\vec{w}}(\vec{x}) \ne h_{\vec{w}*}(\vec{x})\right] \le \overline{C}_1 \theta(\vec{w}, \vec{w}^*), \tag{16.2}$$

where $\overline{C}_1$ is a constant according to property 3 of Theorem 16.3. This region can be partitioned to instances that are within some γ-boundary of $\vec{w}$ (red vertical stripes) and those that are far (blue horizontal stripes). Since the distribution is log-concave, $\Theta(\gamma)$ fraction of it falls within distance γ of the decision boundary of $h_{\vec{w}}$ (see Theorem 16.3, part 4). Moreover, instances that are far from the decision boundary and are classified differently by $h_{\vec{w}}$ and $h_{\vec{w}*}$ form a small fraction of the total disagreement region. Formally, using properties 4 and 5 of Theorem 16.3, for chosen constant $C_3 = \underline{C}_1/8$ and $\gamma := \alpha \cdot \max\left\{C_3', \frac{C_1}{C_2}\right\}$, for any $\vec{w}$ such that $\theta(\vec{w}, \vec{w}^*) \le \alpha$

$$\Pr\left[|\vec{w} \cdot \vec{x}| \le \gamma \text{ and } h_{\vec{w}}(\vec{x}) \ne h_{\vec{w}*}(\vec{x})\right] \le \Pr\left[|\vec{w} \cdot \vec{x}| \le \gamma\right] \le \overline{C}_2 \gamma, \text{ and} \tag{16.3}$$

$$\Pr\left[|\vec{w} \cdot \vec{x}| > \gamma \text{ and } h_{\vec{w}}(\vec{x}) \ne h_{\vec{w}*}(\vec{x})\right] \le C_3 \alpha \le \frac{\overline{C}_2}{8} \gamma. \tag{16.4}$$

Since $h_{\vec{w}}$ has low disagreement far from its decision boundary as shown in Equation 16.4, this suggests that to improve the overall performance one can focus on reducing the error near the decision boundary of $h_{\vec{w}}$. Consider $\vec{w}$, such that $\theta(\vec{w}, \vec{w}^*) \le \alpha$, and any $\vec{w}'$ within angle α of $\vec{w}$. Focusing on instances close to the boundary $\{(\vec{x}, y) : |\vec{w} \cdot \vec{x}| \le \gamma\}$, hereafter called the *band*, and the corresponding distribution of labeled instances in the band denoted by $\mathcal{D}_{\vec{w},\gamma}$, if the disagreement of $h_{\vec{w}'}$ with $h_{\vec{w}*}$ in the band is at most $c_0 = \min\left\{\frac{1}{4}, \frac{C_1}{4C_2 C_3'}\right\}$ then using the rightmost inequality of Equation 16.3 and the leftmost inequality of Equation 16.4, and the fact that $\{\vec{x} : |\vec{w} \cdot \vec{x}| > \gamma, h_{\vec{w}'}(\vec{x}) \neq h_{\vec{w}*}(\vec{x})\} \subseteq \{\vec{x} : |\vec{w} \cdot \vec{x}| > \gamma, h_{\vec{w}}(\vec{x}) \neq h_{\vec{w}*}(\vec{x})$ or $h_{\vec{w}}(\vec{x}) \neq h_{\vec{w}'}(\vec{x})\}$, we have

$$\Pr_{\mathcal{D}}[h_{\vec{w}'}(\vec{x}) \neq h_{\vec{w}*}(\vec{x})] \leq \overline{C}_2 \gamma \cdot \Pr_{\mathcal{D}_{\vec{w},\gamma}}[h_{\vec{w}'}(\vec{x}) \neq h_{\vec{w}*}(\vec{x})] + 2\alpha C_3 \leq \frac{\alpha C_1}{2}. \qquad (16.5)$$

Thus, $\theta(\vec{w}', \vec{w}*) \leq \alpha/2$, by property 3 of Theorem 16.3. That is, given a classifier $h_{\vec{w}}$ that is at angle at most α to the optimal classifier, one can find an even better classifier that is at angle at most $\alpha/2$ by searching over classifiers that are within angle α of $\vec{w}$ and have at most a constant disagreement c_0 with the optimal classifier over the band. This shows that localization reduces the problem of agnostically learning a linear threshold with error opt $+ \epsilon$ on an isotropic log-concave distribution to a learning problem within the band.

In more detail, for the moment let us assume that we have an oracle for the band that returns $\vec{w}'$ within angle α of $\vec{w}*$ such that the disagreement of $h_{\vec{w}'}$ with $h_{\vec{w}*}$ is at most the previously defined constant c_0, whenever the error of $h_{\vec{w}*}$ in the band is small enough compared to c_0, i.e., for some fixed function $g(\cdot)$, $\text{err}_{\mathcal{D}_{\vec{w},\gamma}}(h_{\vec{w}*}) \leq g(c_0)$.

Oracle $\mathcal{O}(\vec{w}, \gamma, \alpha, \delta)$: Given $\vec{w}, \gamma, \alpha, \delta$, and a fixed error tolerance function $g(\cdot)$, such that $\theta(\vec{w}, \vec{w}*) \leq \alpha$ and $\text{err}_{\mathcal{D}_{\vec{w},\gamma}}(h_{\vec{w}*}) \leq g(c_0)$, the oracle takes $m(\gamma, \delta, \alpha)$ samples from $\mathcal{D}$ and returns $h_{\vec{w}'}$ such that $\theta(\vec{w}', \vec{w}) \leq \alpha$ and with probability $1 - \delta$, $\Pr_{\mathcal{D}_{\vec{w},\gamma}}[h_{\vec{w}'}(\vec{x}) \neq h_{\vec{w}*}(\vec{x})] \leq c_0$.

Algorithm 3 uses this oracle repeatedly to find a classifier of error opt $+ \epsilon$. We note that as we localize the problem in narrower bands we may increase the overall noise in the conditional distribution of the band. This inherently makes learning more challenging for the oracle. Therefore, we use function $g(\cdot)$ to emphasize the preconditions under which the oracle should succeed.

Algorithm 3 Localization with an oracle

Input: Given ϵ, δ, sample access to $\mathcal{D}$, an in-band optimization oracle $\mathcal{O}$, and an initial classifier $h_{\vec{w}_1}$ such that $\theta(\vec{w}_1, \vec{w}*) < \pi/2$.

1. Let constant $c_\gamma = \max\left\{C_3', \underline{C}_1/\overline{C}_2\right\}$, $\alpha_k = 2^{-k}\pi$ and $\gamma_k = \alpha_k \cdot c_\gamma$, for all k.
2. For $k = 1, \ldots, \log\left(\frac{\overline{C}_1 \pi}{\epsilon}\right) - 1 = r$, let $h_{\vec{w}_{k+1}} \leftarrow \mathcal{O}\left(\vec{w}_k, \gamma_k, \alpha_k, \frac{\delta}{r}\right)$.
3. Return $h_{\vec{w}_r}$.

Lemma 16.8 (Margin-Based Localization) *Assume that oracle $\mathcal{O}$ and a corresponding error tolerance function $g(\cdot)$ exist that satisfy the post-conditions of the oracle on the sequence of inputs $(\vec{w}_k, \gamma_k, \alpha_k, \delta/r)$ used in Algorithm 3. There is a constant c such that for any distribution $\mathcal{D}$ with an isotropic log-concave marginal, δ, and $\epsilon \geq c$ opt, Algorithm 3, takes*

$$m = \sum_{k=1}^{\log(\overline{C}_1/\epsilon)} m\left(\gamma_k, \alpha_k, \frac{\delta}{\log(\overline{C}_1/\epsilon)}\right)$$

samples from $\mathcal{D}$ and returns $h_{\vec{w}}$ such that with probability $1-\delta$, $\mathrm{err}_{\mathcal{D}}(h_{\vec{w}}) \leq \mathrm{opt}+\epsilon$.

Proof Algorithm 3 starts with $\vec{w}_1$ of angle at most α_1 to $\vec{w}^*$. Assume for now that $\mathrm{err}_{\mathcal{D}_{\vec{w}_k, \gamma_k}}(h_{\vec{w}^*}) \leq g(c_0)$ for all $\vec{w}_k$ and γ_k used by the algorithm, so that the preconditions of the oracle are met. Then, every time the algorithm executes step (2), the oracle returns $\vec{w}_{k+1} \leftarrow \mathcal{O}(\vec{w}_k, \gamma_k, \alpha_k, \delta/r)$ such that with probability $1 - \delta/r$, $\mathrm{Pr}_{\mathcal{D}_{\vec{w}_k, \gamma_k}}[h_{\vec{w}_{k+1}}(\vec{x}) \neq h_{\vec{w}^*}(\vec{x})] \leq c_0$. Using Equation 16.5, $\theta(\vec{w}_{k+1}, \vec{w}^*) \leq \theta(\vec{w}_k, \vec{w}^*)/2 \leq \alpha_{k+1}$, i.e., angle of the candidate classifier to $\vec{w}^*$ is halved. After $r = \log(\overline{C}_1 \pi/\epsilon) - 1$ iterations, we have $\theta(\vec{w}_r, \vec{w}^*) \leq \epsilon/\overline{C}_1$. Using the relationship between the error of $h_{\vec{w}}$ and its angle to $h_{\vec{w}*}$ as described in Equation 16.2, $\mathrm{err}_{\mathcal{D}}(h_{\vec{w}_r}) \leq \mathrm{err}_{\mathcal{D}}(h_{\vec{w}*}) + \overline{C}_1 \theta(\vec{w}^*, \vec{w}_r) \leq \mathrm{opt} + \epsilon$. This approach works for all noise types.

Now, we use the properties of the (adversarial) noise to show that the preconditions of the oracle are met as long as the width of the band is not much smaller than opt. That is, for all $k \leq r$, $\mathrm{err}_{\mathcal{D}_{\vec{w}_k, \gamma_k}}(h_{\vec{w}*}) < g(c_0)$ when $\epsilon > c$ opt. As we focus on a band of width γ_k we may focus on areas where $h_{\vec{w}*}$ is wrong. But, any band of width γ_k constitutes at least $\underline{C}_2 \gamma_k \in \Omega(\epsilon)$ fraction of $\mathcal{D}$ for $k \leq r$. Hence, there is constant c for which $\mathrm{err}_{\mathcal{D}_{\vec{w}_k, \gamma_k}}(h_{\vec{w}*}) \leq \frac{\mathrm{opt}}{\underline{C}_2 \gamma_k} \leq g(c_0)$, for all $\epsilon \geq c$ opt. $\qquad \square$

Lemma 16.8 shows that to get a computationally efficient algorithm for learning over a log-concave distribution, it is sufficient to implement oracle $\mathcal{O}$ efficiently. We use *hinge loss minimization* for this purpose. Formally, hinge loss with parameter τ is defined by $\ell_\tau(\vec{w}, \vec{x}, y) = \max\left\{0, 1 - \frac{y(\vec{w} \cdot \vec{x})}{\tau}\right\}$. Note that whenever $h_{\vec{w}}$ makes a mistake on $(\vec{x}, y)$ the hinge loss is at least 1. Therefore, $\mathrm{err}(h_{\vec{w}}) \leq \mathbb{E}[\ell_\tau(\vec{w}, \vec{x}, y)]$. Thus, it suffices to show that for any distribution $\mathcal{D}_{\vec{w}_k, \gamma_k}$ we can find $\vec{w}_{k+1}$ whose expected τ_k hinge loss is at most c_0. Since hinge loss is a convex function, we can efficiently optimize it over the band using Algorithm 4. So, the main technical challenge is to show that there is a classifier, namely $h_{\vec{w}*}$, whose hinge loss is sufficiently smaller than c_0, and therefore, Algorithm 4 returns a classifier whose hinge loss is also less than c_0. This is done via a series of technical steps, where first the hinge loss of $h_{\vec{w}*}$ is shown to be small when

---

Algorithm 4 Hinge loss minimization in the band

Input: Unit vector $\vec{w}_k$, γ_k, α_k, δ, and sampling access to $\mathcal{D}$.

1. Take a set S of $\tilde{\Theta}\left(\frac{d^2}{\gamma_k c_0^2} \ln\left(\frac{1}{\epsilon}\right) \ln\left(\frac{1}{\delta}\right)\right)$ samples and let $S_k = \{(\vec{x}, y) \mid |\vec{w}_k \cdot \vec{x}| \leq \gamma_k\}$.
2. Let $\tau_k = \gamma_k c_0 \underline{C}_2/4\overline{C}_2$ and for the convex set $\mathcal{K} = \{\vec{v} \mid \|\vec{v}\| \leq 1 \text{ and } \theta(\vec{v}, \vec{w}) \leq \alpha_k\}$ let $\vec{v}_{k+1} \leftarrow \mathrm{argmin}_{\vec{v} \in \mathcal{K}} \mathbb{E}_S\left[\ell_{\tau_k}(\vec{v}, \vec{x}, y)\right]$.
3. Return $\vec{w}_{k+1} = \frac{\vec{v}_{k+1}}{\|\vec{v}_{k+1}\|}$.

---

the distribution has no noise and then it is shown that noise can increase the hinge loss of $h_{\vec{w}*}$ by a small amount only. We refer the reader to the work of Awasthi et al. (2017b) for more details.

Lemma 16.9 (Hinge Loss Minimization) *There is a function $g(z) \in \Theta(z^4)$, such that for any distribution $\mathcal{D}$ with an isotropic log-concave marginal, given $\vec{w}_k, \gamma_k,$ and α_k used by Algorithm 3, such that $\theta(\vec{w}_k, \vec{w}^*) \leq \alpha_k$ and $\mathrm{err}_{\mathcal{D}_{\vec{w}_k, \gamma_k}}(h_{\vec{w}*}) \leq g(c_0)$, Algorithm 4 takes $n_k = \tilde{\Theta}\left(\frac{d^2}{\gamma_k c_0^2} \ln(1/\epsilon) \ln(1/\delta)\right)$ samples from $\mathcal{D}$ and returns $\vec{w}_{k+1}$ such that $\theta(\vec{w}_{k+1}, \vec{w}_k) \leq \alpha_k$ and with probability $1 - \delta$, $\mathrm{Pr}_{\mathcal{D}_{\vec{w}_k, \gamma_k}}[h_{\vec{w}_{k+1}}(\vec{x}) \neq h_{\vec{w}*}(\vec{x})] \leq c_0$.*

Lemmas 16.8 and 16.9 prove the main result of this section.

Theorem 16.10 (Awasthi et al., 2017b) *Consider distribution $\mathcal{D}$ with an isotropic log-concave marginal. There is a constant c such that for all δ and $\epsilon \geq c$ opt, there is $m \in \tilde{O}\left(\frac{d^2}{\epsilon} \ln\left(\frac{1}{\delta}\right)\right)$ for which with probability $1 - \delta$, Algorithm 3 using Algorithm 4 for optimization in the band, takes m samples from $\mathcal{D}$, and returns a classifier $h_{\vec{w}}$ whose error is $\mathrm{err}_{\mathcal{D}}(h_{\vec{w}}) \leq$ opt $+ \epsilon$.*

The Surprising Power of Localization. The localization technique can also be used with stronger malicious adversaries that not only can change the label of a fraction of instances, but also *can change the shape of the underlying distribution.* This noise is commonly referred to as *malicious noise* or *poisoning attack.*

Consider applying Algorithm 3 in the presence of malicious noise when the original distribution has an isotropic log-concave marginal. Since malicious noise changes the marginal distribution of instances, it is not clear if hinge-loss minimization of Lemma 16.9 can find a suitable classifier $h_{\vec{w}_{k+1}}$. To deal with this Awasthi et al. (2017b) introduce a *soft outlier removal* technique that is applied before hinge loss minimization in every step of Algorithm 3. At a high level, this procedure assigns weights to instances in the band, which indicate the algorithm's confidence that these instance were not introduced by "malicious noise." These weights are computed by a linear program that takes into account the variance of instances in the band in directions that are close to $\vec{w}_k$ in angle. The algorithm uses weighted hinge loss minimization to find $\vec{w}_{k+1}$ with similar guarantees to those stated in Lemma 16.9. This shows that when the original distribution has an isotropic log-concave marginal, a variant of Algorithm 3 can deal with malicious adversaries.

Theorem 16.11 (Awasthi et al., 2017b) *Consider a realizable distribution $\mathcal{D}$ with an isotropic log-concave marginal and consider a setting where $(1 - $ opt$)$ fraction of the data comes i.i.d. from $\mathcal{D}$ and the other opt fraction is chosen by a malicious adversary. There is a constant c such that for all δ and $\epsilon \geq c$ opt, there is an algorithm that takes $m \in \mathrm{poly}(d, \frac{1}{\epsilon})$ samples and runs in time $\mathrm{poly}(d, \frac{1}{\epsilon})$ and with probability $1 - \delta$ returns a classifier $h_{\vec{w}}$ whose error is $\mathrm{err}_{\mathcal{D}}(h_{\vec{w}}) \leq \epsilon$.*

Theorem 16.11 shows that localization can extend the guarantees of Theorem 16.10 against stronger adversaries. This result improves over the previously known result of Klivans et al. (2009), which handles only a smaller amount of dimension-dependent noise. Chapter 17 considers malicious noise in the unsupervised setting.

In Section 16.5.2, we will see that localization is also useful in obtaining much stronger learning guarantees in the presence of real-life (and weaker) adversaries that are further constrained in the type of noise they can induce in the data.

16.5 Benefits of Assumptions on the Noise

Learning halfspaces can also be studied in a number of intermediate noise settings. A natural assumption on the noise in classification is that the Bayes optimal classifier belongs to the set of classifiers one considers. That is, any instance is more likely to appear with its correct label rather than the incorrect one, in other words, $f_{bayes}(\vec{x}) = $ sign $(\mathbb{E}[y|\vec{x}]) = h_{\vec{w}*}(\vec{x})$ for some $\vec{w}*$ in the case of learning linear thresholds. This type of noise and its variants are often used to model the noise that is found in crowdsourced data sets, where the assumption on the noise translates to the belief that any given instance would be correctly labeled by majority of labelers. *Random classification noise* with parameter $\nu < \frac{1}{2}$ considers a setting where for all $\vec{x}$, $\mathbb{E}[yh_{\vec{w}*}(\vec{x})|\vec{x}] = (1-2\nu)$. More generally, *bounded noise* with parameter $\nu < \frac{1}{2}$ requires only that for all $\vec{x}$, $\mathbb{E}[yh_{\vec{w}*}(\vec{x})|\vec{x}] \geq (1 - 2\nu)$. Equivalently, random classification noise and bounded noise can be described as noise that is added to a realizable distribution where every instance $\vec{x}$ is assigned the wrong label with probability ν or $\nu(\vec{x}) \leq \nu$, respectively. Unless stated otherwise, we assume that ν is bounded away from $\frac{1}{2}$ by a constant.

In this section, we explore how assumptions on the niceness of the noise allows us to obtain better computational and statistical learning guarantees.

16.5.1 Statistical Improvements for Nicer Noise Models

A key property of random classification and bounded noise is that it tightly upper and lower bounds the relationship between the excess error of a classifier and its disagreement with the optimal classifier. That is, for any classifier h,

$$(1 - 2\nu) \Pr_{\mathcal{D}}[h(\vec{x}) \neq h_{\vec{w}*}(\vec{x})] \leq \operatorname*{err}_{\mathcal{D}}(h) - \operatorname*{err}_{\mathcal{D}}(h_{\vec{w}*}) \leq \Pr_{\mathcal{D}}[h(\vec{x}) \neq h_{\vec{w}*}(\vec{x})]. \tag{16.6}$$

The right-hand side of this inequality holds by triangle inequality regardless of the noise model. However, the left-hand side of this inequality crucially uses the properties of bounded and random classification noise to show that if h and $h_{\vec{w}*}$ disagree on $\vec{x}$, then $\vec{x}$ and its expected label $\mathbb{E}[y|\vec{x}]$ contribute to the error of both classifiers. This results in h incurring only a small excess error over the error of $h_{\vec{w}*}$.

Equation 16.6 is particularly useful because its right-hand side, which denotes the disagreement between h and $h_{\vec{w}*}$, is also the variance of h's excess error, i.e.,

$$\mathbb{E}_{\mathcal{D}} \left[\left(\operatorname*{err}_{(\vec{x},y)}(h) - \operatorname*{err}_{(\vec{x},y)}(h_{\vec{w}*}) \right)^2 \right] = \Pr_{\mathcal{D}}[h(\vec{x}) \neq h_{\vec{w}*}(\vec{x})].$$

Therefore, an upper bound on the disagreement of h also bounds the variance of its excess error and allows for stronger concentration bounds. For example, using

Bernstein's inequality and the VC theory, with probability $1 - \delta$ over the choice of a set S of m i.i.d. samples from $\mathcal{D}$, for all linear thresholds h we have

$$\operatorname*{err}_{\mathcal{D}}(h) - \operatorname*{err}_{\mathcal{D}}(h_{\vec{w}*}) \leq \operatorname*{err}_{S}(h) - \operatorname*{err}_{S}(h_{\vec{w}*}) + \sqrt{\frac{(\operatorname{err}_{\mathcal{D}}(h) - \operatorname{err}_{\mathcal{D}}(h_{\vec{w}*}))\,(d + \ln(\frac{1}{\delta}))}{(1 - 2v)m}} + O\left(\frac{1}{m}\right).$$

That is, there is $m \in O\left(\frac{d + \ln(1/\delta)}{(1 - 2v)\epsilon}\right)$ such that with probability $1 - \delta$ the classifier h' that minimizes the empirical error on m samples has $\operatorname{err}_{\mathcal{D}}(h) \leq \operatorname{opt} + \epsilon$.

This shows that if $\mathcal{D}$ demonstrates bounded or random classification noise it can be learned with fewer samples than needed in the agnostic case. This is due to the fact that we directly compare the error of h and that of $h_{\vec{w}*}$ (and using stronger concentration bounds) instead of going through uniform convergence. While we need $\Omega(d/\epsilon^2)$ samples to learn a classifier of error $\operatorname{opt} + \epsilon$ in the agnostic case, we only need $O(d/\epsilon)$ samples to learn in the presence of random classification or bounded noise. We note that this result is purely information theoretical; i.e., it does not imply existence of a polynomial-time algorithm that can learn in the presence of this type of noise. In the next section, we discuss the issue of computational efficiency in the presence of random classification and bounded noise in detail.

16.5.2 Further Computational Improvements for Nicer Noise Models

In this section, we show that in the presence of random classification or bounded noise there are computationally efficient algorithms that enjoy improved noise robustness guarantees compared to their agnostic counterparts. In particular, one can efficiently learn linear thresholds in the presence of random classification noise.

Theorem 16.12 (Blum et al., 1998) *For any distribution $\mathcal{D}$ that has random classification noise, there is an algorithm that runs in time $\operatorname{poly}(d, \frac{1}{\epsilon}, \ln(1/\delta))$ and with probability $1 - \delta$ learns a vector $\vec{w}$ such that $\operatorname{err}_{\mathcal{D}}(h_{\vec{w}}) \leq \operatorname{opt} + \epsilon$.*

We refer the interested reader to the work of Blum et al. (1998) for more details on the algorithm that achieves the guarantees in Theorem 16.12. Let us note that when in addition to random classification noise, which is a highly symmetric noise, the marginal distribution is also symmetric several simple algorithms can learn a classifier of error $\operatorname{opt} + \epsilon$. For example, when the distribution is Gaussian and has random classification noise the averaging algorithm of Section 16.4.1 recovers $\vec{w}^* \propto \mathbb{E}_{\mathcal{D}}[\vec{x}y]$.

While the random classification noise leads to a polynomial-time learning algorithm, it does not present a convincing model of learning beyond the worst case. In particular, the highly symmetric nature of random classification noise does not lend itself to real-world settings where parts of data may be less noisy than others. This is where bounded noise comes into play – it relaxes the symmetric nature of random classification noise, yet assumes that no instance is too noisy. As opposed to the random classification noise, however, no efficient algorithms are known to date that can learn a classifier of error $\operatorname{opt} + \epsilon$ in the presence of bounded noise when the marginal distribution is unrestricted. Therefore, in the remainder of this section we focus on a setting where, in addition to having bounded noise, $\mathcal{D}$ also has a nice marginal distribution, specifically an isotropic log-concave marginal distribution.

Let us first consider the iterative localization technique of Section 16.4.2. Given that bounded noise is a stronger assumption than adversarial noise, Theorem 16.10 implies that for small enough opt $\in O(\epsilon)$, we can learn a linear threshold of error opt $+ \epsilon$. Interestingly, the same algorithm achieves a much better guarantee for bounded noise and the key to this is that $\text{err}_{\mathcal{D}_{\vec{w},\gamma}}(h_{\vec{w}^*}) \leq \nu$ for any $\vec{w}$ and γ.

Lemma 16.13 (Margin-Based Localization for Bounded Noise) *Assume that oracle $\mathcal{O}$ and a corresponding error tolerance function $g(\cdot)$ exist that satisfy the post-conditions of the oracle on the sequence of inputs $(\vec{w}_k, \gamma_k, \alpha_k, \delta/r)$ used in Algorithm 3. For any distribution $\mathcal{D}$ with an isotropic log-concave marginal and ν-bounded noise such that $\nu \leq g(c_0)$ and any ϵ, δ, Algorithm 3 takes*

$$m = \sum_{k=1}^{\log(\overline{C}_1/\epsilon)} m\left(\gamma_k, \alpha_k, \frac{\delta}{\log(\overline{C}_1/\epsilon)}\right)$$

samples from $\mathcal{D}$, and returns $h_{\vec{w}}$ such that with probability $1 - \delta$, $\text{err}_{\mathcal{D}}(h_{\vec{w}}) \leq$ opt $+ \epsilon$.

The proof follows that of Lemma 16.8, with the exception that the noise in the band never increases beyond $\nu \leq g(c_0)$. This is due to the fact that the probability that an instance $\vec{x}$ is noisy in any band of $\mathcal{D}$ is at most $\nu \leq g(c_0)$. Note that the preconditions of the oracle are met for arbitrarily small bands when the noise is bounded, as opposed to the adversarial setting where the preconditions are met only when the width of the band is larger than $\Omega(\text{opt})$. So, by using hinge loss minimization in the band (Lemma 16.9) one can learn a linear threshold of error opt $+ \epsilon$ when the noise parameter $\nu < g(c_0)$ is a *small constant*. This is much better than our adversarial noise guarantee where the noise has to be at most opt $< \epsilon/c$.

How small $g(c_0)$ is in Lemma 16.9 and how small is ν as a result? As Awasthi et al. (2015) showed, ν has to be almost negligible, of the order of 10^{-6}. So, we ask whether an alternative algorithm can handle bounded noise for *any* $\nu \leq \frac{1}{2} - \Theta(1)$. Note that the key property needed for applying hinge loss minimization in the band is that the noise in $\mathcal{D}_{\vec{w}_k, \gamma_k}$ is at most $g(c_0)$, regardless of the value of ν. So a natural approach for guaranteeing this property is to de-noise the data in the band and reduce the noise from an arbitrary constant ν to a smaller constant $g(c_0)$. Polynomial regression (Algorithm 2) can be used here, as it can learn a polynomial threshold f_{k+1} that has a small constant error in polynomial time. Had f_{k+1} been a linear threshold, we would have set $h_{\vec{w}_{k+1}} = f_{k+1}$ and continued with the next round of localized optimization. However, for general polynomial thresholds we need to approximate f_{k+1} with a linear threshold. Fortunately, f_{k+1} is already close to $h_{\vec{w}^*}$. Therefore, the hinge loss minimization technique of Algorithm 4 can be used to learn a linear threshold $h_{\vec{w}_{k+1}}$ whose predictions are close to f_{k+1}, and thus is close to $h_{\vec{w}^*}$. This is formalized in Algorithm 5 and the following lemma.

Lemma 16.14 (Polynomial Regression with Hinge Loss Minimization) *Consider distribution $\mathcal{D}$ with an isotropic log-concave marginal and bounded noise with parameter ν. For any ϵ, δ, $\vec{w}_k$, γ_k, and α_k stated in Algorithm 3, such that $\theta(\vec{w}_k, \vec{w}^*) \leq \alpha_k$, Algorithm 5 takes $n_k = \text{poly}\left(d^{\text{poly}\left(\frac{1}{1-2\nu}\right)}, \frac{1}{\epsilon}, \ln\left(\frac{1}{\delta}\right)\right)$ samples*

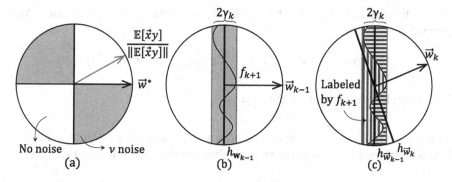

Figure 16.2 Part (a) demonstrates that the averaging algorithm performs poorly on bounded noise, even when the distribution is symmetric. Part (b) demonstrates step 1 of Algorithm 5 where polynomial regression is used to learn f_{k+1}. Part (c) demonstrates the use of hinge loss minimization in step 2 of Algorithm 5 on the distribution labeled by f_{k+1}, where horizontal and vertical stripes denote regions labeled as positive and negative by f_{k+1}.

Algorithm 5 Polynomial regression and hinge loss minimization in the band

---

Input: Unit vector $\vec{w}_k$, γ_k, α_k, δ, c_0, and sampling access to $\mathcal{D}$.

1. Take $n_k = \text{poly}\left(d^{\text{poly}\left(\frac{1}{1-2\nu}\right)}, \frac{1}{\epsilon}, \ln\left(\frac{1}{\delta}\right)\right)$ i.i.d. samples from $\mathcal{D}$ and let S_k include the samples for which $\{\vec{x} \mid |\vec{w}_k \cdot \vec{x}| \leq \gamma_k\}$. Let f_{k+1} be the outcome of Algorithm 2 with excess error of $(1 - 2\nu)g(c_0)$.

2. Take $\tilde{\Theta}\left(\frac{d^2}{\gamma_k c_0^2} \ln\left(\frac{1}{\epsilon}\right) \ln\left(\frac{1}{\delta}\right)\right)$ i.i.d. samples from $\mathcal{D}$ and let S'_k include the samples $(\vec{x}, f_{k+1}(\vec{x}))$ for which $\{\vec{x} \mid |\vec{w}_k \cdot \vec{x}| \leq \gamma_k\}$. Let $\tau_k = \frac{c_0 C_2}{4 C_2} \gamma_k$ and for the convex set $\mathcal{K} = \{\vec{v} \mid \|\vec{v}\| \leq 1 \text{ and } \theta(\vec{v}, \vec{w}) \leq \alpha_k\}$ let $\vec{v}_{k+1} \leftarrow \text{argmin}_{\vec{v} \in \mathcal{K}} \mathbb{E}_{S'_k}\left[\ell_{\tau_k}(\vec{v}, \vec{x}, y)\right]$.

3. Return $\vec{w}_{k+1} = \frac{\vec{v}_{k+1}}{\|\vec{v}_{k+1}\|}$.

---

from $\mathcal{D}$ and returns $\vec{w}_{k+1}$ such that $\theta(\vec{w}_{k+1}, \vec{w}_k) \leq \alpha_k$ and with probability $1 - \delta$, $\Pr_{\mathcal{D}_{\vec{w}_k, \gamma_k}}[h_{\vec{w}_{k+1}}(\vec{x}) \neq h_{\vec{w}*}(\vec{x})] \leq c_0$.

Proof Let $g(c_0) \in \Theta(c_0^4)$ be the error tolerance function of hinge loss minimization according to Lemma 16.9. Note that for log-concave distribution $\mathcal{D}$, the distribution in any band is also log-concave. Therefore, step 1 of Algorithm 5 uses polynomial regression to learn a polynomial threshold f_{k+1} such that $\text{err}_{\mathcal{D}_{\vec{w}_k, \gamma_k}}(f_{k+1}) \leq \text{opt} + (1 - 2\nu)g(c_0)$. Now let distribution $\mathcal{P}$ be the same as $\mathcal{D}$, except that all instances are labeled according to f_{k+1}. Since the noise is bounded, by Equation 16.6

$$\text{err}_{\mathcal{P}_{\vec{w}_k, \gamma_k}}(h_{\vec{w}*}) = \Pr_{\mathcal{D}_{\vec{w}_k, \gamma_k}}[f_{k+1}(\vec{x}) \neq h_{\vec{w}*}(\vec{x})]$$

$$\leq \frac{1}{1 - 2\nu}\left(\text{err}_{\mathcal{D}_{\vec{w}_k, \gamma_k}}(f_{k+1}) - \text{err}_{\mathcal{D}_{\vec{w}_k, \gamma_k}}(h_{\vec{w}*})\right) \leq g(c_0).$$

Then, distribution $\mathcal{P}$ meets the conditions of Lemma 16.9. Therefore, Algorithm 5 returns a $h_{\vec{w}_{k+1}}$ such that

$$\Pr_{\mathcal{D}_{\vec{w}_k, \gamma_k}}\left[h_{\vec{w}_{k+1}}(\vec{x}) \neq h_{\vec{w}^*}(\vec{x})\right] = \Pr_{\mathcal{P}_{\vec{w}_k, \gamma_k}}\left[h_{\vec{w}_{k+1}}(\vec{x}) \neq h_{\vec{w}^*}(\vec{x})\right] \leq c_0.$$

This completes the proof of the lemma. □

Using margin-based localization iteratively while applying polynomial regression paired with hinge loss minimization in the band proves the following theorem.

Theorem 16.15 (Awasthi et al., 2016)   *Let $\mathcal{D}$ be a distribution with an isotropic log-concave marginal and bounded noise with parameter v. For any ϵ and δ there is $m = \text{poly}\left(d^{\text{poly}\left(\frac{1}{1-2v}\right)}, \frac{1}{\epsilon}, \ln\left(\frac{1}{\delta}\right)\right)$ such that Algorithm 3 that uses Algorithm 5 for optimization in the band takes m samples from $\mathcal{D}$, runs in time $\text{poly}(m)$, and with probability $1 - \delta$ returns a classifier $h_{\vec{w}}$ whose error is $\text{err}_{\mathcal{D}}(h_{\vec{w}}) \leq \text{opt} + \epsilon$.*

Theorem 16.15 shows that as long as $v \leq \frac{1}{2} - \Theta(1)$, there is a polynomial-time algorithm that learns a linear threshold of error opt $+ \epsilon$ over isotropic log-concave distributions. However, the sample complexity and runtime of this algorithm is inversely exponential in $1 - 2v$. Note that this sample complexity is exponentially larger than the information theoretic bounds presented in Section 16.5.1. It remains to be seen if there are computationally efficient algorithms that match the information theoretic bound for general log-concave distributions.

16.6 Final Remarks and Current Research Directions

Connecting this chapter to the broader vision of machine learning, let us note that machine learning's effectiveness in today's world was directly influenced by early works on foundational aspects that moved past the worst case and leveraged properties of real-life learning problems, e.g., finite VC dimension and margins (Cristianini and Shawe-Taylor, 2000). We next highlight some of the current research directions in connection to the beyond the worst-case analysis of algorithms.

Adversarial Noise. The polynomial regression of Section 16.4.1 is due to Kalai et al. (2008). The a results of Theorem 16.7 are a variant of the original results of Kalai et al. (2008) that applied to the uniform distribution. Klivans et al. (2009) showed that a variant of the averaging algorithm with a hard outlier removal technique achieves error of opt $+ \epsilon$ for opt $\in O(\epsilon^3 / \ln(1/\epsilon))$ when the distribution is isotropic log-concave. The margin-based localization technique of Lemma 16.8 and its variants first appeared in Balcan et al. (2007) in the context of *active learning*. The combination of margin-based localization technique and hinge loss minimization of Section 16.4.2 is due to Awasthi et al. (2017b), which also works in the active learning setting. Daniely (2015) used this technique with polynomial regression to obtain a polynomial-time approximation scheme (PTAS) for learning linear thresholds over the uniform distribution. Diakonikolas et al. (2018) further extended the margin-based localization results to nonhomogeneous linear thresholds. Going forward, generalizing these techniques to more expressive hypothesis classes is an important direction for future work. The key challenge here is to define an appropriate localization area. For linear separators, we derived margin-based localization analytically. In more general settings, however, such as deep neural networks, a closed-form derivation may not be possible. It would be interesting to see if one can instead algorithmically compute a good localization area using the properties of the problem at hand, e.g., by using unlabeled data.

Bounded Noise. The results of Section 16.5.2 for log-concave distributions with bounded noise are due to Awasthi et al. (2015, 2016). Yan and Zhang (2017) used a variant of this algorithm with improved sample complexity and runtime dependence on $1/(1 - 2\nu)$ for the special case of uniform distribution over the unit ball. Recently, Diakonikolas et al. (2019) presented a polynomial-time algorithm for distribution-independent error bound of $\nu + \epsilon$ when noise is ν-bounded and also showed that their techniques and variants thereof fall short of learning a classier of error $\text{opt} + \epsilon$. This is a significantly weaker guarantee because in typical applications opt is much smaller than ν, which indicates the maximum amount of noise on a given point. To date, the question of whether there are computationally efficient algorithms or hardness results for getting distribution-independent error of $\text{opt} + \epsilon$ in the presence of bounded noise remains an important open problem in the theory of machine learning. On the other hand, one of the main motivations of bounded noise and its variants is crowdsourcing, where every instance is correctly labeled by at least $1 - \nu$ fraction of labelers. If one designs the data collection protocol as well as the learning algorithm, Awasthi et al. (2017a) showed that any set of classifiers $\mathcal{F}$ that can be efficiently learned in the realizable setting using $m_{\epsilon, \delta}^{real}$ samples can be learned efficiently by making $O(m_{\epsilon, \delta}^{real})$ queries to the crowd. This effectively shows that the computational and statistical aspects of *nonpersistent bounded noise* are the same as those of the realizable setting.

In addition to the real-life motivation for this noise model, bounded noise is also related to other notions of beyond the worst-case analysis of algorithms. For example, Equation 16.6, which relates the excess error of a classifier to how its predictions differ from that of the optimal classifier, is a supervised analogue of the *"approximation stability"* assumption used in *clustering*, which states that any clustering that is close in objective value to the optimal classifier should also be close to it in classification. See Chapter 6 for more details on approximation stability.

Robustness to Other Adversarial Attacks. As mentioned, the localization technique introduced in this chapter can also handle malicious noise (Awasthi et al., 2017b). A related model considers *poisoning attacks* where an adversary inserts maliciously crafted fake data points into a training set in order to cause specific failures to a learning algorithm. It would be interesting to provide additional formal guarantees for such adversaries. Another type of attack, called *adversarial examples*, considers a type of corruption that affects the distribution only at test time, thereby requiring one to learn a classifier $f \in \mathcal{F}$ on distribution $\mathcal{D}$ that still achieves a good performance when $\mathcal{D}$ is corrupted by some noise (Goodfellow et al., 2015). By and large, this learning model draws motivation from audio-visual attacks on learning systems, where the goal is to secure learning algorithms against an adversary that is intent on causing harm through misclassification (Kurakin et al., 2017). A beyond the worst-case perspective on test-time robustness could also improve the robustness of learning algorithms to several nonadversarial corruptions, such as distribution shift and misspecification, and therefore is a promising direction for future research.

References

Anthony, Martin, and Bartlett, Peter L. 1999. *Neural Network Learning: Theoretical Foundations*. Cambridge University Press.

Awasthi, Pranjal, Balcan, Maria-Florina, Haghtalab, Nika, and Urner, Ruth. 2015. Efficient learning of linear separators under bounded noise. *Proceedings of the 28th Conference on Computational Learning Theory*, pp. 167–190.

Awasthi, Pranjal, Balcan, Maria-Florina, Haghtalab, Nika, and Zhang, Hongyang. 2016. Learning and 1-bit compressed sensing under asymmetric noise. In *Proceedings of the 29th Conference on Computational Learning Theory*, pp. 152–192.

Awasthi, Pranjal, Blum, Avrim, Haghtalab, Nika, and Mansour, Yishay. 2017a. Efficient PAC learning from the crowd. In *Proceedings of the 30th Conference on Computational Learning Theory*, pp. 127–150.

Awasthi, Pranjal, Balcan, Maria Florina, and Long, Philip M. 2017b. The power of localization for efficiently learning linear separators with noise. *Journal of the ACM*, **63**(6), 50.

Balcan, Maria-Florina, and Long, Phil. 2013. Active and passive learning of linear separators under log-concave distributions. In *Proceedings of the 26th Conference on Computational Learning Theory*, pp. 288–316.

Balcan, Maria-Florina, Broder, Andrei, and Zhang, Tong. 2007. Margin based active learning. In *Proceedings of the 20th Conference on Computational Learning Theory*, pp. 35–50.

Blum, Avrim, Frieze, A., Kannan, Ravi, and Vempala, Santosh. 1998. A polynomial-time algorithm for learning noisy linear threshold functions. *Algorithmica*, **22**(1–2), 35–52.

Cristianini, Nello, and Shawe-Taylor, John. 2000. *An Introduction to Support Vector Machines and Other Kernel-Based Learning Methods*. Cambridge University Press.

Daniely, Amit. 2015. A PTAS for agnostically learning halfspaces. In *Proceedings of the 28th Conference on Computational Learning Theory*, pp. 484–502.

Daniely, Amit. 2016. Complexity theoretic limitations on learning halfspaces. In *Proceedings of the 48th Annual ACM Symposium on Theory of Computing*, pp. 105–117.

Diakonikolas, Ilias, Kane, Daniel M, and Stewart, Alistair. 2018. Learning geometric concepts with nasty noise. *Proceedings of the 50th Annual ACM Symposium on Theory of Computing*, pp. 1061–1073.

Diakonikolas, Ilias, Gouleakis, Themis, and Tzamos, Christos. 2019. Distribution-independent PAC learning of halfspaces with Massart noise. In *Proceedings of 32nd Annual Conference on Neural Information Processing System*, pp. 4751–4762.

Goodfellow, Ian J., Shlens, Jonathon, and Szegedy, Christian. 2015. Explaining and harnessing adversarial examples. In *Proceedings of the 3rd International Conference on Learning Representations*.

Guruswami, Venkatesan, and Raghavendra, Prasad. 2009. Hardness of learning halfspaces with noise. *SIAM Journal on Computing*, **39**(2), 742–765.

Kalai, Adam Tauman, Klivans, Adam R, Mansour, Yishay, and Servedio, Rocco A. 2008. Agnostically learning halfspaces. *SIAM Journal on Computing*, **37**(6), 1777–1805.

Kearns, Michael J., and Li, M. 1988. Learning in the presence of malicious errors. In *Proceedings of the 20th Annual ACM Symposium on Theory of Computing*, pp. 267–280.

Klivans, Adam R., Long, Philip M., and Servedio, Rocco A. 2009. Learning halfspaces with malicious noise. *Journal of Machine Learning Research*, **10**, 2715–2740.

Kurakin, Alexey, Goodfellow, Ian J., and Bengio, Samy. 2017. Adversarial examples in the physical world. In *Fifth International Conference on Learning Representations (Workshop)*.

Lovász, László, and Vempala, Santosh. 2007. The geometry of logconcave functions and sampling algorithms. *Random Structures and Algorithms*, **30**(3), 307–358.

Servedio, Rocco Anthony. 2001. *Efficient algorithms in computational learning theory*. PhD thesis, Harvard University.

Yan, Songbai, and Zhang, Chicheng. 2017. Revisiting Perceptron: Efficient and label-optimal learning of halfspaces. In *Proceedings of the 31st Annual Conference on Neural Information Processing Systems*, pp. 1056–1066.

Exercises

Exercise 16.1 Prove the properties of log-concave distributions, as described in Theorem 16.3, for $\mathcal{D}$ that is a Gaussian distributions with unit variance.

Exercise 16.2 Prove that distribution $\mathcal{D}$ has ν-bounded noise if and only if $\mathbb{E}[y h_{\vec{w}*}(\vec{x})|\vec{x}] \geq (1 - 2\nu)$ for all $\vec{x}$ in the instance space (except for a measure zero subset). Similarly, prove that $\mathcal{D}$ has random classification noise with parameter ν if an only if $\mathbb{E}[y h_{\vec{w}*}(\vec{x})|\vec{x}] = (1 - 2\nu)$ for all $\vec{x}$.

Exercise 16.3 For a distribution with ν-bounded noise prove Equation 16.6.

CHAPTER SEVENTEEN

Robust High-Dimensional Statistics

Ilias Diakonikolas and Daniel M. Kane

Abstract: Learning in the presence of outliers is a fundamental problem in statistics. Until recently, all known efficient unsupervised learning algorithms were very sensitive to outliers in high dimensions. In particular, even for the task of robust mean estimation under natural distributional assumptions, no efficient algorithm was known. A recent line of work gave the first efficient robust estimators for a number of fundamental statistical tasks, including mean and covariance estimation. This chapter introduces the core ideas and techniques in the emerging area of algorithmic high-dimensional robust statistics with a focus on robust mean estimation.

17.1 Introduction

Consider the following basic statistical task: Given n independent samples from an unknown mean spherical Gaussian distribution $\mathcal{N}(\mu, I)$ on $\mathbf{R}^d$, estimate its mean vector μ within small ℓ_2-norm. It is not hard to see that the empirical mean has ℓ_2-error at most $O(\sqrt{d/n})$ from μ with high probability. Moreover, this error upper bound is best possible among all n-sample estimators.

The Achilles heel of the empirical estimator is that it crucially relies on the assumption that the observations were generated by a spherical Gaussian. The existence of even a *single* outlier can arbitrarily compromise this estimator's performance. However, the Gaussian assumption is only ever approximately valid, as real datasets are typically exposed to some source of contamination. Hence, any estimator that is to be used in practice must be *robust* in the presence of outliers.

Learning in the presence of outliers is an important goal in statistics and has been studied in the robust statistics community since the 1960s (Huber, 1964). Classical work in statistics pinned down the sample complexity of high-dimensional robust estimation in several settings of interest. In contrast, until very recently, even the most basic computational questions in this field were poorly understood. For example, the Tukey median (Tukey, 1975) is a sample-efficient robust mean estimator for spherical Gaussian distributions. However, it is *NP*-hard to compute in general (Johnson and Preparata, 1978) and the heuristics proposed to approximate it degrade in the quality of their approximation as the dimension scales.

Until recently, all known computationally efficient high-dimensional estimators could only tolerate a negligible fraction of outliers, even for the basic statistical task of mean estimation. Recent work by Diakonikolas, Kamath, Kane, Li, Moitra, and Stewart (Diakonikolas et al., 2016), and by Lai, Rao, and Vempala (Lai et al., 2016) gave the first efficient robust estimators for various high-dimensional unsupervised tasks, including mean and covariance estimation. Specifically, Diakonikolas et al. (2016) obtained the first robust estimators with *dimension-independent* error, i.e., with error scaling only with the fraction of corrupted samples and *not* with the dimensionality of the data. Since then, there has been significant research activity on designing computationally efficient robust estimators in a variety of settings.

Contamination Model. Throughout this chapter, we focus on the following model of robust estimation that generalizes several other existing models:

Definition 17.1 Given $0 < \epsilon < 1/2$ and a distribution family $\mathcal{D}$ on $\mathbf{R}^d$, the *adversary* operates as follows: The algorithm specifies a number of samples n, and n samples are drawn from some unknown $D \in \mathcal{D}$. The adversary is allowed to inspect the samples, remove up to ϵn of them and replace them with arbitrary points. This modified set of n points is then given to the algorithm. We say that a set of samples is ϵ-*corrupted* if it is generated by this process.

The contamination model of Definition 17.1 is qualitatively similar to the semi-random models studied in Chapters 9 and 10 of this book: First, nature draws a set S of i.i.d. samples from a statistical model of interest, and then an adversary is allowed to change the set S in a bounded way to obtain an ϵ-corrupted set T. The parameter ϵ is the proportion of contamination and quantifies the power of the adversary. Intuitively, among our samples, a $(1 - \epsilon)$ fraction are generated from a distribution of interest and are called *inliers*, and the rest are called *outliers*.

One can consider less powerful adversaries, giving rise to weaker contamination models. An adversary may be (1) adaptive or oblivious to the inliers, and (2) allowed only to add corrupted points, or allowed only to remove existing points, or allowed to do both. For example, in Huber's contamination model (Huber, 1964), the adversary is oblivious to the inliers and is allowed only to add outliers.

In the context of robust mean estimation, given an ϵ-corrupted set of samples from a well-behaved distribution (e.g., $\mathcal{N}(\mu, I)$), we want to output a vector $\widehat{\mu}$ such that the ℓ_2-error is minimized. The goal here is to achieve *dimension-independent* error, i.e., error that scales only with the fraction of outliers ϵ.

Sample Efficient Robust Estimation. The problem of robust mean estimation seems so innocuous that one could naturally wonder why simple approaches do not work. In the one-dimensional case, it is well-known that the median is a robust estimator of the mean in the Gaussian setting. It is easy to show (see Exercise 17.1) that several natural high-dimensional generalizations of the median (e.g., coordinate-wise median, geometric median, etc.) lead to ℓ_2-error of $\Omega(\epsilon\sqrt{d})$ in d dimensions.

It should also be noted that, in contrast to the uncorrupted i.i.d. setting, in the contaminated setting it is not possible to obtain consistent estimators – that is, estimators with error converging to zero in probability as the sample size increases indefinitely. Typically, there is an information-theoretic limit on the minimum error that depends on ϵ and structural properties of the underlying distribution family. In particular, for the one-dimensional Gaussian case, we have:

Fact 17.2 *Any robust estimator for the mean of $\mathcal{N}(\mu, 1)$, must have ℓ_2-error $\Omega(\epsilon)$, even in Huber's contamination model.*

To prove this fact, we proceed as follows: Given two distributions $\mathcal{N}(\mu_1, 1)$ and $\mathcal{N}(\mu_2, 1)$ with $|\mu_1 - \mu_2| = \Omega(\epsilon)$, the adversary constructs two noise distributions N_1, N_2 such that $(1 - \epsilon)\mathcal{N}(\mu_1, 1) + \epsilon N_1 = (1 - \epsilon)\mathcal{N}(\mu_2, 1) + \epsilon N_2$ (see Exercise 17.2).

Ignoring computational considerations, it is not difficult to obtain a sample-efficient robust estimator matching this error guarantee *in any dimension*:

Proposition 17.3 *There exists an (inefficient) algorithm that, on input an ϵ-corrupted set of samples from $\mathcal{N}(\mu, I)$ of size $\Omega((d + \log(1/\tau))/\epsilon^2)$, outputs $\widehat{\mu} \in \mathbf{R}^d$ such that with probability at least $1 - \tau$, it holds that $\|\widehat{\mu} - \mu\|_2 = O(\epsilon)$.*

The algorithm underlying Proposition 17.3 relies on the following simple idea, which is the underlying idea in Tukey's median (Tukey, 1975): It is possible to reduce the high-dimensional robust mean estimation problem to a collection of (exponentially many) one-dimensional robust mean estimation problems. In more detail, the algorithm proceeds by using a one-dimensional robust mean estimator to estimate $v \cdot \mu$, for an appropriate net of $2^{O(d)}$ unit vectors $v \in \mathbf{R}^d$, and then combines these estimates to obtain an accurate estimate of μ (see Exercise 17.2). Tukey's median gives the same guarantee for a spherical Gaussian and can be shown to be robust for more general symmetric distributions. On the other hand, the aforementioned estimator is applicable to nonsymmetric distributions as well, as long as there is an accurate robust mean estimator for each univariate projection.

Structure of this Chapter. In Section 17.2 we present efficient algorithms for robust mean estimation. Section 17.2 is the main technical section of this chapter and showcases a number of core ideas and techniques that can be applied to several high-dimensional robust estimation tasks. Section 17.3 provides a high-level overview of recent algorithmic progress for more general robust estimation tasks. Finally, in Section 17.4 we conclude with a few remarks on the relevant literature.

17.2 Robust Mean Estimation

In this section, we illustrate the main insights underlying recent algorithms for high-dimensional robust estimation by focusing on the problem of robust mean estimation. The objective of this section is to provide the intuition and background required to develop robust learning algorithms in an accessible way. As such, we will not attempt to optimize the sample or computational complexities of the algorithms presented, other than to show that they are polynomial in the relevant parameters.

In the problem of robust mean estimation, we are given an ϵ-corrupted set of samples from a distribution X on $\mathbf{R}^d$ and our goal is to approximate the mean of X, within small error in ℓ_2-norm (Euclidean distance). In order for such a goal to be information-theoretically possible, it is required that X belongs to a suitably well-behaved family of distributions. A typical assumption is that X belongs to a family whose moments are guaranteed to satisfy certain conditions, or equivalently, a family with appropriate concentration properties. In our initial discussion, we will use the running example of a spherical Gaussian, although the results presented here hold in greater generality. That is, the reader is encouraged to imagine that X is of the form $\mathcal{N}(\mu, I)$, for some unknown $\mu \in \mathbf{R}^d$.

Structure of this Section. In Section 17.2.1 we discuss the basic intuition underlying the presented approach. In Section 17.2.2 we will describe a stability condition that is necessary for the algorithms in this chapter to succeed. In the subsequent subsections, we present two related algorithmic techniques taking advantage of the stability condition in different ways. Specifically, in Section 17.2.3 we describe an algorithm that relies on convex programming. In Section 17.2.4 we describe an iterative outlier removal technique, which has been the method of choice in practice.

17.2.1 Key Difficulties and High-Level Intuition

Arguably the most natural idea to robustly estimate the mean of a distribution would be to identify the outliers and output the empirical mean of the remaining points. The key conceptual difficulty is the fact that, in high dimensions, the outliers cannot be identified at an individual level even when they move the mean significantly. In many cases, we can easily identify the "extreme outliers" – via a pruning procedure exploiting the concentration properties of the inliers. Alas, such naive approaches typically do not suffice to obtain nontrivial error guarantees.

The simplest example illustrating this difficulty is that of a high-dimensional spherical Gaussian. Typical samples will be at ℓ_2-distance approximately $\Theta(\sqrt{d})$ from the true mean. That is, we can certainly identify as outliers all points of our dataset at distance more than $\Omega(\sqrt{d})$ from the coordinate-wise median of the dataset. All other points cannot be removed via such a procedure, as this could result in removing many inliers as well. However, by placing an ϵ-fraction of outliers at distance $\sqrt{d}$ in the same direction from the unknown mean, an adversary can corrupt the sample mean by as much as $\Omega(\epsilon\sqrt{d})$.

This leaves the algorithm designer with a dilemma of sorts. On the one hand, potential outliers at distance $\Theta(\sqrt{d})$ from the unknown mean could lead to large ℓ_2-error, scaling polynomially with d. On the other hand, if the adversary places outliers at distance approximately $\Theta(\sqrt{d})$ from the true mean in *random directions*, it may be information-theoretically impossible to distinguish them from the inliers. The way out is the realization that *it is in fact not necessary to detect and remove all outliers*. It is required only that the algorithm can detect the "consequential outliers," i.e., the ones that can significantly impact our estimates of the mean.

Let us assume without loss of generality that there no extreme outliers (as these can be removed via preprocessing). Then *the only way that the empirical mean can be far from the true mean is if there is a "conspiracy" of many outliers, all producing errors in approximately the same direction*. Intuitively, if our corrupted points are at distance $O(\sqrt{d})$ from the true mean in random directions, their contributions will on average cancel out, leading to a small error in the sample mean. In conclusion, it suffices to be able to detect these kinds of conspiracies of outliers.

The next key insight is simple and powerful. Let T be an ϵ-corrupted set of points drawn from $\mathcal{N}(\mu, I)$. If such a conspiracy of outliers substantially moves the empirical mean $\widehat{\mu}$ of T, it must move $\widehat{\mu}$ in some direction. That is, there is a unit vector v such that these outliers cause $v \cdot (\widehat{\mu} - \mu)$ to be large. For this to happen, it must be the case that these outliers are on average far from μ in the v-direction. In particular, if an ϵ-fraction of corrupted points in T move the sample average of $v \cdot (X - \mu)$, where X is the uniform distribution on T, by more than δ (δ should be thought of as small, but substantially larger than ϵ), then on average these corrupted points x must have $v \cdot (x - \mu)$ at least δ/ϵ. This in turn means that these corrupted points will have a contribution of at least $\epsilon \cdot (\delta/\epsilon)^2 = \delta^2/\epsilon$ to the variance of $v \cdot X$. Fortunately, this condition can actually be algorithmically detected! In particular, by computing the top eigenvector of the sample covariance matrix, we can efficiently determine whether or not there is any direction v for which the sample variance of $v \cdot X$ is abnormally large.

The aforementioned discussion leads us to the overall structure of the algorithms we will describe in this chapter. Starting with an ϵ-corrupted set of points T (perhaps weighted in some way), we compute the sample covariance matrix and find the eigenvector v^* with largest eigenvalue λ^*. If λ^* is not much larger than what it should be (in the absence of outliers), by the above discussion, the empirical mean is close to the true mean, and we can return that as an answer. Otherwise, we have obtained a particular direction v^* for which we know that the outliers play an unusual role, i.e., behave significantly differently than the inliers. The distribution of the points projected in the v^*-direction can then be used to perform some sort of outlier removal. The outlier removal procedure can be quite subtle and crucially depends on our distributional assumptions about the clean data.

17.2.2 Good Sets and Stability

In this section, we give a deterministic condition on the uncorrupted data that is necessary for the algorithms in this chapter to succeed (Definition 17.4). We also provide an efficiently checkable condition under which the empirical mean is certifiably close to the true mean (Lemma 17.6).

Let S be a set of n i.i.d. samples drawn from X. We will typically call these sample points good. The adversary can select up to an ϵ-fraction of points in S and replace them with arbitrary points to obtain an ϵ-corrupted set T, which is given as input to the algorithm. To establish correctness of an algorithm, we need to show that with high probability over the choice of the set S, for any choices the adversary makes, the algorithm will output an accurate estimate of the target mean.

To carry out such an analysis, it is convenient to explicitly state a collection of sufficient deterministic conditions on the set S. Specifically, we will define a notion of a "good" or "stable" set, quantified by the proportion of contamination ϵ and the distribution X. The precise stability conditions vary considerably based on the underlying estimation task and the assumptions on the distribution family of the uncorrupted data. Roughly speaking, we require that the uniform distribution over a stable set S behaves similarly to the distribution X with respect to higher moments and, potentially, tail bounds. Importantly, we require that these conditions hold even after removing an arbitrary ϵ-fraction of points in S.

The notion of a stable set must have two critical properties: (1) A set of N i.i.d. samples from X is stable with high probability, when N is at least a sufficiently large polynomial in the relevant parameters; and (2) if S is a stable set and T is obtained from S by changing at most an ϵ-fraction of the points in S, then the algorithm when run on the set T will succeed.

The robust mean estimation algorithms that will be presented in this chapter crucially rely on considering sample means and covariances. The following stability condition is an important ingredient in the success criteria of these algorithms:

Definition 17.4 (Stability Condition) Fix $0 < \epsilon < 1/2$ and $\delta \geq \epsilon$. A finite set $S \subset \mathbf{R}^d$ is (ϵ, δ)-*stable* (with respect to a distribution X) if for every unit vector $v \in \mathbf{R}^d$ and every $S' \subseteq S$ with $|S'| \geq (1 - \epsilon)|S|$, the following conditions hold:

1. $\left| \frac{1}{|S'|} \sum_{x \in S'} v \cdot (x - \mu_X) \right| \leq \delta$, and

2. $\left| \frac{1}{|S'|} \sum_{x \in S'} (v \cdot (x - \mu_X))^2 - 1 \right| \leq \delta^2/\epsilon$.

The aforementioned stability condition or a variant thereof is used in almost every known robust mean estimation algorithm. Definition 17.4 requires that after restricting to a $(1 - \epsilon)$-density subset S', the sample mean of S' is within δ of μ_X and the sample variance of S' is $1 \pm \delta^2/\epsilon$ in every direction. The fact that these conditions must hold *for every* large subset S' of S might make it unclear if they can hold with high probability. However, it is not difficult to show the following:

Proposition 17.5 *A set of i.i.d. samples from a spherical Gaussian of size $\Omega(d/\epsilon^2)$ is $(\epsilon, O(\epsilon\sqrt{\log(1/\epsilon)}))$-stable with high probability.*

We sketch a proof of Proposition 17.5. The only property required for the proof is that the distribution of the uncorrupted data has identity covariance and sub-gaussian tails in each direction; i.e., the tail probability of each univariate projection is bounded from above by the Gaussian tail.

Fix a direction v. To show the first condition, we note that we can maximize $\frac{1}{|S'|} \sum_{x \in S'} v \cdot (x - \mu_X)$ by removing from S the ϵ-fraction of points x for which $v \cdot x$ is smallest. Since the empirical mean of S is close to μ_X with high probability, we need to understand how much this quantity is altered by removing the ϵ-tail in the v-direction. Given our assumptions on the distribution of the uncorrupted data, removing the ϵ-tail only changes the mean by $O(\epsilon\sqrt{\log(1/\epsilon)})$. Therefore, if the empirical distribution of $v \cdot x$, $x \in S$, behaves like a spherical Gaussian in this way, the first condition is satisfied.

The second condition follows via a similar analysis. We can minimize the relevant quantity by removing the ϵ-fraction of points $x \in S$ with $|v \cdot (x - \mu_X)|$ as large as possible. If $v \cdot x$ is distributed like a unit-variance Gaussian, the total mass of its square over the ϵ-tails is $O(\epsilon \log(1/\epsilon))$. We have thus established that both conditions hold with high probability for any fixed direction. Showing that the conditions hold with high probability for all directions simultaneously can be shown by an appropriate covering argument.

More generally, one can show quantitatively different stability conditions under various distributional assumptions. In particular, if the distribution of the uncorrupted data is only assumed to have covariance matrix bounded by the identity (in the Loewner order), then it can be shown that an $\tilde{\Omega}(d/\epsilon)$ sized sample is $(\epsilon, O(\sqrt{\epsilon}))$ stable with high probability. (See Exercise 17.3 for additional examples.)

The aforementioned notion of stability is powerful and suffices for robust mean estimation. For some of the algorithms that will be presented in this chapter, a good set will be identified with a stable set, while others require the good set to satisfy additional conditions beyond stability.

The main reason why stability suffices is quantified in the following lemma:

Lemma 17.6 (Certificate for Empirical Mean)   *Let S be an (ϵ, δ)-stable set with respect to a distribution X, for some $\delta \geq \epsilon > 0$. Let T be an ϵ-corrupted version of S. Let μ_T and Σ_T be the empirical mean and covariance of T. If the largest eigenvalue of Σ_T is at most $1 + \lambda$, then $\|\mu_T - \mu_X\|_2 \leq O(\delta + \sqrt{\epsilon \lambda})$.*

Roughly speaking, Lemma 17.6 states that if we consider an ϵ-corrupted version T of any stable set S such that the empirical covariance of T has no large eigenvalues, then the empirical mean of T closely approximates the true mean. This lemma, or a variant thereof, is a key result in all known robust mean estimation algorithms.

Proof of Lemma 17.6   Let $S' = S \cap T$ and $T' = T \setminus S'$. We can assume w.l.o.g. that $|S'| = (1 - \epsilon)|S|$ and $|T'| = \epsilon|S|$. Let $\mu_{S'}, \mu_{T'}, \Sigma_{S'}, \Sigma_{T'}$ represent the empirical means and covariance matrices of S' and T'. A simple calculation gives that

$$\Sigma_T = (1 - \epsilon)\Sigma_{S'} + \epsilon\Sigma_{T'} + \epsilon(1 - \epsilon)(\mu_{S'} - \mu_{T'})(\mu_{S'} - \mu_{T'})^T.$$

Let v be the unit vector in the direction of $\mu_{S'} - \mu_{T'}$. We have that

$$\begin{aligned}
1 + \lambda \geq v^T \Sigma_T v &= (1 - \epsilon)v^T \Sigma_{S'} v \\
&\quad + \epsilon v^T \Sigma_{T'} v + \epsilon(1 - \epsilon)v^T(\mu_{S'} - \mu_{T'})(\mu_{S'} - \mu_{T'})^T v \\
&\geq (1 - \epsilon)(1 - \delta^2/\epsilon) + \epsilon(1 - \epsilon)\|\mu_{S'} - \mu_{T'}\|_2^2 \\
&\geq 1 - O(\delta^2/\epsilon) + (\epsilon/2)\|\mu_{S'} - \mu_{T'}\|_2^2,
\end{aligned}$$

where we used the variational characterization of eigenvalues, the fact that $\Sigma_{T'}$ is positive semidefinite, and the second stability condition for S'. By rearranging, we obtain that $\|\mu_{S'} - \mu_{T'}\|_2 = O(\delta/\epsilon + \sqrt{\lambda/\epsilon})$. Therefore, we can write

$$\begin{aligned}
\|\mu_T - \mu_X\|_2 &= \|(1 - \epsilon)\mu_{S'} + \epsilon\mu_{T'} - \mu_X\|_2 = \|\mu_{S'} - \mu_X + \epsilon(\mu_{T'} - \mu_{S'})\|_2 \\
&\leq \|\mu_{S'} - \mu_X\|_2 + \epsilon\|\mu_{S'} - \mu_{T'}\|_2 = O(\delta) + \epsilon \cdot O(\delta/\epsilon + \sqrt{\lambda/\epsilon}) \\
&= O(\delta + \sqrt{\lambda \epsilon}),
\end{aligned}$$

where we used the first stability condition for S' and our bound on $\|\mu_{S'} - \mu_{T'}\|_2$. $\qquad\qquad\square$

Lemma 17.6 says that if our input set of points T is an ϵ-corrupted version of a stable set S and has bounded covariance, the sample mean of T must be close to the true mean. Unfortunately, we are not always guaranteed that the set T we are given has this property. In order to deal with this, we will want to find a subset of T with bounded covariance and large intersection with S. However, for some of the algorithms presented, it will be convenient to find a probability distribution over T rather than a subset. For this, we will need a slight generalization of Lemma 17.6.

Lemma 17.7 *Let S be an (ϵ, δ)-stable set with respect to a distribution X, for some $\delta \geq \epsilon > 0$ with $|S| > 1/\epsilon$. Let W be a probability distribution on S that differs from U_S, the uniform distribution over S, by at most ϵ in total variation distance. Let μ_W and Σ_W be the mean and covariance of W. If the largest eigenvalue of Σ_W is at most $1 + \lambda$, then $\|\mu_W - \mu_X\|_2 \leq O(\delta + \sqrt{\epsilon \lambda})$.*

Note that this subsumes Lemma 17.6 by letting W be the uniform distribution over T. The proof is essentially identical to that of Lemma 17.6, except that we need to show that the mean and variance of the conditional distribution $W \mid S$ are approximately correct, whereas in Lemma 17.6 the bounds on the mean and variance of $S \cap T$ followed directly from stability.

Lemma 17.7 clarifies the goal of our outlier removal procedure. In particular, given our initial ϵ-corrupted set T, we will attempt to find a distribution W supported on T so that Σ_W has no large eigenvalues. The weight $W(x)$, $x \in T$, quantifies our belief whether point x is an inlier or an outlier. We will also need to ensure that any such W we choose is close to the uniform distribution over S.

More concretely, we now describe a framework that captures our robust mean estimation algorithms. We start with the following definition:

Definition 17.8 Let S be a $(3\epsilon, \delta)$-stable set with respect to X and let T be an ϵ-corrupted version of S. Let $\mathcal{C}$ be the set of all probability distributions W supported on T, where $W(x) \leq \frac{1}{|T|(1-\epsilon)}$, for all $x \in T$.

We note that *any* distribution in $\mathcal{C}$ differs from U_S, the uniform distribution on S, by at most 3ϵ. Indeed, for $\epsilon \leq 1/3$, we have that

$$d_{\mathrm{TV}}(U_S, W) = \sum_{x \in T} \max\{W(x) - U_S(x), 0\}$$

$$= \sum_{x \in S \cap T} \max\{W(x) - 1/|T|, 0\} + \sum_{x \in T \setminus S} W(x)$$

$$\leq \sum_{x \in S \cap T} \frac{\epsilon}{|T|(1-\epsilon)} + \sum_{x \in T \setminus S} \frac{1}{|T|(1-\epsilon)}$$

$$\leq |T| \left(\frac{\epsilon}{|T|(1-\epsilon)} \right) + \epsilon |T| \left(\frac{1}{|T|(1-\epsilon)} \right)$$

$$= \frac{2\epsilon}{1-\epsilon} \leq 3\epsilon.$$

Therefore, if we find $W \in \mathcal{C}$ with Σ_W having no large eigenvalues, Lemma 17.7 implies that μ_W is a good approximation to μ_X. Fortunately, we know that such a W exists! In particular, if we take W to be W^*, the uniform distribution over $S \cap T$, the largest eigenvalue is at most $1 + \delta^2/\epsilon$, and thus we achieve ℓ_2-error $O(\delta)$.

At this point, we have an *inefficient* algorithm for approximating μ_X: Find *any* $W \in \mathcal{C}$ with bounded covariance. The remaining question is how we can efficiently find one. There are two basic algorithmic techniques to achieve this, which we present in the subsections that follow.

The first algorithmic technique we will describe is based on convex programming. We will call this *the unknown convex programming method*. Note that C is a convex set and that finding a point in C that has bounded covariance is *almost* a convex program. It is not quite a convex program, because the variance of $v \cdot W$, for fixed v, is not a convex function of W. However, one can show that given a W with variance in some direction significantly larger than $1 + \delta^2/\epsilon$, we can efficiently construct a hyperplane separating W from W^* (recall that W^* is the uniform distribution over $S \cap T$) (Section 17.2.3). This method has the advantage of naturally working under only the stability assumption. On the other hand, as it relies on the ellipsoid algorithm, it is quite slow (although polynomial time).

Our second technique, which we will call *filtering*, is an iterative outlier removal method that is typically faster, as it relies on spectral techniques. The main idea of the method is the following: If Σ_W does not have large eigenvalues, then the empirical mean is close to the true mean. Otherwise, there is some unit vector v such that $\mathbf{Var}(v \cdot W)$ is substantially larger than it should be. This can be the case only if W assigns substantial mass to elements of $T \setminus S$ that have values of $v \cdot x$ very far from the true mean of $v \cdot \mu$. This observation allows us to perform some kind of outlier removal, in particular by removing (or down-weighting) the points x that have $v \cdot x$ inappropriately large. An important conceptual property is that one cannot afford to remove only outliers, but it is possible to ensure that more outliers are removed than inliers. Given a W where Σ_W has a large eigenvalue, one filtering step gives a new distribution $W' \in C$ with $d_{\mathrm{TV}}(W', W^*) < d_{\mathrm{TV}}(W, W^*)$. Repeating the process eventually gives a W with no large eigenvalues. The filtering method and its variations are discussed in Section 17.2.4.

17.2.3 The Unknown Convex Programming Method

By Lemma 17.7, it suffices to find a distribution $W \in C$ with Σ_W having no large eigenvalues. We note that this condition *almost* defines a convex program. This is because C is a convex set of probability distributions and the bounded covariance condition says that $\mathbf{Var}(v \cdot W) \leq 1 + \lambda$ for all unit vectors v. Unfortunately, the variance $\mathbf{Var}(v \cdot W) = \mathbf{E}[|v \cdot (W - \mu_W)|^2]$ is not quite linear in W. (If we instead had $\mathbf{E}[|v \cdot (W - \nu)|^2]$, where ν is some fixed vector, this would be linear in W.) However, we will show that finding a unit vector v for which $\mathbf{Var}(v \cdot W)$ is too large, can be used to obtain a separation oracle, i.e., a linear function on W that is violated.

Suppose that we identify a unit vector v such that $\mathbf{Var}(v \cdot W) = 1 + \lambda$, where $\lambda > c(\delta^2/\epsilon)$ for a sufficiently large universal constant $c > 0$. Applying Lemma 17.7 to the one-dimensional projection $v \cdot W$, gives $|v \cdot (\mu_W - \mu_X)| \leq O(\delta + \sqrt{\epsilon\lambda}) = O(\sqrt{\epsilon\lambda})$.

Let $L(Y) := \mathbf{E}_Y[|v \cdot (Y - \mu_W)|^2]$ and note that L is a linear function of the probability distribution Y with $L(W) = 1 + \lambda$. We can write

$$L(W^*) = \mathbf{E}_{W^*}[|v \cdot (W^* - \mu_W)|^2] = \mathbf{Var}(v \cdot W^*) + |v \cdot (\mu_W - \mu_{W^*})|^2$$

$$\leq 1 + \delta^2/\epsilon + 2|v \cdot (\mu_W - \mu_X)|^2 + 2|v \cdot (\mu_{W^*} - \mu_X)|^2$$

$$\leq 1 + O(\delta^2/\epsilon + \epsilon\lambda) < 1 + \lambda = L(W).$$

In summary, we have an explicit convex set $\mathcal{C}$ of probability distributions from which we want to find one with eigenvalues bounded by $1 + O(\delta^2/\epsilon)$. Given any $W \in \mathcal{C}$ which does not satisfy this condition, we can produce a linear function L that separates W from W^*. Using the ellipsoid algorithm, we obtain the following general theorem:

Theorem 17.9 *Let S be a $(3\epsilon, \delta)$-stable set with respect to a distribution X and let T be an ϵ-corrupted version of S. There exists a polynomial time algorithm that given T returns $\widehat{\mu}$ such that $\|\widehat{\mu} - \mu_X\|_2 = O(\delta)$.*

17.2.4 The Filtering Method

As in the convex programming method, the goal of the filtering method is to find a distribution $W \in \mathcal{C}$ so that Σ_W has bounded eigenvalues. Given a $W \in \mathcal{C}$, Σ_W either has bounded eigenvalues (in which case the weighted empirical mean works) or there is a direction v in which $\mathbf{Var}(v \cdot W)$ is too large. In the latter case, the projections $v \cdot W$ must behave very differently from the projections $v \cdot S$ or $v \cdot X$. In particular, since an ϵ-fraction of outliers are causing a much larger increase in the standard deviation, this means that the distribution of $v \cdot W$ will have many "extreme points" – more than one would expect to find in $v \cdot S$. This fact allows us to identity a non-empty subset of extreme points, the majority of which are outliers. These points can then be removed (or down-weighted) in order to "clean up" our sample. Formally, given a $W \in \mathcal{C}$ without bounded eigenvalues, we can efficiently find a $W' \in \mathcal{C}$ so that $d_{\mathrm{TV}}(W', W^*) \leq d_{\mathrm{TV}}(W, W^*) - \gamma$, where $\gamma > 0$ is bounded from below. Iterating this procedure eventually terminates giving a W with bounded eigenvalues.

We note that while it may be conceptually useful to consider the aforementioned scheme for general distributions W over points, in most cases it suffices to consider only W given as the uniform distribution over some set T of points. The filtering step in this case consists of replacing the set T by some subset $T' = T \setminus R$, where $R \subset T$. To guarantee progress toward W^* (the uniform distribution over $S \cap T$), it suffices to ensure that at most a third of the elements of R are also in S, or equivalently that at least two-thirds of the removed points are outliers (perhaps in expectation). The algorithm will terminate when the current set of points T' has bounded empirical covariance, and the output will be the empirical mean of T'.

Before we proceed with a more detailed technical discussion, we note that there are several possible ways to implement the filtering step, and that the method used has a significant impact on the analysis. In general, a filtering step removes all points that are "far" from the sample mean in a large variance direction. However, the precise way that this is quantified can vary in important ways.

Basic Filtering

In this subsection, we present a filtering method that applies to identity covariance (or, more generally, known covariance) distributions whose univariate projections satisfy appropriate concentration bounds. For the purpose of this section, we will restrict ourselves to the Gaussian setting. We note that this method immediately extends to distributions with weaker concentration properties, e.g., subexponential or even inverse polynomial concentration, with appropriate modifications.

We note that the filtering method presented here requires an additional condition on our good set of samples, on top of the stability condition. This is quantified in the following definition:

Definition 17.10 A set $S \subset \mathbf{R}^d$ is *tail-bound-good* (*with respect to* $X = \mathcal{N}(\mu_X, I)$) if for any unit vector v, and any $t > 0$, we have

$$\Pr_{x \sim_u S}(|v \cdot (x - \mu_X)| > 2t + 2) \leq e^{-t^2/2}. \tag{17.1}$$

Since any projection of X is distributed like a standard Gaussian, Equation (17.1) should hold if the uniform distribution over S were replaced by X. It can be shown that this condition holds with high probability if S consists of i.i.d. random samples from X of a sufficiently large size.

Intuitively, the additional tail condition of Definition 17.10 is needed to guarantee that the filter will remove more outliers than inliers. Formally, we have the following:

Lemma 17.11 *Let* $\epsilon > 0$ *be a sufficiently small constant. Let* $S \subset \mathbf{R}^d$ *be both* $(2\epsilon, \delta)$-*stable and tail-bound-good with respect to* $X = \mathcal{N}(\mu_X, I)$, *with* $\delta = c\epsilon \sqrt{\log(1/\epsilon)}$, *for* $c > 0$ *a sufficiently large constant. Let* $T \subset \mathbf{R}^d$ *be such that* $|T \cap S| \geq (1 - \epsilon) \min(|T|, |S|)$ *and assume we are given a unit vector* $v \in \mathbf{R}^d$ *for which* $\mathbf{Var}(v \cdot T) > 1 + 2\delta^2/\epsilon$. *There exists a polynomial time algorithm that returns a subset* $R \subset T$ *satisfying* $|R \cap S| < |R|/3$.

Proof Let $\mathbf{Var}(v \cdot T) = 1 + \lambda$. By applying Lemma 17.6 to the set T, we get that $|v \cdot \mu_X - v \cdot \mu_T| \leq c\sqrt{\lambda\epsilon}$. By (17.1), it follows that $\Pr_{x \sim_u S}(|v \cdot (x - \mu_T)| > 2t + 2 + c\sqrt{\lambda\epsilon}) \leq e^{-t^2/2}$. We claim that there exists a threshold t_0 such that

$$\Pr_{x \sim_u T}(|v \cdot (x - \mu_T)| > 2t_0 + 2 + c\sqrt{\lambda\epsilon}) > 4e^{-t_0^2/2}, \tag{17.2}$$

where the constants have not been optimized. Given this claim, the set $R = \{x \in T : |v \cdot (x - \mu_T)| > 2t_0 + 2 + c\sqrt{\lambda\epsilon}\}$ will satisfy the conditions of the lemma.

To prove our claim, we analyze the variance of $v \cdot T$ and note that much of the excess must be due to points in $T \setminus S$. In particular, by our assumption on the variance in the v-direction, $\sum_{x \in T} |v \cdot (x - \mu_T)|^2 = |T|\mathbf{Var}(v \cdot T) = |T|(1 + \lambda)$, where $\lambda > 2\delta^2/\epsilon$. The contribution from the points $x \in S \cap T$ is at most

$$\sum_{x \in S} |v \cdot (x - \mu_T)|^2 = |S|(\mathbf{Var}(v \cdot S) + |v \cdot (\mu_T - \mu_S)|^2) \leq |S|(1 + \delta^2/\epsilon + 2c^2\lambda\epsilon)$$

$$\leq |T|(1 + 2c^2\lambda\epsilon + 3\lambda/5),$$

where the first inequality uses the stability of S, and the last uses that $|T| \geq (1 - \epsilon)|S|$. If ϵ is sufficiently small relative to c, it follows that $\sum_{x \in T \setminus S} |v \cdot (x - \mu_T)|^2 \geq |T|\lambda/3$. On the other hand, by definition we have

$$\sum_{x \in T \setminus S} |v \cdot (x - \mu_T)|^2 = |T| \int_0^\infty 2t \Pr_{x \sim_u T}(|v \cdot (x - \mu_T)| > t, x \notin S)dt. \tag{17.3}$$

Assume for the sake of contradiction that there is no t_0 for which Equation (17.2) is satisfied. Then the right-hand side of (17.3) is at most

$$|T| \left(\int_0^{2+c\sqrt{\lambda\epsilon}+10\sqrt{\log(1/\epsilon)}} 2t \Pr_{x \sim_u T} (x \notin S) \right.$$

$$\left. + \int_{2+c\sqrt{\lambda\epsilon}+10\sqrt{\log(1/\epsilon)}}^\infty 2t \Pr_{x \sim_u T} (|v \cdot (x - \mu_T)| > t) dt \right)$$

$$\leq |T| \left(\epsilon(2 + c\sqrt{\lambda\epsilon} + 10\sqrt{\log(1/\epsilon)})^2 + \int_{5\sqrt{\log(1/\epsilon)}}^\infty 16(2t + 2 + c\sqrt{\lambda\epsilon})e^{-t^2/2} dt \right)$$

$$\leq |T| \left(O(c^2\lambda\epsilon^2 + \epsilon\log(1/\epsilon)) + O(\epsilon^2(\sqrt{\log(1/\epsilon)} + c\sqrt{\lambda\epsilon})) \right)$$

$$\leq |T|O(c^2\lambda\epsilon^2 + (\delta^2/\epsilon)/c) < |T|\lambda/3,$$

which is a contradiction. Therefore, the tail bounds and the concentration violation together imply the existence of such a t_0 (which can be efficiently computed). $\square$

We note that although exponentially many samples are required to ensure that (17.1) holds with high probability, one can carefully weaken (17.1) so that it can be achieved with polynomially many samples without breaking the aforementioned analysis.

Randomized Filtering

The basic filtering method of the previous subsection is deterministic, relying on the violation of a concentration inequality satisfied by the inliers. In some settings, deterministic filtering seems to fail and we require the filtering procedure to be randomized. A concrete such setting is when the uncorrupted distribution is assumed only to have bounded covariance.

The main idea of randomized filtering is simple: Suppose we can identify a nonnegative function $f(x)$, defined on the samples x, for which (under some high-probability condition on the inliers) it holds that $\sum_T f(x) \geq 2\sum_S f(x)$, where T is an ϵ-corrupted set of samples and S is the corresponding set of inliers. Then we can create a randomized filter by removing each sample point $x \in T$ with probability proportional to $f(x)$. This ensures that the *expected* number of outliers removed is at least the *expected* number of inliers removed. The analysis of such a randomized filter is slightly more subtle, so we will discuss it in the following paragraphs.

The key property the aforementioned randomized filter ensures is that the sequence of random variables (# Inliers removed) − (# Outliers removed) (where "inliers" are points in S and "outliers" points in $T \backslash S$) across iterations is a supermartingale. Since the total number of outliers removed across all iterations accounts for at most an ϵ-fraction of the total samples, this means that with probability at least $2/3$, at no point does the algorithm remove more than a 2ϵ-fraction of the inliers. A formal statement follows:

Theorem 17.12 *Let $S \subset \mathbf{R}^d$ be a $(3\epsilon, \delta)$-stable set (with respect to X). Suppose that T is an ϵ-corrupted version of S. Suppose furthermore that given any $T' \subset T$*

with $|T' \cap S| \geq (1 - 3\epsilon)|S|$ for which $\mathbf{Cov}(T')$ has an eigenvalue bigger than $1 + \lambda$, there is an efficient algorithm that computes a nonzero function $f : T' \to \mathbf{R}_+$ such that $\sum_{x \in T'} f(x) \geq 2 \sum_{x \in T' \cap S} f(x)$. Then there exists a polynomial-time randomized algorithm that computes a vector $\widehat{\mu}$ that with probability at least $2/3$ satisfies $\|\widehat{\mu} - \mu\|_2 = O(\delta + \sqrt{\epsilon\lambda})$.

The pseudocode for the algorithm is

Algorithm 1 Randomized Filtering

---

1. Compute $\mathbf{Cov}(T)$ and its largest eigenvalue ν.
2. If $\nu \leq 1 + \lambda$, return μ_T.
3. Else

- Compute f as guaranteed in the theorem statement.
- Remove each $x \in T$ with probability $f(x)/\max_{x \in T} f(x)$ and return to Step 1 with the new set T.

Proof of Theorem 17.12 First, it is easy to see that this algorithm runs in polynomial time. Indeed, as the point $x \in T$ attaining the maximum value of $f(x)$ is definitely removed in each filtering iteration, each iteration reduces $|T|$ by at least one. To establish correctness, we will show that, with probability at least $2/3$, at each iteration of the algorithm it holds $|S \cap T| \geq (1 - 3\epsilon)|S|$. Assuming this claim, Lemma 17.6 implies that our final error will be as desired.

To prove the desired claim, we consider the sequence of random variables $d(T) = |S \setminus T| + |T \setminus S|$ across the iterations of the algorithm. We note that, initially, $d(T) = 2\epsilon|S|$ and that $d(T)$ cannot drop below 0. Finally, we note that at each stage of the algorithm $d(T)$ increases by (# Inliers removed) $-$ (# Outliers removed), and that the expectation of this quantity is

$$\sum_{x \in S \cap T} f(x) - \sum_{x \in T \setminus S} f(x) = 2 \sum_{x \in S \cap T} f(x) - \sum_{x \in T} f(x) \leq 0.$$

This means that $d(T)$ is a supermartingale (at least until we reach a point where $|S \cap T| \leq (1 - 3\epsilon)|S|$). However, if we set a stopping time at the first occasion where this condition fails, we note that the expectation of $d(T)$ is at most 0. Since it is at least $-\epsilon|S|$, this means that with probability at least $2/3$ it is never more than $2\epsilon|S|$, which would imply that $|S \cap T| \geq (1 - 3\epsilon)|S|$ throughout the algorithm. This completes the proof. $\qquad\square$

Methods of Point Removal. The randomized filtering method requires only that each point x is removed with probability $f(x)/\max_{x \in T} f(x)$, without any assumption of independence. Therefore, given an f, there are several ways to implement this scheme. A few natural ones are given here:

- *Randomized Thresholding*: Perhaps the easiest method for implementing our randomized filter is generating a uniform random number $y \in [0, \max_{x \in T} f(x)]$ and removing all points $x \in T$ for which $f(x) \geq y$. This method is practically useful in many applications. Finding the set of such points is often fairly easy, as this condition may well correspond to a simple threshold.

- *Independent Removal*: Each $x \in T$ is removed independently with probability $f(x)/\max_{x \in T} f(x)$. This scheme has the advantage of leading to less variance in $d(T)$. A careful analysis of the random walk involved allows one to reduce the failure probability to $\exp(-\Omega(\epsilon|S|))$.
- *Deterministic Reweighting*: Instead of removing points, this scheme allows for weighted sets of points. In particular, each point will be assigned a weight in $[0, 1]$ and we will consider weighted means and covariances. Instead of removing a point with probability proportional to $f(x)$, we can remove a fraction of x's weight proportional to $f(x)$. This ensures that the appropriate weighted version of $d(T)$ is definitely nonincreasing, implying correctness of the algorithm.

Universal Filtering

In this subsection, we show how to use randomized filtering to construct a universal filter that works under only the stability condition (Lemma 17.4) – not requiring the tail-bound condition of the basic filter (Lemma 17.11). Formally, we show:

Proposition 17.13 *Let $S \subset \mathbf{R}^d$ be an (ϵ, δ)-stable set for $\epsilon, \delta > 0$ sufficiently small constants and δ at least a sufficiently large multiple of ϵ. Let T be an ϵ-corrupted version of S. Suppose that $\mathbf{Cov}(T)$ has largest eigenvalue $1 + \lambda > 1 + 8\delta^2/\epsilon$. Then there exists an algorithm that, on input ϵ, δ, T, computes a function $f : T \to \mathbf{R}_+$ satisfying $\sum_{x \in T} f(x) \geq 2 \sum_{x \in T \cap S} f(x)$.*

Proof The algorithm to construct f is the following: We start by computing the sample mean μ_T and the top (unit) eigenvector v of $\mathbf{Cov}(T)$. For $x \in T$, we let $g(x) = (v \cdot (x - \mu_T))^2$. Let L be the set of $\epsilon \cdot |T|$ elements of T on which $g(x)$ is largest. We define f to be $f(x) = 0$ for $x \notin L$, and $f(x) = g(x)$ for $x \in L$.

The basic plan of attack is as follows: First, we note that the sum of $g(x)$ over $x \in T$ (which is the variance of $v \cdot Z, Z \sim_u T$) is substantially larger than the sum of $g(x)$ over S (which is approximately the variance of $v \cdot Z, Z \sim_u S$). Therefore, the sum of $g(x)$ over the $\epsilon|S|$ elements of $T \setminus S$ must be quite large. In fact, using the stability condition, we can show that the latter quantity must be larger than the sum of the largest $\epsilon|S|$ values of $g(x)$ over $x \in S$. However, since $|T \setminus S| \leq |L|$, we have that $\sum_{x \in T} f(x) = \sum_{x \in L} g(x) \geq \sum_{x \in T \setminus S} g(x) \geq 2 \sum_{x \in S} f(x)$.

We now proceed with the detailed analysis. First, note that

$$\sum_{x \in T} g(x) = |T|\mathbf{Var}(v \cdot T) = |T|(1 + \lambda).$$

Moreover, for any $S' \subseteq S$ with $|S'| \geq (1 - 2\epsilon)|S|$, we have that

$$\sum_{x \in S'} g(x) = |S'|(\mathbf{Var}(v \cdot S') + (v \cdot (\mu_T - \mu'_S))^2). \tag{17.4}$$

By the stability condition, we have that $|\mathbf{Var}(v \cdot S') - 1| \leq \delta^2/\epsilon$. Furthermore, the stability condition and Lemma 17.6 give

$$\|\mu_T - \mu'_S\|_2 \leq \|\mu_T - \mu\|_2 + \|\mu - \mu'_S\|_2 = O(\delta + \sqrt{\epsilon\lambda}).$$

Since $\lambda \geq 8\delta^2/\epsilon$, this implies that $\sum_{x \in T \setminus S} g(x) \geq (2/3)|S|\lambda$. Moreover, since $|L| \geq |T \setminus S|$ and since g takes its largest values on points $x \in L$, we have that

$$\sum_{x \in T} f(x) = \sum_{x \in L} g(x) \geq \sum_{x \in T \setminus S} g(x) \geq (16/3)|S|\delta^2/\epsilon.$$

Comparing the results of Equation (17.4) with $S' = S$ and $S' = S \setminus L$, we find that

$$\sum_{x \in S \cap T} f(x) = \sum_{x \in S \cap L} g(x) = \sum_{x \in S} g(x) - \sum_{x \in S \setminus L} g(x)$$

$$= |S|(1 \pm \delta^2/\epsilon + O(\delta^2 + \epsilon\lambda)) - |S \setminus L|(1 \pm \delta^2/\epsilon + O(\delta^2 + \epsilon\lambda))$$

$$\leq 2|S|\delta^2/\epsilon + |S|O(\delta^2 + \epsilon\lambda).$$

The latter quantity is at most $(1/2)\sum_{x \in T} f(x)$ when δ and ϵ/δ are sufficiently small constants. This completes the proof of Proposition 17.13. $\square$

Practical Considerations. While the aforementioned point removal methods have similar theoretical guarantees, recent implementations (Diakonikolas et al., 2018c) suggest that they have different practical performance on real datasets. The deterministic reweighting method is somewhat slower in practice as its worst-case runtime and its typical runtime are comparable. In more detail, one can guarantee termination by setting the constant of proportionality so that at each step at least one of the nonzero weights is set to zero. However, in practical circumstances, we will not be able to do better. That is, the algorithm may well be forced to undergo $\epsilon|S|$ iterations. On the other hand, the randomized versions of the algorithm are likely to remove several points of T at each filtering step.

Another reason why the randomized versions may be preferable has to do with the quality of the results. The randomized algorithms produce bad results only when there is a chance that $d(T)$ ends up being very large. However, since $d(T)$ is a supermartingale, this will only ever be the case if there is a corresponding possibility that $d(T)$ will be exceptionally small. Thus, although the randomized algorithms may have a probability of giving worse results some of the time, this will happen only if a corresponding fraction of the time, they also give *better* results than the theory guarantees. This consideration suggests that the randomized thresholding procedure might have advantages over the independent removal procedure precisely because it has a higher probability of failure. This has been observed experimentally in (Diakonikolas et al., 2018c): In real datasets (poisoned with a constant fraction of adversarial outliers), the number of iterations of randomized filtering is typically bounded by a small constant.

17.3 Beyond Robust Mean Estimation

In this section, we provide a brief overview of the ideas behind recently developed robust estimators for more general statistical tasks.

17.3.1 Robust Stochastic Optimization

A simple and powerful idea is that efficient algorithms for robust mean estimation can be used in essentially a black-box manner to obtain robust learners for a range of stochastic optimization problems. Consider the following general stochastic optimization problem: There is some unknown true distribution p^* over (convex) functions $f : \mathcal{W} \to \mathbf{R}$, and the goal is to find an approximate minimizer of $F(w) = \mathbf{E}_{f \sim p^*}[f(w)]$. Here $\mathcal{W} \subseteq \mathbf{R}^d$ is a space of possible parameters. As an example, the problem of linear regression fits in this framework for $f(w) = (1/2)(w \cdot x - y^2)$ and $(x, y) \in \mathbf{R}^d \times \mathbf{R}$ is drawn from the data distribution.

Given a set of clean samples, i.e., i.i.d. set of functions $f_1, \ldots, f_n \sim p^*$, this problem can be efficiently solved by (stochastic) gradient descent. In the robust setting, we have access to an ϵ-corrupted training set of functions $f_1, \ldots, f_n$ drawn from p^*. Unfortunately, even a single corrupted sample can completely compromise standard gradient descent. Charikar et al. (2017) first studied the robust version of this problem in the presence of a majority of outliers. The vanilla outlier-robust setting, where $\epsilon < 1/2$, was studied in two concurrent works (Diakonikolas et al., 2018c; Prasad et al., 2018). The main intuition present in both these works is that robustly estimating the gradient of the objective function can be viewed as a robust mean estimation problem. Diakonikolas et al. (2018c) take this connection a step further: Instead of using a robust gradient estimator as a black box, they apply a filtering step each time the vanilla SGD reaches an approximate critical point of the empirical risk. The correctness of this method relies on properties of the filtering algorithm. Importantly, it turns out that this method is more efficient in practice.

17.3.2 Robust Covariance Estimation

The robust estimation techniques described in this chapter can be generalized to robustly estimate the covariance of high-dimensional distributions. For concreteness, here we consider the Gaussian case; specifically we assume that the inliers are drawn from $G = \mathcal{N}(0, \Sigma)$. (Note that by considering the differences of independent samples we can reduce to the centered case, and that this reduction works in the robust setting as well.) The high-level idea is to filter based on the empirical fourth moment tensor. In more detail, let X be the random variable GG^T and note that $\mathbf{Cov}(G) = \mathbf{E}[X]$.

We can attempt to use the described robust mean estimation techniques on X. However, these techniques require a priori bounds on its covariance, $\mathbf{Cov}(X)$. To handle this issue, we leverage the fact that the covariance of X can be expressed as a function of the covariance of G. Although it might appear that we run into a chicken-and-egg problem, it is in fact possible to bootstrap better and better approximations to the covariance $\mathbf{Cov}(X)$.

In particular, any upper bound on the covariance of G will imply an upper bound on the covariance of X, which can in turn be used to robustly estimate the mean of X, providing a better estimate of $\mathbf{Cov}(G)$. Via a careful iterative refinement, one can show that is possible to learn the covariance $\mathbf{Cov}(G)$ within relative error $O(\epsilon \log(1/\epsilon))$ with respect to the Frobenius norm, which corresponds to robustly estimating G within error $O(\epsilon \log(1/\epsilon))$ in total variation distance.

17.3.3 List-Decodable Learning

In this chapter, we focused on the classical robust setting where the outliers constitute the minority of the dataset, quantified by the fraction of corruptions $\epsilon < 1/2$, and the goal is to obtain estimators with error scaling as a function of ϵ (and is independent of the dimension d). A related setting of interest focuses on the regime when the fraction α of real data is small – strictly smaller than $1/2$. That is, we observe n samples, an α-fraction of which (for some $\alpha < 1/2$) are drawn from the distribution in question, but the rest are arbitrary.

This model was first studied in the context of mean estimation in Charikar et al. (2017). A first observation is that, in this regime, it is information-theoretically impossible to estimate the mean with a single hypothesis. Indeed, an adversary can produce $\Omega(1/\alpha)$ clusters of points each drawn from a good distribution with different mean. Even if the algorithm could learn the distribution of the samples exactly, it still would not be able to identify which of the clusters is the correct one. To circumvent this, the definition of learning must be somewhat relaxed. In particular, the algorithm should be allowed to return a small list of hypotheses with the guarantee that *at least one* of the hypotheses is close to the true mean. Moreover, as opposed to the small ϵ regime, it is often information-theoretically necessary for the error to increase as α goes to 0. In summary, given polynomially many samples, we would like to output $O(1/\alpha)$ many hypotheses, with the guarantee that with high probability at least one hypothesis is within $f(\alpha)$ of the true mean, where $f(\alpha)$ depends on the concentration properties of the distribution in question.

Charikar et al. (2017) used an semidefinite programming-based approach to solve this problem. We note that the techniques discussed in this chapter can be adapted to work in this setting. In particular, if the sample covariance matrix has no large eigenvalues, this certifies that the true mean and sample mean are not too far apart. However, if a large eigenvalue exists, the construction of a filter is more elaborate. To some extent, this is a necessary difficulty because the algorithm must return more than one hypotheses. To handle this issue, one needs to construct a *multifilter*, which may return several subsets of the original sample set with the guarantee that at least one of them is cleaner than the original dataset. Such a multifilter was introduced in Diakonikolas et al. (2018a).

17.3.4 Robust Sparse Estimation

The task of leveraging sparsity in high-dimensional parameter estimation is a well-studied problem in statistics. In the context of robust estimation, this problem was first considered in Balakrishnan et al. (2017), which adapted the unknown convex programming method of Diakonikolas et al. (2016) described in this chapter. Here we describe the filtering method in this setting for the problem of robust sparse mean estimation.

Formally, given ϵ-corrupted samples from $\mathcal{N}(\mu, I)$, where the mean μ is unknown and assumed to be k-sparse, i.e., supported on an unknown set of k coordinates, we would like to approximate μ, in ℓ_2-distance. Without corruptions, this problem is easy: We draw $O(k \log(d/k)/\epsilon^2)$ samples and output the empirical mean truncated in its largest magnitude k entries. The goal is to obtain similar sample complexity and error guarantees in the robust setting.

At a high level, we note that the truncated sample mean should be accurate as long as there is no k-sparse direction in which the error between the true mean and sample mean is large. This condition can be certified, as long as we know that the sample variance of $v \cdot X$ is close to 1 for all unit, k-sparse vectors v. This would in turn allow us to create a filter-based algorithm for k-sparse robust mean estimation that uses only $O(k \log(d/k)/\epsilon^2)$ samples. Unfortunately, the problem of determining whether or not there is a k-sparse direction with large variance is computationally hard. By considering a convex relaxation of this problem, one can obtain a polynomial time version of this algorithm that requires $O(k^2 \log(d/k)/\epsilon^2)$ samples. Moreover, there is evidence (Diakonikolas et al., 2017b), in the form of a lower bound in the Statistical Query model (a restricted but powerful computational model), that this increase in the sample complexity is necessary.

More recently, Diakonikolas et al. (2019) developed iterative spectral algorithms for robust sparse estimation tasks (including sparse mean estimation and sparse principal component analysis). These algorithms achieve the same error guarantees as Balakrishnan et al. (2017), while being significantly faster.

17.3.5 Robust Estimation of High-Degree Moments

Suppose we are interested in robustly estimating the kth order moments of a distribution X. In some sense, this problem is equivalent to estimating the mean of the random variable $Y = X^{\otimes k}$. Unfortunately, in order to estimate the mean of Y robustly, one needs concentration bounds on it, which are rarely directly available. Typically, concentration bounds on Y are implied by upper bounds on the higher moments of X. In particular, upper bounds on the k'th central moments of X for some $k' > k$, imply concentration bounds on Y. Unfortunately, just knowing bounds on the central moments of X is often hard to leverage computationally. Given a set of points, even *determining* whether or not they have bounded central moments is a computationally intractable problem. Instead, known algorithmic approaches (Hopkins and Li, 2018; Kothari et al., 2018) generally require some kind of efficiently certifiable bounded moment conditions (e.g., via a sum of squares proof). This allows one to search for subsets of sample points whose central moments can be similarly certified as bounded, and these will allow us to approximate higher moments of X.

17.4 Notes

The convex programming and filtering methods described in this chapter appeared in (Diakonikolas et al., 2016, 2017a). The idea of removing outliers by projecting on the top eigenvector of the empirical covariance goes back to Klivans et al. (2009), who used it in the context of robustly learning linear separators. Klivans et al. (2009) use a "hard" filtering step which only removes outliers and consequently leads to errors that scale logarithmically with the dimension, even in Huber's model.

The work of Lai et al. (2016) developed a recursive dimension-halving technique for robust mean estimation. Their technique leads to error $O(\epsilon \sqrt{\log(1/\epsilon)} \sqrt{\log d})$ for Gaussian robust mean estimation in Huber's contamination model. Diakonikolas et al. (2016) and Lai et al. (2016) obtained robust estimators for various other statistical tasks, including robust covariance estimation, robust density estimation for mixtures of spherical Gaussians and product distributions, and independent component analysis.

The algorithmic approaches described in this chapter robustly estimate the mean of a spherical Gaussian within error $O(\epsilon\sqrt{\log(1/\epsilon)})$ in the strong contamination model of Definition 17.1. Diakonikolas et al. (2018b) developed a more sophisticated filtering technique that achieves the optimal error of $O(\epsilon)$ in the additive contamination model. For the strong contamination model, it was shown in Diakonikolas et al. (2017b) that any improvement on the $O(\epsilon\sqrt{\log(1/\epsilon)})$ error requires superpolynomial time in the Statistical Query model. Steinhardt et al. (2018) gave an efficient algorithm for robust mean estimation with respect to all ℓ_p-norms.

Finally, we note that ideas from Diakonikolas et al. (2016) have led to proof-of-concept improvements in the analysis of genetic data (Diakonikolas et al., 2017a) and in adversarial machine learning (Diakonikolas et al., 2018c).

References

Balakrishnan, S., Du, S. S., Li, J., and Singh, A. 2017. Computationally efficient robust sparse estimation in high dimensions. Pages 169–212 of: *Proc. 30th Annual Conference on Learning Theory*.

Charikar, M., Steinhardt, J., and Valiant, G. 2017. Learning from untrusted data. Pages 47–60 of: *Proc. 49th Annual ACM Symposium on Theory of Computing*.

Diakonikolas, I., Kamath, G., Kane, D. M., Li, J., Moitra, A., and Stewart, A. 2016. Robust estimators in high dimensions without the computational intractability. In *Proceedings of the 57th IEEE Symposium on Foundations of Computer Science (FOCS)*, pp. 655–664.

Diakonikolas, I., Kamath, G., Kane, D. M., Li, J., Moitra, A., and Stewart, A. 2017a. Being robust (in high dimensions) can be practical. In *Proceedings of the 34th International Conference on Machine Learning (ICML)*, pp. 999–1008.

Diakonikolas, I., Kane, D. M., and Stewart, A. 2017b. Statistical query lower bounds for robust estimation of high-dimensional Gaussians and Gaussian mixtures. In *Proceedings of the 58th IEEE Symposium on Foundations of Computer Science (FOCS)*, pp. 73–84.

Diakonikolas, I., Kane, D. M., and Stewart, A. 2018a. List-decodable robust mean estimation and learning mixtures of spherical Gaussians. In *Proceedings of the 50th Annual ACM Symposium on Theory of Computing (STOC)*, pp. 1047–1060.

Diakonikolas, I., Kamath, G., Kane, D. M., Li, J., Moitra, A., and Stewart, A. 2018b. Robustly learning a Gaussian: Getting optimal error, efficiently. In *Proceedings of the 29th Annual Symposium on Discrete Algorithms*, pp. 2683–2702.

Diakonikolas, I., Kamath, G., Kane, D. M., Li, J., Steinhardt, J., and Stewart, A. 2018c. Sever: A robust meta-algorithm for stochastic optimization. *CoRR*, **abs/1803.02815**. Conference version in ICML 2019.

Diakonikolas, I., Karmalkar, S., Kane, D., Price, E., and Stewart, A. 2019. Outlier-robust high-dimensional sparse estimation via iterative filtering. In *Advances in Neural Information Processing Systems 33, NeurIPS 2019*, pp. 10688–10699.

Hopkins, S. B., and Li, J. 2018. Mixture models, robustness, and sum of squares proofs. *Proc. 50th Annual ACM Symposium on Theory of Computing (STOC)*, pp. 1021–1034.

Huber, P. J. 1964. Robust estimation of a location parameter. *Annals of Mathematical Statistics*, **35**(1), 73–101.

Johnson, D. S., and Preparata, F. P. 1978. The densest hemisphere problem. *Theoretical Computer Science*, **6**, 93–107.

Klivans, A., Long, P., and Servedio, R. 2009. Learning halfspaces with malicious noise. *Journal of Machine Learning Research*, **10**, 2715–2740.

Kothari, P. K., Steinhardt, J., and Steurer, D. 2018. Robust moment estimation and improved clustering via sum of squares. In *Proceedings of the 50th Annual ACM Symposium on Theory of Computing (STOC)*, pp. 1035–1046.

Lai, K. A., Rao, A. B., and Vempala, S. 2016. Agnostic estimation of mean and covariance. In *Proceedings of the 57th IEEE Symposium on Foundations of Computer Science (FOCS)*, pp. 665–674.

Prasad, A., Suggala, A. S., Balakrishnan, S., and Ravikumar, P. 2018. Robust estimation via robust gradient estimation. *arXiv preprint arXiv:1802.06485*.

Steinhardt, J., Charikar, M., and Valiant, G. 2018. Resilience: A criterion for learning in the presence of arbitrary outliers. *Proceedings of the 9th Innovations in Theoretical Computer Science Conference (ITCS)*, pp. 45:1–45:21.

Tukey, J. W. 1975. Mathematics and picturing of data. *Proceedings of ICM* **6**, pp. 523–531.

Exercises

Exercise 17.1 Let S be an ϵ-corrupted set of samples from $\mathcal{N}(\mu, I)$ of sufficiently large size.

(a) The geometric median of a discrete set of points is the point that minimizes the sum of the Euclidean distances to these points. Show that the geometric median of S has ℓ_2-distance $O(\epsilon\sqrt{d})$ from μ with high probability.

(b) Show that this upper bound is tight for a worst-case adversary.

Exercise 17.2 (Sample complexity of Robust Mean Estimation)

(a) Prove Fact 17.2 and Proposition 17.3.

(b) How do Fact 17.2 and Proposition 17.3 change when the distribution of the uncorrupted data has bounded kth moments, for even k?

Exercise 17.3 For what values of (ϵ, δ) do the following distribution families satisfy the stability condition of Definition 17.4: bounded covariance ($\Sigma \preceq I$), bounded covariance and sub-gaussian tails in every direction, identity covariance and log-concave (i.e., the logarithm of probability density function is concave), identity covariance with bounded kth central moments?

Exercise 17.4 Prove Lemma 17.7.

Exercise 17.5 (Diakonikolas et al., 2016) Let S be a sufficiently large ϵ-corrupted set of samples from a binary product distribution on $\{\pm 1\}^d$. Modify the basic filter algorithm of Section 17.2.4 to obtain an estimate of the mean with ℓ_2-distance error $O(\epsilon\sqrt{\log(1/\epsilon)})$. [Hint: Use the modified empirical covariance with its diagonal zeroed out.]

Exercise 17.6 (Robust Estimation of Heavy-Tailed Distributions) Let X be a product distribution on $\mathbf{R}^d$ that is centrally symmetric about a center m. Suppose that, for some constant $c > 0$, each marginal distribution has probability density function bounded below by c at all x within distance one of its median. Give a polynomial-time algorithm that estimates m to within ℓ_2 error $\tilde{O}(\epsilon)$ in the presence of an ϵ-fraction of corruptions. (The $\tilde{O}(\cdot)$ notation hides poly-logarithmic factors in its argument.)

Remark This algorithm applies to distributions that may not even have well-defined means, e.g., products of Cauchy distributions.

[Hint: Reduce the problem to robust mean estimation of a binary product distribution and use the previous exercise.]

Exercise 17.7 (Robust Estimation of a 2-Mixture of Spherical Gaussians) In this exercise, we will adapt the filtering method to robustly learn a 2-mixture of spherical Gaussians. Let $F = (1/2)\mathcal{N}(\mu_1, I) + (1/2)\mathcal{N}(\mu_2, I)$ be an unknown balanced mixture of two identity covariance Gaussians with unknown means. Let T be an ϵ-corrupted set of samples from F.

(a) Show that if the eigenvalue of the empirical covariance in a given direction is $1 + \delta$, then both means in this direction are accurate within $\tilde{O}(\sqrt{\epsilon + \delta})$.

(b) Show that if the empirical covariance has only one large eigenvalue, then there is a simple procedure to learn the means to small error.

(c) Show that if empirical covariance has at least two large eigenvalues, then we can construct a filter.

(d) Combine the above to give a polynomial-time algorithm that with high probability learns the means to error $\tilde{O}(\sqrt{\epsilon})$.

(Remark: This accuracy is essentially best possible information-theoretically. One can have have two mixtures $F^{(i)} = (1/2)\mathcal{N}(\mu_1^{(i)}, I) + (1/2)\mathcal{N}(\mu_2^{(i)}, I)$, $i = 1, 2$ that have $d_{\mathrm{TV}}(F^{(1)}, F^{(2)}) = \epsilon$, where $\mu_1^{(2)}$, $\mu_2^{(2)}$ are at distance $\Omega(\sqrt{\epsilon})$ from $\mu_1^{(1)}$, $\mu_2^{(1)}$.)

CHAPTER EIGHTEEN

Nearest Neighbor Classification and Search

Sanjoy Dasgupta and Samory Kpotufe

Abstract: In both algorithmic analysis of nearest neighbor search and statistical rates of convergence for nearest neighbor classification, the simplest worst-case bounds are pessimistic and discouraging, and do not accurately reflect performance in practice. In this chapter, we discuss some of the more refined types of analysis that have been attempted, and argue that much remains to be done.

18.1 Introduction

Nearest neighbor search is a basic tool of information retrieval: given a new data item (such as the medical record of a new patient, or the latest measurements from a space mission), the task is to find the *most similar* items encountered in the past. These help to place the new item in context, for instance to determine whether it is something familiar that can be handled easily or something novel that demands special attention. In particular, knowledge of the outcomes, or labels, of the nearest neighbors can be used to predict an outcome for the new instance.

Nearest neighbor search raises both algorithmic and statistical questions. How can the nearest neighbor(s) be found quickly? And what is the quality of predictions made using these neighbors? These questions have been studied for many decades, yet remain rich areas of research. A large part of the difficulty is that the simplest worst-case bounds for these problems are so loose as to be meaningless, in the sense that they provide little insight into the behavior observed in reality. Thus it is of great interest to develop methods of analysis that are more refined, that gain accuracy by taking the structure or distribution of data into account.

18.2 The Algorithmic Problem of Nearest Neighbor Search

Given a set S of n points, the nearest neighbor of a query q is the point in S that is closest to q under some distance function of interest. Finding the nearest neighbor naively takes $O(n)$ time, which can be a serious deterrent in many practical settings with large n.[1] To speed this up, can a data structure be built from S that will permit subsequent queries q to be answered quickly?

---

[1] This ignores the time taken to compute distances between points, which is $O(d)$ in d-dimensional Euclidean space, and can be a significant factor when d is large. There is quite a bit of work on mitigating this, for instance using dimensionality reduction, but it is mostly orthogonal to our discussion here and has less of the "beyond worst case" flavor.

For one-dimensional data, there is an easy solution: The data structure is simply a sorted version of S, using which the nearest neighbor of any query can be found in $O(\log n)$ time by binary search. But generalizing this to higher dimension is not straightforward. An especially tricky case is when the points S and query q are all chosen uniformly at random from the surface of the unit sphere in $\mathbb{R}^D$. If $D \gg \log n$, a simple calculation shows that all the points, including the query, will with high probability lie at distance $\sqrt{2} \pm o(1)$ from each other. Thus all points are just a tiny bit further from q than its very nearest neighbor. It is hard to imagine what kind of data structure might permit the nearest neighbor to quickly be identified amid such miniscule differences. In what follows, we will refer to this example as the *canonical bad case*.

There are two ways to banish this nightmare scenario. The first is to be content with a c-approximation to the nearest neighbor, for some small constant c: that is, any point that is at most c times further away from q than its nearest neighbor. For data distributed uniformly on a high-dimensional sphere, anything in S is then an acceptable answer. The second recourse is to think of this particular example as being pathological and unlikely to occur in practice, and to make assumptions about the configuration of the data under which efficient search is possible.

18.2.1 Hashing for Approximate Nearest Neighbor Search

A hugely popular and successful method for nearest neighbor search has been locality-sensitive hashing (LSH), first introduced in the late 1990s (Indyk and Motwani, 1998; Charikar, 2002; Andoni and Indyk, 2008). This is not a specific algorithm but rather a framework for boosting the performance of simple randomized hash functions. The most common instantiation, for data in $\mathbb{R}^D$, uses random linear projections for hashing:

- A point $x \in \mathbb{R}^D$ is mapped to the integer $\lfloor (u \cdot x)/b \rfloor$, where u is a direction chosen at random from the unit sphere and b is the bucket width.
- Taking m such mappings $h_1, \ldots, h_m$, point x then gets stored in an m-dimensional table at location $(h_1(x), \ldots, h_m(x))$; the value of m can be thought of as $O(\log n)$, but would in practice typically be tuned using a set of sample queries. Regardless of m, the table can be stored in $O(n)$ space using standard hashing techniques.
- A query q is answered by looking at all points falling at location $(h_1(q), \ldots, h_m(q))$ and selecting the nearest neighbor among them.

The probability that this fails to return a c-approximate nearest neighbor can be bounded; and by having multiple independently built tables, the failure probability can be made as small as desired.

For n data points in Euclidean space, LSH can be used to create a data structure of size $O(n^{1+1/c^2})$ that is then subsequently able to answer c-approximate nearest neighbor queries in time $O(n^{1/c^2})$ with failure probability that is an arbitrarily small constant (Andoni and Indyk, 2008). For $c = 2$, this translates to space $O(n^{5/4})$ and query time $O(n^{1/4})$. Numerous other variants of LSH have been developed, some that handle other distance and similarity functions (Charikar, 2002; Datar et al., 2004; Andoni et al., 2018), and some that adapt to the particular data distribution (Andoni and Razenshteyn, 2015), but the Euclidean scheme is a useful representative case.

A striking feature of the analysis of LSH is that all the problem-specific character-istics that undoubtedly affect the hardness of NN search – such as the dimension of the data – are swept under the rug and a bound is given entirely in terms of the number of points n and the approximation factor c. This factor itself is somewhat hard to interpret because it means different things for different data sets. Take $c = 2$, for example (values much smaller than this lead to unreasonably large data structures): For some data sets, 2-approximation might yield points very close to the true nearest neighbor and produce usually correct classifications, while on other data sets, 2-approximation might mean that the returned point is essentially a random draw from the data set. In short, this guarantee is not inherently reassuring.

By way of example, here is a table showing the classification error rate of c-approximate nearest neighbors, as a function of c, on the MNIST data set of handwritten digits:

c	1.0	1.2	1.4	1.6	1.8	2.0
Error rate (%)	3.1	9.0	18.4	29.3	40.7	51.4

For each value of c, the error rate shown is that of a classifier that picks a random c-approximate nearest neighbor and predicts with its label. In this case, even a small value like $c = 1.2$ leads to a substantial degradation in classification performance over the true nearest neighbor.

Having a bound that depends only on c is elegant, but the absence of other relevant parameters makes it likely to be too loose to provide guidance on specific data sets of interest. Looking back at the table for MNIST, we might be inclined to believe that we need something like a $c = 1.1$ approximation and that LSH is thus a bad choice because it will require close to quadratic space. But this is far from the truth, which is that even with a much larger setting of c, the LSH scheme described above typically returns the *exact* nearest neighbor on this data set.

Locality-sensitive hashing is a beautiful algorithmic framework that is highly effective in practice. But there is scope for improvement in its analysis. It would be helpful to know the probability with which this data structure returns the exact nearest neighbor, or perhaps one of the 1% closest neighbors. This would likely depend on the configuration of the data points, and it would be interesting to understand what structural properties of the data make for efficient search.

18.2.2 Tree Structures for Exact Nearest Neighbor Search

There is an extensive literature on data structures for *exact* nearest neighbor search. Perhaps the most widely-used of these is the k-d *tree* (Bentley, 1975), a partition of $\mathbb{R}^D$ into hyper-rectangular cells, based on a given set $S \subseteq \mathbb{R}^D$ of data points. The root of the tree is a single cell corresponding to the entire space. A coordinate direction is chosen, and the cell is split at the median of the data along this direction (Figure 18.1). The process is then recursively invoked on the two newly created cells, and continues until all leaf cells contain at most some predetermined number n_0 of points. When there are n data points, the depth of the tree is about $\log_2 (n/n_0)$.

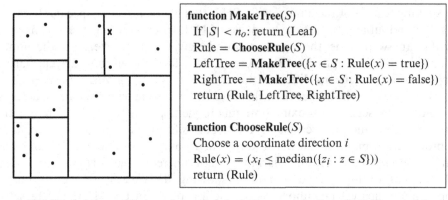

```
function MakeTree(S)
    If |S| < n_o: return (Leaf)
    Rule = ChooseRule(S)
    LeftTree = MakeTree({x ∈ S : Rule(x) = true})
    RightTree = MakeTree({x ∈ S : Rule(x) = false})
    return (Rule, LeftTree, RightTree)

function ChooseRule(S)
    Choose a coordinate direction i
    Rule(x) = (x_i ≤ median({z_i : z ∈ S}))
    return (Rule)
```

Figure 18.1 The k-d tree: example and pseudocode. In the example, the split at the root of the tree is vertical, the two splits at the next level are horizontal, and the next four are a mix of horizontal and vertical. A query point q is marked by a cross.

Given a k-d tree built from data points S, there are two ways to answer a nearest neighbor query q. The quick-and-dirty option is to move q down the tree to its appropriate leaf cell and then return the nearest neighbor in that cell. This *defeatist search* takes time just $O(n_o + \log(n/n_o))$, which is $O(\log n)$ for constant n_o. The problem is that q's nearest neighbor may well lie in a different cell, as is the case in Figure 18.1. Consequently, the failure probability of this scheme (taken over a random choice of queries, say) can be unacceptably high. The alternative is *comprehensive search*, which uses geometric reasoning to decide which other leaf cells might also need to be probed and always returns the true nearest neighbor, but in the worst case can take $O(n)$ time.

Popular prejudice holds that k-d tree performance – whether measured by the success probability of defeatist search or the query time of comprehensive search – deteriorates rapidly with dimension. This remains to be mathematically justified, however. What would be especially interesting is to identify simple conditions on high-dimensional data under which the k-d tree functions well.

Numerous variants of the k-d tree have been developed, attempting to compensate for its perceived weaknesses. One notable such example is the *principal component analysis* (PCA) *tree* (Sproull, 1991; McFee and Lanckriet, 2011), which splits data along directions of largest variance rather than along individual coordinates. Once again, the rigorous analysis of its query complexity remains an open problem, although there have been some attempts in this direction (Abdullah et al., 2014).

In the 1980s and 1990s, a variety of tree structures were introduced that guaranteed running times proportional to $\log n$ but exponential in D; a survey can be found in Clarkson (1999). Notice that this is in line with the canonical bad case described earlier. In $\mathbb{R}^D$, it is possible to have 2^D points that are roughly equidistant from each other, and thus query times proportional to this are not surprising, in the worst case. Interestingly, some of these data structures also work in arbitrary metric spaces. More recent incarnations have tried to move past the pessimism of these worst-case bounds by adapting to situations in which the *intrinsic dimension* of the data is low, even much if its apparent dimension is higher. Before delving into this work, we briefly discuss notions of dimension.

18.2.3 Notions of Intrinsic Dimension

Measures of intrinsic dimension have arisen in a variety of different fields (Cutler, 1993; Clarkson, 2006). The most common notions aim to either quantify the complexity of a (data) space $\mathcal{X}$, or that of a measure μ supported on $\mathcal{X}$ (usually the data-generating distribution). We now look at two such quantities that appear most frequently in analyses of nearest neighbor methods.

For intuition behind the first such quantity, consider the fact that a d-dimensional hypercube of side-length r can be covered by 2^d hypercubes of side length $r/2$.

> **Definition 18.1** A metric space $(\mathcal{X}, \rho)$ is said to have **doubling dimension** d if, for all $r > 0$ and $x \in \mathcal{X}$, the ball $B(x, r)$ can be covered by 2^d balls of radius $r/2$.

Here are some common types of low-dimensional structure that are captured by doubling dimension; see Dasgupta and Freund (2008) for further details.

1. Any k-dimensional affine subspace $\mathcal{X} \subseteq \mathbb{R}^D$ has doubling dimension $\leq c_o k$, for some absolute constant c_o.
2. Any set $\mathcal{X} \subseteq \mathbb{R}^D$ in which each element has at most k nonzero coordinates (that is, a *sparse* set) has doubling dimension at most $c_o k + k \log D$. The same holds when $\mathcal{X}$ is of arbitrary dimension but can be sparsely represented under an unknown *dictionary* of size D, i.e., if there exist vectors $\{a_i\}_{i=1}^{D}$ such that any $x \in \mathcal{X}$ is a linear combination of at most k of them.
3. Let M be a k-dimensional Riemannian submanifold in $\mathbb{R}^D$ with *reach* τ (this is a measure of curvature: It means that every point at distance $< \tau$ of M has a unique nearest neighbor in M). Then every neighborhood of M of radius τ has doubling dimension $O(k)$.

It is also worth remarking that if $\mathcal{X}$, of doubling dimension d, is bounded (i.e., $\sup_{x, x'} \rho(x, x') < \infty$), then for any $r > 0$, $\mathcal{X}$ can be covered by $C_d \cdot r^{-d}$ balls of radius r, for some constant C_d (Exercise 18.1). Any $(\mathcal{X}, \rho)$ with this property is said to have **metric dimension** d.

There is a similar-sounding notion, *doubling measure*, that attempts to capture the intrinsic dimension of a measure (usually a probability measure) on a metric space, by looking at how quickly the measure of a ball grows as its radius increases.

> **Definition 18.2** A measure μ on $(\mathcal{X}, \rho)$ is said to be **doubling** with exponent d, whenever for any x in the support of μ (henceforth denoted supp(μ)), and any $r > 0$, we have $\mu(B(x, r)) \leq 2^d \cdot \mu(B(x, r/2))$.

Unlike the doubling dimension, which depends only on the set $\mathcal{X}$, this varies according to the measure placed on $\mathcal{X}$. The relationship between the two notions is explored in Exercise 18.2.

Remark also that if $(\mathcal{X}, \rho)$ with doubling measure μ is bounded, then for any $r > 0$ and $x \in$ supp(μ), we have $\mu(B(x, r)) \geq C_d r^d$ for some constant C_d (Exercise 18.1). We then say that μ is **homogeneous** (on supp(μ)) with parameters (C_d, d).

18.2.4 Adaptivity to Intrinsic Dimension in Nearest Neighbor Search

One way of going beyond the pessimism of worst-case analysis is to identify families of instances that occur in practice and are also "easier" in the sense of admitting better bounds. For nearest neighbor search, this enterprise has mostly focused on analyzing data sets of low intrinsic dimension. The hope is that the exponential dependence on dimension in worst-case bounds for exact nearest neighbor search can be replaced by a similar dependence on intrinsic dimension, which might be much smaller.

The excellent survey of Clarkson (2006) describes ways in which nearest neighbor data structures can be made adaptive to different types of intrinsic dimension. Perhaps the easiest assumption to work with is a finite-sample version of doubling measure, which we now introduce. Suppose the data lie in a metric space $\mathcal{X}$. We say that a subset $T \subseteq \mathcal{X}$ has *expansion constant* c if for any point $p \in \mathcal{X}$ and any radius $r > 0$, we have $|T \cap B(p, 2r)| \leq c|T \cap B(p, r)|$. The assumption on the data set S is that there exists a small c such that $S \cup \{q\}$ has expansion constant at most c for any query point q. The intrinsic dimension can then be viewed as $\log c$.

One widely used data structure that has been analyzed under this condition is the *cover tree* (Beygelzimer et al., 2006), which can be used for exact nearest neighbor search in any metric space. It works by maintaining a hierarchical covering of the data set, which we will now describe in more detail. Say the data points are $x_1, \ldots, x_n$, and assume for simplicity that all interpoint distances are ≤ 1. Then any point x_i serves as a 1-cover of the entire set; take it to be the root of the tree. The next level will consist of a subset of the x_i's that constitute a $(1/2)$-cover, and the following level will be a $(1/4)$-cover, and so on. Given level $j - 1$, level j can be built as follows: take all the points from level $j - 1$, and repeatedly add in a data point that is not within distance $1/2^j$ of those already chosen. The resulting cover tree on data points $x_1, \ldots, x_n$ is a rooted infinite tree with the following properties:

- Each node of the tree is associated with one of the data points x_i.
- If a node is associated with x_i, then one of its children is also associated with x_i.
- All nodes at depth j are at distance at least $1/2^j$ from each other.
- Each node at depth $j + 1$ is within distance $1/2^j$ of its parent (at depth j).

See Figure 18.2 for an example. In practice, there is no need to duplicate a node as its own child, so the tree takes up $O(n)$ space. Moreover, it is not hard to build the tree on-line, adding one point at a time.

When a query q needs to be answered, it is moved down the tree, one level at a time. At the jth level (call it L_j), geometric reasoning is used to identify a subset of nodes $S_j \subseteq L_j$ whose descendants could possibly include the nearest neighbor of q; this is based on the distance from q to the closest point in L_j, combined with the triangle inequality. At the next level, L_{j+1}, only the children of S_j are examined and these are further restricted to a subset S_{j+1}, and so on. It turns out that with expansion constant c, only $|S_j| = O(\text{poly}(c))$ nodes need to be considered at each level, and the total time to find the exact nearest neighbor is $O(\text{poly}(c) \log n)$.

The cover tree is a popular and effective data structure, especially for non-Euclidean distance metrics. Its analysis, however, is marred by the brittleness of the

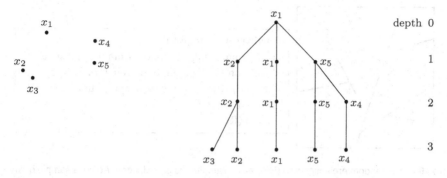

Figure 18.2 A cover tree for a data set of five points. From the structure of the tree we can conclude, for instance, that x_1, x_2, x_5 are all at distance $\geq 1/2$ from each other, since they are all at depth 1, and that the distance between x_2 and x_3 is $\leq 1/4$.

expansion constant assumption. To get a sense of this, observe that even data in $\mathbb{R}^D$, under Euclidean distance, can have arbitrarily high c, unbounded by any function of D. It is thus of interest to devise more reasonable conditions under which to study this scheme.

A weaker and more realistic assumption on a data set is that it has low doubling dimension d. In this case, there are data structures of size $O(n)$ that either yield a $(1+\epsilon)$-approximate nearest neighbor in time $O(2^{O(d)} \log n + (1/\epsilon)^{O(d)})$ (Krauthgamer and Lee, 2004), or, when the query distribution matches the data distribution, yield the correct nearest neighbor in time $O(2^d \log n)$ (Clarkson, 1999, 2006). We will discuss another such data structure in more detail in the next section.

Adaptivity to doubling dimension is nontrivial: k-d trees, for instance, do not have this property (Dasgupta and Sinha, 2015). This makes it technically interesting and has led to quite a bit of computational geometry work around this notion. However, it is really just one specialized way of moving beyond the worst case in nearest neighbor search. The field of unsupervised learning has identified many varieties of geometric structure that commonly exist in data. A few of these, such as manifold structure, are captured by intrinsic dimension; but many others, like cluster structure, are not. Thus it would be useful to move beyond intrinsic dimension when positing structural "niceness" assumptions under which nearest neighbor search can efficiently be performed.

An alternative to bounding the query time of a nearest neighbor data structure in terms of prespecified geometric parameters like intrinsic dimension is to explicitly characterize the types of data on which it is efficient. Ideally, one would be able to achieve tight, instance-specific results in this way. We now turn to such a scheme.

18.2.5 A Randomized Tree Structure with Instance-Specific Bounds

Locality-sensitive hashing has brought a simple and highly effective paradigm to the field of nearest neighbor search: design a data structure that is quick-and-dirty and has nonzero probability of success on any instance; and then boost the success probability by making multiple copies. We now discuss a way of bringing much the same sensibility to k-d trees.

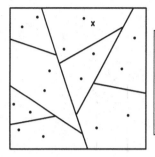

function ChooseRule(S)
Pick U uniformly at random from the unit sphere
Pick β uniformly at random from $[1/4, 3/4]$
Let $v = \beta$-fractile point of the projection of S on U
Rule$(x) = (x \cdot U \leq v)$
return (Rule)

Figure 18.3 The random projection tree (RP tree): example and pseudocode. Again, a sample query point is marked with a cross.

The random projection (RP) tree (Figure 18.3) injects two forms of randomness into a k-d tree: (1) instead of splitting cells along coordinate axes, it picks split directions uniformly at random from the unit sphere, and (2) instead of putting the split point exactly at the median, it is placed at a fractile chosen uniformly at random from the range $[1/4, 3/4]$.

The idea is to answer nearest neighbor queries using defeatist search on this randomized tree structure, which takes time $O((\log(n/n_o)) + n_o)$, where n_o is an upper bound on the number of data points in any leaf. For any data set $x_1, \ldots, x_n \in \mathbb{R}^D$ and any query $q \in \mathbb{R}^D$, the probability of not finding the nearest neighbor, over the randomness in the data structure, can be bounded using an elementary argument (Dasgupta and Sinha, 2015). The bound turns out to be proportional to a simple function of the point configuration,

$$\Phi(q, \{x_1, \ldots, x_n\}) = \frac{1}{n} \sum_{i=2}^{n} \frac{\|q - x_{(1)}\|}{\|q - x_{(i)}\|},$$

where $x_{(1)}, x_{(2)}, \ldots$ denotes an ordering of the x_i by increasing distance from q.

Let's take a closer look at this potential function. If Φ is close to 1, then all the points are roughly the same distance from q, and so we can expect that the NN query is not easy to answer. This is what we get in the canonical bad case discussed at the beginning of Section 18.2. On the other hand, if Φ is close to 0, then most of the points are much further away than the nearest neighbor, so the latter should be easy to identify. Thus the potential function is an intuitively reasonable measure of the difficulty of an instance of nearest neighbor search.

It is not hard to give upper bounds on Φ in situations in which the data have low doubling measure or doubling dimension. This leads to the following results:

- When $x_1, \ldots, x_n$ are drawn i.i.d. from a doubling measure with exponent d, the RP tree is able to answer arbitrary exact nearest neighbor queries in time $O(d)^d + O(\log n)$, with a probability of error that is an arbitrarily small constant.
- When the query q is *exchangeable* with the data $x_1, \ldots, x_n$ – that is, q is a random draw from $\{x_1, \ldots, x_n, q\}$ – and they together form a set of bounded doubling dimension, then a similar result holds, but with an additional dependence on the aspect ratio of the data.

These are close to the best results that have been obtained using other data structures. The failure probability is over the randomization in the tree structure and can be reduced by building multiple trees to get an *RP forest*.

Although RP forests have been found effective in practice (Hyvonen et al., 2016), one would hope to do better by having trees that are still randomized – so that error probability can be reduced by building a forest – but are more attuned to the data, in much the same way that a single PCA tree is (in practice) superior to a single RP tree. It is an interesting open problem to find a way of doing this that both works well empirically and admits a clean analysis.

18.2.6 Wrap-up: Analyzing Nearest Neighbor Search Algorithms

Nearest neighbor search has been the subject of algorithmic research since the 1970s, and many data structures have been developed for it. Some of these, such as locality-sensitive hash tables, k-d trees, and cover trees, are fairly easy to implement and seem to be effective in practice. But in order to understand their relative strengths and weaknesses – to gauge, for instance, which might be preferable for a given type of data – and to develop better algorithms, it is important to have ways of analyzing these schemes. The current state-of-the-art is lacking in this regard.

For some data structures, such as the k-d tree, there is no characterization of the types of data on which it works well. On others, there is analysis that is beautiful but fails to give insight into when and why the scheme works; examples include the bounds for LSH, which are given solely in terms of an approximation factor and are thus very loose, and those for the cover tree, which are based on a dimensionality assumption that is brittle to the point of straining plausibility.

One good open problem is to identify other structural assumptions on data – beyond low doubling dimension – that are likely to hold in many situations and that make nearest neighbor search efficient. A second is to pick any existing practical nearest neighbor algorithm, and to rigorously formulate conditions on the data under which it will work well.

18.3 Statistical Complexity of k-Nearest Neighbor Classification

We now turn to a different aspect of nearest neighbor: its statistical performance when used as a classification strategy. While statistical and computational questions are fundamentally different, and in fact are studied in different communities – machine learning and statistics on one hand, and algorithms on the other – we will see that some of the same ideas were developed to capture notions of favorable *structure* in data with similar upsides and downsides as discussed above.

Nearest neighbor classification is a form of *nonparametric estimation*: That is, it is a prediction strategy whose complexity (e.g., size) is potentially unbounded, and it is capable of modeling any decision boundary. The statistics community has developed a standard framework for analyzing nonparametric estimators, and has obtained basic bounds that provide some insights into general behavior.

18.3.1 The Statistical Learning Framework

Let $\mathcal{X}$ be the space in which data lie, and $\mathcal{Y}$ the space of labels. We will assume for simplicity that $\mathcal{Y} = \{0, 1\}$. The standard model of statistical learning is that there is some (unknown) underlying distribution $P_{X,Y}$ on $\mathcal{X} \times \mathcal{Y}$ from which all data – past, present, and future – is drawn i.i.d. The training data $\{X_i, Y_i\}_1^n \overset{\text{i.i.d}}{\sim} P_{X,Y}$ is useful precisely because it provides some information about $P_{X,Y}$, and any model we build is evaluated according to its performance on $P_{X,Y}$.

A *classifier* is any function $h : \mathcal{X} \to \mathcal{Y}$. It can be evaluated by the *01-risk*

$$R(h) = P_{X,Y}(h(X) \neq Y).$$

There need not exist any classifier with zero risk: consider any scenario with inherent uncertainty, such as a medical prediction problem in which x is a patient's medical record and y is whether the person will suffer a stroke in the next year. Formally, this corresponds to cases in which the conditional distribution of Y given $X = x$, denoted $P_{Y|x}$, assigns nonzero probability to both outcomes, 0 and 1.

Let $\eta(x) = P_{Y|x}(1) = \mathbb{E}[Y|x]$; the 01-risk is minimized by the so-called *Bayes classifier*, which predicts the most likely label at each point x:

$$h^*(x) \doteq \arg\max \left\{ P_{Y|x}(1), P_{Y|x}(0) \right\} = \mathbb{1}\{\eta(x) \geq 1/2\}.$$

We will henceforth evaluate any classifier h by how much its risk exceeds that of h^*, the so-called *excess-risk*,

$$\mathcal{E}(h) \doteq R(h) - R(h^*), \text{ depending on } P_{X,Y}.$$

Now consider any learning procedure that takes n data points sampled i.i.d. from $P_{X,Y}$ and produces a classifier $\hat{h}_n$. The most basic condition we could demand of this procedure is *consistency*: that as n grows to ∞, the excess risk $\mathcal{E}(\hat{h}_n)$ goes to zero. With this assured, the next order of business is to establish the rate of convergence of the excess risk as a function of n and other problem parameters.

Because decision boundaries can be arbitrarily complex, it is well known that in nonparametric estimation there are no universal rates of convergence without conditions on the data distribution (Devroye et al., 1997). But what are reasonable assumptions to make on $P_{X,Y}$? Over the past few decades, a certain set of assumptions has become entrenched in the statistics literature, perhaps more for mathematical convenience than anything else, and has become the standard backdrop for convergence rates. We will talk about these, about the resulting bounds and the estimators that achieve them, and about whether this theory provides an adequate picture of when nearest neighbor classification works well.

18.3.2 Minimax Optimality

We are interested in the limits of performance, assessed in terms of excess risk $\mathcal{E}(\hat{h})$ (as a function of sample size n) achievable by any procedure[2] $\hat{h}$ having little to no

---

[2] We often will not distinguish between the classification procedure $\hat{h}$, which maps data in $\mathcal{X}^n$ to a classifier $\mathcal{X} \to \mathcal{Y}$, and the classifier that it returns. In other words, $\mathcal{E}(\hat{h})$ is the excess risk of the classifier returned by the procedure $\hat{h}$.

information on the Bayes classifier h^*, i.e., little information on $P_{X,Y}$. Assuming $P_{X,Y}$ belongs to some class $\mathcal{P}$, encoding information on h^*, performance limits are captured by the *minimax* classification risk

$$\mathcal{E}^*(\mathcal{P}) \doteq \inf_{\hat{h}} \sup_{P_{X,Y} \in \mathcal{P}} \mathbb{E}_{P_{X,Y}^n} \mathcal{E}(\hat{h}).$$

The sup denotes the worst-case excess risk over $\mathcal{P}$ achievable by any given $\hat{h}$. Any classifier $\hat{h}$ achieving excess risk $O(\mathcal{E}^*)$ for all $P_{X,Y} \in \mathcal{P}$ is called *minimax-optimal* for $\mathcal{P}$. As a classical example, $\mathcal{P} \doteq \{P_{X,Y}\}$ corresponds to assuming $\mathcal{X} \subset \mathbb{R}^D$, while $\eta(x)$ is λ-Lipschitz over $\mathcal{X}$, i.e., $|\eta(x) - \eta(x')| \leq \lambda\|x - x'\|$, for some $\lambda > 0$ – encoding the hope that nearby points in $\mathcal{X}$ have similar Y values. Under these assumptions, $\mathcal{E}^*(\mathcal{P})$ is known to be of order $n^{-1/(2+D)}$; such rate is achieved for instance by k-nearest neighbor (k-NN) classification with a suitable choice of $k \propto n^{2/(2+D)}$. Unfortunately, this is a rather slow rate whenever D is large, since a number of samples $n = \Omega\left(\epsilon^{-(2+D)}\right)$ seems required to achieve excess risk $0 < \epsilon < 1$, a *curse of dimensionality*. While this rate is unavoidable in the worst case over $\mathcal{P}$, one would hope that there are more favorable distributions $P_{X,Y}$ in $\mathcal{P}$ where procedures such as k-NN would do much better. This is indeed the case and is the focus of the rest of this section.

18.3.3 Adaptive Rates versus Worst-Case Rates

As in the preceding discussion, let $\mathcal{P}$ denote the class of all distributions $P_{X,Y}$, with marginal P_X supported on $\mathcal{X} \subset \mathbb{R}^D$ ($\mathcal{X}$ perhaps unknown), with λ-Lipschitz *regression function* $\eta(x)$. For simplicity, in the following discussion, we will let $\mathcal{X}$ be bounded; hence, w.l.o.g., let $\sup_{x,x' \in \mathcal{X}} \|x - x'\| = 1$.

Now note that, $\mathcal{P}$ contains – among other favorable distributions – subclasses $\mathcal{P}_d$ of those distributions $P_{X,Y}$ such that $\mathcal{X} \doteq \text{supp}(P_X)$ (or P_X itself) is of lower intrinsic dimension $d \ll D$, where *intrinsic dimension* is formalized as any of the concepts defined in Section 18.2.3. If we knew a priori that $P_{X,Y} \in \mathcal{P}_d \subset \mathcal{P}$, we could do much better than the minimax rate $\mathcal{E}^*(\mathcal{P}) \propto n^{-1/(2+D)}$: This is immediate to see when d stands for Euclidean dimension, i.e., $\mathcal{X}$ is an affine subspace of dimension d, since as per the preceding discussion, we would then have $\mathcal{E}^*(\mathcal{P}_d) \propto n^{-1/(2+d)} \ll n^{-1/(2+D)}$, which is achieved, e.g., by k-NN with $k \propto n^{2/(2+d)}$. The question is therefore whether such a better rate is achievable (1) under general notions of intrinsic dimension d where $\mathcal{X}$ is nonlinear (e.g., a manifold of dimension d that lies in $\mathbb{R}^D$), and (2) without the knowledge that $P_{X,Y} \in \mathcal{P}_d$. A classification procedure which (nearly) achieves the rates $\mathcal{E}^*(\mathcal{P}_d)$ simultaneously for all $\mathcal{P}_d \subset \mathcal{P}$ (i.e., under (2)) is called *minimax adaptive* over the collection $\{\mathcal{P}_d\}_{d \leq D}$, or colloquially, *adaptive to intrinsic d*.

In the sequel, we will show that this is indeed the case for k-NN for any of the notions of intrinsic dimension d of Section 18.2.3, as it happens that key quantities controlling performance – namely, typical distances to nearest neighbors – depend only on d rather than on the ambient dimension D. To develop this theme, let us first assume that P_X is *homogeneous* on $\mathcal{X}$ with parameters (C_d, d), i.e., balls of radius r have P_X-mass at least $C_d r^d$ (Section 18.2.3).

In this case we have the following theorem. Throughout we assume that the k-NN estimate at any x is defined on exactly $k \leq n$ points; i.e., either there are no ties in distances to x, or a deterministic rule is employed to break ties (e.g. pick the first k ordered indices); we let $k\text{NN}(x)$ be the retained set of k closest neighbors to x.

With this notation, k-NN classification is given by $\hat{h} \doteq \mathbb{1}\{\hat{\eta} \geq 1/2\}$, where

$$\hat{\eta}(x) \doteq \frac{1}{k} \sum_{X_i \in k\text{NN}(x)} Y_i. \tag{18.1}$$

Theorem 18.3 *Let P_X be (C_d, d) homogeneous on bounded support $\mathcal{X} \subset \mathbb{R}^D$, and let $\eta(x)$ be λ-Lipschitz. Let $\hat{h}$ denote a k-NN estimate with $k \propto n^{2/(2+d)}$. We have*

$$\mathbb{E}\,\mathcal{E}(\hat{h}) \leq C\left(\frac{1}{\sqrt{k}} + \left(\frac{k}{n}\right)^{1/d}\right) \leq C' n^{-1/(2+d)},$$

where the expectation is over the random draw of $\{X_i, Y_i\}_{i=1}^n$, and C, C' depend on C_d, d, and λ, but not on D.

Without further distributional assumption, the rate is tight; as it matches the minimax rate for distributions on $\mathbb{R}^d$. The result is obtained by a reduction from classification to regression, where we recall the fact that the Bayes classifier is given by $h^* = \mathbb{1}\{\eta \geq 1/2\}$, $\eta(x) \doteq \mathbb{E}[Y|x]$. Hence, k-NN performance can be assessed through how well $\hat{\eta}$ estimates the *regression function* η. Let $\|\hat{\eta} - \eta\|_1 \doteq \mathbb{E}|\hat{\eta} - \eta|$:

Proposition 18.4 (Regression to Classification) $\mathcal{E}(\hat{h}) \leq 2\|\hat{\eta} - \eta\|_1$.

Proof Let $\mathcal{X}_{\neq} \doteq \{x \in \mathcal{X} : \hat{h}(x) \neq h(x)\}$, and notice that

$$\mathcal{E}(\hat{h}) = \int_{\mathcal{X}_{\neq}} |P_{Y|x}(1) - P_{Y|x}(0)|\,\mathrm{d}P_X = \int_{\mathcal{X}_{\neq}} |2\eta(x) - 1|\,\mathrm{d}P_X,$$

while, whenever $\hat{h} \neq h$, we necessarily have $|\hat{\eta} - \eta| \geq |\eta - 1/2|$. $\square$

Now we aim to bound $\mathbb{E}\,\|\hat{\eta} - \eta\|_1$, one approach being to bound $\|\hat{\eta} - \eta\|_1$ by $\|\hat{\eta} - \eta\|_2 \doteq \left(\mathbb{E}_X|\hat{\eta}(X) - \eta(X)|^2\right)^{1/2}$. We will first condition on $\mathbf{X} \doteq \{X_i\}_{i=1}^n$ while considering just the randomness in $\mathbf{Y} \doteq \{Y_i\}_{i=1}^n$. Let $\tilde{\eta}(x)$ denote the conditional expectation $\mathbb{E}_{\mathbf{Y}|\mathbf{X}}\hat{\eta} = \frac{1}{k}\sum_{X_i \in k\text{NN}(x)} \eta(X_i)$. Clearly, $\tilde{\eta}$ relates most directly to η. Using the fact that, for any random variable Z, $\mathbb{E}[Z - c]^2 = \mathbb{E}(Z - \mathbb{E}Z)^2 + (\mathbb{E}Z - c)^2$, we have the following *bias-variance* decomposition:

$$\mathbb{E}_{\mathbf{Y}|\mathbf{X}}|\hat{\eta}(x) - \eta(x)|^2 = \underbrace{\mathbb{E}_{\mathbf{Y}|\mathbf{X}}|\hat{\eta}(x) - \tilde{\eta}(x)|^2}_{\text{Variance}} + \underbrace{|\tilde{\eta}(x) - \eta(x)|^2}_{\text{Squared Bias}}. \tag{18.2}$$

Variance Bound. Using the independence of Y_i values upon conditioning, we have

$$\mathbb{E}_{\mathbf{Y}|\mathbf{X}}|\hat{\eta}(x) - \tilde{\eta}(x)|^2 = \frac{1}{k^2} \sum_{X_i \in k\text{NN}(x)} \text{Var}(Y_i) \le \frac{1}{k}. \tag{18.3}$$

Bias Bound. Given the Lipchitz assumption on η, we have that

$$|\tilde{\eta}(x) - \eta(x)| \le \frac{1}{k} \sum_{X_i \in k\text{NN}(x)} |\eta(X_i) - \eta(x)| \le \max_{X_i \in k\text{NN}(x)} \lambda \|X_i - x\|.$$

Nearest Neighbor Distances. Let $r_k(x) \doteq \max_{X_i \in k\text{NN}(x)} \|X_i - x\|$ denote the distance from x to its kth closest neighbor in $\mathbf{X}$. As it turns out, typical values of r_k depend on d rather than on the ambient dimension D. For intuition, notice that the ball $B(x, r_k(x))$ will likely have mass at most $c \cdot \frac{k}{n}$ (since it has empirical mass at least $\frac{k}{n}$); we will therefore have the inequality $c \cdot \frac{k}{n} \ge P_X(B(x, r_k(x))) \ge C_d r_k^d(x)$ (following from P_X being (C_d, d) homogeneous), implying that $r_k(x) \le C'_d \left(\frac{k}{n}\right)^{1/d}$. This is formalized as follows.

Let $r_k^*(x) = \inf\left\{1 \ge r > 0 : P_X(B(x, r)) \ge 2\frac{k}{n}\right\}$. First notice that we must have $P_X(B(x, r_k^*(x))) \ge 2\frac{k}{n}$ (by continuity of P_X over monotone sequences of events). Also, since $P_X(B(x, \frac{1}{2}r_k^*(x))) < 2\frac{k}{n}$, we must have that $r_k^*(x) \le C'_d \left(\frac{k}{n}\right)^{1/d}$. Now, we just need to argue that $r_k(x) \le r_k^*(x)$ with high probability, in other words, that the ball $B(x, r_k^*(x))$ contains at least k points; this is certainly the case since empirical masses of balls concentrate around their expectation. Namely, let $P_{X,n}$ denote the empirical distribution induced by $\mathbf{X}$, by a multiplicative Chernoff bound:

$$\mathbb{P}\left(P_{X,n}(B(x, r_k^*(x))) < \frac{k}{n} \le \frac{1}{2} P_X(B(x, r_k^*(x)))\right) \le \exp\left\{-\frac{1}{8}n \cdot P_X(B(x, r_k^*(x)))\right\}$$

$$\le \exp\left\{-\frac{k}{4}\right\} \le \frac{4}{k}.$$

It follows that

$$\mathbb{E}_{\mathbf{X}}\left[r_k^2(x)\right] \le r_k^{*2}(x) + \mathbb{P}\left(r_k(x) > r_k^*(x)\right) \le C_d'^2 \left(\frac{k}{n}\right)^{2/d} + \frac{4}{k}. \tag{18.4}$$

Combining (18.4) and (18.3) by invoking the bias-variance decomposition in (18.2), and then taking expectation over $\mathbf{X}$ yields the result of Theorem 18.3. $\square$

Thus, k-NN classification achieves an excess risk that depends only on $d \ll D$ (for even nonlinear support $\mathcal{X}$) provided k is set according to d. A loose end is therefore whether the parameter k can be set, optimally, without knowledge of d.

Data-Driven Choice of k. The simplest approach is cross-validation, i.e., splitting the sample into two (nearly) equal size independent subsamples, where one subsample is used to define classifiers – corresponding to choices of k – and the other is used to test their performance. W.l.o.g., assume both samples are of size n; define $\hat{h}_k$ as a classifier on subsample $\{X_i, Y_i\}_{i=1}^n$ using the parameter choice $k \in [n]$ (admitting a choice of $k \propto n^{2/(2+d)}$, for unknown d). Now, define the empirical risk $R'_n(h_k) \doteq \frac{1}{n} \sum_i \mathbb{1} \{h(X'_i) \neq Y'_i\}$ on validation sample $\{X'_i, Y'_i\}_{i=1}^n$, and the choice $\hat{k} \doteq \arg\min_{k \in [n]} R'_n(\hat{h}_k)$. Let $k^* \doteq \arg\min_{k \in [n]} R(\hat{h}_k)$; notice that

$$R(\hat{h}_{\hat{k}}) \leq R(\hat{h}_{k^*}) + 2 \max_{k \in [n]} |R(h_k) - R'_n(h_k)|.$$

Combining Chernoff and union bounds, we have that, with probability at least $1 - \delta$:

$$\max_{k \in [n]} |R(h_k) - R'_n(h_k)| \leq \sqrt{\frac{\log(2n/\delta)}{2n}}, \text{ of lower order than } n^{-1/(2+d)}.$$

In other words, picking $\delta = 1/n$, we have with probability at least $1 - 1/n$ that $\mathcal{E}(\hat{h}_{\hat{k}}) \leq \mathcal{E}(\hat{h}_{k^*}) + 2\sqrt{\frac{2\log(2n)}{2n}}$. Now, use the fact that $\mathbb{E}\,\mathcal{E}(\hat{h}_{k^*}) \leq \min_{k \in [n]} \mathbb{E}\,\mathcal{E}(\hat{h}_k)$:

Corollary 18.5 *Under the assumptions of Theorem 18.3, the empirical $\hat{k}$ satisfies*

$$\mathbb{E}\,\mathcal{E}(\hat{h}_{\hat{k}}) \leq C' n^{-1/(2+d)}.$$

Similar arguments extend to more general settings, overviewed next.

General Metrics and Notions of Intrinsic Dimension. First, notice that the preceding arguments extend directly to any metric space $(\mathcal{X}, \rho)$ admitting a (C_d, d)-homogeneous measure P_X. Also, we could have assumed P_X to be doubling, since it is then homogeneous (Section 18.2.3). Suppose instead we only assumed that $(\mathcal{X}, \rho)$ has metric dimension d (allowing spaces of doubling dimension d). The adaptive rate of $n^{-1/(2+d)}$ still holds. However, such a result requires a more refined analysis of k-NN distances r_k: While at any given point x, $r_k(x)$ might not scale with d, it can be shown that $\mathbb{E}\,r_k(X)$ is of the order $(k/n)^{1/d}$ (by adapting a covering argument of Györfi et al. (2006) to metric $\mathcal{X}$), which is sufficient.

Smoothness Conditions on η. The preceding arguments extend easily to the case in which η is Hölder continuous, i.e., $|\eta(x) - \eta(x')| \leq \lambda \rho^\alpha(x, x')$ for some $0 < \alpha \leq 1$, $\lambda > 0$; we would instead obtain the minimax rate $n^{-1/(2+d/\alpha)}$, attained by setting $k \propto n^{2/(2+d/\alpha)}$ (or using $\hat{k}$ as defined earlier). This is obtained by bounding the bias by $\lambda r_k^\alpha(x)$. Notice that the rate $n^{-1/(2+d/\alpha)}$ worsens as $\alpha \to 0$, attesting to the fact that classification is hardest when η changes too fast over $\mathcal{X}$.

While Hölder or Lipschitz conditions on η capture the desired condition that Y should not change too fast over $\mathcal{X}$, they do not allow discontinuities in η, which goes against practical intuition in classification. One way to address this is to instead assume that η is piecewise Hölder, or likely to be *locally* Hölder over $\mathcal{X}$, appropriately formalized (see, e.g., Willett et al., 2006; Urner et al., 2011). More recently Chaudhuri and Dasgupta (2014) formalized the intuition that, all that is needed for k-NN success – irrespective of continuity of η – is that the average Y value in a neighborhood of any x be close to $\eta(x)$ (the average Y at x), especially as the P_X-mass of the neighborhood gets small. This intuition is parameterized as follows: For any set $B \subset \mathcal{X}$, let $\eta(B) = \mathbb{E}[\eta \mid B]$, then it is assumed that

$\forall x \in \mathcal{X}, r > 0, \quad |\eta(B(x,r)) - \eta(x)| \leq C_\gamma \cdot P_X(B(x,r))^\gamma$, for some $C_\gamma, \gamma > 0$.

Intuitively, letting $r = r_k(x)$, we would have $\tilde{\eta}(x) \approx \eta(B(x,r))$, while $P_X(B(x,r)) \approx k/n$, that is, the bias $|\tilde{\eta}(x) - \eta(x)|$ would be of order $(k/n)^\gamma$; this together with a variance of order $1/k$ yields an excess risk of order $n^{-1/(2+\gamma)}$ by optimizing over k.

In particular, under our earlier Hölder conditions, it can be shown that $\gamma = \alpha/d$ holds. This more general condition therefore yields a similar bias bound of order $(k/n)^{\alpha/d}$ and recovers the above minimax rates.

Inhomogeneous Data, and Extensions of k-NN. The preceding distributional conditions, while classical, do not account for spatial variations in $P_{X,Y}$. For instance the density of P_X (e.g., with respect to Lebesgue on $\mathcal{X} = \mathbb{R}^d$) might vary significantly over space; $\mathcal{X}$ might be made up of subregions $\mathcal{X}_i$ of varying intrinsic dimension $d_i \ll D$, and varying complexity in $P_{Y|X}$ (e.g. η might satisfy different Hölder conditions across $\mathcal{X}_i$'s). The support $\mathcal{X}$ might be unbounded, allowing for far outliers. While these situations might be common in practice, they have only now started receiving theoretical attention. In particular, they are commonly handled by extensions of k-NN such as *local k-NN*, where a local choice of $k = k(x)$ is made at every $x \in \mathcal{X}$. While these procedures in essence have *an infinite number of hyperparameters*, e.g. $\{k(x) : x \in \mathcal{X}\}$, they can be shown to *generalize*, i.e., attain nearly minimax rates of convergence, even under data-driven choices of $k(x)$ (see, e.g., Kpotufe, 2011; Samworth et al., 2012; Gadat et al., 2016 for general treatments, that extend to weighted versions of k-NN prediction, under relaxations of traditional assumptions on the marginal P_X).

18.3.4 Low-Noise Conditions and Fast Rates

Another favorable situation in classification is one in which Y labels are deterministic (or nearly so). In particular, suppose $\eta(x)$ has a margin away from $1/2$ at some point x, i.e., $|\eta(x) - 1/2| > \tau$ for some $0 < \tau < 1/2$. Recall that the Bayes classifier satisfies $h^*(x) = \mathbb{1}\{\eta(x) \geq 1/2\}$, while the k-NN estimate $\hat{h}(x) = \mathbb{1}\{\hat{\eta}(x) \geq 1/2\}$, where $\hat{\eta}$ estimates η. Thus, if $|\hat{\eta}(x) - \eta(x)| \leq \tau$, we must have $\hat{h}(x) = h^*(x)$; i.e., the excess risk at x is then 0.

Under the conditions of Theorem 18.3, for $k \propto n^{2/(2+d)}$, and n sufficiently large, we will have $|\hat{\eta}(x) - \eta(x)| \leq Cn^{-1/(2+d)} \leq \tau$ with high probability: This follows from $|\hat{\eta}(x) - \eta(x)| \leq |\hat{\eta}(x) - \tilde{\eta}(x)| + |\tilde{\eta}(x) - \eta(x)|$, and bounding the *variance* and *bias* terms in high probability (by order of $(1/k)$ and $(k/n)^{1/d}$), rather than in expectation. As it turns out, such a result holds uniformly over $x \in \mathcal{X}$: let $0 < \delta < 1$,

$$\mathbb{P}\left(\sup_x |\hat{\eta}(x) - \eta(x)| \leq C\left(\frac{\log(n/\delta)}{n}\right)^{1/(2+d)}\right) \geq 1 - \delta. \tag{18.5}$$

One way to obtain Equation 18.5 is to use uniform Vapnik–Chervonenkis (VC) concentration arguments over the class of balls centered at $x \in \mathcal{X}$; the constant C now also depends on the VC dimension of this class (see, e.g., Kpotufe, 2011).

Now assume the so-called *Massart's noise condition* that $\forall x \in \mathcal{X}, |\eta(x) - 1/2| > \tau$. It then follows from (18.5) that, if n is greater than some $n_0(\tau)$, there is high probability that $\mathcal{E}(\hat{h}) = 0$, which is remarkable. This corresponds to an exponentially fast rate in expectation, i.e., $\mathbb{E}\,\mathcal{E}(\hat{h}) \leq \delta$, for large n, provided $\delta = \omega(e^{-n})$.

A common relaxation of Massart's condition is the so-called *Tsybakov noise condition* which parameterizes the likelihood of having a margin τ:

$$\forall 0 < \tau < 1/2, \quad P_X(x : |\eta(x) - 1/2| \leq \tau) \leq C_\beta \tau^\beta, \text{ for some } C_\beta, \beta > 0.$$

Now, define $\tau_{n,\delta} \doteq C\left(\frac{\log(n/\delta)}{n}\right)^{1/(2+d)} < 1/2$, for n sufficiently large. Under the event of (18.5), the excess risk is 0 at all points in $\mathcal{X}_> \doteq \{x : |\eta(x) - 1/2| > \tau_{n,\delta}\}$. Let $\mathcal{X}_\leq \doteq \mathcal{X} \setminus \mathcal{X}_>$. We therefore have that, with probability at least $1 - \delta$,

$$\mathcal{E}(\hat{h}) \leq \int_{\mathcal{X}_\leq} 2|\eta(x) - 1/2|\, dP_X \leq 2\tau_{n,\delta} \cdot \int_{\mathcal{X}_\leq} dP_X \leq 2C_\beta \cdot \tau_{n,\delta}^{\beta+1}.$$

Thus, we have $\mathbb{E}\,\mathcal{E}(\hat{h}) \leq C\left(\frac{\log(n/\delta)}{n}\right)^{(\beta+1)/(2+d)} + \delta$. In other words, the rate is much faster than $n^{-1/(2+d)}$ for large β. For example, let $\delta = 1/n$, and $\beta \geq d/2$, and the rates are at most $n^{-1/2}$.

Remark (Tension between Parameters) Larger values of $\beta > d$ happen only in restricted situations where η crosses $1/2$ outside of int($\mathcal{X}$), due to the fact that the Lipschitz assumption on η prohibits sharp transitions from $1/2$ (see Audibert and Tsybakov, 2007). Such tension disappears for more general distributions than homogeneous P_X (which corresponds to so-called *strong density* conditions). However, assuming more general conditions on P_X, e.g., only that it has support $\mathcal{X}$ of metric dimension d, minimax rates are slower of the form $n^{-(\beta+1)/(2+d+\beta)}$.

Data-Dependent Choice of k. It remains unclear whether a global choice of k, e.g., by cross-validation, achieves the above rates in terms of β. In particular the above arguments required pointwise guarantees over x as in (18.5), while cross-validation only yields guarantees on global error. However, suitable local choices of $k = k(x)$, e.g., by variants of so-called ICI (Intersecting Confidence Levels), yield the above rates – up to log terms – without prior knowledge of d or β (see, e.g., Kpotufe and Martinet, 2018).

Multiclass Settings. In common classification problems, e.g., object detection, speech, we are in fact dealing with a large number of classes. Therefore, let $Y \in \{1, 2, \ldots, L\}$, and for convenience consider the equivalent encoding $\tilde{Y} \in \{0, 1\}^L$, with coordinate $\tilde{Y}_l = \mathbb{1}\{Y = l\}$. We can now let the regression function $\eta(x) \doteq \mathbb{E}[\tilde{Y}|x]$, with corresponding k-NN estimate $\hat{\eta}(x) = \frac{1}{k}\sum_{X_i \in k\text{NN}(x)} \tilde{Y}_i$.

Now the Bayes classifier is given by $h^*(x) = \arg\max_{l\in[L]} \eta_l(x)$, and similarly obtain the k-NN classifier as $\hat{h}(x) = \arg\max_{l\in[L]} \hat{\eta}_l(x)$. Whether $\hat{h}(x) \neq h^*(x)$ has to do with how well $\hat{\eta}(x)$ estimates $\eta(x)$, as a function of how it is to distinguish the largest coordinate of $\eta(x)$ – say $\eta_{(1)}(x)$ – from the second largest, say $\eta_{(2)}(x)$. Hence, a natural extension to the preceding noise conditions is as follows:

$$\forall 0 < \tau < 1/2, \quad P_X\left(x : \eta_{(1)}(x) \leq \eta_{(2)}(x) + \tau\right) \leq C_\beta \tau^\beta, \text{ for some } C_\beta, \beta > 0.$$

The resulting rates are similar under Lipschitz conditions on η (albeit, with an additional $\log L$ term in the rates; see, e.g., Reeve and Brown, 2018).

18.3.5 Wrap-up: Statistical Complexity

We presented an overview of conditions, or parameterizations of data spaces, going from worst case to more favorable statistical performance:

(a) Notions of dimension similar to those used in analyzing nearest neighbor search algorithms. These are not enough on their own; i.e., rates of convergence can be arbitrarily slow even with this condition, since η (or $P_{Y|X}$) can be arbitrarily complex.

(b) Lipschitz or Holder conditions on the smoothness of η, together with (a), can give bounds of the form $n^{-1/(2+d)}$ that are adaptive to $d \ll D$ for $X \in \mathbb{R}^D$.

(c) Massart/Tsybakov conditions on the "margin": how much of η stays away from $1/2$. Under these conditions, much better rates are possible, e.g., $1/\sqrt{n}$.

Condition (a) is sometimes verifiable, e.g., by appealing to manifold structure or sparsity. But (b) and (c) can be hard to check in practice, although they might be expected to approximately hold.

Together, these conditions alleviate the worst-case nature of the minimax-approach by identifying favorable distributional parameters. Yet, they are still not refined enough, given that many predictors can be shown to be rate-optimal under these conditions (e.g., k-NN, ϵ-NN, various classification trees) but are observed to achieve rather different performance in practice.

Tradeoffs with Fast Search. It is interesting to note that the foregoing analysis and rates remain relevant – up to constants – whenever fast search methods return *approximate* nearest neighbors, since in any case we needed to bound nearest neighbor distances only approximately to obtain these rates. However, changes in constants matter in practice (cf. the discussion of MNIST in Section 18.2.1), but unfortunately are not captured by the type of analysis outlined earlier. There is also a general need for statistical considerations in the design of fast search methods – which largely involve decisions based on marginal X and do not take signal in Y into account, e.g., how slowly labels Y change over X space.

18.4 Notes

References for algorithmic aspects of nearest neighbor search are mostly provided in the main text. The article of Clarkson (1999) on nearest neighbor methods in metric spaces is especially recommended, as is the survey of Cutler (1993) on notions of dimension. For recent developments in locality-sensitive hashing, there is a webpage maintained by Andoni, at www.mit.edu/~andoni/LSH/.

Universal consistency of nearest neighbor methods are first established in Fix and Hodges (1951), Stone (1977), and Devroye et al. (1994) with recent generalizations by Chaudhuri and Dasgupta (2014) and Hanneke et al. (2019) to metric spaces and beyond. Early rates of convergence were given by Cover (1968), Wagner (1971), Fritz (1975), Kulkarni and Posner (1995), and Gyorfi (1981). Various other predictors – local in nature – can be shown to converge at rates adaptive to the unknown intrinsic dimension of data; see, e.g., Scott and Nowak (2006), Bickel and Li (2007), Kpotufe and Dasgupta (2012), Yang and Dunson (2016), and Madrid Padilla et al. (2020). Finally, a recent book of Chen et al. (2018) gives a comprehensive theoretical survey of nearest neighbor methods.

References

Abdullah, A., Andoni, A., Kannan, R., and Krauthgamer, R. 2014. Spectral approaches to nearest neighbor search. In *55th Annual Symposium on Foundations of Computer Science*, pp. 581–590.

Andoni, A., and Indyk, P. 2008. Near-optimal hashing algorithms for approximate nearest neighbor in high dimensions. *Communications of the ACM*, **51**(1), 117–122.

Andoni, A., and Razenshteyn, I. 2015. Optimal data-dependent hashing for approximate near neighbors. In *ACM Symposium on Theory of Computing*, pp. 793–801.

Andoni, A., Naor, A., Nikolov, A., Razenshteyn, I., and Waingarten, E. 2018. Data-dependent hashing via nonlinear spectral gaps. In *ACM Symposium on Theory of Computing*, pp. 787–800.

Audibert, J.-Y., and Tsybakov, A. B. 2007. Fast learning rates for plug-in classifiers. *Annals of Statistics*, **35**(2), 608–633.

Bentley, J. L. 1975. Multidimensional binary search trees used for associative Searching. *Communications of the ACM*, **18**(9), 509–517.

Beygelzimer, A., Kakade, S., and Langford, J. 2006. Cover trees for nearest neighbor. In *Proceedings of the 23rd International Conference on Machine Learning*, pp. 97–104.

Bickel, P. J., and Li, B. 2007. Local polynomial regression on unknown manifolds. In *Complex Datasets and Inverse Problems*. Institute of Mathematical Statistics, pp. 177–186.

Charikar, M. 2002. Similarity estimation techniques from rounding algorithms. In *Proceedings of the 34th ACM Symposium on Theory of Computing*, pp. 380–388.

Chaudhuri, K., and Dasgupta, S. 2014. Rates of convergence for nearest neighbor classification. In *Advances in Neural Information Processing Systems*, pp. 3437–3445.

Chen, George H., Shah, Devavrat, et al. 2018. Explaining the success of nearest neighbor methods in prediction. *Foundations and Trends in Machine Learning*, **10**(5-6), 337–588.

Clarkson, K. 1999. Nearest neighbor queries in metric spaces. *Discrete and Computational Geometry*, **22**, 63–93.

Clarkson, K. 2006. Nearest-neighbor searching and metric space dimensions. In *Nearest-Neighbor Methods for Learning and Vision: Theory and Practice*, pp. 15–59. MIT Press.

Cover, T. M. 1968. Rates of convergence for nearest neighbor procedures. In *Proceedings of the Hawaii International Conference on System Sciences*, pp. 413–415.

Cutler, C. 1993. A review of the theory and estimation of fractal dimension. In Tong, H. (ed), *Dimension Estimation and Models*, pp. 1–107. World Scientific.

Dasgupta, S., and Freund, Y. 2008. Random projection trees and low dimensional manifolds. In *ACM Symposium on Theory of Computing*, pp. 537–546.

Dasgupta, S., and Sinha, K. 2015. Randomized partition trees for nearest neighbor search. *Algorithmica*, **72**(1), 237–263.

Datar, M., Immorlica, N., Indyk, P., and Mirrokni, V. 2004. Locality-sensitive hashing based on p-stable distributions. In *Proceedings of the Twentieth Annual Symposium on Computational Geometry*, pp. 253–262.

Devroye, L., Gyorfi, L., Krzyzak, A., Lugosi, G., et al. 1994. On the strong universal consistency of nearest neighbor regression function estimates. *Annals of Statistics*, **22**(3), 1371–1385.

Devroye, L., Gyorfi, L., and Lugosi, G. 1997. *A Probabilistic Theory of Pattern Recognition*. Springer.

Fix, E., and Hodges, J. 1951. Discriminatory analysis, nonparametric discrimination. *USAF School of Aviation Medicine, Randolph Field, Texas, Project 21-49-004, Report 4, Contract AD41(128)-31*.

Fritz, J. 1975. Distribution-free exponential error bound for nearest neighbor pattern classification. *IEEE Transactions on Information Theory*, **21**(5), 552–557.

Gadat, S., Klein, T., Marteau, C., et al. 2016. Classification in general finite dimensional spaces with the k-nearest neighbor rule. *The Annals of Statistics*, **44**(3), 982–1009.

Gyorfi, L. 1981. The rate of convergence of k_n-NN regression estimates and classification rules. *IEEE Transactions on Information Theory*, **27**(3), 362–364.

Györfi, L., Kohler, M., Krzyzak, A., and Walk, H. 2006. *A Distribution-Free Theory of Nonparametric Regression*. Springer Science+Business Media.

Hanneke, S., Kontorovich, A., Sabato, S., and Weiss, R. 2019. Universal Bayes consistency in metric spaces. *arXiv preprint arXiv:1906.09855*.

Hyvonen, V., Pitkanen, T., Tasoulis, S., Jaasaari, E., Tuomainen, R., Wang, L., Corander, J., and Roos, T. 2016. Fast nearest neighbor search through sparse random projections and voting. In *Proceedings of the 2016 IEEE International Conference on Big Data*, pp. 881–888.

Indyk, P., and Motwani, R. 1998. Approximate nearest neighbors: Towards removing the curse of dimensionality. In *Proceedings of the 30th Annual ACM Symposium on Theory of Computing*, pp. 604–613.

Kpotufe, S. 2011. k-NN regression adapts to local intrinsic dimension. In *Advances in Neural Information Processing Systems*, pp. 729–737.

Kpotufe, S., and Dasgupta, S. 2012. A tree-based regressor that adapts to intrinsic dimension. *Journal of Computer and System Sciences*, **78**(5), 1496–1515.

Kpotufe, S., and Martinet, G. 2018. Marginal singularity, and the benefits of labels in covariate-shift. In *Proceedings of the Conference on Learning Theory (COLT)*, pp. 1882–1886.

Krauthgamer, R., and Lee, J.R. 2004. Navigating nets: Simple algorithms for proximity search. In *ACM-SIAM Symposium on Discrete Algorithms*, pp. 798–807.

Kulkarni, S., and Posner, S. 1995. Rates of convergence of nearest neighbor estimation under arbitrary sampling. *IEEE Transactions on Information Theory*, **41**(4), 1028–1039.

Luukkainen, J., and Saksman, E. 1998. Every complete doubling metric space carries a doubling measure. *Proceedings of the American Mathematical Society*, **126**(2), 531–534.

Madrid Padilla, O. H., Sharpnack, J., Chen, Y., & Witten, D. M. (2020). Adaptive nonparametric regression with the K-nearest neighbour fused lasso. Biometrika, 107(2), 293–310.

McFee, B., and Lanckriet, G. 2011. Large-scale music similarity search with spatial trees. In *12th Conference of the International Society for Music Retrieval*, pp. 55–60.

Reeve, H. W. J., and Brown, G. 2018. Minimax rates for cost-sensitive learning on manifolds with approximate nearest neighbours. *arXiv preprint arXiv:1803.00310*.

Saksman, E. 1999. Remarks on the nonexistence of doubling measures. In *Annales-Academiae Scientiarum Fennicae Series A1 Mathematica*, vol. 24, pp. 155–164. Academia Scientiarum Fennicae.

Samworth, R. J., et al. 2012. Optimal weighted nearest neighbour classifiers. *Annals of Statistics*, **40**(5), 2733–2763.

Scott, C., and Nowak, R.D. 2006. Minimax-optimal classification with dyadic decision trees. *IEEE Transactions on Information Theory*, **52**(4), 1335–1353.

Sproull, R.F. 1991. Refinements to nearest-neighbor searching in k-dimensional trees. *Algorithmica*, **6**(1), 579–589.

Stone, C.J. 1977. Consistent nonparametric regression. *Annals of Statistics*, **5**(4), 595–620.

Urner, R., Shalev-Shwartz, S., and Ben-David, S. 2011. Access to unlabeled data can speed up prediction time. In *Proceedings of the 28th International Conference on Machine Learning (ICML-11)*, pp. 641–648.

Wagner, T. J. 1971. Convergence of the nearest neighbor rule. *IEEE Transactions on Information Theory*, **17**(5), 566–571.

Willett, R., Nowak, R., and Castro, R. M. 2006. Faster rates in regression via active learning. In *Advances in Neural Information Processing Systems*, pp. 179–186.

Yang, Y., and Dunson, D. B. 2016. Bayesian manifold regression. *Annals of Statistics*, **44**(2), 876–905.

Exercises

Exercise 18.1 *Implications of doubling properties.*

(a) Show that if $(\mathcal{X}, \rho)$ is a bounded metric, with doubling dimension d, then it has metric dimension d.

(b) Show that if μ is a doubling measure with exponent d on a bounded metric $(\mathcal{X}, \rho)$, then it is homogeneous (on its support) with parameters (C_d, d) for some C_d.

Exercise 18.2 *Relation between doubling measures and metrics.*

(a) Show that if there exists a doubling measure μ on the metric $(\mathcal{X}, \rho)$ with exponent d, then $(\mathcal{X}, \rho)$ must be *doubling*, with doubling dimension $O(d)$. Hint: Consider maximal packings of a ball by smaller balls.

The reverse is often true, i.e., every *complete* doubling metric admits a doubling measure (Luukkainen and Saksman, 1998; Saksman, 1999).

(b) Show that if there exists a doubling measure μ on the metric $(\mathcal{X}, \rho)$ with exponent d, then $(\mathcal{X}, \rho)$ has metric dimension d (in fact every ball $B(x, r)$ can be covered by $C_d \epsilon^{-d}$ balls of radius ϵr, $\forall \epsilon \in (0, 1]$ and some constant C_d independent of x and r).

Exercise 18.3 *Comprehensive search for k-d trees.* Given a k-d tree built on a data set $S \subset \mathbb{R}^D$ and a query q, a *comprehensive search* begins by finding the nearest point in the leaf cell containing q; call this point x_o. It then expands its search to other leaf cells that might potentially contain an even closer point: namely, those that intersect the ball $B(q, r)$, where $r = \|q - x_o\|$. Along the way, it keeps updating its current-best nearest neighbor and search radius r, and is guaranteed to return the true nearest neighbor. Flesh out an algorithm that implements this logic via a suitable tree traversal.

Exercise 18.4 *ϵ-NN classification.* Under the assumptions of Theorem 18.3, let $\epsilon = Cn^{-1/(2+d)}$, for some $C > 0$. Let $\hat{h}(x) = \mathbb{1}\{\hat{\eta}(x) \geq 1/2\}$, where, for $n_\epsilon(x) \doteq |\mathbf{X} \cap B(x, \epsilon)|$,

$$\hat{\eta}(x) = \frac{1}{n_\epsilon(x)} \sum_{X_i \in B(x,\epsilon)} Y_i \cdot \mathbb{1}\{n_\epsilon(x) \geq 1\}, \; \forall x \in \text{supp}(P_X).$$

(a) Argue that $\mathbb{E}_{Y|X}\|\hat{\eta}(x) - \eta(x)\|^2 \leq \frac{1}{n_\epsilon(x)}\mathbb{1}\{n_\epsilon(x) \geq 1\} + \lambda\epsilon^2 + \mathbb{1}\{n_\epsilon(x) = 0\}$.

(b) Argue that $\mathbb{E}_X \mathbb{1}\{n_\epsilon(x) = 0\} \leq C'/(nP_X(B(x,\epsilon)))$ for suitable C, C'.

(c) Using the fact that for a binomial random variable Z s.t. $\mathbb{E}Z \geq 1$, we have $\mathbb{E}\frac{\mathbb{1}\{Z \geq 1\}}{Z} \leq 3/\mathbb{E}Z$ (Lemma 4.1 of Györfi et al., 2006), bound $\mathbb{E}\,\mathcal{E}(\hat{\langle})$, and conclude that $\hat{h}$ achieves the same rates as derived for k-NN in Theorem 18.3.

CHAPTER NINETEEN

Efficient Tensor Decomposition

Aravindan Vijayaraghavan

Abstract: This chapter studies the problem of decomposing a tensor into a sum of constituent rank one tensors. While tensor decompositions are very useful in designing learning algorithms and data analysis, they are *NP*-hard in the worst case. We will see how to design efficient algorithms with provable guarantees under mild assumptions, and using beyond worst-case frameworks such as smoothed analysis.

19.1 Introduction to Tensors

Tensors are multidimensional arrays and constitute natural generalizations of matrices. Tensors are fundamental linear algebraic entities and widely used in physics, scientific computing, and signal processing to represent multidimensional data or capture multiwise correlations. The different dimensions of the array are called the *modes* and the *order* of a tensor is the number of dimensions or modes of the array, as shown in Figure 19.1. The order of a tensor also corresponds to the number of indices needed to specify an entry of a tensor. Hence every $(i_1, i_2, i_3) \in [n_1] \times [n_2] \times [n_3]$ specifies an entry of the tensor T that is denoted by $T(i_1, i_2, i_3)$ in Figure 19.1.

While we have a powerful toolkit of algorithms such as low-rank approximations and eigenvalue decompositions for matrices, our algorithmic understanding in the tensor world is limited. As we will see soon, many basic algorithmic problems such as low-rank decompositions are *NP*-hard in the worst case for tensors (of order 3 and above). But on the other hand, many higher order tensors satisfy powerful structural properties that are simply not satisfied by matrices. This makes them particularly useful for applications in machine learning and data analysis. In this chapter, we will see how we can indeed overcome this worst-case intractability under some natural nondegeneracy assumptions or using smoothed analysis, and also exploit these powerful properties for designing efficient learning algorithms.

19.1.1 Low-Rank Decompositions and Rank

We start with the definition of a rank one tensor. An order ℓ tensor $T \in \mathbb{R}^{n_1 \times \cdots \times n_\ell}$ is *rank one* if and only if it can be written as an outer product $v_1 \otimes v_2 \otimes \cdots \otimes v_\ell$ for some vectors $v_1 \in \mathbb{R}^{n_1}, \ldots, v_\ell \in \mathbb{R}^{n_\ell}$, i.e.,

$$T(i_1, i_2, \ldots, i_\ell) = v_1(i_1) v_2(i_2) \ldots v_\ell(i_\ell) \quad \forall (i_1, \ldots, i_\ell) \in [n_1] \times \cdots \times [n_\ell].$$

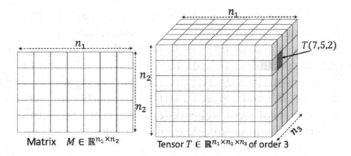

Figure 19.1 A matrix M that is a tensor of order 2 and a tensor T of order 3 with $n_1 = 7, n_2 = 6, n_3 = 5$. The position of the entry $T(7,4,2)$ is highlighted. An order 1 tensor corresponds to a vector, and an order 0 tensor is a scalar.

Note than when $\ell = 2$, this corresponds to being expressible as $v_1 v_2^T$.

Definition 19.1 (Rank-k decomposition) A tensor T is said to have a decomposition of *rank k* iff it is expressible as the sum of k rank one tensors, i.e.,

$$\exists \{u_i^{(j)} | i \in [k], j \in [\ell]\}, \text{ s.t. } T = \sum_{i=1}^{k} u_i^{(1)} \otimes u_i^{(2)} \otimes \cdots \otimes u_i^{(\ell)}.$$

Moreover, T has rank k if and only if k is the smallest natural number for which T has a rank k decompostion.

The vectors $\{u_i^{(j)} : i \in [k], j \in [\ell]\}$ are called the *factors* of the decomposition. To keep track of how the factors across different modes are grouped, we will use $U^{(j)} = (u_i^{(j)} : i \in [k])$ for $j \in [\ell]$ to represent the factors. These "factor matrices" all have k columns, one per term of the decomposition. Finally, we will also consider *symmetric tensors* – a tensor T of order ℓ is symmetric iff $T(i_1, i_2, \ldots, i_r) = T(i_{\sigma(1)}, i_{\sigma(2)}, \ldots, i_{\sigma(r)})$ for every permutation σ over $\{1, 2, \ldots, r\}$ (see Exercise 19.1 for an exercise about decompositions of symmetric tensors).

Differences from Matrix Algebra and Pitfalls. Observe that the definitions of rank and of a low-rank decompositions specialize to the standard notions for matrices ($\ell = 2$). However, it is dangerous to use the intuition we have developed from matrix algebra to reason about tensors because of several fundamental differences. First, an equivalent definition for rank of a matrix is the dimension of the row space, or column space. This is *not true* for tensors of order 3 and above. In fact, for a tensor of order ℓ in $\mathbb{R}^{n \times \ell}$, the rank as we defined it could be as large as $n^{\ell-1}$, while the dimension of the span of n dimensional vectors along any of the modes can be at most n. The definition that we study in Definition 19.1 (as opposed to other notions such as Tucker decompositions) is motivated by its applications to statistics and machine learning.

Second, much of the spectral theory for matrices involving eigenvectors and eigenvalues does not extend to tensors of higher order. For matrices, we know that the best rank-k approximation consists of the leading k terms of the singular value decomposition (SVD). However, this is not the case for tensor decompositions. The best rank-1 approximation may not be a factor in the best rank-2 approximation. Finally, and most importantly, the algorithmic problem of finding the best rank-k

approximation of a tensor is NP-hard in the worst case, particularly for large k;[1] for matrices, this is of course solved using the SVD. In fact, this worst-case NP-hardness for higher order tensors is true for most tensor problems including computing the rank, computing the spectral norm, etc. (Håstad, 1990; Hillar and Lim, 2013).

For all of these reasons, and more,[2] it is natural to ask, why bother with tensor decompositions at all? We will now see a striking property (uniqueness) satisfied by low-rank decompositions of most higher order tensors (but not satisfied by matrices), which also motivates many interesting uses of tensor decompositions.

Uniqueness of Low-Rank Decompositions. A remarkable property of higher order tensors is that (under certain conditions that hold typically) their minimum rank decompositions are unique up to trivial scaling and permutation. This is in sharp contrast to matrix decompositions. For any matrix M with a rank $k \geq 2$ decomposition $M = UV^T = \sum_{i=1}^{k} u_i v_i^T$, there exist several other rank k decompositions $M = U'(V')^T$, where $U' = UO$ and $V' = VO$ for any rotation matrix O, i.e., $OO^T = I_k$; in particular, the SVD is one of them. This *rotation problem* is a common issue when using matrix decompositions in factor analysis (since we can find the factors only up to a rotation).

The first uniqueness result for tensor decompositions was due to Harshman (1970)(who in turn credits it to Jennrich), assuming what is known as the "full rank condition." In particular, if $T \in \mathbb{R}^{n \times n \times n}$ has a decomposition

$$T = \sum_{i=1}^{k} u_i \otimes u_i \otimes u_i, \text{ s.t. } \{u_i : i \in [k]\} \subset \mathbb{R}^n \text{ are linearly independent,}$$

(or the factor matrix U is full rank), then this is the *unique decomposition* of rank k up to permuting the terms. (The statement is actually a little more general and also handles nonsymmetric tensors; see Theorem 19.4). Note that the full rank condition requires $k \leq n$ (moreover, it holds when the vectors are in general position in $n \geq k$ dimensions). What makes this above result even more surprising is that the proof is algorithmic! We will in fact see the algorithm and proof in Section 19.3.1. This will serve as the workhorse for most of the algorithmic results in this chapter. Kruskal (1977) gave a more general condition that guarantees uniqueness up to rank $3n/2 - 1$, using a beautiful nonalgorithmic proof. Uniqueness is also known to hold for *generic* tensors of rank $k = \Omega(n^2)$ (here "generic" means all except a measure zero set of rank k tensors). We will now see how this remarkable property of uniqueness will be very useful for applications such as learning latent variable models.

19.2 Applications to Learning Latent Variable Models

A common approach in unsupervised learning is to assume that the data (input) that are given to us are drawn from a probabilistic model with some latent variables and/or unknown parameters θ that is appropriate for the task at hand, i.e., the structure

---

[1] For small k, there are algorithms that find approximately optimal rank-k approximations in time exponential in k (see, e.g., Bhaskara et al., 2014b; Song et al., 2019).

[2] There are other definitional issues with the rank – there are tensors of a certain rank that can be arbitrarily well approximated by tensors of much smaller rank; i.e., the "limit rank" (or formally, the border rank) may not be equal to the rank of the tensor. See Exercise 19.2 for an example.

we want to find. This includes mixture models such as mixtures of Gaussians, topic models for document classification, etc. A central learning problem is the efficient estimation of such latent model parameters from observed data.

A necessary step toward efficient learning is to show that the parameters are indeed identifiable after observing polynomially many samples. The method of moments approach, pioneered by Pearson, infers model parameters from empirical moments such as means, or pairwise correlations and other higher order correlations. In general, very high order moments may be needed for this approach to succeed, and the unreliability of empirical estimates of these moments leads to large sample complexity (see, e.g., Moitra and Valiant, 2010; Belkin and Sinha, 2015). In fact, for latent variable models such as mixtures of k Gaussians, an exponential sample complexity of $\exp(\Omega(k))$ is necessary, if we make no additional assumptions.

On the computational side, maximum likelihood estimation, i.e., $\text{argmax}_\theta \Pr_\theta[data]$ is *NP*-hard for many latent variable models (see, e.g., Tosh and Dasgupta, 2018). Moreover, iterative heuristics like expectation maximization (EM) tend to get stuck in local optima. Efficient tensor decompositions, when possible, present an algorithmic framework that is both statistically and computationally efficient for recovering the parameters.

19.2.1 Method-of-Moments via Tensor Decompositions: A General Recipe

The method-of-moments is the general approach of inferring parameters of a distribution, by computing empirical moments of the distribution and solving for the unknown parameters. The moments of a distribution over $\mathbb{R}^n$ are naturally represented by tensors. The covariance or the second moment is an $n \times n$ matrix, the third moment is represented by a tensor of order 3 in $\mathbb{R}^{n \times n \times n}$ (the $(i_1, i_2, i_3)th$ entry is $\mathbb{E}[x_{i_2} x_{i_2} x_{i_3}]$), and in general the ℓth moment is a tensor of order ℓ. More crucially for many latent variable models $\mathcal{D}(\bar\theta)$ with parameters $\bar\theta$, the moment tensor, or a suitable modification of it, has a low-rank decomposition (perhaps up to some small error) in terms of the unknown parameters $\bar\theta$ of the model. Low-rank decompositions of the tensor can then be used to implement the general method-of-moments approach, with both statistical and computational implications. The uniqueness of the tensor decomposition then immediately implies *identifiability* of the model parameters (in particular, it implies a unique solution for the parameters)! Moreover, a computationally efficient algorithm for recovering the factors of the tensor gives an efficient algorithm for recovering the parameters $\bar\theta$.

General Recipe. Here is an algorithmic framework for parameter estimation. Consider a latent variable model with model parameters $\bar\theta = (\theta_1, \theta_2, \ldots, \theta_k)$. These could be one parameter each for the k possible values of the latent variable (for example, in a mixture of k Gaussians, the θ_i could represent the mean of the ith Gaussian component of unit variance).

1. Define an appropriate statistic $\mathcal{T}$ of the distribution (typically based on moments) such that the expected value of $\mathcal{T}$ has a low-rank decomposition

$$T = \mathbb{E}_{\mathcal{D}(\theta)}[\mathcal{T}] = \sum_{i=1}^{k} \lambda_i \theta_i^{\otimes \ell}, \text{ for some } \ell \in \mathbb{N}, \text{ and (known) scalars } \{\lambda_i : i \in [k]\}.$$

2. Obtain an estimate $\widetilde{T}$ of the tensor $T = \mathbb{E}[\mathcal{T}]$ from the data (e.g., from empirical moments) up to small error (denoted by the error tensor E).
3. Use tensor decompositions to solve for the parameters $\bar{\theta} = (\theta_1, \dots, \theta_k)$ in the system $\sum_{i=1}^{k} \lambda_i \theta_i^{\otimes \ell} \approx \widetilde{T}$, to obtain estimates $\widehat{\theta}_1, \dots, \widehat{\theta}_k$ of the parameters.

The last step involving tensor decompositions is the technical workhorse of this approach, both for showing identifiability and getting efficient algorithms. Many of the existing algorithmic guarantees for tensor decompositions (that hold under certain natural conditions about the decomposition, e.g., Theorems 19.4 and 19.8) provably *recover* the rank-k decomposition, thereby giving algorithmic proofs of uniqueness as well. However, the first step of designing the right statistic $\mathcal{T}$ with a low-rank decomposition requires a great deal of ingenuity and creativity. In Section 19.2.2 we will see two important latent variable models that will serve as our case studies. You will see another application in the next chapter on topic modeling.

Need for Robustness to Errors. So far, we have completely ignored sample complexity considerations by assuming access to the exact expectation $T = \mathbb{E}[\mathcal{T}]$, so the error $E = 0$ (this requires infinite samples). In polynomial time, the algorithm can access only a polynomial number of samples. Estimating a simple 1D statistic up to $\epsilon = 1/\text{poly}(n)$ accuracy typically requires $\Omega(1/\epsilon^2)$ samples; the ℓth moment of a distribution requires $n^{O(\ell)}$ samples to estimate up to inverse polynomial error (in Frobenius norm, say). Hence, to obtain polynomial-time guarantees for parameter estimation, it is vital for the tensor decomposition guarantees to be noise tolerant, i.e., *robust* up to inverse polynomial error (this is even assuming no model misspecification). Fortunately, such robust guarantees do exist – in Section 19.3.1, we will show a robust analogue of Harshman's uniqueness theorem and related algorithms (see also Bhaskara et al., 2014b, for a robust version of Kruskal's uniqueness theorem). Obtaining robust analogues of known uniqueness and algorithmic results is quite nontrivial and open in many cases (see Section 19.6).

19.2.2 Case Studies

Case Study 1: Mixtures of Spherical Gaussians. Our first case study is on mixtures of Gaussians. They are perhaps the most widely studied latent variable model in machine learning for clustering and modeling heterogeneous populations. We are given random samples, where each sample point $x \in \mathbb{R}^n$ is drawn independently from one of k Gaussian components according to mixing weights $w_1, w_2, \dots, w_k$, where each Gaussian component $j \in [k]$ has a mean $\mu_j \in \mathbb{R}^n$ and a covariance $\sigma_j^2 I \in \mathbb{R}^{n \times n}$. The goal is to estimate the parameters $\{(w_j, \mu_j, \sigma_j) : j \in [k]\}$ up to required accuracy $\epsilon > 0$ in time and number of samples that are polynomial in $k, n, 1/\epsilon$. Existing algorithms based on method of moments have sample complexity and running time that is exponential in k in general (Moitra and Valiant, 2010; Belkin and Sinha, 2015). However, we will see that as long as certain nondegeneracy conditions are satisfied, tensor decompositions can be used to get tractable algorithms that have only a polynomial dependence on k (in Theorem 19.6 and Corollary 19.16).

For the sake of exposition, we will restrict our attention to the uniform case when the mixing weights are all equal and variances $\sigma_i^2 = 1$, $\forall i \in [k]$. Most of these ideas also apply in the more general setting (see Hsu and Kakade, 2013). For the first step of the recipe, we will design a statistic that has a low-rank decomposition in terms of the means $\{\mu_i : i \in [k]\}$.

Proposition 19.2 *For any integer $\ell \geq 1$, one can compute efficiently a statistic T_ℓ from the first ℓ moments such that $\mathbb{E}[T] = T_\ell := \sum_{i=1}^{k} \mu_i^{\otimes \ell}$.*

Let $\eta \sim N(0, I)$ denote a Gaussian r.v. The expected value of the statistic $x^{\otimes \ell}$ is

$$\text{Mom}_\ell := \mathbb{E}[x^{\otimes \ell}] = \sum_i w_i \mathbb{E}_\eta[(\mu_i + \eta)^{\otimes \ell}] = \frac{1}{k} \sum_{i=1}^{k} \sum_{\substack{x_j \in \{\mu_i, \eta\} \\ \forall j \in [\ell]}} \mathbb{E}_\eta \left[\bigotimes_{j=1}^{\ell} x_j \right]. \quad (19.1)$$

Now the first term in the inner expansion (where every $x_j = \mu_i$) is the one we are interested in, so we will try to "subtract" out the other terms using the first $(\ell - 1)$ moments of the distribution. Let us consider the case when $\ell = 3$ to gain more intuition. As odd moments of η are zero, we have

$$\text{Mom}_3 := \mathbb{E}[x^{\otimes 3}]$$

$$= \frac{1}{k} \sum_{i=1}^{k} \left(\mu_i^{\otimes 3} + \mathbb{E}_\eta[\mu_i \otimes \eta \otimes \eta] + \mathbb{E}_\eta[\eta \otimes \eta \otimes \mu_i] + \mathbb{E}_\eta[\eta \otimes \mu_i \otimes \eta] \right)$$

$$= T_3 + \left(\text{Mom}_1 \otimes I + \text{ two other known terms} \right).$$

Hence, we can obtain the required tensor T_3 using a combination of Mom_3 and Mom_1; the corresponding statistic is $x^{\otimes 3} - (x \otimes I + \text{ two other known terms})$. We can use a similar inductive approach for obtaining T_ℓ (or use Iserlis identity that expresses higher moments of a Gaussian in terms of the mean and covariance).[3]

Case Study 2: Learning Hidden Markov Models (HMMs). Our next example is HMMs, which are extensively used for data with a sequential structure. In an HMM, there is a hidden state sequence $Z_1, Z_2, \ldots, Z_m$ taking values in $[k]$ that forms a stationary Markov chain $Z_1 \rightarrow Z_2 \rightarrow \cdots \rightarrow Z_m$ with transition matrix P and initial distribution $w = \{w_j\}_{j \in [k]}$ (assumed to be the stationary distribution). The observation X_t is represented by a vector in $x^{(t)} \in \mathbb{R}^n$. Given the state Z_t at time t, X_t is conditionally independent of all other observations and states. The observation matrix is denoted by $\mathcal{O} \in \mathbb{R}^{n \times k}$; the columns of $\mathcal{O}$ represent the means of the observation $X_t \in \mathbb{R}^n$ conditioned on the hidden state Z_t, i.e., $\mathbb{E}[X_t | Z_t = i] = \mathcal{O}_i$, where $\mathcal{O}_i$ represents the ith column of $\mathcal{O}$. We also assume that X_t satisfies strong enough concentration bounds to use empirical estimates. The parameters are $P, \mathcal{O}, w$.

We now define appropriate statistics following Allman et al. (2009). Let $m = 2\ell + 1$ for some ℓ to be chosen later. The statistic T is $X_{2\ell+1} \otimes X_{2\ell} \otimes \cdots \otimes X_1$. We can also view this $(2\ell + 1)$ moment tensor as a 3-tensor of shape $n^\ell \times n \times n^\ell$. The first mode corresponds to $X_\ell \otimes X_{\ell-1} \otimes \ldots \otimes X_1$, the second mode is $X_{\ell+1}$, and the third mode is $X_{\ell+2} \otimes X_{\ell+3} \otimes \ldots X_{2\ell+1}$. Why does it have a low-rank decomposition? We can think of the hidden state $Z_{\ell+1}$ as the latent variable that takes k possible values.

---

[3] An alternate trick to obtain a statistic T_ℓ that loses only constant factors in the dimension involves looking at an off-diagonal block of the tensor Mom_ℓ after partitioning the n coordinates into ℓ equal sized blocks.

Proposition 19.3 *The aforementioned statistic $\mathcal{T}$ has a low-rank decomposition* $\sum_{i=1}^{k} A_i \otimes B_i \otimes C_i$ *with factor matrices* $A \in \mathbb{R}^{n^{\ell} \times k}$, $B \in \mathbb{R}^{n \times k}$, *and* $C \in \mathbb{R}^{n^{\ell} \times k}$ *s.t.* $\forall i \in [k]$,

$$A_i = \mathbb{E}[\otimes_{j=\ell}^{1} X_j | Z_{\ell+1} = i], \quad B_i = \mathbb{E}[X_{\ell+1} | Z_{\ell+1} = i], \text{ and}$$

$$C_i = \mathbb{E}[\otimes_{j=\ell+2}^{2\ell+1} X_j | Z_{\ell+1} = i].$$

Moreover, O, P, and w can be recovered from A, B, C.

For $\ell = 1$, $C = OP, B = O, A = OP'$, where $P' = \text{diag}(w) P^T \text{diag}(w)^{-1}$ is the reverse transition matrix. Tensor decompositions will allow for efficient recovery of O, P, w in Theorem 19.7 and Section 19.4.4. We leave the proof of Proposition 19.3 as Exercise 19.4. See Allman et al. (2009) for more details.

19.3 Efficient Algorithms in the Full-Rank Setting

19.3.1 Simultaneous Diagonization (Jennrich's Algorithm)

We now study Jennrich's algorithm (first described in Harshman, 1970), that gives theoretical guarantees for finding decompositions of third-order tensors under a natural nondegeneracy condition called the full-rank setting. Moreover, this algorithm also has reasonable robustness properties and can be used as a building block to handle more general settings and for many machine learning applications. Consider a third-order tensor $T \in \mathbb{R}^{n \times m \times p}$ that has a decomposition of rank k:

$$T = \sum_{i=1}^{k} u_i \otimes v_i \otimes w_i.$$

Our algorithmic goal is to recover the unknown factors U, V, W. Of course, we hope to recover the factors only up to some trivial scaling of vectors (within a rank-one term) and permuting terms. Note that our algorithmic goal here is much stronger than usual. This is possible because of uniqueness of tensor decompositions – in fact, the proof of correctness of the algorithm will also give a uniqueness proof! The algorithm considers two matrices M_a, M_b that are formed by taking random linear combinations of the slices of the tensor as shown in Figure 19.2. We will

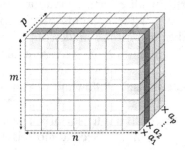

Figure 19.2 A tensor T, and a particular matrix slice highlighted (corresponding to $i_3 = 2$). The linear combination of the slices $T(\cdot, \cdot, a)$ takes a linear combination of these matrix slices weighted according to $a \in \mathbb{R}^p$. The algorithm considers two matrices $M_a = T(\cdot, \cdot, a), M_b = T(\cdot, \cdot, b)$ for two randomly chosen vectors $a, b \in \mathbb{R}^p$.

show later in (19.2) that M_a, M_b both have low-rank decompositions in terms of the unknown factors $\{u_i, v_i\}$. Hence, the algorithm reduces the problem of decomposing one third-order tensor into the problem of obtaining a "simultaneous" decomposition of the two matrices M_a, M_b (this is also called simultaneous diagonalization).

In Jennrich's Algorithm, $M^\dagger$ refers to the pseudoinverse or the Moore–Penrose inverse of M (if a rank-k matrix M has a singular value decomposition $M = U \Sigma V^T$, where Σ is a $k \times k$ diagonal matrix, then $M^\dagger = V \Sigma^{-1} U^T$).

Jennrich's Algorithm
Input: Tensor $T \in \mathbb{R}^{n \times m \times p}$.

1. Draw $a, b \sim N(0, \frac{1}{p})^p \in \mathbb{R}^p$ independently. Set $M_a = T(\cdot, \cdot, a), M_b = T(\cdot, \cdot, b)$.
2. Set $\{u_i : i \in [k]\}$ to be the eigenvectors corresponding to the k largest (in magnitude) eigenvalues of $M_a(M_b)^\dagger$. Similarly let $\{v_i : i \in [k]\}$ be the eigenvectors corresponding to the k largest (in magnitude) eigenvalues of $((M_b)^\dagger M_a)^T$.
3. Pair up u_i, v_i if their corresponding eigenvalues are reciprocals (approximately).
4. Solve the linear system $T = \sum_{i=1}^{k} u_i \otimes v_i \otimes w_i$ for the vectors w_i.
5. Return factor matrices $U \in \mathbb{R}^{n \times k}, V \in \mathbb{R}^{m \times k}, W \in \mathbb{R}^{p \times k}$.

In what follows, $\|T\|_F$ denotes the Frobenius norm of the tensor ($\|T\|_F^2$ is the sum of the squares of all the entries), and the condition number κ of matrix $U \in \mathbb{R}^{n \times k}$ is given by $\kappa(U) = \sigma_1(U)/\sigma_k(U)$, where $\sigma_1 \geq \sigma_2 \geq \cdots \geq \sigma_k \geq 0$ are the singular values. The guarantees (in terms of the error tolerance) will be inverse polynomial in the condition number κ, which is finite only if the matrix has rank k (full rank).

Theorem 19.4 *Suppose we are given tensor $\widetilde{T} = T + E \in \mathbb{R}^{m \times n \times p}$, where T has a decomposition $T = \sum_{i=1}^{k} u_i \otimes v_i \otimes w_i$ satisfying the following conditions:*

1. *Matrices $U = (u_i : i \in [k]), V = (v_i : i \in [k])$ have condition number at most κ,*
2. *For all $i \neq j$, $\|\frac{w_i}{\|w_i\|} - \frac{w_j}{\|w_j\|}\|_2 \geq \delta$.*
3. *Each entry of E is bounded by $\|T\|_F \cdot \epsilon / poly(\kappa, \max\{n, m, p\}, \frac{1}{\delta})$.*

Then Jennrich's Algorithm on input $\widetilde{T}$ runs in polynomial time and returns a decomposition $\{(\widetilde{u}_i, \widetilde{v}_i, \widetilde{w}_i) : i \in [k]\}$ s.t. there is a permutation $\pi : [k] \to [k]$ with

$$\forall i \in [k], \quad \|\widetilde{u}_i \otimes \widetilde{v}_i \otimes \widetilde{w}_i - u_{\pi(i)} \otimes v_{\pi(i)} \otimes w_{\pi(i)}\|_F \leq \epsilon \|T\|_F.$$

We start with a simple claim that leverages the randomness in the Gaussian linear combinations a, b (in fact, this is the only step of the argument that uses randomization). Let $D_a := \text{diag}(a^T w_1, a^T w_2, \dots, a^T w_k)$ and $D_b := \text{diag}(b^T w_1, b^T w_2, \dots, b^T w_k)$.

Lemma 19.5 *With high probability over the randomness in a, b, the diagonal entries of $D_a D_b^{-1}$ are separated from each other, and from 0, i.e.,*

$$\forall i \in [k] \quad \left| \frac{\langle w_i, a \rangle}{\langle w_i, b \rangle} \right| > \frac{1}{poly(p)}, \text{ and } \forall i \neq j \quad \left| \frac{\langle w_i, a \rangle}{\langle w_i, b \rangle} - \frac{\langle w_j, a \rangle}{\langle w_j, b \rangle} \right| > \frac{1}{poly(p)}.$$

The proof just uses simple anti-concentration of Gaussians and a union bound. We now proceed to the proof of Theorem 19.4.

Proof of Theorem 19.4 We first prove that when $E = 0$, the preceding algorithm recovers the decomposition exactly. The robust guarantees when $E \neq 0$ uses perturbation bounds for eigenvalues and eigenvectors.

No-noise Setting ($E = 0$). Recall that T has a rank k decomposition in terms of the factors U, V, W. Hence

$$M_a = \sum_{i=1}^{k} \langle a, w_i \rangle u_i v_i^T = U D_a V^T, \quad \text{and similarly } M_b = U D_b V^T. \qquad (19.2)$$

Moreover U, V are full rank by assumption, and diagonal matrices D_a, D_b have full column rank of k with high probability (Lemma 19.5). Hence

$$M_a (M_b)^{\dagger} = U D_a V^T (V^T)^{\dagger} D_b^{\dagger} U^{\dagger} = U D_a D_b^{\dagger} U^{\dagger}$$

$$\text{and } M_a^T (M_b^T)^{\dagger} = V D_a D_b^{\dagger} V^{\dagger}.$$

Moreover, from Lemma 19.5, the entries of $D_a D_b^{\dagger}$ are distinct and nonzero with high probability. Hence the column vectors of U are eigenvectors of $M_a (M_b)^{\dagger}$ with eigenvalues $(\langle w_i, a \rangle / \langle w_i, b \rangle : i \in [k])$. Similarly, the columns of V are eigenvectors of $(M_b^{\dagger} M_a)^T$ with eigenvalues $(\langle w_i, b \rangle / \langle w_i, a \rangle : i \in [k])$. Hence, the eigendecompositions of $M_a M_b^{\dagger}$ and $(M_b^{\dagger} M_a)^T$ are unique (up to scaling of the eigenvectors), with the corresponding eigenvalues being reciprocals of each other.

Finally, once we know $\{u_i, v_i : i \in [k]\}$ (up to scaling), step 4 of the algorithm solves a linear system in the unknowns $\{w_i : i \in [k]\}$. A simple claim shows that the corresponding co-efficient matrix given by $\{u_i v_i^T : i \in [k]\}$ has "full" rank, i.e., rank of k. Hence the linear system has a unique solution W and algorithm recovers the decomposition.

Robust Guarantees (E Is Nonzero). When $E \neq 0$, we will need to analyze how much the eigenvectors of $M_1 := M_a M_b^{\dagger}$ can change, under the (worst-case) perturbation E. The proof uses perturbation bounds for eigenvectors of matrices (which are much more brittle than eigenvalues) to carry out this analysis. We now give a high-level description of the approach, while pointing out a couple of subtle issues and difficulties. The primary issue comes from the fact that the matrix $M_1 = M_a M_b^{\dagger}$ is not a symmetric matrix (for which one can use the Davis–Kahan theorem for singular vectors). In our case, while we know that M_1 is diagonalizable, there is no such guarantee about $M_1' = M_a M_b^{\dagger} + E'$, where E' is the error matrix that arises at this step due to E. The key property that helps us here is Lemma 19.5, which ensures that all of the nonzero eigenvalues of M_1 are separated. In this case, we know the matrix M_1' is also diagonalizable using a standard strengthening of the Gershgorin disc theorem. One can then use the separation in the eigenvalues of M_1 to argue that the eigenvectors of M_1, M_1' are close, using ideas from the perturbation theory of invariant subspaces (see Chapter 5 of Stewart and Sun, 1990). See also Goyal et al. (2014) and Bhaskara et al. (2014a) for a self-contained proof of Theorem 19.4. □

19.3.2 Implications in Learning Applications

These efficient algorithms that (uniquely) recover the factors of a low-rank tensor decomposition give polynomial time guarantees for learning nondegenerate instances of several latent variable models using the general recipe given in Section 19.2.1. This approach has been used for several problems including, but not limited to, parameter estimation of hidden Markov models, phylogeny models, mixtures of Gaussians, independent component analysis, topic models, mixed community membership models, ranking models, crowdsourcing models, and even certain neural networks (see Anandkumar et al., 2014; Moitra, 2018 for excellent expositions on this topic).

For illustration, we give the implications for our two case studies. For Gaussian mixtures, the k means are assumed to be linear independent (hence $n \geq k$). We apply Theorem 19.4 to the $\ell = 3$ order tensor obtained from Proposition 19.2.

Theorem 19.6 (Hsu and Kakade, 2013) *Given samples from a mixture of k spherical Gaussians, there is an algorithm that learns the parameters up to ϵ error in $poly(n, 1/\epsilon, 1/\sigma_k(M))$ time (and samples), where M is the $n \times k$ matrix of means.*

For hidden Markov models, we assume that the columns of the observation matrix $\mathcal{O}$ and the transition matrix P are linear independent (hence $n \geq k$). We apply Theorem 19.4 to the $\ell = 3$ order tensor obtained from Proposition 19.3.

Theorem 19.7 (Mossel and Roch, 2006; Hsu et al., 2012) *Given samples with $m = 3$ consecutive observations (corresponding to any fixed window of length 3) from an HMM model as in Section 19.2.2, with $\sigma_k(\mathcal{O}) \geq 1/poly(n)$ and $\sigma_k(P) \geq 1/poly(n)$, we can recover $P, \mathcal{O}$ up to ϵ error in $poly(n, 1/\epsilon)$ time (and samples).*

19.4 Smoothed Analysis and the Overcomplete Setting

The tensor decomposition algorithm we have seen in the previous section requires that the factor matrices have full column rank. As we have seen in Section 19.3.2, this gives polynomial-time algorithms for learning a broad variety of latent variable models under the full-rank assumption. However, there are many applications in unsupervised learning in which it is crucial that the hidden representation has much higher dimension (or number of factors k) than the dimension of the feature space n. Obtaining polynomial-time guarantees for these problems using tensor decompositions requires polynomial-time algorithmic guarantees when the rank is much larger than the dimension (in the full-rank setting $k \leq n$, even when the k factors are random or in general position in $\mathbb{R}^n$). Can we hope to obtain provable guarantees when the rank $k \gg n$?

This challenging setting when the rank is larger than the dimension is often referred to as the *overcomplete setting*. The tensor decomposition problem in the overcomplete setting is *NP*-hard in general. However for tensors of higher order, we will see in the rest of this section how Jennrich's algorithm can be adapted to get polynomial-time guarantees even in very overcomplete settings for nondegenerate instances – this will be formalized using smoothed analysis.

19.4.1 Smoothed Analysis Model

The smoothed analysis model for tensor decompositions models the situation when the factors in the decomposition are not worst case.

- An adversary chooses a tensor $T = \sum_{i=1}^{k} u_i^{(1)} \otimes u_i^{(2)} \otimes \cdots \otimes u_i^{(\ell)}$.
- Each vector $u_i^{(j)}$ is randomly "ρ-perturbed" using an independent Gaussian $N(0, \rho^2/n)^n$ with mean 0 and variance ρ^2/n in each direction[4].
- Let $\widetilde{T} = \sum_{i=1}^{k} \tilde{u}_i^{(1)} \otimes \tilde{u}_i^{(2)} \otimes \cdots \otimes \tilde{u}_i^{(\ell)}$.
- The input instance is $\hat{T} = \widetilde{T} + E$, where E is some small potentially adversarial noise.

Our goal is to recover (approximately when $E \neq 0$) the ℓ sets of factors $U^{(1)}, \ldots, U^{(\ell)}$ (up to rescaling and relabeling), where $U^{(j)} = (\widetilde{u}_i^{(j)} : i \in [k])$. The parameter setting of interest is ρ being at least some inverse polynomial in n, and the maximum entry of E being smaller than some sufficiently small inverse polynomial $1/\text{poly}(n, 1/\rho)$. We will also assume that the Euclidean lengths of the factors $\{u_i^{(j)}\}$ are polynomially upper bounded. We remark that when $k \leq n$ (as in the full-rank setting), Theorem 19.4 already gives smoothed polynomial-time guarantees when $\varepsilon < \rho/\text{poly}(n)$, since the condition number $\kappa \leq \text{poly}(n)/\rho$ with high probability.

> **Remarks** There is an alternate smoothed analysis model in which the random perturbation is to each entry of the tensor itself, as opposed to randomly perturbing the factors of a decomposition. The two random perturbations are very different in flavor. When the whole tensor is randomly perturbed, we have n^ℓ "bits" of randomness, whereas when only the factors are perturbed we have ℓn "bits" of randomness. On the other hand, the model in which the whole tensor is randomly perturbed is unlikely to be easy from a computational standpoint, since this would likely imply randomized algorithms with good worst-case approximation guarantees.

Why do we study perturbations to the factors? In most applications each factor represents a parameter, e.g., a component mean in Gaussian mixture models. The intuition is that if these parameters of the model are not chosen in a worst-case configuration, we can potentially obtain vastly improved learning algorithms with such smoothed analysis guarantees.

---

[4] Many of the results in the section also hold for other forms of random perturbations, as long as the distribution satisfies a weak anti-concentration property, similar to the setting in Chapters 13–15; see Anari et al. (2018) for details.

The smoothed analysis model can also be seen as the quantitative analogue of "genericity" results that are inspired by results from algebraic geometry, particularly when we need robustness to noise. Results of this generic flavor give guarantees for all except a set of instances of zero measure. However, such results are far from being quantitative; as we will see later we typically need robustness to inverse polynomial error with high probability for polynomial-time guarantees.

19.4.2 Adapting Jennrich's Algorithm for Overcomplete Settings

We will give an algorithm in the smoothed analysis setting for overcomplete tensor decompositions with polynomial-time guarantees. In the following theorem, we consider the model in Section 19.4.1 where the low-rank tensor $\tilde{T} = \sum_{i=1}^{k} \tilde{u}_i^{(1)} \otimes \tilde{u}_i^{(2)} \otimes \cdots \otimes \tilde{u}_i^{(\ell)}$, and the factors $\{\tilde{u}_i^{(j)}\}$ are ρ-perturbations of the vectors $\{u_i^{(j)}\}$, which we will assume are bounded by some polynomial of n. The input tensor is $\tilde{T} + E$, where E represents the adversarial noise.

Theorem 19.8 *Let $k \leq n^{\lfloor \frac{\ell-1}{2} \rfloor}/2$ for some constant $\ell \in \mathbb{N}$, and $\varepsilon \in [0, 1)$. There is an algorithm that takes as input a tensor $\hat{T} = \tilde{T} + E$ as described in Section 19.4.1, with every entry of E being at most $\varepsilon/(n/\rho)^{O(\ell)}$ in magnitude, and runs in time $(n/\rho)^{O(\ell)}$ to recover all the rank one terms $\{\otimes_{i=1}^{\ell} \tilde{u}_i^{(j)} : i \in [k]\}$ up to an additive ε error measured in Frobenius norm, with probability at least $1 - \exp(-\Omega(n))$.*

To describe the main algorithmic idea, let us consider an order-5 tensor $T \in \mathbb{R}^{n \times n \times n \times n \times n}$. We can "flatten" T to get an order-3 tensor

$$T = \sum_{i=1}^{k} \underbrace{u_i^{(1)} \otimes u_i^{(2)}}_{\text{factor}} \otimes \underbrace{u_i^{(3)} \otimes u_i^{(4)}}_{\text{factor}} \otimes \underbrace{u_i^{(5)}}_{\text{factor}}.$$

This gives us an order-3 tensor T' of size $n^2 \times n^2 \times n$. The effect of the "flattening" operation on the factors can be described succinctly using the following operation.

Definition 19.9 (Khatri–Rao Product) The Khatri–Rao product of $A \in \mathbb{R}^{m \times k}$ and $B \in \mathbb{R}^{n \times k}$ is an $mn \times k$ matrix $U \odot V$ whose ith column is $u_i \otimes v_i$.

Our new order-3 tensor T' also has a rank k decomposition with factor matrices $U' = U^{(1)} \odot U^{(2)}, V' = U^{(3)} \odot U^{(4)}$ and $W' = U^{(5)}$ respectively. Note that the columns of U' and V' are in n^2 dimensions (in general they will be $n^{\lfloor (\ell-1)/2 \rfloor}$ dimensional). We could now hope that the assumptions on the condition number U', V' in Theorem 19.4 are satisfied for $k = \omega(n)$. This is not true in the worst case (see Exercise 19.3 for the counterexample). However, we will prove this is true w.h.p. in the smoothed analysis model!

As the factors in $U^{(1)}, \ldots, U^{(\ell)}$ are all polynomially upper bounded, the maximum singular value is also at most a polynomial in n. The following proposition shows high-confidence lower bounds on the minimum singular value after taking the Khatri–Rao product of a subset of the factor matrices; this of course implies that the condition number has a polynomial upper bound with high probability.

Proposition 19.10 *Let $\delta \in (0, 1)$ be constants such that $k \le (1 - \delta)n^\ell$. Given any $U^{(1)}, U^{(2)}, \ldots, U^{(\ell)} \in \mathbb{R}^{n \times k}$, then for their random ρ-perturbations, we have*

$$\mathbb{P}\left[\sigma_k(\tilde{U}^{(1)} \odot \tilde{U}^{(2)} \odot \cdots \odot \tilde{U}^{(\ell)}) < \frac{c_1(\ell)\rho^\ell}{n^\ell} \right] \le k \exp\left(- c_2(\ell)\delta n \right),$$

where $c_1(\ell), c_2(\ell)$ are constants that depend only on ℓ.

The proposition implies that the conditions of Theorem 19.4 hold for the flattened order-3 tensor T'; in particular, the condition number of the factor matrices is now polynomially upper bounded with high probability. Hence running Jennrich's algorithm to the order-3 tensor T' recovers the rank-one factors w.h.p. as required in Theorem 19.8. The rest of the section outlines the proof of Proposition 19.10.

Failure Probability. We remark on a technical requirement about the failure probability (that is satisfied by Proposition 19.10) for smoothed analysis guarantees. We need our bounds on the condition number or $\sigma_{\min}$ to hold with a sufficiently small failure probability, say $n^{-\omega(1)}$, or even exponentially small (over the randomness in the perturbations). This is important because in smoothed analysis applications, the failure probability essentially describes the fraction of points around any given point that are *bad* for the algorithm. In many of these applications, the time/sample complexity has an inverse polynomial dependence on the minimum singular value. For example, if we have a guarantee that $\sigma_{\min} \ge \gamma$ with probability at least $1 - \gamma^{1/2}$, we have that the probability of the running time exceeding T (upon perturbation) is at most $1/\sqrt{T}$. Such a guarantee does not suffice to show that the expected running time is polynomial (also called polynomial smoothed complexity).

Note that our matrix $\tilde{U}^{(1)} \odot \tilde{U}^{(2)} \odot \cdots \odot \tilde{U}^{(\ell)}$ is a random matrix in which the entries are highly dependent; e.g., there are only $kn\ell$ independent variables but kn^ℓ matrix entries. This presents very different challenges compared to well-studied settings in random matrix theory, where every entry is independent.

While the least singular value can be hard to handle directly, it is closely related to the *leave-one-out distance*, which is often much easier to deal with.

Definition 19.11 Given a matrix $M \in \mathbb{R}^{n \times k}$ with columns $M_1, \ldots, M_k$, the leave-one-out distance of M is

$$\ell(M) = \min_{i \in [k]} \| \Pi^\perp_{-i} M_i \|_2, \text{ where } \Pi^\perp_{-i} \text{ is the projection orthogonal to } \mathrm{span}(\{M_j : j \ne i\}).$$

The leave-one-out distance is closely related to the least singular value, up to a factor polynomial in the number of columns of M, by the following simple lemma.

Lemma 19.12 *For any matrix $M \in \mathbb{R}^{n \times k}$, we have*

$$\frac{\ell(M)}{\sqrt{k}} \le \sigma_{min}(M) \le \ell(M). \tag{19.3}$$

The following (more general) core lemma that lower bounds the projection onto *any* given subspace of a randomly perturbed rank-one tensor implies Proposition 19.10.

Lemma 19.13 *Let $\ell \in \mathbb{N}$ and $\delta \in (0, \frac{1}{\ell})$ be constants, and let $W \subseteq \mathbb{R}^{n \times \ell}$ be an arbitrary subspace of dimension at least δn^ℓ. Given any $x_1, \ldots, x_\ell \in \mathbb{R}^n$, then their random ρ-perturbations $\tilde{x}_1, \ldots, \tilde{x}_\ell$ satisfy*

$$\Pr\left[\|\Pi_W(\tilde{x}_1 \otimes \tilde{x}_2 \otimes \cdots \otimes \tilde{x}_\ell)\|_2 < \frac{c_1(\ell)\rho^\ell}{n^\ell}\right] \leq \exp\left(-c_2(\ell)\delta n\right),$$

where $c_1(\ell), c_2(\ell)$ are constants that depend only on ℓ.

The polynomial of n in the exponent of the failure probability is tight; however, it is unclear what the right polynomial dependence of n in the least singular value bound, and the right dependence on ℓ should be. Lemma 19.13 can be used to lower bound the least singular value of the matrix $\tilde{U}^{(1)} \odot \cdots \odot \tilde{U}^{(\ell)}$ in Proposition 19.10 as follows: We can lower bound the leave-one-out distance of Lemma 19.12 by applying Lemma 19.13 for each column $i \in [k]$, with W being the subspace given by $\Pi_{-i}^\perp$ and $x_1, \ldots, x_\ell$ being $u_i^{(1)}, \ldots, u_i^{(\ell)}$; a union bound over the k columns gives Proposition 19.10. The first version of this lemma was proven in Bhaskara et al. (2014a) with worse polynomial dependencies both in lower bound on the condition number and in the exponent of the failure probability. The improved statement presented here and proof sketched in Section 19.4.3 are based on Anari et al. (2018).

Relation to Anti-concentration of Polynomials. We now briefly describe a connection to anti-concentration bounds for low-degree polynomials and describe a proof strategy that yields a weaker version of Lemma 19.13. Anti-concentration inequalities (e.g., the Carbery–Wright inequality) for a degree-ℓ polynomial $g : \mathbb{R}^n \to \mathbb{R}$ with $\|g\|_2 \geq \eta$, and $x \sim N(0, 1)^n$ are of the form

$$\Pr_{x \sim N(0,1)^n}\left[|g(x) - t| < \varepsilon\eta\right] \leq O(\ell) \cdot \varepsilon^{1/\ell}. \tag{19.4}$$

This can be used to derive a weaker version of Lemma 19.13 with an inverse polynomial failure probability, by considering a polynomial whose coefficients "lie" in the subspace W. As we discussed in the previous section, this failure probability does not suffice for expected polynomial running time (or polynomial smoothed complexity). On the other hand, Lemma 19.13 manages to get an inverse polynomial lower bound with exponentially small failure probability, by considering $n^{\Omega(1)}$ different polynomials. In fact one can flip this around and use Lemma 19.13 to show a vector-valued variant of the Carbery–Wright anti-concentration bounds, where if we have $m \geq \delta n^\ell$ "sufficiently different" polynomials $g_1, g_2, \ldots, g_m : \mathbb{R}^n \to \mathbb{R}$ each of degree ℓ, then we can get $\epsilon^{c(\ell)\delta n}$ for some constant $c(\ell) > 0$ for the bound in (19.4). The advantage is that while we lose in the "small ball" probability with the degree ℓ, we gain an δn factor in the exponent on account of having a vector valued function with m coordinates. See (Bhaskara et al., 2019) for a statement and proof.

19.4.3 Proof Sketch of Lemma 19.13

The proof of Lemma 19.13 is a careful inductive proof. We will sketch the proof for $\ell \leq 2$ to give a flavor of the arguments involved. See Anari et al. (2018) for the complete proof. For convenience, let $\tilde{x} := \tilde{x}^{(1)}$ and $\tilde{y} := \tilde{x}^{(2)}$. The high-level outline is now the following. We will show that there exist $n \times n$ matrices $M_1, M_2, \ldots, M_r \in W$ of bounded length measured in Frobenius norm (for general ℓ these would be order ℓ tensors of length at most $n^{\ell/2}$) that additionally satisfy certain "orthogonality" properties (r will be $\Omega_\ell(\delta n^\ell)$). We will use the orthogonality properties to extract enough "independence" across $\langle M_i, (\tilde{x} \otimes \tilde{y}) \rangle$ for $i \in [r]$ using the randomness in the perturbations; this will allow us to conclude that at least one of these r inner products is at least $\rho/\sqrt{n}$ in magnitude with probability $\geq 1 - \exp(-\Omega(\delta n))$.

What orthogonality property do we want?

Case $\ell = 1$. Let us start with $\ell = 1$. In this case we have a subspace $W \subset \mathbb{R}^n$ of dimension at least δn. Here we could just choose the r vectors $v_1, \ldots, v_r \in \mathbb{R}^n$ to be an orthonormal basis for W, to conclude the lemma, since $\langle v_i, g \rangle$ are independent. However, let's consider a slightly different construction where $v_1, \ldots v_r$ are not orthonormal, which will allow us to generalize to higher $\ell > 1$.

> **Claim 19.14** (for $\ell = 1$) *There exists a set of $v_1, \ldots, v_r \in W$, and a set of distinct indices $i_1, i_2, \ldots, i_r \in [n]$, for $r = \dim(W)$ such that for all $j \in \{1, 2, \ldots, r\}$:*
>
> *(a) $\|v_j\|_\infty \leq 1$,   (b) $|v_j(i_j)| = 1$,   (c) $v_j(i_{j'}) = 0$ for all $j' < j$.*

Hence, each of the vectors v_j has a nonnegligible component orthogonal to the span of $v_{j+1}, \ldots, v_r$. This will give us sufficient independence across the random variables $\langle v_1, \tilde{x} \rangle, \ldots, \langle v_r, \tilde{x} \rangle$. Consider the r inner products in reverse order, i.e., $\langle v_r, \tilde{x} \rangle, \langle v_{r-1}, \tilde{x} \rangle, \ldots, \langle v_1, \tilde{x} \rangle$. Let $\tilde{x} = x + z$, where $z \sim N(0, \rho^2/n)^n$. First $\langle v_r, \tilde{x} \rangle = \langle v_r, x \rangle + \langle v_r, z \rangle$, where $\langle v_r, z \rangle$ is an independent Gaussian $N(0, \rho^2/n)$ due to the rotational invariance of Gaussians. Hence for some absolute constant $c > 0$, from simple Gaussian anti-concentration $|\langle v_r, x \rangle| < c\rho/\sqrt{n}$ with probability $1/2$. Now, let us analyze the event $\langle v_j, x \rangle$ is small, after conditioning on the values of $\langle v_{j+1}, \tilde{x} \rangle, \ldots, \langle v_r, \tilde{x} \rangle$. By construction, $|v_j(i_j)| = 1$, whereas $v_{j+1}(i_j) = \cdots = v_r(i_j) = 0$. Hence

$$\Pr\left[|\langle v_j, \tilde{x} \rangle| < \frac{c\rho}{\sqrt{n}} \,\middle|\, \langle v_{j+1}, \tilde{x} \rangle, \ldots, \langle v_r, \tilde{x} \rangle \right] \leq \sup_{t \in \mathbb{R}} \Pr\left[|z(i_j) - t| < \frac{c\rho}{\sqrt{n}} \right] \leq \frac{1}{2}.$$

$$\text{Hence } \Pr\left[\forall j \in [r], \; |\langle v_j, \tilde{x} \rangle| < \frac{c\rho}{\sqrt{n}} \right] \leq \exp(-r), \text{ as required.}$$

Proof of Claim 19.14 We will construct the vectors iteratively. For the first vector, pick any vector v_1 in W and rescale it so that $\|v_1\|_\infty = 1$; let $i_1 \in [n]$ be an index where $|v_1(i_1)| = 1$. For the second vector, consider the restricted subspace $\{x \in W : x(i_1) = 0\}$. This has dimension $\dim(W) - 1$; so we can again pick an arbitrary vector in it and rescale it to get the necessary v_2. We can repeat this until we get $r = \dim(W)$ vectors (when the restricted subspace becomes empty). $\qquad\square$

Proof Sketch for $\ell = 2$. We can use a similar argument to come up with an analogous set of matrices $M_1, \ldots, M_r$ inductively. It will be convenient to identify each of these matrices M_j with an (row,column) index pair $I_j = (i_j, i'_j) \in [n] \times [n]$. We will also have a total order among all of the index pairs as follows. We first have a ordering among all the valid row indices $R = \{i_j : j \in [r]\}$ (say $i_1 \prec i_2 \prec \cdots \prec i_r$). Moreover, among all index pairs R_{i^*} in the same row i^* (i.e., $R_{i^*} := \{I_j = (i^*, i'_j)\}$), we have a total ordering (note that it could be the case that $(2,4) \prec (2,7)$ and $(3,7) \prec (3,4)$, since the orderings for $i^* = 2$ and $i^* = 3$ could be different).

Claim 19.15 (for $\ell = 2$) *Given any subspace $W \subset \mathbb{R}^{n \times n}$ of dimension $\dim(W) \geq \delta n^2$, there exists r many (row,column) index pairs $I_1 \prec I_2 \prec \cdots \prec I_r$ as outlined earlier, and a set of associated matrices $M_1, M_2 \ldots, M_r$ such that for all $j \in \{1, 2, \ldots, r\}$: (a) $\|M_j\|_{\infty} \leq 1$, (b) $|M_j(I_j)| = 1$, (c) $M_j(I_{j'}) = 0$ for all $j' < j$ and $M_j(i_1, i_2) = 0$ for any $i_1 \prec i_j$ and for all $i_2 \in [n]$ where $I_j = (i_j, i'_j)$.*

Further there are at least $|R| = \Omega(\delta n)$ valid row indices, and each of these indices has $\Omega(\delta n)$ index pairs associated with it.

The approach to proving the above claim is broadly similar to that of Claim 19.14. The proof repeatedly treats the vectors in W as vectors in $\mathbb{R}^{n^2}$ and applies Claim 19.14 to extract a valid row with $\Omega(\delta n)$ valid column indices, and iterates. We leave the formal proof as Exercise 19.5.

Once we have Claim 19.15, the argument for Lemma 19.13 is as follows. First, $\|M_j\|_2 \leq n$ since $\|M_j\|_{\infty} \leq 1$. Hence, we just need to show that there exists $j \in [r]$ s.t. $|\langle M_j, \tilde{x} \otimes \tilde{y}\rangle| \geq c\rho/n$ in magnitude with probability $\geq 1 - \exp(-\Omega(\delta n))$. Consider the vectors $\{M_1 \tilde{y}, M_2 \tilde{y}, \ldots, M_r \tilde{y}\} \subset \mathbb{R}^n$ obtained by applying just $\tilde{y}$. For each valid row $i^* \in R$, consider only the corresponding vectors with row index i^* from $\{M_j \tilde{y} : j \in [r]\}$ and set v_{i^*} to be the vector with the largest magnitude entry in coordinate i^*. By our argument for $\ell = 1$ we can see that with probability at least $1 - \exp(-\Omega(\delta n))$, $|v_{i^*}(i^*)| > \tau := c\rho/\sqrt{n}$, for some constant $c > 0$. Now by scaling these vectors $\{v_i : i \in [R]\}$ by at most $1/\tau$ each, we see that they satisfy Claim 19.14. Hence, using the argument for $\ell = 1$ again, we get Lemma 19.13. Extending this argument to higher $\ell > 2$ is technical, and we skip the details.

19.4.4 Implications for Applications

The smoothed polynomial-time guarantees for overcomplete tensor decompositions in turn imply polynomial-time smoothed analysis guarantees for several learning problems. In the smoothed analysis model for these parameter estimation problems, the unknown parameters θ of the model are randomly perturbed to give $\tilde{\theta}$, and samples are drawn from the model with parameters $\tilde{\theta}$.

However, as we alluded to earlier, the corresponding tensor decomposition problems that arise, e.g., from Propositions 19.2 and 19.3, do not always fit squarely in the smoothed analysis model in Section 19.4.1. For example, the random perturbations to the factors $\{u_i^{(j)} : i \in [k], j \in [\ell]\}$ may not all be independent. In learning mixtures of spherical Gaussians, the factors of the decomposition are $\tilde{\mu}_i^{\otimes \ell}$ for some appropriate $\ell > 1$, where $\tilde{\mu}_i$ is the mean of the ith component. In learning hidden Markov models (HMMs), each factor is a sum of appropriate monomials of the form $\tilde{a}_{i_1} \otimes \tilde{a}_{i_2} \otimes \cdots \otimes \tilde{a}_{i_\ell}$, where $i_1 i_2 \cdots i_\ell$ correspond to *length-ℓ paths* in a graph.

Fortunately the bounds in Proposition 19.10 can be used to derive similar high-confidence lower bounds on the least singular value for random matrices that arise from such applications using *decoupling* inequalities. For example, one can prove such bounds (as in Proposition 19.10) for the $k \times n^\ell$, matrix where the ith column is $\tilde{\mu}_i^{\otimes \ell}$ (as required for mixtures of spherical Gaussians). Such bounds also hold for other broad classes of random matrices that are useful for other applications like HMMs (see Bhaskara et al., 2019, for details).

In the smoothed analysis model for mixtures of spherical Gaussians, the means $\{\mu_i : i \in [k]\}$ are randomly perturbed. The following corollary gives polynomial-time smoothed analysis guarantees for estimating the means of a mixture of k spherical Gaussians. See Anderson et al. (2014) and Bhaskara et al. (2014a) for details.

Corollary 19.16 (Mixture of k Spherical Gaussians in $n \geq k^\epsilon$ Dimensions) *For any $\epsilon > 0, \eta > 0$, there is an algorithm that in the smoothed analysis setting learns the means of a mixture of k spherical Gaussians in $n \geq k^\epsilon$ dimensions up to accuracy $\eta > 0$ with running time and sample complexity $poly(n, 1/\eta, 1/\rho)^{O(1/\epsilon)}$ and succeeds with probability at least $1 - \exp(-\Omega(n))$.*

In the smoothed analysis setting for HMMs, the model is generated using a randomly perturbed observation matrix $\tilde{\mathcal{O}}$, obtained by adding independent Gaussian random vectors drawn from $N(0, \rho^2/n)^n$ to each column of $\mathcal{O}$. These techniques also give similar smoothed analysis guarantees for learning HMMs in the overcomplete setting when $n \geq k^\epsilon$ dimensions (using $O(1/\epsilon)$ consecutive observations), and under sufficient sparsity of the transition matrix. See Bhaskara et al. (2019) for details. Smoothed analysis results have also been obtained for other problems such as overcomplete independent component analysis (Goyal et al., 2014), learning mixtures of general Gaussians (Ge et al., 2015), other algorithms for higher-order tensor decompositions (Ma et al., 2016; Bhaskara et al., 2019), and recovering assemblies of neurons (Anari et al., 2018).

19.5 Other Algorithms for Tensor Decompositions

The algorithm we have seen (based on simultaneous diagonalization) has provable guarantees in the quite general smoothed analysis setting. However, there are other considerations such as running time and noise tolerance, for which the algorithm is suboptimal – for example, iterative heuristics such as alternating least-squares or alternating minimization are more popular in practice because of faster running times (Kolda and Bader, 2009). There are several other algorithmic approaches for tensor decompositions that work under different conditions on the input. The natural considerations are the generality of the assumptions and the running time of the algorithm. The other important consideration is the robustness of the algorithm to noise or errors. I will briefly describe a selection of these algorithms and comment along these axes. As we will discuss in the next section, the different algorithms are incomparable because of different strengths and weaknesses along these three axes.

Tensor Power Method. The tensor power method gives an alternate algorithm for symmetric tensors in the full-rank setting that is inspired by the matrix power method. The algorithm is designed for symmetric tensors $T \in \mathbb{R}^{n \times n \times n}$ with an *orthogonal decomposition* of rank $k \leq n$ of the form $\sum_{i=1}^{k} \lambda_i v_i^{\otimes 3}$, where the vectors $v_1, \ldots, v_k$ are orthonormal. Note that not all matrices need to have such an orthogonal decomposition. However, in many learning applications (where we have access to the second moment matrix), one can use a trick called *whitening* to reduce to the orthogonal decomposition case by a simple basis transformation.

The main component of the tensor power method is an iterative algorithm to find one term in the decomposition that repeats the following power iteration update (after initializing randomly) until convergence $z \leftarrow \frac{T(\cdot, z, z)}{\|T(\cdot, z, z)\|_2}$. Here the vector $T(\cdot, z, z) = u$, where $u(i) = \sum_{i_2, i_3} T(i, i_2, i_3) z_{i_2} z_{i_3}$. The algorithm then removes this component and recurses on the remaining tensor. This method is also known to be robust to inverse polynomial noise, and is known to converge quickly after the whitening. See Anandkumar et al. (2014) for such guarantees.

FOOBI Algorithm and Variants. In a series of works, Cardoso and others (see e.g., Cardoso, 1991; De Lathauwer et al., 2007) devised an algorithm, popularly called the *fourth-order blind only identification (FOOBI) algorithm* for symmetric decompositions of overcomplete tensors of order 4 and above. At a technical level, the FOOBI algorithm finds rank-one tensors in a linear subspace, by designing a "rank-1 detecting gadget." Recently, the FOOBI algorithm and generalizations have been shown to be robust to inverse polynomial error in the smoothed analysis setting for order-2ℓ tensors up to rank $k \leq n^\ell$ (see Ma et al., 2016; Bhaskara et al., 2019).

Alternating Minimization and Iterative Algorithms. Recently, Anandkumar et al. (2017) analyzed popular iterative heuristics such as alternating minimization for overcomplete tensors of order 3 and gave some sufficient conditions for both local convergence and global convergence. Finally, a closely related nonconvex problem is that of computing the "spectral norm," i.e., maximizing $\langle T, x^{\otimes \ell} \rangle$ subject to $\|x\|_2 = 1$; under certain conditions one can show that the global maximizers are exactly the underlying factors. The optimization landscape of this problem for tensors has also been studied recently (see Ge and Ma, 2017). But these results all mainly apply to the case when the factors of the decomposition are randomly chosen, which is much less general than the smoothed analysis setting.

Sum-of-Squares Algorithms. The sum-of-squares (SoS) hierarchy or the Lasserre hierarchy is a powerful family of algorithms based on semidefinite programming. Algorithms based on SoS typically consider a related polynomial optimization problem with polynomial inequalities. A key step in these arguments is to give a low-degree SoS proof of uniqueness; this is then "algorithmicized" using the SoS hierarchy. SoS-based algorithms are known to give guarantees that can go to overcomplete settings even for order-3 tensors (when the factors are random), and are known to have higher noise tolerance. In particular, they can handle order-3 symmetric tensors of rank $k = \tilde{O}(n^{1.5})$, when the factors are drawn randomly from the unit sphere (see Ma et al., 2016). The SoS hierarchy also gives robust variants of the FOOBI algorithm, and get quasi-polynomial time guarantees under other incomparable conditions (Ma et al., 2016). SoS based algorithms are too slow in practice because of large polynomial running times. Some recent works explore an interesting middle ground; they design spectral algorithms that are inspired by these SoS hierarchies, but have faster running times (see, e.g., Hopkins et al., 2016).

19.6 Discussion and Open Questions

The different algorithms for tensor decompositions are incomparable because of different strengths and weaknesses. A major advantage of SoS-based algorithms is their significantly better noise tolerance; in some settings it can go up to constant error measured in spectral norm (of an appropriate matrix flattening), while other algorithms can get inverse polynomial error tolerance at best. This is important particularly in learning applications, since there are significant modeling errors in practice. However, many of these results mainly work in restrictive settings where the factors are random (or incoherent). On the other hand, the algorithms based on simultaneous decompositions and variants of the FOOBI algorithm work in the significantly more general smoothed analysis setting, but their error tolerance is much poorer. Finally, iterative heuristics such as alternating minimization are the most popular in practice because of their significantly faster running times; however, known theoretical guarantees are significantly worse than the other methods.

Another direction where there is a large gap in our understanding is about conditions and limits for efficient recovery. This is particularly interesting under conditions that guarantee that the low-rank decomposition is (robustly) unique, as they imply learning guarantees. We list a few open questions in this space.

For the special case of 3-tensors in $\mathbb{R}^{n \times n \times n}$, recall that Jennrich's algorithm needs the factors to be linearly independent, hence $k \leq n$. On the other hand, Kruskal's uniqueness theorem (and its robust analogue) guarantees uniqueness even up to rank $3n/2 - 1$. Kruskal (1977) in fact gave a more general sufficient condition for uniqueness in terms of what is known as the *Kruskal rank* of a set of vectors. But there is no known algorithmic proof!

Open Problem   *Is there a (robust) algorithm for decomposing a 3-tensor T under the conditions of Kruskal's uniqueness theorem?*

We also do not know if there is any smoothed polynomial time algorithm that works for rank $(1 + \epsilon)n$ for any constant $\epsilon > 0$. Moreover, we know powerful statements using ideas from algebraic geometry that *generic* tensors of order 3 have unique decompositions up to rank $n^2/3$ (Chiantini and Ottaviani, 2012). However, these statements are not robust to even inverse polynomial error. Is there a robust analogue of this statement in a smoothed analysis setting? These questions are also interesting for order ℓ tensors. Most known algorithmic results for tensor decompositions also end up recovering the decomposition (thereby proving uniqueness). However, even for order-3 tensors with random factors, there is a large gap between conditions that guarantee uniqueness vs conditions that ensure tractability.

Open Problem   *Is there a (robust) algorithm for decomposing a 3-tensor T with random factors for rank $k = \omega(n^{3/2})$?*

Acknowledgments

I thank Aditya Bhaskara, Rong Ge, Tim Roughgarden, and Paul Valiant for their comments on an initial draft of the chapter.

References

Allman, Elizabeth S, Matias, Catherine, and Rhodes, John A. 2009. Identifiability of parameters in latent structure models with many observed variables. *The Annals of Statistics*, **37**, 3099–3132.

Anandkumar, Animashree, Ge, Rong, Hsu, Daniel, Kakade, Sham M., and Telgarsky, Matus. 2014. Tensor decompositions for learning latent variable models. *Journal of Machine Learning Research*, **15**(1), 2773–2832.

Anandkumar, Animashree, Ge, Rong, and Janzamin, Majid. 2017. Analyzing tensor power method dynamics in overcomplete regime. *Journal of Machine Learning Research*, **18**, 1–40.

Anari, Nima, Daskalakis, Constantinos, Maass, Wolfgang, Papadimitriou, Christos, Saberi, Amin, and Vempala, Santosh. 2018. Smoothed analysis of discrete tensor decomposition and assemblies of neurons. In *37th Conference on Neural Information Processing Systems (NeurIPS)*, pp. 10880–10890.

Anderson, Joseph, Belkin, Mikhail, Goyal, Navin, Rademacher, Luis, and Voss, James R. 2014. The more, the merrier: The blessing of dimensionality for learning large Gaussian mixtures. *Journal of Machine Learning Research: Workshop and Conference Proceedings*, vol. 35, pp. 1–30.

Belkin, Mikhail, and Sinha, Kaushik. 2015. Polynomial learning of distribution families. *SIAM Journal on Computing*, 44(4), 889–911.

Bhaskara, Aditya, Charikar, Moses, Moitra, Ankur, and Vijayaraghavan, Aravindan. 2014a. Smoothed analysis of tensor decompositions. In *Symposium on the Theory of Computing (STOC)*, pp. 594–603.

Bhaskara, Aditya, Charikar, Moses, and Vijayaraghavan, Aravindan. 2014b. Uniqueness of tensor decompositions with applications to polynomial identifiability. In *Proceedings of 27th Conference on Learning Theory* (Proceedings of Machine Learning Research 35, 742–748).

Bhaskara, Aditya, Chen, Aidao, Perreault, Aidan, and Vijayaraghavan, Aravindan. 2019. Smoothed analysis in unsupervised learning via decoupling. In *Foundations of Computer Science (FOCS)*, pp. 582–610.

Cardoso, J. 1991. Super-symmetric decomposition of the fourth-order cumulant tensor. Blind identification of more sources than sensors. In *Proceedings of International Conference on Acoustics, Speech, and Signal Processing (ICASSP'91)*vol. 5, 3109–3112.

Chiantini, L., and Ottaviani, G. 2012. On generic identifiability of 3-tensors of small rank. *SIAM Journal on Matrix Analysis and Applications*, **33** (3), 1018–1037.

De Lathauwer, L., Castaing, J., and Cardoso, J. 2007. Fourth-order cumulant-based blind identification of underdetermined mixtures. *IEEE Transactions on Signal Processing*, **55**(6), 2965–2973.

Ge, Rong, and Ma, Tengyu. 2017. On the optimization landscape of tensor decompositions. In *Annual Conference on Neural Information Processing Systems*, pp. 3653–3663.

Ge, Rong, Huang, Qingqing, and Kakade, Sham M. 2015. Learning mixtures of Gaussians in high dimensions. In: *Proceedings of the 47th Annual ACM Symposium on Theory of Computing*, pp. 761–770.

Goyal, Navin, Vempala, Santosh, and Xiao, Ying. 2014. Fourier PCA and robust tensor decomposition. In *Proceedings of the 47th Annual ACM Symposium on Theory of Computing*, pp. 584–593.

Harshman, Richard A. 1970. Foundations of the PARAFAC procedure: Models and conditions for an explanatory multimodal factor analysis. CLA Working Papers in Phonetics, 16, 1–84.

Håstad, Johan. 1990. Tensor rank is NP-complete. *Journal of Algorithms*, **11**(4), 644–654.

Hillar, Christopher J., and Lim, Lek-Heng. 2013. Most tensor problems are NP-hard. *Journal of the ACM*, **60**. Article 45.

Hopkins, Samuel B., Schramm, Tselil, Shi, Jonathan, and Steurer, David. 2016. Fast spectral algorithms from sum-of-squares proofs: Tensor decomposition and planted sparse vectors. In *Proceedings of the Forty-eight Annual ACM Symposium on Theory of Computing*, pp. 178–191.

Hsu, Daniel, and Kakade, Sham M. 2013. Learning mixtures of spherical Gaussians: Moment methods and spectral decompositions. In: *Proceedings of the 4th conference on Innovations in Theoretical Computer Science* pp. 11–20.

Hsu, Daniel, Kakade, Sham M., and Zhang, Tong. 2012. A spectral algorithm for learning hidden Markov models. *Journal of Computer and System Sciences*, **78**(5), 1460–1480.

Kolda, Tamara G, and Bader, Brett W. 2009. Tensor decompositions and applications. *SIAM Review*, **51**(3), 455–500.

Kruskal, Joseph B. 1977. Three-way arrays: Rank and uniqueness of trilinear decompositions, with application to arithmetic complexity and statistics. *Linear Algebra and Its Applications*, **18**(2).

Ma, Tengyu, Shi, Jonathan, and Steurer, David. 2016. Polynomial-time tensor decompositions with sum-of-squares. In *IEEE Symposium on the Foundations of Computer Science*, pp. 438–446.

Moitra, Ankur. 2018. *Algorithmic aspects of machine learning*. Cambridge University Press.

Moitra, Ankur, and Valiant, Gregory. 2010. Settling the polynomial learnability of mixtures of Gaussians. In *Foundations of Computer Science (FOCS)*, pp. 93–102.

Mossel, Elchanan, and Roch, Sébastien. 2006. Learning nonsingular phylogenies and hidden Markov models. *The Annals of Applied Probability*, **16**(2), 583–614.

Song, Zhao, Woodruff, David P., and Zhong, Peilin. 2019. Relative error tensor low rank approximation. In *Proceedings of the Thirtieth Annual ACM-SIAM Symposium on Discrete Algorithms (SODA)*.

Stewart, G. W., and Sun, Ji-guang. 1990. *Matrix perturbation theory*. Academic Press.

Tosh, Christopher, and Dasgupta, Sanjoy. 2018. Maximum likelihood estimation for mixtures of spherical Gaussians is NP-hard. *Journal of Machine Learning Research*, **18**, 1–11 .

Exercises

Exercise 19.1 The symmetric rank of a symmetric tensor T is the smallest integer $r > 0$ s.t., T can be expressed as $T = \sum_{i=1}^{r} u_i^{\otimes \ell}$ for some $\{u_i\}_{i=1}^{k}$. Prove that for any symmetric tensor of order ℓ, the symmetric rank is at most $2^\ell \ell!$ times the rank of the tensor.[5] [Hint: For $\ell = 2$, if $u_i \otimes v_i$ was a term in the decomposition, we can express $u_i \otimes v_i + v_i \otimes u_i = \frac{1}{2}(u_i + v_i)^{\otimes 2} - \frac{1}{2}(u_i - v_i)^{\otimes 2}$.]

Exercise 19.2 Let $u, v \in \mathbb{R}^n$ be two orthonormal vectors, and consider the tensor $A = u \otimes u \otimes v + v \otimes u \otimes u + u \otimes v \otimes u$. Prove that it has rank 3. Also prove that it can be arbitrarily well approximated by a rank 2 tensor.
Hint: Try to express A as a difference of two symmetric rank one tensors with large entries (Frobenius norm of $\Theta(m)$), so that the error term is $O(1/m)$.

Exercise 19.3 Construct an example of a matrix U such that the Kruskal-rank of $U \odot U$ is at most twice the Kruskal-rank of U. [Hint: Express the identity matrix as $\sum_i u_i u_i^T$ for two different orthonormal bases.]

Exercise 19.4 Prove Proposition 19.3.

Exercise 19.5 Complete the proof of Claim 19.15 and hence Lemma 19.13 for $\ell = 2$.

---

[5] Comon's conjecture asks if for every symmetric tensor, the symmetric rank is equal to the rank. A counterexample was shown recently by Shitov. It is open what the best gap between these two ranks can be as a function of ℓ.

CHAPTER TWENTY

Topic Models and Nonnegative Matrix Factorization

Rong Ge and Ankur Moitra

Abstract: In this chapter, we introduce nonnegative matrix factorization and topic modeling. We will see that there is a natural structural assumption called *separability* that allows us to circumvent the worst-case NP-hardness results for nonnegative matrix factorization. We will devise a simple algorithm for separable nonnegative matrix factorization and apply it to the problem of learning the parameters of a topic model. Finally we will give an alternative algorithm for topic modeling based on low-rank tensor decomposition.

20.1 Introduction

In this chapter, we introduce topic modeling and nonnegative matrix factorization, which are two classic and interrelated problems where perspectives from beyond worst-case analysis have led to significant algorithmic progress. The goal of topic modeling is to make sense of a large collection of documents by extracting thematic structure. See an example in Figure 20.1, where topics are automatically extracted from a collection of *New York Times* articles. Topic models also have important applications in population genetics and other areas, but in the interest of space, we will not touch on those here.

At the heart of topic modeling is a simple generative model. First, each document is represented as a vector of word frequencies. This may seem like an overly simplistic view because it does not account for any notion of order or syntax. However, intuitively even if you were given this so-called bag-of-words representation you would still be able to tell what the document is about. In this way, the representation is seemingly a good enough approximation for topic modeling. The central assumption is that there is a fixed set of *topics* – numbering, say, a couple hundred – that are shared and recur in different proportions in each document. For example, a news article about legislation related to retirement accounts might be represented as a mixture of 0.7 of the topic *politics* and 0.3 of the topic *personal finance*. Furthermore, each topic is associated with a distribution on words. Note that a word such as *account* can occur in several topics but the probability it is assigned would likely vary from topic to topic. Finally, the topic proportions for each document are generated from some distribution, and then each word is sampled from the document-specific distribution on words.

Let us introduce some notion that we will use throughout the chapter. Let n be the size of the vocabulary. Let k be the number of topics. Then there is an $n \times k$

anthrax, official, mail, letter, worker, attack
president, clinton, white_house, bush, official, bill_clinton
father, family, elian, boy, court, miami
oil, prices, percent, million, market, united_states
microsoft, company, computer, system, window, software
government, election, mexico, political, vicente_fox, president
fight, mike_tyson, round, right, million, champion
right, law, president, george_bush, senate, john_ashcroft

Figure 20.1 Examples of topics automatically extracted from a collection of *New York Times* articles. Each row contains words from one topic in descending order by probability. This is the result of running the algorithm in Arora et al. (2018), which we introduce later in Section 20.3.4.

topic matrix A whose columns represent, for each topic, its distribution on words. Furthermore, let m be the number of documents, and W be a $k \times m$ matrix where each column represents, for each document, its composition as topics. Moreover, we assume that the columns of W are sampled from some distribution on the k-dimensional simplex. Under these notations, if we multiply A and W we can get a document-word matrix $M = AW$. Every column M_i of M represents a document. Since $M_i = \sum_{j=1}^{k} W_{i,j} A_j$, we know the ith document can be represented as a combination (mixture) of topics. Finally, we do not directly observe $M = AW$. Instead for each column of M, we observe L independent samples from the associated distribution. This would correspond to the case in which each document is of length L. We could just as easily allow different sizes, or perhaps sample the sizes from another distribution, but we will suppress these sorts of complications in our discussion.

The basic question we are interested in is: Can we recover the topic matrix A from the collection of documents generated by the topic model? It turns out that there are a wide variety of algorithms that work in practice and extract interesting and useful thematic structure. In this chapter, we will be mostly interested in the theoretical aspects of topic modeling: *Can we design efficient algorithms for topic modeling with provable guarantees?* For us, this quest will go hand-in-hand with making further assumptions about the generative model that are motivated by practical considerations.

The simplest setup is what is called a *pure topic model*:

Definition 20.1 (Pure Topic Model)   There is an unknown $n \times k$ topic matrix A and the columns of W are chosen by sampling a standard basis vector $\{e_i\}_i^k$ with probability $p_1, \ldots, p_k$.

In particular, each document is about just one topic. Pure topic models were also studied under the name of *probabilistic latent semantic indexing* by Hoffman (1999). The model is a mixture of k different monomial distributions. Later we will study more complicated models where columns of W are not basis vectors – or to put it another way, every document can have more than one topic – and we call these the *mixed models*. The pure topic model is already nontrivial. In fact, we will make even stronger assumptions to show our first algorithms for topic modeling. Let us assume that L is infinite so that we really do observe $M = AW$ and do not have to contend with sampling noise. Furthermore, suppose that the columns of A have disjoint support, so that each word appears in only one topic. Papadimitriou et al. (2000) showed that in this setting the singular value decomposition works – it really does recover the topics that were used to generate the documents.

Lemma 20.2 *Suppose $M = AW$, and each column of W and each row of A have exactly one nonzero entry. Furthermore, suppose that the support of each column of A is disjoint. Finally, assume the nonzero singular values of M are distinct. Then the left singular vectors of M are the columns of A (after rescaling).*

Proof Consider the permutation matrix P that permutes the indices of the words so that all the words that appear in the same topic are contiguous. Then

$$PMM^\top P^\top$$

is block diagonal. There is one block for each topic whose dimension is equal to the number of words in that topic. Moreover, each document contributes only to the block corresponding to its topic. And thus each block is rank one. The columns of PM are eigenvectors of $PMM^\top P^\top$, which in turn implies that the columns of A are left singular vectors of M. The fact that M has distinct nonzero singular values means that the singular value decomposition is unique, so the columns of A are the only left singular vectors of M. $\qquad\square$

Papadimitriou et al. (2000) were the first to introduce the natural two-level generative model for documents at the start of the chapter. This model has other applications such as collaborative filtering, where we assume each user is represented by a distribution on interests, and each interest is a distribution on items they may buy. They also gave perturbation bounds that quantify how well the singular value decomposition performs in the presence of sampling noise – i.e., when the documents do not have infinite length. The method of applying the singular value decomposition to the term by document matrix is called *latent semantic indexing* and was introduced in a seminal paper of Deerwester et al. (1990).

There are many assumptions that we made in the preceding text, but perhaps the most egregious is the assumption that the topics are disjoint. Real-world topics have a high degree of overlap. So what happens when we remove this assumption?

Fundamentally, the singular value decomposition is just not the right thing to do anymore. The vectors that it finds are necessarily orthogonal even though the vectors that we are looking for – i.e., the columns of A – are not! The singular value decomposition finds the span of A but the vectors that it spits out are typically dense and often hard to interpret. This brings us to the notion of nonnegative matrix factorization:

Definition 20.3 (Nonnegative Matrix Factorization) A *nonnegative matrix factorization* of inner dimension k of an entrywise nonnegative $n \times m$ matrix M is a decomposition

$$M = AW,$$

where A is $n \times k$, W is $k \times m$ and both are entrywise nonnegative. Moreover, let the *nonnegative rank* $\text{rank}^+(M)$ denote the minimum k so that such a factorization exists.

Nonnegative matrix factorization has been introduced independently in many different contexts. In combinatorial optimization, Yannakakis (1991) showed that the nonnegative rank governs the extension complexity of a polytope. Lee and Seung (1999) found applications in image segmentation. In fact, it was first introduced in chemometrics under the name *self-modeling curve resolution*. While this looks like exactly the right tool to use in the context of topic modeling (at least in the limit where documents are long enough that we do not have to worry about sampling noise), there is a catch. Vavasis (2009) proved:

Theorem 20.4 *It is NP-hard to compute the nonnegative rank of a matrix.*

This chapter is devoted to what you can do in spite of these computational impediments. It turns out that there are natural assumptions we can make, that are motivated by uniqueness and robustness considerations, for which we can give simple algorithms for computing a nonnegative matrix factorization of minimum inner dimension provably and efficiently. These algorithms will also have important implications for topic modeling. There are other methods for topic modeling based on tensor decomposition that we will also cover in detail here.

20.2 Nonnegative Matrix Factorization

In this section we will discuss nonnegative matrix factorization (NMF) in more detail. Recall that a matrix $M \in \mathbb{R}^{n \times m}$ has a nonnegative matrix factorization if we can write

$$M = AW,$$

where $A \in \mathbb{R}^{n \times k}$, $W \in \mathbb{R}^{k \times m}$ are factors with nonnegative entries. The nonnegativity constraints are natural for applications such as topic models. In this section we will see that the nonnegativity constraints naturally lead to a geometric interpretation of NMF. The geometric interpretation is a key step in the NP-hardness proof for NMF; a similar interpretation also gives conditions in which NMF is unique and easy to find and leads to fast algorithms for computing an NMF.

20.2.1 Hardness of Nonngegative Matrix Factorization

Vavasis (2009) showed that finding a nonnegative matrix factorization with smallest possible inner-dimension is NP-hard. His proof revolves around a useful geometric interpretation of NMF and various geometric gadgets.

Vavasis (2009) showed that NMF is in fact equivalent to a geometric problem that is called *Intermediate Simplex*.

Problem 20.5 (Intermediate Simplex) Given a polyhedron $P = \{x \in \mathbb{R}^{k-1} : Ax \geq b\}$, where $A \in \mathbb{R}^{n \times (k-1)}$ and $b \in \mathbb{R}^n$ are such that $[A, b]$ has rank k. Also

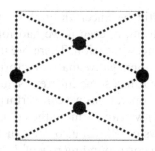

Figure 20.2 Gadget for a variable in the *NP*-hardness reduction. Figure from Vavasis (2009).

given a set $S \subset \mathbb{R}^{k-1}$ of m points that are all contained in P and that are not all contained in any hyperplane (i.e., they affinely span $\mathbb{R}^{k-1}$). The question is whether there exists a $(k-1)$-simplex T such that $S \subset T \subset P$.

Consider the *Exact NMF* problem, where we are given a matrix M and our goal is to determine whether it has a nonnegative matrix factorization of rank k. Vavasis (2009) proved the following:

Theorem 20.6 *There is a polynomial-time reduction from Exact NMF to Intermediate Simplex and vice versa.*

Intuitively, Exact NMF is related to Intermediate Simplex because one can always express a column of M by a nonnegative combination of columns in A:

$$M_i = \sum_{j=1}^{k} W_{i,j} A_j.$$

If the M_i's and A_j's are normalized to have ℓ_1 norm 1 (which is always possible; see Claim 20.9 later), then the column M_i is in the convex hull of $\{A_1, A_2, \ldots, A_k\}$. At a high level, one can think of the columns $\{M_i\}$'s as the set S in Intermediate Simplex, $\{A_j\}$'s as the vertices of T, and the set of all nonnegative vectors as the polyhedron P. The actual reduction is more technical.

Since Exact NMF and Intermediate Simplex are equivalent (with respect to polynomial time reductions), to prove the hardness of Exact NMF we only need to prove the hardness of Intermediate Simplex. The key idea in Vavasis' proof is to construct Intermediate Simplex problems that have exactly two solutions, and use these as gadgets. The gadget is shown in Figure 20.2. In this figure, the bounding box represents the outer polyhedron P, the black dots represent the set S, and the dashed lines represent two possible intermediate simplices.

20.2.2 Uniqueness of Nonnegative Matrix Factorization

In applications such as topic models, often one would hope to find a unique solution that corresponds to the *true* underlying topics for the corpus of text. However, for a matrix $M \in \mathbb{R}^{n \times m}$, its nonnegative matrix factorization is not always unique.

In such cases there would still be uncertainty about whether one has found the correct solution for the application, even if we had found the nonnegative matrix factorization with smallest inner dimension. Therefore it is natural to ask: For a fixed inner dimension, when is the nonnegative matrix factorization unique?

First, we observe that NMF has some inherent symmetries: If $M = AW$, then there are at least two types of operations we can perform that lead to an NMF with the same inner dimension: (1) we can permute the columns of A and and apply the same permutation to the rows of W; (2) also, we can scale one column of A by a positive factor c and scale the corresponding row of W by $1/c$.

These natural symmetries in NMF problems are usually not an issue for the specific applications. If we again consider topic models, the permutation operation only changes the ordering of the topics, which is not relevant to the actual topic model, as we only care about the *set* of topics. Also, we do not have to worry about rescalings because we are interested in one particular scaling where the sum of the entries of each column of A is one. Later when we say an NMF is unique, we will always mean that the NMF is unique up to permutations and scaling operations.

Donoho and Stodden (2004) considered an application to image datasets and gave a set of sufficient conditions for NMF to be unique. Here we will restate their main assumption – *separability* – in the context of general NMF.

Definition 20.7 (Separability)   A nonnegative matrix $A \in \mathbb{R}^{n \times k}$ is *separable* if for every column $i = 1, 2, \ldots, k$, there is a row $a_i \in [n]$ such that the only nonzero entry in this row is at column i. That is, $A_{i, a_i} > 0$, and $A_{j, a_i} = 0$ for all $j \neq i$. Furthermore, we say an NMF $M = AW$ is *separable* if A is separable.

Intuitively, separability requires every component of the NMF (every column of the A matrix) to have a unique coordinate that indicates whether this component is present or not in the NMF. When the matrix M has an exact NMF, separability alone is sufficient to guarantee uniqueness:

Theorem 20.8   *Suppose $M = AW$ is an NMF of M with number of components equal to $\mathrm{rank}^+(M)$. If the matrix A is separable, then the NMF is unique up to permutations and scaling.*

A proof of this theorem can be found in Arora et al. (2016a), where they also gave an algorithm for finding such an NMF efficiently. Although we will not prove the theorem here, in the next section we will explain the geometric intuition behind the proof, and later Theorem 20.11 implies a weaker version of this theorem.

20.2.3 Geometric Interpretation of Separability

Claim 20.9   *If every row of $M \in \mathbb{R}^{n \times m}$ has ℓ_1 norm 1, and M has nonnegative rank k, then there is a nonnegative matrix factorization of $M = AW$ where $A \in \mathbb{R}^{n \times k}$ and $W \in \mathbb{R}^{k \times m}$ such that every row of A or W also has ℓ_1 norm equal to 1.*

We will use $A_{i,:}$ to denote the ith row of A and similarly for matrices M, W. If A is separable, then after normalization each row $A_{a_i,:}$ will be equal to the basis vector e_i.

Now, consider rows of M as points in $\mathbb{R}^m$. Because we can write

$$M_{i,:} = \sum_{j=1}^{k} A_{i,j} W_{j,:},$$

we know every row $M_{i,:}$ is a convex combination of rows in W. If in addition A is separable, we know $M_{a_i,:} = W_{i,:}$ – every row of W actually appears as a row in M! This allows us to restate the problem as follows:

Claim 20.10 (Geometric Interpretation of Separable NMF) *Suppose $M = AW$ is a separable NMF, and the rows of M are normalized to have ℓ_1 norm 1. The NMF problem is equivalent to: Given n points in $\mathbb{R}^m$ (rows of M), find k points (rows of W) out of these n points such that every point is in the convex hull of the k points.*

20.2.4 Algorithm for Separable NMF

Based on the geometric interpretation, there are many ways to design efficient algorithms for finding the factorization $M = AW$. The first polynomial-time algorithm was given in Arora et al. (2016a). Here we give a simpler and more efficient algorithm that appeared in Arora et al. (2013) that also has appealing noise robustness properties that we will discuss later. We will rely on the geometric picture established in Claim 20.10.

Algorithm 1 Separable NMF

Require: n points $v_1, v_2, \ldots, v_n \in \mathbb{R}^m$ that correspond to rows of M that has a separable NMF $M = AW$.

Ensure: k points $w_1, w_2, \ldots, w_k \in \mathbb{R}^m$ that correspond to rows of W.

    Normalize $\{v_1, v_2, \ldots, v_n\}$ so that they have ℓ_1 norm 1.

    Let $w_1 = \arg\min_{v_j} \|v_j\|_2$ (the vector with maximum ℓ_2 norm).

    for $i = 2$ to k **do**

        Let w_i be the vector among $\{v_1, \ldots, v_n\}$ that is furthest (in ℓ_2 distance) from the affine span of $\{w_1, w_2, \ldots, w_{i-1}\}$.

    end for

In this algorithm, the affine span of a set of vectors $\{w_1, w_2, \ldots, w_i\}$ is defined as the set $\text{aff}(\{w_1, w_2, \ldots, w_i\}) = \{w | w = \sum_{j=1}^{i} a_j w_j, \sum_{j=1}^{i} a_j = 1\}$. The ℓ_2 distance between a point v and the affine span is the minimum ℓ_2 distance from v to any point in the span. Once the algorithm finds the w_i's, for every row $M_{i,:}$ one can solve a simple system of linear equations to recover the coefficients $A_{i,:}$.

An example run of Algorithm 1 is given in Figure 20.3. In the figure, the points are the input points $\{v_i\}$'s. The gray points represent vertices of the convex hull, which are the desired outputs of the algorithm. In the second (top right) subfigure, the first vector w_1 is chosen to be the vector with largest ℓ_2 norm; in the third (bottom left) subfigure, w_2 is chosen to be the vector that is farthest from w_1 (as the affine hull $\text{aff}(\{v_1\})$ is just v_1 itself); finally in the fourth (bottom right) subfigure, w_3 is chosen to be the vector that is farthest from the line passing through w_1 and w_2.

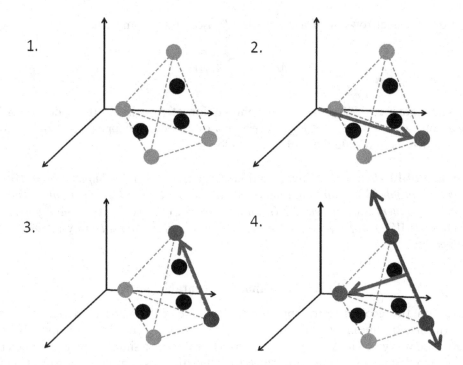

Figure 20.3 Example run of Algorithm 1. Figure from Arora et al. (2018).

The algorithm will run for another iteration after the last subfigure and pick up the remaining grey vertex.

Now we are ready to give the guarantee for this algorithm:

Theorem 20.11 *If M has a separable NMF $M = AW$ of nonnegative rank k, and the rank of W is equal to k, then Algorithm 1 returns k vectors that correspond to the rows of W.*

The theorem can be proved by a simple induction, we leave that as an exercise. Something surprising that has happened here is that the same assumption (separability) that we initially introduced for understanding when NMF is unique turned out to be useful for the seemingly orthogonal goal of designing efficient algorithms for NMF. In fact, in contrast to other chapters in this book, the assumption we are working with is used not merely to analyze some general purpose algorithm but to inspire new algorithms that turn out to be highly practical!

Robustness of Algorithm 1 The analysis in Theorem 20.11 requires the observed matrix M to have an exact NMF. This is a strong assumption: In practice often one can only observe an approximate version of M. The same Algorithm 1 can also be applied when we observe a matrix $\hat{M}$, which is the true matrix $M = AW$ with a small perturbation. In this case we also need the additional assumption that the simplex formed by rows of W is robust:

Definition 20.12 (Robust Simplex) A simplex P is γ-*robust*, if every vertex of P has ℓ_2 distance at least γ with the convex hull of the rest of the vertices.

Of course, when the input is perturbed, we also cannot hope to recover an exact solution. The goal is then to find a set of vertices that are close to the vertices of the simplex, which can be formalized as:

Definition 20.13 (Cover) Let $v_1, v_2, \ldots, v_n \in \mathbb{R}^m$ be a set of points whose convex hull P is a simplex with vertices $w_1, w_2, \ldots, w_k$. Then we say v_i ϵ-*covers* w_j if when v_i is written as a convex combination of the vertices: $v_i = \sum_{l=1}^{k} c_l w_l$, the coefficient $c_j \geq 1 - \epsilon$. Furthermore, we say a set of k points ϵ-*covers* the vertices if each vertex is ϵ-covered by some vertex in the set.

It is easy to see that if $\epsilon = 0$, a set that 0-covers the vertices must be the set of vertices themselves. With these definitions, Arora et al. (2013) proved the following robustness guarantee for Algorithm 1:

Theorem 20.14 Let $v_1, v_2, \ldots, v_n \in \{v \in \mathbb{R}^m, \|v\|_2 \leq 1\}$ be a set of points whose convex hull P is a simplex with vertices $w_1, w_2, \ldots, w_k$. If the convex hull P is γ-robust, and the input to Algorithm 1 are v_i''s where $\|v_i' - v_i\|_2 \leq \epsilon$ for all $i = 1, 2, \ldots, n$, Algorithm 1 returns a subset $\{v_{i_1}', v_{i_2}', \ldots, v_{i_k}'\}$ whose unperturbed version $\{v_{i_1}, v_{i_2}, \ldots, v_{i_k}\}$ $O(\epsilon/\gamma)$-covers the vertices $\{w_1, \ldots, w_k\}$ provided that $20\epsilon k < \gamma^3$.

20.2.5 Further Applications and Discussions

Most of our discussion so far revolved around the separability assumption. We discussed how it leads to uniqueness for NMF, new algorithms for NMF, and has applications to topic modeling. Here we briefly survey some of the other related literature on NMF. First, if one does not make the separability assumption, Arora et al. (2016a) showed that it is hard to compute an exact NMF in time $(mn)^{o(k)}$ assuming the Exponential Time Hypothesis (Impagliazzo and Paturi, 2001); they also give an algorithm that computes an exact NMF in $(mn)^{O(k^2 2^k)}$ time, using tools from the first-order theory of the reals (Basu et al., 1996; Renegar, 1992). This was later improved to $(mn)^{O(k^2)}$ by Moitra (2016). Also, there are many other algorithms for separable NMF that have provable guarantees, including for example Recht et al. (2012) and Gillis and Vavasis (2013). These algorithms are based on the ideas we presented but have different running time and robustness guarantees that are not directly comparable. See more references in the survey by Gillis (2014).

Finally, separability turns out to be a natural assumption in other applications beyond topic modeling. Separability was applied to hyperspectral unmixing (Winter, 1999) under the name of the pure pixel assumption, even before the line of work introduced in this section started (see Ma et al., 2013, for more references). Halpern and Sontag (2013) and Jernite et al. (2013) applied the separability assumptions to noisy-or networks modeling disease–symptom interactions. Cohen and Collins (2014) applied the separability assumptions to learn latent-variable probabilistic context-free grammars, which are a popular model for problems such as parsing. Motivated by applications in biomarkers, Ge and Zou (2016) extended the separability assumption to cases in which there are many points on low-dimensional faces of the simplex (instead of requiring points to exist near vertices).

20.3 Topic Models

In this section, we will study the *Latent Dirichlet Allocation* (LDA) model of Blei et al. (2003). Earlier in the chapter we introduced what we called a pure topic model where each document is about only one topic. This is of course an unrealistic assumption because many documents can be about multiple topics. Blei et al. (2003) proposed that the columns of the topic by document matrix be sampled from a Dirichlet distribution:

Definition 20.15 (Dirichlet Distribution)   A Dirichlet distribution with parameters $\alpha_1, \ldots, \alpha_k$ is a distribution on the k-dimensional simplex and with density function

$$f(x_1, \ldots, x_k) = \frac{\prod_{i=1}^k x_i^{\alpha_i - 1}}{B(\alpha)},$$

where $B(\alpha)$ is a normalizing constant.

On a more intuitive level, we can generate a sample by taking independent samples from k gamma distributions and then renormalizing them so that their sum is one. The expectation of the ith coordinate is equal to α_i / α_0, where $\alpha_0 = \sum_{i=1}^k \alpha_i$. Conditioned on the same expectations, the distribution favors sparse vectors when α_0 is small. One can think of α_0 as an approximate sparsity of the vector (see Telgarsky, 2013). In topic models α_0 is typically a small constant (like 1) which favors very sparse topic vectors (i.e., documents that are about only a small number of different topics). Just as before, the goal is to estimate the underlying topic matrix from a large collection of documents generated by the model. We will give two different types of algorithms – one based on tensor decomposition and one based on nonnegative matrix factorization – which will have different strengths and weaknesses in terms of the technical assumptions they make and their flexibility with respect to different modeling assumptions.

20.3.1 Tensor Decomposition

In this subsection, we will introduce the basics of tensor decompositions as we will need for building algorithms for learning mixed topic models. To keep it simple, we will specialize our discussion to third-order tensors. We can think about these a variety of ways but in their simplest form they are just 3-dimensional grids of numbers $\{T_{a,b,c}\}_{a,b,c}$. For us, the most important parameter associated with a tensor is its rank:

Definition 20.16 (Tensor Rank)   A *rank one* third-order tensor T is the tensor product of three vectors u, v, and w and its entries are

$$T_{a,b,c} = u_a v_b w_c.$$

Moreover, the *rank* of a tensor T is the smallest integer r so that we can write T as the sum of r rank one tensors.

There are numerous subtleties to the notion of rank – things that do not come up with matrices. The most important consideration to keep in mind is that it is *NP*-hard to compute the rank. Håstad (1990) proved:

Theorem 20.17 *It is NP-hard to compute the rank of a tensor.*

But it turns out that the types of tensors that arise in some machine learning applications sometimes avoid these pathologies. This will be the case when we apply it to topic modeling. In particular, there is an important algorithm called *Jennrich's algorithm* that was published in Harshman et al. (1970) that will be the building block of some of our algorithms here. Jennrich's algorithm is covered in detail in Chapter 19, and we summarize its guarantees here:

Theorem 20.18 *Suppose we are given a tensor T that is promised to be of the form*

$$T = \sum_{i=1}^{r} u^{(i)} \otimes v^{(i)} \otimes w^{(i)},$$

where (1) the vectors $\{u^{(i)}\}_i$ are linearly independent, (2) the vectors $\{v^{(i)}\}_i$ are linearly independent, and (3) every pair of vectors in $\{w^{(i)}\}_i$ are linearly independent. Then there is an algorithm that recovers the rank one tensors (up to permutations) in the preceding decomposition in polynomial time.

There are some subtleties to how the guarantees are formulated. We cannot recover the collections $\{u^{(i)}\}_i$, $\{v^{(i)}\}_i$, and $\{w^{(i)}\}_i$ because T remains unchanged when we permute the order of indices in the sum, and even when we rescale any triple of vectors by α, β, and γ factors, where $\alpha\beta\gamma = 1$.

It is also important to know that Jennrich's algorithm works in the presence of noise as well. In particular, if we are given an entrywise approximation to T we can bound the error in how well we recover the rank one terms in terms of other properties of the problem (like how well-conditioned the vectors $\{u^{(i)}\}_i$ are). This is important to us because we will use tensors to store information about the moments of our topic model – how often triples of words co-occur with each other. We will not be able to get these moments exactly with any finite number of samples, but we will be able to approximate them well.

20.3.2 Applications to Pure Topic Models

In this subsection, we will give our first application of tensor methods to topic modeling. These results first appeared in Mossel and Roch (2005), although they studied the more general problem of learning phylogenetic trees and hidden Markov models. Their results were rediscovered later. We will return to the pure topic model setting. Let m be the number of words in the vocabulary. Let A be the topic matrix, and p_i be the probability that a document is about the ith topic. Now suppose we sample a random document from the topic model along with a triple of three words from it (w_1, w_2, w_3). Let T be the $m \times m \times m$ tensor, where $T_{a,b,c}$ is the probability that $w_1 = a, w_2 = b$ and $w_3 = c$.

First, we claim that T can be expressed in terms of the unknown topic matrix A. Let A_ℓ be the ℓth column of A.

Lemma 20.19 *In a pure topic model we have*

$$T = \sum_{\ell=1}^{k} p_\ell A_\ell \otimes A_\ell \otimes A_\ell.$$

Now we can apply Jennrich's algorithm to the tensor representing the third-order moments of the topic model. Sweeping under the carpet issues about how many samples we need and the perturbation bounds for applying Jennrich's algorithm in settings where there is some sampling noise, we get:

Theorem 20.20 *There is a polynomial time algorithm to learn the topic matrix A in a pure topic model provided that A has full rank.*

The point is that if A has full rank the conditions we need to be able to apply Jennrich's algorithm to T will be satisfied. The algorithm will output an estimate of A that converges to the true topic matrix (up to a permutation of its columns) and the rate of convergence will depend polynomially on various parameters in the problem such as the number of words, the number of topics, the condition number of A, etc. But already we can compare the efficacy of tensor methods to spectral methods for learning pure topic models: When we applied the singular value decomposition, we were able to recover the topics only when we made strong assumptions such as having the columns of A have disjoint support (see Lemma 20.2). Now we can get away with a much more reasonable assumption that it has full column rank.

20.3.3 Extensions to Mixed Models

In this subsection, we will show how to apply tensor methods to mixed topic models where a document is allowed to be about more than one topic. We will follow Anandkumar et al. (2012). Recall that in the LDA model the composition of each document is drawn from a Dirichlet distribution.

If we naively try to follow the same recipe as we did for pure topic models and compute the tensor $T^{(3)}$ whose entries are the third-order moments, we would get a different expression for $T^{(3)}$ in terms of A. (Here we have introduced the name $T^{(3)}$ because we will ultimately have to work with a number of different third-order tensors). Just as p_i denoted the probability in a pure topic model that the document is about the ith topic, let $p_{a,b,c}$ denote the probability that the three words we sample were generated from the ath, bth, and cth topics respectively. Explicitly, the correlations between three topics can be written as[1]

---

[1] The computation of these correlations relies on the fact that the Dirichlet distribution is the conjugate prior of categorical distributions, which is also part of the reason why the Dirichlet distribution was used in Blei et al. (2003). See Wikipedia contributors (2019) for more information.

$$p_{a,b,c} = \begin{cases} \frac{\alpha_a(\alpha_a+1)(\alpha_a+2)}{\alpha_0(\alpha_0+1)(\alpha_0+2)} & a = b = c \\ \frac{\alpha_a(\alpha_a+1)\alpha_c}{\alpha_0(\alpha_0+1)(\alpha_0+2)} & a = b \neq c \\ \frac{\alpha_a\alpha_b\alpha_c}{\alpha_0(\alpha_0+1)(\alpha_0+2)} & a, b, c \text{ distinct.} \end{cases}$$

Lemma 20.21 *In a Latent Dirichlet Allocation Model we have*

$$T^{(3)} = \sum_{a,b,c} p_{a,b,c} A_a \otimes A_b \otimes A_c.$$

So we have now hit a roadblock. Before, our approach was to estimate the third-order moments and then apply Jennrich's algorithm. But in our present setting, $T^{(3)}$ is not necessarily low rank. In fact, it is the sum of k^3 rank one tensors. The key idea is that we can form other sorts of third-order tensors that we can use to zero out the off-diagonal entries of $\{p_{a,b,c}\}_{a,b,c}$. For example, if we take three documents sampled from the generative model and select one word uniformly at random out of each of them, their joint distribution can be written as the tensor

$$T^{(1)} = \sum_{a,b,c} p_a p_b p_c A_a \otimes A_b \otimes A_c,$$

where $p_i = \alpha_i/\alpha_0$. These tensors are almost the same. They have the same factors $\{A_i\}_i$ and they differ only in that $T^{(3)}$ puts comparatively more weight on triples with repeated indices. (Intuitively, this is because when the first word comes from the ith topic it makes it more likely for the second word to also come from the same topic.)

We need to introduce one last tensor in order to describe the algorithm. Suppose we sample two documents and take two words uniformly at random from the first and one word uniformly at random from the second. The resulting tensor is

$$T^{(2)}_{\{1,2\}} = \sum_{a,b,c} p_{a,b} p_c A_a \otimes A_b \otimes A_c,$$

where we have

$$p_{a,b} = \begin{cases} \frac{\alpha_a(\alpha_a+1)}{\alpha_0(\alpha_0+1)} & a = b \\ \frac{\alpha_a\alpha_b}{\alpha_0(\alpha_0+1)} & \text{otherwise} \end{cases}.$$

Notice there is now an asymmetry between the indices a, b, c that comes from the fact that the first and second words come from the same document. If instead we want to take (say) the first and third words from the same document and compute the third-order moments we write $T^{(2)}_{\{1,3\}}$. First we introduce some helpful notation:

Definition 20.22 Let $T = \alpha_0(\alpha_0+1)(\alpha_0+2)T^{(3)} - \alpha_0^2(\alpha_0+1)(T^{(2)}_{\{1,2\}} + T^{(2)}_{\{1,3\}} + T^{(2)}_{\{2,3\}}) + 2\alpha_0^3 T^{(1)}$.

Now we are ready to state the key lemma that will allow us to learn the parameters of an LDA model:

Lemma 20.23 *In a Latent Dirichlet Allocation model*

$$T = \sum_{a,b,c} R_{a,b,c} A_a \otimes A_b \otimes A_c \tag{20.1}$$

where $R_{a,b,c}$ is nonzero iff $a = b = c$. In particular $R_{a,a,a} = 2\alpha_a$.

Now we are in a position where we can once again apply Jennrich's algorithm. Let $\widehat{T}^{(3)}$ denote the empirical approximation to $T^{(3)}$ and similarly for the other tensors. The overall algorithm is given as Algorithm 2.

Algorithm 2 Topic modeling via tensor decomposition

Require: m documents of length L generated by a topic model
    Compute the tensors $\widehat{T}^{(1)}, \widehat{T}^{(2)}_{\{i,j\}}, \widehat{T}^{(2)}_{\{i,k\}}, \widehat{T}^{(2)}_{\{j,k\}}$ and $\widehat{T}^{(3)}$.
    Use them to construct $\widehat{T}$.
    Apply Jennrich's algorithm, renormalize the factors so they sum to one, and collect
    them into a matrix A.

The main result of Anandkumar et al. (2012) is:

Theorem 20.24 *There is a polynomial time algorithm to learn the topic matrix A in a Latent Dirichlet Allocation model provided that A has full rank and that all the α_i's are nonzero.*

Again, the algorithm will output an estimate of A that converges to the true topic matrix (up to a permutation of its columns) and the rate of convergence depends polynomially on related parameters such as the number of words, the number of topics, the condition number of A, how close the α_i's are to zero, etc. While this algorithm shows that tensor methods can be extended to some mixed models, there is an important caveat that if we replace the Dirichlet distribution with some other distribution the formula (20.1) would no longer work (and probably there is no way to get a low-rank tensor using just the low-order moments). The main question that we will address in the next subsection is: Are there algorithms for learning mixed models that work without making brittle assumptions about the moments?

20.3.4 Anchor Words Algorithm

In the previous subsection, we showed how to learn parameters of an LDA model by utilizing tensor decompositions. One limitation of this approach is that it requires estimating correlations between a triple of words, which can be costly in practice. In this section we introduce a new algorithm based on separable NMF that works on pairwise correlations, and has the advantage that it works for more general families of topic models.

Topic Models and NMF. Recall that in a topic model, $M \in \mathbb{R}^{n \times m}$ denotes a matrix whose columns represent the intrinsic word distributions of each document. However, we do not observe M in practice. Instead, for every document we observe L words sampled independently from the distribution given by its corresponding column in M. These L words allow us to construct the *empirical* document word matrix

$\widehat{M}$, where $\widehat{M}_{i,j}$ is the relative frequency with which word i appears in document j. It is easy to see that $\mathbb{E}[\widehat{M}] = M$. However, in practice L (usually on the order of hundreds) can be much smaller than the number of words in vocabulary n (usually at least on the order of tens of thousands). Thus $\widehat{M}$ has sparse columns and is a poor approximation of M in standard norms such as ℓ_1 and ℓ_2. This is far too much error to be tolerated by even the robust NMF algorithms that we discussed in Section 20.2.4.

The trouble is that $\widehat{M}$ does not concentrate as we increase the number of documents. Instead we will work with the Gram matrix Q: Let w_1, w_2 be two words from the same document, then for any pair of words i,j we have $Q_{i,j} = \mathbb{P}[w_1 = i, w_2 = j]$. Further, let R denote the topic by topic matrix whose entry in row i, column j is the probability that w_1 was sampled from topic i and w_2 was sampled from topic j. One can relate Q, R, and A using the following claim:

Claim 20.25 $Q = A(RA^{\top})$.

Now, Q is a matrix whose size does not increase as the number of documents increase, so we can hope the empirical estimation $\hat{Q}$ to converge to Q. Further, Claim 20.25 shows that Q admits a convenient decomposition in terms of the matrices we would like to estimate.

Throughout this section, we will assume that A is separable (we will also need to strengthen it so that it is quantitative). Let us translate what this assumption means into the setup of topic modeling:

Definition 20.26 (Anchor Words Assumption)   A topic matrix $A \in \mathbb{R}^{n \times k}$ satisfies *p-anchor words assumption* if for every topic $i = 1, 2, \ldots, k$, there is an *anchor-word* $\pi(i)$ such that $A_{\pi(i),i} \geq p$, and $A_{\pi(i),j} = 0$ for all $j \neq i$.

This does not say that every document about topic i must contain word $\pi(i)$. Rather, what it says is that when word $\pi(i)$ appears the document must be at least partially about that topic. For example, if the word 401k occurs in a document then it is indeed a strong indicator that the document is at least partially about personal finance. Natural language seems to contain many such unambiguous words. (And in fact when the topic matrix is generated using a Dirichlet distribution, as is often assumed, for natural settings of parameters it will produce a separable topic matrix; see Ding et al., 2015.)

While so far we have thought about separability geometrically, we will now turn to a probabilistic interpretation. Let w_1 be the first word in a document and let t_1 denote the topic it was sampled from.

Lemma 20.27   *A word j is an anchor word for topic i if and only if*

$$\mathbb{P}[t_1 = i' | w_1 = j] = 1_{i=i'}.$$

Intuitively, the lemma says that an anchor word j is an indicator that the word must have come from topic i. Similarly we have:

Lemma 20.28   *If j is an anchor word for topic i, w_1, w_2 are two words in the same document, then $\mathbb{P}[w_1 = j | t_2 = i] = \mathbb{P}[w_1 = j | w_2 = \pi(i)]$.*

We leave the proof as an exercise to the reader.

The basic idea behind the algorithm is to use the Gram matrix to set up a system of linear equations to solve for certain posterior probability from which we can compute A. In particular, using the law of total probabilities and Lemma 20.28, we have

$$\mathbb{P}[w_1 = j | w_2 = j'] = \sum_{i'} \mathbb{P}[w_1 = j | w_2 = \pi(i')] \mathbb{P}[t_2 = i' | w_2 = j']. \qquad (20.2)$$

Since the Gram matrix Q satisfies $Q = A(RA^\top)$, we can view A as the first NMF factor and $RA^\top = W^\top$ as the second NMF factor. Therefore we can compute scaled versions of rows of $W = RA^\top$ by solving separable NMF. With these in hand, using Algorithm 1 we can identify the rows that correspond to anchor words $\pi(1), \pi(2), \ldots, \pi(k)$. Now the terms $\mathbb{P}[w_1 = j | w_2 = \pi(i')]$ in Equation (20.2) can be estimated as $\hat{Q}_{j,\pi(i')} / \sum_{j'} \hat{Q}_{j',\pi(i')}$. The left-hand side of Equation (20.2) can also be estimated as $\hat{Q}_{j,j'} / \sum_{j''} \hat{Q}_{j'',j'}$. This gives us a system of equations to solve for the unknowns $\mathbb{P}[t_2 = i' | w_2 = j']$. It turns out that if R has full rank the system has a unique solution so we can solve for these unknowns.

Finally, we can now compute A by using Bayes' Rule:

$$\mathbb{P}[w = j | t = i] = \frac{\mathbb{P}[t = i | w = j] \mathbb{P}[w = j]}{\mathbb{P}[t = i]}$$

$$= \frac{\mathbb{P}[t = i | w = j] \mathbb{P}[w = j]}{\sum_{j'} \mathbb{P}[t = i | w = j'] \mathbb{P}[w = j']}.$$

In summary, the algorithm is the following:

Algorithm 3 Topic modeling via NMF

Require: m documents of length L generated by a topic model with anchor words
  Compute the Gram matrix $\widehat{Q}$.
  Compute the anchor words using Separable NMF (Algorithm 1).
  Solve for $\mathbb{P}[t = i | w = j]$.
  Compute $\mathbb{P}[w = j | t = i]$ using Bayes' Rule.

The main theorem of Arora et al. (2012, 2013) is:

Theorem 20.29 *There is a polynomial-time algorithm to learn the topic matrix A in a general topic model provided that A satisfy the p-anchor words assumption and R has full rank.*

The full analysis requires bounding the errors in each step. The number of documents can be used to bound the error between $\widehat{Q}$ and Q. We can then invoke the guarantees of Separable NMF in the presence of noise to ensure that it finds near-anchor words. We can analyze the stability of the system of linear equations for solving for $\mathbb{P}[t = i | w = j]$ in terms of the condition number of R. Finally we can bound how much the errors blow up when we apply Bayes' Rule.

20.3.5 Further Discussions

Besides Latent Dirichlet Allocation, there are also many other variants of topic models that capture correlations between topics, including Correlated Topic Models

(Blei and Lafferty, 2006) and Pachinko Allocation (Li and McCallum, 2006). It is hard to generalize Algorithm 2 to these models, as their moment structures are more complex. Algorithm 3 can be applied to these models and learns a correct topic matrix (although it's unclear how to learn the additional parameters for generating the topic proportion vectors). There are more extensions to topic models that consider the ordering of words or documents; see the survey by Blei (2012). Designig provable algorithms for these extensions is still an open problem.

Bhattacharya et al. (2016) and Bansal et al. (2014) designed algorithms for topic models that do not rely on the LDA model or the anchor words assumption. They relaxed anchor words to *catch words*, which are words that appear with a higher probability in one topic compared to all the other topics. The assumption on the topic matrix is that every topic has a set of catch words that all together have a large probability in the topic. With stronger assumptions on topic proportions (in particular the existence of pure documents that concern only a single topic) their algorithms can also learn topic models provably.

Even given the topic matrix and parameters for the Dirichlet distribution, computing the posterior of topic proportions can still be a tricky problem. Sontag and Roy (2011) showed that the maximum a posteriori (MAP) estimate problem for LDA is NP-hard. In practice one often wants to compute the expectation over the posterior distribution instead of MAP, but there is also no known algorithm for this in the most general setting. Arora et al. (2016c) gave guarantees for topic inference under conditions inspired by collaborative filtering (Kleinberg and Sandler, 2008).

Variational inference was the algorithm developed in the original paper for LDA (Blei et al., 2003). Similar techniques have been extended to many other probabilistic models. Awasthi and Risteski (2015) gave initial guarantees for variational inference under separability and other assumptions.

20.4 Epilogue: Word Embeddings and Beyond

A topic model can be viewed as mapping every word in the vocabulary to a k-dimensional vector that represents the probabilities of this word in the k topics. Recently, works such as Mikolov et al. (2013) and Pennington et al. (2014) constructed new *word embeddings*, which also map words into vectors in low-dimensional spaces. Unlike topic models, individual entries of these new word embeddings do not have a probabilistic interpretation and are not necessarily nonnegative. The new word embeddings are shown to be effective in a wide range of natural language processing tasks. Perhaps the most interesting property of the new word embeddings is that they can solve analogy tasks (Levy and Goldberg, 2014, Pennington et al., 2014): for analogies like "*man:woman::king:??*", one can just take the vectors v_m, v_w and v_k for words *man, woman, king* respectively, and construct a new vector $v = v_k - v_m + v_w$. The new vector v is very close to the embedding for *queen*, which is the correct answer of the analogy. Arora et al. (2016b) constructed a model that partially explained some properties of word embeddings.

More recently, even more complicated models for representing words using vectors were proposed – such as ELMo in Peters et al. (2018) and BERT in Devlin et al. (2019). These models are dependent on the context of the words and currently do not have a theoretical understanding. We hope future theoretical insights can help explain what information these embeddings might capture, and lead to new practical variants for word embeddings.

References

Anandkumar, Anima, Foster, Dean P., Hsu, Daniel J., Kakade, Sham M., and Liu, Yi-Kai. 2012. A spectral algorithm for latent Dirichlet allocation. In *Advances in Neural Information Processing Systems*, pp. 917–925.

Arora, Sanjeev, Ge, Rong, and Moitra, Ankur. 2012. Learning topic models–going beyond SVD. In *2012 IEEE 53rd Annual Symposium on Foundations of Computer Science*, pp. 1–10. IEEE.

Arora, Sanjeev, Ge, Rong, Halpern, Yonatan, Mimno, David, Moitra, Ankur, Sontag, David, Wu, Yichen, and Zhu, Michael. 2013. A practical algorithm for topic modeling with provable guarantees. In *International Conference on Machine Learning*, pp. 280–288.

Arora, Sanjeev, Ge, Rong, Kannan, Ravi, and Moitra, Ankur. 2016a. Computing a nonnegative matrix factorization – Provably. *SIAM Journal on Computing*, **45**(4), 1582–1611.

Arora, Sanjeev, Li, Yuanzhi, Liang, Yingyu, Ma, Tengyu Ma, and Risteski, Andrej. 2016b. A latent variable model approach to PMI-based word embeddings. *Transactions of the Association for Computational Linguistics*, **4**, pp. 385–399.

Arora, Sanjeev, Ge, Rong, Koehler, Frederic, Ma, Tengyu, and Moitra, Ankur. 2016c. Provable algorithms for inference in topic models. In *International Conference on Machine Learning*, pp. 2859–2867.

Arora, Sanjeev, Ge, Rong, Halpern, Yoni, Mimno, David, Moitra, Ankur, Sontag, David, Wu, Yichen, and Zhu, Michael. 2018. Learning topic models – provably and efficiently. *Communications of the ACM*, **61**(4), 85–93.

Awasthi, Pranjal, and Risteski, Andrej. 2015. On some provably correct cases of variational inference for topic models. In *Advances in Neural Information Processing Systems*, pp. 2098–2106.

Bansal, Trapit, Bhattacharyya, Chiranjib, and Kannan, Ravindran. 2014. A provable SVD-based algorithm for learning topics in dominant admixture corpus. In *Advances in Neural Information Processing Systems*, pp. 1997–2005.

Basu, Saugata, Pollack, Richard, and Roy, Marie-Françoise. 1996. On the combinatorial and algebraic complexity of quantifier elimination. *Journal of the ACM (JACM)*, **43**(6), 1002–1045.

Bhattacharya, Chiranjib, Goyal, Navin, Kannan, Ravindran, and Pani, Jagdeep. 2016. Non-negative matrix factorization under heavy noise. In *International Conference on Machine Learning*, pp. 1426–1434.

Blei, David, and Lafferty, John. 2006. Correlated topic models. *Advances in Neural Information Processing Systems*, **18**, 147.

Blei, David M. 2012. Probabilistic topic models. *Communications of the ACM*, **55**(4), 77–84.

Blei, David M, Ng, Andrew Y, and Jordan, Michael I. 2003. Latent Dirichlet allocation. *Journal of Machine Learning Research*, **3**(Jan), 993–1022.

Cohen, Shay B, and Collins, Michael. 2014. A provably correct learning algorithm for latent-variable PCFGs. In *Proceedings of the 52nd Annual Meeting of the Association for Computational Linguistics (Vol. 1: Long Papers)*, pp. 1052–1061.

Deerwester, Scott, Dumais, Susan T, Furnas, George W, Landauer, Thomas K, and Harshman, Richard. 1990. Indexing by latent semantic analysis. *Journal of the American Society for Information Science*, **41**(6), 391–407.

Devlin, Jacob, Chang, Ming-Wei, Lee, Kenton, and Toutanova, Kristina. 2019. BERT: Pre-training of deep bidirectional transformers for language understanding. In *Proceedings of the 2019 Conference of the North American Chapter of the Association for Computational Linguistics: Human Language Technologies, Vol. 1 (Long and Short Papers)*, pp. 4171–4186.

Ding, Weicong, Ishwar, Prakash, and Saligrama, Venkatesh. 2015. Most large topic models are approximately separable. In *2015 Information Theory and Applications Workshop (ITA)*, pp. 199–203. IEEE.

Donoho, David, and Stodden, Victoria. 2004. When does non-negative matrix factorization give a correct decomposition into parts? In *Advances in Neural Information Processing Systems*, pp. 1141–1148.

Ge, Rong, and Zou, James. 2016. Rich component analysis. In *International Conference on Machine Learning*, pp. 1502–1510.

Gillis, Nicolas. 2014. The why and how of nonnegative matrix factorization. *Regularization, Optimization, Kernels, and Support Vector Machines*, 12(257), 257–291.

Gillis, Nicolas, and Vavasis, Stephen A. 2013. Fast and robust recursive algorithmsfor separable nonnegative matrix factorization. *IEEE Transactions on Pattern Analysis and Machine Intelligence*, 36(4), 698–714.

Halpern, Yoni, and Sontag, David. 2013. Unsupervised learning of noisy-or Bayesian networks. In *Proceedings of the Twenty-Ninth Conference on Uncertainty in Artificial Intelligence*, p. 272–281. UAI'13. Arlington, VA: AUAI Press.

Harshman, Richard A., et al. 1970. Foundations of the PARAFAC procedure: Models and conditions for an" explanatory" multimodal factor analysis. In *UCLA Working Papers in Phonetics*, 16, 1–84.

Håstad, Johan. 1990. Tensor rank is NP-complete. *Journal of Algorithms*, 11(4), 644–654.

Hoffman, Thomas. 1999. Probabilistic latent semantic indexing. In *Proceedings of the 22nd Annual ACM Conference on Research and Development in Information Retrieval, 1999*, pp. 50–57.

Impagliazzo, Russell, and Paturi, Ramamohan. 2001. On the complexity of k-SAT. *Journal of Computer and System Sciences*, 62(2), 367–375.

Jernite, Yacine, Halpern, Yonatan, and Sontag, David. 2013. Discovering hidden variables in noisy-or networks using quartet tests. In *Advances in Neural Information Processing Systems*, pp. 2355–2363.

Kleinberg, Jon, and Sandler, Mark. 2008. Using mixture models for collaborative filtering. *Journal of Computer and System Sciences*, 74(1), 49–69.

Lee, Daniel D, and Seung, H Sebastian. 1999. Learning the parts of objects by non-negative matrix factorization. *Nature*, 401(6755), 788.

Levy, Omer, and Goldberg, Yoav. 2014. Linguistic regularities in sparse and explicit word representations. In *Proceedings of the Eighteenth Conference on Computational Natural Language Learning*, pp. 171–180.

Li, Wei, and McCallum, Andrew. 2006. Pachinko allocation: DAG-structured mixture models of topic correlations. In *Proceedings of the 23rd International Conference on Machine Learning*, pp. 577–584. ACM.

Ma, Wing-Kin, Bioucas-Dias, José M, Chan, Tsung-Han, Gillis, Nicolas, Gader, Paul, Plaza, Antonio J, Ambikapathi, ArulMurugan, and Chi, Chong-Yung. 2013. A signal processing perspective on hyperspectral unmixing: Insights from remote sensing. *IEEE Signal Processing Magazine*, 31(1), 67–81.

Mikolov, Tomas, Chen, Kai, Corrado, Greg, and Dean, Jeffrey. 2013. Efficient estimation of word representations in vector space. In: *Proceedings of the International Conference on Learning Representations*.

Moitra, Ankur. 2016. An almost optimal algorithm for computing nonnegative rank. *SIAM Journal on Computing*, 45(1), 156–173.

Mossel, Elchanan, and Roch, Sébastien. 2005. Learning nonsingular phylogenies and hidden Markov models. In *Proceedings of the Thirty-Seventh Annual ACM Symposium on Theory of Computing*, pp. 366–375. ACM.

Papadimitriou, Christos H, Raghavan, Prabhakar, Tamaki, Hisao, and Vempala, Santosh. 2000. Latent semantic indexing: A probabilistic analysis. *Journal of Computer and System Sciences*, **61**(2), 217–235.

Pennington, Jeffrey, Socher, Richard, and Manning, Christopher. 2014. Glove: Global vectors for word representation. In *Proceedings of the 2014 Conference on Empirical Methods in Natural Language Processing (EMNLP)*, pp. 1532–1543.

Peters, Matthew E., Neumann, Mark, Iyyer, Mohit, Gardner, Matt, Clark, Christopher, Lee, Kenton, and Zettlemoyer, Luke. 2018. Deep contextualized word representations. In *Proceedings of the North American Chapter of the Association for Computational Linguistics.*.

Recht, Ben, Re, Christopher, Tropp, Joel, and Bittorf, Victor. 2012. Factoring nonnegative matrices with linear programs. In *Advances in Neural Information Processing Systems*, pp. 1214–1222.

Renegar, James. 1992. On the computational complexity and geometry of the first-order theory of the reals. Part I: Introduction. Preliminaries. The geometry of semi-algebraic sets. The decision problem for the existential theory of the reals. *Journal of Symbolic Computation*, **13**(3), 255–299.

Sontag, David, and Roy, Dan. 2011. Complexity of inference in latent Dirichlet allocation. In *Advances in Neural Information Processing systems*.

Telgarsky, Matus. 2013. Dirichlet draws are sparse with high probability. *arXiv preprint arXiv:1301.4917*.

Vavasis, Stephen A. 2009. On the complexity of nonnegative matrix factorization. *SIAM Journal on Optimization*, **20**(3), 1364–1377.

Wikipedia contributors. 2019. *Dirichlet distribution*. Wikipedia. [Online; accessed October 1, 2019].

Winter, Michael E. 1999. N-FINDR: An algorithm for fast autonomous spectral end-member determination in hyperspectral data. In *Imaging Spectrometry V*, vol. 3753, pp. 266–275. International Society for Optics and Photonics.

Yannakakis, Mihalis. 1991. Expressing combinatorial optimization problems by linear programs. *Journal of Computer and System Sciences*, **43**(3), 441–466.

Exercises

Exercise 20.1 Prove Claim 20.9: If every row of $M \in \mathbb{R}^{n \times m}$ has ℓ_1 norm 1, and M has nonnegative rank k, then there is a nonnegative matrix factorization of $M = AW$, where $A \in \mathbb{R}^{n \times k}$ and $W \in \mathbb{R}^{k \times m}$ such that every row of A or W also has ℓ_1 norm equal to 1.

Exercise 20.2 Prove Theorem 20.11: If M has a separable NMF $M = AW$ of nonnegative rank k, and the rank of W is equal to k, then Algorithm 1 returns k vectors that correspond to the rows of W.

    (a) Let $v_1, \ldots, v_k \in \mathbb{R}^m$ be k vectors and P be their convex hull. Show that every of $\max_{v \in P} \|v\|_2$ must be one of the k vertices.

    (b) Use (a) to prove Theorem 20.11 by induction.

Exercise 20.3 Prove Lemma 20.28: If j is an anchor word for topic i and w_1, w_2 are two words in the same document, then $\mathbb{P}[w_1 = j | t_2 = i] = \mathbb{P}[w_1 = j | w_2 = \pi(i)]$.

CHAPTER TWENTY ONE

Why Do Local Methods Solve Nonconvex Problems?

Tengyu Ma

Abstract: Nonconvex optimization is ubiquitous in modern machine learning. Researchers devise nonconvex objective functions and optimize them using off-the-shelf optimizers such as stochastic gradient descent and its variants, which leverage the local geometry and update iteratively. Even though solving nonconvex functions is NP-hard in the worst case, the optimization quality in practice is often not an issue – optimizers are largely believed to find approximate global minima. We hypothesize a unified explanation for this intriguing phenomenon: most of the local minima of the practically used objectives are approximately global minima. We rigorously formalize it for concrete instances of machine learning problems.

21.1 Introduction

Optimizing nonconvex functions has become the standard algorithmic technique in modern machine learning and artificial intelligence. It is increasingly important to understand the working of the existing heuristics for optimizing nonconvex functions, so that we can design more efficient optimizers with guarantees. The worst-case intractability result says that finding a global minimizer of a nonconvex optimization problem – or even just a degree-4 polynomial – is *NP*-hard. Therefore, theoretical analysis with global guarantees has to depend on the special properties of the target functions that we optimize. To characterize the properties of the real-world objective functions, researchers have hypothesized that many objective functions for machine learning problems have the property that

$$\text{all or most local minima are approximately global minima.} \qquad (21.1)$$

Optimizers based on local derivatives can solve this family of functions in polynomial time (under some additional technical assumptions that will be discussed). Empirical evidence also suggests practical objective functions from machine learning and deep learning may have such a property. In this chapter, we formally state the algorithmic result that local methods can solve objective with property (21.1) in Section 21.2, and then rigorously prove that this property holds for a few objectives arising from several key machine learning problems: generalized linear models (Section 21.3), principal component analysis (PCA; Section 21.4.1), matrix completion

(Section 24.4.2), and tensor decompositions (Section 21.5). We will also briefly touch on recent works on neural networks (Section 21.6).

21.2 Analysis Technique: Characterization of the Landscape

In this section, we will show that a technical and stronger version of the property (21.1) implies that many optimizers can converge to a global minimum of the objective function.

21.2.1 Convergence to a Local Minimum

We consider a objective function f, which is assumed to be twice-differentiable from $\mathbb{R}^d$ to $\mathbb{R}$. Recall that x is a *local minimum* of $f(\cdot)$ if there exists an open neighborhood N of x in which the function value is at least $f(x)$: $\forall z \in N, f(z) \geq f(x)$. A point x is a *stationary point* if it satisfies $\nabla f(x) = 0$. A *saddle point* is a stationary point that is not a local minimum or maximum. We use $\nabla f(x)$ to denote the gradient of the function and $\nabla^2 f(x)$ to denote the Hessian of the function ($\nabla^2 f(x)$ is an $d \times d$ matrix where $[\nabla^2 f(x)]_{i,j} = \frac{\partial^2}{\partial x_i \partial x_j} f(x)$). A local minimum x must satisfy the first-order necessary condition for optimality, that is, $\nabla f(x) = 0$, and the second-order necessary condition for optimality, that is, $\nabla^2 f(x) \succeq 0$. (Here $A \succeq 0$ denotes that A is a positive semidefinite matrix.) Thus, a local minimum is a stationary point, so is a global minimum.

Under the following strict-saddle assumption, we can efficiently find a local minimum of the function f. A strict-saddle function satisfies that every saddle point must have a strictly negative curvature in some direction:

Definition 21.1 For $\alpha, \beta, \gamma \geq 0$, we say f is (α, β, γ)-*strict saddle* if every $x \in \mathbb{R}^d$ satisfies *at least* one of the following three conditions:

1. $\|\nabla f(x)\|_2 \geq \alpha$.
2. $\lambda_{\min}(\nabla^2 f) \leq -\beta$.
3. There exists a local minimum $x^\star$ that is γ-close to x in Euclidean distance.

This condition is conjectured to hold for many real-world functions, and will be proved to hold for various problems concretely. However, in general, verifying it mathematically or empirically may be difficult. Under this condition, many algorithms can converge to a local minimum of f in polynomial time, as stated.[1]

Theorem 21.2 *Suppose f is a twice differentiable (α, β, γ)-strict saddle function from $\mathbb{R}^d \to \mathbb{R}$. Then, various optimization algorithms (such as stochastic gradient descent) can converge to a local minimum in with ε error in Euclidean distance in time $poly(d, 1/\alpha, 1/\beta, 1/\gamma, 1/\varepsilon)$.*

---

[1] In this chapter, we allow polynomial dependence on $1/\epsilon$, where ϵ is the error. This makes sense for the downstream machine learning applications because very high accuracy solutions are not necessary (there are intrinsic statistical errors, anyway).

21.2.2 Local Optimality vs. Global Optimality

If a function f satisfies the property that "all local minima are global" and the strict saddle property, we can provably find one of its global minima.

Theorem 21.3 *Suppose f satisfies "all local minima are global" and the strict saddle property in a sense that all points satisfying approximately the necessary first-order and second-order optimality condition should be close to a global minimum:*

There exist $\varepsilon_0, \tau_0 > 0$ and a universal constant $c > 0$ such that if a point x satisfies $\|\nabla f(x)\|_2 \leq \varepsilon \leq \varepsilon_0$ and $\nabla^2 f(x) \succeq -\tau_0 \cdot I$, then x is ε^c-close to a global minimum of f.

Then, many optimization algorithms (including stochastic gradient descent and cubic regularization), can find a global minimum of f up to δ error in ℓ_2 norm in domain in time $poly(1/\delta, 1/\tau_0, d)$.

The technical condition of the theorem is often succinctly referred to as "all local minima are global," but its precise form, which is a combination of "all local minima are global" and the strict saddle condition, is crucial. There are functions that satisfy "all local minima are global" but cannot be optimized efficiently. Ignoring the strict saddle condition may lead to misleadingly strong statements.

The condition of Theorem 21.3 can be replaced by stronger ones that may occasionally be easier to verify, if they are indeed true for the functions of interests. One such condition is that "any stationary point is a global minimum." The gradient descent is known to converge to a global minimum linearly, as stated in Theorem 21.4. However, because this condition effectively rules out the existence of multiple disconnected local minima, it can't hold for many objective functions related to neural networks, which guarantees to have multiple local minima and stationary points due to a certain symmetry.

Theorem 21.4 *Suppose a function f has L-Lipschitz continuous gradients and satisfies the Polyak–Lojasiewicz condition: $\exists \mu > 0$ and x^* such that for every x,*

$$\|\nabla f(x)\|_2^2 \geq \mu(f(x) - f(x^*)) \geq 0. \tag{21.2}$$

Then, the errors of gradient descent with step size less than $1/(2L)$ decay geometrically.

It can be challenging to verify the Polyak–Lojasiewicz condition because the quantity $\|\nabla f(x)\|_2^2$ is often a complex function of x. An easier-to-verify but stronger condition is the quasi-convexity. Intuitively speaking, quasi-convexity says that at any point x the gradient should be negatively correlated with the direction $x^* - x$ pointing toward the optimum.

Definition 21.5 (Weak Quasi-convexity) We say an objective function f is τ-*weakly quasi-convex* over a domain $\mathcal{B}$ with respect to the global minimum x^* if there is a positive constant $\tau > 0$ such that for all $x \in \mathcal{B}$,

$$\nabla f(x)^\top (x - x^*) \geq \tau(f(x) - f(x^*)). \tag{21.3}$$

The following one is another related condition, which is sometimes referred to as the restricted secant inequality (RSI):

$$\nabla f(x)^\top (x - x^*) \geq \tau \|x - x^*\|_2^2. \tag{21.4}$$

We note that convex functions satisfy (21.3) with $\tau = 1$. Condition (21.4) is stronger than (21.3) because for smooth function, we have $\|x - x^*\|_2^2 \geq L(f(x) - f(x^*))$ for some constant L.[2] Conditions (21.2), (21.3), and (21.4) all imply that all stationary points are global minimum because $\nabla f(x) = 0$ implies that $f(x) = f(x^*)$ or $x = x^*$.

21.2.3 Landscape for Manifold-Constrained Optimization

We can extend many of the results in the previous section to the setting of constrained optimization over a smooth manifold. This section is useful only for problems in Section 21.5 and casual readers can feel free to skip it.

Let $\mathcal{M}$ be a Riemannian manifold. Let $T_x\mathcal{M}$ be the tangent space to $\mathcal{M}$ at x, and let P_x be the projection operator to the tangent space $T_x\mathcal{M}$. Let $\operatorname{grad} f(x) \in T_x\mathcal{M}$ be the gradient of f at x on $\mathcal{M}$ and $\operatorname{Hess} f(x)$ be the Riemannian Hessian. Note that $\operatorname{Hess} f(x)$ is a linear mapping from $T_x\mathcal{M}$ onto itself.

Theorem 21.6 (Informal) *Consider the constrained optimization problem* $\min_{x \sim \mathcal{M}} f(x)$. *Under proper regularity conditions, Theorems 21.2 and 21.3 still hold when replacing ∇f and $\nabla^2 f$ by $\operatorname{grad} f$ and $\operatorname{Hess} f$, respectively.*

Backgrounds on Manifold Gradient and Hessian. Later in Section 21.5, the unit sphere in d-dimensional space will be our constraint set, that is, $\mathcal{M} = S^{d-1}$. We provide some further background on how to compute the manifold gradients and Hessian here. We view f as the restriction of a smooth function $\bar{f}$ to the manifold $\mathcal{M}$. In this case, we have $T_x\mathcal{M} = \{z \in \mathbb{R}^d : z^\top x = 0\}$, and $P_x = I - xx^\top$. We derive the manifold gradient of f on $\mathcal{M}$: $\operatorname{grad} f(x) = P_x \nabla \bar{f}(x)$, where ∇ is the usual gradient in the ambient space $\mathbb{R}^d$. Moreover, we derive the Riemannian Hessian as $\operatorname{Hess} f(x) = P_x \nabla^2 \bar{f}(x) P_x - (x^\top \nabla \bar{f}(x)) P_x$.

21.3 Generalized Linear Models

We consider the problem of learning a *generalized linear model* and we will show that the loss function for it will be nonconvex, but all of its local minima are global. Suppose we observe n data points $\{(x_i, y_i)\}_{i=1}^n$, where x_i's are sampled i.i.d. from some distribution D_x over $\mathbb{R}^d$. In the generalized linear model, we assume the label $y_i \in \mathbb{R}$ is generated from

$$y_i = \sigma(w_\star^\top x_i) + \varepsilon_i,$$

where $\sigma : \mathbb{R} \to \mathbb{R}$ is a known monotone activation function, $\varepsilon_i \in \mathbb{R}$ are i.i.d. mean-zero noise (independent with x_i), and $w_\star \in \mathbb{R}^d$ is a fixed unknown ground truth coefficent vector. We denote the joint distribution of (x_i, y_i) by D.

---

[2] Readers who are familiar with convex optimization may realize that condition (21.4) is an extension of strong convexity.

Our goal is to recover approximately $w_\star$ from the data. We minimize the empirical squared risk: $\widehat{L}(w) = \frac{1}{2n} \sum_{i=1}^{n} (y_i - \sigma(w^\top x_i))^2$. Let $L(w)$ be the corresponding population risk: $L(w) = \frac{1}{2} \mathbb{E}_{(x,y) \sim D} [(y - \sigma(w^\top x))^2]$.

We will analyze the optimization of $\widehat{L}$ via characterizing the property of its landscape. Our road map consists of two parts: (1) all the local minima of the population risk are global minima; and (2) the empirical risk $\widehat{L}$ has the same property.

When σ is the identity function, that is, $\sigma(t) = t$, we have the linear regression problem and the loss function is convex. In practice, people have taken σ, e.g., to be the sigmoid function and then the objective $\widehat{L}$ is no longer convex.

Throughout the rest of the section, we make the following regularity assumptions on the problem. These assumptions are stronger than what's necessary, for the ease of exposition. However, we note that some assumptions on the data are necessary because in the worst case, the problem is intractable (e.g., the generative assumption (21.4) on y_i's is a key one).

Assumption 21.7 We assume the distribution D_x and activation σ satisfy that

1. The vectors x_i are bounded and nondegenerate: D_x is supported in the ball $\{x : \|x\|_2 \leq B\}$, and $\mathbb{E}_{x \sim D_x}[xx^\top] \succeq \lambda I$ for some $\lambda > 0$, where I is the identity.
2. The ground truth coefficient vector satisfies $\|w_\star\|_2 \leq R$, and $BR \geq 1$.
3. The activation function σ is strictly increasing and twice differentiable. Furthermore, it satisfies the bounds

$$\sigma(t) \in [0,1], \quad \sup_{t \in \mathbb{R}} \{|\sigma'(t)|, |\sigma''(t)|\} \leq 1, \quad \text{and} \quad \inf_{t \in [-BR, BR]} \sigma'(t) \geq \gamma > 0.$$

4. The noise ε_i's are mean zero and bounded: With probability 1, we have $|\varepsilon_i| \leq 1$.

21.3.1 Analysis of the Population Risk

In this section, we show that all the local minima of the population risk $L(w)$ are global minima. In fact, $L(w)$ has a unique local minimum that is also global. (But still, $L(w)$ may likely be not convex for many choices of σ.)

Theorem 21.8 *The objective $L(\cdot)$ has a unique local minimum, which is equal to $w_\star$ and is also a global minimum. In particular, $L(\cdot)$ is weakly quasi-convex.*

The proof follows from directly checking the definition of the quasi-convexity. The intuition is that generalized linear models behave very similarly to linear models from the lens of quasi-convexity: Many steps of the inequalities of the proof involve replacing σ by an identity function effectively (or replacing σ' by 1).

Proof Sketch Using the property that $\mathbb{E}[y|x] = \sigma(w_\star^\top x)$, we have the following bias-variance decomposition (which can be derived by elementary manipulation):

$$L(w) = \frac{1}{2} \mathbb{E}[(y - \sigma(w^\top x))^2] = \frac{1}{2} \mathbb{E}[(y - \sigma(w_\star^\top x))^2] + \frac{1}{2} \mathbb{E}[(\sigma(w_\star^\top x) - \sigma(w^\top x))^2].$$

$$\text{(21.5)}$$

The first term is independent of w, and the second term is nonnegative and equals zero at $w = w_\star$. Therefore, we see that $w_\star$ is a global minimum of $L(w)$.

Towards proving that $L(\cdot)$ is quasi-convex, we first compute $\nabla L(w)$:

$$\nabla L(w) = \mathbb{E}[(\sigma(w^\top x) - y)\sigma'(w^\top x)x] = \mathbb{E}[(\sigma(w^\top x) - \sigma(w_\star^\top x))\sigma'(w^\top x)x],$$

where the last equality used the fact that $\mathbb{E}[y|x] = \sigma(w_\star^\top x)$. It follows that

$$\langle \nabla L(w), w - w_\star \rangle = \mathbb{E}[(\sigma(w^\top x) - \sigma(w_\star^\top x))\sigma'(w^\top x)\langle w - w_\star, x \rangle].$$

Now, by the mean value theorem, and bullet 3 of Assumption 21.7, we have that

$$(\sigma(w^\top x) - \sigma(w_\star^\top x))\langle w - w_\star, x \rangle \geq \gamma(w^\top x - w_\star^\top x)^2.$$

Using $|\sigma'(t)| \geq \gamma$ and $|\sigma'(t)| \leq 1$ for every $|t| \leq BR$, and the monotonicity of σ,

$$\begin{aligned}
\langle \nabla L(w), w - w_\star \rangle &= \mathbb{E}[(\sigma(w^\top x) - \sigma(w_\star^\top x))\sigma'(w^\top x)\langle w - w_\star, x \rangle] \\
&\geq \gamma \mathbb{E}[(\sigma(w^\top x) - \sigma(w_\star^\top x))(w^\top x - w_\star^\top x)] \quad (21.6) \\
&\geq \gamma \mathbb{E}[(\sigma(w^\top x) - \sigma(w_\star^\top x))^2] \geq 2\gamma(L(w) - L(w_\star))
\end{aligned}$$

where the last step uses the decomposition (21.5) of the risk $L(w)$. $\qquad\square$

21.3.2 Concentration of the Empirical Risk

We next analyze the empirical risk $\widehat{L}(w)$. We will show that with sufficiently many examples, the empirical risk $\widehat{L}$ is close enough to the population risk L so that $\widehat{L}$ also satisfies that all local minima are global.

Theorem 21.9 (The empirical risk has no bad local minimum) *Under the problem assumptions, with probability at least $1 - \delta$, for all w with $\|w\|_2 \leq R$, the empirical risk has no local minima outside a small neighborhood of $w_\star$: For any w such that $\|w\|_2 \leq R$, if $\nabla \widehat{L}(w) = 0$, then*

$$\|w - w_\star\|_2 \leq \frac{C_1 B}{\gamma^2 \lambda} \sqrt{\frac{d(C_2 + \log(nBR)) + \log\frac{1}{\delta}}{n}},$$

where $C_1, C_2 > 0$ are universal constants that do not depend on (B, R, d, n, δ).

Theorem 21.9 shows that all stationary points of $\widehat{L}(w)$ have to be within a small neighborhood of $w_\star$. Stronger landscape property can also be proved though: There is a unique local minimum in the neighborhood of $w_\star$.

The main intuition is that to verify quasi-convexity or restricted secant inequality for $\widehat{L}$, it suffices to show that with high probability over the randomness of the data, $\forall w$ with $\|w\|_2 \leq R$

$$\langle \nabla L(w), w - w_\star \rangle \approx \langle \nabla \widehat{L}(w), w - w_\star \rangle. \quad (21.7)$$

Various tools to prove such concentration inequalities have been developed in statistical learning theory and probability theory community, and a thorough exposition of them is beyond the scope of this chapter.

21.4 Matrix Factorization Problems

In this section, we will discuss the optimization landscape of two problems based on matrix factorization: principal component analysis (PCA) and matrix completion. The fundamental difference between them and the generalized linear models is that their objective functions have saddle points that are *not* local minima or global minima. It means that the quasi-convexity condition or Polyak–Lojasiewicz condition does not hold for these objectives. Thus, we need more sophisticated techniques that can distinguish saddle points from local minima.

21.4.1 Principal Component Analysis

One interpretation of PCA is approximating a matrix by its best low-rank approximation. Given a matrix $M \in \mathbb{R}^{d_1 \times d_2}$, we aim to find its best rank-r approximation (in either Frobenius norm or spectral norm). For the ease of exposition, we take $r = 1$ and assume M to be symmetric positive semidefinite with dimension d by d. In this case, the best rank-1 approximation has the form $xx^\top$ where $x \in \mathbb{R}^d$.

There are many well-known algorithms for finding the low-rank factor x. We are particularly interested in the following nonconvex program that directly minimizes the approximation error in Frobenius norm:

$$\min_x \ g(x) := \frac{1}{2} \cdot \|M - xx^\top\|_F^2. \tag{21.8}$$

We will prove that even though g is not convex, all the local minima of g are global, and g also satisfies the strict saddle property. Therefore, local search algorithms can solve (21.8) in polynomial time.[3]

Theorem 21.10 *In the preceding setting, all the local minima of the objective function $g(x)$ are global minima.*[4]

Our analysis consists of two main steps: (1) to characterize all the stationary points of the function g, which turn out to be the eigenvectors of M; and (2) to examine each of the stationary points and show that only the top eigenvector(s) of g can be a local minimum. Step (2) implies the theorem because the top eigenvectors are also global minima of g. We start with step (1) with the following lemma.

Lemma 21.11 *In the setting of Theorem 21.10, all the stationary points of the objective $g()$ are the eigenvectors of M. Moreover, if x is a stationary point, then $\|x\|_2^2$ is the eigenvalue corresponding to x.*

Proof By elementary calculus, we have that

$$\nabla g(x) = -(M - xx^\top)x = \|x\|_2^2 \cdot x - Mx. \tag{21.9}$$

---

[3] In fact, local methods can solve it very quickly. See, e.g., Thereom 1.2 in Li et al. (2018).
[4] The function g also satisfies the (α, β, γ)-strict-saddle property (Definition 21.1) with some $\alpha, \beta, \gamma > 0$ (that may depend on M). We skip the proof of this result for simplicity.

Therefore, if x is a stationary point of g, then $Mx = \|x\|_2^2 \cdot x$, which implies that x is an eigenvector of M with eigenvalue equal to $\|x\|_2^2$. □

Now we are ready to prove (2) and the theorem. The key intuition is the following. Suppose we are at a point x that is an eigenvector but not the top eigenvector; moving in either the top eigenvector direction v_1 or the direction of $-v_1$ will result in a second-order local improvement of the objective function. Therefore, x cannot be a local minimum unless x is a top eigenvector.

Proof of Theorem 21.10 By Lemma 21.11, we know that a local minimum x is an eigenvector of M. If x is a top eigenvector of M with the largest eigenvalue, then x is a global minimum. For the sake of contradiction, we assume that x is an eigenvector with eigenvalue λ that is strictly less than λ_1. By Lemma 21.11 we have $\lambda = \|x\|_2^2$. By elementary calculation, we have that

$$\nabla^2 g(x) = 2xx^\top - M + \|x\|_2^2 \cdot I. \tag{21.10}$$

Let v_1 be the top eigenvector of M with eigenvalue λ_1 and with ℓ_2 norm 1. Then, because $\nabla^2 g(x) \succeq 0$, we have that

$$v_1^\top \nabla^2 g(x) v \geq 0. \tag{21.11}$$

It's a basic property of eigenvectors of positive semidefinite matrix that any pairs of eigenvectors with different eigenvalues are orthogonal to each other. Thus we have $\langle x, v_1 \rangle = 0$. It follows Equations (21.11) and (21.10) that

$$0 \leq v_1^\top (2xx^\top - M + \|x\|_2^2 \cdot I) v_1 = \|x\|_2^2 - v_1^\top M v_1 \qquad \text{(by } \langle x, v_1 \rangle = 0)$$
$$= \lambda - \lambda_1 \qquad \text{(because } v_1 \text{ has eigenvalue } \lambda_1 \text{ and } \lambda = \|x\|_2^2)$$
$$< 0, \qquad \text{(by the assumption)}$$

which is a contradiction. □

21.4.2 Matrix Completion

Matrix completion is the problem of recovering a low-rank matrix from partially observed entries, which has been widely used in collaborative filtering and recommender systems, dimension reduction, and multiclass learning. Despite the existence of elegant convex relaxation solutions, stochastic gradient descent on nonconvex objectives are widely adopted in practice for scalability. We will focus on the rank-1 symmetric matrix completion in this chapter, which demonstrates the essence of the analysis.

Rank-1 Case of Matrix Completion
Let $M = zz^\top$ be a rank-1 symmetric matrix with factor $z \in \mathbb{R}^d$ that we aim to recover. We assume that we observe each entry of M with probability p independently.[5] Let $\Omega \subset [d] \times [d]$ be the set of entries observed.

---

[5] Technically, because M is symmetric, the entries at (i, j) and (j, i) are the same. Thus, we assume that, with probability p we observe both entries and otherwise we observe neither.

Our goal is to recover from the observed entries of M the vector z up to sign flip (which is equivalent to recovering M).

A known issue with matrix completion is that if M is "aligned" with standard basis, then it's impossible to recover it. For example, when $M = e_j e_j^\top$ where e_j is the jth standard basis, we will very likely observe only entries with value zero, because M is sparse. Such scenarios do not happen in practice very often though. The following standard assumption will rule out these difficult and pathological cases:

Assumption 21.12 (Incoherence) without loss of generality, we assume that $\|z\|_2 = 1$. In addition, we assume that z satisfies $\|z\|_\infty \le \frac{\mu}{\sqrt{d}}$. We will think of μ as a small constant or logarithmic in d, and the sample complexity will depend polynomially on it.

In this setting, the vector z can be recovered exactly up to a sign flip provided $\widetilde{\Omega}(d)$ samples. However, for simplicity, in this subsection we aim only to recover z with an ℓ_2 norm error $\epsilon \ll 1$. We assume that $p = \text{poly}(\mu, \log d)/(d\epsilon)$, which means that the expected number of observations is on the order of $d/\epsilon \cdot \text{polylog } d$. We analyze the following objective that minimizes the total squared errors on the observed entries:

$$\text{argmin}_x f(x) := \frac{1}{2} \sum_{(i,j)\in\Omega} (M_{ij} - x_i x_j)^2 = \frac{1}{2} \cdot \|P_\Omega(M - xx^\top)\|_F^2. \tag{21.12}$$

Here $P_\Omega(A)$ denotes the matrix obtained by zeroing out all the entries of A that are not in Ω. For simplicity, we only focus on characterizing the landscape of the objective in the following domain $\mathcal{B}$ of incoherent vectors that contain the ground-truth vector z (with a buffer of factor of 2):

$$\mathcal{B} = \left\{ x : \|x\|_\infty < \frac{2\mu}{\sqrt{d}} \right\}. \tag{21.13}$$

We note that the analyzing the landscape inside $\mathcal{B}$ does not suffice because the iterates of the algorithms may leave the set $\mathcal{B}$. We refer the readers to the original paper (Ge et al., 2016) for an analysis of the landscape over the entire space.

The global minima of $f(\cdot)$ are z and $-z$ with function value 0. In the rest of the section, we prove that all the local minima of $f(\cdot)$ are $O(\sqrt{\varepsilon})$-close to $\pm z$.[6]

Theorem 21.13 *In the aforementioned setting, there are only two local mimina of the function $f(\cdot)$ inside the set $\mathcal{B}$. They are $O(\sqrt{\varepsilon})$-close to $\pm z$.*

It's insightful to compare with the full observation case when $\Omega = [d] \times [d]$. The corresponding objective is exactly the PCA objective $g(x) = \frac{1}{2} \cdot \|M - xx^\top\|_F^2$ defined in Equation (21.8). Observe that $f(x)$ is a sampled version of the $g(x)$, and therefore we expect that they share the same geometric properties. In particular, recall that $g(x)$ does not have spurious local minima and thus we expect neither does $f(x)$.

---

[6] It's also true that the only local minima are exactly $\pm z$, and that f has strict saddle property. However, their proofs are involved and beyond the scope of this chapter.

However, its nontrivial to extend the proof of Theorem 21.10 to the case of partial observation, because it uses the *properties of eigenvectors* heavily. Indeed, suppose we imitate the proof of Theorem 21.10, we will first compute the gradient of $f(\cdot)$:

$$\nabla f(x) = P_\Omega(zz^\top - xx^\top)x. \tag{21.14}$$

Then, we run into an immediate difficulty – how shall we solve the equation for stationary points $f(x) = P_\Omega(M - xx^\top)x = 0$? Moreover, even if we could have a reasonable approximation for the stationary points, it would be difficult to examine their Hessians without using the exact orthogonality of the eigenvectors.

The lesson from this discussion is that we may need to have an alternative proof for the PCA objective (full observation) that relies less on solving the stationary points exactly. Then more likely the proof can be extended to the matrix completion (partial observation) case. In the sequel, we follow this plan by first providing an alternative proof for Theorem 21.10, which does not require solving the equation $\nabla g(x) = 0$, and then extend it via concentration inequality to a proof of Theorem 21.13. The key intuition is:

Proofs that consist of inequalities that are linear in $\mathbf{1}_\Omega$ are often easily generalizable to partial observation case.

Here statements that are linear in $\mathbf{1}_\Omega$ mean the statements of the form $\sum_{ij} \mathbf{1}_{(i,j)\in\Omega} T_{ij} \le a$. We will call these kinds of proofs "simple" proofs in this section. Indeed, by the law of large numbers, when the sampling probability p is sufficiently large, we have that

$$\underbrace{\sum_{(i,j)\in\Omega} T_{ij}}_{\text{partial observation}} = \sum_{i,j} \mathbf{1}_{(i,j)\in\Omega} T_{ij} \approx p \underbrace{\sum_{i,j} T_{ij}}_{\text{full observation}}. \tag{21.15}$$

Then, the mathematical implications of $p\sum T_{ij} \le a$ are expected to be similar to the implications of $\sum_{(i,j)\in\Omega} T_{ij} \le a/p$, up to some small error introduced by the approximation. More precisely, we will use concentration inequalities such as the following theorem:

Theorem 21.14 *Let $\epsilon > 0$ and $p = poly(\mu, \log d)/(d\varepsilon)$. Then, with high probability of the randomness of Ω, we have that for all $A = uu^\top, B = vv^\top \in \mathbb{R}^{d\times d}$, where $\|u\|_2 \le 1, \|v\|_2 \le 1$ and $\|u\|_\infty, \|v\|_\infty \le 2\mu/\sqrt{d}$.*

$$|\langle P_\Omega(A), B\rangle - p\langle A, B\rangle| \le p\epsilon. \tag{21.16}$$

We will provide two claims in the text that follows, the combination of which proves Theorem 21.10. In the proofs of these two claims, all the inequalities are of the form of the left-hand side of Equation (21.15). Following each claim, we will immediately provide its extension to the partial observation case.

Claim 1f Suppose $x \in \mathcal{B}$ satisfies $\nabla g(x) = 0$, then $\langle x, z\rangle^2 = \|x\|_2^4$.

Proof By elementary calculation

$$\nabla g(x) = (zz^\top - xx^\top)x = 0$$
$$\Rightarrow \langle x, \nabla g(x) \rangle = \langle x, (zz^\top - xx^\top)x \rangle = 0 \tag{21.17}$$
$$\Rightarrow \langle x, z \rangle^2 = \|x\|_2^4.$$

Intuitively, a stationary point x's norm is governed by its correlation with z. □

The following claim is the counterpart of Claim 1f in the partial observation case.

Claim 1p Suppose $x \in B$ satisfies $\nabla f(x) = 0$, then $\langle x, z \rangle^2 = \|x\|^4 - \varepsilon$.

Proof Imitating the proof of Claim 1f,

$$\nabla f(x) = P_\Omega(zz^\top - xx^\top)x = 0$$
$$\Rightarrow \langle x, \nabla f(x) \rangle = \langle x, P_\Omega(zz^\top - xx^\top)x \rangle = 0 \tag{21.18}$$
$$\Rightarrow \langle x, \nabla g(x) \rangle = |\langle x, (zz^\top - xx^\top)x \rangle| \le \epsilon \tag{21.19}$$
$$\Rightarrow \langle x, z \rangle^2 \ge \|x\|^4 - \varepsilon,$$

where derivation from line (21.18) to (21.19) follows the fact that line (21.18) is a sampled version of (21.19). Technically, we can obtain it by applying Theorem 21.9 twice with $A = B = xx^\top$ and $A = xx^\top$ and $B = zz^\top$ respectively. □

Claim 2f If $x \in B$ has positive Hessian $\nabla^2 g(x) \succeq 0$, then $\|x\|^2 \ge 1/3$.

Proof By the assumption on x, we have that $\langle z, \nabla^2 g(x)z \rangle \ge 0$. Calculating the quadratic form of the Hessian (which can be done by elementary calculus and is skipped for simplicity), we have

$$\langle z, \nabla^2 g(x)z \rangle = \|zx^\top + xz^\top\|_F^2 - 2z^\top(zz^\top - xx^\top)z \ge 0. \tag{21.20}$$

This implies that

$$\Rightarrow \|x\|^2 + 2\langle z, x \rangle^2 \ge 1$$
$$\Rightarrow \|x\|^2 \ge 1/3 \qquad \text{(since } \langle z, x \rangle^2 \le \|x\|^2\text{).} \quad □$$

Claim 2p If $x \in B$ has positive Hessian $\nabla^2 f(x) \succeq 0$, then $\|x\|^2 \ge 1/3 - \varepsilon$.

Proof Imitating the proof of Claim 2f, calculating the quadratic form over the Hessian at z, we have

$$\langle z, \nabla^2 f(x)z \rangle = \|P_\Omega(zx^\top + xz^\top)\|_F^2 - 2z^\top P_\Omega(zz^\top - xx^\top)z \ge 0. \tag{21.21}$$

Note that Equation is just a sampled version of Equation (21.20), applying Theorem 21.14 for various times (and note that $\langle P_{Omega}(A), P_\Omega(B)\rangle = \langle P_\Omega(A), B\rangle$, we can obtain that

$$\|P_\Omega(zx^\top + xz^\top)\|_F^2 - 2z^\top P_\Omega(zz^\top - xx^\top)z$$
$$= p \cdot \left(\|zx^\top + xz^\top\|_F^2 - 2z^\top(zz^\top - xx^\top)z \pm O(\epsilon)\right).$$

Then following the derivation in the proof of Claim 2f, we achieve the same conclusion of Claim 2f up to approximation: $\|x\|^2 \geq 1/3 - \varepsilon$. $\qquad\square$

With these claims, we are ready to prove Theorem 21.10 (again) and Theorem 21.13.

Proof of Theorem 21.10 (again) and Theorem 21.13 By Claims 1f and 2f, we have x satisfies $\langle x, z\rangle^2 \geq \|x\|^4 \geq 1/9$. Moreover, we have that $\nabla g(x) = 0$ implies

$$\langle z, \nabla g(x)\rangle = \langle z, (zz^\top - xx^\top)x\rangle = 0 \qquad (21.22)$$
$$\Rightarrow \langle x, z\rangle(1 - \|x\|^2) = 0$$
$$\Rightarrow \|x\|^2 = 1. \qquad \text{(by } \langle x, z\rangle^2 \geq 1/9\text{)}$$

Then by Claim 1f again we obtain $\langle x, z\rangle^2 = 1$, and therefore $x = \pm z$. The proof of Theorem 21.13 is analogous (and note that such analogy was by design.) $\quad\square$

21.5 Landscape of Tensor Decomposition

In this section, we analyze the optimization landscape for another machine learning problem, tensor decomposition. The fundamental difference of tensor decomposition from matrix factorization problems or generalized linear models is that the nonconvex objective function here has multiple isolated local minima, and therefore the set of local minima does not have rotational invariance (whereas in matrix completion or PCA, the set of local minima is rotation-invariant). This essentially prevents us to only use linear algebraic techniques, because they are intrinsically rotational invariant.

21.5.1 Nonconvex Optimization for Orthogonal Tensor Decomposition and Global Optimality

We focus on one of the simplest tensor decomposition problems, orthogonal fourth-order tensor decomposition. Suppose we are given the entries of a symmetric fourth-order tensor $T \in \mathbb{R}^{d\times d\times d\times d}$ that has a low-rank structure in the sense that

$$T = \sum_{i=1}^{n} a_i \otimes a_i \otimes a_i \otimes a_i, \qquad (21.23)$$

where $a_1, \ldots, a_n \in \mathbb{R}^d$. Our goal is to recover the underlying components $a_1, \ldots, a_n$. We assume in this subsection that $a_1, \ldots, a_n$ are orthogonal vectors in $\mathbb{R}^d$ with unit norm (and thus implicitly we assume $n \leq d$.) Consider the objective function

$$\text{argmax } f(x) := \langle T, x^{\otimes 4} \rangle \qquad (21.24)$$
$$\text{s.t. } \|x\|_2^2 = 1.$$

The optimal value function for the objective is the (symmetric) injective norm of a tensor T. In our case, the global maximizers of the objective in (21.24) are exactly the set of components that we are looking for.

Theorem 21.15 *Suppose T satisfies Equation (21.23) with orthonormal components $a_1, \ldots, a_n$. Then, the global maximizers of the objective function (21.24) are exactly $\pm a_1, \ldots, \pm a_n$.*

21.5.2 All Local Optima Are Global

We next show that all the local maxima of the objective (21.24) are also global maxima. In other words, we will show that $\pm a_1, \ldots, \pm a_n$ are the only local maxima. We note that all the geometry properties here are defined with respect to the manifold of the unit sphere $\mathcal{M} = S^{d-1}$. (Please see Section 21.2.3 for a brief introduction of the notions of manifold gradient, manifold local maxima, etc.)

Theorem 21.16 *In the same setting of Theorem 21.15, all the local maxima (w.r.t the manifold S^{d-1}) of the objective (21.24) are global maxima.*[7]

Toward proving Theorem 21.16, we first note that the landscape property of a function is invariant to the coordinate system that we use to represent it. It's natural for us to use the directions of $a_1, \ldots, a_n$ together with an arbitrary basis in the complement subspace of $a_1, \ldots, a_n$ as the coordinate system. A more convenient viewpoint is that this choice of coordinate system is equivalent to assuming $a_1, \ldots, a_n$ are the natural standard basis $e_1, \ldots, e_n$. Moreover, one can verify that the remaining directions $e_{n+1}, \ldots, e_d$ are irrelevant for the objective because it's not economical to put any mass in those directions. Therefore, for simplicity of the proof, we make the following assumption without loss of generality:

$$n = d, \text{ and } a_i = e_i, \forall i \in [n]. \qquad (21.25)$$

Then we have that $f(x) = \|x\|_4^4$. We compute the manifold gradient and manifold Hessian using the formulas of $\text{grad} f(x)$ and $\text{Hess} f(x)$ in Section 21.2.3,

$$\text{grad} f(x) = 4P_x \nabla \bar{f}(x) = 4(I_{d \times d} - xx^\top)\begin{bmatrix} x_1^3 \\ \vdots \\ x_d^3 \end{bmatrix} = 4\begin{bmatrix} x_1^3 \\ \vdots \\ x_d^3 \end{bmatrix} - 4\|x\|_4^4 \cdot \begin{bmatrix} x_1 \\ \vdots \\ x_d \end{bmatrix}. \quad (21.26)$$

$$\text{Hess} f(x) = P_x \nabla^2 \bar{f}(x) P_x - (x^\top \nabla \bar{f}(x)) P_x$$
$$= P_x \big(12 \text{diag}(x_1^2, \ldots, x_d^2) - 4\|x\|_4^4 \cdot I_{d \times d}\big) P_x, \qquad (21.27)$$

---

[7] The function also satisfies the strict saddle property so that we can rigorously invoke Theorem 21.6. However, we skip the proof of that for simplicity.

where diag(v) for a vector $v \in \mathbb{R}^d$ denotes the diagonal matrix with $v_1, \ldots, v_d$ on the diagonal. Now we are ready to prove Theorem 21.16. In the proof, we will first compute all the stationary points of the objective and then examine each of them and show that only $\pm a_1, \ldots, \pm a_n$ can be local maxima.

Proof of Theorem 21.16 We work under the foregoing assumptions and simplifications. We first compute all the stationary points of the objective (21.24) by solving grad $f = 0$. Using Equation (21.26), we have that the stationary points satisfy that

$$x_i^3 = \|x\|_4^4 \cdot x_i, \forall i. \tag{21.28}$$

It follows that $x_i = 0$ or $x_i = \pm \|x\|_4^{1/2}$. Assume that s of the x_i's are nonzero and thus take the second choice; we have that

$$1 = \|x\|_2^2 = s \cdot \|x\|_4^4, \tag{21.29}$$

This implies that $\|x\|_4^4 = 1/s$, and $x_i = 0$ or $\pm 1/s^{1/2}$. In other words, all the stationary points of f are of the form $(\pm 1/s^{1/2}, \ldots, \pm 1/s^{1/2}, 0, \ldots, 0)$ (where there are s nonzeros) for some $s \in [d]$ and all their permutations (over indices).

Next, we examine which of these stationary points are local maxima. Let $\tau = 1/s^{1/2}$ for simplicity. This implies that $\|x\|_4^4 = \tau^2$. Consider a stationary point $x = (\sigma_1 \tau, \ldots, \sigma_s \tau, 0, \ldots, 0)$, where $\sigma_i \in \{-1, 1\}$. Let x be a local maximum. Thus Hess $f(X) \preceq 0$. We will prove that this implies $s = 1$. For the sake of contradiction, we assume $s \geq 2$. We will show that the Hessian cannot be negative semidefinite by finding a particular direction in which the Hessian has positive quadratic form.

The form of Equation (21.27) implies that for all v such that $\langle v, x \rangle = 0$ (which indicates that $P_x v = v$), we have

$$v^\top \big((12 \operatorname{diag}(x_1^2, \ldots, x_d^2) - 4\|x\|_4^4 I) v \leq 0. \tag{21.30}$$

We take $v = (1/2, -1/2)$ to be our test direction. Then left-hand side of Equation (21.30) simplifies to

$$3x_1^2 - 3x_2^2 - 2\|x\|_4^4 = 6\tau^2 - 2\|x\|_4^4 = 4\tau^2 > 0, \tag{21.31}$$

which contradicts Equation (21.30). Therefore, $s = 1$, and we conclude that all the local maxima are $\pm e_1 \ldots, \pm e_d$. $\qquad \square$

21.6 Survey and Outlook: Optimization of Neural Networks

Theoretical analysis of algorithms for learning neural networks is highly challenging. We still lack handy mathematical tools. We will articulate a few technical challenges and summarize the attempts and progress.

We follow the standard setup in supervised learning. Let f_θ be a neural network parameterized by parameters θ.[8] Let ℓ be the loss function, and $\{(x^{(i)}, y^{(i)})\}_{i=1}^n$ be

---

[8] For example, a two-layer neural network would be $f_\theta(x) = W_1 \sigma(W_2 x)$, where $\theta = (W_1, W_2)$ and σ are some activation functions.

a set of i.i.d examples drawn from distribution D. The empirical risk is $\widehat{L}(\theta) = \frac{1}{n} \sum_{i=1}^{n} \ell(f_\theta(x^{(i)}), y^{(i)})$, and the population risk is $L(\theta) = \mathbb{E}_{(x,y) \sim D}[\ell(f_\theta(x), y)]$.

The major challenge of analyzing the landscape property of $\widehat{L}$ or L stems from the nonlinearity of neural networks – $f_\theta(x)$ is neither linear in x, nor in θ. As a consequence, $\widehat{L}$ and L are not convex in θ. Linear algebra is at odds with neural networks – a neural network does not have good invariance properties with respect to rotations of parameters or data points.

Linearized Neural Networks Early works for optimization in deep learning simplify the problem by considering linearized neural networks: f_θ is assumed to be a neural network without any activation functions. For example, $f_\theta = W_1 W_2 W_3 x$ with $\theta = (W_1, W_2, W_3)$ would be a three-layer feedforward linearized neural network. Now, the model f_θ is still not linear in θ, but it's linear in x. This simplification maintains the property that $\widehat{L}$ or L is still nonconvex function in θ, but allows the use of linear algebraic tools to analyze the optimization landscapes of $\widehat{L}$ or L.

Baldi and Hornik (1989) and Kawaguchi (2016) show that all the local minima of $L(\theta)$ are global minima when ℓ is the squared loss and f_θ is a linearized feed-forward neural network (but $L(\theta)$ does have degenerate saddle points so that it does not satisfy the strict saddle property). Hardt et al. (2018) and Hardt and Ma (2016) analyzed the landscape of learning linearized residual and recurrent neural networks and showed that all the stationary points (in a region) are global minima. We refer the readers to Arora et al. (2018) and references therein for some recent works along this line.

There are various results on another simplification: neural networks with quadratic activation functions with two hidden layers. In this case, the model $f_\theta(x)$ is linear in $x \otimes x$ and quadratic in the parameters, and linear algebraic techniques allow us to obtain relatively strong theory. See Li et al. (2018), Soltanolkotabi et al. (2018), Du and Lee (2018) and references therein.

Changing the Landscape, by, e.g., Over-parameterization Somewhat in contrast to the clean case covered in earlier sections of this chapter, people have empirically found that the landscape properties of neural networks depend on various factors including the loss function, the model parameterization, and the data distribution. In particular, changing the model parameterization and the loss functions properly could ease the optimization.

An effective approach to changing the landscape is to over-parameterize the neural networks – using a large number of parameters by enlarging the width, often not necessary for expressivity and often bigger than the total number of training samples. It has been empirically found that wider neural networks may alleviate the problem of bad local minima that may occur in training narrower nets. This motivates numerous studies on the optimization landscape of over-parameterized neural networks. Please see Safran and Shamir (2016), Venturi et al. (2018), Soudry and Carmon (2016), Haeffele and Vidal (2015) and the references therein.

Two extremely empirically successful approaches in deep learning, residual neural networks (He et al., 2016) and batch normalization (Ioffe and Szegedy, 2015), are both conjectured to be able to change the landscape of the training objectives and lead to easier optimization. This is an interesting and promising direction with the potential of circumventing certain mathematical difficulties, but existing works often suffer from strong assumptions such as the linearized assumption in Hardt and Ma (2017) and the Gaussian data distribution assumption in Ge et al. (2017).

Connection Between Over-parameterized Model and Kernel Method: The Neural Tangent Kernel (NTK) View Another recent line of work studied the optimization dynamics of learning over-parameterized neural networks (instead of characterizing the full landscape of the objective function.) See Li and Liang (2018), Du et al. (2018), Jacot et al. (2018), and Allen-Zhu et al. (2019) and the references therein. The main conclusion is that, for certain initializations and parameterizations, optimizing over-parameterized neural networks with gradient descent can converge to a zero training error solution.

We dive into a bit more detail to flesh out the strength and limitations of this approach. The key idea is to start with random initialization on a particular scale, and then to optimize the neural networks somewhat locally around the neighborhood of the initialization. Consider a nonlinear model $f_\theta(\cdot)$ and an initialization θ_0. We can approximate the model by a linear model by Taylor expansion at θ_0:

$$f_\theta(x) \approx g_\theta(x) \triangleq \langle \theta - \theta_0, \nabla f_{\theta_0}(x) \rangle + f_{\theta_0}(x) = \langle \theta, \nabla f_{\theta_0}(x) \rangle + c(x), \qquad (21.32)$$

where $c(x)$ depends only on x but not on θ. Ignoring the nonessential shift $c(x)$, the model g_θ can be viewed as a linear function over the feature vector $\nabla f_{\theta_0}(x)$.

Therefore, suppose the approximation in (21.32) is accurate enough throughout the training; then we are essentially optimizing the linear model $g_\theta(x)$. The catch here is that, *for certain settings of initialization and parameterization*, the linear approximation is indeed accurate enough. (We will discuss in the text that follows whether and how much these settings are realistic.)

A concrete and simple setting is the following. Suppose $f_\theta(x) = \sum_{i=1}^{m} a_i [w_i^\top x]_+$, where $a_i \in \mathbb{R}$, $w_i \in \mathbb{R}^d$ and $[t]_+$ is a shorthand for $\max\{t, 0\}$, a.k.a the ReLU activation. Assume that a_i's are generated independently and uniformly from $\{\pm 1/\sqrt{m}\}$, and are fixed throughout the training. (So the model variable $\theta = [w_1, \ldots, w_m]$.) We will let m go to infinity and treat the input dimension as constant. We assume the loss is the mean-squared loss.

We initialize the weights $w_1, \ldots, w_m$ by uniform random vectors on the unit sphere, and denote the initialization as θ_0. The following two statements, which can be obtained by standard tools for linear models, are the keys of the analysis.

1. Suppose that we only optimize the approximated model $g_\theta(x)$; then the loss function is a quadratic function over θ. The Hessian of the loss is the kernel matrix, $H \triangleq [\nabla f_{\theta_0}(x^i), \nabla f_{\theta_0}(x^{(j)})]_{i,j\in[n]}$, induced by the feature map $x \to \nabla f_{\theta_0}(x)$. By standard concentration inequality, we can show that it is well conditioned for sufficiently large m. Therefore, we have a geometric decay of the loss following standard results about the gradient descent. Moreover, a direct calculation shows that the total movement of each of the weight vectors w_i is of norm on the order of $1/\sqrt{m}$. (We can intuitively makes sense of this claim as well – the more neurons we have, the less that each of them needs to move to fit the data.)

2. Within the $1/\sqrt{m}$ neighborhood of the initialization (where the distance is measured by the maximum change of individual weight vectors), the approxima-tion (21.32) is sufficiently good as m goes to infinity. More concretely, for a θ within the neighborhood, let $H(\theta) \triangleq [\nabla f_\theta(x^i), \nabla f_\theta(x^{(j)})]_{i,j\in[n]}$ be the kernel matrix that governs the update of the neural network at θ. We can show that $H(\theta)$ is sufficiently close to H as m goes to infinity, which suggests that the approximation (21.32) is accurate enough within the neighborhood.

The final analysis of optimizing $f_\theta(x)$ will make use of (1) and (2) of the preceding list inductively at every step. We use (2) to show that approximation is accurate, and then use (1) to show that the iterate θ does not leave the neighborhood of $1/\sqrt{m}$.

Discussions about the NTK Approach A common limitation of these analyses based on NTK is that they analyze directly the empirical risk whereas they do not necessarily provide good enough generalization guarantees. This is partially caused by the fact that the approach cannot handle regularized neural networks and the particular learning rate used in practice. In practice, typically the parameter θ does not stay close to the initialization either. When the number of parameters in θ is bigger than n, without any regularization, we cannot expect that $\widehat{L}$ uniformly concentrates around the population risk. This raises the question of whether the obtained solution simply memorizes the training data and does not generalize to the test data. A generalization bound can be obtained by the NTK approach, by bounding the norm of the difference between the final solution and the initialization. However, such a generalization bound can only be effectively as good as what a kernel method can provide. In fact, Wei et al. (2019) show that, for a simple distribution, NTK has fundamentally worse sample complexity than a regularized objective for neural networks.

Regularized Neural Networks Analyzing the landscape or optimization of a regularized objective is more challenging than analyzing the unregularized ones. In the latter case, we know that achieving zero training loss implies that we reach a global minimum, whereas in the former case, we know little about the function value of the global minima. Some progresses had been made for infinite-width two-layer neural networks (Chizat and Bach, 2018; Mei et al., 2018; Rotskoff and Vanden-Eijnden, 2018; Sirignano and Spiliopoulos, 2018; Wei et al., 2019). For example, Wei et al. (2019) show that a polynomial number of iterations of perturbed gradient descent can find a global minimum of an ℓ_2 regularized objective function for infinite-width two-layer neural networks with homogeneous activations. However, likely the same general result won't hold for polynomial-width neural networks, if we make no additional assumptions on the data.

Algorithmic or Implicit Regularization Empirical findings suggest, somewhat surprisingly, that even unregularized neural networks with over-parameterization can generalize (Zhang et al., 2017). Moreover, different algorithms apparently converge to essentially differently global minima of the objective function, and these global minima have *different* generalization performance! This means that the algorithms have a regularization effect, and fundamentally there is a possibility to delicately analyze the dynamics of the iterates of the optimization algorithm to reason about exactly which global minimum it converges to. Such types of results are particular challenging because they requires fine-grained control of the optimization dynamics, and rigorous theory can often be obtained only for relatively simple models such as linear models (Soudry et al., 2018; Woodworth et al., 2019) or matrix sensing (Gunasekar et al., 2017), quadratic neural networks (Li et al., 2018), and special cases of two-layer neural nets with ReLU activations (Li et al., 2019).

Assumptions on Data Distributions The author of the chapter and many others suspect that in the worst case, obtaining the best generalization performance of neural networks may be computationally intractable. Beyond worst case analysis, people have made stronger assumptions on the data distribution such as Gaussian inputs (Brutzkus and Globerson, 2017; Ge et al., 2017) and mixture of Gaussians or linearly separable data (Brutzkus et al., 2017). The limitations of making Gaussian assumptions on the inputs are twofold: (1) they are not realistic assumption; b) it may both overestimate and underestimate the difficulties of learning real-world data in different aspects. It is probably not surprising that Gaussian assumptions can oversimplify the problem, but there could be other non-Gaussian assumptions that may make the problem even easier than Gaussians; e.g., see the early work in deep learning theory (Arora et al., 2014).

21.7 Notes

Hillar and Lim (2013) show that a degree polynomial is *NP*-hard to optimize and Murty and Kabadi (1987) show that it's also *NP*-hard to check whether a point is not a local minimum. Our quantitative definition of quasi-convexity (Definition 21.5) is from (Hardt et al., 2018). Polyak–Lojasiewicz condition was introduced by (Polyak, 1963), and see a recent work (Karimi et al., 2016) for a proof of Theorem 21.4 . The RSI condition was originally introduced in Zhang and Yin (2013).

The strict saddle condition was originally defined in Ge et al. (2015), and we use a variant of the definition formalized in Lee et al. (2016) and Agarwal et al. (2017). Formal versions of Theorems 21.2 and 21.3 for various concrete algorithms can be found in e.g., Nesterov and Polyak (2006), Ge et al. (2015), Agarwal et al. (2017), and Carmon et al. (2018).

Theorem 21.6 is due to Boumal et al. (2019) Theorem 12. We refer readers to the book by Absil et al. (2007) for the definition of gradient and Hessian on the manifolds in Section 21.2.3.[9]

The results covered in Section 21.3 are due to Kakade et al. (2011) and Hazan et al. (2015). The particular exposition was first written by Yu Bai for the statistical learning theory course at Stanford.

The analysis of the landscape of the PCA objective was derived in Baldi and Hornik (1989) and Srebro and Jaakkola (2013). The main result covered in Section 21.4.2 is based on the work of Ge et al. (2016). Please see the reference in Ge et al. (2016) for more references on the matrix completion problem.

Section 21.5 is based on the work of Ge et al. (2015). Recently, there has been work on analyzing more sophisticated cases of tensor decomposition, e.g., using the Kac–Rice formula (Ge and Ma, 2017) for random overcomplete tensors. Please see Ge and Ma (2017) for more references regarding the tensor problems.

References

Absil, P. A., Mahony, R., and Sepulchre, R. 2007. *Optimization Algorithms on Matrix Manifolds*. Princeton University Press.

Agarwal, Naman, Allen Zhu, Zeyuan, Bullins, Brian, Hazan, Elad, and Ma, Tengyu. 2017. Finding approximate local minima faster than gradient descent. In *Proceedings of the 49th Annual ACM SIGACT Symposium on Theory of Computing*, pp. 1195–1199.

---

[9] For example, the gradient is defined in Absil et al. (2007), Section3.6, Equation (3.31), and the Hessian is defined in Absil et al. (2007), Section 5.5, Definition 5.5.1. Absil et al. (2007), Example 5.4.1) gives the Riemannian connection of the sphere S^{d-1}, which can be used to compute the Hessian.

Allen-Zhu, Zeyuan, Li, Yuanzhi, and Song, Zhao. 2019. On the convergence rate of training recurrent neural networks. In *Annual Conference on Neural Information Processing Systems (NeurIPS)*, pp. 6673–6685.

Arora, Sanjeev, Bhaskara, Aditya, Ge, Rong, and Ma, Tengyu. 2014. Provable bounds for learning some deep representations. *International Conference on Machine Learning*, pp. 584–592.

Arora, Sanjeev, Cohen, Nadav, and Hazan, Elad. 2018. On the optimization of deep networks: Implicit acceleration by overparameterization. In *Proceedings of the 35th International Conference on Machine Learning (ICML)*, pp. 244–253.

Baldi, Pierre, and Hornik, Kurt. 1989. Neural networks and principal component analysis: Learning from examples without local minima. *Neural Networks*, **2**(1), 53–58.

Boumal, N., Absil, P.-A., and Cartis, C. 2019. Global rates of convergence for nonconvex optimization on manifolds. *IMA Journal of Numerical Analysis*, 39(1), 1–33.

Brutzkus, Alon, and Globerson, Amir. 2017. Globally optimal gradient descent for a ConvNet with Gaussian inputs. In *Proceedings of the 34th International Conference on Machine Learning (ICML)*, pp. 605–614.

Brutzkus, Alon, Globerson, Amir, Malach, Eran, and Shalev-Shwartz, Shai. 2017. SGD learns over-parameterized networks that provably generalize on linearly separable data. *arXiv preprint arXiv:1710.10174*.

Carmon, Yair, Duchi, John C, Hinder, Oliver, and Sidford, Aaron. 2018. Accelerated methods for non-convex optimization. *SIAM Journal on Optimization*, 28(2), 1751–1772.

Chizat, Lenaic, and Bach, Francis. 2018. On the global convergence of gradient descent for over-parameterized models using optimal transport. In *Annual Conference on Neural Information Processing Systems (NeurIPS)*, pp. 3040–3050.

Du, Simon S, and Lee, Jason D. 2018. On the power of over-parametrization in neural networks with quadratic activation. In *Proceedings of the 35th International Conference on Machine Learning (ICML)*, pp. 1328–1337.

Du, Simon S, Zhai, Xiyu, Poczos, Barnabas, and Singh, Aarti. 2018. Gradient descent provably optimizes over-parameterized neural networks. *arXiv preprint arXiv:1810.02054*.

Ge, Rong, and Ma, Tengyu. 2017. On the optimization landscape of tensor decomposition. In *Annual Conference on Neural Information Processing Systems (NIPS)*, pp. 3653–3663.

Ge, Rong, Huang, Furong, Jin, Chi, and Yuan, Yang. 2015. Escaping from saddle points—online stochastic gradient for tensor decomposition. In *Proceedings of the 28th Conference on Learning Theory (COLT)*, pp. 797–842.

Ge, Rong, Lee, Jason D, and Ma, Tengyu. 2016. Matrix completion has no spurious local minimum. In *Annual Conference on Neural Information Processing Systems (NIPS)*, pp. 2973–2981.

Ge, Rong, Lee, Jason D, and Ma, Tengyu. 2017. Learning one-hidden-layer neural networks with landscape design. *arXiv preprint arXiv:1711.00501*.

Gunasekar, Suriya, Woodworth, Blake E, Bhojanapalli, Srinadh, Neyshabur, Behnam, and Srebro, Nati. 2017. Implicit regularization in matrix factorization. *Advances in Neural Information Processing Systems*, pp. 6151–6159.

Haeffele, Benjamin D, and Vidal, René. 2015. Global optimality in tensor factorization, deep learning, and beyond. *arXiv preprint arXiv:1506.07540*.

Hardt, Moritz, and Ma, Tengyu. 2016. Identity matters in deep learning. *arXiv preprint arXiv:1611.04231*.

Hardt, Moritz, Ma, Tengyu, and Recht, Benjamin. 2018. Gradient descent learns linear dynamical systems. *Journal of Machine Learning Research*, 19, 29:1–29:44.

Hazan, Elad, Levy, Kfir, and Shalev-Shwartz, Shai. 2015. Beyond convexity: Stochastic quasi-convex optimization. *Advances in Neural Information Processing Systems*, pp. 1594–1602.

He, Kaiming, Zhang, Xiangyu, Ren, Shaoqing, and Sun, Jian. 2016. Deep residual learning for image recognition. In *IEEE Conference on Computer Vision and Pattern Recognition (CVPR)*, pp. 770–778.

Hillar, Christopher J., and Lim, Lek-Heng. 2013. Most tensor problems are NP-hard. *Journal of the ACM*, **60**(6), 45.

Ioffe, Sergey, and Szegedy, Christian. 2015. Batch normalization: Accelerating deep network training by reducing internal covariate shift. In *Proceedings of the 32nd International Conference on Machine Learning (ICML)*, pp. 448–456.

Jacot, Arthur, Gabriel, Franck, and Hongler, Clément. 2018. Neural tangent kernel: Convergence and generalization in neural networks. In *Advances in Neural Information Processing Systems (NeurIPS)*, pp. 8580–8589.

Kakade, Sham M, Kanade, Varun, Shamir, Ohad, and Kalai, Adam. 2011. Efficient learning of generalized linear and single index models with isotonic regression. *Advances in Neural Information Processing Systems*, pp. 927–935.

Karimi, Hamed, Nutini, Julie, and Schmidt, Mark. 2016. Linear convergence of gradient and proximal-gradient methods under the polyak-łojasiewicz condition. *Joint European Conference on Machine Learning and Knowledge Discovery in Databases*, pp. 795–811. Springer.

Kawaguchi, Kenji. 2016. Deep learning without poor local minima. In *Advances in Neural Information Processing Systems (NIPS)*, pp. 586–594.

Lee, Jason D, Simchowitz, Max, Jordan, Michael I, and Recht, Benjamin. 2016. Gradient descent only converges to minimizers. In *Proceedings of the 29th Conference on Learning Theory (COLT)*, pp. 1246–1257.

Li, Yuanzhi, and Liang, Yingyu. 2018. Learning overparameterized neural networks via stochastic gradient descent on structured data. *Advances in Neural Information Processing Systems*, pp. 8157–8166.

Li, Yuanzhi, Ma, Tengyu, and Zhang, Hongyang. 2018. Algorithmic regularization in over-parameterized matrix sensing and neural networks with quadratic activations. In *Proceedings of the 31st Conference on Learning Theory (COLT)*, pp. 2–47.

Li, Yuanzhi, Wei, Colin, and Ma, Tengyu. 2019. Towards explaining the regularization effect of initial large learning rate in training neural networks. In *Advances in Neural Information Processing Systems (NeurIPS)*, pp. 11669–11680.

Mei, Song, Montanari, Andrea, and Nguyen, Phan-Minh. 2018. A mean field view of the landscape of two-layers neural networks. *Proceedings of the National Academy of Sciences*, E7665–E7671.

Murty, Katta G, and Kabadi, Santosh N. 1987. Some NP-complete problems in quadratic and nonlinear programming. *Mathematical Programming*, **39**(2), 117–129.

Nesterov, Yurii, and Polyak, Boris T. 2006. Cubic regularization of Newton method and its global performance. *Mathematical Programming*, **108**(1), 177–205.

Polyak, Boris Teodorovich. 1963. Gradient methods for minimizing functionals. *Zhurnal Vychislitel'noi Matematiki i Matematicheskoi Fiziki*, **3**(4), 643–653.

Rotskoff, Grant M, and Vanden-Eijnden, Eric. 2018. Neural networks as interacting particle systems: Asymptotic convexity of the loss landscape and universal scaling of the approximation error. *arXiv preprint arXiv:1805.00915*.

Safran, Itay, and Shamir, Ohad. 2016. On the quality of the initial basin in overspecified neural networks. *International Conference on Machine Learning*, pp. 774–782.

Sirignano, Justin, and Spiliopoulos, Konstantinos. 2018. Mean field analysis of neural networks: A law of large numbers. *arXiv preprint arXiv:1805.01053*.

Soltanolkotabi, Mahdi, Javanmard, Adel, and Lee, Jason D. 2018. Theoretical insights into the optimization landscape of over-parameterized shallow neural networks. *IEEE Transactions on Information Theory*, **65**(2), 742–769.

Soudry, Daniel, and Carmon, Yair. 2016. No bad local minima: Data independent training error guarantees for multilayer neural networks. *arXiv preprint arXiv:1605.08361*.

Soudry, Daniel, Hoffer, Elad, Nacson, Mor Shpigel, Gunasekar, Suriya, and Srebro, Nathan. 2018. The implicit bias of gradient descent on separable data. *The Journal of Machine Learning Research*, **19**(1), 2822–2878.

Srebro, Nathan, and Jaakkola, Tommi. 2013. Weighted low-rank approximations. In *Proceedings of the Twentieth International Conference on Machine Learning (ICML)*, pp. 720–727.

Venturi, Luca, Bandeira, Afonso, and Bruna, Joan. 2018. Neural networks with finite intrinsic dimension have no spurious valleys. *arXiv preprint arXiv:1802.06384*.

Wei, Colin, Lee, Jason D., Liu, Qiang, and Ma, Tengyu. 2019. Regularization matters: Generalization and optimization of neural nets v.s. their induced kernel. *arXiv e-prints*, Oct, In *Advances in Neural Information Processing Systems (NeurIPS)*, pp. 9709–9721.

Woodworth, Blake, Gunasekar, Suriya, Lee, Jason, Moroshko, Edward, Savarese, Pedro, H. P., Golan, Itay, Soudry, Daniel, and Srebro, Nathan. 2019. Kernel and deep regimes in overparametrized models. *arXiv preprint arXiv:1906.05827*.

Zhang, Chiyuan, Bengio, Samy, Hardt, Moritz, Recht, Benjamin, and Vinyals, Oriol. 2017. Understanding deep learning requires rethinking generalization. In *5th International Conference on Learning Representations (ICLR)*.

Zhang, Hui, and Yin, Wotao. 2013. Gradient methods for convex minimization: better rates under weaker conditions. *arXiv preprint arXiv:1303.4645*.

CHAPTER TWENTY TWO

Generalization in Overparameterized Models

Moritz Hardt

Abstract: Simply put, the goal of generalization is to relate the performance of a learned model on seen examples to its performance on *unseen* examples. Traditional generalization bounds relate the gap between the two to various measures of model complexity. In practice, models can generalize well even if they do not enjoy a useful complexity bound by virtue of counting model parameters. Such *overparameterized* models have conquered the state-of-the-art in numerous machine learning benchmarks today. We examine the intriguing empirical phenomena related to overparameterization and generalization in today's machine learning practice. We then review available theory – some old and some emerging – to better understand and anticipate what drives generalization performance.

22.1 Background and Motivation

Generalization in machine learning is an area in which the algorithmic paradigm of worst-case analysis is typically hard to instantiate. When models generalize successfully in practice, it is often due to a subtle interplay of data and algorithm. In this chapter, we will explore why generalization is *beyond worst-case analysis* and what theory we have to reason about generalization nonetheless.

Our focus is on the standard formal setup of supervised learning. We assume there is an underlying distribution D over labeled examples relevant to our learning problem. A labeled *example* is a pair $(x, y) \in X \times Y$, where X is a space of possible data points and Y is some discrete set of class labels. For example, the set X might represent images of a certain dimension, while the set Y contains labels that describe what objects are in an image.

A *predictor* (synonymously, here, *classifier*) is a mapping $f \colon X \to Y$ from points to labels. Predictors are usually specified by a vector of real-valued parameters $w \in \mathbb{R}^d$. We use the term *model* to describe the relationship between parameters and predictor. A linear model, for example, refers to a binary predictor $f_w(x) = \text{sign}(\langle w, x \rangle)$, specified by parameters $w \in \mathbb{R}^d$, that outputs 1 if the inner product $\langle w, x \rangle$ is positive and outputs -1 otherwise. That said, the term "model" has become a colloquialism in machine learning that could refer to either the predictor in its functional form or the parameters describing the predictor.

We measure the quality of a predictor with the help of a *loss function* $\ell\colon Y \times Y \to \mathbb{R}_{\geq 0}$ that maps a pair of labels to a nonnegative real number. An example is the $0/1$-*loss* $\ell_{01}(y,y') = \mathbf{1}\{y \neq y'\}$, which corresponds to classification error. It's often convenient to abuse notation by letting $\ell(f,(x,y)) = \ell(f(x),y)$ denote the loss of predictor f on a labeled example (x,y). Abusing notation one step further, we will use $\ell(w,z)$ denote the loss of the predictor described by the parameters w on labeled example z.

Definition 22.1 (Risk) Define the *risk* of a predictor $f\colon X \to Y$ as

$$R(f) = \mathop{\mathbb{E}}_{(x,y)\sim D}[\ell(f(x),y)].$$

The goal of supervised learning is to find a predictor that minimizes risk. One way to accomplish this is to directly minimize risk, for example, using the *stochastic gradient method* applied to the model parameters with respect to a random sample:

$$w_{t+1} = w_t - \eta \nabla \ell(w_t, z_t) \quad \text{where} \quad z_t \sim D.$$

The scalar $\eta > 0$ is called *step size*. The stochastic gradient method in its many variants is the workhorse of modern machine learning and in recent developments in deep learning. We cannot directly optimize the $0/1$-loss using the gradient method. We therefore use suitable "surrogate" losses during training.

Example 22.2 (Perceptron) The well-known Perceptron algorithm corresponds to the stochastic gradient method applied to linear models with the *hinge loss*:

$$\ell_{\text{hinge}}(w,(x,y)) = \max\{1 - \langle w,x\rangle y, 0\}.$$

Discovered in 1958 by Rosenblatt, the *New York Times* then described the Perceptron as "the embryo of an electronic computer that [the Navy] expects will be able to walk, talk, see, write, reproduce itself and be conscious of its existence."

22.1.1 Empirical Risk and Generalization Gap

It is possible to apply stochastic optimization directly to the risk objective by drawing one fresh example at every step of the algorithm. However, in practice we typically use each training example multiple times. This creates a disconnect between the performance of the model on the training examples compared with its performance on a fresh example. To analyze this gap, we introduce some more terminology.

Definition 22.3 (Empirical Risk) Consider a tuple of n labeled examples,

$$S = ((x_1,y_1),\ldots\ldots,(x_n,y_n)) \in (X \times Y)^n,$$

where $z_i = (x_i,y_i)$ represents the ith labeled example. The *empirical risk* is defined as

$$R_S(f) = \frac{1}{n} \sum_{i=1}^{n} \ell(f(x_i), y_i).$$

Empirical risk minimization seeks to find a predictor f^* in a specified class $\mathcal{F}$ that minimizes the empirical risk:

$$f^* = \arg\min_{f \in \mathcal{F}} R_S(f). \tag{22.1}$$

In the context of empirical risk minimization, the empirical risk is often called *training error* or *training loss*, as it corresponds to the loss achieved by some optimization methods. However, depending on the optimization problem, we may not be able to find an exact empirical risk minimizer and it may not be unique.

Empirical risk minimization is commonly used as a proxy for minimizing the unknown population risk. But how good is this proxy?

Ideally, we would like that the predictor f we find via empirical risk minimization satisfies $R_S(f) \approx R(f)$. However, this may not be the case, since the risk $R(f)$ captures loss on unseen examples, while the empirical risk $R_S(f)$ captures loss on seen examples.

Generally, we expect to do much better on seen examples than unseen examples. This performance gap between seen and unseen examples is what we call *generalization gap*.

Definition 22.4 (Generalization Gap) Define the *generalization gap* of a predictor f with respect to a data set S as

$$\Delta_{\mathrm{gen}}(f) = R(f) - R_S(f).$$

This quantity is sometimes also called *generalization error* or *excess risk*. Note the following tautological, yet important identity:

$$R(f) = R_S(f) + \Delta_{\mathrm{gen}}(f) \tag{22.2}$$

What this shows in particular is that if we manage to make the empirical risk $R_S(f)$ small through optimization, then all that remains to worry about is the generalization gap.

22.2 Tools to Reason About Generalization

So, how can we bound the generalization gap? We will first see a tight characterization in terms of an algorithmic robustness property we call *algorithmic stability*. Intuitively, algorithmic stability measures how sensitive an algorithm is to changes in a single training example. It will give us one powerful and intuitive way of reasoning about generalization.

22.2.1 Algorithmic Stability

To introduce the idea of stability, we introduce two independent samples $S = (z_1, \ldots, z_n)$ and $S' = (z'_1, \ldots, z'_n)$, each drawn independently and identically from the distribution D. We call the second sample S' a *ghost sample*, as it is solely an analytical device. We never actually collect this second sample or run any algorithm on it.

We introduce n *hybrid samples* $S^{(i)}$, for $i \in \{1, \dots, n\}$ as

$$S^{(i)} = (z_1, \dots, z_{i-1}, z'_i, z_{i+1}, \dots, z_n),$$

where the ith example comes from S', while all others come from S.

With this notation at hand, we can introduce a data-dependent notion of average stability of an algorithm. For this definition, we think of an algorithm as a deterministic map A that takes a training sample in $(X \times Y)^n$ to some set model parameters in some output space $\Omega \subseteq \mathbb{R}^d$.

Definition 22.5 (Average Stability) The *average stability* of an algorithm $A \colon (X \times Y)^n \to \Omega$:

$$\Delta(A) = \mathop{\mathbb{E}}_{S, S'} \left[\frac{1}{n} \sum_{i=1}^{n} \left(\ell(A(S), z'_i) - \ell(A(S^{(i)}), z'_i) \right) \right].$$

To parse this definition, note that from the perspective of $A(S)$, the example z'_i is *unseen*, since it is not part of S. But from the perspective of $A(S^{(i)})$ the example z'_i is seen, since it is part of $S^{(i)}$. This shows that the instrument $\Delta(A)$ measures the average sensitivity of the algorithm to replacing one of its training examples by a fresh draw from the distribution. This is the intuition why average stability, in fact, equals expected generalization gap.

Proposition 22.6 (Expected Gap Equals Average Stability)

$$\mathbb{E}[\Delta_{\text{gen}}(A(S))] = \Delta(A).$$

Proof   By linearity of expectation,

$$\mathbb{E}[\Delta_{\text{gen}}(A(S))] = \mathbb{E}\left[R(A(S)) - R_S(A(S))\right]$$
$$= \mathbb{E}\left[\frac{1}{n} \sum_{i=1}^{n} \ell(A(S), z'_i)\right] - \mathbb{E}\left[\frac{1}{n} \sum_{i=1}^{n} \ell(A(S), z_i)\right].$$

Here, we used that z'_i is an example drawn from the distribution that does not appear in the set S, while z_i does appear in S. At the same time, z_i and z'_i are identically distributed and independent of the other examples. Therefore,

$$\mathbb{E}\, \ell(A(S), z_i) = \mathbb{E}\, \ell(A(S^{(i)}), z'_i).$$

Applying this identity to each term in the empirical risk espression, and comparing with the definition of $\Delta(A)$, we conclude $\mathbb{E}[R(A(S)) - R_S(A(S))] = \Delta(A)$. □

22.2.2 Uniform Stability

While average stability gave us an exact characterization of generalization error, it can be hard to work with the expectation over S and S'. Uniform stability replaces the averages by suprema, leading to a stronger but useful notion.

Definition 22.7 (Uniform Stability) The *uniform stability* of an algorithm A is defined as

$$\Delta_{\sup}(A) = \sup_{S,\, S' \in (X \times Y)^n} \sup_{1 \leq i \leq n} |\ell(A(S), z_i') - \ell(A(S^{(i)}), z_i')|.$$

Since uniform stability upper bounds average stability, we know that uniform stability upper bounds the generalization gap (in expectation).

Corollary 22.8 $\mathbb{E}[\Delta_{\text{gen}}(A(S))] \leq \Delta_{\sup}(A).$

This corollary turns out to be surprisingly useful because many algorithms are uniformly stable. For example, strong convexity of the loss function is sufficient for the uniform stability of empirical risk minimization, as we will see next.

22.2.3 Stability of Empirical Risk Minimization

The next theorem shows that empirical risk minimization generalizes provided that the loss function $\ell(w, z)$ is strongly convex in the model parameters w for every example z. A case that meets this assumption would be linear models with the squared loss $\ell(w, (x, y)) = (\langle w, x \rangle - y)^2$ assuming $\|w\| \leq 1$ and $\|x\| \leq 1$.

Theorem 22.9 *Assume that for every z, $\ell(w, z)$ is α-strongly convex in w over the domain Ω, i.e., $\ell(w', z) \geq \ell(w, z) + \langle \nabla \ell(w, z), w - w' \rangle + \frac{\alpha}{2} \|w - w'\|^2$ for all $w, w' \in \Omega$. Further assume that, $\ell(w, z)$ is L-Lipschitz in w for every z, i.e., $\|\nabla \ell(w, z)\| \leq L$.*
Then, empirical risk minimization (ERM) satisfies

$$\Delta_{\sup}(ERM) \leq \frac{4L^2}{\alpha n}.$$

Proof Let $\hat{w}_S = \arg\min_{w \in \Omega} \frac{1}{n} \sum_{i=1}^n \ell(w, z_i)$ denote the empirical risk minimizer on the sample S. Fix arbitrary samples S, S' of size n and an index $i \in \{1, \ldots, n\}$. We need to show that

$$|(\ell(\hat{w}_{S^{(i)}}, z_i') - \ell(\hat{w}_S, z_i'))| \leq \frac{4L^2}{\alpha n}.$$

On the one hand, it follows from strong convexity that

$$R_S(\hat{w}_{S^{(i)}}) - R_S(\hat{w}_S) \geq \frac{\alpha}{2} \|\hat{w}_S - \hat{w}_{S^{(i)}}\|^2. \tag{22.3}$$

On the other hand,

$$
\begin{aligned}
&R_S(\hat{w}_{S^{(i)}}) - R_S(\hat{w}_S) \\
&= \frac{1}{n}(\ell(\hat{w}_{S^{(i)}}, z_i) - \ell(\hat{w}_S, z_i)) + \frac{1}{n} \sum_{i \neq j}(\ell(\hat{w}_{S^{(i)}}, z_j) - \ell(\hat{w}_S, z_j))
\end{aligned}
$$

$$= \frac{1}{n}(\ell(\hat{w}_{S^{(i)}}, z_i) - \ell(\hat{w}_S, z_i)) + \frac{1}{n}(\ell(\hat{w}_S, z_i') - \ell(\hat{w}_{S^{(i)}}, z_i'))$$
$$+ \left(R_{S^{(i)}}(\hat{w}_{S^{(i)}}) - R_{S^{(i)}}(\hat{w}_S)\right)$$
$$\leq \frac{1}{n}|\ell(\hat{w}_{S^{(i)}}, z_i) - \ell(\hat{w}_S, z_i)| + \frac{1}{n}|(\ell(\hat{w}_S, z_i') - \ell(\hat{w}_{S^{(i)}}, z_i'))|$$
$$\leq \frac{2L}{n}\|\hat{w}_{S^{(i)}} - \hat{w}_S\|. \tag{22.4}$$

Here, we used that

$$R_{S^{(i)}}(\hat{w}_{S^{(i)}}) - R_{S^{(i)}}(\hat{w}_S)) \leq 0$$

and the fact that ℓ is L-Lipschitz.

Putting together (22.3) and (22.4), we find $\|\hat{w}_{S^{(i)}} - \hat{w}_S\| \leq \frac{4L}{\alpha n}$. Applying the Lipschitz condition again,

$$\frac{1}{n}|(\ell(\hat{w}_{S^{(i)}}, z_i') - \ell(\hat{w}_S, z_i'))| \leq L\|\hat{w}_{S^{(i)}} - \hat{w}_S\| \leq \frac{4L^2}{\alpha n}.$$

Hence, $\Delta_{\sup}(\text{ERM}) \leq \frac{4L^2}{\alpha n}$. $\qquad\qquad\square$

An interesting point about this result is that there is no explicit reference to the complexity of the model class referenced by Ω.

22.2.4 Regularization

Some empirical risk minimization problems, such as the Perceptron we saw earlier, are convex but not strictly convex. We can turn convex problems into strongly convex problems by adding an ℓ_2-*regularization* term to the loss function:

$$r(w, z) = \ell(w, z) + \frac{\alpha}{2}\|w\|^2. \tag{22.5}$$

The regularized loss $r(w, z)$ is α-strongly convex. The last term is named ℓ_2-*regularization*, *weight decay*, or *Tikhonov regularization* depending on field and context. Regularization gives us the following chain of implications valid for convex empirical risk minimization: regularization $\Rightarrow$ strong convexity $\Rightarrow$ uniform stability $\Rightarrow$ generalization.

A simple argument further shows that solving the regularized objective also solves the unregularized objective. The idea is that assuming $\|w\| \leq B$ we can set the regularization parameter $\alpha \approx \frac{L^2}{B^2 n}$ so that the minimizer of the regularized risk also minimizes the unregularized risk up to error $\mathcal{O}\left(\frac{LB}{\sqrt{n}}\right)$. Moreover, after plugging this choice of α into Theorem 22.9 the generalization gap will also be $\mathcal{O}\left(\frac{LB}{\sqrt{n}}\right)$.

Stability analysis combined with explicit regularization and convexity thus give an appealing conceptual and mathematical approach to reasoning about generalization. However, empirical risk minimization involving nonlinear models is increasingly successful in practice and generally leads to nonconvex optimization problems.

22.2.5 Uniform Convergence

We briefly review other useful tools to reason about generalization. Arguably, the most basic is based on counting the number of different functions that can be described with the given model parameters.

Given a sample S of n independent draws from the same underlying distribution, the empirical risk $R_S(f)$ for a fixed function f is an average of n random variables, each with mean equal to the risk $R(f)$. Assuming for simplicity that the range of our loss function is bounded in the interval $[0, 1]$, Hoeffding's bound gives us the tail bound

$$\Pr\{R_S(f) > R(f) + t\} \leq \exp(-2nt^2).$$

By applying the union bound to a finite set of functions $\mathcal{F}$ we can guarantee that with probability $1 - \delta$, we have for all functions $f \in \mathcal{F}$ that

$$\Delta_{\text{gen}}(f) \leq \sqrt{\frac{\ln|\mathcal{F}| + \ln(1/\delta)}{n}}. \tag{22.6}$$

The cardinality bound $|\mathcal{F}|$ is a basic measure of the complexity of the model family $\mathcal{F}$. We can think of the term $\ln(\mathcal{F})$ as a measure of complexity of the function class $\mathcal{F}$, albeit a rather coarse one. The gestalt of the generalization bound as "$\sqrt{\text{complexity}/n}$" routinely appears with varying measures of complexity.

Bounding the generalization gap from above for all functions in a function class is called *uniform convergence*. A classical tool to reason about uniform convergence is the Vapnik–Chervonenkis dimension (VC dimension) of a function class $\mathcal{F} \subseteq X \to Y$, denoted $\text{VC}(\mathcal{F})$. It's defined as the size of the largest set $Q \subseteq X$ such that for any Boolean function $h: Q \to \{-1, 1\}$, there is a predictor $f \in \mathcal{F}$ such that $f(x) = g(x)$ for all $x \in Q$. In other words, if there is a size-d sample such that the functions of $\mathcal{F}$ induce all 2^d possible binary labelings of S, then the VC dimension of $\mathcal{F}$ is at least d.

The VC dimension measures the ability of the model class to conform to an arbitrary labeling of a set of points. The so-called VC inequality implies that with probability $1 - \delta$, we have for all functions $f \in \mathcal{F}$

$$\Delta_{\text{gen}}(f) \leq \sqrt{\frac{\text{VC}(\mathcal{F})\ln n + \ln(1/\delta)}{n}}. \tag{22.7}$$

We can see that the complexity term $\text{VC}(\mathcal{F})$ refines our earlier cardinality bound, since $\text{VC}(\mathcal{F}) \leq \log|\mathcal{F}| + 1$. However, the VC dimension also applies to infinite model classes. Linear models over $\mathbb{R}^d$ have VC dimension d, corresponding to the number of model parameters. Generally speaking, the VC dimension tends to grow with the number of model parameters for many model families of interest. In such cases, the bound in (22.7) becomes useless once the number of model parameters exceeds the size of the sample.

The generalization bound we saw here is *worst-case* with respect to the data distribution insofar as it only depends on the model class and does not take into account data-dependent properties.

22.2.6 Rademacher Complexity

A weakness of VC dimension is that it's a property of the model class alone that does not take data or problem-specific aspects into mind, such as restrictions on the distribution family or properties of the loss function. Rademacher complexity gives a flexible tool that can mitigate some of these shortcomings. To get a generalization bound in terms of Rademacher complexity, we typically apply the definition not to the model class $\mathcal{F}$ itself but to the class of functions $\mathcal{L}$ of the form $h(z) = \ell(f, z)$ for some $f \in \mathcal{F}$ and a loss function ℓ. By varying the loss function, we can derive different generalization bounds.

Fix a function class $\mathcal{L} \subseteq Z \to \mathbb{R}$, which will later correspond to the composition of a predictor with a loss function, which is why we chose the symbol $\mathcal{L}$. Think of the domain Z as the space of labeled examples $z = (x, y)$. Fix a distribution P over the space Z.

The *empirical Rademacher complexity* of a function class $\mathcal{L} \subseteq Z \to \mathbb{R}$ with respect to a sample $Q = \{z_1, \ldots, z_n\} \subseteq Z$ drawn i.i.d. from the distribution P is defined as

$$\widehat{\mathfrak{R}}_n(\mathcal{L}) = \underset{\sigma \in \{-1, 1\}^n}{\mathbb{E}} \left[\frac{1}{n} \sup_{h \in \mathcal{L}} \left| \sum_{i=1}^{n} \sigma_i h(z_i) \right| \right]. \tag{22.8}$$

We obtain the *Rademacher complexity* $\mathfrak{R}_n(\mathcal{L}) = \mathbb{E}\left[\widehat{\mathfrak{R}}_n(\mathcal{L})\right]$ by taking the expectation of the empirical Rademacher complexity with respect to the sample. Rademacher complexity measures the ability of a function class to interpolate a random sign pattern assigned to a point set.

One application of Rademacher complexity concerns loss functions that are L-Lipschitz in the parameterization of the model class for every example z. This bound shows that with probability $1 - \delta$ for all functions $f \in \mathcal{F}$, we have

$$\Delta_{\text{gen}}(f) \leq 2L\mathfrak{R}_n(\mathcal{F}) + 3\sqrt{\frac{\log(1/\delta)}{m}}. \tag{22.9}$$

Rademacher complexity often leads to better bounds than the VC dimension alone. For example, it depends on both the distribution of the data and the properties of the loss function.

22.3 Overparameterization: Empirical Phenomena

Classical uniform convergence bounds give us no reason to expect good generalization performance when the model complexity exceeds the number of data points. We will now see that such overparameterized models often do generalize well in practice. By taking a tour of the relevant empirical observations we can begin to appreciate what challenges a theory of generalization for overparameterized models must grapple with and why such a theory must go *beyond worst-case analysis*.

22.3.1 Effects of Model Complexity

Figure 22.1 describes the traditional conception of the so-called bias-variance trade-off. As model complexity increases the empirical risk (training risk) decreases due to the model's improved ability to interpolate the training data. However, increasing

---

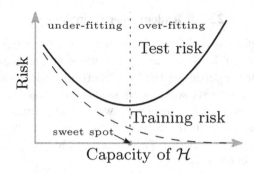

Figure 22.1 The so-called bias-variance trade-off represents a traditional view of generalization consistent with uniform convergence bounds in Section 22.2.5.

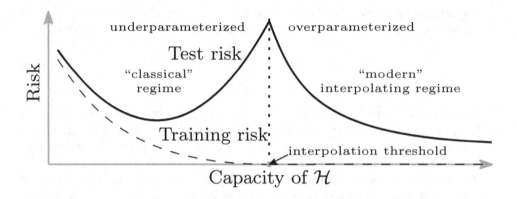

Figure 22.2 An extended picture with a "double descent" shape accounting for the overparameterized regime.

the model complexity too far eventually leads to an increase in risk (test risk) corresponding to signs of *overfitting*.

This kind of picture has been drawn in several textbooks and courses on machine learning. However, practitioners have observed that complex models can often simultaneously achieve close to zero training loss and still generalize well. Moreover, in many cases risk continues to decrease as model complexity grows and training data are interpolated exactly down to (nearly) zero training loss. This empirical relationship between overparameterization and risk appears to be robust and is obtained in numerous model classes, including overparameterized linear models, ensemble methods, and neural networks.

In the absence of regularization and for certain model families, the empirical relationship between model complexity and risk is more accurately captured by a picture like the one in Figure 22.2. There is an interpolation threshold at which a model of the given complexity can fit the training data exactly. The complexity range below the threshold is the *underparameterized regime*, while the one above is the overparameterized regime. Increasing model complexity in the overparameterized regime continues to decrease risk indefinitely, albeit at decreasing marginal returns, toward some convergence point. The double descent curve is not universal. In many cases, in practice we observe a single descent curve throughout the entire complexity range.

22.3.2 Optimization versus Generalization

Training neural networks with stochastic gradient descent, as is commonly done in practice, attempts to solve a nonconvex optimization problem. Reasoning about nonconvex optimization is known to be difficult. As such, theoreticians see a worthy goal in trying to prove mathematically that stochastic gradient methods successfully minimize the training objective of large artificial neural networks. The previous chapter discussed some of the progress that has been made toward this goal.

It is widely believed that what makes optimization easy crucially depends on the fact that models in practice have many more parameters than there are training points. While making optimization tractable, overparameterization puts a burden on generalization.

We can force a disconnect between optimization and generalization in a simple experiment that we will see next. One consequence is that even if a mathematical proof established the convergence guarantees of stochastic gradient descent for training some class of large neural networks, it would not necessarily on its own tell us much about why the resulting model generalizes well to the test objective.

Indeed, consider the following experiment. Fix training data $(x_1, y_1), \ldots, (x_n, y_n)$ and fix a training algorithm A that achieves zero training loss on these data and achieves good test loss as well.

Now replace all the labels $y_1, \ldots, y_n$ by randomly and independently drawn labels $\tilde{y}_1, \ldots, \tilde{y}_n$. What happens if we run the same algorithm on the training data with noisy labels $(x_1, \tilde{y}_1), \ldots, (x_n, \tilde{y}_n))$?

One thing is clear. If we choose from k discrete classes, we expect the model trained on the random labels to have no more than $1/k$ test accuracy, that is, the accuracy achieved by random guessing. After all, there is no statistical relationship between the training labels and the test labels that the model could learn.

What is more interesting is what happens to optimization. The left panel of Figure 22.3 shows the outcome of this kind of *randomization test* on the popular

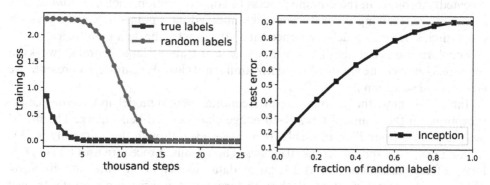

Figure 22.3 Randomization test on CIFAR-10. (Left) How randomization affects training loss. Training still converges to zero loss even on fully randomized labels. (Right) How increasing the fraction of corrupted training labels affects classification error on the test set. At full randomization, the test error degrades to 90%, as good as guessing one of the 10 classes.

Table 22.1 The training and test accuracy (in percentage) with and without data augmentation and ℓ_2-regularization on a representative model architecture called *Inception*. Explicit regularization helps, but is not necessary for non-trivial generalization performance.

No. of params	Random crop	ℓ_2-Regularization	Train accuracy	Test accuracy
1,649,402	yes	yes	100.0	89.05
	yes	no	100.0	89.31
	no	yes	100.0	86.03
	no	no	100.0	85.75

CIFAR-10 image classification benchmark for a standard neural network architecture. What we can see is that the training algorithm continues to drive the training loss to zero even if the labels are randomized. Moreover, the same is true for various other kinds of randomizations. We can even replace the original images by random pixels so as to get a randomly labeled random pixel images $(\tilde{x}_i, \tilde{y}_i)$. The algorithm will continue to successfully minimize the loss function.

The randomization experiment shows that optimization continues to work well even when generalization performance is no better than random guessing, i.e., 10% accuracy in the case of the CIFAR-10 benchmark that has 10 classes. The optimization method is moreover insensitive to the labeling of the data, since it works even on random labels. A consequence of this simple experiment is that a proof of convergence for the optimization method may not reveal any insights into the nature of generalization.

22.3.3 The Diminished Role of Explicit Regularization

Regularization plays an important role in the theory of convex empirical risk minimization. The most common form of regularization used to be ℓ_2-regularization corresponding to adding a scalar of the squared Euclidean norm of the parameter vector to the objective function as we saw in Equation (22.5).

A more radical form of regularization, called *data augmentation*, is common in the practice of deep learning. Data augmentation transforms each training point repeatedly throughout the training process by some operation, such as a *random crop* of the image. Training on such randomly modified data points is meant to reduce overfitting, since the model never encounters the exact same data point twice.

Regularization continues to be a component of training large neural networks in practice. However, the nature of regularization is not clear. We can see a representative empirical observation in Table 22.1.

Table 22.1 shows the performance of a common neural model architecture, called Inception, on the standard CIFAR-10 image classification benchmark. The model has more than 1.5 million trainable parameters, even though there are only 50,000 training examples spread across 10 classes. The training procedure uses two explicit forms of regularization. One is a form of data augmentation with random crops. The other is ℓ_2-regularization. With both forms of regularization the fully trained model achieves close to 90% test accuracy. But even if we turn both of them off, the model still achieves close to 86% test accuracy (without even readjusting any hyperparameters such as the learning rate of the optimizer). At the same time, the model fully interpolates the training data in the sense of making no misclassification errors whatsoever on the training data.

These findings suggest that while explicit regularization may help generalization performance, it is by no means necessary for strong generalization of heavily overparameterized models.

22.4 Generalization Bounds for Overparameterized Models

We turn to some old and some recent theoretical approaches that have the potential to shed light on generalization performance in overparameterized settings.

22.4.1 Margin Bounds for Ensemble Methods

Ensemble methods work by combining many weak predictors into one strong predictor. The combination step usually involves taking a weighted average or majority vote of the weak predictors. Boosting and random forests are two ensemble methods that continue to be highly popular and competitive in various settings. Both methods train a sequence of small decision trees, each on its own achieving modest accuracy on the training task. However, so long as different trees make errors that aren't too correlated, we can obtain a higher accuracy model by taking, say, a majority vote over the individual predictions of the trees.

Researchers in the 1990s already observed that boosting often continues to improve test accuracy as more weak predictors are added to the ensemble. The complexity of the entire ensemble was thus often far too large to apply standard uniform convergence bounds.

A proffered explanation was that boosting, while growing the complexity of the ensemble, also improved the *margin* of the ensemble predictor. Expressing the final ensemble as a function $f : X \to \mathbb{R}$, its *margin* on an example (x, y) is defined as the value $yf(x)$. The larger the margin the more "confident" the ensemble is about the label of the data point. A margin $yf(x)$ just above 0 shows that the weak predictors in the ensemble were nearly split evenly in their weighted votes.

An elegant generalization bound relates the risk of any predictor f to the fraction of correctly labeled training examples at a given margin θ. Below let $R(f)$ be the risk of f w.r.t. classification error. However, let $R_S^\theta(f)$ be the empirical risk with respect to *margin errors* at level θ, i.e., the loss $\mathbf{1}(yf(x) \leq \theta)$ that penalizes errors where the predictor is within an additive θ margin of making a mistake.

Theorem 22.10 *With probability $1 - \delta$, every convex combination f of base classifiers in a given family $\mathcal{H}$ satisfies the following bound for every $\theta > 0$:*

$$R(f) - R_S^\theta(f) \leq O\left(\frac{1}{\sqrt{n}} \left(\frac{\mathrm{VC}(\mathcal{H}) \log n}{\theta^2} + \log(1/\delta) \right)^{1/2} \right).$$

The theorem can be proved using Rademacher complexity we saw in Section 22.2.6. Crucially, the bound only depends on the VC dimension of the base class $\mathcal{H}$ but not the complexity of the ensemble. Moreover, the bound holds for all $\theta > 0$ and so we can choose θ after knowing the margin that manifested during training.

22.4.2 Margin Bounds for Linear Models

Margins also play a fundamental role for linear classification. We'll state the result here for a simple least squares problem:

$$w^* = \arg \min_{w:\, \|w\| \le B} \frac{1}{n} \sum_{i=1}^{n} (\langle x_i, w \rangle - y)^2 .$$

In other words, we minimize the empirical risk w.r.t. the squared loss over norm bounded linear separators; call this class $\mathcal{W}_B$. Further assume that all data points satisfy $\|x_i\| \le 1$ and $y \in \{-1, 1\}$. Analogous to the margin bound in Theorem 22.10, it can be shown that with probability $1 - \delta$ for every linear predictor f specified by weights in $\mathcal{W}_B$ we have

$$R(f) - R_S^\theta(f) \le 4 \frac{\mathfrak{R}(\mathcal{W}_B)}{\theta} + O\left(\frac{\log(1/\delta)}{\sqrt{n}} \right).$$

Moreover, given the assumptions on the data and model class we made, the Rademacher complexity satisfies $\mathfrak{R}(\mathcal{W}) \le B/\sqrt{n}$. What we can learn from this bound is that the relevant quantity for generalization is the ratio of complexity to margin B/θ. Margin is a scale-sensitive notion and it makes sense to talk about it only after suitable normalization of the parameter vector. For linear predictors the Euclidean norm provides a natural and often suitable normalization. Other standard norms make sense and variants of the above result hold.

22.4.3 Margin Bounds for Neural Networks

The margin theory for linear models conceptually extends to neural networks. The definition of margin is unchanged. It simply quantifies how close the network is to making an incorrect prediction. What changes is that for multilayer neural networks the choice of a suitable norm is substantially more delicate.

To see why, a little bit of notation is necessary. We consider multilayer neural networks specified by a composition of L layers. Each layer is a linear transformation of the input, followed by a coordinate-wise nonlinear map:

$$\text{Input } x \to Ax \to \sigma(Ax).$$

The linear transformation has trainable parameters, while the nonlinear map does not. For notational simplicity, we assume we have the same nonlinearity σ at each layer scaled so that the map is 1-Lipschitz. For example, the popular coordinate-wise ReLU $\max\{x, 0\}$ operation satisfies this assumption.

Given L weight matrices $\mathcal{A} = (A_1, \ldots, A_L)$ let $f_{\mathcal{A}} \colon \mathbb{R}^d \to \mathbb{R}^k$ denote the function computed by the corresponding network:

$$f_{\mathcal{A}}(x) := A_L \sigma(A_{L-1} \cdots \sigma(A_1 x) \cdots)). \tag{22.10}$$

The network output $F_{\mathcal{A}}(x) \in \mathbb{R}^k$ is converted to a class label in $\{1, \ldots, k\}$ by taking the $\arg\max$ over components, with an arbitrary rule for breaking ties. We assume $d \ge k$ only for notational convenience.

Our goal now is to define a complexity measure of the neural network that will allow us to prove a margin bound. Recall that margins are meaningless without a suitable normalization of the network. Unfortunately, the complexity measure that we are about to define is somewhat cumbersome and requires a fair bit of notation.

Let $\| \cdot \|_{\mathrm{op}}$ denote the spectral norm. Also, let $\|A\|_{2,1} = \big\| (\|A_{:,1}\|_2, \ldots, \|A_{:,m}\|_2) \big\|_1$ the matrix norm, where we apply the ℓ_2-norm to each column of the matrix and then take the ℓ_1-norm of the resulting vector.

The *spectral complexity* $R_\mathcal{A}$ of a network $F_\mathcal{A}$ with weights $\mathcal{A}$ is defined as

$$
R_\mathcal{A} := \left(\prod_{i=1}^{L} \|A_i\|_{\mathrm{op}} \right) \left(\sum_{i=1}^{L} \left(\frac{\|A_i^\top - M_i^\top\|_{2,1}}{\|A_i\|_{\mathrm{op}}} \right)^{2/3} \right)^{3/2} . \tag{22.11}
$$

Here, the "reference matrices" $M_1, \ldots, M_L$ are free parameters that we can choose to minimize the bound. Random matrices tend to be good choices.

The following theorem provides a generalization bound for neural networks with fixed nonlinearities and weight matrices $\mathcal{A}$ of bounded spectral complexity $R_\mathcal{A}$.

Theorem 22.11 *Given data* $(x_1, y_1), \ldots, (x_n, y_n)$ *drawn i.i.d. from any probability distribution over* $\mathbb{R}^d \times \{1, \ldots, k\}$, *with probability at least* $1 - \delta$, *for every margin* $\theta > 0$ *and every network* $f_\mathcal{A} : \mathbb{R}^d \to \mathbb{R}^k$,

$$
R(f_\mathcal{A}) - R_S^\theta(f_\mathcal{A}) \le \tilde{\mathcal{O}} \left(\frac{R_\mathcal{A} \sqrt{\sum_i \|x_i\|_2^2} \ln(d)}{\theta n} + \sqrt{\frac{\ln(1/\delta)}{n}} \right),
$$

where $R_S^\theta(f) \le n^{-1} \sum_i \mathbf{1}\big[f(x_i)_{y_i} \le \theta + \max_{j \ne y_i} f(x_i)_j \big]$.

The proof of the theorem involves Rademacher complexity and so-called data-dependent covering arguments. Although it can be shown empirically that the complexity measure in $R_\mathcal{A}$ Equation 22.11 somewhat correlated with generalization performance in some cases, there is no reason to believe that it is the "right" complexity measure. The bound has other undesirable properties, such as, an exponential dependence on the depth of the network as well as an implicit dependence on the size of the network. In Section 22.7, we discuss some work that improves on this bound.

22.4.4 Implicit Regularization

In Section 22.3.3 we saw that explicit regularization is not necessary for excellent generalization performance. Researchers therefore believe that a combination of data-generating distribution and optimization algorithm perform *implicit regularization*. Implicit regularization describes the tendency of an algorithm to seek out solutions that generalize well on their own on a given a data set without the need for explicit correction. Since the empirical phenomena we reviewed are all based on gradient methods, it makes sense to study implicit regularization of gradient descent. While a general theory for nonconvex problems remains elusive, there has been progress for linear models.

The theorem holds applies to gradient descent with the *logistic* loss function, a standard loss function whose formal definition we omit.

Theorem 22.12 *For almost all datasets (i.e.; except for a measure zero set) which are strictly linearly separable, unregularized gradient descent with the logistic loss and small enough step sizes converges to the maximum margin solution. That is,*

$$\lim_{t \to \infty} \frac{w_t}{\|w_t\|} = \frac{w^*}{\|w^*\|},$$

where $w^* = \arg\min_{w \in \mathbb{R}^d} \|w\|^2$ *s.t.* $y_i\langle w, x_i \rangle \geq 1$.

A simple exercise shows that the optimizer w^* corresponds to the maximum margin solution when the data are linearly separable, i.e, 0 classification error is possible. What this theorem shows is that gradient descent, on its own, maximizes margin without the need for explicit regularization.

Recent work and ongoing efforts aim to extend this kind of result from the linear case to multilayer neural networks. The key challenge is to establish a norm that induces generalization given margin and to show that gradient descent is biased towards small solutions under this norm.

22.4.5 Interpolation Bounds

Most tools to reason about generalization have the property that they relate risk to empirical risk and end up showing that the generalization gap goes to 0 with more data. Such tools aren't necessarily useful when we expect the learning algorithm to always achieve zero training error, while the risk is bounded away from 0.

An important exception is the theory of nearest neighbor classification that we saw in Chapter 18. To recall, a nearest neighbor classifier, given a test input x, predicts the label of the training point closest to x. Formally, the predicted label for input $x \in \mathbb{R}^d$ is the label y_i such that $i \in \arg\min_j \|x - x_j\|$. We'll take the norm here to be Euclidean, although a nearest neighbor classifier could use any other nonnegative distance measure between points.

A remarkable classical result is that asymptotically (as the number of examples tends to infinity) the risk achieved by the nearest neighbor classifier is at most twice the Bayes optimal risk, i.e., the risk achieved by the classifier that assigns a label based on the conditional expectation $\mathbb{E}[y \mid x]$.

It is tempting to use nearest neighbor classification as a guiding case for reasoning about other model classes, such as neural networks. However, an analogous theory for neural networks is largely missing.

22.5 Empirical Checks and Holdout Estimates

Since theoretical generalization bounds continue to be a weak guide to practical modeling choices, the machine learning community heavily relies on empirical generalization estimates, primarily using a tool called the *holdout method*.

22.5.1 Holdout Method

We can always empirically estimate the risk of a classifier by collecting fresh data and computing the empirical risk of the classifier on the collected data. This leads to the common practice of setting aside a *test set* used for estimating the risk of classifiers trained on a separate *training set*. Sometimes practitioners divide their data into multiple splits, training, holdout, and test. However, for our discussion here that won't be necessary.

The cardinality bound (Equation 22.6) implies that the error of the holdout method on k models is upper bounded by $O(\sqrt{\log(k)/n})$ with high probability, assuming the loss function is bounded. This bound seems to allow for a massive number of classifiers to be evaluated against the test data.

However, there is a catch. The cardinality bound assumed that the k classifiers $f_1, \ldots, f_k$ were fixed independently of the test data. In practice, models incorporate what the analyst learned from previous evaluations against the test data. Model building is an iterative process in which the performance of a model informs subsequent design choices. This iterative process creates a feedback loop between the analyst and the test set. In particular, the classifiers the analyst chooses are not independent of the test set, but rather *adaptive*.

Adaptivity can be interpreted as a form of overparameterization. In an adaptively chosen sequence of classifiers $f_1, \ldots, f_k$, the kth classifier had the ability to incorporate at least $k - 1$ bits of information about the performance of previously chosen classifiers. This suggests that as $k \geq n$, the statistical guarantees of the holdout method become vacuous. This intuition proves correct. Indeed, there is a fairly natural sequence of k adaptively chosen models, resembling the practice of ensembling, on which the holdout estimate is off by at least $\Omega(\sqrt{k/n})$. A matching upper bound shows that the error is never worse.

If this pessimistic bound manifested in practice, holdout data would quickly lose their value. But does it?

22.5.2 Machine Learning Benchmarks

The holdout method is central to the scientific and industrial activities of the machine learning community. In many areas of machine learning, progress is measured on benchmarks based on the holdout method. In computer vision, the CIFAR-10 benchmark is a data set of 50,000 training images from 10 classes, and 10,000 test images. The ImageNet benchmark has 1.2 million training examples from 1,000 classes, and 50,000 test images.

Collectively, these test sets have been used tens of thousands of times. So, it makes sense to ask how much analysts have overfit to these test sets over the years.

In recent replication efforts, researchers carefully recreated new test sets for the CIFAR-10 and ImageNet classification benchmarks, created according to the very same procedure as the original test sets. The researchers then took a large collection of representative models proposed over the years and evaluated all of them on the new test sets. The results are shown in Figure 22.4.

Note that newer models, i.e., those with higher performance on the original test set, had *more* time to adapt to the test set and incorporate more information about it. Nonetheless, the better a model performed on the old test set the better it performs on the new set. Moreover, on CIFAR-10 we can clearly see that the absolute performance drops diminishes with increasing accuracy on the old test set.

These benign effects of adaptivity, as well as the cause of the performance drop, are the subject of ongoing investigation.

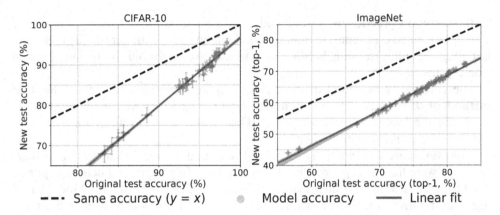

Figure 22.4 Model accuracy on the original test sets vs. new test sets. Each data point corresponds to one model in a test bed of representative models (shown with 95% Clopper–Pearson confidence intervals). The plots reveal two main phenomena: (1) There is generally a significant drop in accuracy from the original to the new test sets. (2) The model accuracies closely follow a linear function with slope greater than 1 (1.7 for CIFAR-10 and 1.1 for ImageNet). This means that every percentage point of progress on the original test set translates into more than one percentage point on the new test set. The two plots are drawn so that their aspect ratio is the same, i.e., the slopes of the lines are visually comparable. The narrow shaded region is a 95% confidence region for the linear fit from 100,000 bootstrap samples.

22.6 Looking Ahead

Despite significant effort and many recent advances, the theory of generalization in overparameterized models still lags behind the empirical phenomenology. What governs generalization remains a matter of debate in the research community.

Existing generalization bounds often do not apply directly to practice by virtue of their assumptions, are quantitatively too weak to apply to heavily overparameterized models, or fail to explain important empirical observations. However, it is not just a lack of quantitative sharpness that limits our understanding of generalization.

Conceptual questions remain open: What is it a successful theory of generalization should do? What are formal success criteria? Even a qualitative theory of generalization, that is not quantitatively precise in concrete settings, may be useful if it leads to the successful algorithmic interventions. But how do we best evaluate the value of a theory in this context?

Our focus in this chapter was decidedly narrow. We discussed how to relate risk and empirical risk. This perspective can capture only questions that relate performance on a sample to performance on the very same distribution that the sample was drawn from. What is left out are important questions of *extrapolation* from a training environment to testing conditions that differ from training. Overparameterized models that generalize well in the narrow sense can fail dramatically even with small changes in the environment. We saw one example in Figure 22.4, where even a carefully collected new test set caused model performance to drop significantly.

22.7 Notes

The tight characterization of generalization gap in terms of average stability, as well as stability of the ERM and regularization, is due to Shalev-Shwartz et al. (2010).

Uniform stability is due to Bousquet and Elisseeff (2002). For additional background on VC dimension and Rademacher, see, for example, Shalev-Shwartz and Ben-David (2014).

The figures in Section 22.3.1 are due to Belkin et al. (2019b). Earlier work pointed out similar empirical risk–complexity relationships (Neyshabur et al., 2014). The empirical findings and figures in Section 22.3.2 are due to Zhang et al. (2017b).

The results in Section 22.4.1 are due to Schapire et al. (1998). Later work showed theoretically that boosting maximizes margin (Zhang and Yu, 2005; Telgarsky, 2013). Results in Section 22.4.2 follow from more general results in Kakade et al. (2009) building on Bartlett and Mendelson (2002) and Koltchinskii et al. (2002). Section 22.4.3 is from Bartlett et al. (2017). See also early work along these lines by Bartlett (1998), and more recent work exploring how other norms shed light on generalization (Neyshabur et al., 2017). Golowich et al. (2018) improve on the bound in Theorem 22.11.

For more on interpolation bounds we discussed in Section 22.4.5, see Belkin et al. (2018, 2019a).

The result on implicit regularization in Section 22.4.4 is due to Soudry et al. (2018). See also Hardt et al. (2016) and subsequent work for attempts to explain the generalization performance stochastic gradient descent in terms of its stability properties. There has been an explosion of work on generalization and overparameterization in recent years. Our exposition is by no means a representative survey of the broad literature on this topic. There are several ongoing lines of work we did not cover: PAC-Bayes bounds (Dziugaite and Roy, 2017), compression bounds (Arora et al., 2018), and arguments about the properties of the optimization landscape (Zhang et al., 2017a).

Adaptivity in holdout reuse was the subject of Dwork et al. (2015) and subsequent work. The results and figures in Section 22.5.2 are due to Recht et al. (2019).

Acknowledgments

We thank Mikhail Belkin for helpful comments and providing Figures 22.1 and 22.2. Ludwig Schmidt generously provided Figure 22.4 as well helpful comments. Thanks to Daniel Soudry and Matus Telgarsky for helpful feedback and comments. The material on stability is in part based on lecture notes from Berkeley's class EE 227C (Spring 2018) – thanks to the student scribes.

References

Arora, Sanjeev, Ge, Rong, Neyshabur, Behnam, and Zhang, Yi. 2018. Stronger generalization bounds for deep nets via a compression approach. In *Proceedings of the 35th International Conference on Machine Learning (ICML)*, pp. 254–263.

Bartlett, Peter L. 1998. The sample complexity of pattern classification with neural networks: The size of the weights is more important than the size of the network. *IEEE Transactions on Information Theory*, **44**(2), 525–536.

Bartlett, Peter L, and Mendelson, Shahar. 2002. Rademacher and Gaussian complexities: Risk bounds and structural results. *Journal of Machine Learning Research*, **3**(Nov), 463–482.

Bartlett, Peter L, Foster, Dylan J, and Telgarsky, Matus J. 2017. Spectrally-normalized margin bounds for neural networks. In *Proceedings of the 31st Conference on Neural Information Processing Systems (NeurIPS)*, pp. 6240–6249.

Belkin, Mikhail, Hsu, Daniel J, and Mitra, Partha. 2018. Overfitting or perfect fitting? risk bounds for classification and regression rules that interpolate. In *Proceedings of the 32nd Conference on Neural Information Processing (NeurIPS)*, pp. 2300–2311.

Belkin, Mikhail, Rakhlin, Alexander, and Tsybakov, Alexandre B. 2019a. Does data interpolation contradict statistical optimality? In *Proceedings of the International Conference on Artificial Intelligence and Statistics (AISTATS)*, pp, 1611–1619.

Belkin, Mikhail, Hsu, Daniel, Ma, Siyuan, and Mandal, Soumik. 2019b. Reconciling modern machine-learning practice and the classical bias–variance trade-off. *Proceedings of the National Academy of Sciences of the USA*, 116(32) 15849–15854.

Bousquet, Olivier, and Elisseeff, André. 2002. Stability and generalization. *JMLR*, **2**(Mar), 499–526.

Dwork, Cynthia, Feldman, Vitaly, Hardt, Moritz, Pitassi, Toniann, Reingold, Omer, and Roth, Aaron. 2015. The reusable holdout: Preserving validity in adaptive data analysis. *Science*, **349**(6248), 636–638.

Dziugaite, Gintare Karolina, and Roy, Daniel M. 2017. Computing nonvacuous generalization bounds for deep (stochastic) neural networks with many more parameters than training data. In *Proceedings of the 33rd Conference on Uncertainty in Artificial Intelligence (UAI)*.

Golowich, Noah, Rakhlin, Alexander, and Shamir, Ohad. 2018. Size-independent sample complexity of neural networks. In *Proceedings of the 31st Conference on Learning Theory (COLT)*, pp. 207–299.

Hardt, Moritz, Recht, Benjamin, and Singer, Yoram. 2016. Train faster, generalize better: Stability of stochastic gradient descent. In *Proceedings of the 33rd International Conference on Machine Learning (ICML)*, pp. 1225–1234.

Kakade, Sham M, Sridharan, Karthik, and Tewari, Ambuj. 2009. On the complexity of linear prediction: Risk bounds, margin bounds, and regularization. In *Proceedings of the 23rd Conference on Neural Information Processing (NeurIPS)*, pp. 793–800.

Koltchinskii, Vladimir, Panchenko, Dmitry, et al. 2002. Empirical margin distributions and bounding the generalization error of combined classifiers. *The Annals of Statistics*, **30**(1), 1–50.

Neyshabur, Behnam, Tomioka, Ryota, and Srebro, Nathan. 2014. In search of the real inductive bias: On the role of implicit regularization in deep learning. *arXiv preprint arXiv:1412.6614*.

Neyshabur, Behnam, Bhojanapalli, Srinadh, McAllester, David, and Srebro, Nati. 2017. Exploring generalization in deep learning. In *Proceedings of the 31st Conference on Neural Information Processing (NeurIPS)*, pp. 5947-5956.

Recht, Benjamin, Roelofs, Rebecca, Schmidt, Ludwig, and Shankar, Vaishaal. 2019. Do ImageNet classifiers generalize to ImageNet? In *Proceedings of the 36th International Conference on Machine Learning (ICML)*, pp. 5389–5400.

Schapire, Robert E, Freund, Yoav, Bartlett, Peter, Lee, Wee Sun, et al. 1998. Boosting the margin: A new explanation for the effectiveness of voting methods. *Annals of Statistics*, **26**(5), 1651–1686.

Shalev-Shwartz, Shai, and Ben-David, Shai. 2014. *Understanding Machine Learning: From Theory to Algorithms*. Cambridge University Press.

Shalev-Shwartz, Shai, Shamir, Ohad, Srebro, Nathan, and Sridharan, Karthik. 2010. Learnability, stability and uniform convergence. *JMLR*, **11**(Oct), 2635–2670.

Soudry, Daniel, Hoffer, Elad, Nacson, Mor Shpigel, Gunasekar, Suriya, and Srebro, Nathan. 2018. The implicit bias of gradient descent on separable data. *JMLR*, **19**(1), 2822–2878.

Telgarsky, Matus. 2013. Margins, shrinkage, and boosting. In *Proceedings of the 36th International Conference on Machine Learning (ICML)*, pp. 307–315.

Zhang, Chiyuan, Liao, Qianli, Rakhlin, Alexander, Sridharan, Karthik, Miranda, Brando, Golowich, Noah, and Poggio, Tomaso. 2017a. *Theory of deep learning III: Generalization properties of SGD*. Tech. rept. Discussion paper, Center for Brains, Minds and Machines (CBMM). Preprint.

Zhang, Chiyuan, Bengio, Samy, Hardt, Moritz, Recht, Benjamin, and Vinyals, Oriol. 2017b. Understanding deep learning requires rethinking generalization. In *Proceedings of the 5th International Conference on Learning Representations (ICLR)*.

Zhang, Tong, and Yu, Bin. 2005. Boosting with early stopping: Convergence and Consistency. *Annals of Statistics*, **33**, 1538–1579.

Exercises

Exercise 22.1 Reproduce the empirical findings of Section 22.3.1.

Exercise 22.2 Reproduce the empirical findings of Section 22.3.2 with a neural network architecture of your choice.

Exercise 22.3 Consider empirical risk minimization for linear models in the case in which the dimension d is greater than the number of samples n. Experiment with the presence and absence of ℓ_2-regularization and its effect on generalization performance.

CHAPTER TWENTY THREE

Instance Optimal Distribution Testing and Learning

Gregory Valiant and Paul Valiant

Abstract: This chapter considers the challenge of saying as much as possible about a probability distribution given a limited number of samples. Traditionally, work has focused on either developing algorithms that are optimal in an asymptotic sense as the amount of data goes to infinity, or developing algorithms that are optimal in a worst-case sense when parameterized by relevant quantities such as the support size. This chapter, by contrast, considers two standard settings – *learning* a discrete distribution from samples, and *testing* whether a set of samples was drawn from a specific distribution – and develops algorithms that are near optimal *on every instance*.

23.1 Testing and Learning Discrete Distributions

This chapter revisits some of the most basic distributional learning and hypothesis testing problems, with the goal of designing algorithms for these tasks that are optimal in stronger senses than classical worst-case analysis. The first portion of the chapter considers the problem of learning a discretely supported distribution from independent draws. To motivate the results presented here, it is worth first considering the naive approach that simply returns the empirical distribution of the samples. The empirical distribution is optimal in a strong worst-case sense: For every error parameter $\epsilon > 0$ and integer k, given $n = k/\epsilon^2$ independent draws from a distribution supported on $\leq k$ elements, the expected total variation distance between the true distribution and the empirical distribution of the samples is bounded by $O(\epsilon)$. Furthermore, for worst-case distributions supported on k elements, there is no algorithm that can achieve expected error ϵ with $n = o(k/\epsilon^2)$ samples. However, despite this worst-case optimality of the empirical estimator, one might hope to do significantly better than this naive algorithm for the many non-worst-case distributions that have exploitable structure. Indeed, this chapter presents an "instance-optimal" algorithm which, in a concrete sense, optimally leverages whatever structure is present in the distribution in question, even without any prior knowledge of this structure.

The second portion of this chapter considers the following basic hypothesis testing problem, sometimes referred to as "identity testing": Given the description of a distribution, p, error tolerance $\epsilon > 0$, and n independent draws from an unknown distribution, q, distinguish the case that $p = q$ versus the case that p and q have total variation distance at least ϵ. Pearson's classical *chi-squared* test is one of the most commonly used algorithms for this problem, though it is far from optimal in the regime in which one expects many domain elements to be observed zero or once among the n samples. Beginning in the early 2000s, new algorithms were developed that pinned down the optimal sample size necessary for performing this test, for worst-case distributions, p, parameterized in terms of their support size. This chapter instead provides a variant of Pearson's chi-squared test that is optimal for every distribution, p, defined over a discrete countable support, and error parameter ϵ. Analyzing this algorithm yields a clean expression representing the sample complexity of testing the identity of a distribution p, as a function of p and ϵ.

Both the instance optimal learning, and the identity testing portions of this chapter, require some machinery that is conceptually and technically interesting beyond the direct applications to the problems at hand. This chapter provides self-contained treatments of this material. Section 23.2.3 describes an algorithm that, given n samples from distribution p, accurately recovers the multiset of the probabilities of the distribution, essentially as accurately as the empirical estimate would be when given $n \log n$ samples. Section 23.4 describes an efficient algorithm for proving inequalities of a certain form; such inequalities arise in the analysis of the identity testing algorithm and in many other settings in theoretical computer science.

23.2 Instance Optimal Distribution Learning

Given independent draws from an unknown distribution over an unknown discrete support, what is the best way to aggregate those samples into an approximation of the distribution? The most obvious approach is to simply return the empirical distribution of the samples. To what extent can one improve over this naive approach?

If one knew, a priori, that the distribution in question possessed some special structure, then that information could plausibly be leveraged to "denoise" the empirical distribution. For example, if one knew that the distribution is uniform over its domain, then one simply needs to identify the support of the distribution and estimate the support size. Both of these tasks may seem easier than estimating the probability of each element. A more realistic scenario might be where one knows that the distribution has a discrete power-law probability profile (where the ith most likely domain element has probability roughly proportional to $1/i^s$ for some constant, s, such as in Zipfian distributions); such information could plausibly be leveraged to "correct" the empirical distribution, by nudging empirical probabilities so that they fit with our prior knowledge of the overall power-law shape.

Is there an algorithm that, for *every* input distribution, optimally leverages whatever "structure" is present, *without any prior information about the type of structure*? This chapter shows that the answer is *yes*, up to a subconstant additive term, if one interprets the "structure" of a distribution to mean any property, such as support size or entropy, that is invariant to permuting or relabeling the domain elements – namely any function of the multiset of probabilities with which elements occur.

For the sake of both the construction of this instance-optimal learning algorithm, as well as its analysis, we will first define an unachievably good benchmark that will quantify how helpful the structure in the given instance actually is. This benchmark will correspond to the expected performance of an algorithm that receives extra information about the distribution in addition to the samples, and then uses this extra information and samples optimally. Specifically, this extra information will be the complete description of the distribution in question, with the labels removed. This extra information can be canonically represented as access to the sorted vector of probabilities with which domain elements occur: $p_1 \geq p_2 \geq p_3 \geq \ldots$. As it turns out, it will not be too difficult to reason about the structure of an algorithm that uses this extra information optimally. The analysis proceeds by designing an algorithm that does not receive this extra information, yet still emulates this unachievably good benchmark. The analysis concludes by showing that this algorithm, on every input distribution, performs nearly as well as the unachievably good benchmark.

Definition 23.1 Let $ErrOpt^*(p, n)$ be the minimum expected ℓ_1 error that any algorithm could achieve on the following learning task: Given the description of p, and n samples drawn independently from a distribution p' that is identical to p up to an arbitrary relabeling of the domain, learn the distribution p'. Let Opt^* be the corresponding algorithm, which takes as input both the samples and the vector of (permuted) probabilities.

The following theorem summarizes the sense in which an instance-optimal algorithm will, for every discrete distribution, learn nearly as well as if it already knew the distribution, up to relabeling the domain.

Theorem 23.2 *The Instance Optimal Learning Algorithm, outlined in Algorithm 1, when given n independent draws from any distribution p of discrete support, outputs a labeled vector q, such that with probability at least $1 - n^{-\omega(1)}$,*

$$\|p - q\|_1 \leq ErrOpt^*(p, n) + 1/polylog(n).$$

The proof of Theorem 23.2 boils down to arguing that if there are sufficient samples for Opt^* to accurately assign the labels of domain elements to the ground truth (unlabeled) vector of probabilities, then one has enough samples to approximately learn the vector of unlabeled probabilities from only the samples. From there the Instance Optimal Learning Algorithm may emulate Opt^*, losing only a $1/polylog(n)$ additive error in comparison to this benchmark. It turns out that the $1/polylog(n)$ additive error term is necessary in the preceding statement. If, however, one allows a multiplicative constant in front of $ErrOpt^*$, then a slightly different algorithm allows the $1/polylog(n)$ error term to be improved to $O(1/poly(n))$. In both cases, this error term is a function of n only, and in particular is independent of the distribution in question.

Theorem 23.3 *The Good–Turing Denoising Algorithm, described in Algorithm 2, when given n independent draws from any distribution p of discrete support, outputs a labeled vector q, such that with probability at least $1 - n^{-\omega(1)}$,*

$$\|p - q\|_1 \leq 2 \cdot ErrOpt^*(p, n) + \tilde{O}(1/n^{1/6}).$$

One surprising implication of Theorems 23.2 and 23.3 is that for large sample sizes, n, prior knowledge of the "shape" of the distribution, or knowledge of the rate of decay of the tails of the distribution, cannot significantly improve the accuracy of the learning task. For example, Theorem 23.2 implies that typical Bayesian assumptions that the frequency of words in natural language satisfy Zipf distributions, or that the frequencies of different species of bacteria in the human gut satisfy gamma distributions or various other power-law distributions, can improve the expected error of the learned distribution by at most a vanishing function of the sample size.

The following two examples highlight the limits and power of these results.

Example 23.4 Let $p = Unif(2)$ denote a distribution supported on two domain elements, with each element having probability $1/2$. The unattainable benchmark Opt^* just needs to learn the support, and hence for $n \geq 1$ the error is simply $1/2$ times the probability of not having observed both elements, namely $ErrOpt^*(Unif(2), n) = \frac{1}{2}\frac{1}{2^{n-1}} = 2^{-n}$. On the other hand, without prior knowledge of the probabilities, no algorithm can use n coin flips to learn the probabilities of a (possibly biased) coin to error $o(1/\sqrt{n})$.

Example 23.4 illustrates that prior knowledge of the vector of probabilities can be very helpful, reducing the expected error from inverse polynomial to inverse exponential. This demonstrates that, in general, one should not hope to achieve a result of the form of Theorem 23.2 without an additive error term. The fact that the error term of Theorem 23.2 vanishes as a function of the sample size, independent of the distribution, implies that for sufficiently large n there is no distribution for which prior knowledge of the probabilities can be leveraged to improve the expected error by a constant. The following example examines a natural extension of the preceding setting, where both Opt^*, as well as the instance-optimal algorithm, achieves significantly less error than the naive algorithm that returns the empirical distribution of the samples.

Example 23.5 Let $p = Unif(k)$ correspond to a uniform distribution over k elements. The Opt^* benchmark needs to learn the support of the distribution, as it knows, a priori, that every domain element that occurs with nonzero probability occurs with probability $1/k$. Hence, given n samples, the expected error is $1/k$ times the expected number of unobserved domain elements:

$$ErrOpt^*(Unif(k), n) = \Pr[Binomial(n, 1/k) = 0] \approx e^{-n/k}.$$

In comparison, the empirical distribution of the samples will have expected error

$$ErrEmp(Unif(k), n) = \frac{k}{n}E[|Binomial(n, 1/k) - n/k|] \approx \min(\sqrt{k/n}, 1).$$

When $n = c \cdot k$, these two expected errors differ drastically, with $ErrOpt^* \approx exp(-c)$ versus $ErrEmp \approx 1/\sqrt{c}$. For example, if $c = 10$, then each domain element will show up 10 times in expectation; if a domain element shows up 9 or 11 times, then the empirical estimator will over- or underestimate its probability respectively, while the optimal estimator will treat such over- or under representation in the samples identically, making an error only in the exponentially ($\approx e^{-10}$) unlikely case that such a domain element is entirely absent from the samples.

Theorem 23.2 shows that the Instance Optimal Learning Algorithm achieves error $exp(-c) + o_n(1)$, which will be close to $ErrOpt^*$ as long as n is large.

23.2.1 Understanding the Benchmark, *Opt**

Rather than directly trying to understand *Opt**, the analysis will instead consider an algorithm that receives *even more* additional information. Suppose you were given a set of samples, and, for each integer $i \geq 1$, you were told the multiset of probabilities of the domain elements observed exactly i times. With this additional information, the optimal algorithm is easy to describe.

First, for all integers i, the optimal algorithm will assign the same probability to all domain elements that are observed exactly i times. If this was not the case, it is not hard to show that there would exist a labeled distribution on which the algorithm would perform suboptimally. Given this, the question is what probability to assign? The following fact, whose proof is left as an exercise (Exercise 23.1), provides the answer.

Fact 23.6 *Given a multiset of real numbers, $S = \{s_1, \ldots, s_m\}$, setting $x = median(S)$ minimizes the sum of absolute differences between elements of S and x:*

$$\sum_{i=1}^{m} |s_i - median(S)| = \inf_{x \in \mathbf{R}} \sum_{i=1}^{m} |s_i - x|.$$

Hence we arrive at the following high-level sketch of the instance-optimal algorithm emulating *Opt**:

Algorithm 1 Sketch of the Instance Optimal Learning Algorithm that emulates *Opt**, achieving the instance-optimal guarantees of Theorem 23.2

Input: A set of n independent draws from an unknown distribution.
Output: A labeled vector of probabilities.

1. Use the samples to accurately reconstruct the unlabeled vector of probabilities, as described in Section 23.2.3.
2. For each $i \geq 1$, leverage the reconstructed vector to approximate the expected median probability of elements occurring i times, and assign that probability to all domain elements that occurred i times.

The most involved component of Algorithm 1 is reconstructing the unlabeled vector of probabilities. This is an extremely useful primitive, independent of our current goals of instance-optimal learning. Section 23.2.3 sketches the approach to this reconstruction problem, and describes some of the other applications of this subroutine. The complete proof of Theorem 23.2 is quite involved, though can be interpreted as arguing that, up to the additive $1/\text{polylog } n$ error term, one can always recover an approximation of the unlabeled vector of probabilities more accurately than one can disambiguate and label such a vector. This chapter will not cover the details of this proof, and we refer the interested reader to Valiant and Valiant (2016).

One of the difficulties in proving Theorem 23.2 is that the median is not especially well behaved, and it is tricky to design unbiased (or little-biased) estimators for the median of a distribution. The *mean*, however, is extremely well behaved, and can be leveraged to construct a simple algorithm that is easy to analyze, which achieves the guarantees of Theorem 23.3. The following fact summarizes the crucial property of the mean used in the analysis (see Exercise 23.2 for its proof):

Fact 23.7 *Given a multiset of numbers, $S = \{s_1, \ldots, s_m\}$, setting $x = mean(S)$ is at most a factor of 2 from minimizing the sum of absolute differences between elements of S and x: $\sum_{i=1}^{m} |s_i - mean(S)| \leq 2 \inf_{x \in \mathbb{R}} \sum_{i=1}^{m} |s_i - x|$.*

The following section describes the *Good–Turing* frequency estimation scheme, which provides an extremely simple estimator for the expected average probability of elements observed i times. This estimator leads to the simple algorithm achieving the guarantees of Theorem 23.3.

23.2.2 Good–Turing Frequency Estimation and Proof of Theorem 23.3

In the context of the British World War II code breaking efforts at Bletchley Park, I. J. Good and Alan Turing developed a slick approach to estimating simple functionals of discrete distributions, including the amount of "missing mass" – the total probability mass comprised by elements that have *not* been observed in a given set of samples. At a high level, their approach is to write an expression for the quantity of interest, and then reexpress that as a linear combination of terms, $\sum_{j \geq 1} c_j E[F_j]$, where F_j denotes the number of elements observed exactly j times. Given that F_j will be tightly concentrated about its expectation, this will yield a good estimate, provided the coefficients, c_j, are not too large.

We begin by instantiating this approach for the task of estimating the expected total probability mass comprised of elements observed exactly i times, yielding a variant of what is often referred to as *Good–Turing Frequency Estimation*.

Proposition 23.8 *Given n independent draws from a distribution p, let F_i denote the number of elements observed exactly i times, and let m_i denote the total probability mass comprised by such elements. Then for $i < n$,*

$$E[m_i] = \frac{i+1}{n-i} E[F_{i+1}] + O((i+1)/(n-i)).$$

Proof We begin by rewriting the expression for $E[m_i]$ in terms of $E[F_{i+1}]$. In the following, the summations are over the domain of the distribution, and $p(x)$ denotes the probability that the distribution assigns to element x.

$$E[m_i] = \sum_x p(x) \Pr[Binomial(n, p(x)) = i]$$

$$= \sum_x p(x)(p(x))^i (1 - p(x))^{n-i} \binom{n}{i}$$

$$= \frac{i+1}{n-i} \sum_x (p(x))^{i+1} (1 - p(x))^{n-i} \binom{n}{i+1}$$

$$= \frac{i+1}{n-i} \sum_x (1 - p(x)) \Pr[Binomial(n, p(x)) = i+1]$$

$$= \frac{i+1}{n-i} E[F_{i+1}] - \frac{i+1}{n-i} \sum_x p(x) \Pr[Binomial(n, p(x)) = i+1].$$

The second term on the last line is bounded by 1, since $\sum_x p(x) = 1$ and each binomial probability is at most 1, yielding the proposition. □

We are now prepared to describe the algorithm to which Theorem 23.3 applies. For elements observed many times, it uses their empirical probabilities, and for elements observed few times, it leverages the above Good–Turing estimate for the expected amount of probability mass comprised by such elements.

Algorithm 2 The Good–Turing Denoising Algorithm, achieving the instance-optimal guarantees of Theorem 23.3

Input: A set of n independent draws from an unknown distribution.
Output: A labeled vector of probabilities.

1. For each $i \geq n^{1/3}$, for every domain element observed exactly i times in the n samples, assign its empirical probability, i/n.
2. For each $i < n^{1/3}$, assign probability $\frac{i+1}{n-i} \cdot \frac{F_{i+1}}{F_i}$ to each of the F_i elements observed exactly i times, where F_j denotes the number of domain elements observed exactly j times in the n samples.

The proof of Theorem 23.3 will rely on the following intuitive concentration results.

Lemma 23.9 *With probability $1 - n^{-\omega(1)}$, for any distribution, p, we have the following tail bounds:*

- *The contribution to the error due to elements occurring more than $n^{1/3}$ times is small:*

$$\sum_{x:\, freq(x) \geq n^{1/3}} |p(x) - \widehat{p(x)}| \leq \sum_{x:\, freq(x) \geq n^{1/3}} \frac{\sqrt{freq(x)}}{n} polylog n \leq \tilde{O}(n^{-1/6}),$$

where $\widehat{p(x)} = freq(x)/n$ denotes the empirical probability of x.
- *For $i \geq 1$, $|F_i - E[F_i]| \leq \sqrt{1 + F_i}\, polylog n$, and the mass comprised of elements seen i times, m_i satisfies $|m_i - E[m_i]| \leq \frac{i}{n}\sqrt{1 + E[F_i]}\, polylog n$, and the contribution to the error from our approximation of the mean probability $m_i/F_i \approx \frac{i+1}{n-i} \cdot \frac{F_{i+1}}{F_i}$ is bounded as*

$$F_i \left| \frac{m_i}{F_i} - \frac{(i+1)F_{i+1}}{(n-i)F_i} \right| = \left| m_i - \frac{(i+1)F_{i+1}}{n-i} \right| \leq \frac{i}{n}\sqrt{1 + E[F_i]}\, polylog n.$$

The proof of Lemma 23.9 is left as an exercise. Proving these concentration bounds is complicated by the fact that the quantities in question cannot be easily represented as a sum of independent random variables – even the quantity F_i representing the number of elements observed exactly i times involves dependencies. Hence, instead of using basic Chernoff bounds to analyze this, which only apply to sums of independent random variables, one must instead apply Azuma's inequality – the standard analogue for martingales and analyze the Doob martingale that considers the expectation of the quantities in question as each of the n draws is successively revealed.

We now complete the proof that the Good–Turing Denoising Algorithm of Algorithm 2 achieves the guarantees of Theorem 23.3. Specifically, with high probability over the choice of the n independent samples, the error of this algorithm is at most $2 \cdot ErrOpt^* + \tilde{O}(1/n^{1/6})$, where $ErrOpt^*$ is the expected error of the optimal algorithm that receives the description of the true distribution without labels, in addition to the samples. We will prove the slightly stronger statement that with high probability, Algorithm 2 achieves an error at most $2 \cdot ErrOpt' + \tilde{O}(1/n^{1/6})$, where $ErrOpt'$ is the expected error of an optimal algorithm that receives a vector of probabilities for each $i \geq 0$, corresponding to the unlabeled vector of probabilities of all elements that occurred exactly i times.

Proof of Theorem 23.3 From Fact 23.6, this even better benchmark algorithm, *Opt'*, simply computes the median of each vector of probabilities and by Fact 23.7, if we instead computed the mean, μ_i of each vector, for $i \geq 1$, and assign μ_i to each element observed i times, we would incur an expected error at most $2ErrOpt'$. The first part of Lemma 23.9 guarantees that the contribution to the error from elements occurring at least $n^{1/3}$ times is bounded by $\tilde{O}(n^{-1/6})$. The second part of Lemma 23.9 shows that the discrepancy between the true and estimated means contribute at most the following quantity to the error: $\sum_{i \in \{1, \ldots, n^{1/3}\}} \frac{i}{n}\sqrt{1 + E[F_i]}$ polylog(n). Because of the constraint that $\sum_{i \geq 1} i F_i = n$, this expression is maximized, up to a constant factor, when $E[F_i] \approx n^{1/3}$ for all $i \leq n^{1/3}$, in which case the bound becomes

$$\sum_{i \in \{1, \ldots, n^{1/3}\}} \frac{i}{n}\sqrt{1 + E[F_i]} \text{ polylog} n \leq n^{1/3}\frac{n^{1/3}}{n}\sqrt{1 + n^{1/3}} \text{ polylog} n = \tilde{O}(n^{-1/6}).$$

$\square$

23.2.3 Estimating the Unseen: Reconstructing a Distribution up to Permutation

In this section we describe an algorithm that accurately approximates the unlabeled vector of probabilities of a distribution, given access to independent samples. This is the main subroutine in the Instance Optimal Learning Algorithm satisfying the guarantees of Theorem 23.2, sketched in Algorithm 1. We also briefly discuss some applications of this subroutine beyond its use in instance-optimal learning.

The recovery guarantee for this reconstruction roughly states that, for any distribution, p, given n independent draws, one can accurately recover the portion of the unlabeled vector of true probabilities comprised of probabilities above $c/n \log n$, for a suitable constant c. This is despite the fact that all the empirical probabilities of elements we observe are integer multiples of $1/n$, and for the elements with probability

$\ll 1/n$, we cannot hope to learn the labels for most of them, as the vast majority of such elements will not be observed in the n samples. The following theorem formalizes the recovery guarantees.

Theorem 23.10 *Let c denote an absolute constant. For a distribution p, let $p_1 \geq p_2 \geq \ldots$ represent the sorted vector of probabilities assigned to domain elements. For sufficiently large n and any $w \in [1, \log n]$, given n independent draws from p,*

a. *One can recover a vector $q = (q_1 \geq q_2 \geq \ldots)$ such that with probability $1 - e^{-n^{\Omega(1)}}$*

$$\sum_{i:p_i \geq w/(n\log n)} |p_i - q_i| \leq \frac{c}{\sqrt{w}}.$$

b. *Letting $cdf_p(v) = \sum_{x:p(x)\leq v} p(x)$ represent that cumulative density function of p, one can recover a distribution q such that with probability $1 - e^{-n^{\Omega(1)}}$*

$$\int_{v=w/(n\log n)}^{1} \frac{1}{v} |cdf_p(v) - cdf_q(v)| \, dv \leq \frac{c}{\sqrt{w}}.$$

In the case that w is a large constant, Theorem 23.10 guarantees that one can accurately learn the multiset of probabilities of the domain elements that occur with probability at least $\Theta(1/n\log n)$. Although many of these elements might not occur in the sample, Theorem 23.10 asserts that one can robustly detect the presence of such elements.

Beyond being interesting in its own right, the ability to reconstruct the unlabeled vector of probabilities as accurately as is guaranteed by Theorem 23.10 has a number of immediate applications for estimating label-invariant properties of the distribution (often referred to as *symmetric* properties). Indeed, any property that is Lipschitz continuous with respect to the distance metrics of Theorem 23.10, can be estimated by evaluating that property value on the recovered distribution, q. Such continuous properties include the expected value of functions of a larger set of independent draws. For example, an easy corollary of Theorem 23.10 is that one can accurately estimate the number of distinct elements that would be observed in a set of $m > n$ independent draws, for m up to $O(n\log n)$:

Corollary 23.11 *Given n samples from an arbitrary distribution p, with probability $1 - e^{-n^{\Omega(1)}}$ over the randomness of the samples, one can estimate the expected number of unique elements that would be seen in a set of m samples drawn from p, to within error $m \cdot c \sqrt{\frac{m}{n\log n}}$ for some universal constant c.*

From a practical standpoint, this corollary has a number of implication for the many settings where data collection is expensive. In (Zou et al., 2016), for example, this framework was fruitfully used to estimate the number of new, medically relevant genetic mutations that would likely be discovered if larger genetic cohorts were sequenced.

The algorithm for learning the unlabeled vector of probabilities will solve an optimization problem that returns a distribution, q, with the property that if the n samples had been drawn from q, one would expect to see similar statistics to the observed statistics of the actual samples. Specifically, the optimization problem will be a linear program, which returns a distribution with the property that the expected number of elements observed once, twice, etc. in a set of n independent draws will closely match the observed quantities $F_1, F_2, \ldots$. Discrepancies between F_i and the expectation of F_i under the returned distribution, are penalized proportionately to the inverse of the standard deviation, which is approximated as $1/\sqrt{F_i + 1}$. This approximation is reasonable because the variance of F_i is roughly equal to the expectation of F_i, as is the case for Poisson random variables.

The linear program will be described in terms of a fine ϵ-mesh of probability values, $x_1, \ldots, x_\ell \in (0, 1]$ that discretely approximate the potential probability values with which elements of the returned distribution may occur. The variables of the linear program, $h_1, \ldots, h_\ell$ will be interpreted so that h_i represents the number of domain elements that occur with probability x_i. Because the goal is to return a distribution, the total probability mass is constrained to equal 1, namely $\sum_i h_i x_i = 1$, which is a linear constraint in terms of the variables h_i. Additionally, by linearity of expectation, the expected values of F_j are also linear in the variables h_i, namely $E[F_i] = \sum_j h_j \Pr[Binomial(n, x_j) = i]$, where the expectation is with respect to the distribution represented by the variable $\{h_i\}$. For the time being, we ignore the fact that the linear program is allowed to return nonintegral values of h_i – as an additional step, the algorithm could perform a rounding/truncation step to deal with this minor issue.

One final subtlety is that this linear program will be used only for the portion of the distribution corresponding to domain elements that are not seen too many times. For large values of i, one would not actually expect F_i to be concentrated about its expectation. For example, even if there is a domain element that occurs with probability $1/2$, one would not expect $F_{n/2}$ to be too tightly concentrated about its expectation – indeed $F_{n/2}$ will either be 0 or 1 (or 2). Fortunately, for elements that occur often, their empirical probabilities are likely to be accurate. Hence, for elements seen frequently (at least n^α times for some appropriately chosen absolute constant $\alpha > 0$) the algorithm can simply use their empirical probabilities. For the potentially large number of elements each observed few times (at most n^α times), the linear program is used to recover the corresponding portion of the distribution. The fact that the linear program will be responsible only for the small portion of the potential distribution means that the linear program will be small, with only $O(n^\alpha)$ constraints corresponding to enforcing that $E[F_i] \approx F_i$ for $i \leq n^\alpha$. This will ensure that, both in theory and in practice, the linear program could be solved in time sublinear in the number of samples, n. For the purposes of this exposition, however, we omit the minor modifications necessary to achieve sublinear runtime.

The algorithm is presented in terms of two positive constants, B, C, which can be defined arbitrarily provided the following inequalities hold: $0.1 > B > C > \frac{B}{2} > 0$.

The proof of correctness of Algorithm 3, establishing Theorem 23.10 is quite involved, and proceeds by directly relating the objective value of the linear program to an appropriate notion of distance between the distribution represented by the returned (x_i, h_i) pairs, and the true vector of probabilities. We refer the reader to the treatment in Valiant and Valiant (2017b) for the details of this analysis.

Algorithm 3 The Frequency Spectrum Recovery Algorithm for reconstructing the unlabeled vector of probabilities, achieving the guarantees of Theorem 23.10

Input: Vector $F_1, F_2, \ldots$ where F_i denotes the number of domain elements observed exactly i times in a set of n samples.
Output: Vector of pairs $(x_1, h_1), \ldots, (x_t, h_t)$.

1. Define the set $X = \{\frac{1}{n^2}, \frac{2}{n^2}, \frac{3}{n^2}, \ldots, \frac{n(n^B + n^C)}{n^2}\}$.
2. For each $x \in X$, define the associated variable h_x, and solve the LP:

$$\text{Minimize} \sum_{i=1}^{n^B} \frac{1}{\sqrt{F_i + 1}} \left| F_i - \sum_{x \in X} h_x \Pr[Binomial(n, x) = i] \right|$$

   Subject to:

   · $\sum_{x \in X} x \cdot h_x + \sum_{i > n^B + 2n^C}^{n} \frac{i}{n} F_i = 1$ (total prob. mass = 1)

   · $\forall x \in X, h_x \geq 0$.
3. Return the set of pairs (x_i, h_{x_i}), together with pairs $(i/n, F_i)$ for those domain elements occuring $i > n^B + 2n^C$ times.

23.3 Identity Testing

We now turn to a basic distributional hypothesis testing problem: Given the description of a distribution p over a discrete support, error tolerance $\epsilon > 0$, and n independent draws from an unknown distribution, q, distinguish the case that $p = q$ versus the case that p and q have total variation distance at least ϵ, with probability of success at least $2/3$ over the randomness of the samples. This success probability of $2/3$ is standard in this literature, and can be exponentially amplified if needed by repeating the test with new samples and returning the majority outcome.

23.3.1 Overview

In contrast to the results of Section 23.2 in which the algorithms presented were instance optimal in terms of the unknown distribution from which the samples were drawn, in this section we will strive for an algorithm that is optimal in terms of the known distribution, p, in a worst-case sense over unknown distributions, q. Since distribution p is known to the algorithm, we will assume, without loss of generality, that it is supported on the positive integers, and will use p_i to denote the probability assigned to element i.

The classic approach to this hypothesis testing problem is via Pearson's chi-squared test. Letting X_i denote the number of times element i appears in the set of n samples, the chi-squared test accepts or rejects according to whether the following quantity exceeds a given threshold: $\sum_i \frac{(X_i - np_i)^2}{p_i}$. For distributions p with large support, this test is far from optimal. For example, if p is a uniform distribution over k elements, for constant ϵ, the chi-squared test requires k samples as compared to the optimal $\sqrt{k}$

---

samples (see Exercise 23.5). *Can one develop an identity test that is optimal for every distribution, p, and every error parameter, ϵ?*

The answer is yes, and the optimal algorithm is a modification of the chi-squared test. As a bonus, the analysis of this algorithm yields an expression, as a function of p and ϵ, characterizing the necessary and sufficient amount of data required to perform this hypothesis test. Before summarizing this result, we introduce the following notation that will be used for the rest of this section.

Notation Given a distribution p, let $p^{-\max}$ refer to the vector of probabilities of the distribution after removing the single highest-probability element; let $p_{-\epsilon}$ refer to the distribution after removing the lowest-probability elements, one-by-one, stopping just before ϵ total probability mass has been removed. We use standard notation for ℓ_p norms, where for real vector, v, and real number a, the ℓ_a norm of v is $\|v\|_a = \left(\sum_i |v_i|^a\right)^{1/a}$; however, unusually, instead of the standard ℓ_1 or ℓ_2 norms, the $a = 2/3$ norm is crucial to the analysis. We slightly abuse notation by using p both to refer to the distribution and to its vector of probabilities, $p = (p_1, p_2, \ldots)$.

Theorem 23.12 *Define the function $f(p, \epsilon) = \max\{\frac{1}{\epsilon}, \frac{\|p_{-\epsilon}^{-\max}\|_{2/3}}{\epsilon^2}\}$. There exists a tester and constants $c_1, c_2 > 0$ such that for any $\epsilon > 0$ and any distribution p, given samples from any unknown distribution q,*

a. *The tester will distinguish $q = p$ from $\|p - q\|_1 \geq \epsilon$ with probability $\geq 2/3$ when run on a set of at least $f(p, c_1 \epsilon)$ samples drawn from q; and*
b. *No tester can accomplish this task with a set of fewer than $f(p, c_2 \epsilon)$ samples.*

23.3.2 Interpretation of the Sample Complexity, $f(p, \epsilon)$

The function $f(p, \epsilon)$ defined in Theorem 23.12 expresses the optimal sample complexity of hypothesis testing distribution p. While the expression may look odd, the fact that it is constant-factor optimal for each and every distribution p means each of the quirks of $f(p, \epsilon) = \max\{\frac{1}{\epsilon}, \frac{\|p_{-\epsilon}^{-\max}\|_{2/3}}{\epsilon^2}\}$ represents a real phenomenon, and this definition is essentially a law of nature.

The $2/3$ norm of p is perhaps the most mysterious part of this expression, though is natural in light of the fact that when p is the uniform distribution on k elements, $\|p\|_{2/3} = \sqrt{k}$, matching the tight bounds for uniformity testing (Batu et al., 2013; Paninski, 2008). Further, for distributions of support at most k, the $2/3$ norm attains its maximum for the uniform distribution, and the "$-max$", "$-\epsilon$" modifiers can only decrease its value meaning that $f(p, \epsilon) \leq \frac{\sqrt{k}}{\epsilon^2}$ for all such distributions, which is a tight worst-case bound for distributions supported on at most k elements.

The $\frac{1}{\epsilon^2}$ multiplier in $f(p, \epsilon)$ shows up repeatedly in statistics, representing the fact that one needs $\frac{1}{\epsilon^2}$ coin flips to estimate the bias of a coin to accuracy $O(\epsilon)$, because the standard deviation of a sample mean decreases with the square root of the number of samples. The maximum with $\frac{1}{\epsilon}$ reflects the fact that, no matter what distribution we start with, it is impossible to distinguish a discrepancy of ϵ probability mass based on fewer than $\Omega(\frac{1}{\epsilon})$ samples; this term becomes relevant only in the "edge case" when $\|p_{-\epsilon}^{-\max}\|_{2/3} < \epsilon$, which can happen only when the maximum probability element has mass at least $1 - 2\epsilon$.

23.3.3 An Instance Optimal Algorithm

The testing algorithm satisfying Theorem 23.12, makes three crucial modifications, term-by-term, to the quantities computed in Pearson's chi-squared test, $\sum_i (X_i - np_i)^2/p_i$: (1) subtract X_i from the numerator to reduce the variance due to rare elements; (2) modify the denominator from p_i to $p_i^{2/3}$ to reduce the penalty for discrepancies in small probabilities; and (3) examine the smallest probability domain elements only in aggregate, while also ignoring the single largest domain element. Before formally stating the algorithm, we briefly motivate the first two of these modifications, which result in the expression $\sum_i \frac{(X_i - np_i)^2 - X_i}{p_i^{2/3}}$, which we refer to as the (instance optimal) test statistic.

The numerator of the ith term, $(X_i - np_i)^2 - X_i$, has two useful properties. First, it gives an *almost* unbiased estimate of $(p_i - q_i)^2$, after scaling: since $E[X_i] = nq_i$ and $E[X_i^2] = n^2 q_i^2 + nq_i(1 - q_i)$, we have

$$E[(X_i - np_i)^2 - X_i] = E[X_i^2] - 2np_i E[X_i] + (np_i)^2 - E[X_i] = n^2(q_i - p_i)^2 - nq_i^2$$

$$\approx n^2(q_i - p_i)^2.$$

Second, domain elements i for which $np_i, nq_i \ll 1$ will contribute very little variance to this expression. For such elements, $(X_i - np_i)^2 - X_i \approx X_i^2 - X_i$, which evaluates to 0 when $X_i = 0$ *and* when $X_i = 1$. Phrased differently, this expression is essentially agnostic to whether a rare element occurs zero times, versus once. The standard chi-squared statistic, by comparison, incurs a significant variance from such elements.

There is not an entirely clean motivation for scaling the ith term by $1/p_i^{2/3}$. Scaling by $1/p_i$, as in the chi-squared test, compensates for the fact that the expectation of the numerator is $(p_i - q_i)^2$, instead of the desired $|p_i - q_i|$. For example, if p_i and q_i differed by a constant factor, then the expected contribution after this scaling would also be proportional to $|p_i - q_i|$. The intuition for scaling by $1/p_i^\alpha$ for some $\alpha < 1$ is that even when $p = q$, we expect proportionately larger deviations between np_i and X_i for smaller values of p_i, and hence we must penalize such deviations less.

The lower bound construction, showing the optimality of this testing algorithm, yields a different perspective on the $1/p_i^{2/3}$ scaling of each term. Roughly speaking, for any distribution p, the most difficult instance of this hypothesis test is distinguishing whether $p = q$, versus a distribution where each element of q has a randomly perturbed probability $q_i = p_i \pm \delta_i$ for some choice of perturbations δ_i that sum to ϵ. From a lower bound standpoint, the question is how to allocate the δ deviation to the different elements. Setting $\delta_i = \epsilon \cdot p_i$, which would be the proportionate allocation, is clearly suboptimal, since the relative accuracy of an empirical estimate of q_i varies inversely with q_i, and thus proportional deviations would be easily detected for large q_i. This motivates setting the magnitude of $\delta_i = |q_i - p_i|$ to be proportional to p_i^α for some $\alpha < 1$. As it turns out, setting $\delta_i = p_i^{2/3}$ is optimal, matching the $1/p_i^{2/3}$ scaling in the statistic $\sum_i \frac{(X_i - np_i)^2 - X_i}{p_i^{2/3}}$.

We conclude by formally describing the testing algorithm in Algorithm 4, and saying a word about the proof of Theorem 23.12.

The proof of Theorem 23.12a, establishing the performance guarantees of the above testing algorithm, is conceptually simple. The core of the analysis is to apply Chebyshev's inequality to the expressions computed in steps 1 and 2 of the algorithm

---

Algorithm 4 The 2/3-Norm Testing Algorithm, which optimally tests whether $p = q$ versus $\|p - q\|_1 \geq \epsilon$

Input: Distribution $p = (p_1, p_2, \ldots)$, parameter $\epsilon > 0$ and a vector $X_1, X_2, \ldots$ where X_i denotes the number of times domain element i occurs in a set of n samples from an unknown distribution q.

Output: Either "$\|p - q\|_1 \geq \epsilon$" or "$p = q$."

0. Assume wlog that the domain elements of p are sorted in nonincreasing order of probability. Define $s = \min\{i : \sum_{j>i} p_j \leq \epsilon/8\}$, and let $S = \{s+1, s+2, \ldots\}$ (the "small" elements) and $M = \{2, \ldots, s\}$ (the "medium" elements).

1. Threshold the test statistic: if $\sum_{i \in M} \frac{(X_i - np_i)^2 - X_i}{p_i^{2/3}} > 4n\|p_M\|_{2/3}^{1/3}$ output "$\|p - q\|_1 \geq \epsilon$."

2. If $\sum_{i \in S} X_i > \frac{3}{16}\epsilon n$ output "$\|p - q\|_1 \geq \epsilon$."

3. Otherwise, output "$p = q$."

---

to show that – with the claimed probability – we accept true hypotheses and reject hypotheses that are far from true. (See Exercise 23.6 for analysis of the complementary roles of these two tests in the algorithm.) Chebyshev's inequality states that a random variable will be more than c standard deviations from its mean with probability at most $\frac{1}{c^2}$. The brunt of the algorithm analysis consists of showing that the expectations of the expressions computed by the algorithm differ significantly when $p = q$ versus when $\|p - q\|_1 \geq \epsilon$, and that this difference is large in comparison to the standard deviation of these quantities. Unfortunately, this simple approach reduces (after some straightforward but tedious algebra that we omit for clarity) to the problem of proving that an extremely messy inequality holds for all distributions p, and all discrepancies from the hypothesis $\Delta = (p_1 - q_1, p_2 - q_2, \ldots,)$:

$$\sum_{i \in M} \left(\frac{p_i^{2/3}\|\Delta_M\|_1^4}{\|p_M\|_{2/3}^2} + 2\frac{\Delta_i\|\Delta_M\|_1^3}{\|p_M\|_{2/3}^{4/3}} + \frac{p_i^{-2/3}\Delta_i^2\|\Delta_M\|_1^2}{\|p_M\|_{2/3}^{2/3}} \right. \tag{23.1}$$

$$\left. + 2\frac{p_i^{-1/3}\Delta_i^2\|\Delta_M\|_1^2}{\|p_M\|_{2/3}} + 2\frac{p_i^{-1}\Delta_i^3\|\Delta_M\|_1}{\|p_M\|_{2/3}^{1/3}} \right) \leq 8 \left(\sum_{i \in M} \Delta_i^2 p_i^{-2/3} \right)^2.$$

In Section 23.4 we describe a way of *automating* the proofs of such inequalities: this yields both a complete characterization of when such inequalities are true, along with a polynomial time algorithm that either produces a proof if the inequality is true, or a refutation if the inequality is not true.

23.4 Digression: An Automatic Inequality Prover

Given a sequence of triples, (a_i, b_i, c_i), is it true that for all positive vectors $x = (x_1, \ldots), y = (y_1, \ldots)$ the following inequality holds?

$$\prod_{i=1}^{r} \left(\sum_j x_j^{a_i} y_j^{b_i} \right)^{c_i} \geq 1. \tag{23.2}$$

Several familiar inequalities, including Cauchy–Schwarz, Hölder, and the monotonicity of ℓ_p norms, can be expressed in this form, as illustrated in the following expressions. Additionally, the proof of the inequality of Equation 23.1 corresponds to proving five inequalities of the above form – each inequality bounding one of the terms on the left-hand side by the right-hand side.

$$\left(\sum_j x_j^2\right)^{1/2} \left(\sum_j y_j^2\right)^{1/2} \left(\sum_j x_j y_j\right)^{-1} \geq 1 \qquad \text{(Cauchy–Schwarz)}$$

$$\left(\sum_j x_j^{1/\lambda}\right)^{\lambda} \left(\sum_j y_j^{1/(1-\lambda)}\right)^{1-\lambda} \left(\sum_j x_j y_j\right)^{-1} \geq 1 \qquad \text{(Hölder)}$$

$$\left(\sum_j x_j^{1/\lambda}\right)^{-\lambda} \left(\sum_j x_j\right) \geq 1. \qquad \text{(ℓ_p monotonicity)}$$

In this section, we show that an inequality of the form of Equation 23.2 is true, if and only if it is expressible as the product of positive powers of Hölder, and ℓ_p monotonicity inequalities. Furthermore, there is an efficient algorithm for automatically proving or disproving such an inequality: Given the triples (a_i, b_i, c_i), the algorithm either produces a derivation of the inequality, or produces a counterexample pair of sequences x, y which falsify the inequality.

Theorem 23.13 *For a sequence of triples $(a,b,c)_i = (a_1, b_1, c_1), \ldots (a_r, b_r, c_r)$, the inequality $\prod_{i=1}^r \left(\sum_j x_j^{a_i} y_j^{b_i}\right)^{c_i} \geq 1$ holds for all finite sequences of positive numbers $(x)_j, (y)_j$ if and only if it can be expressed as a finite product of positive powers of Hölder inequalities of the form $\left(\sum_j x_j^{a'} y_j^{b'}\right)^{\lambda} \cdot \left(\sum_j x_j^{a''} y_j^{b''}\right)^{1-\lambda} \geq \sum_j x_j^{\lambda a' + (1-\lambda)a''} y_j^{\lambda b' + (1-\lambda)b''}$, and ℓ_p monotonicity inequalities of the form $\left(\sum_j x_j^a y_j^b\right)^{\lambda} \leq \sum_j x_j^{\lambda a} y_j^{\lambda b}$, where $\lambda \in [0,1]$. Such a derivation can be found in polynomial time via linear programming whenever the inequality is true; and a compact representation of a refutation can be found whenever the inequality is false.*

Example 23.14 Consider for some $\epsilon \geq 0$ the single-sequence inequality

$$\left(\sum_j x_j^{-2}\right)^{-1} \left(\sum_j x_j^{-1}\right)^3 \left(\sum_j x_j^0\right)^{-2-\epsilon} \left(\sum_j x_j^1\right)^3 \left(\sum_j x_j^2\right)^{-1} \geq 1,$$

which can be expressed in the form of Equation 23.2 via the triples $(a_i, b_i, c_i) = (-2, 0, -1), (-1, 0, 3), (0, 0, -2 - \epsilon), (1, 0, 3), (2, 0, -1)$. This inequality is true for $\epsilon = 0$ but false for any positive ϵ. However, the shortest counterexample sequences have length that grows as $\exp(\frac{1}{\epsilon})$ as ϵ approaches 0. Counterexamples are thus hard to write down, though easy to express—for example, letting $n = 64^{1/\epsilon}$, the sequence x of length $2 + n$ consisting of $n, \frac{1}{n}$, followed by n ones violates the inequality.

23.4.1 Proving Inequalities without Math: A Peg Game

Theorem 23.13 argues that there is a linear-programming based algorithm for efficiently proving or refuting inequalities of the specified form. The intuition underlying
the proof of Theorem 23.13, however, can be used to formulate the task of proving
such an inequality as a simple and intuitive "peg game" played on a 2-d board. This
peg game interpretation allows one to use basic geometric intuitions to easily derive
a proof of many of these inequalities, using only a little bit of pencil and paper!

We describe this peg game in the concrete setting of proving the following inequality (which corresponds to the 4th component of Equation 23.1 from Section 23.3
where Δ has been replaced by x and p has been replaced by y):

$$\left(\sum_j x_j^2 y_j^{-2/3} \right)^2 \left(\sum_j x_j^2 y_j^{-1/3} \right)^{-1} \left(\sum_j x_j \right)^{-2} \left(\sum_j y_j^{2/3} \right)^{3/2} \geq 1, \qquad (23.3)$$

Expressing this inequality in the form of Theorem 23.13, we have the triples
$(a_i, b_i, c_i) = (2, -\frac{2}{3}, 2), (2, -\frac{1}{3}, -1), (1, 0, -2), (0, \frac{2}{3}, \frac{3}{2})$. The peg game – as illustrated
in Figure 23.1 – begins by representing each triple (a_i, b_i, c_i) as the number c_i written
at location (a_i, b_i) in the plane. At any moment, the game board consists of some
numbers written on the plane (with the convention that every point without a number
is interpreted as having a 0), and you "win" if you can remove all the numbers from
the board via a combination of "moves" of the following two types:

1. (Hölder) Any two positive numbers can be moved to the weighted mean of their
   locations. (For example, we can subtract 1 from one location in the plane, subtract
   3 from a second location in the plane, and add 4 to a point $\frac{3}{4}$ of the way from the
   first location to the second location.)
2. (ℓ_p monotonicity) Any negative number can be moved toward the origin by a
   factor $\lambda \in (0,1)$ and scaled by $\frac{1}{\lambda}$. (For example, we can add 1 to one location
   in the plane, and subtract 2 from a location halfway to the origin.)

The rules of the game allow just these two types of moves: you can push positive
numbers together, and push negative numbers towards the origin (scaling them).
Theorem 23.13 translates into the claim that this peg game can be won if, and only if,
the corresponding inequality is true; additionally, a small linear program can either
produce a winning combination of moves, or present a certificate that the game is
unwinnable. Nevertheless, our geometric intuition is quite good at solving these types
of puzzles, even for intricate counterintuitive inequalities like the current example.
(Try it!)

The intuition behind one winning sequence for the game corresponding to
Equation 23.3, illustrated in Figure 23.1, is to first realize that three of the points
lie on a line, with the "−2" halfway between the "$\frac{3}{2}$" and the "2." Thus we take 1
unit from each of the endpoints and cancel out the "−2" via a "Hölder" move. Now,
no three points are collinear, so we need to move one point onto the line formed by
the other two: "−1," being negative, can be moved toward the origin, so we move it
until it crosses the line formed by the two remaining numbers. This moves it $\frac{1}{3}$ of the
way to the origin, thus increasing it from "−1" to "−$\frac{3}{2}$"; amazingly, this number, at

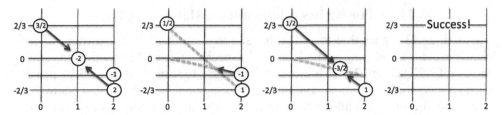

Figure 23.1 Depiction of a successful sequence of "moves" in the game corresponding to the inequality $\left(\sum_j x_j^2 y_j^{-2/3}\right)^2 \left(\sum_j x_j^2 y_j^{-1/3}\right)^{-1} \left(\sum_j x_j\right)^{-2} \left(\sum_j y_j^{2/3}\right)^{3/2} \geq 1$, showing that the inequality is true. The first diagram illustrates the initial configuration of positive and negative weights, together with the "Hölder-type move" that takes one unit of weight from each of the points at $(0, 2/3)$ and $(2, -2/3)$ and moves it to the point $(1, 0)$, canceling out the weight of -2 that was initially at $(1, 0)$. The second diagram illustrates the resulting configuration, together with the "ℓ_p monotonicity move" that moves the -1 weight at location $(2, -1/3)$ toward the origin by a factor of $2/3$ while scaling it by a factor of $3/2$, resulting in a point at $(4/3, -2/9)$ with weight $-3/2$, which is now collinear with the remaining two points. The third diagram illustrates the final "Hölder-type move" that moves the two points with positive weight to their weighted average, zeroing out all weights.

position $\frac{2}{3}(2, -\frac{1}{3}) = (\frac{4}{3}, -\frac{2}{9})$ is now $\frac{2}{3}$ of the way from the remaining "$\frac{1}{2}$" at $(0, \frac{2}{3})$ to the number "1" at $(2, -\frac{2}{3})$, meaning that we can remove the final three numbers from the board in a single move, winning the game. We thus made three moves total, two of the Hölder type, one of the ℓ_p monotonicity type. Reexpressing these moves as inequalities yields the desired derivation of our inequality (Equation 23.3) as a product of powers of Hölder and ℓ_p monotonicity inequalities, explicitly, as the product of the following three inequalities, which are respectively (1) the square of a Cauchy-Schwarz inequality, (2) the $3/2$ power of an ℓ_p monotonicity inequality for $\lambda = 2/3$, and (3) the $3/2$ power of a Hölder inequalty for $\lambda = 2/3$:

$$\left(\sum_j x_j^2 y_j^{-2/3}\right)\left(\sum_j x_j^0 y_j^{2/3}\right)\left(\sum_j x_j^1 y_j^0\right)^{-2} \geq 1$$

$$\left(\sum_j x_j^{4/3} y_j^{-2/9}\right)^{3/2}\left(\sum_j x_j^2 y_j^{-1/3}\right)^{-1} \geq 1$$

$$\left(\sum_j x_j^2 y_j^{-2/3}\right)\left(\sum_j x_j^0 y_j^{2/3}\right)^{1/2}\left(\sum_j x_j^{4/3} y_j^{-2/9}\right)^{-3/2} \geq 1.$$

23.5 Beyond Worst-Case Analysis for Other Testing Problems

There are a wide variety of testing and learning problems that can be considered from perspectives other than worst-case analysis, beyond the two settings highlighted in this chapter. In many cases, a significant part of the challenge is defining a reasonable benchmark or notion of optimality that yields clean, conceptually appealing results and practically meaningful algorithms.

To briefly describe one example, Section 23.3 considers the question of distinguishing whether two distributions, p and q, are equal versus have significant distance, given a description of p and samples drawn from q. The analogous question can also be asked where both distributions p and q are unknown, and one wishes to deduce if $p = q$ versus $\|p - q\|_1 \geq \epsilon$ given samples from both distributions. If p and q are supported on at most n elements, this hypothesis can be tested using $O\left(\max(n^{2/3}/\epsilon^{4/3}, n^{1/2}\epsilon^2)\right)$, which is optimal *in the worst case* (Batu et al., 2013; Chan et al., 2014).

Going beyond worst-case analysis, the works of Acharya et al. (2011, 2012) apply the perspective of *competitive analysis* to this question. Instead of bounding the sample size required for this task in terms of the support size of the distributions, this work bounds the sample size as a (superlinear) function of the sample size that would be required if distributions p and q were known to the algorithm, and the algorithm needed to distinguish whether two sets of samples were drawn from the pair p, q versus both drawn from a single distribution.

The work of Lam-Weil et al. (2019) takes a quite different approach toward this problem of identity testing with two unknown distribution. The authors develop an algorithm that, for every p, q, uses as few samples as would be necessary even if one "approximately" knows distribution q. Specifically, given a vector of probabilities, π, they ask how difficult it is to distinguish $p = q$ versus $\|p - q\|_1 \geq \epsilon$ where distribution q is obtained via the random process of sampling the probabilities of its elements uniformly at random from the multiset π, and p is a worst-case distribution with distance ϵ from q. Here, the goal is to get an optimal sample complexity as a function of π, achieved via an algorithm that does not require knowledge of π.

23.6 Notes

Section 23.2 is based on results from Valiant and Valiant (2016), and Sections 23.3 and 23.4 are based on Valiant and Valiant (2017a). For the problem of instance optimal learning discussed in Section 23.2, the work of Orlitsky and Suresh (2015), which appeared contemporaneously with Valiant and Valiant (2016), considered the problem of learning with respect to KL-divergence, instead of total variation distance (L1 distance). In that setting, they showed a variant of the Good–Turing Denoising Algorithm (Algorithm 2) is instance optimal for learning with respect to KL-divergence in an analogous sense to the results discussed in Section 23.2.

For additional intuition on how the 2/3-norm arises in the sample complexity of instance optimal testing (Theorem 23.12), we refer the reader to Diakonikolas and Kane (2016), who obtained a similar expression with extra polylogarithmic factors, via a general framework for reducing such hypothesis testing questions to the easier task of performing analogous tests in terms of ℓ_2 distance.

For a general introduction to modern questions and perspectives on distributional property testing and estimation, we refer the reader to the survey Canonne (2015), or the slightly older survey Rubinfeld and Shapira (2011). These surveys also provide some historical context for how these fundamental statistical questions came to be studied by the theoretical computer science community, first in the context of testing graph expansion – essentially the question of identity testing with respect to the uniform distribution (Goldreich and Ron, 2011) – and subsequently abstracted and generalized to hypothesis tests and estimates of ℓ_1 and ℓ_2 norms between distributions (Batu et al., 2013).

References

Acharya, J., Das, H., Jafarpour, A., Orlitsky, A., and Pan, S. 2011. Competitive closeness testing. In *Conference on Learning Theory (COLT)*, pp. 47–68.

Acharya, J., Das, H., Jafarpour, A., Orlitsky, A., and Pan, S. 2012. Competitive classification and closeness testing. In *Proceedings of the 25th Conference on Learning Theory (COLT)*, **23**, 22.1–22.18.

Batu, T., Fortnow, L., Rubinfeld, R., Smith, W.D., and White, P. 2013. Testing closeness of discrete distributions. *Journal of the ACM*, 60(1), 4: 1–4: 25.

Canonne, Clément L. 2015. A survey on distribution testing: Your data is big, but is it blue? In *Electronic Colloquium on Computational Complexity (ECCC)*, vol. 22.

Chan, Siu-On, Diakonikolas, Ilias, Valiant, Paul, and Valiant, Gregory. 2014. Optimal algorithms for testing closeness of discrete distributions. In *Proceedings of the Twenty-fifth Annual ACM-SIAM Symposium on Discrete Algorithms*, pp. 1193–1203. SIAM.

Diakonikolas, Ilias, and Kane, Daniel M. 2016. A new approach for testing properties of discrete distributions. In *2016 IEEE 57th Annual Symposium on Foundations of Computer Science (FOCS)*, pp. 685–694. IEEE.

Goldreich, Oded, and Ron, Dana. 2011. On testing expansion in bounded-degree graphs. In *Studies in Complexity and Cryptography. Miscellanea on the Interplay between Randomness and Computation*, pp. 68–75. Springer.

Lam-Weil, Joseph, Carpentier, Alexandra, and Sriperumbudur, Bharath K. 2019. Local minimax rates for closeness testing of discrete distributions. *arXiv preprint arXiv:1902.01219.*

Orlitsky, Alon, and Suresh, Ananda Theertha. 2015. Competitive distribution estimation: Why is Good-Turing good. In *Advances in Neural Information Processing Systems 28*. Curran Associates, pp. 2143–2151.

Paninski, L. 2008. A coincidence-based test for uniformity given very sparsely-sampled discrete data. *IEEE Transactions on Information Theory*, **54**, 4750–4755.

Rubinfeld, Ronitt, and Shapira, Asaf. 2011. Sublinear time algorithms. *SIAM Journal on Discrete Mathematics*, **25**(4), 1562–1588.

Valiant, Gregory, and Valiant, Paul. 2016. Instance optimal learning of discrete distributions. In *Proceedings of the Forty-eighth Annual ACM Symposium on Theory of Computing*, pp. 142–155. STOC '16. ACM.

Valiant, Gregory, and Valiant, Paul. 2017a. An automatic inequality prover and instance optimal identity testing. *SIAM Journal on Computing*, **46**(1), 429–455.

Valiant, Gregory, and Valiant, Paul. 2017b. Estimating the unseen: Improved estimators for entropy and other properties. *Journal of ACM*, **64**(6), 37:1–37:41.

Zou, James, Valiant, Gregory, Valiant, Paul, Karczewski, Konrad, Chan, Siu On, Samocha, Kaitlin, Lek, Monkol, Sunyaev, Shamil, Daly, Mark, and MacArthur, Daniel G. 2016. Quantifying unobserved protein-coding variants in human populations provides a roadmap for large-scale sequencing projects. *Nature Communications*, **7**, 13293.

Exercises

Exercise 23.1 Prove Fact 23.6, that for any multiset of real numbers $S = \{s_1, \ldots, s_m\}$, the *median* minimizes the sum of the absolute distances to elements of S:

$$\sum_{i=1}^{m} |s_i - median(S)| = \inf_{x \in \mathbb{R}} \sum_{i=1}^{m} |s_i - x|.$$

Exercise 23.2 Prove Fact 23.7, that for any multiset of real numbers $S = \{s_1, \ldots, s_m\}$, the sum of the absolute differences between the *mean* and elements of S is at most a factor of two larger than the sum of distances to the median:

$$\sum_{i=1}^{m} |s_i - mean(S)| \leq 2 \cdot \sum_{i=1}^{m} |s_i - median(S)| = 2 \cdot \inf_{x \in \mathbb{R}} \sum_{i=1}^{m} |s_i - x|.$$

Exercise 23.3 Given n independent draws from a distribution with discrete support, for integers $i \geq 1$, let F_i represent the number of domain elements that each appear exactly i times in the samples. Prove that F_i is tightly concentrated about its mean, namely for any $c > 0$, $\Pr[|F_i - E[F_i]| \geq c\sqrt{n}] \leq O(\exp(-\Omega(c^2)))$. (Hint: Letting x_i denote the ith indepedent draw, consider the Doob martingale: $X_0 = E[F_i], X_1 = E[F_i|x_1], X_2 = E[F_i|x_1, x_2], \ldots, X_n = E[F_i|x_1, \ldots, x_n] = F_i$, and apply Azuma's martingale concentration inequality.)

Exercise 23.4 Show that the concentration bound of the previous exercise can be improved if $E[F_i] \ll n$: show that $\Pr[|F_i - E[F_i]| \geq c\sqrt{1 + E[F_i]}] = O(\exp(-\Omega(c^2)))$.

Exercise 23.5 Let $p = (1/2, \frac{1}{2k}, \frac{1}{2k}, \ldots, \frac{1}{2k})$ denote the distribution that puts mass $1/2$ on element 1, and distributes the remaining mass among elements $2, \ldots, k+1$; let $q = (1/2, \frac{1}{k}, \ldots, \frac{1}{k})$ denote an analogous distribution that distributes the remaining mass among $2, \ldots, k/2+1$. Consider using the chi-squared statistic $\sum_i (X_i - np_i)/p_i$ to distinguish the case where n samples were drawn from p versus n samples were drawn from q. Prove that this distinguisher would require $n = \Omega(k)$ samples to have success probability at least $2/3$.

Exercise 23.6 This exercise motivates the two steps of the algorithm of Algorithm 4, with Step 1 detecting discrepancies in "medium" probability elements, and step 2 detecting if the "small" probability elements have too much total probability mass. Recall that the set S of small elements is constructed so that $\sum_{i \in S} p_i \leq \frac{\epsilon}{8}$, and the set M consists of the remaining elements, with the exception of p_{max}. Prove that if $\|p - q\|_1 \geq \epsilon$ then at least one of the following must hold:

- $\sum_{i \in M} |p_i - q_i||_1 \geq \frac{\epsilon}{8}$ (which will likely trigger step 1 of the algorithm), or
- $\sum_{i \in S} q_i \geq \frac{\epsilon}{4}$ (which will likely trigger step 2 of the algorithm).

Exercise 23.7 Show the monotonicity of ℓ_p norms: for a vector x and $\lambda \in (0, 1)$, $||x||_1 \leq ||x||_\lambda$.

Exercise 23.8 Win the "peg game" of Figure 23.1 in a *different* way, where the first move is different from zeroing out the -2 at location $(1, 0)$. Express your winning strategy as a combination of Hölder and ℓ_p monotonicity inequalities.

Exercise 23.9 Prove the inequality of Example 23.14 for $\epsilon = 0$ – or more generally, for any $\epsilon \leq 0$ – via the "peg game" techniques of Section 23.4.1.

PART SIX

Further Applications

CHAPTER TWENTY FOUR

Beyond Competitive Analysis

Anna R. Karlin and Elias Koutsoupias

Abstract: Competitive analysis is frequently unrealistic, because the inputs "in practice" rarely exhibit the worst-case characteristics assumed by the pessimistic adversarial settings of competitive analysis. This chapter discusses approaches that go *beyond competitive analysis* and attempt to bring the analysis of optimization problems under incomplete information within a more realistic realm. We consider various approaches from the literature including restricting the set of inputs the adversary is allowed to provide, giving more power to the online algorithm, changing the way performance is measured, and directly comparing online algorithms.

24.1 Introduction

In competitive analysis, the performance of an online algorithm is compared against an all-powerful adversary on a worst-case input. The *competitive ratio* of a problem – the analog of worst-case asymptotic complexity for this area – is defined as

$$c = \inf_{\mathcal{A}} \sup_{\sigma} \frac{\mathcal{A}(\sigma)}{\mathsf{OPT}(\sigma)} \qquad (24.1)$$

Here $\mathcal{A}$ ranges over all online algorithms and σ over all "inputs"; $\mathsf{OPT}(\sigma)$ and $\mathcal{A}(\sigma)$ denote the cost of an optimum offline algorithm OPT and the cost of the online algorithm A when presented with input σ. This definition is usually adapted by subtracting a constant term from the numerator to account for a possible initial disadvantage of the online algorithm. This clever definition is both the weakness and strength of competitive analysis. It is a strength because the setting is clear, the problems are crisp and sometimes challenging, and the results often elegant and striking. But it is also a weakness for several reasons. First, in the face of the devastating comparison against an all-powerful off-line algorithm, a wide range of online algorithms (good, bad, and mediocre) can fare equally badly; thus the competitive ratio may not be very informative and it may fail to discriminate and to suggest good approaches. Another aspect of the same problem is that, since a worst-case input decides the performance of the algorithm, the optimal algorithms are sometimes unnatural and impractical, and the bounds too pessimistic to be informative in practice. The main argument for competitive analysis over expectation maximization is that *the distribution is usually not known*. However, competitive analysis takes this argument way too far: It assumes that *absolutely nothing* is known about the input and that *any distribution* of the inputs is in principle possible; the worst-case "distribution" prevailing in competitive analysis is, of course, a worst-case input with probability one. Such complete powerlessness seems unrealistic to both the practitioner (we always know, or can learn, *something* about the distribution of the inputs) and the theoretician (the absence of a prior distribution, or some information about it, seems very unrealistic to a probabilist or mathematical economist).

In Chapter 1, we were introduced to the *paging problem,* one of the simplest, most fundamental, and practically important online problems. We saw that an unreasonably wide range of deterministic algorithms (both the good in practice Least-Recently-Used, LRU; the empirically mediocre First-In-First-Out, FIFO; and the ridiculous Flush-When-Full, FWF, which empties the cash at every page fault) have the same competitive ratio – k, the amount of available memory. Even algorithms within more powerful *information regimes* – for example, any algorithm with lookahead $\ell > 0$ pages – provably can fare no better. One approach to improving the competitive ratio of an algorithm is to incorporate *randomization.* For paging, this brings the competitive ratio down to $\ln(k)$ (McGeoch and Sleator, 1991; Achlioptas et al., 2000). However, this improvement doesn't really address the shortcomings of the competitive analysis research program nor has it affected the algorithms used in practice.

We have already seen two ways of going beyond worst-case analysis: In Chapter 1, we saw parameterized bounds in paging, and in Chapter 4, we saw resource augmentation. In this chapter, we survey some of the other approaches that have been taken in the literature.

At a high level, the literature on going beyond worst-case in online algorithms takes three approaches: (1) modifying the resources available to the online algorithm, (2) weakening the adversary/benchmark, and (3) changing the way we measure the performance of the online algorithm.

In the rest of the chapter we give examples of these approaches, primarily in the context of the *paging problem.* We refer the reader to Chapters 1 and 4 for a review of the paging model, the basic results, and basic algorithms.

24.2 The Access Graph Model

Competitive analysis treats the interaction between algorithms and inputs as a zero-sum game, where an adversary generates the inputs. One way to improve over the worst case is to limit the set of inputs the adversary is allowed to provide, ideally in a way that captures the kind of inputs that we are likely to see in practice.

Let's focus on the paging problem and ask what kind of inputs are likely in practice. A natural answer is that most programs exhibit *locality of reference.* Locality of reference, which has been thought to explain the practical success of LRU, means that if a page is referenced, it is more likely to be referenced in the near future (temporal locality) and pages near it in memory are more likely to be referenced in the near future as well (spatial locality). Indeed, a storage hierarchy is only useful if request sequences are *not arbitrary.*

Thus, it is natural to ask how locality of reference can be incorporated into the input model. In Chapter 1, we saw the approach taken by Albers et al. (2005). Borodin et al. (1995) introduced another approach, the so-called *access graph* model, as a way of modeling locality of reference in paging. An access graph $G = (V, E)$ for a program is a graph with a vertex for each page that a program can reference. Locality of reference is imposed by the edge relation – the pages that can be referenced after a page p are just the neighbors of p in G or p itself. In the access graph model a request sequence σ must be a walk on G.

Given an access graph, competitive analysis is unchanged, except for this restriction on the request sequences to walks on G. We denote the competitive ratio of online algorithm $\mathcal{A}$ with k pages of fast memory on the access graph G by

$$c_{\mathcal{A}}(G) := \sup_{\sigma \text{ walk on } G} \frac{\mathcal{A}(\sigma)}{\text{OPT}(\sigma)},$$

where, as before, $\mathcal{A}(\sigma)$ is the number of page faults algorithm $\mathcal{A}$ incurs on input σ and $\text{OPT}(\sigma)$ is the number of page faults OPT incurs on σ. We then define

$$c(G) = \inf_{\text{online algorithms } \mathcal{A}} c_{\mathcal{A}}(G).$$

Thus $c(G)$ is the best competitive ratio that any online algorithm can do on request sequences that are walks on G. If G is an complete graph, then the request sequence is unrestricted and $c(G)$ is the standard competitive ratio. Thus, access graphs provide a flexible way to interpolate between worst-case and highly structured inputs.

An access graph may be either directed or undirected. An undirected access graph might be a suitable model when the page reference patterns are governed by the data structure used by the program. For example, if a program performs operations on a tree data structure, and the mapping of the tree nodes to pages of virtual memory represents a contraction of a tree, then the appropriate access graph might be a tree. Alternatively, if we were to completely ignore data and focus only on the flow of control inherent in the structure of the program, a directed access graph might be a suitable model.

Theorem 24.1 (Borodin et al., 1995) *Let G be any undirected graph on at least $k + 1$ nodes and let H_{k+1} be the set of $(k + 1)$-node connected subgraphs of G. Then the competitive ratio of any deterministic online algorithm on G is*

$$c(T) \geq \max_{T \in \mathcal{T}_{k+1}(G)} (\ell(T) - 1),$$

where

$$\mathcal{T}_{k+1}(G) = \{T \mid \exists H \in H_{k+1} \text{ s.t. } T \text{ is a spanning tree of } H\}$$

and $\ell(T)$ is the number of leaves of tree T.

To prove this theorem, it will be useful for us to partition of the request sequence into phases, defined as follows.

Definition 24.2 (Phases) The first phase of a request sequence begins with the first request. A phase ends just before the request to the $(k + 1)$st distinct node, at which point a new phase begins.

Proof of Theorem 24.1 Let $\mathcal{A}$ be any deterministic algorithm and let T be any tree of $k + 1$ nodes in $\mathcal{T}_{k+1}(G)$. The adversary strategy is the standard one, operating in phases. A phase begins with a request to a page p among the $k+1$ pages covered by T that is not currently in the cache. Next request the pages along the path in the tree between p and the page evicted by $\mathcal{A}$. Repeat this until all the pages in the tree have been requested. (The last page requested is the first request of the next phase.) Assume that $\mathcal{A}$ and OPT start with the same cache state. Then OPT incurs only one fault in the phase (by initially replacing the page that will be requested furthest in the future). On the other hand, any online algorithm $\mathcal{A}$ has at least $\ell(T) - 1$ faults in the phase, since until all leaves are requested, there is always some node in the tree that isn't in $\mathcal{A}$'s cache. $\square$

The next theorem shows that LRU in fact has optimal competitive ratio for trees.

Theorem 24.3 (Borodin et al., 1995) *If the access graph G is a tree, then LRU is optimal, i.e., has competitive ratio equal to*

$$\max_{T \in \mathcal{T}_{k+1}(G)} (\ell(T) - 1).$$

Proof We sketch the proof in the special case that there are $k+1$ nodes in the tree. Consider the partition of the request sequence into phases. Notice that if there are only $k+1$ nodes in total, then OPT incurs only one fault per phase, by replacing the page that will be requested furthest in the future at the beginning of each phase; this page will be the first request of the next phase. Thus, to prove the theorem, it suffices to show that in each phase, LRU incurs at most $\ell(T) - 1$ faults. To see this, observe that the first request of any phase (other than the first) must be to a leaf of the tree, and that the least recently used page at any time during the phase is also a leaf of the tree. (See Figure 24.1 for an explanation.)

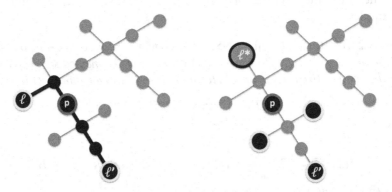

Figure 24.1 The left part of the figure illustrates why an internal node, say p, cannot be the first node requested in a new phase. Since p is on the path between two leaves, e.g., ℓ and ℓ', if p was the first node requested in a new phase, both ℓ and ℓ' would have had to be requested in the previous phase. But that is not possible without requesting p, since the request sequence is a walk on the tree. Thus, the first request in each phase after the first must be to a leaf. Now suppose that the new phase starts with a request, say to ℓ^*. The right figure illustrates why no internal node, say p, can be the least recently used page in the new phase. First, observe that p was requested more recently than ℓ' in the previous phase (and more recently than any of the leaves that are disconnected from ℓ^* by the removal of p.) This is because after the last request to ℓ' in the previous phase, the walk continued back to ℓ^* to start the new phase. Finally, p is requested in the new phase *before* ℓ', since the walk in the new phase starts at ℓ^*. Thus, by the time ℓ' is evicted and then requested again, p is no longer "eligible" to be the least recently requested node.

Finally, since no page is evicted twice in the same phase and a new phase begins when the final leaf in the tree is requested, LRU incurs at most $\ell(T) - 1$ faults per phase. □

Thus, for example, if the graph is a line, LRU is optimal (has competitive ratio 1). In contrast, on a line, FIFO has competitive ratio k. (See Exercise 24.1.) More generally, on trees with few leaves, LRU has low competitive ratio. In contrast, it is possible to show that for all graphs on at least $k + 1$ nodes, FIFO has a competitive ratio of at least $(k + 1)/2$. Moreover, Chrobak and Noga (1998) showed that for every graph G, LRU's performance on inputs that are walks on G is at least as good as FIFO's.

LRU does not have competitive ratio $c(G)$ for all graphs though. For example, suppose that G is a cycle on $k + 1$ nodes and the request sequence consists of repeated traversals of the cycle. Then after a short initial period, LRU will fault on every single request! Notice that this request sequence is arguably realistic, e.g., in any application (such as stochastic gradient descent in machine learning) where multiple passes are taken over a data set.

An alternative to LRU that works well on a cycle is an algorithm introduced by Borodin et al. (1995) known as FAR, which is a *marking algorithm*. (LRU is also a marking algorithm.)

Definition 24.4 (Marking Algorithm) At any time, a page is either marked or unmarked. Initially all pages are unmarked.

A *marking algorithm* is defined by the following rules: All pages are unmarked immediately before the beginning of a phase. When a page is requested within a phase, it is marked. No marked page is ever evicted within a phase.

The unmarked page that FAR chooses to evict on a cache miss is the page that is *furthest in the access graph from the set of marked nodes.*

On a cycle with $k + 1$ nodes, after the first phase,[1] FAR incurs $O(\log_2 k)$ faults per phase. To see this, observe that on the first request in the second phase, the only marked page is the page that caused the new phase to begin. Therefore, the farthest unmarked node is halfway around the cycle, and therefore $k/2$ pages will be requested and marked before the next page fault. When this next page fault occurs, the unmarked node furthest from the set of marked nodes will be about $k/4$ pages away. Therefore $k/4$ additional pages will be marked before the next fault and so on. See Exercise 24.2 for a matching lower bound.

In addition, the proof of Theorem 24.3 that LRU is optimal (in the sense of competitive ratio) for trees applies nearly verbatim to show that FAR is also optimal on trees. It turns out that these two simple cases, trees and cycles, capture pretty much everything that needs to be dealt with when dealing with sequences that correspond to walks on graphs. This is the basis for the proof due to Irani et al. (1996) that, in fact, FAR has competitive ratio that is $O(c(G))$, i.e., matching within a constant factor the performance of an optimal algorithm specialized on graph G. Thus, for instances parameterized by graphs, FAR is an "instance-optimal" algorithm.

---

[1] If the cache is empty initially, there will be a fault on each new page requested in the phase but no evictions.

24.3 The Diffuse Adversary Model

The diffuse adversary model is a generalization of competitive analysis, which attempts to take advantage of the available data for the given problem by assuming that the input comes from a distribution. It departs from classical competitive analysis by removing the assumption that we know nothing about the distribution – without resorting to the equally unrealistic classical assumption that we know all about it. In this model, we assume that the actual distribution D of the inputs is a member of a known class Δ of possible distributions. That is, we seek to determine, for a given class of distributions Δ, the performance ratio

$$R(\Delta) = \inf_A \sup_{D \in \Delta} \frac{\mathbb{E}_D(A(x))}{\mathbb{E}_D(\mathsf{OPT}(x))}. \tag{24.2}$$

Here the adversary picks a distribution D among those in Δ, so that the comparison between the expected performance of the algorithm and the offline optimum algorithm is a bad as possible. Notice that, if Δ is the class of all possible distributions, (24.1) and (24.2) coincide, since the worst possible distribution is the one that assigns probability one to the worst-case input and probability zero everywhere else.

Here we will consider again the paging problem and a particular simple class of distributions Δ_ϵ. This class of distributions essentially weakens the adversary to not being able to select any particular page for next request with probability more than ϵ. It contains those distributions D such that, for any request sequence s and any page a, $\mathrm{Pr}_D(a|s) \leq \epsilon$, where $\mathrm{Pr}_D(a|s)$ denotes the probability that the next request is a given that the sequence so far is s. The parameter ϵ captures the inherent uncertainty of the request sequence and it is assumed to be small, but not smaller that the inverse of the cache size. Of course, a smaller value of this parameter corresponds to a weaker adversary.

We study the competitive ratio of *lazy* marking algorithms, a class of algorithms that contain LRU and FIFO. Lazy means that pages are evicted only when needed to make space on a page fault. Thus, FWF is not lazy (but it is a marking algorithm).

Theorem 24.5 (Young, 2000) *The competitive ratio of any lazy marking algorithm is at most*

$$2 + 2 \sum_{m=1}^{k-1} \frac{1}{\max\{\epsilon^{-1} - m, 1\}}. \tag{24.3}$$

In particular, for $k\epsilon = o(1)$, the competitive ratio is at most $2 + O(k\epsilon)$.

We give here an informal proof of this theorem ignoring subtle issues of conditional probability. For a rigorous treatment, see the original paper by Young (2000). To simplify the presentation, we will assume that $1/\epsilon$ is an integer greater than k. This is essentially equivalent to the model in which, at each step, the adversary selects a set of $1/\epsilon$ potential requests, and then the actual request is drawn uniformly at random from this set.

Consider the execution of a generic lazy marking algorithm DMark that works in phases; at the beginning of each phase all k pages in memory are unmarked; during the phase, each requested page is marked; at a page fault, an unmarked page is removed from memory to make space for the new request; if no such page exists, all pages in memory become unmarked and a new phase begins. There are two types of requests that cause **DMark** to have a page fault: *fresh pages* and *worrisome pages*. Fresh are the pages that do not appear in the previous or current phase, and worrisome are the pages that were in the algorithm's memory at the beginning of the phase but were moved out to deal with some page fault.

One of the nice properties of partitioning the request sequence into phases is that we can bound the optimal cost by the number of fresh pages in each phase. More precisely, for a given request sequence, let f_i be the number of pages that are requested in phase i but not in phase $i - 1$. Then the optimal cost for servicing the request sequence is between $\sum_i f_i/2$ and $\sum_i f_i$. The upper bound is obvious. To see the lower bound note that there must be at least f_i page faults during phases $i - 1$ and i, because together they contain $k + f_i$ requests.

In the analysis that follows, instead of comparing **DMark** against the optimal algorithm, we will compare it against the *optimal amortized cost* $\sum_i f_i/2$. With this handle on the optimal offline cost, it is now intuitively clear that the adversary would prefer to cause a page fault by a worrisome page instead of a fresh page, because fresh pages increase also the optimal amortized cost. As usual, during a phase, we say a page is *marked* if it has been requested during the phase.

To get some intuition, consider the situation when there are m pages marked and w worrisome pages. How should the adversary select the next set of $1/\epsilon$ potential pages? Ideally, from the point of view of the adversary, this set must include only worrisome pages, because they increase the cost of **DMark** without affecting the optimal amortized cost. However, there may not be enough worrisome pages and the adversary will be forced to select other pages as well. Observe also that requests on marked pages are also fine for the adversary, because they don't change anything. But if $1/\epsilon$ is sufficiently large, there will not be enough worrisome or marked pages and the adversary will have to assign probability to other pages. This is exactly where the power of the diffuse adversary model is manifested: The adversary has to deviate from its winning strategy of the original model.

For the analysis, fix a phase and let F be a random variable that indicates the number of requests that are fresh in the phase. The idea is to estimate the cost with respect to F.

The optimal amortized cost of the phase is at least $F/2$. Let us now bound the expected cost of **DMark**. Consider the situation when there are m marked pages and w worrisome pages. Since the probability that the next request will be a marked page is at most $m\epsilon$, the probability that one more page will be marked is at least $1 - m\epsilon$. Conditioned on the event that the request will increase the number of marked pages, the probability that it will be worrisome is at most $w\epsilon/(1 - m\epsilon)$. The trick is to bound this from above by $F\epsilon/(1 - m\epsilon)$, because $w \leq F$ – the number of worrisome requests – can increase only when servicing a fresh request. Therefore the expected cost of **DMark** due to worrisome pages is at most $\mathbb{E}[\sum_{m=1}^{k-1} F\epsilon/(1 - m\epsilon)]$. If we add to this the expected cost from fresh pages $\mathbb{E}[F]$, and divide by the expected amortized cost $E[F/2]$, we get a competitive ratio

$$2 \left(1 + \sum_{m=1}^{k-1} \frac{\epsilon}{1 - m\epsilon} \right) = 2 + 2 \sum_{m=1}^{k-1} \frac{1}{\epsilon^{-1} - m}, \qquad (24.4)$$

as in the statement of Theorem 24.5, when $\epsilon^{-1} \geq k$.

Given that $H_t = 1 + \cdots + 1/t \approx \ln t$ and under the assumption that $k\epsilon = o(1)$, the above expression is approximately $2 + 2(\ln(\epsilon^{-1} - 1)/(\epsilon^{-1} - (k-1)) \approx 2 - 2\ln(1 - k\epsilon) \approx 2 + 2k\epsilon$.

Theorem 24.5 does not differentiate between LRU and FIFO. However, it is not known if the following statement from Koutsoupias and Papadimitriou (2000), which holds for LRU, holds for FIFO.

Theorem 24.6 (Koutsoupias and Papadimitriou, 2000) *LRU has the optimal competitive ratio among all online algorithms for the* Δ_ϵ *diffuse adversary model.*

24.3.1 Discussion

Access graphs and diffuse adversaries are two different ways of restricting the inputs. Both retained some of the worst-case flavor (and hence robustness) of competitive analysis, while attempting to capture some aspects of real-world inputs, thereby limiting the extent to which the results are worst case.

- Both models enabled us to interpolate between very simple and easy to handle inputs and complex, worst-case inputs, thereby defining a hierarchy of ever more powerful adversaries and higher competitive ratios. Putting it another way, both of these are *parameterized analyses* (as discussed in Section 1.3 of Chapter 1): Inputs are defined by a parameter (G for access graphs and ϵ for the diffuse adversary), and the optimal solution for each parameter is provided.
- A unique feature of the access graph model is that it inspired several new and arguably natural algorithms (e.g., FAR) that may in some settings outperform LRU. Fiat and Rosen (1997) have experimented with truly online algorithms[2] inspired by FAR (and by the Markov paging algorithms in Section 24.4.1) and found that in their simulations these new algorithms in fact did outperform LRU. In contrast, the bulk of the research on paging has provided theoretical justification for the beliefs of practitioners (e.g., that LRU is a very effective algorithm), but has not led to new practical algorithms.
- Both the diffuse adversary model and the access graph model restrict the power of the adversary to select the next request. In the access graph model, the restriction forces the next request to come from the (small) set of the neighbors of the most recent request, but in the diffuse adversary model the opposite happens; the selection of the next request is a random page from a set of *at least* $1/\epsilon$ pages. Thus, in the context of paging, the specific choice of Δ_ϵ does not necessarily capture realistic page request sequences that exhibit locality of reference.
- FIFO has provably no better competitive ratio than LRU in both models. However, in the access graph model there are graphs in which LRU is significantly superior to FIFO, while in the Δ_ϵ diffuse adversary model, their competitive ratios are within a factor of 2; this follows from a lower bound that matches Theorem 24.5 within a factor of 2 (Young, 2000). The fact that the access graph model captures locality of reference much better than the diffuse adversary model is a plausible

---

[2] By truly online, we mean algorithms that do not know the graph ahead of time, but rather build it as they see the input.

explanation why the first model has more power to differentiate between these two online algorithms.

- The access graph model is specific to the paging problem. The diffuse adversary model, on the other hand, is a relevant and useful approach for *any* online problem. One merely needs to choose an appropriate class of distributions Δ. The model is also used in Chapter 26 with the same set of distributions Δ_ϵ.

- Finally, a nice feature of both models, perhaps more than a mere coincidence, is that there is a single optimal (LRU for diffuse adversaries) or almost optimal algorithm (FAR for access graphs) for every value of the parameter. This is an indication that the models as well as the corresponding algorithms are robust to perturbations.

24.4 Stochastic Models

Of course, the standard alternative to worst-case analysis is to assume that the inputs are drawn from some known or unknown prior distribution. Many online algorithms have been analyzed from this perspective. The simplest stochastic model, say for paging, is when the requests are i.i.d. draws from some prior distribution. Another common model is to assume that the input is a random permutation of a worst-case sequence chosen by the adversary, as discussed in Chapter 11.

24.4.1 Markov Model

The Markov model for paging is defined by a Markov chain P whose states are the pages that program can reference, with transition probability P_{ij} representing the probability of requesting page j immediately after requesting page i. Notice that now, in contrast to the adversarial setting, the notion of an *optimal online* algorithm is well defined: It is the online algorithm with the smallest expected cost, where the expectation is with respect to the assumed input distribution. In fact, since this is a Markov decision process, it is possible to formulate the optimal policy as the solution to a linear program.[3] However, it has size $O(kn^{k+1})$, where n is the set of possible pages that may be requested and k, as always, is the size of the cache; this sort of running time is prohibitive.

This motivates the search for a simple and approximately optimal online algorithm for the Markov setting. A natural idea is, on a page fault to page p, to find a page to evict that is likely to be requested later than *any* other page in the cache, so as to "simulate" the optimal offline policy. Recall from Chapter 1 that the optimal offline policy is Furthest-in-the-future which, on a page fault, evicts the page that will be requested furthest in the future. For example, one could consider (a) evicting the page q such that the expected number of steps in the Markov chain until q is reached from p is maximum, or (b) evicting the page q such that the probability that q will be requested last is maximum. Unfortunately, it can be shown that both of these algorithms incur $\Omega(k)$ times as many faults as the optimal online algorithm on some Markov chains.

---

[3] There is a variable for each possible cache state, page requested, and choice of page to evict.

Lund et al. (1994) proposed using a randomized approach instead: Whenever there is a page fault, select a page for eviction according to some distribution $\mathbf{y} = \{y_q\}$. Thus, page q in the cache is evicted with probability y_q.

The distribution $\mathbf{y}$ is chosen so that for any other page p that might have been evicted instead of the randomly selected page q, the chance that q will be requested before p is minimized; that is, we seek a distribution $\mathbf{y}$ so that for all pages p in the cache (we use S to denote the set of pages that is in the cache),

$$\sum_{q \in S} y_q \mathbb{P}[q \prec p] \text{ is small} \qquad \text{where } q \prec p := q \text{ is requested before } p.$$

(Define $P(q \prec q) := 0$.) Equivalently, we seek the optimal strategy $\mathbf{y}$ in the two player zero-sum game defined by

$$\min_{\mathbf{y}=\{y_q\}} \max_p \sum_q \mathbb{P}[q \prec p] y_q = \min_{\mathbf{y}=\{y_q\}} \max_{\mathbf{x}=\{x_p\}} \sum_p \sum_q x_p \mathbb{P}[q \prec p] y_q,$$

where $\mathbf{x}$ and $\mathbf{y}$ are both distributions over pages in the cache. By the Minimax Theorem, this is the same as

$$\max_{\mathbf{x}} \min_{\mathbf{y}} \sum_p \sum_q x_p \mathbb{P}[q \prec p] y_q,$$

But the latter is at most 1/2 because if we choose $\mathbf{y} := \mathbf{x}$, we have

$$\sum_p \sum_q x_p \mathbb{P}[q \prec p] x_q = \sum_{\{p,q\} \text{ with } p \neq q} x_p x_q (\mathbb{P}[q \prec p] + \mathbb{P}[p \prec q])$$

$$\leq \frac{1}{2} \sum_p \sum_q x_p x_q = \frac{1}{2},$$

since $\mathbb{P}[q \prec p] + \mathbb{P}[p \prec q] = 1$ (or 0 when $p = q$). We conclude that there is a distribution $\mathbf{y}$ that guarantees that

$$\sum_{q \in S} y_q \mathbb{P}[q \prec p] \leq \frac{1}{2}, \quad \forall p \text{ in cache}$$

and this distribution can be computed efficiently using linear programming. This suggests the following approximately optimal online algorithm ALG:

Given the current cache contents, on a cache miss, select a page to evict according to the distribution $\mathbf{y}$ computed as earlier for the current cache contents S.

Lund et al. (1994) show that the expected number of faults incurred by ALG is at most four times[4] that of the optimal online algorithm OptON.

---

[4] Intuitively, half the time, on an eviction, the page ALG replaces is requested later than what OptON evicted, in which case OptON would have a page fault before ALG. However, this statement is correct only if the cache states of the two algorithms are the same, which of course they will rarely be. Hence, proving this bound on the competitive ratio (against the optimal online) is tricky and requires setting up a charging scheme with the property that each time ALG evicts a page p, that page p places a "charge" on some page q that OptON has evicted but that is likely to be requested no later than p. The charging scheme has to be defined very carefully so that no page has too many charges on it.

Discussion

Stochastic models are perhaps the most obvious way to going beyond worst-case analysis. The concern, as always, is whether or not the stochastic model captures the properties of real-world inputs. Markov paging is a step in the right direction from, say, i.i.d. sequences, but still has limited applicability because of its memoryless nature.

As we discussed, the algorithm for Markov paging described previously was competitive with the optimal *online* algorithm. No comparison was made to the optimal offline. Although using the optimal online algorithm as a benchmark makes perfect sense in stochastic settings, it is not so common in the litereature, largely because we do not have many techniques for getting a handle on the optimal online algorithm or comparing arbitrary online algorithms in stochastic settings.

24.4.2 Best of Both Worlds?

In Sections 24.2 and 24.3, we saw examples of parameterized analysis wherein we considered input restrictions that interpolated between simple inputs and worst-case inputs. However, even when the adversary was very weak, the input was worst-case; we were merely restricting the subset of inputs the adversary could choose from.

An alternative is to try to interpolate between the optimism of stochastic models and the pessimism of adversarial models.[5] For example, one may seek an online algorithm that has the best or nearly the best possible competitive ratio while simultaneously achieving much better performance if the input happens to come from a nice stochastic model. In one example in this direction, Albers and Mitzenmacher (1998) consider the *list update problem*, which addresses the problem of how to rearrange a linked list online in response to a sequence of access requests to items in the list.[6] They showed that an algorithm known as TimeStamp has the optimal competitive ratio of 2 for worst-case inputs, but achieves much better performance when inputs are generated from an i.i.d. source.

A more modern approach proposed by Lykouris and Vassilvitskii (2018) is to augment online algorithms with a machine learned oracle, with an objective of significantly reducing the competitive ratios in those cases where the oracle has low error. See Chapter 30 for more on this approach.

One may also try to directly define input models that interpolate between stochastic and adversarial inputs. For example, Blelloch et al. (2016) proposed the following model for the list update problem: There is a probability distribution $\mathbf{p} = (p_1, \ldots, p_n)$ over the items stored in the list and a parameter ϵ. The input is then generated as follows: For each request, with probability ϵ, let an adversary choose the next item to request and with probability $1 - \epsilon$ sample from the distribution $\mathbf{p}$. Here $\epsilon = 0$ corresponds to pure average case analysis on inputs drawn from a static probability distribution, and $\epsilon = 1$ corresponds to standard worst-case competitive analysis. The hope is to design an algorithm whose performance is better as our "knob"

---

[5] This phrasing is due to R. Ravi (Blelloch et al., 2016).

[6] The cost to access an item in the list is the number of pointers that need to be traversed to reach that item. Once accessed, an item may be moved closer to the front of the list at no cost. In addition, the positions of adjacent items in the list may be swapped at a cost of 1.

moves toward the stochastic case, that is $\epsilon \to 0$. This approach is similar to other semirandom models, such as those discussed in Chapters 16 and 17.

Finally, in Chapters 13–15, we saw smoothed analysis as an approach to going beyond worst-case for offline problems. This notion has also recently been applied to online algorithms: Becchetti et al. (2006) introduced the *smoothed competitive ratio* defined as

$$c := \sup_{\tilde{\sigma}} \mathbb{E}_{\sigma:=\text{pert}(\tilde{\sigma})} \left(\frac{\mathcal{A}(\sigma)}{\text{OPT}(\sigma)} \right),$$

where the supremum is taken over all possible inputs $\tilde{\sigma}$ and the expectation is taken over all inputs σ that are obtained by perturbing $\tilde{\sigma}$ a bit according to some probabilistic model. They applied this notion to the analysis of an online scheduling algorithm.

24.5 Direct Comparison of Online Algorithms

Online algorithms are complicated objects. Evaluating them via projection onto the single-dimensional space of competitive ratios is often uninformative or even misleading. Wouldn't it be better then to compare online algorithms directly rather than through their competitive ratio? This section explores comparative analysis, one specific way to do exactly this.

24.5.1 Comparative Analysis

Suppose that $\mathcal{A}$ and $\mathcal{B}$ are classes of algorithms – typically but not necessarily $\mathcal{A} \subseteq \mathcal{B}$; that is, $\mathcal{B}$ is usually a broader class of algorithms, a more powerful information regime. The *comparative ratio* $R(\mathcal{A}, \mathcal{B})$ is defined as follows:

$$R(\mathcal{A}, \mathcal{B}) = \sup_{B \in \mathcal{B}} \inf_{A \in \mathcal{A}} \sup_{\sigma} \frac{A(\sigma)}{B(\sigma)}. \tag{24.5}$$

This definition is best understood game-theoretically: $\mathcal{B}$ wants to demonstrate to $\mathcal{A}$ that it is a more powerful class of algorithms. To this end, $\mathcal{B}$ proposes an algorithm B among its own. In response, $\mathcal{A}$ comes up with an algorithm A. Then $\mathcal{B}$ chooses an input σ. Finally, $\mathcal{A}$ pays $\mathcal{B}$ the ratio $A(\sigma)/B(\sigma)$. The larger this ratio, the more powerful $\mathcal{B}$ is in comparison to $\mathcal{A}$. Notice that, if we let $\mathcal{A}$ be the class of online algorithms and $\mathcal{B}$ the class of all algorithms – online or offline—then equations (24.1) and (24.5) coincide, and $R(\mathcal{A}, \mathcal{B})$ is the same as the competitive ratio c. Hence comparative analysis is a refinement of competitive analysis.

To illustrate the use of comparative analysis we consider the power of lookahead in the paging problem. If $\mathcal{L}_\ell$ is the class of all paging algorithms with lookahead ℓ – thus in particular $\mathcal{L}_0$ is the class of usual online algorithms – comparative analysis for paging gives

$$R(\mathcal{L}_0, \mathcal{L}_\ell) = \min\{\ell + 1, k\}.$$

It is straightforward to extend the lower bound for the paging problem to show that the comparative ratio is at least $\ell + 1$ (when $\ell + 1 \leq k$). Indeed consider an algorithm with lookahead ℓ that never evicts one of the next ℓ requests. Thus, for every request sequence ρ, this algorithm suffers at most one page fault for every $\ell + 1$ consecutive requests. On the other hand, for any algorithm A with no lookahead, there is a request sequence ρ such that A suffers a page fault for every request.

The next theorem shows that this bound is actually tight.

Theorem 24.7 (Koutsoupias and Papadimitriou, 2000)   *For the paging problem*

$$R(\mathcal{L}_0, \mathcal{L}_\ell) = \min\{\ell + 1, k\}.$$

Proof   Let $m = \min\{\ell, k - 1\}$ and let B be an algorithm for the paging problem in the class $\mathcal{L}_\ell$, that is, with lookahead ℓ. Without loss of generality we assume that B moves pages only to service requests. Consider the following online algorithm A which is a generalization of LRU:

> To service a request r not in its cache, A evicts a page that is not one of the m most recent distinct requests (including r). Among the remaining pages, A chooses to evict a page such that the resulting configuration is as close as possible to the last known configuration of B. A does nothing for requests in its fast memory.

To show that the comparative ratio of A is $m + 1$, it suffices to show that for every $m + 1$ consecutive page faults of A, B suffers at least one page fault. This can be achieved by showing that whenever A suffers m consecutive page faults while B suffers no page fault, A converges to the configuration of B. To do this, we show by induction on the number of requests the stronger claim that if A suffers c consecutive page faults while B does not suffer any page fault, the configurations of A and B differ by at most $m - c$ pages.

Fix a request sequence $\rho = r_1 r_2 \ldots$ and let $A_0, A_1, \ldots$ and $B_0 = A_0, B_1, \ldots$ be the configurations (i.e., set of pages in memory) of A and B that service ρ. The base of the induction is trivial. Assume that the induction hypothesis holds for $t - 1$. We have to deal with a few cases. We treat here the case in which the most recent request r_t is in $B_{t-1} - A_{t-1}$ and algorithm A evicts page $x_t \in A_{t-1} \cap B_{t-1}$ to service it. We leave the other cases for Exercise 24.3.

Since x_t is not one of the m more recent requests, x_t is also in B_{t-m}. It follows that $A_t \subseteq B_{t-m} + \{r_{t-m+1}, \ldots, r_{t-1}, r_t\}$. We also have $B_t \subseteq B_{t-m} + \{r_{t-m+1}, \ldots, r_{t-1}, r_t\}$. If algorithm B has no page fault in the last c requests, the set $B_{t-m} + \{r_{t-m+1}, \ldots, r_{t-1}, r_t\}$ has cardinality at most $k + m - c$. We conclude that $|A_t - B_t| \leq m - c$. $\square$

24.6 Where Do We Go from Here?

Competitive analysis provides a crisp and universal benchmark, the competitive ratio, by which to evaluate the quality of online algorithms. Moreover, its rigorous framework forces us to search the space of online algorithms and discover novel, elegant, and occasionally surprising algorithms.

Nonetheless, there is much to do as we seek to move beyond worst-case analysis. We have introduced a few of the approaches taken in the literature. As we move forward, the key questions we must ask ourselves when evaluating research in this area are:

- Does it help explain the performance of algorithms in practice and give us guidance as to how to choose between algorithms?
- Does it suggest new algorithms that may work better than the currently used algorithms?
- Does the model/benchmark enable an analysis that captures the performance as a function of important parameters of the input?
- Does the performance degrade smoothly as we move from "nice" inputs to "worst-case" inputs, and is the performance on "easy" inputs nearly optimal?

24.7 Notes

For an overview of results on the competitive analysis of online algorithms see the book by Borodin and El-Yaniv (1998) and the surveys, e.g., Albers (2003) and Albers and Leonardi (1999). For the basic models and results for paging and list update, see the seminal paper of Sleator and Tarjan (1985), as well as the surveys by Irani (1998) and Kamali and López-Ortiz (2013).

We can divide the literature on going beyond worst-case in online algorithms into roughly three types: (1) modifying the resources available to the online algorithm, (2) weakening the adversary, and (3) changing the way we measure the performance of the online algorithm.

Modifying the Resources Available to the Online Algorithm In Chapter 4, resource augmentation is covered in the context of paging; there, the online algorithm uses a cache that is larger than that available to the offline algorithm. Perhaps the most well-studied application of resource augmentation is online scheduling where the online algorithm either has more machines or they are faster than those of the offline algorithm, e.g., Kalyanasundaram and Pruhs (2000) and Phillips et al. (2002).

Other ways to modify the resources available include (1) giving the algorithm access to some number of bits of advice (Dobrev et al., 2009; Boyar et al., 2016); (2) giving the online algorithm a small budget to modify prior decisions or ignore some requests , e.g., Albers and Hellwig (2012), Gupta et al. (2014, 2017), Gu et al. (2016), Megow et al. (2016), Boyar et al. (2017), Cygan et al. (2018), Epstein et al. (2018), Feldkord et al. (2018); (3) allowing the algorithm to delay service of some requests, e.g., Emek et al. (2016) and Azar et al. (2017a,b); (4) allowing the algorithm to reorder requests, e.g., Englert et al. (2007, 2008), Adamaszek et al. (2011), Azar et al. (2014), and Englert and Räcke (2017); and (5) giving the online algorithm some amount of lookahead, e.g., Albers (1998).

Weakening the Adversary In Sections 24.2 and 24.3, we discussed weakening the adversary by restricting the set of possible inputs (e.g., using access graphs or diffuse adversaries). Another example of this approach is the working set model from Chapter 1. Panagiotou and Souza (2006) and Albers and Frascaria (2018) consider restricting the adversary to generating inputs that satisfy certain conditions on the inter-request distances between pages and analyze situations in which this leads to improvements in LRU's competitive ratio. Other parameterized analyses include Albers and Lauer (2008) Dorrigiv et al. (2009), and Dorrigiv and López-Ortiz (2012).

Raghavan (1992) proposed the *statistical adversary model*, in which the adversary is required to generate an input that satisfies certain statistical properties. (See also

Chou et al., 1995.) Of course, the extreme version of limiting the adversary is to assume a stochastic model. See Chapter 11 and the references therein.

Markov chain models of the type discussed in Section 24.4.1 were introduced by Shedler and Tung (1972), Lewis and Shedler (1973), and Karlin et al. (1992).

Changing the Way We Measure the Performance of Online Algorithms A head-spinning number of different ways of measuring the performance of online algorithms have been introduced in the literature as alternatives to competitive analysis. For example, the *max/max ratio* proposed by Ben-David and Borodin (1994) considers the online algorithm's maximum cost on any input of length n and the optimal offline's maximum cost on any input of length n, and then measures the supremum of the ratio between them. Thus, it is not comparing the performance of the algorithms on the same inputs. Kenyon et al. (1996) suggest using the *random order ratio*, which considers the worst case over σ of the average cost of the online algorithm on random permutations of σ and the optimal offline cost on σ. For a survey of results in these models and a number of other measures, see the PhD thesis of Dorrigiv (2010), as well as the surveys by Boyar et al. (2015) and Dorrigiv and López-Ortiz (2005).

In Section 24.5, we discussed the comparative ratio as a way to directly compare online algorithms. This is just one of many proposals in the literature. For example, Angelopoulos et al. (2007) introduced *bijective analysis*, which compares algorithms on permutations of the same input. Specifically, suppose that $\mathcal{A}$ and $\mathcal{B}$ are two different online algorithms and let I_n denote the set of request sequences of length n. Then $\mathcal{A} \preceq \mathcal{B}$, that is, $\mathcal{A}$ *is no worse than* $\mathcal{B}$ if for all n sufficiently large, there is a bijection $\pi : I_n \to I_n$ for which $\mathcal{A}(\sigma) \leq \mathcal{B}(\pi(\sigma))$ for all $\sigma \in I_n$.

A number of interesting results have been obtained using this notion. For example, Angelopoulos et al. (2007) showed that LRU with lookahead is strictly better according to bijective analysis than LRU without lookahead and that all *lazy* paging algorithms are equivalent. Angelopoulos and Schweitzer (2013) have shown that LRU is no worse than any other online algorithm if locality is modeled by a concave function (see Section 1.3.1 of Chapter 1).

In this chapter, we have borrowed language from some of our earlier papers including from Karlin et al. (1992) and from Koutsoupias and Papadimitriou (2000).

References

Achlioptas, Dimitris, Chrobak, Marek, and Noga, John. 2000. Competitive analysis of randomized paging algorithms. *Theoretical Computer Science*, **234**(1-2), 203–218.

Adamaszek, Anna, Czumaj, Artur, Englert, Matthias, and Räcke, Harald. 2011. Almost tight bounds for reordering buffer management. In *Proceedings of the Forty-third Annual ACM Symposium on Theory of Computing*, ACM, pp. 607–616.

Albers, Susanne. 1998. A competitive analysis of the list update problem with lookahead. *Theoretical Computer Science*, **197**(1-2), 95–109.

Albers, Susanne. 2003. Online algorithms: A survey. *Mathematical Programming*, **97**(1-2), 3–26.

Albers, Susanne, and Frascaria, Dario. 2018. Quantifying competitiveness in paging with locality of reference. *Algorithmica*, **80**(12), 3563–3596.

Albers, Susanne, and Hellwig, Matthias. 2012. On the value of job migration in online makespan minimization. In *European Symposium on Algorithms*, pp. 84–95. Springer.

Albers, Susanne, and Lauer, Sonja. 2008. On list update with locality of reference. In *International Colloquium on Automata, Languages, and Programming*, pp. 96–107. Springer.

Albers, Susanne, and Leonardi, Stefano. 1999. Online algorithms. *ACM Computing surveys*, **31**(3), Article 4.

Albers, Susanne, and Mitzenmacher, Michael. 1998. Average case analyses of list update algorithms, with applications to data compression. *Algorithmica*, **21**(3), 312–329.

Albers, Susanne, Favrholdt, Lene M, and Giel, Oliver. 2005. On paging with locality of reference. *Journal of Computer and System Sciences*, **70**(2), 145–175.

Angelopoulos, Spyros, and Schweitzer, Pascal. 2013. Paging and list update under bijective analysis. *Journal of the ACM (JACM)*, **60**(2), 7.

Angelopoulos, Spyros, Dorrigiv, Reza, and López-Ortiz, Alejandro. 2007. On the separation and equivalence of paging strategies. In *Proceedings of the Eighteenth Annual ACM-SIAM Symposium on Discrete Algorithms*, pp. 229–237. Society for Industrial and Applied Mathematics.

Azar, Yossi, Englert, Matthias, Gamzu, Iftah, and Kidron, Eytan. 2014. Generalized reordering buffer management. In *31st International Symposium on Theoretical Aspects of Computer Science (STACS 2014)*, pp. 87–94. Schloss Dagstuhl-Leibniz-Zentrum fuer Informatik.

Azar, Yossi, Ganesh, Arun, Ge, Rong, and Panigrahi, Debmalya. 2017a. Online service with delay. In *Proceedings of the 49th Annual ACM SIGACT Symposium on Theory of Computing*, pp. 551–563. ACM.

Azar, Yossi, Chiplunkar, Ashish, and Kaplan, Haim. 2017b. Polylogarithmic bounds on the competitiveness of min-cost perfect matching with delays. In *Proceedings of the Twenty-Eighth Annual ACM-SIAM Symposium on Discrete Algorithms*, pp. 1051–1061. SIAM.

Becchetti, Luca, Leonardi, Stefano, Marchetti-Spaccamela, Alberto, Schäfer, Guido, and Vredeveld, Tjark. 2006. Average-case and smoothed competitive analysis of the multilevel feedback algorithm. *Mathematics of Operations Research*, **31**(1), 85–108.

Ben-David, Shai, and Borodin, Allan. 1994. A new measure for the study of on-line algorithms. *Algorithmica*, **11**(1), 73–91.

Blelloch, G., Dhamdhere, K.and Pongnumkul, S., and Ravi, R. 2016. Interpolating between stochastic and worst-case optimization. *Lecture* at the Simons Institute of Computing.

Borodin, A., and El-Yaniv, R. 1998. *Online Computation and Competitive Analysis*. Cambridge University Press.

Borodin, Allan, Irani, Sandy, Raghavan, Prabhakar, and Schieber, Baruch. 1995. Competitive paging with locality of reference. *Journal of Computer and System Sciences*, **50**(2), 244–258.

Boyar, Joan, Irani, Sandy, and Larsen, Kim S. 2015. A comparison of performance measures for online algorithms. *Algorithmica*, **72**(4), 969–994.

Boyar, Joan, Favrholdt, Lene M, Kudahl, Christian, Larsen, Kim S, and Mikkelsen, Jesper W. 2016. Online algorithms with advice: a survey. *ACM SIGACT News*, **47**(3), 93–129.

Boyar, Joan, Favrholdt, Lene M, Kotrbčík, Michal, and Larsen, Kim S. 2017. Relaxing the irrevocability requirement for online graph algorithms. In *Workshop on Algorithms and Data Structures*, pp. 217–228. Springer.

Chou, Andrew, Cooperstock, Jeremy R, El-Yaniv, Ran, Klugerman, Michael, and Leighton, Frank Thomson. 1995. The statistical adversary allows optimal money-making trading strategies. In *SODA*, vol. 95, pp. 467–476.

Chrobak, Marek, and Noga, John. 1998. LRU is better than FIFO. In *Proceedings of the 9th Symposium on Discrete Algorithms (SODA)*, pp. 78–81. ACM/SIAM.

Cygan, Marek, Czumaj, Artur, Mucha, Marcin, and Sankowski, Piotr. 2018. Online facility location with deletions. In *Proceedings of the 26th Annual European Symposium on Algorithms (ESA)*, pp. 21: 1–21: 15.

Dobrev, Stefan, Královič, Rastislav, and Pardubská, Dana. 2009. Measuring the problem-relevant information in input. *RAIRO-Theoretical Informatics and Applications*, **43**(3), 585–613.

Dorrigiv, Reza. 2010. Alternative measures for the analysis of on-line algorithms. PhD dissertation, University of Waterloo.

Dorrigiv, Reza, and López-Ortiz, Alejandro. 2005. A survey of performance measures for on-line algorithms. *SIGACT News*, **36**(3), 67–81.

Dorrigiv, Reza, and López-Ortiz, Alejandro. 2012. List update with probabilistic locality of reference. *Information Processing Letters*, **112**(13), 540–543.

Dorrigiv, Reza, Ehmsen, Martin R, and López-Ortiz, Alejandro. 2009. Parameterized analysis of paging and list update algorithms. In *International Workshop on Approximation and Online Algorithms*, pp. 104–115. Springer.

Emek, Yuval, Kutten, Shay, and Wattenhofer, Roger. 2016. Online matching: Haste makes waste! In *Proceedings of the forty-eighth annual ACM symposium on Theory of Computing*, pp. 333–344. ACM.

Englert, Matthias, and Räcke, Harald. 2017. Reordering buffers with logarithmic diameter dependency for trees. In *Proceedings of the Twenty-Eighth Annual ACM-SIAM Symposium on Discrete Algorithms*, pp. 1224–1234. SIAM.

Englert, Matthias, Räcke, Harald, and Westermann, Matthias. 2007. Reordering buffers for general metric spaces. In *Proceedings of the Thirty-ninth Annual ACM Symposium on Theory of Computing*, pp. 556–564. ACM.

Englert, Matthias, Özmen, Deniz, and Westermann, Matthias. 2008. The power of reordering for online minimum makespan scheduling. In *2008 49th Annual IEEE Symposium on Foundations of Computer Science*, pp. 603–612. IEEE.

Epstein, Leah, Levin, Asaf, Segev, Danny, and Weimann, Oren. 2018. Improved bounds for randomized preemptive online matching. *Information and Computation*, **259**, 31–40.

Feldkord, Björn, Feldotto, Matthias, Gupta, Anupam, Guruganesh, Guru, Kumar, Amit, Riechers, Sören, and Wajc, David. 2018. Fully-dynamic bin packing with little repacking. In *45th International Colloquium on Automata, Languages, and Programming (ICALP 2018)*, pp. 51:1-51-24.

Fiat, Amos, and Rosen, Ziv. 1997. Experimental studies of access graph based heuristics: Beating the LRU standard? In *ACM-SIAM Symposium on Discrete Algorithms*, pp. 63–72.

Gu, Albert, Gupta, Anupam, and Kumar, Amit. 2016. The power of deferral: maintaining a constant-competitive steiner tree online. *SIAM Journal on Computing*, **45**(1), 1–28.

Gupta, Anupam, Kumar, Amit, and Stein, Cliff. 2014. Maintaining assignments online: Matching, scheduling, and flows. In *Proceedings of the Twenty-fifth Annual ACM-SIAM Symposium on Discrete Algorithms*, pp. 468–479. Society for Industrial and Applied Mathematics.

Gupta, Anupam, Krishnaswamy, Ravishankar, Kumar, Amit, and Panigrahi, Debmalya. 2017. Online and dynamic algorithms for set cover. In *Proceedings of the 49th Annual ACM Symposium on Theory of Computing*, pp. 537–550. ACM.

Irani, Sandy. 1998. Competitive analysis of paging. In *Online Algorithms*, pp. 52–73. Springer.

Irani, Sandy, Karlin, Anna R, and Phillips, Steven. 1996. Strongly competitive algorithms for paging with locality of reference. *SIAM Journal on Computing*, **25**(3), 477–497.

Kalyanasundaram, B., and Pruhs, K. 2000. Speed is as powerful as clairvoyance. *Journal of the ACM*, **47**(4), 617–643.

Kamali, Shahin, and López-Ortiz, Alejandro. 2013. A survey of algorithms and models for list update. In *Space-Efficient Data Structures, Streams, and Algorithms*, pp. 251–266. Springer.

Karlin, Anna R, Phillips, Steven J, and Raghavan, Prabhakar. 1992. Markov paging. In *Proceedings, 33rd Annual Symposium on Foundations of Computer Science*, pp. 208–217. IEEE.

Kenyon, Claire, et al. 1996. Best-fit bin-packing with random order. In *ACM-SIAM Symposium on Discrete Algorithms*, pp. 359–364.

Koutsoupias, Elias, and Papadimitriou, Christos H. 2000. Beyond competitive analysis. *SIAM Journal on Computing*, **30**(1), 300–317.

Lewis, PAW, and Shedler, GS. 1973. Empirically derived micromodels for sequences of page exceptions. *IBM Journal of Research and Development*, **17**(2), 86–100.

Lund, Carsten, Phillips, Steven, and Reingold, Nick. 1994. IP over connection-oriented networks and distributional paging. In *Proceedings 35th Annual Symposium on Foundations of Computer Science*, pp. 424–434. IEEE.

Lykouris, Thodoris, and Vassilvitskii, Sergei. 2018. Competitive caching with machine learned advice. In *Proceedings of the 35th International Conference on Machine Learning (ICML)*, pp. 3302–3311.

McGeoch, Lyle A, and Sleator, Daniel D. 1991. A strongly competitive randomized paging algorithm. *Algorithmica*, **6**, 816–825.

Megow, Nicole, Skutella, Martin, Verschae, José, and Wiese, Andreas. 2016. The power of recourse for online MST and TSP. *SIAM Journal on Computing*, **45**(3), 859–880.

Panagiotou, Konstantinos, and Souza, Alexander. 2006. On adequate performance measures for paging. *Proceedings of the Thirty-eighth Annual ACM Symposium on Theory of Computing*, pp. 487–496. ACM.

Phillips, C. A., Stein, C., Torng, E., and Wein, J. 2002. Optimal time-critical scheduling via resource augmentation. *Algorithmica*, **32**(2), 163–200.

Raghavan, Prabhakar. 1992. A statistical adversary for on-line algorithms. *DIMACS Series in Discrete Mathematics and Theoretical Computer Science*, **7**, 79–83.

Shedler, Gerald S., and Tung, C. 1972. Locality in page reference strings. *SIAM Journal on Computing*, **1**(3), 218–241.

Sleator, D. D., and Tarjan, R. E. 1985. Amortized efficiency of list update and paging rules. *Communications of the ACM*, **28**(2), 202–208.

Young, Neal E. 2000. On-line paging against adversarially biased random inputs. *Journal of Algorithms*, **37**, 218–235. Preliminary version in SODA'98 titled "Bounding the Diffuse Adversary."

Exercises

Exercise 24.1 Show that in the undirected access graph model, FIFO has competive ratio k when the graph is a line consisting of $k + 1$ nodes.

Exercise 24.2 Show that in the undirected access graph model, every online algorithm has competitive ratio $\Omega(\log k)$ on a cycle of length $k + 1$.

Exercise 24.3 Complete the proof of Theorem 24.7.

CHAPTER TWENTY FIVE

On the Unreasonable Effectiveness of SAT Solvers

Vijay Ganesh and Moshe Y. Vardi

Abstract: Boolean satisfiability (SAT) is arguably the quintessential *NP*-complete problem, believed to be intractable in general. Yet, over the last two decades, engineers have designed and implemented conflict-driven clause learning (CDCL) SAT solving algorithms that can efficiently solve real-world instances with tens of millions of variables and clauses in them. Despite their dramatic impact, SAT solvers remain poorly understood. There are significant gaps in our theoretical understanding of why these solvers work as well as they do. This question of "why CDCL SAT solvers are efficient for many classes of large real-world instances while at the same time perform poorly on relatively small randomly generated or cryptographic instances" has stumped theorists and practitioners alike for more than two decades. In this chapter, we survey the current state of our theoretical understanding of this question, future directions, as well as open problems.

25.1 Introduction: The Boolean SAT Problem and Solvers

Boolean satisfiability (SAT) is one of the central problems in computer science and mathematics, believed to be intractable in general. This problem has been studied intensively by theorists since it was shown to be *NP*-complete by Cook (1971). The problem can be stated as follows:

Problem Statement 25.1 (The Boolean Satisfiability Problem) *Given a Boolean formula $\phi(x_1, x_2, \ldots, x_n)$ in conjunctive normal form (CNF) over Boolean variables $x_1, x_2, \ldots, x_n$, determine whether it is satisfiable. We say that a formula $\phi(x_1, x_2, \ldots, x_n)$ is satisfiable if there exists an assignment to the variables of $\phi(x_1, x_2, \ldots, x_n)$ such that the formula evaluates to true under that assignment. Otherwise, we say the formula is unsatisfiable. This problem is also sometimes referred to as CNF-SAT.*

There are many variations of the SAT problem that are all equivalent from a worst-case complexity-theoretic perspective. By SAT, we always refer to the CNF-SAT problem, unless otherwise stated. A SAT solver is a computer program aimed at solving the Boolean satisfiability problem.

More recently, practitioners who work in software engineering (broadly construed to include software testing, verification, program analysis, synthesis), computer security, and artificial intelligence (AI) have shown considerable interest in SAT solvers. This is due to the efficiency, utility, and impact of solvers on software engineering (Cadar et al., 2006), verification (Clarke et al., 2001), and AI planning (Kautz et al., 1992). The success of SAT solvers can be attributed to the fact that engineers have designed and implemented highly scalable conflict-driven clause learning (CDCL) SAT solving algorithms (or simply, SAT solvers[1]) that are able to efficiently solve multimillion variable instances obtained from real-world applications. What is even more surprising is that these solvers often outperform special-purpose algorithms designed specifically for the aforementioned applications. Having said that, it is also known that SAT solvers perform poorly on relatively small randomly generated or cryptographic instances (Balyo et al., 2017). Therefore, the key question in SAT solver research is:

"Why are CDCL SAT solvers efficient for many classes of real-world instances while at the same time perform poorly on randomly generated or cryptographic instances?"

This question has stumped theorists and practitioners alike for more than two decades. In order to address this question we have to go beyond traditional worst-case complexity and develop a parameterized complexity-theoretic understanding of real-world formulas over which CDCL solvers perform well. In this chapter, we survey the state of our knowledge vis-à-vis complexity-theoretic understanding of the power of SAT solvers as well as empirical studies of industrial instances that shed light on this central question.

25.1.1 The Central Questions

Here we list a set of key questions that are essential for a deeper understanding of SAT solvers, followed by sections where we discuss answers to them.

1. **Modeling SAT Solvers as Proof Systems** Perhaps the most important question in this context of understanding SAT solvers is the following: "What is an appropriate mathematical model for CDCL SAT solvers that explains both their efficacy as well as limitations?" This question is of paramount importance not only from a theoretical point of view, but as we argue in the text that follows, critical from a practical solver-design perspective as well. (We discuss detailed answers to this question in Section 25.3.)

   Over the past two decades, a consensus has developed among most theorists and practitioners that SAT solvers are best modeled as proof systems, i.e., a collection of proof rules and axioms. The history of this consensus is quite interesting and goes back to folklore theorems about Davis–Putnam–Logemann–Loveland (DPLL) SAT solvers (Davis et al., 1962) that state that they are essentially equivalent to tree-like resolution (for unsatisfiable inputs). Given that DPLL SAT solvers form the basis for the more powerful CDCL methods, the known connection between DPLL and tree-like resolution naturally led to the conjecture, and

---

[1] While researchers have studied a variety of algorithms for the Boolean SAT problem, in this chapter we focus only on sequential CDCL SAT solvers. The reason is that to date only these solvers seem to scale well for large real-world industrial instances, which is the key mystery addressed here.

subsequent proof, that CDCL (with nondeterministic variable/value selection and restarts) solvers are polynomially equivalent to general resolution, a proof system known to be stronger than tree-like resolution (Atserias et al., 2011; Pipatsrisawat and Darwiche, 2011). This result highlights the mathematical value of modeling solvers as proof systems. First, the "solvers-as-proof-systems" abstraction enables one to leverage powerful methods and results from proof complexity to obtain lower and upper bounds on the length of proofs constructed by solvers. Second, proof complexity suggests many different kinds of proof rules, e.g., extended resolution (Krajíček, 2019), that can be incorporated into solvers, thus strengthening them further. Finally, and perhaps most importantly, proof complexity enables a much deeper understanding of the power of certain solver heuristics (e.g., clause learning), that are best understood in terms of proof rules (general resolution).

While proof systems are a natural and elegant way to model SAT solvers, given that they are designed to construct proofs for unsatisfiable formulas, it is quite legitimate to ask whether they are suitable for studying solver behavior over satisfiable instances as well. It turns out that even when an input formula is satisfiable, SAT solvers generate proofs that establish unsatisfiability of the parts of the search space that do not contain satisfying assignments, thus guiding the solver away from fruitless parts of the search space (the set of all assignments). Hence, one could argue that proof systems are an excellent mathematical model for studying the complexity of SAT solvers for both satisfiable and unsatisfiable instances.

2. **Proof Search and SAT Solvers** While modeling solvers as proof systems enables us to prove upper and lower bounds, it does not quite address the issue of proof search. Proof systems, by their very nature, are best defined as nondeterministic objects. SAT solvers, however, are efficient implementations of proof systems. Hence, in order to properly frame the notion of proof search, we need to view solvers as optimization procedures that attempt to find the optimal (e.g., shortest) proof for a given input. Theorists refer to this as *automatizability of proof systems* (Bonet et al., 2000). Informally, we say that a proof system is automatizable if there exists an algorithm that can find a proof for a unsatisfiable formula with only polynomial overhead (in the size of the formula) over the optimal proof. (We address this in Section 25.4.)

3. **Parameteric Understanding of Boolean Formulas** The topic that has probably received the most attention in the context of understanding solvers is that of parameterization of Boolean formulas (i.e., parameters that enable us to classify formulas as easy or hard for solvers). This question can be restated as "What is a precise mathematical parametric characterization of real-world industrial or application instances over which SAT solvers perform well, and dually, of families of instances over which they perform poorly?" Examples of parameters that have been extensively studied include the clause-variable ratio, backdoors, backbones, community structure, and merge. We discuss the strengths and weaknesses of these parameters. The crucial requirement that these parameters have to satisfy is that they should be amenable to both theoretical analysis (i.e., enable parameterized complexity-theoretic bounds) as well as be relevant in practice (i.e., empirically explain the power of solvers and enable the design of better ones). We address this in Section 25.5. (See also Chapter 2 for a general discussion on parameterized complexity.)

4. **Proof Complexity and Solver Design** In addition to the aforementioned benefits of the "solvers-as-proof-systems" model, proof complexity theory also enables us to systematize practical solver design. Without the aid of proof complexity, practical solvers can seem like an incredibly complicated jumble of heuristics. When viewed, however, through the lens of proof systems, we can discern that certain solver heuristics correspond to proof rules (e.g., clause learning corresponds to the resolution proof rule), while other methods are aimed at optimally sequencing/selecting proof rules (e.g., branching) or (re)-initializing proof search (e.g., restarts). Further, solver heuristics that are aimed at sequencing proof rules or initializing proof search, can be profitably implemented using online, dynamic, and adaptive machine learning (ML) methods. In a series of papers, Liang et al. (2016, 2018) make exactly this point by designing and implementing a series of efficient ML-based CDCL SAT solvers. In Section 25.6, we discuss how theoretical concepts (proof systems) and practical insights (ML-based proof-rule sequencing/selection) can be brought together for better solver design. (See also Chapter 30 for ML-based algorithm design.)

25.2 Conflict-Driven Clause Learning SAT Solvers

In this section, we briefly describe the CDCL SAT solver (Marques-Silva and Sakallah, 1996; Moskewicz et al., 2001), whose pseudo code is presented in Algorithm 1. The CDCL algorithm is built on top of the well known DPLL method developed originally by Davis et al. (1962), and differs from it primarily in its use of the following heuristics: conflict analysis and clause learning (Marques-Silva and Sakallah, 1996), effective variable- and value-election heuristics (Moskewicz et al., 2001; Liang et al., 2016), restarts (Liang et al., 2018), clause deletion (Audemard and Simon, 2013), and lazy data structures (Moskewicz et al., 2001). The CDCL algorithm is a sound, complete, and terminating backtracking decision procedure for Boolean logic. It takes as input a Boolean formula ϕ in CNF and an initially empty assignment μ (aka assignment trail), and outputs SAT if the input formula ϕ has a solution, and outputs UNSAT otherwise.

Given the intricacies of the CDCL algorithm, it is difficult to describe its implementation in great detail in a few short pages. Instead, we focus on a conceptual and theoretically interesting presentation. For example, we discuss subroutines such as clause learning and Boolean constraint propagation (BCP) that are essential for a theoretical explanation of why solvers are efficient, rather than implementation of lazy data structures. Further, all our theoretical models have no clause deletion policy, partly because we have virtually no theoretical understanding of the impact of such policies on solver behavior.

Another important modelling decision often made is to assume that certain solver heuristics (e.g., restarts and variable/value selection) are nondeterministic or all-powerful. That is, for an unsatisfiable input, the dynamic choices made by these heuristics enable the CDCL solver to find the shortest proof (in the number of proof steps) of its unsatisfiability, with only a polynomial time overhead in proof search over the optimal for that input. Such modeling choices are very valuable for two reasons: First, they enable us to establish the strongest possible lower bounds (under nondeterministic assumptions), and second, they simplify the theoretical analysis.

Algorithm 1 The CDCL SAT solving algorithm

1: **function** CDCL(ϕ, μ)
2:   **Input:** A CNF formula ϕ, and an initially empty assignment trail μ
3:   **Output:** SAT or UNSAT
4:
5:   dl = 0;   ▷ : Initially, decision level dl is 0
6:   **if** (CONFLICT == Boolean_Constraint_Propagation(ϕ,μ)) **then**
7:     return UNSAT;
8:   **else if** (all variables have been assigned) **then**
9:     **return** SAT;
10:   **end if**
11:   **do**   ▷ The search loop
12:     x = DecisionHeuristic(ϕ,μ);   ▷ Variable- and value-selection heuristic
13:     dl = dl + 1;   ▷ : Increment dl
14:     $\mu = \mu \bigcup (x, dl)$;   ▷ Add literal x to the assignment trail μ
15:     **if** (CONFLICT == Boolean_Constraint_Propagation(ϕ, μ)) **then**
16:       $\{\beta, C\}$ = ConflictAnalysis(ϕ, μ);
17:                       ▷ Analyze conflict, learn clause C and backjump level β
18:       AddLearnedClause(C)
19:       **if** $\beta < 0$ **then**   ▷ β is the backjump level
20:         return UNSAT;   ▷ Top-level conflict
21:       **else if** (restart condition met) **then**
22:         restart;   ▷ dl is set to 0, and assignment trail μ is emptied
23:       **else**
24:         backtrack(ϕ, μ, β);   ▷ Backjump to start search again
25:         dl = β;
26:       **end if**
27:     **end if**
28:   **while** (all variables have NOT been assigned)
29:   **return** SAT;
30: **end function**

Boolean Constraint Propagation (BCP) The CDCL algorithm first calls the BCP subroutine on input formulas without having branched on variables in it (line 6 in Algorithm 1). If a conflict is detected at this level (i.e., a top-level conflict), then CDCL returns UNSAT. The BCP subroutine (also referred to as unit propagation) is an incomplete SAT solver that takes as input a Boolean formula in CNF, and outputs SAT, CONFLICT, or UNKNOWN. It repeatedly applies the unit resolution rule to the input formula until it reaches a fixpoint. The unit resolution rule is a special case of the general resolution rule, where at least one of the clauses input to the rule is unit (i.e., contains exactly one unassigned literal under the *current partial assignment*). For example, consider the clauses (x) and $(\neg x \vee \alpha)$, which when resolved results in derived clause (α) written as: (x) $(\neg x \vee \alpha) \vdash (\alpha)$. (We choose to use the symbol $\vdash$ to denote a derivation or proof step, with antecedents on its left side and consequent on its right side.)

Repeated applications of the unit resolution rule to an input formula, until reaching a fixpoint, amount to maintaining a queue of unit clauses, simplifying the formula (along with all the learned clauses in the solver's learned clause database) with respect to the "current" unit clause (i.e., all occurrences of the current unit literal in the formula are assigned true, the occurrences of the complement of this unit literal are assigned false, and the clauses in the input formula are appropriately simplified), popping the "current" unit literal from the queue and adding implied units to the unit clause queue, and repeating this process until this queue is empty. A variable x that is assigned a value (alternatively, a variable whose value is set) as a result of applying BCP (one or more application of the unit resolution rule) is said to be *implied/propagated*.

BCP may return CONFLICT (i.e., the current partial assignment is unsatisfying for the input formula) or SAT (i.e., all variables have been assigned values true or false) or UNKNOWN. If BCP returns CONFLICT at the top level, without having made decisions (lines 7 and 20), then this means that the input formula is UNSAT. If, on the other hand, all the variables of the input formula have been assigned, then this means that the solver has found a satisfying assignment and it returns SAT (lines 9 and 29). Else, it means that the BCP subroutine returns UNKNOWN, i.e., it cannot decide by itself whether the formula is SAT or UNSAT. This causes the variable and value-selection heuristics to be invoked, that select an unassigned variable and assign it a truth value (line 12),[2] and iteratively search for a satisfying assignment to the input formula by extending the current partial assignment (line 11).

Variable- and Value-Selection Heuristics Variable selection heuristics[3] are subroutines that take as input the partial state of the solver (e.g., learned clauses and current partial assignment), compute a partial order over the unassigned variables of the input formula, and output the highest ranked variable in this order (line 12). Value-selection heuristics are subroutines that take as input a variable and output a truth value. After a variable selection heuristic selects an unassigned variable to branch on, the selected variable is then assigned a truth value given by a value-selection heuristic and added to the current partial assignment (line 14). Solver researchers have understood for a long time that both variable- and value-selection heuristics play a crucial role in the performance of solvers and a considerable amount of research has gone into their design (Liang et al., 2016, 2018). Unfortunately, due to space limitations we will only present a very brief sketch of the work done on this topic.

Decision Levels, Assignment Trail, and Antecedents On line 5 of the CDCL Algorithm 1, the solver initializes the variable dl (abbrev. for *current decision level*) to 0. The variable dl keeps track of the number of decisions in the *current partial assignment* as the solver traverses paths in the search tree of the input formula. Whenever a variable in the input formula is branched on (a decision variable), the variable dl in the CDCL algorithm is incremented by 1 (line 13). When the solver

---

[2] The variable being assigned by the solver's variable selection heuristic is sometimes also referred to as a branching or decision variable.

[3] Variable selection heuristics are sometimes also referred to as branching, with the variable output by them referred to as branching or decision variables. The term *decision heuristic* typically refers to the combination of variable- and value-selection heuristics. The literal returned by a decision heuristic is referred to simply as a *decision* or *decision literal*. The term *decision variable* refers to the variable that corresponds to a decision.

backjumps after ConflictAnalysis, the current decision level is modified to the level that the solver backjumps to (line 25).

The assignment trail (aka decision stack or partial assignment) μ is a stack data structure, where every entry corresponds to a variable, its value assignment, and its decision level. Whenever a variable x is branched or decided upon, an entry corresponding to x is pushed onto the assignment trail. Further, whenever the solver backjumps from level d to some level $d - \beta$, all entries with decision level higher than $d - \beta$ are popped from the assignment trail. The decision level of a variable is computed as follows: for unassigned variables it is initialized to -1. Unit variables in the input formula are assigned decision level 0. Whenever a variable is decided or branched upon, its decision level is set to dl + 1. Finally, the decision level of an implied literal x_i is the same as the decision level of the current decision variable in the assignment trail.

In addition to the decision level and the truth value assigned to a variable, the solver maintains another *dynamic object* for every variable x, namely, its *antecedent*. As the solver branches, propagates, backjumps, or restarts, the values this object takes may change. The antecedent or the *reason clause* of a variable x is the unit clause c (under the current partial assignment) used by BCP to *imply* x. For variables that are decisions or unassigned, the antecedent is NIL.

The Search Loop in CDCL If there is no conflict at the top level, i.e., dl=0 (line 6), then the algorithm checks whether all the variables of the input formula have been assigned a value (line 8). If so, the solver simply returns SAT. Else, it enters the body of the do-while loop on line 11, decides on a variable of the input formula using its variable- and value-selection heuristics (the DecisionHeuristic subroutine on line 12), increments the decision level (line 13), pushes the decision variable to the partial assignment or the assignment trail μ, along with its decision level (line 14), and performs BCP (line 15). If BCP returns CONFLICT (i.e., the current assignment μ is unsatisfying for the input formula), then conflict analysis is triggered (line 17).

Conflict Analysis and Clause Learning The conflict analysis and clause learning subroutine is perhaps the most important part of a CDCL SAT solver. The ConflictAnalysis subroutine (line 17) determines a reason or root cause for the conflict, learns a corresponding conflict or learned clause, and computes the *backjump level*. Most CDCL solvers implement what are known as *asserting clause learning schemes*, i.e., ones that learn clauses containing exactly one variable from the highest decision level (we discuss this in more detail in Section 25.3). If the backjump level is below 0, then the solver returns UNSAT (line 20), since this corresponds to deriving false. Otherwise, the CDCL solver may jump back several decision levels in the search tree (line 24), unlike in the DPLL case where the solver backtracks only one decision level.

One of the simplest forms of clause learning is the Decision Learning Scheme (DLS). While it is not the most effective (that honor goes to the first-UIP method by Moskewicz et al., 2001), DLS is certainly easy to explain. The key idea behind DLS can be explained as follows: All solvers, irrespective of the asserting learning scheme they implement, maintain a directed acyclic graph of implications whose nodes are variables (either decision or propagated), and there is an edge from node a to node b if setting a caused BCP to set b as well, under the current partial assignment.

Whenever the solver detects a conflict, this graph is analyzed by the ConflictAnalysis subroutine with the goal of determining the root cause of said conflict. In DLS, the ConflictAnalysis subroutine simply takes the negation of the conjunction of decisions responsible for the conflict, and the learned clause thus computed is stored in a learned clause database. Such learned clauses prevent subsequent invocations of BCP from making the same combination of mistakes (i.e., decisions) that led to the conflict. This process is repeated until the solver correctly determines the satisfiability of the input formula.

Backjumping In its simplest form, the backtracking step in a DPLL solver works as follows: on reaching a conflict, these solvers undo the last decision that led to the conflict, which leads the solver to backtrack to the previous decision level and continue its search. In the context of CDCL solvers many backtracking methods have been explored. Perhaps the most well known is called nonchronological backtracking (or simply, backjumping), wherein the solver backjumps to the second-highest decision level over all the variables in the asserting learned clause. Jumping to the second-highest decision level has the benefit that the asserting clause is now unit under the "current" partial assignment (post backjump).[4]

Restarts The original restart heuristic was first proposed by Gomes et al. (1998), in the context of DPLL SAT solvers. The idea behind restart policies is very simple: The assignment trail of a solver is erased at carefully chosen intervals during its run (with the exception of learned unit clauses that are not deleted). It is well known that restarts are a key solver heuristic, both empirically and theoretically. The original idea behind restarts, referred to as the heavy-tailed distribution explanation, is that SAT solvers have variance in their run time due to randomization, and may get unlucky resulting in uncharacteristically long run times. A restart in such cases gives the solver a second chance of getting a shorter run time. This explanation has now been partially discarded in favor of an empirically more robust argument that restarts enable solvers to learn better learned clauses, since they shorten the assignment trail at several intervals during the solver's run (Liang et al., 2018). On the theoretical front, recent work by Bonet et al. (2014) showed that CDCL SAT solvers with no restart (but with nondeterministic variable and value selection) are strictly more powerful than regular resolution. Nevertheless, the question of why restarts are so important for efficiency of CDCL SAT solvers remains open, both from the theoretical and empirical perspectives.

25.3 Proof Complexity of SAT Solvers

25.3.1 Equivalence between CDCL and Resolution

In this subsection, we survey known results regarding the "SAT solver as a proof system" model. Specifically, we discuss the seminal simulation result by Pipatsrisawat and Darwiche (2011) and independently by Atserias et al. (2011), who showed that

---

[4] While we do not discuss clause deletion policies at length, they do deserve mention, since they are an important heuristic in the context of CDCL SAT solvers. The key purpose of deletion policies is removal of derived or learned clauses that have outlived their utility vis-à-vis proof search. As is probably already clear to the reader, predicting the utility of derived clauses is a very difficult problem in general.

CDCL SAT solvers (with nondeterministic branching, restarts, and asserting learning scheme) are polynomially equivalent to the general resolution (Res) proof system. The history of these simulation results go back to the paper by Beame et al. (2004), who first showed that CDCL SAT solvers (under the assumption that a solver can branch on a variable that is already assigned a truth value) are polynomially equivalent to general resolution.

While theorists had long anticipated a polynomial equivalence between CDCL SAT solvers and the general resolution proof system, it was not formally established until 2011 (Atserias et al., 2011; Pipatsrisawat and Darwiche, 2011). In their seminal work, Pipatsrisawat and Darwiche, as well as Atserias et al. realized that CDCL solvers simulate Res not necessarily by producing the Res-proofs exactly, but rather by "absorbing" the clauses of Res-proofs. One should think of the absorbed clauses as being "learned implicitly" – absorbed clauses may not necessarily appear in a formula $\mathcal{F}$ or its proof. If we assign, however, all but one of the literals in the clause to false then unit propagation in CDCL will set the final literal to true. That is, even if the absorbed clause C is not in $\mathcal{F}$, the unit propagation subroutine behaves "as though" the absorbed clause is actually in $\mathcal{F}$. The dual of the notion of absorbed clauses is the concept of 1-empowering clauses.[5] Informally, 1-empowering clauses are ones that have not been "learned implicitly," and may enable BCP to make progress. We now define these notions more precisely, followed by a sketch of the main idea behind the simulation proof.

Definition 25.2 (Asserting Clause)   Recall that an *assignment trail* is a sequence of pairs $\sigma = \{(\ell_1, d_1), (\ell_2, d_2), \ldots, (\ell_t, d_t)\}$ where each literal ℓ_i is a literal from the formula and each $d_i \in \{d, p\}$, indicating that the literal was set by the solver by a decision or by a unit propagation, respectively. The *decision level* of a literal ℓ_i in the branching sequence is the number of decision literals occurring in σ up to and including ℓ_i. The *state* of a CDCL solver at a given point during its run can be defined as $(\mathcal{F}, \Gamma, \sigma)$, where $\mathcal{F}$ is the input CNF formula, Γ is a set of learned clauses, and σ is the assignment trail at the given point during the solver's run. Given an assignment trail σ and a clause C we say that C is *asserting* if it contains exactly one literal occurring at the highest decision level in σ. A clause learning scheme is *asserting* if all conflict clauses produced by the scheme are asserting with respect to the assignment trail at the time of conflict.

Definition 25.3 (Extended Branching Sequence)   An *extended branching sequence* is an ordered sequence $B = \{\beta_1, \beta_2, \ldots, \beta_t\}$ where each β_i is either a branching literal, or a symbol R, denoting a restart. If A is a CDCL solver, we use an extended branching sequence to dictate the operation of the solver A on $\mathcal{F}$: whenever the solver calls the branching scheme, we consume the next β_i from the sequence. If it is a literal, then we branch on that literal appropriately; otherwise restart as dictated by the extended branching sequence. If the branching sequence is empty, then simply proceed using the heuristics defined by the algorithm.

---

[5] The idea of 1-empowering clauses was first introduced by Pipatsrisawat and Darwiche (2011), while its dual notion of absorbed clauses was introduced by Atserias et al. (2011).

Definition 25.4 (Unit Consistency) We say CNF formula $\mathcal{F}$ is unit inconsistent if and only if there is a proof of the unsatisfiability of $\mathcal{F}$ using only unit resolution (alternatively, via BCP). A formula that is not unit inconsistent is said to be unit consistent (sometimes also written as 1-consistent).

Definition 25.5 (1-Empowering Clauses) Let $\mathcal{F}$ be a set of clauses and let A be a CDCL solver. Let $C = (\alpha \Rightarrow \ell)$ be a clause, where α is a conjunction of literals. We say that C is *empowering with respect to* $\mathcal{F}$ at ℓ if the following holds: (1) $\mathcal{F} \models C$, (2) $\mathcal{F} \wedge \alpha$ is unit consistent, and (3) an execution of A on $\mathcal{F}$ that falsifies all literals in α does not derive ℓ via unit propagation (aka, BCP). The literal ℓ is said to be *empowering*. If item (1) is satisfied but one of (2) or (3) is false then we say that the solver A and $\mathcal{F}$ *absorbs* C at ℓ; if A and $\mathcal{F}$ absorbs C at every literal then the clause is simply *absorbed*.

Definition 25.6 (General and Tree-like Resolution Proofs) A general resolution proof can be defined as a directed acyclic graph (DAG), whose nodes are clauses which are either input or derived, and there is an edge from nodes A and B to C if C is derived from A, B via the resolution proof rule. Let $(\alpha \vee x)$ and $(\neg x \vee \beta)$ denote two clauses, where α, β are disjunction of literals. Then, the resolution proof rule derives $(\alpha \vee \beta)$, and is usually written as

$$(\alpha \vee x) \quad (\neg x \vee \beta) \vdash (\alpha \vee \beta).$$

We assume α, β do not contain opposing literals. A tree-like resolution proof is a restricted form of general resolution proof where the proofs may not share sub-proofs, i.e., they are tree-like.

In order for a clause C to be learned by a CDCL solver, it must be *1-empowering at some literal* ℓ at the point in time it is learned by the solver during its run. To see this, consider a trace of a CDCL solver, stopped right after it has learned a clause C. Since we have learned C it is easy to see that it must be the case that $\mathcal{F} \models C$. Let σ be the branching sequence leading to the conflict in which we learned C, and let ℓ be the last decision literal assigned in σ *before* the solver hit a conflict (if CDCL uses an asserting clause learning scheme, such a literal must exist). We can write $C \equiv (\alpha \Rightarrow \neg \ell)$, and clearly $\alpha \subseteq \sigma$. Thus, at the point in the branching sequence σ before we assign ℓ it must be that $\mathcal{F} \wedge \alpha$ is unit consistent, since we have assigned another literal after assigning each of the literals in α. Finally, $\mathcal{F} \wedge \alpha \nvdash_1 \ell$, since $\neg \ell$ was chosen as a decision literal *after* we set the literals in α. (By $\alpha \vdash_1 \beta$ we mean that the literal β is derived from the set of clauses α using only BCP.)

Definition 25.7 (1-Provable Clauses) Given a CNF formula $\mathcal{F}$, clause C is 1-provable with respect to $\mathcal{F}$ iff $\mathcal{F} \wedge \neg C \vdash_1 false$. Put differently, we say a clause C is 1-provable with respect to a CNF $\mathcal{F}$, if C is derivable from $\mathcal{F}$ only using BCP.

Theorem 25.8 *CDCL is polynomially equivalent to general resolution (Res).*

Proof Sketch The high level idea of the simulation is as follows: We need to show that for a Res proof of unsatisfiability of an input formula $\mathcal{F}$, the CDCL solver (with nondeterministic extended branching sequence and asserting clause learning scheme) can simulate that proof with only polynomial overhead in the proof size (in terms of number of clauses). The crucial insight here is that for formulas $\mathcal{F}$ for which BCP alone cannot establish unsatisfiability, there exist empowering clauses implied by $\mathcal{F}$ that, when added to it (i.e., to the solver's database of learned clauses), cause BCP to correctly determine that the input formula is UNSAT. Further, for a general resolution proof π of a 1-consistent formula $\mathcal{F}$, there exists a clause C in π that is both 1-empowering and 1-provable with respect to the formula (at the point in the proof π that C is derived). Finally, such a clause can be absorbed by a CDCL solver in time $O(n^4)$, where n is the number of variables in the input formula. This process is repeated until there are no more clauses that need to be absorbed, and thus we have that CDCL polynomially simulates general resolution. (The reverse direction is trivial.) $\quad\square$

Discussion The value of Theorem 25.8 is threefold: First, we can easily lift lower bounds from the proof complexity literature for Res to CDCL SAT solvers, thus addressing the question of why solvers fail. Further, the polynomial equivalence between CDCL and Res helps explain the power of clause learning, since clause learning in CDCL corresponds to applications of the general resolution rule. In other words, proof complexity enables an improved understanding of certain heuristics in SAT solvers. Finally, proof complexity theory is a storehouse of knowledge on proof systems that can be leveraged to build solvers with varying degrees of strength aimed at different kinds of applications such as cryptography or verification.

25.3.2 Lower and Upper Bounds for Res and CDCL SAT Solvers

Considerable work has been done on the proof complexity of Res. Unfortunately, we cannot possibly do justice to this subject in this chapter. We do, however, sketch a few results that are relevant in the context of CDCL SAT solvers. The first superpolynomial lower bound for resolution was proved by Haken (1985). To be more precise, Haken proved that the family of formulas that encodes the *Propositional Pigeonhole Principle(PHP)* requires resolution proofs of size at least c^n, for some $c > 1$. Another source of hardness for Res comes from randomly generated formulas. Also, Urquhart showed that CNF formulas whose graphs are expanders are hard for Res, and hence for CDCL (Urquhart, 1987).

There is a vast literature on the complexity of proof systems that we have not covered here (Krajíček, 2019). For example, there are many powerful proof systems such as extended resolution with no known lower bounds, that have been studied extensively by theorists (Tseitin, 1983). While there are systems that are stronger than Res, their implementations to date as solvers seem to be useful only in narrow contexts, unlike CDCL SAT solvers that is widely applicable. This suggests that strength of the proof system alone may not lead to powerful solvers. One also has to look into proof search, which we turn to in the next section.

25.4 Proof Search, Automatizability, and CDCL SAT Solvers

Proof complexity gives us powerful tools that enable us to prove lower bounds for SAT solvers (and thus characterize families of formulas where solvers fail spectacularly). It does not, however, quite address the question of proof search. The proof search question for a proof system is: Given an unsatisfiable formula F, does there exist an algorithm that finds proofs in the given proof system with only polynomial overhead? In particular, if the formula F has a short proof, then the question asks whether a solver can find a proof in polynomial time.

This idea of efficient proof search was first formalized by Bonet et al. (2000) via the notion of automatizability of proof systems. (Although there is previous work on proof search by Iwama (1997) in which it was shown that the problem of finding the shortest Res proof is NP-hard.) Recall that the polynomial simulation result in Section 25.3 shows that if there is a short proof π for some formula φ, then there exists a run of a nondeterministic CDCL solver (i.e., a CDCL SAT solver with nondeterministic variable/value selection and restarts) that can produce a proof of size $O(n^4) * |\pi|$. The proof of the theorem relies on the fact that the CDCL solver under consideration has nondeterministic power, yet real-life solvers do not have the same luxury. So, it is natural to ask the following question: "For the class of formulas that do have short proofs, does there exist a solver that always finds such proofs in time polynomial in the size of the input formula?"

In their seminal paper, Bonet et al. (2000) defined the notion of the *automatizability* of proof systems. A proof system P is said to be *automatizable* if there exists a polynomially bounded deterministic algorithm A that takes as input an unsatisfiable formula φ, and outputs a P-proof of φ of size at most polynomially larger (in the size of φ) than the shortest P-proof of φ. There have been several attempts to tackle the automatizability problem for resolution and tree-like resolution. For example, Ben-Sasson and Wigderson (2001) showed that tree-like resolution is automatizable in quasi-polynomial time. A more recent breakthrough result by Atserias and Müller (2019) says that Res is not automatizable in quasi-polynomial time, unless NP is included in SUBEXP.

Automatizability and CDCL SAT Solvers The value of studying the (parametric) automatizability question is that it may eventually shed light on the key question of upper bounds (i.e., why are solvers efficient for certain classes of industrial instances), just as proof complexity of the Res system has helped us better understand lower bounds for CDCL solvers. Automatizability gets to the heart of the proof search question, precisely the task that solvers have been designed for. While we are far from any conclusive answers, we do have promising leads. For example, based on the quasi-automatizability result for tree-like resolution (equivalently, DPLL solvers), we know that if an unsatisfiable formula has a polynomial-sized tree-like proof, DPLL solvers can solve it in quasi-polynomial time. One could ask whether something similar is also (parametrically) true for general resolution and equivalently for CDCL solvers. This naturally leads us to a parameteric study of formulas and their proofs.

25.5 Parameteric Understanding of Boolean Formulas

So far we have addressed the issue of how best to model SAT solvers as proof systems, discussed lower bounds vis-à-vis proof size obtained via an equivalence between solvers and proof systems, and lower bounds for automatizability of Res. While these give us insight into classes of instances over which SAT solvers perform poorly, they do not quite address the central question of solver research, namely, why CDCL SAT solvers are so efficient for instances obtained from real-world applications. In order to better understand this question we need to turn our attention to parameterization of Boolean formulas and their proofs.

There is widespread consensus among SAT researchers that solvers somehow leverage the structure present in real-world CNF formulas (or in their proofs), and that a characterization of this structure can be used to establish a parameteric proof-complexity theoretic and proof search upper bounds. As a consequence, considerable effort has been expended in studying the structure of real-world formulas. We already know that parameterizations such as 2-SAT or Horn clauses that are known to be easy for Res, do not really capture classes of real-world instances over which solvers perform well.

In fact, the challenge for this line of research is to come up with parameters that make sense both in practice (i.e., characterize the structure of real-world instances) and theory (i.e., are amenable to theoretical analysis). While researchers have proposed several parameters, none so far seems to be up to the task of addressing this challenge. The parameters that are easy to work with in theory (e.g., backdoors) do not seem to characterize real-world instances. The ones that do seem to characterize real-world instances (e.g., community structure or modularity) are difficult to work with from a theoretical point of view. Even so, there are many lessons one can learn from the parameters studied so far that may eventually help prove the kind of parameteric upper bounds on proof complexity and proof search that we seek.

Clause Variable Ratio Perhaps one of the first and certainly most widely studied parameter is the *Clause/Variable Ratio (CVR) or Clause Density*, given its intuitive appeal. The CVR of a k-CNF formula is defined as the ratio of the total number of clauses to the number of variables in the formula. The earliest experiments in regards to CVR were performed by Cheeseman et al. (1991), who showed that for randomly generated fixed-width CNF formulas the probability of satisfiability of such instances undergoes a phase-transition around a fixed CVR, which depends only on clause-width (the phase-transition for randomly generated 3-CNF formulas is 4.26). Formulas below the phase transition are more likely to be satisfiable (the asymptotic probability approaches 1 as the CVR goes below 3.52 (Kaporis et al., 2006)), and those above are more likely to be unsatisfiable (the asymptotic probability approaches 1 as the CVR goes above 4.4898 (Díaz et al., 2009)). Further, it was observed that formulas below and above the phase transition are easy to solve, while those around the phase transition are hard (the so-called "easy-hard-easy pattern") (Mitchell et al., 1992).

These results caused a stir when first reported, for it seemed like there was a very simple explanation for the worst-case complexity-theoretic hardness of the Boolean satisfiability problem. It was soon, however, observed that there are many issues with these results. First, it is known that phase transitions exists also for SAT problems that are known to be easy, such as 2-SAT; cf. Chvátal and Reed (1992). Second, when one takes a deeper look at the empirical "easy-hard-easy" pattern of difficulty of solving instances around the phase transition, by keeping the CVR constant and scaling the size of instances, the observed pattern is more like "easy-harder-less hard" (Coarfa et al., 2003), with the transition from "easy" to "harder" occurring well in the satisfiable region. This empirical finding was later confirmed in Achlioptas and Coja-Oghlan (2008), who demonstrated a "shattering" of the solution space around CVR of 3.8.

Treewidth The *treewidth* of a graph measures how close a given graph is to being a tree (Bodlaender, 1994). A tree has treewidth 1. A cycle is the simplest graph that is not a tree, but it can be "squashed" into a path of treewidth 2. A family of graphs is of *bounded treewidth* if there some some $k > 0$ such that all graphs in the family has treewidth at most k. It turns out that many graph problems that are *NP*-hard on general graphs can be solved in polynomial time on bounded-treewidth families of graphs (Freuder, 1990). This idea can also be applied to SAT. Given a CNF forumla ϕ, we can construct a bipartite graph G_ϕ whose nodes are the clauses and the variables of ϕ, and there is an edge between a clause c and a variable v when v occurs in c. The treewidth of ϕ is then the treewidth of G_ϕ. It follows that that SAT can be solved in polynomial time for a bounded-treewidth families of formulas.

If industrial formulas had bounded treewidth, that would perhaps explain the success of CDCL solvers on such formulas. For example, formulas generated by *bounded model checkers* are obtained by unrolling a circuit (Clarke et al., 2001), which yields formulas that have bounded treewidth (in fact, even bounded pathwidth) (Ferrara et al., 2005). It is not clear, however, that this explanation is satisfactory. Polynomial-time algorithms for graph families of treewidth at most k, typically have worst-case time complexity of the form $n^{O(k)}$ (Kolaitis and Vardi, 2000). Thus, such polynomial-time algorithm are feasible in practice only for very small k's, which does not seem to be the case, for example, in bounded model checking.

Backdoors and Backbones The notion of *backdoors* for Boolean formulas was first introduced by Williams et al. (2003). The intuition behind this notion is quite elegant, namely, that for every Boolean formula there is a (small) subset of its variables, which when assigned appropriate values, renders the said formula easy to solve. It was further conjectured that industrial instances must have small backdoors. Williams et al. introduced two kinds of backdoors, namely *weak backdoors* and *strong backdoors*. A weak backdoor B of a satisfiable formula φ is a subset of variables of φ, where there exists a mapping $\delta : B \mapsto \{0, 1\}$, such that the restricted formula $\varphi[\delta]$ can be solved in polynomial time by some subsolver S (e.g., BCP). By contrast, a strong backdoor B of a formula φ is a subset of variables from φ, such that for a mapping $\delta : B \mapsto \{0, 1\}$ from variables in B to truth values, the restricted formula $\varphi[\delta]$ can be solved by a polynomial time subsolver. While weak backdoors are defined only for satisfiable instances, strong backdoors are well defined for both satisfiable and unsatisfiable ones. The *backbone* of a satisfiable Boolean formula φ can be defined as a subset B of variables such that they take the same values in all satisfying assignments and the set B is maximal. Kilby et al. (2005) theoretically proved that backbones are hard to even approximate assuming $P \neq NP$. Unfortunately, both backdoors (and backbones) do not seem to explain why industrial instances are easy. Often industrial instances seem to have large backdoors (Zulkoski et al., 2018b). Further, the hypothesized correlation between the size of backdoors and solver runtime (i.e., smaller the backdoor, easier the problem) seems weak at best for industrial instances (Zulkoski et al., 2018b). It seems like CDCL SAT solvers are not able to automatically identify and exploit small backdoors or backbones.

Modularity and Community Structure Another structure that has been extensively studied is the community structure of the variable-incidence graph or VIG of CNF formulas (formula variables correspond to nodes in the VIG, and there is an edge between two nodes if the corresponding variables appear in the same clause). Informally, community structure of a graph defines how "separable" the clusters of a graph are. An ideal clustering for a VIG would be where every cluster corresponds to a set of clauses that are easy to solve independently and the clusters are "weakly connected" to other clusters. The concept of dividing graphs into natural communities was developed by Clauset et al. (2004). On a high level, we say a graph G has good community structure, that is, there is an optimal decomposition of G (we call each subgraph/component a community/module) such that there are far more intracommunity edges than there are intercommunity ones. Clauset et al. defined the notion of modularity of a graph, denoted Q, more specifically, a graph with high Q value is more "separable" (in the sense that the communities have few intercommunity edges relative to the number of communities) comparing to a graph with low Q value (which is closer to a randomly generated graph).

In their seminal paper, Ansótegui et al. (2012) established that industrial instances have good community structure. Newsham et al. (2014) showed a strong correlation between community structure and solver performance. Specifically, they showed that formulas with good community structure (high Q) correlate with lower solver run time relative to formulas with low Q. Subsequent work has taken advantage of these results in coming up with better solver heuristics. Nevertheless, the promise of community structure as a basis for a theoretical understanding of why solvers perform well has not yet been realized.

Merge Resolution and Mergeability Aside from the parameters we have discussed so far, "merge" is another interesting parameter that researchers have studied from both theoretical (Andrews, 1968) and practical (Zulkoski et al., 2018a) points of view. We motivate the study of merge parameter by recalling the resolution rule given above. Let A denote the antecedent clause $(\alpha \vee x)$, B denote the antecedent clause $(\neg x \vee \beta)$, and C denote the derived clause or consequent $(\alpha \vee \beta)$. For a clause A, let $| A |$ denote the number of literals in it (the length of the clause). It is easy to see that the length $| C |$ of the consequent C is equal to $|A| + |B| - l - 2$, where $l = | A \cap B |$ is the number of literals overlapping in A and B. Put differently, the length of derived clauses in the Res proof system decreases as the number of literals overlapping in the antecedents increase. This number l of overlapping literals in the antecedent of a resolution proof rule application is called *merge*.

We can further make the following observations about the relationship between merge and the completeness of the Res proof system: First observe that derived clauses in a resolution proof decrease in length proportional to the increase in merge (i.e., the overlap between antecedent clauses). Additionally, in order for a Res proof of unsatisfiability to terminate, the length of derived clauses have to start "shrinking" (i.e., the derived clause is strictly smaller than at least one of its antecedent) at some point in the proof, eventually ending in the empty clause. It turns out that repeated application of the resolution rule over clauses with large merge is a powerful way to obtain short clauses, eventually enabling the resolution proof system to obtain complete proofs.

In fact, the power of merge was first observed by Andrews (1968), who defined merge resolution as a refinement of the Res proof system. The merge resolution proof system, which is sound and complete for propositional logic, is designed to bias applications of the resolution proof rule over clauses that have high degree of merge, and thus obtain shorter derived clauses faster relative to a proof system that is not biased in this way. Intuitively, this is a powerful greedy heuristic since maximizing merge likely implies that the *resolution width* of a proof (Ben-Sasson and Wigderson, 2001) also goes down during proof search. Nevertheless, a formal link between merge and resolution width remains to be established.

On the empirical front, Zulkoski et al. (2018a) studied the link between merge and efficiency of CDCL SAT solvers on randomly generated and industrial formulas. They defined a new notion called *mergeability* as follows: Let $m(A, B)$ be the number of overlapping literals in some resolvable pair of clauses A and B, and define M to be $\sum m(A, B)$ for all resolvable pairs of A and B. Additionally, let l be the number of clauses in the input formula ϕ. Then the mergeability of ϕ is defined as $\frac{M}{l^2}$. The empirical hypothesis they posed in their work was: "As the mergeability increases for a formula ϕ (while most of its other key features remains unmodified), the formula becomes easier to solve."

In their paper, Zulkoski et al. (2018a) report that indeed this is the case. They present a random industrial-like instance generator that takes as input a formula and then increases the mergeability of the formula while maintaining other key properties of the formula such as the distribution of variable occurrences, property of the underlying community structures, etc. It turns out, under their notion of mergeability, the runtime of CDCL SAT solvers negatively correlates with mergeability over randomly-generated unsatisfiable instances. Another observation they make is that the CDCL solvers they used in their experiments produce shorter and shorter width clauses on average as the mergeability of the input formula increases. These experiments strongly suggest that merge might be a key parameter that can help explain the power of CDCL solvers on industrial instances.

The jury is still out on how to prove a meaningful upper bound result that is relevant in practice and illuminating from a theoretical point of view. It is clear that we need parameterization. It is not, however, clear which of the aforementioned parameters will do the trick. Our conjecture is that the upper bound is likely to be exponential in both the parameter(s) and the size of the input (n, number of variables). Nevertheless, the parameter(s) and size n may interact in such a way that for relatively small values of n, the upper bound may behave like a polynomial, and for large values of n, the upper bound may behave more like an exponential.

25.6 Proof Complexity, Machine Learning, and Solver Design

For most of this chapter we have focused on a proof-theoretic model of CDCL SAT solvers and questions of lower/upper bounds of proof size and search. As we close, it behooves us to reflect on how these theoretical investigations may help us with practical solver design. If one were to investigate the source code of a typical CDCL SAT solver, without the aid of proof complexity, it is likely they will see a difficult-to-understand jumble of heuristics. Fortunately, a proof complexity-theoretic view can help appropriately abstract solver design.

While SAT solvers are decision procedures, internally they are an interacting set of complex optimization heuristics whose aim is to minimize solver runtime. Many solver heuristics correspond to proof rules (e.g., BCP corresponds to repeated application of the unit-resolution rule, while clause learning correspond to the general resolution rule), while others such as branching heuristics correspond to sequencing or selection of proof rules, and restarts correspond to initialization of proof search. This view suggests a solver-design principle: Solvers are best designed by understanding what kind of proof system best fits the application at hand, and developing optimization procedures to sequence, select, and initialize proof rules. These optimization procedures can be implemented using a rich set of known online and adaptive machine-learning methods. This empirical principle was properly articulated in a series of papers by Liang et al. (2016, 2018) that in turn led to the design and development of MapleSAT, one of the fastest solvers in recent years.

25.7 Conclusions and Future Directions

The question of why CDCL SAT solvers are efficient for industrial instances, while at the same time perform poorly on certain families of crafted and randomly generated instances, is one of the central questions in SAT-solver research (Vardi, 2014). We discussed how proof and parameterized complexity provide the appropriate lens through which we can hope to answer this question. The strongest result to date states that CDCL solvers (with nondeterministic branching and restarts) are as powerful as the Res proof systems. This simulation answers, to some extent, the question of why solvers fail on certain classes of instances by lifting known lower bounds for Res to the CDCL setting. Proof complexity also formalizes the question of proof search via the notion of automatizability, which can be a powerful lens through which to understand paramterized upper bounds on CDCL proof search. We also discussed the search for parameters that may be relevant both in practice and theory. The most promising among them are the merge and community structure parameters. Having said that, much progress needs to be made for we still do not know the right parameterization(s) for industrial instances. Finally, we discussed how solvers can be viewed as a collection of interacting heuristics, some of which implement appropriate proof rules, while others perform the task of proof rule sequencing, selection, and initialization, many of which can be profitably implemented via online and adaptive machine-learning techniques.

While much progress has been made, the central questions remain unanswered. We hope that this chapter suitably captures the progress made thus far, and frames the appropriate ideas that may lead to breakthrough results in the near future. Perhaps the most important unanswered question is that of appropriate parameterization(s) of industrial instances. Despite more than two decades of efforts by a number of leading practitioners and theorists, we still do not have good candidate parameters with which to upper bound the proof size and proof search for industrial instances. Another open problem that has resisted all attempts at solving is the question of the power of restarts (i.e., why are restarts so important in practice, and do they give solvers proof-theoretic power?). Finally, there are mysteries such as power of local branching (a la, the VSIDS heuristic) and first-UIP clause learning schemes. These heuristics seem indispensable and yet no one can convincingly explain why.

References

Achlioptas, Dimitris, and Coja-Oghlan, Amin. 2008. Algorithmic barriers from phase transitions. *2008 49th Annual IEEE Symposium on Foundations of Computer Science*, pp. 793–802. IEEE.

Andrews, Peter B. 1968. Resolution with merging. *Automation of Reasoning*, pp. 85–101. Springer.

Ansótegui, Carlos, Giráldez-Cru, Jesús, and Levy, Jordi. 2012. The community structure of SAT formulas. In Cimatti, Alessandro, and Sebastiani, Roberto (eds), *Theory and Applications of Satisfiability Testing – SAT 2012*, pp. 410–423. Springer.

Atserias, Albert, and Müller, Moritz. 2019. Automating resolution is NP-hard. In *60th IEEE Annual Symposium on Foundations of Computer Science (FOCS)*, pp. 498–509.

Atserias, Albert, Bonet, Maria Luisa, and Esteban, Juan Luis. 2002. Lower bounds for the weak pigeonhole principle and random formulas beyond resolution. *Information and Computation*, **176**(2), 136–152.

Atserias, Albert, Fichte, Johannes Klaus, and Thurley, Marc. 2011. Clause-learning algorithms with many restarts and bounded-width resolution. *Journal of Artificial Intelligence Research*, **40**, 353–373.

Audemard, Gilles, and Simon, Laurent. 2013. Glucose 2.3 in the SAT 2013 competition. In *Proceedings of SAT Competition 2013*, pp. 42–43.

Balyo, Tomás, Heule, Marijn J. H., and Järvisalo, Matti. 2017. SAT competition 2016: Recent developments. In Singh, Satinder P., and Markovitch, Shaul (eds), *Proceedings of the Thirty-First AAAI Conference on Artificial Intelligence*, pp. 5061–5063. AAAI Press.

Beame, Paul, Kautz, Henry, and Sabharwal, Ashish. 2004. Towards understanding and harnessing the potential of clause learning. *Journal of Artificial Intelligence Research*, **22**, 319–351.

Ben-Sasson, Eli, and Wigderson, Avi. 2001. Short proofs are Resolution made simple. *Journal of the ACM*, **48**(2), 149–169.

Bodlaender, Hans L. 1994. A tourist guide through treewidth. *Acta Cybernetica*, **11**(1-2), 1.

Bonet, Maria Luisa, Pitassi, Toniann, and Raz, Ran. 2000. On interpolation and automatization for Frege systems. *SIAM Journal on Computing*, **29**(6), 1939–1967.

Bonet, Maria Luisa, Buss, Sam, and Johannsen, Jan. 2014. Improved separations of regular resolution from clause learning proof systems. *Journal of Artificial Intelligence Research*, **49**, 669–703.

Cadar, Cristian, Ganesh, Vijay, Pawlowski, Peter M., Dill, David L., and Engler, Dawson R. 2006. EXE: Automatically generating inputs of death. In *Proceedings of the 13th ACM Conference on Computer and Communications Security*, pp. 322–335. CCS '06. ACM.

Cheeseman, Peter C, Kanefsky, Bob, and Taylor, William M. 1991. Where the really hard problems are. In *International Joint Conference on Artificial Intelligence (IJCAI)*, pp. 331–337.

Chvátal, Vašek, and Reed, Bruce. 1992. Mick gets some (the odds are on his side)(satisfiability). *Proceedings, 33rd Annual Symposium on Foundations of Computer Science*, pp. 620–627. IEEE.

Clarke, Edmund, Biere, Armin, Raimi, Richard, and Zhu, Yunshan. 2001. Bounded model checking using satisfiability solving. *Formal Methods in System Design*, **19**(1), 7–34.

Clauset, Aaron, Newman, M. E. J., and Moore, Cristopher. 2004. Finding community structure in very large networks. *Physical Review E*, **70**(Dec), 066111.

Coarfa, Cristian, Demopoulos, Demetrios D., Aguirre, Alfonso San Miguel, Subramanian, Devika, and Vardi, Moshe Y. 2003. Random 3-SAT: The plot thickens. *Constraints*, **8**(3), 243–261.

Cook, Stephen A. 1971. The complexity of theorem-proving procedures. *Proceedings of the Third Annual ACM Symposium on Theory of Computing*, pp. 151–158. ACM.

Davis, Martin, Logemann, George, and Loveland, Donald. 1962. A machine program for theorem-proving. *Communications of the ACM*, **5**(7), 394–397.

Díaz, Josep, Kirousis, Lefteris, Mitsche, Dieter, and Pérez-Giménez, Xavier. 2009. On the satisfiability threshold of formulas with three literals per clause. *Theoretical Computer Science*, **410**(30-32), 2920–2934.

Ferrara, Andrea, Pan, Guoqiang, and Vardi, Moshe Y. 2005. Treewidth in verification: Local vs. global. *International Conference on Logic for Programming Artificial Intelligence and Reasoning*, pp. 489–503. Springer.

Freuder, Eugene C. 1990. Complexity of K-tree structured constraint satisfaction problems. In *Proceedings of the 8th National Conference on Artificial Intelligence*, pp. 4–9. AAAI Press / The MIT Press.

Gomes, Carla P., Selman, Bart, and Kautz, Henry. 1998. Boosting combinatorial search through randomization. In *Proceedings of the Fifteenth National/Tenth Conference on Artificial Intelligence/Innovative Applications of Artificial Intelligence*, pp. 431–437. AAAI '98/IAAI '98. American Association for Artificial Intelligence.

Haken, Armin. 1985. The intractability of resolution. *Theoretical Computer Science*, **39**, 297–308.

Iwama, Kazuo. 1997. Complexity of finding short resolution proofs. In *International Symposium on Mathematical Foundations of Computer Science*, pp. 309–318. Springer.

Kaporis, Alexis C, Kirousis, Lefteris M, and Lalas, Efthimios G. 2006. The probabilistic analysis of a greedy satisfiability algorithm. *Random Structures & Algorithms*, **28**(4), 444–480.

Kautz, Henry A, Selman, Bart, et al. 1992. Planning as satisfiability. In *European Conference on Artificial Intelligence (ECAI)*, pp. 359–363. Citeseer.

Kilby, Philip, Slaney, John, Thiébaux, Sylvie, Walsh, Toby, et al. 2005. Backbones and backdoors in satisfiability. In *AAAI Conference on Artificial Intelligence*, pp. 1368–1373.

Kolaitis, Phokion G, and Vardi, Moshe Y. 2000. Conjunctive-query containment and constraint satisfaction. *Journal of Computer and System Sciences*, **61**(2), 302–332.

Krajíček, Jan. 2019. *Proof Complexity* vol. 170. Cambridge University Press.

Liang, Jia Hui, Ganesh, Vijay, Poupart, Pascal, and Czarnecki, Krzysztof. 2016. Learning rate based branching heuristic for SAT solvers. In Creignou, Nadia, and Le Berre, Daniel (eds), *Theory and Applications of Satisfiability Testing – SAT 2016*, pp. 123–140. Springer International Publishing.

Liang, Jia Hui, Oh, Chanseok, Mathew, Minu, Thomas, Ciza, Li, Chunxiao, and Ganesh, Vijay. 2018. Machine learning-based restart policy for CDCL SAT solvers. *Theory and Applications of Satisfiability Testing - SAT 2018 - 21st International Conference, SAT 2018, Held as Part of the Federated Logic Conference, FloC 2018*.

Marques-Silva, João P, and Sakallah, Karem A. 1996. GRASP: A new search algorithm for satisfiability. In *Proceedings of the 1996 IEEE/ACM International Conference on Computer-Aided Design*, pp. 220–227. ICCAD '96. IEEE Computer Society.

Mitchell, David, Selman, Bart, and Levesque, Hector. 1992. Hard and easy distributions of SAT problems. In *AAAI Conference on Artificial Intelligence*, pp. 1368–1373.

Moskewicz, Matthew W., Madigan, Conor F., Zhao, Ying, Zhang, Lintao, and Malik, Sharad. 2001. Chaff: Engineering an efficient SAT solver. In *Proceedings of the 38th Annual Design Automation Conference*, pp. 530–535. DAC '01. ACM.

Newsham, Zack, Ganesh, Vijay, Fischmeister, Sebastian, Audemard, Gilles, and Simon, Laurent. 2014. Impact of community structure on SAT solver performance. Sinz, Carsten, and Egly, Uwe (eds), *Theory and Applications of Satisfiability Testing – SAT 2014*, pp. 252–268. Cham: Springer International.

Pipatsrisawat, Knot, and Darwiche, Adnan. 2011. On the power of clause-learning SAT solvers as resolution engines. *Artificial Intelligence*, **175**(2), 512–525.

Tseitin, Grigori S. 1983. On the complexity of derivation in propositional calculus. *Automation of Reasoning*, pp. 466–483. Springer.

Urquhart, Alasdair. 1987. Hard examples for resolution. *Journal of the ACM (JACM)*, **34**(1), 209–219.

Vardi, Moshe Y. 2014. Boolean satisfiability: Theory and engineering. *Communications of the ACM*, **57**(3), 5–5.

Williams, Ryan, Gomes, Carla, and Selman, Bart. 2003. Backdoors to typical case complexity. In *Proceedings of the International Joint Conference on Artificial Intelligence (IJCAI)*, pp. 1173–1178.

Zulkoski, Edward, Martins, Ruben, Wintersteiger, Christoph M., Liang, Jia Hui, Czarnecki, Krzysztof, and Ganesh, Vijay. 2018a. The effect of structural measures and merges on SAT solver performance. In *Principles and Practice of Constraint Programming - 24th International Conference, CP 2018*, pp. 436–452.

Zulkoski, Edward, Martins, Ruben, Wintersteiger, Christoph M., Robere, Robert, Liang, Jia Hui, Czarnecki, Krzysztof, and Ganesh, Vijay. 2018b. Learning-sensitive backdoors with restarts. *International Conference on Principles and Practice of Constraint Programming*, pp. 453–469. Springer.

CHAPTER TWENTY SIX

When Simple Hash Functions Suffice

Kai-Min Chung, Michael Mitzenmacher, and Salil Vadhan

Abstract: In this chapter, we describe a semirandom data model under which simple, explicit families of hash functions, such as those that are 2-universal or $O(1)$-wise independent, perform in a way that is nearly indistinguishable from idealized random hashing, where each data item is mapped independently and uniformly to the range. Specifically, we show that it suffices for the data to come from a "block source," whereby each new data item has some "entropy" given the previous ones. This provides a possible explanation for the observation that simple hash functions, including 2-universal hash functions, often perform as predicted by analysis for the idealized model of truly random hash functions, despite generally having noticeably weaker worst-case guarantees.

26.1 Introduction

Hashing is at the core of many fundamental algorithms and data structures, including all varieties of hash tables, Bloom filters and their many variants, summary algorithms for data streams, and many others. Traditionally, applications of hashing are analyzed as if the hash function is a truly random function (a.k.a. "random oracle") mapping each data item independently and uniformly to the range of the hash function. However, this idealized model is arguably unrealistic, because a truly random function mapping $\{0,1\}^n$ to $\{0,1\}^m$ requires an exponential (in n) number of bits to describe.

For this reason, a long line of theoretical work has sought to provide rigorous bounds on performance when explicit families of hash functions are used; e.g., families whose description and computational complexity are polynomial in n and m. The first examples used *2-universal hash families*, which have the property that for every two distinct inputs $x \neq x' \in \{0,1\}^n$, if we choose a random hash function H from the family, the probability that x and x' collide under H (i.e., $H(x) = H(x')$) is at most $1/2^m$. There are 2-universal families where each hash function has a description length that is linear (in n) and can be evaluated in nearly linear time, and the 2-universal property can be shown to suffice for a number of applications of hashing. A stronger property sometimes used is s-wise independence, where for every s distinct inputs $x_1, \ldots, x_s \in \{0,1\}^n$, the hash values $H(x_1), \ldots, H(x_s)$ are uniform and independent in

$\{0, 1\}^m$. However, achieving s-wise independence would require the description length and the evaluation time to be at least linear in $s \cdot m$.

While many beautiful results of this type have been obtained, they are not always as strong as we would like. In some cases, the types of hash functions analyzed can be implemented very efficiently (e.g., universal or $O(1)$-wise independent hash functions), but the performance guarantees are noticeably weaker than for ideal hashing. In other cases, the performance guarantees are (essentially) optimal, but the hash functions are more complex and expensive (e.g., with a superlinear time or space requirement). For example, if at most T items are going to be hashed, then a T-wise independent hash function will have precisely the same behavior as an ideal hash function. But a T-wise independent hash function mapping to $\{0, 1\}^m$ requires at least $T \cdot m$ bits to represent, which is often too large. For some applications, it has been shown that less independence, such as $O(\log T)$-wise independence, suffices, but such functions are still substantially less efficient than 2-universal hash functions.

In practice, however, the performance of standard universal hashing often seems to match what is predicted for ideal hashing. Thus, it may not always be necessary to use the more complex hash functions for which this kind of performance can be proven. As in many other examples in this book, this gap between theory and practice may be due to worst-case analysis. Indeed, in some cases, it can be proven that there exist sequences of data items for which universal hashing does not provide optimal performance. But these bad sequences may be pathological cases that are unlikely to arise in practice. That is, the strong performance of universal hash functions in practice may arise from a *combination* of the randomness of the hash function and the randomness of the data.

Of course, doing an average-case analysis, whereby each data item is independently and uniformly distributed in $\{0, 1\}^n$, is also very unrealistic (not to mention that it trivializes many applications). In this chapter, we describe an intermediate model, previously studied in the literature on "randomness extractors," that may be an appropriate data model for some hashing applications. Under the assumption that the data fit this model, we will see that relatively weak hash functions achieve essentially the same performance as ideal hash functions.

26.1.1 The Model

We will model the data as coming from a random source in which the data items can be far from uniform and have arbitrary correlations, provided that each (new) data item is sufficiently unpredictable given the previous items. This is formalized by the notion of a *block source*, where we require that the ith item (block) X_i has at least some k bits of "entropy" conditioned on the previous items (blocks) $X_1, \ldots, X_{i-1}$. There are various choices for the entropy measure that can be used here; *min-entropy* is used most commonly in the literature on randomness extractors, but most of the results presented here hold even for the less stringent measure of *Rényi entropy*. (See Section 26.2.3 for the formal definitions.)

Block sources seem to be a plausible model for many real-life data sources where we believe that there are is some intrinsic randomness in each data item, provided the entropy k required per block is not too large. However, in some settings, the data may have structure that violates the block-source property, in which case the results of this chapter will not apply. See Section 26.1.4 for further discussion about the model.

26.1.2 The Results

Here we give a high-level overview of the results presented in this chapter; see Sections 26.2 and 26.3 for the formal treatment of the definitions and results.

It turns out that standard results in the literature on "randomness extractors"[1] already imply that universal hashing performs nearly as well ideal hashing, provided the data items have enough entropy. Specifically, if we have T data items coming from a block source $(X_1, \ldots, X_T)$ where each data item has (Rényi) entropy at least $m + 2\log(T/\epsilon)$ (all logs are base 2 in this chapter) and H is a random 2-universal hash function mapping to $\{0, 1\}^m$, then $(H(X_1), \ldots, H(X_T))$ has statistical distance at most ϵ from T uniform and independent elements of $\{0, 1\}^m$. Thus, any event that would occur with some probability p under ideal hashing now occurs with probability in the range $[p - \epsilon, p + \epsilon]$. This allows us to automatically translate existing results for ideal hashing into results for universal hashing in the block-source model.

In many hashing applications, it is possible to improve on the preceding analysis and reduce the amount of entropy required from the data items. Assuming our hash function has a description size $o(mT)$, then we must have at least $(1 - o(1))m$ bits of entropy per item for the hashing to "behave like" ideal hashing (because the entropy of $(H(X_1), \ldots, H(X_T))$ is at most the sum of the entropies of H and the X_i's). The standard analysis mentioned earlier requires an additional $2\log(T/\epsilon)$ bits of entropy per block. In the randomness extraction literature, the additional entropy required is typically not significant because $\log(T/\epsilon)$ is much smaller than m. However, it can be significant in our applications. For example, a typical setting is hashing $T = \Theta(M)$ items into $2^m = M$ bins. Here $m + 2\log(T/\epsilon) \geq 3m - O(1)$ and thus the standard analysis requires three times more entropy than the lower bound of $(1 - o(1))m$. (The bounds obtained for the specific applications mentioned in the text that follows are even larger, sometimes due to the need for a subconstant $\epsilon = o(1)$ and sometimes due to the fact that several independent hash values are needed for each item.)

By a finer analysis, the required entropy per block for $(H(X_1), \ldots, H(X_T))$ to be ϵ-close to uniform in statistical distance can be reduced from $m + 2\log(T/\epsilon)$ to $m + \log T + 2\log(1/\epsilon)$, which is known to be tight. The entropy required can be reduced even further for some applications by measuring the quality of the output differently (not using statistical distance) or by using 4-wise independent hash functions (which also have very fast implementations).

26.1.3 Applications

Consider the standard method of *chained hashing*, when T items are hashed into T buckets by a single random hash function. When the hash function is an idealized truly random function, the maximum load of any bucket is known to be $(1 + o(1)) \cdot (\log T / \log \log T)$ with high probability. In contrast, for a natural family of 2-universal hash functions, it is possible for an adversary to choose a set of T items so that the maximum load is always $\Omega(T^{1/2})$. The results of this chapter in turn show that 2-universal hashing achieves the same performance as ideal hashing asymptotically, provided that the data come from a block source with roughly $2\log T$ bits of (Rényi) entropy per item. Similar results for other applications of hashing, such as "linear probing," "balanced allocations," and "Bloom filters," are described in Sections 26.6 and 26.7.

---

[1] See Section 26.2.4 for a brief introduction to and formal definition of randomness extractors.

26.1.4 Perspective

The block source model we consider in this chapter is very much in the same spirit as the other semirandom models covered in this book, in that an adversary can pick a worst-case input distribution from a constrained family of distributions (namely, ones with enough conditional entropy per data item). In fact, the semirandom graph models discussed in Chapter 9 were also inspired by a model of "semirandom sources" in the randomness extractor literature, which amount to block sources where each block consists of one bit, and inspired the later, more general notion of block sources we study. Moreover, the block source model itself (with respect to max probability) is identical to the class of distributions considered for "diffuse adversaries" in the online paging problem in Chapter 24.

In terms of the goals for the analysis of algorithms laid out in Chapter 1, the motivation for the model in the current chapter falls squarely under "performance prediction." Indeed, the goal is to understand when an instantiation of a hashing algorithm with an explicit and efficient family of hash functions will perform similarly to its idealized analysis with truly random functions. The design of an algorithm that optimizes the idealized performance is taken as a given, and the only freedom is in the choice of hash family to instantiate the algorithm.

The block source model seems relatively uncontroversial from the "natural scientist" perspective, where the goal is to explain why previous experiments have not witnessed the gap between universal hashing and idealized analysis predicted by the worst-case theory. Indeed, those experiments may have used input distributions that are block sources or interact with the hash functions in a similar way.

From the "engineering" perspective, where the goal is to select a hash family to achieve good performance in a new application, more care is warranted in judging whether the data distribution is likely to fit the block source model. Even if each data item has sufficient entropy on its own, correlations between data items can make the conditional entropies very small or even zero. An extreme example is when the items are consecutive elements of an interval, i.e., $x_{i+1} = x_i + 1$. If the initial data item x_1 has high entropy, so will all of the other items x_i, but the conditional entropy of x_i given $x_1, \ldots, x_{i-1}$ will be zero. Indeed, such data distributions do sometimes arise in practice, and practical 2-universal hashing families have been found to have poor performance (e.g., when used in linear probing) on such data distributions. Unfortunately, determining whether a distribution is close to a block source is difficult in general; it requires a number of samples that is exponential in the number of blocks (Exercise 26.5).

For this reason, an interesting direction for future work is to identify other families of data distributions (beyond just the block-source model) where simple families of hash functions can be shown to behave like idealized hash functions for a wide class of hashing applications. When that can't be done, there may be no alternative other than to turn to more complex hash families, such as $\omega(1)$-wise independence or cryptographic hash functions.

We remark that the cryptography literature also grapples with a similar issue around the implementation of cryptographic protocols that utilize hashing. It is often easier to provide the security of such protocols by adopting the "random oracle model," where the hash function is modelled as a truly random function that all parties (honest or adversarial) can query as an oracle. But security in the random oracle model does not in general imply security when the hash function is implemented with any explicit polynomial-time instantiation. Thus, there is a large body of work on trying to identify classes of cryptographic protocols and realistic, nonidealized properties of hash families such that the security in the random oracle model is preserved under instantiation (assuming that the hash family actually has the specified properties).

The cryptographic setting is usually much more challenging than the algorithmic one, because an adversary can typically influence the inputs fed to the hash function based on the description of the hash function itself, or at least based on prior observations of input–output behavior. In contrast, even in the worst-case analysis of hashing algorithms, we typically assume that the hash function is chosen randomly and independently of the data items. This assumption should be carefully scrutinized in applications of hashing algorithms (especially when used in a security context), and if it does not hold, then cryptographic hash functions or "pseudorandom functions" may be a safer, albeit more expensive, choice.

26.2 Preliminaries

26.2.1 Notation

$[N]$ denotes the set $\{0, \ldots, N-1\}$. All logs are base 2. For a random variable X and an event E, $X|_E$ denotes X conditioned on E. The *support* of X is $\mathrm{supp}(X) = \{x : \Pr[X = x] > 0\}$. For a finite set S, U_S denotes a random variable uniformly distributed on S.

26.2.2 Hashing

Let $\mathcal{H}$ be a family (multiset) of hash functions $h : [N] \to [M]$ and let H be uniformly distributed over $\mathcal{H}$. We use $h \leftarrow H$ to denote that h is sampled according to the distribution H. We say that $\mathcal{H}$ is a *truly random family* if $\mathcal{H}$ is the set all functions mapping $[N]$ to $[M]$; i.e., the N random variables $\{H(x)\}_{x \in [N]}$ are independent and uniformly distributed over $[M]$. For $s \in \mathbb{N}$, $\mathcal{H}$ is *s-wise independent* (a.k.a. *strongly s-universal*) if for every sequence of distinct elements $x_1, \ldots, x_s \in [N]$, the random variables $H(x_1), \ldots, H(x_s)$ are independent and uniformly distributed over $[M]$. $\mathcal{H}$ is *s-universal* if for every sequence of distinct elements $x_1, \ldots, x_s \in [N]$, we have $\Pr[H(x_1) = \cdots = H(x_s)] \le 1/M^s$. The description size of $H \in \mathcal{H}$ is the number of bits to describe H, which is simply $\log |\mathcal{H}|$.

A standard example of a 2-universal family for a universe $[N]$ being hashed to the range $[M]$ can be obtained by choosing a prime $p \ge \max\{N, M\}$ and using the family

$$h_{a,b}(x) = ((ax + b) \bmod p) \bmod M.$$

Here a and b are integers chosen independently and uniformly at random from $\{1, \ldots, p-1\}$ and $\{0, 1, \ldots, p-1\}$, respectively. We leave it as Exercise 26.2 to show that for $x \ne y$, the probability that $h_{a,b}(x) = h_{a,b}(y)$ is at most $1/M$. A standard example of an s-wise independent family where the domain and range are the same finite field $\mathbb{F}$ is the family of hash functions

$$h_{a_0, a_1, \ldots, a_{s-1}}(x) = a_0 + a_1 x + a_2 x^2 + \cdots + a_{k-1} x^{s-1}. \tag{26.1}$$

Here choosing a hash function from the family corresponds to choosing the a_i's independently and uniformly at random from $\mathbb{F}$; that is, the hash function is a random polynomial of degree at most $s - 1$. Again, we leave it as Exercise 26.3 to show that for a hash function chosen randomly from this family, the hashed values for any s elements of $\mathbb{F}$ are distributed uniformly and independently over $\mathbb{F}$. To obtain a family where the range is smaller than the domain, we can use a field $\mathbb{F}$ of size p^k for a prime p and integer $k > 1$, pick any positive integer $\ell < k$, and compose the hash functions in Equation (26.1) with a fixed mapping $g : \mathbb{F} \to [p^\ell]$, all of whose preimages are of size $\mathbb{F}/p^\ell$ (e.g., $g(y) = y \bmod p^\ell$, after interpreting y as an element of $[p^k]$).

26.2.3 Block Sources

We view the data items as being random variables distributed over a finite set of size N, which we identify with $[N]$. We use the following quantities to measure the amount of randomness in a data item. For a random variable X, the *max probability* of X is $\mathrm{mp}(X) = \max_x \Pr[X = x]$. The *collision probability* of X is $\mathrm{cp}(X) = \sum_x \Pr[X = x]^2$. Measuring these quantities is equivalent to measuring the *min-entropy*

$$\mathrm{H}_\infty(X) = \min_x \log(1/\Pr[X = x]) = \log(1/\mathrm{mp}(X))$$

and the *Rényi entropy*

$$\mathrm{H}_2(X) = \log(1/\Pr[X = X']) = \log(1/\mathrm{cp}(X)),$$

where X' is an i.i.d. copy of X. (These entropy measures are from the family of Rényi q-entropies, defined for positive and finite $q \neq 1$ as

$$\mathrm{H}_q(X) = \frac{1}{1-q} \log \left(\sum_x (\Pr[X = x])^q \right),$$

with $\mathrm{H}_\infty(X)$ obtained by taking the limit as $q \to \infty$, and Shannon entropy by taking the limit as $q \to 1$.) If X is supported on a set of size K, then $\mathrm{mp}(X) \geq \mathrm{cp}(X) \geq 1/K$ (i.e. $\mathrm{H}_\infty(X) \leq \mathrm{H}_2(X) \leq \log K$), with equality if and only if X is uniform on its support. Hence, assuming X has at least k bits of Rényi entropy is strictly weaker than assuming X has at least k bits of min-entropy, and therefore using Rényi entropy makes the positive results stronger. On the other hand, it also holds that $\mathrm{mp}(X) \leq \mathrm{cp}(X)^{1/2}$ (i.e., $\mathrm{H}_\infty(X) \geq \mathrm{H}_2(X)/2$; see Exercise 26.1), so min-entropy and Rényi entropy are always within a factor of 2 of each other.

We model a sequence of data items as a sequence $(X_1, \ldots, X_T)$ of correlated random variables where each item is guaranteed to have some entropy even conditioned on the previous items.

Definition 26.1 (Block Sources) A sequence of random variables $(X_1, \ldots, X_T)$ taking values in $[N]^T$ is a *block source with collision probability p per block* (respectively, *max probability p per block*) if for every $i \in [T]$ and every $(x_1, \ldots, x_{i-1}) \in \mathrm{supp}(X_1, \ldots, X_{i-1})$, we have $\mathrm{cp}(X_i|_{X_1=x_1, \ldots, X_{i-1}=x_{i-1}}) \leq p$ (respectively, $\mathrm{mp}(X_i|_{X_1=x_1, \ldots, X_{i-1}=x_{i-1}}) \leq p$).

When *max probability* is used as the measure of entropy, then this is a standard model of sources used in the randomness extractor literature. We will mainly use the *collision probability* formulation as the entropy measure, since it makes the statements more general.

Definition 26.2 $(X_1, \ldots, X_T)$ is a *block K-source* if it is a block source with collision probability at most $p = 1/K$ per block.

26.2.4 Randomness Extractors

Before obtaining our results on block sources, we need results showing that hashing a single item leads to it being nearly uniformly distributed, which we will then generalize. A *randomness extractor* can be viewed as a family of hash functions with the property that for any random variable X with enough entropy, if we pick a random hash function h from the family, then $h(X)$ is "close" to being uniformly distributed on the range of the hash function. Randomness extractors are a central object in the theory of pseudorandomness and have many applications in theoretical computer science. Thus there is a large body of work on the construction of randomness extractors. A major emphasis in this line of work is constructing extractors where it takes extremely few (e.g., a logarithmic number of) random bits to choose a hash function from the family. This parameter is less crucial for us, so instead our emphasis is on using simple and very efficient hash functions (e.g., universal hash functions) and minimizing the amount of entropy needed from the source X. To do this, we will measure the quality of a hash family in ways that are tailored to our application, and thus we do not necessarily work with the standard definitions of extractors.

In requiring that the hashed value $h(X)$ be "close" to uniform, the standard definition of an extractor uses the most natural measure of "closeness." Specifically, for random variables X and Y, taking values in $[N]$, their *statistical distance* is defined as

$$\Delta(X, Y) = \max_{S \subseteq [N]} |\Pr[X \in S] - \Pr[Y \in S]|.$$

X and Y are called ϵ-*close* (resp., ϵ-far) if $\Delta(X, Y) \le \epsilon$ (resp., $\Delta(X, Y) \ge \epsilon$).

The classic Leftover Hash Lemma shows that universal hash functions are randomness extractors with respect to statistical distance.

Lemma 26.3 (The Leftover Hash Lemma) *Let* $H : [N] \to [M]$ *be a random hash function from a 2-universal family* $\mathcal{H}$. *For every random variable* X *taking values in* $[N]$ *with* $\mathrm{cp}(X) \le 1/K$, *we have*

$$\mathrm{cp}((H, H(X))) \le \frac{1}{|\mathcal{H}|} \cdot \left(\frac{1}{M} + \frac{1}{K} \right),$$

and thus $(H, H(X))$ *is* $(1/2) \cdot \sqrt{M/K}$-*close to* $(H, U_{[M]})$.

Notice that Lemma 26.3 says that the *joint* distribution of $(H, H(X))$ is ϵ-close to uniform (for $\epsilon = (1/2) \cdot \sqrt{M/K}$); a family of hash functions achieving this property is referred to as a "strong" randomness extractor. Up to some loss in the parameter ϵ

(which we will later want to save), this strong extraction property is equivalent to saying that with high probability over $h \leftarrow H$, the random variable $h(X)$ is close to uniform.

Proof Let (H', X') be an i.i.d. copy of (H, X). The bound on the collision probability follows by the following calculation.

$$
\begin{aligned}
\mathrm{cp}(H, H(X)) &= \Pr[H = H' \wedge H(X) = H'(X')] \\
&= \Pr[H = H'] \cdot \Pr[H(X) = H(X')] \\
&\leq (1/|\mathcal{H}|) \cdot (\Pr[X = X'] + \Pr[H(X) = H(X')|X \neq X']) \\
&\leq \frac{1}{|\mathcal{H}|} \cdot \left(\frac{1}{M} + \frac{1}{K} \right).
\end{aligned}
$$

The bound on the statistical distance follows directly by the second statement of the following lemma (we state the more general first statement since it will be useful later). $\qquad\square$

Lemma 26.4 *If X takes values in $[M]$ and $\mathrm{cp}(X) \leq 1/M + 1/K$, then*

1 For every function $f : [M] \to \mathbb{R}$,

$$
|\mathrm{E}[f(X)] - \mu| \leq \sigma \cdot \sqrt{M/K},
$$

where μ is the expectation of $f(U_{[M]})$ and σ is its standard deviation. In particular, if f takes values in the interval $[a, b]$, then

$$
|\mathrm{E}[f(X)] - \mu| \leq \sqrt{(\mu - a) \cdot (b - \mu)} \cdot \sqrt{M/K}.
$$

2 X is $(1/2) \cdot \sqrt{M/K}$-close to $U_{[M]}$.

Proof By the premise of the lemma,

$$
|\mathrm{E}[f(X)] - \mu| = \left| \sum_{x \in [M]} (f(x) - \mu) \cdot (\Pr[X = x] - 1/M) \right|
$$

$$
\leq \sqrt{\sum_{x \in [M]} (f(x) - \mu)^2} \cdot \sqrt{\sum_{x \in [M]} (\Pr[X = x] - 1/M)^2}
$$

$$
\text{(Cauchy–Schwarz)}
$$

$$
= \sqrt{M \cdot \mathrm{Var}[f(U_{[M]})]}
$$

$$
\cdot \sqrt{\sum_{x \in [M]} (\Pr[X = x]^2 - 2\Pr[X = x]/M + 1/M^2)}
$$

$$
= \sqrt{M} \cdot \sigma \cdot \sqrt{\mathrm{cp}(X) - 2/M + 1/M}
$$

$$
\leq \sigma \cdot \sqrt{M/K}.
$$

The "in particular" follows from the fact that $\sigma[Y] \leq \sqrt{(\mu - a) \cdot (b - \mu)}$ for every random variable Y taking values in $[a, b]$ and having expectation μ. (Intuitively, the variance is maximized if Y takes on only the extreme values a and b with appropriate probability masses to make the expectation μ. For a proof: $\sigma[Y]^2 = \mathrm{E}[(Y - a)^2] - (\mu - a)^2 \leq (b - a) \cdot (\mu - a) - (\mu - a)^2 = (\mu - a) \cdot (b - \mu)$.)

Item (2) follows by noting that the statistical distance between X and $U_{[M]}$ is the maximum of $|\mathrm{E}[f(X)] - \mathrm{E}[f(U_{[M]})]|$ over Boolean functions f, since a Boolean function can be viewed as an indicator/characteristic function for a subset S in the definition of statistical distance. Hence, by item (1), the statistical distance is at most $\sqrt{\mu(f) \cdot (1 - \mu(f))} \cdot \sqrt{M/K} \leq (1/2) \cdot \sqrt{M/K}$. $\qquad\square$

26.3 Hashing Block Sources

In this section, we show that when the data is modeled as a block source with sufficient entropy per block, the performance of using 2-universal hash functions is close to that of ideal hashing. More precisely, note that in ideal hashing, the distribution of the hashed values $(H(x_1), \ldots, H(x_T))$ is simply a uniform distribution over $[M]^T$. The following theorem states that when the data is a block source $(X_1, \ldots, X_T)$ with sufficient entropy per block and H is 2-universal, the distribution of the hashed values $(H(X_1), \ldots, H(X_T))$ is close to uniform in statistical distance.

Theorem 26.5 *Let* $H: [N] \to [M]$ *be a random hash function from a 2-universal family* $\mathcal{H}$. *For every block K-source* $(X_1, \ldots, X_T)$, *the random variable* $(H, H(X_1), \ldots, H(X_T))$ *is* $(T/2) \cdot \sqrt{M/K}$*-close to* $(H, U_{[M]^T})$.

Proof The theorem follows by applying the Leftover Hash Lemma (Lemma 26.3) to each block of the source and summing the statistical distance over the T blocks. Specifically, since $(X_1, \ldots, X_T)$ is a block K-source, the Leftover Hash Lemma implies that for every $x_{<i} = (x_1, \ldots, x_{i-1}) \in [M]^{i-1}$, the distribution $(H, H(X_i)|_{X_{<i}=x_{<i}})$ is $(1/2) \cdot \sqrt{M/K}$-close to $(H, U_{[M]})$.

Define hybrid distributions $D_1, \ldots, D_{T+1}$ by

$$D_i = \left(H, H(X_1), \ldots, H(X_{i-1}), U_{[M]}^{(i)}, \ldots, U_{[M]}^{(T)} \right) \text{ for } i \in [T+1].$$

Note that the preceding statement implies that $\Delta(D_i, D_{i+1}) \leq (1/2) \cdot \sqrt{M/K}$ for every $i \in [T]$ (since the statement holds for every $x_{<i} \in [M]^{i-1}$). Also note that $D_1 = (H, U_{[M]^T})$ and $D_{T+1} = (H, H(X_1), \ldots, H(X_T))$. Since statistical distance satisfies the triangle inequality,

$$\Delta(D_1, D_{T+1}) \leq \sum_{i=1}^{T} \Delta(D_i, D_{i+1}) \leq (T/2) \cdot \sqrt{M/K}. \qquad\square$$

Assuming $K \geq MT^2/(4\epsilon^2)$, Theorem 26.5 implies that the distribution of the hashed values $(H(X_1), \ldots, H(X_T))$ is ϵ-close to uniform. Thus, any event that would occur with some probability p under ideal hashing now occurs with probability in the range $[p-\epsilon, p+\epsilon]$. This allows us to readily translate existing results for ideal hashing into results for universal hashing in the block data source model.

A tight version of Theorem 26.5 is known, which improves the linear dependency in T to $\sqrt{T}$:

Theorem 26.6 *Let* $H\colon [N] \to [M]$ *be a random hash function from a 2-universal family* $\mathcal{H}$. *For every block K-source* $(X_1, \ldots, X_T)$, *the random variable* $(H, H(X_1), \ldots, H(X_T))$ *is* $(\sqrt{MT/K})$-*close to* $(H, U_{[M]^T})$.

By Theorem 26.6, it suffices to assume $K \geq MT/\epsilon^2$ to conclude that the hashed values are ϵ-close to uniform. In Section 26.4 we discuss the implication of Theorem 26.6 to chained hashing as an example.

The proof of Theorem 26.6 is quite involved, switching carefully between different distance notions to measure the growth of the distance to the uniform distribution over the T blocks. Thus we omit its proof here.

26.4 Application: Chained Hashing

We first briefly recall the chained hashing algorithm and its results under ideal hashing. A hash table using *chained hashing* stores a set $\bar{x} = \{x_1, \ldots, x_T\} \in [N]^T$ in an array of M buckets. Let h be a hash function mapping $[N]$ to $[M]$. We place each item x_i in the bucket $h(x_i)$. The *load* of a bucket when the process terminates is the number of items in it.

Definition 26.7 Given $h : [N] \to [M]$ and a sequence $\bar{x} = \{x_1, \ldots, x_T\}$ of data items from $[N]$ stored via chained hashing using h, we define the *maximum load* $\mathrm{MaxLoad}_{\mathrm{CH}}(\bar{x}, h)$ to be the maximum load among the buckets after all data items have been placed.

It is known that under ideal hashing, when $M = T$, the expected maximum load is $\log T / \log \log T$ asymptotically. This bound also holds with high probability. More precisely, we have:

Theorem 26.8 *Let H be a truly random hash function mapping* $[N]$ *to* $[T]$. *For every sequence* $\bar{x} \in [N]^T$ *of distinct data items, we have*

$$\Pr\left[\mathrm{MaxLoad}_{\mathrm{CH}}(\bar{x}, H) \leq (1 + o(1)) \cdot \frac{\log T}{\log \log T} \right] = 1 - o(1),$$

where the $o(1)$ *terms tend to zero as* $T \to \infty$.

The calculation underlying this theorem requires that the hash function be $\Omega(\log T / \log \log T)$-wise independent. Indeed, Exercise 26.4 shows that there are 2-universal families and input sets $\bar{x}$ where the maximum load is always at least $\sqrt{T}$. Nevertheless, suppose we model the data as a block source and use 2-universal hashing, Theorem 26.6 allows us to derive the conclusion of Theorem 26.8 assuming the data has sufficient entropy per block.

Theorem 26.9 *Let H be chosen at random from a 2-universal hash family $\mathcal{H}$ mapping $[N]$ to $[T]$. For every block K-source $\overline{X}$ taking values in $[N]^T$ with $K = \omega(T^2)$, we have*

$$\Pr\left[\text{MaxLoad}_{\text{CH}}(\overline{X}, H) \le (1 + o(1)) \cdot \frac{\log T}{\log \log T}\right] = 1 - o(1),$$

where the $o(1)$ terms tend to zero as $T \to \infty$.

Proof Set $M = T$. Note that the value of $\text{MaxLoad}_{\text{CH}}(\overline{x}, h)$ can be determined from the hashed sequence $(h(x_1), \ldots, h(x_T)) \in [M]^T$ alone, and does not otherwise depend on the data sequence $\overline{x}$ or the hash function h. Thus for a function $\lambda : N \to N$, we can let $S \subseteq [M]^T$ be the set of all sequences of hashed values that produce an allocation with a max load greater than $\lambda(T)$. By Theorem 26.8, we can take $\lambda(T) = (1 + o(1)) \cdot (\log T)/(\log \log T)$ so that we have:

$$\Pr[U_{[M]^T} \in S] = \Pr[\text{MaxLoad}_{\text{CH}}(\overline{x}, I) > \lambda(T)] = o(1),$$

where I is a truly random hash function mapping $[N]$ to $[M] = [T]$ and $\overline{x}$ is an arbitrary sequence of distinct data items.

We are interested in the quantity:

$$\Pr[\text{MaxLoad}_{\text{CH}}(\overline{X}, H) > \lambda(T)] = \Pr[(H(X_1), \ldots, H(X_T)) \in S],$$

where H is a random hash function from a 2-universal family. Given $K = \omega(T^2)$, we set $\epsilon = \sqrt{MT/K} = o(1)$. By Theorem 26.6, $(H(X_1), \ldots, H(X_T))$ is ϵ-close to the uniform distribution. Thus, we have

$$\Pr[(H(X_1), \ldots, H(X_T)) \in S] \le \Pr[U_{[M]^T} \in S] + \epsilon$$
$$= o(1). \qquad \square$$

26.5 Optimizing Block Source Extraction

We have seen that, for some applications, when the data comes from a block source with sufficient entropy per block, 2-universal hashing performs nearly as well as ideal hashing. We might naturally ask, how much entropy do we need? The answer can depend on the needs of the application scenario, as well as on the specific hashing algorithm we use and its analysis. With our analysis thus far, the required entropy can range from very reasonable to unrealistic.

In this section, we discuss some general approaches to reduce the required entropy. A main observation is that instead of working with the stringent notion of statistical distance, for several applications it suffices to ensure that the collection of hashed values $(H(X_1), \ldots, H(X_T))$ has (or is statistically close to having) sufficiently small collision probability, say within an $O(1)$ factor of that of the uniform distribution. Theorem 26.10 provides a result of this form with smaller required entropy from the block source, which reduces required entropy for some applications (see Section 26.6).

Theorem 26.10 *Let $H : [N] \to [M]$ be a random hash function from a 2-universal family $\mathcal{H}$. For every block K-source $(X_1, \ldots, X_T)$ and every $\epsilon > 0$,* *the random variable* $(H, \bar{Y}) = (H, H(X_1), \ldots, H(X_T))$ *is ϵ-close to a distribution* $(H, \bar{Z})$ *with collision probability*

$$\mathrm{cp}(H, \bar{Z}) \leq \frac{1}{|\mathcal{H}| \cdot M^T} \cdot \left(1 + \frac{M}{\epsilon K}\right)^T.$$

In particular, if $K \geq MT/\epsilon$, then $(H, \bar{Z})$ has collision probability at most

$$\frac{1}{|\mathcal{H}| \cdot M^T} \cdot \left(1 + \frac{2MT}{\epsilon K}\right).$$

Note that the factor $1/(|\mathcal{H}| \cdot M^T)$ is the collision probability of the uniform distribution $(H, U_{[M]^T})$ and the factors $(1 + (M/\epsilon K))^T$ and $(1 + (2MT/\epsilon K))$ quantify the blow-up in collision probability as compared to ideal hashing. Also note that comparing to Theorem 26.6, the key savings is in the dependency on ϵ. Specifically, to achieve statistical distance ϵ, K only needs to be $\Omega(MT/\epsilon)$ as opposed to $\Omega(MT/\epsilon^2)$. Thus, this is particularly useful in applications where $\epsilon = o(1)$ is required in the analysis.

We omit the proof of Theorem 26.10 here. Roughly, to prove Theorem 26.10, one first shows that a certain average form of the (conditional) collision probability for hashed blocks is small with high probability, using the Leftover Hash Lemma (Lemma 26.3) together with a Markov argument. Then, the theorem follows by showing that the distribution $(H, \bar{Z})$ can be obtained by carefully modifying the distribution of $(H, \bar{Y})$ based on the property established in the first step.

We can further improve the bound by using 4-wise independent hash functions, stated in the following theorem, where the dependency on ϵ is further improved. At a high level, the improvement comes from the fact that 4-wise independent hashing allows us to replace the Markov argument by Chebyshev's inequality in the proof.

Theorem 26.11 *Let $H : [N] \to [M]$ be a random hash function from a 4-wise independent family $\mathcal{H}$. For every block K-source $(X_1, \ldots, X_T)$ and every $\epsilon > 0$, the random variable $(H, \bar{Y}) = (H, H(X_1), \ldots, H(X_T))$ is ϵ-close to a distribution $(H, \bar{Z})$ with collision probability*

$$\mathrm{cp}(H, \bar{Z}) \leq \frac{1}{|\mathcal{H}| \cdot M^T} \left(1 + \frac{M}{K} + \sqrt{\frac{2M}{\epsilon K^2}}\right)^T.$$

In particular, if $K \geq MT + \sqrt{2MT^2/\epsilon}$, then $(H, \bar{Z})$ has collision probability at most $(1 + \gamma)/(|\mathcal{H}| \cdot M^T)$, for $\gamma = 2 \cdot (MT + \sqrt{2MT^2/\epsilon})/K$.

26.6 Application: Linear Probing

In this section, we illustrate that Theorems 26.10 and 26.11 can be used to give a better analysis for some applications than using Theorem 26.6. We first mention that when applied to the "high-probability" statement in chained hashing, Theorems 26.10 and 26.11 do not yield significant improvement over Theorem 26.6. On the other hand, for applications where we only have bounds on expectations, applying

Theorems 26.10 and 26.11 can reduce the required entropy. As we will see in the *linear probing* example that follows, this is because small $\epsilon = o(1)$ is required in the analysis.

We start with a brief review of linear probing (also covered in Chapter 8). A hash table using linear probing stores a sequence $\bar{x} = (x_1, \ldots, x_T)$ of data items from $[N]$ using M memory locations. Given a hash function $h : [N] \to [M]$, we place the data items $x_1, \ldots, x_T$ sequentially as follows. The data item x_i first attempts placement at $h(x_i)$, and if this location is already filled, locations $(h(x_i) + 1) \bmod M$, $(h(x_i) + 2) \bmod M$, and so on are tried until an empty location is found. The ratio $\gamma = T/M$ is referred to as the *load* of the table. The efficiency of linear probing is measured by the insertion time for a new data item as a function of the load. (Other measures, such as the average time to search for items already in the table, are also often studied, and the results here can be generalized to these measures as well.)

Definition 26.12 Given $h : [N] \to [M]$, a set $\bar{x} = \{x_1, \ldots, x_{T-1}\}$ of data items from $[N]$ stored via linear probing using h, and an extra data item $y \notin \bar{x}$, we define the *insertion time* $\text{Time}_{\text{LP}}(h, \bar{x}, y)$ to be the value of j such that y is placed at location $h(y) + (j - 1) \bmod M$.

It is well known that with ideal hashing (i.e., hashing using truly random hash functions), the expected insertion time can be bounded quite tightly as a function of the load.

Theorem 26.13 *Let H be a truly random hash function mapping $[N]$ to $[M]$. For every sequence $\bar{x} \in [N]^{T-1}$ and $y \notin \bar{x}$, we have $\text{E}[\text{Time}_{\text{LP}}(H, \bar{x}, y)] \leq 1/(1 - \gamma)^2$, where $\gamma = T/M$ is the load.*

It is known that the expected lookup time can be bounded in terms of γ (independent of T) using only $O(1)$-wise independence. Specifically, with 5-wise independence, the expected time for an insertion is $O(1/(1 - \gamma)^{2.5})$ for any sequence $\bar{x}$. On the other hand, it is also known that there are examples of sequences $\bar{x}$ and pairwise independent hash families such that the expected time for a lookup is logarithmic in T (even though the load γ is independent of T).

Now, suppose we consider data items coming from a block K-source $(X_1, \ldots, X_{T-1}, X_T)$ where the item $Y = X_T$ to be inserted is the last block. An immediate application of Theorem 26.6, using just a 2-universal hash family, gives that if $K \geq MT/\epsilon^2$, the resulting distribution of the element hashes is ϵ-close to uniform. The effect of the ϵ statistical distance on the expected insertion time is at most ϵT, because the maximum insertion time is T. That is, if we let E_U be the expected time for an insertion when using a truly random hash function, and E_P be the expected time for an insertion using pairwise independent hash functions, we have

$$E_P \leq E_U + \epsilon T.$$

A natural choice is $\epsilon = o(1/T)$, so that the ϵT term is $o(1)$, giving that K needs to be $\omega(MT^3) = \omega(M^4)$ in the standard case where $T = \gamma M$ for a constant $\gamma \in (0, 1)$ (which we assume henceforth). An alternative interpretation is that with probability

$1 - \epsilon$, our hash table behaves exactly as though a truly random hash function was used. In some applications, constant ϵ may be sufficient, in which case $K = \omega(M^2)$ suffices.

Better results can be obtained by applying Lemma 26.4, in conjunction with Theorem 26.10. In particular, for linear probing, the standard deviation σ of the insertion time is known to be $O(1/(1 - \gamma)^2)$. With a 2-universal family, as long as $K \geq MT/\epsilon$, from Theorem 26.10 the resulting hash values are ϵ-close to a block source with collision probability at most $(1 + 2MT/(\epsilon K))/M^T$. We can now apply Lemma 26.4 with this bound on the collision probability to bound the expected insertion time as

$$E_P \leq E_U + \epsilon T + \sigma \sqrt{\frac{2MT}{\epsilon K}}.$$

Choosing $\epsilon = o(1/T)$ gives that E_P and E_U are the same up to lower order terms when K is $\omega(M^3)$. Theorem 26.11 gives a further improvement; for $K \geq MT + \sqrt{\frac{2MT^2}{\epsilon}}$, we have

$$E_P \leq E_U + \epsilon T + \sigma \sqrt{\frac{2MT + \sqrt{\frac{2MT^2}{\epsilon}}}{K}}.$$

Choosing $\epsilon = o(1/T)$ now allows for K to be only $\omega(M^2)$.

In other words, the Rényi entropy needs only to be $2\log(M) + \omega(1)$ bits when using 4-wise independent hash functions, and $3\log(M) + \omega(1)$ bits for 2-universal hash functions. We formalize the result for the case of 2-universal hash functions as follows:

Theorem 26.14 *Let H be chosen at random from a 2-universal hash family $\mathcal{H}$ mapping $[N]$ to $[M]$. For every block K-source $(\overline{X}, Y)$ taking values in $[N]^T$ with $K \geq MT/\epsilon$, we have $E[\text{Time}_{LP}(H, \overline{X}, Y)] \leq 1/(1 - \gamma)^2 + \epsilon T + \sigma \sqrt{\frac{2MT}{\epsilon K}}$. Here $\gamma = T/M$ is the load and $\sigma = O(1/(1 - \gamma)^2)$ is the standard deviation in the insertion time in the case of truly random hash functions.*

26.7 Other Applications

In this section, we survey the application of the methods in this chapter to a couple of other hashing-based algorithms.

With the *balanced allocation* paradigm, it is known that when T items are hashed to T buckets, with each item being sequentially placed in the least loaded of d choices (for $d \geq 2$), the maximum load is $\log \log T / \log d + O(1)$ with high probability. Note that going from $d = 1$ to $d = 2$ yields an exponential saving in the maximum load from $O(\log T / \log \log T)$ to $O(\log \log T)$. Using the methods from this chapter, it can be shown that the same result holds when the hash function is chosen from a 2-universal hash family, provided the data items come from a block source with roughly $(d + 1) \log T$ bits of entropy per data item.

Bloom filters are data structures for approximately storing sets in which membership tests can result in false positives with some bounded probability. It can be

Table 26.1 Entropy required per item

Type of hash family	Required entropy
Linear probing	
2-universal hashing	$3 \log T$
4-wise independence	$2 \log T$
Chained hashing	
2-universal hashing	$2 \log T$
Balanced allocations with d choices	
2-universal hashing	$(d+1) \log T$
Bloom filters	
2-universal hashing	$3 \log T$

Each entry denotes the (Rényi) entropy required per item to ensure that the performance of the given application is "close" to the performance when using truly random hash functions In all cases, the bounds omit additive terms that depend on how close a performance is desired, and we restrict to the (standard) case that the size of the hash table is linear in the number of items being hashed. That is, $m = \log T + O(1)$.

shown that there is a constant gap in the false positive probability for worst-case data when $O(1)$-wise independent hash functions are used instead of truly random hash functions. On the other hand, if the data comes from a block source with roughly $3 \log M$ bits of (Rényi) entropy per item, where M is the size of the Bloom filter, then the false positive probability with 2-universal hashing asymptotically matches that of ideal hashing.

A summary of required (Rényi) entropy per item for the preceding applications can be found in Table 26.1.

26.8 Notes

The material in this chapter is drawn primarily from Chung et al. (2013).

Surveys of algorithmic applications of hashing are given by Knuth (1998), Broder and Mitzenmacher (2005), and Muthukrishnan (2005). Universal and s-wise independent hashing were introduced in Carter and Wegman (1979) and Wegman and Carter (1981), respectively. Analysis of $O(\log T)$-wise independent hashing of T items can be found in Schmidt and Siegel (1990) and Pagh and Rodler (2004). Further coverage of universal and s-wise independent families can be found in many standard texts, e.g., Mitzenmacher and Upfal (2017) and Vadhan (2011). The analysis of maximum load under chained hashing with idealized hash functions (e.g., Theorem 26.8) was done by Gonnet (1981) and Raab and Steger (1998). Worst-case analysis of chained hashing under 2-universal hash families (including Exercise 26.4) was done by Alon et al. (1999). The expected insertion time for linear probing under idealized hash functions (i.e., Theorem 26.13) was analyzed by Knuth (1998), and its variance can be found in Gonnet and Baeza-Yates (1991). Worst-case analysis of linear probing under $O(1)$-wise independence was done by Pagh et al. (2009) and Patrascu and Thorup (2010), with experiments (and fast implementations of 4-wise independent hashing) in Thorup and Zhang (2012). The balanced allocation paradigm is due to Azar et al. (2000) and Bloom filters are due to Bloom (1970). The fact that the performance of standard universal hashing often matches what is predicted for ideal hashing was experimentally observed in (Ramakrishna, 1988, 1989; Ramakrishna et al., 1997; Broder and Mitzenmacher, 2001; Dharmapurikar et al., 2004; Pagh and Rodler, 2004).

Surveys on randomness extractors are given by Nisan and Ta-Shma (1999), Shaltiel (2002), and Vadhan (2011). Block sources were introduced by Chor and Goldreich (1988) (under the name "probability-bounded sources"), generalizing the model of "semirandom sources" introduced by Santha and Vazirani (1986). The Leftover Hash Lemma (Lemma 26.3) is due to Bennett et al. (1988) Impagliazzo et al. (1989), with the proof we present being attributed to Rackoff (Impagliazzo and Zuckerman, 1989). The analysis of universal hashing and randomness extraction on block sources given by Theorem 26.5 follows Chor and Goldreich (1988) and Zuckerman (1996). Semirandom models for graphs were introduced by Blum and Spencer (1995) and diffuse adversaries for online paging by Koutsoupias and Papadimitriou (2000).

The Random Oracle Model in cryptography was introduced by Fiat and Shamir (1987) and Bellare and Rogaway (1993). The fact that security may not be preserved when instantiating the random oracle with explicit hash functions was demonstrated by Canetti et al. (2004). Efforts to find classes of protocols and properties of hash families that allow for secure instantiation can be found in Bellare et al. (2013) and the references therein.

Acknowledgments

Kai-Min is supported in part by Academia Sinica Career Development Award Grant no. 23-17. Michael is supported by NSF grants CCF-1563710 and CCF-1535795. Salil is supported by NSF grant CCF-1763299 and a Simons Investigator Award. We thank Elias Koutsoupias and Tim Roughgarden for their feedback, which has improved this survey.

References

Alon, Noga, Dietzfelbinger, Martin, Miltersen, Peter Bro, Petrank, Erez, and Tardos, Gábor. 1999. Linear hash functions. *Journal of the ACM*, **46**(5), 667–683.

Azar, Yossi, Broder, Andrei Z., Karlin, Anna R., and Upfal, Eli. 2000. Balanced allocations. *SIAM Journal on Computing*, **29**(1), 180–200.

Bellare, Mihir, and Rogaway, Phillip. 1993. Random oracles are practical: A paradigm for designing efficient protocols. In Denning, Dorothy E., Pyle, Raymond, Ganesan, Ravi, Sandhu, Ravi S., and Ashby, Victoria (eds), *CCS '93, Proceedings of the 1st ACM Conference on Computer and Communications Security*, pp. 62–73. ACM.

Bellare, Mihir, Hoang, Viet Tung, and Keelveedhi, Sriram. 2013. Instantiating random oracles via UCEs. In Canetti, Ran, and Garay, Juan A. (eds.), *Advances in Cryptology – CRYPTO 2013–33rd Annual Cryptology Conference*. Lecture Notes in Computer Science, vol. 8043, pp. 398–415. Springer.

Bennett, Charles H., Brassard, Gilles, and Robert, Jean-Marc. 1988. Privacy amplification by public discussion. *SIAM Journal on Computing*, **17**(2), 210–229. Special issue on cryptography.

Bloom, Burton H. 1970. Space/time trade-offs in hash coding with allowable errors. *Communications of the ACM*, **13**(7), 422–426.

Blum, Avrim, and Spencer, Joel. 1995. Coloring random and semi-random k-colorable graphs. *Journal of Algorithms*, **19**(2), 204–234.

Broder, A., and Mitzenmacher, M. 2001. Using multiple hash functions to improve IP lookups. In *INFOCOM 2001: Proceedings of the Twentieth Annual Joint Conference of the IEEE Computer and Communications Societies*, pp. 1454–1463.

Broder, A., and Mitzenmacher, M. 2005. Network applications of Bloom filters: A survey. *Internet Mathematics*, **1**(4), 485–509.

Canetti, Ran, Goldreich, Oded, and Halevi, Shai. 2004. The random oracle methodology, revisited. *Journal of the ACM*, **51**(4), 557–594.

Carter, J. Lawrence, and Wegman, Mark N. 1979. Universal classes of hash functions. *Journal of Computer and System Sciences*, **18**(2), 143–154.

Chor, Benny, and Goldreich, Oded. 1988. Unbiased bits from sources of weak randomness and probabilistic communication complexity. *SIAM Journal on Computing*, **17**(2), 230–261.

Chung, Kai-Min, Mitzenmacher, Michael, and Vadhan, Salil P. 2013. Why simple hash functions work: Exploiting the entropy in a data stream. *Theory of Computing*, **9**, 897–945.

Dharmapurikar, S., Krishnamurthy, P., Sproull, T. S., and Lockwood, J. W. 2004. Deep packet inspection using parallel Bloom filters. *IEEE Micro*, **24**(1), 52–61.

Fiat, Amos, and Shamir, Adi. 1987. How to prove yourself: Practical solutions to identification and signature problems. In *Advances in cryptology—CRYPTO '86*. Lecture Notes in Computer Science, vol. 263, pp. 186–194. Springer.

Gonnet, Gaston H. 1981. Expected length of the longest probe sequence in hash code searching. *Journal of the ACM*, **28**(2), 289–304.

Gonnet, GH, and Baeza-Yates, R. 1991. *Handbook of Algorithms and Data Structures: In Pascal and C*. Addison-Wesley Longman.

Impagliazzo, Russell, and Zuckerman, David. 1989 (Oct. 30 – Nov. 1). How to recycle random bits. In *30th Annual Symposium on Foundations of Computer Science*. IEEE, pp. 248–253.

Impagliazzo, Russell, Levin, Leonid A., and Luby, Michael. 1989 (May 15-17). Pseudo-random generation from one-way functions (Extended Abstracts). In *Proceedings of the Twenty First Annual ACM Symposium on Theory of Computing*, pp. 12–24.

Knuth, D.E. 1998. *The Art of Computer Programming*, vol. 3: *Sorting and Searching*. Addison Wesley Longman.

Koutsoupias, Elias, and Papadimitriou, Christos H. 2000. Beyond competitive analysis. *SIAM Journal on Computing*, **30**(1), 300–317.

Mitzenmacher, Michael, and Upfal, Eli. 2017. *Probability and Computing*, ed. Cambridge University Press. 2nd Randomization and Probabilistic Techniques in Algorithms and Data Analysis.

Muthukrishnan, S. 2005. Data Streams: Algorithms and Applications. *Foundations and Trends in Theoretical Computer Science*, **1**(2), 117–236.

Nisan, Noam, and Ta-Shma, Amnon. 1999. Extracting randomness: A survey and new constructions. *Journal of Computer and System Sciences*, **58**(1), 148–173.

Pagh, Anna, Pagh, Rasmus, and Ruzic, Milan. 2009. Linear probing with constant Independence. *SIAM Journal on Computing*, **39**(3), 1107–1120.

Pagh, R., and Rodler, F. F. 2004. Cuckoo hashing. *Journal of Algorithms*, **51**(2), 122–144.

Patrascu, Mihai, and Thorup, Mikkel. 2010. On the k-independence required by linear probing and minwise independence. In Abramsky, Samson, Gavoille, Cyril, Kirchner, Claude,

Meyer auf der Heide, Friedhelm, and Spirakis, Paul G. (eds), *ICALP (1)*. Lecture Notes in Computer Science, vol. 6198, pp. 715–726. Springer.

Raab, Martin, and Steger, Angelika. 1998. "Balls into bins": A simple and tight analysis. In *Randomization and approximation techniques in computer science (Barcelona, 1998)*. Lecture Notes in Computer Science, vol. 1518, pp. 159–170. Springer.

Ramakrishna, M. V. 1988. Hashing practice: Analysis of hashing and universal hashing. *SIGMOD '88: Proceedings of the 1988 ACM SIGMOD International Conference on Management of Data*, pp. 191–199. ACM Press.

Ramakrishna, M. V. 1989. Practical performance of Bloom filters and parallel free-text searching. *Communications of the ACM*, **32**(10), 1237–1239.

Ramakrishna, M. V., Fu, E., and Bahcekapili, E. 1997. Efficient hardware hashing functions for high performance computers. *IEEE Transactions on Computing*, **46**(12), 1378–1381.

Santha, Miklos, and Vazirani, Umesh V. 1986. Generating quasi-random sequences from semi-random sources. *Journal of Computer and System Sciences*, **33**(1), 75–87.

Schmidt, Jeanette P., and Siegel, Alan. 1990. The analysis of closed hashing unr limited randomness (Extended Abstract). In *Proceedings of the 22nd Annual ACM Symposium on Theory of Computing (STOC)*, pp. 224–234. ACM.

Shaltiel, Ronen. 2002. Recent developments in explicit constructions of extractors. *Bulletin of the European Association for Theoretical Computer Science*, **77**(June), 67–95.

Thorup, Mikkel, and Zhang, Yin. 2012. Tabulation-based 5-independent hashing with applications to linear probing and second moment estimation. *SIAM Journal on Computing*, **41**(2), 293–331.

Vadhan, Salil P. 2011. Pseudorandomness. *Foundations and Trends® in Theoretical Computer Science*, **7**(1-3), front matter, 1–336.

Wegman, Mark N., and Carter, J. Lawrence. 1981. New hash functions and their use in authentication and set equality. *Journal of Computer and System Sciences*, **22**(3), 265–279.

Zuckerman, David. 1996. Simulating BPP using a general weak random source. *Algorithmica*, **16**(4/5), 367–391.

Exercises

Exercise 26.1 Prove $H_\infty(X) \geq H_2(X)/2$ and find a distribution X such that the inequality is (almost) tight. (Hint: Consider X that takes a fixed value with a constant probability, say $1/2$, and is uniform for the rest of the probability mass.)

Exercise 26.2 Prove that the family of hash functions of the form $h_{a,b}(x) = ((ax + b) \bmod p) \bmod M$ is a 2-universal family mapping $[N]$ to $[M]$ for $p \geq \max\{N, M\}$, $a \in \{1, \ldots, p-1\}$, and $b \in \{0, \ldots, p-1\}$.

Exercise 26.3 Prove that for a finite field $\mathbb{F}$ and positive integer s, the family of functions of the form

$$h_{a_0, a_1, \ldots, a_{s-1}}(x) = a_0 + a_1 x + a_2 x^2 + \cdots + a_{k-1} x^{s-1}$$

is an s-wise independent family. [Hint: For every s distinct values $x_1, \ldots, x_s \in \mathbb{F}$ and every $y_1, \ldots, y_s \in \mathbb{F}$, there is a unique polynomial h of degree at most s such that $h(x_i) = y_i$ for all i.]

Exercise 26.4 Let $\mathbb{F}$ be a finite field of size that is a perfect square, and let $\mathbb{F}_0 \subseteq \mathbb{F}$ be its subfield of size $\sqrt{|\mathbb{F}|}$. Consider the family $\mathcal{H}$ of hash functions mapping $\mathbb{F} \times \mathbb{F}$ to $\mathbb{F}$ given by $h_{a,b}(x, y) = ax + by$, where a, b vary over all of $\mathbb{F}$.

(1) Show that $\mathcal{H}$ is a 2-universal family.
(2) Let γ be a fixed element of $\mathbb{F} - \mathbb{F}_0$, and consider the set

$$S = \left\{ \left(\frac{1}{u+\gamma}, \frac{v}{u+\gamma} \right) : u, v \in \mathbb{F}_0 \right\}.$$

Observe that $|S| = |\mathbb{F}_0|^2 = |\mathbb{F}|$. Show that for every $a, b \in \mathbb{F}$, we have

$$\mathrm{MaxLoad}_{\mathrm{CH}}(S, h_{a,b}) \geq |\mathbb{F}_0| = \sqrt{|\mathbb{F}|}.$$

(Hint: When $b = 0$, consider the subset of S where $u = 0$. If $b \neq 0$, then argue that there is a $c \in \mathbb{F}$ such that c/b and $(\gamma c - a)/b$ are both in $\mathbb{F}_0$, and consider the subset of S where $v = (c/b)u + (\gamma c - a)/b$.)

Exercise 26.5 Suppose that there is an algorithm A that takes as input s iid samples $X^{(1)}, \ldots, X^{(s)}$ from an unknown distribution X on $[N]^T$ and has the following properties:

- If X is the uniform distribution on $[N]^T$, then $A(X^{(1)}, \ldots, X^{(s)})$ accepts with probability at least $2/3$, and
- If X has statistical distance at least $1/2$ from every block source with collision probability at most $1/4$ per block, then $A(X^{(1)}, \ldots, X^{(s)})$ accepts with probability at most $1/3$.

Prove that the sample complexity s of A must be at least $\Omega(N^{(T-1)/2})$. (Hint: Consider $X = (X_1, \ldots, X_T)$ where $X_1, \ldots, X_{T-1}$ are uniform and independent, and $X_T = f(X_1, \ldots, X_{T-1})$ for a randomly chosen function $f : [N]^{T-1} \to [N]$, and consider what must occur in the s samples for A to distinguish X from the uniform distribution on $[N]^T$.)

CHAPTER TWENTY SEVEN

Prior-Independent Auctions

Inbal Talgam-Cohen

Abstract: This chapter discusses prior-independent auctions. The goal is to design a single auction which, simultaneously for every distribution in a given class, approximates the expected revenue of the optimal auction designed specifically for that distribution. We consider two main approaches to designing such auctions: The first is *sample-based*, where the problem boils down to learning enough about the distribution (by performing "market analysis on the fly") in order to do almost as well as if the distribution were fully known. The second approach is *competition-based*, where the idea is to increase the competition in the market enough so as to drive up prices, while remaining blissfully ignorant about the distribution.

27.1 Introduction

Auctions as a Meeting Place for Worst- and Average-Case Analysis Auctions are algorithms for resource allocation, with the extra complication that the input ("who values each resource by how much") comes from strategic agents who might misreport. Algorithmic research has only been studying auctions in the past two decades, spurred by their huge importance in the internet age as a main source of revenue for companies like Google. The classic theory of auctions was developed mainly within microeconomics (earning several Nobel prizes along the way).

Unlike the theory of algorithms, which has the worst-case approach at its core, in microeconomics the mainstream approach is average-case analysis. In the context of auctions, this means that buyers' values for different resources are assumed to come from known prior distributions. These priors are hard-coded into the auction in order to maximize the expected revenue from selling the resources. For example, if the known distribution tells us that a potential buyer's value for an item is likely to be high, the auction we design will charge a high price – how high exactly depends on the details of the distribution.

The assumption of distributional knowledge has all the usual downsides of the average-case approach, like being overly brittle to noise. Of course, the worst-case approach has its own downsides like being overly pessimistic. The premise of this chapter is that auctions offer a fascinating meeting place for the average-case economics approach and the worst-case computer science approach. In particular, auctions and other economic mechanisms are a natural testbed of what the algorithmic worst-case approach can contribute to other disciplines, e.g., in making various designs more robust or explaining the prevalence of simple designs in practice; and also of its limitations and how it can be made more suitable for practical applications by drawing closer to average-case analysis.

This chapter is organized as follows. Section 27.2 is a "crash course" in Nobel laureate Roger Myerson's theory of revenue-optimal auctions (which the familiar reader can safely skip). Section 27.3 defines prior-independence – a par excellence example of the semirandom models of Part III. Section 27.4 applies prior-independence to Myerson's theory. Section 27.5 tackles the much more challenging goal of maximizing revenue from selling several different items, to which Myerson's theory no longer applies – luckily resource augmentation (Chapter 4) comes to the rescue. Section 27.6 summarizes.

27.2 A Crash Course in Revenue-Maximizing Auctions

The Basic Problem There is a single item for sale and a set of n bidders participating in an auction for the item. Every bidder i has a value $v_i \in \Re_{\geq 0}$ for winning the item, which is privately known only to the bidder herself. This value is distributed according to a distribution F_i with positive density f_i,[1] and is reported (not necessarily truthfully) to the auctioneer as a *bid* for the item. There are usually two primary objectives when designing an auction: The first is *social welfare*, that is, the total value bidders gain from the auction (in our simple setting, if the item goes to bidder i then the welfare is v_i). The second is *revenue*, that is, the total payments the bidders transfer to the auctioneer (in our setting, what the winner of the item pays for it). An auction is carried out as follows: The auctioneer receives bids $\vec{b} = (b_1, \ldots, b_n)$ from the n bidders, applies an *allocation rule* x to the bids to decide how to allocate (in our setting, $x_i(\vec{b}) \in \{0, 1\}$ indicates whether or not bidder i is allocated the item),[2] and a *payment rule* p to decide how much to charge (where $p_i(\vec{b})$ is the payment of bidder i). An auction is thus an algorithm that gets value-bids as input, and returns an allocation and payments as output, with the goal of maximizing welfare or revenue.

Truthfulness The "twist" in designing auctions compared to other algorithms is that the values are reported by *strategic* bidders, who will not report truthfully unless it's in their best interest. This poses a challenge: For example, for the goal of maximizing welfare, how would you bid in an auction where the item was given for free to the highest bidder? Indeed, you have a strong incentive to bid much higher than your true value for the item! How can the auctioneer find the bidder with the highest value if auction participants have an incentive to overbid to increase their chances of winning? An auction is (dominant-strategy[3]) *truthful* if for every i, no matter what the others bid, bidder i is (weakly) better off bidding her true value than over- or underbidding. A convenient notation for the vector of bids of all other bidders but i is b_{-i}. Using this notation, we can write bidder i's utility from bidding v_i as $v_i \cdot x_i(v_i, b_{-i}) - p_i(v_i, b_{-i})$. Truthfulness means this utility is at least as high as bidder

---

[1] Extensions to discrete distributions are known.

[2] An allocation can also be randomized, in which case $x_i(\vec{b}) \in [0, 1]$ represents the probability with which bidder i is allocated the item.

[3] A weaker requirement than dominant-strategy truthfulness is Bayesian truthfulness, which we return to briefly in Section 27.5.

i's utility $v_i \cdot x_i(b'_i, b_{-i}) - p_i(b'_i, b_{-i})$ if she were to bid $b'_i \neq v_i$. The goal of much of the theory of auction design is to get *truthful* auctions with good welfare or revenue guarantees. From now on we shall focus on truthful auctions and assume that bidders report their values (i.e., $b_i = v_i$ for every i); a discussion of this assumption appears in Section 27.3.1.

27.2.1 Welfare Maximization: The Second Price and VCG Auctions

The problem of designing a truthful auction that maximizes social welfare was solved by Vickrey in 1961. The high-level idea is to use the payments to align the interests of the bidders with those of society. The resulting auction for our single-item setting is very simple: Upon receiving the reported values $\vec{v}$, the allocation rule gives the item to a bidder who values it the most (i.e., bidder $i^* = \arg\max_i\{v_i\}$), and charges the second-highest bid as the item's price. This is called the *second price* auction. For example, if three bidders bid $\vec{v} = (5, 8, 3)$ for an item, then the second bidder wins and pays 5. Intuitively, neither the winner nor losers can gain by bidding higher or lower than their true value, and indeed the second price auction is truthful. Better yet, Vickrey's auction can be generalized beyond a single item to multiple items. The generalization is called the *VCG auction*, after Vickrey, Clarke and Groves. In the generalization, items are partitioned among bidders in a way that maximizes welfare.[4] Each bidder is charged her "externality" on the others (i.e., their lost welfare) caused by her participation in the auction. Notice that for a single item, the winner's externality on the second-highest bidder is precisely this bidder's loss from not being the winner herself, i.e., the second-highest value.

27.2.2 Worst-Case Revenue Maximization

So far, the modeling assumption that v_i is drawn from a distribution F_i played no part in our account. Vickrey's second price auction allocates based only on the reported value profile of the bidders, ignoring the distributions and always choosing the bidder with the highest value as winner. The second price auction thus maximizes welfare *pointwise*, i.e., for every realization of the random values. This ensures worst-case optimality: the auction is guaranteed to maximize welfare for every instance (value profile) of the problem.

Unfortunately, trying to apply the same approach to maximizing revenue rather than welfare is doomed to failure – there is no truthful auction that is worst-case optimal, or even approximately so, for revenue.[5] To see this consider the simplest possible setting with a single bidder interested in the item. Intuitively, all an auction can do to raise revenue is set a take-it-or-leave-it price for the item, which can't depend on the bidder's reported value (to maintain truthfulness). Setting the price to zero is clearly not worst-case optimal, and for any auction that sets a price $p > 0$, there is a worst-case instance on which this auction gets zero revenue (e.g., let the bidder's value be $v = p - \epsilon$). It thus seems to make sense to switch from the worst-case approach to the average-case one, in which the goal is to maximize *expected* revenue

---

[4] One caveat is that this allocation task is in general computationally intractable.

[5] One alternative suggested in the literature in order to stay in the worst-case regime is competitive analysis of online auctions.

over the values' randomness. The average-case approach is indeed the standard one in the economics literature on revenue-maximizing auction design.

27.2.3 Average-Case Revenue-Maximization and Myerson's Theory

For a single item, Myerson solved the problem of designing a truthful auction that maximizes expected revenue in 1981. As discussed above the optimal auction *must* depend on the value distributions $F_1, \ldots, F_n$. The design thus relies on an extra assumption of full distributional knowledge.

In what follows we ignore for simplicity distributions that are "irregular" (e.g., distributions that are "too long-tailed" or bimodal; a formal definition of regularity appears in the text that follows). Essentially what Myerson shows is that the dependence of the optimal auction on the distributions is very specific – they are used to transform the values into new ones called *virtual values*, by subtracting from each value a distribution-dependent "penalty" called the *information rent*. Once we have the virtual values, the allocation rule proceeds by simply maximizing welfare over these new values. In the remainder of the section we give the details of Myerson's theory.

Myerson's Lemma Myerson's first contribution, which we refer to as Myerson's Lemma, is a *characterization* of truthful auctions for the single-item case. It turns out that truthful auctions are precisely those which allocate "monotonically in values," and charge according to a unique payment rule *whose formula depends only on the allocation rule* (provided that bidders who bid zero are not charged). By "allocating monotonically" we mean that for every bidder i and values v_{-i} of the other bidders, bidder i's allocation $x_i(b_i, v_{-i})$ is nondecreasing in her bid b_i. Intuitively, if bidding higher lowers your allocation, you will want to bid lower than your true value, violating truthfulness; Myerson shows that monotonicity is not only necessary but also sufficient, and that once a monotone allocation rule has been fixed, the payments are in effect fixed as well (so we never have to worry about designing payments!).

Application to a Single Bidder Let's now use Myerson's characterization to find the optimal auction (pricing mechanism) for the single-bidder case. We focus for simplicity of exposition on deterministic allocation rules.[6] So a monotone allocation rule must assign 0 ("lose") to all values up to a certain threshold p, and 1 ("win") to all values above the threshold. This is equivalent to presenting the bidder with a price p for the item, and letting her decide whether or not to purchase at this price. We wish to optimize p for expected revenue given the bidder's value distribution F. The expected revenue given price p is $p(1 - F(p))$, since $1 - F(p)$ is precisely the probability that the bidder's value is at least p i.e. she purchases the item.

For simple, regular distributions F, we can maximize the expression $p(1 - F(p))$ – which we refer to as the *revenue curve in value space* – by taking the derivative $(1 - F(p)) - pf(p)$ and setting it equal to zero. We get that the optimal price p^*, known as the *monopoly price* of F, is the solution to $p - \frac{1-F(p)}{f(p)} = 0$. This essentially concludes the single-bidder case. We now give another interpretation of this solution that will be helpful in the multibidder case.

---

[6] One of the conclusions from Myerson's theory is that randomization cannot help extract more expected revenue than deterministic auctions when selling a single item.

Regularity and Virtual Values Call $v - \frac{1-F(v)}{f(v)}$ the *virtual value* corresponding to value v drawn from distribution F. The information rent $\frac{1-F(v)}{f(v)}$ is subtracted from the value and so the virtual value may be negative.[7] We can now formally define *regularity* of a distribution F as the assumption that the virtual value function corresponding to F is (weakly) increasing in v. The uniform, Gaussian and exponential distributions are all examples of regular distributions. Long-tailed distributions like $F(v) = 1 - \frac{1}{\sqrt{v}}$, as well as bimodal distributions, are irregular.

Using the language of virtual values, the auction we ended up with in the single-bidder case maximizes the "virtual welfare" – i.e., the welfare with respect to the virtual value – since it allocates to the bidder iff her virtual value is ≥ 0. In the single-bidder case, we conclude that maximizing the virtual welfare is precisely what's needed in order to maximize the expected revenue. In fact, the revenue from the bidder is equal in expectation to her virtual value.

Multiple Bidders and the I.I.D. Assumption Myerson shows that in the multi-bidder case, the same principle holds, and maximizing the virtual welfare (coupled with the unique payment rule coming from Myerson's Lemma) yields the optimal auction. In fact, the expected revenue of any auction is equal to the expected virtual welfare it induces by its allocation rule.

Perhaps the neatest conclusion from Myerson's theory is what auction to run when the bidder values are i.i.d., that is, all drawn independently from a single (regular) distribution F: In this case, we can skip the transformation to virtual values, since all values would be transformed using the same monotone transformation. We need only set a threshold such that no bidder with value below the threshold (read: virtual value below zero) can win. The optimal auction thus boils down to simply the second price auction with the monopoly price of F set as *reserve price*.[8] This is in fact a well-known auction format in practice, used for example on eBay. The i.i.d. case will play a big role in our account on prior-independence.

Takeaway An important takeaway from the discussion of Myerson's theory in this section is that *the revenue-optimal auction is highly dependent on the value distributions and their knowledge*. In general, the distributional information is used to figure out the precise penalty to subtract from every value in order to get the virtual values. Even in the simple single-bidder or i.i.d. cases, the optimal reserve price closely depends on the distribution.

Beyond a Single Item Unfortunately, the elegant theory of optimal auctions developed by Myerson does not extend (at least not in its simple and clean form) to settings in which buyers have different values for different items. Such settings are formally called *multiparameter* settings, since their complexity stems from the preferences of the bidders being multidimensional rather than from the multiplicity of items per se.[9] In this chapter for simplicity we shall refer to such settings as *multiple item* (*multi-item*) settings, to differentiate them from the single item setting discussed so far. We address the complication introduced by multiple items (multidimensional values) in Section 27.5.

---

[7] This subtracted "penalty" is the inverse of what's known as the *hazard rate* of distribution F.

[8] A reserve price is the lowest price at which the auctioneer is willing to sell.

[9] Myerson's theory does extend to all single-parameter settings, such as settings with multiple identical units of the same item for sale.

27.3 Defining Prior-Independence

A long-time goal of auction design has been to weaken the strong informational assumptions on which revenue-optimal auctions rely. *Robustness* with respect to distributional knowledge has been advocated across disciplines: In economics, Robert Wilson famously called for the weakening of auctions' dependence on the details of the economic environment, a position that has become known in the field as "Wilson's doctrine." In operations research, Herbert Scarf wrote in 1958 that we "have reason to suspect that the future demand will come from a distribution which differs from that governing past history in an unpredictable way." And in computer science, the discipline's general mistrust of average-case solutions (see Chapter 8) immediately extended to auction design.

But what exactly is robustness? Informally, what designers seek is auctions that have performance guarantees that are *in*sensitive to the environment details, i.e., "perform well" for a "large range" of economic environments. We now formally define the robustness notion of *prior-independence*.

Definition We focus for simplicity on the single item case with i.i.d. values. Consider first a particular distribution F from which the bidders' values are independently drawn. Let OPT_F be the optimal expected revenue that a truthful auction, which has full knowledge of F, can achieve in this environment, and let $\alpha \in (0, 1]$ be an approximation factor. An auction is α-*optimal* with respect to F if its expected revenue is at least αOPT_F (so far this is the usual notion of approximation used in algorithms). Now let $\mathcal{F}$ be a family of value distributions, called *priors*. In particular, we shall focus on the family of distributions which satisfy the regularity property of virtual value monotonicity.

Definition 27.1 (Prior-Independence)   An auction is *robustly α-optimal* with respect to the family of priors $\mathcal{F}$ if for every prior $F \in \mathcal{F}$, the auction is α-optimal with respect to F.

Definition 27.1 fills with content the informal terms used earlier to describe robustness: For a prior-independent auction to "perform well," it must achieve expected revenue that approximates the optimal expected revenue simultaneously for every distribution in class $\mathcal{F}$; the "large range" of distributions is usually the class of all regular distributions. The definition extends naturally to multi-item settings.

27.3.1 Discussion of the Definition

The definition of prior-independent robustness is an interesting mixture of average- and worst-case guarantees. On one hand, performance is measured in expectation over the random input (value profile); on the other, it is measured in the worst case over all distributions that belong to a class $\mathcal{F}$.

What are the rationales behind the definition of prior-independent robustness? In particular, why measure whether a robust auction has good performance by comparing it to the optimal auction with the "unfair" advantage of knowing the right distribution from $\mathcal{F}$? And given this measure, why take $\mathcal{F}$ to be the set of regular distributions? This can be split into two subquestions: First, why not take $\mathcal{F}$ to be even bigger? On the other hand, why allow $\mathcal{F}$ to encompass such a large range of distributions?

We begin by addressing the question of why prior-independence is a good idea as a design goal. The first reason is that existence of good prior-independent auctions according to Definition 27.1 is a powerful and useful result. An auction that performs well for all "reasonable" distributions is perfect for situations in which the seller has little to no information about the actual value distribution, such as a newcomer seller entering the market, a new item on the market, or an item whose distribution is constantly shifting. In other cases, the seller may be able to obtain some information regarding the value distribution, but at a prohibitively high cost or subject to substantial noise. Even assuming the seller somehow has reliable, affordable and up-to-date information on the value distribution, hard-wiring it into the auction can harm flexibility, since once an auction becomes the market standard it is not easy to make changes. A second important reason to set prior-independence as a design goal is that as it turns out, it often leads to auctions with a simple and natural format. Prior-independence thus gives a theoretical foundation for well-known auction formats and introduces promising new ones.

A Regularity-Type Assumption on $\mathcal{F}$ Is Necessary and Sufficient The following example taken from (Dhangwatnotai et al., 2015) demonstrates the necessity of some kind of tail-restricting assumption on the class $\mathcal{F}$; regularity is a canonical example of such an assumption. Fix a number n of i.i.d. bidders. Consider an irregular value distribution F_z, with probability $1/n^2$ for value z and probability $1 - 1/n^2$ for value zero. An auction with access to the prior distribution F_z can extract expected revenue of $\Omega(z/n)$ from the n bidders whose values are drawn from F_z. In contrast, any prior-independent truthful auction essentially has to guess the value of z, since using the winning bidder's bid violates truthfulness and all other bids are likely to be zero (therefore providing no information about z). The conclusion is that absent a tail assumption, a prior-independent auction's expected revenue cannot be within a constant factor of z/n simultaneously for every F_z.[10]

On the other hand, the class $\mathcal{F}$ of regular distributions is not "too big": The results presented in this chapter show that the regularity assumption is sufficient to achieve a constant approximation to the ambitious benchmark of OPT_F, even in challenging environments like multi-item settings, for which optimal auctions remain elusive.

Alternative BWCA Models A natural alternative approach to robustness would be, rather than to approximate the optimal auction for every distribution in $\mathcal{F}$, to design an auction that *maximizes the minimum* expected revenue, where the minimum is taken over all distributions in $\mathcal{F}$. This approach is called *robust optimization* in the operations research literature (Bandi and Bertsimas, 2014), and has also been pursued in the context of auctions and mechanism design by economist Gabriel Carroll and others.

The prior-independence and max-min approaches are incomparable and both have already led to interesting insights. For prior-independence, notable successes in identifying natural and interesting mechanisms have been through either *approximation* or *resource augmentation*. Note that the smaller class $\mathcal{F}$ is, the easier it is to achieve a prior-independence result. For max-min, however, some of the most meaningful and interpretable results to date have been through characterizing the mechanism that achieves the *exact* maximum (where the minimum is over a judicious choice of

---

[10] There are alternative tail assumptions to regularity that work too; e.g., Sivan and Syrgkanis (2013) show prior-independence results for convex combinations of a small number of regular distributions.

distributions $\mathcal{F}$). Note that if $\mathcal{F}$ is too small, achieving an exact max-min result can become very challenging. For example, with multiple items, if $\mathcal{F}$ contains only a single distribution then the max-min mechanism is the revenue-optimal one for multiple items, which is known *not* to have a useful characterization. Interestingly, in either of the approaches, typically to single-out natural and interesting mechanisms, the class $\mathcal{F}$ should exhibit sufficient richness.

Another alternative BWCA model to prior-independence is that of *prior-free* auctions. The prior-free approach makes no assumption that values come from an underlying (albeit unknown) distribution, and is thus fundamentally different from prior-independence. Yet there are interesting connections among the two approaches. In particular, prior-free analysis that evaluates mechanisms with respect to an *economically meaningful* benchmark will yield a prior-independent result as a corollary (see Hartline [2019a] for the definition of "economically meaningful"). Also, some techniques are relevant to both approaches, like that of randomly dividing the bidders into two and using one group as a "training set" to learn auction parameters applicable to the other (Balcan et al., 2008). This is similar in spirit to the single-sample methods in Sections 27.4.2 and 27.4.3, which use one bidder as a "training sample" to learn a reserve price applicable to the others. Of course, prior-free guarantees are more demanding than prior-independent ones (since less is assumed), and accordingly have less reach at the moment for settings such as multiple items.

A Note on Truthfulness In our discussion in Section 27.2 of revenue maximization, we focused on truthful auctions. Truthfulness is an important property of auctions in itself – it simplifies participation, thus drawing more competition and leveling the playing field among sophisticated and naïve bidders. For optimal auction design it is remarkably without loss of generality due to a fundamental observation known as the *revelation principle*, by which a truthful mechanism can simulate the bidders' equilibrium strategies in a nontruthful mechanism to obtain the same outcome. Feng and Hartline (2018) note that in Bayesian settings where the agents' equilibrium strategies are a function of the prior, the Bayesian truthful mechanism (a weaker truthfulness guarantee than dominant-strategy) which is constructed via the revelation principle is *not* prior-independent. They show a gap between the robust approximate optimality of nontruthful mechanisms versus that of truthful mechanisms in welfare-maximization settings with budgeted bidders. Existence of a similar gap in revenue-maximization settings is left as an open question.

27.4 Sample-Based Approach: Single Item

In the era of big data, not having knowledge of a bidder's value distribution F may sound like a solvable problem – simply obtain sufficiently many samples, e.g., by interacting with other bidders of the same population (see also Chapter 29). This requires assuming the existence of a population of bidders with the same value distribution so that we can learn about the distribution of one bidder's value from the values of others. Indeed, such an assumption of i.i.d. values seems necessary to get positive prior-independence results. However, relying on large amounts of data is far from ideal in the context of auctions, as we discuss in Section 27.4.1. The main goal of this section is to minimize the required number of samples as much as possible, starting from as little as a single sample from the unknown distribution F (Sections 27.4.2 and 27.4.3). Clearly with so few samples, the empirical distribution will not in general resemble the ground truth one. This differentiates the computer science approach from previous efforts in economics, which typically rely on asymptotically large markets (e.g., Segal, 2003). We discuss a general measure of *sample complexity* in Section 27.4.4, and finish with lower bounds in Section 27.4.5.

27.4.1 How to Get Samples

Limitations on the Number and Nature of Samples As pointed out by Hartline (2019b), optimal auction design is probably most important in "thin" markets, i.e., markets in which there aren't many competitors for the item on sale, and thus insufficient past data. This could result from the nature of the item (say a unique modern art painting), or from deliberate targeting of a small set of bidders for whom the item is particularly well suited (as done in the online ad market). In thick markets we could easily obtain many samples, but the folklore wisdom is that the auction format matters less in such markets (for example, bidders may not be able to effectively strategize regardless of the auction's truthfulness, since every bidder's action has very little influence on the outcome).

Another issue with relying on past data is that once repeated players realize that the seller is learning how to extract revenue from their bids, they have incentive to report untruthfully in order to gain in the long run. There is a growing literature on learning in the presence of strategic behavior, usually requiring behavioral assumptions on the bidders that are outside the scope of this chapter. Tang and Zeng (2018) abstract away from such assumptions, considering instead the equilibria of *distribution-reporting games* in which the distributions are endogenously reported by the bidders. They show that prior-dependent auctions are inferior to prior-independent ones when bidders are strategic about the distributions their bids reflect, a finding they dub as *price of prior-dependence*. If the setting is *not* a repeated one (imagine, e.g., tickets to a one-time event), long-run strategic behavior is less of an issue. But now there is no past data whatsoever.

Using Extra Bidders as Samples In light of the preceding discussion, we shall often assume that the samples come from the bidders themselves. That is, we randomly choose one (or more) of the bidders to excuse from the auction, in which case reporting truthfully becomes a dominant strategy for them. We then use these truthful reports as samples from F.

While providing invaluable information, throwing away bidders also loses a certain fraction of expected revenue. The following lemma shows a bound on how much expected revenue is lost:

Lemma 27.2 *In a single-item setting where the bidders have i.i.d. values, consider the optimal expected revenue OPT as a function of the number of bidders. Then $OPT(k) \geq \frac{k}{k+\ell} OPT(k + \ell)$ for every pair of integers $k, \ell > 0$.*

Lemma 27.2 can be interpreted as saying that the optimal expected revenue is subadditive in the number of bidders. We leave its proof as an exercise (see Exercise 27.1). Applications of Lemma 27.2 include showing that if we start out with a certain number of bidders, say $n = 2$, and throw out one of the bidders at random, we lose no more than $1/2$ of the optimal expected revenue. It can also be applied to analyze the revenue effects of investing marketing efforts in recruiting extra bidders to the auction, then using the extras as data samples.

27.4.2 Single Bidder, Single Sample

Recall from Section 27.2 that the optimal auction for a single bidder and known distribution F maximizes the expected revenue $p(1 - F(p))$ by offering the item at monopoly price p^*. For regular F, p^* is the value at which the corresponding virtual value becomes zero. Now assume we no longer know F but have access to a single sample $p \sim F$. A natural thing to try is to simply set the item's price to be this sample p. It turns out that this method achieves in expectation at least half of the optimal expected revenue. In this section we establish this result using a geometric proof by Dhangwatnotai et al. (2015).

Proposition 27.3 *Consider a single bidder with value drawn from F. Let F be a regular distribution and let p^* be its monopoly price. Then using a random price achieves half of the optimum in expectation:* $\mathbf{E}_{p \sim F}[p(1 - F(p))] \geq \frac{1}{2}p^*(1 - F(p^*))$.

Equivalent Definition of Regularity For simplicity we assume throughout this section that F is continuous and has bounded support (the proof of Proposition 27.3 can be extended beyond these assumptions). In the proof below it will be convenient to use an alternative definition of regularity as follows.

Recall that regularity means that the virtual value function $v - \frac{1-F(v)}{f(v)}$ is (weakly) increasing in v. Recall also that in Section 27.2.3 we referred to $v(1 - F(v))$ as the "revenue curve in value space." We now switch to an equivalent, more convenient formulation for our purpose, which takes place in *quantile space*. The idea is that while the expected revenue can be represented as a function of the price p, where p ranges over all possible values, it can also be represented as a function of the *quantile* of the price, i.e., $q = 1 - F(p)$. The quantile q of p ranges between 0 and 1 and tells us *what fraction of the population would purchase at price p*. We denote by $R(q)$ the expected revenue as a function of the quantile q (also known as the *revenue curve in quantile space*). For example, $R(0.5)$ is the expected revenue if the price is set to be the value at quantile 0.5 – i.e., the median – so that a random bidder would purchase with probability 0.5.

We can now state the alternative definition of regularity: A distribution is regular if and only if its revenue curve in quantile space $R(q)$ is a concave function of q. To verify this one can check that the slope $R'(q)$ of the revenue curve at q is precisely the virtual value corresponding to the value $v = F^{-1}(1 - q)$. We shall use this characterization in the following proof.

Proof of Proposition 27.3 Consider the revenue curve of F in quantile space. We can assume without loss that the lowest value in F's support is zero (this is the hardest case). Thus at the extreme quantiles 0 and 1, the expected revenue is zero (by definition nobody buys at quantile 0, and by assumption everybody buys but pays nothing at quantile 1). We plot the revenue curve in Figure 27.1. Due to regularity of F, the curve is concave. We now use this figure to visualize the two quantities we need to relate in order to prove the proposition.

The optimal expected revenue benchmark $p^*(1 - F(p^*))$ can be written as $R(q^*)$, where q^* is the quantile of p^*. Geometrically, it is the area of the rectangle in the figure (since this rectangle's width is 1, and its height is $R(q^*)$). As for the expected revenue $\mathbf{E}_{p \sim F}[p(1 - F(p))]$ from setting a randomly-drawn price, we

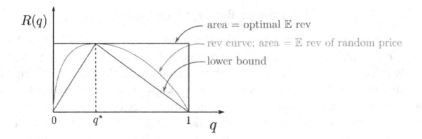

Figure 27.1 Geometric proof of Proposition 27.3.

can rewrite this as $\mathbf{E}_{q \sim U[0,1]}[R(q)]$. This is because randomly choosing a price according to the value distribution F is equivalent to choosing a quantile q uniformly at random and then taking the price $F^{-1}(1-q)$ that corresponds to it. Geometrically, $\mathbf{E}_{q \sim U[0,1]}[R(q)]$ is the area under the revenue curve in Figure 27.1.

To relate these two areas as required, we simply use the concavity of the revenue curve: By concavity, the triangle depicted in Figure 27.1 has area not greater than that under the curve. As its area is exactly half that of the rectangle, this completes the proof. □

The guarantee in Proposition 27.3 is tight: Consider the regular distribution F on the range $[0, H]$ where $F(v) = 1 - \frac{1}{v+1}$ for every $v \in [0, H)$ and $F(H) = 1$. As $H \to \infty$, the revenue curve in quantile space for this distribution is essentially a triangle, and so the analysis in the proof of Proposition 27.3 is tight.

27.4.3 Multiple Bidders, Single Sample

In this section we build upon Proposition 27.3 from the previous section, in order to design a prior-independent auction for *multiple* bidders that is robustly approximately optimal. A slightly more general version of Proposition 27.3 establishes that under the same conditions and for every threshold $t \geq 0$, setting the maximum of t and a sample $p \sim F$ as the bidder's price achieves a $\frac{1}{2}$-approximation to setting the price to the maximum of t and the monopoly price p^* (Exercise 27.2). This can be used to establish that the following prior-independent auction, called the *single sample* auction, is robustly $\frac{n-1}{2n}$-optimal where n is the number of bidders.

Algorithm 27.4 The *single sample* auction has the following allocation rule: (1) Pick a "reserve" bidder i uniformly at random. (2) Run the second-price auction among the non-reserve bidders; let i^* be the tentative winner and let t be the second-highest bid. (3) Allocate the item to i^* if and only if $v_{i^*} \geq v_i$. The payment rule from Myerson's Lemma says that if i^* is allocated she pays $\max\{t, v_i\}$.

The single sample auction is clearly prior-independent as its allocation rule is defined with no mention of the value distributions. It is also not hard to verify its truthfulness using Myerson's Lemma. Its performance guarantee is as follows:

Theorem 27.5 *For every single-item setting with $n \geq 2$ i.i.d. bidders, the single sample auction is robustly $\frac{n-1}{2n}$-optimal with respect to regular distributions.*

Theorem 27.5 follows by first applying Lemma 27.2 to bound the loss from step (1) of the single sample auction, guaranteeing that a factor of $\frac{n-1}{n}$ of the optimal expected revenue is maintained, then applying the generalized version of Proposition 27.3 with random price $p = v_i$ and threshold t to bound the loss from steps (2) and (3) by another $\frac{1}{2}$-factor. The tightness of the guarantee in Theorem 27.5 is discussed shortly (Section 27.4.5).

We end this section by remarking that the single sample auction has also been extended to *multiple samples* – the generalized version is called the "empirical revenue maximization (ERM)" auction[11] – as well as to *multiple items* by Devanur et al. (2011) and Goldner and Karlin (2016).

27.4.4 Multiple Samples: Sample Complexity

The term sample complexity is borrowed from machine learning; in the context of auctions its study was initiated by Cole and Roughgarden (2014) (see also early works like (Elkind, 2007; Balcan et al., 2008), from which certain sample complexity results can be derived). The sample complexity of a family of settings measures how many samples from the prior distribution are needed in order to achieve, with high probability, expected revenue that is close up to a given multiplicative factor (often, $1 - \epsilon$) to the target optimal expected revenue (when the distribution is known). Of course, the number of samples needed will grow with the inverse of the precision parameter ϵ; it is interesting to understand what else it depends on.[12] The sample complexity is an information theoretic measure, related but separate from the question of tractably learning from samples (this is another way in which the study of sample complexity diverges from the concrete prior-independent auctions we saw in previous sections).

There have been two main approaches in the literature to bounding the sample complexity, summarized nicely by Guo et al. (2019) (see references within). The first is to consider a class ("ϵ-net") of auctions, such that for every setting in the relevant family of settings, there always exists an approximately-optimal auction in the class. VC-like learning dimensions from statistical learning theory can then be applied to measure the complexity (or simplicity) of the auction class, telling us how many samples are needed to find the best auction in it.

An alternative approach, closer in spirit to the single sample method described in Sections 27.4.2 and 27.4.3, is to learn enough about the distributions to obtain an auction with approximately optimal expected revenue. The difference from the single sample approach is that the approximation factor is required to be very close to 1. Often the goal is to learn a small set of statistics, for instance sufficiently many quantiles, which are relatively easy to estimate accurately via standard concentration

---

[11] ERM maximizes revenue given the empirical distribution, i.e., the uniform distribution over the samples. For example, for a single bidder, the ERM auction sets the price to be the monopoly price of the empirical distribution, which for a single sample is simply the sample itself.

[12] For example, with multiple nonidentically distributed bidders, the number of samples required from every distributions turns out to depend polynomially on the total number of bidders.

inequalities, and sufficiently robust such that estimation errors don't harm revenue too much. For example, in the single item, single bidder case, it turns out that $\Theta(\log H)$ empirical quantiles suffice for a close-to-1 approximation when the support of the distribution is bounded by H, even without regularity.

We remark that sample complexity has also been studied for the challenging case of multiple items, largely focusing on information-theoretic rather than constructive results (for a single item, many of the most recent results are in fact constructive).

27.4.5 Lower Bounds and Tightness

We discuss lower bounds for the single item case, which has been the main focus of this section. There are three kinds of lower bounds, corresponding to the three types of results we have seen: (1) Robust approximation guarantees with a given number of samples (Proposition 27.3); (2) Robust approximation guarantees with a given number of i.i.d. bidders (Theorem 27.5); (3) Guarantees on the number of samples that suffice to obtain robust $(1 - \epsilon)$-optimal auctions (Section 27.4.4).

For (1), Fu et al. (2015) show that with a single sample, while no deterministic auction can do better than $\frac{1}{2}$, a randomized one can break the $\frac{1}{2}$ barrier. For (2), given $n \geq 2$ i.i.d. bidders, simply running the second-price auction with no reserve achieves an approximation factor of $\frac{n-1}{n}$ (we further discuss this approach of running the welfare-maximizing auction with sufficient competition in Section 27.5). However the $\frac{n-1}{n}$ factor is not tight: in the special case of $n = 2$ bidders, Fu et al. (2015) show a prior-independent randomized auction with a guarantee of 0.512; Allouah and Besbes (2018) show that no auction can guarantee more than 0.556. Finally, for (3), the recent cutting-edge sample complexity results for a single item are all asymptotically tight up to polylogarithmic factors. For example, in (Guo et al., 2019) there is a lower bound of $\Omega(n\epsilon^{-3})$ samples if the prior distribution is regular, and they show a matching upper bound (up to polylogarithmic factors).

27.5 Competition-Based Approach: Multiple Items

We now shift our attention to settings with multiple different items. For such settings Myerson's theory no longer holds, and designing optimal auctions *even given full distributional knowledge* becomes a challenging task.[13]

A way to approach the multi-item challenge – one which we shall not pursue in this section – is to focus on simple, *approximately* optimal auctions. These have been developed for many families of multiple-item markets in recent years. To make these auctions prior-independent, the "market analysis on the fly" methods from the previous section can be applied. The constant-fraction losses in expected revenue by the prior-dependent auctions are of course inherited by their prior-independent counterparts.

To avoid such losses, in this section we explore an alternative approach along the lines of *resource augmentation* (Chapter 4). Note that the model in this section is

---

[13] Indeed, even for a single bidder and two items, revenue-optimal auctions involve various complexities such as intricate menus of lotteries.

still a semi-random one, because the bidders' values are still assumed to be drawn from unknown prior distributions. What are the advantages of combining these two models?

Combining the Semirandom and Resource Augmentation Models Recall that a main source for samples came from "throwing away" part of the demand-side of the market. Given that we are throwing away bidders who, besides being able to provide us with samples from the distributions we're interested in, also have purchasing power and willingness to pay for the items, is this the best way to use these extra bidders? Another idea would be to view extra bidders as increasing the competition for the items on the market. Intuitively, competition drives up revenue naturally, reducing the need to design careful pricing or lotteries. In fact, we can use the extra bidders to get revenue that is competitive with the optimal expected revenue benchmark – without extra bidders and with known distributions (this is the same benchmark approximated by the sample-based approach). This is achieved even while running extremely simple auctions.

VCG The simple auction we mostly focus on is the welfare-maximizing VCG auction. Recall from Section 27.2.1 that the VCG auction is a generalization of the second price auction to multiple items. As in the second price auction, the allocation rule of VCG partitions the items among the bidders in a way that maximizes the social welfare, in this case the bidders' aggregate value. The payment rule is not quite as simple as charging the second highest bid, but it is the natural analog for multiple items: each bidder is charged her externality (for a single item, the winner's externality on the second-highest bidder is precisely this bidder's value). The resulting VCG auction is deterministic, dominant-strategy truthful, and inherently prior-independent. And while our first-order goal is revenue, as an extra bonus by using VCG we get maximum welfare "for free."

27.5.1 Competition Complexity

Warm-up: A Seminal Result from Microeconomics Bulow and Klemperer (1996) were the first to establish positive results using the competition-based approach sketched earlier. The main result in their paper is for a single item setting (they use Myerson's theory in their analysis):

Theorem 27.6 *For every single item setting with n i.i.d. bidders whose values are drawn from a regular distribution F, the optimal expected revenue is at most the expected revenue from running the second price auction with $n + 1$ such bidders.*

In other words, the second price auction with a single additional bidder is robustly optimal. In the case of $n = 1$, Theorem 27.6 says that if we use the distribution-dependent monopoly price to sell the item to a single bidder, we get weakly less expected revenue than if we were to recruit a second bidder and run the second price auction. The proof of Theorem 27.6 for this case of $n = 1$ follows from Proposition 27.3, by observing that each bidder effectively faces a random price p drawn from F.

Multiple Items How far can we push the competition-based approach of Bulow and Klemperer (1996)? Consider complex settings with multiple items; is it always enough to add to the original n bidders a constant, or at least finite, number of extra bidders in order for the VCG auction to surpass the benchmark of optimal expected revenue for n bidders and known distributions? In other words, we seek Bulow–Klemperer-style results of the form: "The revenue of the welfare-maximizing auction with $n + C$ i.i.d. bidders whose values are drawn from a regular distribution F is at least as high in expectation as the optimal revenue with n such bidders." If such a statement holds for a family of auction settings, we call the smallest C for which it holds its *competition complexity* (Eden et al., 2017). Competition complexity falls under the resource augmentation umbrella, since we are comparing the performance of a simple auction with extra resources (bidders) to that of a complex auction with no extra resources.

Our Model We study the competition complexity of multi-item settings in the following model, which generalizes the i.i.d. assumption to multiple items: Consider m items, where each item $j \in [m]$ is associated with a regular distribution F_j. We assume that for every $i \in [n]$, bidder i's value $v_{i,j}$ for item j is drawn independently from F_j.

It is left to specify how to extend item values to values for sets of items. Let set function $v_i : 2^{[m]} \to \Re_{\geq 0}$ be bidder i's valuation function. We consider two cases, where v_i is either *unit-demand*, or *additive*, for every bidder i. In the former case, $v_i(S) = \max_{j \in S}\{v_{i,j}\}$, and in the latter case, $v_i(S) = \sum_{j \in S} v_{i,j}$. As an illustrative example, if the items are different desserts then a bidder on a low-sugar diet can be modeled as having a unit-demand valuation – she will enjoy no more than one dessert. A bidder who is not restricted by a diet can be modeled as additive, since she can enjoy any number of desserts. Notice that in the former case, the welfare-maximizing allocation is simply a maximum-value matching, and in the latter case the welfare-maximizing allocation simply gives every item to the bidder who values it most.

27.5.2 Unit-Demand Bidders

In this section we analyze the competition complexity of settings with n unit-demand bidders and m items. The first competition complexity results for multiple items were obtained by Roughgarden et al. (2019), demonstrating that the classic approach of Bulow and Klemperer (1996) is useful in more complex settings than previously realized. The benchmark used by Roughgarden et al. (2019) is the optimal *deterministic* auction, the expected revenue of which – in the unit-demand context – is up to a small constant fraction away from the optimal randomized auction. The restriction to a deterministic benchmark will be relaxed in Section 27.5.4.

Theorem 27.7 *For every setting with n unit-demand bidders and m items whose distributions $F_1, \ldots, F_m$ are regular, the optimal expected revenue by a deterministic truthful[14] auction is at most the expected revenue from running the VCG auction with $n + m$ such bidders.*

Theorem 27.7 extends Theorem 27.6 beyond $m = 1$, and shows that the VCG auction with m additional bidders is robustly optimal. In the remainder of this section we sketch the proof of Theorem 27.7 in three steps: upper-bounding the optimal expected revenue, lower-bounding the expected revenue of the VCG auction, and relating the two bounds.

---

[14] In this section it is important that we are focusing on the optimal *dominant-strategy* truthful auction.

Proof Sketch   The first part of the proof relies on achieving a sufficient understanding of optimal auctions for multiple items to obtain a reasonable upper bound on their revenue. While no simple closed-form descriptions of these auctions are known, there has been great progress on the approximation front in recent years. One useful bound was obtained for unit-demand bidders by Chawla et al. (2010):

Lemma 27.8   *The optimal expected revenue of a deterministic truthful auction with n unit-demand bidders and regular value distributions is upper-bounded by the expected revenue from selling every item j by the second price auction to $n + 1$ bidders with i.i.d. values from F_j.*

The second part of the proof uses a simple bound on VCG's expected revenue, which follows from charging the winner of an item her externality on the others:

Lemma 27.9   *Let U be the set of unallocated bidders allocated no items by VCG. The expected revenue of the VCG auction is lower-bounded by $\sum_j \max_{i \in U} \{v_{i,j}\}$, i.e., by the sum over all items j of the highest value of a bidder in U for j.*

The third part of the proof relates the two bounds by utilizing the fact that the upper and lower bounds share a similar form. Fix an item j; the upper bound is the expected second-highest among $n + 1$ values drawn independently from F_j; the lower bound is the highest among n values of unallocated bidders for item j, where bidders' values for j are drawn independently from F_j. This is where the proof uses the augmentation of the market with more bidders – in the augmented setting, only m out of $n + m$ bidders are allocated and so there are n unallocated bidders. However, a dependency issue arises: conditioned on the event that a bidder is unallocated by VCG, her value for item j is no longer distributed like a random sample from F_j. In other words, the losers in the VCG auction are likely to have lower values. Luckily, in unit-demand settings VCG allocates according to the maximum matching, and due to combinatorial properties of such matchings, the only thing that can be deduced about a losing bidder's value for item j is that it is lower than the value of item j's winner. Thus, appropriate coupling arguments can relate item j's expected contributions to the upper and lower bounds, completing the proof.

27.5.3 Lower Bounds and Tightness

Before we turn to competition complexity for additive bidders, let's briefly discuss lower bounds.

Unit-Demand Theorem 27.7 is tight, as adding fewer than m extra unit-demand bidders to the VCG auction may fail to guarantee the optimal expected revenue in the original environment. Consider the special case of a single unit-demand bidder ($n = 1$), and m items whose values are all drawn from a point-mass distribution (and thus are identical). If no more than $m - 1$ additional bidders are added to the original single bidder, each of the unit-demand bidders can get one of the m identical items, and so there is no competition to drive up the revenue. In fact, in this particular setting, the expected revenue achieved by the VCG auction with at most m (in total) unit-demand bidders is zero.

Additive Consider again the $n = 1$ case. We now argue that the best lower bound on the extra number of additive bidders needed for the VCG auction to guarantee the optimal expected revenue is $\Omega(\log m)$ (compared to m for unit-demand).

Let the item distributions all be the regular "equal revenue" distribution F on range $[1, m^2]$, where $F(v) = 1 - \frac{1}{v}$ for every $v \in [1, m^2)$ and $F(m^2) = 1$. For sufficiently large m, the optimal expected revenue from selling the items to the original single bidder is $\Omega(m \log m)$.[15] Consider now the expected revenue of VCG with k extra bidders. For additive bidders, VCG is simply a collection of m second price auctions, one per item. Thus the expected revenue is m times the expected second price in a $(k + 1)$-bidder auction with values drawn from F, which is k by direct calculation (omitted). For mk to match the benchmark $\Omega(m \log m)$, the number of extra bidders k must be $\Omega(\log m)$. This lower bound holds even if one is willing to lose an ϵ-fraction of the optimal expected revenue (Feldman et al., 2018).

27.5.4 Additive Bidders

In this section we complete the picture of what's known on competition complexity by discussing settings with additive bidders and m items. For a single additive bidder, Beyhaghi and Weinberg (2019) show that the lower bound from the previous section is tight up to constant factors:

Theorem 27.10 *For every setting with a single additive bidder and m items with regular distributions $F_1, \ldots, F_m$, the optimal expected revenue by a truthful[16] auction is at most the expected revenue from running the VCG auction with $O(\log m)$ additional bidders.*

The proof follows the same general structure as that of Theorem 27.7, but the bounds and the arguments relating them are significantly more intricate.

For n additive bidders, we get an interesting dependence of the competition complexity on n: it is the minimum among $O(n \log \frac{m}{n})$ and $O(\sqrt{nm})$ (where the former is tight when $n \leq m$). Like in sample complexity, understanding which parameters factor into the competition complexity is one of the interesting insights that arise from the study of such complexity measures for auction settings.

27.6 Summary

In this chapter we surveyed prior-independent auctions, a par excellence example of a semirandom model: the objective is to maximize expected revenue, but the distribution over which the expectation is taken is adversarial. We started out with a single item, for which revenue-optimal auctions are well-understood. We saw what can be achieved with very little information about the distribution in the form of either a single sample or, better yet, a single additional bidder with the same value distribution. With so little information about the unknown distribution, we naturally

---

[15] This is achieved by bundling together all m items, whose expected value separately is $\Omega(\log m)$ and so together is concentrated around $\Omega(m \log m)$.

[16] In this section the competition complexity results hold even for the benchmark of the optimal *Bayesian* truthful auction.

aim for approximation results. However losing a constant approximation factor has its downsides, especially in economic context – e.g., companies usually would not be willing to settle for half of the optimal revenue.

One solution is to draw closer to the economics approach of a known distribution, by allowing the auction to learn a lot about the distribution rather than just a single sample. This can be achieved by accessing multiple samples or multiple extra bidders, and these two alternatives each have pros and cons. In particular, samples can be obtained from past data even if additional bidders cannot be recruited. But with extra bidders, the auction format becomes extremely simple and less open to strategic behavior. Perhaps the biggest advantage of the resource augmentation approach of extra bidders is that it does not lose an approximation factor compared to the benchmark; this is the only approach so far that enables such an achievement.

Open Questions We conclude with three directions for future research. The entire range between a single sample (or extra bidder) on the one hand, and an unlimited number of samples (or bidders) on the other, is interesting and relevant for prior-independence and has hardly been explored (see Babaioff et al. (2018) for a starting point). Developing competition complexity bounds for multi-item settings beyond unit-demand and additive presents new challenges (see Eden et al. (2017) for a starting point). In addition to completely eliminating distribution dependence as in prior-dependence, reducing such dependence is an important alternative that is largely open. This comes in two flavors: assuming very limited knowledge of the prior, e.g., just its mean; and allowing the auction to have a limited number of distribution-dependent parameters (see Azar et al. [2013] and Morgenstern and Roughgarden [2016], respectively, for starting points).

27.7 Notes

For an excellent book chapter with an in-depth exposition of prior-independent auctions for mechanism designers, see (Hartline, 2019b). The interested reader is also referred to the PhD theses of Yan (2012) and Sivan (2013) on different aspects of prior-independence. Figure 27.1 is from Roughgarden (2017).

There are many extensions in the prior-independence literature to the results appearing in the chapter, we give here several examples: Utilizing limited, parametric knowledge on the prior distribution (Azar et al., 2013; Azar and Micali, 2013); risk-averse bidders (Fu et al., 2013); interdependent bidders (Roughgarden and Talgam-Cohen, 2016); bidders with nonidentically distributed values (Fu et al., 2019); multiple items beyond additive or unit-demand bidders (Eden et al., 2017); dynamic auctions (Liu and Psomas, 2018); other objectives like makespan minimization in machine scheduling (Chawla et al., 2013); prior-independence for budgeted agents and welfare (Feng and Hartline, 2018); irregular combinations of regular distributions (Sivan and Syrgkanis, 2013); limiting supply instead of adding bidders (Roughgarden et al., 2019).

Acknowledgments

This chapter has greatly benefited from the helpful and insightful comments of Maria-Florina Balcan, Jason Hartline, Balasubramanian Sivan, Qiqi Yan, and Konstantin Zabarnyi. Support by the ISRAEL SCIENCE FOUNDATION (grant No. 336/18) and the Taub Family Foundation is thankfully acknowledged.

References

Allouah, Amine, and Besbes, Omar. 2018. Prior-independent optimal auctions. In *Proceedings of the 19th ACM Conference on Economics and Computation (EC)*, p. 503.

Azar, Pablo Daniel, and Micali, Silvio. 2013. Parametric digital auctions. In *Proceedings of the 4th Innovations in Theoretical Computer Science Conference*, pp. 231–232.

Azar, Pablo Daniel, Daskalakis, Constantinos, Micali, Silvio, and Weinberg, S. Matthew. 2013. Optimal and efficient parametric auctions. In *Proceedings of 24th ACM-SIAM Symposium on Discrete Algorithms (SODA)*, pp. 596–604.

Babaioff, Moshe, Gonczarowski, Yannai A., Mansour, Yishay, and Moran, Shay. 2018. Are two (samples) really better than one? In *Proceedings of the 19th ACM Conference on Economics and Computation (EC)*, p. 175.

Balcan, Maria-Florina, Blum, Avrim, Hartline, Jason D., and Mansour, Yishay. 2008. Reducing mechanism design to algorithm design via machine learning. *Journal of Computer and System Sciences*, **74**(8), 1245–1270.

Bandi, Chaithanya, and Bertsimas, Dimitris. 2014. Optimal design for multi-item auctions: A robust optimization approach. *Mathematics of Operations Research*, **39**(4), 1012–1038.

Beyhaghi, Hedyeh, and Weinberg, S. Matthew. 2019. Optimal (and benchmark-optimal) competition complexity for additive buyers over independent items. In *Proceedings of the 51st ACM Symposium on Theory of Computing (STOC)*, pp. 686–696.

Bulow, Jeremy, and Klemperer, Paul. 1996. Auctions versus negotiations. *American Economic Review*, **86**(1), 180–194.

Chawla, Shuchi, Hartline, Jason D., Malec, David L., and Sivan, Balasubramanian. 2010. Multi-parameter mechanism design and sequential posted pricing. In *Proceedings of the 42nd ACM Symposium on Theory of Computing (STOC)*, pp. 311–320.

Chawla, Shuchi, Hartline, Jason D., Malec, David L., and Sivan, Balasubramanian. 2013. Prior-independent mechanisms for scheduling. In *Proceedings of the 45th ACM Symposium on Theory of Computing (STOC)*, pp. 51–60.

Cole, Richard, and Roughgarden, Tim. 2014. The sample complexity of revenue maximization. In *Proceedings of the 46th ACM Symposium on Theory of Computing (STOC)*, pp. 243–252.

Devanur, Nikhil R., Hartline, Jason D., Karlin, Anna R., and Nguyen, C. Thach. 2011. Prior-independent multi-parameter mechanism design. In *Proceedings of the 7th Conference on Web and Internet Economics (WINE)*, pp. 122–133.

Dhangwatnotai, Peerapong, Roughgarden, Tim, and Yan, Qiqi. 2015. Revenue maximization with a single sample. *Games and Economic Behavior*, **91**, 318–333.

Eden, Alon, Feldman, Michal, Friedler, Ophir, Talgam-Cohen, Inbal, and Weinberg, S. Matthew. 2017. The competition complexity of auctions: A Bulow-Klemperer result for multi-dimensional bidders. In *Proceedings of the 18th ACM Conference on Economics and Computation (EC)*, p. 343.

Elkind, Edith. 2007. Designing and learning optimal finite support auctions. In *Proceedings of the 18th ACM-SIAM Symposium on Discrete Algorithms (SODA)*, pp. 736–745.

Feldman, Michal, Friedler, Ophir, and Rubinstein, Aviad. 2018. 99% revenue via enhanced competition. In *Proceedings of the 19th ACM Conference on Economics and Computation (EC)*, pp. 443–460.

Feng, Yiding, and Hartline, Jason D. 2018. An end-to-end argument in mechanism Design. In *59th IEEE Symposium on Foundations of Computer Science (FOCS)*, pp. 404–415.

Fu, Hu, Hartline, Jason D., and Hoy, Darrell. 2013. Prior-independent auctions for risk-averse agents. In *Proceedings of the 14th ACM Conference on Electronic Commerce (EC)*, pp. 471–488.

Fu, Hu, Immorlica, Nicole, Lucier, Brendan, and Strack, Philipp. 2015. Randomization beats second price as a prior-independent auction. In *Proceedings of the 16th ACM Conference on Economics and Computation (EC)*, p. 323.

Fu, Hu, Liaw, Christopher, and Randhawa, Sikander. 2019. The Vickrey auction with a single duplicate bidder approximates the optimal revenue. In *Proceedings of the 20th ACM Conference on Economics and Computation (EC)*, pp. 419–426.

Goldner, Kira, and Karlin, Anna R. 2016. A prior-independent revenue-maximizing auction for multiple additive bidders. In *Proceedings of the 12th Conference on Web and Internet Economics (WINE)*, pp. 160–173.

Guo, Chenghao, Huang, Zhiyi, and Zhang, Xinzhi. 2019. Settling the sample complexity of single-parameter revenue maximization. In *Proceedings of the 51st ACM Symposium on Theory of Computing (STOC)*, pp. 662–673.

Hartline, Jason D. 2019a. Prior-free mechanisms. *Mechanism Design and Approximation*, Chapter 6. Book draft available at http://jasonhartline.com/MDnA/.

Hartline, Jason D. 2019b. Prior-independent approximation. *Mechanism Design and Approximation*, Chapter 5.

Liu, Siqi, and Psomas, Christos-Alexandros. 2018. On the competition complexity of dynamic mechanism design. *Proceedings of the 29th ACM-SIAM Symposium on Discrete Algorithms (SODA)*, pp. 2008–2025.

Morgenstern, Jamie, and Roughgarden, Tim. 2016. Learning simple auctions. In *Proceedings of the 29th COLT*, pp. 1298–1318.

Roughgarden, Tim. 2017. *Beyond Worst-Case Analysis*. Lecture notes available at http://timroughgarden.org/w17/w17.html.

Roughgarden, Tim, and Talgam-Cohen, Inbal. 2016. Optimal and robust mechanism design with interdependent values. *ACM Transactions on Economics and Comput.*, **4**(3), 18:1–18:34.

Roughgarden, Tim, Talgam-Cohen, Inbal, and Yan, Qiqi. In press. Robust auctions for revenue via enhanced competition. To appear in *Operations Research*.

Segal, Ilya. 2003. Optimal pricing mechanisms with unknown demand. *American Economic Review*, **93**(3), 509–529.

Sivan, Balasubramanian. 2013. *Prior Robust Optimization*. PhD thesis, University of Wisconsin.

Sivan, Balasubramanian, and Syrgkanis, Vasilis. 2013. Vickrey Auctions for Irregular distributions. In *Proceedings of the 9th WINE*. pp. 422–435.

Tang, Pingzhong, and Zeng, Yulong. 2018. The price of prior dependence in auctions. In *Proceedings of the 19th ACM Conference on Economics and Computation (EC)*, pp. 485–502.

Yan, Qiqi. 2012. *Prior Independence: A New Lens for Mechanism Design*. PhD thesis, Stanford University.

Exercises

Exercise 27.1 Prove Lemma 27.2.: In a single-item setting, let $\text{OPT}(\kappa)$ be the optimal expected revenue from κ bidders with i.i.d. values. Show that for every pair of integers $k, \ell > 0$,

$$\text{OPT}(k) \geq \frac{k}{k + \ell} \text{OPT}(k + \ell).$$

Exercise 27.2 Let F be a continuous, regular distribution with bounded support, and let p^* be its monopoly price. Fix a threshold $t \geq 0$. Show that

$$\mathbf{E}_{p \sim F}[\max\{t, p\}(1 - F(\max\{t, p\}))] \geq \frac{1}{2} \max\{t, p^*\}(1 - F(\max\{t, p^*\})).$$

CHAPTER TWENTY EIGHT

Distribution-Free Models of Social Networks

Tim Roughgarden and C. Seshadhri

Abstract: The structure of large-scale social networks has predominantly been articulated using generative models, a form of average-case analysis. This chapter surveys recent proposals of more robust models of such networks. These models posit deterministic and empirically supported combinatorial structure rather than a specific probability distribution. We discuss the formal definitions of these models and how they relate to empirical observations in social networks, as well as the known structural and algorithmic results for the corresponding graph classes.

28.1 Introduction

Technological developments in the twenty-first century have given rise to large-scale social networks, such as the graphs defined by Facebook friendship relationships or followers on Twitter. Such networks arguably provide the most important new application domain for graph analysis in well over a decade.

28.1.1 Social Networks Have Special Structure

There is wide consensus that social networks have predictable structure and features, and accordingly are not well modeled by arbitrary graphs. From a structural viewpoint, the most well studied and empirically validated properties of social networks are:

1. A heavy-tailed degree distribution, such as a power-law distribution.
2. Triadic closure, meaning that pairs of vertices with a common neighbor tend to be directly connected – that friends of friends tend to be friends in their own right.
3. The presence of "community-like structures," meaning subgraphs that are much more richly connected internally than externally.
4. The small-world property, meaning that it's possible to travel from any vertex to any other vertex using remarkably few hops.

These properties are not generally possessed by Erdős–Rényi random graphs (in which each edge is present independently with some probability p); a new model is needed to capture them.

From an algorithmic standpoint, empirical results indicate that optimization problems are often easier to solve in social networks than in worst-case graphs. For example, lightweight heuristics are unreasonably effective in practice for finding the maximum clique or recovering dense subgraphs of a large social network.

The literature on models that capture the special structure of social networks is almost entirely driven by the quest for generative (i.e., probabilistic) models that replicate some or all of the four properties listed earlier. Dozens of generative models have been proposed, and there is little consensus about which is the "right" one. The plethora of models poses a challenge to meaningful theoretical work on social networks–which of the models, if any, is to be believed? How can we be sure that a given algorithmic or structural result is not an artifact of the model chosen?

This chapter surveys recent research on more robust models of large-scale social networks, which assume deterministic combinatorial properties rather than a specific generative model. Structural and algorithmic results that rely only on these deterministic properties automatically carry over to any generative model that produces graphs possessing these properties (with high probability). Such results effectively apply "in the worst case over all plausible generative models." This hybrid of worst-case (over input distributions) and average-case (with respect to the distribution) analysis resembles several of the semirandom models discussed elsewhere in the book, such as in the preceding chapters on pseudorandom data (Chapter 26) and prior-independent auctions (Chapter 27).

Sections 28.2 and 28.3 of this chapter cover two models of social networks that are motivated by triadic closure, the second of the four signatures of social networks listed in Section 28.1. Sections 28.4 and 28.5 discuss two models motivated by heavy-tailed degree distributions.

28.2 Cliques of c-Closed Graphs

28.2.1 Triadic Closure

Triadic closure is the property that, when two members of a social network have a friend in common, they are likely to be friends themselves. In graph-theoretic terminology, two-hop paths tend to induce triangles.

Triadic closure has been studied for decades in the social sciences and there is compelling intuition for why social networks should exhibit strong triadic closure properties. Two people with a common friend are much more likely to meet than two arbitrary people, and are likely to share common interests. They might also feel pressure to be friends to avoid imposing stress on their relationships with their common friend.

The data support this intuition. Numerous large-scale studies on online social networks provide overwhelming empirical evidence for triadic closure. The plot in Figure 28.1, derived from the network of email communications at the disgraced energy company Enron, is representative. Other social networks exhibit similar triadic closure properties.

28.2.2 c-Closed Graphs

The most extreme version of triadic closure would assert that whenever two vertices have a common neighbor, they are themselves neighbors: whenever (u, v) and (v, w)

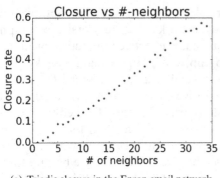

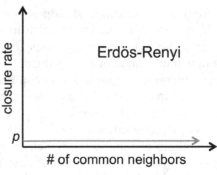

(a) Triadic closure in the Enron email network   (b) Triadic closure in a random graph

Figure 28.1 In the Enron email graph, vertices correspond to Enron employees, and there is an edge connecting two employees if one sent at least one email to the other. In (a), vertex pairs of this graph are grouped according to the number of common neighbors (indicated on the x-axis). The y-axis shows the fraction of such pairs that are themselves connected by an edge. The edge density – the fraction of arbitrary vertex pairs that are directly connected – is roughly 10^{-4}. In (b), a cartoon of the analogous plot for an Erdős–Rényi graph with edge density $p = 10^{-4}$ is shown. Erdős–Rényi graphs are not a good model for networks like the Enron network – their closure rate is too small, and the closure rate fails to increase as the number of common neighbors increases.

are in the edge set E, so is (u, w). The class of graphs satisfying this property is not very interesting – it is precisely the (vertex-)disjoint unions of cliques – but it forms a natural base case for more interesting parameterized definitions.[1]

Our first definition of a class of graphs with strong triadic closure properties is that of *c-closed graphs*.

Definition 28.1 (Fox et al., 2020)   For a positive integer c, a graph $G = (V, E)$ is *c-closed* if, whenever $u, v \in V$ have at least c common neighbors, $(u, v) \in E$.

For a fixed number of vertices, the parameter c interpolates between unions of cliques (when $c = 1$) and all graphs (when $c = |V| - 1$). The class of 2-closed graphs—the graphs that do not contain a square (i.e., $K_{2,2}$) or a diamond (i.e., K_4 minus an edge) as an induced subgraph – is already nontrivial. The c-closed condition is a coarse proxy for the empirical closure rates observed in social networks (like in Figure 28.1), asserting that the closure rate jumps to 100% for vertices with c or more common neighbors.

Next is a less stringent version of the definition, which is sufficient for the main algorithmic result of this section.

Definition 28.2 (Fox et al., 2020)   For a positive integer c, a vertex v of a graph $G = (V, E)$ is *c-good* if whenever v has at least c common neighbors with another vertex u, $(u, v) \in E$. The graph G is *weakly c-closed* if every induced subgraph has at least one c-good vertex.

A c-closed graph is also weakly c-closed, as each of its vertices is c-good in each of its induced subgraphs. The converse is false; for example, a path graph is not

---

[1] Recall that a *clique* of a graph $G = (V, E)$ is a subset $S \subseteq V$ of vertices that are fully connected, meaning that $(u, v) \in E$ for every pair u, v of distinct vertices of S.

Table 28.1 The c-closure and weak c-closure of four well-studied social networks from the SNAP (Stanford Large Network Dataset) collection of benchmarks (http://snap.stanford.edu/)

	n	m	c	weak c
email-Enron	36692	183831	161	34
p2p-Gnutella04	10876	39994	24	8
wiki-Vote	7115	103689	420	42
ca-GrQc	5242	14496	41	9

"email-Enron" is the network described in Figure 28.1; "p2p-Gnutella04" is the topology of a Gnutella peer-to-peer network circa 2002; "wiki-Vote" is the network of who votes on whom in promotion cases on Wikipedia; and "ca-GrQc" is the collaboration network of authors of papers uploaded to the General Relativity and Quantum Cosmology section of arXiv. For each network G, n indicates the number of vertices, m the number of edges, c the smallest value γ such that G is γ-closed, and "weak c" the smallest value γ such that G is weakly γ-closed.

1-closed, but it is weakly 1-closed (as the endpoints of a path are 1-good). Equivalent to Definition 28.2 is the condition that the graph G has an elimination ordering of c-good vertices, meaning the vertices can be ordered $v_1, v_2, \ldots, v_n$ such that, for every $i = 1, 2, \ldots, n$, the vertex v_i is c-good in the subgraph induced by $v_i, v_{i+1}, \ldots, v_n$ (Exercise 28.1). Are real-world social networks c-closed or weakly c-closed for reasonable values of c? Table 28.1 summarizes some representative numbers.

These social networks are c-closed for much smaller values of c than the trivial bound of $n - 1$, and are weakly c-closed for quite modest values of c.

28.2.3 Computing a Maximum Clique: A Backtracking Algorithm

Once a class of graph has been defined, such as c-closed graphs, a natural agenda is to investigate fundamental optimization problems with graphs restricted to the class. We single out the problem of finding the maximum-size clique of a graph, primarily because it is one of the most central problems in social network analysis. In a social network, cliques can be interpreted as the most extreme form of a community.

The problem of computing the maximum clique of a graph reduces to the problem of enumerating the graph's maximal cliques[2] – the maximum clique is also maximal, so it appears as the largest of the cliques in the enumeration.

How does the c-closed condition help with the efficient computation of a maximum clique? We next observe that the problem of reporting all maximal cliques is polynomial-time solvable in c-closed graphs when c is a fixed constant. The algorithm is based on backtracking. For convenience, we give a procedure that, for any vertex v, identifies all maximal cliques that contain v. (The full procedure loops over all vertices.)

1. Maintain a history H, initially empty.
2. Let N denote the vertex set comprising v and all vertices w that are adjacent to both v and all vertices in H.

---

[2] A maximal clique is a clique that is not a strict subset of another clique.

3. If N is a clique, report the clique $H \cup N$ and return.
4. Otherwise, recurse on each vertex $w \in N \setminus \{v\}$ with history $H := H \cup \{v\}$.

This subroutine reports all maximal cliques that contain v, whether the graph is c-closed or not (Exercise 28.2). In a c-closed graph, the maximum depth of the recursion is c – once $|H| = c - 1$, every pair of vertices in $N \setminus \{v\}$ has c common neighbors (namely $H \cup \{v\}$) and hence N must be a clique. The running time of the backtracking algorithm is therefore $n^{c+O(1)}$ in c-closed graphs.

This simplistic backtracking algorithm is extremely slow except for very small values of c. Can we do better?

28.2.4 Computing a Maximum Clique: Fixed-Parameter Tractability

There is a simple but clever algorithm that, for an arbitrary graph, enumerates all of the maximal cliques while using only polynomial time per clique.

Theorem 28.3 (Tsukiyama et al., 1977) *There is an algorithm that, given any input graph with n vertices and m edges, outputs all of the maximal cliques of the graph in $O(mn)$ time per maximal clique.*

Theorem 28.3 reduces the problem of enumerating all maximal cliques in polynomial time to the combinatorial task of proving a polynomial upper bound on the number of maximal cliques.

Computing a maximum clique of an arbitrary graph is an *NP*-hard problem, so presumably there exist graphs with an exponential number of maximal cliques. The *Moon–Moser graphs* are a simple and famous example. For n a multiple of 3, the Moon–Moser graph with n vertices is the perfectly balanced $\frac{n}{3}$-tite graph, meaning the vertices are partitioned into $\frac{n}{3}$ groups of 3, and every vertex is connected to every other vertex except for the 2 vertices in the same group (Figure 28.2). Choosing one vertex from each group induces a maximal clique, for a total of $3^{n/3}$ maximal cliques, and these are all of the maximal cliques of the graph. More generally, a basic result in graph theory asserts that *no n-vertex graph can have more than $3^{n/3}$ maximal cliques.*

Theorem 28.4 (Moon and Moser, 1965) *Every n-vertex graph has at most $3^{n/3}$ maximal cliques.*

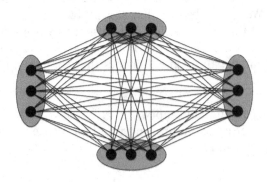

Figure 28.2 The Moon–Moser graph with $n = 12$ vertices.

A Moon–Moser graph on n vertices is not c-closed even for $c = n - 3$, so there remains hope for a positive result for c-closed graphs with small c. The Moon–Moser graphs do show that the number of maximal cliques of a c-closed graph can be exponential in c (since a Moon–Moser graph on c vertices is trivially c-closed). Thus the best-case scenario for enumerating the maximal cliques of a c-closed graph is a fixed-parameter tractability result (with respect to the parameter c), stating that, for some function f and constant d (independent of c), the number of maximal cliques in an n-vertex c-closed graph is $O(f(c) \cdot n^d)$. The next theorem shows that this is indeed the case, even for weakly c-closed graphs.

Theorem 28.5 (Fox et al., 2020) *Every weakly c-closed graph with n vertices has at most*

$$3^{(c-1)/3} \cdot n^2$$

maximal cliques.

The following corollary is immediate from Theorems 28.3 and 28.5.

Corollary 28.6 *The maximum clique problem is polynomial-time solvable in weakly c-closed n-vertex graphs with $c = O(\log n)$.*

28.2.5 Proof of Theorem 28.5

The proof of Theorem 28.5 proceeds by induction on the number of vertices n. (One of the factors of n in the bound is from the n steps in this induction.) Let G be an n-vertex weakly c-closed graph. Assume that $n \geq 3$; otherwise, the bound is trivial.

By assumption, G has a c-good vertex v. By induction, $G \setminus \{v\}$ has at most $(n - 1)^2 \cdot 3^{(c-1)/3}$ maximal cliques. (An induced subgraph of a weakly c-closed graph is again weakly c-closed.) Every maximal clique C of $G \setminus \{v\}$ gives rise to a unique maximal clique in G (namely C or $C \cup \{v\}$, depending on whether the latter is a clique). It remains to bound the number of *uncounted* maximal cliques of G, meaning the maximal cliques K of G for which $K \setminus \{v\}$ is not maximal in $G \setminus \{v\}$.

An uncounted maximal clique K must include v, with K contained in v's neighborhood (i.e., in the subgraph induced by v and the vertices adjacent to it). Also, there must be a vertex $u \notin K$ such that $K \setminus \{v\} \cup \{u\}$ is a clique in $G \setminus \{v\}$; we say that u is a *witness* for K, as it certifies the nonmaximality of $K \setminus \{v\}$ in $G \setminus \{v\}$. Such a witness must be connected to every vertex of $K \setminus \{v\}$. It cannot be a neighbor of v, as otherwise $K \cup \{u\}$ would be a clique in G, contradicting K's maximality.

Choose an arbitrary witness for each uncounted clique of G and bucket these cliques according to their witness; recall that all witnesses are non-neighbors of v. For every uncounted clique K with witness u, all vertices of the clique $K \setminus \{v\}$ are connected to both v and u. Moreover, because K is a maximal clique in G, $K \setminus \{v\}$ is a maximal clique in the subgraph G_u induced by the common neighbors of u and v.

How big can such a subgraph G_u be? This is the step of the proof where the weakly c-closed condition is important: Because u is a nonneighbor of v and v is a c-good vertex, u and v have at most $c - 1$ common neighbors and hence G_u has at most $c - 1$ vertices (Figure 28.3). By the Moon–Moser theorem (Theorem 28.4), each

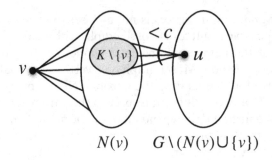

$N(v)$ $G \setminus (N(v) \cup \{v\})$

Figure 28.3 Proof of Theorem 28.5. $N(v)$ denotes the neighbors of v. K denotes a maximal clique of G such that $K \setminus \{v\}$ is not maximal in $G \setminus \{v\}$. There is a vertex u, not connected to v, that witnesses the nonmaximality of $K \setminus \{v\}$ in $G \setminus \{v\}$. Because v is a c-good vertex, u and v have at most $c - 1$ common neighbors.

subgraph G_u has at most $3^{(c-1)/3}$ maximal cliques. Adding up over the at most n choices for u, the number of uncounted cliques is at most $n \cdot 3^{(c-1)/3}$; this sum over possible witnesses is the source of the second factor of n in Theorem 28.5. Combining this bound on the uncounted cliques with the inductive bound on the remaining maximal cliques of G yields the desired upper bound of

$$(n-1)^2 \cdot 3^{(c-1)/3} + n \cdot 3^{(c-1)/3} \leq n^2 \cdot 3^{(c-1)/3}.$$

28.3 The Structure of Triangle-Dense Graphs

28.3.1 Triangle-Dense Graphs

Our second graph class inspired by the strong triadic closure properties of social and information networks is the class of δ-*triangle-dense* graphs. These are graphs where a constant fraction of vertex pairs having at least one common neighbor are directly connected by an edge. Equivalently, a constant fraction of the wedges (i.e., two-hop paths) of the graph belong to a triangle.

Definition 28.7 (Gupta et al., 2016) The *triangle density* of an undirected graph G is $\tau(G) := 3t(G)/w(G)$, where $t(G)$ and $w(G)$ denote the number of triangles and wedges of G, respectively. (We define $\tau(G) = 0$ if $w(G) = 0$.) The class of δ-*triangle-dense graphs* consists of the graphs G with $\tau(G) \geq \delta$.

(In the social networks literature, this is also called the *transitivity* or the *global clustering coefficient*.) Because every triangle of a graph contains three wedges, and no two triangles share a wedge, the triangle density of a graph is between 0 and 1 – the fraction of wedges that belong to a triangle. Triangle density is another coarse proxy for the empirical closure rates observed in social networks (like in Figure 28.1a).

The 1-triangle-dense graphs are precisely the unions of disjoint cliques, while triangle-free graphs constitute the 0-triangle-dense graphs. The triangle density of an Erdős–Rényi graph with edge probability p is concentrated around p (cf., Figure 28.1b). For an Erdős–Rényi graph to have constant triangle density, one would need to set $p = \Omega(1)$. This would imply that the graph is dense, quite unlike social networks. For example, in the year 2011 the triangle density of the Facebook graph was computed to be 0.16, which is five orders of magnitude larger than in a random

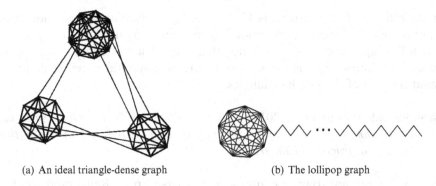

(a) An ideal triangle-dense graph   (b) The lollipop graph

Figure 28.4 Two examples of δ-triangle-dense graphs with δ close to 1.

graph with the same number of vertices (roughly 1 billion at the time) and edges (roughly 100 billion).

28.3.2 Visualizing Triangle-Dense Graphs

What do δ-triangle-dense graphs look like? Can we make any structural assertions about them, akin to separator theorems for planar graphs (allowing them to be viewed as "approximate grids") or the regularity lemma for dense graphs (allowing them to viewed as approximate unions of random bipartite graphs)?

Given that 1-triangle-dense graphs are unions of cliques, a first guess might be that δ-triangle-dense graphs look like the approximate union of approximate cliques (as in Figure 28.4a). Such graphs certainly have high triangle density; could there be an "inverse theorem," stating that these are in some sense the *only* graphs with this property?

In its simplest form, the answer to this question is "no," as δ-triangle-dense graphs become quite diverse once δ is bounded below 1. For example, adding a clique on $n^{2/5}$ vertices to an arbitrary bounded-degree n-vertex graph produces a δ-triangle-dense graph with $\delta = 1 - o(1)$ as $n \to \infty$ (see Figure 28.4b).

Nonetheless, an inverse theorem *does* hold if we redefine what it means to approximate a graph by a collection of approximate cliques. Instead of trying to capture most of the vertices or edges (which is impossible, as the previous example shows), we consider the goal of capturing a constant fraction of the *triangles* of a graph by a collection of dense subgraphs.

28.3.3 An Inverse Theorem

To state an inverse theorem for triangle-dense graphs, we require a preliminary definition.

Definition 28.8 (Tightly-Knit Family) Let $\rho > 0$. A collection $V_1, V_2, \ldots, V_k$ of disjoint sets of vertices of a graph $G = (V, E)$ forms a ρ-*tightly-knit family* if

1. For each $i = 1, 2, \ldots, k$, the subgraph induced by V_i has at least $\rho \cdot \binom{|V_i|}{2}$ edges and $\rho \cdot \binom{|V_i|}{3}$ triangles. (That is, a ρ-fraction of the maximum possible edges and triangles.)
2. For each $i = 1, 2, \ldots, k$, the subgraph induced by V_i has radius at most 2.

In Definition 28.8, the vertex sets $V_1, V_2, \ldots, V_k$ are disjoint but need not cover all of V; in particular, the empty collection is technically a tightly-knit family.

The following inverse theorem states that every triangle-dense graph contains a tightly-knit family that captures most of the "meaningful social structure" – a constant fraction of the graph's triangles.

Theorem 28.9 (Gupta et al., 2016) *There is a function $f(\delta) = O(\delta^4)$ such that for every δ-triangle dense graph G, there exists an $f(\delta)$-tightly-knit family that contains an $f(\delta)$ fraction of the triangles of G.*

Graphs that are not triangle dense, such as sparse Erdős–Rényi random graphs, do not generally admit ρ-tightly-knit families with constant ρ. The complete tripartite graph shows that Theorem 28.9 does not hold if the "radius-2" condition in Definition 28.7 is strengthened to "radius-1" (Exercise 28.4).

28.3.4 Proof Sketch of Theorem 28.9

The proof of Theorem 28.9 is constructive, and interleaves two subroutines. To state the first, define the *Jaccard similarity* of an edge (u, v) of a graph G as the fraction of neighbors of u and v that are neighbors of both:

$$\frac{|N(u) \cap N(v)|}{|N(u) \cup N(v)| - 2},$$

where $N(\cdot)$ denotes the neighbors of a vertex and the "-2" is to avoid counting u and v themselves. The first subroutine, called the *cleaner*, is given a parameter ϵ as input and repeatedly deletes edges with Jaccard similarity less than ϵ until none remain. Removing edges from the graph is worrisome because it removes triangles, and Theorem 28.9 promises that the final tightly-knit family captures a constant fraction of the original graph's triangles. But removing an edge with low Jaccard similarity destroys many more wedges than triangles, and the number of triangles in the graph is at least a constant fraction of the number of wedges (because it is δ-triangle-dense). A charging argument along these lines shows that, provided ϵ is at most $\delta/4$, the cleaner cannot destroy more than a constant fraction of the graph's triangles.

The second subroutine, called the *extractor*, is responsible for extracting one of the clusters of the tightly-knit family from a graph in which all edges have Jaccard similarity at least ϵ. (Isolated vertices can be discarded from further consideration.) How is this Jaccard similarity condition helpful? One easy observation is that, post-cleaning, the graph is "approximately locally regular," meaning that the endpoints of any edge have degrees within a $\frac{1}{\epsilon}$ factor of each other. Starting from this fact, easy algebra shows that every one-hop neighborhood of the graph (i.e., the subgraph induced by a vertex and its neighbors) has constant (depending on ϵ) density in both edges and triangles, as required by Theorem 28.9. The bad news is that extracting a one-hop neighborhood can destroy almost all of a graph's triangles (Exercise 28.4). The good news is that supplementing a one-hop neighborhood with a judiciously chosen subset of the corresponding two-hop neighborhood (i.e., neighbors of neighbors) fixes the problem. Precisely, the extractor subroutine is given a graph G in which every edge has Jaccard similarity at least ϵ and proceeds as follows:

1. Let v be a vertex of G with the maximum degree. Let d_{max} denote v's degree and $N(v)$ its neighbors.
2. Calculate a score θ_w for every vertex w outside $\{v\} \cup N(v)$ equal to the number of triangles that include w and two vertices of $N(v)$. In other words, θ_w is the number of triangles that would be saved by supplementing the one-hop neighborhood $\{v\} \cup N(v)$ by w. (On the flip side, this would also destroy the triangles that contain w and two vertices outside $N(v)$.)
3. Return the union of $\{v\}$, $N(v)$, and up to d_{max} vertices outside $\{v\} \cup N(v)$ with the largest nonzero θ-scores.

It is clear that the extractor outputs a set S of vertices that induces a subgraph with radius at most 2. As with one-hop neighborhoods, easy algebra shows that, because every edge has Jaccard similarity at least ϵ, this subgraph is dense in both edges and triangles. The important nonobvious fact, whose proof is omitted here, is that the number of triangles saved by the extractor (i.e., triangles with all three vertices in its output) is at least a constant fraction of the number of triangles it destroys (i.e., triangles with one or two vertices in its output). It follows that alternating between cleaning and extracting (until no edges remain) will produce a tightly-knit family meeting the promises of Theorem 28.9.

28.4 Power-Law Bounded Networks

Arguably the most famous property of social and information networks, even more so than triadic closure, is a *power-law degree distribution*, also referred to as a heavy-tailed or scale-free degree distribution.

28.4.1 Power-Law Degree Distributions and Their Properties

Consider a simple graph $G = (V, E)$ with n vertices. For each positive integer d, let $n(d)$ denote the number of vertices of G with degree d. The sequence $\{n(d)\}$ is called the *degree distribution* of G. Informally, a degree distribution is said to be a *power-law with exponent* $\gamma > 0$ if $n(d)$ scales as n/d^γ.

There is some controversy about how to best fit power-law distributions to data, and whether such distributions are the "right" fit for the degree distributions in real-world social networks (as opposed to, say, lognormal distributions). Nevertheless, several of the consequences of a power-law degree distribution assumption are uncontroversial for social networks, and so a power-law distribution is a reasonable starting point for mathematical analysis.

This section studies the algorithmic benefits of assuming that a graph has an (approximately) power-law degree distribution, in the form of fast algorithms for fundamental graph problems. To develop our intuition about such graphs, let's do some rough calculations under the assumption that $n(d) = cn/d^\gamma$ (for some constant c) for every d up to the maximum degree d_{max}; think of d_{max} as n^β for some constant $\beta \in (0, 1)$.

First, we have the implication

$$\sum_{d \le d_{max}} n(d) = n \implies cn \sum_{d \le d_{max}} d^{-\gamma} = n. \tag{28.1}$$

When $\gamma \le 1$, $\sum_{d < \infty} d^{-\gamma}$ is a divergent series. In this case, we cannot satisfy the right-hand side of (28.1) with a constant c. For this reason, results on power-law degree distributions typically assume that $\gamma > 1$.

Next, the number of edges is exactly

$$\frac{1}{2} \sum_{d \le d_{max}} d \cdot n(d) = \frac{cn}{2} \sum_{d \le d_{max}} d^{-\gamma+1}. \tag{28.2}$$

Thus, up to constant factors, $\sum_{d \le d_{max}} d^{-\gamma+1}$ is the average degree. For $\gamma > 2$, $\sum_{d < \infty} d^{-\gamma+1}$ is a convergent series, and the graph has constant average degree. For this reason, much of the early literature on graphs with power-law degree distributions focused on the regime where $\gamma > 2$. When $\gamma = 2$, the average degree scales with $\log n$, and for $\gamma \in (1,2)$, it scales with $(d_{max})^{2-\gamma}$, which is polynomial in n.

One of the primary implications of a power-law degree distribution is upper bounds on the number of high-degree vertices. Specifically, under our assumption that $n(d) = cn/d^{\gamma}$, the number of vertices of degree *at least* k can be bounded by

$$\sum_{d=k}^{d_{max}} n(d) \le cn \sum_{d=k}^{\infty} d^{-\gamma} \le cn \int_k^{\infty} x^{-\gamma} \, dx = cnk^{-\gamma+1}/(\gamma - 1) = \Theta(nk^{-\gamma+1}). \tag{28.3}$$

28.4.2 PLB Graphs

The key definition in this section is a more plausible and robust version of the assumption that $n(d) = cn/d^{\gamma}$, for which the conclusions of calculations like those in Section 28.4.1 remain valid. The definition allows individual values of $n(d)$ to deviate from a true power law, while requiring (essentially) that the average value of $n(d)$ in sufficiently large intervals of d does follow a power law.

Definition 28.10 (Berry et al., 2015; Brach et al., 2016)   A graph G with degree distribution $\{n(d)\}$ is a *power-law bounded (PLB) graph with exponent* $\gamma > 1$ if there is a constant $c > 0$ such that

$$\sum_{d=2^r}^{2^{r+1}} n(d) \le cn \sum_{d=2^r}^{2^{r+1}} d^{-\gamma}$$

for all $r \ge 0$.

Many real-world social networks satisfy a mild generalization of this definition, in which $n(d)$ is allowed to scale with $n/(d + t)^{\gamma}$ for a "shift" $t \ge 0$; see the Notes for details. For simplicity, we continue to assume in this section that $t = 0$.

Definition 28.10 has several of the same implications as a pure power law assumption, including the following lemma (cf. (28.2)).

Lemma 28.11 *Suppose G is a PLB graph with exponent $\gamma > 1$. For every $c > 0$ and natural number k,*

$$\sum_{d \leq k} d^c \cdot n(d) = O\left(n \sum_{d \leq k} d^{c-\gamma}\right).$$

The proof of Lemma 28.11 is technical but not overly difficult; we do not discuss the details here.

The first part of the next lemma provides control over the number of high-degree vertices and is the primary reason why many graph problems are more easily solved on PLB graphs than on general graphs. The second part of the lemma bounds the number of wedges of the graph when $\gamma \geq 3$.

Lemma 28.12 *Suppose G is a PLB graph with exponent $\gamma > 1$. Then*

(a) $\sum_{d \geq k} n(d) = O(nk^{-\gamma+1})$.
(b) *Let W denote the number of wedges (i.e., two-hop paths). If $\gamma = 3$, $W = O(n \log n)$. If $\gamma > 3$, $W = O(n)$.*

Part (a) extends the computation in (28.3) to PLB graphs, while part (b) follows from Lemma 28.11 (see Exercise 28.5).

28.4.3 Counting Triangles

Many graph problems appear to be easier in PLB graphs than in general graphs. To illustrate this point, we single out the problem of *triangle counting*, which is one of the most canonical problems in social network analysis. For this section, we assume that our algorithms can determine in constant time if there is an edge between a given pair of vertices; these lookups can be avoided with a careful implementation (Exercise 28.6), but such details distract from the main analysis.

As a warm up, consider the following trivial algorithm to count (three times) the number of triangles of a given graph G ("Algorithm 1"):

* For every vertex u of G:
  - For every pair v, w of u's neighbors, check if u, v, and w form a triangle.

Note that the running time of Algorithm 1 is proportional to the number of wedges in the graph G. The following running time bound for triangle counting in PLB graphs is an immediate corollary of Lemma 28.12(b), applied to Algorithm 1.

Corollary 28.13 *Triangle counting in n-vertex PLB graphs with exponent 3 can be carried out in $O(n \log n)$ time. If the exponent is strictly greater than 3, it can be done in $O(n)$ time.*

Now consider an optimization of Algorithm 1 ("Algorithm 2"):

- Direct each edge of G from the lower-degree endpoint to the higher-degree endpoint (breaking ties lexicographically) to obtain a directed graph D.
- For every vertex u of D:
  - For every pair v, w of u's *out-neighbors*, check if u, v, and w form a triangle in G.

Each triangle is counted exactly once by Algorithm 2, in the iteration where the lowest-degree of its three vertices plays the role of u. Remarkably, this simple idea leads to massive time savings in practice.

A classical way to capture this running time improvement mathematically is to parameterize the input graph G by its *degeneracy*, which can be thought of as a refinement of the maximum degree. The degeneracy $\alpha(G)$ of a graph G can be computed by iteratively removing a minimum-degree vertex (updating the vertex degrees after each iteration) until no vertices remain; $\alpha(G)$ is then the largest degree of a vertex at the time of its removal. (For example, every tree has degeneracy equal to 1.) We have the following guarantee for Algorithm 2, parameterized by a graph's degeneracy:

Theorem 28.14 (Chiba and Nishizeki, 1985) *For every graph with m edges and degeneracy α, the running time of Algorithm 2 is $O(m\alpha)$.*

Every PLB graph with exponent $\gamma > 1$ has degeneracy $\alpha = O(n^{1/\gamma})$; see Exercise 28.8. For PLB graphs with $\gamma > 2$, we can apply Lemma 28.11 with $c = 1$ to obtain $m = O(n)$ and hence the running time of Algorithm 2 is $O(m\alpha) = O(n^{(\gamma+1)/\gamma})$.

Our final result for PLB graphs improves this running time bound, for all $\gamma \in (2, 3)$, through a more refined analysis.[3]

Theorem 28.15 (Brach et al., 2016) *In PLB graphs with exponent $\gamma \in (2, 3)$, Algorithm 2 runs in $O(n^{3/\gamma})$ time.*

Proof Let $G = (V, E)$ denote an n-vertex PLB graph with exponent $\gamma \in (2, 3)$. Denote the degree of vertex v in G by d_v and its out-degree in the directed graph D by d_v^+. The running time of Algorithm 2 is $O(n + \sum_v \binom{d_v^+}{2}) = O(n + \sum_v (d_v^+)^2)$, so the analysis boils down to bounding the out-degrees in D. One trivial upper bound is $d_v^+ \le d_v$ for every $v \in V$. Because every edge is directed from its lower-degree endpoint to its higher-degree endpoint, we also have $d_v^+ \le \sum_{d \ge d_v} n(d)$. By Claim 28.12(a), the second bound is $O(nd_v^{-\gamma+1})$. The second bound is better than the first roughly when $d_v \ge nd_v^{-\gamma+1}$, or equivalently when $d_v \ge n^{1/\gamma}$.

Let $V(d)$ denote the set of degree-d vertices of G. We split the sum over vertices according to how their degrees compare to $n^{1/\gamma}$, using the first bound for low-degree vertices and the second bound for high-degree vertices:

---

[3] The running time bound actually holds for all $\gamma \in (1, 3)$, but is an improvement only for $\gamma > 2$.

$$\sum_{v \in V} (d_v^+)^2 = \sum_d \sum_{v \in V(d)} (d_v^+)^2$$

$$\leq \sum_{d \leq n^{1/\gamma}} \sum_{v \in V(d)} d^2 + \sum_{d > n^{1/\gamma}} \sum_{v \in V(d)} O(n^2 d^{-2\gamma+2})$$

$$= \sum_{d \leq n^{1/\gamma}} d^2 \cdot n(d) + O\left(n^2 \cdot \sum_{d > n^{1/\gamma}} d^{-2\gamma+2} \cdot n(d)\right).$$

Applying Lemma 28.11 (with $c = 2$) to the sum over low-degree vertices, and using the fact that with $\gamma < 3$ the sum $\sum_d d^{2-\gamma}$ is divergent, we derive

$$\sum_{d \leq n^{1/\gamma}} d^2 \cdot n(d) = O\left(n \sum_{d \leq n^{1/\gamma}} d^{2-\gamma}\right) = O(n(n^{1/\gamma})^{3-\gamma}) = O(n^{3/\gamma}).$$

The second sum is over the highest-degree vertices, and Lemma 28.11 does not apply. On the other hand, we can invoke Claim 28.12(a) to obtain the desired bound:

$$n^2 \sum_{d > n^{1/\gamma}} d^{-2\gamma+2} \cdot n(d) \leq n^2 (n^{1/\gamma})^{-2\gamma+2} \sum_{d > n^{1/\gamma}} n(d)$$

$$= O(n^{2/\gamma} \cdot n(n^{1/\gamma})^{-\gamma+1})$$

$$= O(n^{3/\gamma}). \qquad \square$$

The same reasoning shows that Algorithm 2 runs in $O(n \log n)$ time in n-vertex PLB graphs with exponent $\gamma = 3$, and in $O(n)$ time in PLB graphs with $\gamma > 3$ (Exercise 28.9).

28.4.4 Discussion

Beyond triangle counting, which computational problems should we expect to be easier on PLB graphs than on general graphs? A good starting point is problems that are relatively easy on bounded-degree graphs. In many cases, fast algorithms for bounded-degree graphs remain fast for graphs with bounded degeneracy. In these cases, the degeneracy bound for PLB graphs (Exercise 28.8) can already lead to fast algorithms for such graphs. For example, this approach can be used to show that all of the cliques of a PLB graph with exponent $\gamma > 1$ can be enumerated in subexponential time (see Exercise 28.10). In some cases, like in Theorem 28.15, one can beat the bound from the degeneracy-based analysis through more refined arguments.

28.5 The BCT Model

This section gives an impressionistic overview of another set of deterministic conditions meant to capture properties of "typical networks," proposed by Borassi et al. (2017) and hereafter called the *BCT model*. The precise model is technical with a number of parameters; we give only a high-level description that ignores several complications.

To illustrate the main ideas, consider the problem of computing the *diameter* $\max_{u,v \in V} \text{dist}(u,v)$ of an undirected and unweighted n-vertex graph $G = (V,E)$, where $\text{dist}(u,v)$ denotes the shortest-path distance between u and v in G. Define the *eccentricity* of a vertex u by $\text{ecc}(u) := \max_{v \in V} \text{dist}(u,v)$, so that the diameter is the maximum eccentricity. The eccentricity of a single vertex can be computed in linear time using breadth-first search, which gives a quadratic-time algorithm for computing the diameter. Despite much effort, no subquadratic $(1+\varepsilon)$-approximation algorithm for computing the graph diameter is known for general graphs. Yet there are many heuristics that perform well in real-world networks. Most of these heuristics compute the eccentricities of a carefully chosen subset of vertices. An extreme example is the TwoSweep algorithm:

1. Pick an arbitrary vertex s, and perform breadth-first search from s to compute a vertex $t \in \text{argmax}_{v \in V} \text{dist}(s,v)$.
2. Use breadth-first search again to compute $\text{ecc}(t)$ and return the result.

This heuristic always produces a lower bound on a graph's diameter, and in practice usually achieves a close approximation. What properties of "real-world" graphs might explain this empirical performance?

The BCT model is largely inspired by the metric properties of random graphs. To explain, for a vertex s and natural number k, let $\tau_s(k)$ denote the smallest length ℓ so that there are at least k vertices at distance (exactly) ℓ from s. Ignoring the specifics of the random graph model, the ℓ-step neighborhoods (i.e., vertices at distance exactly ℓ) of a vertex in a random graph resemble uniform random sets of size increasing with ℓ. We next use this property to derive a heuristic upper bound on $\text{dist}(s,t)$. Define $\ell_s := \tau_s(\sqrt{n})$ and $\ell_t := \tau_t(\sqrt{n})$. Since the ℓ_s-step neighborhood of s and the ℓ_t-step neighborhood of t act like random sets of size $\sqrt{n}$, a birthday paradox argument implies that they intersect with nontrivial probability. If they do intersect, then $\ell_s + \ell_t$ is an upper bound on $\text{dist}(s,t)$. In any event, we can adopt this inequality as a deterministic graph property, which can be tested against real network data.[4]

Property 28.16 For all $s, t \in V$, $\text{dist}(s,t) \leq \tau_s(\sqrt{n}) + \tau_t(\sqrt{n})$.

One would expect this distance upper bound to be tight for pairs of vertices that are far away from each other, and in a reasonably random graph, this will be true for most of the vertex pairs. This leads us to the next property.[5]

Property 28.17 For all $s \in V$: for "most" $t \in V$, $\text{dist}(s,t) > \tau_s(\sqrt{n}) + \tau_t(\sqrt{n}) - 1$.

The third property posits a distribution on the $\tau_s(\sqrt{n})$ values. Let $T(k)$ denote the average $n^{-1} \sum_{s \in V} \tau_s(k)$.

Property 28.18 There are constants $c, \gamma > 0$ such that the fraction of vertices s satisfying $\tau_s(\sqrt{n}) \geq T(\sqrt{n}) + \gamma$ is roughly $c^{-\gamma}$.

---

[4] The actual BCT model uses the upper bound $\tau_s(n^x) + \tau_t(n^y)$ for $x + y > 1 + \delta$, to ensure intersection with high enough probability.

[5] We omit the exact definition of this property in the BCT model, which is quite involved.

A consequence of this property is that the largest value of $\tau_s(\sqrt{n})$ is $T(\sqrt{n}) + \log_c n + \Theta(1)$.

As we discuss in the text that follows, these properties will imply that simple heuristics work well for computing the diameter of a graph. On the other hand, these properties do not generally hold in real-world graphs. The actual BCT model has a nuanced version of these properties, parameterized by vertex degrees. In addition, the BCT model imposes an approximate power-law degree distribution, in the spirit of power-law bounded graphs (Definition 28.10 in Section 28.4). This nuanced list of properties can be empirically verified on a large set of real-world graphs.

Nonetheless, for understanding the connection of metric properties to diameter computation, it suffices to look at Properties 28.16–28.18. We can now bound the eccentricities of vertices. The properties imply that

$$\text{dist}(u, v) \leq \tau_u(\sqrt{n}) + \tau_v(\sqrt{n}) \leq \tau_u(\sqrt{n}) + T(\sqrt{n}) + \log_c n + O(1).$$

Fix u and imagine varying v to estimate $\text{ecc}(u)$. For "most" vertices v, $\text{dist}(u, v) \geq \tau_u(\sqrt{n}) + \tau_v(\sqrt{n}) - 1$. By Property 28.18, one of the vertices v satisfying this lower bound will also satisfy $\tau_v(\sqrt{n}) \geq T(\sqrt{n}) + \log_c n - \Theta(1)$. Combining, we can bound the eccentricity by

$$\text{ecc}(u) = \max_v \text{dist}(u, v) = \tau_u(\sqrt{n}) + T(\sqrt{n}) + \log_c n \pm \Theta(1). \tag{28.4}$$

The bound (28.4) is significant because it reduces maximizing $\text{ecc}(u)$ over $u \in V$ to maximizing $\tau_u(\sqrt{n})$.

Pick an arbitrary vertex s and consider a vertex u that maximizes $\text{dist}(s, u)$. By an argument similar to the one above (and because most vertices are far away from s), we expect that $\text{dist}(s, u) \approx \tau_s(\sqrt{n}) + \tau_u(\sqrt{n})$. Thus, a vertex u maximizing $\text{dist}(s, u)$ is almost the same as a vertex maximizing $\tau_u(\sqrt{n})$, which by (28.4) is almost the same as a vertex maximizing $\text{ecc}(u)$. This gives an explanation of why the TwoSweep algorithm performs so well. Its first use of breadth-first search identifies a vertex u that (almost) maximizes $\text{ecc}(u)$. The second pass of breadth-first search (from u) then computes a close approximation of the diameter.

The analysis in this section is heuristic, but it captures much of the spirit of algorithm analysis in the BCT model. These results for TwoSweep can be extended to other heuristics that choose a set of vertices through a random process to lower bound the diameter. In general, the key insight is that most distances $\text{dist}(u, v)$ in the BCT model can be closely approximated as a sum of quantities that depend only on either u or v.

28.6 Discussion

Let's take a bird's-eye view of this chapter. The big challenge in the line of research described in this chapter is the formulation of graph classes and properties that both reflect real-world graphs and lead to a satisfying theory. It seems unlikely that any one class of graphs will simultaneously capture all the relevant properties of (say) social networks. Accordingly, this chapter described several graph classes that target specific empirically observed graph properties, each with its own algorithmic lessons:

- Triadic closure aids the computation of dense subgraphs.

- Power-law degree distributions aid subgraph counting.
- ℓ-hop neighborhood structure influences the structure of shortest paths.

These lessons suggest that, when defining a graph class to capture "real-world" graphs, it may be important to keep a target algorithmic application in mind.

Different graph classes differ in how closely the definitions are tied to domain knowledge and empirically observed statistics. The c-closed and triangle-dense graph classes are in the spirit of classical families of graphs (e.g., planar or bounded-treewidth graphs), and they sacrifice precision in the service of generality, cleaner definitions, and arguably more elegant theory. The PLB and BCT frameworks take the opposite view: the graph properties are quite technical and involve many parameters, and in exchange tightly capture the properties of "real-world" graphs. These additional details can add fidelity to theoretical explanations for the surprising effectiveness of simple heuristics.

A big advantage of combinatorially defined graph classes – a hallmark of graph-theoretic work in theoretical computer science – is the ability to empirically validate them on real data. The standard statistical viewpoint taken in network science has led to dozens of competing generative models, and it is nearly impossible to validate the details of such a model from network data. The deterministic graph classes defined in this chapter give a much more satisfying foundation for algorithmics on real-world graphs.

Complex algorithms for real-world problems can be useful, but practical algorithms for graph analysis are typically based on simple ideas like backtracking or greedy algorithms. An ideal theory would reflect this reality, offering compelling explanations for why relatively simple algorithms have such surprising efficacy in practice.

We conclude this section with some open problems.

1. Theorem 28.5 gives, for constant c, a bound of $O(n^2)$ on the number of maximal cliques in a c-closed graph. Fox et al. (2020) also prove a sharper bound of $O(n^{2(1-2^{-c})})$, which is asymptotically tight when $c = 2$. Is it tight for all values of c? Additionally, parameterizing by the number of edges (m) rather than vertices (n), is the number of maximal cliques in a c-closed graph with $c = O(1)$ bounded by $O(m)$? Could there be a linear-time algorithm for maximal clique enumeration for c-closed graphs with constant c?

2. Theorem 28.9 guarantees the capture by a tightly-knit family of an $O(\delta^4)$ fraction of the triangles of a δ-triangle-dense graph. What is the best-possible constant in the exponent? Can the upper bound be improved, perhaps under additional assumptions (e.g., about the distribution of the clustering coefficients of the graph, rather than merely about their average)?

3. Ugander et al. (2013) observe that 4-vertex subgraph counts in real-world graphs exhibit predictable and peculiar behavior. By imposing conditions on 4-vertex subgraph counts (in addition to triangle density), can one prove decomposition theorems better than Theorem 28.9?

4. Is there a compelling algorithmic application for graphs that can be approximated by tightly-knit families?

5. Benson et al. (2016) and Tsourakakis et al. (2017) defined the *triangle conductance* of a graph, where cuts are measured in terms of the number of triangles cut (rather

than the number of edges). Empirical evidence suggests that cuts with low triangle conductance give more meaningful communities (i.e., denser subgraphs) than cuts with low (edge) conductance. Is there a plausible theoretical explanation for this observation?

6. A more open-ended goal is to use the theoretical insights described in this chapter to develop new and practical algorithms for fundamental graph problems.

28.7 Notes

The book by Easley and Kleinberg (2010) is a good introduction to social network analysis, including discussions of heavy-tailed degree distributions and triadic closure. A good if somewhat outdated review of generative models for social and information networks is Chakrabarti and Faloutsos (2006). The Enron email network was first studied by Klimt and Yang (2004).

The definitions of c-closed and weakly c-closed graphs (Definitions 28.1–28.2) are from Fox et al. (2020), as is the fixed-parameter tractability result for the maximum clique problem (Theorem 28.5). Eppstein et al. (2010) proved an analogous result with respect to a different parameter, the degeneracy of the input graph. The reduction from efficiently enumerating maximal cliques to bounding the number of maximal cliques (Theorem 28.3) is from Tsukiyama et al. (1977). Moon–Moser graphs and the Moon–Moser bound on the maximum number of maximal cliques of a graph are from Moon and Moser (1965).

The definition of triangle-dense graphs (Definition 28.7) and the inverse theorem for them (Theorem 28.9) are from Gupta et al. (2016). The computation of the triangle density of the Facebook graph is detailed by Ugander et al. (2011).

The definition of power law bounded graphs (Definition 28.10) first appeared in Berry et al. (2015) in the context of triangle counting, but it was formalized and applied to many different problems by Brach et al. (2016), including triangle counting (Theorem 28.15), clique enumeration (Exercise 28.10), and linear algebraic problems for matrices with a pattern of non-zeroes that induces a PLB graph. Brach et al. (2016) also performed a detailed empirical analysis, validating Definition 28.10 (with small shifts t) on real data. The degeneracy-parameterized bound for counting triangles is essentially due to Chiba and Nishizeki (1985).

The BCT model (Section 28.5) and the fast algorithm for computing the diameter of a graph are due to Borassi et al. (2017).

Acknowledgments

The authors thank Michele Borassi, Shweta Jain, Piotr Sankowski, and Inbal Talgam-Cohen for their comments on earlier drafts of this chapter.

References

Benson, A., Gleich, D. F., and Leskovec, J. 2016. Higher-order organization of complex networks. *Science*, **353**(6295), 163–166.

Berry, J. W., Fostvedt, L. A., Nordman, D. J., Phillips, C. A., Seshadhri, C., and Wilson, A. G. 2015. Why do simple algorithms for triangle enumeration work in the real world? *Internet Mathematics*, **11**(6), 555–571.

Borassi, M., Crescenzi, P., and Trevisan, L. 2017. An axiomatic and an average-case analysis of algorithms and heuristics for metric properties of graphs. *Proceedings of the Twenty-Eighth Annual ACM-SIAM Symposium on Discrete Algorithms (SODA)*, pp. 920–939.

Brach, Pawel, Cygan, Marek, Lacki, Jakub, and Sankowski, Piotr. 2016. Algorithmic complexity of power law networks. *Proceedings of the Twenty-Seventh Annual ACM-SIAM Symposium on Discrete Algorithms (SODA)*, pp. 1306–1325.

Chakrabarti, D., and Faloutsos, C. 2006. Graph mining: Laws, generators, and algorithms. *ACM Computing Surveys*, **38**(1), Article 2.

Chiba, N., and Nishizeki, T. 1985. Arboricity and subgraph listing algorithms. *SIAM Journal on Computing*, **14**(1), 210–223.

Easley, D., and Kleinberg, J. 2010. *Networks, Crowds, and Markets*. Cambridge University Press.

Eppstein, D., Löffler, M., and Strash, D. 2010. Listing all maximal cliques in sparse graphs in near-optimal time. *Proceedings of the 21st International Symposium on Algorithms and Computation (ISAAC)*, pp. 403–414.

Fox, J., Roughgarden, T., Seshadhri, C., Wei, F., and Wein, N. 2020. Finding cliques in social networks: A new distribution-free model. SIAM Journal on Computing, 49(2), 448–464.

Gupta, R., Roughgarden, T., and Seshadhri, C. 2016. Decompositions of triangle-dense graphs. *SIAM Journal on Computing*, **45**(2), 197–215.

Klimt, B., and Yang, Y. 2004. The Enron corpus: A new dataset for email classification research. *Proceedings of the 15th European Conference on Machine Learning (ECML)*, pp. 217–226.

Moon, J., and Moser, L. 1965. On cliques in graphs. *Israel Journal of Mathematics*, **3**, 23–28.

Tsourakakis, Charalampos E., Pachocki, Jakub W., and Mitzenmacher, Michael. 2017. Scalable motif-aware graph clustering. In *Proceedings of the Web Conference (WWW)*, vol. abs/1606.06235, pp. 1451–1460.

Tsukiyama, S., Ide, M., Ariyoshi, H., and Shirakawa, I. 1977. A new algorithm for generating all the maximal independent sets. *SIAM Journal on Computing*, **6**(3), 505–517.

Ugander, J., Karrer, B., Backstrom, L., and Marlow, C. 2011. The Anatomy of the Facebook Social Graph. arXiv:1111.4503.

Ugander, J., Backstrom, L., and Kleinberg, J. 2013. Subgraph frequencies: Mapping the empirical and extremal geography of large graph collections. *Proceedings of World Wide Web Conference*, pp. 1307–1318.

Exercises

Exercise 28.1 Prove that a graph is weakly c-closed in the sense of Definition 28.2 if and only if its vertices can be ordered $v_1, v_2, \ldots, v_n$ such that, for every $i = 1, 2, \ldots, n$, the vertex v_i is c-good in the subgraph induced by $v_i, v_{i+1}, \ldots, v_n$.

Exercise 28.2 Prove that the backtracking algorithm in Section 28.2.3 enumerates all of the maximal cliques of a graph.

Exercise 28.3 Prove that a graph has triangle density 1 if and only if it is a disjoint union of cliques.

Exercise 28.4 Let G be the complete regular tripartite graph with n vertices – three vertex sets of size $\frac{n}{3}$ each, with each vertex connected to every vertex of the other two groups and none of the vertices within the same group.

(a) What is the triangle density of the graph?

(b) What is the output of the cleaner (Section 28.3.4) when applied to this graph? What is then the output of the extractor?

(c) Prove that G admits no tightly-knit family that contains a constant fraction (as $n \to \infty$) of the graph's triangles and uses only radius-1 clusters.

Exercise 28.5 Prove Claim 28.12.

[Hint: To prove (a), break up the sum over degrees into sub-sums between powers of 2. Apply Definition 28.10 to each sub-sum.]

Exercise 28.6 Implement Algorithm 2 from Section 28.4.3 in $O(\sum_v (d_v^+)^2 + n)$ time, where d_v^+ is the number of out-neighbors of v in the directed version D of G, assuming that the input G is represented using only adjacency lists.

[Hint: You may need to store the in- and out-neighbor lists of D.]

Exercise 28.7 Prove that every graph with m edges has degeneracy at most $\sqrt{2m}$. Exhibit a family of graphs showing that this bound is tight (up to lower order terms).

Exercise 28.8 Suppose G is a PLB graph with exponent $\gamma > 1$.

(a) Prove that the maximum degree of G is $O(n^{1/(\gamma-1)})$.
(b) Prove that the degeneracy is $O(n^{1/\gamma})$.

[Hint: For (b), use the main idea in the proof of Exercise 28.7 and Claim 28.12.]

Exercise 28.9 Prove that Algorithm 2 in Section 28.4.3 runs in $O(n \log n)$ time and $O(n)$ time in n-vertex PLB graphs with exponents $\gamma = 3$ and $\gamma > 3$, respectively.

Exercise 28.10 Prove that all of the cliques of a graph with degeneracy α can be enumerated in $O(n 2^\alpha)$ time. (By Exercise 28.8(b), this immediately gives a subexponential-time algorithm for enumerating the cliques of a PLB graph.)

CHAPTER TWENTY NINE

Data-Driven Algorithm Design

Maria-Florina Balcan

Abstract: Data-driven algorithm design is an important aspect of modern data science and algorithm design. Rather than using off the shelf algorithms that only have worst-case performance guarantees, practitioners often optimize over large families of parameterized algorithms and tune the parameters of these algorithms using a training set of problem instances from their domain to determine a configuration with high expected performance over future instances. However, most of this work comes with no performance guarantees. The challenge is that for many combinatorial problems of significant importance including partitioning, subset selection, and alignment problems, a small tweak to the parameters can cause a cascade of changes in the algorithm's behavior, so the algorithm's performance is a discontinuous function of its parameters.

In this chapter, we survey recent work that helps put data-driven combinatorial algorithm design on firm foundations. We provide strong computational and statistical performance guarantees, both for the batch and online scenarios where a collection of typical problem instances from the given application are presented either all at once or in an online fashion, respectively.

29.1 Motivation and Context

The classic approach to designing and analyzing combinatorial algorithms (that has been the backbone of algorithmic research and applications since the field's inception) assumes that the algorithm we design for a given problem will be used to solve worst-case instances of the problem, about which the algorithm has absolutely no information at all. The typical performance guarantees we aim for, in this classic framework, require that the algorithm we design must succeed even for solving just a one-time, worst-case instance of the underlying algorithmic problem. While ideal in principle, for many problems such worst-case guarantees are often weak. Moreover, for many problems, empirically, different methods work better in different settings, and there are often large, even infinite parameterized families of methods that one could try to use. Consequently, rather than using off the shelf algorithms that have weak worst-case guarantees, practitioners often employ a data-driven algorithm design approach; specifically, given an application domain, they use machine learning and instances of the problem coming from the specific domain to learn a method that works best in that domain. This idea has long been used in practice in various communities, including artificial intelligence (Horvitz et al., 2001; Xu et al., 2008), computational biology (Blasio and Kececioglu, 2018), and auction design (Sandholm, 2003). However, so far, most of this work has come with no performance guarantees.

In this chapter we survey recent work that provides formal guarantees for this data-driven algorithm design approach, by building and significantly expanding on learning theory tools. We discuss both the batch and online scenarios in which a collection of typical problem instances from the given application are presented either all at once or in an online fashion, respectively. This includes nearly optimal sample complexity bounds for the batch scenario and no-regret guarantees for the online scenario for a number of important algorithmic families that include classic modules such as greedy, local search, dynamic programming, and semidefinite relaxation followed by rounding. These are applicable to a wide variety of combinatorial problems (e.g., subset selection, clustering, partitioning, and alignment problems) from diverse domains ranging from data science to computational biology to auction design. The key technical challenge is that for many of these problems, a small tweak to the parameters can cause a cascade of changes in the algorithm's behavior, so the algorithm's performance is a discontinuous function of its parameters.

At a technical level, this work draws on insights from some of the other approaches on algorithms beyond the worst case, including perturbation stability discussed in Chapter 5 and approximation stability discussed in Chapter 6. The motivation here is identical: many important optimization problems are unfortunately provably hard even to approximate well on worst-case instances, so using algorithms with worst-case guarantees might be pessimistic. The key difference is that that line of work aims to articulate specific regularities or stability properties that the input instances might satisfy, and to design algorithms that provably exploit them and overcome worst-case hardness results on instances satisfying them. In addition to providing algorithms with provable guarantees when these stability conditions hold, such analyses suggest interesting families of algorithms to learn over in the data-driven algorithm approach, which are even more broadly applicable (including in scenarios where verifying these properties might be hard). Indeed, some of the algorithm families we study in this chapter (in the context of clustering problems in particular) are directly inspired by these analyses.

This topic is related in spirit to several widely popular topics in machine learning, including hyperparameter tuning and meta-learning. The key difference here is that we focus on parametric families of functions induced by algorithms for solving discrete optimization problems, which leads to cost functions with sharp discontinuities. This leads to very interesting challenges that require new techniques that help significantly push the boundaries of learning theory as well.

As discussed in Chapter 12, the goals of data-driven algorithm design are similar to those of self-improving algorithms. The main take away of our chapter is that one can build on and extend tools from learning theory to achieve these goals for a wide variety of algorithmic problems.

29.2 Data-Driven Algorithm Design via Statistical Learning

Gupta and Roughgarden (2016, 2017) proposed analyzing data-driven algorithm design as a distributional learning problem, by using and extending the classic learning theory models, PAC (Valiant, 1984) and Statistical Learning Theory (Vapnik, 1998). In this framework, for a given algorithmic problem, we model an application domain as a distribution over problem instances, and assume that we have access to training instances that are drawn i.i.d from this fixed, but unknown distribution. The formal guarantees we aim for in this framework are generalization guarantees quantifying how many training problem instances are needed to ensure that an algorithm with good performance over the training instances will exhibit good performance on future problem instances. Such guarantees depend on the intrinsic complexity of the search space which in this case is a parameterized family of algorithms for the problem at hand, and this intrinsic dimension is quantified using learning theoretic measures.

The challenge, and the reason that theoretical analysis is needed, is that it could be that parameter settings that work well on past instances perform poorly on future instances due to overfitting to the training data. In particular, even if past and future instances are all drawn i.i.d. from the same probability distribution, if the algorithm family is sufficiently complex, it may be possible to set parameters that capture peculiarities of the training data (or even in the extreme case, memorize specific solutions to training instances), performing well on them without truly performing well on the instance distribution. Sample complexity analysis provides guarantees on how many training instances are sufficient, as a function of the complexity of the algorithm family, to ensure that with high probability no such overfitting occurs. Next, we formally describe the problem setup and how overfitting will be addressed through uniform convergence analysis.

Problem Formulation We fix an algorithmic problem (e.g., a subset selection problem or a clustering problem) and we denote by Π the set of problem instances of interest for this problem. We also fix $\mathcal{A}$ a large (potentially infinite) family of algorithms, and throughout this chapter we assume that this family is parameterized by a set $\mathcal{P} \subseteq \mathbb{R}^d$; we denote by A_ρ the algorithm in $\mathcal{A}$ parameterized by ρ. We also fix a utility function $u : \Pi \times \mathcal{P} \to [0, H]$, where $u(x, \rho)$ measures the performance of the algorithm A_ρ on problem instance $x \in \Pi$. We denote by $u_\rho(\cdot)$ the utility function $u : \Pi \to [0, H]$ induced by A_ρ, where $u_\rho(x) = u(x, \rho)$. Note that u is bounded; for example, for cases in which u is related to an algorithm's running time, H can be the time-out deadline.

The "application-specific information" is modeled by the unknown input distribution $\mathcal{D}$. The learning algorithm is given m i.i.d. samples $x_1, \ldots, x_m \in \Pi$ from $\mathcal{D}$, and (perhaps implicitly) the corresponding performance $u_\rho(x)$ of each algorithm $A_\rho \in \mathcal{A}$ on each input x_i. The learning algorithm uses this information to suggest an algorithm $A_{\hat{\rho}} \in \mathcal{A}$ to use on future inputs drawn from $\mathcal{D}$. We seek learning algorithms that almost always output an algorithm of $\mathcal{A}$ that performs almost as well as the optimal algorithm A_{ρ^*} for $\mathcal{D}$ that maximizes $\mathbb{E}_{x \sim \mathcal{D}}[u_\rho(x)]$ over $A_\rho \in \mathcal{A}$.

Knapsack As an example, a canonical problem we consider in this chapter is the knapsack problem. A knapsack instance x consists of n items, where each item i has a value v_i and a size s_i, together with an overall knapsack capacity C. Our goal is to find the most valuable subset of items whose total size does not exceed C. For this problem we analyze a family of greedy algorithms parameterized by a one dimensional set, $\mathcal{P} = \mathbb{R}$. For $\rho \in \mathcal{P}$, the algorithm A_ρ operates as follows. We set the score of item i to be v_i / s_i^ρ; then, in decreasing order of score, we add each item to the knapsack if there is enough capacity left (breaking ties by selecting the item of smallest index). The utility function $u_\rho(x) = u(x, \rho)$ is defined as the value of the items chosen by the greedy algorithm with parameter ρ on input x.

Uniform Convergence To achieve our desired guarantees, we rely on uniform convergence results, which roughly speaking specify how many training instances we need in order to guarantee that with high probability (over the draw of the training set of instances) we have that, uniformly, for all the algorithms in the class $\mathcal{A}$, their average performance over the sample is additively close to their expected performance on a typical (random) problem instance coming from the same distribution as the training set. It is known from emprical processes and learning theory that these uniform convergence results depend on the intrinsic complexity of the family of real-valued utility functions $\{u_\rho(\cdot)\}_\rho$. In this chapter we consider the pseudo-dimension as a measure of complexity, which roughly speaking quantifies the ability of the class to fit complex patterns.

Definition 29.1 (Pseudo-dimension) Let $\{u_\rho(\cdot)\}_\rho$ be the family of performance measures induced by $\mathcal{A} = \{A_\rho\}_\rho$ and the utility function $u(x, \rho)$.

(a) Let $\mathcal{S} = \{x_1, \ldots, x_m\} \subset \Pi$ be a set of problem instances and let $z_1, \ldots, z_m \in \mathbb{R}$ be a set of *targets*. We say that $z_1, \ldots, z_m$ *witness* the shattering of $\mathcal{S}$ by $\{u_\rho(\cdot)\}_\rho$ if for all subsets $T \subseteq \mathcal{S}$, there exists some parameter $\rho \in \mathcal{P}$ such that for all elements $x_i \in T$, $u_\rho(x_i) \leq z_i$ and for all $x_i \notin T$, $u_\rho(x_i) > z_i$. We say that $\mathcal{S}$ is *shattered* by $\{u_\rho(\cdot)\}_\rho$ if there exist $z_1, \ldots, z_m$ that witness its shattering.

(b) Let $\mathcal{S} \subseteq \Pi$ be the largest set that can be shattered by $\{u_\rho(\cdot)\}_\rho$. Then the pseudo-dimension of the class $\{u_\rho(\cdot)\}_\rho$ is $\mathrm{Pdim}(\{u_\rho(\cdot)\}_\rho) = |\mathcal{S}|$.

When $\{u_\rho(\cdot)\}_\rho$ is a set of binary valued functions, the notion of pseudo-dimension reduces to the notion of VC-dimension, covered in Chapter 16.

Theorem 29.2 *Let $d_\mathcal{A}$ be the pseudo-dimension of the family of utility functions $\{u_\rho(\cdot)\}_\rho$ induced by the class of algorithms $\mathcal{A}$ and the utility function $u(x, \rho)$; assume that the range of $u(x, \rho)$ is $[0, H]$. For any $\epsilon > 0$, any $\delta \in (0, 1)$ and any distribution $\mathcal{D}$ over Π, $m = O\left(\frac{H^2}{\epsilon^2}\left(d_\mathcal{A} + \ln \frac{1}{\delta}\right)\right)$ samples are sufficient to ensure that with probability $1 - \delta$ over the draw of m samples $\mathcal{S} = \{x_1, \ldots, x_m\} \sim \mathcal{D}^m$, for all $\rho \in \mathcal{P}$, the difference between the average utility of the algorithm A_ρ over the samples and its expected utiliy is $\leq \epsilon$, i.e.: $\left|\frac{1}{m}\sum_{i=1}^m u_\rho(x_i) - \mathbb{E}_{x \sim \mathcal{D}}[u_\rho(x)]\right| \leq \epsilon$.*

Theorem 29.2 implies that to obtain sample complexity guarantees it is sufficient to bound the pseudo-dimension of the family $\{u_\rho(x)\}_{\rho \in \mathcal{P}}$. Interestingly, many of the proofs in the literature for doing this proceed by providing (either implicitly or explicitly) a structural result for the dual class of functions, $\{u_x(\rho)\}_{x \in \Pi}$, where $u_x(\rho) = u(x, \rho) = u_\rho(x)$. We present in Lemma 29.3 a simple, but powerful lemma of this form, which we will use throughout the chapter for the case that our parameter vector ρ is just a single real number; this lemma is used implicitly or explicitly in several papers (Gupta and Roughgarden, 2016; Balcan et al., 2017, 2018d).

Lemma 29.3 *Suppose that for every instance $x \in \Pi$, the function $u_x(\rho) : \mathbb{R} \to \mathbb{R}$ is piecewise constant with at most N pieces. Then the family $\{u_\rho(x)\}$ has pseudo-dimension $O(\log N)$.*

Proof Consider a problem instance $x \in \Pi$. Since the function $u_x(\rho)$ is piecewise constant with at most N pieces, this means there are at most $N - 1$ *critical points* $\rho_1^*, \rho_2^*, \ldots$ such that between any two consecutive critical points ρ_i^* and ρ_{i+1}^*, the function $u_x(\rho)$ is constant.

Consider m problem instances $x_1, \ldots, x_m$. Taking the union of their critical points and sorting them, between any two consecutive of these critical points we have that *all* of the functions $u_{x_j}(\rho)$ are constant. Since these critical points break up the real line into at most $(N-1)m+1 \leq Nm$ intervals, and all $u_{x_j}(\rho)$ are constant in each interval, this means that overall there are at most Nm different m-tuples of values produced over all ρ. Equivalently, the functions $u_\rho(x)$ produce at most Nm different m-tuples of values on the m inputs $x_1, \ldots, x_m$. However, to shatter the m instances, we must have 2^m different m-tuples of values produced. Solving $Nm \geq 2^m$ shows that only sets of instances of size $m = O(\log N)$ can be shattered. $\qquad\square$

29.2.1 Greedy Algorithms for Subset Selection Problems

In this section, we discuss infinite parameterized families of greedy algorithms for subset selection problems introduced and analyzed in Gupta and Roughgarden (2016). We start by discussing a specific family of algorithms for the canonical knapsack problem and then present a general result applicable to other problems including maximum weight independent set.

Knapsack For the knapsack problem, let $\mathcal{A}_{knapsack} = \{A_\rho\}$ be the family of greedy algorithms described earlier. For this family $\mathcal{P} = \mathbb{R}_{\geq 0}$, and for $\rho \in \mathcal{P}$, for an instance x where v_i and s_i are the value and size of item i, the algorithm A_ρ adds the items to the knapsack in decreasing order of v_i/s_i^ρ subject to the capacity constraint. The utility function $u(x, \rho)$ is defined as the value of the items chosen by the greedy algorithm with parameter ρ on input x. We can show that the class $\mathcal{A}_{knapsack}$ is not too complex, in the sense that its pseudo-dimension is small.

Theorem 29.4 *The family of utility functions $\{u_\rho(x)\}$ corresponding to $\mathcal{A}_{knapsack}$ has pseudo-dimension $O(\log n)$, where n is the maximum number of items in an instance.*

Proof We first show that each function $u_x(\rho)$ is piecewise constant with at most n^2 pieces, and then apply Lemma 29.3.

To show the first part, fix some instance x. Now, suppose algorithm A_{ρ_1} produces a different solution on x than A_{ρ_2} does for $\rho_1 < \rho_2$. We argue there must exist some critical value $c \in [\rho_1, \rho_2]$ and some pair of items $i, j \in x$ such that $v_i/s_i^c = v_j/s_j^c$. The reason is that if A_{ρ_1} and A_{ρ_2} produce different solutions on x, they must at some point make different decisions about which item to add to the knapsack. Consider the first point where they differ: say that A_{ρ_1} adds item i to the knapsack and A_{ρ_2} adds item j. Then it must be the case that $v_i/s_i^{\rho_1} - v_j/s_j^{\rho_1} \geq 0$ but $v_i/s_i^{\rho_2} - v_j/s_j^{\rho_2} \leq 0$. Since the function $f(\rho) = v_i/s_i^{\rho} - v_j/s_j^{\rho}$ is continuous, there must exist some value $c \in [\rho_1, \rho_2]$ such that $v_i/s_i^c - v_j/s_j^c = 0$ as desired.

Now, for any given pair of items i,j, there is at most one value of $\rho \geq 0$ such that $v_i/s_i^{\rho} = v_j/s_j^{\rho}$; in particular, it is $\rho = \log(v_i/v_j)/\log(s_i/s_j)$.[1] This means there are at most $\binom{n}{2}$ critical values c such that $v_i/s_i^c = v_j/s_j^c$ for some pair of items $i,j \in x$. By the preceding argument, all values of ρ in the interval between any two consecutive critical values must produce the same behavior on the instance x. This means there are at most $\binom{n}{2} + 1 \leq n^2$ intervals such that all values of ρ inside the same interval result in the exact same solution by algorithm A_{ρ}.

Now, we simply apply Lemma 29.3 with $N = n^2$. $\qquad\square$

Maximum Weighted Independent Set Another canonical subset selection problem is the maximum weighted independent set problem (MWIS). An instance x is a graph with a weight $w(v) \in \mathbb{R}_{\geq 0}$ for each vertex v. The goal is to find a set of mutually nonadjacent vertices with maximum total weight. Gupta and Roughgarden (2017) analyze a family $\mathcal{A}_{MWIS}$ of greedy heuristics that at each step selects the vertex maximizing $w(v)/(1 + \deg(v))^{\rho}$, where $\rho \in \mathcal{P} = [0, B]$ for some $B \in \mathbb{R}$, and then removes v and its neighbors from the graph. Using a similar argument as in Theorem 29.4 we can show that the family of utility functions $\{u_{\rho}(x)\}$ corresponding to $\mathcal{A}_{MWIS}$ has pseudo-dimension $O(\log n)$, where n is the maximum number of vertices in an instance.

A General Analysis for Greedy Heuristics We now more generally consider problems in which the input is a set of n objects with various attributes, and the feasible solutions consist of assignments of the objects to a finite set Y, subject to feasibility constraints. The attributes of an object are represented as an element ξ of an abstract set. For example, in the Knapsack problem ξ encodes the value and size of an object; in the MWIS problem, ξ encodes the weight and (original or residual) degree of a vertex. In the Knapsack and MWIS problems, $Y = \{0, 1\}$, indicating whether or not a given object is selected.

Gupta and Roughgarden (2017) provide pseudo-dimension bounds for general greedy heuristics of the following form:

While there remain unassigned objects,

a. Use a scoring rule σ (a function from attributes to $\mathbb{R}$) to compute a score $\sigma(\xi_i)$ for each unassigned object i, as a function of its current attributes ξ_i.
b. For the unassigned object i with the highest score, use an assignment rule to assign i a value from Y and, if necessary, update the attributes of the other unassigned objects. Assume that ties are always resolved lexicographically.

---

[1] Except for the special case that $s_i = s_j$ and $v_i = v_j$, but in that case the order the items are considered in is fixed by the tie breaking rule, so we can ignore any such pair.

Assignment rules that do not modify objects' attributes yield nonadaptive greedy heuristics, which use only the original attributes of each object (like v_i or v_i/s_i in the Knapsack problem, for instance). Assignment rules that modify object attributes yield adaptive greedy heuristics, such as the adaptive MWIS heuristic described earlier. In a *single-parameter* family of scoring rules, there is a scoring rule of the form $\sigma(\rho, \xi)$ for each parameter value ρ in some interval $I \subseteq \mathbb{R}$. Moreover, σ is assumed to be continuous in ρ for each fixed value of ξ. Natural examples include Knapsack scoring rules of the form v_i/s_i^ρ and MWIS scoring rules of the form $w(v)/(1+deg(v))^\rho$ for $\rho \in [0,1]$ or $\rho \in [0, \infty)$.

A single-parameter family of scoring rules is *κ-crossing* if, for each distinct pair of attributes ξ', ξ'', there are at most κ values of ρ for which $\sigma(\rho, \xi') = \sigma(\rho, \xi'')$. For example, all of the scoring rules mentioned above are 1-crossing rules.

For an example assignment rule, in the Knapsack and MWIS problems, the rule simply assigns i to 1 if it is feasible to do so, and to 0 otherwise. In the adaptive greedy heuristic for the MWIS problem, whenever the assignment rule assigns 1 to a vertex v, it updates the residual degrees of other unassigned vertices (two hops away) accordingly. Say that an assignment rule is *β-bounded* if every object i is guaranteed to take on at most β distinct attribute values. For example, an assignment rule that never modifies an object's attributes is 1-bounded. The assignment rule in the adaptive MWIS algorithm is n-bounded, since it only modifies the degree of a vertex (which lies in $\{0, 1, 2, \ldots, n-1\}$). Coupling a single-parameter family of κ-crossing scoring rules with a fixed β-bounded assignment rule yields a (κ, β)-single-parameter family of greedy heuristics. The knapsack greedy heuristic is a $(1,1)$-single-parameter family and the adaptive MWIS heuristic is a $(1,n)$-single-parameter family.

Theorem 29.5 *Let $\mathcal{A}_{greedy}$ be a (κ, β) single parameter family of greedy heuristics and let $\{u_\rho(x)\}$ be its corresponding family of utility functions. The pseudo-dimension of $\{u_\rho(x)\}$ is $O(\log(\kappa \beta n))$, where n is the number of objects.*

Proof Fix an instance x, and consider the behavior of the algorithm as we vary ρ. Because there are n items and the assignment rule is β-bounded, there are a total of at most $n\beta$ distinct attribute values possible over all choices of ρ. For any two such attribute values ξ', ξ'', we know by the κ-crossing assumption there are at most κ distinct *critical values* c such that $\sigma(c, \xi') = \sigma(c, \xi'')$. Thus, there are at most $(n\beta)^2 \kappa$ distinct critical values total. Now, between any two consecutive critical values, the algorithm must behave identically for all ρ in that interval. In particular, if ρ_1 and ρ_2 behave differently on x, there must exist two attribute values ξ', ξ'' such that one has higher score under ρ_1 but the other has higher score under ρ_2, and by continuity of σ this means ρ_1 and ρ_2 must be separated by a critical value. Since the algorithm behaves identically in each interval and there are at most $(n\beta)^2 \kappa + 1$ intervals, this means that that each function $u_x(\rho)$ is piecewise constant with at most $(n\beta)^2 \kappa + 1$ pieces. The theorem then follows from Lemma 29.3. $\qquad\square$

29.2.2 Clustering Problems

In this section we discuss how a data-driven approach can help overcome impossibility results for clustering problems. Clustering is one of the most basic problems in data science; given a large set of complex data (e.g., images or news articles) the goal is to organize it into groups of similar items. Despite significant efforts from different communities, it remains a major challenge. Traditional approaches have focused on the "one-shot" setting, where the goal is to cluster a single potentially worst-case dataset. Unfortunately, there are major impossibility results for such scenarios; first, in most applications it is not clear what objective function to use to recover a good clustering for the given dataset; second, even in cases where the objective can be naturally specified, optimally solving the underlying combinatorial clustering problem is typically intractable. One approach to circumvent hardness of worst-case instances (discussed in Chapters 5 and 6) is to posit specific stability assumptions about the input instances, and to design efficient algorithms with good performance on such instances. Another approach that is particularly suited for settings (including text and image categorization) where we have to solve many clustering problems arising in a given application domain, is to select a good clustering algorithm in a data-driven way. In particular, given a series of clustering instances to be solved from the same domain, we learn a good parameter setting for a clustering algorithm (from a large potentially infinite set of clustering algorithms) that performs well on instances coming from that domain. We can then use the general framework discussed in Section 29.2 to provide guarantees for this approach. We discuss next such guarantees for several parametric families of clustering procedures widely used in practice.

Problem Setup The results we present apply both to objective based clustering (e.g., k-means and k-median) and to an unsupervised learning formulation of the problem. In both cases the input to a clustering problem is a point set V of n points, a desired number of clusters $k \in \{1, \ldots, n\}$, and a metric d (such as Euclidean distance in $\mathbb{R}^d$) specifying the distance between any two points; throughout the rest of this section we denote by $d(i,j)$ the distance between points i and j.

For objective based clustering, the goal is to output a partition $\mathcal{C} = \{C_1, \ldots, C_k\}$ of V that optimizes a specific objective function. For example, in the k-means clustering objective the goal is to output a partition $\mathcal{C} = \{C_1, \ldots, C_k\}$ and a center c_i for each C_i to minimize the sum of the squared distances between every point and its nearest center, i.e., $\text{cost}(\mathcal{C}) = \left(\sum_i \sum_{v \in C_i} d(v, c_i)^2 \right)$, while in the k-median objective the goal is to minimize the sum of distances to the centers rather than the squared distances, i.e., $\text{cost}(\mathcal{C}) = \left(\sum_i \sum_{v \in C_i} d(v, c_i) \right)$. Unfortunately, finding the clustering that minimizes these objectives (and other classic ones such as k-center and min-sum) is NP-hard, so using a data-driven approach can help in identifying solutions with good objective values for specific domains.

In the unsupervised learning or "matching the ground-truth clustering" approach, we assume that for each instance V of n points, in addition to the distance metric d, there is a ground-truth partition of the input points $\mathcal{C}^* = \{C_1^*, \ldots, C_k^*\}$. The goal is to output a partition $\mathcal{C} = \{C_1, \ldots, C_k\}$ in order to minimize some loss function relative to the ground truth; e.g., a common loss function (discussed in Chapter 6) is the fraction of points that would have to be reassigned in $\mathcal{C}$ to make it match $\mathcal{C}^*$ up to reindexing of the clusters, or equivalently $\min_\sigma \frac{1}{n} \sum_{i=1}^{k} |C_i \setminus C_{\sigma(i)}^*|$, where the minimum is taken over all bijections $\sigma : \{1, \ldots, k\} \to \{1, \ldots, k\}$. For the data-driven approach we assume that the ground truth is known for the training instances, but it is unknown and what we want to predict for the test instances.

Linkage-Based Families In the following we discuss families of two stage clustering algorithms, that in the first stage use a linkage procedure to organize data into a hierarchical clustering and then in a second stage use a fixed (computationally efficient) procedure to extract a pruning from this hierarchy. Such techniques are prevalent in practice and from a theoretical point of view, they are known to perform nearly optimally in settings where the data is well-clusterable, in particular perturbation resilient and approximation stable, as discussed in Chapters 5 and 6.

The linkage procedure in the first step takes as input a clustering instance x (a set V of n points and metric d specifying the distance between any pair of the base points) and outputs a cluster tree, by repeatedly merging the two closest clusters. In particular, starting with the base distance d, we first define a distance measure $D(A, B)$ between any two subsets A and B of $\{1, \ldots, n\}$, that is used to greedily link the data into a binary cluster tree. The leaves of the tree are the individual data points, while the root node corresponds to the entire dataset. The algorithm starts with each point belonging to its own cluster. Then, it repeatedly merges the closest pair of clusters according to distance D. When there is only a single cluster remaining, the algorithm outputs the constructed cluster tree. Different definitions for D lead to different hierarchical procedures. For example, the classic linkage procedures single, complete, and average linkage define D as $D(A, B) = d_{\min}(A, B) = \min_{a \in A, b \in B} d(a, b)$, $D(A, B) = d_{\max}(A, B) = \max_{a \in A, b \in B} d(a, b)$, and $D(A, B) = \frac{1}{|A||B|} \sum_{u \in A, v \in B} d(u, v)$, respectively.

The procedure in the second step can be as simple as just "undoing" the last $k - 1$ merges from the first step or a dynamic programming subroutine over the hierarchy from the first step to extract a clustering of highest score based on some measurable objective such as k-means or k-median cost. The final quality or utility (measured by the function $u_\rho(x)$ on clustering instance x) of the solution produced by the algorithm is for the objective-based approach measured by the given objective function (e.g. k-means or k-median objective) or the loss with respect to the ground truth in the unsupervised learning formulation.

We analyze in the text that follows the pseudo-dimension of two parametric families of algorithms of this form (from Balcan et al., 2017). Both of these families use a parameterized linkage procedure in the first step, and the cluster tree produced is then fed into a fixed second-stage procedure to produce a k-clustering. The first family $\mathcal{A}^{scl}$ uses a parameterized family of linkage algorithms with a single parameter $\rho \in \mathcal{P} = [0, 1]$ that helps interpolate linearly between the classic single and complete linkage procedures. For $\rho \in \mathcal{P}$ the algorithm $A_\rho \in \mathcal{A}^{scl}$ defines the distance between two sets A and B as $D_\rho^{scl}(A, B) = (1 - \rho) \, d_{\min}(A, B) + \rho \, d_{\max}(A, B)$. Note that $\rho = 0$ and $\rho = 1$ recover single and complete linkage, respectively.

The second family $\mathcal{A}^{exp}$ uses a parameterized family of linkage algorithms with a single parameter $\rho \in \mathcal{P} = \mathbb{R}$ that helps interpolate not only between single and complete linkage but also includes average linkage as well. For $\rho \in \mathcal{P}$ the algorithm $A_\rho \in \mathcal{A}^{exp}$ defines the distance between two sets A and B as $D_\rho^{exp}(A, B) = \left(\frac{1}{|A||B|} \sum_{u \in A, v \in B} (d(u, v))^\rho \right)^{1/\rho}$. Note that $\rho = 0$ recovers average linkage, $\rho \to \infty$ recovers complete linkage, and $\rho \to -\infty$ recovers single linkage. Balcan et al. (2017) prove that the family of functions $\{u_\rho(x)\}$ corresponding to the family $\mathcal{A}^{scl}$ is not too complex, in the sense that it has pseudo-dimension $\Theta(\log n)$, where n is an upper bound on the number of data points in a clustering instance. Similarly, the family of functions $\{u_\rho(x)\}$ corresponding to the family $\mathcal{A}^{exp}$ has pseudo-dimension $\Theta(n)$. We sketch the upper bounds next.

We start by analyzing the family D_ρ^{scl}-linkage, for which we can prove the following structural result.

Lemma 29.6 *Let x be a clustering instance. We can partition $\mathcal{P}$ into at most n^8 intervals such that all values of ρ inside the same interval result in the exact same solution produced by the D_ρ^{scl}-linkage algorithm.*

Proof First, for any pair of candidate cluster merges (C_1, C_2) and (C_1', C_2'), where C_1, C_2, C_1' and C_2' are clusters, there is at most one critical parameter value c such that $D_\rho^{scl}(C_1, C_2) = D_\rho^{scl}(C_1', C_2')$ only when $\rho = c$. In particular, $c = \Delta_{min}/(\Delta_{min} - \Delta_{max})$, where $\Delta_{min} = d_{min}(C_1', C_2') - d_{min}(C_1, C_2)$ and $\Delta_{max} = d_{max}(C_1', C_2') - d_{max}(C_1, C_2)$. For clarity, we will call this value $c(C_1, C_2, C_1', C_2')$.

Next, the total number of distinct critical values c ranging over all possible 4-tuples of clusters C_1, C_2, C_1', C_2' is at most n^8. The reason is that for any given clusters C_1, C_2, C_1', C_2' there exist 8 points (not necessarily distinct) corresponding to the closest pair between C_1 and C_2, the closest pair between C_1' and C_2', the farthest pair between C_1 and C_2, and the farthest pair between C_1' and C_2', whose distances completely define $c(C_1, C_2, C_1', C_2')$. Since there are at most n^8 possible 8-tuples of such points, this means there are at most n^8 distinct critical values.

Between any two consecutive critical values c, all D_ρ^{scl}-linkage algorithms give the same ordering on all possible merges. This is because for any C_1, C_2, C_1', C_2', the function $f(\rho) = D_\rho^{scl}(C_1, C_2) - D_\rho^{scl}(C_1', C_2')$ is continuous, and therefore must have a zero (creating a critical value) if it switches sign. So, there are at most n^8 intervals such that all values of ρ inside the same interval result in the exact same merges, and therefore the same solution produced by the D_ρ^{scl}-linkage algorithm. $\square$

Lemma 29.6 and Lemma 29.3 imply the following:

Theorem 29.7 *The family of functions $\{u_\rho(x)\}$ corresponding to the family $\mathcal{A}^{scl}$-linkage has pseudo-dimension $O(\log n)$.*

Theorem 29.8 *The family of functions $\{u_\rho(x)\}$ corresponding to the family $\mathcal{A}^{exp}$-linkage has pseudo-dimension $O(n)$.*

Proof Sketch As in the proof of Lemma 29.6, we fix an instance x and bound the number of intervals such that all values of ρ inside the same interval result in the exact same solution produced by the algorithm.

Fixing an instance x, consider two pairs of sets A, B and X, Y that could be potentially merged. Now, the decision to merge one pair before the other is determined by the sign of the expression $\frac{1}{|A||B|} \sum_{p \in A, q \in B}(d(p, q))^\rho - \frac{1}{|X||Y|} \sum_{x \in X, y \in Y}(d(x, y))^\rho$. First note that this expression has $O(n^2)$ terms, and by a consequence of Rolle's Theorem, it has $O(n^2)$ roots. Therefore, as we iterate over the $O\left((3^n)^2\right)$ possible pairs (A, B) and (X, Y), we can determine $O\left(3^{2n}\right)$ unique expressions each with $O(n^2)$ values of ρ at which the corresponding decision flips. Thus, by continuity of the associated functions, we can divide $\mathbb{R}$ into at most $O\left(n^2 3^{2n}\right)$ intervals over each of which the output of the algorithm on input x is fixed.

Finally, we apply Lemma 29.3 using the fact that each function $u_x(\rho)$ is piecewise constant with at most $2^{O(n)}$ pieces. $\qquad\square$

Interestingly, these families of clustering algorithms are also known to have strong analytical properties for stable instances of the type discussed in Chapters 5 and 6. One such condition, called perturbation-resilience, asks that even if distances between data points are perturbed by up to some factor β, the clustering that optimizes a given objective (such as k-means or k-median) does not change. If this condition is satisfied for $\beta \geq 2$, it is known that one can find the optimal clustering efficiently, in fact via a linkage algorithm followed by dynamic programming, further motivating that algorithm family. However, one drawback of all these results is that if the condition does not hold, the guarantees do not apply. Here, we aim to provide guarantees on optimality within an algorithm family that hold regardless of clusterability assumptions, but with the additional property that if typical instances are indeed well-clusterable (e.g., they satisfy perturbation-resilience or some related condition), then the optimal algorithm in the family is optimal overall. This way, we can produce guarantees that simultaneously are meaningful in the general case and can take advantage of settings in which the data are particularly well behaved.

Parameterized Lloyd's Methods The Lloyd's method is another popular technique in practice. The procedure starts with k initial centers and iteratively makes incremental improvements until a local optimum is reached. One of the most crucial decisions an algorithm designer must make when using such an algorithm is the initial seeding step, i.e., how the algorithm chooses the k initial centers. Balcan et al. (2018d) consider an infinite family of algorithms generalizing the popular k-means++ approach (Arthur and Vassilvitskii, 2007), with a parameter α that controls the seeding process. In the seeding phase, each point v is sampled with probability proportional to $d_{\min}(v, C)^\alpha$, where C is the set of centers chosen so far and $d_{\min}(v, C) = \min_{c \in C} d(v, c)$. Then Lloyd's method is used to converge to a local minimum or is cut off at some given time bound. By ranging over $\alpha \in [0, \infty) \cup \{\infty\}$, we obtain an infinite family of algorithms that we call α-Lloyds++. This allows a spectrum between random seeding ($\alpha = 0$), and farthest-first traversal ($\alpha = \infty$), with $\alpha = 2$ corresponding to k-means++. What is different about this algorithm family compared to those studied earlier in this chapter is that because the algorithm is randomized, for this problem the expected cost as a function of α is Lipschitz. In particular, one can prove a Lipschitz constant of $O(nkH \log R)$, where R is the ratio of maximum to minimum pairwise distance, and H is an upper bound on the k-means cost of any clustering. As a consequence, one can discretize values of α into a fine grid, and then try $N = O(\alpha_h nkH(\log R)/\epsilon)$ values of α on a sample of size $O((H/\epsilon)^2 \log N)$ and pick the best, where α_h is the largest value of α one wishes to consider. However, by pushing the randomness of the algorithm into the problem instance (augmenting each problem instance with a random string and viewing the algorithm as a deterministic function of the instance and random string), one can view $u_x(\alpha)$ as a piecewise-constant function with a number of pieces that *in expectation* is only $O(nk(\log n)\log(\alpha_h \log R))$. This allows for many fewer values of α to be tried, making this approach more practical. In fact, Balcan et al. (2018d) implement this approach and demonstrate it on several interesting datasets.

29.2.3 Other Applications and Generic Results

Partitioning Problems via IQPs Balcan et al. (2017) study data-driven algorithm design for problems that can be written as integer quadratic programs (IQPs) for families of algorithms that involve semidefinite programming (SDP) relaxations followed by parameterized rounding schemes. The class of IQP problems they consider is described as follows. An instance x is specified by a matrix $A \in \mathbb{R}^{n \times n}$, and the goal is to solve (at least approximately) the optimization problem $\max_{z \in \{\pm 1\}^n} z^\top Az$. This is of interest, since many classic NP-hard problems can be formulated as IQPs, including max-cut, max-2SAT, and correlation clustering. For example, the classic max-cut problem can be written as an IQP of this form. Recall that given a graph G on n nodes with edge weights w_{ij}, the max-cut problem is to find a partition of the vertices into two sides to maximize the total sum of edge weights crossing the partition. This can be written as solving for $z \in \{\pm 1\}^n$ to maximize $\sum_{(i,j) \in E} w_{ij}\left(\frac{1-z_i z_j}{2}\right)$, where z_i represents which side vertex i is assigned to. This objective can be formulated as $\max_{z \in \{\pm 1\}^n} z^\top Az$ for $a_{ij} = -w_{ij}/2$ for $(i,j) \in E$ and $a_{ij} = 0$ for $(i,j) \notin E$.

The family of algorithms A_ρ^{round} that Balcan et al. (2017) analyze is parameterized by a one-dimensional set $\mathcal{P} = \mathbb{R}$, and for any $\rho \in \mathcal{P}$ the algorithm A_ρ operates as follows. In the first stage it solves the SDP relaxation $\sum_{i,j \in [n]} a_{ij}\langle u_i, u_j \rangle$ subject to the constraint that $\|u_i\| = 1$ for $i \in \{1, 2, \ldots, n\}$. In the second stage it rounds the vectors u_i to $\{\pm 1\}$ by sampling a standard Gaussian $Z \sim \mathcal{N}_n$ and setting $z_i = 1$ with probability $1/2 + \phi_\rho(\langle u_i, Z \rangle)/2$ and -1 otherwise, where $\phi_\rho(y) = y/\rho$ for $-\rho \le y \le \rho$, $\phi_\rho(y) = -1$ for $y < -\rho$, and $\phi_\rho(y) = 1$ for $y > \rho$. In other words, if $|\langle u_i, Z \rangle| > \rho$ then u_i is rounded based on the sign of the dot-product, else it is rounded probabilistically using a linear scale. The utility function $u_\rho(x)$ for algorithm A_ρ maps the algorithm parameter ρ to the expected objective value obtained on the instance x. Note that by design the algorithms A_ρ^{round} are polynomial-time algorithms.

Note that when $\rho = 0$, this algorithm corresponds to the classic Goemans–Williamson max-cut algorithm. It is known that nonzero values of ρ can outperform the classic algorithm on graphs for which the max cut does not constitute a large fraction of the edges.

Theorem 29.9 *Let $\{u_\rho(x)\}$ be the corresponding family of utility functions for the family of algorithms A_ρ^{round}. The pseudo-dimension of $\{u_\rho(x)\}$ is $O(\log(n))$, where n is the maximum number of variables in an instance.*

At a high level, the proof idea is to analyze a related utility function for which we imagine that the Gaussians Z are sampled ahead of time and included as part of the problem instance; in other words we augment the instance to obtain a new instance $\tilde{x} = (x, Z)$. One can then prove that the utility is $u_\rho(\tilde{x}) = \sum_{i=1}^n a_{ii} + \sum_{i \ne j} a_{ij}\phi_s(v_i)\phi_s(v_j)$, where $v_i = \langle u_i, Z \rangle$. Using this form, it is easy to show that this objective function value is piecewise quadratic in $1/\rho$ with n boundaries. The result then follows from a generalization of Lemma 29.3.

Learning to Branch So far we considered families of polynomial-time algorithms and scored them based on solution quality (e.g., clustering quality or objective value). In general, one could also score algorithms based on other important measures of performance. For example, Balcan et al. (2018c) consider parameterized branch-and-bound techniques for learning how to branch when solving mixed integer programs (MIPs) in the distributional learning setting, and score a parameter setting based on the tree size on a given instance (which roughly corresponds to running time). Balcan et al. (2018c) show that the corresponding dual functions are piecewise constant, and then the sample complexity results follow from a high-dimensional generalization of Lemma 29.3. Balcan et al. (2018c) also show experimentally that different parameter settings of these families of algorithms can result in branch and bound trees of vastly different sizes, for different combinatorial problems (including winner determination in combinatorial auctions, k-means clustering, and agnostic learning of linear separators). They also show that the optimal parameter is highly distribution dependent: using a parameter optimized on the wrong distribution can lead to a dramatic tree size blowup, implying that learning to branch is both practical and hugely beneficial.

General Theorem Balcan et al. (2019b) present a general sample complexity result applicable to algorithm configuration problems for which the dual functions are piece-wise structured. The key innovation is to provide an elegant and widely applicable abstraction that simultaneously covers all the types of dual structures appearing in the algorithm families mentioned so far – this includes those in Sections 29.2.1 and 29.2.2 (where $u_x(\rho)$ are piecewise-constant with a limited number of pieces as in Lemma 29.3), and the dual functions appearing in the context of learning to branch mentioned earlier, as well as revenue maximization in multi-item multi-bidder settings. Balcan et al. (2019b) show that this theorem recovers all the prior results and they also show new applications including to dynamic programming techniques for important problems in computational biology, e.g., sequence alignment and protein folding.

Recall that $\mathcal{P}$ denotes the space of parameter vectors ρ (e.g., if ρ consists of d real-valued parameters, then $\mathcal{P} = \mathbb{R}^d$). Let $\mathcal{F}$ denote a family of *boundary functions* such as linear separators or quadratic separators that each partition $\mathcal{P}$ into two pieces, and let $\mathcal{G}$ denote a family of *simple utility functions* such as constant functions or linear functions over $\mathcal{P}$. Balcan et al. (2019b) show the following. Suppose that for each dual function $u_x(\rho)$, there are a limited number of boundary functions $f_1, \ldots, f_N \in \mathcal{F}$ such that within each region[2] defined by these functions, $u_x(\rho)$ behaves as some function from $\mathcal{G}$. Then, the pseudo-dimension of the primal family $\{u_\rho(x)\}$ can be bounded as a function of N, the VC-dimension of the dual class $\mathcal{F}^*$ to $\mathcal{F}$, and the pseudo-dimension of the dual class $\mathcal{G}^*$ to $\mathcal{G}$.[3]

---

[2] Formally, each f_i is a function from $\mathcal{P}$ to $\{0, 1\}$, and a *region* is a nonempty set of ρ that are all labeled the same way by each f_i.

[3] $\mathcal{F}^*$ is defined as follows: for each $\rho \in \mathcal{P}$ define the function $\rho(f) = f(\rho)$ for all $f \in \mathcal{F}$. $\mathcal{G}^*$ is defined similarly.

29.3 Data-Driven Algorithm Design via Online Learning

We now consider an online formulation for algorithm design where we do not assume that the instances of the given algorithmic problem are i.i.d. and presented all at once; instead, they could arrive online, in an arbitrary order, in which case what we can aim for is to compete with the best fixed algorithm in hindsight (Cohen-Addad and Kanade, 2017; Gupta and Roughgarden, 2017; Balcan et al., 2018a), also known as no-regret learning. Since the utility functions appearing in algorithm selection settings often exhibit sharp discontinuities, achieving no-regret is impossible in the worst case over the input sequence of instances.

We discuss a niceness condition on the sequence of utility functions introduced in Balcan et al. (2018a), called dispersion, that is sufficient for the existence of online algorithms that guarantee no regret.

Problem Formulation On each round t the learner chooses an algorithm from the family specified by the parameter vector ρ_t and receives a new instance of the problem x_t; this induces the utility function $u_{x_t}(\rho)$ that measures the performance of each algorithm in the family for the given instance, and the utility of the learner at time t is $u_{x_t}(\rho_t)$. The case where the learner observes the entire utility function $u_{x_t}(\rho)$ or can evaluate it at points of its own choice is called the full information setting; the case where it only observes the scalar $u_{x_t}(\rho_t)$ is called the bandit setting. The goal is to select algorithms so that the cumulative performance of the learner is nearly as good as the best algorithm in hindsight for that sequence of problems. Formally, the goal is to minimize expected regret

$$\mathbb{E}\left[\max_{\rho \in \mathcal{P}} \sum u_{x_t}(\rho) - u_{x_t}(\rho_t)\right],$$

where the expectation is over the randomness in the learner's choices or over the randomness in the utility functions. We aim to obtain expected regret that is sublinear in T, since in that case the per-round average performance of the algorithm is approaching that of the best parameter in hindsight – this is commonly referred as achieving "no regret" in the online learning literature.

As we have seen in the previous sections the utility functions appearing in algorithm selection settings often exhibit sharp discontinuities, and it is known that even for one-dimensional cases, achieving no-regret guarantees for learning functions with sharp discontinuities is impossible, in the worst case. In essence, the problem is that if I is an interval of parameters that have all achieved maximum utility so far, an adversary can choose the next utility function to randomly give either the left or right half of I a utility of 0 and the other half a maximum utility, causing any online algorithm to achieve only half of the optimum in hindsight. Gupta and Roughgarden (2017) show that this is the case for online algorithm selection for the maximum weighted independent set problem for the family of algorithms discussed in Section 29.2.1.

We now describe a general condition on the sequence of utility functions introduced, called dispersion, that is provably sufficient to achieve no-regret, introduced in Balcan et al. (2018a). Roughly speaking, a collection of utility functions $u_{x_1}, \ldots, u_{x_T}$ is dispersed if no small region of the space contains discontinuities for many of these functions. Formally:

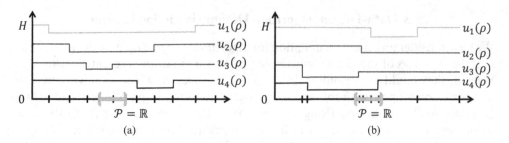

Figure 29.1 The utility functions in figure (a) are dispersed because any small interval has discontinuities for only a few of them. The utility functions in figure (b) are not dispersed because there is a small interval with many discontinuities.

Definition 29.10 Let $u_{x_1}, \ldots, u_{x_T}: \mathcal{P} \to [0, H]$ be a collection of utility functions where u_{x_i} is piecewise Lipschitz over a partition $\mathcal{P}_i$ of $\mathcal{P}$. We say that $\mathcal{P}_i$ splits a set A if A intersects with at least two sets in $\mathcal{P}_i$. The collection of functions is (w, k)-*dispersed* if every ball of radius w is split by at most k of the partitions $\mathcal{P}_1, \ldots, \mathcal{P}_T$. More generally, the functions are (w, k)-*dispersed at a maximizer* if there exists a point $\rho^* \in \text{argmax}_{\rho \in \mathcal{P}} \sum_{i=1}^{T} u_i(\rho)$ such that the ball $B(\rho^*, w)$ is split by at most k of the partitions $\mathcal{P}_1, \ldots, \mathcal{P}_T$.

In many applications, Definition 29.10 holds with high probability for $w = T^{\alpha-1}$ and $k = \tilde{O}(T^\alpha)$ for some $1/2 \leq \alpha \leq 1$, ignoring problem-specific multiplicands.

Continuous Weighted Majority In the full information setting, we can use a continuous version of the classic weighted majority algorithm (Cesa-Bianchi and Lugosi, 2006) to obtain no-regret learning in dispersed settings. In round t, the algorithm samples a vector ρ_t from the distribution $p_t(\rho) \propto \exp(\lambda \sum_{s=1}^{t-1} u_s(\rho))$. The following bound holds for this algorithm (Balcan et al., 2018a).

Theorem 29.11 *Let $u_{x_1}, \ldots, u_{x_T}: \mathcal{P} \to [0, H]$ be a sequence of utility functions corresponding to problem instances $x_1, \ldots x_T$. Assume that these functions $u_{x_1}, \ldots, u_{x_T}$ are piecewise L-Lipschitz functions and (w, k)-dispersed at the maximizer ρ^*. Suppose $\mathcal{P} \subset \mathbb{R}^d$ is contained in a ball of radius R and $B(\rho^*, w) \subset \mathcal{P}$. The continuous weighted majority algorithm with $\lambda = \frac{1}{H}\sqrt{d \ln(R/w)/T}$ has expected regret bounded by $O\left(H\left(\sqrt{Td \log \frac{R}{w}} + k\right) + TLw\right)$.*

When $w = 1/\sqrt{T}$ and $k = \tilde{O}(\sqrt{T})$, this gives regret $\tilde{O}(\sqrt{T}(H\sqrt{d} + L))$.

Proof Sketch Let U_t be the function $\sum_{i=1}^{t-1} u_{x_i}(\cdot)$; let W_t be the normalizing constant at round t, that is $W_t = \int_\mathcal{P} \exp(\lambda U_t(\rho)) \, d\rho$.

The proof follows by providing upper and lower bounds on W_{T+1}/W_1. The upper bound on W_{T+1}/W_1 in terms of the learner's expected payout follows as in the classic weighted majority algorithm, yielding: $\frac{W_{T+1}}{W_1} \leq \exp\left(\frac{P(\mathcal{A})(e^{H\lambda}-1)}{H}\right)$, where $P(\mathcal{A})$ is the expected total payoff of the algorithm.

We use (w, k)-dispersion to lower bound W_{T+1}/W_1 in terms of the optimal parameter's total payout. The key insight is that not only ρ^* the optimal parameter gets a good payoff in hindsight, but all the parameters in the ball of radius w around ρ^* have a good total payoff. Let ρ^* be the optimal parameter and let OPT $= U_{T+1}(\rho^*)$. Also, let $\mathcal{B}^*$ be the ball of radius w around ρ^*. From (w,k)-dispersion, we know that for all $\rho \in \mathcal{B}^*$, $U_{T+1}(\rho) \geq$ OPT $- Hk - LTw$. Therefore,

$$W_{T+1} = \int_{\mathcal{P}} \exp(\lambda U_{T+1}(\rho)) \, d\rho \geq \int_{\mathcal{B}^*} \exp(\lambda U_{T+1}(\rho)) \, d\rho$$

$$\geq \text{Vol}(B(\rho^*, w)) \exp(\lambda(\text{OPT} - Hk - LTw)).$$

Moreover, $W_1 = \int_{\mathcal{P}} \exp(\lambda U_1(\rho)) \, d\rho \leq \text{Vol}(B(0, R))$. Therefore,

$$\frac{W_{T+1}}{W_1} \geq \frac{\text{Vol}(B(\rho^*, w))}{\text{Vol}(B(0, R))} \exp(\lambda(\text{OPT} - Hk - LTw)).$$

Combining the upper and lower bounds on $\frac{W_{T+1}}{W_1}$ gives the result. □

Whether the continuous weighted majority algorithm can be implemented in polynomial time depends on the setting. Assume that for all rounds $t \in \{1, \ldots, T\}$, $\sum_{s=1}^{t} u_s$ is piecewise Lipschitz over at most N pieces. It is not hard to prove that when $d = 1$ and $\mathcal{P} = \mathbb{R}$ and $\exp(\sum_{s=1}^{t} u_s)$ can be integrated in constant time on each of its pieces, the running time is $O(TN)$ per round. When $d > 1$ and $\sum_{s=1}^{t} u_s$ is piecewise concave over convex pieces, Balcan et al. (2018a) provide an efficient approximate implementation by using tools from high-dimensional geometry.

Examples We now show that under natural smoothness conditions about the input instances, dispersion is satisfied for the knapsack and clustering problems discussed in Section 29.2. The proof structure in both cases is to use the functional form of the discontinuities of the corresponding utility functions to reason about the distribution of discontinuity locations that arise as transformations of random problem parameters in algorithm configuration instances. Using this idea one can upper bound the expected number of functions with discontinuities in any fixed interval, and then obtain the final desired result by using a uniform convergence result summarized in the following lemma.

Lemma 29.12 Let $u_{x_1}, u_{x_2}, \ldots, u_{x_T} : \mathbb{R} \to \mathbb{R}$ be piecewise L-Lipschitz functions, each having at most N discontinuities, with independent randomness in their discontinuities.[4] Let $\mathcal{F} = \{f_I : \Pi \to \{0, 1\} \mid I \subset \mathbb{R} \text{ is an interval}\}$, where $f_I : \Pi \to \{0, 1\}$ maps an instance $x \in \Pi$ to 1 if the interval I contains a discontinuity for the utility function u_x, and 0 otherwise. With probability $1 - \delta$ over randomness in the selection of utility functions $u_{x_1}, u_{x_2}, \ldots, u_{x_T}$ we have: $\sup_{f_I \in \mathcal{F}} \left| \sum_{t=1}^{T} f_I(x_t) - \mathbb{E}\left[\sum_{t=1}^{T} f_I(x_t) \right] \right| \leq O(\sqrt{T \log(N/\delta)})$.

Intuitively, Lemma 29.12 states the following. Suppose that instead of a worst-case sequence of utility functions, there is some randomness in the locations of their

---

[4] The independence is between functions. Within a function, the discontinuities may be correlated.

discontinuities, where the randomness is independent between utility functions. Then, with high probability, for every interval I, the actual number of discontinuities in I will be close to its expectation, and in particular within an additive gap of at most $O(\sqrt{T \log(N/\delta)})$. To prove this, the key step is to apply uniform convergence to the class of functions $\mathcal{F}$ defined in the lemma, and to prove that its Vapnik–Chervonenkis (VC)-dimension is $O(\log N)$. This lemma is from Balcan et al. (2020) and it improves over the earlier result in Balcan et al. (2018a).

For the family of greedy algorithms $\mathcal{A}^{knapsack}$ discussed in Section 29.2.2, in the worst case, the associated utility functions might not be dispersed. However, we can perform a smoothed analysis (discussed also in Chapters 13–15 for other applications), and show that if there is some randomness in the item values, then we have dispersion with high probability. Formally, we assume item values are b-smooth: they are random, independent, and each has a density function upper bounded by b. (For example, a canonical b-smooth distribution is a uniform distribution on an interval of width $1/b$.) The dispersion guarantee is given in Theorem 29.13.

Theorem 29.13 *Let $x_1, \ldots, x_T$ be any sequence of knapsack instances with n items and capacity C where instance i has sizes $s_1^{(i)}, \ldots, s_n^{(i)} \in [1, C]$ and values $v_1^{(i)}, \ldots, v_n^{(i)} \in (0, 1]$. Assume that the item values are b-smooth. Then for any $\delta > 0$, with probability at least $1 - \delta$, for any $w > 0$, the utility functions $u_{x_1}, \ldots, u_{x_T}$ are (w, k)-dispersed for $k = O(wTn^2b^2 \log(C) + \sqrt{T \log(n/\delta)})$.*

Proof Sketch Recall from Lemma 29.4 that for a knapsack instance x with item values $v_1, \ldots, v_n$ and sizes $s_1, \ldots, s_n$, the discontinuities of the utility u_x only occur at parameter values where the relative ordering of two items swaps under the score σ_ρ. For items i and j, let $c_{ij} = \log(v_i/v_j)/\log(s_i/s_j)$ be the critical parameter value where their relative scores swap. When the item values are independent and have b-bounded distributions, we are guaranteed that their joint density is also b^2-bounded. Using this Balcan et al. (2018a) prove that each discontinuity is random and has a density function that is upper bounded by $b^2 \log(C)/2$.

Next, fix any ball I of radius w (i.e., an interval of width $2w$). For any function u_{x_i} the probability that any one of its discontinuities belongs to the interval I is at most $wb^2 \log(C)$. Summing over both knapsack instances $x_1, \ldots, x_T$ and the $O(n^2)$ discontinuities for each, it follows that the expected total number of discontinuities in interval I is at most $wTn^2b^2 \log(C)$. This is also a bound on the expected number of functions among $u_{x_1}, \ldots, u_{x_T}$ that are discontinuous on the ball I. Finally, Lemma 29.12 can be used to show that with probability $\geq 1 - \delta$ any interval of radius w has $O(wTn^2b^2 \log(C) + \sqrt{T \log(n/\delta)})$ discontinuous functions. $\square$

Combining the dispersion analysis for the knapsack problem with the regret guarantees for the continuous weighted majority algorithm, we can obtain an upper bound on the algorithm's expected regret. In particular, applying Theorems 29.13 and 29.11 with $\delta = 1/\sqrt{T}$ and $w = 1/(\sqrt{T}n^2b^2 \log(C))$, and using that utilities take values in $[0, C]$, we have the following corollary (from Balcan et al., 2020) which improves over the earlier result (Balcan et al., 2018a):

Corollary 29.14 *Let $x_1, \ldots, x_T$ be any sequence of knapsack instances satisfying the same conditions as in Theorem 29.13. The continuous weighted majority algorithm employed to choose parameters $\rho_1, \ldots, \rho_T \in [0, R]$ for the sequence $x_1, \ldots, x_T$ with $\lambda = \sqrt{\log(R/(\sqrt{T}n^2b^2\log(C))}/C$ has expected regret bounded by*

$$\mathbb{E}\left[\max_{\rho \in [0,R]} \sum_{t=1}^{T} u_{x_t}(\rho) - \sum_{t=1}^{T} u_{x_t}(\rho_t) \right] = O\left(C\sqrt{T\log(RTnb\log(C))}\right).$$

For the $\mathcal{A}^{scl}$-linkage algorithm family analyzed in Section 29.2.2, Balcan et al. (2020) show the following guarantees:

Theorem 29.15 *Let $x_1, \ldots, x_T$ be a sequence of clustering instances over n points and let $D_1, \ldots, D_T \in [0, M]^{n \times n}$ be their corresponding distance matrices. Assume that the pairwise distances for each instance are b-smooth: for all $t \in \{1, \ldots, T\}$ the entries of D_t are random, independent, and have density functions that are bounded by b. Assume further that the utility functions are bounded in $[0, H]$. The continuous weighted majority algorithm employed to choose parameters $\rho_1, \ldots, \rho_T \in [0, 1]$ for the sequence $D_1, \ldots, D_T$ with $\lambda = \sqrt{\log(1/(\sqrt{T}n^8b^2M^2)}/H$ has expected regret bounded by $\mathbb{E}[\max_{\rho \in [0,R]} \sum_{t=1}^{T} u_{x_t}(\rho) - \sum_{t=1}^{T} u_{x_t}(\rho_t)] = O(H\sqrt{T\log(TnbM)})$.*

Proof Sketch Using Lemma 29.6 and properties of b-bounded random variables we can show that for any $\delta > 0$, with probability $1 - \delta$, for any $w > 0$, the utility functions $u_{D_1}, \ldots, u_{D_T}$ are (w,k)-dispersed for $k = O(wTn^8b^2M^2 + \sqrt{T\log(n/\delta)})$. By choosing $w = 1/(\sqrt{T}n^8b^2M^2)$ and using Theorem 29.11, we obtain the result. □

Balcan et al. (2018a) also show good dispersion bounds for the family of algorithms for solving IQPs discussed in Section 29.2 (SDP relaxations followed by parameterized rounding); interestingly, here the dispersion condition holds due to internal randomization in the algorithms themselves (with no additional smoothness assumptions about the input instances).

Extensions Extensions to the results presented here include:

- A regret bound of $\tilde{O}(T^{(d+1)/(d+2)}(H\sqrt{d(3R)^d} + L))$ for the bandit setting. While this is more realistic in terms of feedback per round, the regret bound is significantly worse than that for the full information setting (Balcan et al., 2018a).
- A better regret bound, similar to that of Theorem 29.11, and a computationally efficient implementation for semi-bandit online optimization problems where evaluating the cost function of one algorithm reveals the cost for a range of similar algorithms (Balcan et al., 2020).
- An application of the dispersion condition to the offline learning setting of Section 29.2, specifically the derivation of more refined data-dependent uniform convergence guarantees using empirical Radamacher complexity (Balcan et al., 2018a) (see Chapter 22 for a definition of Rademacher complexity).

29.4 Summary and Discussion

The results in Section 29.2 showing a pseudo-dimension of $O(\log n)$ also lead to computationally efficient learning algorithms, because one can identify and try out a polynomial number of parameter choices. Those with larger pseudo-dimension generally need to use additional problem structure to achieve polynomial-time optimization and learning.

Other Directions Other recent theoretical works (Kleinberg et al., 2017; Weisz et al., 2018) consider data-driven algorithm design for runtime among a finite number of algorithms. Their goal is to select an algorithm whose expected running time, after removing a δ probability mass of instances, is at most $(1 + \epsilon)OPT$, where OPT is the expected running time of the best of the n algorithms on instances from D. The key challenge they address is to minimize the total running time for learning in terms of n, OPT, ϵ, and δ, and without any dependence on the maximum runtime of an algorithm. Note that as opposed to most of the work presented in this chapter these papers do not assume any assume structural relations among the n algorithms. It would be very interesting to combine these two lines of work.

A related line of work presents sample complexity bounds derived for data-driven mechanism design for revenue maximization settings (Morgenstern and Roughgarden, 2015; Balcan et al., 2016, 2018b). The general theorem of Balcan et al. (2019b) (mentioned in Section 29.2.3) can be used to recover the bounds in these papers. Furthermore, the dispersion tools derived in Section 29.3 have been used for providing estimators for the degree of approximate incentive compatibility of an auction, another important problem in modern auction design (Balcan et al., 2019a).

Open Directions Data-driven algorithm design has the potential to fundamentally shift the way we analyze and design algorithms for combinatorial problems. In addition to scaling up the techniques developed so far and also using them for new problems, it would be interesting to develop new analysis frameworks that lead to even better automated algorithm design techniques. For example, it would be interesting to explore a reinforcement learning approach, where we would learn state-based decision policies that use properties of the current state of the algorithm (e.g., the search tree for MIPs) to determine how to proceed (e.g., which variable to branch on next at a given node). It would also be interesting to develop tools for learning within a single problem instance (as opposed to learning across instances).

In addition to providing theoretically sound and practically useful data-driven algorithmic methods, in the long term, this area has the potential to give rise to new algorithmic paradigms of the type humans were not able to design before.

References

Arthur, David, and Vassilvitskii, Sergei. 2007. k-means++: The advantages of careful seeding. In ACM-SIAM Symposium on Discrete Algorithms, pp. 1027–1035.

Balcan, Maria-Florina, Sandholm, Tuomas, and Vitercik, Ellen. 2016. Sample complexity of automated mechanism design. In *Annual Conference on Neural Information Processing Systems*, pp. 2083–2091.

Balcan, Maria-Florina, Nagarajan, Vaishnavh, Vitercik, Ellen, and White, Colin. 2017. Learning-theoretic foundations of algorithm configuration for combinatorial partitioning problems. In *Conference on Learning Theory (COLT)*, pp. 213–274.

Balcan, Maria-Florina, Dick, Travis, and Vitercik, Ellen. 2018a. Dispersion for data-driven algorithm design, online learning, and private optimization. In *Proceedings of the 59th Annual Symposium on Foundations of Computer Science (FOCS)*, pp. 603–614. IEEE.

Balcan, Maria-Florina, Sandholm, Tuomas, and Vitercik, Ellen. 2018b. A general theory of sample complexity for multi-item profit maximization. In *ACM Conference on Economics and Computation*, pp. 173–174.

Balcan, Maria-Florina, Dick, Travis, Sandholm, Tuomas, and Vitercik, Ellen. 2018c. Learning to branch. In *International Conference on Machine Learning (ICML)*, pp. 353–362.

Balcan, Maria-Florina, Sandholm, Tuomas, and Vitercik, Ellen. 2019a. Estimating approximate incentive compatibility. In *ACM Conference on Economics and Computation*, p. 867.

Balcan, Maria-Florina, DeBlasio, Dan, Dick, Travis, Kingsford, Carl, Sandholm, Tuomas, and Vitercik, Ellen. 2019b. How much data is sufficient to learn high-performing algorithms. In *Arxiv*.

Balcan, Maria-Florina, Dick, Travis, and Pegden, Wesley. 2020. Semi-bandit optimization in the dispersed setting. In: Uncertainty in Artificial Intelligence (UAI).

Balcan, Maria-Florina F, Dick, Travis, and White, Colin. 2018d. Data-driven clustering via parameterized Lloyd's families. In *Advances in Neural Information Processing Systems*, pp. 10641–10651.

Blasio, Dan De, and Kececioglu, John D. 2018. *Parameter Advising for Multiple Sequence Alignment*. Springer.

Cesa-Bianchi, Nicolo, and Lugosi, Gábor. 2006. *Prediction, Learning, and Games*. Cambridge University Press.

Cohen-Addad, Vincent, and Kanade, Varun. 2017. Online Optimization Of Smoothed Piecewise Constant Functions. In *International Conference on Artificial Intelligence and Statistics (AISTATS)*, pp. 412–420.

Gupta, Rishi, and Roughgarden, Tim. 2016. A PAC approach to application-specific algorithm selection. In *Innovations in Theoretical Computer Science (ITCS)*, pp. 123–134.

Gupta, Rishi, and Roughgarden, Tim. 2017. A PAC approach to application-specific algorithm selection. *SIAM Journal on Computing*, **46**(3), 992–1017.

Horvitz, Eric J., Ruan, Yongshao, Gomes, Carla P., Kautz, Henry, Selman, Bart, and Chickering, David Maxwell. 2001. A Bayesian approach to tackling hard computational problems. In *Conference in Uncertainty in Artificial Intelligence (UAI)*, pp. 235–244.

Kleinberg, Robert, Leyton-Brown, Kevin, and Lucier, Brendan. 2017. Efficiency through procrastination: Approximately optimal algorithm configuration with runtime guarantees, pp. 2023–2031. *IJCAI*.

Morgenstern, Jamie, and Roughgarden, Tim. 2015. The pseudo-dimension of nearly optimal auctions. In *Conference on Neural Information Processing Systems*, pp. 136–144.

Sandholm, Tuomas. 2003. Automated mechanism design: A new application area for search algorithms. In *International Conference on Principles and Practice of Constraint Programming*, pp. 19–36.

Valiant, L.G. 1984. A theory of the learnable. *Communications of the ACM*, **27**(11), 1134–1142.

Vapnik, V. N. 1998. *Statistical Learning Theory*. John Wiley & Sons.

Weisz, Gellért, György, András, and Szepesvári, Csaba. 2018. Leaps and bounds: A method for approximately optimal algorithm configuration. In *International Conference on Machine Learning (ICML)*, pp. 5254–5262.

Xu, Lin, Hutter, Frank, Hoos, Holger H., and Leyton-Brown, Kevin. 2008. SATzilla: Portfolio-based algorithm selection for SAT. *Journal of Artificial Intelligence Research*, **32**(June), 565–606.

CHAPTER THIRTY

Algorithms with Predictions

Michael Mitzenmacher and Sergei Vassilvitskii

Abstract: We introduce algorithms that use predictions from machine learning applied to the input to circumvent worst-case analysis. We aim for algorithms that have near optimal performance when these predictions are good, but recover the prediction-less worst-case behavior when the predictions have large errors.

30.1 Introduction

In finding ways to go beyond worst-case analysis, previous chapters have described different ways to model the inputs seen by an algorithm in order to avoid fragile bad examples, give better guarantees, or explain the efficacy of methods in practice. Many of these approaches are based on assuming a model of the input that includes randomness in a very specific way. For instance, in average case analysis (Chapter 8) data is drawn from a fixed but unknown distribution, and with random arrival models (Chapter 11) the input is assumed to be randomly permuted. In this chapter, instead of posing a specific model or a set of assumptions on the input, we provide a general framework designed to make use of the rapidly growing power of machine learning techniques. In our framework, we assume that we have a machine learning method that provides us with predictions about the input, and we use the predictions to make a more effective algorithm. We then analyze the performance of the algorithm as a function of how accurate the predictions are; ideally, the better the predictions, the better the performance.

One thing that distinguishes this approach from other work is its natural connection to practice, as for many problems machine learning can be readily applied to provide the necessary prediction for new inputs. Moreover, if we can successfully tie the performance of an algorithm to the quality of the predictions it receives, then as machine learning technology evolves and the quality of predictions improves, we get better performing algorithms essentially for free.

When designing these kinds of algorithms with predictions, there are several new challenges. One is a new goal for our theoretical analysis. We wish to provide formal guarantees of the following form: if our predictor has a given level of performance, our algorithm will achieve a corresponding level of performance. A further challenge is to identify what quantity or quantities to predict, as these will generally be problem specific. Choosing the right quantity to predict can affect both the algorithm's performance and the bounds from our analysis. Finally, an additional challenge is that by nature machine learning methods are imperfect. They have errors that can be large and surprising, and the algorithms we design using machine learning predictions should be robust enough to cope with them.

We start with some very simple examples suggesting why this framework might be useful, and then present some additional examples of more complicated algorithms and data structures that make use of predictions.

30.1.1 Warm-up: Binary Search

As a first example, consider the binary search problem. Given a sorted array A on n elements and a query element q, the goal is to either find the index of q in the array, or state that it is not in the set. The textbook method is binary search: compare the value of q to the value of the middle element of A, and recurse on the correct half of the array. After $O(\log n)$ probes, the method either finds q or correctly returns that q is not in the array.

Binary search optimizes for the worst case, but there are often times when we can do better. For example, most bookstores have books arranged alphabetically by the authors' last name within a particular section. If we were looking for an Agatha Christie mystery, we would likely start our search near the beginning of the section; if, instead, we were to look for a Dorothy Sayers novel, we'd start further toward the end. We first look at the approximate location where we expect to find the book, using our knowledge of the alphabet.

How can we generalize this approach? Let us assume we have a predictor h that, for every query q, returns our best guess for the position of q in the array. To use h, a natural approach is to first probe the location at $h(q)$; if q is not found there, we immediately know whether it is smaller or larger. Suppose q is larger than the element in $A[h(q)]$ and the array is sorted in increasing order. We probe elements at $h(q) + 2, h(q) + 4, h(q) + 8$, and so on, until we find an element larger than q (or we hit the end of the array). Then we apply binary search on the interval that's guaranteed to contain q (if it exists). The bookstore example uses interpolation search as a classifier; since "C" is the third letter out of 26, we start our search for the Agatha Christie book about $3/26 \approx 12\%$ of the way through the Mysteries section.

What is the cost of such an approach, in terms of the number of comparisons? Let $t(q)$ be the true position of q in the array (or the position of the largest element smaller than q if it is not in the array). Suppose the error of the classifier on q is $\eta_q = |h(q) - t(q)|$. The cost of running the above algorithm starting at $h(q)$ is at most $2(\log |h(q) - t(q)|) = 2 \log \eta_q$.

If the queries q come from a distribution, then the expected cost of the algorithm is

$$2\mathbb{E}_q\Big[\log\left(|h(q) - t(q)|\right)\Big] \leq 2\log \mathbb{E}_q\Big[|h(q) - t(q)|\Big] = 2\log \mathbb{E}_q[\eta_q],$$

where the inequality follows by Jensen's inequality. This gives a guarantee on the performance of the algorithm parametrized by the error of the predictor. In particular, even a classifier with an average error of $O(\text{polylog } n)$ leads to an improvement in asymptotic performance. Moreover, since η_q is trivially bounded by n, even an exceptionally bad predictor cannot do much harm.

30.1.2 Online Algorithms: Ski Rental

The binary search example has the nice property that the use of predictions is essentially free. On the one hand, as the prediction error tends to zero, the running time approaches the best possible for this task (a constant). On the other hand, the error is naturally bounded by the number of elements, so even bad predictions will not asymptotically degrade the algorithm's performance. In other situations there can be a more dramatic trade-off between the benefit of using the predictions and the cost incurred when these predictions are wildly incorrect.

Consider the SKIRENTAL problem. At the beginning of the ski season, a new skier has the option to buy skis for b dollars, or to rent them every day for $1 per day. This is one of the simplest settings of decision making under uncertainty – the skier does not know how many days she will ski, yet a simple deterministic strategy will guarantee that she does not spend more than twice as much as she would have had she known the future.

The algorithm achieving that bound rents skis for the first b days, and then buys them on day $b+1$. If the skier skis b or fewer days, she has spent the optimal amount. If, by chance, she stops skiing after day $b+1$, she has spent at most $2b$ in total, which is less than twice the optimal amount.

Suppose the skier has access to a prediction $h(d)$ of how many days she will ski. How should she use this information? Let d^* be the true number of skiing days, and $\eta = |h(d) - d^*|$ be the error in the prediction. It is easy to verify that the algorithm that treats the prediction as truth (i.e., buying skis on day 1 if $h(d) > b$ and renting daily otherwise) has a total cost of $OPT + \eta$. We observe that in this case, the use of predictions is not "free." While the algorithm performs optimally when the prediction is correct, if the skier trusts the prediction and doesn't buy the skis when she should, she can spend arbitrarily more money than if she applies the simple deterministic strategy given earlier.

There is, however, a simple fix. Let $\lambda \in [0, 1]$ be a tunable parameter, and consider the following algorithm. If $h(d) > b$, the skier buys on day $\lceil \lambda b \rceil$, and otherwise, she buys on day $\lceil b/\lambda \rceil$. A case analysis shows that the competitive ratio of this algorithm is bounded by

$$1 + \min\left(\frac{1}{\lambda}, \lambda + \frac{\eta}{(1 - \lambda)OPT}\right). \tag{30.1}$$

In particular, as the error of the prediction drops to 0, the competitive ratio is no more than $1 + \lambda$. On the other hand, even for large errors, the ratio is never worse than $1 + 1/\lambda$. Note that $\lambda = 1$ recovers the algorithm we described originally.

30.1.3 Model

The two preceding examples outline the desiderata that we have for algorithms that use predictions. There are three properties that we highlight.

First, we have isolated the inner workings of the predictor from the algorithm that uses the predictions, instead simply abstracting the predictor as a function h. Our algorithms are accordingly not tied to a specific type of predictor. We can apply decision trees, neural networks, or any other approach to obtain predictions; any h with low error suffices.

Second, the goal is to tie the performance of the algorithm to the observed loss of the predictor. In the setting of our examples, where we used competitive analysis, we further isolated two concepts. We want the algorithms to be *consistent*; that is, ideally their performance should recover that guaranteed by the offline optimal algorithm given an error-free prediction. Additionally, to capture the fact that machine learning systems sometimes have very large errors, we want algorithms to be *robust*; that is, ideally their performance should not be worse than standard online algorithms that use no predictions whatsoever.

While ideal consistency and robustness may be quite challenging, we can loosen the goals using an approximation. Formally, we say that an algorithm is α-*consistent* if its competitive ratio tends to α as the error in the predictions goes to 0, and β-*robust* if the competitive ratio is bounded by β even with arbitrarily bad predictions.

As we saw in the ski-rental example, there is often a tension between consistency and robustness. A practitioner who has high confidence in the predictions may aim for high consistency and low robustness by choosing a small value of λ. On the other hand, a risk-averse decision maker may choose a higher value for λ, limiting the benefit of the predictions but also the additional cost when they turn out to be incorrect.

30.2 Counting Sketches

Another example of a problem where predictions have been shown to boost performance is in the setting of counting sketches for data streams. We briefly describe the Count-Min sketch as an example of a counting sketch. For simplicity, we assume items come in as a data stream one at a time; for example, these could be URLs or IP addresses being accessed. Keeping a separate counter for each item may require too much space, and so we can instead use a sketch that requires less memory at the cost of obtaining only an approximate count for each item, with some chance of failure for each item. The Count-Min sketch sets up a rectangular array of counters with r rows and c columns. Each item hashes to one counter location in each row; when an item passes in the stream, each of its counters is incremented. The approximate count for an item is the minimum counter value associated with the item, which can only yield an overestimate of the actual count for the item. Various results are known that show the error for such a sketch can be small for appropriate values of r and c. Note that if an item has at least one counter where no other item hashes to it, the resulting approximate count will in fact be the exact count. The idea behind the good performance of the Count-Min sketch is that for most items, there will be at least one counter for which the item collides with very few other items, leading to an accurate estimate. In particular, for skewed data streams where item frequencies follow a Zipfian distribution (or more generally for heavy-tailed distributions), so much of the total count is based on a small number of items that the approach can be very accurate, as most collisions introduce only a small error in the counter.

Suppose, however, that we had a predictor that could reasonably accurately predict which items were the "heavy hitters," that is, the most frequent items. Since the idea of using a data sketch is to save space, we do not want to use a separate counter for every item, but we may be willing to use space to keep individual counters for each item that is predicted to have a high count. This assures accuracy for correctly predicted heavy hitters, which is often important, but also importantly it greatly reduces the possibility of a large error for an item with a small count, since removing potential heavy hitters from the larger array greatly reduces the possibility that a small item will have all of its counters collide with a large item.

The works by Aamand et al. (2019) and Hsu et al. (2019) have formalized this high-level argument with provable results for the Count-Min sketch and Count-Sketch for Zipfian frequency distributions, showing they can improve the space/performance tradeoff over sketches without predictions. They also show this improvement holds in practice. While we do not go into further details here, the example of counting sketches provides an intuitive approach for using predictions within algorithms and data structures: If there are a limited set of problematic elements, such as outliers or high weight elements, that greatly affect performance when they are not known in advance, a predictor may allow these elements to be separated out and correspondingly improve overall performance.

30.3 Learned Bloom Filters

An early proposed example of how predictions from machine learning could improve data structures provided a novel variation of the Bloom filter (Kraska et al., 2018).

To start, let us briefly review standard Bloom filters (Bloom, 1970; Broder and Mitzenmacher, 2004), a data structure used to answer set membership queries using small space. A Bloom filter for representing a set $S = \{x_1, x_2, \ldots, x_n\}$ of n elements corresponds to an array of m bits, and uses k independent hash functions $h_1, \ldots, h_k$ with range $\{0, \ldots, m-1\}$. Note that the number of bits per item used by the Bloom filter is given by m/n. Here we assume that these hash functions are perfectly random. Initially all array bits are 0. For each element $x \in S$, the array bits $h_i(x)$ are set to 1 for $1 \le i \le k$; a bit may be repeatedly set to 1. To check if an item y is in S, we check whether all $h_i(y)$ are set to 1. If not, then clearly y is not a member of S. If all $h_i(y)$ are set to 1, we conclude that y is in S, although this may be a *false positive*. A Bloom filter does not produce false negatives.

Let y be an element such that $y \notin S$, where y is chosen independently of the hash functions used to create the filter. Let ρ be the fraction of bits set to 1 after the elements are hashed. Then the probability of a false positive is ρ^k. Now the expected value of ρ is easily calculated, as the probability a specific bit in the filter stays 0 is just

$$\left(1 - \frac{1}{m}\right)^{kn} \approx e^{-kn/m}.$$

Standard techniques show that ρ is close to its expectation with high probability, so using the expectation in place of ρ, we see the false positive probability will be concentrated near

$$(1 - e^{-kn/m})^k$$

when k and m/n are constant. Choosing k appropriately (the optimal value for k is $(m/n) \cdot \ln 2$), we see the false positive probability for an element falls exponentially with m/n, the number of bits per item used in the filter.

The idea of a learned Bloom filter is to train a neural network or other machine learning algorithm to recognize the set S. We represent the algorithm by a function f,

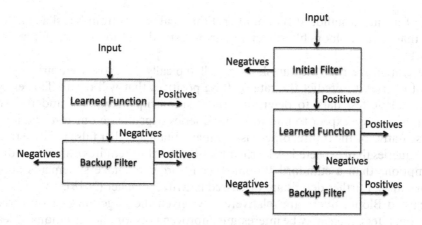

Figure 30.1 The left side shows a learned Bloom filter. Negatives from the learned function are checked against the backup filter to prevent false negatives. The right side shows the sandwiched learned Bloom filter. An initial filter removes many true negatives from reaching the learned function, reducing the false positives from the learned function.

so that on input x the algorithm returns a value $f(x)$ between 0 and 1. The algorithm ideally would return 1 for every element in the set and 0 for every element not in the set. If we had such a predictor, we would not need any data structure, as we could just use the function to represent the set. This is too much to expect in practice; instead, we consider an algorithm that returns a value $0 \leq f(x) \leq 1$. We might intuitively interpret $f(x)$ as an estimate of the probability that x is an element from the set, although this interpretation is not necessary in what follows.

We can choose a threshold τ, and have the algorithm return that any element that satisfies $f(x) \geq \tau$ is in the set and otherwise it is not in the set. Indeed, if we choose $\tau = \min_{x \in S} f(x)$ then there will be no false negatives. But unless the predictor f is very good, it is likely that this value of τ will lead to too many false positives.

The alternative approach we apply is to use the learned function f as a prefilter, selecting a larger value of τ to cut down on false positives, and then using a standard Bloom filter as a backup to prevent false negatives. The setup is shown in Figure 30.1. The initial learned function should correctly identify a substantial number of set elements, with a low false positive rate. The backup Bloom filter then holds all the set elements that are incorrectly rejected by the learned function; to be clear, we determine these in advance and set up the backup Bloom filter accordingly, which means the dataset and the learned function must be fixed before setting up the backup Bloom filter. The backup Bloom filter again yields false positives, but prevents any false negatives.

To see how there might be gains from this approach, imagine a small learned function that correctly identifies half of the original set. Then the backup Bloom filter needs to only correct the erroneous false negatives of the predictor, which means the backup filter needs to represent only half the original set elements. Accordingly, the backup filter could be roughly half the size of a Bloom filter for the entire set with roughly the same false positive rate. If the learned function has a small enough representation, namely less than half the size of a Bloom filter for the entire set, then this combination will be a win in terms of the space versus false positive probability tradeoff against a standard Bloom filter. Empirical results from Kraska et al. (2018) show that learned Bloom filters can outperform standard Bloom filters for real-world datasets.

We emphasize that the threshold τ will typically be chosen empirically, based on test queries, to predict the rate of false positives that will occur. This empirical evaluation of test data to determine the relationship between τ and the rate of false positives we expect to find in future queries depends on our test queries being representative of the future; otherwise we may obtain a higher false positive rate over future queries than expected. A learned Bloom filter thus requires different additional assumptions than a standard Bloom filter in order to make statements about its performance. Further details are discussed in Mitzenmacher (2018).

Learned Bloom filters are relatively new; given the large number of variations of Bloom filters, there may be interesting improvements for and variations of learned Bloom filters that will appear. Indeed, it is already known that a "sandwiched" learned Bloom filter that uses a learned filter between two standard Bloom filters, also shown in Figure 30.1, can yield better performance (Mitzenmacher, 2018).

30.4 Caching with Predictions

The caching or paging problem is both a canonical example of online algorithms and a problem that has necessitated beyond worst-case analysis, as we have seen in Chapters 1, 2, and 24.

Recall the problem setup. We are given a machine with a slow memory that can hold N pages, and a fast memory with k slots. Page requests arrive one at a time, and must be served out of fast memory. If the page is already in fast memory (cache), then a *hit* occurs, and the operation is free. Otherwise, there is a *cache miss*, the page is brought into fast memory, and one of the k existing pages in the cache is evicted. The goal is to minimize the number of cache misses over the sequence of page requests.

30.4.1 What to Predict?

The first question to address is to decide on the quantity that should be predicted by the machine learning subsystem. We look for predictions that are both useful to the algorithm and efficiently learnable. The latter highlights the fact that predictions should be grounded in reality. Specifically, we want to make sure that we only need polynomially many examples to learn a good predictor; formally, we ensure that the function has a low sample complexity. As long as the family of functions specifying the predictor is relatively simple and well behaved, this condition is satisfied. However, an approach to fully predict the whole instance would fail the test and be untenable.

What are good candidates for predictions for the paging problem? As mentioned in Chapter 1, the Furthest-In-Future (FIF) algorithm minimizes the number of cache misses. In order to be able to emulate it online, a useful prediction to be made at the time of each request is the *next* arrival time of this element. Formally, let $next(t)$ be the next arrival time of the element that appeared at time t, and $h(t)$ denote the predicted time of the next arrival of this element.

Armed with such a predictor a natural approach is to plug it into the Furthest-In-Future algorithm, instead of the ground truth. We call this the PFIF for Predicted Furthest-In-Future.

The analysis of the FIF algorithm directly implies that if the predictor h is perfect, that is $h(t) = next(t)$ for all t, then PFIF is optimal. In other words, PFIF is consistent. But is the approach robust?

First we must define an error metric. For a hypothesis h let us define $\eta(h) = \sum_t |h(t) - next(t)|$. The question we want to ask is how the competitive ratio of PFIF scales with $\eta(h)$. The first thing to observe is that, as we defined it, the error grows with the input length. This is undesirable. Suppose we duplicate a request sequence and the predictions. The competitive ratio would remain the same, but the error defined above would double. We can normalize by the input length, but this, too, leads to pathological cases. For instance, take any request sequence of length n, and repeat the last element n times. Since all of these extra requests would be cache hits, the performance of any algorithm remains the same as well. However, if the last n predictions are perfect, then η does not change, but error normalized by sequence length would decrease by a factor of 2. Instead, we will normalize the error by the cost of the optimum solution OPT, which behaves correctly in both of these examples.

We show that the competitive ratio of PFIF grows linearly with the error. Formally, the competitive ratio of PFIF is $\Omega(\eta(h)/\text{OPT})$.

Consider a simple example with a cache of size 2, and three elements, a, b, and c. The true sequence will be $c, a, b, a, b, \ldots, a, b, c$. The predictions will be correct for elements a and b, but the prediction for c will always be at time 0. Hence $\eta(h)$ is the length of the sequence. In this case PFIF will keep c in the cache, and suffer a cache miss almost every time. On the other hand, the optimal solution never misses on a and b once they are in the cache, and has a constant number of misses overall. We note that while it may be tempting to attempt to fix this algorithm by disregarding elements whose predicted appearance time has passed, this also has an $\Omega(\eta(h)/\text{OPT})$ competitive ratio.

30.4.2 Marking Algorithms

A natural question then is whether we can get competitive ratios with a more benign dependence on $\eta(h)/\text{OPT}$.

To proceed we introduce the Marking family of algorithms, first introduced by Fiat et al. (1991). These algorithms proceed in phases. Every phase begins with every cache position "unmarked." Whenever there is a cache miss, an unmarked element is evicted, and the new element is marked. When a cache hit occurs the element is marked as well. This continues until all elements in the cache are marked, at which point the phase ends, and all of the marks are cleared. It is easy to show that any marking algorithm is $O(k)$-competitive, where k is the cache size. Moreover, Fiat et al. (1991) show that if an algorithm evicts a uniformly random unmarked element, then the expected competitive ratio is $O(\log k)$.

To prove a bound on the competitive ratio of the marking algorithm, we must get a lower bound on the optimum. To do so, we partition elements that arrive during a phase into two categories: clean and stale. *Clean* elements in phase i are those that did not appear in phase $i - 1$. In contrast, *stale* elements are those that were seen in the previous phase. Consider the following sequence with a cache of size 3.

$$\underbrace{a, a, b, a, b, c,}_{phase1} \underbrace{b, b, c, b, d,}_{phase2} \underbrace{a, a, d, c}_{phase3}$$

Note that each phase ends as soon as three distinct elements appear. In phase 2, elements b and c are stale (since they appeared in phase 1), and element d is clean. In contrast, in phase 3, d is stale (as is c), and a is clean.

Let C_i be the number of clean elements in phase i. Consider the performance of any algorithm on the clean elements. For some element $j \in C_i$, if it is not present in the cache in the beginning of phase i, then it will incur a cache miss. On the other hand, if it is in the cache at the beginning of the phase, it must have stayed in the cache throughout phase $i-1$, even though it did not appear, thus effectively reducing the working cache size. This argument can be made precise, to show that

$$OPT \geq \frac{1}{2} \sum_i C_i. \tag{30.2}$$

In other words, the number of misses in any strategy is at least half the number of all clean elements. We will relate the misses suffered by our algorithm to the number of clean elements in each phase.

In order to utilize predictions in the marking framework, we modify the eviction strategy of the marking algorithm. If the arriving element is clean, we evict the unmarked element *predicted* to appear furthest in the future. If the arriving element is stale, we proceed as before, and evict a uniformly random unmarked element. We refer to this variant as PREDICTIVEMARKER.

Theorem 30.1 PREDICTIVEMARKER *has a competitive ratio of* $O\left(\log \frac{\eta(h)}{OPT}\right)$.

To prove the theorem, let us try to understand the reason behind cache misses incurred by the algorithm. Suppose an element e arrives and e is not in the cache, causing a cache miss. If the element e is clean, Equation 30.2 tells us we can charge its eviction directly to OPT. Suppose e is stale. By the definition of stale elements, e was in the cache when the phase began, thus it must have been evicted at some point between the beginning of the phase and its arrival. Let $ev(e)$ denote the element whose arrival caused the eviction of e. Either $ev(e)$ is clean, or it is another stale element, e_1, whose arrival time is earlier than e. In this case let us look why e_1 was evicted, i.e., $ev(e_1) = ev(ev(e))$. By the same logic, either $ev(e_1)$ is a clean element, or it is another stale element whose first arrival in this phase was earlier still. Therefore, repeatedly applying the ev function to an element leads to a clean element whose arrival set off this chain of events.

To get a bound on the competitive ratio, we ask how long can this chain be? This gives us the desired bound because each link in the chain represents a cache miss, each chain terminates with a clean element, and the number of clean elements is comparable to OPT by Equation 30.2. It is clear that the length of the chain depends on the eviction rule: If we always evict the element that is latest to arrive (FIF) then each chain is of length 1. If we do the reverse and evict the element that is next to arrive, then a chain can grow to be $\Omega(k)$ in length.

We first analyze the standard marking algorithm which evicts elements uniformly at random.

Lemma 30.2 *When evicting a random unmarked element, the expected length of each chain is $O(\log k)$.*

Proof We need only consider stale elements in every phase, and there may be as many as $k-1$ of them. Order them by their arrival time, with e_1 arriving first, then e_2, and so on. Denote by L_i the length of the chain starting with element e_i. We can write down the recurrence for L_i as

$$L_i = 1 + \frac{1}{k-i} \sum_{j=1}^{k-1} L_j,$$

which solves to $L_0 = \Theta(\log k)$ when $L_{k-1} = 0$. □

On the other hand, in PREDICTIVEMARKER, when a clean element arrives, we evict the element predicted to arrive furthest in the future. Let c be a clean element that arrives at time t_c, s denote the element we chose to evict, and t_s be the next time of arrival of s. Note that any stale element that arrives between t_c and t_s cannot increase the chain started at c. Therefore the only elements that can contribute to the growth of the chain are those that arrive after time t_s. But this is exactly in violation of our prediction, and thus we can charge these cache misses to the error of the predictor. Let $inv_h(s)$ denote the set of elements that arrive after s even though they were predicted by h to arrive before. It is easy to extend Lemma 30.2 to show that the expected length of the chain starting with s is $\Theta(\log inv_h(s))$.

To complete the analysis, we need to bound the number of inversions as a function of the accuracy of the predictor. For any two permutations, the total number of inversions and the ℓ_1 distance of the elements are known to always be within a factor of two by the celebrated Diaconis–Graham inequality (Diaconis and Graham, 1977). The latter is also exactly $\eta(h)$ decomposed across phases. Further, since log is a concave function, to maximize the total length of all chains, we should partition errors equally among them. These two facts imply that the expected error of the above algorithm is $O(\log(\eta(h)/\text{OPT}))$.

30.4.3 Summary of Caching

The caching problem is illustrative of the power of algorithms with predictions and the care that must be taken in designing them. We relied on the offline algorithm to identify the quantity that we wished to predict: the next appearance of every arriving element. We then proved that simply using this prediction as a proxy for the truth in the optimal offline algorithm allowed for pathological examples where the predictions led the algorithm astray. We then showed a different algorithm that, by using the predictions in a more careful manner, leads to a marked improvement in the competitive ratio over the naïve way of using the predictor. In addition, we can show that even if the error is very large, we can guarantee performance within a constant factor of the standard marking algorithm. (See Exercise 30.2.) Finally, as Lykouris and Vassilvitskii (2018) showed, these gains are not just theoretical; even with off-the-shelf prediction models PREDICTIVEMARKER consistently outperformed standard methods like the Least Recently Used (LRU) policy.

30.5 Scheduling with Predictions

In Chapter 4, the problem of scheduling jobs on a single machine was considered in the setting of resource augmentation. One of the key points was that if job times were known, the simple greedy algorithm of Shortest Remaining Processing Time (SRPT) is optimal with respect to minimizing the total flow time. Here we consider the potential of strategies such as SRPT in the context of queueing systems, where arrivals occur over time.

30.5.1 A Simple Model with Predictions

We start with a very simple example. Suppose we have n jobs $j_1, \ldots, j_n$, each of which is either short or long. Short jobs require time s to process and long jobs require time $\ell > s$ to process. Jobs are all available at time 0, and they are to be ordered and then processed sequentially. When the job times are known, shortest job first minimizes the total waiting time over all jobs. If there are n_s short jobs and n_ℓ long jobs, it is easy to check that the average waiting time is

$$\frac{1}{n}\left(n_s \frac{n_s - 1}{2}s + n_\ell \frac{n_\ell - 1}{2}\ell + n_\ell n_s s\right).$$

If one has no information about the job times, then one might randomly order the jobs, in which case the expected waiting time over all jobs is

$$\frac{1}{n}\left(n_s\left(\frac{n_s - 1}{2}s + \frac{n_\ell}{2}\ell\right) + n_\ell\left(\frac{n_s}{2}s + \frac{n_\ell - 1}{2}\ell\right)\right).$$

Finally, suppose we have an algorithm that can predict a job's type. We assume short jobs are misclassified as long jobs with some probability p and long jobs are misclassified as short jobs with some probability q. The natural approach would be to use *shortest-predicted-job-first*; that is, we apply shortest-job-first based on the predictions. Some case arithmetic shows that the expected waiting time is then

$$\begin{aligned}
\frac{1}{n}\bigg(&(1-p)n_s\left(\frac{(1-p)(n_s - 1)}{2}s + \frac{qn_\ell}{2}\ell\right) \\
&+ pn_s\left((1-p)(n_s - 1)s + \frac{p(n_s - 1)}{2}s + \frac{(1-q)n_\ell}{2}\ell + qn_\ell\ell\right) \\
&+ (1-q)n_\ell\left(\frac{(1-q)(n_\ell - 1)}{2}\ell + q(n_\ell - 1)\ell + \frac{pn_s}{2}s + (1-p)n_s s\right) \\
&+ qn_\ell\left(\frac{q(n_\ell - 1)}{2}\ell + \frac{(1-p)n_s}{2}s\right)\bigg).
\end{aligned}$$

With these expressions, one can determine the gain from using predictions over randomly ordering jobs, and the loss from using predictions in place of exact information. Mitzenmacher (2019) suggests that we might also consider the *ratio* between the expected waiting time with imperfect information and the expected waiting time with perfect information. Mitzenmacher (2019) further suggests that for any algorithm where it makes sense to use predicted information in place of exact information one can consider this ratio, which is there referred to as the price of misprediction, using the following definition:

Definition 30.3 Let $M_A(Q; I)$ be the value of some measure (such as the expected waiting time) for a system Q given information I about the system using algorithm A, and let $M_A(Q; P)$ be the value of that metric using predicted information P in place of I when using algorithm A. Then the *price of misprediction* is defined as $M_A(Q; I)/M_A(Q; P)$.

Notice here that (unlike many other uses of the "price of" language in algorithm analysis) the denominator is not necessarily an optimal algorithm, but the corresponding algorithm with exact information. (One could, of course, also compare against an optimal algorithm, as we have seen elsewhere in this chapter.)

30.5.2 More General Job Service Times

We can consider a more general model where a job's actual and predicted times for service are real-valued random variables. A natural probabilistic model is to suppose that the job sizes are governed by some distribution, and correspondingly, for each possible service time x, the output of the predictor y is governed by some distribution that depends only on x. For example, we might model the prediction y as the value x with some additional random noise, where the distribution of the noise might depend on x. Equivalently, we can describe jobs according to a density function $g(x, y)$, giving the density for a job that has service time x and predicted service time y. (For convenience we assume that $g(x, y)$ is "well-behaved" throughout, so that it is continuous and all necessary derivatives exist; the analysis can be readily modified to handle point masses or other discontinuities in the distribution.) This model makes some assumptions, most notably that each job corresponds to an independent instantiation of this density function. However, it does seem sensible to model a machine learning algorithm that has been trained on lots of data as providing an estimated service time that corresponds to a conditional distribution based on the actual service time, as is done here, as long as the future jobs we are going to see can be thought of as coming from the same distribution as the jobs we used for training – that is, roughly speaking, if the future is going to look like the past.

Again, we assume that all jobs are given at time 0, and we simply order the jobs according to the shortest predicted job first. We let $f_s(x) = \int_{y=0}^{\infty} g(x, y)\, dy$ be the corresponding density function for the service time, and $f_p(y) = \int_{x=0}^{\infty} g(x, y)\, dx$ be the corresponding density function for the predicted service time. If there are n total jobs, the expected waiting time for a job using shortest job first given full information is given by

$$(n-1) \int_{x=0}^{\infty} f_s(x) \left(\int_{z=0}^{x} z f_s(z)\, dz \right) dx,$$

while the expected waiting time for a job using predicted information using shortest predicted job first is given by

$$(n-1) \int_{y=0}^{\infty} f_p(y) \left(\int_{x=0}^{\infty} \int_{z=0}^{y} x g(x, z)\, dz\, dx \right) dy.$$

In words, in the full information case, given the service time for a job, we determine its expected waiting time from each other job by taking the expectation conditioned on the other job having a smaller service time. In the predicted information case, to compute the expected waiting time for a job given its predicted service time, we determine its expected waiting time from each other job by taking the expectation based on the other job's actual service time, conditioned on the other job having a smaller predicted service time than the original job.

In this case, the price of misprediction is given by the ratio

$$\frac{\int_{y=0}^{\infty} f_p(y) \left(\int_{x=0}^{\infty} \int_{z=0}^{y} xg(x,z)\, dz\, dx\right) dy}{\int_{x=0}^{\infty} f_s(x) \left(\int_{z=0}^{x} zf_s(z)\, dz\right) dx}; \tag{30.3}$$

while this is not the simplest of expressions, given $g(x,y)$ it can be numerically evaluated. As an interesting albeit not necessarily realistic example, suppose that jobs have service times that are exponentially distributed with mean 1, but the service time prediction for a job with actual service time x is exponential with mean x, so that the mean of the prediction is correct but the prediction itself can be significantly inaccurate. It can be shown that the price of misprediction in this case is 4/3; this is given as Exercise 30.3.

30.5.3 Scheduling Queues

This type of analysis can be extended, with some more involved work, to the case of queues. In the queueing setting, we still just have one machine, but jobs both enter for service and leave after finishing service over time, and we typically first look at the average time in the system when considering performance. For example, in standard queueing theory, the prototypical queue is known as the M/M/1 queue, where arrivals are a Poisson process of rate $\lambda < 1$, service times are independently and identically exponentially distributed with mean 1, and there is a single server serving the customers. (The "M" in the M/M/1 queue stands for memoryless.) One of the fundamental results in queueing theory is that the expected time a customer spends waiting for and obtaining service in equilibrium in an M/M/1 queue with First Come First Served (FCFS) scheduling (also called First In First Out (FIFO)) is given by $1/(1-\lambda)$. In this section we consider queues with Poisson arrivals but general service time distributions, not just exponential.

If one knows the service time for a job, one can try to schedule better than FCFS. Shortest Job First (SJF) is the non-preemptive strategy that schedules the queued job with the shortest service time when a job completes. Preemptive Shortest Job First (PSJF) acts similarly, but will preempt a running job if new job with a smaller service time arrives. Shortest Remaining Processing Time (SRPT) will instead schedule and preempt jobs based on their remaining processing time instead of their service time.

In Mitzenmacher (2019), these strategies are considered in the setting where one has predicted service times instead of actual service times, leading to the strategies Shortest Predicted Job First (SPJF), Preemptive Shortest Predicted Job First (PSPJF), and Shortest Predicted Remaining Processing Time (SPRPT). Equations for all three strategies are provided under the assumption that there is a joint density distribution $g(x,y)$ for jobs with service time x and predicted service time y, and that each job independently yields predicted and actual service times from this distribution.

For example, comparing SJF and SPJF, we first set up the following notation. Let $f_s(x) = \int_{y=0}^{\infty} g(x,y)\, dy$ and $f_p(y) = \int_{x=0}^{\infty} g(x,y)\, dx$ be the corresponding service and predicted service density functions. Finally, the quantity $\rho_x = \lambda \int_{t=0}^{x} tf_s(t)\, dt$ is the rate of work entering the queue from jobs with service time at most x, and $\rho'_y = \lambda \int_{t=0}^{y} \int_{x=0}^{\infty} g(x,t)x\,dx\,dt$ is the corresponding rate of work entering the queue from jobs with predicted service at most y.

For SJF, it is known that $W(x)$, the time spent waiting in the queue (not being served) for jobs with service time x, in the steady state satisfies

$$\mathbf{E}[W(x)] = \frac{\rho \mathbf{E}[S^2]}{2\mathbf{E}[S]\,(1 - \rho_x)^2}.$$

Note that the waiting time for a job with service time x depends on the general service distribution but also specifically on the work from jobs with service time at most x, as one might expect. The overall expected time waiting in a queue, which we denote by $\mathbf{E}[W]$, is then simply

$$\mathbf{E}[W] = \int_{x=0}^{\infty} f_S(x)\mathbf{E}[W(x)]\,dx.$$

It turns out that for SPJF, a similar analysis to that used to derive the performance equations for SJF applies. If we let $W'(y)$ be the distribution of time spent waiting in the queue for a job with predicted service time y in the steady state, then

$$\mathbf{E}[W'(y)] = \frac{\rho \mathbf{E}[S^2]}{2\mathbf{E}[S](1 - \rho'_y)^2}.$$

The price of misprediction for the time waiting in queue for SJF/SPJF is then expressed as

$$\frac{\int_{y=0}^{\infty} \frac{f_p(y)}{(1-\rho'_y)^2}\,dy}{\int_{x=0}^{\infty} \frac{f_s(x)}{(1-\rho_x)^2}\,dx}.$$

Similar analyses can be done for PSJF/PSPJF and SRPT/SPRPT, although the resulting expressions are more complicated.

Simulations show that even fairly weak predictors can provide significant performance gains for queues under high load (that is, as λ gets close to 1), as FIFO queues relatively frequently stack short jobs behind a long job, and this is a primary reason for long expected waiting times. Predictors that simply keep long jobs behind short jobs most of the time therefore greatly improve the expected waiting time over all jobs. For example, a predictor with a multiplicative error can do quite well. Figure 30.2 provides an example with $\lambda = 0.95$ and two types of service distributions: exponential with mean 1, and a Weibull distribution with cumulative distribution $1 - e^{-\sqrt{2x}}$. (The Weibull distribution also has mean 1, but is more heavy-tailed, so longer jobs occur with higher probability.) The results are averaged over 1,000 trials over a time period of 1 million time units, where each trial averages the time in system for jobs that complete after the first $100,000$ time units. A job with service time x has a predicted service time that is uniform over $[(1-\alpha)x, (1+\alpha)x]$ for a parameter α; we try $\alpha = j/10$ for integer j from 0 to 9. We observe that performance degrades gracefully with α, and is much better than without predictions, where the steady-state average time in the system is 20 for the exponential distribution and 58 for the Weibull distribution.

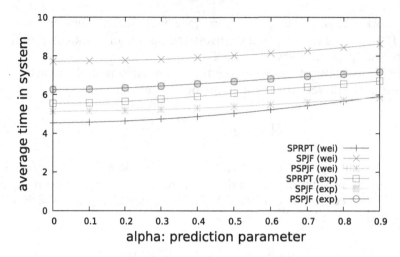

Figure 30.2 Results from simulations at $\lambda = 0.95$ for exponential and Weibull distributions. A job with service time x has predicted service time uniform over $[(1-\alpha)x, (1+\alpha)x]$. Performance degrades gracefully with α.

30.6 Notes

As mentioned in Chapter 24, the use of advice to assist online algorithms has been studied in the past (Boyar et al., 2016). But previous work has focused on minimizing the number of advice bits from omniscient sources to achieve optimal or near-optimal competitive ratios. The motivation of the work in online algorithms using learning-based predictions more closely mirrors the use of machine learning in practice, focusing on improvements in the competitive ratio that can arise with realistic advice.

The idea of learning in order to improve algorithms' performance, especially in the realm of online algorithms, has appeared in some works in the past. For instance, Devanur and Hayes (2009) and Vee et al. (2010) explored how predictions can be used to obtain nearly optimal online matching bounds, while Cole and Roughgarden (2014) and Medina and Vassilvitskii (2017) showed how to learn from samples to maximize revenue in auction settings. In parallel, Kraska et al. (2018) showed that these endeavors are not simply theoretical, building a system that used machine learning to improve retrieval speed for index data structures.

A formal model of learning with predictions, including the notions of α-consistency and β-robustness, was presented by Lykouris and Vassilvitskii (2018). They were also the first ones to analyze this setting for the caching problem. The analysis we presented here is due to Rohatgi (2020). Additionally, Purohit et al. (2018) demonstrated explicit trade-offs between these two concepts in the context of ski-rental and online scheduling.

A good general reference for queueing theory, including derivations for SJF and SRPT with exact information, is Harchol-Balter (2013).

In scheduling for queues, some works have looked at the effects of using imprecise information for load balancing in multiple queue settings. For example, Mitzenmacher (2000) considers using old load information to place jobs in the context of the power of two choices. For single queues, Wierman and Nuyens (2008) look at variations of SRPT and SJF with inexact job sizes, bounding the performance gap based on bounds on how inexact the estimates can be. Dell'Amico, Carra, and Michardi empirically study scheduling policies for queueing systems with estimated sizes (Dell'Amico et al., 2015). As mentioned, Purohit et al. (2018) specifically looked at scheduling with predictions in the standard online setting, where they considered variants of shortest predicted processing time that yield good performance in terms of the competitive ratio, with the performance depending on the accuracy of the predictions.

The Count-Min Sketch (Cormode and Muthukrishnan, 2005) and the Count-Sketch (Charikar et al., 2002) are well-known data structures for finding heavy hitters in data streams, and have found many additional applications.

Bloom filters were originally developed by Bloom (1970), and have proven useful for a number of applications (Broder and Mitzenmacher, 2004). Learned Bloom filters were originally described by Kraska et al. (2018), where other additional possible examples of using learning to improve index data structures were proposed.

References

Aamand, Anders, Indyk, Piotr, and Vakilian, Ali. 2019. (Learned) frequency estimation algorithms under Zipfian distribution. *arXiv preprint arXiv:1908.05198*.

Bloom, Burton H. 1970. Space/time trade-offs in hash coding with allowable errors. *Communications of the ACM*, **13**(7), 422–426.

Boyar, Joan, Favrholdt, Lene M, Kudahl, Christian, Larsen, Kim S, and Mikkelsen, Jesper W. 2016. Online algorithms with advice: A survey. *ACM SIGACT News*, **47**(3), 93–129.

Broder, Andrei, and Mitzenmacher, Michael. 2004. Network applications of Bloom filters: A survey. *Internet Mathematics*, **1**(4), 485–509.

Charikar, Moses, Chen, Kevin, and Farach-Colton, Martin. 2002. Finding frequent items in data streams. In *International Colloquium on Automata, Languages, and Programming*, pp. 693–703. Springer.

Cole, Richard, and Roughgarden, Tim. 2014. The sample complexity of revenue maximization. In *Symposium on Theory of Computing, STOC 2014*, pp. 243–252.

Cormode, Graham, and Muthukrishnan, Shan. 2005. An improved data stream summary: The count-min sketch and its applications. *Journal of Algorithms*, **55**(1), 58–75.

Dell'Amico, Matteo, Carra, Damiano, and Michiardi, Pietro. 2015. PSBS: Practical size-based scheduling. *IEEE Transactions on Computers*, **65**(7), 2199–2212.

Devanur, Nikhil R., and Hayes, Thomas P. 2009. The adwords problem: Online keyword matching with budgeted bidders under random permutations. In *Proceedings 10th ACM Conference on Electronic Commerce (EC-2009)*, pp. 71–78

Diaconis, P., and Graham, R.L. 1977. Spearman's footrule as a measure of disarray. *Journal of the Royal Statistical Society B*, **39**(2), 262–268.

Fiat, Amos, Karp, Richard M., Luby, Michael, McGeoch, Lyle A., Sleator, Daniel Dominic, and Young, Neal E. 1991. Competitive paging algorithms. *Journal of Algorithms*, **12**(4), 685–699.

Harchol-Balter, Mor. 2013. *Performance Modeling and Design of Computer Systems: Queueing Theory in Action*. Cambridge University Press.

Hsu, Chen-Yu, Indyk, Piotr, Katabi, Dina, and Vakilian, Ali. 2019. Learning-based frequency estimation algorithms. In *7th International Conference on Learning Representations*.

Kraska, Tim, Beutel, Alex, Chi, Ed H, Dean, Jeffrey, and Polyzotis, Neoklis. 2018. The case for learned index structures. In *Proceedings of the 2018 International Conference on Management of Data*, pp. 489–504. ACM.

Lykouris, Thodoris, and Vassilvitskii, Sergei. 2018. Competitive caching with machine learned advice. In *Proceedings of the 35th International Conference on Machine Learning, ICML 2018*.

Medina, Andres Muñoz, and Vassilvitskii, Sergei. 2017. Revenue optimization with approximate bid predictions. In *Advances in Neural Information Processing Systems 30: Annual Conference on Neural Information Processing Systems 2017*, pp. 1858–1866.

Mitzenmacher, Michael. 2000. How useful is old information? *IEEE Transactions on Parallel and Distributed Systems*, **11**(1), 6–20.

Mitzenmacher, Michael. 2018. A model for learned bloom filters and optimizing by sandwiching. In *Advances in Neural Information Processing Systems*, pp. 464–473.

Mitzenmacher, Michael. 2019. Scheduling with Predictions and the price of misprediction. In *Proceedings of the 11th Innovations in Theoretical Computer Science Conference (ITCS)*, pp. 14:1–14:18.

Purohit, Manish, Svitkina, Zoya, and Kumar, Ravi. 2018. Improving online algorithms via predictions. In *Advances in Neural Information Processing Systems*, pp. 9661–9670.

Rohatgi, Dhruv. 2020. Near-optimal bounds for online caching with machine learned advice. In *Symposium on Discrete Algorithms (SODA)*, pp. 1834–1845.

Vee, Erik, Vassilvitskii, Sergei, and Shanmugasundaram, Jayavel. 2010. Optimal online assignment with forecasts. In *Proceedings 11th ACM Conference on Electronic Commerce (EC-2010)*, pp. 109–118.

Wierman, Adam, and Nuyens, Misja. 2008. Scheduling despite inexact job-size information. In *ACM SIGMETRICS Performance Evaluation Review*, vol. 36, pp. 25–36. ACM.

Exercises

Exercise 30.1 Prove the competitive ratio bound given in equation 30.1 for the ski rental with predictions algorithm.

Exercise 30.2 Consider the caching problem, and suppose we have two data-dependent eviction algorithms. For an input x, one of them has competitive ratio $a(x)$ while the other has ratio $b(x)$. Develop an algorithm that for every input x has competitive ratio $O(\min(a(x), b(x)))$.

Exercise 30.3 Consider the setting of equation 30.3, where job sizes are exponentially distributed with mean 1, and a job with mean service time x has a predicted service time that is itself exponentially distributed with mean x. Show via numerical evaluation or integration (perhaps using a software package for evaluating integrals) that the "price of misprediction" in this case is 4/3.

Exercise 30.4 Write a simulation to study one of the problems discussed in the chapter. For example, you could write a simulation for a queue that uses predicted service times, and use it to explore how the service time distribution and the quality of the prediction affect the average time spent waiting in the queue. Or you could implement an Count-Min sketch and simulate a predictor for heavy hitter elements, and use it to explore how the accuracy of the sketch improves with the quality of the prediction or varies with how skewed the frequency distribution of items is. Your simulation can use an actual learned function as a predictor, or you could use a synthetic prediction (by, for example, adding noise in some specified way to the ground truth to obtain a prediction).

Index